Frommer's®

Greece

Here's what the critics say about Frommer's:

"Amazingly easy to use. Very portable, very complete."
—*Booklist*

◆

"The only mainstream guide to list specific prices. The Walter Cronkite of guidebooks—with all that implies."
—*Travel & Leisure*

◆

"Complete, concise, and filled with useful information."
—*New York Daily News*

◆

"Hotel information is close to encyclopedic."
—*Des Moines Sunday Register*

Other Great Guides for Your Trip:

Frommer's Greek Islands

Frommer's Greece from $50 a Day

Frommer's Italy

Frommer's Italy from $50 a Day

Frommer's Europe

Frommer's Europe from $50 a Day

Frommer's Gay & Lesbian Europe

The Complete Idiot's Travel Guide to Planning Your Trip to Europe

The Unofficial Guide to Cruises

Frommer's®

Greece

by John S. Bowman,
Fran Wenograd Golden,
Sherry Marker, Mark Meagher
& Robert E. Meagher

MACMILLAN • USA

MACMILLAN TRAVEL USA

A Pearson Education Macmillan Company
1633 Broadway
New York, NY 10019

Find us online at **www.frommers.com**

Copyright © 1999 by Ahsuog, Inc.
Maps copyright © by Ahsuog, Inc.

ISBN 0-02-862608-7
ISSN 1089-6007

Editor: Leslie Shen
Special thanks to Matt Hannafin and Dan Glover
Production Editor: Suzanne Snyder
Photo Editor: Richard Fox
Design by Michele Laseau
Staff cartographers: Jonn Decamillis and Roberta Stockwell
Additional cartography by Mark Reilly
Front cover photo: Ia, Santorini
Back cover photo: Caryatids, Erechtheion, Athens
Page Creation by Carrie Allen, John Bitter, Jerry Cole, and Angel Perez

SPECIAL SALES

Bulk purchases (10+ copies) of Frommer's and selected Macmillan travel guides are available to corporations, organizations, mail-order catalogs, institutions, and charities at special discounts, and can be customized to suit individual needs. For more information write to Special Sales, Macmillan General Reference, 1633 Broadway, New York, NY 10019.

Manufactured in the United States of America

Contents

List of Maps

ABOUT THE AUTHORS

John S. Bowman has been a freelance writer and editor for more than 35 years. He specializes in nonfiction ranging from archaeology to zoology, baseball to biography. He first visited Greece in 1956 and has traveled and lived there over the years. He is the author of numerous guides to regions of Greece and is best known for his *Traveller's Guide to Greece*. He currently resides and works in Northampton, Massachusetts.

Fran Wenograd Golden is cruise editor at *Travel Weekly*, the travel trade newspaper, and is also author of *The Complete Idiot's Travel Guide to Cruise Vacations, Frommer's Alaska Cruises* (coauthored with Jerry Brown), and *TVacations* (Simon & Schuster, 1996). She lives north of Boston with her husband, Ed, and their two kids.

Sherry Marker majored in classical Greek at Harvard, studied archaeology at the American School of Classical Studies in Athens, and did graduate work in ancient history at the University of California at Berkeley. The author of a number of guides to Greece, she has also written for the *New York Times, Travel & Leisure,* and *Hampshire Life*. When not in Greece she lives in Massachusetts, where she teaches a writing seminar at Smith College.

Mark Meagher has passed many fine days exploring the Greek Islands in search of the perfect beach, the most venerable ruin, and the ideal supper. A resident of Boston, he is currently pursuing graduate studies in architecture. Mark also contributes to *Frommer's Ireland, Frommer's Ireland from $50 a Day, Frommer's Portable Dublin,* and *Frommer's Europe from $50 a Day*.

Robert E. Meagher is Professor of Humanities at Hampshire College, Amherst, Massachusetts, where he teaches ancient East Mediterranean history, literature, and religion. He is the author of more than a dozen books, plays, and translations.

An Invitation to the Reader

In researching this book, we discovered many wonderful places—hotels, restaurants, shops, and more. We're sure you'll find others. Please tell us about them, so we can share the information with your fellow travelers in upcoming editions. If you were disappointed with a recommendation, we'd love to know that, too. Please write to:

Frommer's Greece, 2nd Edition
Macmillan Travel
1633 Broadway
New York, NY 10019

An Additional Note

Please be advised that travel information is subject to change at any time—and this is especially true of prices. We therefore suggest that you write or call ahead for confirmation when making your travel plans. The authors, editors, and publisher cannot be held responsible for the experiences of readers while traveling. Your safety is important to us, however, so we encourage you to stay alert and be aware of your surroundings. Keep a close eye on cameras, purses, and wallets, all favorite targets of thieves and pickpockets.

What the Symbols Mean

✪ Frommer's Favorites

Our favorite places and experiences—outstanding for quality, value, or both.

The following abbreviations are used for credit cards:

AE	American Express	EURO	Eurocard
CB	Carte Blanche	JCB	Japan Credit Bank
DC	Diners Club	MC	MasterCard
DISC	Discover	V	Visa
ER	EnRoute		

Find Frommer's Online

Arthur Frommer's Budget Travel Online (www.frommers.com) offers more than 6,000 pages of up-to-the-minute travel information—including the latest bargains and candid, personal articles updated daily by Arthur Frommer himself. No other Web site offers such comprehensive and timely coverage of the world of travel.

The Best of Greece

From Santorini's caldera to the gray pinnacles of rock of the Meteora, Greece is spectacular. There aren't many places in the world where the forces of nature have come together with such dramatic results. Greece is, of course, the land of ancient sites and architectural treasures, the Acropolis in Athens, the Amphitheater of Epidaurus, and the reconstructed palace at Knossos.

It can be bewildering to plan your trip with so many options vying for your attention. Take us along and we'll do the work for you. We've traveled the country extensively, and chosen the very best that Greece has to offer. We've explored the archaeological sites, visited the museums, inspected the hotels, reviewed the tavernas and ouzeries, and scoped out the beaches. Here's what we consider to be the best of the best.

1 The Best Travel Experiences

- **Making Haste Slowly:** Give yourself time to sit in a seaside taverna and watch the fishing boats come and go. If you're visiting Greece in the spring, take the time to smell the flowers: the fields are covered with poppies and daisies. Even in Athens, you'll see hardy species growing through the cracks in concrete sidewalks—or better yet, visit Athens's ancient agora, which will be carpeted in a dazzling variety of wildflowers. See chapter 6.
- **Island-Hopping in the Cyclades:** Though the Cyclades are bound by unmistakable family resemblance, each island has its own unique personality. Distances between islands are small, making travel by ferry pleasant and logistically straightforward (at least in principle). The element of uncertainty inherent to ferry timetables and all island events is part of the experience, and your vacation will be much less stressful if you don't plan too much in advance and allow yourself to "go with the flow." See chapter 10.
- **Going to Extremes:** Persist against your body's and mind's signals that "this is pushing too far" and seek out some obscure church or monastery such as Moni Ayios Nikolaos outside Metsovo—to be rewarded by a moving encounter with the church and its caretaker. It can still happen—but you must overrule common sense! See chapter 14.

- **Leaving the Beaten Path:** You can still relive the age of discovery, even though all the main routes and major attractions are now well marked on any decent up-to-date map. At least once, if you have a car, take a secondary (or for that matter, tertiary!) road and make your own discoveries of landscape, villages, and activities. The back road from Monodendri to Papingo in the Zagori region is only one of many such described in this guide. See chapter 14.

2 The Best of Ancient Greece

- **The Acropolis** (Athens): No matter how many photographs you've seen, nothing can prepare you for watching the light turn the marble of the buildings, still standing after thousands of years, from honey to rose to deep red to stark white. If the crowds get you down, remember how crowded the Acropolis was during religious festivals in antiquity. See chapter 6.
- **Nemea** (Peloponnese): This gem of a site has it all: a beautifully restored stadium, a handsome museum, a romantic temple with three standing columns—and picnic tables where you can enjoy a quiet lunch. See chapter 8.
- **Olympia** (Peloponnese) **& Delphi** (Central Greece): Try to visit both Olympia, where the Olympic Games began, and Delphi, home of the Delphic Oracle. That's the only way you'll be able to decide whether you think Olympia, with its massive temples and shady groves of trees, or Delphi, perched on mountain slopes overlooking olive trees and the sea, is the most beautiful ancient site in Greece. See chapters 8 and 12.
- **Palace of Knossos** (Crete): A seemingly unending maze of rooms and levels and stairways and corridors and frescoed walls—the Minoan Palace of Knossos. It can be packed at peak hours, but it still exerts its power if you enter into the spirit of the labyrinth, where King Minos ruled over the richest and most powerful of Minoan cities and, according to legend, his daughter Ariadne helped Theseus kill the Minotaur and escape. See chapter 9.
- **Delos** (Cyclades): This temple city, on a tiny isle just 2 miles offshore of Mikonos, was considered by the ancient Greeks to be the spiritual center of the Cyclades and its holiest sanctuary. Although in ruins, much of this remarkable site still remains in testament to its former grandeur. From Mount Kinthos (really just a hill, but the island's highest point), you can see the whole archipelago on a clear day. The 3 hours allotted by excursion boats from Mikonos or Tinos are hardly sufficient to explore this vast archaeological treasure. See chapter 10.
- **Vergina** (Northern Greece): In the brilliantly designed museum here, you can peek into what may have been the tomb of Alexander the Great's father, Philip of Macedon, and see the more than 300 burial mounds that stretch for miles across the Macedonian plain. See chapter 16.

3 The Best of Byzantine Greece

- **Mistra** (Peloponnese): This Byzantine ghost town has streets lined with the remains of homes both humble and palatial, as well as some of the most beautiful churches in all Greece. If you have the energy, climb to the top of the defense walls for the superb view over the plain of Sparta. Try to visit in the spring, when Mistra is carpeted with wildflowers. See chapter 8.
- **Church of Panayia Kera** (Kritsa, Crete): If Byzantine art sometimes seems a bit formal and remote, this striking chapel in the foothills of eastern Crete

will reward you with its unexpected intimacy. The 14th- and 15th-century frescoes are not only stunning, but also depict all the familiar Biblical stories. See chapter 9.

- **The Churches of Thessaloniki** (Northern Greece): Thessaloniki's Byzantine churches are the finest not just in Greece, but in the entire world. From the tiny Osios David to the towering Ayios Dimitrios, these churches have mosaics and frescoes that give you an astonishing glimpse of the artistic grandeur of the mighty Byzantine empire. See chapter 16.
- **Nea Moni** (Hios, Northeastern Aegean): Once home to 1,000 monks, this 12th-century monastery high in the interior mountains of Hios is now quietly inhabited by one elderly but sprightly nun and two friendly monks—try to catch one of the excellent tours sometimes offered by the monks. The mosaics in the cathedral dome are works of extraordinary power and beauty; even in the half-obscurity of the nave they radiate a brilliant gold. Check out the small museum, and take some time to explore the extensive monastery grounds. See chapter 17.

4 The Best Beaches

- **Nafplion** (Peloponnese): After a vigorous and tiring day of sightseeing, this small municipal beach can seem like the best in Greece. Handy changing rooms and showers make this a great place for a quick break between exploring the ruins at Mycenae and heading off to take in a play at Epidaurus. See chapter 8.
- **Plaka** (Naxos, Cyclades): Naxos has the longest stretches of sea sand in the Cyclades, and Plaka is the most beautiful and pristine beach on the island. A 3-mile stretch of mostly undeveloped shoreline, you could easily imagine yourself here as Robinson Crusoe in his island isolation (bending the plot somewhat to include a few sunbathing Fridays). If you need abundant amenities and a more active social scene, you can always head north to Ayia Anna or Ayios Prokopios. See chapter 10.
- **Paradise** (Mikonos, Cyclades): Paradise is the quintessential party beach, known for wild revelry that continues through the night. An extensive complex built on the beach includes a bar, taverna, changing rooms, and souvenir shops. This is a place to see and be seen, a place to show off muscles laboriously acquired during the long winter months. Don't miss the opportunity to experience the pure, unrestrained hedonism on which Mikonos has built its international reputation. See chapter 10.
- **Grammata** (Siros, Cyclades): Grammata possesses all the elements of a vision of paradise. The small beach is enclosed by a lush oasis of palm trees at the outlet of a natural spring, sheltered and hidden by a rocky promontory extending into the bay. The beach is only accessible on foot or by boat, so it's rarely crowded. See chapter 10.
- **Lalaria Beach** (Skiathos, Sporades): This gleaming white pebble beach boasts vivid aquamarine water and white limestone cliffs, with natural arches cut into them by the elements. Lalaria is not nearly as popular nor accessible as Skiathos's famous Koukounaries, which is one of the reasons why it's still gorgeous and pristine. See chapter 13.
- **Megalo Seitani** (Samos, Northeastern Aegean): Megalo Seitani and its neighbor, Micro Seitani, are situated on the mountainous and remote northwest coast of Samos. There aren't any roads to this part of the island, so the only way to reach the beaches is a short boat ride or a rather long (and beautiful) hike. You won't regret taking the trouble, since both beaches are superb: Micro Seitani's crescent

of pebbles in a rocky cove, and Megalo Seitani's expanse of pristine sand. See chapter 17.

- **Vroulidia** (Hios, Northeastern Aegean): White sand, a cliff-rimmed cove, and a remote location at the southern tip of the island of Hios combine to make this one of the most exquisite small beaches in the Northeastern Aegean. The rocky coast conceals many cove beaches similar to this one, and it's rare for them to become crowded. See chapter 17.

5 The Best Scenic Villages & Towns

- **Monemvassia & Nafplion** (Peloponnese): Everyone says it, and for once, everyone is right: Nafplion is the loveliest town in the Peloponnese, and Monemvassia is the region's most spectacular village. Thanks to the speedy hydrofoils (Flying Dolphins), you visit both spots and decide for yourself which has the best cafes, castles, and sunsets. See chapter 8.

- **Chania** (Crete): Radiating from its handsome harbor and backdropped by the White Mountains, Chania has managed to hold on to much of its Venetian-Renaissance and later Turkish heritage. This allows you to wander the old town's narrow lanes, filled with a heady mix of colorful local culture, yet still enjoy its charming hotels, excellent restaurants, interesting shops, and swinging nightspots. See chapter 9.

- **Hora** (Folegandros, Cyclades): In this town huddled at the edge of a cliff, one square spills into the next, its green and blue paving slates outlined in brilliant white. On a steep hill overlooking the town is the looming form of Panayia, the church that holds an icon of the Virgin which is paraded through the streets of Hora with great ceremony and revelry each Easter Sunday. Mercifully free of vehicular traffic, Hora is one of the most beautiful and least spoiled villages in the Cyclades. See chapter 10.

- **Yialos** (Simi, Dodecanese): The entirety of Yialos, the main port of the tiny, rugged island of Simi, has been declared a protected architectural treasure, and for good reason. This pristine port with its extraodinary array of neoclassical mansions is a large part of why Simi is known as "the jewel of the Dodecanese." See chapter 11.

- **Skopelos Town** (Skopelos, Sporades): The amazingly well preserved Skopelos, a traditional whitewashed island port town, is adorned everywhere with pots of flowering plants. It has a rather sophisticated local life, several excellent restaurants, some good hotels, and plenty of interesting shopping. See chapter 13.

- **Metsovo** (Western Greece): Steep slopes, ever-green conifers, stone houses with slate and slanted roofs, stolid villagers in traditional clothing speaking a Latin-based language—if this is Thursday you must be in Switzerland. But no, it's Metsovo, in Epirus. Occasionally jammed with excursionists, this mountain town still comes through as an authentic locale, refreshing in the summer and invigorating in the winter ski season. See chapter 14.

- **Corfu Town** (Corfu, Ionian Islands): With its Esplanade framed by a 19th-century palace and the arcaded Liston, its old town a Venice-like warren of structures practically untouched for several centuries, its massive Venetian fortresses, and all this enclosing a lively population and constant visitors, here is urban Greece at its finest. See chapter 15.

- **Piryi & Mesta** (Hios, Northeastern Aegean): These two small towns, in the pastoral southern hills of Hios, are marvelous creations of the medieval imagination. Connected by their physical proximity and a shared history, each is quirkily unique and a delight to explore. In Piryi, every available surface is covered with elaborate geometric black-and-white decorations known as *Ksisti,* a technique that reaches extraordinary levels of virtuosity in the town square. Mesta has preserved its medieval urban fabric, and conceals two fine churches within its maze of narrow streets. See chapter 17.

6 The Best Islands

- **Hydra** (Saronic Gulf Islands): Old-timers keep waiting for Hydra, with its handsome stone mansions overlooking a picture-postcard harbor, to be "spoiled." After all, even before Mikonos and Santorini, Hydra was one of the first Greek islands to be "discovered." So far, so good: donkeys still outnumber motorcycles, and the day-trippers who blitz the appealing harborside shops leave at twilight. That means you can almost always find the table you want at one of Hydra's pleasant small restaurants. See chapter 7.
- **Crete:** Whether for its rugged mountains or its countless beaches, its ancient remains or its ultramodern hotels, its layered history or its intense people, Crete cannot be denied. It is not just a distinctive Greek island—it is a world unto itself. See chapter 9.
- **Santorini** (Cyclades): This is undoubtedly one of the most spectacular islands in the world. The streets of Fira and Ia are carved into the face of a high cliff, facing the circular caldera left by an ancient volcanic eruption and now filled with the deep blue waters of the Aegean. The site of Akrotiri offers a unique glimpse into life in a Minoan city, frozen in time by the eruption 3,600 years ago. Add to this the Fira nightlife scene, and you'll see why this is one of the most popular (and overcrowded) summer vacation spots in the Aegean. See chapter 10.
- **Siros** (Cyclades): This tiny island has it all: a vivacious, cosmopolitan capital town; thriving beach resorts along the west coast; and a starkly beautiful region of farming communities, archaeological remains, and extraordinary remote beaches to the north. Siros is also one of the centers of *rembetika,* a form of Greek traditional music with roots in Asia Minor; the *Fragosiriani,* a classic known throughout Greece, was composed by the Siriot Markos Vamvakaris, and you're sure to hear its simple and infectious rhythms many times during your stay here. See chapter 10.
- **Rhodes** (Dodecanese): The island of Rhodes has everything a visitor could want—dazzling ancient and medieval ruins, great food, spectacular beaches, and the hottest nightlife outside of Athens—the one drawback being that everyone knows it. See chapter 11.
- **Skyros** (Sporades): Winding roads and remote beaches, one main town and a few minor villages, some ancient legends and 20th-century tales: Skyros's charms remain perhaps the most elusive of the four Northern Sporades. But if these have left the island a bit difficult to access and still not overstocked with touristy amenities, Skyros also offers both a living local culture and some natural wildness. See chapter 13.
- **Corfu** (Ionian Islands): Lush vegetation, some still undeveloped interior and unspoiled coast, ancient sites and a 19th-century presence, a dash of Italy and a dose of the cosmopolitan, Corfu is a Greek island like no other. Tourism may be rampant, but Corfu's attractions have survived worse. See chapter 15.
- **Hios** (Northeastern Aegean): You'd think that an island with such gorgeous beaches, exquisite medieval towns, and remarkable scenery wouldn't remain a secret for long. Despite the qualities that attract a small group of devotees year

after year, Hios remains surprisingly quiet. If you like the idea of getting away from the tour buses, being alone on a beach to rival any in the Cyclades, and exploring towns that preserve the contours of medieval life, Hios is for you. Another benefit: The local hospitality hasn't worn thin here, as it has on many of the more heavily touristed islands. See chapter 17.

7 The Best Places to Get Away From It All

- **The National Gardens** (Athens): It's all too easy to overlook this oasis of calm and cool in the heart of Athens. If you explore, you'll discover shady benches, a small cafe, and lots of opportunities to enjoy watching Greek families out for a stroll. See chapter 6.
- **Folegandros** (Cyclades): Many visitors have passed the formidable Folegandros cliffs from the Santorini-Paros ferry, and glimpsed whitewashed Kastro walls perched 300 meters above the sea. The austere beauty of Hora, the fine beaches, and the great walking trails are no longer a secret, but if you arrive off-season, Folegandros still offers a restful retreat. Completely free from the commercialism that has engulfed so many Aegean isles, the only shopping here seems to involve milk, bread, and eggs. There's still no bank; the new addition this year is a taxi that travels up and down the island's only paved road. See chapter 10.
- **Sifnos** (Cyclades): Sifnos is an island of ravines, mountaintops, and pristine beaches. Despite its small size (a hardy walker can explore the entire island on foot), Sifnos has numerous attractive small towns which can be used as bases for your explorations. Apollonia, in the central hills, offers elegant small-town civility, with the added benefit of being the hub of an excellent public transportation system. Kastro, on its seaside rock, is the medieval locus of the island, while Platis Yialos is a quiet beach resort. Don't visit in August, when the island is mobbed with vacationing Athenians. See chapter 10.
- **Zagori & the Vikos Gorge** (Western Greece): If the 40-some tiny villages linked by roads lined with spectacular terrain are not enough, you can venture into at least a section of one of the most spectacular gorges in Europe. Greeks and some Europeans have long appreciated this undeveloped corner of northwestern Greece known as the Zagoria. See chapter 14.

8 The Best Museums

- **The National Archaeological Museum** (Athens): This stunning collection has it all: superb red and black figured vases, bronze statues, Mycenaean gold, marble reliefs of gods and goddesses, and the hauntingly beautiful frescoes from Akrotiri, the Minoan site on the island of Santorini. See chapter 6.
- **The Museum of Greek Popular Musical Instruments** (Athens): Life-size photos of musicians beside their actual instruments and recordings of traditional Greek music make this one of the country's most charming museums to visit. See chapter 6.
- **The Archaeological Museum of Iraklion** (Crete): Few museums in the world can boast of holding virtually all the important remains of a major culture. This museum's Minoan collection is just that, including superb frescoes from Knossos, elegant bronze and stone figurines, and exquisite gold jewelry. The museum also contains Neolithic, Archaic Greek, and Roman finds from throughout Crete. See chapter 9.

- **The Archaeological Museum of Chania** (Crete): Let's hear it for a truly engaging provincial museum, not one full of masterworks but rather of representative works from thousands of years, a collection that lets us see how most people probably experienced their worlds. All this in a former Italian-Renaissance church that makes you feel you're in a special place. See chapter 9.
- **The Archaeological Museum of Thessaloniki** (Northern Greece): This is the place to go to see the gold star of Vergina, a profusion of delicate gold wreaths, and the gold box that may have held the bones of Philip of Macedon, father of Alexander the Great—all found in the royal tombs at and around Vergina. These Macedonian treasures tend to draw the crowds, so you may find that you have the rest of the collection—including fascinating exhibits on the early history of Thessaloniki—almost to yourself. See chapter 16.

9 The Best of Greece's Religious Treasures

- **Panayia Evanyelistria** (Tinos, Cyclades): The most revered Eastern Orthodox shrine in Greece, Evanyelistria is a neoclassical gem, filled to the gills with treasures. It's above the pleasant port of Tinos town, on one of the friendliest, most hospitable islands in Greece. See chapter 10.
- **Patmos** (Dodecanese): For 2 millennia, this small island of more than 300 churches has been hallowed ground, a place of pilgrimage. The Monastery of St. John the Divine and the Cave of the Apocalypse, where St. John is said to have dictated the Book of Revelation, are among the most revered and wondrous Byzantine treasures in the world. See chapter 11.
- **The Monasteries of the Meteora** (Central Greece): Even from a distance, the monasteries perched atop the weird rock formations and mini-mountains of the Meteora are one of the most awesome sights in Greece. Inside, the monasteries are equally impressive, with fine collections of manuscripts, frescoed chapels, shy monks, and chatty nuns. See chapter 12.
- **The Aslan Pasha Mosque & Cami at Ioannina** (Western Greece): Little of Greece's Turkish-Muslim phase has survived beyond the odd minaret, but here on the promontory of the walled quarter of Ioannina are the still-solid fine old mosque (now a museum), minaret, and school. Picturesque from afar, they speak up close of Ioannina's—and Greece's—diverse past. See chapter 14.
- **Mount Athos** (Northern Greece): Only men can visit the Holy Mountain, where monks still live in isolation in some of the most isolated—and beautiful—monasteries in all Greece. If you can't go to Athos itself, take heart: the boats from Ouranopolis that cruise around the peninsula offer excellent views of the rugged, pine-clad promontory and some of the monasteries. See chapter 16.

10 The Best Resorts & Hotels

- **Andromeda Hotel** (Athens; ☎ 01/643-7302): The city's only real "boutique" hotel, located on a wonderfully quiet side street, the classy Andromeda offers charm, comfort, and a reassuringly helpful staff. See chapter 5.
- **Malvasia** (Monemvasia, Peloponnese; ☎ 0732/62-223): Each room in the Malvasia is different, with some of the nicest overlooking the sea; all are tastefully furnished with hand-loomed rugs and antiques. A visit here gives the illusion of staying in the home of wealthy Greek friends of enormous taste—who just happen to be away, but have left the staff behind to tend to your needs. See chapter 8.

- **Atlantis Hotel** (Iraklion, Crete; ☎ 081/229-103): There are many more luxurious hotels in Greece, but few can beat the Atlantis's urban attractions: a central location, modern facilities, and views over a busy harbor. You can swim in the pool, work out in the fitness center, send e-mail via your laptop, and then within minutes be enjoying a fine meal or visiting a museum. See chapter 9.
- **Doma** (Chania, Crete; ☎ 0821/51-772): A former neoclassical mansion east of downtown, the Doma has been converted into a comfortable and charming hotel, furnished with the proprietor's family heirlooms. Although not for those seeking the most modern luxuries, its charms appeal to many. See chapter 9.
- **Astra Apartments** (Santorini, Cyclades; ☎ 0286/23-641): This small hotel with handsomely appointed apartments looks like a miniature whitewashed village—and has spectacular views over Santorini's famous caldera. The sunsets here are not to be believed, the staff is incredibly helpful, and the village of Imerovigli itself offers an escape from the touristic madness that overwhelms the island each summer. See chapter 10.
- **Castro Hotel** (Folegandros, Cyclades; ☎ 0286/41-230): With some rooms perched directly over a 250-meter sea cliff, the simple Castro has one of the best locations in the Cyclades. Situated in a 12th-century Venetian castle, the hotel has lots of character, and a 1993 renovation added the necessary modern comforts. The Danassi family are gracious hosts, and Despo Danassi prepares a delicious breakfast. Come during the off-season to assure yourself one of the remarkable seaside rooms. See chapter 10.
- **Rodos Palace** (Rhodes, Dodecanese; ☎ 0241/25-222): The largest five-star hotel in Greece and possibly in the entire Mediterranean, this is truly a palace, decorated, in fact, by the famed designer of *Ben Hur* and *Quo Vadis.* Located in Iksia, just outside Rhodes city, it offers all the amenities imaginable, and the construction of a new family center was under way at press time. See chapter 11.
- **Hotel Afendoulis** (Kos, Dodecanese; ☎ 0242/25-321): This cozy, unpretentious hotel is a haven of hospitality and calm in Kos town. The only accommodations on a gracious residential street in the heart of Kos center, this family-run establishment offers guests first-class convenience and attention for budget prices. See chapter 11.
- **White Rocks Hotel & Bungalows** (Kefalonia, Ionian Islands; ☎ 0671/28-332): For those who appreciate understated elegance, a shady retreat from all that sunshine, a private beach, and quiet but attentive service, this hotel, located a couple of miles outside Argostoli, can be paradise. See chapter 15.
- **Daphne Hotel** (Samos, Northeastern Aegean; ☎ 0271/94-003): This small hotel is incised into a seaside hill on the steep and densely forested northern coast. It's unusual among new hotels in that it wasn't built for maximum occupancy—every room has the same spacious layout and the same beautiful view of the woods meeting the sea. The proximity to walking paths makes this a perfect base for hikers. See chapter 17.

11 The Best Restaurants

- **Vlassis** (Athens; ☎ 01/646-3060): This small restaurant with a very loyal following, ranging from prominent ambassadors to struggling artists, serves traditional (*paradisiako*) Greek cooking at its very best. A tempting choice if you only have 1 night in Athens—but be sure to make a reservation. See chapter 5.

- **Varoulko** (Piraeus; ☎ 01/411-2043): Everything here is seafood, and everything here is so good that many Athenians believe chef/owner Lefteris Lazarou has created not just the finest restaurant serving only seafood, but the finest restaurant in the greater Athens area. See chapter 5.
- **Taverna Klimataria** (Methoni, Peloponnese; ☎ 0723/31-544): If there's a better restaurant in the Peloponnese, we haven't found it. The Klimataria takes old familiar dishes like fried zucchini and eggplant salad and makes them taste fresh and new—and offers delicacies such as chicken in puff pastry that are unheard of in rural regional restaurants. The staff is congenial, the wine delicious, and eating under the stars in the vine-hung garden is everything that dining out in Greece should be. See chapter 8.
- **Nykterida** (Chania, Crete; ☎ 0821/64-215): We're not denying that the location may influence your tastebuds here, but the spectacular views from this restaurant high above Chania and Soudha Bay can definitely make you feel you're eating a meal like few others in Greece. See chapter 9.
- **Selene** (Santorini, Cyclades; ☎ 0286/22-249): One of the best restaurants on an island with lots of good places to eat, Selene just might be one of the finest restaurants in all Greece. The reason: Owners George and Evelyn Hatzyiannakis are constantly experimenting with local ingredients to turn out their own innovative versions of traditional dishes. Inside, the dining room is elegant, and the terrace has a wonderful view over the caldera. See chapter 10.
- **To Koutouki Tou Liberi** (Siros, Cyclades; ☎ 0281/85-580): Open only 2 days a week and devilishly difficult to find (even the local taxi drivers have a hard time), this restaurant is so popular that you may need to book a table 3 or 4 days in advance. Amazingly, it's worth the trouble—the food is excellent, the view is stunning, and you might even catch an impromptu traditional music session if you're willing to stay around until the early hours of the morning. See chapter 10.
- **Petrino** (Kos, Dodecanese; ☎ 0242/27-251): When royalty come to Kos, this is where they dine. Housed in an exquisitely restored, two-story, century-old stone (*petrino*) private residence, this is hands-down the most elegant taverna in Kos, with cuisine to match. This is what Greek home cooking would be if your mother were part divine. See chapter 11.
- **Venetian Well** (Corfu, Ionian Islands; ☎ 0661/44-761): Rather severe in its setting at the edge of a small enclosed square in Corfu town, with no attempt at the picturesque, this restaurant gets by on its more esoteric and international menu. It's for those seeking a break from the standard Greek scene. See chapter 15.

12 The Best Nightlife

- **Experiencing Theater Under the Stars** (Athens and Epidaurus, Peloponnese): If you can, take in a performance of whatever is on at the Herodes Atticus Theater in Athens or the theater at Epidaurus. You'll be sitting where people have sat for thousands of years to enjoy a play under Greece's magical night sky. See chapters 6 and 8.
- **Barhopping in Mikonos** (Cyclades): Mikonos isn't the only island town in Greece with nightlife that continues through the morning, but it was the first and still offers the most abundant, varied scene in the Aegean. Year-round, the

town's narrow, labyrinthine streets play host to a remarkably diverse crowd—Mikonos's unlimited ability to reinvent itself has assured it of continuous popularity. The spring and fall tend to be more sober and sophisticated, while the 3 months of summer are reserved for unrestrained revelry. See chapter 10.

- **Rhodes** (Dodecanese): From cafes to casinos, Rhodes has not only the reputation, but also the stuff to back it up. A good nightlife scene is ultimately a matter of who shows up—and this, too, is where Rhodes stands out. It's the place to be seen, and, if nobody seems to be looking, you can always watch. See chapter 11.

- **Skiathos Town** (Sporades): With as many as 50,000 foreigners packing this tiny island during the high season, the many nightspots in Skiathos town are often jammed with a mostly younger set. If you don't like the music at one club, just move acros the street. See chapter 13.

- **Corfu** (Ionian Islands): If often-raucous nightspots are what you look for on a holiday, Corfu offers probably the largest concentration in all Greece. Corfu town and its environs have the most, but there are many others at the beach resorts frequented by foreigners. Put simply, Corfu hosts a lot of music and dancing and drinking. See chapter 15.

13 The Best Natural Wonders

- **The Caves of Dirou** (Peloponnese): No one knows just how far these caves run into the seaside cliffs of Dirou in the Peloponnese's Mani peninsula. You can get some idea of how vast they are by taking a tour on one of the boats that explore this underground labyrinth. See chapter 8.

- **Samaria Gorge** (Crete): At 18 kilometers (11 miles) long, the Samaria is the longest gorge in Europe. But although its walls reach up to 500 meters and at one point are only 2 meters apart, it's not the physical dimensions that attract thousands each year. For that, you can credit the wildflowers, the cold stream, and the whole experience of making your way from the heart of Crete to its coast. See chapter 9.

- **The Santorini Caldera** (Cyclades): As you approach Santorini by ferry, the whitewashed clifftop villages of Ia and Fira resemble at first a new dusting of mountain snow. Then the ferry enters the caldera, the cliff walls rise steeply on either side, and you're suddenly enclosed in a fantastic bowl whose sides are formed of red, yellow, and ochre rock, and whose surface is the shimmering blue Aegean. Some 3,600 years ago, the center of the island was blown away in a colossal volcanic eruption, leaving behind a roughly circular depression in the sea floor and the crescent-shaped sliver of rock known as Santorini. The best places to view the caldera are the walking path between Fira and Ia, or the clifftop streets in either of these two towns. See chapter 10.

- **Vikos Gorge** (Western Greece): With its wooded slopes, often taxing terrain, and rugged riverbed, the Vikos Gorge in Epirus is in many ways at least as impressive as the far better known Samaria Gorge of Crete. Its remoteness means that it is also far less frequented—and that much more of a wilderness challenge. See chapter 14.

Getting to Know Greece 2

by Robert E. Meagher

In Greece, you will inevitably lose track of time—and not just what day it is. The timelessness of Greece's mountaintops and beaches, its natural and constructed temples, its glistening waters and slow sunsets bring a cleansing confusion of past and present, a delightful disorientation, even before your first glass of *retsina* (Greek wine). Greece—defined by seas and mountains and a translucent sky—is a land of vistas, a place of spectacle.

That said, it is easy to overlook something you are not prepared to see. One of the oldest and greatest of the Greek philosophers, Heraclitus, known even in his own day as "the obscure," once pointed out that "Reality likes to hide." So does much of Greece. And so the aim of what follows in this chapter is both to excite the imagination and to guide the eyes. Think of it as a collection of trail notes—things to keep in mind and to look for as you make your own way around Greece.

1 The Regions in Brief

Greece is a land of sea and mountains. Over a fifth of the Greek land mass is comprised of islands, numbering several thousand if you count every floating crag—and nowhere in Greece will you find yourself more than 96 kilometers (60 miles) from the sea. It should come as no surprise that the sea molds the Greek imagination, as well as its history.

Mainland Greece, meanwhile, is a great vertebrate, with the Pindos range reaching from north to south, and continuing, like a tail, through the Peloponnese. The highest of its peaks is Mount Olympus, the seat of the gods, nearly 10,000 feet above sea level. Eighty percent of the Greek mainland is mountainous, which you will rapidly discover whether you make your way on foot or on wheels.

ATHENS Whether you're arriving by sea or air, chances are you'll be debarking in Athens. The city is not always pleasant and is sometimes exhausting, yet it's simply invaluable. Its **archaeological sites** and its **museums** alone warrant a couple of days of exploration. Between visits to the sites, a stroll in the **National Garden** will prove reviving. Then, after dark as the city cools, the old city streets of the **Plaka** provide atmospheric strolling, shopping, and informal dining, while the square and lanes of **Kolonaki** provide an upscale version of the same. **Piraeus,** as in antiquity, serves as the port of Athens and the jumping-off point to most of the islands.

reece

0 — 25 mi
0 — 25 km

FORMER YUGOSLAV REPUBLIC OF MACEDONIA

Adriatic Sea

ALBANIA

Kilkis

Giannitsa **MACEDONIA**

Edessa

Pella Thessaloniki

Kastoria Vergina

Kozani

Dion

ZAGORI **Mt. Olympus**

Kalpaki

Metsovo Elassona

Meteora (Kalambaka)

Ioannina

Igoumenitsou Trikkala Larissa

Corfu **EPIRUS** *Lake Pamvotis* **THESSALY** *Pelion Peninsula*

Karditsa

Paxos Volos

Arta

Praveza *Skiathos*

Karpenissi Loutra Edipsou

Vonitsa Lamia

Lefkada Agrinio **CENTRAL GREECE** **Mt. Parnassus**

Astakos Messolongi Delphi Livadia

Kefalonia *Ithaka*

Patras Thebes

Ionian Sea Megara

IONIAN ISLANDS Kyllini **PELOPONNESE** Corinth

Zakinthos **SARONIC GULF ISLANDS**

Pirgos Olympia Mycenae

Argos Nafplion

Tripoli

Andritsena Epidaurus

Mediterranean Sea Megalopolis

Mistra Sparta

Kalamata

Pilos

Githio

Areopolis Monemvassia

CRETE

Sea of Crete

Chania *Kythira*

Rethymnon Ayios Nikolaos

Iraklion

Ayia Galini Ierapetra

BULGARIA

Black Sea

THRACE

Serres

Drama

Xanthi

Komotini

TURKEY

Kavala

Alexandroupolis

Sea of Marmara

Stratoni

Thasos

Samothraki

▲▲ Mt. Athos

Limnos

Aegean Sea

Lesvos

Alonissos

Skopelos

SPORADES

Skyros

NORTHEASTERN AEGEAN ISLANDS

TURKEY

Kimi

EVVIA

Hios

Izmir

Piraeus

Karystos

★ Athens

Sounion

Andros

Samos

Kea

Tinos

Mikonos

Siros

Patmos

Delos

Naxos

Serifos

Paros

Donoussa

Kalimnos

Antiparos

Sifnos

CYCLADES

Amorgos

Kos

Milos

Ios

Folegandros

Simi

Anafi

Santorini

DODECANESE

Rhodes

Legend

Mountain ▲▲

Karpathos

Athens is also a great base for day trips, whether to the temple of Poseidon at **Cape Sounion,** the forested slopes of **Mount Hymettus (Imittos),** the monastery of **Kaisariani (Kessariani),** the sanctuary of Artemis at **Brauron (Vravrona),** the Byzantine monastery of **Daphni,** the legendary plains of **Marathon,** or the ruins of **Eleusis,** place of ancient mysteries.

THE SARONIC GULF ISLANDS   Cupped between Attica and the Peloponnese, in the sheltering Saronic Gulf, these islands offer both proximity and retreat for the nearly four million Athenians who, like their visitors, long for calming waters and cooler breezes. The accessibility of these islands, on any given day or especially weekend in high season, can be their downfall. Choose carefully your day and island, or you may be part of the crowd you're trying to avoid.

Aegina, so near to Athens as to be a daily commute, is the most besieged and yet possesses its own character and charm. The main port town of Aegina is picturesque and pleasant, while across the island to the east, set atop a pine-crested hill, stands the remarkably preserved temple of Aphaia, a Doric gem. **Poros,** next in line proceeding south, is convenient both to Athens and to the Peloponnese. Its beaches and lively port are a real draw, and there's an ancient temple thrown in, scenically situated but mostly in a heap.

Still further to the south lies car-less **Hydra,** remarkable for its natural beauty and Italianate architecture. The port of Hydra has a lot to offer and knows it, all of which is reflected in the prices. It's a great place for pleasant strolls, views, and a swim. **Spetses,** the furthest of these islands from Athens, wins the getaway prize, with its exceptional beaches, comparatively lush interior, and lineup of noteworthy restaurants.

THE PELOPONNESE   Crossing the narrow isthmus—less than 4 miles across at its narrowest point—into the southern peninsula of Greece is a move you will never regret. Once an island, the Peloponnese retains a sense of remove from the north and from the rest of Greece. Its often barren landscape is virtually forested with stunning archaeological remains, each with a richly evocative past: **Mycenae,** the mountain citadel of Agamemnon; **Olympia,** birthplace of the Olympic Games; **Sparta,** home of Helen and Menelaus; the palace of Nestor at **Pylos;** the magnificent and active theater of **Epidaurus;** and the Bema at **Corinth,** where Paul addressed the Corinthians. The small but stately port of **Nafplion** provides a comfortable, convenient base from which to explore the surrounding sites.

At least two drives are worth going out of your way for. One is the spectacular coastal stretch from **Areopoli to Kalamata;** the other is the vertiginous climb and descent of the **Taygetos** mountains en route from Sparta to the monastic ghost city of **Mistra** and on to the western coastal town of Pylos. In fact, the entire three-fingered southern tip of the peninsula is unspoiled and splendid, with first-class destinations at **Monemvassia,** the **Mani,** the caves of **Dirou,** and the Venetian castles of **Koroni** and **Methoni.**

CRETE   The largest of the Greek islands, birthplace of the painter El Greco, possesses a landscape so diverse, concentrated, and enchanting that no description is likely to do it justice. Especially if you rent a car and do your own exploring, a week will pass like a day. More or less circling the island on the national highway (don't imagine an interstate) will take you to a ring of inviting ports like **Rethymnon, Chania, Ayios Nikolaos,** and **Iraklion,** the capital.

Venturing into the heartland of Crete—not far, since Crete's width ranges from 12 to 56 kilometers (7.5 to 35 miles)—you'll find the legendary palaces of the Minoans just as they once were, with a little imagination: **Knossos, Phaestos,** and

Ayia Triadha, to mention only a few. This is not to say that Crete is withou monasteries and Venetian ruins. It's Greece, after all. For the energetic, the **Gorge o Samaria** calls out, as does the sea.

When night falls, remember that Crete has been known for thousands of years for its wines, which complement nicely the fresh goat cheese and olives, all local and all part of Crete's spell.

THE CYCLADES The "Cyclades"—the "encirclers" or "circling islands"—have at their center the ancient spiritual, cultural, and commercial center of the Aegean, the vibrant island of **Delos.** Declared a sanctuary, where both birth and death were pro-hibited, Delos was well on its way to becoming uninhabited in ancient times. At the moment it's a very interesting pile of ruins, well worth a detour. At the other extreme is **Mikonos,** whose reputation as a sacred place is yet to be built, unless worship of beaches, clubs, and the sun counts.

Paros is the transport hub of the Cyclades, the to-and-from-place with its own reputation for windsurfing. From here you can get to **Tinos,** a modern holy place, home to perhaps the most revered of all Orthodox churches; **Naxos,** whose unspoiled forests and mountains lure hikers and campers; **Folegandros,** whose principal port is a beautiful haven for anyone craving a brief respite; and the Cycladic pièce de résistance, magical **Santorini,** to some the lost-and-found Atlantis, to others the here-and-now hot spot of the southern Aegean. Whether you prefer to scamper among ruins or bake on a beach, Santorini does not disappoint.

THE DODECANESE This string of islands, named "the 12" despite the fact that they number more than that, nearly embrace the Turkish shoreline. Except for Rhodes and Kos, all of the Dodecanese are deforested, bare bones exposed to sun and sea. But what bones! Far to the north lies **Patmos,** already in the 5th century nicknamed "the Jerusalem of the Aegean," a holy island where the Book of Revelation is said to have been penned and where the Monastery of St. John still dominates the island. Far to the south basks **Rhodes,** "the city of the Sun," with more than 300 days of sunshine per year. It's the most touristed of the islands, and for obvious reasons. Rhodes has it all: history and hysteria, ruins and resorts, knights and nightlife. There's even peace and quiet—we'll tell you where to find it.

In between these two lie an array of possibilities: from the uncompromised traditional charm of tiny **Simi** to the ruins and well-known beaches of **Kos.** The truth is that part of the popularity of the southern Dodecanese comes from its proximity to Rhodes—a simple matter of overflow for those who can't fit on or afford the most popular package-tour destination in Greece. Just remember that while "close" counts in horseshoes and hand grenades, it often doesn't when planning a holiday. *One other tip:* With Turkey so near, you may want to consider a side trip, quite easy to arrange.

CENTRAL GREECE Central Greece, for our purposes, stretches from the Corinth Canal to Mount Olympus. Its landscape is vastly diverse, from the fertile Boetian plains to the snowy peaks of **Parnassus** and **Olympus.** Enshrined here are the legendary battlegrounds of **Thermopylae** and **Chaironeia.**

Far from the chaos of battle, there is an ineffable stillness that has deep roots in Central Greece. The sanctuary of **Delphi,** especially at either sunset or sunrise, retains its mystery to this day. Then there are the otherworldly heights of **Meteora,** where anyone with vertigo, spiritual or otherwise, best not ascend. If you have a less austere retreat in mind, the lush, gentle slopes of **Pelion,** once roamed by centaurs, may suit. If, confronted with all of these choices, you can't decide what to do, it's best to start with Delphi, where authoritative advice has long been available.

THE SPORADES Whether by ferry or hydrofoil, the Sporades, strewn north and east of the island of Evvia (Euboea), are readily accessible from the mainland and offer verdant forest landscapes, golden-sand beaches, and crystalline waters. That's the good news. The bad news is that they are no secret. **Skiathos** is the most in demand with all that that implies. **Skopelos,** whose lovely port is one of the most striking in Greece, is more rugged and remote than Skiathos, with more trails and fewer nightclubs. Relatively far-off **Skyros** is well worth a visit, offering underwater fishing and diving, sandy beaches, and luminously clear waters. On top of that, it's almost a secret and, for the time being, a bargain.

WESTERN GREECE Northwestern Greece, or **Epirus,** is predominantly mountainous and mostly cut off by those mountains from the sea. You won't likely encounter many tourists here. Much of its appeal is to nature lovers and trekkers, for whom the **Vikos Gorge** and **Perama Cave** pose engaging challenges. Epirus is not, however, without its amenities and attractions.

Ioannina, on the shores of Lake Pamvotis, is the largest and most appealing city in the region; it is one of the few places in Greece where the long Muslim occupation is still manifestly visible. The traditional mountain village of **Metsovo,** perched several thousand feet up in the Pindos mountains, offers a number of local attractions and vista-ridden hiking.

Only 20 miles from Ioannina lie the ruins of one of the most famous of ancient shrines, the Oracle of Zeus at **Dodona,** where the voice of the great lord of Olympus was believed to speak through the rustling leaves of a sacred oak tree, though not the one currently planted there.

THE IONIAN ISLANDS Across centuries, these islands have been the apple of more than one empire's eye. Lush, temperate, blessed with ample rain and sun, and tended like an architectural garden, they are quite splendid. **Corfu,** the most noted and ornamented, is a gem, and is priced accordingly. **Ithaka** is as yet somewhat out of the tourist loop, but needs no introduction for readers of *The Odyssey.* With certain adjustments for the nearly three millennia that have elapsed, Homer's descriptions of the island still hold their own. If you can do without name recognition, **Kefalonia,** still relatively inconspicuous and unspoiled, has a lot to offer: picturesque traditional villages, steep rocks plunging into the sea, fine beaches, and excellent local wine.

THESSALONIKI & NORTHERN GREECE Just as it once was the urban understudy of Constantinople, **Thessaloniki** is modern Greece's second city. With less than 20% of Athens's population, however, it is not a close second. Even so, among Greece's major cities, it may be second to none in visual appeal and international flair. Among the city's many attractions are the legendary White Tower and its archaeological and Byzantine museums. As a home base, it offers comfortable proximity to many of Macedonia's major sites.

Macedonia is Greece's largest geographical region—rich in natural beauty, soaked in history, and mostly removed from the epicenters of the tourist explosion that, in places, has almost leveled the diverse traditions and cultures of Greece. Besides Thessaloniki, Macedon is also home to three major archaeological sites associated with Alexander and his father—**Pella, Vergina,** and **Dion**—as well as to the independent religious state of **Mount Athos.** This mountaintop theocracy, off-limits to women since the year 1060, may be viewed from cruise ships (departing from Thessaloniki) or visited with special permission.

THE NORTHEASTERN AEGEAN ISLANDS The four major islands comprising this group form Europe's sea border with the east. Beyond their strategic and thus richly historic location, they offer a taste of Greece that is less compromised by tourism and more deeply influenced by nearby Asia Minor and modern Turkey. **Samos,** unique among the islands in the extent to which it is covered with trees, also produces from its vineyards some excellent local wine. Its important archaeological sites and opportunities for outdoor activities make it a congenial and interesting destination, and it is an ideal point from which to enter and explore the northwestern Turkish coast. **Hios** is unspoiled and welcoming, offering isolated and quite spectacular beaches, as well as the stunning monastery of Nea Moni, and some of Greece's most striking village architecture. The remaining islands of **Lesvos** and **Limnos,** for various reasons not major tourist destinations, each have their ways of inviting and rewarding those who explore them.

2 History 101

Before asking *who* the Greeks were, it is important to notice *where* they were. Geography, after all, is often destiny. It has certainly been so for the Greeks. By situation and disposition, Greece faces both east and west, both north and south. Its roots and branches reach into three continents. In the ancient world, Greece was in the right place at the right time. It was, indeed, a "corner store," the inevitable meeting place of ancient cultures, European, African, and Asian. Temporally, the coming-of-age and flowering of ancient Greece coincided with arguably the most decisive turning point in human history.

The Greeks, however, have also been at the mercy of their strategic location, finding themselves over and over again in the wrong place at the wrong time. Trapped at the crossroads between east and west, they became a prize everyone else wanted, the battleground where foreigners from several continents fought their wars, wars in which Greeks not infrequently fought on both sides.

THE FIRST GREEK CIVILIZATION   At around 3,000 B.C., the first real flare of Greek civilization began when a wave of Anatolians brought to the islands and mainland a new skill (the working of bronze), a new language (a forefather to Greek), and with them the Aegean age. Their principal areas of settlement were the Cycladic Islands, the eastern shores of Central Greece and the Peloponnese, and Crete. Farmers surrounded by ocean, they became equally at home behind the plow and at the helm. The island civilizations' enchanting art and buried cities easily captivate the imagination. The rich palace culture of Crete, prosperous and unfortified, suggests that for a time the early Aegean farmers and seafarers had little to fear from their neighbors. Mother Nature, however, was another matter. Greece has

Dateline

- **40000 B.C.** The first traceable human incursions into Greece appear in several caves in the Louros Valley.
- **3000 B.C.** Waves of Anatolians introduce bronze-working and an early form of Greek to Crete, the Cyclades, and the mainland, beginning the Bronze Age.
- **1700 B.C.** A massive earthquake on Crete destroys the great Minoan palaces at Knossos and Phaestos. Undeterred, Minoans rebuild even more luxurious digs.
- **1500 B.C.** A volcanic eruption on Santorini (Thira)—one of the most violent on record—buries ancient Akrotiri and helps speed Minoan decline.
- **1400–1100 B.C.** The Mycenaean civilization rises and abruptly collapses, sending Greece into centuries of strife and cultural isolation.
- **800–600 B.C.** Glints of Greece's resurrection appear in the form of city-states. Homer and Hesiod initiate the first great age of Greek poetry.
- **525–485 B.C.** Aeschylus, Sophocles, and Euripides are

continues

born; Athens theater scene markedly improves.

- **490–480 B.C.** Xerxes, emperor of Persia, invades Greece, burning Athens to the ground. Greeks get revenge on land at Marathon and Plataea, and at sea near Salamis and Mycale.
- **431–404 B.C.** Peloponnesian War leads to the fall of Athens and its empire.
- **399 B.C.** Socrates is tried for heresy and sentenced to death. Given the chance to escape, he declines and drinks hemlock potion. Plato immortalizes him in the *Apology* and other philosophical dialogues.
- **338 B.C.** Battle of Chaironeia unifies Greece under Macedon rule.
- **336–323 B.C.** Alexander the Great establishes reign over a kingdom that stretches as far as Egypt and India.
- **323 B.C.** Worn out by a host of dissipations, Alexander dies in Babylon. His successors squabble amongst themselves, squandering great parts of his empire.
- **146 B.C.** After a series of wars, Rome crushes Greece, renaming the northern parts Macedonia, the southern and central parts Achaea.
- **1st & 2nd centuries A.D.** New Testament is written in Greek dialect, the *koine*. Local author John of Patmos gets the last word, in Revelation.
- **A.D. 328** Constantine the Great moves his capital to Byzantium.
- **476** Rome falls to the Goths; Greece is left to fester for 700 years.
- **1204** Fourth Crusade sacks Constantinople and divides up the empire.

continues

always been prey to great seismic events, few more dramatic than the earthquake triggered near Santorini around 1450 B.C., sinking part of the island, leveling Akrotiri, and giving birth to the myth of Atlantis.

But it took more than earthquakes to eclipse the Minoans. Newcomers from the north—the Achaeans or "blow-ins"—were already on their way, full of bold aggression and a few bright ideas. The tongue they spoke and wrote, linear B, was an early form of the Greek spoken today. Within 300 or 400 years, they had developed an extensive and powerful civilization named in retrospect after its supposed capital city, Mycenae, in the Argolis. The **Mycenaean** civilization—a loose confederation of warlords and clan chiefs—combined a form of early feudalism, commerce, and piracy to amass considerable wealth and clout in the world of the eastern Mediterranean. By the mid–second millennium, the Mycenaeans had colonized the Aegean coast of Anatolia and controlled Crete, whose culture they in part absorbed. Their trade connections, whether direct or indirect, extended as far as Britain and Scandinavia. Empire arguably entered the Greek imagination with the Mycenaeans and, like most acquired tastes, was very slow to leave.

After making its mark and wreaking more than its share of havoc in the world, the Mycenaean civilization suffered a mysterious dissolution. By 1100 B.C. most of its great centers had burned to the ground and been all but abandoned. Fortunately, beyond the ruins and artifacts it left behind, the Mycenaean world managed to inspire Greece's greatest poet, Homer, who preserved forever this lost world in his *Iliad* and *Odyssey.*

By the late 12th century B.C., the **Dorians** brought fresh and fierce blood, making the Peloponnese their stronghold and the Eurotas Valley their center. What followed, for several centuries, was a period of cultural isolation and hardship. By the 8th century, however, the Greeks were back on their feet and in their boats. Once again they reached out to the wider Mediterranean and Near Eastern world, founding new colonies and re-establishing old trade connections. Meanwhile, at home, without great upheaval, a revolution was taking place. Increasingly, the freeborn, landholding farmer was calling the shots. Village clusters grew into independent city-states, united in a common cult to their presiding deity who replaced the ancient king. The polis or city-state, which became the standard of Greek social organization, was comprised of a small land mass with a governmental, cultic, cultural, and commercial center. The polis was not a Greek invention. Like so many other ideas, it was something they borrowed, adapted, and brought to full fruition.

The **preclassical** or **archaic** period (800 to 500 B.C.) saw the emergence of hundreds of such city-states, each with its own face. The one common denominator of all Greeks, irrespective of city, was their language, which made them more or less comprehensible to each other. Even so, there was as yet no sense of a unifying government, religion, or race. Greece was a patchwork waiting to be sewn together.

THE CLASSICAL AGE   The classical age is synonymous with the emergence of **Athens** as the preeminent city-state in the Greek world. Peaking in the 5th century, the vision and achievements of this one insanely ambitious city conceived Western civilization. Whether in art or science, athletics or architecture, poetry or philosophy, Athens presided over the splendor that was classical Greece.

Athenian splendor, to be sure, had its dark side. The opportunities it offered were narrowly funneled to a minority of its population. Its radical democracy gave surprising power to the people, but "the people" meant only pure-blooded Athenian men—excluding women, slaves, and landed immigrants. Still more troubling was its foreign policy. After twice playing the crucial hand against Persian invaders, Athens created a permanent military alliance called the **Delian League,** whose members were eventually reduced to subject states. Its founding aim was to deter future Persian aggression, but it also served the convenient purpose of marginalizing Athens's greatest rivals, Corinth and Sparta. This play for power provoked Greece's first civil war, the so-called **Peloponnesian War,** whose scale and duration (431 to 404 B.C.) led to the complete collapse of Athens and its empire, something Greece's most formidable enemies had never come close to accomplishing.

One legacy of the Peloponnesian War was the revival of empire as a Greek aspiration. Sparta, Corinth, Thebes, and a resuscitated Athens were powerhouses in the scramble for domination, but neither one nor all of them proved a match for the armies of **Philip II of Macedon,** who at Chaironeia in 338 B.C. left no doubt who was king. The independent Greek city-state was at this point history. Bound by a common oath to the Macedonian royal house, the Greek people were of one mind and one

- **1453** Constantinople falls to Sultan Mehmet II, initiating more than 350 years of Turkish domination.
- **1571** Turkish fleet destroyed at Lepanto, undermining aura of invincibility.
- **1821–1829** Greeks fight War of Independence, enlisting Britain, Russia, and France as allies.
- **1833** Lacking royal blood of their own, Greeks crown Prince Otto of Bavaria as their first king.
- **1863–1913** Reign of George I sees Greece regain much of its lost territory.
- **1913** King George I is assassinated at Thessaloniki.
- **1917** Greece enters World War I aligned with Britain and France.
- **1919** Greece occupies Izmir; Mustafa Kemal (Atatürk) rises from ranks of military to stir Turkish nationalism.
- **1923** The Greco-Turkish War ends in disaster for Greece.
- **1924–1928** Greece declares itself a republic, but political upheaval leads to 11 military coups.
- **1936–1944** Dictator George Metaxas takes over, modeling his Greece on the examples of Mussolini and Hitler.
- **1940–1941** Italy invades Greece, followed by more determined German forces.
- **1944** Greece is liberated; civil war soon breaks out in Athens and the north.
- **1949** Civil war ends.
- **1952** Greek women win the right to vote.
- **1967** Operation Prometheus establishes military junta; long hair, miniskirts, and Euripides are banned.
- **1974** Turkey invades Cyprus; the junta collapses

continues

and a democratic republic is established.

■ **1981** Greece joins EC; PASOK victory brings Andreas Papandreou to power.

■ **1989** Papandreou government collapses under corruption charges.

■ **1993** After a 3-year hiatus, PASOK and Papandreou are victorious at the polls.

■ **1996** Papandreou resigns and is succeeded by Costas Simitis.

■ **1997** Athens is selected as the site for the 2004 Olympic Games.

will for the first time—and both belonged to Philip, who promised to pay back an ancient debt with the conquest of Persia.

THE HELLENISTIC EPOCH   Philip's promise was kept by his son, **Alexander,** who ascended to his assassinated father's throne in 336 B.C. Alexander— king at 20, conqueror of the Persian empire at 27, and dead at 33—is one of the world's barely believable legends. Like Achilles, he was to live gloriously and die young. But that is where the likeness ends, for the siege of Troy was a turkey shoot compared to the Asian campaigns of Alexander, which brought him south to Egypt and east to India, where his army convinced him to call it a day.

When, in 323 B.C., Alexander drank himself to death at Babylon, 20 years of chaos ensued as his generals fought over his empire. The Greek world was now stretched across the east Mediterranean and was neither confined to nor centered in territorial Greece. Alexandria in Egypt and Pergamon in Asia Minor far outshone any city in Greece as centers of learning and the arts. In these new international centers, the language was Greek while the culture was international.

ROMAN CONQUEST   Without a center, the empire of Alexander unraveled. By the close of the 3rd century B.C., Rome had emerged as the power to be reckoned with. Philip V of Macedon made his first crucial error in allying himself with Carthage, an enemy Rome had resolved to eliminate. Predictably, the Roman army, after defeating Carthage in 201 B.C., moved on to Macedonia. Unpredictably, the Roman commander Flamininus celebrated his victory over Philip by granting independence to the cities of Greece. The Greek cities, in turn, celebrated their new freedom by fighting among themselves and resisting Roman "protection," which they resented as an intrusion. Eventually, after a number of limited military engagements, Roman patience wore thin and Rome crushed Greece, annexing it to the ever-expanding empire. Under Roman occupation, Northern Greece became the province of Macedonia, and Central and Southern Greece the province of Achaea.

Everyone knows that Rome fell, but not until it had been divided. Diocletian began the process of partition in the late 3rd century. Hoping to shore up an unwieldy and threatened empire, he divided it in two, north and south. The imperial power was, in turn, divided four ways, between two emperors (*Augusti*), each with a designated successor (*Caesar*). Diocletian appointed himself the southern *Augustus* and remained in Rome, while his *Caesar*, Galerius, established his own court in Thessaloniki. Each of these decisions bore implications for the future, underlining the preeminence of the southern empire and suggesting that its capital might well move east. As it happened, Diocletian's fragile tetrarchy fell apart amidst civil war, from which Constantine eventually emerged in A.D. 324 as Diocletian's sole successor. Recently crowned and well-disposed to Christianity, Constantine moved his capital in A.D. 328 from Rome to the banks of the Bosporos, to the Greek city of Byzantium, which soon became known as Constantinopolis, "the city of Constantine." The reign of Byzantium had begun and would survive for over a millennium.

RULE BYZANTIUM   **Constantinople** sat atop Byzantium like a crown on a commoner's head. The emperor sacked his own empire to adorn his "Nova Roma," built like the old Rome on seven hills, a city of indescribable splendor dedicated in

A.D. 330 with 40 days of joyous riot and ritual. Seven years later, Constantine lay on his deathbed, his conversion complete, deciding to enter the next life as a Christian. When Rome took the sword from the Goths in A.D. 476, its fall was presumably all but inaudible within the secure walls of Constantinople.

Less than a century later, Muhammad was born in the Arabian desert city of Mecca. His birth was barely noted in Mecca much less in Constantinople, but in his name the walls of Constantinople would a thousand years later come down. In the meantime, Constantinople was the shining center of the Christian world, a unique fusion of the secular and the ecclesiastical.

For reasons more parochial than perceptive, the Byzantine chapter is at best abridged in most Western histories. The story of the Byzantine Empire is far too vast to be even encapsulated here. What is essential to note, however, is that from its Greco-Roman origins it became profoundly multiethnic, interacting with the Islamic Near East as well as the Latin West and becoming in one way or another entangled with regions as far-flung as Sicily, Cyprus, Egypt, Kievan Rus', Georgia, Bulgaria, Syria, and the Holy Land. The identification of "Greece" with Byzantium—the city and the empire—is complex and problematic. The tightest knot here is religion, not race. Byzantium, after all, was not only a political state but also the center of Christian Orthodoxy, whose baptismal waters ran thicker than blood.

THE ECLIPSE OF GREEK CIVILIZATION   The strategic position of Constantinople, as well as its power and wealth, made it a pole of attraction for foreign invaders. The most profound threat came from the **Turks,** who by the end of the 11th century were the controlling power in the east. This provoked the Latin West to intervene with a series of crusades, whose unproclaimed purpose was revealed by the crusaders' plundering of the Byzantine empire while en route to the Holy Land. Finally, in 1204, the Fourth Crusade besieged Constantinople. The Roman Catholic pope and the Orthodox Patriarch of Constantinople had excommunicated each other exactly 50 years earlier, creating a schism which made the sacking of Constantinople and the slaughter of its people a little less unthinkable.

Despite a Byzantine revival in the 13th and 14th centuries, and the brief respite given the Byzantines when Mongol attacks on Ottoman territory forced the sultan to lift his siege on Constantinople, the Turks' conquest of Greece was imminent. In the spring of 1452, a new sultan, Mehmet II, began construction of a massive fortress on the European side of the Bosporos, just north of the city walls. Mehmet cut off every route, by sea or land, to which Constantinople could look for relief, and marshaled 200,000 troops and an awesome array of artillery. It required no imagination to see how this would end.

The siege began in April 1452 and ended in less than two months, when the walls of Constantinople, perhaps the most formidable in the world, were breached and their defenders overwhelmed. Within 8 years of the fall of Constantinople, Mehmet was in complete control of the Greek world, a yoke that would not lighten or loosen for another 3½ centuries, during which time the tenacity of Hellenic memory was put to its ultimate test.

Meanwhile, the Greek people once again found themselves in the wrong place at the wrong time. Caught between the two greatest powers in the eastern Mediterranean—the Ottoman Empire and the Republic of Venice—the Greeks hosted one conflict after another, with the Greek shorelines and islands considered strategic prizes. The Turks had become as formidable on the sea as they were on land, at least until their dramatic defeat in October 1571, in one of the greatest naval battles of all time. There, in the narrow straits west of Corinth, offshore of Lepanto

(Nafpaktos), a combined Spanish and Venetian fleet under the command of Don John of Austria destroyed the Ottoman fleet. On one day, the Ottomans lost not only 25,000 men but also their reputation for invincibility. For Greeks, the outcome was more ambiguous, as they had fought on both sides.

On the mainland, Athens, Nafplion, Thebes, and other landmarks of a glorious Greek past became battlegrounds in which Greeks could only lose. In one such engagement, a Venetian cannonball struck a Turkish store of gunpowder on the acropolis, blowing the roof off of the Parthenon. Mercifully, the majority of Greeks now lived in Asia Minor and in Central and Northern Greece, which rarely saw combat. It fell to them, instead, to finance the sultan's wars with their taxes and to feed them with fresh recruits. Every 4 years, in fact, the Ottomans, until the mid-17th century, imposed on their Greek subjects the *devshirme,* the "children tax," in which a selection of Christian children were taken off to be converted to Islam and trained as an elite corps for the sultan's service, whether in the government bureaucracy or in the army.

While only Muslims could hold public office or positions of power in the empire, everyone else was free to practice the religion of their birth. In fact, the sultan commissioned the Greek Patriarch to administer the common affairs of his Christian subjects. Everyday Greek life, then, fell under the direct jurisdiction of Orthodox priests and primates, who conducted the schools, seminaries, and monasteries. This daily fact of life preserved the Byzantine fusion of the sacred and the secular, and meant that "Greek" remained all but synonymous with "Orthodox Christian." Measured against the atrocities and brutalities of European regimes during the same period, the subjects of the sultan fared no worse and perhaps better than their European counterparts. This is not to say that Greeks were content with their lot, nor that they had forgotten Constantine, still trapped in stone and waiting for resurrection.

A GREEK RESURGENCE   The revolutionary period may be traced to the close of the 17th century, when the Ottoman Empire began losing more battles than it won and thus displaying signs of its mortality. Within the empire, succession became a bloody, unpredictable affair. Soon the central Ottoman authority faced myriad regional and local rivals, managing their own and not the sultan's concerns. And, as the 18th century dawned and developed, revolution was in the air in America and Europe.

The Greeks knew that on their own, they would be no match for the Ottoman Empire, and so they looked around for powerful friends—Russians, British, French— to launch their cause. In addition, a formidable and enthusiastic Greek diaspora stretched from Moscow to Calcutta. In 1814, a band of Greek expatriates in the Russian city of Odessa founded the *Etairia Filike,* the "Friendly Society." This revolutionary society resolved, under the leadership of Alexander Ypsilantis, to strike at the Ottomans simultaneously in the Peloponnese and the Balkans. The fact that the Peloponnesians were not prepared for war and the Serbians not inclined posed, admittedly, a complication.

Not at all according to plan, the Friendly Society was upstaged by Ali Pasha, "the Lion of Janina," a Turkish governor who had become too big for his bloomers and provoked the sultan to war. Hoping that a distracted sultan would be a vulnerable sultan, Ypsilantis and his would-be army crossed the River Prut, dividing the Russian and the Ottoman empires. Only weeks later, in March 1821, Bishop Germanos of Patras, himself a member of the *Etairia Filike,* raised the standard of revolt over the monastery of Ayia Lavra, near Kalavrita (southeast of Patras), which still lays claim to being the first town liberated in the War of Independence. Meanwhile, the army liberation made its way across what is now Hungary. Ypsilantis, its commander, had been an officer in the Russian army; but against the sultan's Janissaries—an elite corps in which Greeks had served for centuries—he would have had to have been a magician. The outcome, in June 1821 at Dragasani (northwest of Bucharest), was simple slaughter, which is not to say that the Greeks lost. Revolution often starts with suicide, with blood made sacred, turning ordinary mayhem into a sacrifice filled with meaning.

The sacrifice at Dragasani provided the needed spark for revolution. One village after another burst into flames. Turks, who had for generations made their homes in the Peloponnese, ran for their lives. One by one the Turkish strongholds in the Peloponnese—all but Nafplion—fell to the Greek rebels, a glorious sight only from a very great distance. Thousands of Turkish men, women, and children were tortuously executed, while many Jews were crucified.

Many Greeks, with conflicting interests and loyalties, were caught in the middle— none more so than the Patriarch of Constantinople, whose excommunication of the rebels was not enough to placate the sultan, who had him hanged on Easter 1821. Similar prominent atrocities followed, as Greeks suspected or accused of rebellious leanings became open game. When the sultan, after dealing with Ali Pasha, finally took the gloves off and dispatched his armies into the Peloponnese, a betting man would have put his money on the Turks—and would have lost. Momentum is a mysterious force, and for now, it was on the Greeks' side.

Despite some setbacks, by 1826 the Turks had taken most of the Peloponnese and were laying siege to the Athenian acropolis. Without European assistance, the Greek cause was clearly lost. The reluctant great powers of the West—Britain, France, and Russia—proclaimed an independent Greek principality at the Treaty of London in 1827. After the allies arrived in force, they annihilated the combined Turkish and Egyptian fleets in Navarino Bay in October. Even after this stunning defeat, the Turks might have mounted further resistance to an independent Greek state had they not found themselves, the following year, at war with Russia. Meanwhile, the Greeks were learning that friendship with great powers comes at a price. With friends like Britain, France, and Russia, they barely needed enemies at all. For the next hundred years, they would be a pawn moved around a board whose edges they could barely envision.

After the allies had helped themselves to some of its choice portions, the lines of the new Greek free state were drawn to include the Peloponnese, Central Greece, and the Cyclades. Its 800,000 inhabitants represented less than a third of the ethnically Greek population, and its first appointed leader was Ioannis Kapodistrias, a former minister of the Tsar. One measure of his popularity was his assassination several years later in October 1831. Midway through the next year, in the Treaty of Constantinople, the signatory powers decided that Greece would not be a republic, but rather a protectorate with a hereditary monarchy. Its king, however, would not be Greek. Greeks, who had discarded monarchy more than 2,000 years earlier, were without royal blood of their own. After casting about the royal houses of Europe, the King of Bavaria offered to the people of Greece his 17-year-old son Otho, a Catholic. Greek gratitude was not overflowing.

All of Otho's instincts ran in the direction of autocracy, and he tried to rule by decree without a constitution. When the army joined antigovernment demonstrators in 1843, Otho reluctantly gave his people a conservative constitution, which he followed some of the time. Under the new constitution, Ioannis Kolettis rose to significance as prime minister and gave voice to an idea, a "Great Idea," which Otho

incapable of realizing. For this and a host of other reasons, including the fact that
e Athenian garrison had taken to the streets against him, Otho was persuaded to
odicate his throne in 1862 and to leave Greece in haste aboard a British naval vessel.

THE GREAT IDEA   Impoverished and humiliated, the Greek people had lost most
everything of any magnitude, except their imaginations. The "Great Idea" (Megali
Idea) was quite simply to reunite the Greek people, not by bringing them to Greece
but by bringing Greece to them. It was—though disguised and diminished—the old
idea of empire, a third Greek civilization "spanning two continents and five seas."
Within the imaginary boundaries drawn by the Great Idea, there lived, of course, not
just Greeks. In fact, in some regions, Greeks were in the minority. But so it had been
in the two previous Greek empires of Alexander and Constantine.

As its contribution to the Great Idea, Britain gave back the Ionian Islands in 1864.
In the same year, Greece received a new constitution, in theory further limiting the
powers of the king and extending franchise to a wider spectrum of Greeks. A major
voice across the next 2 decades was that of Kharilaos Trikoupis, who served seven
terms as prime minister. He implemented major economic and social reforms aimed
at both modernizing and Westernizing Greece. By 1897, Greece—overextended and
watching its major export (currants) plummet in price—fell into national bankruptcy.
Its brief period of reform, out of gas, was stopped in its tracks. The failure of a
revolution in Crete represented a disheartening setback to Greek aspirations, but the
ceding of Thessaly and Arta to Greece, after the Russian-Turkish War of 1877, was an
unexpected boon. Macedonia, an essential yet elusive element of the Great Idea,
remained an obsession and frustration, as it does today.

GREECE IN THE 20TH CENTURY   The new century was marked from the
beginning by upheaval, to which the Athenian garrison once again responded. They
established a Military League in May 1909, which amidst other reforms exiled the
political parties and placed in power a fresh new voice from Crete, Eleftherios
Venizelos, who dominated Greek politics for the next quarter of a century. Like
Trikoupis, Venizelos was a reformer. He was also and foremost a charismatic
expansionist, who soon led the Greeks—the first subject people of the Ottoman
Empire to have won their independence—into war against the Turks, this time with
astounding success. Greece emerged from the Balkan Wars (1912 to 1913) with their
territories increased by two-thirds. Modern Greece now included southern Epirus,
Macedonia, part of western Thrace, and the islands of Samos, Hios, and Crete, in
addition to the Peloponnese, Central Greece, and the Cyclades. These were great
gains, but not as great as the idea implanted in the Greek imagination. Millions of
Greeks were still unredeemed in the Ottoman Empire, and the dream of liberating
them—not by widening Greece's gates but by extending its roof—was very
much alive.

Before long, Europe was at war and Greece's new king, crowned Constantine XII,
favored neutrality (despite the fact that his brother-in-law was the kaiser), while
Venizelos argued for a military alliance with Britain, France, and Russia. The result
was a national schism, in which Venizelos established his own government in
Thessaloniki to rival that of the king's in Athens. Once again the protectors
intervened, this time to remove Constantine; Venizelos returned to Athens as prime
minister alongside a new and slightly more congenial king, Alexander. Venizelos soon
realized his intention to bring Greece into the war on the side of the Entente, and
Greece was amply rewarded for its loyalty. As a result of the postwar negotiations of
1919 and 1920, Greece not only added western and eastern Thrace (except for
Constantinople) and the islands of Imbros and Tenedos to its domain, but was also

authorized to occupy the coastal city of Smyrna (Izmir) and a large swathe of Ottoman Asia Minor. And so Greece—itself a protectorate—became a protector. Greece again occupied two continents and touched five seas.

Venizelos failed to anticipate, however, the new Turkish nationalism which the Greek occupation of Aegean Turkey would ignite. As the Greeks began to secure, with no little brutality, their military grip on coastal Turkey, Mustafa Kemal, Atatürk ("Father of the Turks"), was rallying a new nation to its feet. In 1920, the Turks announced their own state in defiance of Greece and its protectors. The Greek dream was about to become a nightmare. Venizelos was swept out of office, and in the winter of 1921, the Greeks decided to confront Atatürk and to invade Anatolia. Early victories lured the Greek forces deeper and deeper into central Turkey, where they far exceeded their own resources. When they were at their most vulnerable, the Greeks were overwhelmed by a fresh Turkish offensive and driven back to the sea. The Turks then seized Smyrna, massacred some 30,000 defenseless Greeks, and torched the city.

The Greek nation state underwent amputation at the 1923 Treaty of Lausanne, losing eastern Thrace, all territory in Asia Minor, as well as Imbros and Tenedos. More painful, of course, were the deportations and exchange of refugees called for by so vast a redrawing of boundaries. Roughly 1.3 million refugees spilled into Greece, increasing the population by 20%. The boundaries of mainland Greece were now more or less fixed and its population rendered remarkably homogeneous, at least in terms of religion—the decisive factor in determining who belonged in Greece and who did not.

Not surprisingly, Greece entered a period of profound turmoil after the Greco-Turkish War. Punctuated by a series of dictatorships and military coups (11 from 1924 to 1928), Greece lurched towards the republican constitution of 1927, under which an old legend, Eleftherios Venizelos, returned to power and accomplished a number of important domestic reforms and foreign-policy advances. The world economic crisis of the early 1930s translated into more political chaos for Greece, which by a less than manifest logic brought back King George, who called on General George Metaxas to restore order, which he did in his own way with the notorious "Regime of the Fourth of August 1936," modeled after those of his mentors, Mussolini and Hitler. The Greek parliament, to say the least, was out of session and would not reconvene until 1944.

The only good thing to be said of the 1930s was that they were nowhere near as hideous as the 1940s. Ironically, it was Metaxas's famous *"Ochi!"* ("No!") to Mussolini, whom he admired, that helped plunge Greece into World War II, a war Metaxas was trying desperately to sit out. The dramatic Greek victory over Italy's Alpine Division and the ensuing Greek offensive brought a moment of elation followed by years of horror. Provoked by the recent arrival of a British expeditionary force in Greece, Hitler invaded Greece on a massive scale in the spring of 1941. The fall of Greece was rapidly followed by that of Crete, where the Germans would continue to pay a high price for their victory.

There is no describing the sufferings of the Greek people under the wartime occupational forces of Germany, Italy, and Bulgaria. The winter famine of 1941 and 1942, which killed 100,000 people, the massacre of more than 1,400 Greeks at Kalavrita, and the relocation of over 50,000 Jews from Thessaloniki to Auschwitz provided a bitter taste of what the occupation meant. The Greeks made sure, for their part, that their occupiers never slept secure. Regrettably, the Greek resistance was deeply divided against itself. Its two main bodies—ELAS (the National Popular Liberation Army) and EAM (the National Liberation Front)—were both leftist and to a degree communist in their politics, while their right-wing rival, the far less significant EDES (National Greek Democratic League), spent its time undermining both the Germans and ELAS/EAM. Meanwhile, the king, who had fled at the first sign of personal risk, cautioned his people from afar not to resist the occupation. Finally, there were the collaborators, savagely resisting the resistors. Clearly it would take more than the removal of the Germans and their allies to bring peace to Greece.

It was Churchill, not the Greek people, who wanted King George reinstated after the liberation of Greece in 1944. Not surprisingly, Churchill prevailed. Greece had a new set of protectors and a fresh set of problems. Churchill and Stalin had already agreed that postwar Greece would fall under Britain's sphere of influence, which among other things meant that by December 1944, British troops and ELAS resistance fighters were warring against each other in the streets of Athens, leaving 11,000 dead in the Battle of Athens alone. And the ensuing civil war would be allowed to end only when it reached an acceptably anticommunist outcome. When Britain's ability to interfere was exhausted, the United States took its turn, testing the Truman Doctrine and its latest experimental weapon, napalm. There is no easy map through the Greek terror and chaos of the 5 years following World War II. The scars left by those years would confound the course of Greek events for decades.

POSTWAR GREECE   In the shambles that was Greece in 1950, a general election was held, with 44 parties vying for power. As postwar reconstruction got underway, some of the same foreign fists which had helped destroy the country were now opening wide and extending aid. The Dodecanese were ceded to Greece in 1948, comprising the final revision to today's national boundaries. Greece became a charter member of the United Nations in 1946, joined NATO in 1952, and secured associate status in the EC (European Community) in 1962, with the promise of full membership in 1984.

The 1960s brought radical change. After the political right, with considerable support from the United States, had more or less held the Greek stage for a decade (from 1952 to 1963), Georgios Papandreou's Center Union Party rose to power and undertook, with the release of all political prisoners, to close wounds still open since the civil war. Together with his son Andreas (formerly chair of the economics department at the University of California at Berkeley), whom he named minister of the economy, Papandreou also launched a program of ambitious reforms. Furthermore, Greece's new 23-year-old king, Constantine II, seemed congenial to Papandreou's government and its direction. Civil harmony and social progress appeared within reach, until Cyprus—an independent republic since 1959—erupted into violence. Papandreou, already doubtful whether Greece's alliance with the West was in its best interests, was provoked by the Cyprus problem to explore other options. It was when Papandreou attempted to confront and control the Greek military that Greece's demons were again released. The king backed the military, Papandreou resigned, and the king canceled elections. Greek politics were being conducted once more in the streets. In fact, the next regime would come rolling down those streets, in tanks.

The junta of April 21, 1967—code-named "Operation Prometheus"—brought Greece to new depths of repression and despair. "The Colonels," as they were known—Papadoulos, Pattakos, and Makarevzos, by name—were little else than self-serving nonentities, who ruled with a great deal of violence and with very few ideas. They banned any imagined challenge to their political and moral fundamentalism—from long hair to miniskirts to Euripides—and purged the country of every conceivable opponent, including the king. In fact, early on in the regime, one of the three colonels, Georgios Papadoulos, eclipsed the others, appropriating one ministry after another until he became a political one-man band. He in turn was remove Dimitrios Ioannides, the former head of the secret police, who made the regime more repressive. Sensing that he stood for nothing but fear, Ioannides hoped to ra. the Greek people behind him by confronting the Turks in Cyprus. The result was sti another Greek disaster and one more sign that the junta was a savage farce.

Four days after the Turkish invasion of Cyprus in 1974, former prime minister Constantine Karamanlis was summoned from exile in Paris to Athens to pick up the pieces of a shredded democracy. Within a year, the monarchy was abolished and Greece had a new constitution, establishing a democratic republic modeled after that of France. Since that time, Greece has solidified its democratic institutions and realized a new prosperity both as a sovereign state and as a member of the European Union.

3 A Legacy of Art & Architecture

DIGGING UP THE GREEK PAST Whether we dig or dive (being restless mariners, the Greeks lost many of their treasures to the sea) into the Greek past, what we find is mostly things and not words, a rubble of stones and pots. Few of the stones stand on one another as they once did, and most of the pots are broken. Even after vases are reconstructed and walls are rebuilt, they don't speak to us or tell us their stories. At best, they mumble. Like the Oracle at Dodona, whose voice spoke through the sacred oaks, the past speaks through the ruins of cities and wrecks of ships, but not without professional assistance, in our time via the increasingly accurate stories of archaeologists.

Another bridge to the prehistoric past is offered by ancient authors who wrote about what for them was already the remote past. Until recently, Homer's stories of Helen, Achilles, and Odysseus were assumed to be as much works of fantasy as the stories of Tolkien. Troy was assumed to be no more historical than Mirkwood. Likewise, Euripides's stories of human sacrifice, and Plato's accounts of lost Atlantis. Modern archaeology, however, has illuminated and certified the accounts of these and other ancient writers.

THE DIGGERS The most notorious instance of modern shovel being led by ancient book is surely that of **Heinrich Schliemann's** discovery of **Troy.** He wasn't entirely alone in thinking that Homer wrote about real times and real places, but he went further than anyone else to prove it. Schliemann was a man with a single obsession: to unearth Homer's Troy. At age 7 he swore to find Troy, and at 48 he stuck his shovel into the mound at **Hissarlik** in northwestern Turkey, where he eventually unearthed Homer's ancient city. To get there he had used *The Iliad* as a divining rod, leading him from text to stone, from poetry to prehistory.

From Troy, Schliemann went on to other Bronze Age sites straight from the pages of Homer. His excavations at **Mycenae, Tiryns,** and **Orchomenos**—the three cities called "golden" by Homer—were characterized by the same bold and impetuous enthusiasm, genius, and miscalculation. By the time of his death in 1890, the shape and stature of the Mycenaean world had risen from the pages of Homer to open sight.

What Schliemann was to the Mycenaean world, **Arthur Evans** became to the still earlier and more fantastic world of the Minoans. Evans's initial interest in **Crete** was linguistic, and he went there to test a theory of hieroglyphic interpretation. It was to have been a short stay. What he found astounded him and the rest of the world. At **Knossos,** Evans unearthed the all but unknown Minoan civilization, the legendary and splendorous kingdom of Minos. Homer had once again proved to be a man of his

. Indeed, the world of the late Bronze Age—the geographical and cultural
ext of *The Iliad* and *The Odyssey*—as it continues to emerge from excavations in
e Peloponnese, on Crete, and throughout the East Mediterranean, looks more and
ore as Homer described it.

THE SITES   The ancient Greeks were convinced that there are, here and there,
portals or openings into the next world, the world beyond this one. They even found
a few to their satisfaction, like **Eleusis, Dodona,** and **Delphi.** Entrances to the old
world, the world before this one, are still easier to find, especially in Greece. Nowhere
is the archaeological "water table" any higher. A little digging, almost anywhere, and
the past, the ancient past, is uncovered.

There is evidence of human habitation in mainland Greece as early as 40000 B.C.
Several caves in the **Louros River Valley** in Epirus have yielded deposits from the
middle and late Paleolithic period. Hunters and gatherers, however, traveling light, left
only faint traces behind. They drew only the flimsiest of lines between themselves and
nature, and characteristically broke camp in several weeks. By contrast, the settled
communities of the Neolithic period, though 6,000 to 8,000 years old, left enough
evidence behind to be read like a book. This is where the story of ancient Greece
begins, with the first agricultural settlements. The site at **Sesklo,** in Thessaly, has given
its name to a thriving, 6th to 5th millennium agricultural civilization, which found no
need for fortifications, produced fine pottery, and engaged in trade with nearby
islands. Mostly what we find here are private spaces, modest homes of mud brick on
stone foundations.

Only a thousand years later, at the nearby site of **Dimini,** we find signs that life had
changed, dramatically. Fortification walls, arranged in concentric rings, tell of social
division and turbulence. On the hill, a great house, whose plan points towards the later
megara or palaces of the Mycenaeans, indicates that already there was a human heap,
with a few on the top and most at the bottom. Here, in these stones, the focusing of
power, the accumulation of wealth, and the organization of society are recognizably
underway. From here it is only a matter of time and development to the feudal hilltop
citadels and palaces of the Bronze Age—**Mycenae, Athens,** and **Tiryns,** to mention a
few—and from there to the city-states and empires of the archaic and classical periods.
One chapter yields to another, and often one age will literally sit atop another.

The first question to ask of any site is "why here?" Before any people build, they
look around for a place to build—and their choice of site is revealing. Is the construction to be open or closed to its surroundings? Porous or defensible? What will it
reach for or look to, and on what will it turn its back? Before we concern ourselves
with whether a temple is of the Doric, Ionic, or Corinthian order, we need to
remember, for instance, that the word temple (*templum* in Latin, *hiera* in Greek) does
not refer to a building but to something sacred, a sacred place or object, to which the
building is a secondary response. Buildings only mark or point to temples. Nowhere
is this more clear than at **Delphi.** Delphi is first of all itself a *templum,* a sanctuary,
which accounts for all of the constructions located there. While the latter lie in ruins,
the power of the place endures. Thus the absence of temple buildings on **Minoan
Crete** does not mean that the Minoans were without temples. Their temples, their
sacred places or environs, were instead the surrounding mountaintops and caves—
notably **Mount Ida** and the **Dicteon Cave,** by which and in whose embrace they laid
their palaces, such as **Knossos** and **Phaestos.** The Mycenaeans, in contrast, occupied
and fortified the peaks, building mountaintop citadels like **Mycenae** and **Tiryns**
for their royalty. Still later, in the city-states of archaic and classical Greece, the
mountaintops were returned to the gods and goddesses, where they were housed in
royal fashion.

The next thing we notice at most every ancient site is the absence of private or domestic structures. We find stones—not brick or wood, but stones. After the Neolithic period, cut stones were mostly reserved for palaces, temples, public buildings, and fortifications. Private homes were made mostly of wood beams and sunbaked brick. For the most part, these vanished quickly, without a trace, like their inhabitants. What endured were the structures, the pillars, as it were, of society.

GODS & GODDESSES   The ancient Greeks were neither the first nor the last of peoples to acknowledge the existence and activity of forces, personal and impersonal, beyond their grasp and control. Wisdom and piety began, then as always, with knowing where to draw the line between what lay within human control and what lay beyond human control. No line, however, could be in more constant flux and dispute. Birth, death, agriculture, war, travel, commerce, weather, health, beauty, art, love—all of the moments and ingredients of life as we know it—were realms where humans and gods had their hands, as it were, in the same pot. One minute everything seemed to depend on human initiative and energy; the next minute human effort appeared to count for nothing. The controversial 5th-century philosopher Protagoras, a friend of the playwright Euripides, began his famous theological treatise with the confession that everything about the gods—whether or not they exist and what they may be like—outstrips human understanding, both because the subject is so obscure and because life is so short.

In the Greek imagination, then, the world was full of divine forces. Death, sleep, love, fate, memory, laughter, panic, rage, day, night, justice, victory—all of the timeless, elusive forces confronted by generation after generation of humans—were named and numbered among the gods and goddesses with whom the Greeks shared their universe. Understandably, in such a world, the cities, homes, roads, gardens, mountains, caves, forests, and countrysides of ancient Greece were thick with temples, altars, shrines, and consecrated precincts, where people left their offerings and petitions, hoping to be blessed with or spared the gods' interventions. To make these forces more familiar and approachable, the Greeks (like every other ancient people) imagined their gods to be somehow like themselves. They were male and female, young and old, beautiful and deformed, gracious and withholding, lustful and virginal, sweet and fierce.

Most of the myriad divine forces, named and nameless, familiar and faceless, in the Greek tradition can be found in the pages of the two great poets of archaic Greece, Hesiod and Homer—but the "plotlines" driving the poets' stories are dominated by one particular family of divinities, the Olympians, the household of Zeus and Hera ensconced on a great mountain in the northeast corner of Thessaly. Thanks, in part, to the stature and notoriety bestowed on them by their poets, these gods and goddesses were not only cast in leading roles in the theaters of Greece but were also made the focal point for the civic cults of most Greek states and, in sum, became household words.

As told by the ancient poets, the "Lives of the Olympians" is nothing less than a Greek soap opera. They are notoriously petty, quarrelsome, spiteful, vain, frivolous, and insensitive. They resemble nothing so much as a dysfunctional brood of spoiled children, children who have never been taught or made to experience the cost, the consequences, of their own choices and actions. And how could it be otherwise with the Olympians? Never made to pay the ultimate price of death, they cannot know the cost of anything. With *ichor*, not blood, in their veins, their wounds—however deep—heal overnight. Fed on *ambrosia* ("not mortal") and *nektar* ("overcoming death"), they cannot go hungry, much less perish. When life is endless, everything is reversible.

Principal Olympian Gods & Goddesses

Greek Name	Latin Name	Description
Zeus	Jupiter	Son of Kronos and Rhea, high god, ruler of Olympus. Thunderous sky god, wielding bolts of lightning. Patron-enforcer of the rites and laws of hospitality.
Hera	Juno	Daughter of Kronos and Rhea, queen of the sky. Sister and wife of Zeus. Patroness of marriage.
Demeter	Ceres	Daughter of Kronos and Rhea, sister of Hera and Zeus. Giver of grain and fecundity. Goddess of the mysteries of Eleusis.
Poseidon	Neptune	Son of Kronos and Rhea, brother of Zeus and Hera. Ruler of the seas. Earth-shaking god of earthquakes.
Hestia	Vesta	Daughter of Kronos and Rhea, sister of Hera and Zeus. Guardian of the hearth fire and of the home.
Hephaestos	Vulcan	Son of Hera, produced by her parthenogenetically. Lord of volcanoes and of fire. Himself a smith, the patron of crafts employing fire (metalworking and pottery).
Ares	Mars	Son of Zeus and Hera. The most hated of the gods. God of war and strife.
Hermes	Mercury	Son of Zeus and an Arcadian mountain nymph. Protector of thresholds and crossroads. Messenger-god, patron of commerce and eloquence. Companion-guide of souls en route to the underworld.
Apollo	Phoebus	Son of Zeus and Leto. Patron-god of the light of day, and of the creative genius of poetry and music. The god of divination and prophecy.
Artemis	Diana	Daughter of Zeus and Leto. Mistress of animals and of the hunt. Chaste guardian of young girls.
Athena	Minerva	Daughter of Zeus and Metis, born in full-armor from the head of Zeus. Patroness of wisdom and of war. Patron-goddess of the city-state of Athens.
Dionysos	Dionysus	Son of Zeus and Semele, born from the thigh of his father. God of revel, revelation, wine, and drama.
Aphrodite	Venus	Born from the bright sea foam off the coast of Cyprus. Fusion of Minoan tree goddess and Near Eastern goddess of love and war. Daughter of Zeus. Patroness of love.

GREEK THEATER Ancient Greek **tragedy,** a unique art form developed ɾ in the 6th and 5th centuries B.C., was essentially musical. Greek music, the of the Muses," encompassed what we know as poetry, dance, and music. Tɾ represented the fusion of all three—dramatic poetry, music, and dance—in a sɪ art form.

The **Greek theater** was quite literally a "seeing-place," a place of shared spectacɭ and insight, where—during two annual festivals—the citizens of Athens and their guests assembled in the Theater of Dionysos to see the latest original work of their master playwrights. Here, before the eyes of thousands, the great figures of myth and legend—Agamemnon, Helen, Herakles, and others—appeared in open sight and reenacted the stories which had shaped the Greek imagination. The ultimate spectacle of the Greek theater was and is humanity: humanity denied, deified, bestialized, defiled, and restored, which is why the works of Aeschylus, Sophocles, and Euripides play today with undiminished power and poignancy.

In ancient Greece, every city deserving the name had its theater, many of which even today host **festival productions** of the ancient masterworks. The most eminent of these is held every summer in the stunning theater at **Epidaurus.** There are also performances in the ancient theaters of Dodona, Thasos, and Phillipi, as well as the archaeological site at Eleusis, which has an annual "Aeschylia" in honor of the founder of Greek tragedy. Other summer arts festivals include theatrical performances, notably the Athens Festival, held annually in the striking Odeum of Herodes Atticus on the southwest slope of the Acropolis. The Lycabettus Theater also stages a variety of performances. Additionally, the Epirotika Festival in Ioannina, the Hippokrateia Festival on Kos, the Demetria Festival in Thessaloniki, the Aegean Festival on Skiathos, the Molyvos Festival on Lesvos, and the Lefkada Festival include theatrical performances. In September, the Ithaki Theater Festival recognizes the work of the new generation of playwrights.

4 A Taste of Greece

Greek food and drink tell a long story. The ancient Athenians are said to have invented the first *hors d'oeuvre* trolley, and most Greek dinners still start off with *mezedes,* a selection of hot and cold dishes served on small plates and shared from the center of the table. Spit-roasted mutton, goat, and pork were what Patroclus prepared for Achilles's late-night dinner party in *The Iliad,* and you'll still find them featured on Greek menus (though pork, much less boar, has declined in popularity across the millennia and been upstaged by chicken). You'll also find the freshly netted catch of the day, reminiscent of ancient Aegean murals from Santorini or Minoan Crete. Other ancient staples were olives, figs, barley, and almonds—crops still draping the Greek countryside. Take away olive oil from Greek cooks and you might as well cut off their hands.

The distinctive flavor of Greek cuisine—that mix of tastes likely to bring a Proustian flashback years later to some taverna in the Plaka—may be traced to oregano and lemons: oregano from the hillsides of Greece and lemons first hauled from South Asia at the urging of Empress Theodora. As the first lady of Byzantium, she used her imperial clout to encourage the importing of rice, lemons, and eggplant from India, all of which have helped condition the Greek palate. The soups and stews employing various pastas and tomato-based sauces are a Venetian contribution welcomed by Greek households, which until recently had no ovens. The Italians also brought with them a spree of Eastern spices—cinnamon, aniseed, pepper, cloves, and allspice—now well ensconced in the Greek diet. The Turks too left their mark with yogurt, the sent kabob, and an inky sweet syrup imagined to be coffee. Finally, a Greek likely to end with a flaky *filo* pastry—first brought from Persia in Byzantine —soaked in honey, of which the ancient poets sang. There it is: the history of ce on a plate.

DINING PRIMER   You probably already know about the common **taverna,** where you can usually find a number of grilled meats, including *souvlaki* (shish kebab to the Turks), commonly available in lamb, pork, and chicken, and *keftedes* (meatballs), usually fried, but on Hios they may turn out to be made of ground chickpeas and equally delicious. You may also be familiar with many of the other dishes, like the dependable Greek salad with feta cheese, the usually reliable *moussaka* (eggplant casserole, with lots of regional variation, often with minced meat), and *yemista* (tomatoes or green peppers filled with rice and sometimes minced meat), and the often bland but filling *pastitsio* (baked pasta).

Many tavernas still don't serve desserts, which are often very sweet, though there are those who like *baklava* (filo soaked in honey, which some Greeks insist is actually Turkish) or *halva* (a sort of nougat, sweeter yet and undeniably Turkish). Those with a serious sweet tooth may want to stop at a **zaharoplastion** (confectioner) or **patisserie,** as French bakeries are fairly common.

In some places, you'll find that the tavernas don't open for lunch and you may have to settle for a simpler **estiatorio,** where the menu may be not just limited, but nonexistent. Your few choices may all be on display in the kitchen or under steamed-over glass. Yes, it was made earlier and it's probably tepid—hot food is thought to be bad for the stomach—but it's likely to be tasty and even healthful. The oil it's swimming in is olive oil—no cholesterol there.

Another venue is the **ouzeri**—usually informal though not necessarily inexpensive—which serves ouzo, the clear anise-flavored national aperitif. Ouzo is especially intoxicating on an empty stomach—which is why ouzeries serve food, usually an assortment of *mezedes,* hearty appetizers eaten with bread: the common *tzatziki* (yogurt with cucumber and garlic), *taramosalata* (fish-roe dip), *skordalia* (hot garlic and beet dip), *melitzanosalata* (eggplant salad), *yigantes* (giant beans in tomato sauce), *dolmades* (stuffed grape leaves), grilled *kalamarakia* (squid), *oktapodi* (octopus), and *loukanika* (sausage).

There is also the **psarotaverna,** which specializes in fish and seafood. Fish is no longer abundant in Greek waters and trawling with nets is prohibited from mid-May through mid-October, so prices can sometimes be exorbitant. Often you'll have to settle for the smaller fish, such as *barbounia,* which are delicious if not overcooked. Ask locals to recommend a place for a fish dinner, always choose your own fish—in reputable places you shouldn't have to insist—and try to make sure it isn't switched on you.

Fast food is fast becoming common, especially pizza, which can be okay but rarely good. Many young Greeks seem to subsist on *gyros* (thin slices of meat slowly roasted on a vertical spit, sliced off, and served in pita bread). Here's a tip: if the spindle of meat is "skinny" in the morning, you should guess it isn't fresh and pass it by.

Insider Tip

Most restaurants, even very good restaurants, have no objection to meals comprised of multiple appetizers or mezedes, which is both the most interesting and the most economical way of putting a meal together.

Tips on Tipping

The rules for tipping continue to perplex many visitors to Greece—especially in restaurants and cafes. Until the early 1990s, menus in Greek restaurants and cafes usually had two columns—one for the price of the item, the other for its price with the mandatory service/tip included: it was the latter that you always paid. This practice has been abolished, and all you see now is one price. This price now includes a **service charge** (as well as the VAT tax and the local city tax). Although some menus clearly disclose the service charge, many neglect to make it clear. Effectively a tip, the charge is usually 13%. In addition, it remains a tradition to round off, either by telling the waiter to keep the change, or if the change is too much, giving him (or her) some reasonable extra. (A total tip of 15% is a generally acceptable compromise.)

It also used to be the practice in Greek restaurants that a "water boy" serviced your table separately from the main waiter, usually setting and clearing the table as well as providing fresh water. This practice has also pretty much disappeared—you're lucky if anyone brings water!—but if there is an assistant waiter, it is still the custom to leave a couple of hundred drachmas on the table.

A few other warnings: Much of the squid served in Greece is frozen and many restaurants serve dreadful *keftedes, taramosalata,* and *melitzanasalata* made with more bread than any other ingredient. That's the bad news. The good news is that the bad news leaves you free to order things you may not have had before—grilled green or red peppers or a tasty snack of *kokoretsia* (grilled entrails)—or something you probably have had (Greek olives), but never with such variety and pizzazz.

To avoid the ubiquitous favorites-for-foreigners, you may prefer to indicate to your waiter that you'd like to have a look at the food display case, often positioned just outside the kitchen, and then indicate what you'd like to order. Many restaurants are perfectly happy to have you take a look in the kitchen itself, but it's not a good idea to do this without checking first. Not surprisingly, you'll get the best value for your money, and the tastiest food, at establishments serving a predominantly Greek, rather than a transient-tourist, clientele.

When it's not being used as filler, fresh Greek bread is generally tasty, substantial, nutritious, and inexpensive. If you're buying bread at a bakery, ask for *mavro somi* (black bread). It's almost always better than the more bland white stuff. An exception is the white bread in the *koulouria* (pretzel-like rolls covered with sesame seeds); you'll see Greeks buying them on their way to work in the morning, from street vendors carrying wooden trays of these bracelet-shaped snacks.

One of the most reliable of snacks is the ubiquitous *tiropita* (cheese pie), usually made with feta, though there are endless variations. On Naxos, the tiropita may look like the usual flaky round pastry but contain the excellent local cheese, *graviera.* In Metsovo it may resemble cornbread and contain leeks and *metsovella,* a mild local cheese made from sheep milk. On Alonissos, the tiropita may contain the usual feta but be rolled in a big spiral and deep-fried. A close relative to the tiropita is *spanokopita* (spinach pie), which is also prepared in a variety of ways.

MEALS   Breakfast is not an important meal to the Greeks. In the cities, you'll see people grabbing a *koulouri* (pretzel-like roll) as they hurry to work. Most hotels will serve a continental breakfast of bread or rolls with butter and jam, coffee and usually juice (often fresh), and occasionally yogurt. Sometimes an English breakfast will be offered at extra cost. Better hotels will usually serve an American buffet with eggs, bacon, cheese, yogurt, and fresh fruit.

Lunch is typically a heavier meal in Greece than it is in most English-speaking countries, and most Greeks still take a siesta afterwards. Keep siesta hours, about 2 to 5pm, in mind when planning your own day, especially in more provincial destinations. (Even in Athens you should be considerate about contacting friends or acquaintances at home during these hours.)

Dinner is often an all-evening affair for Greeks, starting with mezedes at 7 or 8pm, with the main meal itself as late as 11pm. (You might consider a snack before joining Greek friends in their long evening meal.)

IN THE GLASS   There's also history in the glass. Until classical times, most Greeks drank water at their meals and broke out the wine only for special occasions. Today you'll find both, side by side. The wines for which ancient Greeks were most famous—the wines of Hios and Lesvos—were sweet and thick, almost a sticky paste, requiring serious dilution of up to 20 parts water to 1 part wine, though Alexander the Great is said to have taken his wine "neat" until it killed him. A fine or not so fine Tokay might today come closest to the legendary wines of the Aegean Islands.

Today the most characteristic Greek wine is *retsina* or resinated wine. It is definitely an acquired taste and possibly an addictive one, as you will find yourself years later longing for Greece and a glass of retsina, all in the same breath. At first gulp, however, it's a bit like drinking your Christmas tree. The ancient Greeks were big on adding herbs and spices to their wine, but they threw in pine pitch mostly to wines they considered otherwise undrinkable. Draw your own conclusions. Most every village makes its own home-brewed retsina of which they are fiercely proud. If you prefer a more canonized blend, we recommend Kourtaki, available throughout Greece as well as overseas, in case you learn to crave the resinated cask. Otherwise, ask for *krasi*—Greek wine without the resin—of which there are many.

All of the controlled appellations of origin in Greece (identified by a blue banderole), however, are liqueur wines, such as the Mavrodaphne of Kefalonia or the Muscat of Limnos. Beyond these, 20 areas throughout Greece boast appellations of origin of superior quality (identified by a red banderole), including dry reds from western Macedonia and Crete, and dry whites from Attica, Patras, Crete, and several islands. Local table wines can be full of surprises. Finally, what might be called the Greek national drink is *ouzo,* an 80- to 100-proof anise-flavored aperitif, served with water or ice, for which you can always substitute a glass of Metaxa, which calls itself "the Greek spirit."

5 Recommended Books & Films

BOOKS   Let's begin in the beginning, with the man himself. **Homer,** though reputedly blind, will open your eyes to a Greece that is timeless. *The Iliad* and *The Odyssey* remain *the* imaginative gateways to Greece; and lest you have any doubts that Homer was describing the same landscape you'll be seeing, be sure to read, as a companion to the epics, John V. Luce's *Homer's Troy and Ithaca.*

For a glimpse into **ancient Greek history,** the men on the ground at the time are still the most exciting. *The History* of Herodotus and Thucydides's *Peloponnesian War* hold their own as consummate storytelling and will place you firmly in classical Greece. If you plan on attending any of the country's dramatic festivals, you will want to become familiar in advance with the play(s) you will be seeing and even bring along your favorite translation. And to see Greek temples as you've never seen them before, you might consult Vincent Scully's classic, *The Earth, the Temple and the Gods.*

For the **Byzantine period,** dive into the historical works of Steven Runcim well as the writings of Ernst Kitzinger on Byzantine art. And, if you want an insi account of scandal and splendor in the court of Justinian, pick up *The Secret Hist* of Procopius, a Byzantine soap opera and then some. To put all this in some quic perspective, as well as to follow the full sweep of Greek history down to the present decade, *A Traveller's History of Greece,* by Boatswain and Nicolson, is pocket-sized and quite helpful.

Once into the **modern period,** Nikos Kazantzakis is the name to remember. His *Zorba the Greek* is a must, with *The Odyssey: A Modern Sequel* a close second. They are guaranteed to deliver you to Greece before your plane lands. After that, it's something of a free-for-all, with everyone shouting their own favorites. For sheer enchantment, we still smile every time we think of Gerald Durrell's *My Family and Other Animals,* about childhood on Corfu; and for beach reading, John Fowles's *The Magus* is spellbinding. In a far more serious vein, you will begin to grasp the pain still haunting the eyes of Greece's oldest citizens if you make your way through Nicholas Gage's *Eleni* or the much more recent *Corelli's Mandolin* by Louis de Bernières. Each in its own way is stunning.

FILMS   Of the countless films made in and about Greece, several come to mind, all more or less readily available on video. The films of Michael Cacoyannis—from his Euripides trilogy, including *Trojan Women* and *Iphigenia,* to his famed *Zorba the Greek*—are essential viewing. So too is Costa-Gavras's *Z,* a gripping political thriller inspired by the assassination of Grigorios Lambrakis in 1963. The film version of Gage's *Eleni* manages to be nearly as disturbing as the book. Finally, in the interest of self-knowledge as a tourist, and for a good laugh, you will want to find Irene Papas and Jacqueline Bisset teaming up to confront *High Season* on the island of Rhodes. And don't forget, 007 has "done" Greece (*For Your Eyes Only*), as did Gregory Peck in *The Guns of Navaronne.*

3 Planning a Trip to Greece

by John S. Bowman

Before any trip, most of us like to do a bit of advance planning. When should I go? What is this trip going to cost me? Will there be a special holiday when I visit? What special bits of practical advice might I appreciate? We'll answer these and other questions for you in this chapter.

1 Visitor Information & Entry Requirements

VISITOR INFORMATION

The **Greek National Tourist Organization** (GNTO, or EOT in Greece) has offices throughout the world that can provide you with information concerning all aspects of travel to and in Greece. Look for them at **www.areianet.gr/infoxenios** or contact one of the following GNTO offices:

UNITED STATES   Olympic Tower, 645 Fifth Ave., 5th Floor, New York, NY 10022 (☎ **212/421-5777;** fax 212/826-6940); 168 N. Michigan Ave., Suite 600, Chicago, IL 60601 (☎ **312/782-1084;** fax 312/782-1091); 611 W. Sixth St., Suite 2198, Los Angeles, CA 90017 (☎ **213/626-6696;** fax 213/489-9744).

In the U.S., you can call, fax, or send a self-addressed, stamped envelope to the **Overseas Citizens Emergency Center,** Department of State, Room 4811, Washington, DC 20520 (☎ **202/647-5225;** fax 202/647-3000), for Consular Information Sheets—travel advisories that include security problems and health risks. You can also get the latest information by contacting any U.S. embassy, consulate, or passport office.

AUSTRALIA & NEW ZEALAND   51 Pitt St., Sydney, NSW 2000 (☎ **02/241-1663;** fax 02/235-2174).

CANADA   1300 Bay St., Toronto, ON M5R 3K8 (☎ **416/968-2220;** fax 416/968-6533); 1233 Rue de la Montaigne, Suite 101, Montréal, QC H3G 1Z2 (☎ **514/871-1535;** fax 514/871-1498).

UNITED KINGDOM & IRELAND   4 Conduit St., London W1R ODJ (☎ **0171/734-5997;** fax 0171/287-1369).

ENTRY REQUIREMENTS

Citizens of Australia, Canada, New Zealand, South Africa, the United States, and most other countries are required to have a **valid passport,**

Greece on the Web

Anyone with access to the World Wide Web can obtain a fair amount of information about Greece. Sites are constantly being changed and added, but among the most useful have been:

- www.gtpnet.com
- www.ellada.com

There is also a very helpful free service provided by Matt Barrett in North Carolina: **www.greektravel.com.** Remember that none of these sources can necessarily be counted on for the most up-to-date, definitive, or complete information. We advise that you use all such computer searches as *supplements only,* then check out specific "facts" if you are going to base your travel plans on the information.

which is stamped upon entry and exit, for stays up to 90 days. All U.S. citizens, even infants, must have a valid passport, but Canadian children under 16 may travel without a passport if accompanied by either parent. Longer stays must be arranged with the **Bureau of Aliens,** Leoforos Alexandras 173, 11522 Athens (☎ 01/ 770-5711).

Citizens of the **United Kingdom** and other members of the **European Union** are required to have only a valid passport for entry into Greece, and it is no longer stamped upon entry; they may stay an unlimited period (although they should inquire at a Greek consulate or their embassy in Greece if they intend to stay for an extended period). Children under 16 from EU countries may travel without a passport if accompanied by either parent.

2 Money

The unit of currency in Greece is the **drachma** (*drachmi* in Greek), abbreviated "Dr," and the current exchange rate is about Dr300 (*drachmas*) per U.S. dollar or Dr460 per British pound. Coins come in denominations of Dr5, Dr10, Dr20, Dr50, and Dr100 (with old Dr1 and Dr2 coins still occasionally surfacing). Bills come in denominations of Dr50 (blue), Dr100 (red) (both being taken out of circulation), Dr500 (green), Dr1,000 (brown), Dr5,000 (mostly gray), and Dr10,000 (pinkish).

ATM NETWORKS   Automated teller machines are now almost as abundant in Greece as they are in all economically advanced countries.

Before singing the praises of Greek ATMs, *we must emphasize:* It is always possible that the one or two machines in your immediate locale may not be able to provide cash (incompatibility with your card, a mechanical malfunction, a labor strike, lack of cash due to a long holiday), so you are strongly advised to always have some secondary "fallback" source of cash (traveler's checks or your national currency).

If your bank credit or debit card also is affiliated with one of the major **international credit cards** (such as **MasterCard** or **Visa**), you should not have any trouble getting money in Greece; if in doubt, ask your bank or credit-card company if your card will be acceptable in Greece. For one thing, Greek ATMs usually allow for only a four-digit password; you must get advice from your bank as to how to deal with this if your regular password has more than four. Also note that the punch keys on the Greek ATMs do not use letters, so you must convert your password to numbers. The machines, in case you're wondering, all have some method of allowing you to conduct its operations in English.

The Greek Drachma

At this writing, $1 = Dr300 (or Dr10 = 30¢). This was the rate of exchange used to calculate the dollar values given in the table below and throughout this edition. The £1 at this same time was about Dr460; we give the exchange for that as another aid.

Note: International exchange rates fluctuate from time to time and may not be the same when you travel to Greece. Furthermore, there can be considerable variation in the rate depending on where you make the exchange. Therefore, this table should be used as a guide for approximate values only.

Dr	U.S.$	U.K.£	Dr	U.S.$	U.K.£
5	0.02	0.01	5,000	17	10.87
10	0.04	0.02	7,500	25	16.31
25	0.08	0.05	10,000	33	21.74
50	0.17	0.11	12,500	42	27.17
75	0.25	0.16	15,000	50	32.61
100	0.35	0.22	17,500	59	38.04
125	0.42	0.27	20,000	67	43.48
250	0.83	0.54	22,500	76	48.91
1,250	4.17	2.77	25,000	83	54.35
2,500	8.35	5.43			

Transaction fees are usually built into the exchange rate you get; in any case, exchange rates are usually based on the wholesale rates of the major banks, so you may actually save money by withdrawing larger sums and paying your bills in cash. (However, just as at home, there is usually some limit on how much you can withdraw in a day.) Furthermore, ATMs allow you to obtain cash at any hour of the day and to avoid the often long and slow lines in Greek banks.

In commercial centers, airports, all cites and larger towns, and most tourist centers, you will find at least a couple of machines accepting a wide range of cards; smaller towns will often have only one ATM—and it may not accept your card. The **Commercial Bank** (Emboriki Trapeza) services PLUS and Visa, **Credit Bank** (Trapeza Pisteos) accepts Visa and American Express, **National Bank** (Ethiniki Trapeza) takes Cirrus and MasterCard/Access. Those with access to the World Wide Web can check out ahead of time if the places they are heading to have ATMs: for Visa holders, **www.visa.com/cgi-bin/vee/main.html;** for MasterCard holders, **mastercard.com/atm.**

One final point: If you use your card as a credit card, you are borrowing money and presumably going to pay very high interest; it's better to use it as a debit card, because you are simply taking cash out of your account.

CURRENCY-EXCHANGE MACHINES   In the cities, larger towns, and centers of tourism, some banks also have currency-exchange machines, on the exterior of buildings and open 24 hours a day. You put in your own national currency, press the proper buttons, and get drachmas in exchange. However, they hold back a Dr500 ($1.70) fee for this service.

Commercial foreign-exchange offices are found mostly in Athens.

TRAVELER'S CHECKS   Traveler's checks are still probably the safest means of carrying money while traveling, and in Greece they are accepted by most hotels, some

What Things Cost in Athens	U.K. £	U.S. $
Taxi from airport to the city's center	4.35–7.00	7.00–10.00
Local telephone call	.04	.07
Double room at a B-class hotel	59.00	90.00
Double room, without bathroom, in a pension	16.00	25.00
Lunch for one at a taverna	7.00	10.00
Dinner for one, with wine, at a restaurant	12.00	18.00
Bottle of beer	1.10	1.70
Soda	.65	1.00
Cup of Greek coffee	.30–1.30	.50–$2.00
Roll of ASA 100 Kodacolor film, 36 exp.	3.25	5.00
Admission to National Archaeological Museum	4.35	7.00

restaurants, and some shops—although often with a small commission charged. Do not expect most Greek operations to cash your traveler's checks, however, unless you are paying for their services or goods. Most banks sell traveler's checks with a charge of 1% to 3%. If your bank charges more, you can call the check issuers about more competitive rates. Some organizations sell traveler's checks at reduced rates. (The Automobile Association of America sells American Express checks in several currencies without commission.)

American Express (☎ 800/221-7282 in the U.S. and Canada) is one of the largest and best known issuers of traveler's checks. American Express cardholders and members of AAA can obtain checks without paying a commission.

Citicorp (☎ 800/645-6556 in the U.S. and Canada; elsewhere, contact the local operator and ask to place a collect call to 813/623-1709 in the U.S.) also issues traveler's checks.

Thomas Cook (☎ 800/223-9920 in the U.S.; elsewhere, contact the local operator and ask to place a collect call to 609/987-7300 in the U.S.) traveler's checks, affiliated with MasterCard, are among the better known in Greece.

What Things Cost in Corfu	U.K. £	U.S. $
Taxi from airport to the city's center	3.25–5.00	5.00–8.00
Local telephone call	.04	.07
Double room at a B-class hotel	62.00	80.00
Double room, without bathroom, in a pension	20.00	30.00
Lunch for one at a taverna	7.00	10.00
Dinner for one, with wine, at a restaurant	13.00	20.00
Bottle of beer	1.10	1.70
Soda	.65	1.00
Cup of Greek coffee	.30–1.30	.50–2.00
Roll of ASA 100 Kodacolor film, 36 exp.	3.25	5.00
Admission to Archaeological Museum	1.70	2.70

Interpayment Services (☎ 800/221-2426 in the U.S. or Canada; 800/453-4284 from most places elsewhere) sells Visa checks issued by Barclays Bank and Bank of America.

Most British banks can issue their account holders a **Eurocheque** card and checkbook, which can be used at most cash machines and at Greek banks for an annual fee and a 2% charge.

CREDIT & CHARGE CARDS   Credit cards are accepted in the better hotels and shops, and they are effectively required for renting a car, but most restaurants and smaller hotels still do not accept them. (Indeed, be warned: Even many of the better restaurants in major cities do *not* accept credit.) Visa is the most widely accepted, and MasterCard is usually accepted where you see signs for Access or Eurocard. Diner's Club is also increasingly recognized. American Express is less frequently accepted because it charges a higher commission and is more protective of the cardholder in disagreements.

Most restaurants are reluctant to accept payment in plastic unless the bill is above a certain amount. Many small hotels will accept them only if you agree to pay their commission (usually about 6%); this seems fair enough, especially in some of the more out-of-the-way destinations where negotiating and receiving payment remains difficult and time-consuming.

EMERGENCY CASH   In an emergency, you can arrange to send money from home to a Greek bank. Telex transfers from the United Kingdom usually take at least 3 days and sometimes up to a week, with a charge of about 3%. Bank drafts are more expensive but potentially faster if you are in Athens. From Canada and the United States, money can be wired by **Western Union** (☎ 800/325-6000) or **American Express** (☎ 800/543-4080). In Greece, call Western Union in the United States (☎ 001-314/298-2313) to learn the location of an office; for American Express, go to an American Express agent or the Piraeus Bank. For a fee of 4% to 10% (depending on the sum involved), money can be available in minutes at a local Western Union or American Express office. And, of course, you can always borrow cash on your credit card from an ATM machine (so long as you are prepared to pay the high interest rate).

3 When to Go

THE WEATHER   Greece has a generally mild climate, though in the mountainous northern interior the winters are rather harsh and summers are brief. Southern Greece enjoys a relatively mild winter, with temperatures averaging around 55°F to 60°F (13°C to 16°C) in Athens. Summers are generally hot and dry, with daytime temperatures rising to 85°F to 95°F (30° to 35°C), usually cooled by prevailing north winds (the *meltemi*), especially on the islands, which usually cool appreciably in the evenings. And at some point in most summers, usually July, the temperature will rise to over 100°F (38°C).

The best time to visit is **late April to June,** when the wildflowers are blooming and before summer arrives in force with hordes of tourists, higher prices, overbooked facilities, and strained services. **Orthodox Easter**—close to but usually not exactly concurrent with Western Easter—is a particularly delightful time to visit, though reservations are necessary and service is not the best, as so many Greeks living abroad return for the holiday. After Easter, most of the island resorts crank up for the season. You might plan to visit the mainland attractions first, then see the islands.

Average Monthly Temperature & Precipitation

Month	Athens			Crete		
	ADT		RF	ADT		RF
	F°	C°	Inches	F°	C°	Inches
JANUARY	52	12	2.4	54	13	3.7
FEBRUARY	54	13	2.0	54	13	3.0
MARCH	58	15	1.3	57	14	1.6
APRIL	65	19	0.9	62	17	0.9
MAY	74	24	0.8	68	20	0.7
JUNE	86	30	0.2	74	24	0.1
JULY	92	33	0.1	78	26	0.0
AUGUST	92	33	0.2	78	26	0.1
SEPTEMBER	82	28	1.1	75	24	0.7
OCTOBER	72	23	2.0	69	21	1.7
NOVEMBER	63	18	2.9	63	18	2.7
DECEMBER	56	14	4.1	58	15	4.0

ADT = Average Daytime Temperature, RF = Rainfall

In **July and August,** the temperatures are too high for much but beach and water activities in overcrowded southern Greece and the islands. We strongly recommend you not go unless you have firm reservations and enjoy close encounters with masses of (sometimes raucous) Europeans and footloose students. The higher elevations remain cooler and less crowded, a plus for hikers, bikers, and those who don't demand sophisticated pleasures.

By **mid-September,** temperatures begin to fall and crowds thin, but it can still be hot. The weather remains generally calm and balmy well into October. In **mid-October,** ferry service is reduced and most facilities on the islands begin to close for the winter, but the cooler fall atmosphere makes Athens and the mainland all the more pleasant. If you have the time, visit the islands first, then return for a tour of the mainland archaeological sites.

Winter (say, Nov through Feb) is no time for fun in the sun, unless you want to join the Greeks for skiing and winter sports in the mountains—but some hotels and many good tavernas are open in the winter, prices are at their lowest, and the southern mainland and Crete are still inviting, especially for those interested in archaeology and authentic local culture.

HOLIDAYS   The legal national holidays of Greece are: **New Year's Day,** January 1; **Epiphany** (Baptism of Christ), January 6; **Clean Monday** (Kathari Deftera), day before Shrove Tuesday, 41 days before Easter (which in Greece may come in late Mar to late Apr; every few years it coincides with Easter Sunday in Western Christian lands); **Independence Day,** March 25; **Good Friday to Easter,** including Monday; **May Day** (Labor Day), May 1; **Whitmonday** (Holy Spirit Monday), day after Whitsunday (Pentecost), the 7th Sunday after Easter; **Assumption of the Virgin,** August 15; **Ochi Day,** October 28; **Christmas,** December 25 and 26.

On these holidays, government offices, banks, post offices, most stores, and many restaurants are closed; a few museums and attractions may remain open. Meanwhile, visitors are often included in the celebration. Consult the "Calendar of Events," below, if you are in the planning stage. If you are already in Greece, ask at your hotel or find one of the current English-language publications, such as the *Athens News,* the *Kathimerini* insert in the *International Herald Tribune,* the weekly brochure *Athens Today,* or the *Athenscope* section of the weekly *Hellenic Times.*

GREECE CALENDAR OF EVENTS

January

- **Feast of St. Basil** (Ayios Vassilios). St. Basil is the Greek equivalent of Santa Claus. Gifts are exchanged, and a special cake, *vassilopita,* is made with a coin in it; the person who gets the piece with the coin will have good luck. January 1.
- **Epiphany** (Baptism of Christ) is celebrated with the blessing of baptismal fonts and water. A priest may throw a cross into the harbor and young men will try to recover it; the finder wins a special blessing. Children, who have been kept good during Christmas with threats of the *kalikantzari* (goblins), are allowed on the 12th day to help chase them away. January 6.
- **Gynecocracy** (Gynaikokratia, Rule of Women) is celebrated in some villages in Thrace, when women take over the cafes and the men stay home and do the housework. January 8.

February

- ✪ **Carnival (Karnavali)** is celebrated with parades, marching bands, costumes, drinking, dancing, and more or less loosening of inhibition, depending on the locale. Some scholars say the name comes from the Latin for "farewell meat," while others hold that it comes from "car naval," the chariots celebrating the ancient sea god Poseidon (Saturn, to the Romans). The city of Patras shows its support of the latter theory with its famous chariot parade and wild Saturnalia, private parties and public celebrations. Masked revels are also widely held in Macedonia. On the island of Skyros, the pagan "Goat Dance" is performed, reminding us of the primitive Dionysiac nature of the festivities. Crete has its own colorful versions, while in the Ionian islands, festivities are more Italian. In Athens, people bop each other on the head with plastic hammers. Celebrations last the 3 weeks before the beginning of Lent.

March

- **Independence Day and the Feast of the Annunciation** are celebrated simultaneously with military parades, especially in Athens. The religious celebration is particularly important on the islands of Tinos and Hydra and in churches or monasteries named *Evanyelismos* ("Bringer of Good News") or *Evanyelistria* (the feminine form of the name). March 25.

April

- **Sound-and-light performances** begin on the Acropolis in Athens and the Old Town on Rhodes. Nightly to October.
- ✪ **Procession of St. Spyridon (Ayios Spyridon)** is held in Corfu town on Palm Sunday. (St. Spyridon's remains are also paraded through the streets of Corfu town on Holy Saturday, Aug 1, and the 1st Sun in Nov.)
- **Feast of St. George** (Ayios Yioryios), the patron saint of shepherds, is an important rural celebration with dancing and feasting. Arachova, near Delphi, is famous for its festivities. The island of Skyros also gives its patron saint a big party. April 23. (If the 23rd comes before Easter, the celebration is postponed until the Mon after Easter.)

May

- **May Day** is an important urban holiday when families have picnics in the country and pick wildflowers, which are woven into wreaths and hung from balconies and over doorways. Labor Day is still celebrated by Greek Communists and socialists as a working-class holiday. May 1.

Holy Week Celebrations

Orthodox Easter, a time of extraordinary festivities in Greece, usually falls one more weeks after Easter in the West—inquire ahead! The Good Friday exodus from Athens is truly amazing, and you can remain and enjoy the deserted city or, if you're fortunate—and have made reservations—you can be among the celebrants in any town or village. Holy Week is usually marked by impressive solemn services and processions; serious feasting on roasted lamb, the traditional margaritsa soup, and homemade wine; and dancing, often in traditional costumes. One unique celebration occurs on Patmos, where the Last Supper is reenacted at the monastery of St. John the Divine. *Tip:* Tourists should remember to dress appropriately, especially at this Easter time (shorts, miniskirts, and sleeveless shirts will all cause offense).

- **Folk-dance performances** begin in the amphitheater on Filopappos Hill in Athens and continue to September.
- ✪ Ritual recitations of the **Hippocratic Oath** by the citizens of Kos honor their favorite son Hippocrates. Young girls in ancient dress, playing flutes, accompany a young boy in procession until he stands and recites in Greek the timeless oath of physicians everywhere. May through September.
- **Sound-and-light shows** begin in Corfu town and continue to mid-September.
- **Feast of St. Constantine** (Ayios Konstandinos)—the first Orthodox emperor, and his mother **St. Helen** (Ayia Eleni)—is celebrated, most interestingly, by fire-walking rituals (*anastenaria*) in four villages in Macedonian Greece: Ayia Eleni, Ayios Petros, Langada, and Meliki. It's a big party night for everyone named Costa and Eleni. (Name-days, rather than birthdays, are celebrated in Greece.) The anniversary of the Ionian reunion with Greece is also celebrated, mainly in Corfu. May 21.

June

- **Athens Festival** features superb productions of ancient drama, opera, orchestra performances, ballet, modern dance, and popular entertainers in the handsome Odeum of Herodes Atticus, on the southwest side of the Acropolis. June through September.
- **Folk-dance performances** are given in the theater in the Old Town of Rhodes.
- **Wine Festival** is held annually at Daphni, about 10 kilometers (7 miles) west of Athens; other wine festivals are held on Rhodes and elsewhere.
- **Lycabettus Theater** presents a variety of performances at the amphitheater on Mount Likavitos (Lycabettus) overlooking Athens, from mid-June to late August.
- The **Miaoulia,** celebrated on a mid-June weekend on Hydra, honors Hydriot Admiral Miaoulis, who set much of the Turkish fleet on fire by ramming them with explosives-filled fireboats.
- **Aegean Festival** on Skiathos presents ancient drama, modern dance, folk music and dance, concerts, and art exhibits in the Bourtzi Cultural Center in the harbor of Skiathos town. June through September.
- **International Classical Musical Festival** is held annually for 1 week in June or July at Nafplion, in the Peloponnese.
- **Midsummer Eve** (June 23 to 24) is celebrated by burning the dry wreaths picked on May Day to drive away witches, a remnant of pagan ceremonies now associated with the birth of John the Baptist on Midsummer Day, June 24.
- **The Feast of the Holy Apostles** (Ayii Apostoli, Petros, and Pavlos) is another important name-day. June 29.

Navy Week is celebrated throughout Greece. In Volos, the voyage of the Argonauts is reenacted. On Hydra, the exploits of Adm. Andreas Miaoulis, naval hero of the War of Independence, are celebrated. Fishermen at Plomari on Lesvos stage a festival. End of June and beginning of July.

July

- Hydra's annual **puppet festival,** in recent years, has drawn puppeteers from countries as far away as Togo and Brazil. Early July.
- **Dodoni Festival** presents classical dramas at the ancient theater of Dodoni, south of Ioannina. July through September.
- **Epidaurus Festival** of classical Greek drama begins in the famous amphitheater and continues to early September. For information, contact the **Athens Festival Office,** Odos Stadiou 4 (☎ **01/322-1459** or 01/322-3111 to 3119, ext. 137).
- The **Northern Greece National Theater** performs classical drama in the amphitheaters in Phillipi and on the island of Thasos. Here's a way to see these productions free of the hassles of Athens. For information, call ☎ **051/22-354** or 051/227-820). July and August.
- **Hippokrateia Festival** brings art, music, and theater to the medieval castle of the Knights of St. John, in the main harbor of Kos. July and August.
- **Dionysia Wine Festival** is held on the island of Naxos. Not a major event, but fun if you're there. For information, call ☎ **0285/22-923**. Mid-July.
- ✪ **Wine Festival** at Rethymnon, Crete, continues throughout the month. Rethymnon also hosts a **Renaissance Festival** starting in early July and running into early September. There are now wine festivals and arts festivals all over Greece, but among the more engaging are those held in Rethymnon. Sample the wines, then sample something of the Renaissance theatrical and musical performances.
- **Feast of Ayia Marina,** protector of crops, is widely celebrated in rural areas. July 17.
- **Feast of the Prophet Elijah** (Profitis Elias) is celebrated in the hilltop shrines formerly sacred to the sun god Helios, the most famous of which is on Mount Taygetos, near Sparta. July 18 to 20.
- **Feast of Ayia Paraskevi** continues the succession of Saint Days celebrated at the height of summer, when agricultural work is put on hold. July 26.

August

- **Feast of the Transfiguration** (Metamorphosi) is celebrated in the numerous churches and monasteries of that name, though it isn't much for name-day parties. August 6.
- **Aeschylia festival** of ancient drama stages classical dramas at the archaeological site of Eleusis, home of the ancient Mysteries and birthplace of Aeschylus, west of Athens. August to mid-September.
- ✪ **Feast of the Assumption of the Virgin** (Apokimisis tis Panayias) is an important day of religious pilgrimage. Many take the opportunity to go home for a visit, so rooms are particularly hard to find. The holiday reaches monumental proportions in Tinos; thousands of people descend on the small port town to participate in an all-night vigil at the cathedral of Panayia Evanyelistria, in the procession of the town's miraculous icon, and in the requiem for the soldiers who died aboard the Greek battleship *Elli* on this day in 1940. August 15.
- **Epirotika Festival** in Ioannina presents theatrical performances, concerts, and exhibitions. August.

- **Olympus Festival** presents cultural events in the Frankish Castle of Platamonas, near Mount Olympus. August.
- **Santorini Festival of classical music** features international musicians and singers in outdoor performances for 2 weeks beginning at the end of the month.

September

- **Feast of the Birth of the Virgin** (Yenisis tis Panayias) is another major festival, especially on Spetses, where the anniversary of the Battle of the Straits of Spetses is celebrated with a re-enactment in the harbor, fireworks, and an all-night bash. September 8.
- **Feast of the Exaltation of the Cross** (Ipsosi to Stavrou) marks the end of the summer stretch of feasts, and even Stavros has had enough for a while. September 14.
- **Thessaloniki International Trade Fair.** This is one of the world's major trade fairs. Rooms are scarce in the city, so if the fair's not your destination, try to come to Thessaloniki at another time. For information, call ☎ **031/271-888**. Mid-September.
- **Thessaloniki Film Festival and Festival of Popular Song.** That lively and sophisticated city continues to live it up. End of September.

October

- **Feast of St. Demetrius** (Ayios Dimitrios) is particularly important in Thessaloniki, where he is the patron saint, and the Demetrius Festival features music, opera, and ballet. New wine is traditionally untapped. October 26.
- **Ochi Day,** when General Metaxa's negative reply (*ochi* is Greek for "no") to Mussolini's demands in 1940 gives a convenient excuse for continuing the party with patriotic outpourings, including parades, folk music and dancing, and general festivity. October 28.

November

- **Feast of the Archangels Gabriel and Michael** (Gavriel and Mihail), with ceremonies in the many churches named for them. November 8.
- **Feast of St. Andrew** (Ayios Andreas), patron saint of Patras, is another excuse for a party in that swinging city. November 30.

December

- **Feast of St. Nikolaos** (Ayios Nikolaos). This St. Nick is the patron saint of sailors. Numerous processions head down to the sea and the many chapels dedicated to him. December 6.
- **Christmas.** The day after Christmas honors the Gathering Around the Holy Family (Synaksis tis Panayias). December 25 and 26.
- **New Year's Eve,** when children go out singing Christmas carols (*kalanda*) while their elders play cards, talk, smoke, eat, and imbibe. December 31.

4 The Active Vacation Planner

BICYLING   Increasing numbers of foreigners are choosing to travel in Greece by bicycle, and those interested in the possibility can get more information from the **Greek Cycling Federation,** Odos Bouboulinas 28, 11742 Athens (☎ 01/883-1414).

  Trekking Hellas, Odos Filellinon 7, 10557 Athens (☎ 01/323-4548; fax 01/325-1474), can also assist you in arranging mountain-biking trips. But Greece is not the place to start learning how to tour on a bicycle; Greek drivers have little experience in accommodating bicyclists, road shoulders in Greece are often non-existent and even at best are not generous, and roads are not especially well maintained.

In the United States, **Classic Adventures,** Box 153, Hamlin, NY 14464 (☎ 800/777-8090 or 716/964-8488), offers bicycle tours, such as a 14-day tour that follows the coast and includes Corinth, Epidaurus, Mycenae, Olympia, and the island of Zakinthos, or a 12-day tour of Crete.

Mountain bikes are better suited for Greek terrain, and you can even bring your own along by train (for a small fee) or plane (free, though not easy), and you can take them along on Greek ferries and trains, usually at no extra cost. You should also bring along spare parts, as they are rarely available outside the major cities.

If you insist on trying a bicycle in Greece, you can rent an old bike for very little in most major resorts, and good mountain bikes are increasingly available. On Crete, mountain bikes are available for rent in Iraklion at **Creta Travel,** Odos Epimenidou 20–22 (☎ 081/227-002), which also has offices in Rethymnon and Ayios Nikolaos. In Chania, try **Athanasakis Tours,** Odos Halidon 25 (☎ 0821/24-965). On Paros, the **Mountain Bike Club,** near the post office in Parikia (☎ and fax 0284/23-778), rents good mountain bikes. On Rhodes, they are available at **Mike's Motor Club,** Odos Kazouli 23 (☎ 0241/37-420). Kos is also well suited to cycling, and bicycles are widely available for rent there.

CAMPING Greece offers a wide variety of camping facilities throughout the country. Rough or freelance camping—setting up your camp on some apparently unoccupied land—is forbidden by law but may be overlooked by some local authorities. The **Greek National Tourist Organization** should have further information on its many licensed facilities, as well as a very informative booklet, *Camping in Greece,* published by the **Greek Camping Association,** Odos Solonos 102, 10680 Athens (☎ 01/362-1560; fax 01/346-5262).

DIVING Scuba diving is currently restricted throughout most of Greece because of potential harm to sunken antiquities and the environment. There is some legal diving off the coast of Attica, off the Peloponnese peninsula, and off Halkidiki and a few other places in the north. There is also limited diving off the islands of Corfu, Crete, Kalimnos, Kefalonia, Mikonos, Rhodes, and Zakinthos. In general, though, you cannot dive in Greek waters unless you have signed on with a recognized sponsor. For more information, contact the **Organization of Underwater Activities** (☎ 01/982-3840) or the **Union of Greek Diving Centers** (☎ 02/922-9532). If you are a serious underwater explorer, contact the **Department of Underwater Archaeology,** Odos Kalisperi 30, 11741 Athens (☎ 01/924-7249).

There are diving schools on both Corfu—**Calypso Scuba Divers,** Ayios Gordis (☎ 0661/53-101; fax 0661/34-319)—and Rhodes—the **Dive Med Center,** Odos Dragoumi 5, Rhodes town (☎ 0241/33-654). There are diving and underwater-activity centers on Crete—**Paradise Dive Center,** Odos Giamboudaki 51, 74100 Rethymnon (☎ and fax 0831/53-258)—and Mikonos—**Lucky Scuba Divers,** Ornos Beach (☎ 0289/22-813; fax 0289/23-764). Even if you are qualified, you must dive under supervision. And above all, you are forbidden to even photograph, let alone remove, anything that might possibly be regarded as an antiquity.

Snorkeling, however, is permitted, and the unusually clear water makes it a special pleasure. Simple equipment is widely available for rent or sale.

FISHING Opportunities for fishing abound. Contact the **Amateur Anglers and Maritime Sports Club,** Akti Moutsopoulou, 18537 Piraeus (☎ 01/451-5731).

GOLF There are relatively few golf courses in Greece, although several more are s. to be in the planning stage. Those now in existence are in Glifada (along the coast ou side of Athens), Halkidiki, Corfu, and Rhodes. Any travel agent will supply the details.

HIKING Greece offers endless opportunities for hiking, trekking, and walking. Greeks themselves are now showing interest in walking for pleasure, and there are a number of well-mapped and even signed routes.

Probably the best and most up-to-date source for information on tours or groups that specialize in the natural aspects of Greece are the ads in the various magazines that appeal to people with these interests—*Audubon Magazine,* for instance, for birders.

In Greece itself, we recommend **Trekking Hellas,** Odos Filellinon 7, 10557 Athens (☎ 01/323-4548; fax 01/325-1474), and in Thessaloniki at Odos Aristotelous 11 (☎ 031/242-190), for both guided tours and help in planning your own private trek. Other Greek travel agencies specializing in nature tours include **Athenogenes,** Plateia Kolonaki 18, 10673 Athens (☎ 01/361-4829); **F-Zein Ltd.,** Leoforos Syngrou 132, 11743 Athens (☎ 01/921-6285); and in the Sporades, **Ikos Travel,** Patitiri, 37005 Alonissos (☎ 0424/65-320).

In the United States, the **Appalachian Mountain Club,** 5 Joy St., Boston, MA 02108 (☎ 617/523-0636), often organizes hiking tours in Greece. **Classic Adventures,** Box 253, Hamlin, NY 14464 (☎ 800/777-8090 or 716/964-8488), offers hiking tours of Crete and the Zagori region of Epirus. **Mountain Travel-Sobek,** 6420 Fairmount Ave., El Cerrito, CA 94530 (☎ 800/227-2384 or 510/527-8105), sometimes conducts summer hikes in the Pindos Mountains and the Zagori. **Avenir Travel and Adventures,** 2029 Sidewinder Drive, Park City, Utah 84060 (☎ 800/367-3230), is another agency that conducts its own walking tours through regions of Greece.

Birders and nature lovers should contact **Pharos Travel and Tourism, Inc.,** 230 W. 31st St., New York, NY 10001 (☎ 800/999-5511), or the **Hellenic Ornithological Society,** Odos Emmanouil Benaki 53, 10681 Athens (☎ 01/381-1271). **Questers Worldwide Nature Tours,** 381 Park Ave. S., Suite 1201, New York, NY 10016 (☎ 800/468-8668 or 212/251-0444), sometimes offers nature tours in Greece. Another group specializing in walking tours is **Alternative Travel Group,** 69–71 Banbury Rd., Oxford, OX2 6PE England (☎ 44/1865-315665, or 800/527-5997 in the U.S.).

HORSEBACK RIDING There is some opportunity for horseback riding in Greece. Near Athens you'll find the **Athletic Riding Club** of Ekali (☎ 01/813-5576); the **Hellenic Riding Club,** Maroussi (☎ 01/682-6128); and the **Riding Club of Parnitha** (☎ 01/240-2413); call for directions and reservations. Good facilities are also found near Thessaloniki, and on Corfu, Crete, Rhodes, and Skiathos, with many smaller stables elsewhere (inquire at local travel agencies).

In the United States, **Equitour,** Box 807, Dubois, WY 82513 (☎ 800/545-0019 or 307/455-3363), offers an 8-day riding tour of the beautiful Mount Pelion coast.

MOUNTAINEERING Those interested in more strenuous trekking and mountain climbing should contact the **Hellenic Federation of Mountaineering Clubs,** Odos Milioni 5, 10673 Athens (☎ 01/364-5904 or 01/364-4687).

SKIING There are a number of attractive skiing centers in Greece. They can't compare to those further north in deep snow and posh facilities, but they don't approach them in steep prices either, and there is much charm in their little hotels and lively après-ski life. The season generally begins after Christmas and continues until the end of April, depending on the weather.

he best developed is the **Parnassos Ski Center,** near Arachova, on Mount :nassus, which has 20 ski slopes, chairlifts, tow bars, classes, equipment rental, snack .ars and restaurants, and even child care. For more information, contact the **Greek Tourist Organization (EOT)** or the Parnassos Ski Center itself, at 320 04 Arachova, Viotias (☎ **0234/22-689** or 0234/22-493; fax 0234/22-695).

There is also skiing on the gentler slopes of Mount Pelion and at charming Metsovo, in Epirus northeast of Ioannina, where the season is somewhat shorter. Other centers are found on the Peloponnese at Helmos, near Kalavrita; in central Greece at Velouhi, near Karpenissi; and in Macedonia, at Pisoderi, near Florina, and Vermion, near Naoussa. For more information, contact the **Hellenic Federation of Skiing Clubs,** Odos Karayioryi Servias 7, 10563 Athens (☎ **01/323-0182;** fax 01/323-0142).

SPELUNKING   If you don't know what the word refers to, then you won't be wanting to do it. It refers to cave exploring, and there are numerous caves in Greece and numerous individuals who are skilled in exploring them. For details contact the **Hellenic Speleological Society,** Odos Sina 32 (☎01/361-1782; fax 01/364-3476).

WATER SPORTS   Water sports of various kinds are available at most major resort areas, and we will mention the more important facilities in our individual reviews. Parasailing is possible at the larger resorts in the summer. Although some of these facilities are limited to patrons of the hotels/resorts, in many places they are available to anyone willing to pay.

River rafting and kayaking are definite possibilities, especially in Epirus, with more limited opportunities on the Peloponnese peninsula. Contact the **Alpine Club,** Leoforos Syngrou 28, 11743 Athens (☎ **01/924-5218**). One very special opportunity— a 12-day kayaking trip through several of the Ionian islands—is conducted by the American agency **Mountain Travel–Sobek,** 6420 Fairmount Ave., El Cerrito, CA 94530 (☎ **800/227-2384** or 510/527-8105).

Waterskiing facilities are widely available; there are several schools at Vouliagmeni, south of Athens, and usually at least one on each of the major islands. Contact the **Hellenic Water-Ski Federation,** Leoforos Poseidonos, 16777 Athens (☎01/ 894-7413).

Windsurfing has become increasingly popular in Greece, and boards are widely available for rent. The many coves and small bays along Greece's convoluted coastline are ideal for beginners, and instruction is usually available at reasonable prices. The best conditions and facilities are found on the islands of Corfu, Crete, Lefkada, Lesvos, Naxos, Paros, Samos, and Zakinthos. There are a number of excellent schools. Contact the **Hellenic Wind-Surfing Association,** Odos Filellinon 7, 10557 Athens (☎ **01/323-0068** or 01/323-0330).

5   Special-Interest Vacations

ARCHAEOLOGICAL DIGS   The **American School of Classical Studies at Athens,** 6–8 Charlton St., Princeton, NJ 08540 (☎ 609/683-0800), often sponsors tours, focused on archaeology and guided by archaeologists and historians, in Greece and adjacent Mediterranean lands. **Archaeological Tours,** 30 E. 42nd St., Suite 1202, New York, NY 10017 (☎ 212/986-3054; e-mail: archtours@aol.com), offers tours led by expert guides; typical tours might be to classical Greek sites or to Cyprus/Crete/Santorini. **FreeGate Tourism,** 585 Stewart Ave., Suite 3190, Garden City, NY 11530 (☎ 800/223-0304 or 516/222-0855; fax 516/222-0848), also specializes in guided trips in Greece. **Educational Tours and Cruises,** 9 Irving St.,

Medford, MA 02111 (☎ 800/275-4109; e-mail: edtours@ars.nep.gr), is another agency experienced in arranging specialized tours in Greece; it can be reached in Greece at Odos Artemidos 1, Glyfada, 16674 Athens (☎ 01/898-1741; fax 01/895-5419).

ART   International Study Tours, 225 W. 34th St., No. 1020, New York, NY 10122 (☎ **800/833-2111** or 212/563-1202; fax 212/594-6953), offers studies in the architecture, art, and culture of Greece, led by professionals. Especially attractive are the **Aegean Workshops** run by Harry Danos, a Greek-American architect and watercolorist; in the spring and autumn, he leads groups to various regions of Greece, where he provides instruction in drawing and watercolors (and also ends up teaching some of the language). To learn more, call ☎ **860/739-0378.**

The **Athens Center for the Creative Arts,** Odos Archimidou 48, Pangrati, 11636 Athens (☎ **01/701-2268**), offers summer programs. The **Hellas Art Club** on the island of Hydra, at the Leto Hotel, 18040 Hydra (☎ **0298/53-385;** fax 01/361-2223 in Athens), offers classes in painting, ceramics, music, theater, photography, Greek dancing, and cooking.

MODERN GREEK   There are numerous courses offered at both formal educational institutions and private language institutes throughout the English-speaking world; there are also several quite decent courses on tape for self-study. Just be sure that it is modern Greek that you want to study—and not classical Greek! If you are already in Greece, the **Athens Center for the Creative Arts,** Odos Archimidou 48, Pangrati, 11636 Athens (☎ **01/701-2268**), is highly recommended. The **School of Modern Greek Language of Aristotle University in Thessaloniki** also offers summer courses.

PERSONAL GROWTH   The **Skyros Center,** which can be contacted in the United Kingdom at 92 Prince of Wales Rd., London NW5 3NE (☎ **0171/267-4424**), offers "personal growth" vacations on the island of Skyros, with courses in fitness, holistic health, creative writing, and some handicrafts.

6 Health & Insurance

STAYING HEALTHY   There are no immunization requirements for getting into the country, though it's always a good idea to have polio, tetanus, and typhoid covered when traveling anywhere.

Diarrhea can be a minor problem with all travelers everywhere, so it's wise to take along some of your favorite remedy. Cola soft drinks are said to be helpful for those having digestive difficulties stemming from too much olive oil in their food. Milk is pasteurized, though refrigeration is sometimes not the best, especially in out-of-the-way places—you might also want to take some care with meat. Allergy sufferers should carry along some antihistamines, especially in the spring. And everyone should be aware that overexposure to the much-lauded Greek sun can cause sun poisoning or sunstroke.

Health services are good, if not as noticeable as they are in most English-speaking countries. The hospitals in the large cities are excellent. Virtually all doctors in Greece can speak English or some other European language. For minor health problems, go first to the nearest **pharmacy** (*pharmakio*), which will be marked with a green cross. (In the larger cities, if it is closed, there should be a sign in the window directing you to the nearest open one. Newspapers also list the pharmacies that are open late or all night.) Pharmacists are well trained and usually speak English quite well, and many medications are available without prescription. You should bring along a sufficient quantity of any prescription medication you are taking, and keep it in your carry-on luggage. Just in case, ask your doctor to write you new prescriptions, using the generic—not the brand—name.

For more serious medical problems, your embassy or consulate or hotel management can recommend an English-speaking doctor. In an emergency, call a **first-aid center** (☎ **166**), the nearest **hospital** (☎ **106**), or the **tourist police** (☎ **171**).

Perhaps the best source of information regarding potential medical problems while traveling is the **International Association for Medical Assistance for Travelers (IAMAT).** They not only have a list of English-speaking doctors in some 120 cities abroad, but also put out specialized publications about diseases such as malaria, climate charts, etc. They can be reached in the United States at 417 Center St., Lewiston, NY 14092 (☎ **716/754-4883**); in Canada at 40 Regal Road, Guelph, ON N1K 1B5 (☎ **519/836-1002**); or you can write the office at 57 Voirets, 1212 Grand-Lancy, Geneva, Switzerland.

Those with chronic illnesses should discuss their travel plans with their physician. Those with epilepsy, diabetes, or significant cardiovascular disease should wear a Medic Alert identification tag or bracelet, which will alert a health-care provider to the condition and provide the telephone number of the 24-hour hot line from which your medical record can be obtained. Contact the **Medic Alert Foundation,** P.O. Box 819008, Turlock, CA 95381-1009 (☎ **800/344-3226**).

Emergency treatment is usually given free of charge in state hospitals, but be warned that only basic needs are met. (Citizens of EU nations should inquire before leaving, but their policies will probably cover treatment in Greece.) The care in outpatient clinics, which are usually open in the mornings (from 8am to noon), is usually somewhat better; you can find them next to most major hospitals, on some islands, and occasionally in rural areas, usually indicated by prominent signs.

INSURANCE   Before you purchase any additional insurance, check your current medical, automobile, and homeowner's policies as well as any insurance provided by credit-card companies and auto and travel clubs. You may already have adequate off-premises theft coverage, and your credit-card company may provide cancellation coverage on tickets paid for with their card. If you are prepaying for your trip or taking a flight that has cancellation penalties, consider cancellation insurance.

The following companies can provide you with insurance and further information:
Mutual of Omaha (Tele-Trip), 3201 Farnam St., Omaha, NE 68131 (☎ **800/228-9792** or 402/342-7600).
Travel Guard International, 1145 Clark St., Stevens Point, WI 54481 (☎ **800/782-5151**).
Travel Insurance International, P.O. Box 285568, East Hartford, CT 06128 (☎ **800/243-3174** or 860/528-7663).
Wallach and Co., 107 W. Federal St., P.O. Box 480, Middleburg, VA 22117 (☎ **800/237-6615** or 540/687-3166; fax 540/687-3172). They offer a special plan called HealthCare Abroad.

7 Tips for Travelers with Special Needs

FOR TRAVELERS WITH DISABILITIES   Few concessions exist for the disabled in Greece: steep steps, uneven pavement, almost no cuts at curbstones, narrow walks, slick stone, and traffic congestion can cause problems. Archaeological sites by their very nature are usually difficult to navigate, and crowded public transportation can be all but impossible. More modern and private facilities are only now beginning to provide ramps, but little else has been done. (That said, foreigners in wheelchairs accompanied by companions—are becoming a more common sight in Greece, and v have read a first-person account of a wheelchair-using individual who found a cruise ship well designed to service her needs.) The **Greek National Tourist Organization** can provide you with a short list of hotels that may be suitable, and we will mention the special facilities in those few hotels that have them. In Greece, the **Hermes Association,** Odos Patriarchou 13, Argiroupoli, 16542 Athens (☎ **01/996-1887**), also offers advice.

One of the best sources of free travel information for the disabled is **Access-Able Travel Source,** P.O. Box 1796, Wheatridge, CO 80034 (☎ **303/232-2979;** www.access-able.com; e-mail: carol@access-able.com), which issues occasional informative sheets but above all can refer you to travel agencies that handle arrangements for the disabled. Another good source for information is the **Society for the Advancement of Travel for the Handicapped,** 347 Fifth Ave., Suite 619, New York, NY 10016 (☎ **212/447-7284;** fax 212/725-8253; www.sath.org), which also publishes the quarterly ($13 a year) *Open World,* with lots of useful information on travel. **Moss Rehabilitation Hospital** in Philadelphia maintains a Web site that offers help and references for people with disabilities: **www.mossresourcenet.org.** The **American Foundation for the Blind,** 15 W. 15th St., New York, NY 10011 (☎ **800/232-5463**), is the best source of information for those with visual impairment. **New Directions,** 5276 Hollister Ave., No. 207, Santa Barbara, CA 93111 (☎ **805/967-2841;** fax 805/964-7344), arranges tours for people with disabilities.

FOR GAY & LESBIAN TRAVELERS A most helpful source is *Our World,* a magazine designed specifically for gay and lesbian travelers (10 issues a year, $35), at 1104 N. Nova Rd., Suite 251, Daytona Beach, FL 32117 (☎ **904/441-5367**); it not only is full of ads for travel agencies and facilities that accommodate gays and lesbians, but also carries firsthand accounts of visits to locales all around the world. (Its May 1997 issue is devoted to Greece; it can be purchased for $4.95.) The **International Gay Travel Association,** 4331 Federal Hwy., Suite 304, Fort Lauderdale, FL 33308 (☎ **800/448-8550**), can advise you about travel opportunities, agents, and tour operators. A monthly newsletter, *Out and About,* also has information about gay travel, and can be ordered by phone (☎ **800/929-2268**). Available in early 1999, *Frommer's Gay & Lesbian Europe*—sponsored by *The Advocate* magazine—will cover gay-, lesbian-, and bisexual-friendly destinations in Greece and nine other countries.

In Athens, the gay and lesbian organizations **EOK & AKOE-AMPHI** can be found at Odos Patission 21 (☎ **01/523-9017**). The **Autonomous Group of Gay Women** can be contacted through The Women's House, Odos Romanou Melodou 4, Likavitos, 10022 Athens (☎ **01/281-4823**). The *Greek Gay Guide,* published by Kraximo Press, P.O. Box 4228, 10210 Athens (☎ **01/362-5249**), can be purchased at some kiosks.

FOR SENIORS There are a number of "senior-citizen discounts" available in Greece. At press time, Olympic was offering about a 10% discount on all airfares for people ages 60 or over. Some museums and archaeological sites also offer discounts (up to 50%) on admissions for those 60 and over, but the practice seems unpredictable; for example, some places claim that you must be a citizen of an EU nation.

For general information before you go, Americans can acquire *Travel Tips for Older Americans,* available for $1.25 from the Superintendent of Documents, U.S. Government Printing Office, Washington, DC 20402 (☎ **202/512-1800**). Another

...klet, *101 Tips for Mature Travelers,* is available free from **Grand Circle Travel,** ...ich specializes in service to seniors, 347 Congress St., Boston, MA 02210 (☎ **800/ ...8-3737**). **Vantage Travel,** 111 Cypress St., Brookline, MA 02146 (☎ **800/ 322-6677**), offers a free booklet, *99 Travel Tips for Mature Travelers.* A monthly newsletter, *The Mature Traveler,* is available for $29.95 a year by contacting P.O. Box 50400, Reno, NV 89513 (☎ **702/786-7419**).

The **American Association of Retired Persons (AARP),** 1909 K St. NW, Washington, DC 20049 (☎ **800/424-3410** or 202/872-4700), offers members information on discounts on airfares, car rentals, and hotels. **Saga International Holidays,** 222 Berkeley St., Boston, MA 02116 (☎ **800/343-0273**), specializes in all-inclusive tours in Greece for seniors 50 and older.

Elderhostel, 75 Federal St., Boston, MA 02110 (☎ **617/426-7788**), offers study cruises in Greece for people over 55.

Interhostel, University of New Hampshire, 6 Garrison Ave., Durham, NH 03824 (☎ **800/733-9753** or 603/862-1147), offers 2-week programs in more than three dozen countries for people over 50. In Greece, they typically settle in one area for a week or so, with excursions that focus on getting to know the history and culture.

FOR STUDENTS In the United States, the largest travel service for students is the **Council on International Education Exchange (CIEE),** 205 E. 42nd St., New York, NY 10017 (☎ **212/822-2700**), with branches in Boston (☎ **617/266-1926**), Los Angeles (☎ **310/208-3551**), Miami (☎ **305/670-9261**), and many other college towns. CIEE provides details about such matters as budget travel, study abroad, and work permits; it sells special student medical insurance, as well as ISIC, Go 25, and ITIC cards; it also publishes a number of helpful publications, such as *Student Travels* magazine (free on request). An agency that specializes in students' travel needs is **STA Travel,** with over 150 offices around the world; in the United States, it's best to start with their toll-free number (☎ **800/777-0112**) and see where they direct you.

In Greece, students with proper identification (ISIC and IYC cards) are given reduced entrance fees to archaeological sites and museums, as well as discounts on admission to most artistic events, theatrical performances, and festivals.

A Hostelling International membership can save students money in some 5,000 hostels in 70 countries, where sex-segregated, dormitory-style sleeping quarters cost about $8 to $25 a night. In the United States, membership is available through **Hostelling International–American Youth Hostels,** 733 15th St. NW, Suite 840, Washington, DC 20005 (☎ **202/783-6161**). Membership (valid 1 year from purchase) is $10 for ages 17 and under, $25 for ages 18 to 54, and $15 for ages 55 and over.

In Greece, an International Guest Card can be obtained at the **Greek Association of Youth Hostels (OESE),** in Athens at Odos Botassi 11 near Kaningos Square, behind Omonia (☎ **01/330-2340**). Information on various student arrangements in Greece can also be had from the **International Student and Youth Travel Service,** Odos Nikis 11, 10557 Athens (☎ **01/323-37676**).

8 Getting There

The vast majority of travelers reach Greece by plane. Many also come by ferry from Italy. There is still bus service from Europe, but few except the young are interested in the arduous journey. Train service from Europe has been disrupted by the trouble in the Balkans, and even when running, it's slow and uncomfortable in the summer—and a Eurail Pass is valid only for connections via the ferry service from Italy. There are sometimes, however, special passes allowing rail travel in Greece and several other countries: see **www.raileurope.com,** or in the U.S. call ☎ **888/382-7245.**

BY PLANE
FROM NORTH AMERICA

UNITED STATES   At press time, only two regularly scheduled airlines offer direct, nonstop flights from the States to Athens—Olympic and Delta. Some travelers find the personnel brusque and the frequent strikes and delays aggravating, but **Olympic Airways** (☎ 800/223-1226; agn.hol.gr/info/olympic1.htm) has long offered nonstop service daily from New York, twice weekly from Boston, and twice weekly from Chicago via New York. **Delta Air Lines** (☎ 800/241-4141; www.delta-air.com) has satisfactory service from throughout the United States, with all flights connecting to their nonstop Athens flights at JFK in New York. All the other airlines make stops at some major European airport, where they usually require a change of planes. **Alitalia** (☎ 800/223-5730; www.alitalia.com) offers flights from JFK that go to Greece via Rome. **British Airways** (☎ 800/247-9297; www.british-airways.com) has service to Athens from a number of major U.S. cities, all stopping in London (most at Heathrow, but some at Gatwick). **KLM Royal Dutch Airlines** (☎ 800/374-7747; www.klm.nl) has superior service from 10 major cities in the United States to Athens, with all flights stopping in Amsterdam. **Lufthansa** (☎ 800/645-3880; www.lufthansa.com) has superior service to Athens, Thessaloniki, and Crete from 10 U.S. cities, via Frankfurt. **Sabena** (☎ 800/955-2000; www.sabena-usa.com) has good service to Athens from Atlanta, Boston, Chicago, and New York, with all flights stopping in Brussels. **Virgin Atlantic Airways** (☎ 800/862-8621; www.fly.virgin.com) offers excellent service at fair prices, especially its low-cost promotional fares, with daily service from Los Angeles and from New York or Newark, several times weekly from several other cities, to London and then to Athens.

CANADA In addition to the various airlines flying out of the United States, Canadians have a number of their own choices. **Olympic Airways** (☎ 800/ 223-1226; agn.hol.gr/info/olympic1.htm) offers the only direct flights from Canada to Athens—two flights a week from Montréal and Toronto. **Air Canada** (☎ 800/ 776-3000; www.aircanada.ca) flies from Calgary, Montréal, Toronto, and Vancouver to various airports in Europe, with connections on Olympic to Athens. **Air France** (☎ 800/667-2747; www.airfrance.com), **British Airways** (☎ 800/668-1059; www.british-airways.com), **CSA Czech Airlines** (☎ 800/223-2365; www.csa.cz), **Iberia** (☎ 800/423-7421; www.iberia.com), **KLM Royal Dutch Airlines** (☎ 800/ 361-5073; www.klm.nl), **Lufthansa** (☎ 800/645-3880; www.lufthansa.com), **Sabena** (☎ 800/955-2000; www.sabena-usa.com), **Swissair** (☎ 800/221-4750; www.swissair.com), and **TAP Air Portugal** (☎ 800/221-7370; www.tap-airportugal.pt) all have at least one flight a week from Calgary, Montréal, Toronto, or Vancouver via other European cities to Athens.

FROM EUROPE

IRELAND **Aer Lingus** (☎ 01/844-4777 in Dublin; www.aerlingus.ie) and **British Airways** (☎ 0345/222-111 in Belfast; www.british-airways.com) both fly to Athens via London's Heathrow. Less-expensive charters operate in the summer from Belfast and Dublin to Athens, less frequently to Corfu, Crete, Mikonos, and Rhodes. Contact **Balkan Tours,** 37 Ann St., Belfast BT1 4EB (☎ 01/232/236795), or **Joe Walsh Tours,** 8 Baggot St., Dublin (☎ 01/676-0991). Students should contact **USIT,** at Aston Quay, O'Connell Bridge, Dublin 2 (☎ 01/679-8833), or at Fountain Centre, College Street, Belfast (☎ 01232/324073).

UNITED KINGDOM **British Airways** (☎ 0181/897-4000; www.british-airways. com), **Olympic Airways** (☎ 0181/846-9080; agn.hol.gr/info/ olympic1.htm), and **Virgin Atlantic Airways** (☎ 01293/747-747; www.fly.virgin.com) have several flights daily from London's Heathrow Airport. For the smaller companies that offer no-frill flights, check some of the following sites on the Web: **www.easyjet.co.uk,** **www.go-fly.com, www.ryanair.co.uk.** Eastern European airlines, such as **CSA Czech Airlines** (☎ 0171/255-1898; www.csa.cz), **Balkan Bulgarian Airlines** (☎ 0171/ 637-7637; www.balkan.com), and **Malev Hungarian Airlines** (☎ 0171/439-0577; www.malev-airlines.com), offer service to Athens via their capitals at good prices, but with frequent delays. There are also connecting flights to Athens and some to Thessaloniki from Aberdeen, Belfast, Birmingham, Bristol, Edinburgh, Glasgow, Leeds, Liverpool, Newcastle, and Southampton; as well as flights to Athens and the major islands from Birmingham, Cardiff, Gatwick, Glasgow, Luton, and Manchester.

FROM AUSTRALIA & NEW ZEALAND

AUSTRALIA Service to Athens is offered daily from Perth and Sydney and several times weekly from Brisbane and Melbourne by **Alitalia** (☎ 02/247-1308 in Sydney; www.alitalia.com), via Bangkok and Rome; **KLM Royal Dutch Airlines** (☎ 800/ 505-747 throughout Australia; www.klm.nl), via Singapore and Amsterdam; **Lufthansa** (☎ 02/367-3800 in Sydney; www.lufthansa.com), via Frankfurt; and **Olympic Airways** (☎ 02/251-2204 in Sydney; agn.hol.gr/info/olympic1.htm), via

Bangkok. The lowest fares generally offered are on weekly service from Sydney. **Aeroflot** (☎ 02/233-7148 in Sydney; www.aeroflot.org), via Moscow, and on **Tr Airways** (☎ 02/844-0900 in Sydney; www.thaiair.com), from Brisbane, Melbourn Perth, and Sydney via Bangkok. **British Airways** (☎ 02/258-3000 in Sydney, www.british-airways.com) and **Qantas Airways** (☎ 02/957-0111 in Sydney; www.qantas.com) have regular service to London, and a "Global Explorer Pass" that allows you to make up to six stopovers wherever the two airlines fly, except to South America.

NEW ZEALAND **Singapore Airlines** (☎ 09/303-2506 in Auckland; www. singaporeair.com), via Singapore, and **Thai Airways** (☎ 09/377-3886 in Auckland; www.thaiair.com), via Bangkok, presently offer the least-expensive fares to Athens. **Air New Zealand** (☎ 09/309-6171 in Auckland; www.airnz.co.nz) and **Qantas Airways** (☎ 09/303-3209 in Auckland; www.qantas.com) offer connections through Lufthansa (☎ 09/303-1529 in Auckland) to Athens. **British Airways** (☎ 09/ 367-7500 in Auckland; www.british-airways.com) and **Qantas** can get you to Europe and they offer a "Global Explorer Pass," with up to six stopovers, for very little more. **Alitalia** (☎ 09/379-4457; www.alitalia.com) also flies to Athens, via Rome.

FROM SOUTH AFRICA

Olympic Airways (☎ 11/880-1614; agn.hol.gr/info/olympic1.htm) offers the only direct flights from Johannesburg to Athens—about three a week, each way. **Air France** (☎ 01/880-8040; www.airfrance.com), **Alitalia** (☎ 01/880-9254; www.alitalia.com), **British Airways** (☎ 01/975-3931; www.british-airways.com), and **Ethiopian Airlines** (☎ 01/616-7624; www.ethiopianairlines.com) also offer occasional flights to and from Johannesburg, with connections via other foreign cities en route.

FINDING THE BEST AIRFARE

BUCKET SHOPS & CONSOLIDATORS Bucket shops—those companies you see advertising the very low prices—buy unused seats in bulk from the various airlines at even lower prices and sell them at a profit. You must usually be prepared to leave on short notice. Not all of them are entirely trustworthy, and some will not make refunds, so take precautions: pay for tickets with a credit card, consider taking out cancellation insurance, and always confirm the reservation with the airline itself. Some frequently recommended consolidators that seem to stay in business are **Travac** (☎ 800/872-8800) and **Unitravel** (☎ 800/325-2222).

CHARTER FLIGHTS There are a number of companies that charter less-expensive flights to Athens from the United States; generally you must book through a travel agent and at least a month in advance to get on a flight in the summer. Flights are less expensive in the spring and fall, least expensive in the winter, and slightly less expensive during the week. One company we continue to recommend is **Homeric Tours** (☎ 800/223-5570 or 212/753-1100), which at press time charged $560 for a round-trip from New York in the winter, $690 in the spring, and from $499 to $699 during the summer. They may have several flights a week between June and September, only one flight a week during the rest of the year. **Tourlite International** (☎ 800/272-7600 or 212/599-2727) charges similar fares for its flights between New York and Athens. Both companies also offer low-cost tours, car rentals, cruises, and hotel accommodations at considerable savings.

Note: Greece prohibits visitors on charter flights from leaving and reentering the country—to prevent visitors from taking advantage of subsidized landing fees only to spend their time and money in, say, Turkey—and you should determine if this rule is being enforced before you break it.

INTERNET TRAVEL AGENCIES & FARE-FINDERS Increasingly more travel services are being offered on the Internet. Not everyone will feel comfortable ordering their tickets this way—it may seem impersonal, final, and even risky. But some travelers might like to look to see what is offered. Among the better known and more useful Web sites are: **expedia.msn.com**, **www.travelocity.com**, **www.priceline.com**, and **www.cheaptickets.com**.

BY BOAT

Most people who travel by ship to Greece from foreign ports come from Italy, although there is occasional service from Cyprus, Egypt, Israel, and Turkey. Brindisi to Patras is the most common ferry crossing, about a 20-hour voyage, with as many as seven departures a day in summer. There is also regular service, twice a day in summer, from Ancona and Bari, once daily from Otranto, and two or three times a week from Trieste or Venice. Most ferries stop at Corfu or Igoumenitsou, often at both; in summer, occasionally a ship will also stop at Kefalonia. If you want to learn more about the various ferry services between Greece and foreign ports, try the London-based agency **Viamare Travel,** Graphic House, 2 Sumatra Rd., London NW6 1PU (☎ **0171/431-4560;** fax 0171/431-5456; www.viamare.com; e-mail: ferries@ viamare.com). There is also the new **Superfast Ferries Line,** Leoforos Alkyonidon 157, 16673 Athens (☎ **01/969-1100;** fax 01/969-1190; www.superfast.com; e-mail: superfast@superfast.com, which offers service between Ancona and Patras (20 hr.) or Bari and Patras (17 hr.).

On the regular ferries, one-way fares from Brindisi to Patras at press time cost from about Dr13,500 ($45) for a tourist-class deck chair to about Dr30,000 ($100) for a cabin with a view. Vehicles cost at least another Dr15,000 ($50). Fares to Igoumenitsou are considerably cheaper, but by no means a better value unless your destination is nearby. The number of shipping lines involved and variations in schedules doesn't permit us to provide more concrete details. Consult a travel agent about the possibilities, book well ahead of time in summer, and reconfirm with the shipping line on the day of departure.

9 Getting Around

BY CAR

Driving in Greece is a bit of an adventure, but it's the best way to see the country at your own pace. Greece has the highest accident rate in Europe, probably due more to treacherous roads, mountain terrain, and poor maintenance of older cars than to reckless driving—although Greeks are certainly aggressive drivers. Athens is a particularly intimidating place to drive in at first, and parking spaces are practically nonexistent in the center of town. Several of the major cities are linked by modern expressways with tolls: Athens to Corinth, for instance, is Dr500 ($1.70). Accidents must be reported to the police for insurance claims.

The **Greek Automobile Touring Club (ELPA),** Odos Mesoyion 2, Athens (☎ 01/779-1615), with offices in most cities, can help you with all matters relating to your car, issue an international driver's license, and provide you with maps and information (☎ 174, 24 hr. daily). The emergency road service number is ☎ 104, and the service provided by the able ELPA mechanics is free for light repairs, but you should definitely give a generous tip.

CAR RENTALS   There is an abundance of rental cars, with considerable variation in prices. However, many cars have a standard shift; if you must have an automatic, you are strongly advised to make your reservation before leaving home and well in advance. Always ask if the quoted price includes insurance; many credit cards make the collision-damage waiver unnecessary, but you will find that most rental agencies simply include this in their rates. You can usually save by booking at home before you leave, and this is especially advisable during the summer. When shopping around for a bargain, be sure to carry along and display a number of brochures from competitors.

Most companies require that the renter be at least 21 years old (25 for some models, and sometimes no older than 70 to 75: inquire!); possess a valid Australian, Canadian, EU-nation, U.S., or international driver's license; and have a major credit card or leave a large cash deposit.

The major rental companies in Athens are **Avis** (☎ 01/322-4951), **Budget** (☎ 01/ 922-6666), **HellasCars** (☎ 01/923-5353), **Hertz** (☎ 01/922-0102), and

Street Names

The Greek word for "street" is *odos*—think of our word "odometer"—and the word for "avenue" is *leoforos,* often abbreviated *Leof.,* usually applied to major thoroughfares. Numbers are written after rather than before the street name.

Plateia—think "place" or "plaza"—is Greek for square, and usually means a large public square, such as Syntagma (Constitution) Square in Athens, though sometimes a *plateia* may be little more than a wide area where important streets meet.

InterRent/EuropeCar (☎ 01/921-5789), all with offices in major cities, at most airports, and on most islands. Smaller local companies usually have lower rates, though their vehicles are often older and not as well maintained. If you prefer to combine your car rental with your other travel arrangements, we can recommend **Galaxy Travel,** Odos Voulis 35, at Apollonos, near Syntagma Square (☎ 01/ 322-9761; fax 01/322-9538; e-mail: galaxy_trvl@matrix.kapatel.gr), open Monday through Saturday.

Daily rates start at about $40 per day, plus 40¢ per kilometer, or $400 a week with unlimited mileage for the smaller Fiat or Suzuki in the high season, but at other times rates are negotiable. And be prepared to have about 18% in taxes added to the quoted price! (There's also a hefty surcharge for pickup and drop-off at airports.) *Note:* You must have written permission from the car-rental agency to take your car on a ferry or into a foreign country.

DRIVING YOUR OWN VEHICLE   To drive your own vehicle, valid registration papers, an international third-party insurance certificate, and a driver's license are required. Valid American and EU licenses are accepted in Greece. A free entry card allows you to keep your car in the country up to 4 months, after which another 8 months can be arranged without having to pay import duty.

DRIVING RULES   You drive on the right in Greece, pass on the left, and yield right-of-way to vehicles approaching from the right except where otherwise posted. Greece has adopted international road signs, though many Greeks apparently haven't learned what they mean yet. The maximum speed limit is 100 kilometers per hour (65 m.p.h.) on open roads, and 50 kilometers per hour (30 m.p.h.) in town, unless otherwise posted. Seat belts are required. The police have become increasingly strict in recent years, especially with foreigners in rental cars; alcohol tests can be given and fines imposed on the spot. (Worse things have been known to happen to foreign tourists in rental cars, but if you feel you have been treated unfairly, get the officer's name and report him at the nearest tourist police station.) Honking is illegal in Athens, but you can hear that law broken by tarrying at a traffic signal.

PARKING   Parking a car has become a serious challenge in the cities and towns of Greece. If you stay at the better hotels, they will probably provide parking, either on their premises or by some arrangement with a nearby lot. There are few parking garages or lots in Greece. Follow the blue signs with their white *"P"* and you may be lucky enough to find an available space. Most Greek city streets have restricted parking of one kind or another. But in some cities, signs—usually yellow, and with the directions in English as well as Greek—will indicate that you can park along the street but must purchase a ticket from the nearest kiosk. Otherwise, be prepared to park fairly far from your base or destination. If you lock your car and remove all obvious valuables from sight, you should not have to worry about it being broken into.

CAR FERRIES   Car ferry service is available on most larger ferries, and there's regular service from Piraeus to Aegina and Poros in the Saronic Gulf, most of the Cyclades, Chania and Iraklion on Crete, Hios, Kos, Lesvos, Rhodes, and Samos. For the Cyclades, crossing is shorter and less expensive from Rafina, an hour east of Athens. From Patras, there's daily service to Corfu, Ithaka, and Kefalonia. In the summer, there are four car ferries daily from Kyllini to Zakinthos. The Sporades have service from Ayios Konstandinos, Kimi, and Volos (and then among the several islands). The short car ferry across the Gulf of Corinth from Rio to Antirio can save a lot of driving for those traveling between the northwest and the Peloponnese or Athens. There's also service between many of the islands, even between Crete and

Rhodes, as well as car crossing to and from Turkey between Hios and Çesme, Lesvos and Dikeli, and Samos and Kusadasi.

BY PLANE

Compared to the cheaper classes on ships and ferries, air travel within Greece can be expensive, but we recommend it for those pressed for time and/or heading for the more distant destinations (even if the planes don't always hold strictly to schedule). **Olympic Airways** maintains a virtual monopoly on domestic air travel and thus has little incentive to improve service (although there has been talk in recent years that the airline will be privatized). One major exception in recent years is **Air Greece,** a line that operates between Crete and several major destinations (see "Essentials" in chapter 9); at press time Air Greece had also introduced several flights a week between Thessaloniki and Patras. Better computerized booking has reduced the possibility of finding out at the last minute that you don't actually have a seat, but delayed flights are still common; although the quality of the service is criticized by some, Olympic actually has one of the best safety records of any major airline. (Their domestic flight attendants tend to be more pleasant than their international counterparts.) Book as far ahead of time as possible (especially in the summer), reconfirm your booking before leaving for the airport, and try to arrive at the airport at least an hour before departure; the scene at a check-in counter can become quite hectic. *Note:* Tickets are nonrefundable, and changing your flight can cost you up to 30% within 24 hours of departure and 50% within 12 hours.

Olympic Airways (☎ 01/966-6666; fax 01/921-9933) has a number of offices in Athens, though most travel agents also sell tickets. It offers service on the **mainland** to Aktaion Preveza, Alexandroupolis, Ioannina, Kalamata, Kavala, Kozani, Kastoria, and Thessaloniki; and for **islands,** to Astipalea, Corfu (Kerkira), Crete (Iraklion, Chania, Sitia), Hios, Ikaria, Karpathos, Kassos, Kastellorizo, Kefalonia, Kos, Kithira, Leros, Limnos, Milos, Mikonos, Mitilini (Lesvos), Naxos, Paros, Rhodes, Samos, Santorini, Skiathos, Skyros, Siros, and Zakinthos. All domestic flights leave from Athens's West Terminal, often called Olympiki. Most flights are to or from Athens, though there is some inter-island service. The baggage allowance is 15 kilos (33 lb.) per passenger, except with a connecting international flight; even the domestic flights generally ignore the weight limit unless it is way over. Smoking is prohibited on all domestic flights.

Round-trip tickets are sold as two one-way fares. Some sample one-way fares (including taxes) at this writing are: Athens–Corfu, Dr20,400 ($68); Athens–Ioannina, Dr18,100 ($60); Athens–Iraklion, Dr21,600 ($72); Athens–Mikonos, Dr18,800 ($63); Athens– Rhodes, Dr24,600 ($82); Athens–Santorini, Dr21,900 ($73); Iraklion–Rhodes, Dr21,600 ($72). As you can see, the shorter trips, such as to Mikonos or Santorini, are not cheap, and though you'll probably save a little time, you'll miss all the scenery. But there's no denying that for those with limited time in Greece, air travel may be the best way to go.

BY TRAIN

Greek trains are generally slow but inexpensive and fairly pleasant. The **Railway Organization of Greece (OSE)** also operates some bus service from stations adjacent to major terminals. (Bus service is faster, but second-class train fare is nearly 50% cheaper, and trains are more comfortable and scenic.) If you are interested in some of the special arrangements involving rail passes for Greece (sometimes in combination with Olympic flights within Greece), check out **www.raileurope.com** or call ☎ 888/ 382-7245 (in the U.S. only).

For information and tickets in Athens, visit the **OSE office** at Odos Karolou 1–3 (☎ 01/524-0601), or Odos Sina 6 (☎ 01/362-4402), both near Omonia Square. Information is available at Odos Filellinon 17 (☎ 01/323-6747), near Sytagma Square.

Purchase your ticket and reserve a seat ahead of time, as a 50% surcharge is added to tickets purchased on the train and some lines are packed, especially during the summer. A first-class ticket may be worth the extra cost, as seats are more comfortable and less crowded. There is sleeper service (costly, but a good value if you can sleep on a train; you must be prepared to share a compartment with three to five others) on the Athens–Thessaloniki run, and express service (6 hr.) twice a day, at 7am and 1pm.

Trains to northern Greece (Alexandroupolis, Florina, Kalambaka, Lamia, Larissa, Thessaloniki, Volos, etc.) leave from the Larissa Station (Stathmos Larissis). **Trains to the Peloponnese** (Argos, Corinth, Patras) leave from the nearby Peloponnese Station (Stathmos Peloponnisou). Take trolley no. 1 or 5 from Syntagma Square to both stations.

The Peloponnese circuit from Corinth to Patras, Pirgos (near Olympia), Tripolis, and Argos is one way to experience this scenic region, though the Athens–Patras stretch is often crowded. The spectacular spur between Diakofto and Kalavrita is particularly recommended for train enthusiasts.

BY BUS

Public buses are inexpensive but often overcrowded. Local buses vary from place to place, but on most islands the bus stop is usually fairly central with a posted schedule; destinations are (usually—so ask!) displayed on the front of the bus. Fare is collected after departure by a conductor. In Athens and other large cities, a ticket must be purchased before boarding—kiosks usually have them, as well as schedule information—and validated after boarding.

Greece has an extensive **long-distance bus service (KTEL),** an association of regional operators with green-and-yellow buses that usually leave from convenient central stations. Current information can usually be found at a Greek Tourist Organization (EOT) or municipal tourist office.

In Athens, **most destinations within Attica** leave from the Mavromate terminal, north of the National Archaeological Museum; **most buses to central Greece** leave from Odos Liossion 60, 5 kilometers (3.1 miles) north of Omonia Square (take local bus no. 024 from Leoforos Amalias in front of the entrance to the National Garden and tell the driver your destination); **most buses to the Peloponnese, Western, and Northern Greece** leave from the terminal at Odos Kifissou 100, 4 kilometers (2.5 miles) northeast of Omonia Square (take local bus no. 051 from 2 blocks west of Omonia, near the big church of Ayios Konstandinos, at Zinonos and Menandrou).

Express buses between major cities, usually air-conditioned, can be booked through travel agencies. Make sure you're pronouncing your destination properly, or at least are being understood—you wouldn't be the first to see a bit more of Greece than bargained for—and determine the bus's schedule and comforts before purchasing your ticket. Many buses are not air-conditioned, take torturous routes, and make frequent stops. (NO SMOKING signs are generally disregarded by drivers and conductors, as well as by many older male passengers.)

Organized and guided **bus tours** are widely available; some of them will pick you up at your hotel. Ask at your hotel or almost any travel agent in Athens. One that is especially recommended is **CHAT Tours,** the oldest and probably most experienced in providing a wide selection of bus tours led by highly articulate guides. Almost any travel agent can book its tours, but if you want to deal with them directly, contact their office at 214 Bedford Rd., Toronto, Ontario M5R 2K9 (☎ 800/268-1180).

BY BOAT

BY FERRY   Ferries are the most common, cheapest, and generally the most authentic way to visit the islands, though the slow roll of a ferry can be authentically stomach-churning. A wide variety of vessels sail Greek waters—some huge, sleek, and new, with comfortable TV lounges, discos, and good restaurants; some old and ill-kept, but pleasant enough if you stay outside. Ferries often don't hold to their schedules, but they can be fun if you enjoy opportunities to meet people. Drinks and snacks are almost always sold, but the prices and selection are never good, so you may want to bring along your own.

The map of Greece offered by the Greek Tourist Organization (EOT) is very useful in planning your sea travels because the common routes are indicated. Once you've learned what is possible, you can turn your attention to what is available. Remember that the summer schedule is the fullest, spring and fall have reduced service, and winter schedules are skeletal.

There are dozens of shipping companies, each with its own schedule, which by the way are regulated by the government. Your travel agent might have a copy of *Hellenic Travelling,* a monthly travel guide published by GNTO, or another similar summary of schedules, *Greek Travel Pages.* While in the United States, you might purchase *Greece by Rail with Major Ferry Routes,* by Zane Katsikis (Globe Pequoit Press, $17.95).

Photos can give you some idea of the ships, but remember any photo displayed was probably taken when the ship was new, no matter when it was reproduced, and it is unlikely that anyone will be able (or willing) to tell you its actual age. The bigger ferries offer greater stability during rough weather. Except in the summer, you can usually depend on getting aboard a ferry by showing up about an hour before scheduled departure—inter-island boats sometimes depart before their scheduled time—and purchasing a ticket from a dockside agent or aboard the ship itself, though this is often more expensive.

Your best bet is to buy a ticket from an agent ahead of time. In Athens we recommend **Galaxy Travel,** Odos Voulis 35, at Apollonos, near Syntagma Square (☎ 01/322-9761; fax 01/322-9538), open Monday through Saturday. Right on the square is **HellasTours,** the Thomas Cook representative, at Odos Karayioryi Servias 4 (☎ 01/322-0005; fax 01/323-3487), a full-service agency that changes Cook Travel Cheques without commission. Just down the street, in the arcade at no. 10, **Summertime Tours** (☎ 01/323-4176) offers discounts on its services. But you must be warned: Different travel agencies sell tickets to different lines—this is usually the policy of the line itself—and one agent might not know or bother to find out what else is being offered (although we believe that if you press reputable agencies like those above, they will at least tell you of the other possibilities). The port authority is the most reliable

Early-Season Ferries

In the early weeks of the tourist season, from April to early May, the boat services are altogether unpredictable. Boat schedules, at the best of times, are tentative—but during this time, they are wish lists, nothing more. Our best advice is to wait until you get to Greece, and then go to a major travel agency and ask for help.

source of information, and the shipping company itself or its agents usually offer better prices and may have tickets when other agents have exhausted their allotment. It often pays to shop around a little to compare vessels and prices.

First class usually has roomy air-conditioned cabins and its own lounge and on some routes costs almost as much as flying; but consider that on longer overnight hauls, you're essentially on a comfortable floating hotel and thus save that cost. Second class has smaller cabins (which you will probably have to share with strangers) and its own lounge. The tourist-class fare entitles you to a seat on the deck or in a lounge. (Tourists usually head for the deck, while the Greeks stay inside, watch TV, and smoke copiously.) Hold on to your ticket; crews usually conduct ticket-control sweeps.

Note: Those taking a ferry to Turkey from one of the Dodecanese islands must submit their passport and payment to an agent the day before departure.

We include more details on service and schedules with the fuller discussion of each island, as well as suggested travel agencies and sources of local information. But just to give some sense of the fares, here are examples for first class at press time (compare with airfares during this same time, p. 59). Between Piraeus and Crete (Iraklion), Dr17,700 ($59); Kos, Dr23,100 ($77); Mitilini (Lesvos), Dr16,300 ($54); Mikonos, Dr9,000 ($30); Naxos, Dr10,000 ($33); Rhodes, Dr25,300 ($84); Santorini, Dr12,500 ($42). A small embarkation tax and value-added tax (VAT) of 8% will be added.

BY HYDROFOIL　　Hydrofoils (often referred to by the principal line's "trade name," **Flying Dolphins,** or by Greeks as *to flying*) are nearly twice as fast as ferries, and have comfortable airline-style seats. Their stops are much shorter, and they are less likely to cause seasickness. Although they cost nearly twice as much as ferries, are frequently fully booked in the summer, can be quite bumpy during rough weather, and give little or no view of the passing scenery, they're the best choice for those with limited time, and everyone should try one of the sleek little craft at least once. There is presently regular hydrofoil service to nearly all the major islands, with new service appearing every year. Longer trips over open sea, such as between Santorini and Iraklion, Crete, may make them well worth the extra expense. (Smoking is prohibited, and actually less likely to be indulged in, possibly because the cabins seem so much like those of an aircraft.) The forward compartment offers better views, but is also bumpy.

Flying Dolphins are operated by **Ceres,** Odos Filellinon 3, 10557 Athens (☎ 01/ 324-4600). The service from Zea Marina in Piraeus to the Saronic Gulf islands and the Peloponnese is especially good, and the new Super Cats are truly super. (The fare to Spetses is about Dr5,700/$19, as compared to about Dr3,000/$10 for tourist-class ferry service, but because of the number of stops in between, it's better than twice as fast.) Flying Dolphin service in the Sporades is also recommended for its speed and regularity. Hydrofoil service to the Cycladic Islands is operated by **Ilios Lines,** Rafina (☎ 0294/25-100).

BY SAILBOAT & YACHT　　Increasing numbers of people are choosing to explore Greece by sailboat or yacht. Sailing and yachting require such specialized skills and equipment that it is unlikely that anyone wanting to undertake either of these activities in Greece will depend on a general guide such as this. But clearly there are numerous facilities and possibilities for both. Experienced sailors interested in renting a boat in Greece can contact the **Hellenic Professional and Bareboat Yacht Owners' Association,** Zea Marina, 18536 Piraeus (☎ 01/452-6335). One possibility is to sign up for one of the "flotillas"—a group of usually eight or more sailboats that sail about as a group led by a boat crewed by experienced sailors; the largest of such organizations is **Sunsail,** 980 Awald Rd., Annapolis, MD 21403 (☎ 800/327-2276), but travel agencies should be able to put you in touch with one of these organizations. At the other extreme, those who want to charter a yacht with anything from a basic skipper to a full crew should probably first contact the **Hellenic Professional Yacht Owners' Association** (listed above) or the **Greek Yacht Brokers and Consultants Assoc.,** Odos Filellinon 7, 10557 Athens (☎ **01/322-3221;** fax 01/322-3251). If you feel competent to make your own arrangements, contact an agency such as **Hellenic Holidays,** 1501 Broadway, New York, NY 10036 (☎ **212/944-8388**), or **Valef Yachts Ltd.,** P.O. Box 391, Ambler, PA 19002 (☎ **215/641-1624;** fax 215/641-1746; www.valefyachts.com; e-mail: VALEF@ix.netcom.com). In Greece, either contact one of these associations, or a private agency such as **Alpha Yachting,** Leoforos Vasileos Yioryios 67, 16674 Glyfada (☎ **01/968-0486**); **Aris Drivas Yachting,** Odos Neorion 147, Piraeus (☎ **01/411-3194**); or **Thalassa Charter and Yacht Brokers,** Odos Grypari 72, Kallithea, Athens (☎ **01/956-6866**).

BY TAXI

Taxis are the most expensive and often the most exasperating means of travel in Greece, though there have been improvements in recent years. You no longer have to negotiate for a cab at most airports; just find the line. Cabs are considerably less expensive in Athens than they are in London, New York, or Toronto. There are probably no greater percentage of cheats among the drivers than in all major cities around the world—and many Greek taxi drivers are good-natured, helpful, and informative. Language and cultural difficulties, however, can make it easier for them to gouge you, and many drivers take advantage of the opportunity. The converse, though, is sometimes true: language gaps often lead to genuine misunderstandings. There are some legitimate surcharges—for heavy luggage, from midnight to 5am (almost twice the regular rate!), on holidays, from (but *not* to) airports and docks, etc.

Get your hotel desk to help you in hailing or booking a taxi. Radio cabs cost Dr500 ($1.70) extra, but you'll have some leverage. Restaurants and businesses can also help in calling or hailing a cab, negotiating a fare, and making sure your destination is understood. Take a card from your hotel, have your destination written down, or learn to pronounce it at least semicorrectly. Be willing to share a cab with other passengers picked up on the way, especially during rush hour; think of it as your contribution to better efficiency and less pollution (and you are not supposed to pay more than your proportion of the shared fare). Always have some vague idea of where you're going on the map, so you don't end up going to Plaka from Syntagma by way of Kolonaki. (There are, however, several ways of getting to Plaka from Syntagma.) Don't be bothered by bullying or bluster; try to find it amusing and counter with your own bluff, showing your superiority by keeping your cool. See "Typical Taxi Tricks," below.

BY MOPED, MOTORBIKE & MOTORCYCLE

There seems to be no end to the number of mopeds available for rent in Greece. They can be an inexpensive way to sightsee, especially in the islands, but they are not recommended for everyone: Greek hospitals admit scores of tourists injured on mopeds or motorbikes every summer, and there are a number of fatalities. Roads are often poorly paved and shoulderless; loose gravel or stones are another common problem. Make sure you have insurance and that the machine is in good working condition before you take it. Helmets are required by law and strongly recommended, although you will rarely see Greeks wearing one.

Some of us wish the larger motorbikes and motorcycles were forbidden on all the islands, as Greek youths seem to delight in punching holes in the muffler and tearing around all hours of the day and night. (Some islands are wisely banning them from

Typical Taxi Tricks

- The meter is left off, and the driver hopes you won't notice and will try to extort a much larger fare. Check the meter, and even if you don't speak a word of Greek besides "taxi," point at the meter and say "meter."
- The meter is on, but the little window next to the drachma display will be on "2"—which indicates a late-night/early-morning or outside-the-city-limits rate. If that's not the case, reach over and indicate that you notice.
- With a group of tourists, a driver may insist that each person pay the full metered fare. Pay one fare only. (In pairs or groups, have a designated arguer; the others can write down names and numbers, stick with the luggage, or look for help—from a policeman, maitre d', or desk clerk.)
- Late at night, especially at airports, ferry stops, and bus and railroad stations, a driver will refuse to use his meter and demand an exorbitant fare. Smile, shake your head, and look for another cab; if there is none available, begin to write down the license number of the first driver and you will probably see that he relents.
- A driver will want more than the legal surcharge for a service such as pickup from an airport (Dr300/$1); pickup from bus, train, or seaport terminals (Dr150/50¢); or luggage (Dr100/35¢ per piece). Ask to see the official rate sheet that he is required to carry.
- A driver will say that your hotel is full, but he knows a better and cheaper one. Laugh, and insist you'll take your chances at your hotel.
- A driver may want to let you off where it's most convenient for him. Be cooperative if it's easier and quicker for you to cross a busy avenue than for him to get you to the other side, but you don't have to get out of the cab until you're ready.

If things are obviously not going well for you, conspicuously write down the driver's name and number and by all means report him to the **tourist police** (☎ 171) if he has the nerve to call your bluff. One of the best countertactics is to simply reach for the door latch and open the door slightly; he won't want to risk damaging it. (Two of you can open a door.)

Our final advice: don't sweat the small change. So the driver is charging you Dr2,300 ($8) for a ride you have been told should be Dr2,000 ($7): are you prepared to go to court for $1? But any difference from Dr500 ($2) up probably should be questioned. Most cabbies are honest and we don't want to make you paranoid, just aware of the possibilities. And please be sure to reward good service with a tip.

certain areas and restricting the hours of use, as they are the single most common cause of complaint from tourists and residents alike.) The motorcycles rented to tourists are usually a bit quieter, but they are more expensive and at least as dangerous; a driver's license is usually required to rent one.

BY BICYCLE

Bicycles are not nearly as common in Greece as they are throughout most of Europe, as they are not well suited to the terrain (or temperament) and would be downright dangerous in traffic. Older bikes are usually available for rent at very modest prices in

Warning

Although mopeds are the vehicle of choice in Greece, especially on the islands, be aware that a law was recently passed in Greece (prompted by a huge number of accidents) requiring a motorcycle license for anyone driving a moped. Agencies offering moped rentals rarely tell tourists this, because very few tourists have motorcycle licenses. This makes for a whirlwind of troubles if an accident occurs and the rider is found not to have been licensed. The rider will not be covered by insurance and will have broken the law.

---

most resort areas, and good mountain bikes are increasingly available. (See "The Active Vacation Planner," above, for more information.)

FAST FACTS: Greece

Area Code   The international telephone country code for Greece is **30.** To call Greece from abroad, dial the international access code from your base country plus 30 (Greece's code) plus the Greek area (or city) code *minus* the first zero, then the number. The international access code from Australia is **0011;** from Ireland, New Zealand, and the United Kingdom, **00;** from the United States and Canada, **011.** See also "Telephone," below.

ATMs   See "Money," earlier in this chapter.

Banks   Banks are open to the public Monday through Thursday from 8am to 2pm, Friday from 8am to 1:30pm. Some banks have additional hours for foreign currency exchange. All banks are closed on the long list of Greek holidays. (See "Holidays," earlier in this chapter.)

Business Hours   Greek business and office hours take some getting used to, especially in the afternoon, when most English-speaking people are accustomed to getting things done in high gear. Compounding the problem is that it is virtually impossible to pin down the precise hours of opening. We can start by saying that almost all stores and services are still closed on Sunday—except, of course, tourist-oriented shops and services. On Monday, Wednesday, and Saturday, hours are usually 9am to 3pm; Tuesday, Thursday, and Friday, 9am to 2pm and 5 to 7pm. The afternoon siesta is still generally observed from 3 to 5pm, though many tourist-oriented businesses have a minimal crew during nap time and may keep extended hours, often from 8am to 10pm. (In fact, in tourist centers, shops may be open at all kinds of hours.) Most government offices are open Monday through Friday only, from 8am to 3pm. We suggest you call ahead to check the hours of businesses you need to deal with and that you not disturb Greek friends during siesta hours. Final advice: Anything you really need to accomplish in a government office, business, or store should be done on weekdays between about 9am and 1pm.

Car Rentals   See "Getting Around," earlier in this chapter.

Climate   See "When to Go," earlier in this chapter.

Crime   Crime is not a significant concern in Greece. Athens is probably the safest capital in Europe. Pocket-picking and purse snatching may be slightly on the rise, especially in heavily touristed areas, but breaking into cars remains rare. Tourists, however, are conspicuous and much more likely to be carrying

A Word on Hotel Bathrooms

The bathrooms in all the newer and higher-grade Greek hotels are now practically "state of the art," but there are a few things travelers might appreciate knowing in advance. Few hotels ever provide washcloths, and the soap is often the old-fashioned minibar. Many hotels still don't offer generous-sized towels, and even many mid-priced hotels provide only cramped showers. As it happens, the one thing the Greeks are generous with is slippery marble: be very careful getting in and out of tubs or showers.

valuables, so take normal precautions—lock the car, don't leave cameras and such gear visible, etc.

Currency See "Money," earlier in this chapter.

Customs You are allowed to bring into Greece duty-free personal belongings including clothes, camping gear, and most sports equipment. (Certain water-sports equipment, such as Windsurfers, can be brought in only if a Greek citizen residing in Greece guarantees they will be reexported. Scuba diving is presently restricted to a very few areas, and divers will have difficulty bringing in equipment.) You may bring two cameras with 10 rolls of film each, a movie or video camera, a portable radio, a phonograph or tape recorder, a typewriter, a laptop computer, and new articles (including electronic equipment) worth up to Dr10,000 ($33) or Dr40,000 ($134) for EU members, provided they are not for resale.

Visitors from outside the European Union are allowed up to 10 kilos of food and beverage, 200 cigarettes (300 for EU members), 50 cigars (75, EU), 250 grams of tobacco (400, EU), 1 liter of distilled alcohol or 2 liters of wine (1½ liters of alcohol or 5 liters of wine, EU), 50 grams of perfume (75 grams, EU), 500 grams of coffee (1 kilo, EU), and 100 grams of tea (400 grams, EU).

There are presently no restrictions on the amount of traveler's checks either arriving or departing, though amounts over $1,000 must be declared, and if you plan to leave the country with more than $500 in bank notes (or its equivalent in other currency) you must declare at least that sum on entry. No Greek moneys more than Dr10,000 per traveler may be imported or exported.

Explosives, weapons, and narcotics are prohibited; violations are subject to severe punishment. Medication, except for limited amounts properly prescribed for your own use, and plants with soil are prohibited. Passengers from the United States and the United Kingdom arriving in Athens aboard international flights are generally not searched, and if they have nothing to declare, continue through a green lane. (Because of the continuing threat of terrorism, baggage is x-rayed before boarding domestic flights.)

Dogs and cats may be brought in with proper health documentation, including rabies inoculation, not newer than 6 days before arrival nor older than 12 months for dogs and 6 months for cats.

Greek antiquities are strictly protected by law, and no genuine antiquities may be taken out of Greece without prior special permission from the **Archaeological Service,** Odos Polignotou 3, Athens. Also, you should expect to explain how you acquired any genuinely old objects—in particular, icons or religious articles.

Remember to keep receipts for all merchandise purchased in Greece for clearing customs on your return home.

Dentists & Doctors   Ask your embassy or consulate in a major city or your hotel's management to direct you to a dentist or doctor who speaks either English or some other well-known European language.

Driving Rules   See "Getting Around," earlier in this chapter.

Drugs   Greek authorities and law are reputed to be extremely tough when it comes to finding foreigners with drugs—starting with marijuana. Don't attempt to bring any illicit drugs into or out of Greece.

Drugstores   See "Pharmacies," below.

Electricity   Electric current in Greece is 220 volts AC, alternating at 50 cycles. (Some larger hotels have 110-volt low-wattage outlets for electric shavers, but they aren't good for hair dryers and most other appliances.) Electrical outlets require Continental-type plugs with two round prongs. U.S. travelers will need an adapter plug *and* a converter, unless their appliances are dual-voltage. (These can be bought in stores like Radio Shack.) Laptop-computer users will want to check their specs; a converter may be necessary, and surge protectors are recommended.

Embassies & Consulates   See "Fast Facts: Athens" in chapter 5 for a list of embassies and consulates. U.S. citizens can get emergency aid by calling ☎ 01/ 723-6211 during the day; at night, try ☎ 01/723-7727 or 01/724-1331. United Kingdom citizens can get emergency aid by calling ☎ 01/721-2951 during the day; at night, try ☎ 01/729-4301 or 01/729-4444.

Emergencies   These numbers can be used throughout Greece. For the regular **police,** dial ☎ **100;** for **tourist police,** dial ☎ **171.** For **fire,** dial ☎ **199.** For **medical emergencies** and/or first-aid and/or an ambulance, dial ☎ **166.** For **hospitals,** dial ☎ **106.** For **automobile emergencies,** put out a triangular danger sign and telephone ☎ **104** or **174.**

Faxes   Almost all hotels of a certain category, many telephone offices, some post offices, and some travel agencies will send and receive faxes locally and internationally for you at set fees. But don't forget: sending a fax is the equivalent of making a phone call, so you must be prepared to pay for that plus the extra service of the fax machine (about Dr1,500/$5 per page to the U.S.).

Holidays   See "When to Go," earlier in this chapter.

Information   See "Visitor Information," earlier in this chapter.

Internet Access   Increasingly popular throughout the world, these cafes-with-computers are springing up in Greece's cities and resort towns. We indicate their location wherever they are known. For a set fee—about Dr1,500 ($5) an hour, with a Dr500 ($1.70) minimum—you get to log on to the Internet. (It is not required that you buy a drink while using the computer, but why not enjoy the experience?) Most travelers will want one particular service—to gain access to their **e-mail,** a cheaper and more convenient way of keeping in touch than the telephone.

Before you leave for Greece, visit one of the Web sites dedicated to listing Internet cafes worldwide. They're bound to be more up-to-date than a printed guide could ever be. The best of these guides at press time was **www. netcafeguide.com.**

A number of **free e-mail services** have established themselves on the Web in the last year or two (try www.excite.com or www.hotmail.com). These services allow you to establish an account in exchange for viewing their ads, and do not charge a fee to the user. Any traveler with this kind of account can access e-mail from any computer worldwide that has Internet access. Simply enter your ID and password, and hope for rapid and reliable access.

Language   Language is usually not a problem for English speakers in Greece, as so much of the population has lived abroad, where English is the primary language; meanwhile, young people learn it in school, from Anglo-American–dominated pop culture, and in special classes meant to prepare them for the contemporary world of business. Many television programs are also broadcast in their original language, and American prime-time soaps are very popular, nearly inescapable. Even advertisements have an increasingly high English content.

Don't let all this keep you from trying to pick up at least a few words of Greek; your effort will be rewarded by your hosts, who realize how difficult their language is for foreigners and will patiently help you improve your pronunciation and usage. There are various taped programs, including **Berlitz's Greek for Travelers** and **Passport's Conversational Greek in 7 Days,** which can be very helpful.

Our Appendix, "Making Your Way in Greek," will teach you the basics.

Laundry & Dry Cleaning   All cities and towns of any size will have both laundry and dry-cleaning establishments. Many travelers will prefer to make arrangements through their hotel desks; this is fine, but be prepared to pay heavily for even the smallest bundle. (Then again, everything including socks will have been ironed!) If you are more ambitious (or frugal), you can seek out one of the laundries that we try to locate wherever available. In most instances, these are attended and you can leave your laundry to be picked up later (be sure you are in agreement as to the time it will be ready). A medium-size bag of laundry may cost about Dr2,400 ($8), washed, dried, and neatly folded.

Mail   You can receive mail addressed to you % Poste Restante, General Post Office, City (or Town), Island (or Province), Greece. You will need your passport to collect this mail. Many hotels will accept, hold, and even forward mail for you also; ask first. American Express clients can receive mail at any Amex office in Athens, Corfu, Iraklion, Mikonos, Patras, Rhodes, Santorini, Skiathos, and Thessaloniki, for a nominal fee and with proper identification.

Newspapers & Magazines   All cities, large towns, and major tourist centers now have at least one shop and/or kiosk that carries a selection of foreign-language publications; most of these are flown or shipped in on the very day of publication. English-language readers have a wide selection, including most of the British papers—*Daily Telegraph, Financial Times, Guardian, Independent, Times*—the *International Herald Tribune* (with its inserted English-language version of the well-known Athens newspaper, *Kathimerini*), or *USA Today.* A quite decent alternative is the English-language paper published in Athens, *Athens News,* widely available throughout Greece.

Pets   See "Customs," above.

Pharmacies   The *pharmakio,* identified by a green cross, is the first place to go with minor medical problems, as pharmacists usually speak English well and many medications can be dispensed without prescription. Ask for directions at your hotel. In larger cities, if the one you find is closed, look in the window for a sign giving the address of one that might be open.

Photographic Needs   Cameras, film, accessories, and photo developing (including express service) are widely available, though more expensive, in Greece.

Booking a Room

Try to make reservations by fax so that you have a written record of what room and price were agreed upon. Also, a double room in Greece does not mean a room with a double bed, but a room with two twin beds. Double beds in Greece are, at least on the islands, called matrimonial beds. And rooms with double beds are most often designated not as doubles but as honeymoon rooms. This leads to many disputes and misunderstandings.

Note that room prices, no matter what people say officially, are negotiable, especially at the edges of the season. Because of Greek law and OTE regulations, hotel keepers are very reluctant to give out any rates in advance and often quote prices higher than their actual rates. When you bargain, don't cite our prices, which may be too high, but ask instead for the best current rate. Off-season prices may be as much as 40% lower than the lowest rate given to us for the book.

Police   To report a crime or medical emergency, or for information or other assistance, first contact the local tourist police (telephone numbers will be found under "Essentials" in the particular destinations' chapters that follow), where an English-speaking officer is more likely to be found. If there is no tourist police officer available (☎ **171**), contact the local police. The telephone number for emergencies throughout Greece is ☎ **100.**

Radio & Television   The Greek ERT 1 radio has weather and news in English at 7:40am. The BBC World Service can be picked up on short-wave frequencies, often at the frequencies of 9.140, 15.07, and 12.09 Mhz; on FM it is usually at 107.1. Antenna TV, CNN, Eurochannel, and other cable networks are widely available. Many better hotels have cable television.

Rentals (Apartments & Houses)   An increasingly popular way to experience Greece is to rent an apartment or house; the advantages include freedom from the formalities of a hotel, often a more desirable location, and a kitchen that allows you to avoid the costs and occasional crush of restaurants. Such rentals do not come cheap, but if you calculate what two or more people might pay for a decent hotel, not to mention all the meals eaten out, it can turn out to be a good deal. (Costs per person per day in really nice apartments run about $75; in the fancier villas, about $150.) Any full-service travel agency in your home country or in Greece should be able to put you in touch with an agency specializing in such rentals. Among those in the United States are **Greek Island Connection,** 889 Ninth Ave., New York, NY 10019 (☎ 800/241-2417; fax 212/581-5890); **Rent a Home Int'l,** 7200 34th Ave. NW, Seattle, WA 98117 (☎ 800/488-7368; fax 206/789-9379); **Villas International,** 605 Market St., San Francisco, CA 94105 (☎ 800/221-2260; fax 415/281-0919). In Canada, try **CTI Carriers,** 65 Overlea Blvd., Toronto, Ontario M4H 1P1 (☎ 800/363-8181; fax 416/429-7159), or **Grecian Holidays,** 75 The Donaway West, Don Mills, Ontario M3C 2E9 (☎ 800/268-6786; fax 416/510-1509). In the United Kingdom, try **Simply Travel Ltd.,** 598–608 Chiswick High Rd., London W4 5XY (☎ 0181/994-4462), or **Pure Crete,** 90–92 Southbridge Rd., Croydon, Surrey CRO 1AF (☎ 0181/760-0879; fax 0181/680-8521). A similar possibility is to rent a traditional house in 1 of about 12 relatively rural or remote villages or settlements throughout Greece. These small traditional houses have been restored by the Greek National Tourist Organization (GNTO); to learn more about this possibility, contact the GNTO office nearest you. (See "Visitor Information," earlier in this chapter, or go to www.areianet.gr/infoxenios).

Rest Rooms   Public rest rooms are not widespread in Greece, and they are sometimes crude, but there is usually at least one in any good-size Greek town and they usually do work. (Old-fashioned squat facilities are still found.) Carry some toilet tissue with you at all times. In most places—even quite modern restaurants and hotels—you are told not to flush it down the toilet; use the receptacles provided. In an emergency, you can ask to use the facilities of a restaurant or shop, though near major attractions they are sometimes denied to all but customers because the generosity is abused. If you are permitted the use of such facilities, keep in mind the needs of future travelers, respect your benefactor, and leave a small tip to the attendant.

Smoking   As mentioned above under discussions of various modes of travel, Greeks continue to be among the most persistent smokers. Smoking is prohibited on all domestic flights and in certain areas or types of ships, but elsewhere, Greeks—and foreigners—feel free to puff away at will. (The Olympic airport in Athens is virtually a cancer culture lab.) We are not aware of any hotels that set aside rooms for nonsmokers, but you can ask. If you are really bothered by smoke while eating, about all you can do is position yourself as best as possible—and then be prepared to move if it gets really bad.

Taxes & Service Charges   Unless otherwise noted, all hotel prices include a service charge, usually 12%, a 6% value-added tax (VAT), and a 4½% community tax. In most restaurants, a 13% service charge, an 8% VAT, and some kind of municipal tax (in Athens it is 5%) are also included in the prices and final bill. (By the way, don't confuse any of these charges with a standard "cover charge" that may be Dr100 to Dr250 (35¢ to 80¢) per setting. Also see "Tipping," below.) A VAT of 18% is added to rental-car rates.

All purchases also include a VAT tax of anywhere from 4% to 18%. If you have purchased an item that costs Dr40,000 ($133) or more and are a citizen of a non–European Union nation, you can get at least most of this refunded (provided you are exporting it within 90 days of time of purchase). The easiest thing to do is to shop at stores that display the sign "TAX-FREE FOR TOURISTS." But any store should be able to provide you with a Tax-Free Check Form, which you complete in the store. As you are leaving the country, you present a copy of this to the refund desk (usually with the Customs office); be prepared to show both the goods and the receipt as proof of purchase, and be prepared to spend a fair amount of time before you get the refund.

Telephone   In the cities and larger towns, many kiosks have telephones from which you can make local calls for Dr20 (7¢). (In remote areas, they will let you make long-distance calls from these phones.) Older public telephones require a Dr20 coin—which are in short supply, so hold onto several if they come your way. Deposit the coin and listen for a dial tone, an irregular beep. A regular beep indicates the line is busy.

In the old days, most foreigners went to the offices of the **Telecommunications Organization of Greece** (*Organismos Tilepikinonion tis Ellados*), **OTE**—pronounced *oh*-tay—to place most of their phone calls, especially overseas calls. But because card phones are now so widespread throughout Greece, this is no longer necessary, once you get the hang of using them. You must first purchase a phone card at an OTE office or at most kiosks. (You are advised to buy one at the

OTE office at the airport on first arriving.) These come in three denominations: Dr1,700 ($6) for 100 units; Dr7,000 ($23) for 500 units; and Dr11,500 ($39) for 10,000 units.

A local call of up to 3 minutes costs Dr20 (7¢) or one unit off a phone card; for each minute beyond that, it costs another Dr20 or one unit off the card (so that a 10-min. local call costs eight units).

Long-distance calls, both domestic and international, can be quite expensive in Greece, especially at hotels, which may add a surcharge up to 100%, unless you have a telephone credit card, which can reduce your expense considerably by avoiding hotel surcharges.

If you still prefer to make your call from an OTE office, these are usually centrally and conveniently located. (Local offices are given under "Essentials" for the destinations in the chapters that follow.) At OTE offices, you must first go to one of the clerks, who will assign you a booth with a metered phone. You can make collect calls, but this can take much longer, so it's easier to pay cash, unless you have a phone card or intend to use your own international credit card.

To call Greece from abroad, follow your long distance provider's directions for making a long distance call. For AT&T, for instance, to reach Greece, this means dialing 011 + 30 + the city code + telephone number. We provide these city codes and local numbers throughout our text. Note, however, that when calling from abroad, you *drop* the 0 that precedes the city code.

To make an international long distance call from Greece, the easiest and cheapest way is to make use of your long-distance service provider; call your company before leaving home to determine the access number that you must dial in Greece. The principal access codes in Greece are: **AT&T,** ☎ **00800-1311; MCI,** ☎ **00800-1211;** and **Sprint,** ☎**00800-1411.** Most companies also offer a recorded-message service in case the number you're calling at home is busy or doesn't answer.

To make a direct call abroad from Greece—whether placing the call from an OTE office, a card phone, or a coin phone—dial the country code plus the area code, omitting the initial zero (if any), then the number. Some country codes are: **Australia,** 0061; **Canada,** 001; **Ireland,** 00353; **New Zealand,** 0064; **United Kingdom,** 0044; and **United States,** 001. Note that if you are going to put all the charges on your phone card (that is, not on your long-distance provider), you are being charged at quite a high rate per minute (at least Dr1,000/$3.30 to North America), so you should not start a call unless your phone card has a fair number of drachmas still valid. However, if you use the phone card simply to get access to the international code required by the long-distance provider whose special access numbers you are using (see above), you will be charged only at the rates for local calls: one unit for the first 3 minutes, then one unit for each subsequent minute.

Time Zone   Greece is 2 hours ahead of Greenwich mean time. With reference to North American time zones, it's 7 hours ahead of eastern standard time, 8 hours ahead of central standard time, 9 hours ahead of mountain standard time, and 10 hours ahead of Pacific standard time.

The European system of a 24-hour clock is used officially, and on schedules you'll usually see noon written as 1200, 3:30pm as 1530, and 11pm as 2300. In informal conversation, however, Greeks express time much as we do—though noon may mean anywhere from noon to 3pm, afternoon is 3 to 7pm, and evening is 7pm to midnight.

Tipping   A 10% to 15% service charge is included in virtually all restaurant bills. (It is no longer shown in a second column of prices next to the menu item. Prices are, by the way, to some extent controlled by the government.) Nevertheless, it's customary to leave an additional 5% to 10% for the waiter, especially if there has been some special service. Even on small bills, change up to the nearest Dr100 is left. Good taxi service merits a tip of 10% or so. (Greeks rarely tip taxi drivers, but tourists are expected to.) Hotel chambermaids should be left about Dr300 ($1) per night (Dr500/$1.70 per couple). Bellhops and doormen should be tipped Dr200 to Dr500 (60¢ to $1.70), depending on the services provided.

Water   The public drinking water in Greece is safe to drink, though it can be salty or brackish in some locales near the sea. Many people prefer the bottled water commonly available at restaurants, hotels, cafes, food stores, and kiosks. The days when Greek restaurants automatically served glasses of cold fresh water are gone; you are now usually made to feel that you must order bottled water, at which point you will have to choose between natural or carbonated (*metalliko*), and domestic or imported. Cafes, however, still tend to provide a glass of natural water.

Cruising the Greek Islands 4

by Fran Wenograd Golden

A cruise around the Greek islands affords travelers an easy and convenient way to enjoy the spectacular scenery and ancient historic sites without the hassle of ferry schedules and changing hotel rooms.

You get on the ship, you unpack once, and you're transported to a world of whitewashed villages, volcanic shorelines, and lost cities surrounded by very blue sea. The ship—your floating hotel—goes with you, providing accommodations and food, attentive service, and a familiar retreat to return to after a day of touring or just kicking back in the Greek sun. As Dolphin Hellas (Golden Sun) Cruises puts it on its Internet site, "Every moment of your experience reminds you that Western civilization began with the Greeks, and apparently so too did relaxation and pampering."

The Greek Islands are one of the best cruise destinations in the world. The seas are relatively calm and the islands individual in character, offering travelers a satisfying mix of local culture, gorgeous scenery, and ancient and medieval ruins to explore.

Most Greek Island itineraries highlight the region's history with optional guided tours, called **shore excursions,** that take in the major sights. In addition, passengers have the option of joining organized diversions such as visits to beaches, meals at local restaurants, and fishing or sailing excursions.

Of course, you can also choose to get off the ship at each port of call and head off on your own to explore the sights, hit the beach, or check out the local color at the nearest taverna.

1 Choosing the Right Cruise for You

In choosing your cruise, you need to think about what you want to see and in what level of comfort you want to see it.

We recommend you first decide **what you want to see.** Are you looking to visit the most popular islands—Mikonos, Santorini, and Rhodes—or are you interested in places off the beaten path? Whichever it is, you'll want to make sure the itinerary you choose allows enough time for you to really experience the place. Some ships visit a port and spend the full day, while others visit two or even three, meaning your sightseeing time is very limited.

Because of the Greek laws, only Greek-flagged ships have in the past been allowed to cruise within Greece. This law officially changes in 1999, allowing any European-flagged ship to sail between Greek ports.

But for now many Greek Islands cruises either embark or disembark in Italy or Turkey. You'll have to consider embarkation and disembarkation points in making your decision. Do you mind flying to Venice or Istanbul to catch your ship?

Greece is also visited by ships as part of European itineraries where Greece is not the sole focus, but only one of several countries visited. If you're looking for a trip that includes several countries, that's fine. But if you're looking to spend most of your time in Greece, make sure you choose an appropriate itinerary.

Next, consider **how long you want to spend on the ship**—3 days, a week, 2 weeks? If you have the time, you may want to consider a **cruisetour,** which combines a cruise to the islands with a guided tour of important sights on the mainland. This is made easy in Greece by the fact that some lines offer cruises of only 3 or 4 days, which you can combine with a land tour into a 1-week vacation.

Also consider **when you want to cruise.** While Greece has traditionally been a summer destination, the season has been stretched in recent years, and some lines now offer cruises here year-round (although most of the action on the islands still takes place from Apr through Oct). Some months have their drawbacks. For instance, temperatures can reach 100°F in July and August, and, due to the wind, August tends to be a particularly bumpy month on the high seas. It tends to rain in April and November. In contrast, May and October are relatively problem-free, making them particularly nice times to sail in Greece.

You'll want to think about **what you want out of the cruise experience.** Is the purpose of your cruise to see as much as you can of the islands, or to relax by the ship's pool? And what level of comfort, entertainment, onboard activities, and so forth do you require? Some ships spend a day or more at sea, meaning they don't visit a port at all that day. Experienced cruises will tell you these are among the most favored itineraries, giving them a chance to truly relax and unwind. But if your goal is seeing as much of Greece as you can, these itineraries may not be for you.

CHOOSING YOUR SHIP

Ships cruising the Greek Islands range from small yacht-type vessels to traditional midsize ships to resortlike 2,000-passenger megaships. Which you choose has a lot to do with your personality and vacation goals.

MEGASHIPS & LARGE SHIPS   These ships focus as much on the ship and onboard offerings as they do on the destination they're visiting. The ships are floating resorts—sometimes of the glitzy variety—offering American-style luxury and amenities and attentive service. In its brochure, Holland America Line unabashedly says that "When asked which European city he liked best, one guest replied 'My Holland America ship—that was my favorite city.'" We think that kind of says it all. These ships, which tend to be newer, feature Las Vegas–style shows, lavish casinos, big spas and gyms, plenty of bars, extravagant meals, lots of daytime activities (such as games, contests, cooking lessons, wine tastings, and sport tournaments), and generally few ethnic Greek offerings.

CLASSIC & MIDSIZE SHIPS   Ships in this category include older, classic vessels as well as some newer ships. Destination is more a focus than on the bigger ships, and itineraries may be very busy, with the ship visiting an island a day, or sometimes two. This leaves little time for onboard daytime activities, although some will be offered. In the Greek market, some of these ships feature Greek crews and cuisine, and service tends to be a big area of focus. Because these ships are popular with Europeans, many languages are likely to be spoken. The ships offer a variety of bars and lounges, have entertainment generally in a main show lounge, and feature at least one swimming pool and a small casino, a spa and gym, and plenty of open deck space. Some also have movie theaters. Accommodations are generally good-sized, and range from rather plain to quite lavish.

SMALL SHIPS & YACHTS   Small ships and yachts tend to offer more of a relaxed pace and may seek itineraries that focus on smaller, alternative ports (which they can get into because of their smaller size and shallow draft). They may offer a "soft adventure" cruise experience, or they may offer more of a luxury yacht experience. Some of the ships feature Greek crews and Greek cuisine. There will typically be more interaction with fellow passengers than on larger ships—partially because there will be less entertainment, and there may or may not be a swimming pool, casino, spa, or gym. Cabins range from small and comfortable on some of these ships to very luxurious on others. Ditto for public rooms. Some are sailing vessels, although the sails are typically more for show than for power.

2 Calculating the Cost

Cruises in the Greek Islands range from 3 days to 2 weeks, with per diem prices ranging from around $99 to over $1,000 per person, double occupancy. To determine the real value of the cruise, though, you have to examine what you get for your money.

The prices include three meals a day (with a couple exceptions, which we've noted in the ship reviews below), accommodations, onboard activities and entertainment, and, if you book your airfare through the cruise line, a transfer from the airport to the ship. Some rates include tips, shore excursions, pre- and postcruise hotel rooms, and airfare—though these are generally offered at an extra charge. Some cruises are packaged as cruisetours, meaning they include both hotel stays and land tours. Rarely included in the price are alcoholic beverages or—at the opposite end of the spectrum—spa and beauty treatments. Port charges, taxes, and other fees are also typically extra, though they're sometimes included in the fare.

Cruise brochures typically state the highest rate the line will charge for the cruise, but cruises rarely actually sell for that rate. Think of it as the **sticker price.** Various discounts and deals are calculated off this price, including early-bird savings, group deals, and last-minute deals. Seasonal sales are also offered, usually in the early spring and late fall. Cruise prices quoted in this chapter are brochure rates.

Cruise prices are based on two people sharing a cabin. Some lines have special **single supplement** prices, which are generally higher than shared-cabin rates. At the opposite end, some lines offer highly discounted rates for a third or fourth person sharing a cabin with two full-fare passengers.

Senior citizens may be able to get extra savings on their cruise. Some lines will take 5% off the top for those 55 and over, and the senior rate applies even if the second person in the cabin is younger. Membership in groups such as AARP is not required, but such membership may bring additional savings.

Some of the more upscale lines will reward customers willing to pay their full fare in advance (thus giving the cruise line cash in hand) with savings of as much as 10%.

If your package does not include **airfare,** you should consider booking air transportation with the cruise line. The rates tend to be discounted, and booking through the line allows the cruise company to keep track of you if, for instance, your flight is delayed. The cruise lines also negotiate special deals with hotels at port cities if you want to come in a few days before your flight or stay after.

3 Booking Your Cruise

There are a lot of nuances to booking a cruise vacation, and the best way to assure you get what you paid for is to work with an experienced travel agent. The agent can help you find the best deal on the cruise itself as well as airfare, and can clue you in on the latest discounts to help you decide whether, for instance, you want to combine your cruise with a land tour.

To find an agent, ask friends for advice. Try to find someone who is experienced in selling cruises and who has cruised before, preferably in Greece. Work with a cruise-only agency (an agency that specializes in cruises) or a cruise specialist (an agent that specializes in cruises).

Cruise specialists are in frequent contact with the cruise lines and are kept informed by the lines about the latest and greatest deals and special offers. Some agencies buy blocks of space that they sell at a special price.

A good and easy rule of thumb in finding an experienced agent is to seek a member of the **Cruise Lines International Association** (CLIA) (☎ **212/921-0066;** www.ten-io.com/clia) or the **National Association of Cruise Oriented Agencies** (☎ **305/663-5626;** www.nacoa.com). Members of both groups are cruise specialists.

Be wary of high-volume operators who advertise in the Sunday newspaper. You may get a decent price, but you will probably not get a high level of service and expertise. Also, since these operators work by buying up large blocks of space on ships, they're not likely to offer a great variety of options—you'll be conforming to their schedules rather than them conforming to yours.

CHOOSING A CABIN

One of your biggest decisions once you choose the ship you want to sail on is what type of cabin you desire. Will you be happy with a slightly cramped space without a window, or do you require a suite with a private veranda?

Obviously price will be a determinant here. If you aren't planning to spend time in your cabin except to sleep, shower, and change clothes, an **inside cabin** (that is, one without a porthole or window) might do just fine. If you get claustrophobic, however, or insist on sunshine first thing in the morning, pay a bit more and take an **outside cabin** (one with a window).

When you book your cabin, you generally will not be choosing a specific cabin number but rather a cabin category, within which all units have the same amenities. With this in mind, one concern if you do go the window route is **obstructed views.** Check to make sure none of the cabins in the category you've selected have windows that directly face lifeboats or other objects that may stand between you and the clear blue sea. You can determine this by looking at a diagram of the ship (included in the cruise brochure) or through consultation with your travel agent.

Most ships offer cabins for two with private bathrooms and showers (bathtubs are considered a luxury on most ships, and are usually offered only in the most expensive cabins), and twin beds that may be converted to a queen. There are other variations, of course: For instance, a number of ships have some cabins with bunk beds, many ships have cabins designed for three or four people, and some have connecting cabins for families.

Cabin amenities vary by line, and might include TVs (with a closed system of pro-grammed movies and features), hair dryers, safes, minirefrigerators, and VCRs. If any of these are must-haves, let your agent know.

Cruising the Web

The Internet is a good tool for researching your cruise, and we include the Web addresses of the cruise lines in our cruise reviews (see below). Most of these feature pictures of the ships and their cabins, and some even offer virtual tours. A few allow you to actually book your cruise on the spot, but keep in mind that if you do this and goof up, you have no one to blame but yourself. You can also use the Web to find a good, experienced, cruise-savvy travel agent. The following sites, operated by cruise and travel-agent trade associations, include listings of agents by zip code, telephone area code, and special areas of expertise.

- **Cruise Lines International Association (CLIA):** www.ten-io.com/clia
- **National Association of Cruise Oriented Agents (NACOA):** www.nacoa.com
- **American Society of Travel Agents (ASTA):** www.asta.net.com
- **Institute of Certified Travel Agents (ICTA):** www.icta.com

Usually the higher on the ship the cabin is located, the more expensive it is. But upper decks also tend to be rockier in rough seas than the middle or lower parts of the ship (a factor to consider if you're prone to seasickness).

Size of cabin is determined in terms of square feet. As a rough guide, 120 square feet is low-end and cramped; 180 square feet is midrange and the minimum for people with claustrophobia; 250 square feet and larger is suite-sized.

A recent and popular innovation is private verandas or balconies, where you can enjoy the sea breezes in your own lounge chair—but you pay for the privilege.

If noise bothers you, try to pick a cabin away from the engine room and nowhere near the disco.

CHOOSING A MEAL TIME

Because most ship dining rooms are not large enough to accommodate all passengers at one dinner seating, times and tables are assigned. When you book your trip, you will have to indicate your preferred meal time. Early, or "main," seating is usually 6 or 6:30pm; late seating, 8 or 8:30pm.

There are advantages to both times. **Early seating** is usually less crowded, and the preferred time for families and older passengers who want to get to bed early. Food items are fresher (they don't have to sit in warmers), but the waiters may be rushed, waiting for the next wave. Early diners get first dibs on nighttime entertainment venues, and might be hungry again for the midnight buffet. **Late seating** allows time for a nap or late spa appointment before dinner. Service is slower paced. You can linger with after-dinner drinks. You can catch the late show at 10pm.

On most ships, breakfast and lunch are open seating, but you may be requested to eat at an assigned time. (Early means breakfast at 7 or 8am, lunch at noon; late, breakfast 8:30 to 9am, lunch at 1:30pm.)

The cruise line should be informed at the time you make your reservations about any **special dietary requests** you have. Some lines offer kosher menus; all will have vegetarian, low-fat, low-salt, and sugar-free options available.

You also need to consider **table size** (on most ships, you can request to be at a table of 1, 2, 4, 8, 10, or 12) and whether you want to sit at a **smoking or nonsmoking table**—a particularly important factor in Europe, where smoking is still quite popular.

DEPOSITS, CANCELLATIONS & EXTRAS

After you've made your decision as to which ship you will vacation on, you will be required to put a deposit on your trip, with the remaining fare usually paid no later than 2 months in advance of your departure date.

Cruise lines have varying policies regarding cancellations, and it's important to look at the fine print in the line's brochure to make sure you understand the policy. Most lines allow you to cancel for a full refund on your deposit and payment any time up to 76 days before the sailing, after which you have to pay a penalty. If you cancel at the last minute, you will typically be refunded only 75% of what you've paid.

Your agent will discuss with you optional **airfare programs** offered by the lines, **transfers from the airport to the pier,** and any **pre- or postcruise hotel or tour programs.** Some lines also let you purchase **shore excursions** in advance (for more on shore excursions, see below). And there may also be prebookable spa packages available.

If you are not booking airfare through the cruise line, make sure to allow several hours between the plane's arrival and when you need to get on the ship. It may be best, in terms of reducing anxiety, to come in a day before and spend the night in a hotel.

4 Cruise Preparation Practicalities

About 1 month before your cruise and no later than 1 week before, you should receive your **cruise documents,** including your airline tickets (if you purchased them from the cruise line), a boarding document with your cabin number and sometimes dining choices on it, boarding forms to fill out, luggage tags, and your prearranged bus transfer vouchers and hotel vouchers (if applicable).

There will also be information about **shore excursions** and additional material detailing things you need to know before you sail.

Read all of this carefully. Make sure your cabin category and dining preferences are as you requested and that your airline flight and arrival times are what you were told. If there are problems, call your agent immediately. Make sure there is enough time so you can arrive at the port no later than an hour before departure time.

You will be required to have a passport for your trip (see chapter 3 for more on this). If you are flying into Istanbul you will also be required to have a Turkish visa.

We recommend you confirm your flight 3 days before departure. Also, before you leave for the airport, tie the tags provided by the cruise line onto your luggage and fill in your boarding cards. This will save you time when you arrive at the ship.

CASH MATTERS

You have already paid the lion's share of your cruise vacation, but you will need a credit card or traveler's checks to handle your **onboard expenses** on the ship (such as bar drinks, dry cleaning and laundry, phone calls, massage and other spa services, beauty parlor services, photos taken by the ship's photographer, baby-sitting, wine at dinner, and souvenirs) as well as **shore excursions** and **tips** (see below for tips on tipping).

You will want cash for taxis, drinks, small purchases, and tips for guides in port.

Some ships, but not all, will take a personal check. If you want to pay in cash or by traveler's check, you will be asked to leave a deposit, usually $250 for a 1-week sailing. Some ships have ATMs if you need to get cash while aboard, and some (but not all) offer currency-exchange services.

We suggest you keep careful track of your onboard expenses to avoid an unpleasant surprise at the end of your cruise. Some ships make this particularly easy by offering interactive TV. By pushing the right buttons, you can check your account from the comfort of your own stateroom. On others you can get this information at the purser's office or guest-relations desk.

PACKING

Generally, ships describe their daily recommended attire as **casual, informal,** and **formal,** prompting many people to think they'll have to bring a steamer trunk full of clothes just to get through their trip. Not true; you can probably get along with about half of what you think you need. Also, almost all ships offer laundry and dry-cleaning services, and some have coin-operated self-serve laundries aboard, so you have the option of packing less and just having your clothes cleaned midway through your trip.

During the day, the onboard style is casual, but keep in mind some ships do not allow swimsuits or tank tops in the dining room. For dinner, there are usually two formal nights and two informal nights during a 5- to 7-day cruise, with the rest casual. There will usually be proportionally more formal nights on longer cruises.

The daily bulletin delivered to your cabin each day will advise you of the proper dress code for the evening. **Formal** means a tux or dark suit with tie for men, and a nice cocktail dress, long dress, gown, or dressy pantsuit for women. **Informal** is a jacket, tie, and dress slacks or a light suit for men (jeans are frowned upon), and a dress, skirt and blouse, or pants outfit for women. **Casual** means a sports shirt or open dress shirt with slacks for men (some will also wear a jacket); women should wear a dress, pants outfit, or skirt and blouse.

Check your cruise documents to determine the number of formal nights (if any) during your cruise. Men who don't own a tuxedo might be able to rent one in advance through the cruise line's preferred supplier (who delivers the tux right to the ship). Information on this service often is sent with your cruise documents. Also, some cruises offer **theme nights,** so you may want to check your cruise documents to see if there are any you'll want to bring special clothes for. (For instance, Greek night means wear blue and white—the national colors.)

We recommend you bring costume jewelry instead of the real stuff, but if you must bring the crown jewels, be careful. If you're not wearing them, leave them either in your in-room safe (if there is one) or with the purser.

In general, for Greece you're best off packing loose and comfortable cotton or other lightweight fabrics. You'll also want to pack a swimsuit, a sun hat, sunglasses, and plenty of sunscreen—the Greek sun can be intense. Obviously, you should adjust your wardrobe depending on when you plan to travel (summer is hotter than spring and fall). Even if you're traveling in August, though, you should bring a sweater, as you'll be in and out of air-conditioning. And don't forget an umbrella.

For shore excursions, comfortable walking shoes are a must, as some involve walking on stone or marble. Also, some tours may visit religious sites that have a "no shorts or bare shoulders" policy, so it's best to bring something to cover up with. (If you're taking the tour through the cruise line, you'll be advised of this before you go.)

If you plan on bringing your own hair dryer, electric razor, curling iron, or other electrical device, you will want to check out the electric current available on the ship in advance. An adapter may be required.

Travel Tip

For customs purposes, we recommend you carry a receipt for jewelry, cameras, or other expensive items, so you can prove you didn't buy them on your trip. (And speaking of cameras, don't forget to pack plenty of film.)

5 Embarkation

Check-in is usually 2 to 3 hours before sailing. You will not be able to board the ship before the scheduled embarkation time. You have up until a half hour (on some ships it's 1 hr.) before departure to board.

At check-in, your boarding documents will be checked and your passport will likely be taken for immigration processing. You will get it back sometime during the cruise (you might want to carry a photocopy as backup). Depending on the cruise line, you may establish your **onboard credit account** at this point by turning over a major credit card to be swiped or making a deposit in cash or traveler's checks (usually $250). On other ships you need to go to the purser's office onboard to establish your account.

You may be given your **dining-room table assignment** in advance of your sailing (on your tickets), or advised of your table number as you check in, or find a card with your table number waiting for you in your stateroom. If you do not receive an assignment by the time you get to your stateroom, you will be directed to a maitre d's desk. This is also the place to go to make any changes if your assignment does not meet with your approval.

Once aboard you'll be shown to your cabin by a crew member, who will probably offer to help carry your hand luggage. No tip is required for this service.

In your cabin you will find a **daily program** detailing the day's events, mealtimes, and so forth, as well as important information on the ship's **safety procedures** and possibly a **deck plan** of the ship. There are also deck plans and directional signs posted around the ship, generally at main stairways and elevators.

If you are planning to use the ship's **spa services,** it's best to stop by early to make appointments so you can get your preferred times (the best times go fast, and some popular treatments sell out).

Note the ship's casino and shops are always closed when the ship is in port. While in the port, the swimming pool(s) will also likely be tarped. They will be filled with either fresh or saltwater after the ship sets sail.

Some lines offer **escorted tours** of the public rooms to get you acquainted with the ship. If you aren't comfortable roaming on your own the first day, check the daily program in your cabin for details.

LIFEBOAT/SAFETY DRILL

Ships are required by law to conduct safety drills the first day out. Most do this either right before the ship sails or shortly thereafter. Attendance is mandatory. A notice on the back of your cabin door will list the procedures and advise as to your assigned **muster station** and how to get there. You will also find directions to the muster station in the hallway. You will be alerted as to the time in both the daily program and in repeated public announcements (and probably by your cabin steward as well).

At the start of the drill, the ship will broadcast its emergency signal. At this time, you will be required to return to your cabin, grab your **life jacket** (which you're shown as soon as you arrive in your cabin), and report to your assigned muster station—usually in a lounge, the casino, or other public room. If you're traveling with children, make sure your cabin is equipped with special children's life jackets. If not, alert your steward.

During the drill, crew members will review how to use the life jackets and explain the ship's safety procedures. Some drills last only a few minutes, while others are quite detailed. If you have any questions about safety procedures, you can address them to a crew member or officer at this time.

Dealing with Seasickness

If you suffer from seasickness, plan on packing some **Bonine** or **Dramamine** in case your ship encounters rough seas. Keep in mind that with both these medications it is recommended you not drink alcohol; Dramamine in particular can make you drowsy. Both can be bought over the counter, and ships also stock supplies onboard, available at either the purser's office or the medical center (in both cases it's usually free).

Another option is the **Transderm patch,** available by prescription only, which goes behind your ear and time-releases medication. The patch can be worn for up to 3 days, but comes with all sorts of side-effect warnings. Some people have also had success in curbing seasickness with **ginger capsules** available at health-food stores. If you prefer not to ingest anything, you might try the **acupressure wristbands** available at most pharmacies. When set in the proper spot on the wrist, they effectively ease seasickness, although if the seas are particularly rough they may have to be supplemented with some medication.

6 Disembarkation

Your shipboard account will close in the wee hours before departure, but prior to that time you will receive a preliminary bill in your cabin. If you are settling your account with your credit card, you don't have to do anything but make sure all the charges are correct. If there is a problem, you will have to report to the purser's office.

If you are paying by cash or traveler's check, you will be asked to settle your account either during the day or night before you leave the ship. This will require you to report to the purser's office. A final invoice will be delivered to your room before departure.

TIPS

You will typically find tipping suggestions in your cabin on the last day of your cruise. These are only suggestions, but, since service personnel make most of their salaries through tips, we don't recommend tipping less—unless, of course, bad service warrants it.

(Usually, when ships operate on a **no-tipping-required** basis, the staff will still accept a tip, but on some very upper-scale lines, tipping is strictly forbidden.)

Each passenger should usually tip his or her cabin steward and waiter about $3 to $3.50 per day each, and the bus boy $1.50 to $2. On some ships you are also encouraged to tip the maitre d'. That totals up to about $56 for a 7-night cruise (you do not have to include disembarkation day). On Greek ships, all tips are pooled and later divvied up among the crew. The recommended amount in these cases is about $9 per person per day.

You may have to pay tips in cash (U.S. dollars are okay), although some lines let you put the tips on your charge account.

Bar bills automatically include a 15% tip, but if the wine steward, for instance, has served you exceptionally well, you can slip him or her a bill, too. If you have spa or beauty treatments, you can tip that person at the time of the service (you can even do it on your shipboard charge account).

Don't tip the captain or other officers. They're professional, salaried employees. The porters at the pier will likely expect a tip.

PACKING UP

Because of the number of bags being handled, big ships require guests to pack the night before departure and leave their bags in the hallway, usually by midnight. (Be sure they're tagged with the cruise line's luggage tags, which are color-coded to indicate deck number and disembarkation order.) The bags will be picked up overnight and removed from the ship before passengers are allowed to disembark. You'll see them again in the cruise terminal, where they'll most likely be arranged by deck number.

Pack all your purchases made during the trip in one suitcase. This way you can easily retrieve them if you are stopped at customs.

7 The Cruise Lines & Their Ships

In this section, we describe the ships offering Greek Islands cruises. Ships that focus on Greece are first, followed by ships that visit Greece as part of longer itineraries.

The lines are listed alphabetically. Rates are 1999 **brochure prices.** As we said earlier, various discounts and deals are calculated off this price, including early-bird savings, group deals, and last-minute deals. Prices given are per person, per day, based on double occupancy. Itineraries are also for the 1999 season. Both prices and itineraries are subject to change.

We've listed the **sizes of ships** in two ways: **passenger capacity** and **gross registered tons (GRTs),** which describes not actual tonnage but is, rather, a measure that takes into account interior space used to produce revenue on each vessel. One GRT = 100 cubic feet of enclosed, revenue-generating space.

AIRTOURS

SHIPS   Seawing

Airtours c/o Sun Cruises, Wavell House, Holcombe Rd. Helmshore, Lancashire, UK BB4 4NB.
☎ 8701/577775.

This large British tour firm has big U.S. connections. Carnival Corp., parent company of Carnival Cruise Lines, is a major investor, and the ship the line operates in the Greek market, the *Seawing,* was once operated in North America by Norwegian Cruise Line as the *Southward.*

The *Seawing* (built in 1971; 727 passengers, 16,607 GRTs) offers an informal experience with a decidedly British appeal and mostly British passengers. Many of the passengers are first-timers, attracted by the line's affordable prices.

Cabins have radios and phones; some have a picture window and sitting area.

Entertainment and dancing are offered at the ship's lounge and nightclub. There's also a casino, an outdoor pool, two saunas, a gym, spa, and library. Special activities are offered for teens.

ITINERARIES & RATES

SEAWING   Two different itineraries: (1) **7-day round-trip from Limmasol, Cyprus,** visiting Crete, Santorini, Rhodes, Piraeus, and Antalya (Turkey); (2) **7-day round-trip from Limmasol,** visiting Volos, Lesvos, and Kos as well as Kusadasi and Istanbul (Turkey). Both are offered May through October, sailing on alternating weeks. **Per diem rates:** $119–$140 inside, $141–$248 outside, no suites. Rates include airfare from the U.K. and port taxes.

CLASSICAL CRUISES & TOURS

SHIPS   Clelia II • Panorama
c/o Travel Dynamics, 132 E. 70th St., New York, NY 10021. ☎ 800/252-7745.

This operator of small yachts offers a number of interesting itineraries that include Greek ports. The journeys are tailored to be unique and are complemented by high-quality educational programs.

The *Clelia II* (built in 1990; 84 passengers, 4,077 GRTs) is the newest addition to the Classical fleet. The luxury all-suite yacht was purchased in 1996 for private use by one of Greece's most prominent shipping families (the ship is named for owner Clelia Hadjiioannou) and is chartered by Classical. The owners recently completed a $3-million upgrade, creating clublike interiors and a full-size gym, and outfitting the deluxe cabins and public rooms with designer fabrics and original art. All cabins on the *Clelia II* offer ocean views and a sitting area or separate living room, TV/VCR, and minibar. The penthouse offers 520 square feet of space.

The *Panorama* (built in 1993; 44 passengers, 599 GRTs) is a three-masted sloop with teak decks, a dining room and salon with picture windows, and a bar. Cabins are all outside, with picture windows, and have lower beds, radio, phone, and writing area. Three cabins include a pull-down child's berth. Passengers can swim directly from the ship's stern if weather permits.

ITINERARIES & RATES

CLELIA II   Three different itineraries. (1) **12-day Piraeus-to-Istanbul** cruisetours include a 7-day cruise and 4 nights in a hotel in Loutraki. Ports include Santorini, Ayios Nikolaos (Crete), Lindos/Rhodes, and Kusadasi (Turkey). A special Young Explorers program is offered on this tour for those ages 8 to 17. June, July, and August. (2) **12-day Athens-to-Istanbul** cruisetours include a 7-day cruise and four nights at a hotel in Athens. Ports include Santorini, Iraklion, Lindos/Rhodes, Patmos, Kusadasi (Turkey), Volos, Limnos, and Samothraki. April, May, Aug, October. (3) **14-day Istanbul-to-Piraeus** cruise traces places recounted in Homer's epic *Odyssey.* Ports in Greece include Nafplion, Pilos, Ithaka, and Corfu. June and October. The ship also sails other tours combining Greece and Turkey with visits to other countries, including Italy and Croatia. **Per diem rates:** $333–$1,159 suites. No standard cabins. Kids' rates on Piraeus-to-Istanbul cruisetours are $166. Fares include shore excursions as well as hotel stays for land tours.

PANORAMA   Two different itineraries. (1) **13-day, Istanbul-to-Piraeus** cruisetour includes a 7-night cruise and a hotel stay in Istanbul and Athens. Greek ports include Lindos/Rhodes, Kusadasi (Turkey), Patmos, and Santorini. April and May. (2) 13-day **Athens-to-Istanbul** cruisetour includes a 7-day cruise, three nights in Athens, and two nights in Istanbul. Ports include Delos/Mikonos, Santorini, Ayios Nikolaos (Crete), Lindos/Rhodes, Simi, Patmos, and Kusadasi (Turkey). It's offered in April and May. **Per diem rates:** $448–$559 outside (no suites). Fares include shore excursions as well as hotel stays for land tours. Also being introduced in 1999 is a Greek Islands "walking tour" cruise, round-trip from Athens, in which passengers sail between ports (Serifos, Kamares, Santorini, Crete, Kithira, and Momemvasia), with a walking tour included at each. Itinerary includes a 7-day cruise and two nights in Athens. September and October.

COSTA CRUISE LINES

SHIPS   CostaClassica • CostaVictoria

World Trade Center, 80 SW 8th St., Miami, FL 33130-3097. ☎ **800/462-6782.**
www.costacruises.com.

This Italian line traces its origins back to 1860 and the Italian olive-oil business. Today Carnival Corporation, parent of Carnival Cruise Lines, is a major investor. Onboard, Italy shows through in nearly everything Costa offers, from the great food to the Italian design of the vessels to the Italian-speaking crew (although they are not all from Italy) to the mostly Italian entertainers. The Italian experience is presented in casual elegance, in a warm and humorous manner. You'll feel like you're a part of one big Italian family.

The line's six ships represent one of the newest fleets in the industry, sporting blue-and-yellow smokestacks emblazoned with a huge letter *C.* They are popular in the U.S./Caribbean market but are not designed strictly for a North American audience, and therein lies their charm. In Europe, the ships attract a good share of Italian and French passengers.

Entertainment includes puppet and marionette shows, mimes, and acrobatics, all presented in showrooms designed to look like 18th-century opera houses. Opera singers sometimes come aboard to entertain. The line also offers a well-developed activities program for kids and teens.

The *CostaClassica* (built in 1991; 1,300 passengers, 54,000 GRTs) offers spacious public rooms done up in contemporary Italian design, with Italian marble and original artwork, including sculptures, paintings, murals, wall hangings, and hand-crafted furnishings. The ship's 446 cabins average almost 200 square feet (that's big by industry standards). There are also 10 spacious suites with verandas.

The *CostaVictoria* (built in 1996; 1,928 passengers, 76,000 GRTS) is the ship that brought Costa into the megaship era. It is technologically advanced, sleek, and stylish, with spacious and dramatic interiors. A grand gallery at the ship's forward end offers viewing with large glass walls. Among the cabins are 26 suites, four grand suites, and special rooms for nonsmokers.

ITINERARIES & RATES

COSTACLASSICA 7-day Greek Islands itinerary, round-trip from Venice, includes visits to Katakolon, Santorini, Mikonos, and Rhodes, as well as Bari (Italy) and Dubrovnik (Croatia). May through October. **Per diem rates:** $365–$514 inside, $422–$585 outside, $537–$671 suites. Rates include airfare from New York and other selected gateway cities, as well as port charges.

COSTAVICTORIA 7-day Eastern Mediterranean itinerary, round-trip from Venice, visits Katakolon, Piraeus, Kusadasi and Istanbul (Turkey), and Bari (Italy). May to November. **Per diem rates:** $365–$514 inside, $422–$585 outside, $537–$671 suites.

CUNARD

**SHIPS   Sea Goddess I • Sea Goddess II • Vistafjord •
              Royal Viking Sun**

6100 Blue Lagoon Dr., Suite 400, Miami, FL 33126. ☎ **800/5-CUNARD.** www.cunardline.com.

Cunard is the grande dame of the cruise industry, with a pedigree that includes the *Mauritania, Queen Mary,* and *Queen Elizabeth.* Under its new ownership by Carnival

Corporation, it is a sister line to the very posh Seabourn line, to which some of its ships—namely the yachtlike *Sea Goddess* vessels and the elegant *Royal Viking Sun*—are expected to be transferred in the third quarter of 1999. At this time, the *Sea Goddesses* will be renamed *Seabourn Goddess I* and *Seabourn Goddess II* and the *Royal Viking Sun* will be renamed *Seabourn Sun*. The classic *Vistafjord* (soon to be renamed *Caronia*) and the famous QE2 will remain with Cunard, which has also announced plans to build at least one brand-new ocean liner in the next few years, probably by 2002.

In late 1998, the line announced a rate reduction across the board for 1999 sailings, with savings of 30 to 45 percent and even greater discounts for repeat passengers.

The atmosphere on Cunard ships is both formal and traditional, and these ships are definitely not glitzy or party ships. Customers can expect ever-so-polite white-gloved service, a tasteful if not dramatic setting, and food that's high in quality and presented with flawless service. There will be many British among the passengers, and they will take such offerings as high tea very seriously.

Guest lecturers include noted chefs, wine connoisseurs, economic advisers, professors, authors, and authorities on the ports visited.

The *Sea Goddess I* and *Sea Goddess II* (built in 1984 and 1985; 116 passengers each, 4,250 GRTs each) are twin ships that boast some of the most luxurious cruise experiences afloat. According to the *Sea Goddess* brochure, waiters will wade "through the shallows off a tropical beach to hand you a glass of champagne." And they really *will*.

But these small ships are not for those who get claustrophobic. The cabins are all outside suites, but they aren't particularly large. And the ships are not suitable for kids.

The *Vistafjord* (built in 1973; 675 passengers, 24,492 GRTs) is a classic ocean liner right down to her brass and mahogany and her formal atmosphere. She's luxurious, tasteful, and spacious, and has a following that includes British and Germans as well as Americans.

In addition to these three ships, the *Royal Viking Sun* also offers Greece as part of 14-day cruises between Barcelona and Piraeus in June and September. These also visit Malta, Israel, Egypt, Turkey, or France, Italy, and Turkey. Greek stops include Santorini and Mikonos, plus Kusadasi in Turkey. Another itinerary sailing in June also adds a stop at Lesvos (Mitilini), as well as calls in Turkey and Italy.

ITINERARIES & RATES

SEA GODDESS I   Five different itineraries include calls at Greek ports. (1) **7-day Venice-to-Piraeus** cruise includes visits to Corfu, Itea, Santorini, Mikonos, and Dubrovnik (Croatia), plus a transit of the Corinth Canal. (2) **7-day Venice-to-Istanbul** includes visits to Corfu, Kefalonia, Lesvos (Mitilini), and Dubrovnik (Croatia), plus a transit of the Corinth Canal. (3) **7-day Piraeus-to-Venice** visits Nafplion, Gythion, Katakolon, and Dubrovnik (Croatia). (4) **7-day Istanbul-to-Piraeus** visits Limnos and Mikonos as well as Kusadasi, Bodrum, and Marmaris (all in Turkey). (5) **11-day Istanbul-to-Venice** visits Kamena Vourla, Marathon, Piraeus, Nisos Idhra, Delos, Pilos, and Praveza, as well as Canakkale (Turkey) and Marina di Ravenna (Italy). **Per diem rates:** $1,078–$1143 outside, $2,156–$2,281 suite. Rates include tips and drinks.

SEA GODDESS II   Two itineraries include Greek port calls. (1) **7-day Piraeus-to-Venice** visits Nafplion, Gythion, Katakolon, and Dubrovnik (Croatia). (2) **7-day Venice-to-Piraeus** visits Corfu, Itea, Skiathos, and Mikonos, and includes a transit of the Corinth Canal. Several other sailings make one or more Greek stops. **Per diem rates:** $1,078–$1,143 outside, $2,156–$2,281 suite. Rates include tips and drinks.

VISTAFJORD　Four different itineraries. (1) **14-day round-trip from Venice** visits Itea, Gythion, Mikonos, Piraeus, and Corfu, as well as Istanbul and Kusadasi (Turkey). (2) **8-day Venice-to-Istanbul** includes Zakinthos, Iraklion, Rhodes, and Mikonos, as well as Kusadasi (Turkey). (3) **14-day round-trip from Venice** visits Zakinthos, Mikonos, Piraeus, Crete, and Rhodes, as well as Canakkale and Bodrum, both in Turkey. (4) **14-day round-trip from Venice** visits Zakinthos, Gythion, Crete, Nafplion, and Itea, as well as Istanbul and Canakkale (Turkey). Other itineraries call at only one or two Greek ports. **Per diem rates:** $294–$396 inside, $327–$745 outside, $744–$1,368 suites.

DOLPHIN HELLAS (SEE ZEUS TOURS)
FIRST EUROPEAN CRUISES
SHIPS　Azur • Mistral
95 Madison Ave., Suite 1203, New York, NY 10016. ☎ **888/983-8767** or 212/779-7168.

First European is the name adopted by Greece-based Festival Cruises for U.S. marketing purposes. The company was established in 1992 in Piraeus by Greek entrepreneur George Poulides, who has ambitious growth plans.

The line currently operates four older, classic ships, including the *Azur,* that have been extensively refurbished and cater to a diverse European audience, with Americans a more recent addition to the passenger roster.

In June 1999, First European will launch its first brand-new vessel, the *Mistral,* a 1,200-passenger, 48,000 GRT ship built in France at a cost of $240 million. When completed, the *Mistral* will be the largest ship to sail under the French flag. It will be staffed by Greek officers and an international crew and will offer a contemporary interior design, created by leading international architects and designers. Each deck will be named after a European city: Paris, Rome, London, Berlin, Brussels, Athens, Cannes, and Madrid.

The ship will offer several dining options, a show lounge, a ballroom, and a disco, plus a full casino and numerous other public rooms and lounges, as well as a solarium, health spa, and thalassotherapy center. Cabins include 80 large suites with private verandas.

The line's other ship sailing Greek Islands itineraries is the *Azur* (built in 1971; 750 passengers, 15,000 GRTs)), which was built as a ferry but has been remodeled into a cruise ship with classic appeal. There's plenty of open deck space, several bars, and lots of activities. Some cabins have picture windows and sitting areas.

ITINERARIES & RATES
AZUR　**7-day round-trip from Venice** visits Itea, Santorini, Mikonos, Rhodes, Piraeus, and Dubrovnik (Croatia), and includes a crossing of the Corinth Canal. May, June, and July. **Per diem rates:** $409–$459 inside, $430–$486 outside, $486–$561 suites. Children 2–17 pay $175 per cruise plus port taxes.

MISTRAL　**7-day round-trip from Venice** visits Katakolon, Santorini, Mikonos, Rhodes, and Dubrovnik (Croatia). July through October. **Per diem rates:** $316–$411 inside, $419–$486 outside, $499 suites. Children 2–17 pay $175 per cruise plus port taxes.

GALILEO CRUISES (SEE ZEUS TOURS)
GOLDEN SUN CRUISES (SEE ZEUS TOURS)
ORIENT LINES
SHIPS   Marco Polo

1510 SE 17th St., Suite 400, Fort Lauderdale, FL 33315. ☎ **800/333-7300.** www. orientlines.com.

Orient Lines is a one-ship line that was owned by a British entrepreneur until he decided to sell to Norwegian Cruise Line in 1998.

The *Marco Polo* (formerly the *Alexandr Pushkin;* built in 1965; 800 passengers, 22,080 GRTs) was built in East Germany and completely refitted in 1993, offers classic style, and is comfortable and upscale, with art-deco interiors featuring Oriental art and antiques and decent-sized cabins, all with both bathtub and shower.

Cuisine is continental/American, and passengers tend to dress up at night. A high level of service is offered by the Scandinavian officers and Filipino crew.

Passengers tend to be American and older, experienced travelers, but there are also first-timers attracted by the value the line offers.

Orient Lines's cruises are designed to be destination-oriented, to present cruising as an enriching experience. This is achieved thanks to expert lecturers and a special focus on shore excursions. Local entertainers are brought on at various ports to add local color.

ITINERARIES & RATES
MARCO POLO   12-day Athens-to-Istanbul and Istanbul-to-Athens cruisetours include hotel stays and tours in Athens and Istanbul and a 6-day cruise with stops that include Piraeus, Delos, Mikonos, Santorini, Iraklion, Rhodes, and Kusadasi and Istanbul (Turkey). A similar itinerary includes Itea and Nafplion (with a hotel stay in Nafplion). April through October. **Per diem rates:** $145–$227 inside, $181–$312 outside, $270–$411 suite. Pre- and postcruise hotel stays, transfers, and sightseeing included.

RADISSON SEVEN SEAS CRUISES
SHIPS   Radisson Diamond • Song of Flower

600 Corporate Dr., Suite 410, Fort Lauderdale, FL 33334. ☎ **800/477-7500.** www.rssc.com.

In 1992, Radisson Hotels Worldwide decided to translate its hospitality experience to the cruise industry, offering to manage and market upscale ships for their international owners. The ships all offer itineraries geared towards affluent travelers, plus excellent cuisine, service, and amenities. A no-tipping policy is employed aboard all their ships.

The line assumes most of its passengers want to entertain themselves, so organized activities are limited, though they do include lectures by well-known authors, producers, and oceanographers, among others. There are also card and board games, shuffleboard, and dance lessons.

The *Radisson Diamond* (built in 1992; 350 passengers, 20,295 GRTs) is to the cruise industry what the DeLorean was to the car industry, sporting one unusual design concept—in this case two side-by-side hulls, with the main passenger areas perched above and across them, creating a ship that is in essence a giant catamaran. The $125-million, twin-hulled vessel is a very wide ship. Only 420 feet long, she is nonetheless only 2 feet narrower (at 102 ft.) than the QE2 (which is 963 ft. long).

Thanks to her design, the *Diamond* is roomy and also probably the most stable ship afloat (it's a good choice for those fearing seasickness). The ship's cabins are all large and luxurious suites, and there are two VIP master suites that are even bigger and more luxurious. All the suites are outside, 121 offering balconies and 53 offering bay windows.

The smaller *Song of Flower* (built in 1986; 172 passengers, 8,292 GRTs) offers good-size cabins, all with outside views. They include a bathtub or shower, TV/VCR, radio, phone, hair dryer, refrigerator, and fully stocked complimentary minibar. Some cabins offer sitting areas. There are also 20 suites, 10 with private verandas.

Both ships have a pool, gym, spa, and casino. The *Diamond* also has a free-floating retractable marina that provides easy access to water sports including sailing, windsurfing, and waterskiing.

Radisson is also in the process of building a new ship, the *Seven Seas Navigator,* that will be in the Mediterranean in August and September 1999, calling at Greek ports. An all-suite luxury vessel, the *Navigator* will feature 245 large ocean-view suites, 80% with private balconies, and will be both the largest and fastest vessel in the Radisson fleet.

ITINERARIES & RATES

RADISSON DIAMOND 7-night Athens-to-Istanbul and Istanbul-to-Athens cruises visit Santorini, Rhodes, and Mikonos/Delos, plus Kusadasi, Hios, and Dikili (Turkey), and, on some cruises, Patmos/Samos. September and October. **Per diem rates:** $682–$1,199 suites (no standard cabins). Prices include airfare.

SONG OF FLOWER 7-night Athens-to-Istanbul and Istanbul-to-Athens cruises visit Delos/Mikonos, Rhodes, Santorini, Itea (transit Corinth Canal), plus Hios and Kusadasi (Turkey). April and September. **Per diem rates:** $595–$842 outside, $1,056–$1,085 suites (no inside cabins). Prices include airfare.

OTHER ITINERARIES Both the *Diamond* and *Song of Flower* offer Greek ports of call on itineraries that also include Italy, and the *Song of Flower* offers Greece as part of longer itineraries that include the Middle East. The new *Seven Seas Navigator* will also call at Greek ports including Naxos and Corfu as part of longer itineraries, and offer some sailings from Piraeus.

RENAISSANCE CRUISES

SHIPS R1 • Renaissance VIII

1800 Eller Dr., Fort Lauderdale, FL 33335. ☎ **800/525-5350.** www.renaissancecruises.com.

Renaissance Cruises is a bit of a renegade in the cruise industry. Owned by parties including Edward Rudner, an American travel entrepreneur, the company markets to consumers as much through direct mail and the Internet as through travel agents. This has angered agents, some of whom have vowed not to sell the line. In fact, the company's aggressive marketing tactics in 1998 caused Renaissance to be the first cruise line to be expelled from membership in the American Society of Travel Agents.

Renaissance has in the past been known for its fleet of small luxury ships, but the firm is in the process of replacing that fleet with sleek, new 684-passenger vessels, the first of which debuted in 1998. The new ships are very simply named—*R1, R2,* and so forth—and at least six are believed to be on order.

The *R1* (built in 1998; 684 passengers, 30,200 GRT) and her sister ships are state-of-the-art luxury vessels featuring four restaurants with open seating, including two specialty restaurants. Other public rooms include a specialty dessert cafe and a complete spa and fitness center. Some 66% of the cabins have private verandas. The deluxe suites are particularly spacious.

Something for nonsmokers to note in smoke-happy Europe: The *R1* is a completely smoke-free ship.

Also offering Greek Islands cruises is the smaller, more yachtlike *Renaissance VIII* (built in 1992; 114 passengers, 4,280 GRT), which features all outside suite accommodations and meals served at one open seating. Service is low-key (some say too low-key) and the overall ambiance casually elegant.

Renaissance sells the cruise experience as part of cruisetour packages that include land tours and hotel stays. The packages include round-trip air from New York (with add-ons available from other airports); 1, 2, or 3 nights at a hotel in Athens; and 1, 2, or 3 nights at a hotel in Istanbul.

ITINERARIES & RATES

R1   Athens to Istanbul cruisetours include a 10-day cruise with calls at Rhodes, Crete, and Kusadasi (Turkey), as well as Israel and Cyprus. Year-round. **Per diem rates:** $219–$269 inside, $279–$399 outside, $499–$649 suites.

Renaissance VIII   Sails on the above itinerary as well as 5-day cruises with calls at Santorini, Rhodes, and Kusadasi (Turkey). February and March, with two additional 5-day cruises in November. **Per diem rates:** $499–$649 suites (no standard cabins).

ROYAL OLYMPIC CRUISES

SHIPS   Odysseus • Olympic Countess • Stella Oceanis • Stella Solaris • Triton • World Renaissance

805 Third Ave., New York, NY 10022. ☎ **800/872-6400.** www.royalolympiccruises.com.

Royal Olympic is to Greece what Carnival Cruise Line is to the Caribbean: the dominant market giant. The line was formed in 1995 by the merger of top Greek lines Sun Line and Epirotiki, and in 1999 will have six ships offering Greek Islands itineraries.

The line's current fleet offers a variety of older, classic vessels, but shortly after going public in 1998, Royal Olympic announced that for the first time it would build some brand-new ships. The new orders will begin with 836-passenger, high-speed vessels that will be introduced in 2000 and 2001 (the line also has an option for a third).

The Royal Olympic ships focus on destination as much as the shipboard experience (the line makes more onboard revenue on its shore excursions than on selling drinks), and passengers usually have a goal of seeing as much of the islands as is possible in 3, 4, or 7 days. Some of the itineraries are consequently quite loaded, visiting as much as two ports a day.

The line packages its shore excursions so that you can book several and save. Royal Olympic also offers special shore-excursion rates for kids.

The onboard atmosphere is relaxed. Passengers tend to go to bed pretty early, exhausted from busy days of sightseeing (although the ships do offer late-night discos for those who want to stay up late).

The Royal Olympic cruise experience includes a friendly and accommodating Greek crew who offer a talent show complete with Greek music and Zorba-style dancing at least once during each cruise. Food on the ships is continental but with Greek specialties. On these ships, you won't forget you are in Greece.

The cruises are affordably priced and attract about 60% Americans, with the other 40% predominantly Europeans. Most tend to be seasoned travelers, but these ships, with their intimate atmosphere, are also suitable for first-timers and families. Children's and teens' activities are offered based on need (if there are enough kids booked, the line will put a youth counselor onboard).

The ships vary in style and design. The *Stella Solaris* and *Olympic Countess* (formerly a Cunard ship) are the fanciest. All the ships have classic features like teak and brass, and expansive decks, and the line has been busy lately renovating and upgrading. Cabins are comfortably furnished but can be a bit cramped. They are bigger on the *Stella Solaris* than on the other ships. The *Olympic Countess* and *Stella Solaris* offer in-room TVs, while the others offer cabins equipped with radios and phones. All the ships offer at least a few suites. Public rooms are comfortable and there are plenty of quiet nooks to get away from it all, including libraries on all the vessels and movie theaters on the *Olympic Countess, Stella Solaris, Triton,* and *World Renaissance*

Entertainment is low-key, presented in the main lounge, and includes headline performers such as Leroy Schultz (formerly of The Platters) plus cabaret acts. Daytime activities are minimal but include bingo, dance classes, lectures, movies, exercise classes, and shuffleboard. All the ships have a swimming pool (in some cases two), a small gym, spa, beauty parlor, and casino, and offer expansive deck space for taking in the Greek sun (the *Olympic Countess* also offers tennis and a golf driving range).

The fleet consists of the *Olympic Countess* (built in 1976; 840 passengers, 18,000 GRTs), *Triton* (built in 1971; 620 passengers, 14,000 GRT), *Stella Solaris* (built in 1973; 620 passengers, 18,000 GRTs), *World Renaissance* (built in 1966; 400 passengers, 12,000 GRTs), *Odysseus* (built in 1962; 400 passengers, 12,000 GRT), and *Stella Oceanis* (built in 1965; 300 passengers, 5,500 GRTs).

ITINERARIES & RATES

OLYMPIC COUNTESS   **7-day round-trip from Piraeus** visits Santorini, Iraklion, Rhodes, Patmos, Kusadasi (Turkey), Mikonos, and Istanbul (Turkey). March through October. **Per diem rates:** $190–$286 inside, $290–$327 outside, $390–$426 suites.

ORPHEUS   **7-day round-trip from Piraeus** visits Nafplion, the Corinth Canal, Itea, Ithaka, Corfu, Saranda, Butrint, Zakinthos, Katakolon, Rethymnon, Santorini, and Mikonos. May through October. **Per diem rates:** $190–$226 inside, $286–$310 (no suites).

STELLA OCEANIS   Three different itineraries. (1) **7-day round-trip from Piraeus** visits Santorini, Iraklion, Port Said (Egypt), Ashod (Israel), Patmos, and Kusadasi (Turkey), and includes a day at sea. April through October. (2) **7-day round-trip from Piraeus** traces the footsteps of St. Paul, round trip, with stops including Rhodes, Patmos, Thessaloniki, plus Kusadasi, Dikili, and Istanbul (Turkey). April through October. (3) **7-day round-trip from Piraeus** visits Nafplion, the Corinth Canal, Itea, Ithaka, Corfu, Saranda, Butrint, Zakynthos, Katakolon, Rethymnon, Santorini, and Mikonos. May to October. **Per diem rates:** $199–$297 inside, $320–$353 outside, $390 suites.

STELLA SOLARIS   A variety of **7- and 14-day cruises,** as well as two **21-day cruises,** round-trip from Piraeus, combine stops in Greece with Egypt and Israel, the Black Sea, and/or Turkey. The **7-day round-trip from Piraeus** (May through Oct) visits Patmos, Mikonos, Rhodes, Iraklion, and Santorini, plus Kusadasi and Istanbul (Turkey). The **14-day round-trip from Athens** (Aug) visits Lesvos (Mitilini), Patmos, Mikonos, Rhodes, Iraklion, and Santorini, plus Kusadasi and other stops in Turkey, Odessa, and Yalta. **Per diem rates:** $199–$298 inside, $320–$353 outside, $390–$426 suites.

TRITON   3- and 4-day round-trip from Piraeus. The 3-day itinerary visits Mikonos, Rhodes, Patmos, and Kusadasi (Turkey), while the 4-day itinerary visits Mikonos, Patmos, Rhodes, Iraklion, Santorini, and Kusadasi (Turkey). February through November. **Per diem rates:** $188–$220 inside, $220–$311 outside, $361–$371 suites.

WORLD RENAISSANCE   3- and 4-day round-trip from Piraeus are the same as those followed by the *Triton* (above). April through November. **Per diem rates:** $195–$230 inside, $230–$325 outside, $351–$428 suites.

SEABOURN CRUISE LINE
SHIPS   Seabourn Spirit
55 Francisco St., Suite 710, San Francisco, CA 94133. ☎ **800/929-9595.** www.seabourn.com.

Seabourn is what it was created to be: the best cruise line in the world in terms of food, service, ship design, itineraries, and refined environment. That said, the Seabourn cruise experience is not for everyone. These cruises are very pricey and the customers who can afford them are often very discriminating, even about who they choose to chat with on their vacation. Most passengers have household incomes that exceed $200,000.

Discretion is key on these ships, and the discreet environment and decor prove it. Staff and crew, like the passengers, are well mannered.

The three ships in the fleet—including the line's primary Greece ship for 1999, the *Seabourn Spirit* (built in 1989; 204 passenger, 10,000 GRTs)—are all small and ultra-modern, with a yachtlike appeal, but they are also designed to allow passengers plenty of space to stretch out and feel at home (remembering that most of these people live in really big houses).

Cuisine is innovative, with French influences, and the dining room follows an open-seating policy, allowing passengers to sit with whomever they choose. Men wear jackets at dinner, and everyone dresses up for formal nights.

The line enhances its cruises with guest lecturers, past examples of which have included celebrities like Walter Cronkite and Art Linkletter. Nighttime entertainment is very low-key, with the ship's soloist doubling as social host or hostess.

The ships have marinas hidden in their hulls that, when lowered, provide a platform for water sports. There's also a mesh net that becomes a saltwater swimming pool.

All the cabins are outside suites, and each has a 5-foot-wide picture window and comes with a fully stocked complimentary bar. Owner's suites are very plush, and offer private verandas.

In 1998, Carnival Corporation, parent of Carnival Cruise Lines and a majority owner of Seabourn, also acquired a majority interest in Cunard, and at this point it's expected that the Cunard ships *Sea Goddess I, Sea Goddess II,* and *Royal Viking Sun* will be moved to the Seabourn fleet in late 1999 and renamed the *Seabourn Goddess I, Seabourn Goddess II,* and *Seabourn Sun.*

ITINERARIES & RATES
SEABOURN SPIRIT   A number of cruises visit some of the less-populated ports (and some popular ones, too), from April through November. Some focus on Greece and Turkey, while others visit Greece as part of longer itineraries. In July, the ship sails on a **10-day Istanbul-to-Piraeus** itinerary that includes Mikonos, Santorini, Monemvassia, Nafplion, and Despotiko, as well as Kusadasi, Fethiye, and Bodrum

(Turkey). The reverse sailing, **10-day Piraeus-to-Istanbul,** includes Ayios Nikolaos (Crete), Santorini, Despotiko, and Mikonos as well as Fethiye, Bodrum, and Kusadasi (Turkey). A **14-day round-trip from Istanbul,** sailing in August, visits Volos, Skopelos, Nafplion, Monemvassia, Despotiko, Tinos, Mikonos, and Limnos, plus Kusadasi and Mudanya (Turkey) and Nesebur (Bulgaria). This cruise also features a solar eclipse observation. A **14-day round-trip from Istanbul** in May visits the Ukraine and Bulgaria in the 1st week, but passengers can join for the 2nd week in Piraeus for a 7-day sailing that includes Santorini, Nafplion, Mikonos, and Volos, plus Kusadasi (Turkey). **Per diem rates:** $570–$1,212 suites (no standard cabins).

SEA CLOUD CRUISES

SHIPS   Sea Cloud

c/o Abercrombie & Kent, 1520 Kensington Rd., Oak Brook, IL 60523-2141. ☎ **800/ 323-7308,** or 171/730-9600 in the U.K. www.abercrombiekent.com.

Owned today by a German firm that also operates the European river ship *River Cloud*, the sailing ship *Sea Cloud* (built in 1931; 68 passengers, 2,532 GRT) is a millionaire's yacht—literally. Formerly named the *Hussar*, it was built by desire of American financier E. F. Hutton as a wedding present for his bride, Marjorie Merriweather Post.

History is a big part of this elegant vessel's appeal; the Duchess of Windsor really did sleep here, and so did Zsa Zsa Gabor.

The ship's four masts carry 29 sails, and it is a glorious presence on the open seas. Cabins include some of the ship's original quarters (these cabins are on the small side), and two plush owner's suites with marble fireplaces and antique furnishings. All cabins are outside, and some have bathtubs.

Public rooms include the dining room, which boasts restored wood paneling. The ship also offers a teak deck with brass trim, and there are two bars and a library. The cuisine is German.

ITINERARIES & RATES

SEA CLOUD   Three itineraries. (1) **13-day Istanbul-to-Athens cruisetour** in September features a 7-day cruise with visits to Kusadasi, Dikili, Delos, Mikonos, Santorini, Crete, and Monemvassia, plus a 6-day land package in Istanbul and Athens. (2) **13-day Athens-to-Istanbul cruisetour** includes 7-day cruise and five nights ashore. Port calls include Santorini, Delos, and Mikonos, plus Kusadasi and other ports in Turkey. September. (3) **12-day Athens-to-Catania** cruisetour in October visits Greek ports Hydra, Nafplion, Gythion, Katakolon, and Kefalonia during its 7-day cruise portion. **Per diem rates:** $599–$1,000 outside, $1,200 suite (no inside cabins).

OTHER ITINERARIES   **Elegant Cruises,** 31 Central Dr., Port Washington, NY 11050 (☎ **800/683-6767**), also offers a 14-day Istanbul-to-Kusadasi cruisetour on the *Sea Cloud.* This trip includes visits to Lesvos, Dikili/Pergamon, and Patmos.

SILVERSEA CRUISES

SHIPS   Silver Cloud • Silver Wind

110 E. Broward Blvd., Fort Lauderdale, FL 33301. ☎ **800/722-9955,** ext. 1.

The luxurious sister ships *Silver Cloud* and *Silver Wind* (both built in 1994; 296 passengers, 16,800 GRTs) carry their guests in true splendor, in an atmosphere that's elegant but low-key, and in a milieu that's sociable rather than stuffy. Passengers are generally experienced cruisers, not necessarily American, and certainly are well traveled. Most are in the over-50 group. These ships are not for kids.

All accommodations are in outside suites with picture windows, writing tables, sofas, walk-in closets, marble bathrooms, and all the amenities you'd expect of a top-of-the-line ship. Throughout both ships, there is more space allotted to each passenger than on most other ships at sea. There's also more crew, with the large staff at your service, ready to cater to your every desire on a 24-hour-a-day basis.

The fine accoutrements that complement the luxurious accommodations include Limoges china, Christofle silverware, Frette bed linens, and soft down pillows. If you don't know these brands, a Silversea cruise is probably not going to be right for you.

Activities offerings include bridge and other games, aerobics, dance lessons, wine tastings, lectures (including a *National Geographic Traveler* series), and yes, even bingo and quiz shows. Nighttime entertainment includes productions featuring resident and local talent in the ships' showrooms, plus dancing, a piano bar, and a small casino.

Both ships offer five-star cuisine served in a single seating, with guests able to dine when, where, and with whom they choose.

The relatively small size and design of the *Silver Cloud* and *Silver Wind,* which includes a shallow 18-foot draught, allow the ships to dock in intimate harbors that are off-limits to large vessels.

ITINERARIES & RATES

SILVER CLOUD 13-day Athens-to-Rome cruisetour in May visits Nafplion, the Corinth Canal, and Itea, plus Kusadasi and Istanbul (Turkey), as well as ports in Italy and Malta, and includes an overnight in Athens. **Per diem rates:** $771–$1,842 suites (no standard cabins). Rates include wine, spirits, and champagne; tips; a shore-side event; airfare; hotel accommodations; port charges; and transfers.

SILVER WIND 14-day itineraries can be broken up into weeklong segments. For instance, a 14-day Rome-to-Istanbul sailing in May can be booked as a **7-day Rome-to-Piraeus** cruise that visits Katakolon, Kithira, Santorini, Nafplion, as well as Kusadasi (Turkey) and Taormina (Italy), or a **7-day Piraeus-to-Istanbul,** with stops in Mikonos, Volos, and Kusadasi (Turkey). The second half of a Barcelona-to-Piraeus itinerary in June can be booked as a **7-day cruise from Valletta (Malta) to Piraeus,** with visits to Kithira, Rhodes, and Patmos, plus Marmaris and Kusadasi (Turkey). A 14-day Istanbul-to-Piraeus sailing in September can be broken into a **7-day Istanbul-to-Valletta** cruise, with calls at Mikonos, Rhodes, and Crete, as well as ports in Turkey, or as a **7-day Valletta-to-Piraeus,** with stops in Santorini and Patmos as well as several ports in Turkey. An **8-day Valletta-to-Piraeus** sailing in October visits Crete and Rhodes, as well as Kusadasi, Marmaris, and Bodrum (Turkey). **Per diem rates:** $771–$1,842 suites (no standard cabins). Rates include wine, spirits, and champagne; tips; a shore-side event; airfare; hotel accommodations; port charges; and transfers.

OTHER ITINERARIES The *Silver Wind* also offers Greece on **11- to 14-day summer/fall itineraries** combined with Italy, Turkey, Croatia, and Monaco; Spain, Italy, Malta, and Turkey; Turkey, Lebanon, Cyprus, Italy, and Monte Carlo; Italy and Croatia; or Turkey, Bulgaria, and Ukraine.

STAR CLIPPERS

SHIPS   Star Flyer

4101 Salzedo St., Coral Gables, FL 33146. ☎ **800/442-0551.** www.star-clippers.com.

The *Star Flyer* (built in 1991; 170 passengers, 3,025 GRTs), which operates in Greece, and its twin ship *Star Clipper* are replicas of the big 19th-century clipper sailing ships (or barkentines) that once circled the globe. Their tall square rigs carry enormous sails and are glorious to look at, and a particular thrill for history buffs.

But these ships are not just window dressing. The *Star Clipper* and *Star Flyer* were constructed using original drawings and the specifications of a leading 19th-century naval architect, but updated with modern touches so that today they are the tallest and among the fastest clipper ships ever built (they've reached speeds of more than 19 knots).

The atmosphere onboard is akin to being on a private yacht rather than a mainstream cruise ship. It's casual in an L. L. Bean sort of way, and friendly. Passengers generally fall into the 30-to-60 age range.

Cabins are pleasant, and decorated with wood accents. There is one owner's suite. The public rooms include a writing room, an open-seating dining room, and an Edwardian-style library with a belle-epoque fireplace and walls lined with bookshelves. There are two swimming pools.

Local entertainment is sometimes brought on at night, and the ships also have a pianist and a makeshift disco in the Tropical Bar. Movies are piped into passenger cabins.

Activities on the ships tend toward the nautical, such as visiting the bridge, observing the crew handle the sails, and participating in knot-tying classes.

It should be noted that despite stabilizers, movement of the ships may be troublesome to those who get seasick.

ITINERARIES & RATES

STAR FLYER Two **7-day round-trip itineraries from Athens.** (1) **Northern Cyclades itinerary** visits Delos/Mikonos, Patmos, and Serifos, as well as Kusadasi, Bodrum, and Cesme (Turkey). (2) **Southern Cyclades itinerary** visits Paros, Rhodes, Astipalea, and Santorini, as well as Bodrum and Dalyn River (Turkey). May through September. **Per diem rates:** $210–$239 inside, $239–$360 outside, $500 suite.

SWAN HELLENIC

SHIPS **Minerva**

77 New Oxford St., London WCIA IPP. ☎ 44-**171-800-2200.**

This British firm is owned by Peninsular and Orient Steam Navigation Company (P&O), the company that also owns U.S.-based Princess Cruises.

With its one ship, *Minerva* (built in 1996; 300 passengers, 12,000 GRTs), Swan Hellenic offers a small-ship experience that is both high-quality and enriching. All the itineraries feature acclaimed guest lecturers who are authorities in their fields, and the passengers—a mix of British and Americans—tend to be experienced, inquisitive travelers.

Public rooms are spacious, and include two open-seating restaurants, a large library, and a variety of lounges and bars done up in understated, English-country decor, complete with cushy upholstered chairs. The ship does not have a casino. Every cabin has a TV, phone, and fax. All feature private bathrooms with showers, and some cabins have full-size bathtubs. The ship's luxurious suites offer private verandas.

ITINERARIES & RATES

MINERVA **15-day Athens-to-Istanbul** in August/September is one of the most comprehensive offerings available in Greece, with visits to the Corinth Canal, Ithaka, Katakolon, Kithira, Gythion, Nafplion, Delos, Mikonos, Chios, Lesvos (Mitilini), and Samothraki. A **15-day Rhodes-to-Kusadasi** itinerary in April visits Rethymnon, Katakolon, the Corinth Canal, Piraeus, and Kusadasi (Turkey). An

8-day Kusadasi-to-Athens sailing in April visits Rhodes, Iraklion, and Santorini. **Other 8- or 15-day cruises** in April and May include Delos, Thessaloniki, and Kavala, or Nafplion, Gythion, Kalamata, Katakolon, and Praveza. **Per diem rates:** $231–$279 inside, $259–$307 outside, $307–$388 suite. Rates include shore excursions, tips, transfers, and airfare from London.

WINDSTAR

SHIPS   Wind Song • Wind Spirit
300 Elliott Ave. W., Seattle, WA 98110. ☎ **800/258-7245.** www.windstarcruises.com.

While they look like sailing ships of yore, the *Wind Song* (built in 1987; 148 passengers, 5,350 GRTs) and *Wind Spirit* (built in 1988; 144 passengers, 5,350 GRTs) are more like luxury floating resorts, complete with top-notch service and extraordinary cuisine. Million-dollar computers operate the sails, and stabilizers allow for a smooth ride.

Casual, low-key elegance is the watchword on these vessels. There's no set regime, unless you consider pampering a regime. Most of the passengers are well heeled and range in age from 30 to 70. Passengers can visit the bridge whenever they want.

Cabins are all outside, with teak-decked bathrooms and large portholes, and include owner's suites. Amenities include VCRs and CD players.

A water-sports platform at the stern allows for a variety of activities when the ships are docked. Nighttime entertainment is low-key and sometimes includes local entertainers brought onboard at ports of call. The ships also have small casinos.

The line is owned by Carnival Corporation, which is also the parent of Carnival, Holland America Line, Costa, Seabourn, and Cunard.

ITINERARIES & RATES

WIND SONG 7-day Athens-to-Istanbul (and Istanbul-to-Athens) itinerary from May through October, visiting Mikonos, Santorini, and Rhodes, plus Kusadasi and Bodrum (Turkey). A **7-day Athens-to-Rome** cruise in October visits Monemvassia, Zakinthos, and Fiskardo. **Per diem rates:** $556–$656 outside, $853 suite (no inside cabins).

WIND SPIRIT Same as **7-day Athens-Istanbul** itineraries above. The ship also offers a **7-day Rome-to-Athens** cruise in May that visits Fiskardo, Gythion, and Hydra. **Per diem rates:** $556–$656 outside, $853 suite (no inside).

ZEUS TOURS & YACHT CRUISES

SHIPS   Aegean I • Arcadia • Galileo Sun • Zeus I • Zeus II • Zeus III
566 Seventh Ave., New York, NY 10018. ☎ **800/447-5667.** www.zeustours.com.

This 50-year-old firm represents several lines, including its own fleet of yachts known as Zeus Cruises, the sailing ship *Galileo Sun,* and two classic vessels operated by Golden Sun Cruises. The yachts, the *Zeus I, II,* and *III* (built in 1995; 40 passengers), all offer a casual, reasonably priced, soft-adventure cruise experience with an international group of passengers, visiting both popular and out-of-the-way ports.

The *Zeus I* and *III* have sails, although they are also motor-powered. The *Zeus II* is a motorized yacht.

The ships feature outside cabins that are small but comfortable and fitted with picture windows. Some have upper and lower beds. There's also a dining room, bar, and lounge.

Two meals are served each day, breakfast and either lunch or dinner (passengers are in port for the third meal). And, for the first time in 1999, local wine, beer, ouzo, and soft drinks are free.

The crew is Greek and adds much to the ambiance. An English-speaking cruise leader is also aboard each yacht. Each cruise features a Beach BBQ, a Greek night with Greek dancing, and a Captain's Dinner.

The *Galileo Sun* (built in 1994; 34 passengers,), on the other hand, provides a more upscale yacht experience. Cabins are all outside and some have double beds. A special emphasis is put on cuisine, served in a wood-paneled dining room. Public rooms also include a bar/lounge. Again, the crew is Greek, with an English-speaking cruise leader.

Zeus is also the preferred representative for Golden Sun/Dolphin Hellas's *Aegean I* (built in 1973; 570 passengers, 13,000 GRTs) and *Arcadia* (built in 1968; 278 passengers, 5,200 GRTs), cruises aboard which are also sold through other tour operators. Both ships are older vessels, with numerous public rooms and a casual ambiance.

ITINERARIES & RATES

Zeus Tours offers 7-day cruises on the *Zeus* ships and *Galileo Sun* that can be purchased as cruise-only or with a 3-night hotel stay in Athens. Cruises on the *Aegean I* and *Arcadia* combine a 3-, 4-, or 7-day cruise with a 3-night hotel stay in Athens, or can be booked as cruise-only. You get a better deal if you take both the cruise and hotel package.

AEGEAN I　3-, 4- and 7-day cruises round-trip from Athens. The **3-day cruises** visit Mikonos, Rhodes, and Patmos, plus Kusadasi (Turkey). The **4-day cruises** visit Mikonos, Kusadasi, Patmos, Rhodes, Crete, and Santorini. The **7-day cruises** visit Crete, Santorini, Rhodes, Patmos, Delos, Mikonos, and Kusadasi, plus Istanbul (Turkey). Zeus combines the cruises into cruisetours with 3 nights in a hotel in Athens, and into longer packages that include land tours. March through November. **Per diem rates:** $89–$160 inside, $122–$173 outside (no suites).

**ARCADIA　** Same itineraries and rates as Aegean I (above).

GALILEO SUN　7-day round-trip from Athens visits Delos, Santorini, Mikonos, Samos, Amorgos, Rhenia, Cape Sounion, Patmos, and Kusadasi (Turkey). May through October. **Per diem rates:** $257–$314 outside (no inside cabins or suites).

ZEUS I/ZEUS II/ZEUS III　** Three different itineraries. (1) **7-day round-trip from Athens visits Paros, Santorini, Ios, Naxos, Mikonos, Delos, Tinos, Kea, and Cape Sounion (on the mainland). April through October. (2) **7-day round-trip from Corfu** visits Paxi, Lefkada, Kefalonia, Ithaka, Zakinthos, and Parga (on the mainland). May through September. (3) **7-day round-trip from Rhodes** visits Kalimnos, Kos, Patmos, Lipsi, Leros, Simi, and Marmaris (Turkey). May through October. **Per diem rates:** $151–$188 outside (no inside cabins or suites).

8　Ships Sailing Longer Mediterranean Itineraries

The following lines and ships visit Greece as part of longer itineraries.

Celebrity Cruises. 5201 Blue Lagoon Dr., Miami, FL 33125. ☎ **800/437-3111.** www.celebrity-cruises.com.

Celebrity, an upscale U.S. operator, offers Greece as part of three 11- and 12-day Italy and Greek Isles itineraries aboard the *Century* (built in 1995; 1,750 passengers, 70,606 GRTs), sailing round-trip from Italy (Venice or Genoa), in May, September, and

October. The ship visits Katakolon, Piraeus, Crete, Santorini, and Gythion, plus Kusadasi (Turkey) and ports in Italy and Malta.

Club Med Cruises. 40 W. 57th St., New York, NY 10019. ☎ **800/4-LE-SHIP.** www.clubmed.com.

This line, operated by Club Med, did not have its Greek and Turkey schedules available at press time, but in 1998, the *Club Med II* (built in 1989; 376 passengers, 14,745 GRTs), a sailing ship along the lines of the Windstar vessels, offered 7-night cruises in July and August from Kusadasi (Turkey) to Athens that included Kaunos, Kekova, and Antalya (Turkey), Rhodes, Santorini, and Nafplion. That itinerary could change in 1999.

Crystal Cruises. 2049 Century Park E., Suite 1400, Los Angeles, CA 90067. ☎ **310/ 785-9300.**

This luxury operator offers Greece on the *Crystal Symphony* (built in 1997; 940 passengers, 51,004 GRTs) as part of 12-day cruises in May, September, and October. Departures are either from Rome or Athens, with the itinerary including Italy; Italy and Malta; or Italy, France, and Spain. Greece-area stops are either Corfu, Mikonos, and Kusadasi (Turkey), or Santorini, Rhodes, Mikonos, and Kusadasi (Turkey).

Peter Deilmann EuropAmerica Cruises. 1800 Diagonal Rd., Suite 170, Alexandria, VA 22314. ☎ **800/348-8287.** www.deilmann-cruises.com.

This German company, which operates river ships in Europe as well as ocean-going vessels, offers Eastern Mediterranean sailings in July and August on the *Lili Marleen* (built in 1994; 50 passengers, 750 GRTs), a luxury sailing yacht that's a re-creation of a 19th-century tall ship. A 9-day sailing from Antalya (Turkey) to Piraeus includes visits to Megisti, Simi, Samos, and Mikonos, plus Kusadasi (Turkey). A 12-day sailing from Piraeus to Nice includes Serifos, Milos, and Kithira.

EuroCruises/Fred Olsen Cruise Lines. 303 W. 13th St., New York, NY 10014-1207. ☎ **800/688-3876.** www.eurocruises.com.

EuroCruises offers two 18-day sailings round-trip from Dover, England, on its *Black Watch* (built in 1972; 798 passengers, 28,000 GRTs), a classic, upscale, European-style ship. In the spring, the ship visits Corfu and Katakolon; in the fall, Santorini, Piraeus, Mikonos, and Iraklion.

Holland America Line–Westours. 300 Elliott Ave. W., Seattle, WA 98119. ☎ **800/ 426-0327.** www.hollandamerica.com.

Holland America offers Greece on 12-day itineraries aboard the modern *Maasdam* (built in 1993; 1,266 passengers, 55,451 GRTs). In April, the ship sails round-trip from Venice, visiting Piraeus, Nafplion, and Katakolon in addition to Dubrovnik (Croatia) and Kusadasi and Istanbul (Turkey). In May and September, the ship sails from Venice to Istanbul, stopping in Piraeus and Kusadasi (Turkey), as well as ports in Croatia, Ukraine, Romania, and Bulgaria. In October the ship stops in Piraeus and Kusadasi (Turkey) on an Istanbul-to-Venice cruise that also includes Egypt, Israel, and Croatia. Also in October the ship visits Katakolon, Piraeus, and Kusadasi (Turkey) on a Venice-to-Barcelona itinerary that also includes port calls in Malta, Italy, and Monaco.

The line's flagship, the *Rotterdam* (built in 1997; 1,316 passengers, 62,000 GRTs), offers a 12-day itinerary in September and October from Piraeus to Rome, with visits to Rhodes, Patmos, and Katakolon, plus ports in Egypt, Israel, Cyprus, and Malta. Another itinerary offered in September, from Rome to Istanbul or vice versa, includes Italy, Greece, Croatia, and Turkey, with Greek stops in Corfu, Katakolon, and Iraklion, plus Kusadasi (Turkey). A 12-day Rome-to-Athens itinerary in September has port calls in Greece, Turkey, Bulgaria, Romania and Ukraine, with Greek stops in Nafplion and Patmos, plus Kusadasi (Turkey).

Mediterranean Shipping Cruises. 420 Fifth Ave., New York, NY 10018-2702. ☎ **800/ 666-9333,** or 081/554-5411 in Italy.

Mediterranean Shipping, which offers "classic Italian cruising," was still refining its 1999 schedules at press time. The line's *Rhapsody* (built in 1974; 768 passengers, 16,852 GRTs) was expected to sail on 13-day cruises round-trip from Genoa (Italy) in April, May, and September, visiting Santorini, Volos, and Piraeus, plus Istanbul and Kusadasi (Turkey) and ports in Italy. The ship is also expected to offer an alternative 12-day itinerary from Genoa in June with visits to Santorini, Crete, Piraeus, and Katakolon, plus Palma (Spain), Tunis, and Malta.

The *Monterey* (built in 1952; 576 passengers, 20,046 GRTs) is tentatively set to offer 12-day itineraries April through October from Genoa, round-trip, visiting Santorini, Volos, and Iraklion, plus Istanbul and Kusadasi (Turkey) and ports in Italy.

Norwegian Cruise Line. 7665 Corporate Center Dr., Miami, FL 33126. ☎ **800/327-7030.** www.ncl.com.

Norwegian, a midpriced American line, offers Greece aboard the *Norwegian Dream* (built in 1992; 1,726 passengers, 46,000 GRTs) as part of a 12-day sailing between Rome and Istanbul, in September and October, and as part of a 12-day sailing between Athens and Rome, offered in November. The Rome-Istanbul itinerary includes visits to Rhodes, Santorini, and Piraeus, plus ports in the Ukraine, Bulgaria, Turkey, and Italy. The Athens-Rome itinerary visits Crete and Rhodes, as well as ports in Italy, Israel, Egypt, and Cyprus.

P&O Cruises. 77 New Oxford St., London, WC1A 1PP England ☎ **44-171-800-2345,** or ☎ 800/426-0359 in the U.S. (Princess Tours).

British operator P&O Cruises visits Greece on several sailings. The *Arcadia* (built in 1989; 1,500 passengers, 63,500 GRTs) offers a 16-night sailing from Southampton (U.K.) that includes Piraeus, Crete, and Katakolon. The *Oriana* (built in 1995; 1,800 passengers, 69,000 GRTs) offers a 16-night cruise from Southampton in May that visits Piraeus and Lesvos, and a 15-day sailing in October that stops at Katakolon and Corfu. The *Victoria* (built in 1965; 726 passengers, 27,670 GRTs) cruises in October from Venice to Athens on a 14-night sailing that includes stops in Rhodes, Santorini, and Volos.

Princess Cruises. 10100 Santa Monica Blvd., Suite 1800, Los Angeles, CA 90067. ☎ **800/ 421-0522.** www.princesscruises.com.

Premium U.S. operator Princess, which is owned by P&O, offers several 12- to 13-day itineraries that include Greece. The *Grand Princess* (built in 1998; 2,600 passengers, 109,000 GRTs), at present the world's largest ship, sails between Venice and Istanbul in June, July, and September, with a stop in Athens, then Italy, Monte Carlo, Barcelona, and Kusadasi and Istanbul (Turkey).

The considerably smaller *Island Princess* (built in 1972; 610 passengers, 20,000 GRTs) offers sailings in April and October from Athens to Istanbul, visiting Santorini, Rhodes, and Volos, plus Kusadasi (Turkey), the Ukraine, and Bulgaria. The ship also offers an Athens-to-Istanbul itinerary in April, November, and December that includes Rhodes, Santorini, and Kusadasi (Turkey), along with port calls in Egypt and Israel. In November, the *Island Princess* also sails from Rome to Istanbul on an itinerary that includes Athens, Rhodes, and Kusadasi (Turkey), along with calls in Italy, Israel, and Egypt. Another itinerary between Istanbul and Rome (in May, Sept, and Oct) includes Mikonos, Crete, Athens, and Kusadasi (Turkey), along with calls in Malta, Spain, France, and Italy.

Sister ship *Pacific Princess* (built in 1971; 620 passengers, 20,000 GRTs) offers an Athens-to-Istanbul itinerary in April, November, and December that includes Rhodes, Santorini, and Kusadasi (Turkey), as well as Israel and Egypt. A Rome-to-Istanbul itinerary in April and November includes Athens, Rhodes, and Kusadasi (Turkey), as well as Israel and Egypt. In April and October, an Athens-to-Istanbul itinerary includes Santorini, Rhodes, Volos, and Kusadasi (Turkey), as well as Bulgaria and the Ukraine. An itinerary offered in May, September, and November from Istanbul to Rome includes Mikonos, Crete, Athens, and Kusadasi (Turkey), as well as calls in Malta, Spain, France, and Rome.

Royal Caribbean International. 1050 Caribbean Way, Miami, FL 33132. ☎ **800/ALL-HERE.** www.royalcaribbean.com.

Big Caribbean operator Royal Caribbean offers one 10-day sailing in October on the megaship *Legend of the Seas* (built in 1995; 1,804 passengers, 70,000 GRTs). The itinerary is from Barcelona to Piraeus, with calls at Crete, Santorini, Rhodes, and Kusadasi (Turkey).

Special Expeditions. 720 Fifth Ave., New York, NY 10019. ☎ **800/762-0003.** www.specialexpeditions.com.

Soft-adventure operator Special Expeditions offers four sailings on its expedition ship *Caledonia Star* (built in 1966; 110 passengers, 3,905 GRTs) in September and early October on an itinerary from Malta to Kusadasi (Turkey) that includes Italy, Greece, and Turkey. Greek ports include Katakolon, Itea, Skiros, Hios, Delos, and Santorini.

9 Best Shore Excursions in the Ports of Call: Greece

Shore excursions are designed to help you make the most of your limited time in port, taking you by various transport to sites of historical or cultural value or natural or artistic beauty. The tours are usually booked on the first day of your cruise, are sold on a first-come, first-served basis, and are nonrefundable. Some lines allow bookings in advance, and some include shore excursions in their cruise fares.

Generally, shore excursions that take you well beyond the port area are the ones most worth taking—you'll get professional commentary and avoid having to hassle with local transportation. In ports that have attractions within walking distance of the pier, however, you may be best off touring on your own.

Keep in mind that shore excursions are a revenue-generating area for the cruise lines, and the tours may be heavily promoted onboard the ship. They aren't always offered at bargain prices.

When touring in Greece, remember to wear comfortable walking shoes and bring a hat, sunscreen, and bottled water to ward off the effects of the hot sun (most lines make bottled water available as you disembark, usually for a fee).

Below we highlight a selection of shore-excursion offerings at the major cruise ports. Keep in mind that not all the tours will be offered by every line. We also offer a description of the ports for those of you who want to tour on your own.

For more information on many of these ports, consult the relevant chapters in this book.

Greek Ports & The Cruise Lines That Visit Them

Corfu	Classical, Crystal, Cunard, EuroCruises, Holland America, P&O, Royal Olympic, Zeus
Crete	Airtours, Celebrity, Classical, Cunard, EuroCruises, Golden Sun, Holland America, Mediterranean Shipping, Norwegian, Orient Lines, Princess, Renaissance, Royal Caribbean, Royal Olympic, Sea Cloud, Seabourn, Silversea, Swan Hellenic, Zeus
Itea (Delphi)	Classical, Cunard, Golden Sun, Radisson, Royal Olympic, Silversea, Special Expeditions
Katakolon (Olympia)	Celebrity, Costa, Cunard, EuroCruises, First European, Holland America, Mediterranean Shipping, P&O, Royal Olympic, Sea Cloud, Silversea, Special Expeditions, Swan Hellenic
Lesvos (Mitilini)	Airtours, Cunard, P&O, Royal Olympic, Swan Hellenic
Mikonos/Delos	Classical, Costa, Cunard, First European, Galileo, Golden Sun, Orient Lines, Princess, Radisson, Royal Olympic, Sea Cloud, Seabourn, Silversea
Nafplion	Classical, Club Med, Cunard, Holland America, Orient Lines, Royal Olympic, Sea Cloud, Sea Cloud, Seabourn, Silversea, Swan Hellenic
Patmos	Classical, Galileo, Golden Sun, Holland America, Royal Olympic, Silversea, Star Clippers, Zeus
Piraeus/Athens	Airtours, Celebrity, Classical, Club Med, Costa, Crystal, Cunard, EuroCruises, First European, Galileo, Golden Sun, Holland America, Mediterranean Shipping, Norwegian, Orient Lines, P&O, Peter Deilmann, Princess, Radisson, Renaissance, Royal Caribbean, Royal Olympic, Sea Cloud, Seabourn, Silversea, Star Clippers, Swan Hellenic, Windstar, Zeus
Rhodes	Airtours, Classical, Club Med, Costa, Crystal, Cunard, First European, Golden Sun, Holland America, Norwegian, Orient, P&O, Princess, Radisson Lines, Renaissance, Royal Caribbean, Royal Olympic, Silversea, Star Clippers, Swan Hellenic, Windstar, Zeus
Santorini	Airtours, Celebrity, Classical, Club Med, Costa, Crystal, Cunard, EuroCruises, First European, Galileo, Golden Sun, Mediterranean Shipping, Norwegian, Orient Lines, P&O, Princess, Radisson, Renaissance, Royal Caribbean, Royal Olympic, Sea Cloud, Seabourn, Silversea, Special Expeditions, Star Clippers, Swan Hellenic, Windstar, Zeus
Volos	Airtours, Classical, Mediterranean Shipping, P&O, Princess, Seabourn, Silversea

CORFU (KERKIRA)

See chapter 15 for complete sightseeing information.

Achilleion Palace & Paleokastritsa (4 hr., $42): Visit Achilleion Palace and see the statues of Achilles. Continue on to Paleokastritsa to visit the 13th-century Monastery of the Virgin Mary. There's usually free time and an opportunity to swim in Paleokastritsa. Stop in Corfu town and visit St. Spyridon Church, named for the patron saint of Corfu, or stroll the narrow streets

IRAKLION & AYIOS NIKOLAOS (CRETE)

See chapter 9 for complete sightseeing information.

The Palace of Knossos (3 hr., $47): Travel by motor coach from Iraklion to Knossos, once the capital of the prehistoric Minoan civilization, and thought to be the basis for the original labyrinth housing the mythological Minotaur. Visit the excavation of the palace of King Minos. Return to Iraklion for a museum tour or free time. (Similar tour offered from Rethymnon, Crete—5 hr.; $53.)

Exploring Crete (4 hr., $47): Ride by bus to Ayios Nikolaos, stopping for photos outside the archaeological site of Mallia, home of King Radamanthys. Travel to the Greek Orthodox monastery of St. George Selinaris. Take photos at scenic Elounda Bay. Free time in Ayios Nikolaos.

ITEA (DELPHI)

See chapter 12 for complete sightseeing information.

Delphi Excursion (4 hr., $55): Delphi is located on the slope of Mount Parnassus. Visit the Sanctuary of Apollo to see the Temple of Apollo, the theater, the treasury buildings, and the Sacred Way. Visit the Archaeological Museum. There's usually a short stop at Castalian Spring.

KATAKOLON (OLYMPIA)

See chapter 8 for complete sightseeing information.

Excursion to Olympia (4 hr., $52): Visit the site of the original Olympic Games, held from 776 B.C. to A.D. 393. See the Temple of Hera, in front of which burns the Olympic Flame; the Temple of Zeus, which once housed the gold-and-ivory statue of Zeus that was one of the Seven Wonders of the Ancient World; and the original stadium and *bouleuterion*, where Olympic competitors swore an oath to conform to the rules of the Games. Also visit the famous Archaeological Museum of Olympia to see the marble statue of the Temple of Zeus and the statue of Hermes. Also included is a short stop in the town of Olympia.

LESVOS (MITILINI)

See chapter 17 for complete sightseeing information.

Mitilini-Limnos Monastery & Folk Dances (4½ hr., $50): Depart in buses from Mitilini and drive along the Gulf of Gera to the Monastery of Limnos. Tour the monastery and church, and visit the Ecclesiastical Museum. Stop at a local taverna for a glass of Mitilini ouzo, mezedes, and a dance performance.

Mitilini-Ayiassos Village & Folk Dances (4½ hr., $50): Travel by bus from Mitilini to the traditional mountain village of Ayiassos. Take a walking tour of the village, including the Church of the Virgin Mary and the museum. Stop at a local taverna near the Gulf of Gera for ouzo, mezedes, and a folk-dance performance.

MIKONOS (& DELOS)

See chapter 10 for complete sightseeing information.

Delos Apollo Sanctuary (3–4½ hr., $37–$55): Travel by small boat from Mikonos harbor to Delos for a 2-hour guided walking tour of the tiny island that was once the religious and commercial hub of the Aegean, but now is home only to ancient ruins and their caretakers. View the Agora; the Sacred Way, which leads to the Sanctuary of Apollo; and the Terrace of the Lions, where marble beasts from the 7th century B.C. guard the now-dry Sacred Lake. View the remains of the Maritime Quarter with its harbors, water houses, and villas (including the House of Cleopatra) and the renowned mosaic floors in the House of the Masks and the House of Dionysos. Also visit the Archaeological Museum (if it's open).

NAFPLION

See chapter 8 for complete sightseeing information.

Palamidi Castle & Mycenae (4 hr., $56): Visit the area ruled by Agamemnon. Visit the Palamidi Castle, which was built by Venetians and seized by the Turks. The path up consists of nearly a thousand steps (motor coaches can drive up to the gate). At Mycenae you walk through the Lion Gate to view the ruins, which will remind you of Homer's *Iliad.*

Epidaurus & Palamidi Castle (4 hr., $56): See the countryside as you travel to Epidaurus, the town dedicated to Asklepios, god of healing. Visit the 4th-century B.C. theater with its remarkable acoustics. On the way back, stop by Palamidi Castle, located on a hill above Nafplion.

Combo tour of Epidaurus & Mycenae (7 hr., $89): Includes lunch at a traditional restaurant.

Ancient Corinth (4 hr., $49): Visit the ancient city where the most impressive relic is the 6th-century B.C. Doric temple of Apollo. You can also view the canal from 200 feet up on the bridge that stradles the waterway.

PATMOS

See chapter 11 for complete sightseeing information.

The Monastery of St. John & Cave of the Apocalypse (2½ hr., $32): Depart the port of Skala and travel by bus to the village of Hora and the 900-year-old Monastery of St. John. Visit the main church and view the ecclesiastical treasures in the museum. Continue on by bus to the nearby Cave of the Apocalypse to see the silver niches in the wall that mark the pillow and ledge used as a desk by the author of the Book of Revelation and the crack made by the Voice of God.

Exploration of Hora (3½ hr., $42): Depart the port of Skala by bus to visit the Cave of the Apocalypse (see above). Walk uphill to Hora where you will visit Plateia Xanthos, which houses the City Hall and the bust of Emmanuel Xanthos, one of the Greek independence leaders (in 1821). Also visit Symantiri House, a typical Patmian Mansion, and the historical chapel and museum of the Monastery of St. John. The trip includes a visit to a local tavern to sample mezedes (Greek hors d'oeuvres) and ouzo, and to be entertained by local musicians.

Afternoon at the Beach (2 hr., $15): Depart the ship on tenders to Kambos beach, where you'll have 2 hours to swim and tan. Changing facilities are available and sun beds and umbrellas will be provided, along with soft drinks.

PIRAEUS/ATHENS

See chapter 6 for complete sightseeing information.

Athens City Tour (8½–9 hr., $90–$92): Includes a guided tour of the Acropolis, Athens's most prominent historical and architectural site; the Temple of Poseidon, located high on a cliff overlooking the Aegean Sea; shopping in the Plaka; and a Greek lunch. May also include a visit to the National Archaeological Museum.

Athens, the Acropolis & the Corinth Canal (9 hr., $91): Visit the Acropolis and, by bus, tour past other sights in Athens, then take the highway from Athens to the Corinth Canal (about 96km/60 miles) for views of the canal and to visit Ancient

Corinth, once a grand city with a forum larger than that of Rome. Also visit the Corinth Museum.

Mycenae, Epidaurus & Corinth Canal (10 hr., $89): This long trip combines a visit to the Corinth Canal with a visit to the ruins at Mycenae and Epidaurus (see "Nafplion," above). Lunch with wine is included at a restaurant in Mycenae.

RHODES
See chapter 11 for complete sightseeing information.

Rhodes & Lindos Combined (4–4½ hr., $47–$56): Travel by bus through the scenic countryside to Lindos, an important city in ancient times. At Lindos, view the medieval walls which were constructed by the Knights of St. John in the 14th century. Walk or take a donkey up to the ancient Acropolis, where there are ruins and great views (you'll pass souvenir shops on the way). The trip may include a walking tour of Old Town Rhodes (see description below), a stop at a workshop selling Rhodian ceramics, and/or a visit to Mount Smith to view the ruins of ancient Rhodes, the Temple of Apollo, and Diagoras Stadium.

Lindos with Lunch by the Beach (8 hr., $65): Drive to Lindos and explore the city (see above). Continue on to a secluded beach for some swimming and sunning. Changing facilities, rest rooms, and showers are available. Enjoy lunch at a beachfront restaurant. Return to Rhodes, driving along the walls of the medieval city and stopping at Port d'Amboise for a walk through Old Town. View the Palace of the Knights and the medieval houses, as well as the Hospital of the Knights of St. John. The tour may stop at a ceramics workshop to view how Rhodian ceramics are made.

SANTORINI (THIRA)
See chapter 10 for complete sightseeing information.

Akrotiri Excavations & Fira Town (3 hr., $47–$57): Visit Akrotiri, an excavation site that dates back to the 2nd millennium B.C. See pottery, two- and three-story houses, and a variety of rooms, all 3,600 years old. Visit Fira, perched on the caldera rim, and take a stroll through town. Take a cable car ride or mule back to the ship (down the slope).

VOLOS
See chapter 12 for complete sightseeing information.

The Monasteries of the Meteora (9 hr., $99): Visit the Meteora, where incredible granite rocks soaring hundreds of feet in the air served as a refuge for medieval monks. Originally the only way to get to the site was via net baskets operated by rope pulley, but now a road leads close to the base of the site, and many steps have been cut into the stone, leading to the top. You'll visit monastic buildings that contain Byzantine artifacts, icons, and wall paintings, and enjoy sweeping views of the low plains and neighboring monasteries. Shopping time is offered in Kalambaka, and lunch at a local hotel is included.

Volos & Makrinitsa Village (3½ hr., $36): Visit the Volos Archaeology Museum, which houses a collection of ancient treasures. Also visit Makrinitsa village, located on the slopes of Mount Pelion. The narrow cobblestone streets are filled with small shops selling candied fruit, herbs, spices, and the like. The village square offers a stunning view of the surrounding countryside. Free time to shop is always included.

10 Best Shore Excursions in the Ports of Call: Turkey

The following Turkish ports of call are commonly visited on Greek itineraries.

ISTANBUL

Highlights of Istanbul (7 hr., $65): Includes the Hippodrome, once the largest chariot race grounds of the Byzantine Empire; Sultanahmet Mosque, also known as the Blue Mosque for its 21,000 blue Iznik tiles; the famous St. Sophia, once the biggest church of the Christian world; and Topkapi Palace, the official residence of the Ottoman Sultans and home to treasures that include Spoonmaker's Diamond, one of the biggest diamonds in the world. Also visit the Grand Bazaar, with its 4,000 shops. Stop during the tour for lunch on the ship. The same tour is sometimes offered with lunch in a first-class restaurant (8 hr., $80). Shorter versions of the tour sometimes visit only St. Sophia, the Blue Mosque, and the Grand Bazaar (4½ hr., $30), or Topkapi Palace and the Grand Bazaar (4 hr., $27).

Byzantine Underground Cistern and Grand Bazaar (3 hours, $22): Visit the underground cistern which dates from the 6th century and is supported by 336 Corinthian columns. The cistern is also known as "The Underground Palace." You reach the water-filled cavern by traveling with a guide down steep steps and along a raised walkway. Also visit the Grand Bazaar and view the outside of St. Sophia.

Beylerbeyi Palace (2½ hr., $34): Visit Istanbul's grandest seaside mansion, built by Sultan Abdulaziz on the Asian side of the Bosphorous in 1865. The tour includes the palace's harem, men's quarters, and grand central hall.

Istanbul Nightlife with Dinner (4 hr., $55): Enjoy traditional Turkish cuisine and belly dancing in a city nightclub.

Dolmabahce Palace & Chora Museum (8 hr., $75): Visit the 285-room 19th-century palace, the principal imperial residence of the late years of the Ottoman Empire. Drive across the Bosphorus Bridge to enjoy a panoramic view of Istanbul from the Asian side. Drive past gardens, old mansions, fortresses, and fishermen's villages. Return to the European side via Faith Bridge, arriving at the suburb of Tarabya for a Turkish seafood lunch. After lunch, drive to the modern part of Istanbul and across the Golden Horn to visit the Chora Museum and a Byzantine church that dates back to the 11th century and features mosaics and frescoes. The tour ends at the Grand Bazaar.

KUSADASI

Ephesus (3–4 hr., $40–$42): Visit one of the best-preserved ancient cities in the world. Your guide will take you down the city's actual marble streets to the baths, theater, and incredible library building, and along the way you'll pass columns, mosaics, monuments, and ruins. The tour may include a stop at a shop for a presentation of Turkish carpets (with an emphasis on getting you to buy).

Ephesus & the House of the Virgin Mary (3½ hr., $47): This tour combines a visit to Ephesus with the House of the Virgin Mary, a humble chapel located in the valley of Bulbuldagi. Located there is the site where the Virgin Mary is believed to have spent her last days. The site was officially sanctioned for pilgrimage in 1892.

Ephesus, St. John's Basilica & the House of the Virgin Mary (4½ hr., $52): This tour combines the above two with a visit to St. John's Basilica, another holy pilgrimage site. It is believed to be the site where St. John wrote the fourth book of the New Testament. A church at the site, which is now in ruins, was built by Justinian over a 2nd-century tomb believed to contain St. John the apostle. This tour may also be offered as a full-day excursion, including lunch at a local restaurant and a visit to the museum of Ephesus (7½ hr., $75).

Three Ancient Cities (6 hr., $67): This tour takes in the ruins that surround the region of Ephesus, including Priene, known for its Athena Temple bankrolled by Alexander the Great; Didyma, known for the Temple of Apollo; and Miletus, which includes a stadium built by the Greeks and expanded by the Romans to hold 15,000 spectators. A light lunch at a restaurant in Didyma is included.

Ephesus, Priene & Didyma (7½ hr., $75): Includes the above plus Ephesus and a buffet lunch at a five-star hotel.

5 Settling into Athens

by Sherry Marker

Athens is the city that Greeks love to hate, complaining that it's too expensive, too crowded, too polluted. Some 40% of the country lives here, making the city burst at the seams with five million inhabitants, a rumored 15,000 taxis—but try to find one that's empty—and streets so congested that you'll suspect that each of the five million Athenians has a car. Meanwhile, work continues on the new metro (subway line), with the tunneling turning once-lovely Syntagma Square into a construction site while disrupting traffic throughout central Athens.

Knowing this, you may be wondering if Athens, with all its fabled glories, is the place for you. Don't despair: Quite soon, you'll almost certainly develop your own love-hate relationship with Athens, snarling at the traffic and gasping in wonder at the Acropolis, fuming at the taxi driver who tries to overcharge you—and marveling at the stranger who realizes that you're lost and walks several blocks out of his way to take you where you're going.

Even though you've probably come here to see the "glory that was Greece," perhaps best symbolized by the Parthenon and the superb statues and vases in the National Archaeological Museum, allow some time to make haste slowly in Athens. Your best moments may come sitting at a small cafe, sipping a tiny cup of the sweet sludge that the Greeks call coffee, or getting hopelessly lost in the Plaka—only to find yourself in the shady courtyard of an old church, or suddenly face to face with an ancient monument you never knew existed. With only a little advance planning, you should find a good hotel here, eat well in convivial restaurants, enjoy local customs such as the refreshing afternoon siesta and the leisurely evening *volta* (promenade or stroll)—and leave Athens planning to return, as the Greeks say, *Tou Chronou* (Next Year).

And if you do get caught in an Athenian gridlock, just remember what it was like when the Parthenon was built: Teams of mules dragged carts laden with 12-ton blocks of marble from Mount Pendeli along today's Queen Sophia Avenue to the Acropolis. If an axle broke, traffic stopped for several days until the damage was repaired.

If you take a look at "Suggested Itineraries for First-Time Visitors" in the beginning of chapter 6, you'll get some good ideas on how to approach the city. As far as when to go, from March through May it's almost always pleasant and mild in Athens, although Greeks say that the March wind can have "teeth." Between June and August, the temperature usually rises steadily, making August a good month to emulate Athenian practice and try to avoid the city. Although sometimes almost as hot as August, September is usually balmy, with occasional light rain. October usually offers beautiful summer/autumn weather, with rain and some high winds likely, and it might be intermittently chilly. Most rain falls between November and February, when Athens can be colder and windier than you might expect. Average daytime temperatures range from 52°F in January to 92°F in August. Stretches when it's well over 100°F are not uncommon in summer, when anyone with health problems such as asthma should be wary of Athens's *nefos* (smog). The city can be very hot and exhausting—be sure to give yourself time off for a coffee or a cold drink in a cafe. After all, you're on vacation!

1 Orientation

ARRIVING
BY PLANE
Athens's **Hellenikon International Airport** is only 11 kilometers (7 miles) south of central Athens, but traffic to and from the airport is often so heavy that you should allow an hour for the trip. The **East (*Anatoliko*) Air Terminal** on the eastern side of the airport runways handles non-Olympic flights and some charters. The **West Airport (*Dhitiko,* usually called *Olympiakon*)**, handles all Olympic flights. A third, smaller terminal handles most charter flights.

Both the East and West terminals have free luggage trolleys, exchange and banking facilities, ATMs, post office and telephone offices, luggage storage, cafes, taxi and bus stands, tourist information offices, and hotel-booking agencies.

In the East Terminal, the **Greek National Tourist Organization** (abbreviated **GNTO** in English-speaking countries and **EOT** in Greece) tourist information desk, slightly to the left as you come out of customs, is officially open Monday through Friday from 9am to 7pm, Saturday from 9am to 2pm (but, as with everything in Greece, the official hours do not always reflect reality). This office usually has maps of Athens and a selection of pamphlets on various regions of Greece. **Pacific Travel,** located by the EOT desk, can help you book a hotel room. There's a poorly signposted **luggage storage facility** charging Dr1,000 ($3.35) per piece per day across from the parking lot near the entrance of the East Terminal entrance.

Numbers for the East Air Terminal include **Switchboard** (☎ 01/969-4111), **Arrival/Departure Information** (☎01/949-4466 or 01/949-4467), and **Tourist Information** (☎ 01/969-4500 or 01/961-2722).

If you arrive at the West Air Terminal, you will see the **GNTO office** after you clear customs; beside it is the **hotel reservations** office. The **luggage storage office** is (poorly) signposted on the sidewalk outside the terminal.

A New Airport

Athens's new airport, **Eleftherios Venizelos International,** is currently under construction and scheduled to open at Spata, 23 kilometers (14 miles) outside Athens, in March 2001, well in advance of the 2004 Olympics. If you are traveling around that time, be sure to check with your travel agent to see whether the airport has, in fact, opened.

Numbers for the West Air Terminal include **Switchboard** (☎ 01/926-9111 or 01/936-9111), **Arrival/Departure Information** (☎ 01/936-3363) and **Tourist Information** (☎ 01/969-4500 or 01/961-2722).

Flight information on Olympic flights is sometimes available at ☎ **01/966-6666** or 01/926-9111; both numbers are usually busy.

Many charter flights now use the **Charter Terminal,** the former U.S. military facility, to the south of the main terminals. There sometimes is, and sometimes is not, bus service directly from this terminal to Piraeus and Athens; sometimes, buses from the East and West terminals stop here to pick up passengers. The information numbers for the Charter Terminal are ☎ **01/997-2581** and 01/997-2686.

There is no shuttle bus between any of these terminals, but they are usually linked by bus nos. 091 and 91, which run into Athens and Piraeus.

GETTING TO ATHENS   Since buses run on erratic schedules, the easiest way into town is to take a **taxi** from immediately outside the terminal. This is not as simple as it sounds: Greeks regard waiting in line with amusement, and getting a cab is usually a fiercely competitive sport. A cab into the center (*kentro*) of town will cost you about Dr2,000 to Dr3,000 ($7 to $10), double that between midnight and 5am. Depending on traffic, the cab ride can take less than 30 minutes or well over an hour—something to remember when you return to the airport.

If you want to take a **bus** from the airport into central Athens, be prepared for what may be a substantial wait and a slow journey. In theory, bus no. 091 runs to Syntagma and Omonia squares before continuing to Piraeus every half hour from 7am to 10pm (Dr200/65¢), and then every hour from about 10:15pm to 6:30am (Dr400/$1.35). (Because of Metro construction, the bus sometimes stops first near Omonia Square and then doubles back to Syntagma Square.)

GETTING BETWEEN THE AIRPORT & PIRAEUS (PIREAS)   A taxi from the airport to Piraeus should cost Dr2,000 to Dr2,500 ($7 to $8). It's important to know that island boats leave from *several different Piraeus harbors*. Most ferryboats and hydrofoils (Flying Dolphins) for Aegina leave from the **Main Harbor.** Hydrofoils for other islands leave from **Marina Zea,** a vigorous half-hour walk from the Main Harbor. All this makes Piraeus a good place to take a taxi to and from the airport. If you do not know which harbor your boat is leaving from, tell your taxi driver your destination and he can probably find out the harbor and even the pier you are leaving from.

In theory, **bus no. 19** runs from the East to the West Terminal and then to Piraeus every hour from 5am to midnight (Dr200/65¢), and every 2 hours from midnight to 5am (Dr400/$1.35). The bus will leave you in Karaiskaki Square, several blocks from the harbor.

AIRLINE OFFICES   Most international carriers have ticket offices in or near Syntagma Square. Try to find out the location of your airline's Athens office before you leave home, as these offices can move without warning. The **Air Canada** office is at Odos Othonos 10 (☎ 01/322-3206). The **American Airlines** office is located at

---

Insider Tip

A word about making air connections after an island trip: It is unwise—even foolhardy—to allow anything less than 24 hours between your return to Piraeus by island boat and your departure by air, as rough seas can make for significant delays.

Athens & Environs

0 _____ 50 mi
0 _____ 50 km

Notios Envoikos Kolpos
(South Evvian Gulf)

44

1

44

Inefyta

Avion

E75

Pyli

Mt. Parnitha (Parnes)

Lake Marathon

1

1 **Rhamnous**

2 **Marathon**

A T T I C A

Dekelia

Mt. Pentelicus (Pendeli)

Nea Makri

E962

Aspropyrgos

Kolpos Petalion *(Petalian Gulf)*

Elefsina 3

8A

83

ATHENS

Rafina

4 **Daphni**

Salamis

Perama

89

6

Brauron (Vravrona) 7

5 **Piraeus**

Mt. Hymettus (Imittos)

SALAMIS

Glyfada

Markopoulo

Vouliagmeni

Varkiza

Keratea

Saronikos Kolpo *(Saronic Gulf)*

91

Lavrio

Aegina

AEGINA

8

Sounion

Legend

Airport ✈

Cruise Ship Terminal

Mountain ⛰

GREECE

⭐

Athens & Environs

Ferries to the islands at the port of Piraeus (Pireas) 5

Sanctuary of Artemis at Brauron (Vravrona) 7

Marathon Battlefield & Burial Mound 2

Sanctuary of Eleusis (Elefsis) at Elefsina 3

Monastery of Daphni (Dafni) 4

Sanctuary of Nemesis at Rhamnous 1

Monastery of Kaisariani (Kessariani) 6

Temple of Poseidon at Sounion 8

Odos Panepistimiou 15 (☎ 01/331-1045 or 01/331-1046). The **British Airways** office is at Odos Themistokleous 1, at Leoforos Vouliagmenis 130 (☎ 01/890-6666). The **Delta Air Lines** office is at Odos Othonos 4 (☎ 01/331-1668). The **Lufthansa Airlines** office is at Leoforos Vas. Sofias 11 (☎ 01/617-5200). The **Qantas Airways** office is at Odos Nikodimou 2 (☎ 01/323-9063). The **Swissair** office is at Odos Othonos 4 (☎ 01/323-5811). The **Turkish Airlines** office is at Odos Filellinon 19 (☎ 01/324-6024). The **Virgin Atlantic Airways** office is at Odos Tzireon 8–10 (☎ 01/924-9105).

Olympic, the national carrier, offers both international and domestic service and has offices just off Syntagma Square at Odos Othonos 6 (☎ **01/926-7444**), and at Leoforos Syngrou 96 (☎ **01/926-7251** to 7254). The main reservations numbers are ☎ **01/961-6161** and 01/966-6666. The **Olympic Office** (☎ **01/926-7445**) in the Athens Hilton hotel, Leoforos Vas. Sofias 6, is usually less crowded and easier to use than their main offices.

BY CAR

If you arrive by car **from Corinth** (to the southwest), the signs into Athens will direct you fairly clearly into Omonia Square, which you will enter from the west along Odos Ayiou Konstandinou. In Omonia, signs *should* direct you on towards Syntagma Square and other points in central Athens (signs in Omonia disappear mysteriously). If you arrive **from Thessaloniki** (to the north), the signs pointing you into central Athens are few and far between. It is not a good idea to attempt this for the first time after dark, as you may well miss the turning for Omonia Square. If this happens, your best bet is to try to spot the Acropolis and head toward it as best you can until you pick up signs for Omonia Square or Syntagma Square.

BY BUS

Before you start out on any bus trip, check with the **Tourist Police** (☎ **01/171**) or the **Greek National Tourist Organization (EOT)** office (☎ **01/331-9437** or 01/331-0561) for current schedules and fares. If possible, get someone to write down the name and address of your bus station in Greek; this will be a great help to you when you take a taxi or bus to the station.

There are two principal stations for the national bus company, **KTEL. Terminal A,** Odos Kifissou 100 (☎ **01/512-9233**), off the road out of Athens toward Corinth, handles buses **to and from the Peloponnese and parts of Northern Greece.** A taxi here from Syntagma Square should cost Dr1,000 to Dr1,500 ($3.35 to $5); allow an hour for the journey. If you don't have much to carry, take public bus no. 51 to the terminal (Dr100/35¢). It leaves from the corner of Odos Zinonos and Odos Menandrou, several blocks off Omonia Square; you can catch the same bus at the terminal for the trip into town.

Terminal B, Odos Liossion 260 (☎ **01/831-7096**), handles buses **to and from Central Greece** (including Delphi, Thebes, Evvia, and Meteora) and some destinations **to the north and east of Athens.** Bus no. 24, which stops at Leoforos Amalias in front of the entrance to the National Garden (a block south of Syntagma Square), will take you to and from the terminal for Dr100 (35¢). If you take this bus, tell the driver you want to get off at the bus terminal and then head right onto Odos Yousiou to reach the terminal.

The **Mavromateon terminal** at Patission and Alexandras, a few hundred meters north of the Archaeological Museum, handles buses for most **destinations in Attica.**

BY TRAIN

Trains **from the south and west,** including Eurail connections via Patras, arrive at the **Peloponnese Station** (Stathmos Peloponnisou), about a mile northwest of Omonia Square. Trains **from the north** arrive at **Larissa Station** (Stathmos Larissis), just across the tracks from the Peloponnese Station. The Larissa Station has both an **exchange office,** usually open daily from 8am to 9:15pm, and **luggage storage,** usually open from 6:30am to 9pm and charging Dr500 ($1.65) per bag per day.

To get to the train stations, a taxi from the center of town should cost no more than Dr1,000 ($3.35). Trolley 1 runs from Larissa Station to Omonia, Syntagma, and Koukaki for Dr100 (35¢). The most central place from which to catch it is the stop in front of the Parliament Building in Syntagma Square.

You can purchase train tickets just before your journey at the station (running the risk that all seats may be sold); at the Omonia Square ticket office, Odos Karolou 1 (☎ 01/524-0647); at Odos Filellinon 17 (☎ 01/323-6747), off Syntagma Square; or at most travel agents.

BY BOAT

Piraeus, the main harbor of Athens's main seaport, 11 kilometers (7 miles) southwest of central Athens, is a 15-minute subway (metro) ride from Monastiraki and Omonia squares. The subway runs from about 5am to midnight and costs Dr100 (35¢). The far-slower bus no. 040 runs from Piraeus to central Athens (with a stop at Odos Filellinon, off Syntagma Square) every 15 minutes between 5am and 1am and hourly from 1am to 5am for Dr200 (65¢).

You may prefer to take a **taxi** to avoid what can be a long hike from your boat to the bus stop or subway terminal. Be prepared for some serious bargaining. The normal fare on the meter from Piraeus to Syntagma should be about Dr1,800 to Dr2,000 ($6 to $7), but many drivers simply offer a flat fare, which can easily be as much as Dr5,000 ($17). Pay it if you're desperate, or walk to a nearby street, hail another taxi, and insist that the meter be turned on.

If you arrive at Piraeus by hydrofoil (Flying Dolphin), you'll probably arrive at the **Zea Marina** harbor, about a dozen blocks south across the peninsula from the main harbor. Even our Greek friends admit that getting a taxi from Zea Marina into Athens can involve a wait of an hour or more—and that drivers usually drive a hard (and exorbitant) bargain. To avoid both the wait and big fare, you can walk up the hill from the hydrofoil station and catch bus no. 905 for Dr100 (35¢), which connects Zea to the Piraeus subway station, where you can complete your journey into Athens. You must buy a ticket at the small ticket stand near the bus stop or at a newsstand before boarding the bus. *Warning:* If you arrive late at night, you may not be able to do this, as both the newsstand and the ticket stand may be closed.

If you've landed at the port of **Rafina** (about an hour's bus ride east of Athens), you'll see a bus stop with several buses in line up the hill from the ferryboat pier. Inquire about the bus to Athens; it runs often and will return you within the hour to the **Areos Park Terminal,** Odos Mavromateon 29, near the junction of Leoforos Alexandras and Odos Patission (about 25 min. by trolley from Syntagma Square or 1 block from the Victoria Square Metro stop). From the terminal, there are buses to Rafina every half hour.

VISITOR INFORMATION

The **Greek National Tourist Organization** (EOT, also known as the Hellenic Tourism Organization) has closed its central office in Syntagma Square; the new

Athens at a Glance

American Express Office ❸
EOT (Greek National
    Tourist Organization) ❷
First Aid Station ❶
Olympic Airways Office ❹

Legend
Church ✝
OTE ⎡C⎤
Post Office ✉

central office has no clearly visible sign or street number, but is behind the street-level plate-glass windows at Odos Amerikis 2 (☎ **01/331-0437** or 01/331-0561), 2 blocks west of Syntagma between Odos Stadiou and Odos Venizeliou. Open Monday through Friday from 9am to 7pm and Saturday from 9:30am to 2pm.

Information about Athens, free city maps, transportation schedules, hotel lists, and other booklets on many regions of Greece are available in Greek, English, French, and German—although when we stopped by, many publications we asked for were already "all gone," according to the staff, which consistently appears bored with their jobs and irritated by any questions.

Information on Greece is also available on the Internet at **www.arelanet.gr/ infoxenios.**

Available 24 hours a day, the **Tourist Police** (☎ **01/171**) speak English, as well as other languages, and will help with problems or emergencies.

CITY LAYOUT

As you begin to explore Athens, you may find it helpful to look up to the **Acropolis,** west of Syntagma Square, and **Mount Likavitos** (Lycabettus), to the northeast. You can see both Acropolis and Likavitos, whose marble lower slopes give way to pine trees and a summit crowned with a small white church, from most parts of the city.

Central Athens forms an almost perfect equilateral triangle, with points at **Syntagma (Constitution) Square, Omonia (Harmony) Square,** and **Monastiraki (Little Monastery) Square.** This area is technically defined as a commercial center, from which cars are banned (in theory, if not in practice) except for several cross streets.

At press time, all three squares were, alas, construction sites for the new subway line, known as the **metro.** In July 1988, Prime Minister Costas Simitis and a group of dignitaries took the official first ride on the metro, and reaffirmed their hopes that it will be fully operational by the end of 1999.

Most Greeks think of **Omonia Square**—Athens's commercial hub—as the city center, but most visitors take their bearings from **Syntagma Square**, site of the House of Parliament. The two are connected by the parallel **Odos Stadiou** and **Odos Panepistimiou.** (Panepistimiou is also known as Eleftheriou Venizelou.) Flanking the Parliament Building is Athens's largest park, the **National Garden.** West of Syntagma Square, **Odos Ermou** and **Odos Mitropoleos** lead slightly downhill to **Monastiraki Square,** home of the city's famous flea market. From Monastiraki Square, **Odos Athinas** leads north back to Omonia past the modern Central Market. The old warehouse district of **Psirri**—now the home of many chic galleries, cafes, and restaurants—is between Odos Athinas and Odos Ermou.

If you stand in Monastiraki Square and look south, you'll see the Acropolis. At its foot are the **Ancient Agora** (Market) and the **Plaka,** Athens's oldest neighborhood, many of whose street names honor Greek heroes, many from either classical antiquity or the Greek War of Independence. The twisting labyrinth of streets in the Plaka can challenge even the best navigators. Don't panic: The Plaka is small enough that you can't go far astray and its side streets with small houses and neighborhood churches are so charming that you won't mind being lost. One excellent map may help: the *Historical Map of Athens,* produced by the Greek Archaeological Service, which has a map of the Plaka in addition to a map of the city center showing the major archaeological sites. The map costs about Dr500 ($1.65) and is sold at many bookstores, museums, ancient sites, and newspaper kiosks. (Those whose map skills are minimal can take comfort in the fact that many Athenians speak some English and almost all are helpful to direction-seeking strangers.)

FINDING AN ADDRESS   If possible, have the address you want to find written out in Greek so that you can show it to your taxi driver or ask for help from pedestrians. Most street signs are given both in Greek and a transliteration, which is a great help. Most taxi drivers carry a good Athens street guide in their glove compartment, and can usually find any destination, although a certain number of Athenian cabbies are newcomers to the capital, and may have trouble with out-of-the-way addresses.

STREET MAPS   As already mentioned, you can get a free map of central Athens from the **Greek National Tourist Office** at Odos Amerikis 2, off Syntagma Square. With its small print and poor-quality paper, this is not a great map, and you may prefer to stop at a newspaper kiosk or bookstore to pick up a copy of the *Historical Map of Athens* or another congenial city map (see "Books" under "Shopping A to Z," in chapter 6).

NEIGHBORHOODS IN BRIEF

It's not easy to see that this sprawling city is divided into distinct districts and neighborhoods, each with its own character and associations, each with its favorite cafe and bakery. If you have the time to explore Athens, here are some of the neighborhoods that await you. Unless you have a specific goal and limited time, why not just stroll, get lost—and be pleasantly surprised when you discover that you're on a street where almost all the shops sell only icons or sugared almonds (essential to give to guests at weddings and baptisms), or find a little park where you can sit on a bench and study your map.

CENTRAL ATHENS

The Commercial Center   This area (a name no one uses and that appears on no map) lies between **Omonia, Syntagma,** and **Monastiraki** squares, and includes the **Plaka** and **Psirri** districts. In theory, vehicles are mostly forbidden here; in practice, they're endemic. Nonetheless, certain streets—and which they are today says nothing about tomorrow—are pedestrian, which makes parts of the area quite pleasant. Keep in mind that many motorists and virtually all motorcycle riders assume that pedestrian-only regulations do not apply to them.

Omonia Square is the heart of the working city of Athens, a tumultuous square around a circular fountain that's currently but a memory, thanks to the ongoing subway construction. You'll probably pass through Omonia when you walk to the National Archaeological Museum or head out of Athens by car or bus. Take a look at the increasingly decrepit 19th-century building facades around Omonia. Once, many housed some of Athens nicest hotels, now abandoned or desultory at best. One thing that hasn't changed much: **Odos Athinas,** between Omonia and Monastiraki squares. This is where you'll find Athens's **Central Market,** where you can browse the fish and meat halls, buy vegetables and fruits from all over Greece, sample cheeses from distant islands—or buy a pair of shoes or sunglasses from a street vendor. By day, this is the best street in town to get a sense of Athens's nonstop bustle. By night, most of the Omonia area has something of the tacky ambiance of New York's Times Square in the mid-1980s, and is one of Athens's few high-crime areas, with a vigorous and often violent drug trade. Omonia attracts a good number of wanderers, including refugees from Albania and Eastern Europe, who will try to sell you pirated CDs, leather jackets, and, sometimes, themselves.

Syntagma (Constitution) Square is, for most visitors, the heart of Athens. This is where you'll find the major banks, travel agencies, American Express and Thomas

The Plaka

As you'd expect from the oldest continuously inhabited section of Athens, the Plaka has a good number of archaeological sites, including the Greek and Roman agoras. It also has the charming district of Anafiotika, high on the slopes of the Acropolis, founded in the 19th century by emigrants from the island of Anafi. This is still a villagelike community, where on twisting streets like Epimenidou and Epikharmou, you could almost think you'd been whisked out of Athens to a Cycladic island.

But let's face it: This is probably not the Plaka you've heard of and come to see. That Plaka is the Plaka of restaurants, cafes, nightclubs, and nonstop souvenir shops on Odos Hadrian and Odos Kidathineon. It's the Plaka that's not unlike Boston's Quincy Market, or London's Covent Garden Market—both of which, until quite recently, actually were real markets. Similarly, shops aimed at the tourist market have displaced most of the Plaka's neighborhood shops—although, if you look closely, you'll find one or two corner groceries.

If you find the hustle and bustle and hard sell of the Plaka overwhelming, try to come back in the early morning, when the streets are being washed, the caged canaries are trilling their hearts out, and the shopkeepers have a smile, rather than a sales pitch, for passersby.

Cook, and several fine hotels, including the **Grande Bretagne,** the grand old lady of Greek hotels. The **central post office** is at the corner of Odos Mitropoleos. For years, the sidewalk cafes here were popular places to watch the world go by, but with the center of Syntagma Square torn up for subway construction, and a proliferation of fast-food joints, you'll probably not want to linger. Syntagma is also where many young (and not so young) Greek men, known colloquially as "spearmen," hone their skills at picking up foreign women.

Syntagma is the home of much of governmental Athens: the handsome neoclassical building at the head of the square is the **Greek Parliament building,** formerly the Royal Palace. That's where you'll see the changing of the guard several times a day and may hear a band playing on Sundays around 11am. The soldiers who march in front of the parliament building and the **Tomb of the Unknown Soldier** often wear the *evzone* uniforms (frilly white skirts and pom-pommed red shoes) of their ancestors who fought to gain Greece's freedom during the War of Independence (from 1821 to 1828). Most foreigners find the evzones' uniforms rather droll; Greeks do not, something to remember when you watch the changing of the guard. Laughing at this ceremony is equivalent to snickering when taps is played at the Tomb of the Unknowns at Arlington Cemetery in the United States, or when wreaths are laid at the Cenotaph in London on Remembrance Day.

If you're in Athens when there are street demonstrations, you'll probably see the marchers mass in Omonia Square to show their solidarity with workers, and then march to Syntagma Square, to make their representatives inside the House of Parliament take notice.

South of Syntagma Square, **Monastiraki Square** and the **Plaka** area are Athens's two main tourist destinations. Monastiraki's flea markets are open every day, but are usually best—and most crowded—on Sundays. In the Plaka, wall-to-wall shops and restaurants have displaced many of the Plaka's elegant 19th-century homes, especially along Odos Adrianou (Hadrian) and Odos Filellinon.

Psirri is the district between Odos Athinas and Odos Hermou which until only a few years ago would not have merited any mention. Now, it's where you'll find some of Athens's newest and most popular restaurants, cafes, and galleries. The district is being reclaimed by young entrepreneurs drawn here by relatively low rents. The area can still be rather deserted at night, but is usually perfectly safe—although walking alone late at night is not a great idea, as Odos Athinas has a vigorous drug and prostitution trade.

Kolonaki   This is the posh area in town, on the slopes of **Mount Likavitos** (Lycabettus), a few blocks northwest of Syntagma Square, spreading out around a central square. The square is officially named Plateia Filikis Eterias (Square of the Friendly Society), but is usually called Kolonaki, after the fragmentary marble column in the square.

Although many Athenians have fled the city's smog and congestion for northern suburbs, Kolonaki remains one of *the* places to live—or at least see and be seen—in Athens. If you're here on a Friday, try to take in the street market snaking along Odos Xenokratous. You may be surprised at how many Asian women you see shopping here: most of these young women, usually from the Philippines, work as maids and nannies in the homes of the Kolonaki elite.

If you're in Kolonaki on a Saturday, you can't miss seeing the beautiful people and the wanna-bes promenading up and down the streets, thronging in front of favorite boutiques to ogle the latest fashions before collapsing into street-side cafes to revive their spirits with cool drinks. There are more shoe stores per inch in Kolonaki than almost anywhere else in Greece, a nation that takes its footwear *very* seriously.

If you tire of window-shopping, you may want to take the funicular railway up Mount Likavitos to take in the panoramic view (smog permitting) of the entire metropolitan area and the sea and mountains beyond. If you walk down, you'll end up passing through some of central Athens's nicest and greenest streets, that wind around Likavitos's lower slopes.

The University Area   Kolonaki gradually merges to the northwest with the university area, spread loosely between the 19th-century university buildings on Panepistimiou and the Polytechnic some 10 blocks to the northwest. Lots of publishers have their offices in this area, and bibliophiles may enjoy the window displays of everything from children's books on Hercules to mathematical texts. A few blocks from the Polytechnic, **Exarchia Square,** with its many sandwich shops, cafes, and bars, is usually full of students. When there are demonstrations at any of Athens's institutions of higher learning, Exarchia Square is often where speeches are made.

Koukaki & Makriyanni   Koukaki, once the working-class counterpart to Kolonaki, has been increasingly gentrified. The district lies at the base of **Filopappos Hill** (Lofos Filopappou), also known as the Hill of the Muses (Lofos Mousseon). There are a number of pleasant paths leading from streets at the base of Filopappos

Plaka Tram Rides

In spring 1998, a tram service leaving from and returning to Palia Agora Square in the Plaka was initiated. The tram does a loop through the Plaka, out onto Odos Dionissiou Areopayitou, past the Acropolis, and back into the Plaka. The ride lasts 30 to 40 minutes, costs Dr1,000 ($3.35), and is offered from 10am to 10pm in summer and sometimes on weekends the rest of the year.

up through its pine-clad slopes, some ending at the Dora Stratou Theater or the Observatory. The main road through Koukaki is Veïkou, along which buses and trolleys run, and where there are some unpretentious cafes and restaurants as well as reasonably priced hotels. This is a nice area to stay in if you want to be out of tourist Athens, enjoy shopping in neighborhood groceries and shops—and don't mind the walk back into tourist Athens.

Makriyanni, the neighborhood just north of Koukaki, at the southern base of the Acropolis, is more upscale, probably because it's that little bit closer to the city center. There are some quite luxurious hotels here, as well as some middle-of-the-road places and several good restaurants, including the increasingly popular **Socrates's Prison.** This is a good area to stay in if you want to be almost as centrally located as you would be in the Plaka or Syntagma, but a bit out of the tourist maelstrom.

Pangrati & Mets Surrounding the reconstructed Athens Stadium known to the Greeks as **Kallimarmaro** (Beautiful Marble), **Pangrati** is popular with those who can't afford Kolonaki, and seems to have a high percentage of foreigners, including academics attached to various schools of archaeology in Athens. If you enjoy baroque funerary monuments, don't miss the sprawling **First Cemetery,** where luminaries such as the late Prime Minister Andreas Papandreou are buried. If you prefer your green spaces without tombs, explore Pangrati's lovely **green park,** almost a miniforest in the heart of Athens. There are lots of neighborhood restaurants and tavernas scattered in Pangrati, so you won't go hungry here.

Mets is southeast of Pangrati, on the other side of the Stadium, between the temple of Zeus and the First Cemetery. There are still some elegant private homes here, although most of Mets has Athens's typical low, concrete apartment buildings. Mets takes its name from a popular 19th-century cafe, the Metz, that once flourished here. Appropriately, the district still has some elegant bars and good restaurants—including the longtime favorite, Manesis, and the newcomer Bajazzo, the first Greek restaurant to be awarded a Michelin star.

Embassy District Leoforos Vas. Sofias (Queen Sophia Boulevard) runs from Syntagma Square toward Athens's fashionable northeastern suburb of Kifissia. If you walk along Vas. Sofias and explore the side streets that run uphill from it into Kolonaki, you'll notice the national flags of many countries on elegant office buildings and town houses. This is the Embassy District, which stretches as far as the Hilton Hotel, where many embassy workers head for a snack at the Byzantine Cafe.

THE NORTHEAST SUBURBS

Athens is growing every-which-way, but much of its expansion is to the northeast, in the valley between the mountains of Penteli to the east and Parnitha to the west. Two major roads—the **National Road** to the west and **Leoforos Kifissias** to the east—run north from Athens through wall-to-wall bedroom suburbs before reaching fashionable **Kifissia,** some 12 kilometers (8 miles) from the center of Athens.

Kifissia Cooler than Athens, thanks to its elevation, Kifissia was fashionable enough for the Royal Family to have a villa here. Until recently, many wealthy Athenian mothers and children decamped to the elegant villalike hotels in Kifissia for the summer, leaving the men behind to work (and, some said, play) in Athens. Now, Kifissia has a distinctly suburban feel, with large supermarkets and incipient malls, although its spreading plane trees still give many streets a rural feel. There are some good restaurants, but there's no reason to trek out here until you've spent a lot of time in central Athens.

PIRAEUS (PIREAS)

The main port of Athens, Piraeus is a city very much in its own right—although even locals have trouble telling precisely where Athens ends and Piraeus begins. Piraeus prides itself on being rough and tough—a stronghold of communism, the home of *rembetika* (street-slang songs of political protest), and the workplace of a profusion of prostitutes. Probably none of this will be particularly obvious when you come here to catch a boat to the islands from the **Main Harbor,** or Megas Limani (Great Harbor), or **Zea Marina,** also called Pasalimani. (For ferry information, see "Getting Around," below.) What will be obvious if you go to any of the many fish tavernas in the little harbor of **Mikrolimani** (Little Harbor), which is also still called by its former name of Turkolimani (Turkish Harbor), is the prices, which range from exorbitant to extortionate.

THE SOUTHERN SUBURBS

Heading southeast out of Athens along the coast are a string of once-pleasant suburbs, now virtually entirely absorbed into Athens. This used to be a good place for a swim, but now there are frequent pollution alerts for these, and virtually no other, beaches in Greece.

Palco Faliro, a once-lovely coastal suburb, has become almost a city by the sea, full of apartment buildings in the occasionally deafening flight path to the airport. South of the large yacht harbor of Kalamaki along Leoforos Poseidonos, the coast road, there's a big, busy public beach at **Ayios Kosmas.** Farther south, **Glyfada,** Attica's largest resort, with a yacht harbor, has lots of restaurants, bars, discos, food and clothing stores—and an almost always crowded, but decent, public beach.

Voula, farther southeast, has another public beach. The major resort area of **Vouliagmeni,** 23 kilometers (14 miles) south of Athens, has two good public beaches and several hotels, notably the luxury Astir Palace.

2 Getting Around

BY PUBLIC TRANSPORTATION
BY METRO

The new Metro (subway), designed to allow travel in much of central Athens and beyond, is very much under construction, with a scheduled completion date of the end of 1999. This date replaces several earlier, more optimistic dates, and it remains to be seen whether the 1999 date will itself prove to have been optimistic. The existing tram line runs from **Piraeus to Kifissia,** covering only the western part of the city. Most visitors encounter the subway when they take it from Omonia or Monastiraki to Piraeus to catch a boat to the islands. (Don't miss the spectacular view of the Acropolis as the subway comes above ground by the Agora). Buy your tickets at the station, validate them in the machines as you enter, and hang on to the ticket. The fare at press time was Dr100 (35¢). If you're not carrying much luggage, the harbor in Piraeus is a 5-minute walk left from the station.

BY BUS & TROLLEY BUS

The public transportation system is cheap—and, if you use it, you may think deservedly so. Although you can get almost everywhere you want to in central Athens and the suburbs by bus or trolley, you would need more time than you will probably have to figure out which bus to take. Once you have figured this out, you will usually have a long wait before you catch your bus, which will almost certainly be packed to the seams. The bus service does has an information number (☎ 01/185), but it's usually busy.

If you find none of this daunting, tickets cost Dr100 (35¢) each and can be bought from the kiosks (*periptera*) scattered throughout the city. The tickets are sold in packets of 10, though sometimes you can buy them individually. They are good for a ride anywhere on the system. Be certain to validate yours when you get on, and keep it until you get off. Occasionally, inspectors board the bus and check to see that everybody has paid the fare.

If you're heading out of town and take a blue A-line bus for transferring to another blue A-line bus, your ticket will still be valid on the transfer bus. In central Athens, the minibuses numbered 60 and 150 serve the commercial area free of charge.

Buses heading out to farther points of Attica leave from **Odos Mavromateon** on the western edge of the Pedion tou Areos park at the western end of Leoforos Alexandras.

BY TAXI

It's rumored that there are more than 15,000 taxis in Athens, but finding one empty is almost never easy. Especially if you have travel connections to make, it's a good idea to reserve a radio taxi (see below). Fortunately, taxis are inexpensive in Athens and most drivers are honest men trying to wrest a living by maneuvering through Athens's endemic gridlock. However, some drivers, notably those working Piraeus, the airports, and popular tourist destinations, can't resist trying to overcharge obvious foreigners. When you get into a taxi, check to see that the meter is turned on and set on "1" rather than "2"; the meter should be set on "2" (double fare) only between midnight and 5am, or if you take a taxi outside the city limits (if you plan to do this, try to negotiate a flat rate in advance). Unless your cab is caught in very heavy traffic, a trip to the center of town from the airport between 5am and midnight should not cost more than Dr3,000 ($10). Don't be surprised if your driver picks up other passengers en route; the driver will work out everyone's fair share of the fare.

Keep in mind that your driver may have difficulty understanding your pronunciation of your destination: if you are taking a taxi from your hotel, a staff member can assist you by telling the driver your destination or writing down the address for you to show to a driver. If you carry a business card from your hotel with you, you can show it to the taxi driver for your return.

If you suspect that you have been overcharged, before you pay the fare, ask for help at your hotel or other destination.

At press time, the minimum fare is Dr200 (65¢), and the "1" meter rate is Dr62 (20¢) per kilometer, with a surcharge of Dr150 (50¢) for service from a port or rail or bus station, Dr300 ($1) for service from the airport, and a luggage fee of Dr50 (15¢) for every bag over 10 kilograms (22 lb.). These prices will almost certainly be higher by the time you visit Greece, as increases were scheduled to go into effect in autumn 1998.

There are about 15 **radio taxi** companies in Athens, including **Aris** (☎ 01/346-7137), **Express** (☎ 01/993-4812), **Kosmos** (☎ 01/801-9000), **Parthenon** (☎ 01/581-4711), and **Piraeus** (☎ 01/413-5888). If you're trying to make travel connections or traveling during rush hours, the service will be well worth the Dr300 ($1) surcharge. Again, your hotel can make the call for you and make sure that the driver knows where you want to go. Most restaurants will call a taxi for you without charge.

The Hellenic Tourism Organization's pamphlet *Helpful Hints for Taxi Users* has information on taxi fares as well as a complaint form, which you can send to the

Ministry of Transport and Communication, Xenophondos 13, 10191 Athens. Replies to complaints should be forwarded to the *Guinness Book of Records.* See also the "Typical Taxi Tricks" feature in chapter 3 of this book.

BY CAR

In Athens a car is more trouble than convenience. The traffic is heavy and finding a parking place is so difficult that we once, in desperation, drove to the airport, left the car in the long-term parking lot there, and took a cab back into town.

If you want to drive outside Athens, there are plenty of rental agencies south of Syntagma Square. Here's a list of some of the better agencies: **Athens Cars,** Odos Filellinon 10 (☎ 01/323-3783 or 01/324-8870); **Autorental,** Leoforos Syngrou 11 (☎ 01/923-2514); **Avis,** Leoforos Amalias 46–48 (☎ 01/322-4951 to 4957); **Budget Rent a Car,** Leoforos Syngrou 8 (☎ 01/921-4771 to 4773); **Eurodollar Rent a Car,** Leoforos Syngrou 29 (☎ 01/922-9672 or 01/923-0548); **Hellascars,** Leoforos Syngrou 148 (☎ 01/923-5353 to 5359); **Hertz,** Leoforos Syngrou 12 (☎ 01/922-0102 to 0104) and Leoforos Vas. Sofias 71 (☎ (01/724-7071 or 01/722-7391); **Interrent-Europcar/Batek SA,** Leoforos Syngrou 4 (☎ 01/921-5789 or 01/921-5789); and **Thrifty Hellas Rent a Car,** Leoforos Syngrou 24 (☎ 01/922-1211 to 1213). Prices for rentals range from about Dr15,000 to Dr30,000 ($50 to $100) per day. *Warning:* Be sure to take full insurance.

ON FOOT

Since most of what you want to see and do in Athens is in the city center, it's easy to do most of your sightseeing on foot. Fortunately, Athens has created pedestrian zones in sections of the **Commercial Triangle** (the area bounded by Omonia, Syntagma, and Monastiraki squares), the **Plaka,** and **Kolonaki,** making strolling, window-shopping, and sightseeing infinitely more pleasant. Still, don't relax completely even on pedestrian streets: Athens's multitude of kamikaze motorcyclists seldom respects the rules, and you should remember that a red traffic light or stop sign is no guarantee that cars will stop for pedestrians.

Wheelchair users will find Athens a major challenge, although curbs on some streets are being redesigned, and the government announced plans in 1998 to make the Acropolis more easily accessible for those in wheelchairs.

FAST FACTS: Athens

American Express   The office at Odos Ermou 2, near the southwest corner of Syntagma Square (☎ **01/324-4975**), is open Monday through Friday from 8:30am to 4pm and Saturday from 8:30am to 1:30pm. For lost or stolen credit cards and checks, you can call collect during off-hours to the American Express office in London (☎ **0044/273/675-975**).

ATMs   Automatic teller machines are increasingly common at banks throughout Athens, and the **National Bank of Greece** operates a 24-hour ATM in Syntagma Square.

Banks   Banks are generally open Monday through Thursday from 8am to 2pm and Friday from 8am to 1:30pm. All banks are closed on the long list of Greek holidays (See "When to Go," in chapter 3). Most banks exchange currency at the rate set daily by the government. This rate is usually more favorable than that offered at unofficial exchange bureaus. Still, it's worth doing a little comparison shopping. Some hotels offer better-than-official rates, usually only for cash, as do some stores, usually only when you are making an expensive purchase.

A Warning about ATMs

It is *not* a good idea to rely on using ATMs exclusively in Athens, since the machines here are often out of service when you need them most: on holidays or during bank strikes.

Banks on Syntagma Square include the **National Bank of Greece** (☎ 01/ 322-2255) and **Citibank** (☎ 01/322-7471); other centrally located banks include **Bank of America,** Odos Panepistimiou 39 (☎ 01/324-4975), and **Barclays Bank,** Voukourestiou 15 (☎ 01/364-4311).

Business Hours   Even Greeks get confused by their complicated and changeable business hours. In winter, Athens's shops are generally open Monday and Wednesday from 9am to 5pm; Tuesday, Thursday, and Friday from 10am to 7pm; and Saturday from 8:30am to 3:30pm. In summer, shops are generally open Monday, Wednesday, and Saturday from 8am to 3pm; and Tuesday, Thursday, and Friday from 8am to 2pm and 5:30 to 10pm.

Most food stores are open Monday and Wednesday from 9am to 4:30pm, Tuesday from 9am to 6pm, Thursday from 9:30am to 6:30pm, Friday from 9:30am to 7pm, and Saturday from 8:30am to 4:30pm.

Many shops geared to visitors stay open late into the night—but often only if the shop owner thinks that business will be good. In other words, the shop that was open late yesterday may close early today.

Dentists & Doctors   Embassies (see below) usually have a list of dentists and doctors; some English-speaking physicians advertise in the daily *Athens News.*

Drugstores   See "Pharmacies," below.

Embassies & Consulates   Australia, Leoforos Dimitriou Soutsou 37 (☎ 01/ 645-0404); **Canada,** Odos Ioannou Yenadiou 4 (☎ 01/723-9511 or 01/ 725-4011); **Ireland,** Odos Stratigou Kalari 16, Psychiko (☎ 01/723-2771); **New Zealand,** Odos Semitelou 9 (☎ 01/771-0112); **South Africa,** Odos Seferi 4, Psychiko (☎ 01/680-6645); **United Kingdom,** Odos Ploutarchou 1 (☎ 01/ 723-6211); **United States,** Leoforos Vas. Sofias 91 (☎ 01/721-2951; emergency number 01/729-4301). Embassies are usually closed on their own important national holidays and sometimes on Greek holidays as well.

Emergencies   In an emergency, dial ☎ **100** for the **police** and ☎ **171** for the **tourist police.** Dial ☎ **199** to report a **fire** and ☎ **166** for an **ambulance** and the **hospital.** If you need an English-speaking doctor or dentist, call your embassy for advice or try **SOS Doctor** at ☎ **01/331-0310.** The English-language daily *Athens News* lists some American- and British-trained doctors and hospitals offering emergency services. Most of the larger hotels have doctors whom they can call for you in an emergency, and embassies will sometimes recommend local doctors.

KAT, the emergency hospital in Kifissia (☎ **01/801-4411** to 4419), and **Asklepion Voulas,** the emergency hospital in Voula (☎ **01/895-3416** to 3418), both have emergency rooms open 24 hours a day. If you need medical attention fast, don't waste time trying to telephone these hospitals: just go. Their doors are open and they will see to you as soon as you enter.

In addition, one of the major hospitals takes turns each day being on emergency duty. A recorded message in Greek at ☎ **01/106** tells which hospital is open for emergency services and gives the telephone number.

The **SOS Doctor** in Athens can be reached at ☎ **01/331-0310** or 01/ 331-0311; this is a 24-hour service that can send you a physician promptly for a fee of approximately Dr20,000 ($66).

Eyeglasses   If anything happens to your glasses, **Optical,** Odos Patriarchou Ioakim 2 (☎ **01/724-3564**), has a wide range of designer shades and specs at designer prices, and can provide a fast replacement.

Hospitals   Except for emergencies, hospital admittance is gained through a physician. See "Dentists & Doctors," above.

Information   See "Visitor Information," earlier in this chapter.

Internet Access   One block off Omonia Square, the **Astor Internet Café,** Odos Patission 17 (☎ **01/523-8546**), is open Monday through Saturday from 10am to 10pm and Sunday from 10am to 4pm, and charges Dr1,500 ($5) per hour to use e-mail, the Internet, and word-processing. Across from the National Archaeological Museum, the **Central Music Coffee Shop,** Odos Octobriou 28 (also called Odos Patission; ☎ **01/883-3418**), is open daily from 9am to 11pm and charges Dr1,500 ($5) per hour for similar services. **Inforama,** Odos 28 Octobriou 302a, offers similar services for Dr1,800 ($6) an hour; it's open Monday through Saturday from 10am to 10:30pm.

Laundry & Dry Cleaning   The **self-service launderette** at Odos Angelou Yeronda 10, in Filomouson Square, off Odos Kidathineon, Plaka, is open daily from 8:30am to 7pm; it charges Dr2,000 ($7) for wash, dry, and soap. The **National Dry Cleaners and Laundry Service,** Odos Apollonos 17 (☎ **01/ 323-2226**), next to the Hermes Hotel, is open Monday and Wednesday from 7am to 4pm and Tuesday, Thursday, and Friday from 7am to 8pm; laundry costs Dr1,500 ($5) per kilo (2.2 lb.). Hotel chambermaids will often do laundry for you at a reasonable price. Dry cleaning in Athens is reasonable, about Dr900 ($3) for a pair of slacks, and next-day service is usually possible.

Lost & Found   If you lose something on the street or on public transport, contact the **police lost and found,** Leoforos Alexandras 173 (☎ **01/642-1616**), open Monday through Saturday from 9am to 3pm. Lost passports and other documents may be returned by the police to the appropriate embassy, so check there as well. It's a good idea to travel with a photocopy of all important documents.

Luggage Storage/Lockers   If you're coming back to stay, many hotels will store excess luggage while you travel. Just southwest of Syntagma Square, **Pacific Ltd.,** Odos Nikis 26 (☎ **01/324-1007** or 01/322-3213), has a per-piece charge of Dr500 ($1.65) per day, Dr1,000 ($3.35) per week, Dr2,500 ($8) per month. Open Monday through Saturday from 8am to 8pm. **Bellair Travel and Tourism Inc.,** Odos Nikis 15 (☎ **01/323-9261** or 01-321-6136; e-mail: bellair@ travelling.gr), is open Monday through Friday from 9am to 5pm and has similar charges. There are storage facilities at the Metro station in Piraeus, at both train stations, and across from the entrance at the East Air Terminal.

Newspapers & Magazines   The *Athens News* is a daily newspaper published locally in English, with a weekend section ("Scope") listing events of interest; it's available at kiosks everywhere for Dr250 (80¢). Most central Athens newsstands also carry the *International Herald Tribune,* which has an English-language insert of highlights from the Greek daily *Kathimerini,* and *USA Today.* Local weeklies include the *Hellenic Times,* with its entertainment listings. The free magazine *Athens Today,* with information on restaurants, shopping, museums and galleries, is published about six times a year and is usually available in major hotels and sometimes from the Greek National Tourist Organization.

Pharmacies　Pharmakia, identified by green crosses, are scattered throughout Athens. Hours are usually Monday through Friday from 8am to 2pm. In the evening and on weekends most are closed, but usually post a notice listing the names and addresses of pharmacies that are open or will open in an emergency. Newspapers, including the *Athens News,* list the pharmacies open outside regular hours.

Police　In an **emergency,** dial ☎ **100.** For help dealing with a troublesome taxi driver, hotel, restaurant, or shop owner, stand your ground and call the **tourist police** at ☎ **171.**

Post Offices　The main post offices in central Athens are at Odos Eolou 100, just south of Omonia Square, and in Syntagma Square on the corner of Odos Mitropoleos. These are open Monday through Friday from 7:30am to 8pm, Saturday from 7:30am to 2pm, and Sunday from 9am to 1pm. The two post offices at the East and West air terminals also keep these extended hours. Oddly, mail posted at the air terminals almost always takes longer to arrive than mail posted in Athens itself.

All the post offices can accept parcels, but the **parcel post office** is at Odos Stadiou 4, inside the arcade (☎ **01/322-8940**), open Monday through Friday from 7:30am to 8pm. They sell cardboard shipping boxes in four sizes. Parcels must be open for inspection before you seal them at the post office.

You can receive correspondence in Athens in care of **American Express,** Odos Ermou 2, 102 25 Athens, Greece (☎ **01/324-4975**), near the southwest corner of Syntagma Square, open Monday through Friday from 8:30am to 4pm and Saturday from 8:30am to 1:30pm. If you have an American Express card or traveler's checks, the service is free; otherwise, each article costs a steep Dr600 ($2).

Radio & Television　There are 11 major Greek TV stations in Athens and at least two local stations. In addition, foreign-language channels from Italy, Spain, and Germany can be seen, as well as CNN around the clock. Most foreign-language films shown on Greek TV are not dubbed, but have the original sound-tracks with Greek subtitles. All current-release foreign-language films shown in Greek cinemas have the original soundtracks with Greek subtitles.

Rest Rooms　There are public rest rooms in the underground station beneath Omonia Square and beneath Kolonaki Square, but you'll probably prefer a hotel or restaurant rest room. (Toilet paper is often not available; carry some tissue with you. Do not flush paper down the commode; use the receptacle provided.)

Safety　Athens is among the safest capitals in Europe, and there are few reports of violent crimes. **Pickpocketing,** however, is not uncommon, especially in the Plaka and the Omonia Square area, on the Metro and buses, and in Piraeus. We advise travelers to avoid the side streets of Omonia and Piraeus at night. As always, leave your passport and valuables in a security box at the hotel. Carry a photocopy of your passport, not the original.

Taxes　A VAT (value-added tax) of between 4% and 18% is added onto every-thing you buy. Some shops will attempt to cheat you by quoting you one price and then, when you hand over your credit card, adding on a hefty VAT charge. Be wary. In theory, if you are not a member of a Common Market/EU country, you can get a refund on major purchases at Hellenikon airport when you leave Greece. In practice, you would virtually have to arrive at the airport a day before your flight to get to the head of the line, do the paperwork, get a refund, and catch your flight.

Telephone/Telegrams/Faxes   Many of the city's public phones now accept only phone cards, available at newsstands and OTE offices in several denominations starting at Dr1,700 ($5.65). The card works for 100 short local calls (or briefer long distance or international calls). Some kiosks still have metered phones; you pay what the meter records. Local phone calls cost Dr20 (6¢). North Americans can phone home directly by contacting **AT&T** (☎ **00-800-1311**), **MCI** (☎ **00-800-1211**), or **Sprint** (☎ **00-800-1411**); calls can be collect or billed to your phone charge card. You can send a telegram or fax from offices of the **Telecommunications Organization of Greece (OTE).** At press time, the OTE office at Stadiou 15, near Syntagma, was temporarily closed, leaving the Omonia Square OTE office and the Victoria Square Office at Odos Patission 85 as Athens's most central OTE offices.

Tipping   Athenian restaurants include a service charge in the bill, but many visitors add a 10% tip. Most Greeks do not give a percentage tip to taxi drivers, but often round out the fare to Dr1,000, for example, on a fare of D1950.

3 Accommodations

While virtually all Greek hotels are clean and acceptably comfortable, few are charming or cozy, and fewer still are elegant or distinctive. If shower and tub facilities are important to you, be sure to have a look at the bathroom of the room you are offered: many Greek tubs are tiny, and the showers hand-held and capricious. Another warning: Decent reading lamps are virtually unknown here—consider using one of the little traveler's night-lights that clips onto your book.

The **Syntagma Square** area and the **Plaka/Monastiraki** district are the most convenient locations for sightseeing. If you only have a few days in Athens, you should seriously consider staying here. There are also good choices in **Makriyanni** and the **Embassy District,** as well as some good budget choices near the National Archaeological Museum. We've enjoyed staying in **Kolonaki,** the upscale Athenian neighborhood on the slopes of Mount Likavitos, although there were times we didn't look forward to the uphill walk back to the hotel. We have friends who always stay in the **Koukaki** district, near Filopappos Hill and off the non-Acropolis side of Dionissiou Areopayitou. They love the quiet residential streets and the bonus of being out of the heart of tourist Athens in a real Greek neighborhood. If you do stay there, you'll be doing extra walking to get to almost everything you want to do.

In summer, we strongly advise that you reserve ahead of time to avoid the hassle of searching when you arrive. If you do arrive without a reservation, you can usually book a room at the **tourist information booth** in the West Air Terminal. It's run by a private tourist agency and is open daily from 7am to 1am; the service costs a small fee.

Note: Although the rates below were accurate at press time, increases of 10% to 15% may occur in 1999 and 2000.

THE PLAKA
EXPENSIVE

Electra Palace. Odos Nikodimou 18, Plaka, 10557 Athens. ☎ **01/337-0000** or 01/324-1407. Fax 01/324-1875. 106 units. A/C MINIBAR TV TEL. Dr45,000 ($150) double. Rates include breakfast. AE, DC, MC, V.

Athens Accommodations

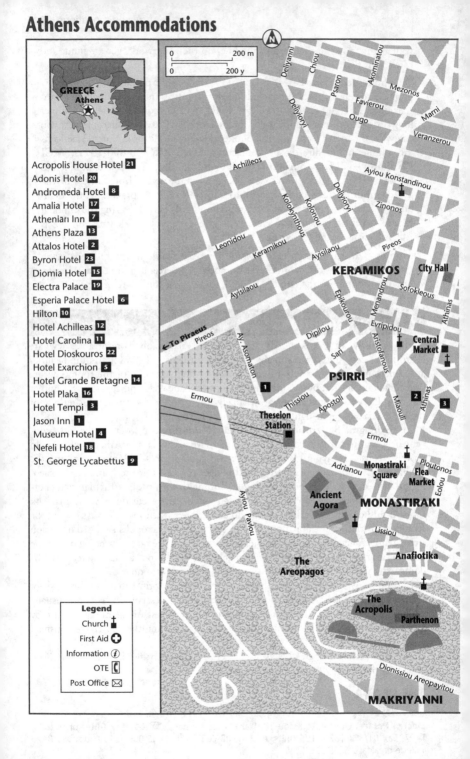

Acropolis House Hotel **21**
Adonis Hotel **20**
Andromeda Hotel **8**
Amalia Hotel **17**
Athenian Inn **7**
Athens Plaza **13**
Attalos Hotel **2**
Byron Hotel **23**
Diomia Hotel **15**
Electra Palace **19**
Esperia Palace Hotel **6**
Hilton **10**
Hotel Achilleas **12**
Hotel Carolina **11**
Hotel Dioskouros **22**
Hotel Exarchion **5**
Hotel Grande Bretagne **14**
Hotel Plaka **16**
Hotel Tempi **3**
Jason Inn **1**
Museum Hotel **4**
Nefeli Hotel **18**
St. George Lycabettus **9**

GREECE
Athens

Legend

Church ✝
First Aid ✚
Information ⓘ
OTE 🄲
Post Office ✉

0   200 m
0   200 y

← To Piraeus

KERAMIKOS   City Hall

Central
Market

PSIRRI

Theseion
Station

Monastiraki
Square   Flea
                Market

Ancient
Agora   **MONASTIRAKI**

The
Areopagos   **Anafiotika**

The
Acropolis   Parthenon

MAKRIYANNI

Bargaining for a Room

Room prices, no matter what people say officially, are negotiable, especially at the edges of the season. Because of Greek law and OTE regulations, hotel keepers are very reluctant to give out any rates in advance and often quote prices higher than their actual rates. When you bargain, don't cite our prices, which may be too high, but ask instead for the best current rate. Off-season prices may be as much as 40% lower than the lowest rate given to us for the book.

The Electra, just a few blocks southwest of Syntagma Square on a relatively quiet side street, is the most modern and stylish Plaka hotel. Top-floor rooms are smaller, but they're where you want to be, both for the view of the Acropolis and to escape traffic noise. (Ask for a top-floor unit when you make your reservation. Your request will be honored "subject to availability.") Guest rooms here are hardly drop-dead elegant, but they are pleasant, decorated in soft pastels. Don't miss the rooftop pool with a terrific view of the Acropolis. If you're too tired to go out for dinner, the hotel restaurant is quite decent.

MODERATE

Acropolis House Hotel. Odos Kodrou 6–8, 10558 Athens. ☎ **01/322-2344.** Fax 01/324-4143. 25 units, 15 with bathroom (3 with tub/shower; 12 with shower only); 4 suites (2 with tub/shower, 2 with shower only). A/C TEL. Dr15,000 ($50) double without bathroom; Dr21,593 ($68) double with bathroom. Rates include continental breakfast. Add Dr4,000 ($13) for use of air-conditioning. V.

This small hotel in a handsomely restored 150-year-old villa retains many of its original classical architectural details. It offers a central location—just off Odos Kidathineon in the heart of the Plaka, a 5-minute walk from Syntagma Square—and the charm of being on a quiet pedestrian side street. Room nos. 401 and 402 have good views and can be requested (but not guaranteed) when making a reservation. The newer wing, only 60 years old, isn't architecturally special; each unit's spartan bathroom is across the hall. There's a book-swap spot and a washing machine, free after a 4-day stay.

If the Acropolis House is full, try the **Adonis Hotel,** on the same street at Odos Kodrou 3 (☎ **01/324-9737;** fax 01/323-1602); it's architecturally undistinguished, but does have an appealing location and a rooftop garden cafe with a view of the Acropolis.

Byron Hotel. Odos Vyronos 19, 10558 Athens. ☎ **01/325-3554.** Fax 01/323-0327. 20 units. TEL. Dr22,000 ($73) double. Rates include breakfast. No credit cards.

The Byron has a convenient and reasonably quiet Plaka location just off busy Odos Dionissiou Areopayitou. You can negotiate having the TV in the lobby cafe turned off (or on) at breakfast. The small rooms are pleasant, if spare, and the ones in the back overlooking apartments and gardens are usually quieter than the six in front (but lack balconies and partial views of the Acropolis). Eight rooms have air-conditioning for a supplement of Dr2,500 ($8).

✪ **Hotel Plaka.** Odos Kapnikareas 7 and Mitropoleos, 10556 Athens. ☎ **01/322-2096.** Fax 01/322-2412. 67 units. A/C TV TEL. Dr28,000 ($93) double. Rates include breakfast. AE, DC, EURO, MC, V.

This hotel is popular with Greeks, who prefer its modern conveniences to the old-fashioned charms of most other hotels in the Plaka area. It has a terrific location just off Syntagma Square. Most guest rooms have balconies; those on the fifth and sixth floors in the rear (where it's usually quieter) have views of the Plaka and the Acropolis, also visible from the roof-garden (snack-bar).

✪ **Nefeli Hotel.** Odos Iperidou 16, 10558 Athens. ☎ **01/322-8044.** Fax 01/322-5800. 18 units. TEL. Dr18,000 ($60) double. Rates include breakfast. AE, V.

The charming little Nefeli ("Cloud") is central but quiet; its quietest rooms overlook pedestrian Odos Angelikes Hatzimihali. The entire hotel has been completely redecorated. The rooms—most with A/C—are small (as are the bathrooms) and somewhat monastic, but we found them to have character, unlike so many Athenian hotels. We also found the staff courteous and helpful.

INEXPENSIVE

Hotel Dioskouros (also known as the Dioskouros Guest House). Odos Pittakou 6, Plaka, 10558 Athens. ☎ **01/324-8165.** 12 units, none with bathroom. Dr0,000 ($27) double. Breakfast Dr800 ($2.70). MC, V

This is as good a deal as you'll get in the Plaka. Student friends who have stayed here found the staff very helpful and didn't mind the small, spare rooms, the Plaka noise, or the lack of air-conditioning and ceiling fans. Ah, to be young again!

MONASTIRAKI
MODERATE

Attalos Hotel. Odos Athinas 29, 10554 Athens. ☎ **01/321-2801.** Fax 01/324-3124. E-mail: atthot@hol.gr. 80 units. A/C TEL. Dr18,000 ($60) double (ask for the 10% discount for Frommer's readers). Rates include buffet breakfast. AE, V. Walk about 1½ blocks north from Monastiraki Sq. on Odos Athinas; the hotel (large sign) is on the left.

One of the pleasures of staying at the six-story (with elevator) Attalos is taking in the frenzied street life of the nearby Central Market. Things quiet down at night, although the market opens around 5am, making the early morning hours lively. The clean, recently repainted rooms are plain, but many have framed color photos of archaeological sites and antiquities, and 44 have balconies. One real plus: the roof garden, with its fine views of the city and the Acropolis.

✪ **Jason Inn Hotel.** Odos Ayion Assomaton 12, 10553 Athens. ☎ **01/325-1106.** Fax 01/523-4786. 57 units. A/C TV TEL. Dr16,500 ($55) double. Rates include American buffet breakfast. DC, MC, V.

This newly renovated hotel (admittedly on a dull street, but just a few blocks from the Agora and the Plaka) offers attractive, comfortable rooms with double-paned windows for extra quiet. If you don't mind walking a few extra blocks to Syntagma, this is currently one of the best values in Athens, with an eager-to-help staff.

If the Jason Inn is full, staff may be able to find you a room in one of their other hotels: the similarly priced **Adrian Hotel,** on busy Odos Hadrian in the Plaka, or the slightly less expensive **King Jason** or **Jason Hotels,** both a few blocks from Omonia Square.

INEXPENSIVE

Hotel Tempi. Odos Eolou 29, 10551 Athens. ☎ **01/321-3175.** Fax 01/325-4179. 24 units. Dr8,500 ($28) double without shower; Dr9,500 ($32) double with shower. AE, MC, V.

For those who need no frills and few comforts, the Tempi is an excellent value choice in a charming location. The three-story hotel faces the flower market by the church of Ayia Irini on a basically pedestrian-only street. The Tempi has very simply furnished rooms (bed, table, chair), but the beds are decent, the ceilings high, and the showers (usually) hot. Ten rooms have balconies from which (if you lean) you can see the Acropolis. There's a rooftop lounge, laundry facilities, free luggage storage, and a book exchange that includes a number of travel guides. Not surprisingly, this hotel is popular with students.

SYNTAGMA
VERY EXPENSIVE

Athens Plaza. Syntagma Sq., 10564 Athens. ☎ **01/325-5301.** Fax 01/323-5856. 207 units. A/C MINIBAR TV TEL. Dr120,000 ($400) double. AE, DC, MC, V.

The Athens Plaza, managed by the Grecotel group, reopened its glitzy doors in March 1998 after a complete remodeling, and we were pretty excited to stay here shortly thereafter. There are acres of marble in the lobby, and almost as much in some bathrooms, which have their own phones and hair dryers. Many of the bedrooms are larger than our own living room, and many have balconies overlooking Syntagma Square. Hardly a place where you'd expect bare wires dangling from the ceiling in your bathroom, or a bedside table with a small hole cut out of its side and covered in aluminum foil. Mysterious. No doubt former senator Gary Hart, whom we saw lounging in the lobby, had no such problems in his room, but at $400 a night, should anyone?

Hotel Grande Bretagne. Syntagma Sq., 10563 Athens. ☎ **01/321-5555.** Fax 01/322-0211. 398 units. A/C MINIBAR TV TEL. Dr63,000–Dr125,650 ($210–$418) double; from Dr92,000 ($306) suite. AE, CB, DC, MC, V.

Built in 1864 with an elegant beaux arts decor, the Grande Bretagne has hosted everyone from Churchill to Sting. Although Greek political and social movers and shakers still pass through the lobby with its ornately carved wood paneling, soaring ceilings, and polished marble floors for power lunches at the popular GB Corner, so increasingly do the tour groups staying here. Although many bedrooms were renovated in 1992, too many inner-courtyard units look the worse for wear and utterly lack the elegance of the rooms fronting on Syntagma Square with Acropolis views. Let's hope that the renovations scheduled to begin when work on the metro in Syntagma Square ends will restore this hotel to its former glory. For now, you may prefer to have a look at the lobby or a drink in the GB Corner, but stay elsewhere— although of late the Grande Bretagne has had some very good off-season prices. (You can make reservations for the Grande Bretagne through Sheraton Hotels at ☎ **800/325-3535** in the U.S.)

EXPENSIVE

Electra Hotel. Odos Ermou 5, 10563 Athens. ☎01/322-3223. Fax 01/322-0310. 110 units. A/C TV TEL. Dr34,800–Dr40,400 ($116–$135). Rates include buffet breakfast. DC, MC, V.

If Odos Ermou remains pedestrian, the Electra has a location that is both central (steps from Syntagma Square) and quiet. Most of the guest rooms have comfortable armchairs, large windows, and modern bathrooms with hair dryers. Be sure to have a look at your room before you accept it: although most are large, some are quite tiny. The front desk is sometimes understaffed, but the service is generally acceptable.

Esperia Palace Hotel. Odos Stadiou 22, 10561 Athens. ☎01/323-8001. 185 units. A/C MINIBAR TV TEL. Dr35,650–Dr46,450 ($119–$154) double. Rates include buffet breakfast. AE, DC, MC, V.

This is a good-value hotel with a convenient location near Syntagma Square. The rooms are rather plain, but large and comfortable. The extensive buffet breakfast is a plus. Many tour groups stay here, which you may find a drawback if you are on your own. (You can make reservations through Best Western at ☎ 800/528-1234 in the U.S.)

MODERATE

You might consider as a fall-back option the 98-unit **Amalia Hotel,** Leoforos Amalias 10 (☎ 01/323-7301 to 7309; fax 01/323-8792). Although it's overdue for a complete renovation, it has a convenient location and fair price for the area.

Diomia Hotel. Odos Diomias 5, 10562 Athens. ☎ **01/323-8034.** Fax 01/323-8034. 71 units. A/C TV TEL. Dr22,000 ($73) double. AE, DC, MC, V.

The location can't be beat: front rooms overlook a pedestrian street steps from Syntagma Square, and back rooms on the top two floors look out across office and apartment buildings to the Acropolis. The Diomia repainted most of its bedrooms in 1996, and while they still lack charm, the fresh paint certainly helps. The bathrooms retain their original inconveniences, such as minuscule shower curtains, ancient tubs (usually without plugs), and hand-held showers. News freaks will appreciate having CNN both on the lobby TV and in their rooms.

Hotel Achilleas. Odos Lekka 21, 10562 Athens. ☎ **01/323-3197.** Fax 01/324-1092. 34 units. A/C TV TEL. Dr22,000 ($74) double. Rates include breakfast. AE, DC, EURO, MC, V.

The Achilleas (Achilles), on a relatively quiet side street steps from Syntagma Square, was fully renovated in 1995. Although the entrance lacks charm, the central location and fair prices make this a good choice. The bedrooms are good-sized, cheerful and light; some rear units have small balconies. Breakfast is served in the first-floor dining room, which has lots of green plants.

INEXPENSIVE

Hotel Carolina. Odos Kolokotroni 55, 10560 Athens. ☎ **01/324-3551.** Fax 01/324-3350. 31 units, 15 with shower and toilet. TEL. Dr8,000 ($27) double without shower and toilet; Dr10,000 ($34) double with shower and toilet. AE, EURO, MC, V.

At press time, word came in that the Carolina, a 5-minute walk from Syntagma Square, had repainted and refurnished all its rooms. We haven't seen the renovations, but can vouch that they were badly needed. We look forward to hearing how readers find the hotel, whose prices have always been excellent, but whose facilities had been allowed to slide in recent years. The hotel has been, and presumably will continue to be, very popular with students.

KOLONAKI
VERY EXPENSIVE

Saint George Lycabettus Hotel. Odos Kleomenous 2, 10675 Athens. ☎ **01/729-0711.** Fax 01/721-0439. 167 units. A/C TV TEL. Dr54,000–Dr73,000 ($180–$243) double. Rates include breakfast. AE, DC, MC, V.

The rooftop pool is a plus, and the hotel is just steps from the chic Kolonaki restaurants and shops. The nicely appointed rooms look toward Mount Likavitos or a small park, although the surrounding street traffic keeps this from being a real oasis of calm. As yet, the Saint George Lycabettus does not get many tour groups, which helps it to maintain its tranquil tone.

MODERATE

✪ **Athenian Inn.** Odos Haritos 22, Kolonaki, 10675 Athens. ☎ **01/723-8097.** Fax 01/724-2268. 28 units. A/C TEL. Dr33,000 ($110) double. Rates include breakfast. AE, DC, V.

The Athenian Inn's quiet location 3 blocks from Kolonaki Square is a blessing, as are the clean accommodations and friendly staff. (A quote in the guest book from Hellenophile Lawrence Durrell: "At last the ideal Athens hotel, good and modest in scale but perfect in service and goodwill.") Some of the balconies look out on Mount Likavitos. Breakfast is served in a small lounge with a fireplace, piano, and TV. Between stays, we tend to forget how small the rooms are, which suggests that the staff is doing a good job of making guests feel comfortable and at home.

EMBASSY DISTRICT
VERY EXPENSIVE

✪ **Andromeda Hotel.** Odos Timoleontos Vassou 22 (off Plateia Mavili), 115 21 Athens. ☎ **01/643-7302.** Fax 01/646-6361. 30 units. A/C MINIBAR TV TEL. Dr60,000–Dr85,500 ($200–$285) double. AE, DC, EURO, MC, V. Special rates sometimes available.

The city's only boutique hotel is easily the most charming in Athens, with a staff that makes you feel at home. Rooms are large and elegantly decorated, with furniture and paintings you'd be happy to live with. The quiet hotel overlooks the garden of the American ambassador's home. The only drawback : it's a serious hike (20 to 30 min.) or at least a 10-minute taxi ride to Syntagma, and there are few restaurants in this residential neighborhood (although the Andromeda has its own small restaurant).

The Hilton. Leoforos Vas. Sofias 46, 11528 Athens. ☎ **800/445-8667** in the U.S., 01/725-0210, or 01/725-0393. Fax 01/721-3110. 446 units. A/C MINIBAR TV TEL. Dr114,300–Dr125,400 ($381–$418) double; Dr134,100 ($447) Plaza Executive double. AE, DC, EURO, MC, V.

The Hilton, near the U.S. Embassy, is a brisk 10-minute walk from Syntagma Square. It's something of an Athenian institution, where businessmen and diplomats meet for a drink or a meal. A number of small shops, a salon, and cafes and restaurants surround the glitzy lobby. The guest rooms (looking toward either the hills outside Athens or the Acropolis) have large marble bathrooms and are decorated in the generic (but comfortable) international Hilton style, with some Greek touches. The Plaza Executive floor of rooms and suites offers a separate business center and higher level of service. Facilities include a pool and health club. The Hilton often runs promotions, so ask about special rates before booking.

KOUKAKI & MAKRIYANNI (NEAR THE ACROPOLIS)
Keep in mind that with all the Makriyanni/Koukaki hotels, you'll be doing some extra walking and crossing busy Odos Dionissiou Areopayitou to get to most places you want to visit.

VERY EXPENSIVE

✪ **Divani-Palace Acropolis.** Odos Parthenonos 19–25, Makriyanni, 11742 Athens. ☎ **01/922-2945.** Fax 01/921-4993. 253 units. A/C MINIBAR TV TEL. Dr52,000–Dr72,000 ($173–$240) double. AE, DC, MC, V.

For luxury, comfort, and quiet location, you'd have a hard time beating this hotel, just 3 blocks south of the Acropolis. The rooms are quietly elegant, and service is professional. The spacious, modern lobby contains copies of classical sculpture, and sections of the actual walls built by Themistocles during the Persian Wars are visible in the basement. The hotel has a small, handsome pool, a bar, a good restaurant, and a lovely roof garden with a view. The same hotel group operates the more glamorous **Divani Caravel Hotel,** Leoforos Vas. Alexandrou 2 (☎ 01/725-3725; fax 01-725-3770), near the National Art Gallery.

Accommodations & Dining South of the Acropolis

ACCOMMODATIONS
Acropolis View Hotel 3
Art Gallery Hotel 10
Austria Hotel 9
Byron Hotel 1
Divani-Palace Acropolis 7

Herodion Hotel 5
Hotel Hera 11
Hotel Philippos 8
Marble House Pension 13
Parthenon Hotel 2
Tony's Pension 12

DINING
Socrates's Prison 6
Strofi Tavern 4

MODERATE

✪ **Acropolis View Hotel.** Odos Webster 10, 11742 Athens. ☎ **01/921-7303.** Fax 01/923-0705. 32 units. A/C TV TEL. Dr27,000 ($90) double. Rates include generous breakfast. Substantial reductions Nov–Mar. AE, EURO, MC, V.

This lovely old hotel, popular with repeat visitors to Athens, is on a winding side street off Odos Rovertou Galli, not far from the Herodes Atticus theater. The quiet neighborhood, at the base of Filopappos Hill, is a 10- to 15-minute walk from the heart of the Plaka. The rooms (many recently renovated) are small, but clean and pleasant, with good bathrooms. Some units, such as no. 405, overlook Filopappos Hill, and others, such as no. 407, face the Acropolis. The rooftop bar also has a bead on the Acropolis.

Art Gallery Hotel. Odos Erechthiou 5, Koukaki, 11742 Athens. ☎ **01/923-8376.** Fax 01/923-3025. E-mail: ecotec@atenet.gr. 22 units. TEL. Dr16,800 ($56) double. Breakfast Dr1,500 ($5).

As you might expect, this small hotel—in a half-century-old house that has been home to several artists—has an artistic flair (and a nice old-fashioned cage elevator). Rooms are small and plain, but comfortable, with polished hardwood floors and ceiling fans. There's a nice Victorian-style breakfast room on the fourth floor, with heavy marble-topped tables and old velvet-covered chairs.

Austria Hotel. Odos Mousson 7, Filopappou, 11742 Athens. ☎ **01/923-5151.** Fax 01/924-7350. E-mail: austria@topservice.com or austria@hol.gr. 37 units. A/C TEL. Dr20,500 ($68) double. Rates include breakfast. AE, DC, EURO, MC, V.

This quiet, well-maintained hotel at the base of Filopappos Hill is operated by a Greek-Austrian family, who offer guests use of the hotel safe-deposit box and fax services, will exchange your foreign money into drachmas (which not all small hotels are prepared to do), and can point you to the convenient neighborhood laundromat. Guest rooms are rather spartan (the linoleum floors are not enchanting), but tidy. There's a great view over Athens and out to sea (we could see the island of Aegina the day we visited) from the rooftop, where you can sun or sit under an awning in the shade.

Herodion Hotel. Odos Rovertou Galli 4, Makriyanni, 11742 Athens. ☎ **01/923-6832** or 01/923-6836. Fax 01/923-5851. 90 units. A/C TV TEL. DR30,000 ($100) double. Rates include breakfast. AE, DC, MC, V.

An archaeologist friend who always stays at this attractive hotel a block south of the Acropolis, near the Herodes Atticus theater, begged us not to mention it, as she was afraid that she might have trouble getting a room if the word got out. Many of the large rooms have balconies, some with good views. The lobby leads to a lounge and patio garden where you can have drinks and snacks under the trees. The same owners run the nearby **Hotel Philippos,** Mitseon 3, Makriyanni (☎ **01/922-3611**; fax 01/922-3615).

✪ **Hotel Hera.** Odos Falirou 9, Makriyani, 11742 Athens. ☎ **01/923-6682.** Fax 01/924-7334. E-mail: hhera@hol.gr. 49 units. A/C TEL. Dr30,000 ($100) double. Rates include breakfast. AE, MC, V.

The Hera boasts a garden behind the breakfast room and great views of the Acropolis from the rooftop garden. That's a lot of greenery in Athens, and since the bland bedrooms have balconies with hanging plants and are perfectly comfortable, you may find that the location out of the heart of tourist Athens is just what you want. If you have a car, you'll appreciate the garage here.

Parthenon. Odos Makri 6, 11527 Athens. ☎ **01/923-4594.** Fax 01/644-1084. 79 units. TEL. Dr15,000 ($50) double. MC, V.

This modern, recently refurbished hotel has an excellent location just steps from the Plaka and the Acropolis. The carpeted bedrooms have bright, cheerful bedspreads and decent-sized bathrooms, and some have TVs. The hotel has a bar, restaurant, and small garden. The Parthenon is one of a group of four hotels; if it's full, the management will try to get you a room in the **Christina,** a few blocks away, or at the **Riva** or **Alexandros,** near the Megaron (the Athens Concert Hall).

INEXPENSIVE

Another option is **Tony's Pension,** Zacharitsa 26, Koukaki (☎ **01/923-6370** or 01/923-5761), which attracts students and frugal travelers. Located between Filopappos Hill and Leoforos Syngrou, Tony's has a communal lounge and kitchen on each floor and a roof garden with a barbecue.

✪ **Marble House Pension.** Odos Zinni 35A, Koukaki, 11741 Athens. ☎ **01/923-4058.** Fax 01/922-6461. 17 units, 9 with bathroom. TEL. Dr12,000 ($40) double without bathroom; Dr13,500 ($45) double with bathroom. From Oct–May, double rooms can be rented by the month for Dr100,000 ($333). No credit cards.

Named for its marble façade, which is usually covered by fuchsia and bougainvillea, this small hotel is on a cul-de-sac near the church. It's famous among budget travelers for its friendly, helpful staff. Rooms (some with A/C and minibars) are clean, with wood-frame beds, stone floors, ceiling fans, and balconies overlooking the quiet residential neighborhood. If you're spending more than a few days in Athens and don't mind being out of the center, this is a fine homey base for sightseeing.

UNIVERSITY AREA (NEAR EXARCHIA SQUARE/ ARCHAEOLOGICAL MUSEUM)
INEXPENSIVE

Hotel Exarchion. Odos Themistokleous 55, 10683 Athens. ☎ **01/360-1256.** Fax 01/ 360-3296. 49 units. TEL. Dr10,000 ($33) double. No credit cards.

The no-frills Hotel Exarchion has comfortable, decent-size rooms, most of which have balconies. You can drink and snack at the rooftop bar while you watch University of Athens students debating and sometimes demonstrating in the square below.

Museum Hotel. Odos Bouboulinas 16, 10682 Athens. ☎ **01/360-5611.** Fax 01/380-0057. 58 units. TEL. Dr11,500 ($38) double. Rates include breakfast. AE, DC, V.

This venerable hotel is so close to the Archaeological Museum that all its balconies overlook the museum's relatively quiet, tree-filled park. The rooms are bland and could use a lot of sprucing up (saggy mattresses). In short, this is a you-get-what-you-pay-for good-value place in a good location, although the traffic here is, as almost everywhere in Athens, pretty steady.

4 Dining

Most restaurants have menus in Greek and English, but many don't keep their printed (or handwritten) menus up-to-date. If a menu is not in English, there's almost always someone working at the restaurant who will either translate or rattle off suggestions for you in English. Consequently, you may be offered some fairly repetitive suggestions, as restaurant staff tend to suggest what most tourists request. In Athens, that means *moussaka* (baked eggplant casserole, usually with ground meat), *souvlaki* (chunks of beef, chicken, pork, or lamb grilled on a skewer), *pastitsio* (baked pasta, usually with ground meat and a béchamel sauce), or *dolmadakia* (grape leaves stuffed usually with rice and ground meat). Although these dishes can be delicious—you may have eaten them outside of Greece and looked forward to enjoying the real thing here—you may end up cherishing your memories and regretting your meal. All too often, restaurants catering to tourists tend to serve profoundly dull moussaka and unpleasantly chewy souvlaki. We hope that the places we're suggesting do better.

In the last few years, a number of Athenian restaurants have begun to experiment with a "nouvelle Greek" cuisine. Usually, this involves aspects of *paradisiako* (traditional) cooking, but with a lighter hand on the olive oil and an adventurous combination of familiar ingredients. In our reviews, we draw attention to these restaurants.

THE PLAKA

Some of the most charming old restaurants in Athens are in the Plaka—as are some of the worst tourist traps. Here are a few things to keep in mind when you head off for a meal in the Plaka.

Some Plaka restaurants station waiters outside who don't just urge you to come in and sit down, but virtually pursue you down the street with an unrelenting sales pitch. The hard sell is almost always a giveaway that the place caters to tourists. (That said, remember that announcing what's for sale is not invariably a ploy reserved for tourists. If you visit the Central Market, you'll see and hear stall owners calling out the attractions of their meat, fish, and produce to passersby—and even waving particularly tempting fish and fowl in front of potential customers.)

In general, it's a good idea to avoid places with floor shows; many charge outrageous amounts (and levy surcharges not always openly stated on menus) for drinks and food.

Athens Dining

L'Abreuvoir 34
Abyssinia Cafe 9
Aprooto 26
Athinaikon 4
Bajazzo 23
Damigos (Bakaliarakia) 20
Daphne's 19
Dimokritos 31
Diporto 5
Eden Vegetarian
  Restaurant 14
GB Corner 28
Gerofinikas 29
Kalliste 30
Kouklis Ouzeri
  (To Yerani) 18
Manesis 25
Myrtia 24
Neon (Kolonaki) 32
Neon (Omonia) 3
Neon (Syntagma) 27
Papandreou 5
Platanos Taverna 13
Restaurant Kostoyannis 1
Rodia 33
Socrates's Prison 17
Strofi Tavern 15
Symbosio 16
Taki 13 6
Taverna Ipiros (Epirus) 10
Taverna Sigalas 11
Taverna Xinos 21
Taygetos 2
Thanasis 12
To Kafenio 36
To Ouzadiko 35
To Tristato 22
Vitrina 7
Zeidoron 8

Legend

Church ✝
Information (i)
OTE C
Post Office ✉

KERAMIKOS
City Hall
Central Market
PSIRRI
Theseion Station
MONASTIRAKI
Monastiraki Square
Ancient Agora
Anafiotika
The Areopagos
The Acropolis
Parthenon
MAKRIYANNI

← To Piraeus
Dionissiou Areopayitou

A Note on Credit Cards

Many Athenian restaurants do not accept credit cards. Each year, some restaurants that formerly accepted credit cards stop accepting them. Be prepared to pay with cash or traveler's checks at even the finest establishments. If you want to pay with a credit card, double-check to make sure the restaurant will accept your credit card before going.

If you get burned, stand your ground, phone the **Tourist Police** (☎ 171), and pay nothing before they arrive. Often the mere threat of calling the Tourist Police has the miraculous effect of causing a bill to be lowered.

EXPENSIVE

✪ **Daphne's.** Odos Lysikratous 4. ☎ **01/322-7971.** Main courses Dr4,500–Dr8,500 ($15–$28), with some fish priced by the kilo. No credit cards. Daily 1:30–6pm and 9pm–2am. ELEGANT GREEK/NOUVELLE.

There are frescoes on the walls and sophisticated Athenians and foreigners at the tables (this is where Hillary Clinton dined in Athens), and the "nouvelle Greek" cuisine gives you all the old favorites with new distinction. Try the zesty eggplant salad and the delicious hot pepper and feta-cheese dip. We could have gone on eating the mezedes all night—but were glad to have saved room for the *stifado* (stew) of rabbit in *mavrodaphne* (sweet wine) sauce, and the tasty prawns with toasted almonds.

Symbosio. Odos Erechthiou 46. ☎ **01/922-5321.** Fax 01/923-2780. Main courses Dr2,500–Dr8,000 ($8–$27). No credit cards. Mon–Sat about 8pm–midnight. ELEGANT GREEK/CONTINENTAL.

This is a very pretty place to eat: a lovingly cared for 19th-century Plaka town house. The food here, although delicious, can be fussy, with a bit too much lily gilding and use of sauces. That said, friends of ours make a point of eating here every time they get to Athens, and swear by the quality of the fish, the delicate seasonings used in meat dishes, the fresh veggies, and the excellent wine list.

MODERATE

Aprooto. Odos Nikis 48. ☎ **01/322-0521.** Main courses Dr1,800–Dr4,800 ($6–$16). No credit cards. Mon–Sat about 11am–2pm and about 7pm–midnight. GREEK/MEZEDES.

This is a good place to head in the Plaka and make a meal of familiar Greek mezedes like tzatziki and taramosalata (or that American and British standby, the baked potato). Main courses include grills and a nice pork stew with mushrooms (an unusual touch in Greece). The ambiance is cozy, the food good—and the place is not yet overwhelmed by tourists.

Eden Vegetarian Restaurant. Odos Lissiou 12. ☎/fax **01/324-8858.** Main courses Dr1,200–Dr3,200 ($4–$11). AE, DC, MC, V. Daily noon–midnight. GREEK/VEGETARIAN.

You can find vegetarian dishes at almost every Greek restaurant, but if you want to experience soy (rather than eggplant) moussaka, mushroom pie with a sturdy whole-wheat crust, and freshly squeezed juices, join the young Athenians and Europeans who patronize the Eden. The prices are reasonable, if not cheap, and the decor, with 1920s-style prints and wrought-iron lamps, is engaging.

✪ **Platanos Taverna.** Odos Dioyenous 4. ☎ **01/322-0666.** Main courses Dr 2,500–Dr3,500 ($8–$12). No credit cards. Mon–Sat noon–4:30pm and 8pm–midnight. GREEK.

In good weather, this traditional taverna, on a quiet pedestrian square near the Tower of the Winds, has tables outdoors beneath a spreading *platanos* (plane tree). Locals usually congregate indoors to escape the summer sun at midday and the tourists in the evening. The Platanos has been serving good *spitiko fageto* (home cooking) since 1932, and has managed to keep steady customers happy while enchanting visitors. If artichokes or spinach with lamb are on the menu, you're in luck: they're delicious. The house wine is tasty, and there's a wide choice of bottled wines from many regions of Greece.

Taverna Xinos. Odos Agelou Geronta 4 (just off Odos Kidathineon, and signposted in the cul-de-sac). ☎ **01/322-1065.** Main courses Dr2,000–Dr4,000 ($7–$13). No credit cards. Daily about 8pm–midnight; not always open Sun and usually closed part of July and Aug. GREEK.

Despite the forgivable lapse in spelling, Xinos's business card says it best: "In the heart of old Athens there is still a flace where the traditional Greek way of cooking is upheld." The stews here (including lamb with spinach in egg lemon sauce) are hearty and tasty, and the "flace" is charming. In summer, there are tables outside in the courtyard; in winter, you can warm yourself by the coal-burning stove and admire the frescoes showing Greek soldiers, gypsies, and what appears to be a camel. While the strolling musicians aren't the Three Tenors, they sing wonderful Greek golden oldies, accompanying themselves on the guitar and bouzouki. (If you are serenaded, you may want to give the musicians a small tip. If you want to hear the theme from *Never on Sunday,* ask to hear "Ena Zorbas.") Most evenings, tourists predominate until around 10pm, when locals begin to arrive—as they have since Xinos opened in 1935.

INEXPENSIVE

✪ Damigos (The Bakaliarakia). Odos Kidathineon 41. ☎ **01/322-5084.** Main courses Dr1,000–Dr2,500 ($3.35–$8). No credit cards. Daily about 7pm–midnight. Usually closed part of Aug and Sept. GREEK/CODFISH.

This basement taverna, with enormous wine barrels in the backroom and an ancient column supporting the roof in the front room, has been serving delicious deep-fried codfish and eggplant, as well as chops and stews, since 1865. The wine comes from the family vineyards, and there are few pleasures greater than sipping retsina while you watch the cook turn out unending meals in his absurdly small kitchen. Don't miss the delicious *skordalia* (garlic sauce), which is equally good with the cod, eggplant, bread—well, you get the idea.

Kouklis Ouzeri (To Yerani). Odos Tripodon 14. ☎ **01/324-7605.** Mezedes Dr500–Dr1,500 ($1.65–$5). No credit cards. Daily 11am–2am. GREEK/MEZEDES.

In addition to "Kouklis Ouzeri" and "To Yerani" (Geranium), Greeks also call this popular old favorite "Skolario" because of the nearby school. Find a seat, and a waiter will present a large tray with about a dozen plates of mezedes: appetizer portions of fried fish, beans, grilled eggplant, taramosalata, cucumber-and-tomato salad, olives, fried cheese, sausages, and other seasonal specialties. Accept the ones that appeal to you. If you don't order all 12, you can enjoy a tasty and inexpensive meal, washed down with the house *krasi* (wine).

To Tristato. Odos Dedalou 34 and Ay. Yeronda 12. ☎ **01/324-4472.** Main courses Dr1,000–Dr2,000 ($3.35–$7); desserts Dr800–Dr1,500 ($2.65–$5). No credit cards. Mon–Fri 11am–after midnight; Sat–Sun 10am–after midnight. Closed Aug 10–Sept 10. SNACKS/DESSERTS.

This New Age cafe/tearoom by a rose garden serves fresh fruits and yogurt, omelets, fresh-squeezed juices, and scrumptious cakes—everything healthful and homemade. This is an excellent choice for late breakfast, afternoon tea, light supper, or late-night dessert—and a place where women traveling alone will feel especially comfortable.

MONASTIRAKI
INEXPENSIVE

✪ Abyssinia Cafe. Plateia Abyssinia, Monastiraki. ☎ **01/321-7047.** Appetizers and main courses Dr1,500–Dr4,000 ($5–$13). No credit cards. Tues–Sun 10:30am–6pm. Closed for a week at Christmas and Easter, and for 2 weeks in Aug. GREEK.

This small cafe in a ramshackle building has a nicely restored interior, featuring lots of gleaming dark wood and polished copper. It faces lopsided Abyssinia Square (off Odos Ifaistou), where furniture restorers ply their trade and you can buy anything from gramophones to hubcaps in the "antiques" shops. You can sit indoors or outside and have just a coffee, but it's tempting to snack on *saganaki* (fried cheese), fried eggplant, or *keftedes* (meatballs).

Diporto. Athens Central Market. No phone. Main courses Dr800–Dr2,000 ($2.65–$7). No credit cards. Mon–Sat 6am–6pm. GREEK.

This little place, sandwiched between olive shops, serves up salads, stews, and delicious *revithia* (chickpeas), a Greek winter dish popular among stall owners, shoppers, and Athenians who make their way to the market for cheap and delicious food.

Papandreou. Meat hall, Central Market, Odos Athinas. ☎ **01/321-4970.** Main courses about Dr1,500 ($5). No credit cards. Mon–Sat from about 8am–5pm. GREEK.

The butcher, the baker, and the office worker duck past the sides of beef hanging in the Meat Hall and head to this hole-in-the-wall for zesty tripe dishes. Don't like tripe? Don't worry: There's usually something on the menu that doesn't involve it. Papandreou has a virtually all-male clientele, but a woman alone need not hesitate to eat here.

Taverna Ipiros (Epirus). Plateia Ayiou Philippou 15 (2 blocks southwest of the Monastiraki metro station). ☎ **01/324-5572.** Main courses Dr1,200–Dr2,000 ($4–$7). No credit cards. Most days noon–midnight. GREEK.

This is a great budget spot on a crowded little square not far from the entrance to the ancient Agora in the heart of the Flea Market district. The food is standard Greek fare, the portions generous, and the prices fair. Be sure to take a table that belongs to unpretentious little Ipiros, rather than to a nearby competitor taking advantage of this place's reputation.

Taverna Sigalas. Plateia Monastiraki 2. ☎ **01/321-3036.** Main courses Dr1,000–Dr2,500 ($3.35–$8). AE, MC, V. Daily 7am–2am. East across the square from Metro station. GREEK.

This longtime Plaka taverna, housed in a vintage 1879 commercial building with a newer outdoor pavilion, boasts that it is open 365 days a year. Its lively interior has huge old retsina kegs in the back and dozens of black-and-white photos of Greek movie stars on the walls. After 8pm nightly, there's Greek muzak. At all hours, Greeks and tourists wolf down large portions of stews, moussaka, grilled meatballs, baked tomatoes, gyros, and other hearty dishes, washed down with the house red and white retsinas.

✪ Thanasis. Odos Mitropoleos 69. (just off the northeast corner of Monastiraki Sq.). ☎ **01/ 324-4705.** Main courses Dr500–Dr2,500 ($1.65–$8). No credit cards. Daily 9am–2am. GREEK/SOUVLAKI.

Quick Bites in Syntagma

In general, Syntagma Square is not known for good food, but there are a number of places in the area to get a snack. The **Apollonion Bakery,** Odos Nikis 10, and the **Elleniki Gonia,** Odos Karayioryi Servias 10, make sandwiches to order and sell croissants, both stuffed and plain. **Ariston** is a small chain of *zaharoplastia* (confectioners), with a branch at the corner of Karayioryi Servias and Voulis (just off Syntagma Square) selling snacks as well as pastries. **Floca** is another excellent pastry-shop chain; look in the arcade on Panepistimiou near Syntagma Square. As always, you pay extra to be served at one of their tables.

For the quintessentially Greek *loukoumades* (round donut-center–like pastries that are deep-fried, then drenched with honey and topped with powdered sugar and cinnamon), nothing beats **Doris,** Odos Praxitelous 30, a continuation of Odos Lekka, a few blocks from Syntagma Square. If you're still hungry, Doris serves hearty stews and pasta dishes for absurdly low prices Monday through Saturday until 3:30pm. **Everest** is another chain worth trying; there's one a block north of Kolonaki Square at Tsakalof and Iraklitou. Also in Kolonaki Square, **To Kotopolo** serves succulent grilled chicken to take out or eat in. In the Plaka, the **K. Kotsolis Pastry Shop,** Odos Adrianou 112, serving excellent coffee and sweets, is an oasis of old-fashioned charm in the midst of the souvenir shops. The **Oraia Ellada** ("Beautiful Greece") cafe at the Center of Hellenic Tradition, opening both onto Odos Pandrossou 36 and Odos Mitropoleos 59 near the flea market, has a spectacular view of the Acropolis where you can revive yourself with a cappuccino and a few pastries.

Thanasis serves very good souvlaki and pita—and exceptionally good french fries—both to go and at its outdoor and indoor tables; as always, prices are higher if you sit down to eat. On weekends, it often takes the strength and determination of an Olympic athlete to get through the door and place an order here. It's worth the effort: this is both a great budget choice and a great place to take in the local scene.

SYNTAGMA
EXPENSIVE

GB Corner. In the Grande Bretagne Hotel, Syntagma Sq. ☎ **01/323-0251.** Reservations required for lunch. Main courses Dr5,000–Dr12,000 ($17–$40). AE, DC, EURO, MC, V. Daily about 10am–1am. INTERNATIONAL.

We always envy the people whom we glimpse through the windows here. There we are, foot-weary and hot outside; there they are, lounging in the dark leather booths and toying with salads and shrimp while waiters hover nearby. When we have eaten here, it's been very pleasant—and very expensive. The menu has a full international/continental range, as well as breakfast, tea, and late-night offerings.

MODERATE

Gerofinikas. Odos Pindar 10. ☎ **01/363-6710.** Reservations strongly recommended. Main courses Dr3,000–Dr5,200 ($10–$17). Fixed-price menu Dr6,000 ($20), not including beverage. AE, DC, MC, V. Daily usually noon–2pm and 7pm–midnight. GREEK/INTERNATIONAL.

For years, this was *the* place to go for a special lunch or dinner. The food is still very good—which is why tour groups have, alas, discovered it. Still, it's always pleasant to walk down the passageway into Gerofinikas ("the old palm tree"), look at the long display cases of tempting dishes, and try to decide between the shrimp with feta cheese, the rabbit stew with onions, and the tasty eggplant dishes—all the while keeping room for one of Gerofinikas's rich desserts. If you stick to the fixed-price menu, or order carefully, Gerofinikas is not expensive; if you throw caution to the wind, it is.

INEXPENSIVE

Neon. Odos Mitropoleos 3 (on the southwest corner of Syntagma Sq.). ☎ **01/322-8155.** Snacks Dr200–Dr650 (65¢–$2.15); sandwiches Dr450–Dr1,200 ($1.50–$4); main courses Dr1,000–Dr3,200 ($3.35–$11). No credit cards. Daily 9am–midnight. GREEK/INTERNATIONAL.

This new addition to the Neon chain is convenient, though not as charming as the original restored kafenion (coffeehouse/bar) on Omonia Square or the Kolonaki Neon (see below). You're sure to find something to your taste—maybe a Mexican omelet, spaghetti bolognese, choices from the salad bar, or sweets ranging from Black Forest cake to tiramisu.

KOLONAKI
EXPENSIVE

L'Abreuvoir. Xenokratous 51. ☎ **01/722-9106.** Reservations recommended. Main courses Dr5,200–Dr8,500 ($17–$28). MC, V. Daily 12:30–4:30pm and 8:30pm–midnight. FRENCH/INTERNATIONAL.

A tranquil spot for lunch or dinner, this fine French restaurant has tables both indoors and outside under mulberry trees. From the fluffy spinach tart or smoked trout to the steak au poivre and *entrecôtes provençals* (a fillet cooked in a marvelous garlic, mushroom, and parsley sauce) to the soufflé au Grand Marnier or chocolate mousse, it's all usually excellent—but only if you want a break from Greek food.

MODERATE

Dimokritos. Odos Dimokritou 23. ☎ **01/361-3588.** Main courses Dr3,200–Dr4,200 ($11–$14). No credit cards. Mon–Sat 1–5pm and 8pm–1am. Off Odos Skoufa, marked only by the word TAVERNA on the doors. GREEK.

Overlooking the Church of Ayios Dionysios, this cozy taverna serves good food to a dedicated clientele. The large menu features grilled veal, rabbit, fish, and lamb, and usually has excellent swordfish souvlaki. A variety of Greek salads and hors d'oeuvres are often on display in a case by the entrance, and you can usually point out what you want for starters on your way to your table.

Rodia. Odos Aristipou 44. ☎ **01/722-9883.** Main courses Dr2,000–Dr3,500 ($7–$12). No credit cards. Mon–Sat 8pm–2am. GREEK.

This well-established taverna in a handsome old house has tables in its small garden in good weather—although the interior, with its tile floor and old prints, is charming enough to tempt you to eat indoors. The Rodia is a favorite of visiting archaeologists from the nearby British and American Schools of Classical Studies, as well as of local residents. It may not sound like just what you'd always hoped to have for dinner, but the octopus in mustard sauce is terrific, as are the perhaps less intimidating veal or *dolmades* (stuffed grape leaves) in egg lemon sauce. The house wine is excellent, as is the halva, which manages to be both creamy and crunchy.

✪ To Kafenio. Odos Loukianou 26. ☎ **01/722-9056.** Main courses Dr1,800–Dr5,200 ($6–$17). No credit cards. Mon–Sat 11am to around midnight. GREEK/INTERNATIONAL.

This is hardly a typical rough-and-ready *kafenio* (coffeehouse/bar): there are pictures on the walls, pink tablecloths, and a clientele of ladies who lunch and staff members from the many embassies in Kolonaki. In short, a great people-watching place. If you relax you can easily run up a substantial tab, but you can also eat here more modestly, and equally elegantly. Try the artichokes *à la polita* (cooked in the manner of Constantinople) or leeks in crème fraîche, washed down with draft beer or the house wine—and save room for the delectable profiteroles. This is an especially congenial spot if you're eating alone.

To Ouzadiko. Alopekis 28 (in the Lemos International Shopping Center), Kolonaki. ☎ 01/ 729-5484. Mezedes and main courses Dr2,000–Dr4,000 ($7–$13). No credit cards. Mon–Sat 12:30pm–12:30am. OUZERI/MEZEDES.

This cozy ouzo bar has at least 40 kinds of ouzo and as many mezedes, including fluffy *keftedes* (meatballs) that make all others taste leaden. A great place for a snack or a full meal, if you can find a seat at this popular Kolonaki hangout. A serious foodie friend comes here especially for the wide variety of *horta* (greens), which she says are the best she's ever tasted.

INEXPENSIVE

Neon. Odos Tsakalof 6, Kolonaki Sq. ☎ 01/364-6873. Snacks Dr200–Dr650 (65¢–$2.15); sandwiches Dr450–Dr1,200 ($1.50–$4); main courses Dr1,000–Dr3,200 ($3.35–$11). No credit cards. Daily 9am–midnight. GREEK/INTERNATIONAL.

The Kolonaki Neon serves the same food as the Syntagma and Omonia branches, but the reasonable prices are especially welcome in this pricey neighborhood. Tsakalof is a shady pedestrian arcade, and you can usually sit indoors or outdoors.

OMONIA SQUARE & UNIVERSITY AREA (NEAR EXARCHIA SQUARE/ARCHAEOLOGICAL MUSEUM)
EXPENSIVE

✪ **Restaurant Kostoyannis.** Odos Zaimi 37 (2 blocks behind the Archaeological Museum). ☎ 01/822-0624. Main courses Dr2,500–Dr6,800 ($8–$23). No credit cards. Mon–Sat 8pm–2am. GREEK.

It's not easy to simply walk into Kostoyannis and sit down: just inside the entrance is a show-stopping display of shrimp, mussels, fresh fish, seemingly endless appetizers, tempting stews in ceramic pots, and yards of chops. You can choose the items you'd like to sample, and you may decide to make an entire meal just from the mezedes, which we think are even better than the entrees. Don't be put off by this restaurant's slightly out-of-the-way location on a rather uninteresting street: it's well worth the trip.

MODERATE

Athinaikon. Themistokleous 2, Omonia. ☎ 01/383-8485. Main courses Dr2,000–Dr4,000 ($7–$13). No credit cards. Mon–Sat 10am–midnight. Closed Aug. GREEK.

This is a favorite haunt of lawyers and businesspeople working in the Omonia Square area. You can have just some appetizers (technically, this is an ouzeri) or a full meal. Obviously, the way to have a reasonably priced snack is to stick to the appetizers and pass on the grilled shrimp or swordfish.

INEXPENSIVE

Neon. Dorou 1, Omonia Sq. ☎ 01/522-9939. Snacks Dr200–Dr650 (65¢–$2.15); sandwiches Dr450–Dr1,200 ($1.50–$4); main courses Dr1,000–Dr3,200 ($3.35–$11). No credit cards. Daily 9am–midnight. GREEK/INTERNATIONAL.

In a handsome 1920s building, the Neon serves up cafeteria-style food, including cooked-to-order pasta, omelets, and grills, as well as salads and sweets. Equally good for a meal or a snack, the Neon proves that fast food doesn't have to be junk food.

Taygetos. Odos Satovriandou 4. ☎ **01/523-5352.** Main courses Dr1,000–2,300 ($3.35–$8). No credit cards. Mon–Sat 9am–1am. GREEK/SOUVLAKI.

This is a great place to stop on your way to or from the museum. Service is swift, and the souvlaki and fried potatoes are excellent, as are the grilled lamb and chicken (priced by the kilo). The menu sometimes also includes delicious *kokoretsia* (grilled entrails). The **Ellinikon Restaurant** next door is also a good value.

METS
VERY EXPENSIVE

✪ **Bajazzo.** At Odos Tyrteou 1 and Odos Anapafseos 14, Mets. ☎ and fax **01/921-3013.** Reservations required Fri–Sat, and always a good idea. Dinner for 2 from Dr45,000 ($150). AE, DC, MC, V. Mon–Sat 8pm–1am. INTERNATIONAL.

Bajazzo put Greek cuisine on the map when it won its Michelin star in 1998. Chef Klaus Feuerbach's specialties include a feta tart, langostino souvlaki, kid with Peloponnesian herbs, and sea bass with mustard sauce—perhaps not all to be eaten at one sitting. The menu changes from night to night, so part of the fun is finding out what's being prepared on any given night.

Myrtia. Odos Trivonianou 32–34. ☎ **01/924-7175.** Reservations recommended. Fixed-price menu Dr12,000–Dr22,500 ($40–$75). AE, DC, EURO, MC, V. Mon–Sat 8:30pm–2am. Closed Aug. GREEK.

The Myrtia is a bit too kitschy for our taste, but lots of visitors love this famous fixed-menu taverna, up the hill behind the Olympic Stadium in Mets. The atmosphere, with strolling musicians, is either charmingly bucolic or a bit artificial, depending on your frame of mind. You'll be served a full array of mezedes, tender roast chicken, delicious lamb, fruit, sweets, various wines, and much more—all you can eat (and all you can drink of the house wine)—although there are rumors that this may change.

MODERATE

Manesis. Markou Mouzourou 3. ☎ **01/922-7684.** Main courses Dr2,200–Dr3,800 ($7–$13). No credit cards. Daily about 7pm–midnight. GREEK.

This longtime favorite, with a pleasant garden and wide range of delicious mezedes, continues to be popular with locals, and increasingly attracts visitors (including the occasional group). The swordfish souvlaki here is usually excellent, the *loukanika* (sausage) tasty, and the stews nicely seasoned with dill and lemon. The basic menu hasn't changed in years, although more nonmeat dishes have been added, including an excellent, creamy hummus.

KOUKAKI & MAKRIYANNI (NEAR THE ACROPOLIS)
See the "Accommodations & Dining South of the Acropolis" map on p. 133 to locate these restaurants.

MODERATE

✪ **Socrates's Prison.** Odos Mitseon 20. ☎ **01/922-3434.** Main courses Dr1,250–Dr3,200($4.15–$11). V. Mon–Sat 11am–4pm and 7pm–1am. Closed Aug. GREEK.

This is a favorite with both Greeks and American and European expatriates living in Athens, who lounge at tables outdoors in good weather and in the pleasant indoor rooms year-round. Some long tables are communal, and there are also tables for four. The food here is noticeably more imaginative than average Greek fare (try the veggie croquettes), and includes continental dishes such as salade niçoise and pork roll stuffed with vegetables. The retsina is excellent and there's a wide choice of bottled wines and beers. This is a good place to head if you don't want to eat in the Plaka but enjoy strolling through it on your way to or from dinner.

Strofi Tavern. Odos Rovertou Galli 25, Makriyianni. ☎ **01/921-4130.** Reservations recommended. Main courses Dr2,400–Dr3,500 ($8–$12). DC, MC, V. Mon–Sat 8pm–2am. Located 2 blocks south of Acropolis. GREEK.

The Strofi serves standard Greek taverna fare, but the view of the Acropolis is so terrific that everything tastes particularly good. This is a good place to know about if you're staying south of the Acropolis, an area that is not packed with restaurants.

HERE & THERE—AND WORTH THE JOURNEY
EXPENSIVE

Kalliste. Odos Asklepiou 137, off Odos Akadimias above the University of Athens. ☎ **01/ 645-3179.** Reservations recommended. Main courses Dr3,200–Dr5,700 ($10–$19). No credit cards. Mon–Sat about noon–2pm and 8pm–midnight. ELEGANT GREEK.

In a beautifully restored 19th-century house with polished wooden floors and ornamental plaster ceilings, Kalliste manages to be both cozy and elegant. The menu features traditional dishes with a distinctive flair, such as lentil soup with pomegranate, and chicken with hazelnuts and celery purée. Even that old standby crème caramel is enlivened by the addition of rose liqueur.

✪ **Varoulko.** Deligeorgi 14, Piraeus. ☎ **01/411-2043.** Fax 01/422-1283. Reservations necessary (arrange several days in advance). Dinner for 2 around Dr30,000 ($100); fish priced by the kilo. No credit cards. Mon–Sat about 8pm–midnight. SEAFOOD/NOUVELLE.

In a most unlikely location on a side street in Piraeus, chef/owner Lefteris Lazarou has created what many consider not just the finest restaurant serving only seafood, but the finest restaurant in the greater Athens area. We had one of the best meals of our lives here, tasting smoked eel, artichokes with fish roe, crayfish with sun-dried tomatoes, monkfish livers with soy sauce, honey, and basalmic vinegar—and the best sea bass and monkfish we have ever eaten. Everything is beautifully presented here, but nothing is fussy—and it's all delicious. We liked the austere brick walls enlivened by paintings of the old warehouse that Varoulko inhabits, although some find the style a bit too understated.

Vitrina. Odos Navarchou Apostoli 7, in the Psirri district. ☎ **01/321-1200.** Reservations necessary. Main courses Dr3,800–Dr8,000 ($13–$27). No credit cards. Oct–May Tues–Sat about noon–4pm and about 8pm–midnight; Sun about noon–4pm; closed rest of year. ELEGANT GREEK/NOUVELLE.

Who would expect to find this drop-dead fashionable restaurant in the old warehouse district of Psirri, off Odos Ermou? The walls are pale gold, the tablecloths and chairs are pale gray, and many of the pale young waiters and waitresses are aspiring actors and writers. The kitchen seems to try too hard (shrimp in muscatel and lavender sauce, for example), but the food is usually both delicious and beautifully presented, and there's a serious wine list. The fashion accessory of choice here is a cell phone—so useful for calling people at the next table—and almost no one arrives before 10pm.

MODERATE

Another rising star in the newly fashionable Psirri district is **Taki 13,** Odos Taki 13 (☎ 01/325-4707), where the food is less the thing than the bar, the music, and the stylish young Athenians who gather here.

✪ **Vlassis.** Odos Paster 8 (off Plateia Mavili in the Ilissia district). ☎ **01/646-3060** or 01/ 642-5337. Reservations necessary. Main courses Dr1,500–Dr3,600 ($5–$12). No credit cards. Mon–Sat about 7pm–midnight. ELEGANT TRADITIONAL GREEK.

Greeks call this kind of food *paradisiako* (traditional), but paradisiacal is just as good a description. This is traditional food fit for the gods: delicious fluffy vegetable cro-quettes, eggplant salad that tastes like no other eggplant salad you've had, hauntingly tender lamb in egg lemon sauce. It's a sign of Vlassis's popularity with Athenians—the last time we ate there, we were the only obvious foreigners in the place—that there's not even a discreet sign announcing its presence in a small apartment building on hard-to-find Odos Paster. Take a taxi; you may feel so giddy with delight after eating that you won't mind the half-hour walk back to Syntagma Square.

Zeidoron. Taki 10 and Ayion Anaryiron, Psirri. ☎ **01/321-5368.** Mezedes Dr1,500–Dr3,500 ($5–$12). No credit cards. Mon–Sat usually about 2pm–midnight. GREEK/MEZEDES.

This *mezedopolio* (hors d'oeuvres place) is one of a number of restaurants springing up in the old warehouse district of Psirri (off Odos Ermou and Odos Athinas), which is now on the verge of being reclaimed and Guppified, as the Greeks term their own ver-sion of Yuppification. There are lots of delicious mezedes, including vegetable cro-quettes, several eggplant dishes, and some heartier meat dishes, such as pork in mustard. You can have a varied and delicious meal here by eating a range of these appetizers.

Exploring Athens 6

by Sherry Marker

It's quite likely that you'll arrive in Athens in the late afternoon, groggy and disoriented after a seriously long flight. The ride into town from the airport is unlikely to help your spirits: You'll creep through Athens's ferocious traffic along an outstandingly ugly road lined with garish furniture and chandelier shops. Somewhere, you know, not far away, must be the blue Aegean and the lofty Acropolis. But where? Surrounded by cars that are either stuck in gridlock or maniacally racing along a three-lane highway with no observable (or observed) lanes, deafened by the explosions of hordes of mufflerless kamikaze motorcycles, you'll almost certainly be considering asking your cab driver to make a U-turn and take you back to the airport.

Don't despair. When you get to your hotel, jump in the shower, take a nap, and then set off for an evening stroll past the House of Parliament in **Syntagma (Constitution) Square.** If it's warm out, escape into the shade of the National Gardens, and join the Athenians feeding pigeons. Then head into the **Plaka,** the old neighborhood on the slopes of the Acropolis that has more restaurants, cafes, and souvenir shops than private homes. Still, if you get off the Plaka's main drags, Kidathineon and Adrianou, and follow one of the streets such as Thespidos that run up the slope of the Acropolis, you'll find yourself in **Anafiotika.** This Plaka district, built in the 19th century by immigrants from the Cycladic island of Anafi, retains much of its old village character. From time to time as you stroll, look up: You're bound to see the Acropolis, probably floodlit, and the best possible reminder of why you came.

After you have your first Greek meal, perhaps washed down with some astringent retsina wine, head back to your hotel and get a good night's sleep so that you'll be ready for your first real day in Athens.

SUGGESTED ITINERARIES FOR FIRST-TIME VISITORS

If You Have 1 Day

Something to check as soon as you arrive: In June 1998, plans were announced to keep all major attractions open in the summer until 7pm. If this plan is in effect, you will have a lot of extra opportunities to see the sites and museums that currently close in midafternoon.

Athens does not wear its heart on its sleeve, and has neither the grand boulevards of Paris, the acres of green parks of London, nor the

Athens Attractions

Academy of Arts & Letters **18**
Acropolis Museum **11**
Athens Cathedral **20**
Ayios Yioryios **19**
Benaki Museum **21**
Byzantine Museum **23**
Goulandris Museum of
  Cycladic Art **22**
Greek Folk Art Museum **24**
Hadrian's Arch **27**
Hadrian's Library **6**
Ilias Lalaounis
  Jewelry Museum **13**
Kerameikos Cemetery **1**
Monastiraki Church **5**
National Archaeological
  Museum **14**
National Historical
  Museum **15**
National Library **16**
National Picture Gallery **26**
Parthenon **10**
Presidential Palace **25**
Roman Agora **7**
Stoa of Attalos **4**
Stoa of Zeus **3**
Temple of Olympian Zeus **28**
Theater of Dionysos **12**
Theseion
  (Temple of Hephaistos) **2**
Tower of Winds (Aerides) **8**
University **17**

Legend
Church ✝
First Aid ✚
Information *i*
OTE **C**
Post Office ✉

An Important Warning

Strikes that close museums and archaeological sites can occur without warning. Decide what you most want to see, and go there as soon as possible after your arrival. The fact that something is open today says nothing about tomorrow. If you're visiting in the off-season, check with the **Greek National Tourist Organization** (☎ 01/331-0437) for the abbreviated **winter hours** of sites and museums. Keep in mind that the opening hours posted at sites and listed at the tourist office often vary considerably. Alas, no information is utterly reliable.

---

consistently engaging architecture of most other European capitals. Consequently, if you only have 1 day here, you'll probably want to concentrate on the major attractions.

Since lots of other first-time visitors will also be determined to "do" the **Acropolis** and the **National Archaeological Museum**—usually in that order—in their day here, decide which of these two major attractions you most want to see, and get there just before opening time, or an hour before closing time. That way you'll have a good chance of escaping the crowds, which take over by 10am but usually diminish substantially toward closing time.

If you visit the Acropolis first, finish by strolling downhill to the **Agora,** the heart of ancient Athens's political and commercial center. The Agora is steps from the Monastiraki and Plaka districts, each filled with shops, cafes, and restaurants, where over lunch you can digest all that you've seen. When you get your second wind, grab a taxi to the **National Archaeological Museum** to see the Mycenaean gold, the classical bronze statues, and the hauntingly beautiful frescoes from Akrotiri, the Minoan Pompeii on the island of Santorini. Then, grab another cab back to your hotel for a siesta, before heading back into the Plaka for dinner and some shopping at the multiplicity of stores that stay open until at least 10pm. If you've had your fill of the Plaka, stroll up to the fashionable Kolonaki district to people-watch in a cafe, eat dinner, or do some serious window-shopping at the boutiques and galleries lining the district's streets.

If You Have 2 Days

If you didn't make it to the **National Archaeological Museum** on your first day, take a taxi, arriving just before it opens so that you'll beat the tour groups. Then, to get a sense of Greek life since antiquity, take in some of Athens's smaller museums, such as the enchanting **Museum of Greek Popular Musical Instruments** or the **Folk Art Museum.** If you need a change of pace, head up **Mount Likavitos** (Lycabettus) on the funicular that leaves from the top of Odos Ploutarchou about every 20 minutes from 8am to 10pm in summer (Dr500/$1.65). If Athens's habitual *nefos* (smog) isn't too bad, you'll have a wonderful view of Athens, Piraeus, and the Saronic Gulf. Smog or no smog, you can relax at the summit-top **Dionysos Café** with a coffee or snack (best not to eat a full meal here: the food is undistinguished and overpriced). If you feel like stretching your legs, take one of the paths from the summit and stroll down, enjoying the scent of the pine trees and the changing views of the city. You'll end up in Kolonaki, another good spot to choose a cafe and watch the world go by.

If You Have 3 Days or More

For your first 2 days in Athens, follow the suggestions above. Then, since you've spent a good deal of time visiting Athens's museums and ancient sites, you might want to explore the city. If you want to see how Athens is fed, head to the **Central Market** on Odos Athinas, and wander through the fish and meat halls before having a coffee and (if you're in the mood) a bowl of tripe stew at **Papandreou,** a hole-in-the-wall market restaurant where the butcher, the baker, and the office worker all meet to eat (for a review, see page 140). If tripe stew isn't your snack of choice, you may prefer to head from the Central Market to **Zonar's,** the venerable sweet shop and restaurant on Odos Panepistimiou, where you can spy on elegant matrons reviving themselves with cups of tea after the exertions of their shopping expeditions. Then you could wander through the National Gardens, watching Greek toddlers watching the ducks and peacocks in the small zoo. If your conscience begins to bother you at this point, head back into the Plaka and visit the **Roman Agora** or ancient Athens's cemetery, the **Kerameikos,** with its handsome marble funerary monuments.

If a day wandering Athens is too unstructured for your tastes, consider taking a day trip to one of the great sites of antiquity, such as **Delphi** (see page 423) or **Sounion** (see page 179). You can even go on a dawn-to-dusk whirlwind day trip to Corinth, Mycenae, and Epidaurus (best done on a bus tour). If you've had your fill of ancient monuments, visit the Byzantine monasteries of **Daphni** (see page 184) or **Kaisariani** (see page 180).

If you don't want to leave Athens without seeing one of the "isles of Greece," you can take a day trip by boat from Piraeus to one or more of the islands of the Saronic Gulf. **Aegina** (Egina), **Poros,** and **Hydra** (Idra) are all feasible day trips—all covered in chapter 7—but best not done the day before you leave Athens, lest bad weather strand you on an island. Whatever you do, be sure to give yourself time to sit in cafes and watch the world go by.

1 The Top Attractions

✪ **The Acropolis.** ☎ **01/321-0219.** Admission Dr2,000 ($7) adults, Dr1,500 ($5) seniors, Dr1,000 ($3.35) students with ID. Free on Sun. Admission includes entrance to the **Acropolis Museum,** which sometimes closes earlier than the site. Summer Mon–Fri 8am–6pm; Sat–Sun and holidays 8:30am–3pm (sometimes to 6pm). You can reach the path up first to the ticket booth and thence to the entrance for the Acropolis by following Dionissiou Areopayitou, Odos Theorias, or the path up through the Ancient Agora.

The Acropolis is one of a handful of places in the world that are so well known it's hard not to be nervous when you finally get here. Will it be as beautiful as its photographs? Will it be, ever so slightly, a disappointment? Rest assured: The Acropolis does not disappoint—but it usually *is* infuriatingly crowded. What you want here is some time—time to watch as the columns of the Parthenon appear first beige, then golden, then rose, then stark white in changing light; time to stand on the Belvedere and take in the view over Athens—and listen for the muted sounds of conversations floating up from the Plaka; time to realize that you really are here, and to think of all those who have been here before you.

A little history: When you climb up the Acropolis—the heights above the city— you know that you're on your way to see Greece's most famous temple, the **Parthenon.** What you may not know is that people lived on the Acropolis as early as 5,000 B.C. The Acropolis's sheer sides made a superb natural defense, just the place to avoid enemies and be able to see any invaders coming across the sea or the plains of Attica. And, of course, it helped that in antiquity there was a spring here.

In classical times, when Athens's population had grown to around 250,000, people had moved down from the Acropolis, which had become the city's most important religious center. The city's **civic and business center**—the Agora—and its **cultural**

center, with several theaters and concert halls, bracketed the Acropolis. When you peer over the sides of the Acropolis at the houses in the Plaka, and the remains of the ancient Agora and the theater of Dionysos, you'll see the layout of the ancient city. Syntagma and Omonia squares, the heart of today's Athens, were well out of the ancient city center.

Even the Acropolis's superb heights couldn't protect it from the Persian invasion of 480 B.C., when most of its monuments were burned and destroyed. You may notice some immense column drums built into the Acropolis's walls. When the great Athenian statesman Pericles ordered the monuments of the Acropolis rebuilt, he had these drums from the destroyed Parthenon built into the walls lest Athenians forget what had happened—and so they would remember that they had rebuilt what they had lost. Pericles's rebuilding program began about 448 B.C.; the new Parthenon was dedicated 10 years later, but work on other monuments continued for a century.

The **Parthenon,** dedicated to Athena Parthenos (Athena the Virgin), patron goddess of Athens, was, of course, the most important religious shrine here, and you won't have any trouble spotting it. There were also shrines to many other gods and goddesses on the Acropolis's broad summit. Most have been almost completely destroyed, but here are some that you'll still be able to see.

Visiting the Acropolis: As you enter the Acropolis, you'll first go through the **Beulé Gate,** built by the Romans, and named for the French archaeologist who discovered it in 1852. After that, you'll pass through the **Propylaia,** the monumental 5th-century B.C. entranceway. It's characteristic of the Roman mania for building that they found it necessary to build an entranceway to an entranceway!

Just above the Propylaia is the little temple of **Athena Nike** (Athena of Victory); this beautifully proportioned Ionic temple was built in 424 B.C. and heavily restored in the 1930s. To the left of the Parthenon is the **Erechtheion,** which the Athenians honored as the tomb of Erechtheus, a legendary king of Athens. A hole in the ceiling and floor of the northern porch indicates the spot where Poseidon's trident struck to make a spring gush forth during his contest with Athena to have the city named in his honor. Athena countered with an olive tree; the olive tree planted beside the Erechtheion reminds visitors of her victory—as, of course, does Athens's name.

Give yourself a little time to enjoy the delicate carving on the Erechtheion, and be sure to see the original Caryatids in the Acropolis Museum. The Caryatids presently holding up the porch of the Erechtheion are the casts put there when the originals were moved to prevent further erosion by Athens's acid *nefos* (smog).

However charmed you are by these elegant little temples, you're probably still heading resolutely toward the Parthenon, and you may be disappointed to realize that visitors are not allowed inside, both to protect the monument and to allow restoration work to proceed safely. If you find this frustrating, keep in mind that in antiquity only priests and honored visitors were allowed in to see the monumental—some 36 feet tall—**statue of Athena** designed by the great Phidias, who was in charge of Pericles's building program. Nothing of this huge gold-and-ivory statue remains, but there's a small Roman copy in the National Archaeological Museum—and horrific renditions on souvenirs ranging from T-shirts to ouzo bottles. Admittedly, the gold-and-ivory statue was not understated; the 2nd-century A.D. traveler Pausanias, one of the first guidebook writers, recorded that the statue stood "upright in an ankle-length tunic with a head of Medusa carved in ivory on her breast. She has a Victory about 8 feet high, and a spear in her hand and a shield at her feet, with a snake beside the shield, possibly representing Erechtheus." The floor of the room in which the statue stood was covered in olive oil, so that the gold and ivory reflected through the dimly lit space.

If you look over the edge of the Acropolis toward the **Temple of Hephaistos** (now called the **Theseion**) in the ancient Agora, and then at the Parthenon, you can't help but be struck by how much lighter and more graceful the Parthenon is. Scholars tell us that this is because Ictinus, the architect of the Parthenon, was something of a magician of optical illusions. The columns and stairs—the very floor—of the Parthenon all appear straight because all are minutely curved. The exterior columns are slightly thicker in the middle (a device known as *entasis*), which makes the entire column appear straight. That's why the Parthenon, with 17 columns on each side and eight at each end (creating an exterior colonnade of 46 relatively slender columns), looks so graceful, while the Temple of Hephaistos, with only six columns at each end and 13 along each side, seems so squat and stolid.

Of course, one reason the Parthenon looks so airy is that it is, quite literally, open to the air. The Parthenon's entire roof and much of its interior were blown to smithereens in 1687, when the Venetians attempted to capture the Acropolis from the Turks. A shell fired from nearby Mouseion Hill struck the Parthenon—where the Turks were storing gunpowder and munitions—and caused appalling damage to the building and its sculptures. Most of the remaining sculptures were carted off to London by Lord Elgin in the first decade of the 19th century. Those surviving sculptures—known as the Elgin Marbles—are on display in the British Museum, causing ongoing pain to generations of Greeks, who continue to press for their return. Things heated up again in the summer of 1988, when English historian William St. Clair's book *Lord Elgin and the Marbles* received a lot of publicity. According to St. Clair, the British Museum "over-cleaned" the marbles in the 1930s, removing not only the outer patina, but also many sculptural details. The British Museum countered by saying that the damage wasn't all that bad—and that the marbles would remain in London.

The Parthenon originally had sculpture on both of its pediments, as well as a frieze running around the entire temple. The frieze was made up of alternating **triglyphs** (panels with three incised grooves) and **metopes** (sculptured panels). The east pediment showed scenes from the birth of Athena, while the west pediment showed Athena and Poseidon's contest for possession of Athens. The long frieze showed the battle of the Athenians against the Amazons, scenes from the Trojan war, and the struggles of the Olympian gods against giants and centaurs. The message of most of this sculpture was the triumph of knowledge and civilization—that is, Athens—over the forces of darkness and barbarians. An interior frieze showed scenes from the Panathenaic Festival each August, when citizens processed through the streets, bringing a new tunic for the statue of Athena. Only a few fragments of any of these sculptures remain in place, and every visitor will have to decide for himself whether it's a good or a bad thing that Lord Elgin removed so much before the nefos became endemic in Athens and ate away much of what he left here.

If you're lucky enough to visit the Acropolis on a smog-free and sunny day, you'll see the gold and cream tones of the Parthenon's handsome Pentelic marble at their most subtle. It may come as something of a shock to realize that in antiquity, the Parthenon—like most other monuments here—was painted in gay colors that have since faded, revealing the natural marble. If it's a clear day, you'll also get a superb view of Athens from the Belvedere at the east end of the Acropolis.

Near the Belvedere, the **Acropolis Archaeological Museum** hugs the ground to detract as little as possible from the ancient monuments. Inside, you'll see the four original Caryatids from the Erechtheion still in Athens (one disappeared during the Ottoman occupation and one is in the British Museum). Other delights here include sculpture saved from the Parthenon burned by the Persians, and statues of smiling

Korai (maidens) and *Kouroi* (young men). You'll have to decide whether you find their smiles insufferably smug or becomingly modest.

While you're deciding, don't miss the graceful 5th-century relief called the **Mourning Athena,** the athletic **Calfbearer,** and the three-headed figure of the **Tryphon,** whose tripartite body ends in a snaky tail. You can see clear traces of the ancient paint that decorated much ancient sculpture on the Tryphon.

As you leave the Acropolis, you probably feel that you've seen a great many monuments. In fact, almost all of what you've seen comes from Athens's heyday in the mid-5th-century B.C., when Pericles rebuilt what the Persians destroyed. In the following centuries, every invader who came built monuments, most of which were resolutely destroyed by the next wave of invaders. If you had been here a century ago, you could have seen the remains of mosques and churches, and a Frankish bell tower. The great archaeologist Schliemann, the discoverer of Troy and excavator of Mycenae, was so offended by the bell tower that he paid to have it torn down.

If you'd like to know more about the Acropolis and its history, as well as the Elgin Marbles controversy, you can visit the **Center for Acropolis Studies,** on Odos Makriyanni just southeast of the Acropolis (☎ 01/923-9381), open daily from 9am to 2:30pm; admission is free. On display are artifacts, reconstructions, photographs, drawings, and plaster casts of the Elgin Marbles that Greeks hope will someday return to Athens and be put on display in the museum presently under construction near the center.

Work slowed in summer 1998, when excavations unearthed the remains of homes from an early Christian community. After archaeologists excavate and document the remains, they will be destroyed so that the museum can be built. A pity—but less of a pity than what happens all too often in central Athens, when ancient remains found during construction are illicitly destroyed.

If you've found the Acropolis too crowded, you can usually get a peaceful view of its monuments from one of three nearby hills (all signposted from the Acropolis): the **Hill of the Pnyx,** where the Athenian assembly met; the **Hill of the Areopagus,** where the Athenian upper house met; and the **Hill of Filopappos** (also known as the Hill of the Muses), named after the 2nd-century A.D. philhellene Filopappos, whose funeral monument tops the hill.

✪ **Ancient Agora.** Below the Acropolis on the edge of Monastiraki (entrance on Odos Adrianou, near Ayiou Philippou Sq., east of Monastiraki Sq.). ☎ 01/321-0185. Admission Dr1,200 ($4) adults, Dr900 ($3) seniors, Dr600 ($2) students. Tues–Sun 8:30am–3pm.

The Agora was Athens's commercial and civic center. Its buildings were used for a wide range of political, educational, philosophical, theatrical, and athletic purposes—which may be why it now seems such a jumble of ancient buildings, inscriptions, and fragments of sculpture. This is a nice place to wander and enjoy the views up toward the Acropolis and take in the herb garden and flowers planted around the 5th-century B.C. Temple of Hephaistos and Athena (the Theseion).

Find a shady spot by the temple, sit a while, and imagine the Agora teeming with merchants, legislators, and philosophers—but very few women, who didn't often go into public places. Athens's best-known philosopher, **Socrates,** often strolled here with his disciples, including **Plato,** in the shade of the Stoa of Zeus Eleutherios, asking questions that alternately infuriated and delighted his friends. In 399 B.C., Socrates was accused of "introducing strange gods and corrupting youth," and sentenced to death. He drank his cup of hemlock in a prison in the southwest corner of the Agora—where excavators centuries later found small, clay cups, just the right size for a fatal drink of hemlock. Another figure who spoke in the Agora and irritated

The Acropolis & Monastiraki Square

ATHENS

Acropolis & Monastiraki

Flea Market 1
Greek Orthodox Cathedral (Metropolis) 4
Panayia Gorgoepikoos (Little Metropolis) 5
Propylaia 7
Roman Agora 2
Temple of Athena Nike 6
Tower of the Winds 3

most Athenians was **St. Paul,** who rebuked them as superstitious when he saw an inscription here to the "Unknown God."

The one monument you can't miss in the Agora is the 2nd-century B.C. **Stoa of Attalos,** built by King Attalos of Pergamon, in Asia Minor, and totally reconstructed by American archaeologists in the 1950s. (You may be grateful that they chose to include an excellent modern toilet in the stoa.) The museum in the stoa's ground floor has finds from 5,000 years of Athenian history, including sculpture and pottery, as well as a voting machine and a child's potty seat, all with labels in English. The stoa is open Tuesday through Sunday from 8:30am to 2:45pm; admission is included with the site admission.

As you leave the stoa, take a moment to look at the charming little 11th-century Byzantine **Church of the Holy Apostles,** also restored by the Americans. The church is almost always closed, but its delicate proportions come as a relief after the somewhat heartless facade of the Stoa of Attalos.

The Kerameikos. Odos Ermou 148. ☎ 01/346-3552. Admission Dr500 ($1.65) adults, Dr400 ($1.35) seniors, Dr300 ($3) students. Tues–Sun 8:30am–3pm. Take Odos Ermou west from Monastiraki Sq. past the Thisio metro station; the cemetery is on the right.

You may not immediately think that you want to visit ancient Athens's most famous cemetery, located just outside the city walls—but this is a lovely spot. Many handsome monuments from the 4th century B.C. and later are still lined up along the Street of the Tombs, and relatively few visitors come here. This can be a nice spot to sit and imagine **Pericles** putting the final touches on his **Funeral Oration** for the Athenian soldiers killed during the first year's fighting in the Peloponnesian War. Athens, Pericles said, was the "school of Hellas" and a "pattern to others rather than an imitator of any." Offering comfort to the families of the fallen, he urged the widows to remember that the greatest glory belonged to the woman who was "least talked of among men either for good or for bad"—which must have caused a few snickers in the audience, since Pericles's own mistress, Aspasia, was the subject of considerable gossip.

The Kerameikos was a major crossroads in antiquity, rather like today's Omonia Square, where major roads from outside Athens converged before continuing into the city. You can see remains of the massive **Dipylon Gate,** where most roads converged, and the **Sacred Gate,** where marchers in the Panathenaic Festival converged before marching through the ancient Agora and climbing up to the Parthenon. What you can't see is the remains of **Plato's Academy,** which was in this district, but has thus far eluded archaeologists.

Very often ancient Greek words turn out to hide familiar English words, and that's true of the Kerameikos. The name honors the hero Keramos, who was something of a patron saint of potters, giving his name both to the ceramics they made here and to the district itself.

The **Oberlaender Museum,** with a collection of terra-cotta figures and finds from the Kerameikos, is usually open when the site is.

If you like cemeteries, ancient and modern, be sure to visit Athens's enormous **First Cemetery,** near the Athens Stadium, which has acres of monuments, many as elaborate as anything you'll see at the Kerameikos.

The Roman Agora (Forum). Enter from corner of Pelopida and Eolou. Admission Dr500 ($1.65). Tues–Sun 8:30am–2:45pm.

One of the nicest things about the Roman Agora is that, if you don't want to inspect it closely, you can take it in very nicely from one of the cafes and restaurants on its periphery.

In addition to building a number of monuments on the Acropolis, and in the ancient Agora, Roman leaders, beginning with Julius Caesar, built their own agora, or forum, an extension of the Greek agora. If the area between the Greek agora and the Roman forum were to be excavated, we'd have lots more of both. That's just what some archaeologists want, and precisely what Plaka merchants and fans of the district do not want. At present, the Roman Agora is a pleasant mélange of monuments from different eras, including a mosque built here after the Byzantine Empire was conquered by Mehmet II in 1453.

The Roman Agora's most endearing monument is the octagonal **Tower of the Winds,** with its relief sculptures of eight gods of the winds, including Boreas blowing on a shell. Like so many monuments in Athens—the Parthenon itself had a church inside it for centuries—the Tower of the Winds has had a varied history. Built by a 1st-century B.C. astronomer as a combination sundial and water-powered clock, it became a home for whirling dervishes in the 18th century. When Lord Byron visited Athens, he lodged near the tower, spending much of his time writing lovesick poetry to the beautiful "Maid of Athens."

You can usually find the remains of the Roman latrine near the Tower of the Winds by following the sound of giggles and seeing where people are taking pictures of each other in the seated position. The less-well-preserved remains of the **Emperor Hadrian's** enormous and once-famous **library** go largely unnoticed. Draw your own conclusions.

The Theater of Dionysos. Odos Dionissiou Areopayitou, on the south slope of the Acropolis. ☎ 01/322-4625. Admission Dr500 ($1.65). Daily 8:30am–2:30pm.

This theater was built in the 4th century B.C. to replace and enlarge the earlier theater in which the plays of the great Athenian dramatists were first performed. The new theater seated some 17,000 spectators in 64 rows of seats, 20 of which survive. Most spectators sat on limestone seats—and probably envied the 67 grandees who got to sit in the handsome Pentelic marble thronelike seats in the front row. The most elegant throne belonged to the priest of Dionysos, the god of wine, revels, and theater; appropriately, carved satyrs and bunches of grapes ornament the priest's throne.

The Odeum (Odeion; also known as the Irodio) of Herodes Atticus. Odos Dionissiou Areopayitou, on the south slope of the Acropolis.

This Odeum (Music Hall) was one of an astonishing number of monuments built in Greece by the wealthy 2nd-century A.D. philhellene Herodes Atticus. If you think it looks suspiciously well preserved, you're right: it was reconstructed in the 19th century. Since the Odeum is usually closed, the best way to see it is either looking down from the Acropolis or, better yet, during one of the performances staged here during the Athens Festival each summer. If possible, bring a cushion if you attend a performance here: Marble seats are as hard as you'd expect, and the cushions provided are lousy.

Hadrian's Arch. On Leoforos Amalias, near the Temple of Olympian Zeus, and easily seen from the street.

The Roman emperor Hadrian built a number of monuments in Athens, including this enormous triumphal arch with its robust, highly ornamental Corinthian columns. Although Hadrian was a philhellene, he didn't hesitate to use his arch to let the Athenians know who was boss: An inscription facing the Acropolis side reads THIS IS ATHENS, THE ANCIENT CITY OF THESEUS. On the other side it states THIS IS THE CITY OF HADRIAN, NOT OF THESEUS. Ironically, much more of ancient Athens is visible today than of Hadrian's Athens, and much of Roman Athens lies unexcavated under modern Athens.

Hadrian's Arch is still a symbolic entrance to Athens: a number of times when demonstrations were blocking traffic from the airport into central Athens, our taxi driver has told us that he can get us as far as Hadrian's Gate, and that we'll have to walk into town from there.

The Temple of Olympian Zeus (the Olympieion, also known as the Kolonnes [the columns]). At Leoforos Vas. Olgas and Amalias and easily seen from the street. ☎ **01/922-6330.** Admission Dr500 ($1.65). Tues–Sun 8:30am–3pm.

Hadrian also built this massive temple—or, rather, he finished the construction that had begun in the 6th century B.C. and continued on and off (more off than on) for 700 years. At 360 feet long and 143 feet wide (110m by 44m), this was one of the largest temples in the ancient world. The 13 56-foot-high Pentelic marble columns that remain standing, as well as the one sprawled on the ground, give a good idea of how impressive this forest of columns must have been—although we have a sneaking suspicion that it may be more appealing as a ruin than it ever was as a contender for the title "mother of all temples."

✪ **National Archaeological Museum.** Odos Patission 44. ☎ **01/821-7717.** Admission Dr2,000 ($7) adults, Dr1,000 ($3.35) students. Mon 12:30–5pm; Tues–Fri 8am–5pm; Sat–Sun and holidays 8:30am–3pm. (The museum is sometimes open to 7pm, but you cannot count on this.) The museum is a third of a mile (10 min. on foot) north of Omonia Sq. on the road named Leoforos 28 Octobriou but usually called Patission.

This is an enormous and enormously popular museum; try to be at the door when it opens so that you can see the exhibits, and not just the backs of other visitors. Early arrival, except in high summer, should give you at least an hour before most tour groups arrive; alternatively, get here an hour before closing, or at lunchtime, when the tour groups often are not as dense. If possible, come several times, so that your time here is a pleasure rather than an endurance contest.

Immediately ahead of you as you enter is the **Mycenaean Hall,** with gold masks, cups, dishes, and jewelry unearthed from the site of Mycenae by Heinrich Schliemann in 1876. Many of these objects are small and delicate, and very hard to see when the gallery is crowded.

Don't miss the stunning **burial mask** that Schliemann misnamed the "Mask of Agamemnon" when he found it at Mycenae. Alas, Schliemann was wrong: Spoilsport archaeologists are sure that the mask is not Agamemnon's, but belonged to an earlier, unknown monarch. In the same gallery are the stunning **Vaphio cups,** showing mighty bulls, unearthed in a tomb at a seemingly insignificant site in the Peloponnese. If little Vaphio could produce these riches, what else remains to be found in future excavations?

Just off the Mycenaean Gallery, **Cycladic figurines,** named after the island chain, are on display. Although these figurines are among the earliest known Greek sculpture (about 2,000 B.C.), almost everyone is struck by how modern they look, often comparing the idols' faces to those wrought by Modigliani. One figure, a musician with a lyre, seems to be concentrating on his music, cheerfully oblivious to his onlookers.

The museum's staggeringly large sculpture collection spreads through much of the rest of the ground floor. You may simply want to wander along, stopping when something catches your fancy. Almost everyone's fancy is captured by the **bronzes,** from the tiny jockey to the monumental figure variously identified as Zeus or Poseidon. Much ink has been spilt trying to prove either that the god was holding a thunderbolt (which would make him Zeus) or a trident (which would mean that he was Poseidon). And who could resist the bronze figures of the staggeringly handsome young men, perhaps athletes, seemingly about to step forward and sprint away through the crowds?

Upstairs, the museum has more Greek vases than you may have suspected existed, or wanted to see, and you might want to head instead for the **frescoes** from the site of Akrotiri on the island of Santorini (Thira). Around 1450 B.C., the volcanic island exploded, destroying not just most of the island itself but also, some say, the Minoan civilization of Crete. Could Santorini's virtual disappearance have given rise to the legend of the lost civilization of Atlantis? Perhaps. Fortunately, these beautiful frescoes survived and were brought to Athens for safekeeping and display. Just as Athens wants the Elgin Marbles back, the present-day inhabitants of Santorini want their frescoes back, hoping that the crowds who come to see them in Athens will come instead to Santorini.

There are as many theories on what these frescoes show as there are tourists in the museum on any given day. Who are the boxing boys? Were there monkeys on Santorini, or does the scene show another land? Are the ships sailing off to war, or returning home? No one knows, but it's impossible to see these lilting frescoes and not envy the people of Akrotiri who looked at such beauty every day.

✪ **N. P. Goulandris Foundation Museum of Cycladic Art.** Odos Neofytou Douka 4. ☎ **01/722-8321.** Admission Dr800 ($2.65) adults, Dr400 ($1.35) students. Mon and Wed–Fri 10am–4pm; Sat 10am–3pm. From Syntagma Sq., walk 7 blocks east along Vas. Sofias and turn left on Neofytou Douka; the museum is on the right.

This handsome museum opened its doors in 1986 and houses the astonishing collection of Nicolas and Aikaterini Goulandris, the largest collection of Cycladic art outside the National Museum. There are some 230 stone and pottery vessels and figurines from the 3rd millennium B.C. on display, and if you didn't make up your mind at the National Museum that the faces of the idols remind you of the work of Modigliani, here's your chance. The museum's elegant little shop, which takes most major credit cards, has reproductions of a number of items from the collection, including a pert Cycladic pig.

Despite the impressive number of displays, this museum is as congenial as the National Museum is overwhelming. It helps that the Goulandris does not usually get the huge crowds that go to the National Museum, and it also helps that the galleries here are small and well lit, with labels throughout in Greek and English. The collection of Greek vases is both small and exquisite—the ideal place to find out if you prefer black or red figure vases.

When you've seen all you want to here (and perhaps refreshed yourself with something in the basement snack bar), be sure to walk through the courtyard into the museum's newest acquisition: the elegant 19th-century **Stathatos Mansion,** with some of its original furnishings. There's usually a temporary exhibit here, but even if there's not, this is a wonderful chance to get a glimpse of how wealthy Athenians lived a hundred years ago.

✪ **Greek Folk Art Museum.** Odos Kidathineon 17, Plaka. ☎ **01/322-9031.** Admission Dr500 ($1.65) adults, Dr400 ($1.35) seniors, Dr300 ($1) students. Tues–Sun 10am–2pm.

This endearing small museum has dazzling embroideries and costumes from all over the country, and a small room with zany frescoes of gods and heroes done by the eccentric artist Theofilos Hadjimichael, who painted in the early part of this century. We visit here every time we're in Athens, always finding something new, always looking forward to our next visit—and always glad we weren't born Greek women 100 years ago, when we would have spent endless hours embroidering, crocheting, and weaving. Much of what is on display here was made by young women for their *proikas* (dowries) in the days when a bride was supposed to arrive at the altar with enough embroidered linen, rugs, and blankets to last a lifetime.

⚙ **Museum of Greek Popular Musical Instruments.** Odos Dioyenous 1–3 (around the corner from the Tower of the Winds). ☎01-325-0198. Free admission. Tues and Thurs–Sun 10am–2pm; Wed noon–6pm.

Photos show the musicians, while recordings let you listen to the tambourines, Cretan lyres, lutes, pottery drums, and clarinets on display here. Not only that, but this museum is steps from the excellent **Platanos restaurant,** so you can alternate the pleasures of food, drink, and music. The last time we were here, an elderly Greek gentleman listened to some music, transcribed it, stepped out into the courtyard, and played it on his own violin! The shop has a wide selection of CDs and cassettes.

2 More Museums

The Athens City Museum. Paparigopoulou 7 (Klathmonos Sq., off Odos Stadiou). ☎ 01/323-0168. Admission Dr400 ($1.35). Mon, Wed, and Fri–Sat 9am–1:30pm.

This handsomely restored 19th-century Athenian town house is where modern Greece's first king, young King Otho, and his bride, Amalia, lived while a more spacious royal palace (now the Parliament) was built. Poor Otho attempted to ingratiate himself with his Greek subjects by wearing the *foustanella* (short pleated skirt); most thought him dotty. He and Amalia were sent packing in 1862 and Greece imported a new king, George I, from Denmark.

The museum has a wonderful collection of watercolors of 19th-century Athens, including many by the English painter—and author of *The Owl and the Pussy-Cat*—Edward Lear. Amalia's piano is still here, along with some nice portraits of the royal couple. There's even a mini–throne room where the royal couple received important visitors—and a wonderful model of provincial Athens in 1842.

Benaki Museum. Odos Koumbari 1 (at Leoforos Vas. Sofias, Kolonaki, 5 blocks east of Syntagma Sq.). ☎ 01/361-1617.

The Benaki Museum has been closed for several years for major alterations, although there are occasionally special exhibitions in one gallery here. If the museum has reopened by the time you're here, you're in luck. The costume collection is superb, and the relics of Greece's 1821 War of Independence, including Lord Byron's writing desk and pen, fascinating.

Byzantine Museum. Leoforos Vas. Sofias 22. ☎ 01/723-1570 or 01/721-1027. Admission Dr500 ($1.65) adults, Dr250 (85¢) students. Tues–Sun 8:30am–3pm. At Leoforos Vas. Konstandinou, 12 long blocks east of Syntagma Sq.

This museum in a 19th-century Florentine-style villa is devoted to the art and history of the Byzantine era. Greece's most important collection of icons and religious art, along with sculptures, altars, mosaics, religious vestments, bibles, and a small-scale reconstruction of an early Christian basilica, are exhibited on several floors around a courtyard. The museum hopes to reopen all its galleries by 1999.

Ilias Lalaounis Jewelry Museum. Odos Kalisperi 12. ☎ 01/922-1044. Fax 01/923-7358. E-mail: ioannal@acropolis.gr. Admission Dr800 ($2.65) adults; Dr500 ($1.65) students, seniors, and children. Mon and Thurs–Sat 9am–4pm; Wed 9am–9pm; Sun 10am–4pm. At Karyatidon, 1 block south of the Acropolis between the Theater of Dionysos and the Odeum.

The 3,000 pieces of jewelry on display here are so spectacular that even those with no special interest in baubles will enjoy this glitzy new museum, founded by one of Greece's most successful jewelry designers. The first floor has a boutique and small workshop. The second and third floors display pieces honoring ancient, Byzantine, and Cycladic designs, as well as plants, animals, and insects. The museum shop has copies of some of the displays, and jewelers in the museum's workshop take orders, in case you want your own gold necklace inspired by insect vertebrae.

The Jewish Museum. Odos Nikis 39 (on the left-hand side of Nikis as you walk away from Syntagma Square). ☎ **01/322-5582.** Fax 01/323-1577. Admission Dr500 ($1.65) adults, Dr250 (85¢) students and children. Mon–Fri 9am–2:30pm; Sun 10am–2pm.

Greece's Jewish community, a strong presence throughout the country, and a dominant force in Thessaloniki, was essentially obliterated in the Holocaust. Heartrending exhibits here include the wedding photograph of Yosef Levy and Dona Habif, who married in April 1944 and a month later were sent to Auschwitz, where they were killed. Although many of the Jewish Museum's very helpful English labels seem to have disappeared, the handsome reconstruction of the Patras synagogue is still on display, as are articles of daily life and religious ceremony.

If you contact museum curator Zanet Battinou in advance of your visit, she will try to have a staff member show you the exhibits.

The Kanellopoulos Museum. Odos Theorias and Odos Panos, Plaka. ☎ **01/321-2313.** Admission Dr500 ($1.65). Tues–Sun 8:30am–3pm.

The Kanellopoulos, in a former private home with a wonderful position high on the slopes of the Acropolis, is another nice place to visit when you've had your fill of big museums. This private collection has some superb red and black figure vases, stunning Byzantine and post-Byzantine icons, and even some Mycenaean pottery baby bottles. The house itself, with some fine painted ceilings, is a delight.

3 Ancient Monuments

One small, graceful monument that you might easily miss is the 4th-century B.C. **Choregic Monument of Lysikrates** on Odos Lysikratous in the Plaka, handily located just a few steps from the excellent **Daphne's** restaurant (see page 173). This circular monument with Corinthian columns and a domed roof bears an inscription stating that Lysikrates erected it when he won the award in 334 B.C. for the best musical performance with a "chorus of boys." There's a lovely frieze showing Dionysos busily trying to turn evil pirates into friendly dolphins.

Three hills near the Acropolis deserve at least a respectful glance: the **Areopagus,** the **Pnyx,** and **Filopappos** Hill. The **Areopagus** is the bald marble hill across from the entrance to the Acropolis. The Areopagus is so slippery, despite its marble steps, that it is never an easy climb, and is positively treacherous in the rain. This makes it hard to imagine the distinguished Athenians who served on the Council and Court making their way up here to try homicide cases. Still harder to imagine is St. Paul thundering out criticisms of the Athenians for their superstitious devotion to the Unknown God from this slippery perch.

From the Areopagus and Acropolis you can see two nearby wooded hills. The one with the monument visible on its summit is **Filopappos** (also known as the Hill of the Muses), and the monument is the funeral stele of the Roman consul after whom the hill is named. There are some nice walks on the wooded slopes of this hill, one nice Byzantine church (**Ayios Demetrios**), and the **Dora Stratou Theater** where folk dances take place (see page 172). If you climb to the summit (don't try this, or any wanderings here or on the Pnyx, alone at night) and face the Acropolis, you can imagine the wretched moment in 1687 when the Venetian commander Morosini shouted "Fire!"—and his cannon shells struck the Parthenon.

Syntagma Square & Plaka

Legend

✝ Church
⊠ Post Office

ATHENS

Syntagma Square & Plaka

Grande Bretagne ❶
Greek Folk Art Museum ❺
Greek Orthodox Cathedral (Metropolis) ❸
Hadrian's Gate ❽
Monument of Lysikrates ❼
Panayia Gorgoepikoos ❹
Souvenir shops and outdoor tavernas ❻
Tomb of the Unknown Soldier & Parliament ❷

The **Pnyx,** crowned by the Athens Observatory, is where Athens's citizen assembly met. The Pnyx, as much as any spot in Athens—which is to say, any place in the world—is the "birthplace of democracy." Here, for the first time in history, every citizen could vote on every matter of common importance. True, citizens did not include women, and there were far more slaves than citizens in Athens—but that was the case in most of the world for a very long time after democracy was born in Athens.

4 Historic Buildings

Athens was a small village well into the mid–19th century, and did not begin to grow until it became capital of Independent Greece in 1834. It's hard to believe in today's traffic-clogged Athens, but the **Byzantine Museum,** at Vas. Sofias 22, occupies the Renaissance-style villa that the Duchess of Plaisance built—imagine this, in today's Athens—as her country retreat in the 1840s. Several other buildings from the same period, including the **Parliament House** (the former royal palace) and the **Grande Bretagne Hotel** (a former mansion) are still standing in Syntagma Square. Unfortunately, all too many of the neoclassical buildings built in the 19th century were torn down in Athens's rapid expansion after World War II. Here are a few suggestions of some buildings you may pass on your explorations of central Athens.

One historic and handsome building is the **Iliou Melathron** (Palace of Troy) on Odos Stadiou, by the Catholic Church of Saint Denis, a few blocks from Syntagma Square. This was the Athenian home of Schliemann, the discoverer of Troy, and its arcaded and painted facade is as outrageous as Schliemann himself.

In the Plaka, several 19th-century buildings have survived, tucked between the T-shirt shops and restaurants on busy Odos Adrianou (Hadrian) and Odos Kidathineon. **Adrianou 96** is thought to be the oldest surviving prerevolutionary house in Athens, dating from the Turkish occupation, and the nearby 19th-century **Demotic School** has a pleasant neoclassical facade. Over on Kidathineon is the house in which mad **King Ludwig** of Bavaria stayed when he visited Athens in 1835 (there's no number on the house, but a small plaque identifies it), and several other buildings here are former houses from the same period.

Finally, if you climb up through the Plaka to the **Anafiotika district** on the slopes of the Acropolis, you'll find yourself in a delightful neighborhood with many small 19th-century homes. This district is often compared to an island village, and small wonder; most of the homes were built by stonemasons from the Cycladic island of Anafi, who came to Athens to work on the buildings of the new capital of independent Greece.

5 Churches & Synagogues

As you stroll through Athens, you'll discover scores of charming churches. Many date from the Byzantine era of A.D. 330 to A.D. 1453—although virtually nothing survives from the early centuries of that Christian empire. Alas, vandals and thieves have forced many churches to lock their doors, so you may not be able to go inside unless a caretaker is present. If you do go inside, **remember to dress suitably:** Shorts, miniskirts, and sleeveless shirts cause offense. If you wish, you can leave a donation in the collection boxes. Below we list a few churches to keep an eye out for on your travels.

Athens's 19th-century **Greek Orthodox Cathedral** (Metropolis) on Odos Mitropoleos gets almost universally bad press: too big, too new, too . . . well, ugly. It also suffers terribly in comparison with the adjacent 12th-century **Little Metropolis,** with the wonderful name of the **Panayia Gorgoepikoos** ("the Virgin Who Answers Prayers Quickly"). The little church has a number of fragments of classical masonry, including inscriptions, built into its walls that create a delightful crazy-quilt effect.

The square in front of the cathedral is a great place to people-watch on summer weekends, when nonstop weddings often take place, usually in the evening. As one bride leaves the church, the next one (and her flowers, attendants, and guests) are poised to enter. It's a very Greek assembly line, with limousines pulling up, horns blaring, and everyone having a fantastic time.

Also on Mitropoleos, crouched on the sidewalk below an ugly modern building, is the minuscule chapel of **Ayia Dynamis,** a good place for women to light a candle if they want to become pregnant.

If you like spying (from a respectful distance) on weddings and baptisms, continue on to the 12th-century **Church of Ayia Aikaterini,** in the little square off Odos Frinihou. The church sits well below ground level, an indication of just how Athens has grown over the centuries. You'll notice some ancient columns strewn around the courtyard, and may even decide to sit on one while you watch the comings and goings.

If you walk from Syntagma to Monastiraki Square, you can take in a few more churches.

A few blocks from Syntagma Square, on Odos Skouleniou, the little 11th-century Church of St. Theodore is also below street level, another reminder of how the ground level has risen over the centuries. Over on Odos Hrissopileotissis, the small Church of the Virgin is a good place to stop and buy some incense from one of the street vendors usually here. At the Square of St. Irene, off Odos Eolou, there's a very nice flower market in front of the church, and on Monastiraki Square, the Church of the Pantanassa is all that remains of a convent on this spot. And, a short walk away on busy Odos Ermou, the 11th-century Kapnikarea Church sits right in the middle of the road.

If you're walking along busy Leoforos Vas. Sofias, you may want to sit for a bit and rest in the courtyard of the **Church of Ayios Nikolaos.** A few blocks further along on Odos Gennadius, the 12th-century **Church of the Taxarchi** is in a small park.

Beth Shalom, the Athens synagogue, on Odos Melidoni, stands in what was, before World War II, a vibrant Jewish neighborhood. Across the street from Beth Shalom is the old synagogue, which Beth Shalom, with its marble facade, replaced. You can get information on visiting the synagogue, and on services, from the **Jewish Museum,** Odos Nikis 39 (☎ **01/322-5582;** fax 01/323-1577).

6 Parks & Gardens

In addition to the parks and gardens listed here, see "Especially for Kids," below.

The **National Garden,** between Leoforos Amalias and Irodou Attikou, south of Vas. Sofias, was once the royal family's palace garden. Now a public park, the area combines a park, a garden, and a small, rather sad zoo with shady trees, benches, a cafe, and small lakes and ponds with ducks, swans, and a few peacocks. There are several cafes tucked away in the garden, and you can also picnic here. The large neoclassical exhibition/reception hall in the garden was built by the brothers Zappas and so is known as the Zappion. The garden is open daily from 7am to 10pm. This is not a good place to loiter alone at night.

Mount Likavitos (Lycabettus), which dominates the northeast of the city, is a favorite retreat for Athenians and a great place to get a bird's-eye view of Athens and its environs—if the *nefos* (smog) isn't too bad. Even when the nefos is bad, sunsets can be spectacular here. On top, there's a small **Chapel of Ayios Yioryios** (St. George), whose name-day is celebrated on April 23. Each summer, there are performances at the Lykavitos Theater here, and the (expensive) **Dionysos Café** on the summit is usually open all year. You can take the funicular from the top of Odos Ploutarchou (Dr500/$1.65) between 8am and 10pm (it leaves every 20 min. in summer), or walk up from Dexameni Square, which is the route preferred by young lovers and the energetic.

7 Especially for Kids

The **National Garden** off Syntagma Square has a small zoo, several duck ponds, a playground, and lots of room to run around. There's also a **Children's Library** with books in English and some toys and coloring material (adults are usually not allowed to stay with their children). The library is usually open Tuesday through Saturday from 8:30am to 3pm, and is closed in August. The National Garden is open from sunrise to well after sunset.

There are other small parks and gardens scattered through Athens, but this is the best for children. That said, if you're staying in Kolonaki, try **Dexamini Square,** which has a small playground and several cafes and is below the St. George Lycabettos hotel off Odos Kleomenous.

The ride up **Mount Likavitos** on the cable-car railway (*teleferique*) is often a hit with children. It usually operates every 20 minutes from 10am to 10pm in summer (Dr500/$1.65). There's a cafe on top that sells ice cream, and children can let off steam by running along any number of paths downhill.

A good place to check to see if there are any special activities going on is the **Museum of Greek Children's Art,** Odos Kodrou 9, Plaka (☎ 01/331-2621), where admission is Dr500 ($1.65). It's open Tuesday through Saturday from 10am to 2pm and Sunday from 11am to 2pm; closed in August. This small museum has changing displays of children's art from throughout Greece, and your children may enjoy seeing what Greek kids like to draw. Workshops for children are offered here, and conducted in Greek. There are also workshops at the **Children's Museum,** around the corner at Odos Kidathineon 14, but usually no exhibitions. In addition, there are sometimes **Karaghiozis Puppet Shows** (shadow theater) a few doors away at the **Greek Folk Art Museum,** Odos Kidathineon 17. You don't need to understand Greek to appreciate the slapstick comedy of Karaghiozis.

There are usually lots of new-release American **movies** showing in central Athens, and a couple of hours in an air-conditioned theater is not a bad way to pass a hot afternoon. Check the English-language daily *Athens News* or the daily *Kathimerini* insert in the *International Herald Tribune* for listings.

The "Scope" section in the weekly *Hellenic Times* lists activities of interest to children in Athens, including Girl Scout meetings, hiking excursions, and day camps, in its "Kids Corner."

The beaches nearest to Athens are a fair trek—and crowded and often polluted. Consider buying a day pass for the **Hilton pool** (at press time, Dr7,500/$25 Mon through Fri and Dr10,000/$34 Sat and Sun; information available at ☎ 01/725-0201).

8 Organized Tours

Many independent travelers (ourselves included) tend to turn up their noses at organized tours. Nonetheless, this can be an efficient and easy way to get an overview of an unfamiliar city. We're impressed by how many people we know who have confessed that they were very glad they had taken one of these tours, which helped them orient themselves and find out what they wanted to go back and see thoroughly. Almost all the tour guides have passed stiff tests to get their licenses.

The best-known Athens-based tour groups are **CHAT Tours,** Odos Stadiou 4 (☎ 01/322-3137 or 01/322-3886); **GO Tours,** Odos Voulis 31–33 (☎ 01/322-5951); and **Key Tours,** Odos Kaliroïs 4 (☎ 01/923-3166). Each offers half- and full-day tours of Athens, Athens by Night tours, and day excursions from Athens. Expect to pay about $40 for a half-day tour, $60 for a full-day tour, and at least $60 for Athens by Night (including dinner, and sometimes a folk-dancing performance at the Dora Stratou Theater). With all these tours, you must book, and usually pay, in advance. At that time, you will be told what time you will be picked up at your hotel, or where you should meet the tour.

Each company also offers excursions from Athens, including the **Temple of Poseidon at Sounion** (usually about $30 for a half-day trip including swimming and a meal), **Delphi** (usually about $60 for a full day, including a stop at the Monastery of Osios Loukas and the village of Arachova), and the **Peloponnese** (usually about $80 for a very full 1-day trip to Corinth, Mycenae, and Epidaurus).

If your time in Greece is limited, you may find one of these day trips considerably less stressful than renting a car for the day and driving yourself.

Educational Tours & Cruises, Odos Artemidos 1, Glyfada (☎ 01/898-1741), can arrange tours in Athens and throughout Greece, including individual tours.

Amphitriton Holidays, Karayiorgi Servias 2 (☎ 01/322-8884), offers tours with an emphasis on history and education.

If you want to hire a private guide, you can speak to the concierge at your hotel or contact the **Association of Guides,** Apollonas 91 (☎ 01/322-9705). Expect to pay about $100 for a 5-hour tour.

9 Spectator Sports

The Greeks are passionately devoted to soccer and basketball, and betting (legal and nationwide) on sports events is heavy. All sports events are listed in the Greek press and sometimes in the English-language daily *Athens News*. You can also try to get information by stopping by the **Greek National Tourist Office,** Odos Amerikis 2, and asking if anyone is playing (Unless you speak Greek, do not try this by phone). The best-known soccer teams are the fierce rivals **Olympiakos** (Piraeus) and **Panathanaikos** (Athens).

The Greek national basketball team endeared itself to the nation when it won the European Championship by defeating Russia in 1987. Celebrations went on all night. (We should know: We were among the few people in Greece trying to sleep that night). The championships take place in July or August in different venues in Europe. You may also be able to catch a game between Greek teams in Athens.

If you're in Greece when major international sports events in the world of football or basketball take place, you probably will be able to see them on Greek television or CNN. If you're in Greece during Wimbledon, you may have to settle for listening to the live radio coverage on the BBC.

10 Shopping

THE SHOPPING SCENE

You may find a copy of the monthly magazine *Athens Today,* which has a shopping section, in your hotel room, or you can pick one up at the **Greek National Tourist**

Office, Odos Amerikis 2. Keep in mind that most of the restaurants and shops featured pay for the privilege.

You're in luck shopping in Athens, because almost everything you'll probably want to buy can be found in the central city. As you might expect, the **Commercial Triangle,** bounded by Omonia, Syntagma, and Monastiraki squares, contains most of the shops frequented by Athenians, including a number of large **department stores** (see below).

Monastiraki has its famous **flea market,** which is especially lively on Sundays. Although there's a vast amount of ticky-tacky stuff for sale here, there are also still some real finds, including retro clothes and old copper. Many Athenians furnishing new homes head here to try to pick up old treasures.

The **Plaka** has pretty much cornered the market on souvenir shops, with enough T-shirts, reproductions of antiquities (including obscene playing cards, drink coasters, bottle openers, and more), fishermen's sweaters (increasingly made in the Far East), and jewelry (often not real gold) to circle the globe.

In the Plaka-Monastiraki area, several shops worth seeking out include **Stavros Melissinos,** the Poet-Sandalmaker of Athens, Odos Pandrossou 89 (☎ 01/321-9247); **Iphanta,** the weaving workshop, Odos Selleu 6 (☎ 01/322-3628); **Emanuel Masmanidis' Gold Rose Jewelry Shop,** Odos Pandrossou 85 (☎ 01/321-5662); the **Center of Hellenic Tradition,** Odos Mitropoleos 59 and Odos Pandrossou 36 (☎ 01/321-3023), which sells arts and crafts; and the **National Welfare Organization,** Odos Ipatias 6 and Apollonos, Plaka (☎ 01/325-0524), where a portion of the proceeds from everything sold here (including handsome woven and embroidered carpets) goes to the National Welfare Organization, which encourages traditional crafts.

Kolonaki, up on the slopes of Mount Likavitos, is boutique heaven—but a better place to window-shop than buy, since much of what you see here is imported and heavily taxed. If you're here during the January or August sales, you may find some bargains. If not, it's still a lot of fun to work your way up pedestrian Odos Voukourestiou, along Odos Tsakalof and Odos Anagnostopoulou (with perhaps the most expensive boutiques in Athens), before collapsing at a cafe by one of the pedestrian shopping streets in Kolonaki Square. Then you can engage in the other really serious business of Kolonaki: people watching. Give yourself about 15 minutes to figure out the season's must-have accessory. Since it was Timberland boots and spaghetti-strap, semitransparent tops at press time, it's bound to be something else soon.

SHOPPING A TO Z
ANTIQUES

Warning: If you're hoping to take home an antique—perhaps an icon or a wood carving—keep in mind that not everything sold as an antique is genuine, and that it's illegal to take antiquities and icons more than 100 years old out of Greece without a hard-to-obtain export license.

If you're looking for first editions, prints showing 19th-century Athens, or a silver sword or amber worry beads, try **Antiqua,** Leoforos Vas. Sofias 2–4, just off Syntagma Square (☎ 01/323-2220). This is one of Athens's oldest antiques stores, and perhaps the best, with handsome ancient coins and old icons—but take heed of the warning above.

Also near Syntagma Square, **Giannoukos,** Vas. Amalias 4 (☎ 01/324-1700), has a sound reputation, and the small but tempting **Mati,** Odos Voukourestiou 20 (☎ 01/362-6238), has some antiques as well as icons, and a range of items in blue glass to ward off the evil eye, including eyes, vases, and bowls. If you're near Syntagma

Museum Shops

Keep in mind that most museums have shops. Especially good are those at the National Archaeological Museum, the Goulandris Museum of Cycladic Art, and the Museum of the Musical Instrument.

Square and looking for antiquarian books, maps, and prints, try **Salaminia,** with branches at Panepistimiou 47 (☎**01/321-8155**) and Odos Stadiou 22 (☎ **01/ 331-3944**).

Over in Monastiraki on Odos Pandrossou, there are any number of pseudo-antiques shops, and one or two good ones. **Martinos,** Odos Pandrossou 50 (☎ **01/ 321-3110**), has Venetian and ancient glass, embroidery and kilims, swords and side tables. **Anita Patrikiadon,** Odos Pandrossou 58 (☎ **01/324-6325**), also has a good selection of weavings and wood carvings. If you're more interested in reproductions than the real thing, **Orpheus,** Odos Pandrossou 28B (☎ **01/324-5034**), has museum copies of classical and Byzantine art.

Up in Kolonaki, the eponymous proprietor of **Argyriadis,** Patriarchou Ioakim 42 (☎ **01/725-1727**), specializes in 18th-century furniture and also has a variety of more transportable bibelots. **Mihalarias Art,** Odos Alopekis 1–3 (☎ **01/721-3079**), in a gorgeous neoclassical Kolonaki mansion, has museum-quality furniture, paintings, and just about anything else you can imagine.

BOOKS

✪ **Eleftheroudakis,** with its old quarters still open at Odos Nikis 4 (☎ **01/ 322-2255**), has a new eight-story headquarters at Leoforos Panepistimiou 17 (☎ **01/ 331-4480**), with Athens's widest selection of English-language books and a good selection of CDs, including much Greek music. There's also a cafe (with some free newspapers and journals to read) and clean rest rooms. The staff seems amazingly tolerant of tourists who stop by to read, but not buy, their wide selection of books on Greece. Check the bulletin board by the cafe to see if there are any readings by local authors (sometimes in English) or upcoming concerts.

Compendium, Odos Nikis 28 (☎ **01/322-1248**), on the edge of the Plaka near Syntagma Square, is a small but fine English-language bookstore, selling both new and used fiction and nonfiction, plus magazines and maps. Just off Panepistimiou and steps from Syntagma Square, **Reymondos,** Voukourestiou 18 (☎ **01/364-8189**), has a good selection in English (including some dazzling photo books on Greece), stocks English-language magazines and newspapers, and is often open after usual shop hours. In the stoa, one floor up, **Kakoulides** (The Book Nest), Panepistimiou 25–29 (☎ **01/ 323-1703**), has a wide selection of books on Greece, as does **Pantelis,** Amerikis 11, up from Panepistimiou (☎ **01/362-3673**).

In Kolonaki, try **Rombos,** Kapsali 6, off Kolonaki Square (☎ **01/724-2082**), for English-language books, including books on Greece.

CRAFTS

There are lots of mass-produced "crafts" for sale in Athens, which is why it's good to know about some shops that have quality work. **Center of Hellenic Tradition,** Mitropoleos 3 and Pandrossou 36 in the Plaka (☎ **01/321-3023**), is a wonderful place for quality traditional Greek art, including icons, pottery, wood carvings, embroideries, and prints. Best of all, you can take a break from shopping and look at the Acropolis while you have coffee and a snack at the cafe here.

Also in the Plaka, **Anoyi,** Sotiros 1 (☎ **01/322-6487**), is an absolute delight, with old prints, furniture, reproduced icons, and fabrics. On the fringes of the Plaka, the **National Welfare Organization** (Ethnikos Organismos Pronias), Ypatias 6 and Apollonos, just east of the Cathedral (☎ **01/325-0524**), has gorgeous embroideries, rugs, pottery, icons, and, usually, very bored and unhelpful salespeople. The **Greek Women's Institution,** Kolokotroni 3 (☎ **01/325-0524**), specializes in embroidery from the islands and copies of embroideries from the Benaki Museum.

DEPARTMENT STORES

Head toward Omonia Square to see the city's best-known department stores: **Lambropoulos,** Eolou 99 (☎ 01/324-5811); **Minion,** Veranzerou 17 at Patission (☎ 01/523-8901); **British Home Stores** (BHS) and **Klaudatos,** Kratinou 3–5 at Odos Athinas (☎ 01/324-1915). BHS occupies the first two floors including mezzanine; Klaudatos all the upper floors. The building faces north on Kotzia Square 3 blocks south of Omonia on Athinas and isn't easy to see until you're right at one of the two entrances. The self-service restaurant on the eighth floor is just a bit lower than the Acropolis and treats the startling view casually.

FASHION

If you do any window-shopping in Athens, you'll soon see how expensive most things are, except during the January and August sales. Not surprisingly, Athens's poshest clothing stores are in **Kolonaki.** Much of what you'll see here is American or European and carries a hefty import duty; most of the rest is Greek designer wear. Good streets to browse include Voukourestiou, Kanari, Milioni, Tsakalof, Patriarchou Ioakim, and the most expensive street in town, Anagnostopoulou—where Versace, Ferre, Lagerfeld, and Guy Laroche have boutiques, as do well-known Athenian designers such as Aslanis, Nikos, Filemon, and Sofos. If shoes are your thing, head for Tsakalof, with a heavy concentration of the shoe stores that most Athenians find irresistible.

Here are a few individual shops near Kolonaki Square: **Artisti Italiani,** Kanari 5 (☎ 01/363-9085), has Italian-designed clothes for men and women. The well-known French firm **Lacoste** has men's and women's sportswear at Solonos 5 (☎ 01/361-8030). **Jade,** Anagnostopoulou 3 (☎ 01/364-5922), **Ritsi,** Tsakalof 13 (☎ 01/363-8677), and **Sofos,** Anagnostopoulou 5 (☎ 01/361-8713), all sell designer women's clothing. **Desmina,** Koubare 5 (☎ 01/364-1010), has sportier women's clothing, with lots of pantsuits and casual wear. **New Man,** Solonos 25, corner of Voukourestiou (☎ 01/360-8876), has casual men's clothes. See also "Shoes" and "Sweaters," below.

JEWELRY

All that glitters most definitely is not gold in Athens's myriad jewelry shops. Unless you know your gold very well, you'll want to exercise caution in shopping here, especially in the stores that cater to tourists in the Plaka and Monastiraki.

We've been pleased with the quality and prices at Emanuel Masmanidis's small **Gold Rose Jewelry shop,** Odos Pandrossou 85 (☎ **01/321-5662**). Others report satisfaction in dealings with **Stathis,** Pa. Venizelou 2, Mitropoleos Square (☎ **01/322-4691**).

Greece's best-known jewelry stores are **Zolotas,** Odos Panepistimiou 10 (☎ **01/361-3782**), and **Lalaounis,** Odos Panepistimiou 6 (☎ **01/362-1371**), both at the foot of pedestrian Odos Voukourestiou. Both shops have gorgeous reproductions of ancient and Byzantine jewelry, as well as their own designs. You can see more of the

---

Pack & Send

Pallis, Odos Ermou 8 (☎ 01/324-2115), has a good selection of envelopes, tape, wrapping paper, and pens and pencils—everything you might need to wrap and send a package home.

Lalaounis designs at their own museum (see section 2, "More Museums," above). Up on Voukourestiou, there are at least five excellent jewelers, of which we prefer **Mati,** Voukourestiou 20 (see "Antiques," above). A bit further along, **Ioannidis,** Valaoritou 9 (☎ 01/361-0677), is the place to head if you want a Faberge egg or Piaget watch.

One of the best shops for silver is **Nisiotis,** Lekka 23, just off Syntagma Square (☎ 01/324-4183). Off Syntagma, but toward Plaka, **Pantelis Mountis,** Odos Apollonos 27 (☎ and fax 01/324-4574), has reproductions of Byzantine icons and religious medals.

MARKETS & GROCERIES

✪ **The Central Market** (fish, meat, vegetables, and more) on Odos Athinas is open Monday through Saturday from about 8am to 6pm. You may not want to take advantage of all of the bargain prices (two sheeps' heads were going for the price of one when we were last here), but this is a great place to buy Greek spices and herbs, cheeses, and sweets—and to see how Athens is fed.

Every Friday from about 8am until 2pm, **Odos Xenokratous** in Kolonaki turns into a street market selling flowers, fruits, and vegetables. This is a very different scene from the rowdy turmoil of the Central Market, although it's lively enough. Many Kolonaki matrons come here with their Filipino servants, then let the servants lug their purchases home while they head off for some shopping and light lunch (perhaps at the fashionable **To Kafenio**).

MUSIC

You won't have trouble finding **Metropolis,** Odos Panepistimiou 66 and Odos Tsakalof 15 (☎ 01/361-1463), Athens's largest music store: just follow the booming vibrations. At **Slammin',** Odos Asklepiou 22 (☎ 01/361-3611), you can buy CDs and clothes. The excellent bookstore **Eleftheroudakis** (see above) has a wide selection of CDs.

SHOES

If you walk along Odos Tsakalof or Odos Patriarchou Ioakim in Kolonaki, or almost any street in central Athens, you'll begin to get an idea of how serious Greeks are about their shoes. Sometimes the biggest crowds in town on a Saturday night are the window-shoppers eyeing the shoes on Odos Ermou off Syntagma Square. Some good-quality stores include **Kaloyirou,** Pandrossou 12, Plaka (☎ 01/331-0727), or Patriarchou Ioakim 4, Kolonaki (☎ 01/722-8804); **Mouriadis,** Odos Stadiou 4 (☎ 01/322-1229); and **Moschoutis,** Voulis 12 at Ermou (☎ 01/324-6504).

SWEATERS

Several travelers recommend **Nick's Corner,** Pandrossou 48, Monastiraki (☎ 01/321-2990), for the heavy-knit sweaters that are usually bargains in Greece. Look downstairs. You'll see many more sweaters along Odos Adrianou in the Plaka and, if you don't mind that many of these "authentic" Greek sweaters are made by machines and imported from third-world countries, you can find decent prices almost every-where.

SWEETS

Greeks love sweets, and you will have no problem satisfying your sweet tooth here. If anything, you'll come up gasping for air as you eat the seriously sweet sweets that most Greeks adore.

The long-established **Aristokratikon,** Karayioryi Servias 9, just off Syntagma Square (☎ 01/322-0546), has excellent chocolates, glazed pistachio nuts, and *loukoumia* (Turkish delight). Beware—even chocoholics may find the truffles coated with white chocolate too sweet. Next, head over to **Karavan,** the hole-in-the-wall at Voukourestiou 11 (no phone), with the best Levantine delights in town.

Serving excellent coffee and sweets, **K. Kotsolis Pastry Shop,** Odos Adrianou 112, is an oasis of old-fashioned charm in the midst of the Plaka souvenir shops.

Loukoumades are the Greek donut with a difference—they are about the size of an American donut hole, served hot, drenched in honey, and covered with cinnamon. Delicious. If you're near Syntagma Square, try **Doris,** Praxitelous 30 (☎01/323-2671), and if you're nearer Omonia Square, try **Aigina,** Panepistimiou 46 (☎ 01/381-4621). Better yet, try both.

11 Athens After Dark

Greeks enjoy their nightlife so much that they take an afternoon nap to rest up for it. The evening often begins with a leisurely *volta* (stroll); you'll see this in most neighborhoods, including the main drags through the Plaka and Kolonaki Square. Most Greeks don't think of dinner until at least 9pm in winter, 10pm in summer. Around midnight the party may move on to a club for music and dancing.

Check the daily *Athens News,* or the daily *Kathimerini* insert in the *International Herald Tribune* sold at most major newsstands, for current cultural and entertainment events, including films, lectures, theater, music, and dance. The weekly *Hellenic Times* and monthly *Now in Athens* list nightspots, restaurants, movies, theater, and much more.

FESTIVALS

THE ATHENS FESTIVAL   During the Athens Festival (from the beginning of June to the end of September), famous Greek and foreign artists perform on the slopes of the Acropolis. You may catch an opera, concert, drama, or ballet here—and, usually, see the Acropolis illuminated over your shoulder at the same time. To enjoy the performance to the fullest, bring some kind of cushion to sit on (the cushions available are often minimal). Schedules are usually available at the **Athens Festival Office,** Odos Stadiou 4 (☎ 01/322-1459, 01/322-3111, or 01/322-3110, ext. 137). The office is open Monday through Saturday from 8:30am to 2pm and 5 to 7pm, Sunday from 10am to 1pm. If available—and that's a big if—tickets can also be purchased at the **Odeon of Herodes Atticus** (☎ 01/323-2771) several hours before a performance. Shows usually begin at 9pm.

THE LYCABETTUS (LIKAVITOS) FESTIVAL   There are usually pop-music concerts and other special events at the outdoor amphitheater near the top of Likavitos during the summer. For information, check with the **Athens Festival Office,** Odos Stadiou 4 (☎ 01/322-1459 or 01/322-3111 to 3119, ext. 137).

THE EPIDAURUS FESTIVAL   From late June to late August, performances of ancient Greek tragedies and comedies (usually given in modern Greek translations) take place at Epidaurus in Greece's most beautiful ancient theater. This makes for a long evening, but a memorable one—and since you don't have to do the driving (about 2 hr. each way), it doesn't have to be exhausting. For information, check with the **Athens Festival Office** (see above). (You can also sometimes get tickets at Epidaurus just before a performance.)

THE PERFORMING ARTS

The acoustically marvelous new **Megaron Mousikis Concert Hall,** Leoforos Vas. Sofias 89 (☎ 01/729-0391 or 01/728-2333), hosts a wide range of classical-music programs that include quartets, operas in concert, symphonies, and recitals. On performance nights, the box office is open Monday through Friday from 10am to 6pm, Saturday from 10am to 2pm, and Sunday from 6pm to 10:30pm. Tickets run Dr1,000 to Dr20,000 ($3.35 to $67), depending on the performance. The Megaron has a limited summer season, but is in full swing the rest of the year.

The **Greek National Opera** performs at the **Olympia Theater,** Odos Akadimias 59, at Mavromihali (☎ 01/361-2461). The summer months are usually off-season.

The **Pallas Theater,** Odos Voukourestiou 1 (☎ 01/322-8275), has many jazz and rock concerts, as well as some classical performances. Prices vary from performance to performance, but you can usually get a cheap ticket for about Dr3,000 ($10).

The **Hellenic American Union,** Odos Massalias 22 between Kolonaki and Omonia squares (☎ 01/362-9886), often hosts performances of English-language theater and American-style music (tickets are usually about Dr3,000/$10). If you arrive early, check out art shows or photo exhibitions in the adjacent gallery.

Since 1953, the **Dora Stratou Folk Dance Theater** has been giving performances of traditional Greek folk dances. Athenians were alarmed in 1998 when Dora Stratou announced that she might have to close her company at the end of the 1998 season unless a promised government subvention materialized. The Dora Stratou troupe is such an institution that it's almost impossible to imagine that performances at the Dora Stratou Theater on Filopappos Hill won't continue. At present, performances take place May through September at 10:15pm, with additional performances at 8:15pm on Wednesday and Sunday. There are no performances on Monday. You can buy tickets at the **box office,** Odos Scholio 8 in the Plaka, from 8am to 2pm (☎ 01/924-4395, or 01/921-4650 after 5:30pm). Prices range from Dr2,500 to Dr3,500 ($8 to $12). Tickets are also usually available at the theater before performances.

Seen from the Pnyx, **Sound and Light Shows** illuminate (sorry) Athens's history by telling the story of the Acropolis. As lights pick out monuments on the Acropolis and the music swells, the narrator tells of the Persian attack, the Periclean days of glory, the invidious Turkish occupation—you get the idea. Shows are held April through October. Performances in English begin at 9pm and last 45 minutes. Tickets can be purchased at the **Athens Festival Office,** Odos Stadiou 4 (☎ 01/322-7944), or at the entrance to the Sound and Light (☎ 01/922-6210). Tickets are Dr1,500 ($5) for adults and Dr600 ($2) for students. You'll hear the narrative best if you do not sit too close to the very loud public address system.

THE CLUB, MUSIC & BAR SCENE

This scene changes *very* quickly, with last year's hot spot becoming this year's ho-hum. Your best bet here is to have a local friend; failing that, try asking someone at your hotel. The listings in the weekly *Hellenic Times* can be very helpful. If you ask a taxi driver, he's likely to take you to either his cousin George's joint or the place that gives him drinks for bringing you.

RUNNING THE GAUNTLET   Wherever you go, you're likely to face an entrance fee of at least Dr2,000 ($7). Thereafter, each drink will cost—ouch!—between Dr2,000 and Dr5,000 ($7 to $17). Many clubs plop down a bottle on your table that's

Open in August

A great many popular after-dark spots close in August, when much of Athens flees the summer heat to the country. Some places that stay open include a number of bars, cafes, ouzeries, and tavernas on the pedestrian **Iraklion Walkway** near the Theseion. **Stavlos,** the restaurant, bar, and disco popular with all ages, remains open on August weekends. Nearby, **Berlin Booze,** which caters to a young crowd and specializes in rock and roll, is open most nights; **Ambibagio** has quite genuine Greek music. The sweet shop **Aistisis** has great views of the Acropolis and stays open as late as the nearby bars.

labeled as, but doesn't necessarily contain, Johnny Walker Red or Black, and then try very hard to charge you about Dr30,000 ($100) whether you drink it or not. It's best to go to these clubs with someone *trustworthy* who knows the scene.

TRADITIONAL MUSIC

Walk the streets of the Plaka on any night and you'll find plenty of tavernas offering pseudo-traditional live music. As noted, many are serious clip joints, where if you sit down and ask for a glass of water, you'll be charged $100 for a bottle of scotch. At most of these places, there's an entrance charge (usually at least Dr3,000/$10). We've had good reports on **Taverna Mostrou,** Odos Mnissikleos 22 (☎ 01/324-2441), which is large, old, and best known for traditional Greek music and dancing. Shows begin around 11pm and usually last until 2am. The entrance fee of Dr5,000 ($17) includes a fixed-menu supper. A la carte fare is available but expensive (as are drinks). Nearby, **Palia Taverna Kritikou,** Odos Mnissikleos 24 (☎ 01/322-2809), is another lively open-air taverna with music and dancing.

Several tavernas that usually offer low-key music include fashionable **Daphne's,** Odos Lysikratous 4 (☎ 01/322-7971); **Nefeli,** Odos Panos 24 (☎ 01/321-2475); **Dioyenis,** Odos Sellei (Shelley) 4 (☎ 01/324-7933); **Stamatopoulou,** Odos Lissiou 26 (☎ 01/322-8722); and longtime favorite **Xinos,** Odos Agelou Geronta 4 (☎ 01/322-1065).

For more intimate and unusual entertainment, climb Mnissikleos toward the Acropolis, turn right on Tholou, and find **Apanemia** and **Esperides,** two smoky little cafes that are usually filled with hip young Athenians nursing drinks from Dr1,500 ($5) and enjoying music that's both traditional and innovative.

POP MUSIC

For Greek pop music, try **Zoom,** Odos Kidathineon 37, in the heart of the Plaka (☎ 01/322-5920). Performers, who are likely to have current hit albums, are showered with carnations here by adoring fans. The minimum order is Dr5,000 ($17). If you want to check out the local rock and blues scene along with small doses of metal, Athenian popsters play at **Memphis,** Odos Ventiri 5, near the Hilton Hotel east of Syntagma Square (☎ 01/722-4104); open Tuesday through Friday from 10:30pm to 2:30am.

REMBETIKA & BOUZOUKIA

Those interested in authentic *rembetika* (music of the urban poor and dispossessed) and *bouzoukia* (traditional and pop music featuring the *bouzouki,* a kind of guitar, today almost always loudly amplified) should consult their hotel receptionist, the listings in the weekly *Hellenic Times,* or listings in *Kathimerini,* the daily insert in the *International Herald Tribune,* to find out what's going on. Shows usually don't start until nearly midnight, and though there's rarely a cover charge, drinks can cost as much as Dr5,000 ($17). Many clubs are closed during the summer, and many are far from the center of town, so budget another Dr2,500 to Dr5,000 ($8 to $17) for round-trip taxi fare. Among these more distant upscale bouzoukia are the **Dioyenis Palace,** Syngrou 259 (☎ 01/942-4267), a lot farther out than you might think, and **Poseidonio,** Poseidonos 18, Elliniko, way out by the airport (☎ 01/ 894-1033).

One of the more central places for rembetika is the **Stoa Athanaton,** Sofokleous 19, in the Central Meat Market (☎ 01/321-4362), which serves good food and has live rembetika from 3 to 6pm and after midnight. It's closed Sunday; the minimum is Dr3,000 ($10). The smoke-filled **Rembetiki Istoria** (☎ 01/642-4937), housed in a neoclassical building at Odos Ippokratous 181, features old-style rembetika music, played to a mixed crowd of older regulars and younger students. The music usually doesn't start until at least 11pm, but the seats go earlier. **Taximi,** Odos Isavron 29, Exarchia (☎ 01/363-9919), is consistently popular; drinks cost Dr3,500 ($12) and it's closed Sunday and in July and August. Open Wednesday through Monday, **Frangosyriani,** Odos Arachovis 57, Exarchia (☎ 01/360-0693), specializes in the music of rembetika legend Markos Vamvakaris.

JAZZ

The fine ✪ **Half-Note Jazz Club,** Trivonianou 17, Mets, near the Athens First Cemetery (☎ 01/921-3310), brings in good artists from Europe and the United States. **Jazz Bar** (☎ 01/360-5889) serves up music at Tsakalof 10 in Kolonaki. **Rock and Roll** (☎ 01/721-7127) is at Loukianou 6 in Kolonaki.

DANCE CLUBS & DISCOS

You can find most Athenian dance clubs by following the sound of booming music. On the outskirts of the Plaka, the second-floor **Booze,** Odos Kolokotroni 57 (☎ 01/ 324-0944), blasts danceable rock to a hip student crowd. There's art on every wall, gelled stage lights, and two bars. Admission is Dr1,500 ($5); drinks are Dr1,000 ($3.35).

If it's disco you're craving, head east to **Absolut,** Odos Filellinon 23. If you feel a bit too old here, head north to **The Wild Rose,** in the arcade at Odos Panepistimiou 10 (☎ 01/364-2160). Up the street, **Mercedes Rex,** Odos Panepistimiou 48 (☎ 01/ 361-4591), has even more diversity.

GAY & LESBIAN BARS

The gay and lesbian scene here is vigorous, but not always easily accessible to foreigners. Some gay and lesbian groups advertise get-togethers in the English-language press. **Granazi,** Odos Lebesi 20 (☎ 01/325-3979), is popular, and the best-known alternative is **E . . . Kai?** ("So What?"), across Syngrou at Iossif ton Rogon 12 (☎ 01/ 922-1742). In upscale Kolonaki, **Alexander's,** Anagnostopoulou 44 (☎ 01/ 364-6660), is more sedate and has more variety. See also "For Gay & Lesbian Travelers" in chapter 3.

There's also a lively transvestite cruising scene along Leoforos Syngrou in Makriyanni.

MOVIES

Central Athens has lots of air-conditioned theaters showing new-release Greek, American, and European films. Listings appear in the *Athens News* and in the weekly *Hellenic Times.*

If you're in Athens in summer, keep an eye out for listings of neighborhood open-air cinemas, still a very pleasant way to pass an evening, although some old favorites have closed in recent years. Many of the open-air cinemas are family owned and run, and all are great places to watch Athenian families watching films—which is to say, talking to each other, pursuing toddlers who are trying to run away, munching snacks and sipping cold drinks, all the while keeping up a running commentary on the film. We're fond of the **Dexameni** (☎ 01/362-3942) in Dexameni Square, Kolonaki, where there always seems to be a little breeze on a hot evening.

12 Piraeus: A Jumping-Off Point to the Islands

Piraeus has been the port of Athens since antiquity and is still where you catch most island boats and cruise ships. What's confusing is that Piraeus has **three harbors:** the main harbor (**Megas Limani**), where you'll see everything from tankers to island boats and cruise ships; Zea Marina (**Zea Limani**), the port for most of the swift hydrofoils that dart to the islands; and **Mikrolimano** (Little Harbor, also called Turkolimano, or Turkish Harbor), with a yacht harbor and a number of fish restaurants. As if that weren't confusing enough, the absence of helpful signs at both the main harbor and Zea Limani and the constant hustle and bustle here mean that this is not an easy place to navigate. To be on the safe side, even if you have your tickets, try to get here an hour before your ship sails—and don't be surprised if it leaves late. And since schedules depend on the weather, and sailings are often delayed or canceled, it's not a good idea to plan to return to Athens by boat less than 24 hours before your flight home.

As in antiquity, today's Piraeus has the seamier side of a sailors' port of call and the color and bustle of an active harbor—both aspects, somewhat sanitized, were portrayed in the film *Never on Sunday*. Piraeus also has a sprawling street market just off the main harbor, where you can buy produce brought each day on island boats, including bread baked that morning on distant islands. There are a number of fish restaurants here, but many are overpriced and serve fish that's less fresh than the bread. You're probably not going to fall in love with Piraeus, but if you have some time to kill, here are some suggestions.

ESSENTIALS

GETTING THERE   By Metro   The fastest and easiest way to Piraeus is to take the metro from Omonia Square or Monastiraki to the last stop (Dr75/25¢), which will leave you 1 block from the domestic port. (This can feel like a very long block if you are carrying heavy luggage.)

By Bus   From Syntagma Square take the Green Depot bus no. 40 from the corner of Odos Filellinon; it will leave you 1 block from the international port, about a 10-minute walk along the water from the domestic port. From the airport, bus no. 19 goes to Piraeus; the fare is Dr300 ($1).

By Taxi   A taxi from Syntagma Square will cost up to Dr2,000 ($7). A taxi from the airport to the port costs about Dr3,000 ($10).

A Word of Caution

Piraeus is not a good place for men or women to explore at night. Stick to the harbor front.

RETURNING TO ATHENS   The easiest way is to take the metro to central Athens, to either Monastiraki or Omonia Square. Most taxi drivers will try to overcharge tourists disembarking from the boats. They often offer a flat rate two or three times the legal fare. If you stand on the dock, you'll get no mercy. The only option is to pay up, try to get a policeman to help you, or walk to a nearby street, hail a cab, and hope for a fair rate.

VISITOR INFORMATION   For boat schedules, transit information, and other tourist information 24 hours a day, dial ☎ **171.** The *Athens News* and the *Kathimerini* insert in the *International Herald Tribune* print major ferry schedules. The closest **Greek National Tourist Organization (EOT)** office (☎ **01/453-7107**) is inconveniently located on the street above Zea Marina (the hydrofoil port) on the second floor of a shopping arcade stocked with yacht supplies. It's open Monday through Friday from 9am to 2:30pm, but its limited resources probably won't warrant the 20-minute walk from the ferry piers. You'd do better to try to get a ferry schedule from the **GNTO** office in central Athens at Odos Amerikis 2 (☎ **01/331-0437**).

FAST FACTS   There are several **banks** in Piraeus along the waterfront. The **National Bank,** on Odos Ethniki Antistaseos, has extended hours in summer. A portable **post office** opposite the Aegina ferry pier also offers currency exchange; it's open Monday through Saturday from 8am to 8pm, Sunday from 8am to 6pm. The **main post office** is at Ethniki Antistaseos and Dimitriou streets; it's usually open from 8am to 4pm. The **telephone office (OTE)** is a block away from the post office and is usually open 24 hours a day. There is another branch by the water, on Akti Miaouli at Odos Merarchias, open daily from 7am to 9:30pm. You'll find secure **luggage storage** in the metro station at the **Central Travel Agency** (☎ **01/411-5611**); the cost is Dr1,000 ($3.35) per piece per day, and hours are usually 6am to 8pm.

TICKETS TO THE ISLANDS   The quay of the main harbor is lined with **ticket agents,** many concentrated in Plateia Karaiskaki; some sell tickets for one or two lines or destinations only, some for more. Usually, there's a sign in the window telling you what the agent sells. Almost every agent will tell you that you're getting a good deal; almost no agent will give you one. Some readers have reported good luck dealing with **Explorations Unlimited,** Odos Kapodistriou 2 (☎ **01/411-6395** or 01/411-1243), just off Akti Poseidonos near the metro station, open Monday through Friday from 8am to 7pm and Saturday from 9am to 2pm.

FERRIES TO THE ISLANDS   You will be confused as to where to catch your boat; this is inevitable. Allow plenty of time. Even the person you buy your ticket from may give you a bum steer. Any information below may change at any moment. Sorry—but we thought you should know the truth!

Ferry tickets can be purchased at a ticket office up to 1 hour before departure; after that they can usually be bought on the boat. To book first-class cabins or buy advance-sale tickets, see one of the **harborside travel agents** (around Karaiskaki Square by the domestic ferries and along Akti Miaouli, opposite the Crete ferries). Most open at 6am and some will hold your baggage for the day (but without security). The **GNTO** publishes a list of weekly sailings, and the **tourist police** (☎ **01/171**) or the **Port Authority** (☎ **01/451-1311**) can provide you with schedule information.

Boats for the eastern Cyclades (including Mikonos and Santorini) usually leave in the morning from Akti Tzelepi across from Plateia Karaiskaki. Aegina boats usually leave from Akti Poseidonos. Boats for Rhodes usually sail in the afternoon from Akti Miaouli. Boats for the western Cyclades (including Sifnos) usually sail in the early evening from Akti Kalimassioti near Plateia Karaiskaki. Boats for Crete usually sail in

Aegean Ferries ②
Crete Ferries ⑤
Cyclades Ferries ④
Flying Dolphins to
  Poros, Hydra, Spetses ⑦
International Ferries ⑥
Northeast Aegean Ferries ③
Saronic Gulf Ferries,
  Flying Dolphin to Aegina ①

the early evening from Akti Kondyli. Many additional island boats leave from the quay opposite the metro station. Boats heading out of Greece leave from the quay on Akti Miaouli farthest away from the quays near the metro and train stations. Boats for Aegina, Poros, Hydra, Spetses, Peloponnesian ports, and Kithira go from Zea Marina, across the Piraeus peninsula and opposite the great harbor, from which it is a good 30-minute walk.

WHAT TO SEE & DO

If you're stuck between boats, you may not want to do anything except pass the time as quietly as possible. If so, you might simply walk inland from the harbor on Odos Demosthenous to Plateia Korai and sit at a cafe. Or, if you want to be by the sea, take the no. 904 bus (Dr100/35¢) from the main harbor to Akti Themistokleous, where there are also cafes.

More energetic suggestions include finding out if there's an **open-air theatrical performance** at the Kastella Theater, a few blocks inland from Mikrolimano. In the winter, performances are staged indoors, at the Public Theater on the green at Leoforos King Constantine. The **Sunday flea market** on and around Odos Alipedou and Odos Skylitsi is an equally crowded variation on the Monastiraki flea market with generally lower-quality goods. The daily **street market** just off the main harbor is a good place to get picnic supplies for your boat trip.

The **Maritime Museum,** Akti Themistokleous, near the pier for the hydrofoils (☎ 01/452-1598), has handsome models of ancient and modern ships. Don't miss the classical warship (*trireme*); scholars are still trying to figure out just how all those oarsmen rowed in unison. Open Tuesday through Saturday from 9am to 2pm; admission is Dr500 ($1.65). If you have time, stop by the **Archaeological Museum,** Odos Harilaou Trikoupi 32 (☎ **01/452-1598**), to see three superb monumental bronzes depicting a youth (some say Apollo) and two goddesses (some say Athena and Artemis). Open Tuesday through Sunday from 8:30am to 3pm; admission is Dr500 ($1.65).

WHERE TO STAY

We don't recommend an overnight stay in Piraeus, but if it makes sense in your travel plans, try one of these decent, moderately priced choices: the 103-unit **Hotel Mistral,** Odos Vassileos Pavlou 105, Kastella, 18533 Piraeus (☎ **01/411-7150**; fax 01/ 412-2096), with a nice roof garden; or the 29-unit **Ideal Hotel,** Odos Notara 142, 18531 Piraeus (☎ **01/451-1727**).

WHERE TO DINE

While there are some good restaurants in Piraeus, the places to eat along the harbor are generally mediocre at best. You'll do better if you walk in a few blocks along Odos Demosthenous to Plateia Korai, where there are a number of small cafes and restaurants actually patronized by Greeks. If you do decide to try one of the seafood restaurants in central Piraeus or Mikrolimani, make sure you know the price before ordering; some of these places prey on the unwary. If the final tab seems out of line, insist on a receipt, phone the tourist police, and sit tight.

For the best, freshest, most inventively prepared seafood you can imagine, see page 145 for a review of ✪ **Varoulko,** Deligeorgi 14 (☎ **01/411-2043**; fax 01/ 422-1283).

Aschimopapo (The Ugly Duckling). Odos Ionon 61, Ano Petralona. ☎ **01/346-3282.** Reservations suggested. Meals Dr2,500–Dr4,000 ($8–$13). No credit cards. Mon–Sat 8:30pm–1am. GREEK.

Ano Petralona is the neighborhood between the western edge of the Filopappos Hill and the Athens-Piraeus train line, technically in Piraeus. It's not far from the center of town, but you'll need a cab driver who either knows this taverna or has the Athens street guide to get here. The Aschimopapo is on the last stretch of Ionon before the ring road around the Filopappos Hill, and the entrance is marked only by a light. This place offers much more than the regular taverna fare, and it's worth the trouble. Their specialties are lamb cooked in a clay pot, snails, and *eksohiko* (pork baked in aluminum foil in individual servings), and they have many other good dishes, good mezedes, and wine from the barrel.

Dourambeis. Odos Dilaveri 29, Piraeus. ☎ **01/412-2092.** Reservations suggested. Fish prices (by the kilo) change daily, ranging from about Dr9,000–Dr14,000 ($30–$47). No credit cards. Mon–Sat noon–5pm and 8pm–1am. SEAFOOD.

This fish taverna near the Delphinario theater in Piraeus is where locals go when they want a good fish dinner. The decor is simple, the food excellent. The crayfish soup alone is worth the trip, but the whole point of going is for the excellent grilled fish.

Vasilainas. Etolikou 72, Ayia Sofia. ☎ **01/461-2457.** Reservations recommended Fri–Sat. Meals Dr5,000 ($17). No credit cards. Mon–Sat 8pm–midnight. SEAFOOD/GREEK.

There's no menu at this restaurant, located in an old grocery store in a suburb just north of Piraeus; for a flat fee of Dr5,000 ($17) per person you're presented with a steady flow of more than 15 dishes. Come here hungry, and even then you probably won't be able to eat everything set before you. There's plenty of seafood, plus good Greek dishes. This is a good place to come with friends, so you can compare notes on favorite dishes.

13 Day Trips from Athens

Although there are a number of tempting excursions from Athens, simply getting in and out of Athens is so unpleasant that we suggest you visit most of these places as you head off to the Peloponnese (**Daphni** and **Eleusis** are on the way) or visit Central or Northern Greece (you could take in Marathon, Brauron, or Rhamnous this way). Nonetheless, there are two excursions—the Monastery at Kaisariani and the Temple of Poseidon at Sounion—that are easily done as day trips from Athens.

All these excursions take you into Attica, today, as in antiquity, the name of the countryside around Athens. According to legend, the hero Theseus unified the 12 towns of Attica under Athens. Although by no means one of the most fertile areas of Greece, the Attic countryside provided Athens with wine grapes, olives, honey, grains, fruits, marvelous marble from **Mount Pentelicus** (Pendeli) and **Mount Hymettus** (Imittos), and silver from the mines at Laurium, near Sounion. Today the Attic *Mesogeion* (the word means "the middle of the earth" and refers to the Attic plain) is still known for its fine grapes, most often used in making white retsina.

Sadly, fires raged through much of Attica in summer 1998. Some forests on Mounts Pentelicus and Hymettus were totally destroyed. Much farmland was destroyed, and the museum at Marathon was almost lost. Be prepared to see the signs of these terrible fires for some years when you visit Attica.

THE TEMPLE OF POSEIDON AT SOUNION
70km (43 miles) E of Athens

One of the easiest and most popular day trips from Athens is to the 5th-century B.C. Temple of Poseidon on the cliffs above Cape Sounion, about 2 hours by bus outside Athens. This is a very popular place at sunset for individuals, families, and tour groups—so popular that, if at all possible, you should not come on a weekend.

The easiest way to visit Sounion is on an **organized tour** run by CHAT, Key, or GO tours (see Section 8, "Organized Tours," above). If you want to go on your own for far less money, take the Sounion bus leaving from Odos Mavromateon along the west side of the Pedion tou Areos park (off the eastern end of Leoforos Alexandras). Buses leave about every half hour, take 2 hours to reach Sounion, and cost under Dr1,200 ($4). To verify times, ask a Greek speaker to telephone the **local ticket office** (☎ 01/823-0179). Once you're in Sounion, you can catch a cab or walk the remaining kilometer to the temple.

If you drive to Sounion, heading out of Athens on Syngrou or Vouliagmenis boulevards, you'll probably fight your way through heavy traffic almost all the way, in both directions. Signs for Sounion appear around the Athens Airport.

WHAT TO SEE & DO
The Temple of Poseidon. ☎ **0292/39-363.** Admission Dr800 ($2.65). Daily 10am–sunset (sometimes in summer from 8am–sunset).

Cape Sounion is the southernmost point of Attica, and in antiquity, as today, sailors knew they were getting near Athens when they caught sight of the Temple of Poseidon's slender Doric columns. According to legend, it was at Sounion that the great Athenian hero Theseus's father, King Aegeus, awaited his son's return from his journey to Crete to slay the Minotaur. The king had told his son to have his ship return with white sails if he survived the encounter, with black sails if he met death in the Cretan labyrinth. In the excitement of his victory, Theseus forgot his father's words, and the ship returned with black sails. When Aegeus saw the black sails, he threw himself, heartbroken, into the sea—forever after known as the Aegean.

One of the things that makes Sounion so spectacular, other than its site, is that 15 of the temple's original 34 columns are still standing. A popular pastime here is trying to find the spot on one column where Lord Byron carved his name. After you find Byron's name, you may wish to sit in the shade of a column, enjoy the spectacular view over the sea, envy the solitude and quiet Byron found here, and recite these lines on Sounion from the poet's *Don Juan:*

> *Place me on Sunium's marbled steep,*
> *Where nothing, save the waves and I*
> *May hear our mutual murmurs sweep . . .*

It's easy to think that this sanctuary was purely a religious spot in antiquity. Nothing could be more wrong: the entire sanctuary (of which little remains other than the temple itself) was heavily fortified during the Peloponnesian War because of its strategic importance overlooking the sea routes. Much of the grain that fed Athens arrived from outside Attica in ships that had to sail past Cape Sounion. In fact, Sounion had something of an unsavory reputation as the haunt of pirates in antiquity; it would be uncharitable to think that their descendants run today's nearby souvenir shops, restaurants, and cafes.

If you wish, you can take a swim in the sea below Sounion and a snack at one of the overpriced restaurants. Better yet, bring a picnic to enjoy on the beach.

THE MONASTERY OF KAISARIANI (KESSARIANI) & MOUNT HYMETTUS (IMITTOS)
16km (10 miles) E of central Athens

The beautiful **Kaisariani Monastery** (☎ 01/723-6619) stands in a cool, bird-inhabited grove of pines and cypresses on the lower slopes of Mount Hymettus, famous for its beautiful marble and delicious honey. In fact, the 4th-century A.D. philosopher Synesius of Cyrene tells the story that the Sophists lured students to their lectures "not by the fame of their eloquence, but by pots of honey from Hymettus." This has long been a lovely place to escape the heat of Athens, especially after most of the bees left Hymettus and no longer vexed visitors. Alas, the forests were damaged in the fires of 1998, when four firemen died fighting the blazes. Keep in mind that the remaining pine groves here are a potential tinderbox. As always, be very careful if you smoke or use matches.

The easiest way to visit Kaisariani is to take a **taxi** from central Athens for about Dr4,000 ($13). Then, if you wish, you can return by bus, having spotted the bus stop on your way up to Kaisariani.

Every 20 minutes, **bus no. 224** leaves from Panepistimiou and Vas. Sofias, northeast of Syntagma Square, to the suburb of **Kaisariani.** It's a pleasant 2-kilometer walk (follow the signs) up the road to the wooded site, or you can take one of the cabs that waits for business by the bus stop.

We suggest that you do not drive unless you want to explore Mount Hymettus, which is no longer the woodsy place fabled in antiquity, but has become bleak after its recent fires. Kaisariani is irritatingly poorly signposted, and you may have trouble finding it, even with a good map.

AT&T Direct® Service

AT&T Access Numbers

Australia	1-800-881-011	Fiji	004-890-1001
Austria ○	022-903-011	Finland ●	9800-100-10
Belgium ●	0-800-100-10	France	0-800-99-0011
Brazil	000-8010	Germany	0-800-2255-288
China, PRC ▲	10811	Greece ●	00-800-1311
Colombia	980-11-0010	Guam	1-800-2255-288
Czech Rep. ▲	00-42-090-101	Honduras	800-0-123
Denmark	8001-0010	Hong Kong	800-96-1111
Ecuador ▲	999-119	Indonesia →	001-801-10
Egypt (Cairo) ●	510-0200	Ireland ✓	1-800-550-000

AT&T Direct® Service

AT&T Access Numbers

Australia	1-800-881-011	Fiji	004-890-1001
Austria ○	022-903-011	Finland ●	9800-100-10
Belgium ●	0-800-100-10	France	0-800-99-0011
Brazil	000-8010	Germany	0-800-2255-288
China, PRC ▲	10811	Greece ●	00-800-1311
Colombia	980-11-0010	Guam	1-800-2255-288
Czech Rep. ▲	00-42-090-101	Honduras	800-0-123
Denmark	8001-0010	Hong Kong	800-96-1111
Ecuador ▲	999-119	Indonesia →	001-801-10
Egypt (Cairo) ●	510-0200	Ireland ✓	1-800-550-000

Country	AT&T Access Number	Country	AT&T Access Number
Israel •	1-800-94-94-949	Portugal ▲	0800-800-128
Italy •	172-1011	Singapore ■	800-0111-111
Japan ▲	005-39-111	South Africa	0-800-99-0123
Japan ▲	0066-55-111	Spain	900-99-00-11
Korea, Republic •	0072-911	Sweden	020-799-111
Luxembourg ×	0-800-0111	Switzerland •	0-800-89-0011
Malaysia ◇	1-800-80-0011	Turkey •	00-800-12277
Netherlands •	0800-022-9111	Thailand †	001-999-111-11
New Zealand	000-911	U.K. ★✦	0800-89-0011
Norway	800-190-11	Venezuela	800-11-120
Panama	109	Vietnam ◇	1-201-0288
Philippines •	105-11		

FOR EASY CALLING WORLDWIDE

1. Just dial the AT&T Access Number for the country you are calling from.
2. Dial the phone number you're calling. 3. Dial your card number.

For access numbers not listed ask any operator for **AT&T Direct®** Service.
In the U.S. call 1-800-331-1140 for a wallet guide listing all worldwide AT&T Access Numbers.

Visit our Web site at: **www.att.com/traveler**

Bold faced countries permit country-to-country calling outside the U.S.

- ♦ Public phones require coin or card deposit.
- ▲ When calling from public phones use phones marked "Lenso".
- ■ May not be available from every phone/public phone.
- ○ **AT&T Direct** Service calls cannot be placed to this country from outside the U.S.
- × Public phones require local coin payment during call.
- ★✦ Use U.S. access number in N. Ireland.
- ◇ If call does not complete, use 0800-013-0011.
- Collect calling from public phones.
- ⬇ Service available in calling centers in Hanoi, Da Nang, Quang Ninh and post offices and select hotels in Ho Chi Minh City. Use phones allowing international access.

When placing an international call *from* the U.S., dial 1 800 CALL ATT.

© 4/99 AT&T

Country	AT&T Access Number	Country	AT&T Access Number
Israel •	1-800-94-94-949	Portugal ▲	0800-800-128
Italy •	172-1011	Singapore ■	800-0111-111
Japan ▲	005-39-111	South Africa	0-800-99-0123
Japan ▲	0066-55-111	Spain	900-99-00-11
Korea, Republic •	0072-911	Sweden	020-799-111
Luxembourg ×	0-800-0111	Switzerland •	0-800-89-0011
Malaysia ◇	1-800-80-0011	Turkey •	00-800-12277
Netherlands •	0800-022-9111	Thailand †	001-999-111-11
New Zealand	000-911	U.K. ★✦	0800-89-0011
Norway	800-190-11	Venezuela	800-11-120
Panama	109	Vietnam ◇	1-201-0288
Philippines •	105-11		

FOR EASY CALLING WORLDWIDE

1. Just dial the AT&T Access Number for the country you are calling from.
2. Dial the phone number you're calling. 3. Dial your card number.

For access numbers not listed ask any operator for **AT&T Direct®** Service.
In the U.S. call 1-800-331-1140 for a wallet guide listing all worldwide AT&T Access Numbers.

Visit our Web site at: **www.att.com/traveler**

Bold faced countries permit country-to-country calling outside the U.S.

- ♦ Public phones require coin or card deposit.
- ▲ When calling from public phones use phones marked "Lenso".
- ■ May not be available from every phone/public phone.
- ○ **AT&T Direct** Service calls cannot be placed to this country from outside the U.S.
- × Public phones require local coin payment during call.
- ★✦ Use U.S. access number in N. Ireland.
- ◇ If call does not complete, use 0800-013-0011.
- Collect calling from public phones.
- ⬇ Service available in calling centers in Hanoi, Da Nang, Quang Ninh and post offices and select hotels in Ho Chi Minh City. Use phones allowing international access.

When placing an international call *from* the U.S., dial 1 800 CALL ATT.

© 4/99 AT&T

(it's a breeze)

with **AT&T Direct®** Service. With the world's most powerful network you get fast, clear, reliable connections from anywhere. Plus you'll always have the option of an operator who speaks your language. All it takes is your AT&T Calling Card or credit card, and you're well on your way.

For a list of **AT&T Access Numbers,** take the attached wallet guide.

t's all within your reach.

For Travelers
who want more than
the Official Line

For Travelers Who Want More Than the Official Line

the Unofficial Guide to Florida with Kids

♦ Tips for Saving Time
Family-Friendly Hotels & R...
Attractions Rated for Each ...

For Travelers Who Want More Than the Official Line

the Unofficial Guide to Walt Disney World

The Series with More Than 3 Million Copies Sold!

♦ Tips & Warnings
♦ Save Money & Time
♦ All Attractions Candidly Rated & Ranked, Including Disney's New Animal Kingdom

Bob Sehlinger

For Travelers Who Want More Than the Official Line

the Unofficial Guide to Las Vegas

The Series with More Than 3 Million Copies Sold!

♦ Save Time & Money
♦ Insider Gambling Tips
♦ Casinos & Hotels
Candidly Rated & Ranked

Bob Sehlinger

Also Available:

- The Unofficial Guide to Branson
- The Unofficial Guide to California with Kids
- The Unofficial Guide to Chicago
- The Unofficial Guide to Cruises
- The Unofficial Disney Companion
- The Unofficial Guide to Disneyland
- The Unofficial Guide to the Great Smoky & Blue Ridge Region
- The Unofficial Guide to Miami & the Keys
- Mini-Mickey: The Pocket-Sized Unofficial Guide to Walt Disney World
- The Unofficial Guide to New Orleans
- The Unofficial Guide to New York City
- The Unofficial Guide to San Francisco
- The Unofficial Guide to Skiing in the West
- The Unofficial Guide to Washington, D.C.

Macmillan Publishing USA

Reminder

Kaisariani is still an active church and should not be visited in shorts or sleeveless or skimpy shirts.

WHAT TO SEE & DO

The Kaisariani Monastery. ☎ 01/723-6619. Admission Dr800 ($2.65). Tues–Sun 8:30am–3pm.

When a spot is holy in Greece, it has usually been holy for a very long time indeed. Today's monastery occupies the site of an ancient temple to Aphrodite, probably built here because of the spring that still flows. You'll see the water pouring forth through the open mouth of the marble goat's head at the monastery's entrance. Incredibly, this spring once supplied much of Athens with drinking water. Now, Greek brides who wish to become pregnant often journey here to drink from the spring, whose waters are believed to speed conception.

This monastery was built in the 11th century over the ruins of a 5th-century Christian church, itself built over the temple. The monks supported themselves by bee-keeping and selling the honey, much as some religious orders today sell jams and liqueurs. The monastery's kitchen and refectory, which now house some sculptural fragments, are on the west side of a paved, flower-filled courtyard. To the south, the old monks' cells and a bathhouse are being restored (exploration at your own risk is usually permitted). The well-preserved church, built like so many in Greece in the shape of a Greek cross, has a dome supported by four ancient Roman columns. Most of the frescoes are relatively late, dating from the 17th century; the distinctive bell tower is from the 19th century.

THE SANCTUARY OF ARTEMIS AT BRAURON (VRAVRONA)

38km (22 miles) E of central Athens between Porto Rafti and Loutsa on the east coast of Attica

This little shrine to Artemis in the Attic hills is not much visited; more's the pity, since it's a lovely tranquil spot.

Take the **bus** for Ayia Paraskevi from Odos Akadimias and get off at the end of the line in front of the Greek national television station. From here, take bus no. 305 to Loutsa, asking the driver to let you off at the Vravrona intersection about 300 yards from the site.

By car, drive through Peania and Markopoulo towards Porto Rafti, which the road signs also call Mesoyia. Turn left at the first turn after Markopoulo. The sign indicates Mesoyia's Port (Porto Rafti) straight ahead 6 kilometers (3.7 miles) and has an arrow to the left toward Vravrona and Artemida, written only in Greek. The ancient sanctuary is just over 4 kilometers (2.5 miles) from this turn. On the left about 600 meters before the site are the remains of a 6th-century church. Traffic often backs up on the road between Stavrou and Markopoulo, particularly in Peania, so the trip probably will take the better part of an hour.

WHAT TO SEE & DO

The Sanctuary of Artemis. ☎ 0294/71-020. Site admission Dr500 ($1.65); museum admission Dr500 ($1.65). Both open Tues–Sun 8:30am–3pm.

Just when you think that you are beginning to understand the ancient Greeks a little bit, you encounter something like the cult of Artemis at Brauron. According to legend, Agamemnon's ill-fated daughter Iphigenia served as a priestess here, and was buried here after her ritual sacrifice on the eve of the expedition to Troy. That's the easy part.

The hard part is understanding why Iphigenia and Artemis were honored here with a quadrennial festival in which little girls were dressed as bear cubs. According to one story, the custom began when an epidemic broke out after a youth killed a bear that had attacked his sister. An oracle suggested that a purifying ceremony take place in which young girls dressed like bears, and this continued every 4 years throughout antiquity.

As you sit on a shady slope, you may want to imagine the procession of little girls who came here in saffron-colored robes, and their bear-like antics. Just to confuse matters further, these ceremonies were believed to assist women in childbirth.

The most striking structure at Brauron is the **stoa,** restored in 1961. The stoa was built in the shape of an incomplete Greek letter "p" facing south toward the hill. Six rooms on the north of the stoa contained 11 small beds for the children, with stone tables by the beds. Four rooms on the west of the stoa may also have been used as bedrooms for the children.

You can also see the foundations of the 5th-century **Temple of Artemis** here, as well as a cave, usually called the **Tomb of Iphigenia.** There's also a sacred spring and two chapels in this altogether delightful spot. The five-room museum is very charming, with a number of marble portrait heads of the little girls, plus some bear masks.

We've enjoyed picnicking on the site, and there are also a number of tavernas nearby, including several fish tavernas.

THE SANCTUARY OF NEMESIS AT RHAMNOUS
53km (33 miles) NE of Athens

In antiquity, Rhamnous was a fortress town on the northern borders of Attica with an important sanctuary of Nemesis, the goddess of revenge. For the last several years, the Greek Archaeological Society has been carrying out extensive excavations in the area. The ancient entrance road to the site has now been cleared, and several tombs at the beginning of this road have been reconstructed.

Rhamnous can be visited easily only **by car,** and it can be handily combined with a trip to **Marathon,** as it is only 12 kilometers (7.4 miles) beyond the site of the famous battle. From Athens, take the Neo Makri–Marathona road, turning right toward Kato Souli. The unmarked road to Rhamnous branches left 3 kilometers (1.9 miles) from Kato Souli and continues another 2.5 kilometers (1.6 miles) beside vineyards to the site. There's only the fence and the small ticket stand to indicate that you have reached the archaeological site.

WHAT TO SEE & DO
Sanctuary of Nemesis. ☎ 0294/69-477. Admission Dr500 ($1.65). Daily 8:30am–3pm.

The Sanctuary of Nemesis has the remains of two temples, one built after Athens's victory over the Persians in 490 B.C. and one built in the mid–5th century B.C. Only the foundations of each remain, and this is another site to visit more for its pleasant location near the sea than for its ancient remains.

The smaller, older temple was dedicated to Themis (Justice), while the larger was dedicated to Nemesis (Revenge). The tireless 2nd-century A.D. traveler Pausanias tells a nice story about the temple of Nemesis. "The Persians," Pausanias wrote, "were so sure that nothing could stop them from taking Athens that they carried with them a block of Parian marble to raise a victory trophy after the battle." When the Athenians defeated the Persians in 480 B.C., the great sculptor Phidias used the Persians' block of Parian marble for a colossal figure of Nemesis for the temple here.

Nemesis, by the way, was one of many goddesses to catch the eye of Zeus. In her attempts to flee him, she changed herself into a goose, but Zeus was not fooled.

According to one legend, the result of their union was an egg from which Helen, the wife of Menelaos and the cause of the Trojan War, eventually was born. Nemesis gave the egg to Leda, who raised Helen and often is considered Helen's mother. According to other legends, Leda herself was Helen's mother, impregnated by Zeus when the King of the Gods turned himself into a swan.

Because excavations are going on at Rhamnous, you may not be able to visit the fortress above the site, but you may get to see some recently excavated tombs.

MARATHON
42km (26 miles) NE of Athens between the villages of Nea Makri and Marathona

In 490 B.C., the vastly outnumbered Athenians and their allies from the little Boeotian town of Plataea defeated the invading Persian army on the plain of Marathon, and saved Athens and much of Greece (some say, much of Europe) from Persian rule. In honor of their valor, the 192 Athenians who fell here were buried on the battlefield in an enormous burial mound. Beyond that, there's little to see at Marathon, as there is little to see at Gettysburg and Runnymede, but such sites are moving because of the battles that once tore up the ground and shaped the course of history. When Lord Byron came to Greece to fight in the War of Independence, he came to Marathon and wrote

> *The mountains look on Marathon,*
> *And Marathon looks on the sea.*
> *And musing there an hour alone,*
> *I dreamed that Greece might still be free . . .*

Alas, before he could fight to free Greece, Byron succumbed to fever in the boggy, cholera-infested town of Mesolongi, where he died on April 19, 1824.

Buses leave for Marathon from Odos Mavromati along the east side of the Pedion tou Areos Park approximately every half hour in the morning and every hour in the afternoon. The trip costs about Dr700 ($2.35) and takes about 2½ hours. For departure times, call the **tourist police** at ☎ **01/171,** or ask a Greek speaker to call the **local ticket office** (☎ **01/821-0872).**

By car, you can reach Marathon by driving north from Athens along Leoforos Kifissias, the more scenic route that rounds Mount Pendeli through Dionissos to the sea at Nea Makri, or along the National Highway toward Thessaloniki, from which signs will direct you to Marathon. Marathon is very close to the **Sanctuary of Nemesis** (see above); consider pairing the two sites on your day trip.

WHAT TO SEE & DO
Marathon Battlefield & Burial Mound. ☎ **0294/55-155.** Admission of Dr500 ($1.65) includes both the mound and museum. Museum open Tues–Sun 8:30am–3pm.

By September of 490 B.C., the advancing force of Persia—then the most powerful empire in the world—reached Marathon, anchored its fleet in the bay, and made plans to attack Athens by land and by sea. The Athenians sent their swiftest runner, Pheidippides, to Sparta to ask for help, and marched their entire army of perhaps 9,000 men north to Marathon. When Pheidippides reached Sparta (most think it took him about a day and a half), the Spartans said they would be delighted to join the Athenians—as soon as an important Spartan religious festival observing the full moon was concluded. This was widely thought to be a delaying tactic, and Athens prepared to stand alone—and did, except for a small contingent of perhaps 1,000 soldiers from the little town of Plataea in Boeotia. The Persian force was at least 24,000 strong.

For some days, the two forces eyed each other, but neither attacked. Then, before dawn on September 12, the Athenians launched a surprise attack. As the Athenian right and left wings forged forward, the center gave way—but when the Persians pressed forward, the Athenian flanks surrounded them and the serious slaughter began. Many of the Persians tried to flee to the safety of their ships, anchored offshore, but were cut down in the marshy plain that lay between the battlefield and the sea. By nightfall, the victory was won, and Pheidippides was again dispatched, this time to run to Athens with news of the victory at Marathon. Pheidippides ran flat out, burst into the Athenian Agora, shouted "We have won"—and fell dead from exhaustion. Today's marathons commemorate Pheidippides's run.

Although the Athenians won the battle at Marathon, the Persian navy had not been harmed, and it set sail for Athens. The weary Athenian army marched post-haste back to Athens and prepared to do battle again, but the Persians, for whatever reason, after sailing up and down the coast of Attica, reversed course and returned to Asia Minor. Ten years later, they would be back—only to be defeated decisively in the Battle of Salamis.

The Athenian victory at Marathon, against such great odds, became the stuff of legend. Some said that the Athenian hero Theseus himself fought alongside his descendants. Others said that the god Pan had bewitched and confused the Persians, leading them to plunge to their deaths in the marshy swamp—leading them, in short, to panic, the word derived from the god's name. According to one legend, Pan also appeared to Pheidippides as he ran with news of the victory to Athens. Pointedly, Pan asked why the Athenians built so few shrines to him—a situation that was quickly rectified throughout Attica.

Although it was customary to bury war casualties in the Kerameikos cemetery in Athens, the 192 Athenian dead from this astonishing victory were cremated and buried together in the mound, which still stands on the battlefield. When the Athenian mound was excavated in the late 19th century, quantities of ashes and burnt bones were found.

Half a millennium after the battle, when the traveler Pausanias visited Marathon, he wrote, "Here every night you can hear the noise of whinnying horses and of men fighting." Indeed, there are those today who claim to have heard sounds of battle on moonlit nights at Marathon.

The mound where the Plataeans were buried, and the small archaeological museum with finds from the site and area, are both 2 kilometers (1.25 miles) from the battle-field in the village of **Marathona** (Plataean mound and museum signposted at Marathon). This area was one of many severely threatened in the fires that swept across Greece in the summer of 1998.

If you're not bothered by swimming near where so many Persians drowned in the marshy swamp, there are lots of opportunities to swim and enjoy a bite at a taverna along the coast here.

THE MONASTERY OF DAPHNI (DAFNI)
9km (5.5 miles) W of Athens on the highway to Corinth

If you've never seen Byzantine mosaics and wonder what all the fuss is about, Daphni is the place to come. Daphni is one of the greatest masterpieces of the Byzantine empire, which was founded by the first Christian emperor, Constantine, in the 4th century A.D. and conquered by the Turks in 1453. The great art historian of Byzantine Greece, Sir David Talbot-Rice, has called Daphni "the most perfect monument" of the 11th century—and this sober scholar was not given to hyperbole.

Unfortunately, getting here is an ordeal. If possible, see Daphni on your way to or from the Peloponnese; if you're driving, you can easily stop here; if you're traveling with a tour, most stop at Daphni. (You could brave a taxi, but it's a very ugly ride and can take an hour from central Athens.)

By bus, take no. 860 from Odos Panepistimiou north of Sina (behind the university); nos. 853, 862, 873, or 880 from Eleftheria Square off Leoforos Pireos (northwest of Monastiraki); or no. A15, marked Elefsina, from Odos Sachtouri, southeast of Eleftheria Square (this trip can be combined with a visit to **Eleusis,** reviewed below). The trip will take about an hour, and the bus stop at Daphni is about 150 meters from the monastery, which is behind the wall where you see trees.

If you are **driving,** follow the signs for Corinth out of Omonia Square. You will be on a very ugly and very crowded road for the entire journey of at least half an hour. After you go cross an overpass over the National Road that runs north to Thessaloniki (Salonika), the road rises steadily for 5 kilometers (3 miles) to the gentle crest of a hill. There is a traffic light just over the crest and another traffic light approximately 500 yards further on. Turn left at the second traffic light and then right along the parallel road some 300 yards to the monastery. *Warning:* Due to the heavy traffic, turning off the National Road is not always easy, so allow yourself plenty of time to get to the left to make the turn.

WHAT TO SEE & DO

The Monastery of Daphni. ☎ **01/581-1558.** Admission Dr800 ($2.65). Daily (except on major holidays) 8:30am–2:45pm.

When you reach Daphni, you may want to take a few minutes in the courtyard to look at the church's lovely brickwork and think about the long history of this sacred spot. There have been shrines here since antiquity, when there was a temple to Apollo. The temple is long since gone (except for one column near the entrance), but the name "Daphni" (Greek for "laurel," Apollo's favorite plant), still honors that god.

In the 6th century, a small monastery was built here, later greatly expanded in the 11th century. The monastic buildings have been almost entirely destroyed, but the domed church dedicated to the Virgin Mary remains. This is something of a miracle: Over the centuries, Daphni has been repeatedly damaged by invaders and earthquakes, and repeatedly rebuilt. You'll see an example of that rebuilding in the twin gothic arches in front of the church's west entrance. These were added by the Cistercian monks who turned Daphni into a Catholic monastery after the Crusaders captured Constantinople in 1204. During the long period of the Turkish occupation, there was no functioning monastery here—indeed, for a while, the buildings were used as army barracks. After the Greek War of Independence, Daphni was reclaimed by the Greek Orthodox church and restored to its former glory.

A severe earthquake in the 1980s prompted another round of restoration in which the church was strengthened and its dazzling mosaic cycle repaired. When you step inside and let your eyes become accustomed to the dark, here's some of what you'll see:

The **central dome** has the commanding mosaic of Christ Pantocrator (the Almighty). This image of Christ as an awesome judge is quite different from the Western tradition of Christ as a suffering mortal.

If you are familiar with the Old and New Testament, you'll be able to pick out familiar stories in the mosaics throughout the rest of the church. As is traditional in Greek Orthodox churches, the Annunciation, Nativity, Baptism, and Transfiguration are in the squinches supporting the dome, and the 16 major prophets are displayed between the windows of the dome. The Adoration of the Magi and the Resurrection are in the **barrel vault** inside the main (southern) entrance of the church, and the Entry into Jerusalem and the Crucifixion are in the **northern barrel vault**. Mosaics showing scenes from the life of the Virgin are in the **south bay** of the narthex (passage between the entrance and nave). Even if you're not familiar with Biblical stories, and even if you find the mosaic of Christ Pantocrator grim rather than awesome, you may well be enchanted by the charming details in scenes such as the Adoration of the Magi.

Daphni is also known for the **Wine Festival** which is usually held on the grounds every year from mid-August to mid-September. Unfortunately, you can't combine a visit to the monastery with a visit to the Wine Festival, which runs from 8pm to midnight. Admission is Dr1,000 ($3.35); for Dr2,000 ($7) you get a glass and can sample as many of the wines as you deem wise. Check with the **Athens Festival** box office, Odos Stadiou 4, near Syntagma Square (☎ 01/322-7944), for more information.

THE SANCTUARY OF ELEUSIS (ELEFSIS)
22.5km (14 miles) W of central Athens on the highway to Corinth

Although Eleusis was the site of the most famous and revered of all the ancient Mysteries, the present-day site is so grim (surrounded by the horrors, and horrible smells, of the industrial city of Elefsina), that you'll need a very keen interest in either archaeology, mystery cults, or oil refineries to enjoy a visit here.

That said, we must admit that we have one friend who says that Eleusis is her favorite site near Athens. This makes absolutely no sense to us, but if you come here, you can see if she has a point.

To get here **by bus**, take no. 853 or 862 from Eleftheria Square off Leoforos Pireos (northwest of Monastiraki), or no. A15, marked Elefsina, from Odos Sachtouri, southeast of Eleftheria Square. (This trip can be combined with a visit to Daphni Monastery.) Ask the driver to let you off at the Sanctuary (Heron), which is off to the left of the main road, before the center of town.

If you're **driving**, take the national road and exit at Elefsina. At press time, the signs pointing to the site had been removed; if they have not been replaced, you will have to ask (repeatedly, as the site is little known) for directions.

WHAT TO SEE & DO
The Sanctuary Of Eleusis. Elefsina. ☎ 01/554-6019. Admission Dr500 ($1.65), free Sun. Tues–Sun 8:30am–3pm.

The unknown and the famous were initiated into the sacred rites here, yet we know almost nothing about the Eleusinian Mysteries. What we do know is that the Mysteries commemorated the abduction of Demeter's daughter Persephone by the god of the underworld, Hades (Pluto). Demeter was able to strike a bargain with the god, who allowed Persephone to leave the underworld and rejoin her mother for 6 months each year. The Mysteries celebrated this—and the cycle of growth, death, and rebirth of each year's crops.

Despite its substantial remains and glorious past—this was already a religious site in Mycenaean times—the sanctuary's present surroundings make it difficult to warm to the spot. Admittedly, there are the considerable remains of a Temple of Artemis, a 2nd-century A.D. **Roman Propylaea** (monumental entrance), and triumphal arches dedicated to the Great Goddesses and to the emperor Hadrian. Hadrian's arch here, by the way, inspired the Arc de Triomphe, on the Champs-Elysées in Paris. Nearby is the **Telesterion,** the Temple of Demeter, where only initiates of the cult knew what really happened—and they kept their silence.

One poignant spot at the Sanctuary is the **Kallichoron Well,** where the goddess Demeter wept over the loss of her daughter Persephone, whom Hades (Pluto) spirited away to the Underworld. The dark god may have dragged Persephone with him through the cave here known as **Ploutonion,** which was believed to be an entrance to the Underworld. It seems ironic that modern Elefsina itself is so ghastly that it has become something of a hell on earth.

The small **museum** has finds from the site, including several **figures of Demeter** and a lithe **statue of Antinous,** the beautiful boy who won the emperor Hadrian's heart.

7

The Saronic Gulf Islands

by Sherry Marker

The islands of the Saronic Gulf, which lies between Attica and the Peloponnese, are so close to Athens that each summer they are inundated with Athenians—all of whom, of course, are seeking to avoid the crowds of Athens. In addition, these islands are popular destinations for travelers whose time is limited, but who are determined to see at least one Greek island.

The easiest island to visit is **Aegina,** a mere 30 kilometers (17 nautical miles) from Piraeus. The main attractions here are the graceful Doric temple of **Aphaia,** one of the best-preserved Greek temples, several good beaches, and some pleasant pine and pistachio groves. That's the good news. The bad news is that Aegina is so close to the metropolitan sprawl of Athens and Piraeus that you're unlikely to get any real sense of why the Greek islands are so beloved.

Poros is hardly an island at all: only a narrow (370m) inlet separates it from the Peloponnese. The landscape is wooded, gentle, and rolling, like the adjacent mainland, and there are several good beaches. Young Athenians and tour groups head here in profusion. On summer nights, the waterfront is either very lively or hideously crowded, depending on your point of view.

Hydra (Idra), with its bare hills, superb natural harbor, and elegant stone mansions, is the most strikingly beautiful of all the Saronic Gulf islands. One of the first Greek islands to be "discovered," it has an air of sophistication that many islands lack. Hydra has been declared a national monument and vehicles have been banished here, which makes this island a particular delight. One drawback: There's almost no decent beach, but lots of places to swim off the rocks. Despite the hydrofoils that link Hydra all too often with other islands and the mainland, this island manages to maintain a certain sense of resolute individuality.

Spetses has always been popular with wealthy Athenians, who built handsome villas on the island. There are several good beaches, but most are home to the large hotels that house tour groups. If you like your islands wooded, you'll love Spetses; if you think an island should be bare and austere, you may find Spetses a bit too bland for your taste.

STRATEGIES FOR SEEING THE ISLANDS   If at all possible, do not visit here from late June through August—unless you have a hotel reservation and think that you'd enjoy the hustle and bustle of high season.

0   50 mi
0   50 km

To Athens

Salamis   Perama

Ambelakia   Piraeus

SALAMIS

Peristeria   Perani   Glyfada

Saronikos Kolpos
(Saronic Gulf)

DIAPORIA

LAOUSSES

IPSILI

Souvala   Vaia

Korfos

Aegina ①

Messagros

②

Paleohora

Ayia
Marina

KIRA

Marathonas

Portes

AEGINA

Epidaurus

MONI

Perdika

ANGISTRI

Kounoupitsa

*Epidaurikos
Kolpos*
*(Gulf of
Epidaurus)*

Vathy

Methana

POROS

Methana

③

Kaloni

Poros

THE PELOPONNESE

Trizina ④
(Ancient Troezen)

Galatas

⑤

Didima

Loukaiti

TSELEVINIA

Piepi   Metochi

Ermioni

Zourvas

Kranidi

Dokos

Hydra

DOKOS

Episkopi

⑥

HYDRA

Legend

Airport ✈
Ferry Routes
Archeological Site
Prehistoric Site

Spetses

SPETSES

SPETSOPOULA

GREECE
Athens
★
**The
Saronic
Gulf**

Lemon Groves of Limonodassos ⑤
Monastery of Ayios Nektarios ①
Monastery of the Prophet Elijah (Profitis Elias) ⑥
Monastery of Zoodoches Piyi ④
Temple of Aphaia ②
Temple of Poseidon ③

Insider Tip

If you visit the islands of the Saronic Gulf in July and August, keep an eye out for posters announcing exhibitions at local museums and galleries. Many Athens galleries close for part of July and August, and some have shows on the islands.

If you go to one of these islands on a **day trip,** remember that the hydrofoils that serve them cannot travel when the sea is rough. You may find yourself an unwilling overnight island visitor, grateful to be given the still-warm bed in a private home that a family member has surrendered to make some money. We speak from experience.

There are frequent **hydrofoils** from Piraeus to all these islands, and from island to island, and you can visit any of the islands for no more than Dr12,000 ($40) round-trip. It is usually impossible to buy a round-trip ticket, which means that as soon as you arrive at your destination, you should rush to a ticket agent to book your return.

Several cruises offer day trips to Hydra, Poros, and Aegina; for details, see chapter 4, "Cruising the Greek Islands," and below under "Essentials" for Aegina.

1 Aegina

30km (17 nautical miles) SW of Piraeus

Triangular Aegina (Egina), the largest of the Saronic Gulf islands, continues to be the most visited island of Greece, due to its proximity to Athens. In fact, many of the 10,000 who live here commute daily to Athens. If you have only one day for one island, you may decide on a day trip here to see the famous Doric temple of **Aphaia.** Most ships arrive and depart from the main port and capital of Aegina town on the west coast, though there are a few that stop at the resort town of Ayia Marina on the east coast. Ayia Marina is about as charmless as it's possible to be, but this port is your best choice if your principal destination here is the temple of Aphaia.

Despite massive tourism and the rapid development that is devouring much farmland, there are still almond, olive, and, especially, pistachio orchards here. In fact, the island has an endemic water problem simply because of watering the pistachio groves. When you buy pistachios in Greece, the vendor will often assure you that they are from Aegina to indicate their superior quality.

ESSENTIALS

GETTING THERE   Car ferries and **excursion boats** to Aegina usually leave from Piraeus's main harbor; **hydrofoils** leave from Marina Zea harbor. Hydrofoil service is particularly efficient; the Ceres Flying Dolphins are twice as fast as ferries and about 40% more expensive. The sleek little yellow-and-blue hydrofoils are outfitted like broad aircraft with airline seats, toilets, and a minimum of luggage facilities. (The fore sections offer better views, but they are also bumpier.) The newer Super Cats are bigger, faster, and more comfortable, with food and beverage service.

By Organized Tour   A good way to see the Saronic Gulf is via a three-island day cruise, which can be booked through a travel agent, such as **Viking Star Cruises** (☎ 01/898-0729 or 01/898-0829), or at your hotel desk. **Epirotiki Lines** (☎ 01/429-1000) provides transportation to and from your hotel in Athens to Flisvos Marina, where their *Hermes* departs daily around 8:30am for **Hydra** (swimming and shopping), **Poros** (lunch and sightseeing), and **Aegina** (visiting the Temple of Aphaia or swimming); returning to Athens about 7:30pm. Lunch is served onboard, and there's a small pool. For about Dr30,000 ($100) you get a good tour and an introduction to travel aboard a cruise ship.

Ferry and excursion boat tickets can be purchased at the pier. Call the **Piraeus Port Authority** (☎ 01/451-1456) for schedule and departure pier information. Hydrofoil tickets can be purchased in advance from **Ceres Hydrofoils,** Akti Themistokleous 8 (☎ 01/428-0001), midway on the waterfront in Piraeus, or at the nearby departure pier.

VISITOR INFORMATION   There are several travel agents on Aegina. **Pipins Tours,** Odos Kanari 2 (☎ 0297/24-456; fax 0297/26-656), 1 block inland from the hydrofoil pier, is the Ceres Hydrofoil agent. **Aegina Island Holidays,** Demokratias 47 (☎ and fax **0297/25-860**), near the church, is also good. Both Pipins Tours and Aegina Island Holidays are also good sources for rooms to let around the island.

We recommend Anne Yannoulis's *Aegina* (Lycabettus Press), usually on sale on the island, for those wanting to pursue Aegina's history.

GETTING AROUND   The **bus station** is on Plateia Ethneyersias, to the left from the ferry pier. There is good service to most of the island, with trips every hour in summer to the Temple of Aphaia and Ayia Marina, for Dr350 ($1.15); tickets must be purchased at the small temporary office before boarding. **Taxis** are available nearby; fare to the temple should cost about Dr3,000 ($10). You can sometimes negotiate a decent rate for a round-trip with an hour's wait at the temple. **Bikes, mountain bikes,** and **mopeds** can be rented at the opposite (south) end of the waterfront, near the beach. Careful: Prices can be exorbitant. An ordinary bike should cost no more than Dr1,500 ($5) a day, and mopeds should cost about Dr4,500 to Dr6,000 ($15 to $20) a day.

FAST FACTS   You can change currency at the **National Bank of Greece,** on the paralia (waterfront), which has an ATM as well; some travel agents also exchange money both during and after normal bank hours, usually at less favorable rates. For medical emergencies, the island **clinic** (☎ **0297/22-251**) is on the northeast edge of town. The **police** (☎ **0297/22-391**) are on Odos Leonardou Lada, about 200 meters inland from the port. The **tourist police** (☎ **0297/22-462**) are in the same building as the police. The **post office** is in Plateia Ethneyersias, around the corner from the hydrofoil pier. The **telephone office (OTE)** is 5 blocks inland from the port, on Odos Aiakou.

WHAT TO SEE & DO
EXPLORING AEGINA TOWN

Aegina town has a legacy of neoclassical buildings from its brief stint as the first capital of newly independent Greece (from 1826 to 1828), but your primary impression of this harbor town will be of fishing boats and the small cargo vessels that ply back and forth to the mainland. If you take a horse-drawn carriage (about Dr6,000/$20) or wander the streets back from the port, you'll easily see the neoclassical buildings, including the restored **Markelos Tower,** where the first Greek parliament met. Fans of Nikos Kazantzakis may want to take a cab to **Livadi,** just north of town, to see the house where he lived when he wrote *Zorba the Greek.*

North of the harbor, behind the town beach, and sometimes visible from boats entering the harbor, is the lone worn Doric column that marks the site of the **Temple of Apollo,** open Tuesday through Sunday from 8:30am to 3pm; admission is Dr500 ($1.65). The view here is nice, the ruins very ruined.

SEEING THE TEMPLE OF APHAIA

The **Temple of Aphaia,** set on a pine-covered hill 12 kilometers (7.5 miles) east of Aegina town (☎ 0297/32398), is one of the best-preserved and most handsome Greek temples. No one really knows who Aphaia was, although it seems that she was a very old, even prehistoric, goddess, who eventually became associated both with the huntress goddess Artemis and with Athena, the goddess of wisdom. According to some legends, Aphaia lived on Crete, where King Minos, usually preoccupied with his labyrinth and Minotaur, fell in love with her. When she fled Crete, he pursued her, and she finally threw herself into the sea off Aegina to escape him. At some point in the late 6th or early 5th centuries B.C., the temple was built (on the site of earlier shrines) to honor Aphaia.

Thanks to the work of restorers, 25 of the original 32 Doric columns still stand. The pedimental sculpture, showing scenes from the Trojan war, was carted off in 1812 by King Ludwig of Bavaria. Whatever you think about the removal of art treasures from their original homes, Ludwig probably did us a favor by taking it to the Glyptothek in Munich: When Ludwig had the sculpture removed, locals were busily burning much of the temple to make lime and hacking up other bits to use in building their homes. Admission to the site is Dr1,000 ($3.35); it's open Monday through Friday from 8:30am to 7pm, Saturday and Sunday from 8:30am to 3pm.

WHERE TO STAY

✪ **Eginitiko Archontiko** (Traditional Hotel). Odos Eakou 1 and Ayiou Nikolaou, 18010 Aegina. ☎ and fax **0297/24-968.** 13 units. Dr18,000 ($60) double. AE, MC, V.

This mansion, near the Markelos Tower, was built in 1820 and renovated in 1988 with some loss of original detail, although some lovely painted ceilings remain. The rooms are rather small, but traditionally furnished, comfortable, and quiet. The pleasant downstairs lobby retains much 19th-century charm. The owners care about this handsome building (Greece's first president, Ioannis Kapodistrias, was a guest here) and try to make guests comfortable.

Eleni Rooms to Let. Odos Kappou, 18010 Aegina. ☎ **0297/26-450.** 7 units, 4 with bathroom. Dr10,000 ($33) single/double without bathroom; Dr12,000 ($40) single/double with bathroom. No credit cards.

This excellent budget choice is in part of a house built in 1888. Rooms are cool, quiet, and exceptionally clean, with refinished pine floors and whitewashed walls. Each unit is different, and the second-floor rooms with bathrooms are the best.

Hotel Apollo. Ayia Marina, 18010 Aegina. ☎ **0297/32-271.** Fax 0297/32-688. 107 units. TV TEL. Dr30,000 ($100) double. Rates include breakfast buffet. AE, DC, MC, V.

Ayia Marina, with lots of resort hotels, is not our cup of tea. That said, friends who stayed at this beach hotel in 1998 were pleased with their large bathroom and bedroom (with balcony). Most of the rooms at this glitzy resort hotel (fresh- and saltwater swimming pools, minigolf, tennis) have balconies overlooking the sea.

Moondy Bay Bungalows. Profitis Elias, Perdika, 18010 Aegina. ☎ **0297/61-146,** or 01/380-3745 in Athens. Fax 0297/61-147. 80 units. A/C TEL. Dr24,000 ($80) double. Rates include breakfast. AE, V.

This bungalow complex, 7 kilometers (4.5 miles) south of Aegina town in well-kept grounds overlooking the sea, is a good place for families. The bungalows have the usual pine furniture, and the bathrooms are decent sized. Facilities include a good seawater pool, tennis court, minigolf, and children's playground.

WHERE TO DINE

Estiatorion Economou. Odos Demokratias. ☎ **0297/25-113.** Main courses Dr900–Dr3,600 ($3–$12). AE, EURO, MC, V. Daily 9am–1am. GREEK.

A reader suggested this excellent port-side taverna with a dark-blue canopy about midway along the waterfront, and several visits have confirmed its high quality. We recommend the lemony fish soup, grilled fish, and tender lamb souvlaki with decent chips. Grilled local lobster is sometimes available; expect to pay at least Dr18,000 ($60) a kilo.

Maridaki. Odos Demokratias. ☎ **0297/25-869.** Main courses Dr1,500–Dr1,800 ($5–$6). No credit cards. Daily 8am–midnight. GREEK.

This lively port-side spot has a wide selection of fish, grilled octopus, and the usual taverna fare of souvlaki and moussaka. The mezedes here are usually very good, and you can make an entire meal of them if you wish.

Taverna Vatsoulia. Odos Ayii Assomati. ☎ **0297/22-711.** Dr600–Dr1,500 ($2–$5). No credit cards. Wed and Sat–Sun 6pm–1am. GREEK.

This local favorite is about a 10-minute walk out of town on the road to the Temple of Aphaia, but call ahead before you go to make sure it's open. The menu is limited; rabbit is a specialty. Sometimes there's live music.

AEGINA AFTER DARK

At sunset the harbor scene gets livelier as everyone comes out for an evening **volta** (stroll). Kanella's **Piano Restaurant** usually has live pop music, and **N.O.A.,** a port-side ouzeri, offers a more traditional scene. Dancers will want to find **Disco Elpianna** or the **Inoi Club** in Faros for Greek music, and the scene in Ayia Marina is sure to be lively, if a bit sordid (some holidaymakers attempt to set records for amount of beer and retsina they consume). For more sedentary entertainment, there are two outdoor cinemas, the **Anesis** and **Olympia,** and several bars, including the **Bel Epoque,** at the corner of Aiandos and Pileos, and the **Rainbow,** on Mitropoleos.

2 Poros

55km (31 nautical miles) SW of Piraeus

Poros shares the gentle, rolling landscape of the adjacent Peloponnesian coastline, and has several good beaches, some decent tavernas, and a lively summer nightlife. If that sounds like lukewarm praise, we're afraid it is: Poros does not have enough of the atmosphere of an island to make us want to return often.

As someone once said, "Geography is destiny": Poros (the word means "straits" or "ford") is separated from the Peloponnese by a narrow channel only 370 meters wide. This makes this island so easy to reach from the mainland that weekending Athenians and many tourists (including many package-holiday groups) flock here each summer. In fact, there's a car ferry across the straits almost every 20 minutes in summer—which means there are a *lot* of cars here.

If you wish, you can use Poros as a base for visiting the nearby attractions on the mainland, including Epidaurus, ancient Troezen (modern Trizina), and the lemon groves of Limonodassos. In a long day trip, you can visit Nafplion (Nafplio), Mycenae, and Tiryns.

ESSENTIALS

GETTING THERE   **Hydrofoils** to Poros, Hydra, and Spetses leave from Zea Marina in Piraeus. Most people come and leave on ferries or hydrofoils from Piraeus or the other Saronic islands, but others cross the narrow strait to and from Galatas by ferry, which costs Dr100 (33¢) and takes only a few minutes. For information call the **Piraeus Port Authority** (☎ 01/45-11-311), **Ceres Hydrofoils** (☎ 01/42-80-001) in Piraeus, or **Marinos Tours** (☎ 0298/23-423) in Poros.

The other Saronic islands are all easy to reach from Poros, and Marinos Tours also runs a weekly **round-trip hydrofoil excursion** to Tinos (3½ hr. each way) for Dr21,000 ($70), and to Mikonos via Hydra (4 hr. each way) for Dr30,000 ($100). (The one-way fare to Mikonos is Dr22,500/$75.)

VISITOR INFORMATION   The waterfront hotels are generally too noisy for all except heavy sleepers, so if you want to stay in town we suggest you check with **Marinos Tours** (☎ 0298/22-977; fax 0298/25-325), which handles several hundred rooms and apartments, as well as many island hotels. We've also had good reports of **Tan Tours,** Odos Papadopoulou 36 (☎ 0298/22-112).

The best guide to the island is Niki Stavrolakes's enduring classic, *Poros* (Lycabettus Press), usually on sale here.

GETTING AROUND   You can walk anywhere in Poros town. The **island's bus** can take you to the beaches; the conductor will charge you according to your destination. The **taxi station** is near the hydrofoil dock, or you can call for one at ☎ 0298/ 23-003; the fare to or from the beach at Askeli should cost about Dr1,500 ($5). **Kostas Bikes** (☎ 0298/23-565), opposite the Galatas ferry pier, rents bicycles for about Dr1,500 ($5) a day and mopeds from about Dr2,400 ($8) a day; helmets are provided free.

FAST FACTS   You can change currency at the **National Bank of Greece,** on the paralia (waterfront), which has an ATM as well; some travel agents also exchange money both during and after normal bank hours, usually at less favorable rates. The **police** and **tourist police** (☎ 0298/22-462) are on the paralia. The **post office** and **telephone office (OTE)** are also on the waterfront; their hours are Monday through Friday from 8am to 2pm. In summer, in addition to the normal weekday hours, the OTE is usually open Saturday and Sunday from 8am to 1pm and 5 to 10pm.

WHAT DO SEE & DO
ATTRACTIONS IN POROS TOWN

As you cross over to the island, you'll see the streets of Poros town, the capital, climbing a hill topped with a clock tower. Poros town is itself an island, joined to the rest of Poros by a causeway. The narrow streets along the harbor are usually crowded with visitors inching their way up and down past the restaurants, cafes, and shops. At night, the adjacent hills are, indeed, alive to the sound of music; unfortunately, even the "Greek" music is usually heavily amplified pop.

Poros town has a **Naval Training School**—which means that there are usually a lot of young men looking for company here. Anyone wishing to avoid their attention might try to visit the small **Archaeological Museum** (☎ 0298/23-276), with finds from ancient Troezen. It's usually open Monday through Saturday from 9am to 3pm; admission is free.

EXPLORING THE ISLAND

The island's best-known antiquity, the **Temple of Poseidon** near Kalavria, is one of those sites best described as "of most interest to the specialist." In other words, the remains are mostly ankle-high. In part, this is because the inhabitants of the nearby island of Hydra plundered the temple and hauled away most of the marble to build their harborside Monastery of the Virgin. Despite the lack of remains, the Temple of Poseidon is a pleasant, shady spot.

Poros's beaches are not an enchantment. The beach northwest of town, at **Neorio**, is not always unpolluted; the better beaches are found southeast of town at **Askeli** and **Kanali.**

OFF THE ISLAND: A FESTIVAL, ANCIENT TROEZEN & LEMON GROVES

If you're in Poros in mid-June, you might want to catch the ferry across to Galatas and take in the annual **Flower Festival,** when there are parades with floats and marching bands and floral displays. (There are usually lots of posters up in Poros town advertising the festival.)

From Galatas you can catch a bus the 8 kilometers (5 miles) west to **Trizina** (ancient Troezen), birthplace of the great Athenian hero Theseus, and the scene of the tragedy of his wife, Phaedra, and son, Hippolytus. Phaedra, in one of the misogynistic fables beloved of the Greeks, fell in love with her stepson. When the dust settled, both she and Hippolytus were dead and Theseus was bereft. There's the remains of a temple to Asklepius here—but again, these ruins are very ruined.

About 4 kilometers (2.5 miles) south of Galatas near the beach of Aliki, you'll find the olfactory wonder of **Limonodassos** (Lemon Grove), where more than 25,000 lemon trees fill the air with their fragrance each spring. Alas, many were harmed in a harsh storm in March 1998, but it is hoped that most will survive and bloom again. There are several tavernas nearby where you can get freshly squeezed lemonade for about Dr600 ($2).

WHERE TO STAY

Hotel Latsi. Odos Papadopoulou 74, 18020 Poros, Trizinias. ☎ **0298/22-392.** 39 units, most with bathroom. Dr10,500 ($35) without bathroom; Dr13,500 ($45) with bathroom. No credit cards.

The Latsi is on the quieter north end of the port, near the Naval School, opposite the Galatas ferry, with balconies overlooking the port and the Peloponnese. Rooms are worn but clean and comfortable. If you want an up-to-date bathroom, this hotel is not for you; otherwise, it may be just the spot.

Hotel Sirena. Monastiri, Askeli, 18020 Poros, Trizinias. ☎ **0298/22-741.** Fax 0298/22-744. 120 units. A/C TEL. Dr30,000 ($100) double. Half-board (Dr6,000/$20) optional. MC.

If you're talking creature comforts, the Sirena, on the beach east of town beyond Askeli, is the best hotel on the island. Those creature comforts mean that the Sirena is very popular with tour groups; if you want to stay here, you must book a room early, even though you may be one of the few non–group members. Just about all the spacious rooms in this six-story building have excellent views, and there's a nice saltwater pool near the private beach.

Maria Christofa Rooms to Let. 18020 Poros, Trizinias. ☎ **0298/22-392.** 6 units, none with bathroom. Dr9,000 ($30) double. No credit cards.

Our favorite budget choice is the home of Maria Christofa, in a narrow lane high above Poros town. Many of the spare but high-ceilinged rooms here have great views of the town and harbor. The bathrooms are perfectly acceptable.

WHERE TO DINE

Caravella Restaurant. Paralia, Poros town. ☎ **0298/23-666.** Main courses Dr1,500–Dr4,200 ($5–$14). No credit cards. Daily 10am–1am. GREEK.

This port-side taverna specializes in seafood and traditional dishes such as veal stifado, moussaka, souvlaki, and stuffed eggplant.

Lucas Restaurant. Paralia, Poros town. ☎ **0298/22-145.** Main courses Dr1,800–Dr4,200 ($6–$14). No credit cards. GREEK.

You'll find this pleasant outdoor place across from the private yacht marina. Fresh seafood and traditional dishes are well prepared and reasonably priced, especially for this upscale area.

POROS AFTER DARK

There's plenty of evening entertainment in Poros town, especially if you're in the mood to dance. The best disco is probably still **Scirocco,** about a kilometer south of town. The elegant music bar **Artemis,** in Askeli, draws a more sophisticated crowd, including the yachting set.

3 Hydra (Idra)

65km (35 nautical miles) S of Piraeus

Hydra is one of a handful of places in Greece that seemingly can't be spoiled. Even in summer, when the waterfront teems with day-trippers, many side streets remain quiet. If you can, arrive here in the evening, when most of the day-trippers have left.

With the exception of a handful of municipal vehicles, there are no cars on Hydra. You'll probably run into at least one example of a popular form of local transportation: the donkey. When you see Hydra's splendid 18th- and 19th-century stone **archontika** (mansions) along the waterfront and on the steep streets above, you won't be surprised to learn that the entire island has been declared a national treasure by both the Greek government and the Council of Europe. You'll probably find Hydra town so charming that you'll forgive its one serious flaw: no beach. You may wish to do as the Hydriotes do, and swim from the rocks at Spilia, just beyond the main harbor.

Whatever you do, be sure to be out on the deck of your ship as you arrive, so you can see Hydra's bleak mountain hills suddenly reveal a perfect horseshoe harbor. This really is a place where arrival is half the fun.

ESSENTIALS

GETTING THERE   Several ferries and excursion boats make the 4-hour voyage between Piraeus and Hydra daily, and there is connecting service to several ports on the Peloponnese peninsula, as well as with the other Saronic islands. Contact the **Piraeus Port Authority** (☎ 01/451-1311) or the **Hydra Port Authority** (☎ 0298/ 52-279) for schedules. **Ceres Hydrofoils** (☎ 01/428-0001) has several daily Flying Dolphins, some of them direct (a 1¼-hr. trip), as well as Super Cat service between Piraeus's Zea Marina (the southwest corner) and Hydra. It's a good idea to make reservations in summer and on weekends; if at all possible, have the concierge at your hotel do this for you.

VISITOR INFORMATION   The free publication *This Summer in Hydra* is widely available and contains much useful information; keep in mind that shops and restaurants pay to appear here. **Saitis Tours** (☎ 0298/52-184), in the middle of the harbor

Festivals in Hydra

On a mid-June weekend, Hydra celebrates the **Miaoulia,** honoring Hydriot Admiral Miaoulis, who set much of the Turkish fleet on fire by ramming them with explosives-filled fireboats. In early July, Hydra has an annual **puppet festival** which, in recent years, has drawn puppeteers from countries as far away as Togo and Brazil. As these two festivals are not on set dates, you should attempt to get additional information from the **Hydra tourist police** (☎ 0298/52-205).

front, can exchange money, provide information on rooms and villas, book excursions, and help you make long-distance calls or send faxes.

To reach the **Ceres Flying Dolphin** hydrofoil office, take the street that runs uphill at the foot of the main quay, which is at the far left of the harbor if you are standing with your back to the harbor. The office is up a flight of stairs; you will probably spot it by the foreigners hanging around before you see its minuscule sign.

We recommend Catherine Vanderpool's *Hydra* (Lycabettus Press), usually on sale on the island, to those wanting to pursue Hydra's history.

GETTING AROUND   Walking is the only means of getting around on the island itself, unless you bring or rent a donkey or bicycle. **Caïques** provide water-taxi service to the island's beaches (Molos, Avlaki, Bitsi, and Limnioniza are the best) and the little offshore islands of Dokos, Kivotos, and Petasi, as well as to secluded restaurants in the evening; rates run from about Dr300 to Dr3,000 ($1 to $10) depending on destination, with an extra Dr600 ($2) charge if booked by phone.

FAST FACTS   The **National Bank of Greece** and the **Commercial Bank** both have offices on the harbor; in addition to normal bank hours, both are sometimes open on Saturday from 11am to 2pm in July and August. The National Bank has an ATM. Several travel agents, including **Saitis Tours** on the harbor, will exchange money from about 9am to 8pm, usually at a less favorable rate. Hydra's small health **clinic** is signposted on the harbor; cases requiring surgery or complicated treatment are taken by boat or helicopter to the mainland. The **tourist police** (☎ 0298/52-205) are on the second floor at Odos Votsi 9 (signposted in the harbor). They often have the free publication *This Summer in Hydra,* which has a map, a list of rooms to rent, and other useful information. The **post office** is just off the harbor front on Odos Ikonomou, the street between the two banks. The **telephone office (OTE),** across from the police station on Odos Votsi, is open Monday through Saturday from 7:30am to 10pm, Sunday from 8am to 1pm and 5 to 10pm.

WHAT TO SEE & DO
ATTRACTIONS IN HYDRA TOWN

In the 18th and 19th centuries, ships from Hydra transported cargo around the world and made Hydra very rich indeed. Just as on the American island of Nantucket, ships' captains demonstrated their wealth by building the fanciest houses money could buy. The captains' lasting legacy is the handsome stone mansions (*archontika*) that give Hydra town its distinctive character.

One archontiko that you can hardly miss is the **Tombazi house,** which dominates the hill that stands directly across the harbor from the main ferry quay. This is now a branch of the School of Fine Arts, with a hostel for students, and you can usually get a peek inside. Call the **mansion** (☎ 0298/52-291) or the **Athens Polytechnic** (☎ 01/619-2119) for information about the program or exhibits.

The nearby **Ikonomou-Miriklis** (sometimes called the Voulgaris) **mansion** is not open to the public, nor is the hilltop **Koundouriotis mansion,** built by an Albanian family that contributed generously to the cause of independence. If you wander the side streets on this side of the harbor, you will see many more handsome houses, some of which are being restored so that they can once again be private homes, while others are being converted into stylish hotels.

Some of Hydra's nicest boutiques and jewelry shops are concentrated on the waterfront, especially in the area below the Tombazi house. **Hermes Art Shop** (☎ **0298/ 52-689**) has a wide array of jewelry, some good antique reproductions, and a few interesting textiles. **Vangelis Rafalias's Pharmacy** is a lovely place to stop in, even if you don't need anything, just to see the jars of remedies from the 19th century.

Like many islands, Hydra boasts that it has 365 churches, one for every day of the year. The most impressive, the mid-18th-century **Monastery of the Assumption of the Virgin Mary,** is by the clock tower on the harbor front. This is the monastery built of the marble blocks that were hacked out of the (until then) well-preserved Temple of Poseidon on the nearby island of Poros. The buildings here no longer function as a monastery, and the cells are now municipal offices. The church itself has rather undistinguished 19th-century frescoes, but the elaborate 18th-century marble iconostasis (altar screen), is terrific. Like the marble from Poros, this altar screen was "borrowed" from another church and brought here. Seeing it is well worth the donation requested, Dr150 (50¢).

Exploring the Island: A Monastery, a Convent & Beaches

If you want to take a vigorous, uphill walk (with no shade), head up Odos Miaouli past Kala Pigadia (Good Wells), still the town's best local source of water. If you keep going, a walk of about an hour will bring you to the **Convent of Ayia Efpraxia** and the **Monastery of the Prophet Elijah** (Profitis Elias). Both religious foundations have superb views of the town and beyond, both are still active, and the nuns sell their hand-woven fabrics. (*Note:* Men and women in shorts and tank tops will not be allowed inside. Both nuns and monks observe the mid-day siesta and usually lock their doors to visitors between 1 and 5pm.)

There are a number of other monasteries and convents deeper in the countryside on Hydra; if you are interested in visiting them, get a copy of Catherine Vanderpool's *Hydra*, or ask for directions at the Tourist Police.

The only real **beach** on the island is at **Mandraki,** a 20-minute walk east of town, where a large hotel has been built. Just outside town, you can swim at the rocks at **Spilia** or **Kamini.** Farther west along a donkey trail you'll find **Kastello,** with the small fort that gives it its name, and another rocky beach with less crowded swimming. Still farther west is the pretty pine-lined cove of **Molos,** a favorite anchorage for yachts. The donkey path continues west to the cultivated plateau at **Episkopi,** from which a faint trail leads on west to **Bisti** and **Ayios Nikolaos** for more secluded swimming. (Most of these beaches are best reached by water taxi from the main harbor.)

One fairly good beach on the south coast, **Limioniza,** can be reached with strong legs, sturdy shoes, and a good map from Ayia Triada, though it's much easier to take a water taxi here and to Molos, Avlaki, and Bisti. The island of **Dokos,** northwest off the tip of Hydra, an hour's boat ride from town, has a good beach and excellent diving conditions—it was here that Jacques Cousteau found a sunken ship with cargo still aboard, believed to be 3,000 years old. You may want to take a picnic with you, as the taverna here keeps unpredictable hours.

WHERE TO STAY

As most Hydra hotels are rather small, you would be wise to book well ahead of time; reservations in summer are almost invariably a necessity. You'll have the best chance of success if you can avoid weekends. All hotels are open from early April until late October unless otherwise noted. Low-season prices should be 20% to 30% less.

In addition to the following choices, you might also consider the 15-unit **Pension Efi,** Odos Sachini (☎ **0298/52-371**), in a handsome stone building with good views of the harbor; or the 19-unit **Hotel Greco,** Odos Kouloura (☎ **0298/53-200**; fax 0298/53-511), a former fishing-net factory in a quiet neighborhood. The Greco's taverna on the large enclosed stone patio is a pleasant place for fresh grilled meats and Greek fare in the evenings.

Hotel Angelika. Odos Miaouli 42, 18040 Hydra. ☎ **0298/53-202.** Fax 0298/53-698. 22 units. Dr22,200 ($74) double. Rates include breakfast. MC, V.

This friendly pension, a 10-minute walk from the port, is open most of the year. The rooms are simple, clean, and a good value, all overlooking a quiet arbor courtyard, where breakfast is served. Room nos. 6, 8, 9, and 10 have large rooftop terraces with panoramic views.

✪ **Hotel Bratsera.** Odos Tombazi, 18040 Hydra. ☎ **0298/53-971.** Fax 0298/53-626. 23 units. A/C TEL. Dr29,000–Dr36,000 ($96–$120) double; Dr45,000–Dr53,000 ($150–$176) suite. Rates include breakfast. AE, DC, EURO, MC, V. Closed mid-Jan to mid-Feb.

The Bratsera keeps turning up on everyone's list of the best hotels in Greece, which says a lot about the state of hotels in Greece. True, this small hotel, in a lovingly restored 1860 sponge factory a short stroll from the harbor, is one of Hydra's nicest hotels. The rooms—most are good sized, but a few are quite small—are all different, distinctively decorated in typical Hydriot style. The small pool, with wisteria-covered trellises, is very welcoming; meals are sometimes served poolside in fair weather. The hotel restaurant (about Dr10,000/$33 per person) offers such slightly off-beat treats as fisherman's linguine.

So, what's the problem? For one thing, we've had reports that room-service trays left in the hall after breakfast were still not collected by late afternoon and that messages left for guests were not always delivered. And surely a fisherman's linguine should be topped with more than a solitary shrimp and one forlorn crayfish. We're eager to hear more from readers on this hotel.

Hotel Hydra. Odos Voulgari 8, 18040 Hydra. ☎ **0298/52-102.** Fax 0298/52-102. 13 units, 8 with bathroom. TEL. Dr18,000 ($60) double without bathroom; Dr21,600 ($72) double with bathroom. Rates include breakfast. MC, V. Open year-round.

This is one of the best bargains in town if you don't mind the steep walk up to a beautifully restored two-story, gray-stone mansion on the western cliff, to the right as you get off the ferry. The rooms are carpeted, high ceilinged, and simply furnished, many with balconies overlooking the town and harbor.

Hotel Leto. 18040 Hydra. ☎ **0298/53-385,** or ☎ 01/801-2855 in Athens. Fax 0298/53-806, or 01/801-9995 in Athens. 30 units. TEL. Dr17,500 ($58) double; Dr20,000 ($67) double with A/C; Dr27,900 ($93) suites with A/C (for 3–4 persons). Rates include buffet breakfast. AE, V.

The recently renovated Leto, just off the harbor, has new hardwood floors, large bathrooms, and contemporary furnishings, including modern-art posters on the walls. The staff is young and eager to please (there's a serious attempt to create smoke-free zones for guests at breakfast). The Leto also has a very nice garden.

✪ **Hotel Miranda.** 18040 Hydra. ☎ **0298/52-230.** Fax 0298/53-510. 16 units. TEL. Dr19,600 ($65) double without A/C; Dr27,600 ($92) double with A/C; Dr31,600 ($105) double with A/C and balcony; Dr32,600 ($109) suite. Rates include breakfast. AE, V.

Once, when we were trapped for the night on Hydra by bad weather, we were lucky enough to get the last room at the Miranda. The room was small, with a tiny bathroom and no real view—and it's a tribute to this hotel that we have wonderful memories of that visit. Most of the rooms here are good sized, with nice views of the lovely garden courtyard and town. Throughout, this handsome 1820 sea-captain's mansion is decorated with oriental rugs, antique cabinets, worn wooden chests, marble tables, contemporary paintings, and period naval engravings. There's even a small art gallery—in short, this is a very classy place.

Hotel Mistral. 18040 Hydra. ☎ **0298/52-509.** Fax 0298/53-412. 19 units. TEL. Dr19,500 ($65) double; Dr20,500 ($68) double with A/C. Rates include breakfast.

The three-story Mistral (named for the strong northerly winds that cool the late summer) is another small hotel in a nicely restored, traditional Hydriot house. The furnishings here are standard hotel contemporary, with some nice watercolors of local views. One plus here: the large courtyard, where the proprietor Sophia will serve dinner—but only to hotel guests. This is a pleasant place to sit and enjoy some fresh seafood at reasonable prices, just a few minutes walk from the harbor.

Hotel Orloff. Odos Rafalia 9, 18040 Hydra. ☎ **0298/52-564.** Fax 0298/53-532. 10 units. A/C TEL. Dr25,500–Dr39,000 ($85–$130). Rates include breakfast. AE, MC, V.

This mansion was built in the 18th century by a Russian philhellene, Count Orloff. Now the recently restored 200-year-old mansion, just a short walk from the port, is a pleasant small hotel, distinctively decorated with antique furnishings and professionally and graciously managed. Each room is unique, quiet, and comfortable (with good-sized bathrooms), and there's a very nice basement lounge with a bar. Breakfast is excellent.

WHERE TO DINE

The harborside eateries are predictably expensive and not very good, although the view is so nice that you may not care. There are also a number of cafes along the waterfront, including **To Roloi** (The Clock), by the Clock Tower. Just off the harbor, the **Ambrosia Cafe** serves vegetarian fare and good breakfasts.

Bratsera. Odos Tombazi, Hydra. ☎ **0298/52-794.** Reservations recommended in summer and on weekends. Main courses Dr1,500–Dr4,200 ($5–$14). AE, DC, EURO, MC, V. Daily 8am–11pm. GREEK/INTERNATIONAL.

This restaurant in the Hotel Bratsera just off the harbor is getting generally favorable reviews, although we've heard complaints of terribly slow service. The indoor dining area is charmingly rustic and decorated with antique maps, but sitting outdoors under the wisteria-covered trellis beside the pool may be more enjoyable. The menu is small but varied, with pastas, fresh seafood, grilled meats, and even a few Chinese specialties. (See also the Hotel Bratsera under "Where to Stay," above.)

Marina's Taverna. Vlihos. ☎ **0298/52-496.** Main courses Dr1,000–Dr3,200 ($4.25–$11). No credit cards. Daily noon–11pm. GREEK.

Several readers report that they have enjoyed both the food and the spectacular sunset at this seaside taverna, appropriately nicknamed the Iliovasilema ("Sunset"). Perched on the rocks west of the swimming place at Kamini, it's a Dr3,000 ($10) water-taxi ride from town. The menu is basic, but the food is fresh and carefully prepared by the lovely Marina; her *kleftiko* (pork pie, an island specialty) is superb.

O Kipos (The Garden). Hydra. ☎ **0298/52-329.** Reservations recommended in the summer. Main courses Dr1,800–Dr3,600 ($6–$12). No credit cards. Daily 7pm–midnight. GREEK.

This very popular *psisteria* (grill) is in a tree-filled garden behind whitewashed walls, several blocks up from the quay side of the harbor. Grilled meat is, of course, the specialty, but there is also excellent swordfish souvlaki. The mezedes alone will be enough for many. The specialty is *eksohiko*—lamb wrapped in filo (thin leaves of pastry). We've always enjoyed eating here, except on one or two occasions when boisterous tour groups were in evidence.

To Steki. Odos Miaouli. ☎ **0298/53-517.** Main courses Dr1,200–Dr2,400 ($4–$8); daily specials Dr2,200–Dr3,500 ($7–$12). No credit cards. GREEK.

This small taverna, a few blocks up from the quay-side end of the harbor, has simple food at reasonable prices. The walls inside have framed murals showing a rather idealized traditional island life. The daily specials, including moussaka and stuffed tomatoes, sometimes include locally caught seafood; they come with salad, vegetables, and a dessert.

HYDRA AFTER DARK

The **Veranda** is up from the right (west) end of the harbor, near the Hotel Hydra; look for the sign SAVVAS ROOMS TO LET. It's an excellent place to sip a glass of retsina and watch the sunset. There are several discos, most of them fairly low-key and usually open from June to September. **Heaven** (☎ 0298/52-716), which has grand views, is up the hill on the west side of town, and **Kavos** (☎ 0298/52-716), west above the harbor, has a pleasant garden for a rest from the dancing. The louder **Scirocco** is well outside of town, on the way to Kamini.

Port-side, there are plenty of bars. **The Pirate** (☎ 0298/52-711), near the Clock Tower, is the best known, though nearby **To Roloi** is probably a quieter place for a nightcap. Friends report enjoying a drink at the **Amalour,** just off the harbor, where they were surrounded by hip, black-clad 20- and 30-somethings. There are also a few local haunts left around the harbor; if you see them, you'll recognize them.

4 Spetses

98km (53 nautical miles) SW of Piraeus; 3km (2 nautical miles) from Ermioni

Despite a series of dreadful fires, Spetses's pine groves still make it the greenest of the Saronic Gulf islands. In fact, this island was called "Pityoussa" (pine-tree island) in antiquity. Although the architecture here is less impressive than on Hydra, there are some handsome **archontika** (mansions), built by wealthy 18th- and 19th-century sea captains, and the island has long been popular with wealthy Athenians.

Many Spetses homes have handsome pebble mosaic courtyards; if you're lucky, you'll catch a glimpse of some when garden gates are open. One real plus for visitors here: Cars are not allowed to circulate freely in Spetses town, which would make for a good deal of tranquillity if motorcycles were not increasingly endemic.

In recent years Spetses has become increasingly popular with foreign tourists, especially the British. Some are pilgrims to see the island where John Fowles set his novel *The Magus,* but more are with tour groups. Consequently, there are times here when you can hear as much English as Greek spoken in cafes and restaurants. As always, if you come here off-season, you're bound to have a more relaxed time and get a better sense of island life—even though some restaurants, shops, and small hotels will be closed.

ESSENTIALS

GETTING THERE   Several **ferries** and **excursion boats** make the 5-hour voyage from Piraeus daily, connecting with the other Saronic islands; contact the **Piraeus Port Authority** (☎ 01/451-1311) for schedules. (*Note:* Cars are not allowed on the island without express permission.) Several **hydrofoils** (Flying Dolphins and Supercats) leave Piraeus's Zea Marina daily, most connecting with the other Saronic islands; express service takes 90 minutes. Contact **Ceres Hydrofoils** (☎ 01/ 42-80-001) in Piraeus for schedules. (Reservations are recommended on weekends.)

There is less frequent service from Spetses to the island of Kithira and various ports on the Peloponnese.

VISITOR INFORMATION   **Pine Island Tours** (☎ 0298/72-464; fax 0298/ 73-255), across from the water-taxi stop, can help you with day tours, ferry tickets, travel plans, and yacht charters; the manager, Kostas, is exceptionally well-informed about the island, and handles rentals for the Villa Yasemia, the home of the Magus in John Fowles's novel.

Andrew Thomas's *Spetses* (Lycabettus Press), usually on sale on the island, is recommended to those wanting to pursue Spetses's history.

GETTING AROUND   The island's limited public transportation consists of two municipal **buses** and three or four **taxis**. **Mopeds** can be rented everywhere, beginning at about Dr4,500 ($15) per day. **Bikes** are also widely available, and the terrain along the road around the island makes them sufficient means of transportation; three-speed bikes cost about Dr1,500 ($5) a day, while newer 21-speed models go for about Dr3,000 ($10).

Horse-drawn carriages can take you away from the busy port into the quieter back streets where most of the island's handsome old mansions are to be found. (Take your time choosing a driver; some are friendly and informative, others are surly and bent on getting the trip over with. Fares are highly negotiable.)

The best way to get to the various beaches around the island, as well as to the beach at Kosta, on the Peloponnese, is by **water taxi** (locally called a *venzina*, "gasoline"); these little powered boats can hold about eight to 10 people. A tour around the island should cost about Dr7,500 ($25), and shorter trips, such as from Dapia to the Old Harbor, should cost about Dr3,000 ($10). Schedules are posted on the pier.

FAST FACTS   You can exchange currency at the **National Bank of Greece,** on the harbor; it has an ATM. Most travel agencies (usually open from 9am to 8pm) will also exchange money, usually at a less favorable rate than the bank. The health **clinic** (☎ 0298/72-201) is signposted inland from the east (left) side of the port. The local **police** (☎ 0298/73-100) and **tourist police** (☎ 0298/73-744) are to the left off the Dapia pier, where the hydrofoils dock, on Odos Botassi. The **post office** is on Odos Botassi near the police station; it's open from 8am to 2pm. The **telephone office (OTE),** open daily from 7:30am to 3pm, is to the right off the Dapia pier, behind the Hotel Soleil.

WHAT TO SEE & DO
EXPLORING SPETSES TOWN (KASTELLI)

Spetses Town (also called Kastelli) meanders along the harbor and inland in a lazy fashion, with most of its neoclassical mansions partly hidden from envious eyes by high walls and greenery. Much of the town's street life takes place on the Dapia, the square where the ferries and hydrofoils now arrive; the old harbor, Baltiza, largely silted up, is just east of town, before the popular swimming spots at Ayia Marina.

If you sit at a cafe on the Dapia, you'll see pretty much everyone here coming and going. The handsome black-and-white pebble mosaic commemorates the moment during the War of Independence when the first flag with the motto "Freedom or Death" was raised. Thanks to its large fleet, Spetses played an important part in the War of Independence, and the biggest and most colorful celebration of the year falls on the weekend closest to September 8, the anniversary of the island's victory over the Turks in the Straits of Spetses in 1822.

One of the greatest heroes of the War of Independence was, in fact, a heroine: Laskarina Bouboulina, the daughter of a naval captain from Hydra. Bouboulina built the warship *Agamemnon,* served as its captain, and was responsible for several naval victories. Some said she could drink any man under the table and that she was so ugly, the only way she could keep a lover was with a gun. You can see where Bouboulina lived when she was ashore by visiting the **Laskarina Bouboulina House (☎ 0298/ 72-077)** in Pefkakia, just off the port. It's open to the public Monday through Saturday from 10am to 5:30pm, with an English-speaking guide giving a half-hour tour; admission is Dr800 ($2.65). You can even see her bones, along with archaeological relics and more recent folk objects, at the **Mexis Museum,** beyond the post office, behind the clinic, open daily from 9:30am to 2:30pm; admission is Dr500 ($1.65). Stop by her statue as well, on the Dapia waterfront by the Hotel Possidonion.

The **Hotel Possidonion** itself figures in Spetses's history. The hotel was built in 1911, as one of Greece's first "European"-style hotels, by the island's greatest benefactor, Sotiris Anaryiros. He also built Anaryiros College, just outside town, modeled on an English public school. It's now most famous because John Fowles taught here, and is closed most of the year except during August, when it hosts the Anaryiria festival of art exhibits.

The harbor front has the usual tourist shops, but you might have a look by the OTE, behind the Hotel Soleil, at **Pityoussa** (no phone), which has a collection of decorative folk paintings, ceramics, and interesting gift items.

If you head east away from the Dapia, you'll come to the picturesque **Old Harbor** (the Baltiza, or Paleo Limani), where the wealthy moor their yachts. The **Cathedral of Ayios Nikolaos** (St. Nicholas) here is the oldest church in town; it has a lovely bell tower on which the Greek flag was first raised on the island. A pebble mosaic here shows the event, as do a number of similar pebble mosaics in Spetses town. While you're at the old harbor, have a look at the boatyards where you can usually see caïques (*kaikia*) being made with tools little different from those used when Bouboulina's mighty *Agamemnon* was built here.

BEACHES

Ayia Marina, signposted and about a 30-minute walk east of Spetses town, is the best town beach. There are also a number of tavernas, cafes, and discos here. On the south side of the island, **Ayii Anaryiri** has the best sandy beach anywhere in the Saronic Gulf, a perfect C-shaped cove lined with trees, bars, and several tavernas (we prefer the Taverna Tassos). The best way to get here is by water taxi.

Some prefer the beach at **Ayia Paraskevi,** which is smaller and more private because it's more closely bordered by pine trees. There's a cantina and the **Villa Yasemia,** residence of the Magus himself, which can now be rented, for a price (see "Visitor Information," above). West over some rocks is the island's official nudist beach. **Zogeria,** on the northwest coast, has a few places to eat and some pretty rocky coves for swimming. West of Spetses Town, **Paradise Beach** is usually crowded, littered, and to be avoided.

WHERE TO STAY

Finding a good, quiet, centrally located room in spread-out Spetses is not easy. Below are some suggestions.

Hotel Faros. Plateia Kentriki (Central Sq.), 18050 Spetses. ☎ **0298/72-613.** 50 units. TEL. Dr11,400 ($38) double. No credit cards.

Though there's no *faros* (lighthouse) nearby, this older hotel shares the busy central square with a Taverna Faros, a Faros Pizzeria, and other establishments whose tables and chairs curb the flow of vehicular traffic. Try for the top floor, where simple, comfortable, twin-bedded rooms are quietest, with balcony views of the island.

✪ **Hotel Possidonion.** Dapia, 18050 Spetses. ☎ **0298/72-208** or 0298/72-006. Fax 0298/72-208. 55 units. TEL. Dr25,500 ($85) double; Dr30,000 ($100) double with sea view. Rates include breakfast. AE, DC, MC, V.

The landmark Poseidon (as we would call it) is a grand and gracious hotel that was built in 1911 and, under new management, was completely renovated in the early 1990s. This belle-epoque classic boasts two grand pianos in its lobby and the statue of Bouboulina guarding the plaza in front. The high-ceilinged rooms are spacious, and sparsely but elegantly furnished. The old-fashioned bathrooms have large tubs. The view over the harbor from the tall front windows is superb.

Spetses Hotel. 18050 Spetses. ☎ **0298/72-602.** Fax 0298/72-494. 77 units. A/C TEL. Dr28,000 ($93). MC, V.

The Spetses sits on its own beach and has its own restaurant, which makes it a good choice if you don't want to hassle with other restaurants, which are usually very crowded in the summer. The rooms here are furnished with the standard Greek hotel twin beds and bedside tables, and the bathrooms are standard. If you stay for more than a week, there is usually a discount of about $10 a night.

✪ **Star Hotel.** Plateia Dapia, 18050 Spetses. ☎ **0298/72-214** or 0298/72-728. Fax 0298/72-872. 37 units. TEL. Dr15,000 ($50) double. No credit cards.

This blue-shuttered five-story hotel, the best in its price range, is fortuitously situated on a pebbled mosaic, making it off-limits to vehicles. All rooms have balconies, the front ones with views of the harbor. The large bathrooms contain bathtub, shower, and bidet. Breakfast is available à la carte in the large lobby.

WHERE TO DINE

Spetses's restaurants can be packed with Athenians on weekend evenings, and you may want to eat unfashionably early (about 9pm) to avoid the Greek crush. The island also has some of the best **bakeries** in the Saronic Gulf, and all serve an island specialty called *amygdalota,* small cone-shaped almond cakes flavored with rosewater and covered with powdered sugar.

For standard Greek taverna food, usually including a number of vegetable dishes, try the rooftop taverna **Lirakis,** Dapia (☎ **0298/72-188**), over the Lirakis supermarket, with a nice view over the harbor.

The Bakery Restaurant. Dapia. No phone. Main courses Dr1,500–Dr3,900 ($5–$13). EURO, MC, V. Daily 6:30pm–midnight. GREEK/CONTINENTAL.

This restaurant is on the deck above one of the island's more popular patisseries. The food is prepared fresh, with little oil, and served hot. The chef obviously understands foreign palates and offers smoked trout salad, grilled steak, roasted lamb with peas, and the usual Greek dishes.

Exedra Taverna. Paleo Limani. ☎ **0298/73-497.** Main courses Dr1,500–Dr4,200 ($5–$14). No credit cards. Daily noon–3pm and 7pm–midnight. GREEK/SEAFOOD.

This traditional taverna on the Old Harbor, where yachts from all over Europe moor, is also known by locals as Siora's, after the proprietor. The specialties are fish Spetsiota (a broiled fish-and-tomato casserole) and Argo (shrimp and lobster baked with sharp feta cheese). The freshly cooked zucchini, eggplant, and other seasonal vegetables are also excellent. If you can't find a table for supper, try the nearby **Taverna Liyeri,** also known for good seafood.

Lazaros Taverna. Dapia. No phone. Main courses Dr1,000–Dr3,200 ($3.35–$11). No credit cards. Daily 6:30pm–midnight. GREEK.

This traditional place is decorated with potted ivy, family photos, and big kegs of homemade retsina lining the walls. It's popular with a lively local crowd that comes here for the good, fresh, reasonably priced food. The menu is small and features grilled meats and daily specials, such as goat in lemon sauce. The Lazaros is inland and uphill about 400 meters from the water.

SPETSES AFTER DARK

There's plenty of nightlife on Spetses, with bars, discos, and bouzouki clubs from the Dapia to the Old Harbor to Ayia Marina, and even the more remote beaches.

For bars, try **Socrates** in the heart of Dapia. The **Anchor** is more upscale, and there's the **Bracera Music Bar** on the yachting marina. For something a little more sedate, try the **Halcyon** or the **Veranda,** with softer Greek music. To the west of town, in Kounoupitsa, near the popular Patralis Fish Taverna, **Zorba's** and **Kalia** are popular bars.

As for discos, there's the trendy and hot **Figaro,** with a seaside patio and international funk until midnight, when the music switches to Greek and the dancing follows step. The **Delfina Disco,** opposite the Dapia town beach on the road to the Old Harbor, has become increasingly popular. **Disco Fever,** with its flashing lights, draws the British crowd, while **Naos,** which looks more like a castle than a temple, features techno pop. The **Fox** often has live Greek music and dancing; obvious tourists are usually encouraged to join in—information that may help you decide either to go here, or to stay away!

8 The Peloponnese

by Sherry Marker

What's special about the Peloponnese? It's tempting to answer, "Everything." With the exception of Athens and Delphi, just across the Gulf of Corinth, virtually every famous ancient site in Greece is in the Peloponnese—the awesome Mycenaean palaces of Kings Agamemnon and Nestor at Mycenae and Pylos (Pilos); the mysterious thick-walled Mycenaean fortress at Tiryns; the magnificent classical temples at Corinth, Nemea, Vassae, and Olympia; and the monumental theaters at Argos and Epidaurus, still used for performances today.

But the Peloponnese isn't just a grab bag of famous ancient sites. This peninsula, divided from the mainland by the Corinth Canal, is studded with medieval castles and monasteries, bounded by sand beaches, and dominated by two of Greece's most impressive mountain ranges: Taygetos and Parnon. Tucked away in the valleys and hanging precipitously from the mountainsides are hundreds of the villages that are among the Peloponnese's greatest treasures. An evening under the plane trees in tiny Andritsena, where the sheep bells are the loudest sound at night and oregano and flowering broom scent the hills, is every bit as memorable as a visit to one of the famous ancient sites. This is perhaps especially true in the mountains of Arcadia and deep in the Mani peninsula, where traditional Greek hospitality hasn't been eroded by too many busloads of visitors.

While many of the Aegean islands sag under the weight of tourists from May until September, the Peloponnese is still relatively uncrowded, even in midsummer. That doesn't mean that you're going to have Olympia all to yourself if you arrive at high noon in August, but it does mean that if you get to Olympia early in the morning, you may have a quiet hour under the pine trees. If you're traveling with a car and can set your own pace, you can visit even the most popular tourist destinations of Corinth, Mycenae, Epidaurus, and Olympia early in the morning or late in the afternoon—and have them virtually all to yourself.

Still, even the most avid tourists do not live by culture alone, and one of the great delights of spending time in the Peloponnese comes from the quiet hours spent in seaside cafes, watching fishermen mend their nets while Greek families settle down for a leisurely meal. *Leisurely* is the word to remember in the Peloponnese, an ideal place to make haste slowly. And what better place to watch shepherds on the hills or fishing boats on the horizon as you wait for dinner?

Peloponnesian culinary favorites include rabbit stew (*kouneli stifado*) with a surprising hint of cinnamon, or fish à la Spetsai (fish baked with tomato sauce). In summer—when it seems that every tree on the plain of Argos hangs with apricots and every vine is heavy with tomatoes—Peloponnesian food is at its freshest and best. If you're here in the spring, look for delicious fresh artichokes and delicate little strawberries. Even in winter, the fresh lettuce grown here is superb, citrus fruits are at their peak, and there's less competition in restaurants to get the best and freshest fish.

A few suggestions for your trip to the Peloponnese: Don't forget sunscreen, a broadbrimmed hat, good walking shoes, and some books to read while you're sitting in that cafe. Bookstores with a good selection of English titles are few and far between here, although you will find excellent stores in Nafplion and Olympia. In the summer of 1998, many Peloponnesian banks were installing ATMs, and all banks, most hotels, and many post offices changed money at competitive rates.

Speaking of competitive rates, don't hesitate to ask if there's a cheaper rate for a room than the one first quoted at hotels. This is especially true off-season, when many hotels are willing to be quite flexible in their prices.

You'll probably be pleasantly surprised at how very impressed locals are if you master the linguistic basics of hello (*yassas*) and thank you (*efcharisto*). If you have trouble pronouncing "efcharisto," here's a suggestion: It sounds a lot like the name "F. Harry Stowe." If you're still having trouble, try *merci* (French for "thank you"), which most Greeks use interchangeably with *eucharisto*.

And however relaxed you get on your Peloponnesian holiday, it's a good idea to remember that this is still one of the more conservative areas of Greece, and virtually the only area where there's strong sentiment to restore the monarchy and bring back the good old days. Most Peloponnesians are at best amused and at worst deeply offended by public drunkenness, elaborate displays of affection, and swimsuits or shorts and halters worn anywhere but on the beach. That said, *kalo taxidi* (bon voyage) on your trip to the Peloponnese, the most beautiful and historic part of Greece.

STRATEGIES FOR EXPLORING THE REGION   If you look at our map of the Peloponnese, you'll realize that you can go around the region clockwise or counterclockwise. Whichever approach you choose, at some point you'll probably head into the center of the Peloponnese, to see the Byzantine ghost town of Mistra outside ancient Sparta, or to take in some of the lovely mountain villages of Arcadia and the temple of Apollo at Vassae. Here's one suggested itinerary based on the assumption that you have your own car. If you don't, and are going to travel by public transportation, you can still do everything we're suggesting, but you'd be wise to double the time allowed. Even if you do have a car, don't let yourself be deceived by the short distances between what you want to see in the Peloponnese. You'll be astonished at how long even a short drive on a winding mountain road can take—especially when you have to stop repeatedly to let flocks of goats cross the road!

In 2 days, you can see most of the important sites in the northern Peloponnese as well as the lovely harbor town of Nafplion. Head from Athens to **Corinth,** have a look at the canal and visit the ancient site, as well as **Acrocorinth,** the sugarloaf mountain that looms over the plain of Corinth. Then, head on to **Mycenae,** before ending up for the night in **Nafplion,** where you may feel like a swim at the public bathing beach there. In the morning, explore Nafplion and drive over to **Epidaurus,** to see the famous theater and site, before heading back along the coast to Athens.

If you have a couple of more days to spend here, you can head from Nafplion to **Tripolis** and **Olympia,** taking in some of the Arcadian mountain villages, and perhaps the **temple of Vassae,** en route. Then, you can head back to Athens along the **Gulf of Corinth,** which offers lots of chances for a swim. At this point, you still will have missed a great deal in the Peloponnese—so we hope you have at least a week to spend here.

Tour Alternatives

If you don't want to travel through the Peloponnese on your own, but hate the thought of a conventional tour, you might want to contact two English companies that run "green" tours to various sections of Greece, including the Peloponnese. **Grecofile,** Sourdock Hill, Barkisland, Halifax, West Yorkshire HX4 OAG (☎ **0422/375-999** or 0422/371-796; fax 0422/310-340), has fly-drive trips to the Peloponnese for small groups. **Zoe Holidays,** 34 Thornhill Rd., Surbiton, Surrey, KT6 7TL 9 (☎ **081/390-7623**), specializes in "alternative" Greece, arranging stays in monasteries, restored homes, and women's cooperatives in several villages.

1 Corinth

89km (55 miles) W of Athens

Today, as in antiquity, Corinth, along with Patras, is one of the two major gateways to the Peloponnese. Still, gates are there to pass through, not to linger in. There's no reason not to stop to see the ships slipping through the impressive Corinth Canal that cuts across the isthmus, and then head straight for ancient Corinth, bypassing the modern city altogether. Mycenae and Nafplion both have excellent hotels and restaurants—and are only about an hour's drive from Corinth.

In fact, the entire modern town of Corinth (population 24,000) has remarkably little to recommend it. The town was moved here in 1834, after an earthquake devastated the settlement at ancient Corinth; successive earthquakes in 1858, 1928, and 1981 destroyed virtually every interesting building in the new town. As a result, Corinth is now a thicket of undistinguished, flat-roofed buildings, supposedly built to withstand future quakes.

All this makes modern Corinth a far cry from ancient Corinth, which was famously splendid and lively. As one Greek proverb had it, "See Corinth and Die," suggesting that there was nothing to look forward to after visiting the splendid monuments (and fleshpots) of the city that dominated trade in Greece for much of the 7th and 8th centuries B.C. and had a second golden age under the Romans in the 2nd century A.D.

A LOOK AT THE PAST   Historians are fond of saying that "Geography is destiny," and much of Corinth's power and prosperity came from its strategic location overlooking the sea and land routes into the Peloponnese. No enemy could sneak across the isthmus without being spotted by the soldiers stationed on Corinth's towering acropolis, Acrocorinth (1,863 ft.).

During the 8th and 7th centuries B.C., Corinth controlled much of the trade in the Mediterranean and founded colonies as far away as Syracuse in Sicily. This was when Corinth made and exported the distinctive red-and-black figured pottery decorated with lively animal motifs, examples of which are on display in the excavation museum. Great sailors, the Corinthians were credited with refining the design of the *trireme,* the standard warship in Greek antiquity. The only obstacle Corinth couldn't overcome was the isthmus itself: ships had to be dragged from the port of Kenchreai on the east to the port of Lechaion on the west.

Although Corinth's greatest period of prosperity was between the 8th and 5th centuries B.C., most of the ancient remains here are from the Roman period. Razed and destroyed when the Romans conquered Greece in 146 B.C., Corinth was refounded by Julius Caesar in 44 B.C. and began a second period of wealth and prosperity. When Saint Paul visited here in A.D. 52, he found Corinth all too sophisticated and chastised the Corinthians for their wanton ways.

By the 2nd century A.D., with some 300,000 citizens and 500,000 slaves, Corinth was much larger and more powerful than Athens. During the next hundred years, a series of barbarian invasions and attacks undermined Corinth's prosperity. Thereafter, although the long series of invaders—Normans, Franks, Venetians, and Turks—fought for control of the strategic citadel of Acrocorinth, Corinth itself was a provincial backwater with a glorious past.

ESSENTIALS

GETTING THERE   By Train   There are several trains a day from Athens's Stathmos Peloponnisou (Train Station for the Peloponnese) to the Corinth station off Odos Demokratias (☎ 0741/22-522). These trains are almost invariably late, often taking 3 hours or more. For information on schedules and fares, call ☎ 01/ 512-4913.

By Bus   There are at least 15 buses a day, taking 2 to 2½ hours from the **Stathmos Leoforia Peloponnisou** (Bus Station for the Peloponnese) in Athens, Odos Kifissou 100 (☎ 01/51-34-110), to the Corinth station at Odos Ermou and Odos Koliatsou (☎ 0741/25-645), where you can catch a bus (15 to 20 min.) to Archaia Korinthos. For information on Athens-Corinth-Athens schedules and fares, call ☎ 01/51-28-233.

Buses for the Peloponnese leave Corinth from the station at the corner of Odos Konstantinou and Odos Aratou (☎ 0741/244-03). For most destinations beyond Tripolis, you'll find yourself changing buses at Tripolis.

By Car   The National Highway runs from Athens to Corinth. The toll is Dr400 ($1.35). The highway is in the process of being widened to seven lanes, but still contains some three-lane stretches that are particularly dangerous. The highway now sweeps over the Corinth Canal; if you want to stop here, look for the signs indicating the Canal Tourist Area. Shortly after the canal, you'll see signs for Corinth (the modern town and ancient site), Isthmia (site of the Isthmian Games), and Patras. Allow at least 1½ hours for the journey from Athens.

FAST FACTS   You can find **ATMs** and exchange currency at the **National Bank of Greece,** Ethniki Antistaseos 7, and several banks on Leoforos Vas. Konstantinos. The **hospital** (☎ 0741/25-711) is clearly signposted in town and has English-speaking doctors on staff. The **police** (☎ 0741/22-143) and the **tourist police** (☎ 0741/ 23-282) are both at Ermou 51, near the Athens bus station. The **telephone office (OTE),** Odos Kolokotroni 33 (open from 6am to midnight), and the **post office,** by the park on Odos Adimantou (open Mon through Fri from 7:30am to 2pm), are both signposted.

WHAT TO SEE & DO

The new highway rushes you over the **Corinth Canal** very quickly, and unless you're vigilant you can miss the turnoff to the **Canal Tourist Area.** Before the new road was completed in 1997, almost everyone stopped here for a coffee, a souvlaki, and a look at the Corinth Canal that separates the Peloponnese from the mainland. Now, much traffic hurtles past, and the cafes, restaurants, and shops here are hurting. There's a small post office at the canal, along with a kiosk with postcards and English-language newspapers; most of the large souvlaki places have clean toilet facilities (and very tough souvlaki). One word of warning that is necessary here and almost nowhere else in Greece: Be sure to lock your car door. This is a popular spot for thieves to prey on unwary tourists.

The French engineers who built the Corinth Canal between 1881 and 1893 used lots of dynamite, blasting through 285 feet of sheer rock to make this 6.4-kilometer-long (4 miles), 30-yard-wide passageway. The Corinth Canal utterly revolutionized shipping in the Mediterranean: Ships that previously had made their way laboriously around Cape Matapan at the southern tip of the Peloponnese could dart through the canal. The journey from Brindisi, Italy, to Athens was immediately shortened by more than 320 kilometers (200 miles).

Although it took modern technology to build the canal, the Roman emperors Caligula and Nero had tried, and failed, to dig a canal with slave labor. Nero was obsessed with the project, going so far as to lift the first shovelful of earth with a dainty golden trowel. That done, he headed back to Rome and left the real work to the 6,000 Jewish slaves he had brought here from Judea.

The Archaeological Museum. Old Corinth, on the site of ancient Corinth. ☎ **0741/ 31-207.** Admission Dr1,200 ($4) includes admission to the site. Summer Mon–Fri 8am–7pm; Sat–Sun 8am–3pm. Winter Mon–Fri 8:45am–3pm; Sat–Sun 8:30am–3pm.

As you'd expect, the museum has a particularly fine collection of the famous Corinthian pottery that is often decorated with charming red-and-black figures of birds and animals. In addition, there are a number of statues of Roman worthies and several mosaics, including one in which Pan is shown piping away to a clutch of cows. The museum also has an extensive collection of finds from the shrine of Asklepios; as many of these are graphic representations of intimate body parts, they are kept in a room that is usually locked. If you express a scholarly interest, a guard may unlock the room. The museum courtyard is a shady spot to sit and read up on the ancient site.

Ancient Corinth. Old Corinth. ☎ **0741/31-207.** Admission Dr1,000 ($3.35), includes admission to the museum (see above). Summer Mon–Fri 8am–7pm; Sat–Sun 8am–3pm. Winter Mon–Fri 8:45am–3pm; Sat–Sun 8:30am–3pm.

If at all possible, visit here first thing in the morning or late in the afternoon: there will be fewer tourists, and the sun on this virtually shadeless site will be less fierce.

The most conspicuous—and the most handsome—surviving building at ancient Corinth is clearly the 6th-century B.C. **Temple of Apollo,** which stands on a low hill overlooking the extensive remains of the **Roman Agora** (marketplace). Only seven of the temple's 38 monolithic Doric columns are standing, the others having long since been toppled by earthquakes.

From the temple, ancient Corinth's main drag, a 40-foot-wide marble-paved road that ran from the port of Lechaion into the heart of the marketplace, is clearly visible. Pottery from Corinth was carried down this road to the ships that took it around the world; back along the same road came the goods Corinthian merchants bought in every corner of the Mediterranean. Everything made here and brought here was for sale in countless shops, many of whose foundations are still clearly visible in the agora.

Two spots in the agora are especially famous: the **Bema** and the **fountain of Peirene.** In the 2nd century A.D., the famous Roman traveler, philhellene, and benefactor Herodes Atticus rebuilt the original modest fountain house. Like most Romans, Herodes seemed to think that bigger was better: when he was done, the spring was encased in an elaborate two-storied building with arches and arcades and a 50-square-foot courtyard. Peirene, by the way, was a woman who wept so hard when she lost her son that she finally dissolved into the spring that still flows here. As for the Bema, this was the public platform where St. Paul had to plead his case when the Corinthians, irritated by his constant criticisms, hauled him up in front of the Roman governor Gallo in A.D. 52.

Acrocorinth. Old Corinth. Admission Dr500 ($1.65). Tues–Sun 8:30am–6pm.

A road twists from the ancient site to the summit of Acrocorinth, the rugged limestone sugarloaf mountain that looms 1,885 feet above the plain. On a clear day, the views from the summit are superb, although it's been a long time since the atmosphere was clear enough to spot the glistening columns of the Parthenon on the Athenian acropolis.

A superb natural acropolis, Acrocorinth was fortified first in antiquity. Everyone who came later—the Byzantines, Franks, Venetians, and Turks—simply added to the original walls. Today, there are three courses of outer walls, massive gates with towers, and a jumble of ruined houses, churches, and barracks. Before you head down, you might like to have a cold drink at the small cafe here and reflect on the fact that there was a Temple of Aphrodite on this summit in antiquity, staffed by an estimated 1,000 temple prostitutes—some of whom worked the streets in Corinth, but others who worked here, awaiting those hardy customers who walked up from Corinth.

WHERE TO STAY

As noted, if at all possible, do not stay in Corinth, a noisy and unappealing town. If you must, try the 19-unit **Hotel Bellevue,** Odos Damaskinou 41 (☎ **0741/22-088**), overlooking the harbor. The rooms in front have the best views, but also the most street noise; a double goes for Dr13,500 ($45).

Kalamaki Beach Hotel. P.O. Box 22, 20100 Corinth. ☎ **0741/37-653,** or 01/323-5605 in Athens. Fax 0741/37-652, or 01/324-1092 in Athens. 82 units. TV TEL. Dr25,500–Dr30,000 ($85–$100) double. No credit cards.

This sprawling beach resort, with its own restaurant, two pools, gardens, and tennis courts, is about 9.6 kilometers (6 miles) outside Corinth near Isthmia. The rooms are plainly furnished, with tile floors, decent beds, semi-comfortable reading chairs, and good-sized balconies and bathrooms. This is a popular place with tour groups and Greek families. If you're exploring the archaeological sites in the northern Peloponnese and want to stay on the water, you might consider the Kalamaki—but remember that independent travelers are in the minority here.

WHERE TO DINE

None of the cafes or restaurants along the Corinth Canal out of town or the water-front in town deserves to be singled out; most deserve to be avoided. Similarly, the restaurants near the ancient site tend to have high prices and mediocre food. That said, here are some suggestions if you find yourself hungry in Corinth (and can't wait until you get to Nafplion, where there are lots of good places to eat).

Archaeologists of the American School of Classical Studies who excavate here give the nod to the grandly named **Splendid** restaurant across from the site; a lunch or dinner of simple stews, chops, and salads costs around Dr2,400 ($8).

In the modern town, locals speak well of the **Pantheon Restaurant,** Odos Ethniki Antistaseos, Corinth (☎ **0741/25-780**), which serves standard Greek fare such as chops, salads, moussaka, and *pastitsio* (macaroni with cream sauce); lunch or dinner goes for around Dr2,400 ($8). If you like sardines, try **Theodorakis Taverna,** on the waterfront. Lunch or dinner of sardines, salad, and wine or beer costs around Dr2,000 ($7).

SIDE TRIPS FROM CORINTH
ISTHMIA

Isthmia was one of the four places in Greece where Panhellenic Games were held (the others being Delphi, Olympia, and Nemea). According to legend, the games here were founded in 582 B.C. in honor of a certain Meliertes, whose body was carried ashore by a dolphin at the very moment that the Delphic Oracle had revealed that a harsh famine would end only when the Corinthians honored someone who had died at sea. The Isthmian Games took place every 2 years at the Sanctuary of Poseidon, of which regrettably little remains.

From ancient Corinth, drive back toward the canal. Isthmia is signposted on your right just before you reach the canal.

The **Site and Museum of Isthmia** are officially open Wednesday through Monday from 9am to 3pm. Admission costs Dr500 ($1.65) for each. The principal **temple** in Isthmia was dedicated to Poseidon; foundations remain of the structure built in the

7th century B.C., first rebuilt after a fire in the 5th century B.C., and then rebuilt once again when the Romans refounded Corinth in 44 B.C. Even the excavator here, Oscar Broneer, admitted of the temple that, "The casual visitor will marvel chiefly, perhaps, at the thoroughness of its destruction." The **ancient stadium,** with its elaborate starting gate, which Broneer lovingly reconstructed, is better preserved.

Isthmia's interesting small **museum** seems to be closed at least as often as it is open. If you do get in, you'll see exhibits on the Isthmian Games and some handsome **glass-mosaic panels** showing land- and townscapes and the figure of a philosopher, sometimes identified as Plato. These panels were found carefully packed in wooden crates, which preserved them for posterity after the ship they were on sank in the harbor of Kenchreai. Archaeologists speculate that the panels may have been intended to decorate the elegant home of one of the Roman officials who lived at Corinth.

LOUTRAKI & PERACHORA

To get to Loutraki from Corinth, cross the Corinth Canal. Once you are on the mainland, you'll see that Loutraki is signposted on your left. For Perachora, continue through Loutraki to Perachora, 32 kilometers (20 miles) or 30 minutes away by car.

Loutraki is the famous Greek spa whose springs churn out a good deal of the bottled water you'll see in restaurants. If possible, don't visit Loutraki or Perachora on summer weekends: It's slow going getting through Loutraki, which bursts at the seams with the Athenians who stream here each weekend to enjoy the beaches and "take the waters" at the **Hydrotherapy Thermal Spa,** Odos G. Lekka 26; open Monday through Saturday from 8am to 1pm.

En route to Perachora from Loutraki, you'll see signs of the severe fires that raged here during the summer of 1998. You'll also pass **Lake Vouliagmeni,** a saltwater inlet from the Gulf of Corinth. There are a number of equally good fish restaurants along the lake; make your choice depending on what's on the menu.

After sprawling Corinth, **Perachora** will seem like a miniature model of an ancient site. The site was founded in the 8th century B.C. and had several temples to Zeus's wife Hera, several stoas, and a number of useful water cisterns. Perched at the end of the peninsula, around a tiny cove, this is an idyllic spot, with just enough to see; there's also a picturesque lighthouse chapel here. There would be more antiquities to see if the Romans hadn't dismantled the temples and stoas and ferried the stones across the gulf to rebuild Corinth.

The **Site of Perachora** is open daily, in summer from 8am to 7pm; in winter from 8am to 5pm. Admission is Dr500 ($1.70). The ancient Corinthians called this spot Perachora, which means "the land beyond," meaning the land beyond the gulf. From here on a clear day, you can see the land beyond just about everything: there are superb views south across the Gulf to Acrocorinth and the mountains of the Peloponnese and along the north coast to the mountains of Central Greece.

This is an ideal spot to spend a few lazy hours swimming and picnicking (but not on weekends, when too many other people have the same idea). You may prefer simply to dangle your toes in the water and not swim in the cove: sharks are not unknown just outside the harbor in the gulf.

2 Nafplion

145km (90 miles) SW of Athens

It's easy to overlook contemporary Greece as you travel from one ancient site to another in the Peloponnese. Nafplion (population 10,000) brings you face to face with the beginnings of modern Greece. For several years after the Greek War of Independence (from 1821 to 1828), this was Greece's first capital. Although the palace of Greece's young King Otto—a mail-order monarch from Bavaria—burned down in the 19th century, you can still see the former mosque off Syntagma (Constitution) Square where Greece's first parliament met. Another legacy of those years is the impressive number of handsome neoclassical civic buildings and private houses, as well as the generous number of commemorative statues of revolutionary heroes in Nafplion's squares and parks.

All this would be reason enough to visit this port on the east coast of the Gulf of Argos, but Nafplion also has two hilltop Venetian fortresses, a miniature castle on an island in the harbor, shady parks, an interesting assortment of small museums, and better-than-average hotels, restaurants, and shops.

In short, Nafplion is far and away the most charming town in the Peloponnese. You could spend several pleasant days here simply enjoying the port town itself, but you'll probably want to use Nafplion as your home base for day trips to the ancient sites at Argos, Nemea, Mycenae, Tiryns, Epidaurus, and—if you didn't see it on the way to Nafplion—Corinth.

ESSENTIALS

GETTING THERE   By Train   Unless you are a totally dedicated train buff, it makes no sense to come here by train. That said, there are several trains a day from Athens to Corinth and Argos, where you can catch a bus to Nafplion. Information on schedules and fares is available from the **Stathmos Peloponnisou** (railroad station for the Peloponnese) in Athens (☎ **01/513-1601**).

By Bus   There are at least a dozen buses a day to Nafplion from the **Stathmos Leoforia Peloponnisou** (Bus Station for the Peloponnese) in Athens, Odos Kifissou 100 (☎ **01/513-4110** or 01/513-4588). The trip is a slow one (about 4 hr.) because the bus goes into both Corinth and Argos before reaching Nafplion.

By Boat   Monday through Saturday, there is Flying Dolphin hydrofoil service from Marina Zea, Piraeus, to Nafplion, weather permitting. The hydrofoil makes a number of stops and takes almost as long as the bus to reach Nafplion. The hydrofoil usually leaves Athens for Nafplion in the late afternoon and leaves Nafplion for Athens in the early morning. For information on fares and schedules, call ☎ **01/324-2281** or 01/453-6107.

By Car   From Athens, head south to the Corinth Canal. If you want to stop at Mycenae and/or Nemea en route, take the winding old road to Nafplion. If you want to stop at Epidaurus en route, turn left just after the canal at the sign for Epidaurus. If you want to get to Nafplion as quickly as possible, take the new Corinth-Tripolis road as far as the Argos exit. Follow the signs first into Argos itself, about 10 kilometers (6 miles) from the exit and thence on to Nafplion. You will almost certainly get lost at least once in Argos, which has an abysmal system of directional signs. Allow at least 3 hours for the drive from Athens to Nafplion, including a brief stop at the Corinth Canal and some time thrashing around in Argos.

When you reach Nafplion, leave your car—and be sure to lock it—in the large municipal **parking** lot (no charge) by the harbor.

VISITOR INFORMATION   The municipal tourist office is at Odos 25 Martiou, catercorner from the bus station in Plateia Nikitara. The tourist office is usually open Monday through Friday from 9am to 2pm (☎ **0752/24-444**). Ask if they have the useful brochure *Nafplion Day and Night.* Information and tickets for special events,

---

Insider Tip: Hairdressers

Women travelers might like to know that Dimitra Panagopoulou and Angeliki Skiada at **AD Hair Studio** (☎ **0752/24-861**), at the corner of Ypsilanti and Kotsonopoulou 5, both speak excellent English and do good work. There's another hairdresser nearby, so make sure that you get this one.

---

such as the concerts in the **Nafplion Music Festival,** usually held during the first half of June, are sometimes available from the Town Hall (Demarkeion) in the old high-school building on Iatrou Square (☎ **0752/23-332**). There are a number of travel agencies in Nafplion, such as **Staikos Travel** by the harbor (☎ **0752/27-950**), where you can get information on car rentals and day trips from Nafplion.

FAST FACTS   The **National Bank of Greece** on Plateia Syntagma (Constitution Square) has an ATM and currency exchange, as do most other banks in Nafplion. The **hospital** (☎ **0752/27-309**), clearly signposted in town, is at Kolokotroni and Asklepiou streets. The **police** are in National Assembly Square (☎ **0752/27-269**). The **tourist police** (☎ **0752/28-131**) are at Odos 25 Martiou, next to the Municipal Tourist Information Office. The **post office,** Odos Sidiras Merarhias 1, and the **telephone office (OTE),** Odos Polizoidou 2, are signposted from the bus station.

WHAT TO SEE & DO

Nafplion is a stroller's delight; one of the great pleasures here is simply wandering along the harbor, through the parks, and up and down the stepped side streets, discovering unexpected Turkish fountains and small churches. Don't make the mistake of ending your harborside stroll when you come to the last of the large seaside cafes by the Hotel Agamemnon: if you continue on, you can watch fishing boats putting in at the pier, explore several cliff-side chapels, and wind your way past the small beach on a cliff-side path under the Acronafplia. And don't ignore Nafplion's lush green parks at the foot of the Palamidi: You can usually find a cool spot to sit here even at midday. Nafplion is so small that you can't get seriously lost, so have fun exploring. Here are some suggestions on how to take in the official sights after you've had your initial stroll.

ACRONAFPLIA & PALAMIDI

Nafplion's two massive fortifications, the **Acronafplia** and the **Palamidi,** dominate the skyline. As you'll realize when you visit these fortresses, whoever held the heights here could keep a close watch on both the gulf and the plain of Argos. The Greeks began to fortify Acronafplia and Palamidi, and the Romans, Byzantines, Venetians, Franks, and Turks added a wall here and a turret there, with the results you see today. If you're here in the summer, try to visit the fortresses in the relative cool of either the morning or the evening; there's no admission cost to visit Acronafplia. If you're in Nafplion in June during the **Music Festival,** check to see if any evening concerts are being held at the Palamidi, which is open in summer, Monday through Friday from 8am to 7pm; in winter, Monday through Friday from 8:30am to 5pm. Admission is Dr500 ($1.65).

The easiest way to get up to the cliffs above Nafplion, known as the Acronafplia, is to drive or hitch a ride on the elevator that conveys guests from the lower town to the Xenia Palace Hotel. If you want to walk up, follow signs in the lower town to the **church of St. Spyridon;** one of its walls has the mark left by one of the

---

Take a Dip

The best place to swim is at the beach beneath the Palamidi. With the Bourtzi on your right, walk as far as you can along the quay until you come to the beach.

---

bullets that killed Ioannis Kapodistrias, the first governor of modern Greece. From Saint Spyridon, follow signs further uphill to the Catholic **church of the Metamorphosis.**

This church is as good a symbol as any for Nafplion's vexed history. Built by the Venetians, it was converted into a mosque by the Turks, and then reconsecrated as a church after the War of Independence. Inside, an ornamental doorway has an inscription listing philhellenes who died for Greece, including the nephews of both Lord Byron and George Washington. Greece's first King, young Otto of Bavaria, worshipped here wearing the Greek national costume, the short pleated skirt known as the *foustanella,* which he adopted to show solidarity with his new subjects. Ironically, while Otto wore his foustanella, the more fashion-conscious of his subjects here abandoned their Greek costumes and copied the Western clothes worn by the members of Otto's court.

As you continue to climb toward Acronafplia, you may see several **carvings of the winged lion** that was the symbol of Saint Mark, the protector of Venice. The most important fortifications on Acronafplia were built during the first (1388 to 1540) and second (1686 to 1715) Venetian occupations. In the days before the Greek historical preservation movement dug in its tentacles, both the Xenia and the Xenia Palace Hotels were built over the fortifications, one reason that the original structures have been obscured. Unless you are a military historian, you may have to take it on faith that what you're looking at here is a Frankish castle and Venetian defense tower to the east and a Byzantine castle to the west. Nafplion retained its strategic importance well into this century: during World War II, the German occupying forces had gun emplacements here.

If you're not staying in the **Xenia Palace Hotel,** where bedrooms overlook the harbor, be sure to enjoy the view from Acronafplia of the **Bourtzi fortress** in the harbor. The Venetians built the Bourtzi to guard the entrance to the harbor in the 15th century. Since then, it's had a checkered career, serving as a home for retired executioners in the 19th century and briefly as a small hotel in this century.

From Acronafplia, you can look down at the Bourtzi and up at the Palamidi. If you are not in the mood to climb the 800-plus steps to the **summit of Palamidi,** you can take a taxi up and then walk down. The Venetians spent 3 years building the Palamidi, only to be conquered the next year by the Turks in 1715. You'll enter the fortress the way the Turkish attackers did, through the main gate to the east. Once inside, you can trace the course of the massive wall that encircled the entire summit and wander through the considerable remains of the five defense fortresses that failed to stop the Turkish attack. Kolokotronis, the hero of the Greek war of Independence who later tried to subvert the new nation and seize power for himself, was held prisoner for 20 months in **Fort Miltiades,** the structure to your right as you enter the Palamidi. It's open daily from 9am to about sunset; admission is Dr800 ($2.65).

MUSEUMS

✪ **The Folk Art Museum.** Odos Vas. Alexandros 1. ☎ **0752/28-379.** Admission not known at press time. Scheduled to reopen in early 1999, with open hours Wed–Mon 9am–2:30pm. Closed Feb. Until then, the museum shop remains open at Odos Vas. Olgas 36 (☎ **0752/25-267**); its official hours are daily 10am–1pm and 6–10pm.

It's hard to imagine that this wonderful museum could be even better when it reopens, but, no doubt, it will be. Everything about the original museum was charming: It was housed in an elegant 18th-century house with a shady courtyard, welcome snack bar, and a superb shop, and contained one of the finest collections of costumes in Greece. Throughout, labels were in English as well as Greek, which means that you could learn just how cotton was harvested and silk was spun and what kind of loom was used to make what type of costume. Life-sized photos of women spinning, men shearing sheep, and a wide-eyed bridal couple posing in front of their wedding bed made the exhibits here come alive. The excellent museum shop had interesting books, records, old embroidery, and rugs, as well as inexpensive but stylish small purses made from old fabrics. We look forward to the reopening of the museum.

The Archaeological Museum. Syntagma Sq. ☎ **0752/27-502.** Admission Dr500 ($1.65). Year-round Tues–Sun 8:30am–1pm.

The Archaeological Museum is housed in the handsome 18th-century Venetian arsenal that dominates Syntagma Square. The thick walls make this a deliciously cool place to visit on even the hottest day. Displays are from sites in the area and include pottery, jewelry, and some quite horrific Mycenaean terra-cotta idols as well as a handsome bronze Mycenaean suit of armor.

The Military Museum. Leoforos Amalias. ☎ **0752/25-591.** Free admission. Year-round Tues–Sun 9am–2pm.

If you like old prints and old photographs, not to mention muskets, you'll enjoy strolling through the exhibits here, which cover Greek wars from the War of Independence to World War II.

The Museum of Childhood. Stathmos, Kolokotronis Park. Admission Dr400 ($1.35). Year-round Mon–Fri 4–8pm; Sat 9am–1pm. Frequent unscheduled closings.

An offshoot of the Folk Art Museum, this museum has an eclectic collection of dolls, baby clothes, and toys. It seems to keep especially fluid hours; if you arrive and the door is locked, you can see a fair amount by peering through the windows.

SHOPPING

Nafplion has not escaped the invasion of mass-produced-souvenir shops that threatens to overwhelm Greece, but there are also some genuinely fine shops here, many on or just off **Odos Spiliadou,** the street immediately above Plateia Syntagma. As in most Greek towns heavily dependent on tourism, many of these shops are closed in winter.

On Saturdays the weekly **market** occupies most of the road alongside Kolokotronis Park, from around 7am to 1pm. You can buy everything from handsaws to garlic here.

For a wide range of handsome jewelry, try **Preludio,** Vas. Constantinou 2, just off Syntagma Square (☎ **0752/25-277**), with a very helpful staff. **Aelios,** Vas. Konstantinou 4 (☎ **0752/28-149**), sometimes has unusually distinctive rings and bracelets. Virtually everything here is a pleasant departure from the mass-produced gold jewelry on sale elsewhere in Nafplion.

You can find lovely scarves and throws made from interesting hand-loomed fabrics and natural dyes at **Agnythes,** Ath. Siokou 10 and Vas. Alexandrou (☎ **0752/ 21-704**). **The Corner,** Staikopoulou and Koletti, just off Syntagma Square (☎ **0752/ 21-359**), has old prints, copper, and, sometimes, handsome old embroidered aprons and vests from traditional costumes.

Helene Papadopoulou, Odos Spiliadou 5, near the watefront (☎ **0752/25-842**), sells dolls made of brightly painted gourds and traditional weavings, priced from around Dr12,000 ($40). You'll know that you've found **To Enotion,** Odos

Staikopoulou (no phone and no visible street number), when you see a window full of handsome museum-quality reproductions of characters from the Greek shadow theater, from country bumpkins to damsels in distress. The smallest of the colorful marionettes begin at about Dr12,000 ($40).

The fascinating **Komboloi Museum,** Odos Staikopoulou 25 (☎/fax **0752/ 21-618**), sells komboloi, usually referred to as "worry beads"; the owner will lovingly explain the differences between the grades of amber and wood used to make them. **Konstantine Beselmes,** Ath. Siokou 6 (☎ **0752/27-274**), has magical paintings of village scenes, sailing ships, and idyllic landscapes. Although new, the paintings are done on weathered boards, which gives them a pleasantly aged look.

The **Odyssey,** Syntagma Square, has a wide selection of newspapers, magazines, and books in English, as well as a startling collection of pornographic drink coasters. This is also a good place to pick up a copy of Timothy Gregory's *Nafplion* (Lycabettus Press), the best guide to the city.

The Wine Shop, Amalias 5 (☎/fax **0752/24-446**), is one of the best wine shops in the Peloponnese, and an excellent place to head if you want to browse and learn about Greek wines.

WHERE TO STAY

Nafplion has enough hotels that you can usually find a room here, although you may end up on the outskirts of town in high season. Be sure to make a reservation if you want a view of the harbor, or if you are going to be here when there is a performance at Epidaurus, when tour groups reserve entire hotels.

EXPENSIVE

✪ **Xenia Palace Hotel.** Acronafplia, 21000 Nafplion. ☎ **0752/28-981.** Fax 0752/28-987. 57 units, 54 bungalows. A/C MINIBAR TV TEL. Dr60,000–Dr78,000 ($200–$260) double. Off-season reductions possible. Rates include breakfast and either lunch or dinner. AE, DC, EURO, MC, V.

The Palace has the best view in town; whether you think it has the best location depends on whether you want to be in town or up here on the slopes of Acronafplia, looking across the harbor to the Bourtzi and the mountains of the Peloponnese. This may be the only hotel in the Peloponnese where you'll find such luxurious touches as a telephone in your bathroom; that said, the rugs and chairs in many of the bedrooms are showing signs of wear. The dining room has indifferent "international" and Greek cuisine, but people watching can be fun here when elegant Athenian families appear on weekends. One big plus: a pool, which is the perfect place to cool off after a day of sightseeing. You can sometimes make arrangements to use the pool here if you're staying at the nearby **Xenia Hotel,** the Xenia Palace's less-expensive sister hotel, where rooms are usually at least $20 cheaper (same phone number and fax).

MODERATE

✪ **Byron Hotel.** Plateia Ayiou Spiridona, 21100 Nafplion. ☎ **0752/22-351.** Fax 0752/ 26-338. E-mail: byronhotel@otenet.gr. 13 units. TEL. Dr21,000 ($70) double. AE, EURO, MC, V.

This very pleasant small hotel, painted a distinctive pink with blue shutters, is in a quiet, breezy location overlooking the Church of Ayiou Spiridona, a short, steep hike up from the main plateia. The sitting rooms and bedrooms (some of which are quite small for two) contain a number of nice bits of Victoriana, including marble-topped tables. Word has gotten out about the Byron's charm, and it's almost impossible to stay here in July or August without a reservation.

Hotel Agamemnon. Akti Miaouli 3, 21100 Nafplion. ☎ **0752/28-021.** Fax 0752/28-022. 40 units. TV TEL. Dr30,000 ($100) double. Rates include breakfast and either lunch or dinner. AE, EURO, MC, V.

The Agamemnon is on the harbor just past the string of cafes, which means that you're bound to hear voices if you have a front room with a balcony. Still, friends who have stayed here claim they were not bothered by noise and loved the view. The guest rooms are of the generic variety found in hotels throughout Greece. They're furnished with two single beds with pine bed frames and bedside tables. This is a good deal, especially when you consider that the price includes lunch or dinner, as well as breakfast.

Hotel Amphitriton. Plateia Speliadon, 21100 Nafplion. ☎ **0752/27-366.** 42 units. TEL. Dr26,000 ($87) double. Rates include breakfast. AE, MC, V.

If you arrive in Nafplion without a reservation, you might check to see if the promised renovations have taken place at the Amphitriton, which recent owners neglected badly. If the bathrooms and bedrooms have been spruced up, the views of the harbor and Bourtzi castle may persuade you to stay here. Keep in mind that Nafplion's new parking lot is just past the hotel, which means that this once tranquil location can be noisy.

INEXPENSIVE

✪ **Epidaurus Hotel.** Odos Kokkinou 2 (beside the Commercial Bank), 21100 Nafplion. ☎ and fax **0752/27-541.** 15 units, all with shower only. Dr12,000 ($40) double. No credit cards.

The Epidaurus is currently expanding, adding an annex across the street as well as nearby pension quarters (Dr7,000/$23 double). The rooms here are small, but very pleasant, with good, firm beds. The location, on a quiet street just off the main square, is excellent; the staff, although not wildly welcoming, is helpful.

King Otto. Farmakopoulou 4, 21100 Nafplion. ☎ **0752/27-585.** 12 units, 4 with shower only. Dr12,000 ($40) double. AE, MC, V.

The small, venerable King Otto Hotel, in a pleasant neoclassical building with a handsome suspension staircase, is still an excellent bargain. Don't expect frills here, but the rooms have high ceilings and some overlook a pleasant small garden.

✪ **Omorphi Poli Pension.** Odos Sofroni 5, 21100 Nafplion. ☎ **0752/21-565.** 10 units, all with shower only. TV TEL. Dr15,000 ($50) double. Rates include breakfast. MC, V.

What a lovely place! This small pension/hotel above the charming cafe by the same name (Beautiful City) has gone all out: Their restoration of the building gives guests the sense that they are staying in a Nafplion home—but with their own privacy. There's nothing to fault here—the beds are good, and the tile floors and prints on the walls are nice. This makes a very pleasant base for touring the area. Families will like the rooms with fridges and sleeping lofts for children (Dr18,000/$60 for three).

WHERE TO DINE

Oddly enough, the restaurants in and just off Syntagma Square are not the tourist traps you'd expect. Furthermore, you'll see a good number of Greeks at the big harborside cafes on Akti Miaouli. In short, Nafplion has lots of good restaurants—as well as one superb pastry shop and any number of ice-cream parlors selling elaborate gooey confections.

Hellas Restaurant. Syntagma Sq., Nafplion. ☎ **0752/27-278.** Main courses Dr1,500–Dr2,400 ($5–$8). AE, MC, V. Daily 9am–midnight. GREEK.

Shady trees and awnings make this a cool spot to eat outdoors; there's also an inside dining room, where locals tend to congregate year-round. Excellent dolmades with egg lemon sauce are usually on the menu, as well as stuffed tomatoes and peppers in season. Just about everyone in town passes through Syntagma Square, so this is a great spot to watch the world go by.

Karamanlis. Bouboulinas 1, Nafplion. ☎ **0752/27-668.** Main courses Dr1,500–Dr2,500 ($5–$8); fresh fish priced by the kilo. AE, EURO, MC, V. Usually daily, 11am to about midnight. GREEK.

This simple harbor-front taverna several blocks east of the cluster of harbor-front cafes tends to get fewer tourists than most of the places in town and serves up good grills and several kinds of meatballs (keftedes, sousoutakia, and yiouvarlakia). If you like the food here, you'll probably also enjoy the **Kanares Taverna** and the **Hundalos Taverna,** both also on Bouboulinas.

✪ **Noufara.** Plateia Syntagma, Nafplion. ☎ **0752/23-648.** Fax 0752/23-945. Main courses Dr1,000–Dr4,000 ($3–$13). EURO, MC, V. Usually daily, about 8am–1am. INTERNATIONAL/ GREEK.

If you're not sure that you can face another stuffed tomato, head for the Noufara, which has a wide range of Italian dishes as well as the usual Greek favorites. You can sit under the umbrellas here and have a cool drink or a full meal—or you can retreat inside to the cool, air-conditioned dining room.

The **Noufara** also has a branch with the same menu (but a wider offering of fish) just outside Nafplion, on the shore in Nea Chios (☎ 0752/52-314).

The Pharos. Akti Miaouli (by the children's playground), Nafplion. ☎ **0752/26-043.** Ouzo and standard mezedes plate from Dr600 ($2); ouzo and a meal of mezedes from Dr2,400 ($8). No credit cards. Daily from around 10am–midnight. OUZO BAR.

It's easy to stop at the Pharos for a drink and a snack and end up eating enough octopus, *keftedes* (meatballs), and *saganaki* (fried cheese) to make a meal. This is a great spot for enjoying the waterfront away from the main tourist bustle.

Savouras Psarotaverna. Leoforos Bouboulinas 79, Nafplion. ☎ **0752/27-704.** Fish priced by the kilo according to availability. AE, EURO, MC, V. Daily from about noon–11pm. FISH.

This restaurant has been here for more than 20 years; its fresh fish attracts Greek day-trippers from Tripolis and even Athens. What you eat depends on what was caught that day. Expect to pay at least $50 for two fish dinners, a salad, and some house wine. On summer weekends, this restaurant can be terribly crowded.

Ta Phanaria. Staikopoulo 13, Nafplion. ☎ **0752/27-141.** Main courses Dr1,500–Dr3,000 ($5–$10). MC, V. Daily about noon–midnight. GREEK.

The shaded tables under Ta Phanaria's enormous scarlet bougainvillea are one of the prettiest places in town for lunch or dinner. Ta Phanaria usually has several inventive vegetable dishes on the menu in addition to such standbys as moussaka. The stews and chops here are also good, and in winter there are usually hearty bean dishes available. Like the Hellas, Ta Phanaria continues to attract steady customers, despite doing much of its business with tourists.

OUZERIES, CAFES & SWEET SHOPS

✪ **Aladdin.** Amalias 19 (across from the Military Museum), Nafplion. ☎ **0752/21-331.** Pastries from Dr3,000 ($10) a kilo. No credit cards. Usually daily, about 9am–10pm. ANATOLIAN SWEETS/SNACKS/ICE CREAM/COFFEE.

When you tire of museums, head into the Aladdin. The different varieties of honey-drenched Anatolian pastries here are the next best thing to the pastries sold at the superb Karavan pastry shops in Athens. You can eat your pastries at the shop or get them to go—or both.

The Pink Panther. Odos Staikopoulou, Nafplion. No phone. Ice-cream sundaes from Dr1,500 ($5). No credit cards. Daily from about 10am–midnight. SWEETS/ICE CREAM.

There are those who swear that this place has the best ice cream in town. Anyone wanting to test the assertion might do a comparison taste test at the Fantasia, also on Odos Staikopoulou, and then try the mango sherbet at the Napoli di Romania cafe on Akti Miaouli—although perhaps not all in one day!

Sokaki. Odos Ethnossinelefseos (National Assembly) 8, Nafplion. ☎ **0752/26-032.** Drinks and snacks from Dr600–Dr1,800 ($2–$6). No credit cards. Daily from about 8am–8pm (until midnight in summer). COFFEE/DRINKS/SNACKS/BREAKFAST.

In the morning, tourists tuck into the full American breakfast here, while locals toy with a tiny cup of Greek coffee. In the evening, young men lounge here, some eyeing the women who pass by, others eyeing the men. A nice place to take a break and watch people watching people.

✪ **Stathmos Cafe.** Nafplion (the old railroad station). No phone. Coca-Cola Dr500 ($1.65); bag of potato chips Dr300 ($1); mezedes from Dr900 ($3). No credit cards. Daily from about 9am–midnight. DRINKS/SNACKS.

This is a nice shady spot to sit and take a break from tourist Nafplion, perhaps after visiting the Museum of Childhood next door. The old train station is decorated with a splendid painting of an old steam engine, and has elaborate wooden gingerbread trim, comfortable chairs under shady trees, and a cozy inside room for cold weather.

SIDE TRIPS FROM NAFPLION
AYIA MONI CONVENT
3km (1.5 miles) outside Nafplion

Although this peaceful hillside convent is just minutes outside Nafplion, it seems a world away. To get there by car, head out of Nafplion on the Epidaurus road. Turn right at the sign for Ayia Moni and continue on a partly bumpy road to the convent. Don't go during the afternoon siesta time, when the convent is usually closed.

Ayia Moni was founded in the 12th century, and the church is a fine example of Byzantine church architecture, with nice brickwork. Many of the other buildings here are modern and were built after a series of fires destroyed much of the original convent. The nuns sometimes have embroidery to sell and are usually more than willing to show you the church and garden.

The spring that feeds a small pond just outside the convent walls is one of a number of springs in Greece identified as the one in which Zeus's wife Hera took an annual bath to restore her virginity and renew Zeus's ardor. Today, the spring water is considered both holy and delicious; pilgrims here often fill bottles to take home.

TIRYNS
5km (3 miles) outside Nafplion on the Argos road

From the moment that you see Tiryns, you'll understand why Homer called this Mycenaean citadel "well-walled." The **Archaeological Site of Tiryns** is usually open in summer daily from 8am to 7pm, in winter Monday through Saturday from 8am to

5pm. Admission is Dr500 ($1.65). If you have a car, this is an easy drive; if you don't, take one of the Argos-Nafplion-Argos buses and ask to be let off at Tiryns. Taxi drivers in both Argos and Nafplion will take you to Tiryns and wait while you visit; expect to pay around Dr10,000 ($30).

Tiryns stands on a rocky outcropping 87 feet high and about 330 yards long, and the entire citadel is encircled by the massive walls that so impressed Homer. Later Greeks thought that only the giants known as Cyclopes could have positioned the wall's 14-ton red limestone blocks, and archaeologists still call these walls "cyclopean." Even today, Tiryns's walls stand more than 30 feet high; originally, they were twice as tall—and as much as 57 feet thick.

According to Greek legend, the great hero Heracles (Hercules) was born at Tiryns after Zeus deceived and impregnated Alkmene, one of many maidens to catch his fancy. Zeus's wife Hera, infuriated that her attempts to win back her husband's love had failed yet again, sent serpents to strangle the infant Hercules in his cradle. Instead, Hercules strangled the serpents. Hera, however, was nothing if not determined; years later she made Hercules kill his wife and children in a fit of temporary insanity.

As at Mycenae, people seem to have lived at Tiryns virtually forever. And, as at Mycenae, Tiryns seems to have increased its fortifications around 1,400 B.C. and been destroyed around 1,200 B.C. Most scholars assume that Tiryns was a friendly neighbor to the more powerful Mycenae, and some have suggested that Tiryns was Mycenae's port. Even today, Tiryns is only a mile from the sea; and in antiquity, before the plain silted up, it would have been virtually on the seashore.

Tiryns is a good deal better preserved than Mycenae: Once you climb the ramp and pass through the two gates, you'll find yourself in an impressive **series of storage galleries and chambers** on the east side of the citadel. Ahead, there are more galleries and chambers, including one long passageway with a corbelled arch whose walls have been rubbed smooth, probably by the generations of sheep that took shelter here after Tiryns fell.

The citadel is crowned by the **palace,** whose **megaron** (great hall) has a well-preserved circular hearth and the base of a putative throne. This room would have been gaily decorated with frescoed walls; you can see the surviving frescoes, some with scenes of elegant women riding in a chariot, in the National Archaeological Museum in Athens. These women, who would have lived in the royal apartments west of the megaron, probably freshened up in the bathroom, whose floor is a massive 20-ton limestone slab. Lesser folk would have lived below the citadel on the plain. Two tunnels led from the lower slopes of Tiryns out into the plain to the large **subterranean cisterns** that held the secret water supply that allowed Tiryns to withstand even a lengthy siege.

As at Mycenae, there's no knowing why Tiryns finally fell into decline, with some scholars suggesting civil wars, others natural disasters, still others invasions by the mysterious "People of the Sea," sometimes credited with invading Greece about this time.

3　Mycenae

50km (31 miles) S of Corinth; 115km (71 miles) SW of Athens

According to Greek legend and the poet Homer, King Agamemnon of Mycenae was the most powerful leader in Greece at the time of the Trojan War. It was Agamemnon, Homer says, who led the Greeks from Mycenae, which he called "rich in gold," to Troy (ca. 1250 B.C.). There, the Greeks fought for 10 years to reclaim fair Helen, the wife of Agamemnon's brother Menelaus, from her seducer, the Trojan prince Paris.

The German archaeologist Heinrich Schliemann, who found and excavated Troy, began to excavate at Mycenae in 1874. Did Schliemann's excavations here prove that what Homer wrote was based on an actual event—and not myth or legend? Scholars are suspicious, although most admit that Mycenae could have been built to order from Homer's descriptions of Mycenaean palaces.

After you visit here, see if you agree with something that the English philhellene Robert Liddell once wrote: "Mycenae is one of the most ancient and fabulous places in Europe. I think it should be visited first for the fable, next for the lovely landscape, and thirdly for the excavations."

ESSENTIALS

GETTING THERE   By Bus   There is frequent bus service from the **Stathmos Leoforia Peloponnisou** (Bus Station for the Peloponnese), at Odos Kifissou 100 in Athens (☎ 01/513-4100), to Corinth, Argos, and Nafplion (allow 3 to 4 hr.). From any of these places you can travel on by bus to Mycenae (allow an hour).

By Car   From Corinth, take the old Corinth-Argos highway south from Corinth for about 48 kilometers (30 miles), and then take the left turn to Mycenae, which is about 8 kilometers (5 miles) down the road. **From Nafplion,** take the road out of town toward Argos. When you reach the Corinth-Argos highway, turn right and then, after about 16 kilometers (10 miles), right again at the sign for Mycenae. (If you are going to Nafplion when you leave Mycenae, try the very pleasant back road that runs through villages and rich farmland. You'll see the sign for Nafplion on your left shortly after you leave Mycenae.)

FAST FACTS   You can buy stamps and change money at the **mobile post office** at the ancient site, Monday through Friday from 8am to 2pm. This office is sometimes open on weekends and after 2pm, but don't count on it. There is a **pay phone** near the mobile post office.

WHAT TO SEE & DO

The Citadel and the Treasury of Atreus. Admission Dr1,500 ($5). Summer Mon–Fri 8am–7:30pm; Sat–Sun 8am–3pm. Winter Mon–Fri 8am–5pm; Sat–Sun 8am–3pm.

As you walk uphill to Mycenae, you begin to get an idea of why people settled here as long ago as 3,000 B.C.: Mycenae straddles a low bluff between two protecting mountains and is a superb natural citadel. The site overlooks one of the richest plains in Greece, and whoever held Mycenae could control all the land between the narrow Dervenakia Pass to the north and the Gulf of Argos, some 16 kilometers (10 miles) to the south.

By about 1,400 B.C., Mycenae controlled not just the Plain of Argos, but much of mainland Greece, as well as Crete, many of the Aegean islands, and outposts in distant Italy and Asia Minor. Then, some unknown disaster struck Mycenaean Greece; by about 1,100 B.C., the Mycenaeans were on the decline. By the time of the classical era, almost all memory of the Mycenaeans had been lost, and Greeks speculated that places like Mycenae and Tiryns had been built by the Cyclopes. Only those enormous giants, people reasoned, could have moved the enormous rocks used to build the ancient citadels' defense walls.

You'll enter Mycenae through just such a wall, passing under the massive **Lion Gate,** whose two lions probably symbolized Mycenae's strength. The door itself

---

Insider Tip ───

If at all possible, visit Mycenae early in the morning and wear a hat and sturdy shoes: There's no shade at the site (except in the cistern and the beehive tombs), and the rocks are very slippery. Bring a flashlight if you plan to explore the cistern.

(missing, like the lions' heads) would have been of wood, probably covered with bronze for additional protection; cuttings for the door jambs and pivots are clearly visible in the lintel. Soldiers stationed in the **round tower** on your right would have shot arrows down at any attackers who tried to storm the citadel. Since soldiers carried their shields on their left arms, the tower's position made the attackers vulnerable to attack on their unprotected right side.

One of the most famous spots at Mycenae is immediately ahead of the Lion Gate: the so-called **Grave Circle A,** where Schliemann found the gold jewelry now on display at the National Museum in Athens. When Schliemann opened the tombs and found some 14 kilos of gold here, including several solid-gold face masks, he concluded that he had found the grave of Agamemnon himself. At once, Schliemann fired off a telegram to the king of Greece saying, "I have looked upon the face of Agamemnon bare." More sober scholars have concluded that Schliemann was wrong, and that the kings buried here died long before Agamemnon was born.

From the grave circle, head uphill past the low remains of a number of **houses.** Mycenae was not merely a palace, but a small village, with the palace at the crest of the hill and administrative buildings and homes on the slopes. The **palace** was considerably grander than these small houses and had several court rooms, bedrooms, a throne room, and a large megaron (ceremonial hall). You can see the imprint of the **four columns** that held up the roof in the megaron, as well as the outline of a **circular altar** on the floor.

If you're not claustrophobic, head to the northeast corner of the citadel and climb down the flight of stairs to have a look at Mycenae's enormous **cistern.** You may find someone here selling candles, but it's a good idea to bring your own flashlight. Along with Mycenae's great walls, this cistern, which held water channeled here from a spring 500 meters away, helped to make Mycenae impregnable for several centuries.

If it's not too hot when you visit, try to give yourself some time to sit on the citadel and contemplate the sad history of the House of Atreus and enjoy the view of the farm fields below. On your way back down, take a look at the **little bathtub** in the palace, which Schliemann thought was the very bathtub where Agamemnon was stabbed to death by his wife, Clytemnestra.

There's one more thing to see before you leave Mycenae: the massive tomb known as the **Treasury of Atreus,** the largest of the tholos tombs found here. You'll see signs for it on your right as you head down the modern road away from Mycenae. This treasury may have been built around 1300 B.C., at about the same time as the Lion Gate, in the last century of Mycenae's real greatness.

This enormous tomb, with its 118-ton lintel, is 43 feet high and 47 feet wide. To build it, workers first cut the 115-foot-long passageway into the hill and faced it with stone blocks. Then the tholos chamber itself was built, by placing slightly overlapping courses of stone one on top of the other until a capstone could close the final course. As you look up toward the ceiling of the tomb, you'll see why these are called "beehive tombs." Once your eyes get accustomed to the poor light in the tomb, you can make out the bronze nails that once held hundreds of bronze rosettes in place in the ceiling.

This tomb was robbed even in antiquity, so we'll never know what it contained, although the contents of Grave Circle A give an idea of what riches must have been here. If this was the family vault of Atreus, it's entirely possible that Agamemnon himself was buried here.

WHERE TO STAY & DINE

Most of the restaurants in Mycenae specialize in serving up fixed-price, set meals to groups. You won't starve if you eat at one of these big, impersonal roadside restaurants, but you're likely to be served a bland, lukewarm meal. You'll have better luck trying the smaller restaurants at **La Petite Planete** or **La Belle Helene** hotels (see below). It's also sometimes possible to avoid tour groups at the **Achilleus,** on the main street (☎ 0751/76-027), where you can eat lunch or dinner, priced from Dr3,000 ($10).

La Belle Helene. Mycenae, Argolis, 21200. ☎ **0751/76-225.** 8 units, none with bathroom. Dr15,000–Dr19,500 ($50–$65) double, sometimes less in the off-season. Rates include breakfast. DC, V.

The real reason to stay here is to add your name to that of Schliemann and other luminaries in the guest book. Sentiment aside, this small hotel, one of the most famous in Greece, is usually very quiet; the simple rooms are clean and comfortable. If you stay here, be sure to drive or walk up to the ancient site at night, especially if it's a full moon.

✪ **La Petite Planete.** Mycenae, Argolis, 21200. ☎ **0751/76-240.** 30 units. TEL. Dr22,500 ($75) double, sometimes less in the off-season. Rates include breakfast. AE, V.

This would be a nice place to stay even without its swimming pool, which is irresistible after a hot day's trek around Mycenae. We've usually found it quieter here than at La Belle Helene, and friends who stayed here recently praised the restaurant and enjoyed the view over the hills from their window.

4 Epidaurus

32km (20 miles) E of Nafplion; 63km (39 miles) S of Corinth

The Theater of Epidaurus is one of the most impressive sights in Greece. Probably built in the 4th century, possibly by Polykleitos, the architect of the Tholos, this theater seated—and still seats—some 14,000 spectators. Unlike so many ancient buildings, including almost everything at the Sanctuary of Asklepios, the theater was not pillaged for building blocks in antiquity. As a result, it is astonishingly well preserved; restorations have been both minimal and tactful.

The village of Palea Epidaurus, a beach resort 10 kilometers (6 miles) from Epidaurus, is sometimes signposted ANCIENT EPIDAURUS; the theater and sanctuary are usually signposted ANCIENT THEATER.

To confuse things further, Palea Epidaurus has its own small theater and festival. If you want a swim, Palea Epidaurus is the nearest beach—but is heavily developed.

ESSENTIALS

GETTING THERE   By Bus   Two buses a day run from the **Stathmos Leoforia Peloponnisou** (Bus Station for the Peloponnese) in Athens, Odos Kifissou 100 (☎ 01/513-4110), to Epidaurus. Buses take about 3 hours. There are three buses a day from the Nafplion bus station, off Plateia Kapodistrias (☎ 0752/27-323), to Epidaurus, as well as extra buses when there are performances at the Theater of Epidaurus. The bus takes about an hour.

By Car   If you're coming from Athens or Corinth, turn left for Epidaurus immediately after the Corinth Canal and take the coast road to the Theatro (ancient theater), not to Nea Epidaurus or Palaia Epidaurus. From Nafplion, follow the signs for Epidaurus. If you drive to Epidaurus from Nafplion for a performance, be alert: the road will be clogged with tour buses and other tourists who are driving the road for the first time.

FAST FACTS   There is a **mobile post office** and a **pay phone** at the ancient site.

WHAT TO SEE & DO

✪ **The Sanctuary, Museum, and Theater at Epidaurus.** Combined admission Dr1,500 ($5). Hours for all 3: summer Mon–Fri 8am–7pm; Sat–Sun 8:30am–3:15pm. Winter Mon–Fri 8am–5pm; Sat–Sun 8:30am–3:15pm.

Although it's pleasant to wander through the shady **Sanctuary of Asklepios,** it's not at all easy to decipher the scant remains here—visit the excavation museum first (see below). As at Olympia, the Asklepion had accommodations for visitors, several large bathhouses, civic buildings, a stadium, gymnasium, and several temples and shrines. The remains here are so meager that you may have to take this on faith, but try to find the round **tholos** that you'll pass about halfway into the sanctuary. The famous 4th-century B.C. architect Polykleitos, who built similar round buildings at Olympia and Delphi, was the architect here. If you wonder why the inner foundations of the tholos are so convoluted and labyrinthine, you're in good company: scholars still aren't sure what went on here, although some suspect that Asklepios's healing serpents lived in the labyrinth.

Next to the tholos are the remains of **two long stoas,** where patients slept in the hopes that Asklepios would reveal himself to them in a dream. Those who had dreams and cures dedicated the votive offerings and inscriptions now in the museum.

As you wander around the site, you'll probably notice signs of recent excavation and restoration work on the early 4th-century B.C. **altar of Apollo Maleatas.** Archaeologists think that the altar was destroyed in the 1st century B.C. by a band of Cilician pirates, irritated when they couldn't find any buried treasure here. The Greek Archaeological Service hopes to finish restoring the altar by 2000. So far, no hidden treasure has been found.

At the entrance to the site, the **excavation museum** helps to put some flesh on the bones of the confusing remains of the sanctuary. It has an extensive collection of architectural fragments from the sanctuary, including lovely acanthus flowers from the mysterious tholos. The terra-cotta body parts are votive offerings that show precisely what part of the anatomy was cured. The display of surgical implements will send you away grateful that you didn't have to go under the knife here, although hundreds of inscriptions record the gratitude of satisfied patients.

If you climb to the top of the **ancient theater,** you can look down over the 55 rows of seats, divided into a lower section of 34 rows and an upper section with 21 rows. The upper seats were added when the original theater was enlarged in the 2nd century B.C. The theater's acoustics are famous: you'll almost certainly see someone demonstrating how a whisper can be heard all the way from the round orchestra to the topmost row of seats. Just as the stadium at Olympia brings out the sprinter in many visitors, the theater at Epidaurus tempts many to step stage center and recite poetry, declaim the opening of the Gettysburg Address, or burst into song. Still, there's almost always a respectful silence here when a performance of a classical Greek play begins, as the sun sinks behind the orchestra and the first actor steps onto the stage (see "Epidaurus After Dark," below).

WHERE TO STAY & DINE

There are several kiosks selling snacks and cold drinks near the ticket booth at Epidaurus. In Nea and Palaia Epidaurus, you'll find a number of boring restaurants, most of which cater to large groups. In other words, you won't starve, but there's no place worth seeking out.

Epidaurus Xenia Hotel. Ligourio, Nafplias, 21059 Peloponnese. ☎ **0753/22-005.** 26 units, 12 with bathroom. TEL. Dr22,500 ($75) double, sometimes less in the off-season. Rates include breakfast. No credit cards.

The best place to stay overnight at Epidaurus is this hotel, at the site itself. Once everyone leaves, this is a lovely, quiet spot in a pine grove. The 26 bungalowlike units go quickly on the night of a performance, so book well in advance. The bungalows are, admittedly, absolutely undistinguishcd as to decor: here, as so often, it's location, location, location that makes this the place to stay. The restaurant serves bland but acceptable food.

EPIDAURUS AFTER DARK

Classical performances at the **ancient theater** are usually given Saturday and Sunday from June through September. Many productions are staged by the **National Theater of Greece,** some by foreign companies. For information and ticket prices, contact the **Athens Festival Box Office,** Odos Stadiou 4 (☎ **01/322-1459**), or the **Epidaurus Festival Box Office** (☎ **0753/22-006**). It's also possible to buy tickets at most of the travel agencies in Nafplion and at the theater itself, from 5pm on the day of a performance. The performance starts around 9pm. The ancient tragedies are usually performed either in classical or modern Greek; programs (Dr1,400/$5) usually have either a full translation or a full synopsis of the play. The excellent Odyssey bookstore in Nafplion (see "Shopping" in Section 2, above) usually has English translations of the plays being performed at Epidaurus.

Beginning in 1995, the Society of the Friends of Music have sponsored the **"Little Epidaurus" Music Festival** during the last 2 weekends of July at the recently restored 4th-century theater at Palea Epidaurus, 7 kilometers (4.5 miles) from Epidaurus. Check with the **Greek National Tourist Office** or the **Municipality of Palea Epidaurus** (☎ **0753/41-250**) for the schedule of performances. The **Athens Concert Hall,** the Megaron Musikis (☎ **01/728-2333**), also sometimes has information. In 1998, a number of poetry readings were also held in July at the Little Epidaurus theater, and there are plans to continue this in future summers.

5 Nemea

25km (15 miles) SE of Corinth; 35km (21 miles) N of Argos

Panhellenic Games were held every 4 years at Olympia and Delphi and every 2 years at Isthmia, near Corinth, and at Nemea, in a gentle valley in the eastern foothills of the Arcadian mountains. The first Olympic Games were held in 776 B.C. and didn't begin at Nemea until 573 B.C. By about 100 B.C., Nemea's powerful neighbor Argos moved the festival from Nemea to Argos itself, putting an end to the games here. But, thanks to the Society for the Revival of the Nemean Games, Games were held here for the first time in 2,000 years on June 1, 1996, when 1,000 contestants from around the world, ranging in age from 12 to 90, raced here. The next Games will take place again on June 3 and 4, 2000. So, when you visit Nemea, you won't just see the stadium where athletes once contended, but the site of the new Nemean Games.

Cooling Down

If you want to swim, check to see if the municipal pool (*piscina*), about 1 mile from the stadium, is open (☎ **0726/22-168**); the entrance fee is Dr600 ($2).

Contestants will be barefoot, as in antiquity, but will wear short tunics, rather than running naked. If you want to know more about the Nemean Games, contact the **Society for the Revival of the Nemean Games,** Nemea, 20500, Greece (☎ **510/ 642-5924** in the U.S.).

Two excellent site guides are on sale at the museum: *Nemea* (Dr3,500/$12) and *The Ancient Stadium of Nemea* (Dr500/$1.65). You'll find shady spots to read them both at the site and at the stadium.

ESSENTIALS

GETTING THERE　By Car　From Athens, take the National Road to Corinth and then follow signs for Argos and Tripolis. The road divides just after the sign for Ancient Corinth. The speedy new Corinth-Tripolis toll road has green signposts with a drawing of a highway. The toll is Dr700 ($2.35). Take the Nemea turnoff and then follow signs to the site. If you take the old road, you'll see signs for Nemea just after the Nemea train station, where the main road bends sharply left, and you continue straight toward Nemea. Allow 30 minutes from Corinth to Nemea on the new road and an hour on the old road.

By Bus　There are about five buses a day from the **Stathmos Leoforia Peloponnisou** (Bus Station for the Peloponnese) in Athens, Odos Kifissou 100 (☎ **01/513-4110**), to Nemea. Allow about 2 hours for the trip and ask to be let off at the ancient site of Nemea (*Ta Archaia*) on the outskirts of the hamlet of Archaia Nemea, not in the village of Nea Nemea.

By Train　It's possible to take the train from Athens to the station several kilometers from the ancient site. The train, however, is very slow; it makes better sense to take the bus.

FAST FACTS　There's a **post office** and a **telephone office** in Nea Nemea, but it's unlikely that you'll want to go there. There's a **pay phone** by the ancient site.

WHAT TO SEE & DO

The Museum and Ancient Site. Admission Dr500 ($1.65). Year-round Tues–Sun 8:30am–3pm.

The Nemea Museum, set on an uncharacteristically Greek green lawn, is one of the most charming small museums in Greece. You'll get an excellent picture of the history of the excavation of Nemea and the Nemean Games, as well as the early Christian village here, much of which was built from material pillaged from ancient Nemea.

A display map just inside the museum's main gallery shows all the cities in the Greek world whose coins were found at Nemea and illustrates just how far people came to see these games. There are a number of excellent photographs of the excavations and enlarged photos of important finds, such as the small bronze figure of the infant Opheltes, in whose honor the Nemean Games may have been founded.

According to legend, the Seven Theban Champions founded the games in memory of the infant, who—not as agile as Hercules (Heracles)—was killed by a serpent. Because the Games were perceived as funeral games, the judges wore black mourning robes, just as they will in June 2000 at the revived Nemean Games. Another legend says that the Games were established not to honor Opheltes but to honor Heracles, who killed a fierce lion that had his lair in one of the caves in Evanyelistria hill, just behind the stadium. Fortunately, lions are unknown in today's Greece.

While you're in the museum, be sure to take a look out of one of the large picture windows that overlook the ancient site where the coins, vases, athletic gear, and architectural fragments on display were found. A raised stone path tactfully suggests the route from the museum to the site, passing a carefully preserved early Christian burial tomb and skirting a large Christian basilica and Roman bath before arriving at the Temple of Zeus.

This temple was built of local limestone around 330 B.C. on the site of an earlier temple, which may have burned down. Today, only three of the original 32 exterior Doric columns are still standing: the drums of the others are scattered on the ground. When Pausanias came by here in the 2nd century A.D., he felt that the temple was worth seeing but complained "that the roof has collapsed." Sometime later, the columns followed suit, perhaps when early Christian squatters pillaged the temple for building blocks, or after one of the many earthquakes that rocked the Peloponnese.

The Stadium. Admission Dr500 ($1.65). Year-round Tues–Sun 8:30am–3pm.

To reach the stadium, leave the site and head several hundred yards back along the road that brought you into Nemea.

The Ancient Stadium of Nemea, on sale at the ticket booth, contains a self-guided tour of the stadium. The locker room just outside the stadium caused quite a stir when it was discovered in 1991, with few journalists able to resist cracks about what a locker room must smell like after 2,500 years.

Athletes would have stripped down in the locker room, oiled their bodies with olive oil, and then entered the stadium through the vaulted tunnel, just as football players today rush onto the playing field. Once you pass through the tunnel, you'll see where the judges sat while spectators sprawled on earthen benches carved out of the hillside itself. When they got thirsty, they could have a drink from the water carried around the racetrack in a stone channel. If you want, walk down onto the 178-meter race course and stand at the stone starting line where the athletes took their places for the footraces. Running naked and barefoot, the athletes kept their balance at the starting line by gripping the indentations in the stone with their toes.

WHERE TO STAY & DINE

There's no hotel here as yet. The **Pisina Restaurant,** in New Nemea next to the swimming pool, keeps irregular hours.

6 Argos

48km (30 miles) S of Corinth

Argos was the most powerful city in the Peloponnese in the 7th century B.C. when it was ruled by its skillful tyrant, Pheidon, often credited with inventing coinage in Greece. There should be lots of impressive remains to visit here, but since modern Argos (population 20,000) is built precisely on top of the ancient city, there's little to see in town except the 4th-century theater and the excellent museum. Out of town is a different story: the fortifications on Argos's twin citadels, the Aspis and the Larissa, are very impressive.

A Word of Caution

Argos's confusing system of one-way streets and potentially lethal three-way intersections makes driving here almost as chaotic as the night in 272 B.C. when Pyrrus of Epirus stormed the city with a large force—including two war elephants, one of which overturned and blocked the main gate into the city. In short, drive with particular care here.

As for the modern town itself, repeated earthquakes have left Argos with an undistinguished agglomeration of flat-roofed buildings, with only the occasional neoclassical house as a reminder of how nice this town once was. That said, the central plateia is very lively and the street market on Wednesday and Saturday mornings is one of the largest in the Peloponnese.

If your time in the Peloponnese is limited, you might consider saving Argos for a return trip. If you can spend a few hours here, give the theater a passing glance, concentrate on the museum, and try to drive up to the Larissa and Aspis citadels to take in the Venetian fortifications and the view over the plain.

ESSENTIALS

GETTING THERE   By Train   There are about five trains a day from Athens to Argos. Information on schedules and fares is available from the **Stathmos Peloponnisou** (Railroad Station for the Peloponnese) in Athens (☎ 01/513-1601) or at the Corinth train station (☎ 0751/27-212). Trains take at least 3 hours. The Argos train station on Leoforos Vas. Sofias is about a kilometer from the central square.

By Bus   There are five buses a day to Argos from the **Stathmos Leoforia Peloponnisou** (Bus Station for the Peloponnese) in Athens, Odos Kifissou 100 (☎ 01/513-4110). Buses usually take just under 3 hours. Argos is also served by frequent buses from Nafplion (buses take about 30 min.). Argos has two bus stations: the Athinon Station (buses to and from Athens) is on Leoforos Vas. Georgiou B. (☎ 0751/673-24); the Arcadia-Laconia Station (buses for Tripolis) is at Odos Peithonos 24 (☎ 0751/67-324).

By Car   From Athens, take the National Road to Corinth, and then follow signs for Argos and Tripolis. The road divides just after the sign for Ancient Corinth. The speedy new Corinth-Tripolis toll road has green signposts with drawings of highways. The toll is Dr700 ($2.35). Take the Argos exit (the second exit) and follow the exit road until it reaches an obvious main road (the old Corinth-Argos road). Turn right, cross the bridge, and you'll soon enter Argos. If you take the old road to Argos, it runs straight into the town.

It's never easy to park in Argos, but you'll probably find a place on one of the side streets off the central square or by the ancient theater.

FAST FACTS   You can exchange currency at several **banks** on the main square, Plateia Ayios Petros, including the **National Bank of Greece** (which also has an ATM). The **hospital,** signposted on the main road into town from Athens, has English-speaking staff. The **police** are at Odos Agelou Bobou 10 (☎ 0751/67-222); there's often someone who speaks English. The **post office,** Odos Danaou 16, off the central square, is open Monday through Friday from 7am to 2pm. The **telephone office (OTE),** Odos Nikitara 8, is usually open Monday through Friday from 7am to midnight.

WHAT TO SEE & DO

The Theater at Argos. Admission Dr500 ($1.65). Year-round Mon–Sat 9am–6pm; Sun 10am–3pm. Sometimes closed unexpectedly.

If you've already seen the theater at Epidaurus, you'll find it hard to believe that Argos's 4th-century theater was not just larger, but probably the largest in classical Greece. Twenty thousand spectators could sit here, in 89 tiers of seats, many of which were carved from the hillside itself.

The thronelike seats in the front rows were added by the Romans and reserved for visiting bigwigs, including the Roman emperor himself. The Romans remodeled the theater, so that the orchestra (stage) could be flooded and mock naval battles staged here. Fortunately, the Romans had a genius for building the aqueducts needed to channel enough water here to create a temporary inland sea. There was enough water left over to service the baths, whose remains are next to the theater.

The Museum at Argos. Admission Dr500 ($1.65). Tues–Sun 8:30am–3pm.

This small museum has a handful of superlative pieces that you'll want to take in, including the fragment of a 7th-century B.C. clay krater showing a determined Ulysses blinding the one-eyed Cyclops Polyphemus. Nearby are a handsome lyre made from a tortoise shell and a stunning late geometric bronze helmet and suit of body armor. Downstairs, in the Lerna room, the tiny, stout Neolithic clay figure of a woman or goddess found at Lerna is one of the oldest known sculptural representations of the human body yet found in Europe. Nearby is a handsome pitcher in the shape of a bird with its head thrown back in song—and ornamental breasts on its chest.

Outside, in the museum's shady courtyard with rose bushes, there are some terrific Roman mosaics showing the god Dionysos and the seasons. The figures in the seasons mosaics are bundled up in cloaks and heavy leggings in the cold months and casually dressed in light tunics and filmy cloaks in the summer months.

If you visit the museum (which has a welcome icy cold water fountain and very clean toilets) on Wednesday or Saturday morning, don't miss the **street market** that runs for several blocks to your left as you leave. This is the place to get anything from water glasses, baseball caps, and farm implements to live chickens and every possible seasonal fruit and flower.

If you're here on a nonmarket day and need supplies, there's a large **supermarket** (Pharmatetras) just off the main square. To reach the supermarket, turn right as you leave the museum and then right again in the plateia.

The Larissa and the Aspis. Free admission. Usually open from sunrise to sunset.

You can climb up to the Larissa from the theater (allow at least an hour), and then hike across the ridge called the Deiras to the Aspis. If you drive, ask for directions to the Kastro, or castle, as the Larissa is called, at the museum or the police station, as roads in Argos are in a seemingly constant state of flux.

Argos was famous in antiquity for its two citadels; the 905-foot-high Larissa was well fortified by the 6th century B.C. When you reach the Larissa summit, you'll be able to spot the more elegant ancient blocks that were reused in the medieval battlements. There's an inner and outer system of walls here, with several towers and the ruins of a church. The view's the thing here, and you get a bird's-eye view of the plain, Argos, the Gulf of Nafplion, and the lower citadel, the Aspis (328 ft. high).

The Greek word *Aspis* means "shield," which is what the Argives thought this hill looked like. This was the city's first acropolis, abandoned when the higher Larissa was fortified. With the exception of one tower, the summit here really is a confusing jumble of low walls and the indeterminate depressions in the earth that mark building foundations. Still, the views are tremendous. If you're properly dressed and not here at siesta time, you may want to stop at the convent of the Panayia tou Brakou, although the building is not of enormous architectural interest.

You can wander around the Larissa or Aspis as you wish. Not many visitors come here, so be especially cautious about doing any dangerous climbing on the walls if you're here alone.

WHERE TO STAY & DINE

With Nafplion just down the road, there's really no reason to stay overnight in Argos unless you prefer the bustle of this crowded Greek market town to Nafplion's more sybaritic pleasures. If you do stay here, the **Hotel Mycenae,** Plateia Ayio Petrou (Saint Peter's Square) 10, 21200 Argos (☎ **0751/28-569**), is probably your best bet; doubles with breakfast start from Dr21,000 ($70). Although the Hotel Mycenae is on Argos's energetic main square, the rooms are relatively quiet and you're certainly where the action is.

None of the small cafes and restaurants in Argos is worth seeking out, but the conveniently located **Aigle,** on the main square between the General Bank and the Ionian Bank, has the usual chops, salads, and souvlaki. Lunch or dinner costs from Dr3,000 ($10). If you want a sweet, try the place directly across from the Archaeological Museum; in 1998, they were installing a very promising-looking cappuccino machine.

SIDE TRIPS FROM ARGOS

The two sites of Argive Heraion and Lerna are easy to reach from Argos, and although neither has spectacular remains, each is worth visiting for its lovely locale, stirring legends, and great antiquity.

THE ARGIVE HERAION

The Argive Heraion is a lovely spot to come in the early evening, when the heat haze has diminished and the views over the plain are particularly fine. The earliest settlement here probably dates from the Neolithic era, but the remains you see are from an important sanctuary to Zeus's long-suffering wife, Hera; it was built between the 7th and 4th centuries B.C., although the Romans constructed the inevitable bath here in later years.

The Argive Heraion is about 13 kilometers (8 miles) outside Argos. To get here, head out of Argos on the inland road to Nafplion and take the left-hand turn toward Prosimna. At Nea Irea, the road divides; turn left for the Heraion.

As is often the case at the smaller ancient sites in the Peloponnese, you'll probably enjoy the setting here more than the actual remains, which include several stoas, two temples, an altar, and the Roman baths. Admission is Dr500 ($1.65), and the site is open Tuesday through Sunday from 8am to 5pm. The sanctuary occupied three terraces, and the 7th-century B.C. temple on the highest terrace may have been the first building in the Peloponnese to be built with columns on all sides, rather than just in front. The 5th-century temple on the middle terrace contained a massive chryselephantine statue of Hera made by the sculptor Polykleitos that rivaled Phidias's similar statue of Zeus at Olympia. Nothing of these temples remains but low foundations, and you'll probably have more fun finding the nicely carved doves that ornament some building blocks than trying to decipher the ruins.

According to legend, Agamemnon was officially named leader of the Greek expedition against Troy at the Argive Heraion. And, according to the historian Herodotus, two of the happiest mortals ever to have lived died here: Cleobis and Biton. Herodotus tells us that when King Croesus of Lydia asked the Athenian statesman and sage Solon who was the happiest mortal in the world, Solon named Cleobis and Biton, whose mother was a priestess at the Argive Heraion. One day, when the oxen customarily yoked to the family chariot failed to turn up, the devoted Argive youths pulled their mother's chariot here from Argos so that she would arrive in time for a festival of Hera. Moments after they arrived, Herodotus says, "The two boys fell asleep in the temple and never awoke." As Solon pointed out to King Croesus, "Call no man happy until his death"—words Croesus would remember years later when he lost his great empire.

If you think this is only a pretty story, and that there never was a Cleobis or a Biton, consider this: Herodotus says that the Argives dedicated statues of the two boys at Delphi; the statues are lost, but their bases, inscribed in honor of Cleobis and Biton, were found in the excavations at Delphi and are now on display in the museum there.

LERNA

As you travel around the Peloponnese, you're often told that the sites you are visiting were occupied as long ago as the Neolithic era, but you very seldom see any actual building remains from that period. That's what makes Lerna's 4th-millennium B.C. palace, known as the House of the Tiles, so special. People lived at Lerna from the Neolithic period through the Mycenaean era, and pottery from as far away as Troy has been found here.

From Argos, take the old road to Tripolis to Myloi. Lerna is just outside Myloi on the left-hand side of the road. The sign is very modest. Look for a straight path running through citrus groves to the site, which is protected by a metal roof.

The **Archaeological Site at Lerna** is open Tuesday through Sunday from 8am to 3pm; admission is Dr500 ($1.65). Although Lerna's remains are scant, the final fire that destroyed the House of the Tiles calcified its mud brick walls, leaving the remains you see today, including several enormous pottery-storage vessels. According to legend, Hercules killed the nine-headed Lernan Hydra in a nearby swamp. The swamp, long since drained, is now a fertile plain with citrus and fruit trees.

WHERE TO DINE   If you're hungry when you visit Lerna, head back into Myloi. Just as you enter the hamlet, drive steeply downhill to the nameless **souvlaki place** on the right-hand side of the road across from the blue-and-white house that serves as the Nea Demokratia headquarters. The souvlaki is delicious and, at the time of our visit, the french fries were still homemade, not the increasingly ubiquitous flabby prepackaged frozen fries. A stick of souvlaki is Dr150 (50¢); Dr1,800 ($6) will get you four souvlaki, salad, fries, and an ice-cold beer. Accept no substitutes: the souvlaki here is much better than that peddled at the other souvlaki stands in Myloi.

If you'd rather have fish, try **To Mouragio** (☎ 0751/47-198), one of a string of fish tavernas on the water at Myloi (follow the signs for Nea Chios and Nafplion). This is a pleasant spot to sit, under shady trees, and enjoy some grilled fish. As always, make sure you know how much the fish is per kilo before you order: you could easily spend Dr15,000 ($50) for two for lunch here.

7 Sparta (Sparti)

248km (153 miles) SW of Athens; 58km (36 miles) S of Tripolis

Few sights in the Peloponnese are more imposing than the immense bulk of Mount Taygetos towering above Sparta. There's often snow on Taygetos until well into the summer, and when the sun sinks behind the mountain, the temperature seems to plummet instantly. The rich plain watered by the bottle-green Eurotas River that has made Sparta prosperous since antiquity stretches between the Taygetos and Parnon mountain ranges. Lush olive and citrus groves run for miles between the ranges, and there are even ornamental orange trees planted along Sparta's main avenues.

In a famously accurate prediction, the 5th-century B.C. Athenian historian Thucydides wrote that if Sparta were ever "to become desolate, and the temples and the foundations of the public buildings were left, no one in future times would believe that this had been one of the preeminent cities of Greece." The ancient remains here are so meager that only the truly dedicated will seek them out. Others will prefer to take in the small archaeological museum, enjoy the bustling town of Sparta itself, and head 8 kilometers (5 miles) down the road to the very impressive remains of the Byzantine city of Mistra (see "A Side Trip from Sparta: Mistra," below).

A LOOK AT THE PAST   The Spartans earned their reputation for courage and military heroism in 580 B.C., when the Spartan general Leonidas and a band of only 300 soldiers faced down the invading Persian army at Thermopylae. From 431 to 404 B.C. Sparta and Athens fought the Peloponnesian War; Sparta finally won, but was exhausted by the effort. From then on, Sparta was a sleepy provincial town with a great future behind it. Greece's first king, young Otto of Bavaria, paid tribute to Sparta's past by redesigning the city with the wide boulevards and large central square that make it still charming today.

ESSENTIALS

GETTING THERE   By Bus   From Athens, seven buses a day depart from the **Stathmos Leoforia Peloponnisou** (Bus Station for the Peloponnese), Odos Kifissou 100 (for information call **01/512-4913**), for the Sparta bus station at Odos Vrasidou (☎ **0731/26-441**). There are frequent buses from Sparta to Mistra.

By Car   From Athens, allow 5 hours; from Corinth, 3 hours; from Patras, 3 hours; from Tripolis, 2 hours. From Athens or Corinth, the new Corinth-Tripolis road is well worth taking.

VISITOR INFORMATION   It is usually possible to get visitor information in the Town Hall on the Main Square (open Mon through Fri from 8am to 3pm). In recent years, there has been a **summer music and drama festival** in Sparta; information is available at the Town Hall.

FAST FACTS   The **National Bank of Greece,** on Paleologou, exchanges currency and was installing an ATM machine in 1998. The **hospital** (☎ **0731/28-671**) is signposted in the town. There are usually English-speaking doctors on the staff. The **police** and **tourist police** are both at Odos Hilonos 8 (☎ **0731/26-229**). Both the **post office,** on Odos Kleombrotou, and the **telephone office (OTE),** at Odos Kleombrotou 11, are signposted.

WHAT TO SEE & DO

The Acropolis and Ancient Theater. Free admission. Usually open sunrise to sunset.

The ancient Spartans boasted that they didn't need fortifications because the Taygetos and Parnon mountains were their defense walls. In addition, as Thucydides reminds us, Spartans did not go in for much building. Consequently, there's not a lot to see on the Spartan acropolis.

The acropolis is at the north end of town, just beyond the monumental statue of Leonidas near the supposed site of his tomb. The grove of trees here makes this a pleasant place to sit and read at sunset, but you'll probably enjoy the view of Taygetos more than the scattered remains of the 2nd-century B.C. theater. Originally, this was one of the largest theaters in Greece, seating 16,000. The theater was dismantled and the blocks were carted off for reuse when the Franks built Mistra in the 13th century. In 1998, there were signs of restoration work here, and perhaps by the time you visit, you'll be able to enjoy a play in this ancient theater.

The Temple of Artemis Orthia. Free admission. Usually open sunrise to sunset.

If you continue out of town on the Tripolis road, you'll see a small yellow sign for the Temple of Artemis Orthia, where little Spartan boys were whipped to learn courage and endurance. Today the site, which dates from the 10th century B.C. but was extensively remodeled by the Romans, is often crowded with gypsy children, aggressively begging for money. This is not a pleasant place to visit, especially alone.

The Menelaion. Free admission. Usually open sunrise to sunset.

To visit the Menelaion, take the Tripolis road north out of town and turn right immediately after the bridge; the Menelaion is signposted about 5 kilometers (3 miles) down the road. The shrine, in honor of Helen of Troy's long-suffering husband, Menelaus, has three terraces of gray limestone blocks and is about a 10-minute walk uphill from the chapel, where you'll park your car.

Beside the shrine are the low remains of several Mycenaean houses, none of which seems remotely grand enough to have belonged to Menelaus. Again, as with the acropolis of ancient Sparta, the real reason to come here is for the view of the plain and Taygetos.

The Archaeological Museum. Admission Dr500 ($1.65). Tues–Sat 8:30am–3pm; Sun 8:30am–12:30pm. Entrance usually free in Jan.

The prize of this museum is a handsome 5th-century marble bust, believed to show Leonidas and to have stood on his tomb. The Spartans, however, were famous as soldiers, not as artists, and the museum's collection reflects Sparta's lack of a lively

The Volta, Spartan Style

Sit in the square almost any evening, and around 9pm you'll start to see the famous Spartan volta, or promenade. For years, this was a highly stylized affair, with men and women walking on separate sides of the square. It was where much courting went on under the watchful eye of parents; today, most young men and women stroll in couples with no attending chaperones. Especially on weekends, this is a lively scene, as entire families stroll up and down and up and down again, sometimes taking a break to sit at one of the cafes for an ice cream.

artistic tradition. Still, it's worth stopping here to see the statue of Leonidas, several fine Roman mosaics, and a small collection of objects found at Mycenaean sites in the countryside near Sparta. The museum's rose garden, peopled with decapitated Roman statues, is a nice spot to sit and read. *Be warned:* This museum has no rest rooms.

WHERE TO STAY

Hotel Byzantion. 23100 Mistra, Laconia. ☎ **0731/83-309.** Fax 0731/20-019. 26 units, 22 with full bathroom. TEL. Dr15,000 ($50) double; less off-season. EURO, MC, V. Usually closed Nov 1–Mar 1.

This is the place to stay if you want to be poised to visit Mistra first thing in the morning. There's very little traffic on the road through Mistra at night, but whatever there is passes the Hotel Byzantion, which may make you decide to opt for a back room. Bedrooms and bathrooms are on the small side, but are very clean, and the staff is helpful. There are several small tavernas in Mistra if you don't want to go to Sparta for dinner.

Hotel Maniatis. Odos Paleologou 72, 23100 Sparta, Laconia. ☎ **0731/22-665.** Fax 0731/29-994. 80 units. A/C TV TEL. Dr15,000 ($50) double. MC, V.

Despite its location at the corner of Paleologou and Lycourgou, Sparta's two main streets, the Maniatis is reasonably quiet (the rooms in back are by far the best). The marble-and-glass lobby is considerably grander than the bedrooms, which, if not spartan, are simple, with functional bedside tables, a straight chair, and a small bathroom. The hotel restaurant, the Dias, is decorated in pastels that should be soothing but somehow aren't. The food here is okay, but the restaurant is often filled with noisy tour groups and it's worth walking a block or two to the excellent Diethnes restaurant.

Hotel Melelaion. Odos Paleologou 91, 23100 Sparta, Laconia. ☎ **0731/22-161.** Fax 0731/26-332. 48 units. A/C MINIBAR TV TEL. Dr28,000 ($93) double. Rates include breakfast. EURO, MC, V.

It's good to see the handsome neoclassical Menelaion, built in 1935, looking good again. For too many years, this once-elegant hotel, with high ceilings and stylish architectural detail, let itself go. Now redone, with a very nice swimming pool in the central courtyard, the Menelaion is once more an appealing place to stay. Friends who visited in 1998 had no complaints, although they think travelers who like extra-firm mattresses might find the beds a bit soft.

Hotel Sparta Inn. Thermopilion 109, 23100 Sparta, Laconia. ☎ **0731/21-021,** or 416/362-4342 in Toronto. Fax 0731/24-855. 150 units. A/C TV TEL. Dr18,000 ($60) double. MC, V.

This large hotel has a quiet location on a side street, but is often taken over by not-so-quiet tour groups. Guest rooms are air-conditioned, with firm beds, decent reading lights, and good-size bathrooms. There's nothing charming about this hotel, whose muted color scheme is rather gloomy, but its quiet location and two (small) pools are real pluses in Sparta, which tends to be noisy and hot in the summer. Ask for the hotel's handy English printout of area attractions.

Shopping

The weekly **market** in Sparta is on Saturday. **Lampropoulou,** on Odos Paleologou, stocks English-language guides, newspapers, magazines, and books.

WHERE TO DINE

✪ Diethnes. Paleologou 105, Sparta. ☎ **0731/28-636.** Main courses Dr1,500–Dr2,400 ($5–$8). No credit cards. Daily from about 8am–midnight. GREEK.

On summer Saturdays, all of Sparta seems to eat lunch in the Diethnes's shady garden after shopping at the street market around the corner. If you're only going to eat one meal in Sparta, it should be here; in fact, unless you really don't like eating in the same place more than once, why go anywhere else? The grills (including local loukanika sausages) are excellent; the vegetables are drizzled, not drenched, in oil; and the waiters move with the speed of light through the crowds.

Elysse Restaurant. Odos Paleologou 113. ☎ **0731/29-896.** Main courses from Dr1,550–Dr2,400 ($5–$8). No credit cards. Daily from about 11am–11pm. GREEK.

If the Diethnes Restaurant wasn't just a few doors away, this would be a very tempting place to eat. The food is good, the staff is efficient, but in the summer it's much more pleasant to sit in the garden at the Diethnes than in the Elysse's indoor dining room. If you are tired of Greek food by the time you reach Sparta, check to see whether any of the continental dishes listed on the Elysse's menu are actually being served: chicken Madeira has been known to appear here.

The Stoa Cafeteria. Lycourgou 140. No phone. Coffee and loukoumades Dr900 ($3). Daily 8am–late evening. LOUKOUMADES/SNACKS.

This little hole-in-the-wall next to a florist is the place to go for a Spartan favorite: *loukoumades,* airy deep-fried puffs of pastry drenched in honey syrup.

A SIDE TRIP FROM SPARTA: MISTRA

The deserted medieval city of Mistra, now Greece's most picturesque ghost town, sprawls down a distinctive conical hill on Taygetos's lower slopes. So much remains of Mistra and so little of ancient Sparta that it's not surprising that the early travelers here identified Mistra as ancient Sparta, lovingly describing the 13th-century A.D. Palace of the Despots, now undergoing restoration, as Menelaus's Mycenaean palace— a cautionary tale for all travelers trying to make sense of Greek ruins.

To reach Mistra, leave Sparta on Odos Lycourgou and follow the signs for Mistra 8 kilometers (5 miles). If you arrive here alone by car, you'll have to decide whether to park at the main gate and climb up to the castle (Kastro), or park at the castle entrance, work your way downhill to the main gate, and then climb back up to your car. If you are not traveling alone, try to persuade your companion to let you out at the castle entrance and meet you at the main gate. There are frequent buses from the main square in Sparta to Mistra.

If you visit Mistra in the summer, try to go in the relative cool of the morning. There's little shade, and you'll find yourself climbing up and down a very steep hill for several hours. *Be warned:* There are no toilet facilities at Mistra. Vendors sometimes sell water and soft drinks outside the Kastro and main entrances to Mistra.

A LOOK AT THE PAST   In 1204, the Frankish leader William de Villehardouin chose this site as the headquarters for his Greek empire. De Villehardouin crowned Mistra with a fortress and defense walls, built himself a palace on the slopes below, and had 10 good years here, until the Byzantine Greeks defeated him at the Battle of Pelagonia in 1259. According to legend, de Villehardouin would have escaped capture if a Greek soldier had not identified him by his famously protruding buck teeth.

Mistra's real heyday came under the Byzantine Greeks, when most of its churches and more than 2,000 houses, as well as the enormous Palace of the Despots, were built. Some 25,000 people lived in Mistra—twice the population of Sparta today. Among them were the philosophers, writers, architects, and artists who made Mistra something of an international center of culture.

Mistra was such an important city that many Byzantine emperors sent their heirs here for some on-the-job training. After Constantinople and the Byzantine empire fell to the Turks in 1453, Mistra held out; the last emperor of Byzantium was crowned in the Cathedral at Mistra, which finally fell to the Turks in 1460.

The Venetians captured Mistra from the Turks in 1687 and ruled here for a half century, during which time Mistra swelled to an enormous city of more than 40,000, largely supported by a flourishing silk industry. When the Turks regained power, Mistra began its long decline into what it is today: Greece's most picturesque ghost town.

THE ARCHAEOLOGICAL SITE OF MISTRA

The site is open from 8am to 3pm and sometimes later in summer. Admission is Dr1,500 ($5). If you start your tour of Mistra at the top, you can orient yourself by taking in the fine view over the entire site from de Villehardouin's **Castle** (the Kastro). As you head down, you'll begin to pass Mistra's **churches,** most of which have elaborate brickwork decoration, a multiplicity of domes, and superb frescoes. Despite Mistra's "picturesque incoherence," the churches are signposted, and you should be able to find the most beautiful ones—the **Saint Sophia,** the **Pantannasa,** the **Panayia Hodegetria,** the **Peribleptos,** and the **Cathedral.**

Give your eyes time to adjust to the poor light inside the churches; once they do, you'll be able to pick out vivid scenes, such as the *Raising of Lazarus* and the *Ascension* in the 15th-century frescoes in the Pantannasa Monastery, the *Marriage of Cana* in the 14th-century Panayia Hodegetria, and the stunning *Birth of Christ* in the 14th-century Peribleptos Monastery. The frescoes that decorated Greek churches have been described as the "Books of the Illiterate"; any devout Byzantine Greek could have "read" these frescoes and identified every New and Old Testament scene, just as their descendants can today.

8 Vassae & Andritsena

45km (27 miles) from Megalopolis to Andritsena; 24km (15 miles) from Andritsena to Vassae

Vassae is one of the most impressive 5th-century Greek temples, its gray granite columns the perfect complement to its remote mountain setting. Unfortunately, the temple, badly damaged by time and earthquakes, is now hidden under a bizarre protective tent that looks rather like the Sydney opera house. When fires threatened to engulf Vassae in August 1998, the staff here hosed the tent all day and all night and successfully protected both tent and temple from the flames. Every year the guard here says that he hopes that Vassae will be mended and the tent removed "next year," a phrase that in Greek does not carry the specificity that its English translation suggests.

Although it's perfectly possible to visit Vassae on a day trip from Olympia, Andritsena, with the scent of oregano and the sound of sheep bells everywhere, is one of the most charming of the Peloponnesian mountain villages. There's one decent hotel here and a number of small restaurants. The main street is punctuated by enormous plane trees, several of which have been fitted with pipes gushing forth the delicious local spring water. In the evening, villagers stroll the main street while sheep bells echo in the hills. In short, if you want to get away from it all and spend the night in a Greek mountain village, try to make it Andritsena.

ESSENTIALS

GETTING THERE   By Bus   There are several buses a day to Andritsena from Athens and from Argos, Tripolis, Olympia, and Megalopolis. The Greek National Tourist Office in Athens should have information on these services.

By Car   All the routes to Andritsena go through spectacular mountain countryside. The roads are excellent, but each winding mile takes about twice as long to drive as you might have anticipated.

FAST FACTS   Everything you might need—the **bus station,** the **OTE,** the **post office,** the **bank,** the **police**—is clearly signposted on or just off Andritsena's main street.

WHAT TO SEE & DO

The Temple of Vassae. Admission Dr500 ($1.65). Usually open daily 8am–7pm.

Coming around the last turn in the road and suddenly seeing the severe gray limestone columns of this 5th-century Doric temple to Apollo used to be one of the great sights in the Peloponnese. It seemed almost impossible that such a staggeringly impressive building should have been built in such a remote location—and designed by none other than Ictinus, the architect of the Parthenon. Evidently, the temple was built by the inhabitants of the tiny hamlet of Phigaleia, to thank Apollo for saving them from a severe plague.

If you saw the temple before it disappeared under its tent, cherish your memories and don't bother to visit there now. The tent fits so snugly that the only way to get a sense of what the temple actually looks like is to buy a postcard.

If you haven't seen Vassae, you'll have to decide whether you want to see it this way, or hope that the guard will be right and that "next year" the tent will be gone.

THE VILLAGE OF ANDRITSENA

Tiny Andritsena has one of the finest libraries in Greece, the legacy of a 19th-century philhellene. If you like old books, check to see if the **library,** recently moved into a grand new building just off the main street, has opened.

The small **folk museum,** on the plateia below the main street, is usually locked, despite its posted hours. Admission is Dr200 (65¢); contributions are welcome. To see the endearing collection of local wedding costumes, rugs, farm tools, and family photographs, ask to be let in at the house nearest to the museum.

If you can, plan to be in Andritsena on Saturday, when the main street is taken over by the weekly **market,** an excellent place to buy every manner of sheep, goat, and cow bells, mountain tea, and herbs.

WHERE TO STAY

Theoxenia Hotel. 27061 Andritsena, Eleia. ☎ **0626/22-219.** 45 units. TEL. Dr11,500 ($38) double. MC, V.

This 1950s hotel has clearly seen better days, and it was heartening to see that some public rooms and bedrooms were being freshly painted during our visit—less heartening to see that the painting hadn't been completed a month later. Still, the views from the front rooms overlooking the valley below Andritsena more than compensate for the basically shabby decor, and students of kitsch will appreciate the needlework pictures. The sometimes less-expensive rooms in back have almost as good a view and are much quieter; trucks and buses tend to turn around in front of the hotel. The room rates here are somewhat flexible; you might bargain if you are quoted a high rate. Avoid the restaurant, and hold onto your room key, as there's often no one at the front desk.

If the Theoxenia is full, consider the small, tidy **Pan Hotel,** 27061 Andritsena (☎ **0626/22-213**), and try to ignore its unfortunate location (next to the Shell station and its fumes and traffic).

WHERE TO DINE

The Andritsena Kafezakeroplasteion (Coffee-Sweet Shop). Main St. ☎ **0626/22-004.** Full breakfast Dr1,500 ($5). No credit cards. Daily from about 7am–11pm. COFFEE/SWEETS.

You can avoid your hotel breakfast by coming here for bread and honey, yogurt, or an omelet. In nice weather, you can sit outside under the red-and-white–striped umbrellas, looking at the elegant lace curtains in the cafe's six decorative fan windows.

Sigouri. Odos Sofokleos (across from the metalworker's shop above the main plateia), Andritsena. No phone. Lunch or dinner Dr2,400 ($8). No credit cards. Open most days for lunch and dinner, usually closing by 10pm. GREEK HOME COOKING.

Kyria Vasso's *briam* (vegetable stew) is excellent, as are her stuffed tomatoes and barrel wine. A meal here consists of a salad, main course, and the local wine. If you like *kourouloudes* (rag rugs), ask to see the ones she makes and sells by the meter; for about Dr7,500 ($25), you can take home a colorful hand-loomed bedside rug.

The Trani Brisi. Main St. No phone. Lunch or dinner Dr2,400 ($8). No credit cards. Open most days for lunch and dinner, usually closing by 10pm. GREEK.

This small restaurant has tables outside under extra-large beach umbrellas, in a widening of the road between the two upper plateias (squares). The menu varies from day to day, but often features some kind of lamb stew, fresh vegetables, and the local wine. If you like the wine here, you can usually buy some to take away with you.

9 Monemvassia

97km (60 miles) S of Sparta; 340km (210 miles) S of Athens

Nicknamed "the Gibraltar of Greece" because of its strategic importance during the Middle Ages, Monemvassia was a virtual ghost town by the 20th century. Today, this rocky island just off the easternmost tip of the Peloponnese has a new lease on life: Wealthy foreigners and Greeks are buying and restoring old houses here. Furthermore, word is getting out that in addition to its medieval fortress, handsome churches, and drop-dead sunsets, Monemvassia has several of the most stylish small hotels in the Peloponnese.

Unfortunately, an increasing number of round-the-Peloponnese bus tours make a brief stop here; try to arrive in the late afternoon or evening, have a swim, relax, and do your sightseeing in the early morning before the first bus tour arrives.

Although Monemvassia is an island, it's connected to the mainland by a causeway that you can drive or stroll across. Once you step through the massive Venetian Gate that is Monemvassia's only entrance (*mone emvasis* means "one entrance" in Greek), you're in a separate world. Cars are banned here—a wise decision, since the only approximation of a street on "the rock" is barely wide enough for two of the donkeys that bring in supplies to squeeze past each other.

ESSENTIALS

GETTING THERE   By Bus   There is one direct bus a day from the **Stathmos Leoforia Peloponnisou** (Bus Station for the Peloponnese), at Odos Kifissou 100 in Athens, to Monemvassia, and six daily buses via Sparta. Call ☎ **01/24-913** for schedule information.

By Car   Take the National Road from Athens-Corinth-Tripolis. Then head south to Monemvassia via Sparta. Allow at least 6 hours for the trip.

By Boat   The Flying Dolphin hydrofoil leaving from Marina Zea in Piraeus links Athens and Monemvassia for most of the year and is the fastest way to reach Monemvassia from Athens. For information call ☎ **01/61-219.**

FAST FACTS   At press time, the **bank** in the new town of Monemvassia (on the shore across the causeway from the old town) exchanged currency, but had no ATM. You'll find the **post office** and the **OTE** in the town of new Monemvassia, on the shore across the causeway from the old town. The **Malvasia Travel Agency** (☎ **0732/61-432**) has several helpful English-speaking staff members.

WHAT TO SEE & DO
A STROLL THROUGH MONEMVASSIA

Monemvassia is a great place to wander. Sure, you'll get lost in the winding cobbled lanes, but how lost can you get on an island 1,600 feet long and half as wide? The answer (at least at night) is pretty lost: It's a good idea to wear decent walking shoes, bring along a flashlight, and save the 880-foot ascent of the citadel for daytime.

From the **citadel,** there are truly spectacular views down to the red-tile roofs of Monemvassia, out across the sea, and deep into the mountains of the Mani peninsula. While you're on the citadel, try to figure out just how the 13th-century **Church of Ayia Sophia** (Holy Wisdom) was built not just on, but virtually over, the edge of the cliffs.

After taking on the climb to the citadel, you'll probably want a swim, so head down to the **bathing jetty.** En route, you'll pass the **Church of Christos Elkomenos** (Christ in Chains), across from a Venetian canon, as well as a tumbledown **mosque** and the **Venetian chapel of Panayia Chryssafiotissa.** The churches sometimes are and sometimes are not locked; if they're locked, content yourself with the thought that the **handsome stone houses** lining Monemvassia's winding lanes are the real treat to see here.

On the subject of treats, Monemvassia is one place in the Peloponnese where you don't have to contemplate yet another moussaka. Strung out along Monemvassia's main street are a number of restaurants: **Martina's** has a varied Greek menu, and **To Canoni** has pasta, including spaghetti Carbonara. No wonder knowledgeable travelers come back to Monemvassia every year: excellent food, marvelous sunsets, medieval ruins—and, as yet, relatively few tourists.

SHOPPING

There's no shop on "the rock" that's truly outstanding, but those strung out along **Odos Ritsos** have thus far avoided the infestation of T-shirts and cheap museum reproductions so common elsewhere. Just inside Monemvassia's gate, **Costas Lekakis** has a good selection of books in English, including R. Klaus and U. Steinmuller's excellent guide *Monemvassia* ($6). **Bentouraki** has nice linen caps and straw boaters from around $40—a hat is a necessity to ward off the harsh sun here. **Ioanna**

Angelatou's shop, next to the Byzantion hotel, often has a good selection of the deep-blue glassware made in Greece and well-done reproductions of antique wood carvings and copper.

WHERE TO STAY

There are so few rooms on "the rock" that this is one place where it's a good idea to try to make a reservation. We say "try" because records of reservations sometimes disappear mysteriously, even after several phone calls.

If the Byzantion and the Malvasia are full, you might consider the **Kellia,** by the Panayia Chrysafiotissa church (☎ **0732/61-520**). This former convent is run as a hotel by the GNTO, which, alas, does not seem to be keeping an eye on the place. The rooms are nicely furnished, but the service is haphazard.

Byzantion. Odos Ritsos, Monemvassia. ☎ **0732/61-351.** Fax 0732/61-352. 18 units. Dr13,500–Dr24,000 ($45–$80) double or suite. DC, EURO, MC, V.

There's only one problem with staying in this small hotel in a beautifully restored and furnished house: A number of the rooms are built flush against a hillside, do not get cross-ventilation, and can be stuffy, with a strong odor of mildew. Ask for a room with a balcony and cross-ventilation. Some rooms have air-conditioning, televisions, and refrigerators.

✪ **Malvasia.** Headquarters on Odos Ritsos, Monemvassia. ☎ **0732/62-223.** Fax 0732/ 61-722. 35 units. From Dr24,000 ($80) double; from Dr75,000 ($250) suite; substantial reductions possible off-season. EURO, MC, V.

This is far and away the finest hotel in Monemvassia and one of the most charming in Greece. Over the years, the owners have bought up a number of old houses, restored them, and furnished the rooms with old copper, hand-loomed rugs and bedspreads, and handsome wooden furniture. This would be a wonderful place to stay a week, or a month (long-term reduced rates available). If you can't do that, at least stay for 1 night and hope for a sea-view room in the Stellaki Mansion on the ramparts, or in the hotel's original building on Odos Ritsos. If you're here in the winter, ask for a room with a fireplace. Some rooms have phones and refrigerators; some suites have full kitchens.

10 The Mani

Githio is 301km (186 miles) S of Athens and 45km (27 miles) S of Sparta; Areopoli is 32km (20 miles) W of Githio

The innermost of the Peloponnese's three tridentlike prongs, the Mani is still one of the least-visited areas in Greece. That's changing fast, as word gets out about the good beaches near Githio and Kardamili and the haunting landscape of the Inner Mani (the southernmost Mani). Good roads mean that you can now drive the circuit of the entire Mani in a day, but it's more fun to spend at least 1 night here in one of the restored tower-house hotels.

A LOOK AT THE PAST　The Inner Mani's barren mountains are dotted with tiny olive trees and enormous prickly pear cactuses. It's hard to believe that 100 years ago, this was a densely populated area, with almost every hillside cultivated. If you squint, you can still make out the stone walls and terraces that farmers built on the deserted hillsides.

Now that most Maniotes have moved away, to Athens or abroad, many of the handsome gray-stone tower houses are deserted. Originally, the Maniotes chose to live in tower houses because they were easy to defend, an important consideration for these constantly feuding Peloponnesians, who spent much of their time until the 20th century lobbing cannonballs at their neighbors. Fortunately, many tower houses survived, and the towers of the virtually deserted villages of Koita and Nomia look like miniature skyscrapers from a distance.

When the Maniotes weren't trying to destroy their neighbors' homes, they seem to have atoned by building churches: The area is dotted with tiny medieval chapels tucked in the folds of the hills. Keep an eye out for the stands of cypress trees that often mark the chapels, many of which have decorative brickwork and ornately carved marble doors. If you don't want to tramp around the countryside in search of chapels, at least take a look at the **Church of the Taxiarchoi (Archangels)** in Areopoli. Don't miss the droll figures of the saints and signs of the zodiac carved on the church's facade.

ESSENTIALS

GETTING THERE   By Bus   It's possible to get a bus from Athens to Sparta and from Sparta to Githio or Areopoli, but this is a trip that takes a full day. For schedule information call ☎ 01/24-913.

By Car   Again, a long trip, but not as tedious as the bus, which makes many stops. Take the National Road Athens-Corinth-Tripolis, and then head south to Githio and Areopoli via Sparta.

GETTING AROUND   Longtime visitors to Greece wax nostalgic about the days when they had to hoof it around the Mani. You can get around today by local bus, but by far the most efficient method is by car.

FAST FACTS   There are **banks** in both Githio and Areopoli, but no ATMs. Do not count on finding banks elsewhere in the Mani. The **GNTO Mani office** is on the main square in the capital of Areopoli, as is a **bank** (usually open Tues and Thurs from 9am to noon), the **post office,** the **OTE,** the **bus station,** and several **restaurants.** The **police** are signposted on the main square in Areopoli. There are no tourist police in Areopoli or Githio.

WHAT TO SEE & DO

✪ **The Caves of Dirou.** Pirgos Dirou, The Mani. ☎ **0733/52-222.** Fax 0733/52-223. Admission Dr3,500 ($12). The visiting hours for the caves vary unpredictably; in general, the caves are open 9am–5pm in summer, with shorter hours off-season.

These caves, a very popular holiday destination for Greeks, are mobbed in summer, so try to arrive as soon as they open. Guided tours through the Glyfada cave take about 30 minutes and are not recommended for the claustrophobic: you take your place in a small boat that your guide poles through the clammy caverns. The crystal-studded stalactites (the ones hanging from the ceilings like icicles) and stalagmites (the ones rising up from the cave's floor) are spectacular, in shades of rose, green, amber, black, blood red, and purple. It may be best not to trail your fingers in the cool water: Giant eels live just beneath the surface.

The Pirgos Dirou Caves were discovered in 1955 by a dog that crawled through a hole into the caves and returned several days later coated in red clay. Fortunately, his owner, spelunker Anna Petroclides, was curious about the red clay and followed her dog when he next set off on explorations. What she found was a vast network of caves, of which some 5,000 meters have now been explored. The caves themselves are impressive, but what has made them famous is the Paleolithic and Neolithic remains found here. In short, the Pirgos Dirou caves are one of the oldest inhabited spots in Greece, and the pottery, bone tools, and even garbage found here has shed light on Greece's earliest history.

Before you leave Pirgos Dirou, check to see if the small **Neolithic Museum** (☎ 0733/52-233), with displays of artifacts found in the caves, is open. Admission is Dr500 ($1.65).

The Demaglion Folklore Museum. Thalames, The Mani. Admission Dr900 ($3). Usually open May 1–Sept 30 daily 9:30am–5pm.

This small private collection in the village of Thalames, some 20 kilometers (12 miles) north of Areopoli, has old prints, costumes, olive presses, farm tools, ceramic plates commemorating various Greek monarchs—and just about anything else you'd expect to find if you cleaned out a number of Maniote attics. The owner, Mr. Demaglion, is a local schoolteacher who speaks a little English and a lot of German and enjoys lecturing visitors. From time to time, Mr. Demaglion sells duplicate items from his collection; you may be able to buy an inexpensive antique wood carving or piece of embroidery here. Items for sale are usually on display in front of the museum.

WHERE TO STAY

Hotel Itilo. Neo Itilo, 23062 Lakonia, Mani. ☎ **0733/59-222.** Fax 0733/29-234. 26 units. TEL. Dr22,500 ($75) double. Rates include breakfast. AE, MC, V.

This beachfront family-run hotel on the Gulf of Itilo, just north of Areopoli, attracts lots of families, whose children enjoy the little beachside playground. Many of the large bedrooms overlook the sea. If you show up here for just a night or two in high season, you may be relegated to the annex, just across the road from the beach. The hotel food, with lots of fresh fish, is excellent, but, as always with fish, expensive.

Kapetanakou Tower Hotel. Areopoli, 26062 Laconia, Mani. ☎ **0733/51-233.** 8 units (2 bathrooms on each floor). Dr15,000 ($50) double. AE, EURO, MC, V.

One of the first of the traditional settlement hotels managed by the Greek National Tourist Organization, the 180-year-old Kapetanakou Tower stands in a walled garden just off the main street in Areopoli. Some of the rooms have sleeping lofts, and most have colorful rag rugs and locally handmade weavings. This is a wonderful place to stay to get an idea of what it was like to live in a Maniote tower—despite the intrusive TV in the breakfast room. There's no restaurant here, but it's only a 5-minute stroll to Areopoli's restaurants.

Limeni Village Hotel. Areopoli, Limeni, 23062 Laconia, Mani. ☎ **0733/51-111.** Fax 0733/51-182. 32 units. TV TEL. Dr19,500 ($65) double. AE, EURO, MC, V.

With the Mani filled with deserted tower-house villages, it's hard not to wonder whether this new hotel, built as a Maniote tower village north of Areopoli, isn't a glaring example of bringing coals to Newcastle. Some of the bedrooms here are quite charming, with nice rag rugs, stone floors, and balconies overlooking the Bay of Itilo. For several years, we've been told that the pool will be open "next year." At the time of our visit, this hotel was marvelously quiet with only a handful of guests, but be warned: The management is trying to attract groups.

Tsimova Guesthouse. Areopoli, 26062 Laconia, Mani. ☎ **0733/51-301.** 10 units, 8 with bathroom. Dr10,500 ($35) double. Reductions possible off-season. No credit cards.

If you speak some Greek and want to find out about the Mani, this private home in a 300-year-old tower with gun slits is the place to stay. Owner George Bersakos has lived all his life in the Mani and turned much of his house into a small museum, stuffed with Maniote memorabilia. If you don't speak Greek, Mr. Bersakos will entertain you in his distinctive English, French, or German. You'll be beautifully taken care of here, but you'll inevitably have less privacy than you would in a hotel. Two of the rooms have TVs.

Tsitsiris Castle. Stavri, 23071 Laconia, Mani. ☎ **0733/56-297.** Fax 0733/56-296. 20 units. TEL. Dr15,000–Dr19,500 ($50–$65) double. Rates include breakfast. MC, V. Usually closed Nov 1–Apr 15.

This tower-house hotel—10 kilometers (6.2 miles) south of Areopoli, in the virtually deserted hamlet of Stavri—has its lobby and dining room in a 200-year-old restored tower, with most of the bedrooms in two new wings flanking a lush rose garden. The lobby and dining room are handsome, with lots of exposed stone walls and interesting woven rugs. The bedrooms are more mundane, although when we stayed here, we had our own icon shrine and wonderful views across the hills. Not many independent travelers make their way here; you may either have the place to yourself, or be surrounded by tour groups. The restaurant is excellent when there are a good number of guests; otherwise, choice is limited and the cooking is desultory.

WHERE TO DINE
GITHIO

We've eaten at most of the seaside seafood restaurants on the harbor in Githio—and still haven't found one that's good enough to make us come back again and again. You should get good, fresh fish at any one of these restaurants, so you may want to make your choice based on factors such as how best to avoid the loud Greek pseudo-folk music at some establishments.

AREOPOLI

The three basically interchangeable restaurants on Areopoli's main square serve equally good—or bad, depending on your point of view—food, featuring grilled meats and salads. Lunch or dinner at any one of these costs from about Dr2,700 ($9).

✪ **Fish Taverna To Limeni.** Limeni, Areopoli. ☎ **0733/51-327.** Starters from Dr600 ($2); fish priced by the kilo. No credit cards. Usually open for lunch and dinner; sometimes closed in winter. SEAFOOD.

The superb fresh fish in this small restaurant in Limeni, the harbor of Areopoli, draws customers from as far away as Kalamata. If you can, choose your fish from the live tanks floating just offshore rather than from the refrigerated display case inside. This is not the place to eat if you are squeamish about seeing fish cleaned a few feet away from where you are eating. The price per kilo varies from day to day and is never cheap; be sure to check the price before you order.

11 Pylos (Pilo/Navarino)

50km (31 miles) W of Kalamata; 108km (67 miles) W of Sparta; 317km (196 miles) SW of Athens

We must admit that all too often in the Peloponnese, the modern village with a famous ancient name—Olympia or Corinth, for example—is a disappointment. That's not the case at Pylos (also known as Navarino), where the modern harbor town has considerable charm. Pylos is developing some sprawling suburbs, and a few of the nearby beaches are being developed with a vengeance, but the harbor and leafy main square are still very pleasant—so pleasant that it's hard to realize that Pylos's harbor has seen some very bloody battles. The Athenians trapped a Spartan force on the offshore island of Sfaktiria in 424 B.C., and in 1827, a combined French, Russian, and British armada defeated the massed Ottoman fleet here. More than 6,000 Ottoman sailors were butchered in what proved to be one of the critical battles of the Greek War of Independence. There's a monument to the three victorious admirals in Pylos's main square, which is understandably called the Square of the Three Admirals.

Ancient Pylos, site of the Mycenaean palace of King Nestor, is located about 17 kilometers (10 miles) north of the town. Homer described Pylos as "sandy Pylos, rich in cattle," and the hilltop palace still overlooks sandy beaches flanked by rich farmland. Ancient Pylos seems to be a site that people take to—or don't. For every visitor who complains about the protective plastic roof over the site, another raves about the palace's idyllic setting. Some call the remains here "scanty," while others find the low walls remarkably "evocative." You decide.

ESSENTIALS

GETTING THERE   By Bus   There are several buses a day to Pylos from the **Stathmos Leoforia Peloponnisou** (Bus Station for the Peloponnese) in Athens, Odos Kifissou 100 (☎ **01/51-34-293**). There is also bus service to Pylos from Kalamata (☎ **0721/28-581**).

By Car   Pylos is a full day's drive from Athens and 3 to 4 hours from either Patras or Sparta. The drive from Sparta to Pylos is via the Langada pass to Kalamata, one of the most beautiful mountain roads in the Peloponnese.

FAST FACTS   Both **banks** in the main square offer currency exchange; the National Bank of Greece has an ATM. The **hospital** (☎ **0723/22-315**) is signposted in town. The **post office** and **telephone office** (**OTE**) are signposted in the main plateia. The **police** (☎ **0723/22-100**) and **tourist police** (☎ **0723/23-733**) are also signposted in the main plateia.

WHAT TO SEE & DO

Neokastro. Pylos. Admission Dr800 ($2.65). Daily 8am–7pm.

The Turkish fortress known as Neokastro, to distinguish it from an earlier fortress, now contains a splendid small museum in a restored 19th-century barracks. The museum features the extensive collection of maps, prints, and watercolors of the French philhellene Rene Puaux, as well as a number of marvelously kitschy porcelain figurines of the English philhellene, Lord Byron. Neokastro also contains a small church, clearly a former mosque, and some impressive fortification walls.

Ancient Pylos (Nestor's Palace) and Museum. ☎ **0763/31-358.** Admission to each Dr500 ($1.70). Tues–Sat 8:30am–3pm; Sun 9:30am–2:30pm. Head north out of Pylos on the main road and follow the signs for Chora.

The palace at Pylos belonged to Nestor, the garrulous old king who told stories and gave unsolicited advice while the younger warriors fought at Troy. The palace was rediscovered in 1939 by the American archaeologist Carl Blegen, who had the unbelievable good fortune of discovering the palace archives on his first day working here. Blegen uncovered some 600 clay tablets written in a mysterious language initially called Linear B, and later shown to be an early form of Greek.

Unlike Mycenae and Tiryns, Pylos was not heavily fortified: you'll see a sentry box, but no massive walls here. The royal apartments are well preserved, and include a more-than-adequate bathroom with the tub still in place. The palace, with its central courtyard, was originally two stories high and richly decorated with frescoes, some of which are on display at the small archaeological museum a mile away in the village of Chora.

WHERE TO STAY

Hotel Miramare. Odos Paralia, 24001 Pylos, Messenia. ☎ **0723/22-751.** Fax 0723/22-226. 30 units, all with shower only. TV TEL. Dr16,200 ($54) double. AE, EURO, MC, V.

The Miramare is just above Pylos's public bathing beach and has its own small restaurant. The rooms are simply furnished, but most have balconies overlooking the harbor. Some units have minibars. This hotel is usually considerably quieter than the Karalis Hotel, but not as quiet as seaside rooms at the Karalis Beach Hotel.

Hotel Zoe. Yalova Pylou 24001, Messenia. ☎ **0723/22-025.** Fax 0723/22-026. 35 units. Dr15,000 ($50). No credit cards.

This pleasant seaside hotel about 5 kilometers (3 miles) north of Pylos is very popular with German families. If you are traveling with children, the chance to begin and end a day of sightseeing with a swim here might be the salvation of a family holiday. The rooms are decent sized, spare, and ferociously clean.

Karalis Beach Hotel. Odos Paralia, 24001 Pylos, Messenia. ☎ **0723/23-021.** Fax 0723/22-970. 14 units, 4 with shower only. TV TEL. Dr15,600 ($52) double. Rates include breakfast. AE, DC, EURO, MC, V. Usually closed Nov 1–May 1.

With the best location in town, at the end of the harbor below the Turkish kastro, far from most traffic, this used to be the nicest place to stay in Pylos. Suddenly, the management has become dreadful: It takes forever to get a room cleaned and there's seldom anyone at the desk. The lobby is often filled with young friends of staff members. Speaking of the lobby, perhaps someone could persuade the owners that placing an enormous television in front of the lobby picture window so that it blocks a good deal of the sea view is not the way to please guests. Nor is it clever to have TV brackets but no TVs in some rooms. In short, at press time, there's only one reason to stay here: getting one of the seaside rooms with a balcony. If that's not available, you'd probably be happier at the Hotel Miramare (see above).

The Karalis Beach Hotel often sends its overflow to the **Karalis Hotel,** Odos Kalamateas 26 (☎ **0723/22-980**), which is under the same management. Rooms here are pleasant, but suffer from traffic noise.

Navarone Hotel/Bungalows. Petrochori, 24001 Pilias, Messenia. ☎ **0723/41-571.** Fax 0723/41-575. 17 units, 41 bungalows. TEL. Dr21,000–Dr28,000 ($70–$93). DC, MC, V.

Friends who stayed here in the summer of 1998 report enjoying this new hotel, about 5 kilometers (3 miles) north of Pylos and a 5-minute walk from an excellent sand beach. Many of the rooms have seafront balconies and most have good reading lights and handy desks; since the hotel is new, everything in it is also, which means that the mattresses are nice and firm.

WHERE TO DINE

Diethnes Taverna. Odos Paralia. No phone. Fish priced by the kilo. No credit cards. Mid-May to mid-Sept daily noon to at least 11pm. GREEK/SEAFOOD.

In bad weather, you can eat indoors, but in good weather, tables are set up on the quay overlooking the harbor. As you'd expect from a restaurant on the sea and next to the government fish-inspection station, the seafood here is very fresh. Fish in Greece is never cheap, so be sure to ask how much your meal will cost before ordering. There are usually a number of chicken and meat dishes on the menu as well.

Philip Restaurant. On Pylos-Kalamata road. ☎ **0723/22-741.** Fax 0723/23-262. Main courses from Dr1,500 ($5). MC, V. Daily about noon–2pm and about 7pm–midnight. GREEK.

This good restaurant that prides itself on its "traditional home cooking" has an unfortunate location on the main road into town. It's not easy to park here; if you walk uphill from town, you're all too aware of trucks thundering past you downhill. That said, the food is a bit more imaginative here than at many Pylos restaurants, with swordfish shish kebab, inventive vegetable dishes, and the occasional European entree on the menu.

SIDE TRIPS FROM PYLOS: METHONI & KORONI
Methoni is 13km (8 miles) from Pylos; Koroni is 30km (18 miles) from Pylos

Methoni and Koroni are two of the most impressive medieval fortresses in Greece and would be worth seeing for that reason alone. But that's not the only reason to come here: Methoni has one of the best restaurants in Greece, and the drive through the lush Messenian countryside between Methoni and Koroni is ravishing. The route from Pylos to Koroni via Longa is especially blissful; by contrast, the southerly seaside route takes in the village of Finikounda, which is in the throes of overdevelopment.

The long, sandy **Methoni beach** has won several awards for its eco-sensitivity, including Greece's Golden Starfish and the Common Market's Blue Flag. Happily, eco-sensitivity seems to include not only a clean beach, but also an absence of loud music at the children's playground and beachside cafes. Although it's perfectly possible to visit both Methoni and Koroni on a day trip from Pylos, the superb ✪ **Taverna Klimataria** (see below) makes it tempting to spend the night here.

The Venetians built Methoni on the Ionian Sea and Koroni on the Gulf of Messenia in the 13th century to safeguard their newly acquired Greek empire. In some of the bloodiest fighting on record, the fortresses, almost immediately nicknamed "the twin eyes of empire," passed back and forth between various powers for the next several centuries. In 1500, the Turks slaughtered all 5,000 Venetian defendants at Methoni; in 1685, the Venetians wiped out the 1,500-man garrison at Koroni.

Methoni stands at the end of a spit of land and covers enough ground to have contained a city of several thousand inhabitants during the Middle Ages. Ships filled with pilgrims bound for the Holy Land put in here for supplies; in 1571, Miguel de Cervantes was an unwilling visitor here, one of many Spanish seamen captured and forced to work as galley slaves by the Turks after the Battle of Lepanto. Methoni's **exterior walls** are stupendous, although little remains inside the fortress itself. Don't worry about being locked in here when the gates close at 7pm: A very officious guard on a motorcycle rounds up any stragglers. The fortress is usually open from 8am to 7pm; admission is free.

Whereas Methoni's fortress is deserted except for visitors, the fortress at **Koroni** encloses a number of **village houses,** a flourishing **convent,** and several small **cemeteries.** Although the main road in town leads directly to the fortress gate, park before the road heads steeply uphill to the gate, unless you'd enjoy backing up over a sheer drop to the sea. The grounds inside the fortress walls are lovingly planted with roses and very welcome shade trees; piles of cannonballs and the occasional cannon remind visitors of Koroni's bloody past. There's a string of seafood restaurants at the harbor below, but nothing here to compare with Methoni's Klimataria. This is a good place to avoid on summer weekends, when there's an influx of day-trippers from Kalamata.

WHERE TO STAY
Hotel Amalia. 24006 Methoni, Messenia. ☎ **0723/12-931.** Fax 0723/31-195. 36 units. TV TEL. Dr18,000 ($60) double. AE, DC, EURO, MC, V.

This new hotel, with its large lobby and dining room, straddles a low hill outside Methoni, with fine views of the sea and fortress. The bedrooms here are larger than usual, as are the bathrooms. Each unit faces the sea and is entered through a freshly planted rose garden that is coming along nicely. The only drawbacks here: Although you can see the sea, you aren't *on* the sea—and the Amalia does a brisk tour-group business.

Hotel Korakakis Beach. 24006 Finikounda, Messenia. ☎ **0723/71-221.** Fax 0723/ 71-232. 25 units. TEL TV. Dr15,000 ($50) double. Reductions for stays of a week or more. No credit cards.

Finikounda, about halfway between Methoni and Koroni, is not our cup of tea: too developed, too many hotels, too many people. That said, Finikounda has lots of fans because of its lovely sand beach and small seaside hotels and restaurants. If this sounds appealing, try the Hotel Korakakis Beach, many of whose rooms have seafront balconies. Beach-loving friends who stayed here one night in 1998 are planning to come back for a month in 1999, so this hotel must be doing something right!

WHERE TO DINE

The Akroyiali. Waterfront, Methoni. No phone. Snacks from Dr600 ($2); fish priced by the kilo. No credit cards. Open all day in summer. FISH/SNACKS.

This is a pleasant spot for a snack by the sea. Even though this place has good fresh fish, it's hard to resist the Klimataria (see below) at mealtime.

The Kaggelarios. Waterfront, Koroni. No phone. Snacks from Dr600 ($2); ouzo and octopus Dr1,500 ($5). No credit cards. OUZO/SNACKS/LIGHT MEALS.

This cafe seems to attract more locals than the other waterfront fish tavernas in Koroni. The octopus is certainly fresh—the day's catch can be seen hanging on a line at the restaurant.

✪ Taverna Klimataria. Methoni. ☎ **0723/31-544.** Main courses from Dr1,150 ($3.85). MC, V. May 15 to about Oct 20 daily 1:30–6:30pm and 8pm–midnight. GREEK/ANATOLIAN & VEGETARIAN.

This restaurant, serving the best food we've eaten in the Peloponnese, is reason enough to visit Methoni. The chef somehow manages to take standard dishes familiar from any Greek menu (fried zucchini, eggplant salad, briam) and turn them into elegant delights. Then there are the delicately seasoned stews, the chicken breasts in puff pastry, and the fresh fish and lobster. The restaurant is in a pleasant garden, and the service is fast and attentive. It's easy to be seduced by the wide variety of food here, and this is one of the few nonhotel restaurants in the Peloponnese where it's not difficult for a couple to spend more than $50 for dinner—and be eager to come back the next day and do it all over again.

12 Messene (Ithomi/Mavromati)

25km (16 miles) N of Kalamata; 60km (39 miles) E of Pylos

Between 370 and 369 B.C., the great Theban general and statesman Epaminondas built the sprawling city of Messene and its almost 9.5 kilometers (6 miles) of walls below Mount Ithomi in the hopes of checking the power of Sparta. Today, the defense wall, with its two-story towers and turreted gates, is the best preserved classical fortification in the Peloponnese.

GETTING THERE   By Car   From Pylos, Kalamata, or Tripolis, take the main Kalamata-Pylos road to the modern town of Messini, where the road to ancient

Messene is signposted. The site of ancient Messene (also called Ithomi) is in the village of Mavromati, approximately 20 kilometers (13 miles) north of Messini.

WHAT TO SEE & DO

Ancient Messene. Admission Dr500 ($1.65). Tues–Sun 8am–3pm. (In reality, admission is seldom charged and the site is usually open.)

The most impressive stretches of the ancient wall are outside the site, north of the village of Mavromati. As you drive there through Mavromati, you can pick up a copy of the excellent site guide at the postcard shop next to the village spring for Dr1,000 ($3). Even at a distance, the sheer size of the wall, with its towers and gates, makes most visitors gasp. The **Arcadian Gate** is especially well preserved, with the grooves cut in the marble pavement by ancient chariot wheels still clearly visible.

As you drive back toward Mavromati, you'll pass more of the defense wall and the site museum, which has been closed for some time and shows no signs of reopening.

The excavated ruins of Messene are clearly signposted past the museum. This is a vast, sprawling site, with a **Sanctuary of Asklepios** so large that it was originally thought to be the agora (marketplace). The partially excavated **Stadium,** with many of its marble benches well preserved, lies along the dirt road beyond the Asklepeion. To walk the entire site takes a minimum of several hours, but it's possible to see the Asklepeion alone in an hour.

WHERE TO STAY & DINE

Pension Zeus. Mavromati-Ithome, 24200 Messenia. ☎ **0724/51-025.** 5 units, 3 with bathroom. Dr15,000 ($50) double. Rates include breakfast. No credit cards.

This small family-run pension—which is about as far from the Greece of tour-group hotels as you can get—has several small rooms with balconies. The family is very helpful and pleasant and the rooms are perfectly acceptable. The only problem: You're on the one road through town, and will hear whatever traffic there is.

The Ithome Restaurant. Mavromati-Ithome (across from the Spring of Gramatikon). ☎ **0724/51-298.** Lunch or dinner with a beer from Dr2,400 ($8). No credit cards. GREEK.

This very simple restaurant has a terrific view over the ancient site and serves souvlaki, grills, salads, french fries, and the occasional vegetable dish. It's not a bad idea to check the prices on the menu here and compare them with the bill when it comes.

13 Olympia

311km (199 miles) W of Athens; 90km (55 miles) S of Patras; 21km (13 miles) E of Pirgos

With its shady groves of pine, olive, and oak trees, the considerable remains of two temples, and the stadium where the first Olympic races were run in 776 B.C., Olympia is the most beautiful major site in the Peloponnese—although the forest fires of 1998 badly damaged neighborhood groves and almost engulfed the site itself. When you realize that the archaeological museum is one of the finest in Greece, you'll see why you can easily spend a full day here.

A LOOK AT THE PAST   There's really no modern equivalent for ancient Olympia, which was both a religious sanctuary and an athletic complex, where the Games took place every 4 years from 776 B.C. to A.D. 393. Thereafter, the sanctuary slipped into oblivion, and buildings were toppled by repeated earthquakes and covered by the flooding of the Alfios and Kladeos rivers. When the English antiquarian Richard

The Ancient Olympic Games

The 5-day Olympic festival was held every 4 years between 776 B.C. and A.D. 393 at full moon in mid-August or September, after the summer harvest. Participants came from as far away as Asia Minor and Italy, and the entire Greek world observed a truce to allow athletes and spectators to make their way to Olympia safely. During all the years that the Games took place, the truce was broken only a handful of times.

By the time the Games opened, literally thousands of people had poured into Olympia; much of the surrounding countryside was a tent city. Women were barred from watching or participating in the games, although they had their own games in honor of Hera, Zeus's long-suffering wife, in non-Olympic years. Any woman caught sneaking into the Olympic Games was summarily thrown to her death from a nearby mountain.

No one knows precisely what the order of events was at the Games, but the 5 days included footraces, short and long jumps, wrestling and boxing contests, chariot races, the arduous pentathlon (discus, javelin, jumping, running, and wrestling), and the vicious pankration, which combined wrestling and boxing techniques.

The 3rd-century A.D. writer Philostratos recorded that participants in the pentathlon "must have skill in various methods of strangling." The most prestigious event was the *stade,* or short footrace, which gave its name to the stadium. Each Olympiad was named after the winner of the stade, and athletes like the 2nd-century B.C. Leonidas of Rhodes, who won at four successive Olympics, became international heroes. In addition to the glory, each victor won a crown made of olive branches and free meals for life in his hometown.

Chandler rediscovered the site in 1766, most of Olympia lay under 10 feet of mud and silt. The Germans began to excavate here in 1852 and are still at it today.

Reports of the rediscovery of Olympia prompted the French Baron de Coubertin to work for the reestablishment of the Olympic Games in 1896. The first modern Games were held in Athens in 1896, and Greece was very sorry to lose the 1996 100th-anniversary Games to Atlanta.

OLYMPIA TODAY   The straggling modern village of Olympia (confusingly known as Ancient Olympia) is bisected by its one main street, Leoforos Kondili. The town has the usual assortment of tourist shops selling jewelry, T-shirts, and reproductions of ancient pottery and statues, as well as more than a dozen hotels and restaurants. Two things worth visiting in town: the Museum of the Olympic Games and the excellent Galerie Orphee bookstore (see below).

The ancient site of Olympia lies an easily walkable 15 minutes south of the modern village, but if you have a car, you might as well drive: the road teems with tour buses and the walk is less than relaxing.

ESSENTIALS

GETTING THERE   By Train   There are several trains a day from Athens to Pirgos, where you change to the train for Olympia. Information on schedules and fares is available from the Stathmos Peloponnisou (Railroad Station for the Peloponnese) in Athens (☎ 01/513-1601).

By Bus   There are three buses a day to Olympia from the **Stathmos Leoforia Peloponnisou** (Bus Station for the Peloponnese) in Athens, Odos Kifissou 100 (☎ 01/513-4110). There are also frequent buses from Patras to Pirgos, with connecting service to Olympia. In Patras, KTEL buses leave from the intersection of Odos Zaimi and Odos Othonos (☎ 061/273-694).

By Car   Olympia is at least a 6-hour drive from Athens, whether you take the coast road that links Athens-Corinth-Patras and Olympia or head inland to Tripolis and Olympia on the new Corinth-Tripolis road. Heavy traffic in Patras means that the drive from Patras to Olympia can easily take 2 hours.

VISITOR INFORMATION   Olympia is basically a one-street town; the few things you do not find on that main street, **Praxitelous Kondili,** will be just off it. The **tourist office (EOT),** on the way to the ancient site near the south end of the main street, is usually open daily, in summer from 9am to 10pm, and in winter from 11am to 6pm. This is the place to ask for a map of the site and town and information on accommodations and transportation (☎ 0624/23-100 or 0624/23-125).

FAST FACTS   The **National Bank of Greece,** on Odos Praxitelous Kondili (the main drag), exchanges currency and was installing an ATM machine in 1998. The **health clinic** (☎ 0624/22-222) is signposted in town. The **police** (☎ 0624/22-100) are at Odos Ethnossinelefseos 6. Both the **post office** and the **telephone office (OTE)** are located on the main street, Praxitelous Kondili; the OTE usually stays open until 10pm in summer.

WHAT TO SEE & DO

The Archaeological Museum. Admission Dr1,200 ($4). Summer Mon noon–6pm; Tues–Sat 8am–5pm. Winter Mon noon–6pm; Tues–Sat 11am–5pm.

If ever a building should not be judged by its facade, this is it: From outside, the museum has all the charm of a small factory. Inside, one of the finest collections in Greece is beautifully displayed in well-lit rooms, some of which look onto an interior courtyard. In August 1998, when forest fires were less than half a kilometer from both the site and museum, it was revealed that the museum owned, but had not installed, a fire-extinguishing system. Subsequent statements from the archaeological service suggested that the only thing unusual here was that a fire-extinguishing system had actually been purchased.

Even though you'll be eager to see the ancient site, it's a good idea to begin your visit to Olympia with the museum whose collection makes clear Olympia's astonishing wealth and importance in antiquity: Every victorious city and almost every victorious athlete dedicated a bronze or marble statue here. Nothing but the best was good enough for Olympia, and many of these superb works of art are on view here. Most of the exhibits are displayed in rooms to the right and left of the main entrance and follow a chronological sequence from severe Neolithic vases to baroque Roman imperial statues, neither of which will probably tempt you from heading straight ahead to see the museum's superstars.

The monumental **sculpture from the Temple of Zeus** is probably the finest surviving example of archaic Greek sculpture. The sculpture from the west pediment shows the battle of the Lapiths and Centaurs raging around the magisterial figure of Apollo, the god of reason. On the east pediment, Zeus oversees the chariot race between Oinomaos, the king of Pisa, and Pelops, the legendary figure who wooed and won Oinomaos's daughter by the unsporting expedient of loosening his opponent's chariot pins. On either end of the room, sculptured metopes show scenes from the

Labors of Hercules, including the one he performed at Olympia: cleansing the foul stables of King Augeus by diverting the Alfios River.

Just beyond the sculpture from the Temple of Zeus are the 5th-century B.C. **winged victory,** done by the artist Paionios, and the 4th-century B.C. figure of Hermes and the infant Dionysos, known as the **Hermes of Praxitelous.** The Hermes has a room to itself—or would, if tourists didn't make a beeline to admire Hermes smiling with amused tolerance at his chubby half-brother Dionysos. If you want to impress your companions, mention casually that many scholars think that this is not an original work by Praxitelous, but a Roman copy.

In addition to several cases of glorious bronze heads of snarling griffins and the lovely terra-cotta of a resolute Zeus carrying off the youthful Ganymede, the museum has a good deal of **athletic paraphernalia** from the ancient games: stone and bronze weights that jumpers used, bronze and stone discuses, and even an enormous stone with a boastful inscription that a weight lifter had raised it over his head with only one hand.

Before you leave the museum, have a look at the two excellent **site models** just inside the main entrance. As the models make clear, ancient Olympia was quite literally divided by a low wall into two distinct parts: the Altis or religious sanctuary, containing temples and shrines, and the civic area, with athletic and municipal buildings.

The Ancient Site. Admission Dr1,200 ($4). Usually open summer Mon–Fri 7:30am–7pm; Sat–Sun 8:30am–3pm. Winter Mon–Fri 8am–5pm; Sat–Sun 8:30am–3pm.

In antiquity between festivals, Olympia was crowded with thousands of statues, but every 4 years during the Games, so many people thronged here that it was said by the time the Games began, not even one more spectator could have wedged himself into the stadium. So, if the site is very crowded when you visit, just remember that it would have been much worse in antiquity.

Olympia's setting is magical. Pine trees shade the little valley, dominated by the conical Hill of Kronos, that lies between the Alfios and Kladeos rivers. The handsome temples and the famous stadium that you've come here to see, however, are not immediately apparent as you enter the site. Immediately to the left are the unimpressive low walls that are all that remain of the **Roman baths,** where athletes and spectators could enjoy hot and cold plunges. The considerably more impressive remains with the slender columns on your right mark the **gymnasium** and **palestra,** where athletes practiced their footracing and boxing skills. The enormous gymnasium had a roofed track, precisely twice the length of the stadium, where athletes could practice in bad weather. Still ahead on the right are the fairly meager remains of a number of structures, including a **swimming pool** and the large square **Leonidaion,** which served as a hotel for visiting dignitaries until a Roman governor decided it would do nicely as his villa. If you want, you can continue around the outskirts of the site, identifying other civic buildings, but you'll probably want to enter the sanctuary itself.

The **religious sanctuary** was, and is, dominated by two temples: the good-sized temple of Hera and the massive temple of Zeus. The **Temple of Hera,** with its three standing columns, is the older of the two, built around 600 B.C. If you look closely, you'll see that the temple's column capitals and drums are not uniform. That's because this temple was originally built with wooden columns, and as each column decayed, it was replaced; inevitably, the new columns had variations. The Hermes of Praxitelous was found here, buried under the mud that covered Olympia for so long due to the repeated flooding of the Alfios and Kladeos rivers.

The **Temple of Zeus,** which once had a veritable thicket of 34 stocky Doric columns, was built around 456 B.C. The entire temple—so austere and gray today—was anything but austere in antiquity: gold, red, and blue paint decorated it everywhere, and inside stood the enormous gold-and-ivory statue of Zeus, seated on an ivory-and-ebony throne. The statue was so ornate that it was considered one of the Seven Wonders of the Ancient World—and so large that people joked that if Zeus stood up, his head would go through the temple's roof. In fact, the antiquarian Philo of Byzantium suggested that Zeus had created elephants simply so that the sculptor Phidias would have the ivory to make the statue of Zeus.

Not only do we know that Phidias made the 13-meter-tall statue, we know where he made it: the **Workshop of Phidias** was on the site of the well-preserved brick building clearly visible west of the temple, just outside the sanctuary. How do we know that this was Phidias's workshop? Because a cup with "I belong to Phidias" written on it and artists' tools were found here.

Between the temples of Zeus and Hera you can make out the low foundations of a round building. This is all that remains of the **shrine** that Philip of Macedon, never modest, built here to pat himself on the back after conquering Greece in 338 B.C.

Beyond the two temples, built up against the Hill of Kronos itself, are the curved remains of a once-elegant **Roman fountain** and the foundations of 11 **treasuries** where Greek cities stored votive offerings and money. In front of the treasuries are the low bases of a series of bronze **statues of Zeus,** dedicated not by victorious athletes but by those caught cheating in the stadium. These statues would have been the last thing that competitors saw before they ran through the vaulted tunnel into the stadium.

Ancient tradition clearly shows that the Olympic Games began here in 776 B.C. and ended in A.D. 395, but is less clear on just why they were held every 4 years. According to one legend, Hercules (Herakles) initiated the games to celebrate completing his 12 labors, one of which took place nearby when the hero diverted the Alfios River to wash out the fetid Augean stables that King Augeas had neglected for more than a decade. With the stables clean, Hercules paced off the stadium and then ran its entire length of 600 Olympic feet (192.27m) without having to take a single breath.

The Museum of the Olympic Games. Admission Dr500 ($1.65). Mon–Sat 8am–3:30pm; Sun and holidays 9am–2:30pm.

When you head back to town, try to set aside half an hour to visit the Museum of the Olympic Games. Not many tourists come here, and the guards are often glad to show visitors around. Displays include victors' medals, commemorative stamps, and photos of winning athletes, such as former King Constantine of Greece and the great African-American athlete Jesse Owens. There's also a photo of the bust of the founder of the modern Olympics, Baron de Coubertin. (The bust itself stands just off the main road east of the ancient site and marks the spot where de Coubertin's heart is buried.)

A Worthwhile Shop

✪ **Galerie Orphee,** Antonios Kosmopoulos's bookstore on the main street in Ancient Olympia (☎ **0624/23-463**), carries an extensive range of cassettes and CDs of Greek music, plus frequent displays of contemporary art. It's a pleasant contrast to Olympia's other shops, which have all too many T-shirts, museum reproductions, and machine-made rugs and embroideries sold as genuine handmade crafts.

WHERE TO STAY

Olympia has more than 20 hotels, which means that you can almost always find a room—although if you arrive without a reservation in July or August, you may not get your first choice. In the winter, many hotels are closed.

Grecotel Lakopetra Beach. Kato Achaia, 25200 Achaia. ☎ **0693/51-713.** Fax 0693/ 51-045. 192 units. MINIBAR TV TEL. Dr30,000 ($100) double. MC, V.

This resort hotel, with tennis courts, fresh- and saltwater pools, saunas, exercise facilities, restaurants, and boutiques, is set in extensive gardens a short walk from the beach. With a car, you can be at ancient Olympia in less than 30 minutes. The rooms here are large, with balconies or terraces, and the bathrooms are well appointed. In short, a comfortable place to come home to after a day's sightseeing.

Hotel Europa. 27065 Ancient Olympia, Peloponnese. ☎ **800-528-1234** in the U.S., 0624/22-650, or 0624/22-700. Fax 0624/23-166. 80 units. A/C TV TEL. Dr33,000 ($110) double. Breakfast Dr2,000 ($7) extra. AE, DC, MC, V. The Europa plans to be open year-round.

This member of the Best Western Hotel chain, a few minutes' drive out of town on a hill overlooking both the modern village and the ancient site, is clearly the best hotel in town—and one of the best in the entire Peloponnese. The only reason not to stay here is if you want to be able to walk out the door and be in the village of Ancient Olympia. The lobby and large restaurant gleam with marble and boast great views out the picture windows. Most of the guest rooms overlook the large pool and garden, and several overlook the ancient site itself. The rooms are large, with colorful rugs, extra-firm mattresses, and generous balconies. Friends who travel through the Peloponnese every summer rave about the Hotel Europa's unusual tranquillity.

Hotel Neda. Odos Praxitelous, 27065 Ancient Olympia, Peloponnese. ☎ **0624/22-563.** Fax 0624/22-206. 43 units. TEL. Dr22,500 ($75) double. AE, V.

With a pleasant rooftop cafe, comfortable lobby, serviceable restaurant, and a distinctive red-and-white facade, the Neda offers good value. The double rooms, many decorated in shades of pink and rose, are large, with colorful shaggy flokati rugs on the floor and good bedside reading lamps. Some of the double rooms have double beds, but most have twin beds, so specify which you want. All units have balconies, and are usually quieter than at hotels on the main street.

✪ **Hotel Pelops.** Odos Varela 2, 27065 Ancient Olympia, Peloponnese. ☎ **0624/22-543.** Fax 0624/22-213. E-mail: hospiti@ermis.gr. 25 units, 16 with shower only. TEL. Dr16,500 ($55) double. EURO, MC, V. Closed Nov–Feb.

The English-speaking owner, Susanna Spiliopoulou, described by many visitors here as especially helpful, makes this one of the most welcoming hotels in Olympia. There are flokati rugs on the floors, good mattresses on the beds, and plants and vines shading the terrace.

Hotel Praxitelous. Odos Spiliopoulou 7, 27065 Ancient Olympia, Peloponnese. ☎ **0624/ 225-92.** 10 units. Dr9,000 ($30) double. AE, EURO, V.

This small, family-run hotel is the best bargain in town. It's just one street back from Olympia's main street, and the neighborhood has a nice feel, with children often playing ball in the street in front of the police station. Although guest rooms are small and very spare, the beds are decent and the front rooms have balconies. If you want to avoid the murmurs of conversation from the Praxitelous's excellent restaurant on the sidewalk below the balconies, ask for a room at the back.

WHERE TO DINE

There are almost as many restaurants as hotels in Olympia. The ones on and just off the main street with large signs in English and German tend to have indifferent food and service, although it's possible to get good snacks of yogurt or *tiropites* (cheese pies) in most of the cafes.

Taverna Ambrosia. Behind the train station in Ancient Olympia. ☎ **0624/23-755.** Main courses Dr1,500–Dr3,600 ($5–$12). AE, MC, V. Daily 8–11pm. Lunch served every weekend. GREEK.

This large restaurant with a pleasant outside veranda continues to attract locals, although it does a brisk business with tour groups as well. You'll find the usual grilled chops and souvlaki here, but the vegetable dishes are unusually good, as is the lamb stew with lots of garlic and oregano.

✪ Taverna Kladeos. Behind the train station in Ancient Olympia. ☎ **0624/23-322.** Main courses Dr1,500–Dr2,500 ($5–$8). No credit cards. Daily 7–11pm. GREEK.

The charming Kladeos, with the best food in town, is at the end of the little paved road that runs steeply downhill past the Ambrosia restaurant. You may not be the only foreigner, but you probably will find lots of locals here. In good weather, tables are set up under canvas awnings and roofs made of rushes. If you sit in the hillside, you'll be serenaded by the frogs that live beside the river. The menu varies according to what's in season. In summer, the lightly grilled green peppers, zucchini, and eggplant are especially delicious. The house wine, a light rose, is heavenly. If you want to buy a bottle to take with you, give your empty water bottle to your waiter and ask him to fill it with *krasi* (wine).

Taverna Praxitelous. Odos Spiliopoulou 7, Ancient Olympia. ☎ **0624/23-570** and 0624/22-592. Main courses Dr900–Dr3,000 ($3–$10). AE, EURO, V. Daily, about 11am–3pm and about 7pm–midnight. GREEK.

The reputation of the Hotel Praxitelous's excellent and reasonably priced restaurant has spread rapidly—and it's packed almost every evening, first with foreigners, eating unfashionably early for Greece, and then with locals, who start showing up around 10pm. Although the main courses are very good, especially the rabbit stew with onions (*stifado*), you can make an entire meal out of the delicious and varied mezedes, which may include octopus, eggplant salad, taramosalata, fried cheese, and a handful of olives. In good weather, tables are set outside on the sidewalk; the rest of the time, meals are served in the pine-paneled dining room.

14 Patras (Patra)

207km (128 miles) SW of Athens

The third-largest city in Greece and far and away the largest in the Peloponnese, Patras's unappealing urban sprawl now extends for miles north and south of the city center. Although Patras does have sights worth seeing—the Cathedral of Saint Andrew, the Archaeological Museum, a Roman Odeon (music hall) on the slopes of the ancient Acropolis, and a medieval castle on the summit—there's nothing here worth lingering over unless you have to mark time until catching the ferry to Italy.

ESSENTIALS

GETTING THERE **By Train** There are frequent trains from the **Stathmos Peloponnisou** (Railroad Station for the Peloponnese) in Athens (☎ **01/513-1601**

for schedule information). If you are catching a ferryboat, keep in mind that Greek trains usually run late.

By Bus There are some 15 buses to Patras daily from the **Stathmos Leoforia Peloponnisou** (Bus Station for the Peloponnese) in Athens, Odos Kifissou 100 (☎ 01/522-4914 for schedule information). The Patras train station, at Odos Othonos Amalias 14, is on the waterfront near the boat departure piers.

By Car The drive on the National Highway from Athens to Patras takes about 6 hours. *Note:* In the city center, the system of one-way streets, not always obviously marked, means that you should drive with particular care.

VISITOR INFORMATION The **Greek National Tourist Office (EOT)** is at Odos Iroon Polytechniou 1, on the harbor near ferryboat gate no. 6 (☎ 061/653-358); it's usually open Monday through Friday from 7am to 9pm, Saturday and Sunday from 2 to 9pm.

FAST FACTS A number of **banks** on the waterfront and on Plateia Georgiou exchange currency and have ATMs. There are also a number of around-the-clock **currency exchanges** on the harbor front; rates are invariably not as good as the official rate. Most of the **car-rental agencies** (Avis, Hertz, Kemwell) have clearly marked offices on the waterfront. The main **hospital** is signposted in the town. As you might expect in a city with lots of sailors, there is also an **emergency first-aid station** (☎ 061/277-386) at the corner of Karolou and Ayiou Dionysion. The **tourist police** are at Odos Patreos 53, off Plateia Georgiou (☎ 061/220-902).

The Ferry to the Ionian Islands & Italy

The major ferryboat and shipping companies all have offices on the waterfront. There is usually daily ferryboat service from Patras to the **Ionian islands** and **Corfu.** There are many daily services from Patras to the Italian towns of **Brindisi** and **Ancona.** The fastest service to Italy is the 18-hour **Super Ferry Crossing** from Patras to Ancona, offered by **Superfast Ferries** (☎ **061/622-500,** or 01/969-1100 in Athens, or 310/544-3551 in the U.S.; fax 061/623-547, or 301/541-0166 in the U.S.; e-mail: superfaxt@superfast.com). In 1998, a deluxe cabin for two costed Dr75,000 ($250); a bunk in a shared four-bunk cabin costed Dr6,000 ($20).

WHAT TO SEE & DO

If you find yourself with a few hours in Patras, here are some suggestions: first, head for **Plateia Yioryiou** (George Square). Sit at one of the cafes and take in the facades of the handsome neoclassical theater and banks on the square. Patras has been hit repeatedly by earthquakes, and these buildings are among the few that remain from the 19th century, when the city was famous for its arcaded streets and neoclassical architecture.

Then, head down to the waterfront to the **Cathedral of Saint Andrew.** Although the present rather hideous church was only built after World War II, the mosaics give a vivid picture of old Patras. Be sure to dress appropriately to visit the cathedral, a major pilgrimage shrine thanks to the presence of Saint Andrew's skull in an ornate gold reliquary to the right of the altar. There are several pleasant cafes in the shaded park across from the cathedral.

If you're in Patras in July or August, you may be able to take in one of the concerts or plays given during the **International Patras Festival of the Arts.** Or you may prefer to concentrate on the **Wine Festival,** featuring wine tastings at the Achaia Clauss winery. (Schedule information is available from the EOT.) Patras also has a vigorous **carnival** that lasts nearly a month, with parades, costumes, and floats, ending the Monday before Lent.

WHERE TO STAY

Astir Hotel. Ayiou Andreas 16, 26223 Patras. ☎ **061/277-502.** Fax 061/271-644. 120 units. MINIBAR TV TEL. Dr33,000 ($110) double. No credit cards.

If you arrive too late to continue your journey or have an early-morning boat to catch, this is a convenient hotel whose best feature is its roof garden with pool. The bedrooms are nothing special, and many seem to have been decorated by someone who couldn't decide on just which color to go with, although others have a fairly soothing blue-and-green color scheme. Some units have harbor views, as does the rooftop terrace. For Patras, this is a quiet place to spend the night—which is to say that the street noise here is usually endurable.

Porto Rio Hotel. 26500 Rion. ☎ **061/992-102.** Fax 061/992-115. 269 units, 48 bungalows. A/C TV TEL. Dr30,000–Dr51,000 ($100–$170) double. Full board supplement Dr7,500 ($25) per person. AE, MC, V.

This sprawling hotel complex on the beach, a 20-minute drive north of Patras, does a brisk business with business conventions, tour groups, and European families on holiday. The Rio has several pools, a health club (with saunas and Jacuzzi), and two tennis courts. The guest rooms are large, and most have either a terrace or a balcony overlooking the extensive gardens. This is a good place to stay if you have a day to kill before catching a ferry in Patras. The only drawback is the unimaginative food.

WHERE TO DINE

The restaurants along the harbor near the train station serve consistently mediocre food to the hordes of tourists arriving from and departing for Italy. You won't starve at any one of these places, but you can do better. If you just want an ouzo before dinner or a sweet after, head for any of the cafes in the main square, Plateia Yioryiou.

One place we recommend is **Trikoyia,** Amalias 46 (no phone), a hole-in-the-wall taverna that serves up excellent fresh fish and octopus. Chops and one or two other meat dishes are usually available as well. It's a 15-minute walk along the harbor from the main port.

Next door at Amalias 48 (the number is not posted on the building) is the **Pharos Fish Taverna** (☎ 061/336-500), with equally fresh fish. There are usually lots of locals eating here—always a good sign. Head inside first and choose your fish; if you arrive and sit at a table, the waiter will probably ignore you, thinking that you haven't made up your mind yet.

SIDE TRIPS FROM PATRAS

ARCHAIA CLAUSS WINERY

This winery is located above Patras in the hills, which are usually noticeably cooler than Patras itself, and can be reached by bus no. 7 from Odos Kolokotroni and Kanakari. Free tours of the winery, with its old barrels and grape presses, are given most weekdays (☎ 061/325-051 or 061/620-353 for information). The German vintner Clauss named his sweet dessert wine "Mavrodaphne" in memory of his beloved Greek wife, who died young. You may be offered a free sample of Mavrodaphne at the end of your tour. *Take note:* The wine is as sweet as molasses.

THE CASTLE AT CHLEMOUTSI

This is an astonishingly well-preserved 13th-century Frankish castle with crenelated walls, cavernous galleries, and an immense hexagonal keep. Like most castles in the Peloponnese, it passed back and forth between the Franks, Venetians, Turks, and Greeks. The gaps in the outer wall were caused by Ibrahim Pasha's cannon during the Greek War of Independence. The castle is open most days from sunrise to sunset. Admission is free. The turnoff to the castle is signposted some 55 kilometers (34 miles) out of Patras on the main Patras-Olympia road.

9

Crete

by John S. Bowman

Does anyone need to be sold on the glories of the Minoan culture of Crete? But how many know that Crete also offers visitors cities with layers of at least 4,000 years of continuous inhabitation, including the vibrant heritage of centuries of Orthodox Christianity and the distinctive imprint left by 700 years of Venetian and Turkish rule? Not to mention endless beaches and magnificent mountains, intriguing caves and resonant gorges, and countless villages and sites that provide unexpected and unforgettable experiences. Per square mile, Crete must be one of the most "loaded" places in the world—loaded, that is, in the diversity of history, archaeological sites, natural attractions, tourist amenities, and more. In a world where increasing numbers of travelers have "been there, done that," Crete remains an endlessly fascinating and satisfying destination.

Every year, thousands of foreigners visit Crete, and an elaborate service industry has grown up to please them. There are facilities now for everyone's taste, ranging from luxury resorts to guest rooms in villages that have hardly changed over several centuries. You can spend a delightful day in a remote mountain environment where you're treated to some fresh goat cheese and olives; then within an hour, you can be back at your hotel on a beach and enjoying a cool drink.

Crete isn't always and everywhere a gentle Mediterranean idyll—its terrain can be raw, its sites austere, its tone brusque. But for those looking for a distinctly defined place, Crete will be rewarding.

STRATEGIES FOR SEEING THE ISLAND If possible, go in June or September, even late May or early October (unless you seek only a sun-drenched beach): Crete has become an island on overload during July and August (it is also very hot!). The overnight ferry from Piraeus is still the purists' way to go, but the hour-long flights give you more time for activities. There's enough to do on Crete to fill up a week, if not a lifetime of visits; by flying, you could actually see the major sites in two packed days. (By the way, you can fly into Iraklion and out of Chania.)

The following selection of destinations is designed to fill 5 to 7 days—allowing for a mix of activities and even time for collapsing on a beach at the end of the day. Iraklion is a must, what with its archaeological museum and nearby Knossos. An excursion to Phaestos and its associated sites could occupy most of a second day; if you don't need to see that second Minoan palace, we recommend you move on

Legend
Hiking

Sea of Crete

Sea of Libya

Elassa
Palekastro
Kato Zakros
Koufonissi

Sitia Bay
Sitia
Orno
Makriyialos

Spinalonga
Gulf of Mirambelo
Psira
Gournia
Ierapetra

Mallia
Ayios Nikolaos
Mikronissi

Gulf of Malia
Kritsa
Chryssi

Kouloukonas
Lassithi Plain
Dikti (Lassithiotika)
Myrtos

Dia
Gulf of Iraklion
Iraklion
Knossos Site

Idi (Psiliritis)
Gortyra Site
Phaestos Site

Rethymnon
Plain of Messara

Monastery of Arkadhi
Ayia Galini
Mires
Matala

Spili
Ayia Triadha Minoan Site

Siderotas
Messaras Bay
Paximadia

Plakias

Angathies

Lefk Ori
Kastro
Loutro
Frangokastello
Gavdopoula

Samaria Gorge
Ayia Roumeli
Gavdos

Chania
Soudha

Kolymbari
Tavronitis
Kastelli-Kissamou

Ghonia
Gulf of Chania
Soudha Bay
Almiros Bay

Gulf of Kastelli
Fallasarna
Platanos
Sfinario
Paleochora

GREECE
Athens
Crete

25 mi
25 km
0

to Chania or Rethymnon. The walk through the famed Samaria Gorge requires one long day for the total excursion, hotel-to-hotel. Those seeking less strenuous activity might prefer a visit to Ayios Nikolaos and its nearby attractions. None of these trips require a car, as public transportation or tour groups are so frequent. At some point, however, you might want to rent a car (although definitely not in the cities or towns)—this allows you to leave the overdeveloped tourist trail and gives you access to countless villages, spectacular scenery, beaches at the end of the roads, and lesser known archaeological, historical, and cultural sites.

A LOOK AT THE PAST   Crete's diversity and distinction begins with its history, a past that has left far more remains than the Minoan sites many people first associate with the island. After being settled by humans around 6500 B.C., Crete passed through the late Neolithic and early Bronze ages, sharing the broader eastern Mediterranean culture.

Sometime after 3000 B.C., new immigrants came over; by about 2500 B.C., there began to emerge a fairly distinctive culture that has been named Early Minoan. By about 2000 B.C., the Minoans were moving into a far more ambitious phase, the Middle Minoan—the civilization that gave rise to the palaces and other structures and the superb works of art and artifacts that now attract thousands of visitors to Crete every year.

Mycenaean Greeks appear to have taken over the palaces by 1500 B.C., and by about 1200 B.C., this Minoan-Mycenaean civilization had pretty much gone under. For several centuries, Crete was a relatively marginal player in the great era of Greek classical civilization.

When the Romans conquered the island in 67 B.C., they revived certain centers (including Knossos) as imperial colonies. Early converts to Christianity, the Cretans slipped into the shadows of the Byzantine world, but the island was pulled back into the light when Venetians in 1204 broke up the Byzantine Empire and took over Crete. The Venetians made Crete a major colonial outpost, revived trade and agriculture, and eventually built quite elaborate structures.

By the late 1500s, however, the Turks were conquering the Venetians' eastern Mediterranean possessions, and in 1669 they captured the last major holdout on Crete, the city of Candia—today's Iraklion. Cretans suffered considerably under the Turks, and although some of Greece finally threw off the Turkish yoke in the late 1820s, Crete was left behind. A series of rebellions marked the rest of the 19th century, resulting in the Great Powers' sponsoring a sort of independent Crete in 1898.

Finally in 1913, Crete was for the first time formally joined to Greece. Crete had yet another cameo role in history when the Germans invaded it in 1941 with gliders and parachute troops; the ensuing occupation was another low point for the people of Crete.

Since 1945, Crete has advanced amazingly in the economic sphere, powered by its agricultural products as well as by its tourist industry. Not all Cretans are pleased by the development, but all would agree that, for better or worse, Crete owes much to its history.

1 Iraklion (Iraklio)

Iraklion is home to the world's only comprehensive collection of Minoan artifacts, and it's the gateway to Knossos, the major Minoan palace site. Beyond that, it has magnificent fortified walls and several other testimonies to the Venetians' time of power.

0 ____ 250 m
0 ____ 250 y

Sea of Crete

Harbor Fort (The Koules)

Sof. Venizelou

Sof. Venizelou

Skordilon

Historical Museum of Crete

Palelogou

Theotokopoulou

25 Avgusto

Epimenidou

To Bus Terminals

Odos 1878

Delimarkou

Giamalaki

Handaka

Plateia Venizelou

Idis

Police

Dikeossinis

Hatzimihali Gianari

Archaeological Museum

Panthoudidou

Kissamou

Valestra

Makari

Papadopoulou

Kounkerinou

1821

1866

Evans

Averof

Ioustinianou

Chania (Panigra) Gate

Nikolaou Plastira

Vikela

Glamboudi

Vikela

Evans

Pediados

Spinalongas

Kounali

Thenon

Nikolaou Plastira

Nikolaou Plastira

Kainouriya (Gesu) Gate

Kondiliaki

Tomb of Nikos Kazantzakis

Georgladi

Grigoraki

Eroflis

Akadimias

Neas Ionias

Kastrinaki

Knossou

Papandreou G.

ACCOMMODATIONS
Atlantis Hotel **4**
Atrion Hotel **1**
Lato Hotel **3**

DINING
Giovanni **6**
Ionia **7**
Ippocampus **2**
Kyriakos **9**
Louloukos **5**
Pantheon **8**

CRETE — Iraklion

Legend
Church †
First Aid ✚
Information *i*
OTE **C**
Post Office ✉

Iraklion is also big enough (Greece's fifth-largest city) and confident enough to have its own identity as a busy modern city. It often gets bad press simply because it's bustling with traffic and commerce and construction—the very things most travelers want to escape. At any rate, give Iraklion a chance. If you follow some of the advice we proffer, you just may come to like it.

ESSENTIALS

GETTING THERE   By Plane   Most people fly from the **Athens Airport** to Iraklion on an **Olympic Airlines** flight at a cost of some Dr21,600 ($72) one-way. Reservations are a necessity in high season. In summer, Olympic also offers service between Iraklion and Corfu, Mikonos, Rhodes, Santorini, and Thessaloniki—again, these are heavily booked in high season.

An alternative to Olympic is **Air Greece,** a privately owned airline that offers flights between Iraklion and Athens, Thessaloniki, and Rhodes, and between Chania and Athens. Ask your travel agent to look into these flights, or contact Air Greece's head office in Iraklion (☎ **081/330-074;** fax 081/330-534).

Iraklion's airport is about 5 kilometers (3 miles) east of the city, along the coast. Major car-rental companies have desks at the airport. A taxi to Iraklion costs about Dr1,500 ($5), and the public bus is Dr200 (70¢).

To get back to the airport, you have the same two choices—taxi or public bus no. 1. You can take both from Plateia Eleftheria (Liberty Square) or at other points along the way. Inquire in advance at your hotel about the closest possibility.

By Boat   Throughout the year, there is at least one ship (and as many as two or three) a day from Piraeus to Iraklion, and other ships to Chania and Rethymnon. Less frequent ships link Crete to Rhodes (and Karpathos, Kassos, and Khalki, the islands between the two); Santorini and some of the other Cycladic islands en route to or from Piraeus; and even to Thessaloniki and various Greek ports en route. During high season, occasional ships from Italy, Cyprus, and Israel put into Iraklion. For information about all ships, call the **Port Authority** in Iraklion at ☎ **081/244-912.**

If you have arrived at Iraklion's harbor by ship, you'll probably want to take a taxi up into the town, as it's a steep climb. Depending on where you want to go, the fare may be Dr700 to Dr1,500 ($2.35 to $5).

By Bus   The third common mode of arrival in Iraklion is by public bus from one of the other Cretan cities or towns. Where you end up depends on where you've come from. Those arriving from points to the west or east or southeast—Chania or Rethymnon, for instance, or Ayios Nikolaos or Sitia to the east—end up down along the harbor and will have a choice of three approaches to the center of town: walking (although you're only a couple hundred yards closer to the town than if you got off a ship), taking a taxi, or catching the public bus. The bus starts its route at the terminal where buses from the east and southeast stop; directly across the boulevard is the station for the Rethymnon-Chania buses. Those arriving from the south—Phaestos, Matala, and such—will end up at the Chania Gate on the southwest edge of town; walking will not appeal to most, but you have the choice of a public bus or a taxi.

VISITOR INFORMATION   The **National Tourist Office Information Desk** is at Odos Xanthoudidou 1 (opposite the entrance to the Archaeological Museum), 71202 Iraklion (☎ **081/244-462,** 081/244-633, 081/228-203, or 081/228-225). It's open Monday through Friday from 8am to 2pm.

As in any Cretan city, you might consider turning to one of the many travel agencies. Among the oldest and most reliable in Iraklion are **Adamis Tours,** Odos 25

Avgusto 23, 71202 Iraklion (☎ 081/346-202; fax 081/224-717); **Creta Travel Bureau,** Odos Epimenidou 20–22, 71202 Iraklion (☎ 081/227-002; fax 081/223-749); and **Arabatzoglou Travel,** Odos 25 Avgusto 54, 71202 Iraklion (☎ 081/226-697; fax 081/222-184).

GETTING AROUND   By Bus   Public buses remain a solid possibility for seeing much of Crete. They are cheap, relatively frequent, and connect to all but the most isolated locales. The downside is that the schedules are not always the most convenient for travelers with limited time. Certainly you can take them between all major points. The "long distance" bus system is operated by the KTEL that services all of Greece. Travel agents can give advice, or call ☎ **081/221-765** to find out more about KTEL buses to Rethymnon-Chania and points west. For buses to Mallia, Ayios Nikolaos, Sitia, Ierapetra, and points east, call ☎ **081/245-019.** For buses to Phaestos and other points to south, call ☎ **081/255-965.**

By Car & Moped   A car gives maximum flexibility in seeing the island, and there is no shortage of rental agencies in all the main centers of Crete (including the airports). In Iraklion we recommend **Hertz,** Odos 25 Avgusto 34 (☎ **081/341-734**). As for mopeds and motorcycles, be *very* sure you can control such a vehicle in chaotic urban traffic and/or dangerous mountain roads (with few shoulders but many potholes and much gravel). If you want to go this way, there are rental agencies all over town; we can recommend the **Motor Club,** Plateia Agglon 18, at the bottom of Odos 25 Avgusto, overlooking the harbor (☎ **081/222-408;** fax 081/222-862).

By Taxi   Don't overlook taxis as a reasonable means for two or three people to share a trip to a site: No place on Crete is more than a day's round-trip from Iraklion. Ask a travel agent to find you a driver who speaks at least rudimentary English; he can then serve as your guide as well.

By Boat   There are now several excursion boats that take visitors on day trips to offshore islands or isolated beaches; inquire at a travel agency.

FAST FACTS   The official **American Express** agency is Adamis Travel Bureau, Odos 25 Avgusto 23 (☎ **081/346-202;** fax 081/224-717). There are numerous **banks** and **ATMs** (as well as several currency-exchange machines) throughout the center of Iraklion, with many along Odos 25 Avgusto. The **British Consul** is at Odos Papa Alexandrou 16 (opposite the Archaeological Museum); there is no American consulate in Iraklion. The **Venizelou Hospital** (☎ **081/237-502**) is on Knossos Road. For general **first-aid** information, call ☎ **081/222-222.** For **medical emergencies,** call ☎ **166.** For **Internet access,** the Istos Cyber Cafe, Odos Malikouti 2 (☎ **081/222-120;** www.istos-cafe.gr; e-mail: general@ns-istos.otenet.gr), is open Tuesday through Sunday from 10:30am to 12:30am.

The most convenient **laundry** is at Odos Merebellou 25 (one street behind Archaeological Museum); open Monday through Friday from 9am to 2pm and 5 to 7pm, Saturday from 9am to 2pm. You can leave **luggage** at the airport for Dr1,000 ($3.35) per piece per day; most hotels will also hold luggage for brief periods. The **tourist police,** Odos Dikiosenis 10, the main street linking top of Odos 25 Avgusto to Plateia Eleftheria (☎ **081/283-190**), is open daily from 7am to 11pm; in an emergency, call ☎ **171.** The main **post office** (☎ **081/289-995**) is on Plateia Daskaloyiannis; open daily from 7:30am to 8pm. There's a branch post office on El Greco Square, open Monday through Friday from 7:30am to 8pm. The **telephone office (OTE),** Odos Minotaurou 10 (the far side of El Greco Park), is open daily from 6am to 11pm.

WHAT TO SEE & DO
ATTRACTIONS

✪ **The Archaeological Museum.** Odos Xanthoudidou (far corner of Plateia Eleftheria), Iraklion. ☎ **081/226-092.** Admission Dr1,500 ($5) adults, Dr750 ($2.50) students with official ID and EU citizens 65 and over; free on Sun. Apr to mid-Oct Tues–Sun 8am–8pm; Mon 12:30–8pm. Mid-Oct to Mar, closes daily at 5pm.

This is the world's premier collection of art and artifacts from the Minoan civilization. Although many of its most spectacular objects are from Knossos, it does have finds from other sites. The variety of objects, styles, techniques, and materials will amaze all who have not previously focused on the Minoans. Among the most prized objects are the **snake goddesses** from Knossos, the **Phaestos Disc** (with its still undeciphered inscription), the **bee pendant** from Mallia, the **carved vases** from Ayia Triadha and Kato Zakros, and various objects testifying to the famous bull-leaping. Upstairs are the **original frescoes from Knossos** and other sites, their restored sections clearly visible (the frescoes now at Knossos are copies of these).

Tip: To avoid the tour groups in high season, plan to visit either very early or late in the day (allowing 1 to 2 hrs. for your visit); there are also fewer groups on Sunday. Most displays have decent labels in English, but you may want to invest in one of the guidebooks on sale in the lobby.

✪ **The Palace of Knossos.** Knossos Rd., 5km (3 miles) south of Iraklion. ☎ **081/231-940.** Admission Dr1,500 ($5); free on Sun. Apr to mid-Oct daily 8am–8pm. Mid-Oct to Mar Mon–Fri 8am–5pm; Sat–Sun 8:30am–3pm.

Until Arthur Evans began excavating here in 1900, little was known about this ancient people. Using every possible clue and remnant, he rebuilt large parts of the palace—walls, floors, stairs, windows, and columns. Visitors can now wander through these rooms. Realize that you are seeing the remains of two major palaces plus several restorations that were made from about 2000 B.C. to 1250 B.C. Understand, too, that this was not a palace in the modern sense of a royal residence, but a combination of that and the Minoans' chief religious-ceremonial center as well as their administrative headquarters and royal workshops.

Tip: The latter part of the day tends to be less crowded; Sunday also is far less frequented by tour groups. Here is one place where a guided tour might be worth the expense; your hotel or a travel agency can arrange for this.

Historical Museum of Crete. Odos Kalokorinou 7 (street behind Xenia Hotel on coast road), Iraklion. ☎ **081/283-219.** Admission Dr1,000 ($3.35) adults, Dr750 ($2.50) students with official ID. Mon–Fri 9am–5pm; Sat 9am–2pm.

This museum picks up where the Archaeological Museum leaves off, displaying artifacts and art from the early Christian era up to the present. You get some sense of the role the Cretans' long struggle for independence still plays in their identity. On display are traditional Cretan **folk arts;** the re-created study of **Nikos Kazantzakis,** Crete's great modern writer; and works attributed to the painter **El Greco,** another of the island's admired sons. Even if you take only an hour for this museum, it will reward you with some surprising insights on Crete.

Harbor Fort (The Koules). At mole on old harbor. ☎**081/288-484.** Admission Dr500 ($1.70). Daily 9am–1pm and 4–7pm.

The harbor fort, built on the site of a series of earlier forts, went up between 1523 and 1540, and although greatly restored, is essentially the Venetian original. Both its exterior and interior are impressive in their dimensions, workmanship, and details: thick walls, spacious chambers, great ramparts, cannonballs, the Lion of St. Mark plaques—you may feel that you are walking through a Hollywood set! Young people will love it.

Venetian Walls and Tomb of Nikos Kazantzakis. The tomb is on the Martinengo Bastion, at the southern corner of the walls, along Odos Plastira. Free admission. Open sunrise to sunset.

These great walls and bastions were part of the fortress-city the Venetians called Candia. Two of the great city gates have survived fairly well: the Pantocrator or Panigra Gate, better known now as the Chania Gate (dating from about 1570), at the western edge; and the Gate of Gesu, or Kainouryia Gate (dated to about 1587), at the southern edge. You can walk around the outer perimeter of almost the entire walls and get an impression of their sheer massiveness. They were built, of course, by the forced labor of Cretans.

But one non-Venetian presence has now come to rest on one of the bastions, the Martinengo Bastion at the southern corner. Here is the grave of Nikos Kazantzakis (1883 to 1947), a native of Iraklion and author of *Zorba the Greek* and *The Last Temptation of Christ*. From Kazantzakis's tomb is one of the best views to the south of Mount Iouktas, which appears in profile to be the head of a man. According to one ancient myth, this is the head of the buried god Zeus.

A STROLL AROUND IRAKLION

Start your stroll at **Fountain Square** (a.k.a. Lions Square, officially Plateia Venizelou), perhaps fortified with a plate of *bougatsa* at one of the two cafes serving this distinctive filled pastry—it's not Cretan but was introduced by Greeks from Armenia. The fountain was installed here in 1628 by the Venetian governor of Crete, Francesco Morosini. Note the now fading but still elegant relief carvings around the basin. Across from the fountain is the **Basilica of St. Mark,** restored to its original 14th-century Italian style and used for exhibitions and concerts.

Proceeding south 50 meters to the crossroads, you see before you the **market street** (officially Odos 1866), now, alas, increasingly taken over by tourist shops but still harboring some purveyors of fresh fruits and vegetables, meat, and wine.

At the far end of the market street, you come out onto **Kornarou Square,** with its lovely Turkish fountain; beside it is the **Venetian Bembo Fountain** (1588). The modern statue in the center of the square commemorates the hero and heroine of Vincenzo Kornarou's Renaissance epic poem *Erotokritos,* a Cretan-Greek classic.

Turning right onto Odos Vikela, you proceed (always bearing right) until you come out at the imposing, if not artistically notable, **Cathedral of Ayios Menas,** dedicated to the patron saint of Iraklion. Below and to the left is the medieval **Church of Ayios Menas,** which boasts some old wood carvings and icons.

At the far corner of the cathedral (to the northwest) is the 15th-century **Church of St. Katherine.** During the 16th and 17th centuries, this hosted the Mount Sinai Monastery School, where Domenico Theotokopoulou is alleged to have studied before moving on to Venice, Spain, and fame as **El Greco;** it now houses a small museum of icons, frescoes, and wood carvings. It's open Monday through Saturday from 10am to 1pm; Tuesday, Thursday, and Friday also from 4 to 6pm. Admission is Dr400 ($1.35).

Taking the narrow street that's directly perpendicular to the facade of St. Katherine's—Odos Ayii Dheka—you come out onto **Leoforos Kalokerinou,** the main shopping street for locals. Turn right onto it and proceed on up to the crossroads of the market and 25 Avgusto. Turn left and proceed back down past Fountain Square and, on the right, the (totally reconstructed) **Venetian Loggia,** originally dating from the early 1600s. Here the leading Venetians met to conduct affairs; it now houses offices of the city government.

A little farther down 25 Avgusto, also on the right, is the **Church of Ayios Titos;** dedicated to the patron saint of all Crete (the Titus of the Bible, who introduced Christianity to Crete). Proceed down to the **harbor** (with a side visit to the **Venetian fort,** or *Koules,* if you have the energy at this time; see description above), then pass, along the right, the two sets of great **Venetian arsenali**—where ships were built and repaired (the sea then came in this far). Climbing the stairs just past the arsenali, you turn left onto Odos Bofort and curve up under the **Archaeological Museum** to **Plateia Eleftheria (Liberty Square)**—where you can take a much deserved refreshing drink at any one of the numerous cafes at the far side.

SHOPPING

Costas Papadopoulos, the proprietor of **Daedalou Galerie,** Odos Daedalou 11, between Fountain Square and Plateia Eleftheria (☎ 081/246-353), has been offering his tasteful selection of traditional Cretan-Greek arts and crafts for several decades—icons, jewelry, porcelain, silverware, pistols, and more. Some of it is truly old, and he'll tell you when it isn't.

Eleni Kastrinoyanni-Cretan Folk Art, Odos Ikarou 3, opposite the Archaeological Museum (☎ 081/226-186), is the premier store in Iraklion for some of the finest in embroidery, weavings, ceramics, and jewelry; all new pieces but reflecting traditional Cretan folk methods and motifs. Get out your credit card and go for something you'll enjoy for years to come. Closed October through February.

For one of Crete's finest selections of antique and old Cretan textiles (rugs, spreads, coverlets, and more) along with some unusual pieces of jewelry, try **Eva and Helmut Grimm Handicrafts of Crete,** Odos 25 Avgusto 96, opposite the Venetian Loggia (☎ 081/282-547). The finest objects are not cheap, but you get what you pay for here, and the textiles are stunning.

Popi's Shop, Odos Xanthoudidou 9, just below the entrance to the Archaeological Museum (☎ 081/229-490), is part of a new wave on Crete: It offers local agricultural products such as olive oil (rated as among the finest in the world), honey, wines and spirits, raisins, olives, herbs, and spices.

WHERE TO STAY

Iraklion has actually been losing rooms and overnight visitors in recent years as the trend moves toward beach hotels, but there is still a good selection of choices, and you may still need reservations in high season. Single rates are always available, as are special arrangements for families.

Iraklion lies annoyingly close to the flight patterns of commercial airliners and occasional jet fighters of the Greek Air Force. Not to deny the nuisance element, but the total time of the overhead noise adds up to probably less than 30 minutes every 24 hours—and the sound of scooters and motorcycles outside your hotel at night is more annoying. There are plans to add a runway out into the sea to eliminate the flights over Iraklion; it will take some years for this to happen. All we can say is that we have made the search for quiet a major criterion in our selection of hotels; in any case, air-conditioning promises the best defense.

INSIDE THE CITY
Expensive

✪ **Atlantis Hotel.** Odos Iyias 2 (behind the Archaeological Museum), 71202 Iraklion. ☎ 081/229-103. Fax 081/226-265. 160 units. A/C MINIBAR TV TEL. High season Dr34,000 ($114) double; low season Dr30,000 ($100) double. Rates include buffet breakfast. Surcharge of

Dr1,000 ($3.35) for 1 night's stay, but reductions possible for longer stays. Special rates for business travelers and half-board rates (which include breakfast and dinner) available. AE, DC, EURO, MC, V. Parking on nearby streets (with special arrangements for conference groups).

There are many more luxurious hotels in Greece, but few can beat the Atlantis's urban attractions: a central location, modern facilities, and views over a busy harbor. This superior Class A hotel is in the heart of Iraklion, yet just enough removed from the noise of the city (especially if you use the air-conditioning). The staff is friendly and helpful, and although the Atlantis is especially popular with conference groups, individuals will still get individual attention. Guest rooms are not plush, but are certainly comfortable. The Atlantis is probably your best bet if you can afford it and want to be in the center of things. You can swim in the pool, work out in the fitness center, send e-mail via your laptop, and then within minutes be enjoying a fine meal or visiting a museum.

Amenities include a restaurant, two bars, a rooftop garden, concierge, room service, laundry, massage, baby-sitting, pickup at airport by arrangement, video rentals, Jacuzzi, sundeck, fitness center, small pool, outdoor tennis court (across the street), bicycle rentals, children's playground (across the street), conference rooms for up to 1,000, car-rental and tour arrangements, hairdresser, and boutiques.

Galaxy Hotel. Leoforos Demokratias 67 (about $^1/_2$ mile out main road to Knossos), 71306 Iraklion. ☎ **081/238-812.** Fax 081/211-211. www.compulink.gr/galaxy. E-mail: galaxyir@otenet.gr. 140 units, some with shower only, some with tub only. A/C MINIBAR TV TEL. High season Dr36,000 ($120) double; low season Dr28,000–Dr30,000 ($94–$100) double. Buffet breakfast Dr3,000 ($10). AE, DC, EURO, JCB, MC, V. Parking on street. Frequent bus to center within yards of entrance.

In recent years, this has gained the reputation as one of the finer hotels in Iraklion, and it *is* classy—once you get past its rather forbidding exterior. The main-level public areas are striking, and the Galaxy boasts (for now at least) the largest pool in Iraklion, as well as saunas. Guest rooms are stylish; ask for an interior unit, since you lose nothing in a view and gain in quietness.

The restaurant serves the standard Greek and international menu. The pastry shop and ice-cream parlor attract outsiders, as their fare is so delicious. Although one of our readers has reported a less than gracious tone, the front desk does handle all the usual requests for special services.

Moderate

Atrion Hotel. Odos Paleologou 9 (behind the Historical Museum), 71202 Iraklion. ☎ **081/229-225.** Fax 081/223-292. 65 units, some with tub only, some with shower only. A/C TEL. High season Dr19,500 ($65) double; low season Dr18,000 ($60) double. Rates include buffet breakfast. Reductions for children. AE, EURO, JCB, MC, V. Parking on street. Public bus within 200m.

This hotel has well-appointed public areas—a lounge, restaurant, cafeteria, bar, and refreshing patio garden. Its rooms are good sized and pleasant, while its suites offer color TV and a minibar. The front desk can arrange for such services as laundry, baby-sitting, and rentals. Best of all, the location offers quiet while still leaving you within a 10-minute walk to the center of town. The adjacent streets are not that attractive but perfectly safe, and once inside you can enjoy your oasis of comfort and peace.

Lato Hotel. Odos Epimenidou 15, 71202 Iraklion. ☎ **081/228-103.** Fax 081/240-350. 50 units (some with shower only, some with tub only). A/C TV TEL. High season Dr22,800 ($76) double; low season Dr20,500 ($69) double. Rates include continental breakfast. AE, DC, EURO, MC, V. Parking on street.

One of several hotels on this street (east off the bottom of Odos 25 Avgusto), this one offers many rooms with an especially fine view of the harbor. Its buffet breakfast is among the best we've enjoyed in a hotel of its category. The Lato can host meetings of up to 50 (and will arrange to feed them). Once again, what earns this otherwise standard hotel its inclusion here is its harbor-view rooms, offering relatively more quiet at night.

Inexpensive

Poseidon. Odos Poseidonos 46, Poros (about 2.5km/1½ miles from Plateia Eleftheria, off the main road to the east), 71202 Iraklion. ☎ **081/222-545.** Fax 081/245-405. 26 units, all with shower only. TEL. High season Dr16,500 ($55) double; low season Dr12,000 ($40) double. Rates include continental breakfast. Ask about a 10% reduction for Frommer's users when making reservations. AE, V. Frequent public buses 200m at top of street.

We include the Poseidon because it's a favorite of Frommer's loyalists, and for a reason. Its owner/host, John Polychronides, and the desk staff (fluent in English) provide useful support and show genuine concern for your stay on Crete. Yes, it's on a not especially elegant street—but that's true of most of the city hotels, and few can match the fresh breezes and the view over the port. Yes, it gets the airplane noise—but so do virtually all the other places nearby. And it is a budget hotel—no elevator, small rooms, basic showers—but everything is clean and functional. Frequent buses and cheap taxi fares let you come and go into Iraklion center (a 20-min. walk).

OUTSIDE THE CITY

One solution to avoiding the city noise is to stay on the coast. We're assuming that you want to be fairly close to Iraklion—if you just want a remote beach on Crete, such accommodations are described elsewhere. Although the hotels below can be reached by public bus, a car or taxi would save you some valuable time.

Expensive

Candia Maris. Amoudara, Gazi (on beach about 3km/2 miles west of Iraklion center), 71303 Iraklion. ☎ **081/314-632.** Fax 081/250-669. 258 units. A/C TV TEL. High season Dr21,000–Dr24,000 ($70–$80) room; Dr27,000–Dr33,000 ($90–$110) seafront bungalow. Low season Dr10,000–Dr12,000 ($35–$40) room; Dr12,000–Dr16,000 ($40–$53) bungalow. All rates are per person per day, buffet breakfast included. Reductions for extra person in room and for children; half-board plan (including breakfast and dinner) available for additional Dr5,500 ($18). AE, DC, EURO, JCB, MC, V. Public bus every half hr. to Iraklion.

Although the beach on the west coast is not always as pleasant as that on the east, and you have to pass through a rather dreary edge of Iraklion to get here, this area has the advantage of being really close to town. The grandest and newest of the west coast hotels is the luxury Candia Maris, which offers just about everything. It was also one of the first hotels in Greece to be handicapped accessible. The rooms are good sized and cheerful, but the exterior and layout are rather severe. If it looks like a brick-factory owner's idea of a hotel, it's because the owner is just that. Considering that you won't be spending much time looking at the outside of the building, this shouldn't deter you from trying this first-class resort hotel.

Amenities include three restaurants and four bars, with special Cretan nights of traditional music and dancing; concierge, room service, laundry, baby-sitting, airport transport arrangements, three pools, children's pool, health club, sundeck, tennis, squash court, volleyball, bowling, water-sports center, bicycle rentals, game room, children's program, conference facilities for up to 1,000, car-rental and tour arrangements, hairdresser, and boutiques.

Moderate

✪ **Minoa Palace.** Amnisos Beach (about 11km/7 miles east of Iraklion), 71110 Iraklion. ☎ **081/380-404.** Fax 081/380-422. E-mail: minoaplc@iraklio.hellasnet.gr. 127 units.

A/C TV TEL. High season Dr33,000 ($110) double; low season Dr19,000 ($63) double. Rates include buffet breakfast. Half-board plan (including breakfast and dinner) may be arranged for Dr3,500 ($12) extra. AE, DC, EURO, MC, V. Closed Nov–Mar. Public bus every half hr. to Iraklion or points east.

Everything here is deluxe, but what makes the Minoa Palace truly special is its location: east of that airport yet only 11 kilometers (7 miles) from the center of Iraklion. The comfortable rooms have views of the sea, the beach is beautifully maintained, and there are as many activities as you care to engage in. With your own vehicle, you are only a couple of hours from any point of interest on the whole island. This is your chance to visit the Minoans while living in a palace with greater comfort than anything they ever knew.

Amenities include a restaurant with a view of the sea, a more informal taverna, a weekly "Cretan Night" of traditional music and dancing, concierge, room service, laundry, baby-sitting, airport transport arrangements, children's playground and supervised activities, pool, children's pool, aerobics, sundeck, tennis court (lit at night), volleyball, water polo, water-sports equipment, bicycle rentals, table tennis, billiards, video games, fully equipped conference rooms hosting 180, car-rental and tour arrangements, hairdresser, gift shop, and minimart.

Xenia-Helios. Kokkini Hani (about 13km/8 miles east of Iraklion), 71500 Iraklion. ☎ **081/761-502.** Fax 081/418-363. 108 units. A/C TEL. High season Dr24,000 ($80) double; low season Dr18,000 ($60) double. Rates include half-board plan. EURO. Closed Oct–Mar. Buses every half hr. to Iraklion or points east.

We single out the Xenia-Helios because it's one of three such hotels run by the Greek Ministry of Tourism to train young people for careers in the hotel world (one is outside Athens, the other outside Thessaloniki). There's a pool as well as a beautiful beach, two tennis courts, a hairdresser, water-sports equipment, a fine restaurant, and a conference room for up to 200. The physical accommodations may not be quite as glitzy as some of the other beach resorts, but they're certainly first class and the service is especially friendly. You can pamper yourself, be convenient to any place on the island, and help support the young Greeks in training for the future—and save a bit of money!

WHERE TO DINE

Avoid eating a meal on either Fountain Square or Liberty Square (Plateia Eleftheria) unless you simply want to have the experience, because the food at those establishments is, to put it mildly, nothing special. Save these squares for a coffee or beer break.

EXPENSIVE

✪ **Kyriakos.** Leoforos Demokratias 53 (about ¹/₂ mile from center on the road to Knossos). ☎ **081/224-649.** Reservations recommended for dinner in high season. Main courses Dr1,400–Dr4,200 ($3.70–$14). AE, DC, EURO, MC, V. Thurs–Tues noon–4pm and 8pm–2am; Wed noon–4pm only. Closed Sun in July–Aug. Frequent public bus service to the restaurant. GREEK.

In recent years, this restaurant has gained the reputation of offering the most style as well some of the finest cooking in Iraklion. The menu is essentially traditional Greek, but it offers several specialties such as pork with celery, octopus with onions, and aubergines stuffed with feta. Snails are another specialty, and if that doesn't tempt you, come back at Christmas for their turkey. The wine choices are appropriately fine (and expensive). A couple should expect to drop Dr15,000 to Dr20,000 ($50 to $67) for the full works here, but think what you'd pay at home for such a meal.

Louloukos. Odos Korai 5 (1 street behind Daedalou). ☎ **081/224-435.** Reservations recommended for dinner in high season. Main courses Dr1,500–Dr5,000 ($5–$17); fixed-price lunch about Dr3,500 ($12). AE, DC, V. Mon–Sat noon–1am; Sun 6:30pm–midnight. ITALIAN/GREEK.

Another restaurant that has gained a stylish reputation, this is almost the opposite of the Kyriakos in that it's cramped into a tiny patio on a back street and features fanciful umbrellas over the tables. But the chairs are comfortable, and the table settings lovely. The selection of mezedes (or mezes) is varied, and the creative Italian menu features lots of pasta dishes, such as a delicious rigatoni with a broccoli-and-Roquefort-cream sauce. Treat yourself to Iraklion's "in" place.

MODERATE

Giovanni. Odos Korai 12 (on street behind Daedalou). ☎ **081/246-338.** Main courses Dr1,000–Dr2,800 ($3.35–$9); fixed-price meal Dr2,100–Dr3,300 ($7–$11). AE, EURO, MC, V. Mon–Sat 12:30pm–2am; Sun 5pm–1:30am. GREEK.

A taverna with some pretensions to chic, this appeals to a slightly younger and more informal set than its neighbor, Louloukos (described above). For some reason, it, instead of Louloukos, has the Italian name while its fare is traditional Greek. House specialties include shrimp in tomato sauce with cheese, baked eggplant with tomato sauce, and *kokhoretsi* (a sort of oversize sausage made from the innards of lamb; much better than it may sound)—all quite tasty.

Pantheon. Odos Theodosaki 2 ("Dirty Alley," connecting the market street and Odos Evans). ☎ **081/241-652.** Main courses Dr1,200–Dr2,400 ($4–$8). No credit cards. Mon–Sat 11am–11pm. GREEK.

Anyone who spends more than a few days in Iraklion should take at least one meal in "Dirty Alley." The menus (all much the same at the half-dozen "Dirty Alley" locales) offer the taverna standards—stews of various meats, chunks of meat or chicken or fish in tasty sauces, vegetables such as okra or zucchini or stuffed tomatoes. These places are not especially cheap—you're paying for atmosphere—but it's all tasty. If you sit in the Pantheon, on the corner of the market street, you get a choice view of the passing scene.

INEXPENSIVE

Ionia. Odos Evans 3 (just to the left of the market street). ☎ **081/28-313.** Main courses Dr800–Dr2,400 ($2.70–$8). EURO, JCB, MC, V. Mon–Fri 8am–10:30pm; Sat 8am–4pm. GREEK.

Founded in 1923, Ionia has served generations of Cretans as well as all the early archaeologists. The food is as good as ever, and the staff encourages foreigners to step into the kitchen area and select from the warming pans. You may find more refined food and fancier service elsewhere on Crete, but you won't taste heartier dishes than the Ionia's green beans or lamb joints in sauce. We recommend a visit to what is clearly a fading tradition.

Ippocampus. Odos Mitsotaki 3 (off to left of traffic circle as you come down Odos 25 Avgusto). ☎ **081/282-081.** Main courses Dr800–2,000 ($2.70–$7). No credit cards. Mon–Fri 1–3:30pm and 7pm–midnight. SEAFOOD/GREEK.

This is something of an institution among locals, who line up for a typical Cretan meal of little appetizers. The zucchini slices, dipped in batter and deep-fried, are fabulous. A plate of tomatoes and cukes, another of sliced fried potatoes, some small fish, perhaps the fried squid—that's it. You can assemble a whole meal for as little as $10. Go early.

IRAKLION AFTER DARK

To spend an evening the way most Iraklians themselves do, stroll about (the famous Mediterranean **volta**), then sit in a cafe and watch others stroll by. The prime locations for the latter have been Plateia Eleftheria (Liberty Square) or Fountain Square, but the packed-in atmosphere of these places—and the overly aggressive solicitation of your presence by some waiters—has considerably reduced their charm.

For far more atmosphere, go down to the old harbor and the **Marina Cafe** (directly across from the restored Venetian arsenals). For as little as Dr350 ($1.20) for a coffee or as much as Dr1,200 ($4) for an alcoholic drink, you can enjoy the breeze as you contemplate the illuminated Venetian fort looking much like a stage set.

Another alternative is the **Four Lions Roof-Garden Cafe** (☎ 081/222-333), entered by an interior staircase in the shopping arcade on Fountain Square. It attracts a younger set of Iraklians, but adult foreigners are welcome. The background music is usually Greek. You get to sit above the crowded crossroads, and with no cover or minimum, enjoy anything from a coffee (Dr300/$1) or ice cream (Dr900 to Dr1,100/$3 to $3.70) to an alcoholic drink (Dr600 to Dr1,200/$2 to $4).

There is no end to the number of **bars** and **discos** featuring rock-and-roll and/or Greek popular music, although they come and go from year to year to reflect the latest fads. **Disco Athina,** Odos Ikarou 9, just outside the wall on the way to the airport, is an old favorite with the young set; a newer favorite is **Veneto Bar,** Odos Epimenidou 4. For just plain modern Greek popular music, the **Doré Club,** on Plateia Eleftheria (☎ 081/229-970), is a popular bar/restaurant.

For those seeking **traditional Cretan music** and **dancing**—and by the way, almost every Class A hotel now has a **Cretan night,** when performers come to the hotel—there are a couple of clubs: the **Aposperides,** out on the road toward Knossos, and **Sordina,** about 5 kilometers (3 miles) to the southwest of town, are well regarded; take a taxi to either.

For many years now, Iraklion has hosted an **arts festival** that, although hardly competitive with the major festivals of Europe, certainly provides some interesting possibilities for those spending even a few nights in town. The schedule usually begins in late June and ends about mid-September. Some of the performers have world-class reputations—ballet troupes, pianists, and such—but most come from the Greek realm and perform ancient and medieval-renaissance dramas, dances based on Greek themes, and Greek music both traditional and modern. Most performances take place outdoors in one of three venues: on the roof of the **Koules** (the Venetian fort in the harbor), the **Kazantzakis Garden Theater,** or the **Hadzidaksis Theater.** Ticket prices vary so from year to year and for individual events that it's meaningless to list them here, but they are well below what you'd pay at such cultural events elsewhere. Maybe you didn't come to Crete expecting to hear Vivaldi, but why not enjoy it while here?

Films Alfresco

Another delight during the long summers is attending an outdoor movie. There are now three such theaters in Iraklion—the **Romantika,** the **Pallas,** and the **Galaxy**—and a fourth in nearby Halikarnassos, the **Studio.** The current films are posted at several bulletin boards around the center of town. The movies start only as darkness settles. (As throughout Greece, most foreign films are shown in their original language, with Greek subtitles.)

SIDE TRIPS FROM IRAKLION

Travel agencies arrange excursions setting out from Iraklion to virtually every point of interest on Crete—from the **Samaria Gorge** in the far southwest to the Minoan palace at **Kato Zakros** in the far southeast. In that sense, Iraklion can be used as the home base for all your touring on Crete. If you have only one extra day on Crete, we recommend the following trip.

GORTYNA, PHAESTOS, AYIA TRIADHA, KOMMOS & MATALA

If you have an interest in history and archaeology, this is probably the trip to make if you have only one other day after visiting Knossos and Iraklion's museum. The distance isn't that great—a round-trip of some 165 kilometers (100 miles)—but it would be a full day indeed to take it all in. If you don't have your own car, a taxi or guided tour is advisable as bus schedules won't allow you to fit in all the stops. (You can, of course, stay at one of the hotels down at the south coast, but they're usually booked up in high season.)

The road south takes you right up and across the **mountainous spine** of central Crete, and at about the 25th mile you get the experience of leaving the **Sea of Crete** (to the north) behind and seeing the **Libyan Sea** to the south. You then descend onto the **Messara,** the largest plain on Crete (some 32km/20 miles by 5km/3 miles), long a major agricultural center. At about 45 kilometers (28 miles), you see on your right the **remains of Gortyna;** many more lie scattered in the fields off to the left. Gortyna (or Gortyn or Gortys) first emerged as a center of the Dorian Greeks who moved onto Crete after the end of the Minoan civilization. By 500 B.C., it was advanced enough to have a law code that was inscribed in stone. The inscribed stones were found in the late 19th century and reassembled here, where you can see this unique—and to scholars, invaluable—document testifying to the legal and social arrangements of this society.

Then, after the Romans took over Crete (after 67 B.C.), Gortyna enjoyed yet another period of glory: it was the capital of Roman Crete and Cyrenaica (Libya), and as such was endowed with the full selection of Roman structures—temples, a stadium, and all. They are the ones to be seen in the fields to the left. On the right, along with the **Code of Gortyna,** you will see a small **Hellenistic odeon,** or theater, as well as the remains of the **Basilica of Ayios Titos**—dedicated to the Titus commissioned by Paul to head the first Christians on Crete; the church was begun in the 6th century but was later greatly enlarged.

Proceeding down the road another 15 kilometers (10 miles), you turn left at the sign and ascend to the ridge where the **palace of Phaestos** sits in all its splendor. Regarded by scholars as the second most powerful Minoan center, it is also regarded by many visitors as the most attractive because of its setting—on a prow of land that seems to float between the plain and the sky. Italians began to excavate Phaestos soon after Evans began at Knossos, but they made the decision to leave the remains pretty much as they found them. The **ceremonial staircase** is as awesome as it must have been to the ancients, while the **great court** remains one of the most resonant public spaces anywhere.

Leaving Phaestos, you continue down the main road 4 kilometers (2½ miles) and turn left onto a side road, where you park and make your way to at least pay your respects to another Minoan site, a mini-palace complex known as **Ayia Triadha.** To this day, scholars cannot be certain exactly what it was—something between a satellite of Phaestos or a semi-independent palace. Several of the most impressive artifacts now in the Iraklion Museum were found here, including the painted sarcophagus (on the second floor).

Back on the road, follow the signs to **Kamilari** and then **Pitsidia.** And now you have earned your rest and swim, and at no ordinary place: the nearby **beach at Matala.** It's a small cove enclosed by bluffs of age-old packed earth in which humans—possibly beginning under the Romans but most likely no earlier than A.D. 500—have dug **chambers,** some complete with bunk beds. Cretans long used them as summer homes, the German soldiers used them as storerooms during World War II, and hippies took them over in the late 1960s. Now they are off-limits except for looking at during the day. Matala has become one more overcrowded beach in peak season, so after a dip and a bit of refreshment, you'll be glad to depart and make your way back to Iraklion (going up via **Mires** and so bypassing the Phaestos-Kommos stretch).

2 Chania (Hania/Xania/Canea)

150km (95 miles) W of Iraklion

Until the 1980s, Chania was one of the best-kept secrets of the Mediterranean: a delightful seaside town, nestled between mountains and sea, a labyrinth of atmospheric streets and structures from its Venetian-Turkish era. Since then, tourists have flocked here, and there's hardly a square inch of the Old Town, which fans back from the harbor, that's not dedicated to satisfying them. Chania was heavily bombed during World War II; ironically, some of its atmosphere is due to still-unreconstructed buildings that are now used as shops and restaurants.

What's amazing is how much of Chania's charm has persisted since the Venetians and Turks effectively stamped the old town in their own image between 1210 and 1898. Try to visit any time except July and August, but whenever you come, dare to strike out on your own and see the old Chania.

ESSENTIALS

GETTING THERE   By Plane   Olympic Airways (☎ 01/966-6666) offers at least three flights daily to and from Athens in high season. Olympic also has one flight weekly to and from Thessaloniki. **Air Greece** (☎ 0821/75-000) offers a few flights weekly to and from Athens. The airport is located 15 kilometers (10 miles) out of town on the Akrotiri. Public buses meet all flights except for the last one at night, but almost everyone takes a taxi (about Dr2,500/$8).

By Boat There is one ship sailing daily between Piraeus and Chania (and back), usually leaving early in the evening. This ship arrives at and departs from Soudha, a 15-minute bus ride from the stop outside the Municipal Market. Many travel agents around town sell tickets. In high season, those with vehicles should make reservations well in advance.

By Bus There are frequent buses from early in the morning until about 9 or 10pm (depending on the season), connecting Chania to Rethymnon and Iraklion. There are less frequent (and often inconvenient) buses between destinations in western Crete. The main **bus station** (to points all over Crete) is at Odos Kidonias 25 (☎0821/ 93-306).

VISITOR INFORMATION The **National Tourist Office (EOT)** is located in the new town (off Plateia 1866) at Odos Kriari 40, on the ground floor (☎ 0821/ 92-943; fax 0821/92-624). It's open Monday through Friday from 8am to 3pm.

Of the many travel agencies around town, we like **Lissos Travel,** Plateia 1866 (☎ 0821/93-917; fax 0821/95-930). A useful source of insider's information is **The Bazaar,** Odos Daskaloyiannis 46, the main street down to the new harbor (to the right

---

A Taxi Tip

To get a taxi driver accustomed to dealing with English speakers, call **Mikhali** at
☎ **0821/46-855.**

---

of the Municipal Market). This shop sells used foreign-language books and assorted
"stuff." Owned and staffed by non-Greeks, it maintains a listing of all kinds of helpful
services.

GETTING AROUND   Almost any place you will want to visit in Chania itself is
best reached by foot. There are public buses to both nearby points and all the main
destinations in western Crete. If you want to explore the countryside or more remote
points in western Crete, a rented car is advisable to make the best use of your time.

FAST FACTS   Banks in the new city have ATMs. For the **tourist police,** dial
☎ **171.** For **medical emergencies,** dial ☎ **166.** The **hospital** (☎ **0821/27-231**) is
on Odos Venizelou in the Halepa Quarter. The Cafe Sante, which provides **Internet
access,** was under renovation in 1998 but should be open again; it's on the far (west)
corner of the old harbor. The **Speedy Laundry,** Odos Kordiki 17, on the corner of
Koroneou, a block west of Plateia 1866 (☎ **0821/88-411**), promises wash and dry
in 90 minutes, will pick up and deliver for free, and makes small repairs and alterations. The only organized place for **luggage storage** is at the KTEL Bus Station on
Odos Kidonias. The main **post office** is on Tzanakaki (leading away from the Municipal Market); open Monday through Friday from 8am to 8pm, Saturday from 8am to
noon. The yellow branch office in front of the Cathedral on Odos Halidon deals only
in stamps and foreign exchange; it's open April through October, Monday through
Saturday from 8am to 8pm; November through March, Monday through Saturday
from 8am to 2pm. The **telephone office (OTE)** is at Odos Tzanakaki (beside the post
office); open daily from 7:30am to 11:30pm.

WHAT TO SEE & DO
A WORTHWHILE MUSEUM

Archaeological Museum. Odos Halidon 20. ☎ **0821/90-334.** Admission Dr500 ($1.70).
Mon 12:30–7pm; Tues–Sun 8:30am–3pm.

Even short-term visitors should stop in here, if only for a brief walk-through.
The museum is housed in the 16th-century Venetian Catholic Church of St. Francis
(carefully restored in the early 1980s), and gives a fascinating glimpse of the different
cultures that have played out on Crete, from the Neolithic through the Minoan, on
to the Romans and early Christians. You'll come away with a sense of how typical
people of these periods lived, as opposed to the various elites.

A WALK AROUND OLD CHANIA

As good a place as any to start is **Plateia Santrivani,** the large clearing at the far curve
of the old harbor. Head along the east side for the prominent domed **Mosque of
Djamissis** (or of Hassan Pasha), erected soon after the Turks conquered Chania in
1645.

Proceeding around the **waterfront** toward the **new harbor,** you come to
what remains of the great *arsenali,* where the Venetians made and repaired ships;
exhibitions are sometimes held inside. If you have time, go to the far end of this
inner harbor and walk out along the breakwater to the lighthouse, which is from the
19th century.

Chania

Korai

Akti Miaouli

SPLANTZIA

Minoos

Karou

Sifaka

Vourdouba

A. Melidoni

Plateia
1821

Nikiforou Episkopou

El. Venizelou

Nikitos Foka

Konstantinou

Tzanakaki

Daskaloyiannis

Apokoronou

Grigoriou E.

Kalergon

Arholeon

Akti Enoseos

Karaoli - Dimitriou

Tsouderon

Municipal
Market

Hadzimikhali Giannari

Knari

Plateia
1866

Stakianaki K.

Ziminrakidon

Skir-dlof

Halidon

Kondilaki

Zambeliou

Atki Kountounioutou

Theotokopouli

Pireos

Aapede 'G

NEA HORA

Apostolidou

Patriarhou Nikfoui

Akti Kanari

Patriarhou Gerasimou

Metaxaki

Manousogianakidon

Skalidi

Kidonias

Bus
Terminal

Konstantinoupoleos

Margoniou

Legend
Information
OTE
Post Office

CRETE

Chania

ATTRACTIONS
Archaeological Museum ❺
Mosque of Djamissis ❽
Nautical Museum ❶
Orthodox Cathedral ❻

ACCOMMODATIONS
Amphitri Hotel ❾
Casa Delfino ❹
Hotel Palazzo ❷
Hotel Porto Veneziano ⓭

DINING
Amphora Restaurant ❸
Antigone Restaurant ⓬
O Anemos ❿
O Mathios ⓫
Remezzo Cafe ❼
The Well of the Turk ⓮

Turning inland at the near end of the arsenali onto Odos Arnoleon, and proceeding up Odos Daskaloyiannis, you'll come, on the left, to **Plateia 1821** and the present-day **Orthodox Church of St. Nicholas.** Begun as a Venetian Catholic monastery, it was converted by the Turks into a mosque—thus its campanile and minaret! The square is a pleasant place to sit and have a cool drink. Proceeding along, you come to Odos Tsouderon, where you turn right and (passing another minaret) come to the back steps of the great **Municipal Market** (1911)—definitely worth a walk-through. If you exit at the opposite end of where you entered, you'll come out on the edge of the **new town.** Proceed right along Hadzimikhali Giannari till you come to the top of **Odos Halidon,** the main tourist shopping street. As you make your way down, you pass on the right the now famous **Odos Skridlof,** with its leather workers; then the **Orthodox Cathedral,** the Church of the Three Martyrs (from the 1860s); and then on the left the **Archaeological Museum** (see above).

As you come back to the edge of Plateia Santrivani, turn left one street before the harbor onto **Odos Zambeliou.** You can turn left onto any of the streets and explore the **old quarter** (now, alas, somewhat overwhelmed by very modern tourist enterprises). Continuing along Zambeliou (taking a slight diversion on Odos Moskhou to view the **Renieri Gate** of 1608), you will ascend slightly until you come up to **Odos Theotokopouli;** turn right here to enjoy the structures and shops of this Venetian-style street as you make your way down to the sea. You are now just outside the harbor; turn right and pass below the walls of the **Firkas,** the name given to the fort here that was a focal point in Crete's struggle for independence at the turn of the century. If you're into naval history, the **Nautical Museum** (☎ **0821/26-437**) located here has some interesting displays and artifacts (open daily from 10am to 4pm; admission is Dr400/$1.35); or you can just sit at the **Cafe Meltemi,** on the slope just before the entrance to the museum, and join Chania's smart set in a much-deserved refreshment.

SHOPPING

Jewelers, leather-goods shops, and souvenir stores are everywhere—but it's hard to find that very special item that's both tasteful and distinctively Cretan. Our choices below offer authentic Cretan objects—or at least items you will not find anyplace else. Unless otherwise noted, the following shops are open daily.

Anatolia, Odos Halidon 5, at end of the street, just above Plateia Santrivani on the harbor (☎ **0821/41-218**), boasts a fabulous selection of jewelry from around the world—principally from the Middle East, Asia, and Africa; closed Sundays. **Carmela,** at Odos Anghelou 7, the narrow street across from the entrance to the Naval Museum (☎ **0821/90-487**), has some of the finest ceramics, jewelry, and works of art in all of Crete—all original, but inspired by ancient works of art and even employing some of the old techniques.

To step into **Cretan Rugs and Blankets,** Odos Anghelou 5 (☎ **0821/98-571**), is to enter a realm probably not to be experienced anywhere else on Crete—an old Venetian structure filled with gorgeously colored rugs, blankets, and kilims. Prices range from Dr 30,000 to Dr 400,000 ($100 to $1,335). Visit **Roka Carpets,** Odos Zambeliou 61 (☎ **0821/74-736**), even if only to see a traditional weaver at his trade. The proprietors produce an endless succession of varied rugs, blankets, coverlets, and wall hangings. There are patterns and colors and sizes for every taste, with prices from Dr 4,000 ($13) and up. These are not artsy textiles but traditional Cretan weaving.

Although **Khalki,** Odos Zambeliou 75, near the far end of the street (☎ **0821/ 75-379**), is one of many little shops that sell ceramics along with other trinkets and souvenirs, it's worth seeking out. Khalki carries the work of several local and Greek ceramists who produce some distinctive work—not in the modern vein, but using traditional Greek motifs and colors that both dazzle and refresh. Some platters are stunning. Finally, for a truly different souvenir or gift, try **Aquarrelles,** Odos Zambeliou 15 (☎**0821/40-654**), a tiny shop with a nice selection of original and delicate watercolors depicting scenes in and around Chania.

WHERE TO STAY
EXPENSIVE

✪ **Casa Delfino.** Odos Theofanous 8, 73100 Chania, Crete. ☎ **0821/87-400.** Fax 0821/96-500. E-mail: casadel@cha.forthnet.gr. 19 units. A/C TV TEL. Dr39,000–60,000 ($130–$200) double. Breakfast extra. AE, EURO, MC, V. Free parking in nearby area. Open year-round (with central heating).

This mansion was converted into stylish independent suites and studios, whose tastefully decorated rooms are among the most spacious and elegant you will find on Crete. All units (most with bed on an upper level) have modern bathrooms, fridges, and stoves. Services of all kinds are provided, from airport transport to tour arrangements. You're only a block or so behind the harbor, but are far removed from the harbor's bustle and noise. This is an ideal way to combine a convenient location and comfortable amenities with old-world charm in a 17th-century neighborhood.

✪ **Creta Paradise Beach Resort Hotel.** P.O. Box 89, Gerani, Crete (19km/12 miles west of Chania on coast road). ☎ **0821/61-315.** Fax 0821/61-134. www.vacation.forthnet.gr/cretpara.html. E-mail: cretpar@vacation.forthnet.gr. 186 units. A/C TEL. High season Dr44,000–Dr53,000 ($147–$177) double; Dr59,000 ($197) bungalow for 2. Low season Dr26,000–Dr48,000 ($87–$160) double; Dr37,000–Dr54,000 ($123–$180) bungalow for 2. Rates include buffet breakfast. Considerably lower rates for tour groups include half-board plan (breakfast and dinner). AE, DC, EURO, MC, V. Ample parking. Taxi or bus to Chania.

This luxurious hotel resort is perfect for those who want to sun on a beach or tour western Crete. Among its more unusual charms is a small petting zoo—in general, kids would have a fine time here. A unique delight are the turtles that come onto the hotel's beach to lay their eggs from May to June; these hatch in late August. The hotel boasts the largest and most technically advanced conference facilities in western Crete (for up to 600 delegates). Guest rooms are a bit severe for Americans accustomed to upholstered luxury (don't expect plush beds), but everything is tasteful and modern. (TVs and refrigerators are free in bungalows only; each requires a charge in rooms.) Beautifully landscaped in the style of a Mediterranean villa, the resort lives up to its image.

The hotel has multiple restaurants, weekly "theme nights" with Greek music and dance troupes, and an in-house orchestra. Virtually anything can be provided on request, from a TV or minibar in your room to baby-sitting or a massage. The hotel can arrange secretarial and other business services, vehicle rentals, tours, laundry, and dry cleaning. A doctor and a dentist are on call. Facilities include a large pool, children's pool, small health club and sauna, tennis and volleyball courts, water sports (with professional instruction available), children's video games and TV, salon, and boutiques.

Louis Creta Princess Club Hotel. P.O. Box 9, 73014 Platanias, Crete (19km/12 miles west of Chania on coast road). ☎ **0821/62-7023.** Fax 0821/62-406. www.vacation.forthnet.gr/maleme.html. E-mail: maleme-beach@cha.forthnet.gr. 414 units. A/C TEL. High season Dr41,000 ($137) double; low season Dr26,000 ($87) double. Rates include buffet breakfast and dinner. Children under 2 stay free, ages 2–12 stay for half price. AE, DC, EURO, JCB, MC, V. Ample parking. Closed Oct–Mar. Taxis and frequent buses to Chania.

Close to the Creta Paradise in both its location and facilities, this hotel tends to be more family oriented and even a bit like a Club Mediterrané. That means it has an "animation team" of young people who lead an endless round of activities and diversions, from water polo to impromptu games, for both children and adults. The turtles (described under Creta Paradise, above) also come to this beach, which has been awarded a Blue Flag of the European Community for its fine condition. Its rooms are not plush, but are comfortable and modern—a stripped-down holiday mode. (TVs cost extra.)

The main restaurant serves buffet breakfast and dinner; the dinner menu is the now-standard International cuisine, with some Greek specialties. Also on site are a beach taverna, bars in the lounge and at the pool, and a disco. A weekly "Greek night" brings music and dancing. The desk clerks can arrange laundry, dry cleaning, baby-sitting, secretarial assistance, car rentals, and tours. Facilities include a large pool and small children's pool; tennis, basketball, and volleyball courts; a minigolf course; table tennis; water sports including waterskiing, windsurfing, water-parachuting, and canoeing; and a 600-person conference room.

MODERATE

Amphitri Hotel. Odos Lithinon 31, 73100 Chania, Crete. ☎ **0821/52-980.** 22 units. TEL. High season Dr22,000 ($73) double with A/C; Dr20,000 ($67) without A/C. Low season Dr20,000 ($67) double. Rates include continental breakfast. EURO. Parking on nearby streets.

This unpretentious hotel is an old favorite of regular visitors to Chania, who value the spectacular views over the harbor enjoyed by some rooms, its quiet street but closeness to the very heart of Chania's action, and its comfortable rooms and homey atmosphere. Decidedly low-key, but it should appeal to those who prize convenience above all. And you can enjoy your breakfast on a balcony with a view to die for.

✪ **Doma.** Odos Venizelou 124 (3km/2 miles from town center along coastal road to airport), 73100 Chania, Crete. ☎ **0821/51-772** or 0821/51-773. Fax 0821/41-578. 25 units, all with bathroom (22 with shower only). TEL. Dr24,000 ($80) double; Dr37,000–Dr47,000 ($123–$157) suite (with A/C and TV). Rates include continental breakfast. Reduced rates for longer stays and/or more than 2 persons in suite. EURO, MC, V. Free parking on nearby streets. Closed Nov–Mar. Bus to Halepa or Chania center; can be reached by taxi, car, or on foot.

The Doma has long been cited as one of the most distinctive hotels on Crete, in part because it was one of the first in Greece to locate in a converted fine old building. In this case, it is a neoclassical mansion from the turn of the century that was once, among other things, the British consulate; its public areas are decorated with authentic Cretan heirlooms. Guest rooms are not especially large, and bathrooms are a bit dated. Front units have the great view of the sea but also the sound of passing traffic, although the hotel is far from the noise of the center of town. Amenities are there for the asking, including laundry on the premises, plus an elevator for those who can't take stairs. The new ground-floor bar offers a civilized ambiance. Among the Doma's attractions is the third-story dining room, with fresh breezes and a superb view of Old Chania; breakfast here includes several homemade delights, while evening dinner brings Cretan specialties. The Doma is not for those seeking luxury, but should appeal to travelers who appreciate a discreetly laid-back atmosphere.

Halepa Hotel. Odos Eleftherios Venizelou 164 (on the street in Halepa just past the right turn to the airport), 73133 Chania, Crete. ☎ **0821/28-440.** Fax 0821/28-439. 50 units, all with bathroom (some with tub only, some with shower only). A/C TEL. High season Dr22,200–27,700 ($74–$93) double; low season Dr19,400–23,800 ($65–$80) double. Rates include continental breakfast. AE, DC, MC, V. Parking nearby. Open year-round with central heating. Frequent public buses to Chania (a 20-min. walk along the coast).

Like the better-known Doma, this hotel is in a converted neoclassical mansion. The Halepa is located in a quiet neighborhood, buffered from the street by its front garden. It's a restful oasis, with classical music often wafting through the air. Bedrooms are fair sized, bathrooms modern; most units have TVs. The owners can take care of your every need, from laundry to car rentals. There's a full bar, and a sunroof that offers a spectacular view of Chania and the bay. *Tip:* Ask for a room in the main, or traditional, mansion—otherwise you must settle for a room (albeit quiet and comfortable) in the rather nondescript new wing.

Hotel Porto Veneziano. Enetikos Limin, 73122 Chania, Crete. ☎ **0821/27-100.** Fax 0821/ 27-105. www.one-world.net/hotels/portoven/portoven.html. E-mail: portoven@otenet.gr. 57 units, all with bathroom (51 with shower only). A/C TV TEL. High season Dr27,200 ($91) double; Dr43,800 ($146) suite for 2. Low season Dr16,500 ($55) double; Dr36,400 ($121) suite. Rates include buffet breakfast. AE, DC, EURO, MC, V. Free parking nearby. Within walking distance to everything.

This fine hotel is located at the far end of the so-called Old Harbor (follow the walkway from the main harbor all the way around to the east, or right) and gives proximity to the center with a minimum of noise. The tasteful bedrooms are relatively large, and many have a fine view of the harbor. Meals are served only to organized groups, but refreshments from the hotel's own Cafe Veneto may be enjoyed in the garden. The desk personnel are genuinely helpful and will make any arrangements, from car rentals to laundry. All in all, an excellent choice for those who appreciate being down on an old harbor.

INEXPENSIVE

Hotel Palazzo. Odos Theotokopoulou 54 (around the corner of the far left/west arm of harbor), 73100 Chania, Crete. ☎ **0821/93-227.** Fax 0821/93-229. 11 units, some with shower only, some with tub only. High season Dr14,000 ($47) double; low season Dr12,000 ($40) double. Rates include breakfast. EURO, MC, V. Ample parking 100m away. Closed Nov–Mar (but will open for special groups). Within easy walking distance to all of Chania.

This Venetian town house, now a handsome little hotel, gives the feel of old Crete, but various amenities make it a first-class hotel—a fridge in every room, TV in the bar, a roof garden with a spectacular view of the mountains and sea. Rooms are good sized; those on the front have balconies. It's generally quiet, and if occasionally the still night air is broken by rowdy youths (true of all Greek cities), that seems a small price to pay for staying on Odos Theotokopoulou—the closest some will come to living on a Venetian canal. The owners will graciously help with all your wants—including laundry services, car rentals, and tours.

WHERE TO DINE
EXPENSIVE

✪ **Nykterida.** Korakies, Crete (about 6.4km/4 miles from town on road to airport, left turn opposite NAMFI Officers Club). ☎ **0821/64-215.** Reservations recommended for parties of 7 or more. Main courses Dr1,200–Dr3,600 ($4–$12). MC, V. Mon–Sat 6pm–1am. Parking on site. Open year-round. Taxi required if you don't have a car. GREEK.

Many would nominate this as the finest restaurant in all Crete. Certainly none can beat its setting, high on a point providing spectacular nighttime views of Chania or Soudha Bay. The cuisine is traditional Cretan-Greek, but many of the dishes have an extra something. For an appetizer, try the *kalazounia* (cheese pies with specks of spinach) or the *dolmades* (made with squash blossoms stuffed with a spiced rice and served with yogurt). Any of the main courses is going to be well done, from the basic steak fillet to the chicken with okra. Complimentary *tsoukoudia* (a potent Cretan liqueur) is served at the end of the meal. On Monday, Thursday, and Friday evenings through the high season (until the end of Oct.), traditional Cretan music is performed.

O Anemos. Akti Tombazi (at corner where the new and old harbors meet), Chania. ☎ and fax **0821/58-330.** Reservations accepted for large parties. Main courses Dr1,300–Dr3,900 ($4.35–$13); seafood platter for 2 Dr9,900 ($33). MC, V. Daily 10am–midnight. Closed Dec–Jan. GREEK.

Competing with the Nykterida (see above) for title of the finest restaurant in Chania, the food lives up to expectations. Try one of its specialties—chicken santos (boned breast of chicken stuffed with spinach, cheese, and bacon) or, if you're adventurous, stuffed goat. The special seafood platter is a bargain anyplace else in the world. (Purists might ask them to hold the sauces.) Having a meal here as you overlook the harbor is the epitome of stylish Mediterranean dining.

MODERATE

Amphora Restaurant. Akti Koundouriotou 49 (near the far right/western curve of the harbor), Chania. ☎ **0821/73-131.** Fax 0821/93-224. Main courses Dr1,200–Dr3,600 ($4–$12); fixed-price meals Dr2,300–Dr6,500 ($8–$22); combination plates Dr1,800–Dr5,000 ($6–$17). EURO, MC, V. Daily 11:30am–midnight. Closed Oct–Apr. GREEK.

This is a favorite when it comes to balancing price with quality, choice with taste. As with any Greek restaurant, if you order the lobster or steak, you'll pay a hefty price. But you can also assemble a delicious meal here at modest prices. To start, try the aubergine croquettes and the specialty of the house, a lemony fish soup. This restaurant belongs to the Amphora Hotel, a Category A, and although its tables and location suggest a basic harbor taverna, its food and friendly service make it first class.

Antigone Restaurant. Akti Enoseos (at farthest corner of new Harbor), Chania. ☎ **0821/ 45-236.** Main courses Dr1,200–Dr3,800 ($4–$13). No credit cards. Daily 11am–midnight. Parking at side of restaurant if you approach from behind; otherwise walk from the harbor. GREEK/SEAFOOD.

Start off here with an unusual appetizer such as a dip made of limpets and mussels, then move on to a specialty such as stuffed crab or whatever is the catch of the day, and you'll be eating fresh produce of the sea. Trust the staff to direct you to whatever is best that day. With its colorful interior, fresh flowers on your table, and a view of the harbor, this can be a most pleasant dining experience.

The Well of the Turk. Kalinikou Sarpaki 1–3 (a small street off Odos Daskaloyiannis), Chania. ☎ **0821/54-547.** Reservations recommended for parties of 7 or more. Main courses Dr1,700–Dr3,500 ($6–$12). No credit cards. Wed–Mon 6pm–midnight. MIDDLE EASTERN/ MEDITERRANEAN.

This restaurant, located in the heart of the old Turkish quarter (Splanzia), is in a historic old building with an interior well. Diners may choose to sit outside in a quiet street-court. The chef brings to the cuisine imaginative touches that make it more than standard Middle Eastern. In addition to tasty kebabs, there are such specialties as meatballs with eggplant mixed in, and the *laxma bi azeen,* a pita-style bread with a spicy topping. Middle Eastern musicians sometimes play here, and you can settle for a quiet drink at the bar.

INEXPENSIVE

You might also consider **Apostolis II,** Akti Enoseos 6, near the far end of the new harbor (☎ **0821/41-767**), for a typical family-run harbor taverna with decent traditional food; open daily from 10am to midnight.

O Mathios. Akti Enoseos 3 (about midway along new harbor), Chania. ☎ **0821/54-291.** Main courses Dr900–Dr2,700 ($3–$9). No credit cards. Daily 11am–2:30am. GREEK.

At this traditional harborside taverna, you can enjoy a decent meal while watching the boats bobbing at the quay and the cats stalking beneath the tables. In general, it has not been patronized by that many foreigners, but this is no reflection on its service (prompt no-nonsense) or food (as good as any in its class). Try the basic tzatziki and Greek salad, moussaka, or stuffed tomatoes—you can't go wrong. Fish dishes are their specialty (and as elsewhere can cost considerably more).

Remezzo Cafe. Venizelou 16A (on corner of main square at old harbor), Chania. ☎ **0821/52-001.** Main courses Dr900–2,000 ($3–$7). No credit cards. Daily 7am–2am. Must approach on foot. INTERNATIONAL.

Sooner or later, every tourist will say, "Enough of Greek salads!" and want to indulge in a club sandwich or tuna salad. Remezzo, at the very center of the action on the old harbor, is a great choice for breakfasts and light meals, and also offers a full range of coffee, alcoholic drinks, and ice-cream desserts. Sitting in one of the heavily cushioned chairs as you sip your drink and observe the lively scene, you'll feel like you have the best seat in the house.

CHANIA AFTER DARK

Chania's nightlife mostly comes down to two options: Head for a club/bar/disco packed with young people, or walk around the harbor and Old Town and enjoy the passing scene—the ritual known in Greece as the **volta.** Wander into the back alleys and see both the old Venetian and Turkish remains and the modern tourist enterprises. Sit in a quayside cafe and enjoy a coffee or drink, or treat yourself to a ride in a horse-drawn carriage down at the harbor. Or at the other extreme, stroll through the new town and be surprised at the modernity and diversity (and prices) of the stores patronized by typical Chaniots.

Clubs come and go, from year to year, of course, so there is no use getting excited over last year's "in" place. Some popular spots include **El Mondo** and **Nota Bene** on Kondilaki (the street leading away from the center of old harbor); **Idaeon Andron** at Odos Halidon 26; and **Ariadne** on Akti Enoseos (around the corner where the old harbor has become the new). On Odos Anghelou (up from the Naval Museum) is **Fagotta,** a bar that sometimes offers jazz music. **Meltemi,** at the far left (west) corner of the new harbor, is one of the more cosmopolitan cafes, attracting both locals and foreigners, some young, some old.

There are several **movie houses** around town, too—both outdoor and indoor. They usually show foreign movies in the original language. (The one in the Public Gardens is especially enjoyable.) Viewing a movie on a warm summer night in an outdoor cinema in Greece is one of life's simpler pleasures.

In recent years there's been an effort to provide a **summer cultural festival** of sorts—occasional performances from July into September of dramas, symphonic music, jazz, dance, and traditional music. These performances take place at several venues: the **Firka** fortress at the far left of the harbor; the **Venetian arsenals** along the old harbor; the **East Moat Theater** along Odos Nikiforou Phokas; or in the **Peace and Friendship Park Theater** on Odos Demokratias, just beyond the Public Gardens. For details, inquire at one of the tourist information offices as soon as you arrive in town.

The longtime favorite nightclub of the gay community is the **Triiris,** on Odos Mousourou (on Plateia Horatsou, on the west side of the Municipal Market). (It sports a PRIVATE CLUB sign, but it is not.) A newer club is **Ta Padia Paizei,** on

Odos Archoleon, at the far (east) end of the new harbor; the club has no street address but is distinguished by wheelbarrows with flowers at the door.

TWO SPECIAL CAFES

Pallas Roof Garden Cafe-Bar. Akti Tobazi (right at the corner where the new harbor meets the old harbor). ☎ **0821/45-688.** No cover or minimum. No credit cards. Daily 6pm–1am. Closed mid-Sept to June.

In some ways, the Pallas Roof Garden is the best-situated locale on the harbor: it's a place for anyone seeking to get away from the crowds, celebrate a special occasion, or just enjoy a lovely vista and a refreshing drink. This cafe-bar offers everything from coffee to ice-cream sundaes to champagne. With little lanterns at each table, you sit high above the harbor, watch the blinking lighthouse, and listen to the murmur of the crowds and the mellow background music. There has to be some drawback here, and there is—you must climb 44 stairs to get here. But as the sign says, it's worth it.

Tzamia–Krystalla. Odos Skalidi 35. ☎ **0821/71-172.** No cover or minimum. EURO, MC, V. Mon–Fri 10am–2pm and 5–10pm; Sat 10am–2pm. In winter, open daily until midnight.

Here's a most unusual addition to the scene in Chania, a combination art gallery/cafe/performance space. The gallery hosts changing exhibits by Greek artists, as well as the award-winning ceramics of one of the owners. The cafe serves a standard selection of alcoholic and nonalcoholic drinks, and at times these are complemented by performances of live music. This is a most welcome alternative to the usual tourist diversions.

A SIDE TRIP FROM CHANIA: THE SAMARIA GORGE

Everyone with an extra day on Crete—and steady legs and solid shoes—should consider the descent through the Gorge of Samaria. First, this involves getting to the top of the gorge, a trip of some 42 kilometers (26 miles) from Chania. Second comes the descent by foot and passage through the gorge itself, some 18 kilometers (11 miles). Third, a boat takes you from the village of Ayia Roumeli, at the end of the gorge, to Khora Sfakion; from there, it's a bus ride of about 75 kilometers (46 miles) back to Chania. (Some boats go westward to Paleochora, approximately the same distance by road from Chania.)

Most visitors do it all in a long day, but there are modest hotels and rooms at Ayia Roumeli, Khora Sfakion, Paleochora, and elsewhere along the south coast where you can put up for the night. We advise most travelers to sign up with one of the many **travel agencies** in Chania that get people to and from the gorge. This way, you are assured of guaranteed seats on the bus and boat.

In recent years, the Gorge of Samaria has been so successfully promoted as one of the great natural splendors of Europe that on certain days it seems that half of the continent is trekking through. It's only open from about April through October (depending on weather conditions), so your best chance for a bit of solitude is near those two extremes. On the most crowded days, you can find yourself walking single file with several thousand other people many of those 11 miles. As a hike or trek, it rates as relatively easy, but here and there you will scramble over some boulders. Bring your own water and snacks and wear comfortable shoes.

After all this, is it worth it? We think so. The gorge has enough "breathing space" that you can still break away from the crowds in places. You'll be treated to the fun of crisscrossing the water, not to mention the sights of wildflowers and dramatic geological formations, the sheer height of the gorge's sides, and several chapels that you come across—it will all add up to a worthwhile experience, even a metaphor of your visit to Crete.

3 Rethymnon (Rethimno)

72km (45 miles) E of Chania; 78km (50 miles) W of Iraklion

Whether visited on a day trip from Chania or Iraklion or used as a base for a stay in western Crete, Rethymnon can be a most pleasant town—provided you pick the right Rethymnon.

The town's defining centuries came under the Venetians in the late Middle Ages and the Renaissance, then under the Turks from the late 17th century to the late 19th century. Its maze of streets and alleys are now lined with shops, its old beachfront is home to restaurants and bars, and its new beach-resort facilities (to the east of the old town) offer a prime (some might say appalling) example of how a small town's modest seacoast can be exploited. Assuming you have not come to see these "developments," however, we show how you can focus your time and attention on the old town—the side of Rethymnon that can still work its charm.

ESSENTIALS

GETTING THERE Rethymnon lacks an airport but is only about 1 hour from Chania's and 1½ hours from Iraklion's.

By Boat Rethymnon does have its own ship line, offering daily trips direct to (about 7:30pm) and from Piraeus (about 7pm).

By Car Many people now arrive by car, taking the highway from either Iraklion (some 79km/49 miles) or Chania (72km/45 miles).

By Bus If you don't have your own vehicle, the bus offers frequent service to and from Iraklion and Chania—virtually every half hour from early in the morning until midevening (in high season, buses have departed Rethymnon as late as 10pm). The fare has been about Dr1,500 ($5) one-way. The KTEL bus line (☎ 0831/22-212) that provides service to and from Chania and Iraklion is located at Akti Kefaloyianithon, at the west edge of the city (so allow an extra 10 min. to get there).

By Taxi One-way taxi fares are about Dr15,000 ($50) from Iraklion and Dr10,000 ($33) from Chania.

VISITOR INFORMATION The **National Tourist Information office (☎ 0831/ 29-148)** is on Odos Venizelou, near the center of the town beach; it's open Monday through Friday from 8am to 4pm, Saturday from 9am to 2pm. Of the numerous private travel agencies in town, one of the oldest is **Creta Travel Bureau,** Odos Venizelou 3 (☎ 0831/22-915), which can arrange trips to virtually anywhere on the island.

GETTING AROUND Rethymnon is a walker's town—bringing a car into the maze of streets and alleys is more trouble than it's worth. The sites you'll want to see are never more than a 20-minute walk from wherever you are. Taxis, meanwhile, are there for anyone who can't endure a short walk—especially in the heat of the day.

To see the countryside of this part of Crete, unless you have unlimited time to use the buses, you'll need to rent a car. Among the major agencies with offices in

For Wine Lovers

Rethymnon's annual wine festival takes place in the last 10 or so days of July, centered in the Public Gardens, with music and dancing to accompany the samplings of local wines. It's a modest affair, but we find it a welcome change from some of the more staged festivals.

Rethymnon are **Europcar** (☎ 0831/54-440), **Europrent** (☎ 0831/26-302), **Hertz** (☎ 0831/51-772), **Kosmos** (☎ 0831/25-206), and **Reliable International** (☎ 0831/72-172).

FAST FACTS   Several **banks** in both the old town and new city have both ATMs and currency-exchange machines. The town **hospital** is at Odos Trantallidou 7–9, behind the municipal gardens in the new town (☎ **0831/27-491**). For **medical emergencies**, dial ☎ **166.** The most convenient **laundry** is next to the Youth Hostel, Odos Tombazi 45; open Monday through Saturday from 8am to 8pm. For **police emergencies**, dial ☎ **171.** The **tourist police** (☎ 0831/28-156) share the same building with the Tourist Information Office, along the town beach. The **post office** is at Kountourioti 100 (☎ 0831/22-571); open Monday through Friday from 8am to 8pm, Saturday from 8am to noon. The **telephone office (OTE)** is at Kountourioti 40; open daily from 7:30am to midnight.

WHAT TO SEE & DO
ATTRACTIONS
The Venetian Fortezza. ☎ **0831/28-101.** Admission Dr500 ($1.70). Daily 8:30am–7pm. On foot, climb Odos Katehaki, a fairly steep road opposite the Hotel Fortezza on Odos Melissinou; by car, ascend the adjacent Odos Kheimara.

Dominating the headland at the western edge of town, this massive fortress is the one site everyone should take time to visit. Built under the Venetians (but *by* Cretans) from about 1573 to 1580, its massive walls, some 1,130 meters in perimeter, were designed to deflect the worst cannon fire of the day. In the end, of course, the Turks simply went around it and took the town in 1646 by avoiding the fort. There's a partially restored mosque inside as well as a Greek Orthodox chapel. It's in this vast area, by the way, that most of the performances of the annual **Rethymnon Renaissance Festival** take place (see below).

Historical and Folk Art Museum. Odos Vernadou 30. ☎0831/23-398. Admission Dr400 ($1.35). Mon–Sat 9am–1pm.

Housed in a Venetian mansion, this small museum displays ceramics, textiles, jewelry, artifacts, implements, clothing, and other vivid reminders of the traditional way of life of most Cretans across the centuries.

A STROLL THROUGH THE OLD TOWN
Rethymnon's attractions are best appreciated by walking through the old town and focusing on whatever appeals to you. Start by getting a free map from the tourist office, located down along the beachfront.

If you have limited time, the first place you should visit is the **Fortezza** (see above). Then make your way back along Odos Melissinou to the corner of Odos Mesologiou, with the Catholic church at the corner. Proceeding down Odos Salaminos, you'll come to Odos Arkadiou; a left there brings you out to the western edge of the **old harbor.** Curving right down to that harbor brings an unexpected sight: the wall of restaurants and bars that effectively obliterates the quaint harbor that drew them there in the first place. Making your way through that, you'll emerge at the southeast corner of this curved harbor and come to a square that faces the town's long beach, its broad boulevard lined with even more restaurants and cafes. Turn right up Odos Petikhaki, and at the first crossroads you'll see the **Venetian Loggia** (ca. 1600)—for many years the town's museum and now a Ministry of Culture gallery that sells officially approved reproductions of ancient Greek works of art. Continue up past it on Odos Paleologou to the next crossroads, where you'll come, on the right, to the **Rimondi Fountain** (1623).

Rethymnon

Legend
- Information ⓘ
- OTE ☎
- Post Office ✉

CRETE
Rethymnon

ATTRACTIONS
Entrance to Venetian Fortezza ❶
Historical & Folk Art Museum ❽
Mosque of Nerantzes ❾
Orthodox Church of the Four Martyrs ⓫
Porta Guora ❿
Rimondi Fountain ❼

ACCOMMODATIONS
Hotel Fortezza ❺
Hotel Ideon ❹

DINING
Famagusta ❸
Fanari ("The Lantern") ❷
Taverna Mourayiou Maria ❻

The Rethymnon Renaissance Festival

Rethymnon's cultural festival offers varied events—mostly musical and theatrical—from early July to early September. Productions range from ancient Greek dramas to more contemporary artistic endeavors (and now include folk and rock concerts). Most performers are Greek; some are foreigners. The majority of performances are staged in the Fortezza itself; there's nothing quite like listening to 17th-century music or seeing a Renaissance drama in this setting. For details, inquire at the tourist information office on first arriving.

Leaving the fountain at your back, proceed onto Odos Antistaseos toward the 17th-century **Mosque of Nerantzes** with its minaret (open for climbing Mon through Fri from 11am to 7:30pm, Sat from 11am to 3pm; closed in Aug). If you follow Antistaseos to its top, you'll come to the **Porta Guora,** the only remnant of the Venetian city walls.

Across the main east-west road and to the right are the **Municipal Gardens.** On your left is the **Orthodox Church of the Four Martyrs,** worth a peek in as you walk east along Odos Gerakari, until you come to a large open crossroad that serves as the border of the old town and the new beachfront development.

Turning back into the old town on Odos Arkadiou, you will see on your left the **Mosque of Kara Pasha,** now restored and used as a botanical museum (open daily from 9am to 6pm). As you continue along Arkhadiou, in addition to the modern shops and their offerings, note the several remains of the Venetian era that survive—for instance, the **facade of no. 154.** From this point on, you're on your own to explore the various narrow streets, to shop, or to simply head for the waterfront and enjoy some refreshment.

OUTDOOR PURSUITS

Among the newer diversions offered in Rethymnon are the daily **excursion boats** that take people on a day trip for **swimming** on the beach either at **Bali** (to the east) or **Marathi** (on the Akrotiri to the west). The price (which has been about Dr7,000/$23 for adults) includes a midday meal at a local taverna as well as all the wine you care to drink. **Nias Tours,** Odos Arkadiou 4 (☎ **0831/23-840**), also offers an **evening cruise** with refreshments that provides a view of Rethymnon glittering in the night. If you're interested in **horseback riding,** try the **Riding Center,** located southeast of town at Platanias, Odos N. Fokas 39 (☎ **0831/28-907**).

SHOPPING

Here, as in Chania and Iraklion, you may be overwhelmed by the sheer number of gift shops offering largely the same objects—mostly souvenirs. Those looking for something a bit different might try Nikolaos Papalasakis's shop, **Palaiopoleiou,** Odos Souliou 40, which is crammed with some genuine antiques, old textiles, jewelry, and curiosities such as the stringed instruments made by the proprietor. At **Olive Tree Wood,** Odos Arabatzoglou 51, the name says it all—the store carries various bowls, containers, and implements carved from olive wood.

For a nice selection of Cretan embroidery, see **Haroula Spridaki,** Odos Souliou 36. Those interested in modern ceramics should stop into **Omodamos,** Odos Souliou 3, where the original works reflect imaginative variations on traditional Greek pottery. And **Talisman,** Odos Arabatzoglou 32, offers a most interesting selection of blown glass, ceramics, plaques, paintings, and other handmade articles.

WHERE TO STAY

There is no shortage of accommodations in and around Rethymnon—but it has become increasingly harder to find a place that offers a convenient location, some authentic atmosphere, and a good night's sleep. Our choices try to satisfy the last-mentioned criterion first. Note that many places in Rethymnon shut down in winter.

EXPENSIVE

✪ **Rethymna Beach Grecotel.** P.O. Box 23, 74100 Rethymnon, Crete (7km/4 miles east of Rethymnon on the old road to Iraklion). ☎ **0831/71-002.** Fax 0831/71-668. E-mail: grecotel@hol.gr. 568 units (including bungalows and villas, 7 with private pools). A/C TV TEL. High season Dr30,450–Dr32,550 ($102–$109) double; Dr34,650–Dr38,950 ($116–$130) bungalow. Low season Dr17,750 ($60) double; Dr18,800 ($63) bungalow. All rates are per person but include breakfast and 1 other meal. Reduction for 3rd person sharing room of 2 persons paying full rates; babies stay free. AE, DC, EURO, MC, V. Parking on premises. Buses to and from Rethymnon (and Chania or Iraklion) about every half hr.

This luxury beach hotel is one of the finest on the island, and offers an escape from the noise of the city. The bedrooms are standard for even luxury hotels in Greece—modest in size and furnishings but with fine bathrooms and views. This hotel's particular strength is the supervised activities for children. If you like to mix occasional sightseeing with luxurious facilities, pampered relaxation, and water-based activities, consider this rather glitzy hotel.

There are many restaurants on site, and amenities such as concierge, room service, dry cleaning and laundry, newspaper delivery, massage, baby-sitting, secretarial services, courtesy car, and children's activities. Facilities include four pools, health club, aerobics, Jacuzzi, sauna, sun areas, bridge room, video room, five outdoor tennis courts (two with lights), squash court at nearby Creta Palace, water-sports equipment (and instruction), bicycle rentals, nature trails, children's programs, conference rooms (for up to 600), car-rental desk, tour desk, beauty salon, and boutiques.

MODERATE

✪ **Hotel Fortezza.** Odos Melissinou 16 (at western edge of town, just below the Venetian Fortezza, which is approached by this road), Rethymnon, Crete. ☎ **0831/23-828.** Fax 0831/54-073. 54 units. High season Dr24,200 ($81) double; low season Dr19,800 ($66) double. Rates include continental breakfast. Surcharge for 3rd person sharing room with 2 persons paying full rates; babies stay free. AE, DC, EURO, MC, V. Parking nearby. Public bus service 100m.

This is one of the more appealing hotels in Rethymnon, for its location isolates it from the noise of the inner town. This is especially true of its inside rooms, which overlook the modest but welcome pool. You're only a few blocks from the inner old town and then another couple of blocks to the town beach or the Venetian harbor. All guest rooms are good sized with modern bathrooms, and most have balconies. Half of the rooms have air-conditioning and telephones. This relatively new hotel has become so popular that you're advised to make reservations for the high season.

Hotel Ideon. Plateia Plastira 10 (on coast road just east of the Venetian harbor), Rethymnon, Crete. ☎ **0831/28-667.** Fax 0831/28-670. 86 units, some with shower only, some with tub only. A/C TEL. High season Dr20,600 ($69) double; low season Dr13,600 ($45) double. Rates include buffet breakfast; 5 full meals can be had for Dr14,000 ($47). Reduced rates for 3rd person in room and children ages 2–12. AE, DC, EURO, MC, V. Parking on adjacent street. Closed Nov to mid-March.

This old favorite now boasts a new pool and a sunbathing area as well as a conference room that can handle up to 80 persons. The friendly desk staff can arrange for everything from laundry to car rental. Guest rooms are the standard modern of Greek hotels. We like this place because it offers an increasingly rare combination in a Cretan hotel: it's near the active part of the town and near the water (although it doesn't have a beach), yet it's relatively isolated from night noises. A solid choice for sheer convenience.

Kournas Village Hotel Bungalows. Kavros (20 min. west of Rethymnon, on the main road to Chania), Crete. ☎ and fax **0831/61-416.** 141 units. A/C TEL. High season Dr26,000 ($87) double; low season Dr18,000 ($60). No credit cards. Rates include breakfast and dinner. Parking on site. Closed Nov–Mar.

Here's an alternative for those who want to focus their Cretan stay on Rethymnon and Chania and western Crete, yet prefer to be based on a beach that's not an annex to a noisy town. Everything about this place is first class, yet you'll feel like you're living on a remote Cretan beach with the sea before you and the mountains behind. The village of Georgioupolis is close enough for an evening stroll. Guest rooms are of moderate size but with fully modern bathrooms, and if lacking the luxury of the grand resorts to the east of Rethymnon, the Kournas Village is more than adequate.

Amenities include concierge, dry cleaning and laundry arrangements, and car-rental and tour arrangements. Facilities include two pools, children's pool, health club, sauna, massage, sundeck, tennis court (with flood lights), table tennis, water-sports equipment, bicycle rentals, playground nursery, conference room (for 150), video games, safe-deposit boxes, and boutiques. The complex has a restaurant, cafeteria, and bar, but many other options are within walking distance.

WHERE TO DINE
MODERATE

Famagusta. Plateia Plastira 6 (near Ideon Hotel, on coast road just to the west of Venetian harbor), Rethymnon. ☎ **0831/23-881.** Main courses Dr1,100–Dr3,200 ($3.70–$11); daily combination plates Dr1,700–Dr2,200 ($6–$7). AE, DC, EURO, MC, V. Daily 10am–midnight. Parking nearby. Closed during Christmas to New Year holidays. GREEK/INTERNATIONAL.

This well-tested restaurant is removed from the hustle of the harbor, yet it's convenient to the center's attractions and enjoys a view of the sea. The menu offers several Cretan specialties as appetizers—try breaded zucchini deep-fried with yogurt and lightly flavored with garlic. Grilled fish and steak fillets are the core of the main courses, but the adventurous chef also includes such dishes as Chinese-style mandarin beef. Eating here makes you feel like you're at an old-fashioned seaside restaurant, not some tourist confection.

Taverna Mourayiou Maria. Odos Nearchou 45 (Venetian harbor). ☎ **0831/26-475.** Main courses Dr1,000–Dr2,700 ($3.35–$9). AE, EURO, MC, V. Daily 9am–midnight. Closed Nov–Mar. GREEK.

Like all of the restaurants on the Venetian harbor, this one specializes in lobster and fish in season, but it also offers a choice of traditional Greek dishes at the lower end of the price scale. The popularity of the area has somewhat overwhelmed the picturesque charm that originally attracted restaurants such as this one, but everyone will want to try at least one meal on the harbor—and this is as good a choice as any.

INEXPENSIVE

Fanari ("The Lantern"). Odos Kefaloyianithon 16 (on coast road just west of Venetian harbor—past Ideon Hotel and Famagusta Restaurant), Rethymnon. ☎ **0831/54-849.** Main courses Dr1,000–Dr2,600 ($3.35–$9); daily special combination plates about Dr1,500 ($5). No credit cards. Daily 11am–1:30am. Parking nearby. Closed late Nov to early Jan. GREEK TAVERNA.

We list this place not because its menu or cooking are so exceptional, but because its location is so pleasant, overlooking the sea and well removed from the bustle of the center of Rethymnon. It also offers prompt and pleasant service. The old harbor and the old beach strip have now become so geared to tourism that an unpretentious taverna like this comes as a relief and a retreat. Take a table at the railing, order a cool drink, and enjoy your meal: you can't go wrong with the standard fare, and fish here can be as tasty as at most of the more expensive locales.

A SIDE TRIP FROM RETHYMNON: MONASTERY OF ARKADHI

Anyone who wants some sense of modern Cretans should visit the **Monastery of Arkadhi.** It sits some 23 kilometers (15 miles) southeast of Rethymnon and can be reached by public bus. A taxi might be in order if you don't have a car, and you'll only need the driver to wait about an hour—it should cost about Dr10,000 ($33). What you see when you arrive is a surprisingly Italianate-looking church façade, for although it belongs to the Orthodox priesthood, it was built under Venetian influence in 1587.

Like many monasteries on Crete, Arkadhi provided support for the rebels against Turkish rule. During a major uprising in 1866, many Cretan insurgents, along with their women and children, took refuge here. Realizing they were doomed to fall to the far larger besieging Turkish force, the abbot, it is claimed, gave the command to blow up the powder storeroom. Whether an accident or not, hundreds of Cretans and Turks died in the explosion. This occurred on November 9, 1866, and the event became known throughout the Western world, inspiring writers and revolutionaries and statesmen of several nations to protest at least with words. To Cretans it became and remains the archetypal incident of their long struggle for "freedom or death." (An ossuary outside the monastery contains the skulls of many who died in the explosion.) Even if you have never had occasion to think about Cretan history, a brief visit to Arkadhi should go a long way in explaining the Cretans you deal with.

4 Ayios Nikolaos

220km (135 miles) E of Iraklion

Ayios Nikolaos tends to inspire strong reactions, depending on what you're looking for. Until the 1970s, it was a lazy little coastal settlement, with no archaeological or historical structures of any interest. Then the town got "discovered," and the rest is the history of organized tourism in our time.

For about 5 months of the year, Ayios Nikolaos becomes one gigantic resort town, taken over by the package-tour groups who stay in beach hotels along the adjacent coast, but come into town to eat, shop, and stroll. During the day, Ayios Nikolaos vibrates with people. At night, it vibrates with music—the center down by the water is like one communal nightclub.

Yet somehow Ayios Nikolaos remains a pleasant place to visit, and serves as a fine base for excursions to the east of Crete. And if you're willing to stay outside the very center of town, you can take only as much of Ayios Nikolaos as you want—and then retreat to your beach or explore the east end of the island.

ESSENTIALS

GETTING THERE   By Plane   Ayios Nikolaos does not have its own airport but can be reached in 1½ hours by taxi or bus from the Iraklion airport. Olympic Airways also offers several flights weekly to Sitia, the town to the east of Ayios Nikolaos, but the drive from there to Ayios Nikolaos is a solid 2 hours.

By Boat   There are several ships a week each way (at least during tourist season) that link Ayios Nikolaos to Sitia (just east along the coast) and on, via the islands of Kassos, Karpathos, and Khalki, to Rhodes. In summer, there are also several ships that link Ayios Nikolaos to the islands of Santorini, and then via several other Cycladic islands to Piraeus. Schedules and even ship lines vary so much from year to year that you should wait until you get to Greece to make specific plans.

By Bus   Bus service almost every half hour of the day each way (during the tourist season) links Ayios Nikolaos to Iraklion; almost as many buses go to and from Sitia. The **KTEL** bus line (☎ 0841/22-234 or 0841/28-284) has its terminal at Akti Atlantidos, by the town marina, around the headland.

VISITOR INFORMATION   The **Municipal Information Office** (☎ 0841/ 22-357) is one of the most helpful in all of Greece, perhaps because it's staffed by eager young employees instead of jaded veterans. It is open April 1 through the end of October, daily from 8:30am to 10pm. In addition to providing maps and other ready services, it issues a **Visitor's Card,** which entitles you to certain free items and discounts when presented at the Municipal Beach.

Among the scores of travel agencies and ticket offices, we recommend **Creta Travel Bureau,** at the corner of Odos Paleologou and Odos Katehaki, just opposite Lake Voulismeni (☎ 0841/28-496; fax 081/223-749).

GETTING AROUND   The town is so small that you can walk to all points, although there are taxis available. The KTEL buses (see above) service towns, hotels, and other points along the coast highway.

If you want to explore this end of the island on your own, it seems as though car and moped/motorcycle rentals are at every other doorway. We found some of the best car rates at **Alfa Rent a Car,** Odos Kap. Nik. Fafouti 3, the small street between the lake and harbor road (☎ 0841/24-312; fax 0841/25-639). Fotis Aretakis is the man to deal with.

FAST FACTS   There are several **ATMs** and **currency-exchange machines** along the streets leading away from the harbor. Dial ☎ 100 for all **emergencies**. The town's **hospital** (☎ 0841/25-221) is on the west edge of town, at the junction of Odos Lasithiou and Odos Paleologou. Peripou, an **Internet cafe,** is at Odos 28 Octobriou 25 (☎ 0841/24-76; e-mail: peripou2@agn.forthnet.gr); open daily in high season from 9am to 9pm. The one **laundry** in town is the Xionati Laundromat, Odos Chortatson 10 (a small street leading up from Akti Nearchou, down by the bus terminal and beach there); open Monday through Friday from 8am to 2pm and 5 to 8pm, Saturday from 8am to 4pm. **Luggage** may be stored at the main bus station, Akti Atlantidos (around headland and down by Town Marina). The charge is Dr400 ($1.35) per piece per 24 hours. The **tourist police** (☎ 0841/26-900) are at Odos Koundoyianni 34. The **post office** is at Odos 28 Octobriou 9 (☎ 0841/22-062). In summer, it's open Monday through Saturday from 7:30am to 8pm; in winter, Monday through Saturday from 7:30am to 2pm. The **telephone office (OTE),** Odos Sfakinaki 10, at the corner of Odos 25 Martiou (☎ 0841/1-31), is open Monday through Saturday from 7am to midnight, Sunday and holidays from 7am to 10pm.

WHAT TO SEE & DO

The main point of interest here is the little pool, formally called **Lake Voulismeni,** just inside the harbor—you can sit on the edge of it while enjoying a meal or drink. Inevitably, it has given rise to all sorts of tales: that it's bottomless (it's known to be about 65m deep); that it's connected to Santorini, the island some 104 kilometers

Archaeological Museum

Milatou

Koritsas

Koraka

Prigipos Georgiou

Paleologou

Ethniks Antistaseos

Theotokouloud

Kobnarouv

D. Solomos

Akti Koundourou

Quay

Kantanoleontos

Katehaki

Kondilaki

Lake Voulismeni

Titou

Plastira

Filellinon

Omirou

28 Octobriou

Plateia Venizelou

Koundourou

25 Martiou

K. Sfakianaki

Polytechniou

Manousogianakis

El. Venizelou

Bus Station

Tavla

Koziri

Akti Atlantidos

Koundourou

Lasthenous

Pasilias

M. Sfakianaki

Ebans

Ariadnis

Milou

Alexomanoli

Kitroplatia Beach

Legend

Information ⓘ

OTE 🄲

Post Office ✉

ACCOMMODATIONS
Hotel Hermes **2**
Minos Beach **1**

DINING
Hollands—De Molen (The Mill) ◆
Itanos ◆
La Casa ◆
Pelagos ◆

CRETE
Ayios Nikolaos

(65 miles) to the north; and that it was the "bath of Athena." Originally it was a fresh-water pool, probably fed by some subterranean river draining water from the mountains inland. The channel was dug sometime early in the 20th century, so now the freshwater mixes with seawater.

Archaeological Museum. Odos Paleologou 74, Ayios Nikolaos. ☎ **0841/24-943.** Admission Dr500 ($1.70). Tues–Sun 8am–2:30pm.

This is a fine example of one of the relatively new provincial museums that are appearing all over Greece in an effort to decentralize the country's rich holdings and also allow the local communities to profit from the finds from their region. It contains a growing collection of Minoan artifacts and art that is being excavated in eastern Crete. Its prize piece is the eerily modern ceramic **Goddess of Myrtos,** a woman clutching a jug, found at a Minoan site of this name down on the southeastern coast. It's worth at least a brief visit.

SHOPPING

Definitely make time to visit **Ceramica,** Odos Paleologou 28 (☎0841/234-075); you will see many reproductions of ancient Greek vases and frescoes for sale throughout Greece, but seldom will you have a chance to visit the workshop of one of the masters of this art, Nikolaos Gabriel. His authentic and vivid vases range from Dr7,500 to Dr45,000 ($25 to $150).

Sofia Kana, the proprietor of **Marieli,** Odos 28 Octobriou 33 (☎ 0841/28-813), studied law and then worked as a journalist until 1972, when she decided her true vocation was weaving. Until recently, her shop featured her distinctive woven rugs—but the work eventually became too demanding. Now she carries interesting ceramics, candlesticks, jewelry, and other crafts, all chosen with the same style she brought to her weaving. **Pegasus,** Odos Sfakianakis 5, on the corner of Koundourou, the main street up from the harbor (☎ 0841/24-347), carries an interesting selection of jewelry, knives, icons, and trinkets. Some of these are old, some not, and you have to trust the owner, Kostas Kounelakis, to tell you which is which.

For something truly Greek, what could be better than an icon, a religious painting on a wooden plaque? The tradition is kept alive at **Petrakis Workshop for Icons,** Elounda, on the left as you come down the incline from Ayios Nikolaos, just before the town square (☎ 0841/41-669). Here in their studio/store, Georgia and Ioannis Petrakis work seriously at maintaining this art. Their icons are in demand from Orthodox churches in North America as well as in Greece. Stop by and watch the artists at their painstaking work. You don't have to be Orthodox to admire or own one. They also have a selection of original jewelry, blown glass, and ceramics.

Lato Cultural Festival

Ayios Nikolaos's modest arts festival usually runs from late July to early September, with Cretan choral groups, Cretan traditional dance troupes, both classic and modern plays (usually in Greek), and concerts by Greek instrumentalists and vocalists. Admission is from Dr1,200 to Dr3,000 ($4 to $10), usually less for kids. To show their appreciation for the foreigners who visit the town and support these and other events, the sponsors have also given parties about midway through the season and then at the end of September—a nice touch, suggesting that perhaps mass tourism need not totally wipe out local customs.

WHERE TO STAY
INSIDE TOWN

Hotel Hermes. Akti Koundourou (on the shore road around from the inner harbor), 72100 Ayios Nikolaos, Crete. ☎ **0841/28-253.** Fax 0841/28-754. 207 units. A/C TEL. High season, Dr32,000 ($107) double; low season, Dr23,000 ($77) double. Rates include half-board plan (breakfast and dinner); cheaper rate for breakfast only; special rate for longer stays. AE, DC, EURO, MC, V. Parking on adjacent street. Closed Nov–Mar.

This is perhaps the best you can do if you want to stay as close to the center of town as possible, yet be free from as much of the noise as possible. It's just far enough and around the corner from the inner harbor to escape the nightly din. This won't be attractive to everyone, but it's a compromise between the deluxe beach resorts and the cheaper in-town hotels. Guest rooms are done in the standard style, and most enjoy a view over the sea. There's a private terrace (not a beach) on the shore, just across the boulevard. On the roof is a pool, with plenty of space to sunbathe. There's also a sauna and exercise room. All rooms have fridges, and suites have TVs. Other diversions include video games and billiards. The main restaurant is on the fifth floor. A conference room can accommodate up to 250.

If the Hermes is booked, you might try the **Hotel Coral,** Akti Koundourou (next door to the Hermes on the shore road), 72100 Ayios Nikolaos (☎ 0841/28-253), which is under the same management.

Minos Beach. Amoudi (a 10-min. walk from center), 72100 Ayios Nikolaos, Crete. ☎ **0841/ 22-345.** Fax 0841/22-548. 12 units (in main building), 118 bungalows. A/C MINIBAR TEL. High season Dr37,000–Dr39,500 ($123–$132) double; low season Dr16,100–Dr28,500 ($53–$95) double. All rates include buffet breakfast. Special rates for children. 1 meal a day for Dr6,000 ($20). AE, DC, EURO, MC, V. Closed end of Oct to early Apr. Frequent public buses to Ayios Nikolaos center or Elounda.

This was the first of the luxury beach-bungalow resorts on Crete and remains a favorite among many loyal returnees. Its grounds now look a bit cramped, and the common areas are not as glitzy as at newer resorts. As with almost all Greek deluxe hotels, the mattresses seem a bit thin (to Americans, at least). But the hotel has a civilized air, enhanced by the original works by world-famous modern sculptors located around the grounds. It's a great place to enjoy complete peace and quiet and yet not be that far from Ayios Nikolaos.

The resort has several restaurants and bars. Amenities include concierge, room service, laundry, newspaper delivery, baby-sitting, secretarial services, valet parking, airport transportation arrangements, TVs in VIP Bungalows and large TV room, saltwater pool, sauna, sundecks, outdoor tennis court lit at night, water-sports equipment, bicycle rentals, table tennis, snooker table, video games, conference center (for up to 60), car-rental desk, tour arrangements, hairdresser, and boutiques.

OUTSIDE TOWN

✪ **Elounda Beach.** 72053 Elounda (about 6.4km/4 miles from center of Ayios Nikolaos), Crete. ☎ **0841/41-412.** Fax 0841/41-373. E-mail: elohotel@compulink.gr. 268 units (including 21 suites and bungalows with private swimming pools). A/C MINIBAR TV TEL. High season Dr42,800–Dr74,600 ($143–$249) double; Dr89,900–Dr144,800 ($300–$483) bungalow suite. Low season Dr28,500–Dr56,900 ($95–$190) double; Dr59,000– Dr111,000 ($197–$370) bungalow suite. Rates are per person per day and include breakfast. (1 meal supplement costs Dr8,000/$27.) AE, DC, EURO, MC, V. Closed early Nov to late Mar. Public buses to Ayios Nikolaos or Elounda every hr.; Elounda is a 15-min. walk.

This is truly a world-class resort. It offers even more extras than we can list, including the gala dinner every Sunday and open-air movies on Monday nights. There's not much more to say about such a place except that it's truly grand. From the prunes at the breakfast buffet to the mini-TV at your bathroom mirror, they've thought of everything. Yes, we stayed there and the meals are fabulous. And oh, in case you're concerned, they do have their own heliport, so you can arrive that way if you please.

Restaurants and bars are located throughout the vast property. Amenities include concierge, room service, laundry, newspaper delivery, nightly turndown, baby-sitting, secretarial services, airport transport arrangements, VCRs and videos available from desk, pool, health and fitness center, Jacuzzi, sauna, sundecks, two floodlit tennis courts, water-sports equipment, bicycle rentals, table tennis, billiards, basketball, volleyball, minigolf, supervised children's activities during the day, business support by arrangement, conference center for up to 450 (at adjacent sister hotel, Elounda Bay), car-rental and tour arrangements, hairdresser, and boutiques.

✪ Istron Bay. 72100 Kato Chorio (13km/8 miles east of Ayios Nikolaos), Crete. ☎**0841/61-347.** Fax 0841/61-383. E-mail: istron@agn.forthnet.gr. 145 units (including bungalows). A/C. High season Dr47,400 ($158) double; Dr64,400 ($215) suite or bungalow. Low season 25,400 ($85) double; Dr36,400 ($122) suite or bungalow. Rates include buffet breakfast. Special rates for extra beds in room, for children, and for half-board plan (breakfast and dinner). AE, DC, MC, V. Closed Nov–Mar. Public buses every hr. to Ayios Nikolaos or Sitia.

Still another new and beautiful beach resort, this one is a few miles to the east of Ayios Nikolaos and is nestled against the slope on its own bay. It's the resort's location, plus its own beach and the sense of being in some tropical paradise, that makes this such a special place. Plus, it's family owned and thus maintains a touch of the traditional Cretan hospitality—inviting newcomers to a cocktail party to meet others, for instance. Guest rooms are comfortable with modern bathrooms; all have spectacular views. If you can tear yourself away from here, you're well situated to take in all the sights of eastern Crete.

The main dining room, high up the "sloped" hotel, has a fabulous view to go with its award-winning cuisine; it takes special pride in its selection of Greek wines. Amenities include concierge, room service, laundry, baby-sitting, children's activities, pool, children's pool, aerobics, sundeck, outdoor tennis court (lit at night), water-sports equipment, table tennis, volleyball, video games, bicycle rentals, conference rooms for 30, car-rental and tour arrangements, hairdresser, and boutique.

WHERE TO DINE

Ayios Nikolaos and nearby Elounda have so many restaurants that it's hard to know where to start or stop. When deciding where to go, consider location and atmosphere; those factors have governed our recommendations below.

MODERATE

Hollands Restaurant—De Molen (The Mill). Odos Dionysos Solomos 10 (the road at the highest point above the lake). ☎ **0841/25-582.** Main courses Dr1,100–Dr3,000 ($3.70–$10); combination plates offered. EURO, V. Daily 10am–11:30pm. Closed Nov–Mar. A taxi is your only choice if you can't make it up the hill. DUTCH/INDONESIAN.

Who would go to Crete to eat Dutch cuisine? But aside from offering a new experience for your palate, this place commands the most dramatic nighttime view of Ayios Nikolaos. Specialties include pork fillet in a cream sauce. Vegetarian? Try the crepe with eggplant, mushrooms, carrots, and cabbage, tied up with leeks. We tasted something even more exotic: one of their Indonesian dishes, Nasi Goreng—a heaping plate of rice with vegetables and pork, in a satay (peanut) sauce. Somehow it seemed to go with our perch overlooking exotic Ayios Nikolaos.

La Casa. Odos 28 Octobriou 31. ☎**0841/26-362.** Main courses Dr1,300–Dr2,900 ($4.35–$10). AE, DC, DISC, EURO, JCB, MC, V. Daily 9am–midnight. No parking in immediate area. GREEK/INTERNATIONAL.

With its lakeside location, tasty menu, and friendly Greek-American proprietress, this might be many tourists' first choice in Ayios Nikolaos. Despite its address and interior rooms, most people will head straight for the tables overlooking the water. There you can enjoy any of the fine meals Marie Daskaloyiannis cooks up, including such specialties as fried rice with shrimp, lamb with artichokes, and rabbit stifado. Or try the "Greek sampling" plate for only Dr1,300 ($4.35): moussaka, dolmades, stuffed tomato, meatballs, and whatever other goodies Marie heaps on. Perhaps it's her American side, but there's always a slightly special twist to the food here.

Pelagos. Corner of Odos Koraka and Katehaki 10 (1 block up from the waterfront). ☎**0841/25-737.** Reservations recommended in high season. Main courses Dr900–Dr3,000 ($3–$10). No credit cards. Daily 11am–3pm and 7pm–midnight. Parking on adjacent streets—but all but impossible in high season. SEAFOOD.

Looking for a change from the usual touristy seafront restaurant—something a bit more cosmopolitan? Try Pelagos, in a handsome old house a block up from the bustle and hustle of the harbor. As its name suggests, it specializes in seafood, and from squid to lobster (expensive, as always in Greece), it's all done with a special flair. You can sit indoors in a subdued atmosphere or out in the secluded garden; either way you'll be served with style. This restaurant lets you get away from the crowd and share an intimate meal.

Vritomartes. Elounda (on the breakwater). ☎ **0841/41-325.** Reservations recommended for evenings in high season. Main courses Dr900–Dr3,500 ($3–$12); fish platter special Dr3,000 ($10). EURO, MC, V. Daily 10am–11pm. Closed Nov–Mar. SEAFOOD/GREEK.

This taverna, out in Elounda, involves a slight amount of effort to get to—but there are buses every hour as well as taxis for the 12-kilometer (8-mile) trip, and everyone who's come as far as Ayios Nikolaos should get out to Elounda, too. You can't beat dining at this old favorite—there's been at least a lowly taverna here long before the beautiful people discovered the area. (They're the reason you should either come early or make a reservation.) The specialty, no surprise, is the seafood. (You may find the proprietor literally "out to sea," catching that night's fish dinners.) If you settle for the red mullet and a bottle of Cretan white Xerolithia, you can't go wrong. The dining area itself is pretty plain, but this is still one dining experience you won't forget.

INEXPENSIVE

Itanos. Odos Kyprou 1 (just off Plateia Iroon, at top of Koundourou). ☎ **0841/25-340.** Reservations not accepted, so come early in high season. Main courses Dr900–Dr2,400 ($3–$8). No credit cards. Daily 10am–midnight. GREEK.

A now familiar story on Crete: A simple local taverna where you go to experience "the authentic" gets taken up by the tourists, changing the scene somewhat. But the fact is, the food and prices haven't changed *that* much. It's still standard taverna oven dishes—no-nonsense chicken, lamb, and beef in tasty sauces with hearty vegetables—and grilled meats. The house wine comes out of barrels. During the day, you sit indoors, which is characterized by no-nonsense decor and service. But at night during the hot months, tables appear on the sidewalk, a roof garden is opened up on the building across the narrow street, and your fellow tourists take over. Come here, though, if you need a break from the harbor scene and want to feel you're in a place that still exists when all the tourists go home.

SIDE TRIPS FROM AYIOS NIKOLAOS

Almost everyone who comes to Ayios Nikolaos makes the two short excursions to Spinalonga and Kritsa. Each can easily be visited in a half day.

SPINALONGA

Spinalonga is the **fortified islet** in the bay off Elounda. The Venetians built another of their fortresses there in 1579, and it enjoyed the distinction of being their final outpost on Crete, not taken over by the Turks until 1715. When the Cretans took possession in 1903, it was turned into a leper colony, but this ended after World War II, and now Spinalonga has become a major tourist attraction. In fact, there's not much to do here except walk around and soak in the atmosphere and "ghosts" of the past. Boats depart regularly from both Ayios Nikolaos harbor and Elounda as well as from certain hotels.

KRITSA

Although a walk through Spinalonga can resonate as an historical byway, if you have time to make only one of these short excursions, we advise taking the 12-kilometer (8-mile) trip up into the hills behind Ayios Nikolaos to the village of Kritsa and its 14th-century ✪ **Church of Panayia Kera.** Not only is the church of some interest architecturally, but its **frescoes,** dating from the 14th and 15th centuries, are also regarded as among the jewels of Cretan-Byzantine art. They have been restored, but the power emanates from the original work. Scenes depict the life of Jesus, the life of Mary, and the Second Coming. Guides can be arranged in Ayios Nikolaos at any travel agency or the Town Information Office. After seeing the church, go into the village of Kritsa itself and enjoy the view and the many fine handcrafted goods for sale.

The Cyclades 10

by Mark Meagher

From the summit of Mount Kinthos, the islands of the Cyclades lie close up and low to the horizon, sprawled across windswept Aegean waters to the place where the sea turns a deeper blue with distance. The landscape is bare white rock and dust, poppies grow from crevices, and the air is redolent with the aroma of wild herbs. Immediately below lie the ruins of an ancient temple city; across the bay are beaches blazing white in the sun, and somewhat further off the brilliant form of Panayia Evanyelistria, a church that draws pilgrims from all of Greece.

This low hill on the tiny isle of **Delos** is the center of the Cyclades, in more ways than one. For the ancient Greeks, this island was the still point around which the chain of islands slowly turned (*kiklos* means "circle," thus the *Kiklades* are the circling islands). Geographically too, Delos is the near center of the Cyclades, and for this reason it's a great place to get your bearings.

The islands of **Mikonos, Paros,** and **Santorini** are rightfully acclaimed for their beaches, lively nightlife, abundant shops, and fine restaurants. The culture of bars and beaches isn't foreign to the Greek character, and many of those packing the streets of Hora, Parikia, and Fira are young Greeks.

STRATEGIES FOR SEEING THE ISLANDS We recommend planning your island-hopping tour of the Cyclades so that you experience both the high-paced cosmopolitan scene and the world of the villages, which has changed little in past centuries. There's a good reason for this—strange to say, both these worlds are somehow inherently Greek. The smallest villages in Greece are often remarkably urbane, and that old man walking his donkey through cobbled streets is very likely more widely traveled than your average New York cosmopolite. Similarly, even the most touristy islands haven't yet become a parody of the island culture they've replaced, but have somehow kept enough of the old to preserve their dignity and integrity.

Although the Cyclades are bound by unmistakable family resemblance, each island is rigorously independent and unique, making this archipelago an island-hopper's paradise. Ease of travel is facilitated by the frequent ferries that traverse the narrow straits between islands with admirable reliability. Hydrofoils, on the other hand, are notoriously irregular, and service is often canceled at the whim of the meltemi winds. You should also keep in mind that service to most islands is highly seasonal, with frequency dropping off

The Cyclades

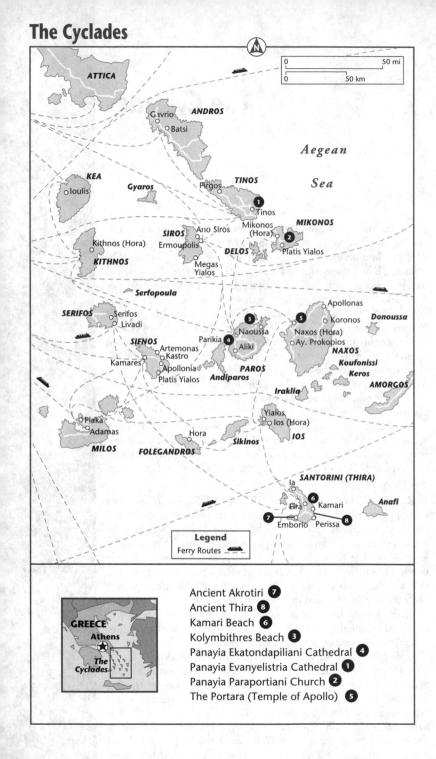

ATTICA

ANDROS

Gavrio
Batsi

Aegean

Sea

KEA
Ioulis

Gyaros

TINOS

Pirgos

Tinos 1

KITHNOS
Kithnos (Hora)

SIROS
Ano Siros
Ermoupolis

Mikonos
(Hora)

MIKONOS
2
Platis Yialos

DELOS

Megas
Yialos

Serfopoula

SERIFOS
Serifos
Livadi

Apollonas

Koronos

Donoussa

SIFNOS
Artemonas
Kastro
Apollonia
Platis Yialos
Kamares

Parikia 4

Naoussa 3
Aliki

Naxos (Hora) 5
Ay. Prokopios

NAXOS

Koufonissi

Keros

AMORGOS

PAROS

Andiparos

Iraklia

Plaka
Adamas

MILOS

Hora

FOLEGANDROS

Sikinos

Yialos
Ios (Hora)

IOS

SANTORINI (THIRA)

Ia

Fira

6 Kamari

Anafi

7

Emborio Perissa 8

Legend
Ferry Routes

GREECE
Athens
The
Cyclades

Ancient Akrotiri 7
Ancient Thira 8
Kamari Beach 6
Kolymbithres Beach 3
Panayia Ekatondapiliani Cathedral 4
Panayia Evanyelistria Cathedral 1
Panayia Paraportiani Church 2
The Portara (Temple of Apollo) 5

significantly between October and April. Between May and September, you can go just about anywhere you want, whenever you want, although winds can sometimes upset the most carefully arranged plans.

1 Santorini (Thira)

233km (126 nautical miles) SE of Piraeus

Santorini is that rare thing, a place where legend is matched by reality. One of the most spectacular islands in the world, Santorini's cliff-faced crescent isle graces tourist brochures and posters in Greek restaurants the world over. The real wonder is that the place itself meets and exceeds all glossy picture-postcard expectations. Like an enormous mandible, Santorini encloses the pure blue waters of its caldera, the core of an ancient volcano. Its two principal towns, **Fira** and **Ia,** perch at the summit of the caldera, their whitewashed houses resembling from an approaching ship a dusting of new snow on the mountaintop.

The eruption that blew out the center of this once circular island some 3,600 years ago buried the cosmopolitan city of **Akrotiri** under tons of ash, and sent tidal waves that may have inundated the Minoan cities of Crete and very nearly destroyed its civilization. Was Akrotiri the origin of the Atlantis legend? Don't miss the opportunity to visit the extensive excavations of this vast ancient city, and decide for yourself.

Ancient Thira is another of Santorini's archaeological wonders, spectacularly situated atop a high promontory. There is a paved road to the site, but the steep hike up from Kamari is abundantly rewarding. Arid Santorini isn't known for its agriculture, but the rocky island soil has long produced a plentiful grape harvest, and the local wines are among the finest in Greece; be sure to visit one of the island wineries for a tasting. Among the many other obligatory Santorini experiences are the **Ia sunset** (best seen from the ramparts of Lontza Castle or the footpath between Fira and Ia) and the **volta (stroll) in Fira,** whose nighttime streets seem steeped in the caldera's sublime stillness.

The best advice we can offer is to visit some time other than July or August. Santorini experiences an even greater transformation during the peak season than other Cycladic isles. With visitors far in the excess of the island's small capacity, trash collects in the squares and crowds make movement through the streets of Fira and Ia next to impossible. Accommodation rates will also be as much as 50% less if you can travel in May, June, or September.

ESSENTIALS

GETTING THERE   By Plane   Olympic Airways has daily flights (several daily in July and Aug) between Athens and the Santorini airport at Monolithos (which also receives European charters). There is also daily connection with Mikonos, service three or four times a week to and from Rhodes, and service two or three times a week with Iraklion, Crete. For schedule information and reservations, check with the Olympic Airways office in Fira on Odos Ayiou Athanassiou (☎ **0286/22-493**), just southeast of town on the road to Kamari, or in Athens at ☎ **01/966-6666.** There's no public transport between the airport and Fira, so a taxi is the only option.

By Ferry   There is ferry service to and from Piraeus at least twice daily; the trip takes 10 to 12 hours, but it's relaxing and a good opportunity to see most of the Cyclades. Ferries connect several times a day with **Ios, Mikonos, Naxos,** and **Paros;** once daily with **Anafi** and **Siros;** and five or six times a week with **Folegandros** and **Sikinos.** Service to **Thessaloniki** is four to five times per week, and to **Skiathos** (Sporades) two to three times per week. There is almost daily connection by excursion boat with **Irak-**

lion in Crete, but because this is an open sea route, the trip can be an ordeal in bad weather. Check schedules with **Tourist Information in Athens** (☎ 01/171), the **Port Authority in Piraeus** (☎ 01/451-1310), or the **Port Authority in Santorini** (☎ 0286/22-239).

Almost all ferries now dock at **Athinios,** where buses meet each boat, returning directly to the Fira station (the fare to Fira is Dr450/$1.50). From the Fira station, buses depart for numerous other island destinations. Taxis are also available from Athinios, at nearly 10 times the bus fare. Most ferry tickets can be purchased at **Nomikos Travel** (☎ 0286/23-660), with offices in Fira, Karterados, and Perissa. The exposed port at **Skala,** directly below Fira, is unsafe for the larger ferries, but is often used by cruise ships, yachts, and excursion vessels. If your boat docks at Skala you can choose between the cable car (Dr800/$2.70), a mule or donkey ride (Dr900/$3), and a tough 45-minute uphill walk (be prepared to share the narrow path with the mules). We recommend a mule up and the cable car down.

VISITOR INFORMATION   Among the many travel agencies here, we recommend **Kamari Tours** (☎ 0286/22-666; fax 0286/22-971; e-mail: kamaritours@santonet.gr), 2 blocks south of the main square on the right, which offers day excursions by boat or bus to most of the island's sites and can help you find a room or rent a car; open daily from 8am to 11pm in summer. **Dakoutros Travel** (☎ 0286/22-958; fax 0286/ 22-686), just down the hill from the Pelican Hotel, offers a full range of guided tours; open daily from 9am to 9pm.

GETTING AROUND   By Bus   Santorini has reliable and frequent bus service, a rarity in the Cyclades. The island's **central bus station** is just south of the main square in Fira; all routes branch out radially from this point. Schedules are posted here: most routes are serviced every half hour from 7am to 11pm between June and August; at other times of the year, the frequency drops to every 2 to 3 hours on most routes. (Jot down the return times from your destination, as they will probably not be displayed there.) Destinations are displayed on the front of the bus, and fares are collected by a conductor after the bus is underway. Fares range from Dr450 to Dr900 ($1.50 to $3). Destinations include **Akrotiri, Athinios** (the ferry pier), **Ia, Kamari, Monolithos, Perissa,** and **Vourvoulos.** Excursion buses travel to all the island's major attractions; inquire with a travel agent for schedules and prices.

By Car   Most travel agents will be able to help you rent a car. Of the car-rental agencies in Fira, we recommend **Budget** (☎ 0286/22-900; fax 0286/22-887), a block below the bus-stop square in Fira, where an economy car should cost about Dr19,000 ($63) a day with insurance and unlimited mileage. In Ia you can rent a car at **Vazeos Car Rental** (☎ 0286/71-200), where the rates are somewhat lower.

By Moped   Roads on the island are notoriously treacherous, narrow, and winding, with shoulders that give way easily on steep slopes. There are a number of serious accidents and several fatalities every year. Nevertheless, you won't have any trouble finding a moped to rent (assuming that you can show a valid motorcycle license); expect to pay Dr3,000 to Dr6,000 ($10 to $20) per day.

By Taxi   The **taxi stand** (☎ 0286/22-555) is just south of the main square, though in the high season you should book ahead by phone. The drivers are better organized here than elsewhere in the Cyclades, and prices are standard from point to point. If you call for a taxi outside Fira, you'll be required to pay a pickup fee of Dr500 ($1.70).

FAST FACTS   The **American Express** agent is X-Ray Kilo Travel Service, at the head of the steps to the old port facing the caldera, opposite the Tropical Bar and above Franco's Bar (☎ 0286/22-624; fax 0286/23-600); open daily from 8:30am to

9pm. The **National Bank** (open Mon through Fri from 8am to 2pm), with an ATM, is a block south from the main square on the right near the taxi station. Many travel agents also change money; most are open daily from 8am to 9:30pm. The **health clinic** (☎ 0286/23-123) is on the southeast edge of town on Odos Ayiou Athanassiou, to the left after the children's playground. The local **Internet center** is P.C. Club, on the main square in Fira, above Markozannes Tours (☎ 0286/24-600). Transmission is very slow—count on spending up to an hour to retrieve your e-mail, and forget about browsing the Web. Open Monday through Saturday from 9am to 2pm and 5 to 9pm; the rate is Dr1,500 ($5) per hour. You can drop off **laundry** at the Pelican Hotel, just below the main square in Fira, or go to the self-service laundry at the edge of Fira on the road to Ia, north of the main square. The **police station** (☎ 0286/22-649) is several blocks south of the main square, near the post office. The **port police** can be reached at ☎ 0286/22-239. The **post office** (☎ 0286/22-238), open Monday through Friday from 8am to 1pm, is up to the right from the bus station. The **telephone office (OTE)** is just off Odos Ipapantis, up from the post office; open Monday through Saturday from 8am to 3pm.

THE TOP ATTRACTIONS

✪ **Ancient Akrotiri.** Akrotiri. ☎ **0286/81-366.** Admission Dr1,200 ($4) adults, Dr600 ($2) students. Tues–Sun 8:30am–3pm.

Since the beginning of excavations in 1967, this site has provided the world with a fascinating look at urban life in the Minoan period. This city, whose elaborate

---

Insider Tip

Akrotiri is enclosed by a massive metal shed that magnifies the afternoon heat. This, combined with the growing crowds, is a good argument for arriving as early as possible.

---

architecture and vivid frescoes demonstrate a high level of culture, was frozen in time 3,600 years ago by a cataclysmic eruption of the island's volcano. Many of the implements and artifacts can be seen on site, as their owners left them before abandoning the town (the absence of human remains indicates that the residents had ample warning of the town's destruction). You enter the Akrotiri site along the ancient town's main street, and on either side are the stores or warehouses of the ancient commercial city: numerous large earthen jars, or *pithi*, were found here, some with traces of olive oil, fish, and onion inside. You can get the best sense for the scale and urban nature of this town in the triangular plaza, near the exit, where buildings rise to two stories and create a spacious gathering place. There are descriptive plaques in four languages at various points along your path through the town, but unfortunately only a few poor reproductions of the magificent frescoes found here and since moved to the Archaeological Museum in Athens. These frescoes are an essential companion to any tour of this site—they depict the town's inhabitants in moments both mundane and immemorial, giving life to what could otherwise be yet another dusty archaeological site. We recommend either a tour or the purchase of a guidebook with color reproductions of the frescoes, available at the ticket booth.

✪ **Ancient Thira.** Kamari, 84700 Santorini. ☎ **0286/31-366.** Admission Dr1,200 ($4) adults, Dr600 ($2) students. Daily 8am–2:30pm. On a hilltop 3km (1.8 miles) south of Kamari by road.

The two popular beaches of Kamari and Perissa are separated by a high rocky headland called Mesa Vouna, on which stand the ruins of Ancient Thira. It's an incredible site, with cliffs dropping precipitously to the sea on three sides and dramatic views of Santorini and neighboring islands. The hilltop was first inhabited by the Dorians in the 9th century B.C., though most buildings date from the Hellenistic era when the site was occupied by Ptolemaic forces; there are also Roman and Byzantine remains. One main street runs the length of the site, passing first through two agoras. The arc of the theater embraces the town of Kamari, Fira beyond, and the open Aegean. It's an extensive group of ruins, and like all ruins it requires some imagination to bring it to life; in fact, a good tour guide wouldn't hurt. Tours leave from Kamari every hour in the peak season, for Dr2,000 ($7) per person; contact **Kamari Tours** (☎ **0286/ 31-390**) for information. You can reach the site by taxi, or even better, on foot— passing on the way a cave that holds the only spring on the island (see "Walking" under "Outdoor Pursuits," below).

Boutari Winery. Megalohori. ☎ **0286/81-011.** Admission Dr1,500 ($5). Daily 9am–sunset. Located 1½ km (0.9 mile) south of Akrotiri village. Just outside Megalohori, on the main road to Perissa.

Boutari is the island's largest winery, and Greece's best known wine export. The admission cost includes a tasting of six wines, with mezedes or light snacks. There are three grape varieties grown on Santorini: Asirtiko, Aidani, and Athiri. From these are made the three whites for which the island is known: Nichteri, with its high alcohol content; Kalliste, a wine aged in smoked oak barrels; and Vin Santo, a sweet dessert wine traditionally used for communion in the local churches. Rounding out the tasting are reds and whites from Northern Greece.

EXPLORING THE ISLAND
FIRA

Fira, the island's capital, is also its busiest and most commercial town. The abundance of **jewelry stores** on these streets is matched in the Cyclades only by Mikonos, as are the crowds in July and August. The town has a spectacular location on the rim of the caldera, a fact you can quickly verify by walking uphill from the main square. Odos M. Nomikou follows the edge of the caldera, and the evening volta (stroll) along this street is one of the most exquisite in the Cyclades—the chanted tones of evening prayer resound from the Orthodox Cathedral, and the streets are corridors of light and sound within the silent expanse of the dark sea. The town supports a wild bar scene that continues throughout the night, banishing all thought or hope of sleep in peak season.

At the north end of Odos Ipapantis (also known as "Gold Street" for its abundant jewelry stores), you'll find the **cable-car station.** The Austrian-built system, the gift of wealthy shipowner Evangelos Nomikos, can take you down to the port of Skala in 2 minutes. The cable car makes the trip every 15 minutes from 6:45am to 8:15pm for Dr800 ($2.70), and it's worth every cent, especially on the way up.

Up and to the right from the cable-car station is the small **Archaeological Museum** (☎ **0286/22-217**), which has some early Cycladic figurines, vases from Ancient Thira, some interesting Dionysiac figures, and finds from Akrotiri. It's open Tuesday through Sunday from 8:30am to 3pm. Admission is Dr800 ($2.70) for adults, Dr600 ($2) for seniors, and Dr400 ($1.35) for students. A new archaeological museum is being built next to the post office, below the bus stop, and may be completed as early as summer of 1999.

IA

Ia is the most beautiful and pleasantly unconventional village on the island, if not in the whole Cyclades. It was severely damaged by the 1956 earthquake, and there aren't many buildings remaining from before that time. A few notable exceptions are the fine **19th-century mansions** at the top of the town near the castle—one example is the building housing the **Restaurant-Bar 1800.** Much of the reconstruction continues the ancient Santorini tradition of dwellings excavated from the cliff face, and many of the island's most beautiful cliff dwellings can be found here. There are basically only two streets, the one with traffic and the much more pleasant inland pedestrian lane, Odos Nikolaos Nomikou (the other end of the Nomikos street that began in Fira), paved with marble and lined with an increasing number of jewelry shops (as if there weren't enough in Fira), tavernas, and bars. The battlements of the ruined **Lontza Castle** at the western end of town is the best place to catch the famous Ia sunset. Below the castle, a long flight of steps leads down to the pebble beach at **Ammoudi,** which is okay for swimming and sunning. To the west is the more spacious and sandy **Kolumbus Beach.** To the southeast below Ia is the fishing port of **Armeni,** where ferries sometimes dock and you can catch an excursion boat around the caldera.

One thing English-speaking foreigners can do in Ia more easily than just about anywhere in Greece is **get married.** Markos Karvounis, of **Karvounis Tours** (☎ **0286/71-290** or 0286/71-209; fax 0286/71-291) has proven himself as good at arranging weddings (not marriages) as he is at making travel and accommodations arrangements. Visit his office on the marble pedestrian street to change money, make

Fira

Legend

- **†** Church
- **✚** Clinic
- **C** OTE
- **⊠** Post Office
- **P** Parking
- **▥** Steps

ACCOMMODATIONS

- Hotel Aressana **13**
- Hotel Kavalari **7**
- Hotel Keti **8**
- Hotel Tataki **4**
- Loucas Hotel **2**
- Pension Blue Sky **6**

DINING

- Barbara's Café-Brasserie **9**
- Crêperis House **5**
- Meridiana Restaurant Bar **10**
- Naoussa Restaurant **1**
- Selene **12**
- Sphinx Restaurant **11**
- Taverna Nikolas **3**

To Karterados,
Kamari & Perissa →

New Archaeological Museum

Mitropoleos

Orthodox Cathedral

Bus Station

Ipapantis

Main Square (Plateia Theotokopoulou)

25 Martiou

Port Police

Ayiou Athanassiou

← To Ia

Ipapantis

Nomikos

Archaeological Museum

Catholic Cathedral

Cable-Car Station

Ayiou Ioannou

Walking Path to Imerovigli & Ia ↙

Walking Path to Fira Skala ↙

CLIFFS

a long-distance call, rent a villa or room, book island day trips, or purchase ferry and plane tickets. You can also call if you have questions, from 10am to 2pm and 6:30 to 10pm, his time, from April through October.

THE VILLAGES

At the south end of the island, on the road to Perissa, is the handsome old village of **Emborio.** Life here moves at a much slower pace than elsewhere on the island, and traditions have been maintained that were long ago abandoned in the commercial centers of Fira and Ia. In the 17th century the town was fortified, and you can still see the towers of this fortified village as well as modern-day homes built into the ruins of the citadel.

Pirgos, a village on a steep hill just above the island's port at Athinios, is a maze of narrow pathways, steps, chapels, and squares. Near the summit of the village is the crumbling Venetian Kastro, plus several public squares with excellent views of the surrounding countryside. There is a merciful absence of tourism, and the central square, just off the main road, has the only shops and cafes in town. **Pirgos Taverna** (☎ 0286/31-346), at the entrance to town, is known as a good place for traditional Greek food and music.

THE CALDERA ISLETS

Thirassia is a small inhabited island west across the caldera from Santorini, originally part of the same circular island. A clifftop village of the same name faces the caldera, and is still a quiet retreat from Santorini's summer crowds. The village is reached from the caldera side by a long flight of steep steps, as Fira and Ia were originally. **Full-day boat excursions** departing daily from the port of Fira (accessible by cable car, donkey, or on foot) make a brief stop at Thirassia, just long enough to have a quick lunch in the village; the cost of the excursion (which also includes Nea Kameni, Palea Kameni, and Ia) is about Dr5,000 ($17) per person. Another alternative is **local caïques,** which sometimes make the trip from Armeni, the port of Ia. The local ferry is impractical, because it only visits Thirassia once a week.

The two smoldering dark islands in the middle of the caldera are **Palea Kameni** ("Old Burnt"), the smaller and more distant one, which appeared in A.D. 157; and **Nea Kameni** ("New Burnt"), which began its appearance sometime in the early 18th century. There are many more interesting places to visit, but unfortunately the day excursion to Thirassia (a far more exciting destination) happens to include these litter-strewn volcanic isles.

OUTDOOR PURSUITS

BEACHES Santorini's beaches aren't exceptional. The island's black sand isn't particularly plentiful, and quickly heats up in the afternoon sun. Still, there are a few places to catch those rays.

Kamari, a little over halfway down the east coast, has the best beach on the island. It's also the most developed, lined by hotels, restaurants, shops, and clubs. The black pebbled beach does tend to get overcrowded, but it's preferable to the scruffier beach at **Perissa,** to the south.

There are small beaches all along the east coast of the island, though none of them is anything to rave about, including **Paradise** and **Kolumbus** near the north end. **Monolithos,** near the end of the road to the airport, has a small beach and a couple of tavernas. The **Red Beach,** or Paralia Kokkini, at the end of the road to Ancient Akrotiri, has space on its cobbles for a few tanning bodies. There's also a fine taverna on the beach: **Melina's** (☎ 0286/82-764), open from 9am to 11pm.

BICYCLING Santorini's roads are in fairly good condition, and although the island's topography is notoriously extreme, the roads have gentler slopes than you'd expect. Mountain bikes can be rented at **Moto Chris** (☎ 0286/23-431) in Fira for Dr2,000 ($7) a day; the day's rental is from 8am to 9pm. In Ia you can rent a mountain bike at **Moto Piazza** (☎ 0286/71-055), on the main road about a mile outside the town; the rates are the same as Moto Chris, but here you can rent for a full day. At both places, the bikes are in sorry shape and receive almost no maintenance.

WALKING The path from **Fira to Ia** follows the edge of the caldera, passing several churches and climbing two substantial hills along the way. Beginning from Fira, follow the pedestrian path on the caldera rim, climbing past the Catholic Cathedral to the villages of Firostephani and Imerovigli. In Imerovigli there are some signs on the footpath pointing the way to Ia—you'll be okay so long as you continue north, eventually reaching a dirt path along the caldera rim which parallels the vehicular road in its descent from Ia. The trail leaves the vicinity of the road with each of the next two ascents, returning to the road in the valleys. The descent into Ia eventually leads you to the main pedestrian street in town. The distance is 10 kilometers (6.2 miles); allow yourself 2 hours for the walk. The walk is especially beautiful around sunset.

In **Imerovigli** there is a rocky promontory jutting into the sea, known locally as **Skaros.** In the last century this was the site of an elaborate building complex which housed all the administrative offices of the island; these all collapsed into the sea during the 1956 earthquake. Skaros now offers a fantastic view of the caldera, and a tranquil haven from the crowds and bustle of the adjacent towns. The trail begins from the terrace of a church just below the Blue Note Taverna. From here it descends steeply to the isthmus connecting Skaros with the mainland. The path wraps around the promontory, reaching after a mile a small chapel with a unique panoramic view of the caldera. On the way, note the cliffs of glassy black obsidian, beautifully reflective in the brilliant sun—this is the material with which so many of the older buildings on Santorini were built and decorated.

The trail from Kamari to the site of **Ancient Thira** is quite steep but worth the trouble, since it passes the beautiful site of the island's only freshwater spring. To reach the trail from Kamari, follow the car road to Ancient Thira, turning right into the drive of a group of new villas at the base of the climb, opposite the Hotel Annetta. The trail begins just behind these villas; the trailhead may be partially obscured in coming years by this new construction. Climbing quickly by means of sharp switchbacks, the trail soon reaches a small chapel with a terrace and olive trees at the mouth of a cave. You can walk back into the cave, which echoes with the purling water, a surprising and miraculous sound in this arid place. Continuing up, the trail rejoins the car road after a few more switchbacks, about 500 meters from Ancient Thira. The full ascent from Kamari takes about an hour.

SHOPPING

In the summer months, Fira never sleeps, and most stores remain open until midnight or later. Ia's shopping day is almost as long. In the towns with little tourism, like Pirgos and Emporio, many stores close at 5 or 6pm.

If you're interested in fine **jewelry,** the prices in Fira are just a little higher than they are in Athens, but the selection is fantastic. **Porphyra** (☎ 0286/22-981), in the Fabrica Shopping Center near the cathedral, has some impressive work. Santorini's best known jeweler is probably **Kostas Antoniou** (☎ 0286/22-633), on Odos Ayiou Ioannou, north of the cable-car station. And there are plenty of shops between the two. Generally the further north you go, the higher the prices, the less certain the quality, and the greater the pressure to buy.

In Firostephani, **Cava Sigalas Argiris** (☎ 0286/22-802) stocks all the local wines, including their own. They also sell several locally grown and prepared foods, often served as mezedes, or snacks: *fava*, a spread made with chickpeas; *tomatahia*, small pickled tomatoes; and *kapari*, or capers. The store is open from 8am to midnight.

The main street in Ia, facing the caldera, has many quirky and interesting stores in addition to the inevitable proliferation of souvenir shops. **Replica** (☎ 0286/71-916) is a source for contemporary statuary and pottery as well as museum replicas; they will ship purchases to your home at Greek post-office rates. Further south on the main street is **Nakis** (☎ 0286/71-813), specializing in amber jewelry; they also have a collection of insects in amber. Ia doesn't rival Fira's gold trade, but it does have enough gold merchants to keep the streets glittering.

WHERE TO STAY

Santorini is packed in July and August; try to make a reservation with a deposit at least 2 months in advance or be prepared to accept pot luck. Don't accept rooms offered at the port unless you're exhausted and don't care how meager the room and how remote the village you wake up in the next morning.

The barrel-vaulted **cave houses,** built for earthquake resistance and economy, may at first strike you as rather cramped, dark, and stuffy, but like most visitors you'll probably soon find them another part of the island's special charm. The best of them are designed with enough cross-ventilation that they always have fresh air, and since they are carved into the cliff face, these rooms have the welcome quality of remaining cool throughout the summer.

Many apartments and villas have efficiency kitchens, but for the most part these are extremely minimal facilities—a minifridge, hotplate, and a few utensils. You'll probably find yourself frustrated if you try to prepare anything much more elaborate than a coffee.

Unless otherwise noted, the hotels listed remain open from about mid-April to mid-October.

FIRA

Due to the noise in Fira, light sleepers may want to consider one of the more remote possibilities.

In addition to the choices below, you might consider **Pension Blue Sky** (☎ 0286/ 24-351 or 0286/25-121; fax 0286/25-120), a humble but comfortable place on the edge of town.

Hotel Aressana. Fira, 84700 Santorini. ☎ **0286/23-900.** Fax 0286/23-902. www.santonet.gr/hotels/aressana. E-mail: aressana@santonet.gr. 48 units. A/C TEL. Dr40,000 ($133) double; from Dr50,000 ($167) suite. Rates include breakfast. AE, DC, MC, V.

This newer hotel has just about everything you could ask for except a caldera view—though it's only a block away, just beyond the Orthodox Cathedral, across a small plaza from the Atlantis Hotel. The rooms are large, attractively furnished, and very comfortable, with a small balcony or shared terrace; some have the high, barrel-vaulted ceiling typical of this island. The suites have spacious private balconies, a benefit that simply isn't offered on the caldera side of town, where space is so precious. The breakfast room opens onto the large pool terrace, as do most of the rooms. The Aressana also maintains seven nearby apartments facing the caldera, beginning at Dr33,000 ($110) for a two-person unit, which includes use of the hotel pool.

Hotel Kavalari. P.O. Box 17, Fira, 84700 Santorini. ☎ **0286/222-347** or 0286/22-603. Fax 0286/22-603. 18 units. TEL. From Dr32,000 ($107) double; from Dr47,000 ($157) triple. AE, MC, V.

This excellent hotel just below Odos Ipapantis has traditionally styled accommodations. Each room faces the caldera and is unique, comfortably furnished, and colorfully decorated. There are shared patios for enjoying the view. Some rooms have kitchenettes and cost a bit more.

Hotel Keti. Fira, 84700 Santorini. ☎ **0286/22-324** or 0286/22-380. 7 units. TEL. Dr14,000 ($47) double; 18,000 ($60) triple. No credit cards.

This tiny hotel is very plain, but does offer one of the best bargains on the caldera. All rooms have traditional vaulted ceilings and open onto shared terraces overlooking the extraordinary beauty of the Santorini caldera; bathrooms are at the back of the rooms, carved into the rock of the cliff face. The furnishings are plain, even a bit flimsy; rooms are small and clean. This place offers an experience more authentic than that of the slick hotels that surround it: laundry hangs on the terrace, local children play on the stairs, and the proprietress speaks only a few words of English.

Hotel Tataki. Fira, 84700 Santorini. ☎ **0286/22-389.** 10 units. Dr18,000 ($60) double. No credit cards.

This simple hotel is built above the home of an older couple. They maintain their small, plain rooms well, and though short on English offer a friendly welcome to guests. All rooms are situated around a courtyard; two shared terraces have views across the roofs of Fira to the distant sea. It's a good value for the central location, just off the main square on the lane behind Pelican Travel.

✪ Loucas Hotel. Fira, 84700 Santorini. ☎ **0286/22-480** or 0286/22-680. Fax 0286/24-882. 22 units. A/C TV TEL. Dr32,300 ($108) double; Dr40,800 ($136) triple. Rates include breakfast. MC, V.

This is one of the oldest and best hotels on the caldera. Its terraces cascade down the side of the cliff, connected by a giddily steep flight of steps—definitely not for the acrophobic, or those who have a hard time negotiating stairs. The impeccably maintained rooms have barrel-vaulted ceilings, and the bathrooms are often carved into the rock of the cliff wall. They're furnished with handsome blue furniture, and although the terraces overlooking the caldera are often shared between rooms, thoughtful design provides a surprising degree of privacy. The Renaissance Bar is situated on a broad terrace above the rooms, and the unexceptional Aris Restaurant is immediately below.

FIROSTEPHANI

This quieter and less-expensive neighborhood is just a 10-minute walk from Fira. The views of the caldera are just as good, if not better.

Dana Villas. Firostephani, 84700 Santorini. ☎ **0286/24-641** or 0286/24-643. Fax 0286/22-985. 30 units. A/C TV TEL. Dr43,600 ($145) double; Dr46,600 ($155) apt; Dr54,600 ($182) suite; Dr76,600 ($255) VIP suite. AE, DC, MC, V.

These meticulously maintained terrace villas cling to the cliff face, perched vertiginously over the sea. They stand out from most of the villas on the caldera by virtue of their simple and tasteful furnishings and thoughtful design: each villa has a small terrace, and more than a few (highly coveted) villas have private terraces. Most are one room (studios), while a few have a separate bedroom or a loft (apartments). The suites have two bedrooms, and can sleep four adults comfortably; VIP suites come with a few added amenities that don't seem to justify the higher price. All villas have the same minimal kitchen. The pool is quite large by local standards, and there's a poolside bar. Villa nos. 20 and 22 are the studios to reserve well in advance, while no. 21 is the best apartment (all have private terraces).

IMEROVIGLI

The next village north along the caldera rim is so named because it is the first place on the island from which one can see the rising sun: the name translates to "day vigil." By virtue of its height, Imerovigli also has the best views on this part of the caldera.

Altana Traditional Houses. Imerovigli, 84700 Santorini. ☎ **0286/23-240.** Fax 0286/ 23-204. In winter, call Athens: ☎ 01/277-4374; fax 01/275-4636. 10 units. TEL. Dr43,000– Dr48,000 ($143–$160) studio; Dr58,000 ($193) 1-bedroom; Dr68,000 ($227) 2-bedroom. AE, MC, V.

These traditional cave houses are located high on the cliff in Imerovigli, and have great views across the roofs of the town toward Fira and the waters of the caldera. Each apartment is unique, with furniture built into the walls of the cave and simple, tasteful pieces. All have incredible views, although the terrace for each apartment is either shared or serves as the path to another apartment as well. Units are on three levels; the apartments on the top level have the most privacy and the best views. On the street level is a cozy, bright breakfast room with terrace, which serves as a bar in the evening. Bathrooms are a bit cramped. Although these apartments have a simple elegance that's very appealing, they are somewhat overpriced.

✪ **Astra Apartments.** Post Office Box 45, Imerovigli, 84700 Santorini. ☎ **0286/ 23-641.** Fax 0286/24-765. 18 units, all with shower only. A/C MINIBAR TV TEL. Dr36,000–Dr43,500 ($120–$145) studio; Dr75,000–Dr90,000 ($250–$300) 2-bedroom. Rates include breakfast. AE, V. Closed from about Nov 15 to Mar 20.

This is one of the nicest places to stay in all of Greece. The 18 units of the Astra Apartments look like a tiny, whitewashed village (flanking an elegant small pool) in still-sleepy Imerovigli. Every detail here is perfect: the floors are paved with handsome flagstones, the windows hung with hand-embroidered curtains, the bath towels luxuriously thick. The apartments are decorated in rich earth tones and deep Aegean blue. Best of all, although each unit has its own kitchenette, breakfast is served on your private terrace or balcony, and you can order delicious salads and sandwiches from the bar day and night. Manager George Karayiannis is always at the ready to arrange car rentals, recommend a wonderful beach or restaurant—or even help you plan your wedding and honeymoon here. Our only problem when we stayed here: We didn't want to budge from our terrace, especially at sunset, when the view over the offshore islands is dazzling.

KARTERADOS

Just 2 kilometers (1.2 miles) southeast of Fira, this attractive whitewashed traditional village offers a more sedate setting, if not the views. The island buses stop at the top of Karterados's main street on their way to Kamari, Perissa, and Akrotiri. Karterados also has its own small beach, a 3-kilometer (2-mile) walk from the center of town; the longer beach of Monolithos is accessible by continuing south along the water's edge another half mile.

Pension George. Karterados, Santorini. ☎ **0286/22-251.** Fax 0286/22-351. 10 units. Dr14,000 ($47) double; Dr19,000 ($63) triple. No credit cards.

The pension is surrounded by new homes, and the views aren't great—what is exceptional here is the generosity and genuine kindness of George Halaris and his English wife, Helen, who are both great sources of information on the island. George will meet you at the port or the airport if given advance notice. The 10 guest rooms are located on the upper two stories of their house; all are simply and comfortably furnished, all have small fridges, and six units are equipped with air-conditioning. Most rooms have a small balcony, and the two rooms at the north side of the house have large private terraces with an abundance of luxuriant plants.

IA

Ia is quieter and somewhat less crowded than Fira, but also less convenient as a base if you're getting around the island by bus. Accommodation rates tend to be higher here than anywhere else on the island.

Canaves Ia Traditional Houses. Ia, 84702 Santorini. ☎ **0286/71-453.** Fax 0286/71-195. 15 units. A/C TEL. Dr72,000 ($240) double; Dr95,000 ($317) 2-bedroom suite. MC, V.

These houses are fashioned in traditional island style, with vaulted ceilings and curvaceous walls; the two-bedroom apartments are especially spacious and sumptuous. All apartments have views of the caldera, and some also have private terraces. There are two complexes within 200 meters of each other, each with a swimming pool and bar. There is private parking within a short distance of the apartments. Other amenities include safe-deposit boxes in each apartment, room service, and fully equipped kitchens, which even have small ovens.

✪ **Chelidonia.** Ia, 84702 Santorini. ☎ **0286/71-287.** Fax 0286/71-649. www.chelidonia.com. 10 units. Weekly rates: Dr189,000 ($630) studio; Dr231,000 ($770) 1-bedroom; Dr283,500 ($945) 2-bedroom; daily rates also available—call for information. No credit cards.

There are many thoughtful details that combine to make these the most appealing traditional apartments in Santorini. Most apartments have truly private terraces, and in one instance two. The rooms are spacious and the bathrooms luxuriously large. Every apartment has a kitchenette, and most have small gardens on the terrace with flowering plants and herbs for cooking. The interiors are simple and highly elegant: slabs of white marble combine with extensions of the walls to form tables and shelves, and the beds are enclosed by a low arch. These are all cave dwellings, and each has its own unique geometry, some with skylights like bulbous tubes of light illuminating rooms from above. Each apartment has the best of the famous Ia view across the caldera toward Imerovigli, Fira, and the southern end of the island. Although there is little luxury here, there is clearly a great understanding of what makes guests feel at home—an amenity that is extremely rare.

Hotel Finikia. Finikia, 84702 Santorini. ☎ **0286/71-373;** winter ☎ 01/654-7944. Fax 0286/71-118. 15 units. Dr18,500 ($62) double; Dr22,000 ($73) suite (sleeps up to 3 persons). Rates include breakfast. MC, V.

About 1.5 kilometers (1 mile) south of the bus stop in Ia on the main road, you'll find this small, appealing hotel. Rooms are sparsely and tastefully furnished, and several have the traditional domed ceiling. Most rooms have semiprivate balconies or terraces with views toward the water—the hotel is on the gentle east sloping side of the island, so the view isn't spectacular. There's a large pool and a restaurant/bar that remains open all day. Irene and Thodoris Andreadis are your very helpful and friendly hosts.

Perivolas Traditional Settlement. Ia, 84702 Santorini. ☎ **0286/71-308.** Fax 0286/71-309. 16 units. TEL. Dr84,000 ($280) studio; Dr96,000 ($320) 1-bedroom suite. Rates include breakfast. No credit cards.

The interiors of these traditional cave dwellings are highly refined, with wall niches, skylights, and stonework providing a very personal touch. Some of the suites are quite spacious, with a separate bedroom and sunken living room with fireplace; the design and layout of each apartment is unique. All apartments have kitchenettes. A bar opens onto a terrace and incredible pool—the edge of which disappears into the bay, its horizon merging with the horizon of the sea below. A buffet breakfast is served in the bar. The only downside here is that just a couple of the units have terraces with any degree of privacy.

Villa Ritsa. Ia, 84702 Santorini. ☎ and fax **0286/71-055.** 15 units. Dr10,000 ($33) double; Dr12,000 ($40) triple. No credit cards.

The rooms here are spare but comfortable, the best budget option in this pricey town. All rooms have a fridge, and several have balconies with views of the Aegean—not the jaw-dropping caldera view, but the gentler, more pastoral view of the island's east side. Nine of the units benefit from a good location just off the main pedestrian street in the center of town; the others are 200 meters away in an annex on the automobile road. The helpful proprietor is Dimitrios Vazeos, who also operates **Moto Piazza,** a moped- and bicycle-rental outfit in Ia.

MEGALOHORI

One of the island's most charming villages has Santorini's finest hotel.

✪ **Vedema Hotel.** Megalohori, 84700 Santorini. ☎ **0286/81-796** or 0286/81-797. In the U.S. and Canada 800/525-4800; in Australia 008-251-958; in Great Britain 0800-964-470. Fax 0286/81-798. 42 units. A/C MINIBAR TV TEL. Dr75,000–Dr95,000 ($250–$317) 1-bedroom apt; Dr106,000–Dr135,000 ($353–$450) 2-bedroom apt; Dr170,000 ($567) 3-bedroom apt. Minimum 3-night stay. AE, DC, EURO, MC, V.

This member of "Small Luxury Hotels of the World" is justly proud of its attentive but unobtrusive service. The residences are set around several irregular courtyards much like those found in the village itself. Each apartment is unique, comfortable, and tastefully furnished; they have separate living rooms, marble bathrooms, central heat, refrigerators and bars, and twice-daily maid service. The complex has a swimming pool with a bar, the medieval chic **Vedema restaurant** with fine Mediterranean cuisine, the charming **Canava Bar** in a 300-year-old wine cellar, a souvenir and sundry shop, in-house laundry service, and an interesting art gallery with a new exhibition each month. The only false note is the poor acoustics in the conference hall.

KAMARI

Most of the hotels at Santorini's best and best-known resort are booked by tour groups in the summer. In addition to the following choices, you might also try the 27-unit **Matina Hotel** (☎ **0286/31-491**; fax 0286/31-860), which has no views to speak of but is just a 2-minute walk from the beach; a double here goes for Dr24,000 ($80). If you can't find a room, try the local office of **Kamari Tours** (☎ **0286/31-390** or 0286/31-455), which may be able to find you a vacancy.

Kamari Beach Hotel. Kamari, 84700 Santorini. ☎ **0286/31-216** or 0286/31-243, or 01/482-8826 in Athens. Fax 0286/31-243. 92 units. Dr32,000 ($107) double. Rates include breakfast. AE, DC, MC, V.

This superior hotel has the best beachfront location, close by the small village. All of its spacious balconied rooms take advantage of the view over the Aegean and the lovely pool below. It looks like a resort, and it's run like one, too.

Rooms Hesperides. Kamari, 84700 Santorini. ☎ **0286/31-670.** Fax 0286/31-423. 21 units. TEL. Dr15,000 ($50) double. Rates include breakfast. AE, MC, V.

This neat, modern pension in the middle of the pistachio orchard is owned by the same man who runs the Akis Hotel across the street; go to the Akis reception to book a room. It's 200 meters from the beach, near the Kamari bus stop. All the simple rooms have a balcony with a view of the sea or of Mount Profitis Elias. Breakfast is served at the Akis on a sunny terrace. Excavations around the pension have revealed buried Byzantine ruins.

Venus and Aphrodite Hotels. Kamari, 84700 Santorini. ☎ **0286/31-183.** 125 units. TEL. Venus: Dr27,000 ($90) double. Aphrodite: Dr33,000 ($110) double; Dr49,000 ($163) suite. Rates include breakfast. DC, MC, V.

These two beach hotels recently merged and now share the two pools found in the courtyard of the Aphrodite. The Venus rooms are plain and bright, while the Aphrodite rooms are somewhat more plush, with marble surfaces and a pastel color scheme. Breakfast at the Aphrodite is a buffet in the poolside restaurant, while the Venus offers a simple continental breakfast in a breakfast room facing the beach. In our opinion the Venus is a better value, since the rates are considerably less than those of the Aphrodite, and the Venus rooms are the only ones in the complex with a view of the beach.

WHERE TO DINE
FIRA

The closer you are to the cable car in Fira, the steeper the tabs at restaurants (someone has to pay the outrageous rents) and the smaller the incentive for quality (those tourists will never be back). The better restaurants on Odos Ipapantis are nearer the cathedral.

If all you want is breakfast or a light, cheap meal, try **Crêperis House,** Theotokopoulou Square (no phone), or **Barbara's Café-Brasserie,** in the Fabrica Shopping Center up from the bus station toward the cathedral (no phone). After 7pm, Barbara's becomes one of the least expensive bars in town.

Meridiana Restaurant Bar. Odos Ipapantis. ☎ **0286/23-427.** Reservations recommended for dinner. Main courses Dr3,000–Dr8,000 ($10–$27). AE, MC, V. Daily 11am–3pm and 7pm–1am. INTERNATIONAL.

On the second story of the Fabrica Shopping Center, near the cathedral, this excellent restaurant has views of both the caldera and the town and island. The decor is informal and the service is relaxed. The food is meticulously prepared with little oil and salt, so that the subtle flavors of the distinctive spices can come through. The menu is large and varied, including piquant paella, chicken curry, pasta, teriyaki beef, and traditional Santorini dishes. Desserts are also excellent.

✪ **Selene.** Just past the Hotel Aressana, facing the caldera. ☎ **0286/22-249.** Reservations recommended for dinner. Main courses Dr4,300–Dr5,500 ($14–$18). AE, MC, V. Daily noon–3pm and 7pm–midnight. GREEK.

This is one of the best restaurants on the island, and definately merits a visit. Some establishments possess such a remarkable combination of outstanding qualities that it's difficult to assess any attribute individually. Take the setting: a coveted position along the caldera rim, on a terrace that wraps the hillside, with the heartbreaking beauty of island and bay. Or the dining room, with a lofty vaulted stone ceiling and massive walls—an unusually elegant space in this town. And the service? Excellent. As for the food, it's ultimately up to you to decide whether it lives up to expectations. Locally grown capers add a welcome pungency to several dishes, such as pork baked with fava and capers, or monkfish on caper leaves.

Sphinx Restaurant. Odos Mitropoleos, near the Atlantis Hotel. ☎ **0286/23-823.** Reservations recommended. Main courses Dr1,800–Dr6,000 ($6–$20). AE, DC, MC, V. Daily noon–3pm and 7pm–2am. INTERNATIONAL.

This more formal restaurant is especially recommended for those who like to get dressed up for dinner. A restored old mansion has been decorated with antiques, sculpture, and ceramics by local artists. The seafood specials and imaginative Greek dishes are fresh and superbly prepared.

Taverna Nikolas. Fira. No phone. Main courses Dr1,000–Dr2,000 ($3.35–$7). No credit cards. Daily noon–midnight. GREEK.

There are no menus in this taverna just up from the main square in Fira: the night's offerings are proclaimed (in Greek) on a blackboard over the kitchen, and the waiters gladly translate into the four or five languages they have at their disposal. This is one of the few restaurants in Fira where locals queue up alongside throngs of travelers for a table. There aren't any surprises here, just traditional Greek dishes prepared very well. There are some unfortunate concessions to economy—the baklava seems to be made with a sugar syrup rather than honey—but overall the food is hearty and delicious, well worth every drachma. The dining room is always busy, so arrive early or plan to wait.

IA

Katina Fish-Taverna. Port of Ia (Ammoudi). ☎ **0286/71-280.** Main courses Dr1,500–Dr4,200 ($5–$14). No credit cards. Daily 9am–1am. SEAFOOD.

One of the best places to eat in Ia isn't in town but rather down in the port of Ammoudi, best reached by donkey (Dr950/$3.20 one-way). Katina Pagoni is considered one of the very best local cooks, and the restaurant's setting beside the glittering Aegean is simply stunning. The specialty is fresh seafood, and she grills it to perfection. To return, you can climb several hundred steps to the caldera rim (a breathtaking option in more than one sense), but by midsummer the long path is thick with donkey droppings; calling a taxi might be a better way to conclude a romantic evening.

Neptune Restaurant. Odos Nikolaos Nomikos, Ia. ☎ **0286/71-294.** Main courses Dr1,200–Dr3,900 ($4–$13). MC, V. Daily 6pm–midnight. GREEK.

This very good choice is on the pedestrian lane near the church square. It has a rooftop garden with a partial sunset view. All their typical Greek dishes are well prepared, and the vegetable specials are made with the season's best.

Restaurant-Bar 1800. Odos Nikolaos Nomikos, Ia. ☎ **0286/71-485.** Main courses Dr2,100–Dr6,000 ($7–$20). AE, DC, EURO, MC, V. Daily 6pm–midnight. INTERNATIONAL.

This establishment in a restored captain's mansion is certainly the most attractive restaurant in town. It has a large and varied menu that includes fresh mussels, spaghetti with fresh crabmeat, and cold chicken with walnut sauce.

KAMARI

✪ **Camille Stephani.** Kamari Beach. ☎ **0286/31-716.** Reservations recommended July–Sept. Main courses Dr2,500–Dr6,000 ($8–$20). AE, DC, MC, V. Daily noon–midnight (Fri–Sun in winter). Open year-round. GREEK/INTERNATIONAL.

Even if you're not staying at Kamari, it's worthwhile to make a trip there to this excellent, more formal restaurant on the north end of the beach, 500 meters from the bus stop. You can take a moonlight stroll along the beach afterward. The special is a tender beef fillet with green pepper in Madeira sauce.

SANTORINI AFTER DARK

Fira has nightlife aplenty and in some variety. We suggest starting the evening with a drink on the caldera, taking in the spectacular sunset. **Franco's** (☎ **0286/22-881**) is still the most famous and best place for this magic hour, but be prepared to pay about Dr2,500 ($8) per drink. For more reasonable prices, a bit more seclusion, and the same fantastic view, continue through the Canava Café and below the Loucas Hotel to the **Renaissance Bar** (☎ **0286/22-880**). Underneath the square, the **Kirathira Bar** plays jazz at a level that permits conversation. Cross the main street and wander around the shopping area to find a number of smaller bars that come alive after 9pm. The **Town Club** appeals to clean-cut rockers, while the **Two Brothers** pulls in the biggest, chummiest, and most casual crowd on the island. **Tithora** is popular with a young, heavy-drinking crowd. A bit further north, the outdoor **Tropical Bar** attracts a louder, rowdier gang. For bouzouki, find **Bar 33.** Discos come and go, and you only need to follow your ears to find them. The **Koo Club** is the biggest, and the **Enigma** is still popular with those interested in good music. There's usually no admission charge, but drinks start at Dr2,000 ($7).

In Ia, **Zorba's** is a good cliffside pub. **1800** is a more sophisticated bar, without the view.

Kamari has its share of bars. The **Yellow Donkey Disco** (☎ **0286/31-462**) is popular with younger partiers, and the more sophisticated usually seek the chic **Valentino's,** near the bus stop.

Those visiting in August and September may be able to catch a performance of classical music at the **Santorini Festival** (☎ **0286/22-220** for details), where international singers and musicians perform at the open-air amphitheater.

<hr>

2　Folegandros

181km (98 nautical miles) SE of Piraeus

Most travelers who know of Folegandros have seen it only when passing its forbidding northern coast, where precipitous cliffs rise to a height of 250 meters. So far, relatively few have ventured up to experience the spare beauty of its capital, **Hora.** In this town huddled at cliff's edge, one square spills into the next, with green and blue paving slates outlined in brilliant white. On a steep slope overlooking the town is the looming form of **Panayia,** the church whose icon of the Virgin is paraded through Hora's streets with great ceremony and revelry each Easter Sunday.

The rugged northern slopes of Folegandros offer a contrast to the austere civility of Hora's streets and squares. Here the hills are ribboned with the terraced fields that allow local farmers to grow barley on the island's steep slopes. Rocky coves shelter pristine cobble beaches, and many trails weave their way through the hills, some of them ancient paths paved with marble or carved from the bedrock. If you want to explore Folegandros, you'll have to walk—there's simply no other way to see the many beautiful sites outside Hora.

Ferry connections are reasonably frequent during the summer, but plan carefully in the off-season, when infrequent service and bad weather could easily keep you here longer than you'd intended.

ESSENTIALS

GETTING THERE　By Ferry　Three ferries a week (five in the high season) stop at Folegandros on the Piraeus-Ios-Santorini route. Two or three ferries (five in the high season) a week stop on the Naxos-Paros route. Two ferries (four in the high season) stop on the Serifos-Sifnos-Milos run. Ferries connect twice a week (three to four times a week in the high season) with Kimolos, Kithnos, Sikinos, and Siros. The local **Port Authority** can be reached at ☎ **0286/41-249.**

VISITOR INFORMATION   The **Maraki Travel Agency** (☎ **0286/41-273**), just around the southwest corner of the bus-stop square in Hora, exchanges money, helps with travel arrangements, and sells maps of the island for Dr600 ($2). **Sotto Vento Travel** (☎ **0286/41-444;** fax 0286/41-430) is another travel agency in Hora, near the stop for the Angali and Ano Meria bus, where you can book trips by caïque to the beaches, arrange boat tours of the island, book accommodations, buy ferry tickets, and store luggage.

GETTING AROUND   By Bus   The bus meets all ferries in peak season, and most ferries during the rest of the year; it also makes eight or nine trips a day along the main road, which runs along the spine of the island between Hora and Ano Meria at the island's northern end. The bus fare is Dr250 (85¢).

By Moped   There are two fledgling moped-rental outfits on Folegandros: **Jimmy's Motorcycle** (☎ **0286/41-448**) in Karavostassis, and **Moto Rent** (☎ **0286/41-316**) in Hora, near Sotto Vento Travel.

FAST FACTS   Folegandros has neither bank nor ATM, but you can exchange money at **Maraki Travel** in Hora (☎ **0286/41-273**) or at **Sotto Vento** (☎ **0286/41-444**), near the stop for the Angali bus in Hora. Arrangements can also be made for left luggage at Sotto Vento. The **post office** and **telephone office (OTE)** are right off the central square in Hora, open Monday through Friday from 8am to 3pm. The **police station** (☎ **0286/41-249**) is behind the post office and OTE. There's one **taxi** (☎ **0286/41-048;** mobile 094/693-957) on the island, but with the frequency of bus service and dearth of places to drive, you're unlikely to need it.

WHAT TO SEE & DO

Visitors arrive in the unimpressive port of **Karavostassis,** where there's a decent beach and a few hotels and rooms to let. Most will jump aboard the bus that's waiting to chug the 4 kilometers (2½ miles) up to Hora.

✪ **Hora** is one of the most beautiful capitals in the Cyclades. Above it, the Panayia Church beckons you to climb the hillside for a closer look and incredible views. Even from the bus-stop square, the sheer drop off the cliff offers an awesome sight. On the right in the next square, you'll find the **Kastro:** two narrow pedestrian streets connected by tunnel-like walkways, squeezed between the town and the sea cliffs. The town is centered around five closely connected squares, along and around which you'll find churches, restaurants, and shops.

Continue west from Hora by foot or bus to reach the village of Ano Meria. The small farms there are so widely dispersed that they're barely recognizable as a community, though **Ano Meria** is the island's second largest town. There's an interesting **Folk Museum,** open in the afternoons, with exhibits on local life.

BEACHES

Swimmers will want to get off the bus to Ano Meria at the first crossroad and walk down to **Angali,** the best fine-sand beach on the island. There are a few tavernas on the beach and rooms to let. **Ayios Nikolaos,** another good beach, is a couple of kilometers farther west—a well-used path follows the coast west from Angali. At the far northwest end of the island is the beach at **Ayios Yeoryios,** a pristine choice sheltered in a rocky cove; it's a great walk, but the beach is often too windy for swimming and sunning. In the summer there's caïque service to these beaches from Karavostassis for those who aren't keen on walking; inquire at Sotto Vento Travel (see above) for more information.

WALKING

The footpaths through the northern part of the island are well used and for the most part easy to follow. Numerous paths branch off to the southwest from the paved road through Ano Meria; the region of hills traversed by these trails, between the road and the sea, is particularly beautiful. One path that's particularly easy to follow leads **from Ayios Andreas to the bay at Ayios Yioryios.** Take the bus to the next to last stop, at the northern end of Ano Meria; it's next to the church of Ayios Andreas, and next at the stop is a sign reading AG. GEORGIOS 1.5, and pointing to the right. Follow the sign, and continue along a road which quickly becomes a path and descends steeply toward the bay. Follow the main path at each of several intersections; you'll be able to see the bay for the last 20 minutes of the walk. The bay of Ayios Yioryios holds a small pebble beach; there's no fresh water here, so be sure to bring plenty. Allow 2 hours round-trip.

WHERE TO STAY

Most visitors will choose to stay in beautiful cliff-top Hora. Keep in mind that the island's limited facilities are fully booked in July and August, and advance reservations will be necessary.

Anemomilos Apartments. Hora (just up from the central bus stop), 84011 Folegandros. ☎ **0286/41-309.** Fax 0286/41-407. 17 units. TEL. Dr24,000–Dr28,000 ($80–$93) studio; Dr36,000 ($120) suite. Continental breakfast Dr1,800 ($6) extra. V.

Hora's best luxury apartments—in a spectacular location at the edge of a cliff overlooking the open Aegean—are simply elegant, spacious, and bright. All apartments have a kitchenette; the suite has a separate bedroom, and can sleep four comfortably. Half the apartments have views of the sea, a few of these with private terraces; the rest look out over the rooftops of the village. One apartment is wheelchair accessible. Transport to and from the port is available for Dr1,000 ($3.35) one-way, a convenient option in the off-season.

✪ **Castro Hotel.** Hora, 84011 Folegandros. ☎ **0286/41-230,** or 01/778-1658 in Athens. Fax 0286/41-230. 12 units. TEL. Dr16,000 ($53) double; Dr20,000 ($67) triple. Continental breakfast Dr1,500 ($5) extra. AE, V.

The Castro is in the oldest part of Hora, in a Venetian castle built in 1212. The hotel was opened in 1972 and fully renovated in 1993, preserving features like the exposed ceiling timbers in several rooms, which date to the 17th century. Guest rooms are small but comfortable, and seven are on the phenomenal cliff side of the hotel—the windows of these units overhang cliffs that drop hundreds of feet into the sea. The two most desirable rooms have balconies surveying the extraordinary view; these don't cost extra, and are a great bargain. (Try to reserve room no. 3, 4, 5, 13, 14, 15, or R1if you'd like a sea view.) For those units without the view, a shared rooftop terrace offers the same magnificent prospect. The charming Despo Danassi, whose family has owned this house for five generations, will make you feel at home here—her homemade fig jam is fabulous.

Hotel Odysseus. Hora, 84011 Folegandros. ☎ **0286/41-276,** or 01/342-3545 in Athens. Fax 0286/41-366. 13 units. TEL. Dr15,000 ($50) double; Dr18,000 ($60) triple. Continental breakfast Dr1,200 ($4) extra. No credit cards. On the west side of town, a few blocks beyond the OTE/post office, then left.

This hotel received a dramatic face-lift in 1998, when the existing building was renovated and a new wing added. Each room now has its own small terrace, and the large shared terrace has an expansive sea view. All rooms but one face the sea; those on the second floor have the best view. Although the facilities are rather spartan, rooms are reliably quiet, comfortable, and clean.

Polikandia Hotel. Hora, 84011 Folegandros. ☎ **0286/41-322** or 0286/41-404; 01/ 682-5484 in Athens. Fax 0286/41-323. 31 units. Dr17,000 ($57) double. Rates include breakfast. No credit cards.

This handsome new traditional-style hotel is on the left as you enter town. The rooms are large and comfortable, with balconies overlooking the bright courtyard and hotel cafe. The hotel quickly fills up in July and August with group tours.

WHERE TO DINE

Main courses for all the restaurants listed here are Dr800 to Dr2,000 ($2.70 to $7); hours are generally from 9am to 3pm and 6pm to midnight.

The local specialty is a dish called *matsata*, made with fresh pasta and rabbit or chicken. The best place to sample it is **Mimi's** in Ano Meria (☎ 0286/41-377), where the pasta is made on the premises. Hora has a number of tavernas along the central squares. On the bus-stop square, **Pounda** (☎ **0286/421-063**) serves a delicious breakfast of crepes, omelets, yogurt, or coffee cakes; they also serve lunch and dinner, including a variety of vegetarian dishes. **Nikolaos** (☎ **0286/41-216**) is on the second square—its owner is especially friendly and informative. **Piatsa** (☎ **0286/41-274**), on the third square, is a simple, family-run taverna. **O Kritikos** (☎ **0286/41-219**) is another local favorite, known for its grilled chicken.

3 Sifnos

172km (93 nautical miles) SE of Piraeus

Presenting an austere face to ferries arriving at the unexciting port of Kamares, Sifnos keeps its riches concealed within a hilly interior. Elegantly ornamented dovecotes rest in the cool green hollows, and ancient fortified monasteries and watchtowers occupy the arid summits of the island's hills. A trio of beaches along the southern coast offer long stretches of fine amber sand; several smaller rocky coves are also excellent for swimming.

The island is sufficiently small that any town can be used as a base for touring; the most beautiful are the **seven settlements** spread across the central hills (notably Apollonia and Artemonas) and **Kastro,** a small medieval fortified town atop a rocky pinnacle on the eastern shore. A combination of bus rides and some short walks will allow you to visit the top attractions: the ancient acropolis at **Ayios Andreas,** the town of Kastro and its tiny but excellent archaeological museum, the **southern beaches,** and for the ambitious the **walled monastery of Profitis Elias** on the summit of the island's highest mountain. While you're on the island, don't miss the **pottery workshops:** Sifnos is renowned for its ceramics, and some of the island's best practitioners are in Kamares and Platis Yialos.

ESSENTIALS

GETTING THERE   By Boat   There's at least one boat daily from Piraeus; contact tourist information in Athens (☎ **01/1-71** or 01/322-2545) or the Port Authority in Piraeus (☎ **01/451-1310**) for information. Ferries travel daily (twice daily June through Aug) to nearby islands such as **Serifos, Milos, Kimolos,** and **Kithnos.** They

A Note on Ferries

Outside the summer months, ferry connections to Sifnos are particularly sparse.

depart two or three times a week for Folegandros, Ios, Mikonos, Paros, Santorini, Sikinos, Siros, and Tinos. Call the **Sifnos Port Authority** (☎ **0284/31-617**) for more information.

VISITOR INFORMATION   Your first stop should be the excellent **Aegean Thesaurus Travel and Tourism office** on the port (☎ **0284/31-804;** www.travelling. gr/sifnos-aegean-thesaurus; e-mail: thesaurus@travelling.gr). Located 20 meters north of the square, this is a one-stop center where you can cash traveler's checks, book a flight, or arrange a boat tour of the island for about Dr3,000 ($10). A packet of island information including bus schedule, hydrofoil schedule, and a brief local history is offered for Dr200 (70¢); an excellent island map with walking trails is Dr400 ($1.35). Open daily from 9am to midnight (reduced hours in the off-season). The main office of **Aegean Thesaurus** is in Apollonia (☎ **0284/33-151;** fax 0284/32-190).

Note that Aegean Thesaurus Travel only provides tickets and schedules for the Flying Dolphin hydrofoils; for all other companies you'll have to inquire at **Ventouris Ferries,** next door to Aegean Thesaurus in Kamares (☎ **0284/31-700**), or at **Xidis Travel,** just off the main square in Apollonia (☎ **0284/31-895**).

GETTING AROUND   Given the island's small size and the presence of a reliable bus system, renting a car or moped shouldn't be necessary.

By Bus   Apollonia's central square, **Plateia Iroon,** is the main bus stop for the island. Buses run regularly to and from the port at Kamares, north to Artemonas, east to Kastro, and south to Faros, Platis Yialos, and Vathi. Pick up a schedule at Aegean Thesaurus Travel (see "Visitor Information," above).

By Car   Cars can be rented in Apollonia at **FS** (☎ **0284/31-795;** fax 0284/33-089) and **Aegean Thesaurus** (☎ **0284/33-151**). In Kamares, **Sifnos Car** (☎ and fax **0284/33-052**) is a good choice. The daily rate for an economy car with full insurance is about Dr18,000 ($60).

By Moped   Apollonia has a few moped dealers; try **Yannis** (☎ **0284/31-155**) on the main square.

By Taxi   Apollonia's main square is the island's primary taxi stand. There are about 10 taxis on the island, each privately owned, so you'll have to use the **mobile phone numbers** and hope someone's phone is turned on: try ☎ **094/642-680,** 094/444-904, 094/761-210, or 094-936-111.

FAST FACTS   Visitor services are centered around Plateia Iroon, the main square in Apollonia. The **National Bank** (☎ **0284/31-317**) is open Monday through Thursday from 8am to 2pm, Friday from 8am to 1:30pm. The **post office** (☎ **0284/31-329**) is open Monday through Friday from 8am to 3pm, Saturday and Sunday from 9am to 1:30pm in summer. The **telephone center (OTE),** just down the vehicle road, is open daily from 8am to 3pm, and in summer from 5 to 10pm as well. (The news kiosk on the square has a metered phone for after-hours calls.) There's a **self-service laundry** in the courtyard of the Hotel Anthousa in Apollonia; inquire at Yerontopoulos patisserie, on the ground floor of the hotel. The **police station** (☎ **0284/31-210**) is just east of the square, and a **first-aid station** is nearby; for **medical emergencies** call ☎ **0284/31-315.**

WHAT TO SEE & DO

The capital town of the island, **Apollonia,** is one of the **seven settlements,** which have grown together on these lovely interior hills. It's 5 kilometers (3 miles) inland from Kamares; a local bus makes the trip hourly in summer. The town's central square, Plateia Iroon (Heroes' Square), is the transportation hub of the island: all the vehicle roads converge here, and this is where you'll find the bus stop and taxi stand. Winding pedestrian paths of flagstone and marble slope up from the square and lead through this beautiful village. **Lakis Kafeneion,** an open-air cafe on the square, is the island's principal hangout. Also on Plateia Iroon is the small **Popular and Folk Art Museum;** it's open July 1 to September 15 from 10am to 1pm and 6 to 10pm, and admission is Dr400 ($1.35).

✪ **Kastro** is the finest medieval town on Sifnos, built on the dramatic site of an ancient acropolis. The walk from Apollonia (2km/1.2 miles) is easy, except under the midday sun: start out on the footpath that passes under the main road in front of Hotel Anthousa, and continue through the tiny village of Kato Petali, finishing the walk into Kastro on a paved road. Whitewashed houses, some well preserved and others eroding, adjoin each other in a defensive ring abutting the sheer cliff. Venetian coats of arms are still visible above the doorways of the older houses. Within its maze are a few tavernas, some beautiful rooms to let, and a gem of an **Archaeological Museum** (☎ **0284/31-022**) housing pottery and sculpture found on the island; open Tuesday through Saturday from 9am to 3pm, Sunday and holidays from 10am to 2pm. Admission is free. Below the town is a small pebble beach that's suitable for swimming.

About 2 kilometers (1.2 miles) south of Apollonia on the road to Vathi is a trail leading to the hilltop church of **Ayios Andreas** and the excavations of an **ancient acropolis.** It's hard to see the sign (in Greek only) for Ayios Andreas; it's across from a road sign reading KADES, at the top of a long uphill. Broad stone steps begin a long climb to the summit; count on at least 20 minutes ascending and 15 minutes coming down. At the top of the hill the ruins of the acropolis are on your left: Excavations haven't been completed and there's no interpretive information on the site, but the location is stirring—it's well worth a visit if only for the view. These ruins are the outer walls and a block of houses from a Mycenaean fortified town.

BEACHES

The central part of **Kamares** cove harbors a sandy beach lined with tamarisk trees and dune grass. There are some fine isolated beaches north and south of Kamares that can be reached by boat; contact **Thesaurus Travel** (☎0284/31-804 or 0284/33-151) for information on its summer-only caïque excursions.

The southern end of the island shelters a trio of coves with fine-sand beaches. The most popular of these is **Platis Yialos,** and a slew of hotels, tavernas, and shops have grown up around the beach. This town is more upscale than Kamares, and attracts the yachting crowd in the summer. From here, it's a half-hour walk east through the olive groves and intoxicating oregano and thyme patches over the hill to **Panayia Chrissopiyi,** a double-vaulted whitewashed church on a tiny island. There's good swimming immediately below the monastery and along the coast, where secluded bays protect swimmers from rough water. A short walk to the east, **Apokofto** has a good long sand beach, and nude bathing is permitted at nearby **Fasolou.**

Until 1997 the beach at **Vathi** was accessible only by foot or boat, but a new automobile road is now open and permits regular bus service. There are a few tavernas (but not yet the dense development of Kamares and Platis Yialos), plus one of the best beaches on the island. The excellent beach at **Fikiada** has no services, and is still accessible only on foot (see "Walking," below).

WALKING

Like many of the Cyclades, the hills of Sifnos are traced with countless walking paths, many of them paved with slabs of limestone or schist. Sadly, the continuity of these fine paths has been interrupted in many places by the construction of new roads and houses. The following walks, on a combination of road and path, are fairly easy to follow.

APOLLONIA TO PROFITIS ELIAS   This is the best walk on the island, taking you through a remote valley of extraordinary beauty to the summit of the island's highest mountain, with a short detour to the church and ruined monastery at Skafis. From the center of Apollonia, walk south along the main pedestrian road, past Sifnos Taverna and the cathedral. About 1 kilometer (0.6 miles) from the center of Apollonia you'll reach the small village of Katavati; look out for the small black arrow pointing to the right, painted with the words PR. ELIAS in Greek. From here the trail descends toward a paved road, makes a short jog to the right on the road, then turns left onto a footpath (with another PR. ELIAS arrow at the left turn). After about 1 kilometer (0.6 miles) of walking along the base of a valley, the path to the summit branches to the right. From here it's another hour or so to the summit. The 12th-century walled monastery is a formidable citadel. The interior courtyard is lined with the monks' cells, and contains a lovely chapel with a fine marble iconostasis. If you continue straight from the point where the summit path branches right, and walk straight through the next intersection, you'll soon reach the church of Skafis. The church is situated within the ruins of an old monastery, and looks out over a small valley shaded by olive trees. Allow yourself 4 hours for the round-trip to Profitis Elias, with an additional hour for the detour to Skafis.

VATHI TO FIKIADA   Fikiada is a small cove 3 kilometers (2 miles) south of Vathi. There's a good beach here, but no water or facilities, and its accessible only on foot or by boat; as a result, it doesn't ever get very crowded. You can walk from Vathi or Platis Yialos, but the walk from Vathi is a bit shorter. No single path goes all the way, so you should be confident of your navigational abilities. A good place to begin is the southernmost hairpin turn on the road in to Vathi; from here head south, following a stream valley to the height of land and then find one of the several paths in the vicinity that will make the going easier. Allow yourself 1½ hours each way. You can also continue around the headland to Platis Yialos, an additional distance of about 4 kilometers (2½ miles).

SHOPPING

Sifnian ceramics are exported throughout Greece; they're in wide use because of their durability and charming folk designs. One of the most interesting shops is the ceramics workshop of **Antonis Kalogirou** (☎ **0284/31-651**), on the main harborside lane in Kamares. Antonis sells folk paintings of island life and the typical pottery of Sifnos, which is manufactured in his showroom from the deep gray or red clay mined in the inland hill region. Another fine ceramics workshop is that of **Simos and John Apostolidis** (☎ **0284/71-258**), on the main street in Platis Yialos.

In Apollonia, **Hersonissos** (☎ **0284/32-209**) has a choice selection of contemporary jewelry and ceramics. There are several other contemporary ceramics galleries featuring the excellent work of Greek artisans in the town's winding back streets.

WHERE TO STAY
APOLLONIA

Hotel Anthousa. Apollonia, 84003 Sifnos. ☎ **0284/31-431.** 15 units. A/C TV TEL. Dr14,000 ($47) double; Dr18,000 ($60) triple. Continental breakfast Dr1,500 ($5) extra. MC, V.

This hotel is above the excellent and popular Yerontopoulos cafe-patisserie. Although the street-side rooms offer wonderful views over the hills, they're recommended only to night owls in the high season, as they overlook the late-night sweet-tooth crowd. The back rooms are quieter and overlook a beautiful bower of bougainvillea.

Hotel Sifnos. Apollonia, 84003 Sifnos. ☎ and fax **0284/31-624** or 024/33-067. 7 units. A/C TV TEL. Dr15,000 ($50) double; Dr18,000 ($60) triple. AE, EURO, MC, V. Open year-round.

This is the best hotel in Apollonia, and it's the most traditional choice in terms of island architecture, even though it was built in the 1970s. The hotel is located southeast of the main square, on the pedestrian street leading to the cathedral. The hotel's manager, Helen Diareme, and her son Apostolos will do their best to make your stay comfortable.

Hotel Sofia. Apollonia, 84003 Sifnos. ☎ **0284/31-238.** 11 units. TEL. Dr10,000 ($33) double. No credit cards. Breakfast not offered.

This was one of the first hotels in town, and continues to offer basic rooms for a decent price. Most rooms open onto a narrow courtyard, and the ones on the second floor don't get much light; ask for a top-floor or street-front room. All rooms have a fridge, ceiling fan, and spacious bathroom. The reception is in the minimarket on the ground floor. To get there from the main square in Apollonia, follow the main vehicular road 50 meters north (toward Artemonas); the hotel will be on your left.

ARTEMONAS

Hotel Artemon. Artemonas, 84003 Sifnos. ☎ **0284/31-303** or 0284/33-158. Fax 0284/32-385. 23 units. MINIBAR TEL. Dr15,100 ($50) double. Continental breakfast Dr1,500 ($5) extra. AE, EURO, MC, V.

This quiet, comfortable hotel is on the road to Apollonia, just beyond the central plateia of Artemonas. Rooms on the ground floor have patios and views of the small hotel gardens; the units above have balconies and a view of wheat fields and olive groves sloping down to the sea. The Artemon has a large terrace shaded by a luxuriant grape arbor; breakfast is served here or in the adjoining dining room. The restaurant also serves lunch and dinner.

KASTRO

Aris Rafeletos Apartments. ☎ and fax **0284/31-161.** 5 units. Dr10,000–13,000 ($33–$43) room; Dr17,000–27,500 ($57–$92) apt. No credit cards.

These traditional rooms and apartments are all within the medieval town of Kastro. Most have exposed ceiling beams, stone ceilings and floors, and the long narrow rooms typical of this fortified village. The two small rooms are somewhat dark and musty, but the three apartments are spacious and charming. All apartments have kitchenettes and terraces; two have splendid sea views. The largest apartment is on two levels, and could comfortably sleep four. If the antiquity and charm of this hilltop medieval village appeals to you, then these apartments may be the perfect base for your explorations of the island. The rental office is at the north end of the village, about 50 meters past the archaeological museum—the sign says TRADITIONAL ROOMS FOR RENT—and the apartments are distributed throughout the village.

KAMARES

Kamares has the biggest concentration of hotels and pensions on the island, but unfortunately it has little of the beauty of Sifnos's traditional villages.

Hotel Boulis. Kamares, 84003 Sifnos. ☎ **0284/32-122.** Fax 0284/32-381. 45 units. TEL. Dr17,000 ($57) double; 20,400 ($68) triple. Rates include breakfast. AE.

This recently built hotel is right on the port's beach. The large, carpeted rooms have balconies or patios, most with beach views; all have fridges and ceiling fans. There's a spacious, cool marble-floored reception area and a bright breakfast room.

Hotel Kamari. Kamares, 84003 Sifnos. ☎ **0284/32-383.** Fax 0284/31-709. 18 units. TEL. Dr16,000 ($53) double. Rates include breakfast. AE, MC, V.

This is a clean, attractive lodging with balconied rooms at the quiet end of town, 300 meters from the ferry pier, where the road and beach meet. The friendly and attentive management offers car rentals and transportation to other island villages by minibus.

PLATIS YIALOS

Hotel Benakis. Platis Yialos, 84003 Sifnos. ☎ **0284/71-263** or 0284/71-368. Fax 0284/71-334. 34 units. Dr18,400 ($61) double; Dr22,080 ($74) triple. Rates include breakfast. No credit cards.

This small, plain hotel with a lovely sea view from its place on the beach is run by the friendly, helpful Benakis family. The rooms are spotless, quiet, and comfortable.

Hotel Philoxenia. Platis Yialos, 84003 Sifnos. ☎ **0284/71-221.** Fax 0284/71-222. 9 units. Dr18,000 ($60) double; Dr20,000 ($67) triple. Rates include breakfast. No credit cards.

This simple hotel on the main street has large, clean rooms, some with balconies offering sea views. A few rooms have air-conditioning (add Dr2,000/$7).

✪ Hotel Platis Yialos. Platis Yialos, 84003 Sifnos. ☎ **0284/31-324,** or 0831/22-626 in winter. Fax 0284/31-325, or 0831/55-042 in winter. 29 units. MINIBAR TV TEL. Dr40,000 ($133) double; Dr60,000 ($200) 4-person suite; Dr80,000 ($267) 6-person suite. Rates include breakfast. No credit cards.

The island's best hotel is ideally situated overlooking the beach on the west side of the cove. Originally a government-owned Xenia hotel, the design is functional rather than beautiful, and the place is even something of an eyesore from across the bay. The hotel is set apart from the rest of the town's densely populated beach strip, and is surrounded by a small garden. The ground-floor rooms, with patios facing the garden and the water, are especially desirable; rooms on the upper stories have balconies. Frescoes and small paintings of all sorts are displayed throughout the hotel, the work of a local artist. The Platis Yialos's flagstone sundeck extends from the beach to a dive platform at the end of the cove. A bar and restaurant share the same Aegean views. A new six-person suite has flagstone floors, beamed ceilings, a separate bedroom, and two bathrooms, one with Jacuzzi; it is on the ground floor, and opens to a private terrace and views of the bay.

WHERE TO DINE

APOLLONIA

Apostoli's Koutouki Taverna. Apollonia. ☎ **0284/31-186.** Main courses Dr1,200–Dr3,000 ($4–$10). No credit cards. Daily noon–midnight. GREEK.

There are several tavernas in Apollonia, but this one on the main pedestrian street is the best for Greek food. The service, though, is usually leisurely. The vegetable dishes, most made from locally grown produce, are delicious.

Mama Mia. Apollonia. ☎ **0284/33-086.** Main courses Dr1,200–Dr6,000 ($4–$20). No credit cards. Daily 5pm–midnight. SPAGHETTERIA/PIZZERIA.

When you need a break from taverna fare, try this trattoria on the path between Apollonia and Artemonas. The food is simple but surprisingly good. House specialties include a variety of veal and lobster dishes; humbler fare includes pasta, risotto, or pizza. The pizzas can also be ordered for takeout. The large outdoor terrace in back is a very pleasant spot to enjoy a leisurely dinner.

Sifnos Cafe-Restaurant. Apollonia. ☎ **0284/31-624.** Main courses Dr1,000–Dr3,000 ($3.35–$10). AE, EURO, MC, V. Daily 8am–midnight. GREEK.

You'll find the best all-around place to eat in Apollonia along the main pedestrian street toward the cathedral. It's under a grape arbor, between the Sifnos Hotel and a quiet plaza. The breakfast menu offers fresh fruit juice and a dozen coffees. Choose from a variety of snacks, light meals, and desserts during the day. At sunset, have ouzo and mezedes. When you're ready for a big evening meal, go in and check out the refrigerator case displaying the catch of the day and other main courses.

ARTEMONAS

✪ **To Liotrivi (Manganas).** Artemonas. ☎ **0284/32-051.** Main courses Dr900–Dr3,300 ($3–$11). No credit cards. Daily noon–midnight. GREEK.

Find out why the Sifnians, who pride themselves on their fine, distinctive cooking, consider Yannis Yiorgoulis one of their finest chefs. Try his delectable *kaparosalata* (minced caper leaves and onion salad), *revidokeftedes* (croquettes of ground chickpeas), or *ambelofasoula* (crisp local black-eyed peas in the pod). Or go for something ordinary like the beef fillet with potatoes baked in foil. The taverna has a handsome new building, with dining in the cellar, on the roof, or by the street.

KAMARES

Captain Andreas. Kamares. ☎ **0284/32-356.** Main courses Dr1,000–Dr1,800 ($3.35–$6); fish Dr3,000–Dr17,000 ($10–$57) per kilo. No credit cards. Daily 1–5pm and 7:30pm–12:30am. SEAFOOD.

Captain Andreas, a favorite place for seafood, has tables right on the town beach. Andreas, the proprietor and fisherman, serves the catch of the day. It's usually simply prepared and accompanied with terrific chips or a seasonal vegetable dish.

Pothotas Taverna O Simos. Kamares. ☎ **0284/31-697.** Main courses Dr900–Dr2,100 ($3–$7). No credit cards. Daily 11am–midnight. GREEK.

This unobtrusive portside place has a basic Greek menu, and everything is done well. The bread brought to your table is sprinkled with sesame seeds, their *horiatiki* salad is made with locally aged *mizithra* cheese, the fish is fresh and not expensive, and the individually baked pots of moussaka are delicious.

PLATIS YIALOS

Sofia Restaurant. Platis Yialos. ☎ **0284/71-202.** Main courses Dr900–Dr2,700 ($3–$9). No credit cards. Daily 9pm–1am. GREEK.

At the east end of the beach is the town's best restaurant for Greek peasant fare. It's popular for an outdoor terrace and large wine list. For many in Apollonia, the casual seaside ambiance warrants an evening outing.

SIFNOS AFTER DARK

In Apollonia, the **Argo Bar, Botzi,** and **Volto** on the main pedestrian street are good for the latest European and American pop music at very loud volumes. In

A Special Feast

The celebration in mid-July of the Prophet Elijah's feast day is a special tradition on Sifnos, which has had a monastery dedicated to this saint for at least 800 years. The celebration begins with a mass outing to the monastery of Profitis Elias on the summit of the island's highest mountain, and continues through the night with dancing and feasting.

summertime, the large **Dolphin Pub** becomes a lively and elegant nightspot; it closes for the season in mid-September.

In Kamares at sunset, you can seek relative tranquillity near the beach at the picturesque **Old Captain's Bar.** Or join the yacht set drinking Sifnos Sunrises at the rival **Collage Club.** Later, the **Mobilize Dance Club** and the more elegant **Follie-Follie,** right on the beach, start cranking up the volume for dancing.

In summer, the **Cultural Society of Sifnos** sometimes hosts concerts in Artemonas, and local festivals offer folk music and dance.

4 Paros

168km (91 nautical miles) SE of Piraeus

Every island-hopper in the Cyclades is likely to pass at some point through Paros, the transportation hub of the archipelago. With a few good beaches, and nightlife to rival Mikonos or Santorini, it's not surprising that Paros has become a tremendously popular destination in its own right. **Parikia,** its lively capital, offers an eclectic marketplace, the remains of a Venetian castle, a fine Byzantine cathedral, and some of the best culinary options of any town in the Cyclades.

On the north coast of the island, the fishing village of **Naoussa** has grown into a full-scale resort, and is almost as crowded as Parikia during July and August; the most popular Paros beaches are within easy commuting distance of Naoussa's hotels. Charming **Lefkes,** set within the island's inland hills, has preserved many of its medieval buildings amidst a maze of steep narrow streets. The west coast of the island has long stretches of fine sand, and wind conditions that have made this the site of the World Cup windsurfing championship every year since 1993.

We recommend taking a day or two to explore the island and visit its attractions before moving on. Rent a car or moped for an around-the-island tour that includes a morning visit to **Petaloudes,** enough time in Lefkes to get lost and find your way again, a stop for a good lunch in Naoussa, a swim at your beach of choice, and a night of shopping and barhopping in hectic Parikia.

ESSENTIALS

GETTING THERE   By Plane   Olympic Airlines has at least two flights daily (up to 10 in summer) between Paros and Athens. For schedules and reservations call ☎ **01/966-6666** in Athens, 0284/21-900 in Parikia, or 0284/91-257 at the airport.

By Ferry   Paros has more connections with more ports than any other island in the Cyclades. The main port, Parikia, has ferry connections at least once daily (four times daily in the peak season) with Piraeus; the travel time is about 6 hours. Confirm schedules with **tourist information** in Athens (☎ **01/171** or 01/322-2545) or the **Port Authority** in Piraeus (☎ **01/451-1310**). **Ilio Lines** (☎ **01/422-4980** in Piraeus) has hydrofoil service daily or almost daily from Rafina. Daily ferry service links Paros with Ios, Mikonos, Naxos, Santorini (Thira), and Tinos. Several times a week ferries depart for Folegandros, Sifnos, and Siros. There are daily excursion tours from Parikia or Naoussa (the north coast port) to Mikonos. The **Golden Veryina** has overnight service to Ikaria and Samos four times a week. (From Samos you can arrange a next-day excursion to Ephesus, Turkey.) During the peak season there is hourly caïque service to Andiparos.

For general ferry information, call the **port authority** in **Parikia** (☎ **0284/ 21-240**). Ferry tickets are sold by several agents around Mavroyenous Square and along the port; schedules are posted along the sidewalk.

VISITOR INFORMATION   There is a **visitor information office** on Mavroyenous Square, just behind and to the right of the windmill at the end of the pier. This office is often closed, but there are numerous travel agencies on the seafront, including the most helpful **Paros Travel** (☎ **0284/21-582;** fax 0284/22-582), just to the left as you walk off the pier. Also try **Santorineos Travel** (☎ **0284/24-245;** fax 0284/ 23-922), run by friendly and knowledgeable Nikos Santorineos, located along the seafront, 100 meters south of the pier (to the right as you get off the boat). The island has a fledgling Web site, **parosweb.com,** which is growing rapidly and should be a very helpful resource in the near future.

GETTING AROUND   By Bus   The **bus station** (☎ **0284/21-395**) in Parikia is on the waterfront, left from the windmill. There is hourly public bus service between Parikia and Naoussa between 8am and midnight (outside peak season the last bus is at 8pm). The other public buses from Parikia run hourly from 8am to 9pm in two general directions: **south** to Aliki or Pounda, and **southeast** to the beaches at Piso Livadi, Chrisso Akti, and Drios, passing the Marathi Quarries and the town of Lefkes along the way. Schedules are posted at the stations.

By Car   Paros is large enough that renting a car makes sense; there are several agencies along the waterfront, and except in July and August you should be able to bargain. We recommend **Rent-A-Car Acropolis** (☎ **0284/21-830**), left from the windmill on the waterfront, which has a basic two-door car for Dr15,000 ($50) per day with full insurance, and Suzuki Jeeps for about Dr31,000 ($103) per day. **Budget Rent-a-Car** (☎ **0284/22-320**), also on the waterfront, is another good choice.

By Moped   There are several moped dealers along the waterfront, left from the windmill. Depending on size, mopeds should cost about Dr4,000 to Dr6,000 ($13 to $20) per day.

By Taxi   Taxis can be booked (☎ **0284/21-500**) or hailed at the windmill taxi stand. If you're coming off the ferry with lots of luggage and are headed for a hotel in Naoussa, it's worth the Dr2,000 ($7) to take a taxi directly there.

FAST FACTS   The local **American Express** agent is Santorineos Travel, on the seafront 100 meters south of the pier (☎ **0284/24-245;** fax 0284/23-922). There are three **banks** in Parikia on Mavroyenous Square (to the right behind the windmill), and one in Naoussa; open Monday through Thursday from 8am to 2pm, Friday from 8am to 1:30pm. The new private **Medical Center of Paros** (☎ **0284/24-410**) is to the left (north) of the pier, across from the post office; the public **Parikia Health Clinic** (☎ **0284/22-500**) is on the central square, just down the road from the Ekatondapiliani Cathedral.

The island's only **Internet center** is in Parikia at the Sindemeno Cafe on Market Street (☎ **0284/22-003**); the fee is Dr2,500 ($8) per hour. Connection speeds here tend to be quite good. Drop-off **laundry** service is available at the Laundry House, on the paralia near the post office (☎ **0284/24-898**). To reach the **police,** call ☎ 0284/ 100 or 0284/23-333. In Marpissa, call ☎ **0284/ 41-202;** in Naoussa ☎ **0284/ 51-202.** The **Tourist Police** (☎ **0284/21-673**) are in Parikia behind the windmill on the port. The **post office** in Parikia (☎ **0284/21-236**) is left from the windmill on the waterfront road, open Monday through Friday from 7:30am to 2pm, with extended hours in July and August. The **telephone office (OTE)** in Parikia (☎ **0284/ 22-135**) is just to the right from the windmill; open from 7:30am to midnight. (If the front door is closed, go around to the back, as wind direction determines which door is open.) There's a branch in Naoussa with similar hours.

WHAT TO SEE & DO
THE TOP ATTRACTIONS

Panayia Ekatondapiliani Cathedral. Parikia, 84400 Paros. Museum ☎ **0284/21-243.** Admission Dr500 ($1.70). Daily 8am–1pm and 4–9pm. On the central square of Parikia, opposite and north of the ferry pier.

The town's most famous sight is the Byzantine cathedral of Panayia Ekatondapiliani (Our Lady of a Hundred Doors). The cathedral is surrounded by a high white wall built as protection from pirates; in the thickness of the wall are rows of monk's cells, now housing a small shop and ecclesiastical museum. After you step through the outer gate, the noise of the town vanishes, and you enter a garden with lemon trees and flowering shrubs. The cathedral contains several icons dating back as far as the 15th century, and a fine cruciform baptismal font from the 4th century. The museum (to the right as you enter the front gate) contains many 16th- to 19th-century icons and beautiful objects used to celebrate the varied ceremonies of the Orthodox Church; although the museum is small, it's well worth the entrance fee.

Archaeological Museum. Parikia, 84400 Paros. ☎ **0284/21-231.** Admission Dr500 ($1.70) adults, Dr300 ($1) students. Tues–Sun 8:30am–2:30pm. Behind the cathedral, opposite the playing fields of the local school.

The museum's most valued holding is a fragment of the famous Parian Chronicle; the Ashmolean Museum at Oxford University has a larger portion. The chronicle, carved on marble tablets, was found in the 17th century and contains valuable information from which many of the events of Greek history are dated. (Interestingly, it gives us information about artists, poets, and playwrights, but doesn't bother to mention political leaders or battles.) The museum also contains a Winged Victory from the 5th century B.C.; some objects found at the local temple of Apollo; and part of a marble monument with a frieze of **Archilochus,** the important 7th-century B.C. lyric poet known as the inventor of iambic meter and for his ironic detachment— "What breaks me, young friend, is tasteless desire, lifeless verse, boring dinners."

The Valley of Petaloudes. Petaloudes, 84400 Paros. Admission Dr800 ($2.70). Daily 8am–1pm and 4–8pm. Head 4km (2½ miles) south of Parikia on the coast road, turn left at the sign for the nunnery of Christou sto Dassos, and continue another 2½ km (1½ miles).

Another name for this oasis of plum, pear, fig, and pomegranate trees is *Psychopiani* ("soul softs"). The butterflies, actually tiger moths (*Panaxia quadripunctaria poda*), look like black-and-white–striped arrowheads until they fly up to reveal their bright red underwings. They have been coming here for at least 300 years because of the freshwater spring, flowering trees, dense foliage, and cool shade, and are most numerous in May and June. Kostas Gravaris, the custodian of this place, recommends that you come in the early morning or evening when the butterflies are most active. There's a small snack bar. Donkey or mule rides from Parikia to the site along a back road cost about Dr2,000 ($7). You can take the Pounda and Aliki bus, which drops you off at the turnoff to the nunnery; you'll have to walk the remaining 2½ kilometers (1½ miles) in to Petaloudes.

Marathi Marble Quarries. Marathi, 84400 Paros. Open site.

The inland road to Lefkes and Marpissa will take you up the side of a mountain to the marble quarries at Marathi, source of the famous Parian marble. This marble was prized for its translucency and fine, soft texture, and was used by ancient sculptors for their best work, including the *Hermes* of Praxitelous and the *Venus de Milo*. The turnoff to the quarries is signposted, and a path paved with marble leads up the valley toward a group of deserted buildings. These once belonged to a French mining company, the last to operate here, which in 1844 quarried the marble for Napoleon's tomb. There isn't much to see now unless you're a spelunker at heart, in which case you'll find it irresistible to explore the deep caverns opened by the miners high above the valley. Take a flashlight, or if you haven't got one, a ball of thread might be a reasonable substitute.

BEACHES

The beaches of Paros are small and overcrowded in comparison with nearby Naxos, but there is an abundance of sea sand to be found, as well as a few exceptional beaches. One of the island's best and most famous beaches, picturesque ✪ **Kolimbithres** ("Fonts"), is an hour's walk or a 10-minute moped ride west from Naoussa. It has smooth giant rocks, some reminiscent of baptismal fonts, that divide the smooth golden-sand beach into several tiny coves. There are a few tavernas nearby; we recommend the **Dolphin Taverna**, to the south, open from 7am to 2am, for traditional Greek food. North of the beach at Kolimbithres, by the Ayios Ioannis Church, is **Monastery Beach**, with some nudism, and the Monasteri Club, a bar-restaurant with music and beach service. Most of the other beaches west of Naoussa are overcrowded because of all the new hotels. Caïques depart from Naoussa to Kolimbithres, Monastery, and Langeri beaches, and cost about Dr1,000 ($3.35) round-trip.

About 2½ kilometers (1½ miles) north of Naoussa on an unimproved road is the popular **Langeri Beach.** A 10-minute walk further north will bring you to the nudist beach, with a gay and straight crowd.

Before you reach Langeri, the road forks to the right and leads to ✪ **Santa Maria Beach,** one of the most beautiful on the island. It has particularly clear water and shallow dunes (rare in Greece) of fine sand along the irregular coastline. It also offers some of the best windsurfing on the island. The excellent **Aristophanes Taverna** serves grilled fresh fish and meats and sometimes a feast of superb grilled *astakos* (local lobster) with wine, cheese, and salad for about Dr12,500 ($42) for two. The Aristophanes also offers villas for rent. The nearby **Santa Maria Surf Club** provides windsurfing gear and lessons. There's bus service to Santa Maria beach from Naoussa twice a day; caïque day trips from Naoussa are about Dr1,700 ($6) round-trip.

Southeast of Naoussa, connected by public bus, is the fishing village of **Ambelas,** which has a good beach and some inexpensive tavernas. About a half-hour's hike south of Ambelas along the east coast, past several undeveloped beaches, brings you to **Glyfades** and just beyond it **Tsoukalia,** which are said to be the place for "radical" windsurfers. Both beaches have a few studios to rent and a restaurant. The main north-south road is nearly 1 kilometer (0.6 miles) inland at this point.

The better beaches on the east coast can be reached by public bus from Parikia and Naoussa; buses leave hourly in the summer. Unfortunately, the road is inland and you can't scope out the beaches from the bus window. Ask around about crowd conditions on the several beaches; once you've reached a beach, it's several miles to the next one.

Molos, at the tip of a small peninsula, is beautiful and convenient to the attractive inland villages of Marmara and Marpissa, where there are rooms to let, so it can sometimes get crowded.

The next major beach, ✪ **Chrissi Akti (Golden Beach),** a kilometer of fine golden sand, is generally considered the best beach on the island. It's also the windiest, although the wind is usually offshore. As a result, this has become the primary windsurfing center on the island, and has hosted the World Cup windsurfing championship every year since 1993. Many overnight visitors head south to nearby **Drios,** a pretty village that is fast becoming a resort town, with hotels, luxury villas, waterside tavernas, and rooms to let. Buses run from Drios to Parikia five times daily, hourly in the summer.

The next beach south of Drios, **Loloantonis,** is about 200 meters long and protected from the meltemi winds by a rocky headland. The beach is usually uncrowded, and has a small taverna and a snack shop. If you take the bus you'll have to walk in 1.5 kilometers (1 mile) along a gravel road, signposted from the Drios-Parikia road.

Just south of Aliki, on the south shore of the island, is beautiful, sheltered **Faranga Beach,** a short walk in from the main road.

TOWNS & VILLAGES

Until recently **Naoussa** was a fishing village with simple white houses in a labyrinth of narrow streets, but it's now a growing resort center with good restaurants, trendy bars, and sophisticated boutiques. Most of the new building has been concentrated along the nearby beaches, and the town itself still retains much charm, with colorful caïques in its harbor, the nearby half-submerged ruins of a Venetian fortress, and fishermen still calmly going about their work. There are a number of good beaches within walking distance of town, or you can catch a caïque to the more distant ones.

The ruins of the Venetian fortress on the east end are most impressive when lighted at night. The most colorful **local festival** is held on August 23, when the battle against the pirate Barbarossa is reenacted by torch-lit boats converging on the harbor; this is followed by feasting, dancing, and general merriment.

The ever helpful **Nissiotissa Tours** (☎ **0284/51-480** or 0284/52-094; fax 0284/51-189) can be found off the left side of the main square near the bus station, across the lane from the Naoussa Sweet Shop. Cathy and Kostas Gavalas, Greek Americans who are experts on this area of the island, can help you find accommodations, book Olympic flights, and arrange other plane, ferry, and excursion tickets, island tours, and rental cars.

Buses to Parikia leave the main square in Naoussa on the half hour from 8:30am to 8:30pm, more frequently in July and August. Service to other villages on narrow dirt roads is infrequent (check the schedule at the station). There are daily excursion tours from Naoussa to Mikonos; inquire with a local travel agent.

Hilltop **Lefkes** is the medieval capital of the island. Its whitewashed houses with red-tile roofs form a maze around the central square. Lefkes was built in such an inaccessible location and with an intentionally confusing pattern of streets to thwart pirates. Test your own powers of navigation by finding the famous **Ayia Triada** (Holy Trinity) **Church,** whose carved marble towers are visible above the town.

OUTDOOR PURSUITS

BICYCLING   Paros's interior roads are too hilly for most cyclists; the rolling coastal road which circles the island's periphery is more suited to cycling, and has few long

The Cave of Andiparos

If you're looking to get away from all the crowds in Parikia, you might appreciate a visit to **Andiparos** ("Opposite Paros"). This islet, about a kilometer (0.6 miles) off the western coast of Paros, was once connected to it by a natural causeway. In recent years, Andiparos has begun to attract its own crowds—but even though you may not be able to completely escape civilization, this smaller, quieter island still has much to offer, including a huge cave full of fantastic stalactites. It was discovered on Andiparos during the time of Alexander the Great, and it's been a compelling reason to visit ever since.

Excursion caïques leave the port of Parikia regularly (hourly in the summer), beginning at 8am for the 45-minute ride to the busy little port of Andiparos. There is also a shuttle barge for vehicles as well as passengers that crosses the channel between the southern port of Pounda and Andiparos continuously from 9am; the fare is Dr500 ($1.70), and you can take along your bicycle for no extra charge. There are also round-trip caïque excursions that include a visit to the cave from Parikia for about Dr3,000 ($10), and from Naoussa for Dr2,100 ($7).

The impressive **cave** is a half-hour walk up from the boat landing or a 2-hour hike from the port of Andiparos. From the church of Ayios Ioannis, you'll have an excellent view of Folegandros (farthest west), Sikinos, Ios, and part of Paros. Tourists once entered the cave by rope, but a concrete staircase now offers more convenient—if less adventuresome—access. The cave is about 90 meters (300 ft.) deep, but the farthest reaches are now closed to visitors. Through the centuries, visitors have broken off parts of stalactites as souvenirs and left graffiti to commemorate their visit, but the cool, mysterious cavern is still worth exploring. An hour spent in the dark, echo-filled chamber trying to decipher some of the inscriptions offers a unique contrast to all your hours devoted to lying on a sun-drenched beach. You'll also be in the company of such distinguished guests as Lord Byron and King Otto of Greece, who each left behind evidence of his visit. The Marquis de Nointel celebrated Christmas mass here in 1673 with 500 paid attendants, plus explosions to add drama.

Andiparos town, with a permanent population of about 700, has several travel agents, a bank with limited hours, a post office, and a small telephone office (OTE). You'll find a plentiful selection of shops and tavernas along the harbor front, and inland a fine **Kastro,** the remains of the medieval fortified town.

If you're spending the night, we suggest the comfortable **Hotel Artemis,** at the end of the paralia (☎ **0284/61-460;** fax 0284/61-472); or the **Hotel Mantalena** (☎ **0284/61-206**), which offers rooms with views of the sea and port. There's also **Camping Andiparos** (☎ **0284/61-221**), with full facilities about a 10-minute walk north from the port.

Of the several eateries to choose from, we recommend the **Anargyros** taverna, on the port below the hotel of the same name; **Klimataria,** inland about 100 meters; and the more expensive **Marios Taverna,** near the square, which features seafood dinners and local wine.

climbs. Road quality on the peripheral road is good, and there are many unpaved roads that are popular with local mountain bikers—ask at **Mountain Bike Club Paros** (☎ 0284/23-778) for recommendations of trails to match your skill level. A beater bike, suitable for getting around the town or travel to nearby beaches, will cost about Dr2,000 ($7) per day. For Dr4,500 ($15) a day you can rent a specialized mountain bike, tuned up and ready to ride; the rental includes helmet, pump, repair kit, water bottle, and a map of island trails. Guided rides are also organized during the summer. Mountain Bike Club Paros is north of the bus station, just off the waterfront, facing a fenced archaeological site.

WALKING   Paros has numerous old roads connecting the interior towns, many of which are still in good condition and perfect for walking. The best trail maps are the *Map of Paros,* for sale at the **Foreign Press Agency** (see "Shopping," below), and the *Mountain Bike Club Paros* map (see "Bicycling," above). One of the best known trails is the **Byzantine Road** between Lefkes and Prodromos, a narrow path paved along much of its 4-kilometer (2½-mile) length with marble slabs. It's best to begin in Lefkes, since from there the way is mostly downhill. There isn't an easy way to find the beginning of the Byzantine Road among the labyrinthine streets of Lefkes; the best we can suggest is to begin at the church square, from which point you can see the Byzantine road in a valley at the edge of the town, to the west. Having fixed your bearings, plunge into the maze of streets and spiral your way down and to the right. After a 2-minute descent, you emerge into a ravine, with open fields beyond, and a sign indicates the beginning of the Byzantine Road. It's easy going through terraced fields, a leisurely hour's walk to the Marpissa Road, from which point you can catch the bus back to Parikia (check the schedule and exact pick-up point beforehand). This also makes a good (and technically challenging) mountain-bike outing.

WINDSURFING   The continuous winds on Paros's east coast have made it a favorite destination for windsurfers, and there are several equipment-rental and instruction outfitters. The best months are July and August, but since the beaches are packed at these times, serious windsurfers may want to plan their travel for earlier or later in the season. The **World Cup** has been held on Golden Beach for the past six consecutive years, bringing Paros to the attention of windsurfers from around the globe. The *Paros Windsurfing Guide* has a good small map of the island, maps of several beaches, and a wealth of useful information for windsurfers; you can pick up your free copy at most of the tourist offices in Parikia or Naoussa. On Golden Beach you can rent a board at **Sunwind BIC Center** (☎ 0284/42-900; fax 0284/42-384; www.ultranet.com/~sunwind; e-mail: sunwind@otenet.gr), where there's a surf shop and cafe. For Dr4,500 ($15), you'll get a board, sail, harness, and wet suit for 1 hour; instruction is an additional Dr1,000 ($3.35) per hour. Weekly packages are also available, including board rental and accommodation. In Naoussa, you can rent equipment from **Club Mistral** (☎ 0284/52-010; fax 0284/51-720) at the Porto Paros Hotel near Kolimbithres Beach.

SHOPPING

Market Street in Parikia is the shopping hub of the island, with many interesting alternatives to the ubiquitous souvenir stores. A good selection of English-language periodicals is available at Marcos Bizas's **Foreign Press Agency** (☎ 0284/21-247) on Market Street (there isn't a sign—just look for the books and magazines in the window). At **Geteki** (☎ 0284/21-855), you'll find a collection of paintings and sculpture by French artist Jacques Fleureaux, now a full-time resident of Paros. He makes use of local materials (clay, driftwood) and motifs (Cycladic figurines) in his work. Also for sale here are Afghani rugs and local ceramics by other artists. **Pali Poli** (☎ 0284/21-909), opposite the Apollon Restaurant in the agora, has a fine selection of antique vernacular furniture from the islands and the Greek mainland. There are also many smaller items, such as finely decorated mirror frames, water jugs hollowed from solid wood, and handmade household utensils.

In Naoussa, be sure to visit the **Metaxas Gallery** (☎ 0284/52-667), in the old town, which has exhibitions of paintings by local artists (sometimes for sale) and a collection of locally crafted jewelry in gold and silver. Perched above the village of Kostos, on the road between Parikia and Lefkes, you'll find **Studio Yria** (☎ 0284/ 29-007), where local craftspersons Stelio and Monika Ghikis produce functional earthenware that incorporates indigenous designs, including an abstract octopus motif. They also sell weavings and objects of cast bronze, forged iron, and Parian marble.

WHERE TO STAY
PARIKIA

The port town has three basic hotel zones: the **agora,** the **harbor,** and the **beach.** The agora is the heart of Parikia, and can get noisy; accommodations in the quiet back streets are most enticing. The harborside near the windmill is a convenient and lively place, but it's often too noisy for a good night's rest. The strip of hotels along Livadi beach—north of the windmill, left coming from the ferry—have three common features: bland decor, proximity to the crowded town beach, and sea views.

The gauntlet of room hawkers that meet you at the port gets increasingly daunting. We recommend ignoring them unless you're absolutely desperate—the rooms offered are usually a considerable distance from the town and many don't meet basic standards of comfort and cleanliness.

In addition to the choices below, you might consider the small, simple, and inexpensive **Hotel Captain Manolis,** in the center of the agora (☎ 0284/21-244).

Hotel Argonauta. Agora, Parikia, 84400 Paros. ☎ **0284/21-440.** Fax 0284/23-442. 15 units. A/C TEL. Dr14,000 ($47) double. EURO, MC, V.

This charming and comfortable hotel is at the far end of Mavroyenous Square, opposite the Ethniki (National) Bank, so it's refreshingly quiet. The rooms are modern and well equipped with a few traditional touches; they're built around an inner second-floor courtyard. The owners, Soula and Dimitri Ghikas, make their spacious and attractive lobby feel like home.

Hotel Asterias. Parikia, 84400 Paros. ☎ **0284/21-797.** Fax 0284/22-172. 36 units. TEL. Dr16,500 ($55) double. Rates include breakfast. MC, V.

A buffet breakfast is served in the breakfast room, the only room with some degree of character in this rather bland hotel. The hotel is just across the street from the bay, and most units have balconies facing the water; those on the other side of the building have views toward the interior hills of the island.

✪ **Hotel Dina.** Market St., Parikia, 84400 Paros. ☎ **0284/21-325** or 0284/21-345. Fax 0284/23-525. 8 units. Dr11,500 ($38) double. No credit cards. The entrance is just off Market St., next to the Apollon Restaurant and across from the Pirate Bar.

More pension than hotel, these cozy rooms are reached through a narrow, plant-filled courtyard, off one of the finest small plazas in Parikia. Dina Patelis has been the friendly proprietor for nearly 3 decades, and she has created an excellent establishment with a personal quality that keeps her guests coming back year after year. Three guest rooms open to the square, and room no. 2, with a private balcony, is especially desirable. The rest of the units face a small garden courtyard, and room no. 8 has the additional benefit of a view toward the hills and a private terrace.

Hotel Oasis. Harbor, Parikia, 84400 Paros. ☎ **0284/21-227.** Fax 0284/23-257. 20 units. TV TEL. Dr15,000 ($50) double; Dr18,000 ($60) triple. Continental breakfast Dr800 ($2.70) extra. AE, MC, V. Just north of the windmill, on the central square.

This is the best hotel on the harbor, with an ideally central but rather noisy location. All but one of the rooms have balconies looking out over the square, the port, and the bay. The rooms are spare and comfortable, a little short on character, with marble floors and contemporary furnishings. Breakfast is available at the Oasis Cafe next door, which is also open throughout the day and night for drinks and light meals. Fondas Vaggelis is the jovial proprietor.

Hotel Platanos. Parikia, 84400 Paros. ☎ and fax **0284/24-262.** 12 units. TEL. Dr17,000 ($57) double. Continental breakfast Dr1,000–Dr1,500 ($3.35–$5) extra. No credit cards. Located 800 meters south of the windmill and 200 meters in from the beach.

This small hotel is an attractive blend of traditional stonework and modern construction. The neighborhood is quiet, the rooms are comfortable, and Ursula and Anestis Antonionou are gracious hosts. Call ahead and they'll pick you up at the port—a good idea, since it's a 10-minute walk, and the place can be hard to find. The beach and the agora are 2 minutes from the hotel on foot. All rooms but one have a balcony, looking toward the sea or over the neighboring fields. The pine furnishings are simple and tasteful, floors are marble, and the bathroom is tiled in a deep blue. This is a casual place where children are most welcome.

✪ **Pension Vangelistra.** Parikia, 84400 Paros. ☎ **0284/21-482.** Fax 0284/22-464. 10 units. Dr12,000 ($40) double; Dr15,000 ($50) apt. No credit cards. Follow the central square to the cathedral, and continue back on a road just to the right of the town school, with the small Catholic church on your right. You'll reach an intersection in about 100m—turn right, and the pension will be on your left.

Call Yorgos and Voula Maounis, and one of their friendly English-speaking kids will help you find this cozy and attractive lodging in a quiet neighborhood, a 5-minute walk from the pier. All rooms have balconies, with views over the rooftops or toward the hills behind the town; most rooms have kitchenettes, and all have small fridges. The best option is the apartment in the back garden, a small cottage with kitchen and bedroom/dining room, and a semiprivate terrace.

SOUTH OF PARIKIA

Hotel Yria. Parasporos, 84400 Paros. ☎ **0284/24-154.** Fax 0284/21-167. 68 units. A/C MINIBAR TV TEL. Dr35,800 ($119) double; Dr42,600 ($142) suite. Lunch or dinner Dr5,000 ($17) extra. AE, DC, MC, V. Located 2½ km (1½ miles) south of the port.

This new bungalow complex is just too good to be ignored. The architecture is traditional with a villagelike plan, and while not all rooms have a sea view, the grounds are so beautifully landscaped and well maintained that you won't feel deprived if your room faces inward. Facilities include a big handsome freshwater pool, a fair beach nearby, tennis and basketball courts, a children's playground, a spacious lounge, and a good dining room. The hotel offers an information desk, currency exchange, car rental, travel arrangements, laundry, and fax and mail service. The staff is well trained, friendly, courteous, and exceptionally helpful.

NAOUSSA

If you haven't made reservations in the high season and are unable to find a room, try **Nissiotissa Tours** (☎ **0284/51-480**), just off the east (left) side of the main square. In addition to the following choices, you might try the moderately priced

Captain Dounas Apartments (☎ **0284/52-525** or 0284/52-585; in winter 01/ 894-4047; fax 0284/52-586; e-mail: dounas@par.forthnet.gr), which stand on a rocky promontory between Naoussa and Ayii Anaryiri Beach; about half of the units directly face the sea.

Astir of Paros. Kolimbithres Beach (west of Naoussa, off the south end of the beach), 84401 Paros. ☎ **0284/51-976** or 0284/51-707. Fax 0284/51-985. agn.hol.gr/hotels/astir/astir.htm. E-mail: astir@prometheus.hol.gr. 61 units. A/C MINIBAR TV TEL. Dr50,000 ($167) double; Dr56,000–Dr135,000 ($187–$450) suite. AE, DC, MC, V.

The most extravagant hotel on the island is built like a Cycladic village and has a sumptuous garden. There's a small private beach, a three-hole golf course, a good pool, Jacuzzi, tennis court, gym, and art gallery. Contemporary Greek art is on display in the elegant reception area. The staff is especially attentive. Double rooms are unexceptional, but the suites are spacious and elegantly furnished; the suite bathrooms are paneled in marble, and are also very roomy. Four rooms offer handicapped access.

Hotel Fotilia. Naoussa, 84401 Paros. ☎ **0284/52-581** or 0284/52-582. Fax 0284/52-583. 14 units. TEL. Dr20,000 ($67) double; Dr24,000 ($80) triple. Rates include breakfast (except studios). No credit cards.

Climb to the top of the steps at the end of town, and to the left of the hilltop church you'll see a restored windmill behind a stone archway. The companionable Michel Leondaris will probably meet you with a cup of coffee or glass of wine. The rooms are spacious and furnished in an elegant country style, with crisp blue-and-white curtains that open to balconies overlooking the old harbor and bay. Studio apartments with kitchenette are available for the same price as a room; breakfast is not included with the studios.

Hotel Petres. Naoussa, 84401 Paros. ☎ **0284/52-467.** Fax 0284/52-759. 16 units. A/C MINIBAR TEL. Dr22,000 ($73) double; Dr27,900 ($93) triple. Rates include breakfast. No credit cards.

Clea Hatzinkolakis has decorated her charming reception area with antiques and her guest rooms with loving care. The beds have handsome woven covers, hand-crocheted lace is draped over the lamps, and the walls are adorned with prints from the Benaki Museum. Her "honeymoon suite" contains her grandmother's marriage bed. The breakfast buffet is unusually extensive, and dinner is available on request; every Saturday in summer there's a barbeque at the poolside grill. Clea is a source of extensive knowledge concerning the island and its inhabitants. Free transportation to and from the airport or port is available on request. Since the hotel is 1 kilometer (0.6 miles) from Naoussa, it's very quiet but somewhat disconnected from the life of the town.

Kalypso Hotel. Ayii Anaryiri Beach, 84401 Paros. ☎ **0284/51-488.** Fax 0284/51-607. agn.hol.gr/hotels/kalypso/kalypso.htm. E-mail: kalypso@otenet.gr. 40 units. TV TEL. Dr18,000 ($60) double; Dr19,000 ($63) studio. Rates include breakfast. AE, MC, V.

A 10-minute walk along the coast from Naoussa brings you to this traditional-style hotel, built right on the sand of the pleasant Ayii Anaryiri Beach. You enter the hotel through a cobblestone courtyard, surmounted by a wooden mezzanine. About three-quarters of the rooms have balconies overlooking the sea; the remaining units face a narrow street behind the hotel. A row of shaded beachfront tables is a great place to have breakfast or just enjoy the salt air and view across the bay.

✪ **Papadakis Hotel.** Naoussa, 84401 Paros. ☎ **0284/51-643** or 0284/52-504. Fax 0284/51-269. 19 units. Dr18,000 ($60) double. Breakfast Dr1,700 ($6) extra. No credit cards.

A brisk 5-minute walk uphill from the main square brings you to the new Papadakis, which offers the best views in town—the view over the village and bay is exceptional from every room. The large guest rooms were renovated in 1998, with new wardrobes, beds, and desks in dark walnut; several units have sofas that can sleep another person. Ten rooms have satellite TV and minibars, five are air-conditioned, and several have kitchenettes. The excellent breakfast includes homemade baked goods.

WHERE TO DINE
PARIKIA

Walk along the bed of the dry river that cuts through Mavroyenous Square's north side to **Symposium** (☎ 0284/24-147), an elegant coffeehouse perched on a bridge. Enjoy a slow cup of coffee or tea here, or try the dependable continental breakfast or crepes.

Apollon. Agora. ☎ **0284/21-875.** Main courses Dr2,000–Dr5,000 ($7–$17). MC, V. Daily 5pm–midnight. GREEK/CONTINENTAL.

This popular restaurant in the heart of the agora inhabits the halls and garden courtyard of an old olive-pressing factory. The menu includes a range of traditional Greek dishes and a variety of steaks; the specialties include a veal fillet with white-wine cream sauce, *dolmadakia* (stuffed grape leaves), and *bourekakia* (a fried purée of roasted eggplant, feta, and ham). Both the food and the service possess a degree of sophistication that is hard to find elsewhere on this island. Host Theo Maniatis owns a farm in his native Sparta, where the excellent olives and olive oil for his restaurant are produced.

Bountaraki. Paralia. ☎ **0284/22-297.** Main courses Dr1,200–Dr4,000 ($4–$13). No credit cards. Daily 1–5pm and 7pm–midnight. Walk all the way to the southern extremity of the paralia, where a bridge spans the dry streambed and the road curves up to the right toward the Xenia hotel; Bountaraki is on the left, just after the bridge. GREEK.

Many small details set this taverna apart from its neighbors: fresh brown bread that's refreshingly flavorful and almost a meal in itself, and simple main courses that don't drown the taste of the food in too much oil. There's a small porch in front, facing the quieter southern end of the paralia. As with all the local tavernas, don't bother with the desserts, which are clearly an afterthought.

✪ **Happy Green Cow.** Agora. ☎ **0284/24-691.** Main courses Dr700–Dr2,000 ($2.35–$7). No credit cards. Daily noon–3pm and 6pm–2am. VEGETARIAN.

Four tables huddle in the tiny dining room of the Happy Green Cow, a funky place with simple vegetarian dishes, thoughtfully prepared. Traditional Greek dishes are available, if you can call "souvlaki soya" traditional, and are joined by tacos, felafel, burritos, and curries; all the above are also available at the restaurant's take-out window, the only option if you feel like eating outside.

Porphyra. Paralia. ☎ **0284/22-693.** Main courses Dr1,500–Dr3,000 ($5–$10). AE, V. Daily 6:30pm–midnight. Closed Jan–Feb. Between the pier and the post office, just back from the waterfront. GREEK/FISH.

The small Porphyra serves the best fish in town. The nondescript, utilitarian service and decor are typical of your average taverna; the difference here is that the owner cultivates the shellfish himself, resulting in an exceptional Mussels Saganaki (mussels cooked with tomato, feta, and wine). The tzatziki and other traditional cold appetizers are also very good. The fish is predictably fresh, and offerings vary with the season.

✪ **Tamarisco.** Agora. No phone. Reservations recommended July–Aug. Main courses Dr1,400–Dr4,000 ($4.70–$13). AE, V. Daily 7pm–midnight. Closed Jan–Feb. Follow the signs from Market Street to this quiet back plaza of busy Parikia. GREEK/VEGETARIAN.

Although most summer diners will sit outside in the garden courtyard, the indoor dining room here is particularly pleasant: exposed ceiling beams, a flagstone floor, simple comely furniture, and tapestried walls combine to create a space of unusual comfort and warmth. Eleni, co-owner of the restaurant with her husband, Menios, is a native of Paros and uses many local recipes that you won't find elsewhere. The menu features subtle and delightful use of fresh herbs, innovative vegetable dishes, fresh pasta, and a variety of fish. If you're looking for traditional Greek food that's full of surprises and refreshingly contemporary, this is the place.

NAOUSSA

Naoussa's main square has plenty of casual eateries. The **Naoussa Pâtisserie,** on the east side of the square, has delicious cheese pies, pastries, biscuits, and espresso. The village's **bread bakery** is past the church near Christo's Taverna. The beautiful **Kavarnis Bar,** Odos Archilochus, just around the corner from the post office (☎ **0284/51-038**), takes you back to Paris in the 1920s, serving up elaborate cocktails and delectable crepes (try the famous cognac crepe) along with modern jazz.

Barbarossa Ouzeri. The waterfront. ☎ **0284/51-391.** Appetizers Dr550–Dr1,200 ($1.85–$4). No credit cards. Daily 1pm–1am. GREEK.

This authentic ouzeri is right on the port. Old, wind-burned fishermen sit for hours nursing their milky ouzo in water and their miniportions of grilled octopus and olives. If you haven't partaken of this experience yet, this is the place to try it.

Christo's Taverna. Odos Archilochus. ☎ **0284/51-442.** Reservations recommended July–Aug. Main courses Dr1,200–Dr3,500 ($4–$12). No credit cards. Daily 7:30–11:30pm. EURO-GREEK.

Christo's is known for its eclectic menu and Euro-Greek style. Dinner-only is served in a beautiful garden filled with red and pink geraniums. The color of the dark purple grape clusters dripping through the trellised roof in late summer is unforgettable. Classical music soothes as you dine on elegantly prepared, freshly made veal, lamb, or steak dishes.

Lalula. Naoussa. ☎ **0284/51-547.** Reservations recommended July–Aug. Main courses Dr2,000–Dr3,600 ($7–$12). No credit cards. Daily 7–11:45pm. Take a left at the post office; the Lalula is across from the Minoa Hotel. GREEK/MEDITERRANEAN/VEGETARIAN.

We like this special place for the delicious and distinctive food, subdued decor, and interesting but unobtrusive music. There's a lovely little garden in the back. The cooking is lighter and more refined than usually found in Greece, and the menu is imaginative and eclectic, depending upon what's fresh at the market. Regular items include vegetable quiche, sweet-and-sour chicken with rice and ginger chutney, and fish steamed in herbs.

Pervolaria. Naoussa. ☎ **0284/51-598.** Main courses Dr1,900–Dr4,200 ($6–$14). AE, V. Daily 7pm–midnight. GREEK.

This good restaurant is set in a lush garden with geraniums and grapevines behind a white stucco house decorated with local ceramics, about 100 meters back from the port. Favorite courses here include schnitzel à la chef (veal in cream sauce with tomatoes and basil) and tortellini Pervolaria (with pepperoni and bacon), but the Greek plate with souvlaki and varied appetizers is also recommended.

MARPISSA

Corina Taverna. Marpissa. ☎ **0284/41-049.** Main courses Dr1,300–Dr2,900 ($4.35–$10). No credit cards. Daily 9am–4pm and 7pm–midnight. GREEK.

Beware the *Bomba*

Several places on the strip in Parikia offer very cheap drinks or "buy one, get one free"—this is usually locally brewed alcohol that the locals call *bomba*. It's illegal, and it makes one intoxicated quickly and very sick afterward.

A convivial atmosphere reigns at this small taverna, operated by French/American Corina, who draws a loyal following. There is a variety of traditional Greek dishes, including the specialty of the house: a platter of 12 mezedes for two with wine, for Dr6,500 ($22). Several vegetable dishes are also offered. Corina has lived in Greece for more than 2 decades, and is a great source of information on the islands. Ask for her excellent photocopied map of attractions on Paros (in French).

PAROS AFTER DARK

Just behind the windmill in Parikia is a local landmark, the **Port Cafe,** a basic kafenio lit by bare incandescent bulbs and filled day and night with tourists waiting for a ferry, bus, taxi, or fellow traveler. The cafe serves coffee, pastry, and drinks; it's a good place for casual conversation.

The ✪ **Pebbles Bar** on the paralia plays classical music at sunset; it's a highly congenial place, as popular with locals as it is with visitors. The **Saloon d'Or** (☎ 0284/22-176), south of Parikia's port, is more touristy, but it is a popular place for starting the evening with fairly inexpensive drinks. Continue south from Parikia along the coast road, turn left at the bridge, and about 100 meters later you should have no difficulty finding a complex with the **Dubliner** (☎ 0284/22-759), which has loud live rock several nights a week and appeals to a young crowd.

If you're not in the mood to party, Parikia offers several more-elegant alternatives. The **Pirate Bar** (☎ 0284/21-114), a few doors away from the Hotel Dina in the agora, is a tastefully decorated nightspot with a stone interior and dark wooden beams; it plays mellow jazz, blues, and classical music. Back on the paralia, **Evinos Bar** has a great view of the harbor—it's above the retaining wall south of the OTE, high enough above the madding crowd that you can hear the music and enjoy the scenery. For partiers in Parikia, there's **Black Bart's** (☎ 0284/21-802), midway on the paralia in Parikia, a good place for loud music and boisterous big drinkers. The outdoor **Ciné Rex** (☎ 0284/21-676) in Parikia shows two features, often in English.

There seems to be little traditional Greek entertainment on Paros, but if you're interested, ask about the possibility of seeing a performance by **N.E.L.E.** This group performs traditional dances in costume, usually in Naoussa.

Bars in Naoussa tend to be more sophisticated and considerably less raucous than in Parikia. The hot spot is still **Banana Moon,** about a 10-minute walk up the main street. There's also an outdoor movie theater in Naoussa, **Makis Cinema** (☎ 0284/ 22-221), with nightly features usually at 10pm and midnight; these are often action films in English.

5 Naxos

191km (103 nautical miles) SE of Piraeus

Fertile, self-sufficient Naxos is not yet as developed for tourism as neighboring Paros, but it's working hard to catch up. A wealthy agricultural island, Naxos exports an abundant harvest of olives, grapes, and potatoes throughout the Aegean, and until recently showed little interest in promoting itself as a tourist destination. That's all changed in the past 10 years—a new airport has increased the flow of visitors, and big new hotels keep sprouting up to either side of the port. The harbor front in Hora has undergone massive reconstruction, successfully erasing whatever individual character this part of the town once possessed.

Thankfully, the character of the island still isn't completely dominated by the recent development. The inland mountain villages, huddled on the lower slopes of imperious Mount Zas, still preserve the rhythms of agrarian life. In Apiranthos, you can taste bread redolent with the smoky aroma of a wood oven, and in Filoti sample local wines under the magisterial arms of a venerable plane tree. The locals still have an attitude of friendly indifference (which could be misconstrued as surliness) to the visitors who pass through.

The architecture of Naxos is distinct from that of any other Cycladic isle. You'll notice immediately the fortified Venetian towers, or *piryi,* punctuating the hillsides. Also specific to Naxos is the remarkable abundance of small Byzantine chapels, many of which contain exceptional frescoes dating from the 9th to the 13th centuries. The Kastro of Hora is one of the finest medieval fortified towns in the Cyclades, and a delight to explore.

Naxos is very well connected to other islands by ferry, so you shouldn't have any trouble getting here at most times of year. It's possible to catch a bus to a village that interests you, then explore it leisurely on foot; keep in mind that island buses are reliable but infrequent. A bike may be all the transport you need to the island's beaches, which happen to be among the best in the Cyclades.

ESSENTIALS

GETTING THERE   By Plane   Olympic Airways has two flights daily (three daily in summer) between Naxos and Athens. For information and reservations, call the office in Athens (☎ **01/966-6666**) or Naxos (☎ **0285/23-043**).

By Ferry   There is one ferry daily (more in summer) from Piraeus; schedules can be checked with tourist information in **Athens** (☎ **01/171** or 01/322-2545), the **Athens Port Authority** (☎ **01/451-1310**), or the **Naxos Port Authority** (☎ **0285/22-300**). **Ilio Lines** (☎ **0285/422-4980** in Piraeus) has daily hydrofoil service from Rafina (summer only). There is at least once-daily ferry connection with Ios, Mikonos, Paros, and Santorini. There is ferry connection several times weekly with Siros, Tinos, and Sifnos, and somewhat less frequently with Folegandros, Rhodes, and Samos.

VISITOR INFORMATION   The privately operated **Naxos Tourist Information Center** (☎ **0285/22-993;** fax 0285/25-200), across the plaza from the ferry pier (not to be confused with the small office on the pier itself, which is often closed), is the most reliable and helpful source on the island for accommodations and general information. Under the energetic direction of Despina Kittini, this office provides ferry information, books inexpensive charter flights between various European airports and Athens, arranges island excursions, sells island maps, exchanges money, holds luggage, helps make card and collect phone calls, provides 2-hour laundry service, and offers a **24-hour emergency number** (☎ **0285/24-525**) for travelers on Naxos who need immediate assistance.

For ferry tickets and Olympic Airways tickets, the best place is **Zas Travel** (☎ **0285/23-330**), next to the Naxos Tourist Information Center on the paralia; they aren't very helpful with questions unrelated to ticket sales. You will want to find a good map as soon as possible, as Hora (Naxos town) is old, large (with a permanent population of more than 3,000), and complex. The free *Summer Naxos* magazine has the best map of the city. The new *Harms-Verlag Naxos* is the best map of the island, but somewhat expensive at Dr2,000 ($7) a copy.

GETTING AROUND   By Bus   You can't miss the bus station right in the middle of the port plaza at the north end of the harbor. Ask at the nearby KTEL office, across the plaza to the left, for specific schedules. There's regular service throughout most of the island two or three times a day, more frequently to the more important destinations. In summer there's hourly service to the nearby south coast beaches at Ayios Prokopios and Ayia Anna. One of the most popular day trips is to Apollonas, near the northern tip of the island. The bus only makes this 2-hour trip twice a day, and the competition for seats is often fierce, so get to the station well ahead of time. In addition to the public buses, there are various excursion buses that can be booked through travel agents.

By Bicycle   Moto Naxos (☎ 0285/23-420), on Protodikiou Square south of the paralia, has the best mountain bikes on the island. A basic bike is Dr1,500 ($5) a day; aluminum-frame mountain bikes range from Dr2,500 to Dr5,000 ($8 to $17) a day (2 days' advance notice is required for clipless pedals and shoes). **Anna's Bikes** (☎ 0285/41-778), on Ayios Prokopios Beach, has aluminum-frame bikes with front suspension for Dr2,500 ($8). All of the above rentals come with helmet, water bottle, pump, tire-repair kit, and lock.

By Moped   Moto Naxos (☎ 0285/23-420), on Protodikiou Square, and **Stelios Rent-A-Bike** (☎ 0285/25-480), near the police station, have good selections. Expect to pay Dr4,000 to Dr6,000 ($13 to $20) a day, including insurance, depending on size. Naxos has some major inclines that require a strong motor and good brakes, so a larger bike (80cc or greater) is recommended.

By Car   This is the ideal mode of transport on Naxos, and most travel agents rent them. At **AutoTour** (☎ 0285/25-480), near the police station, or at **Auto Naxos** (☎ 0285/23-420), on Protodikiou Square, a basic four-door car is about Dr12,000 ($40) per day, and a Suzuki jeep is Dr24,000 ($80) per day; both prices include full insurance.

By Taxi   A half-day round-the-island tour should cost you about Dr15,000 ($50). The taxi station (☎ 0285/22-444) is on the port. Find a compatible driver who speaks English well enough to act as a guide, then bargain and agree on a price before you depart.

FAST FACTS   Banks all keep the same hours—Monday through Thursday from 8am to 2pm, Friday from 8am to 1:30pm—but travel agencies change money during extended hours. Several banks have ATMs, the most central being the Commercial Bank (Emporiki Trapeza) on the paralia. Naxos has a good **health center** (☎ 0285/23-333), open 24 hours, just outside Hora on the left off Odos Papavasiliou, the main street off the port just after the OTE. **Holiday Laundry** offers drop-off service—you can leave your laundry with most hotels and some tourist offices, and they'll return it clean the same day. Holiday is located on Periferiakos Road, Grotta area (☎ 0285/23-988); open daily from 9am to 11pm, and the cost per load is Dr2,500 ($8). The **town police** (☎ 0285/23-280) are off the north end of the port, up from the bus station, across from the elementary school. The **tourist police** (☎ 0285/22-100) are 2 blocks behind the Panayia Pantanassa Church, just before the Agrarian Bank, about 200 meters south from the ferry pier; there's a list of hotels and private rooms here, and they can make reservations for you. To find the **post office,** continue south on the paralia past the OTE to a playground and basketball court; it is opposite the court on the left. Open from 8am to 2pm. The **telephone office (OTE)** is at the south end of the port; summer hours are daily from 7:30am to midnight.

WHAT TO SEE & DO
THE TOP ATTRACTIONS
The Portara. Hora, 83400 Naxos. Open site.

Naxos harbor is dominated by the picturesque silhouette of the Portara ("Great Door"), all that remains of an ancient Temple of Apollo. The ruin stands on the islet of Palatia, accessible by a causeway off the northern tip of the harbor. The temple was once thought to honor Dionysos, the island's patron, and is associated in the popular imagination with his rescue of Ariadne after she was abandoned on Naxos by the ungrateful Theseus. The temple is now believed to be dedicated to Apollo, due to a brief reference in the Delian Hymns and because it directly faces Delos, Apollo's birthplace. Most of the temple was carted away to build the Kastro, but fortunately the massive posts and lintel of the Portara were too big for the Venetians to handle. The small cafe/ouzeri at the end of the causeway, below the Portara, is a superb spot to watch the sunset.

✪ **Kastro/Archaeological Museum.** Hora, 84300 Naxos. Museum ☎ **0285/22-725.** Admission Dr500 ($1.70), Dr300 ($1) students. Tues–Sun 8:30am–3pm.

The museum is located in the heart of the exquisite Venetian Kastro, the medieval citadel that dominates the town—the Kastro is Hora's greatest treasure, and you should allow yourself several hours to explore it. The high walls of this hilltop citadel rise above the rooftops of the town. The Kastro ("Castle") was built in the 13th century by Marco Sanudo, nephew of the doge of Venice, and was the domain of the Catholic aristocracy.

By walking up from the seafront in Hora you'll soon reach the outer wall of the castle, which has three entryways. The most remarkable of these is the north entry, known as the Trani Porta or Strong Gate, a narrow marble arched threshold marking the transition to the Kastro's medieval world. Look for the incision on the right column of the arch, which marks the length of a Venetian yard, and was used to measure the cloth brought here for the ladies of the Venetian court. At the center of the Kastro is the 16th-century **Catholic cathedral,** with its brilliant white marble facade; it contains an icon of the Virgin which is thought to be older than the church itself. To the right behind the cathedral is the French School of Commerce and the Ursuline Convent and School.

The French School has housed schools run by several religious orders, and among its more famous students was the Cretan writer Nikos Kazantzakis, who studied here in 1896. It now houses the ✪ **Archaeological Museum.** There have been many archaeological finds on Naxos, and this museum has a great diversity of objects from several different periods. Among the highlights are the early Cycladic figurines in white marble, the earliest example of sculpture in Greece. The other prize of this museum is its collection of late Mycenaean period (1400 to 1100 B.C.) artifacts found near Grotta, including vessels with the octopus motif that still appears in local art. The museum occupies long vaulted chambers in the walls of the Kastro, with a great view from its terrace and balconies to the hills of Naxos. There is little in the way of interpretive information, and almost all of it is in Greek; serious museum-goers will appreciate the descriptive booklet available at the ticket desk for Dr1,500 ($5).

Temple of Demeter. Ano Sangri. Open site. Depart from Hora on the road to Filoti, and turn off after about 10km (6.2 miles) on the signposted road to Ano Sangri and the Temple of Demeter. From here it's another 3½ km (2.2 miles) to the temple, primarily on dirt roads (all the major turnings are signposted).

Until recently the temple, built in the 6th century B.C., was in a state of complete ruin; it had been partially dismantled in the 6th century A.D. to build a chapel on the site, and what was left was plundered repeatedly over the years. It was discovered a few years ago that virtually all the pieces of the original temple were on the site, either buried or integrated into the chapel. Then began a long process of reconstruction, which continues at present. Most of the work has been completed, and it's possible to see the basic form of the temple—this is one of the few known temples to be perfectly square in plan. Perhaps as early as 1999 the site will be officially open to the public.

BYZANTINE CHURCHES

There is a remarkable number of small Byzantine chapels on Naxos, most dating from the 9th to the 15th centuries. The prosperity of Naxos during this period of Byzantine rule meant that sponsorship existed for elaborate frescoes, many of which can still be seen on the interior walls of the chapels. Restoration has revealed multiple layers of frescoes, and whenever possible the more recent ones have been removed intact during the process of revealing the initial paintings. Several frescoes removed in this way from the churches of Naxos can be seen at the Byzantine Museum in Athens.

Just south of Moni, near the middle of the island, is the important 6th-century monastery of ✪ **Panayia Drossiani** ("Our Lady of Refreshment"), which contains some of the finest frescoes on Naxos. Visits are allowed at all hours during the day; when the door is locked, the custom is to ring the church bell to summon the caretaker (remember to dress appropriately). To get here, drive about 1 kilometer (0.6 miles) south from Moni and look for the low, grey rounded form of the church on your left.

About 8 kilometers (5 miles) from Hora along the road to Sangri, you'll see a sign on the left for the 8th-century Byzantine cathedral of Ayios Mamas, which fell into disrepair during the Venetian occupation but has recently been partly restored. South of the pretty little village of Ano ("Upper") Sangri is the small Byzantine chapel of Ayios Ioannis Yiroulas. It was built over an ancient temple of Demeter and is accessible on foot or by an unimproved road off the main road south from Sangri. About 1 kilometer (0.6 miles) west of Sangri on the road to Halki is the ✪ **Kaloritsa chapel,** a cave inside the hilltop ruins of a Byzantine chapel. The earliest of the frescoes seen here date from the 10th century. The chapel is accessible only on foot; for directions see "Walking" under "Outdoor Pursuits," below.

EXPLORING THE VILLAGES OF NAXOS

The expansive interior of Naxos holds many small villages within the folds of its hills. Each is quite unique, and you could easily spend several days exploring them. The bus between Hora and Apollonas makes stops at each of the villages mentioned below, but because are only two buses daily, you'll have considerably more freedom if you can arrange your own transportation.

Halki, 16 kilometers (9.9 miles) from Hora, has a lovely central square shaded by a magnificent plane tree. The 19th-century neoclassical homes of this town lend the streets a certain grandeur. The fine 11th-century white church with the red-tiled roof, **Panayia Protothronos** ("Our Lady Before the Throne"), is sometimes open in the morning. Turn right to reach the Frankopoulos (or Grazia) tower. The name says it's Frankish, but it was originally Byzantine; a marble crest gives the year of 1742, when it was renovated by the Venetians. Climb the steps for an excellent view of Filoti, one of the island's largest inland villages.

The brilliant white houses of **Filoti** (2km/1.2 miles up the road from Halki) are draped elegantly along the lower slopes of Mount Zas, the highest peak in the

Cyclades. The center of town life is the ample main square, shaded by a massive plane tree; the kafenion at the center of the square and two tavernas within 50 meters are all authentic and welcoming. In the center of town is the church of **Kimisis tis Theotokou** ("Assumption of the Mother of God"), with a lovely marble iconstasis and a Venetian tower.

Apiranthos (10km/6.2 miles beyond Filoti), the most enchanting of the mountain villages, is remarkable for the fact that its buildings, streets, and even domestic walls are built of the brilliant white Naxos marble. The people of Apiranthos were originally from Crete, and fled their home during a time of Turkish oppression. Be sure to visit **Taverna Lefteris,** the excellent cafe/restaurant just off the main square (see "Where to Dine," below).

Apollonas, at the northern tip of the island, is a small fishing village on the verge of becoming a rather depressing resort. It has a sand cove, a pebbled public beach, plenty of places to eat, rooms to let, and a few hotels. From the town a path takes you about 1 kilometer (0.6 miles) south to the famous **kouros;** you can also drive, turning right on the road to Hora just south of town. The kouros is a colossal statue some 20 meters tall, begun in the 7th century B.C. and abandoned probably because of the fissures that time and the elements have exacerbated. Some archaeologists believe it was meant for the nearby temple of Apollo, but the beard suggests that it's probably the island's patron deity, Dionysos.

BEACHES

Naxos has the longest and some of the best beaches in the Cyclades, although you wouldn't know it looking at the crowded **Ayios Yioryios** beach just south of Hora. The next beach south is **Ayios Prokopios,** around the headland of Stellida. This fine-sand beach is less crowded at its northern end. **Ayia Anna,** the next cove south, is much smaller, with a small port for the colorful caïques that transport beachgoers from the main port. **Taverna Gorgona** (☎ 0285/23-799), at the pier where the caïques dock, has an excellent buffet dinner daily, with fresh grilled fish and meat, salads, vegetables, and complimentary wine. Both Ayios Prokopios and Ayia Anna are accessible over dirt roads by public bus in the summer, when school buses run vacation routes. They run almost hourly from Hora and cost Dr340 ($1.15). Ayia Anna has caïque service from the small caïque jetty south of the Myrtidiotissa church islet in Hora, hourly from 9:30am to 5:30pm for about Dr700 ($2.35) each way.

South of Ayia Anna you'll find ✪ **Plaka Beach,** the best on the island, a 5-kilometer (3.1-mile) stretch of almost uninhabited shoreline where clothing is optional. You can reach it by caïque from Hora in the summer or by walking south from Ayia Anna. Further south (16km/9.9 miles from Hora) are **Micri Vigla,** known for its windsurfing center, and **Kastraki Beach,** with waters recently rated the cleanest in the Aegean and a 7-kilometer (4½-mile) stretch of beach; both remain relatively uncrowded, even in peak season. Further still (21km/13 miles from Hora), **Pyrgaki,** the last stop on the coastal bus route, offers excellent swimming in the large protected bay. The 150 meters of sand and cobble beach in the sheltered cove of **Abrami,** about 6 kilometers (4 miles) past Apollonas at the north end of the island, is secluded and

---

Remember the Repellent

Note that both Ayios Prokopios and Ayia Anna have a mosquito problem in the summer due to several stagnant ponds behind the beach that serve as breeding grounds.

uncrowded. It's 500 meters in from the main road on a rough one-lane dirt track. There's a pension with a small taverna—the tables are on a patio overlooking the beach.

OUTDOOR PURSUITS

WALKING If you're going to spend some time on the island, we recommend buying a copy of Christian Ucke's *Walking Tours on Naxos,* an excellent guide offering many fine walks with varying lengths and levels of difficulty. Most of the start and finish points for the walks can be reached by island bus. It's available for Dr3,500 ($12) at **Naxos Tourist Information Center** on the paralia. As with all the Cyclades, you should be equipped with a map and a good sense of direction.

One fascinating Naxos site that can only be reached on foot is the ✪ **Kaloritsa Chapel,** near the town of Ano Sangri. Inside the ruins of this Byzantine Church is a cave containing an iconostasis and some fine 13th-century frescoes—it's best seen in the late afternoon, when the low sun illuminates the cave's interior. You can take the bus to Ano Sangri and walk from there, or you can drive—200 meters past Ano Sangri on the road to Filoti, there's a fork to the right at a JetOil station, signposted for Kaloritsa. Another 200 meters brings you to the striking **Pirgos Timios Stavros;** park just past this medieval tower, where another sign for Kaloritsa points up the side of the hill. Look up the hillside in the direction of the sign, and you'll see the ruined remains of the Kaloritsa Chapel about halfway up. There isn't a trail, but there are some goat paths that make the going easier. Make your way to a low stone wall that climbs in the direction of the chapel—there's a path along its base that goes most of the way. The cave itself is blocked off, but you can get a good view of the interior from above; binoculars are helpful for making out the details of the icons and frescoes inside.

WINDSURFING The **Micri Vigla Hotel** (☎ 0285/75-241) has a windsurfing center, offering lessons and equipment rental. This is one of the least crowded of the island's best beaches, and has a consistent offshore wind.

SHOPPING

Hora is a fine place for shopping, both for value and variety. Toward the north end of the paralia, near the bus station, you'll find **O Kouros** (☎ 0285/25-565), which has excellent copies of Cycladic figurines in Naxian marble, other reproductions, and interesting modern ceramics. To the right and up from the entrance to the Old Market is **Techni** (☎ 0285/24-767), which has two shops within 20 meters of each other. The first shop contains a good array of silver jewelry at fair prices; above it the second and more interesting of the two has textiles, many handwoven, and some by local women. Many are from earlier in the century, when the traditions of weaving and embroidery were still flourishing. There are also hand-painted copies of icons made at Mount Athos.

On the paralia next to Grotta Tours is tiny **Galini** (☎ 0285/24-785), with a collection of local ceramics. Continue south along the paralia to the OTE, turn left on the main inland street, Odos Papavasiliou, and continue up on the left side of the street until your nose leads you into the **Tirokomika Proïonia Naxou** (☎ 0285/ 22-230). This delightful old store is filled with excellent local cheeses (*kephalotiri,* a superb sharp one, and milder *graviera*), barrels of olives, spices, and other dried comestibles. It's also a good place to pick up a bottle of *kitron,* the island's famous sweet citron liqueur.

In the interior of Naxos, on the stretch of road between Sangri and Halki, you'll see a sign pointing toward the **Damalas Pottery Workshop** (☎ 0285/32-890).

Two hundred meters along this one-lane road brings you to the small workshop, operated by a father-and-son team. The father learned his trade on Sifnos, an island renowned for its pottery, and now father and son produce a variety of forms, some of them specific to Naxos. No English is spoken.

In Apiranthos some local weaving and needlework is sold by the village women, and **Stiasto** (☎ 0285/61-392) has a good selection of popular art, including good ceramics.

WHERE TO STAY

Hora's broad paralia is too busy for quiet accommodations, so we recommend hotels in four nearby areas, all within a 10-minute walk of the port: **Bourgo,** the old section of town just above the harbor below the Kastro; **Grotta,** a development of newer houses left (north) and up from the port; behind the town; and **Ayios Yioryios,** a beach resort just south (right from the harbor) of town.

BOURGO

Chateau Zevgoli. Bourgo, Hora, 84300 Naxos. ☎ **0285/22-993** or 0285/26-123. Fax 0285/25-200. 14 units. Dr20,000 ($67) double (hotel and Kastro); Dr25,000 ($83) honeymoon suite (Kastro). Hotel rates include breakfast. AE, MC, V.

This small hotel is easily the most attractive in Bourgo, and is located at the foot of the Kastro walls. The lobby/dining area has been charmingly decorated with antiques and family heirlooms by the gracious and discerning owner, Despina Kitini. All guest rooms open onto a central atrium with a lush garden. The units are small but distinctively furnished, with many thoughtful touches like lace curtains and brightly ornamented carpets; room no. 8 features a canopy bed and a private terrace, and several units have views of the distant harbor. For those interested in an experience of medieval grandeur, Despina Kitini also has four apartments in a 12th-century house in the Kastro, just 100 meters from the hotel: these share a magisterial sitting room with 5-meter-high ceilings, stone walls and floors, and appropriately antiquated and austere furnishings. The bedrooms here are simple and unremarkable, with the exception of the honeymoon suite, which shares the grandeur of the sitting room and has a balcony overlooking the town and the sea. (Inquire at the Naxos Tourist Information Center on the paralia.)

Hotel Anixis. Bourgo, Hora, 84300 Naxos. ☎ **0285/22-932** or 0285/22-782. Fax 0285/22-112. 19 units. Dr12,000 ($40) double; Dr14,400 ($48) triple. Continental breakfast Dr900 ($3) extra. V. From the bus station, take the nearest major street (with traffic) off the port and turn right through the lancet archway into the Old Market area; follow the stenciled blue arrows to the hotel.

This simple hotel near the Kastro's Venetian tower offers comfortable accommodations in a desirable old neighborhood of Hora. Located on a narrow pedestrian street, the entrance leads through a small, luxuriant garden to a terrace overlooking town and sea. Dimitris Sideris is the friendly manager—he knows the island well, so be sure to ask him about excursions to uncrowded beaches, Byzantine chapels, and ancient sites. The rooms on the top floor have the best view of the sea, and six of them have their own small balcony; all rooms have minifridges. The breakfast terrace enjoys a splendid sea view.

GROTTA

Hotel Grotta. Grotta, Hora, 84300 Naxos. ☎ **0285/22-215** or 0285/22-201. Fax 0285/22-000. E-mail: grotta@naxos-island.com. 20 units. TEL. Dr13,800 ($46) double. Rates include breakfast. V.

Follow the east coast road to the left after the school, and you'll find the friendly Lianos family's hotel off to the left. Guests are greeted by Dimitris or Nicoletta Lianos, both exceptional hosts. Spotless rooms have polished marble floors, large balconies, and fridges. The attractive dining area has a gallery overlooking the sea and the Portara. The rooms without sea views face a pleasant garden courtyard. You can call ahead and arrange to be picked up at the ferry or the airport.

AYIOS YIORYIOS

Another option is the unexciting but reliable **Galaxy Hotel,** 75 meters from the beach at Ayios Yioryios (☎ **0285/22-422** or 0285/22-423; fax 0285/22-889); some of the rooms have balconies or terraces facing the water.

Hotels Galini and Sofia. Ayios Yioryios, Hora, 84300 Naxos. ☎ **0285/22-516** or 0285/ 22-114. Fax 0285/22-677. www.naxos-island.com/hotels/galini. E-mail: h-galini@ naxos-island.com. 30 units. MINIBAR TEL. Dr15,000 ($50) double. Rates include breakfast. AE, V.

The hotels Galini and Sofia share the same building, the same friendly management, and the same sea views. In fact, they represent the curious phenomenon of one hotel with two names. There are some differences: the Sofia's bedrooms are decorated in bright pastels, while those in the Galini are a more conservative white. All but two unfortunate units on the interior courtyard have balconies with excellent sea views: the view from rooms 11 and 14 is especially good. The hotels are both run by the charming Sofia, who has a green thumb, and her amiable son George. Guests are free to send and receive e-mail from the hotel computer. Transportation is provided to and from the port if you make arrangements in advance.

Hotel Nissaki. Ayios Yioryios, Hora, 84300 Naxos. ☎ **0285/25-710.** Fax 0285/23-876. nissaki@naxos-island.com. 68 units. A/C TV TEL. Dr20,000 ($67) double; Dr35,000 ($117) 4-person suite. Rates include breakfast. AE, DC, EURO, MC, V.

Just down the street from the Hotels Galini and Sofia, the Papadopoulos family owns and runs this comfortable hotel, which has its own beachfront restaurant and a swimming pool. The pool doesn't offer much privacy—it's open to the street on one side—but it is fairly spacious, and is one of the few hotel pools in Hora. The rooms are somewhat characterless, but they do have balconies, many of which enjoy beach and sea views. The large restaurant serves three meals a day, with seating available under a shaded awning at the edge of the sand. The buffet breakfast includes omelets, several varieties of fruit juice, and cake.

OUTSIDE HORA

Mathiassos Village Bungalows. Hora, 84300 Naxos. ☎ **0285/22-200,** or 01/291-8749 in winter. Fax 0285/24-700. 110 bungalows. TEL. Dr20,000 ($67) double; Dr28,000 ($93) for 4 persons. AE, EURO, MC, V.

This resort complex on the ring road behind the town has semiattached bungalows spread through well-landscaped grounds. There's a pool and sundeck, tennis court, cafeteria, taverna, an ouzeri, and a chapel. The bungalows are spacious, with patios or balconies. Refrigerators are available, making them especially suitable for families. The complex doesn't have sea views, but there is bus service to the beach.

Naxos Beach Two. Ayios Prokopios, 84300 Naxos. ☎ **0285/26-591.** Fax 0285/24-197. 50 units. A/C TV TEL. Dr35,000 ($117) double. MC, V.

Built on a steep slope overlooking Hora, the Naxos Beach Two is the most attractive complex of villas on the island. The surfaces of the buildings are tile, stone, and whitewashed plaster, and in the sunlight they beautifully evoke the traditional architecture of local villages. Each group of houses is built around a small flagstone courtyard, and one court is connected with another by steep steps curving through low archways. The rooms have been designed with many elements typical of vernacular buildings: exposed wooden ceiling beams, stone floors, and wooden shutters, all effective in keeping the spaces cool in summer even without the aid of the air-conditioning. Units tend to be rather small, but all have a balcony or terrace, plus a kitchenette with fridge. The downside of this place is that the immediately surrounding landscape is particularly desolate and packed with new development, making it necessary to rent a car to go to Hora, 3½ kilometers (2 miles) away; the nearest good beach, Ayios Prokopios, is about 2 kilometers (1.2 miles) by road or footpath.

WHERE TO DINE
HORA

The Bakery (☎ 0285/22-613) on the paralia has baked goods at fair prices. Further north, across from the bus station, **Bikini** is a good place for breakfast and crepes.

For hearty, simple Greek fare, try **Boulamatsis,** toward the north end of the paralia, up a short flight of stairs adjacent to Posto Travel Office (☎ 0285/24-227).

Christos' Grill. Hora. ☎ **0285/23-072.** Main courses Dr1,400–Dr2,900 ($4.70–$10). No credit cards. Daily 6pm–1am. GREEK.

This small family-run taverna is one street up from the paralia, just off the district road (next to the church that was once a synagogue). Christos and his wife serve fresh grilled fish and meat with a large assortment of side dishes. We recommend the delicious Naxos potatoes fried in olive oil.

Nikos. Paralia (above the Commercial Bank), Hora. ☎ **0285/23-153.** Main courses Dr1,500–Dr3,000 ($5–$10). MC, V. Daily 8am–1am. GREEK.

This is one of the most popular restaurants in town. The owner, Nikos Katsayannis, is himself a fisherman, and the range of seafood available will amaze you. It's all excellent, but if you're not in the mood for fish, try the *eksohiko,* fresh lamb and vegetables with fragrant spices wrapped in crisp filo (pastry leaves). The wine list is quite long, with lots of local and Cyclades wines. The ice-cream desserts are also delightful.

The Old Inn. Hora. ☎ **0285/26-093.** Main courses Dr1,000–Dr3,500 ($3.35–$12). AE, DC, EURO, MC, V. Daily 6pm–2am. INTERNATIONAL.

Dieter Ranizewski, who operated for 12 years the popular Faros Restaurant on the paralia, has now moved 100 meters in from port to open this new place. The courtyard is entered through a wooden gate, and offers a green shaded haven from the noise and crowds of the paralia. The restaurant inhabits several buildings around the courtyard, once a small monastery, and the wine cellar is situated in a former chapel. Another vaulted room houses the "fleamarket," a bizarre and eclectic collection of old objects from the island and from Dieter's native Berlin. The Germanic menu offers an alternative to standard taverna fare, and the food is simple, hearty, and abundant. Although there's a complete lack of formality, the service is also good.

Taverna To Kastro. Hora. ☎ **0285/22-005.** Main courses Dr1,400–Dr3,000 ($4.70–$10). No credit cards. Daily 7pm–2am. GREEK.

Just outside the Kastro's south gate you'll find the small Braduna square, named after a Naxiot soldier who died in Macedonia early in this century. On summer evenings the square is packed with tables, and word has gotten out about the fine food and wine. There's an excellent view from here toward the bay and St. George's beach, and toward dusk the place is pervaded with a pacifying calm. The specialty here is rabbit stewed in red wine with onions, spiced with pepper and a suggestion of cinnamon. The local wines, served by the carafe, are surprisingly light and delicious.

APIRANTHUS

✪ **Taverna Lefteris.** Apiranthos. ☎ **0285/61-333.** Main courses Dr1,300–Dr2,100 ($4.35–$7). No credit cards. Daily 11am–11pm. GREEK.

Find your way to Apiranthos, the most beautiful town in Naxos, where you'll find one of the island's best restaurants. The small menu features the staples of Greek cooking, prepared in a way that reminds you how good this food can be. The dishes highlight the freshest of vegetables and meats, prepared with admirable subtlety. The bread is delicious, a hearty loaf that's redolent of wood smoke from the wood-burning oven in which it's baked. A cozy marble-floored room faces the street, and in back steps climb down to a flagstone terrace and the magnificent shade of two massive trees. The homemade sweets are an exception to the rule that you should avoid dessert in tavernas—it's worth making the trip for the sweets alone.

NAXOS AFTER DARK

Naxos certainly doesn't compare to Mikonos or Santorini for wild nightlife, but it has a lively and varied scene.

Apostolis (☎ 0285/24-781), an ouzeri on the port near the ferry pier, or **Portara,** just below its namesake at the far end of the harbor, are both excellent places to enjoy the sunset. **Fragile** (☎ 0285/25-336), through the arch in the entrance to the Old Town, is worth a stop. **Remezzo** and **Relax** are also recommended. You can always join the evening volta (stroll) along the paralia. Behind the Rendezvous (Panteboy) Fast Food, you'll find **Dolphini,** which begins the evening with classical music and then segues into jazz or rock subdued enough for conversation. Up in Kastro, **Notos** offers an even more sedate evening with mellow jazz.

Day and Night, opposite the OTE, has a good blend of music which becomes more purely Greek in the early morning. At the end of the waterfront past the National Bank, you'll find the more sophisticated **Vengera** (☎ 0285/23-567), which doesn't open until 9pm and doesn't get warmed up until much later; there's a garden if the rock gets a little much for you. Next door, **Ecstasis** has a more eclectic blend of music.

Naxos By Night, back closer to town, has bouzouki music and dancing. More authentic Greek music is at **O Platanos,** 4 kilometers (2½ miles) east of town on the road to Melanes.

6 Mikonos (Mykonos)

177km (96 nautical miles) SE of Piraeus

Mikonos is an island that lives well with contradiction. Depending on the season, Mikonos, a place with multiple personalities, can be an island of partyers, of sophisticated travelers, of students, of "Greece for the Greeks"—what you experience depends largely on when you go. The most remarkable thing about Mikonos is that through all the transformations and responses to changing fashions, it has somehow managed to hold on to much of its charm and self-respect.

In July and August the island is occupied by legions of young travelers attracted by Mikonos's reputation as *the* party destination in the Aegean, which it *is* during those

Mikonos Town

ACCOMMODATIONS

Hotel Aegean **1**
Hotel Anastassios
  Sevasti **8**
Hotel Belvedere **7**
Hotel Carbonaki **5**
Hotel Matina **6**
Hotel Poseidon **9**
Hotel Terra Maria **13**
Kouros Hotel **2**
Pension Stelios **3**

DINING

Chez Catherine **14**
Edem Restaurant **4**
El Greco/Yorgos **10**
Philippi **12**
Remvi **7**
Sesame Kitchen **11**
Taverna Caprice **15**

Island
Ferries

Archaeological
Museum

North
Bus Station

**Aegean
Sea**

Boats to
Delos

Harbor

Beach

Polikandhrioti

Ayiou Stefanou

Folklore
Museum

Tourist
Police

Taxi Square
(Plateia Mantos
Mavroyenous)

Al Mavroyenous

† **Panayia Paraportiani
Church**

LITTLE VENICE

Ayion Anaryiron

Drakopoulou

Delia Travel
(American Express)

Matoyianni

Legend

OTE **C**
Post Office ✉
Rest Rooms 👫

Kaloyera

Mikonos
Accommodations
Center

To Ano
Mera ↓

Ayiou Ioannou

**Cathedral
(Mitropolis)**

**Maritime
Museum**

Enoplan Dinameon

Beach

Mitropoleos

**Plateia
Tria Pigadia**

Rohari

Ipirou

Windmills

Xenias

**Plateia
Laka**

✉

**South
Bus Station**

Ayiou Ioannou

↓ **To Ornos**

months. In May and June the nightlife is active on weekends, but you can walk through the streets at night without having to negotiate a sea of revellers. In September—perhaps the best month to visit—the sea is warm, the debris that fills the streets throughout the summer has mostly been cleared away, and you can actually eat in a restaurant without a reservation. Mikonos remains active year-round, and during the winter the island hosts numerous cultural events, including a small film festival. Many who are scared off by the summer crowds find a different, tranquil Mikonos during this off-season, drawn by the deserved reputation of Hora as one of the most beautiful towns in the Cyclades. Mikonos is one of the only islands in the Aegean where scuba diving is permitted, and there are several diving centers that rent equipment and offer instruction.

During the peak season (July and Aug), the overcrowding is truly overwhelming. The best way to avoid the crowds is to get up early, visiting the beaches before noon and exploring the streets of Hora in the late afternoon, when almost everyone in town wakes up and heads for the beach. We strongly recommend that you not plan a stay on Mikonos without reservations in the high season, unless you enjoy sleeping out of doors.

ESSENTIALS

GETTING THERE   By Plane   Olympic Airways has several flights daily (once daily in the low season) between Mikonos and Athens. Olympic also has one flight daily between Mikonos and Iraklion, Crete; Rhodes; and Santorini. It's difficult to get a seat on any of these flights, so make reservations early and reconfirm them at the Olympic office in Athens (☎ **01/966-6666**) or Mikonos (☎ **0289/22-490**). The Mikonos office is near the south bus station, by Plateia Laka. You can also buy tickets at **Sea and Sky Travel** (☎ **0289/22-853**).

By Ferry   From Piraeus, there are departures for Mikonos at least once daily, usually at 8am, with a second in the afternoon in the summer. Check schedules in Piraeus with the **Port Authority** (☎ **01/451-1310**), or with **tourist information** in Athens (☎ **01/171** or 01/322-2545). From Rafina, there is daily ferry and hydrofoil service to Mikonos; schedules can be checked with the local **Port Authority** at ☎ **0294/22-300.** There is daily ferry connection between Mikonos and Paros, Naxos, Siros, and Tinos. **Sea and Sky Travel** (☎ **0289/22-853;** fax 0289/24-753), on Taxi Square, represents all ferry lines, as well as Olympic Airways; this travel agency also offers excursions to Delos.

By Hydrofoil   Dolphin Sea Lines has daily hydrofoil service to Mikonos from Rafina. Hydrofoil (catamaran) service from Mikonos to Crete, Ios, Naxos, Paros, and Santorini is often irregular. For tickets call **Sea and Sky Travel** (see above). For information call the **Piraeus Port Authority** (☎ **01/451-1310**), **Rafina Port Authority** (☎ **0294/22-300**), or **Mikonos Port Authority** (☎ **0289/22-218**).

VISITOR INFORMATION   The **Mikonos Tourist Office** (☎ **0289/23-990**) is on the west side of the port near the excursion boats to Delos. Look for a copy of the free *Mikonos Summertime* magazine. The **Veronis Agency** (☎ **0289/22-687;** fax 0289/23-763), also on Taxi Square, offers information, safekeeping of baggage, and other services.

GETTING AROUND   One of the best things to happen to Mikonos was the government decree that made Hora an architectural landmark and prohibited motorized traffic from its streets. You will see a few small delivery vehicles, but the only way to get around town is to walk. There's a busy peripheral road, along which many of the

Parking

If you park in town or in a no-parking area, the police will remove your license plates, and you, not the rental office, will have to find the police station and pay a steep fine to get them back. There is free parking on the north side of the port.

---

town's large hotels are found. Much of the rest of the island is served by a good transportation system.

By Bus   Mikonos has one of the best-organized bus systems in the Greek islands. Buses run frequently and cost Dr200 to Dr800 (70¢ to $2.70) one-way. There are two bus stations in Hora. The **north station** is near the middle of the harbor below the Leto Hotel. From there, buses leave for Tourlos, Ayios Stefanos, the northwest coast hotels, the inland village of Ano Mera, and the far east coast beaches of Elia, Kalo Livadi, and Kalafatis. Schedules are posted, though subject to change, and buses often leave when they're full. Ask the driver when there will be bus service back to Hora from your destination.

The **south station** is a 10-minute walk inland from the harbor, near Plateia Laka. From this stop, buses leave for the airport, Ayios Ioannis, Ornos, Psarou, and Platis Yialos.

By Boat   Caïques (skiffs) to Super Paradise, Agrari, and Elia depart from the town harbor every morning, weather permitting. Caïques to the same beaches leave somewhat more frequently from Platis Yialos; there is also service from Ornos during the peak season (July and Aug) only. Caïque service is highly seasonal, with almost continuous service during the peak season, and no caïques from October through May. Excursion boats to Delos depart Tuesday through Sunday from the west side of the harbor near the tourist office between 8:30 and 9:30am. (For more information see a travel agent; guided tours are available.)

By Car & Moped   Rental cars are available from about Dr15,000 ($50) per day in high season, including full insurance; most agencies are near one of the two bus stops in town. One reliable shop with average prices is **Apollon** (☎ 0289/24-136), with offices at the south bus station, the airport, and at Ornos Beach. The largest concentration of moped shops is just beyond the south bus station. Expect to pay about Dr3,500 to Dr11,000 ($12 to $37) a day for a moped, depending on engine size. Take great care when driving: the roads on the island can be treacherous.

By Taxi   There are two types of taxis in Mikonos: your standard **car taxi** for destinations outside town, and the tiny **scooters with a cart in tow** that buzz through the narrow streets of Hora. The latter type are seen primarily at the port, where they wait to bring new arrivals to their lodgings in town—a good idea, if you're staying in town and don't want to lug your bags 800 meters. Getting a car taxi in Hora is easy; walk to Taxi (Mavro) Square, near the statue, and join the line. There's a notice board that gives rates for each destination for both high and low seasons. You can also call ☎ 0289/22-400. For late hours and out-of-town service, call ☎ 0289/23-700.

FAST FACTS   The local **American Express** branch is at **Delia Travel** (☎ 0289/24-300) on the harbor; open daily from 8am to 9pm. The **Commercial Bank** and the **National Bank of Greece** are conveniently located on the harbor a couple of blocks west of Taxi Square. Both are open Monday through Friday from 8am to 2pm. ATMs are available throughout the town. The **health center** (☎ 0289/23-944) handles minor medical complaints. The **hospital** (☎ 0289/23-994) offers 24-hour emergency service. The **Mykonos Cyber Cafe** (☎ 0289/27-684; www.mykonos-cyber-cafe.com) is at M. Axioti 26, on the road between the south bus station and the Windmills, open daily from 9am to 10pm. The rate is Dr1,500 ($5) for 15 minutes; other computer services include scanning and color printing. **Ace Laundry,** on Ayios Efthimiou, 100 meters toward the port from the south bus station (☎ 0289/28-389), offers drop-off service. The **tourist police** (☎ 0289/22-482) are on the west side of the port near the ferries to Delos; the **local police** (☎ 0289/22-235) are behind the grammar school, near Plateia Laka. The **post office** (☎ 0289/22-238) is next to the police station; open Monday through Friday from 7:30am to 2pm. The **telephone office (OTE)** is on the north side of the harbor beyond the Hotel Leto (☎ 0289/22-499).

WHAT TO SEE & DO
BEACHES
The beaches on the **south shore** of the island have the best sand, views, and wind protection, but these days they're so popular that you'll have to negotiate a forest of beach umbrellas to find your square meter of sand. A few (**Paradise, Super Paradise**) are known as party beaches, and guarantee throbbing music and loud revelry until late at night. Others (**Platis Yialos, Psarrou, Ornos**) are quieter and more popular with families. With all the south coast beaches, keep in mind that most people begin to arrive in the early afternoon, and you can avoid the worst of the crowds by going in the morning. The **north coast beaches** are less developed but just as beautiful. Since the buses and caïques don't yet make the trip, you'll have to rent a car or scooter, and you'll be more than compensated for the trouble by the quiet and lack of commercial development.

For those who can't wait to hit the beach, the closest to Mikonos town is **Megali Ammos** ("Big Sand"), about a 10-minute walk south—it's very crowded and not particularly scenic. The nearest to the north is 2 kilometers (1.2 miles) away at **Tourlos,** with extensive industrial development just offshore. **Ornos,** about 2½ kilometers (1.6 miles) south of Mikonos town, has a fine-sand beach in a sheltered bay with extensive hotel development along the shore; buses run hourly from the south station between 8am and 11pm. This beach is popular with families.

Platis Yialos is the best first stop: although the beach is unexceptional and likely to be extremely crowded, from here you can catch a caïque to the more distant beaches of Paradise, Super Paradise, Agrari, and Elia. The bus runs every 15 minutes from 8am to 8pm, then every 30 minutes until midnight. Nearby **Psarou** is less overwhelmed by resort hotels and has a lovely pale-sand beach that you can actually see except in the high season. Its water-sports facilities include the **Diving Center Psarou,** waterskiing, and windsurfing. **Paranga,** further east, can be reached easily by foot on an inland path from Platis Yialos; this small cove is popular with nudists, and usually isn't too crowded.

✪ **Paradise,** the island's most famous beach, is accessible by footpath from Platis Yialos (about 2km/1.2 miles), by bus, or by caïque. This was the original nude beach of the island, and many nudists come here to continue the tradition. A stand of small trees provides some shade, and it's well protected from the predominant north winds. Several bars line the waterfront, and pump out loud music throughout the day and night.

Beach Note

Activity on the beaches is highly seasonal, and all the information offered here pertains only to the months of June through September.

Super Paradise (Plindri) is in a rocky cove just around the headland from Paradise; it's somewhat less developed than its neighbor, but no less crowded. The beach is accessible on foot, by bus, or by caïque; if you take your car or moped, be very careful on the extremely steep and narrow access road. The beach is predominantly gay and bare, and there's a cafeteria-style taverna with nonstop pop music. Further east across the little peninsula is **Agrari,** a lovely cove sheltered by lush foliage, with all states of dress common and a good little taverna.

Elia, a 45-minute caïque ride from Platis Yialos and the last regular stop, is a sand-and-pebble beach with crowds nearly as overwhelming as at Paradise. The protection from sun and wind is minimal. Nevertheless, this is a beautiful beach, and one of the longest on the island. It's also accessible by bus. The next major beach is **Kalo Livadi,** which means "Good Pasture." In a farming valley, this long, beautiful beach is accessible by a scramble over the peninsula east from Elia and by bus from the north station. There's a taverna and a few villas and hotels on the hills adjacent to the beach.

The last resort area on the southern coast accessible by bus from the north station is at ✪ **Kalafatis.** This fishing village was once the port of the ancient citadel of Mikonos, which dominated the little peninsula to the west. A line of trees separates the beach from the rows of buildings which have grown up along the road. This is one of the longest beaches on Mikonos, and less crowded than its neighbors to the west. Adjacent to Kalafatis in a tiny cove is lovely **Ayia Anna,** a short stretch of sand with a score of umbrellas. Several kilometers further east, accessible by a fairly good road from Kalafatis, is **Lia,** which has fine sand, clear water, bamboo wind breaks, and a small taverna.

Most of the north coast beaches are too windy to be of interest to anyone other than windsurfers—the long fine-sand beach at **Ftelia** would be one of the best on the island if it didn't receive the unbroken force of the meltemi wind. There are, however, two well-sheltered northern beaches, and because you can only reach them by car or moped, they're much less crowded than the southern beaches. Head east from Mikonos town on the road to Ano Mera, turning left after 1½ kilometers (0.9 miles) on the road to Ayios Sostis and Panormos. At **Panormos** you'll find a cove with 100 meters of fine sand backed by low dunes. There are two tavernas, the better of which is the **Panormos Restaurant** on a hill above the beach; it's one of the few tavernas on the island to bake its own bread. Another 1.2 kilometers (0.75 miles) down the road is the beach of ✪ **Ayios Sostis,** a lovely small beach just below a village. There isn't any parking, so it's best to leave your vehicle along the main road and walk 200 meters down through the village. There's a taverna on the beach that operates without electricity, so it's open only during daylight hours. Both Panormos and Ayios Sostis have few amenities—no beach umbrellas, bars, or snack shops—but they do offer a break from the crowds.

DIVING

Mikonos is known throughout the Aegean as a place for diving—it's one of the few islands where this sport hasn't been forbidden to protect undersea archaeological treasures from plunder. The best month is September, when the water temperature is typically 24°C and visibility is 30 meters. Certified divers can rent equipment and participate in guided dives, and first-time divers can rent snorkeling gear or take an introductory beach dive. The best established diving center on the island is at **Psarou Beach** (☎/fax **0289/24-808;** e-mail: diving_center_psarou@myk.forthnet.gr). PADI certification courses (offered in English) are 2 to 5 days in duration and cost Dr100,000 to Dr160,000 ($333 to $533) with equipment rental; certified divers can join guided dives for Dr12,000 ($40) per dive; and beginners can take a 2-hour class and beach dive for Dr15,000 ($50). There is a nearby wreck at a depth of 20 meters to 30 meters, and wreck dives are offered for Dr14,000 ($47). Another diving center offering lessons and full equipment rental is **Dive Adventures** (☎ and fax **0289/ 26-539**) on Paradise Beach.

ATTRACTIONS

Getting ineluctably lost in the labyrinthine alleys of Hora is an essential element of every Mikonian holiday. Searching for the right bar, a good place to eat, or your hotel is sure to be twice as difficult as you'd expected and twice as enjoyable. Despite its intense commercialism and seething crowds during the peak season, Hora is still the quintessential Cycladic town, and is worth a visit to the island in itself.

The best way to see the town is to simply venture inland from the port and wander. Just keep in mind that the town is bounded on two sides by the bay, and on the other two by the busy vehicular District Road, and that all paths funnel eventually into one of the few main squares: **Plateia Mantos Mavroyenous** on the port (called "Taxi Square" because it's the main taxi stand); **Plateia Tria Pigadia;** and **Plateia Laka** (near the south bus station). Among the experiences you should be sure to sample during your stay are the sunset from one of the bars in **Little Venice;** the evening **volta (stroll),** which is quietly civilized in the off-season and frenziedly hysterical in July and August; and a visit to some of the fine **art galleries** and **workshops** that populate the back streets of the town, and make this a cultural center as well as a party town.

The museums of Mikonos aren't among the island's main attractions, but as a rainy-day outing, consider the **Archaeological Museum** (☎ **0289/22-325**), on the north side of town beyond the OTE, across from the bus stop. It contains ceramic vases dating from 2,500 B.C.; a large 7th-century B.C. storage jar with Trojan war reliefs; and a Parian marble statue of Hercules. It's open Wednesday through Saturday and Monday from 9am to 3:30pm, Sunday and holidays from 10am to 3pm; admission is Dr600 ($2).

The only other town on Mikonos is **Ano Mera,** 7 kilometers (4 miles) east of Hora near the center of the island, a quick bus ride from the north station. We especially recommend this trip to those interested in religious sites—the **Monastery of Panayia Tourliani** southeast of town dates from 1580 and has a handsome carved steeple. Inside the church are a huge Italian baroque iconostasis (altar screen) with icons of the Cretan school, an 18th-century marble baptismal font, and a small museum containing liturgical vestments, needlework, and wood carvings. One kilometer (0.6 miles) southeast is the 12th-century **Monastery of Paleokastro,** in one of the greenest spots on the island. Ano Mera also has the most traditional atmosphere on the island, with a fresh-produce market on the main square selling excellent local cheeses, and it's the island's place of choice for Sunday brunch.

SHOPPING

Mikonos has a large community of artists, and several galleries selling their work. At ✪ **Apocalypse** (☎ **0289/24-267**), on Ayios Vlasis, just in from the port, you'll find the icon workshop of Maria Adama and Mercourios Dimopoulos. Their materials and techniques are drawn from the ancient tradition of icon painting. Much of their exquisite work is done on commission for churches and individuals; there is also a selection of icons for sale on the walls of the tiny workshop.

Orama Art Gallery (☎ **0289/26-339;** fax 0289/24-016) features the work of local painters Luis Orozco and Dorlies Schapitz. Orozco is originally from Mexico City, and has been living and painting on Mikonos since 1960. Many of the paintings depict local scenes, but this is not tourist art: the delightful use of color and joyous quality of the paintings is consistent, regardless of their subject. The **Scala Gallery,** Odos Matoyianni 48 (☎ **0289/23-407;** fax 0289/26-993), is one of the best art galleries in town. All the artists represented are from Greece, many of them quite well known. There is a selection of jewelry, plus an interesting collection of recent works by Yorgos Kypris, an Athenian sculptor and ceramic artist. Nearby on Odos Panahrandou is **Scala Stock Gallery** (☎ **0289/26-993**), where the overflow from the Scala Gallery is sold at reduced prices.

The best bookstore on Mikonos is **To Vivlio** (no phone), on Odos Zouganeli, one street over from Odos Matoyianni. The selection of books in English is good, including many works of Greek writers in translation; they also have some art and architecture books, and a few travel guides.

Mikonos has an abundance of jewelry shops, most of them unexceptional and more expensive than their Athenian counterparts. There are, however, some excellent local jewelers. The best-known is **Elias Lalaounis,** Odos Polykandrioti 14 (☎ **0289/ 22-444**), near the taxi station, who has an international reputation for superb crafts-manship and design, especially in classical, Byzantine, and natural motifs. **Vildiridis,** Matoyianni 12 (☎ 0289/23-245), has designs based on ancient jewelry as well as contemporary styles.

Works of culinary art can be found at **Skaropoulos,** on Matoyianni (☎ **0289/ 24-983**), including almond sweets such as amygdalota and almond biscuits, claimed to be a favorite of Winston Churchill.

WHERE TO STAY

Greece's most popular resort destination seems to have developed every possible spot, and yet there's still a shortage of desirable and affordable accommodations in high season. Needless to say, Mikonos is a much easier and more pleasant place to visit in the spring or fall; the best month is September, when the water is warm and the crowds have departed. Those determined to visit the hottest spot during the hottest season should make reservations at least a month and if possible 3 months in advance. If you want to save the time and effort of making a booking yourself, contact the **Mikonos Accommodations Center (MAC),** Odos Enoplon Dinameon at Malamatenias (near Tria Pigadia), 84600 Mikonos (☎ **0289/23-160** or 0289/ 23-408; fax 0289/24-137; e-mail: mac@mac.myk.forthnet.gr). The helpful multi-lingual staff will correspond, talk by phone, or meet with you to determine the best accommodation for your budget. The service is free of charge when booking hotel stays of 3 nights or longer; shorter stays or bookings of budget accommodations will bring a fee of Dr7,000 ($23).

IN HORA

In addition to those listed below, another option to consider is the 15-unit **Hotel Terra Maria,** Odos Kaloyera 18, Hora, 84600 Mikonos (☎ **0289/24-212;** fax 0289/27-112).

✪ **Hotel Belvedere.** Rohari, 84600 Mikonos. ☎ **0289/25-122** or 0289/25-125. Fax 0289/25-126. www.belvederehotel.com. E-mail: belvedere@myk.forthnet.gr. 41 units. A/C MINIBAR TV TEL. Dr52,000 ($173) double; Dr61,000 ($203) triple; Dr81,000 ($270) suite. Rates include breakfast. AE, DC, MC, V. Just below the District Road and across from the School of Fine Arts.

This brand-new hotel is easily the finest in Hora. It has large bathrooms with full tubs, balconies overlooking the town and sea, and some rooms are even equipped with fire-places. Rooms are tastefully decorated in traditional island style; all have specially designed double-pane doors and windows for extra quiet. Ten units are wired for direct Internet connection, a bonus for those traveling with laptops. The courtyard contains a handsome pool, bar, and a faithfully restored 1850 mansion where a buffet breakfast is served; during the afternoon and evening the mansion is the home of Remvi, one of the town's best restaurants (see "Where to Dine," below). A new exercise room offers fitness machines, Jacuzzis, and a sauna. Check out the fine Web site, where you can find many photos of the hotel and several excellent off-season special offers, available only with Internet booking.

Hotel Carbonaki. Odos Panahrandou 23, Hora, 84600 Mikonos. ☎ **0289/22-461** or 0289/24-124. Fax 0289/24-102. E-mail: scala@otenet.gr. 21 units. A/C TV TEL. Dr25,000 ($83) double; Dr30,000 ($100) triple. Look for this hotel in a narrow lane, not far from Tria Pigadia and just toward the port from the Hotel Matina.

The Carbonaki's rooms are clustered around a bright courtyard, verdant with an abundance of trees and potted plants. There's a small pool here, and a terrace for sunning. A higher terrace has fine views across the rooftops of Mikonos, and a glimpse of the sparkling bay. Rooms are small and tastefully equipped with hardwood furniture; they don't have stellar views, opening either to the courtyard or the street. This is a primarily residential neighborhood, so it remains fairly quiet. Andonis and Theo Rousselonis have run this hotel for nearly 30 years; they speak little English, but their son Dimitris, who runs the Scala Stock Gallery across the street, speaks English perfectly. Dimitris also has studios and apartments for rent in several locations in town; prices are comparable to those at the hotel.

Hotel Marios. Odos Kaloyera 24, Hora, 84600 Mikonos. ☎ **0289/22-704.** 13 units. A/C TV TEL. Dr21,500 ($72) double. No credit cards.

This basic hotel has spotless doubles with modern facilities. The rooms are tiny, as are the bathrooms. A few fortunate units have balconies overlooking a small, verdant garden with a massive palm tree and a table where you can sit and enjoy the luxuriant shade. Rooms facing the street can be noisy at night, but those facing the garden are admirably quiet. Breakfast is not available.

Hotel Matina. Odos Fournakion 3, Hora, 84600 Mikonos. ☎ **0289/22-387** or 0289/26-433. Fax 0289/24-501. 19 units. TEL. Dr27,000 ($90) double. Continental breakfast Dr1,900 ($6) extra. AE, V.

Rooms are small but clean, modern, and inside a walled garden that makes them especially quiet for their central location. Most units have balconies or small terraces. The owner, Yannis Kontizas, was born on Mikonos—he's generous in offering information about the island.

Pension Stelios. Odos Apollonos 9, Hora, 84600 Mikonos. ☎ **0289/24-641.** 21 units. Dr18,000 ($60) double; Dr22,000 ($73) triple. Continental breakfast Dr1,200 ($4) extra. No credit cards.

Conveniently located near the ferry pier on the northeast end of the harbor, on the hill above the OTE office, this place is easily reached by broad stone steps above the road. The new building cascades down the hillside in three steps—all rooms have balconies with stunning views of the port, and a few have large private terraces. The rooms are clean and very basic, with pine furniture and stone floors; all have fridges. You should note that Stelios speaks very little English.

ON THE EDGE OF TOWN

Most of the new hotel construction in town in recent years has been along the District Road (Odos Ayiou Ioannou), which is the road that circles the older Hora.

There also are new hotels along two other roads: the one that leads south to Platis Yialos and that leading north to Ayios Stefanos; this latter road is particularly scenic and quiet, although you have to be willing to walk 10 to 15 minutes to town. All three areas have good views of Hora and the sea; they're easily accessible by car, and it's an easy walk down to the nightlife spots.

In addition to the following listings, also consider the rather dull but reliable **Hotel Poseidon,** Hora, 84600 Mikonos (☎ **0289/24-441** or 0289/24-442; fax 0289/ 23-812), which has 58 units, some with fine sea views (avoid the rooms that face the busy District Road).

Hotel Aegean. Tagou, 84600 Mikonos. ☎ **0289/23-544** or 0289/22-869. Fax 0289/24-927. 42 units. TV TEL. Dr28,000 ($93) double; Dr53,000 ($177) suite. Rates include breakfast. AE, EURO, MC, V. Located beyond the north bus stop above the road to Ayios Stefanos.

This pleasant bungalow hotel offers large, comfortable rooms. The view of the sea from the pool terrace is truly stellar—the bay opens in a bowl of azure, with Tinos and Delos on the horizon. Some rooms have the same view, although several look back toward the hills. The hotel has an attentive staff. Transportation to and from the airport or port is free if you arrange it at the time of booking.

Hotel Anastassios Sevasti. Hora, 84600 Mikonos. ☎ **0289/23-545** or 0289/24-334. Fax 0289/24-336. www.greekhotel.com/cyclades/myconos.sevasti. 42 units. A/C TV TEL. Dr32,000 ($107) double; Dr38,900 ($130) triple. AE, EURO, MC, V.

The Anastassios Sevasti is the best of the many hotels on a steep hill overlooking Mikonos town from above the peripheral District Road. Although it's only 100 meters from the edge of the old town, you'll want to have a car or the will to climb the 100 steps to the hotel's lofty perch. The large pool has a fine view of the town and the bay. Guest rooms are plain and somewhat larger than the average hotel room in town; all have balconies or terraces with views of the sea or the hills behind Mikonos town. The bathrooms are small, but all have a decent shower and some have half-bathtubs. The rooms and common areas are decorated with many paintings of local scenes, several painted by the owner's sister.

Kouros Hotel. Tagou, 84600 Mikonos. ☎ **0289/25-381** or 0289/25-383. Fax 0289/ 25-379. 25 units. A/C MINIBAR TV TEL. Dr55,000 ($183) double; Dr70,000 ($233) triple; Dr90,000 ($300) suite. Children under 12 stay half price in parents' room; children under 2 stay free. AE, DC, EURO, MC, V.

This new apartment hotel just outside of town above the road to Ayios Stefanos isn't as well known as the nearby Cavo Tagoo, but its rooms are much more spacious. All have kitchenettes, large modern bathrooms with tubs, and large balconies with sea views. Its pool is filled with fresh water, the staff is friendly, and it's a good place for families. The sea views from here are superb.

AROUND THE ISLAND

There are hotels clustered around many of the more popular beaches on the island, but most people prefer to stay in town and commute to the beaches. Following each review is a short description of the beach the hotel serves.

Apollonia Bay Hotel. Ayios Ioannis, 84600 Mikonos. ☎ **0289/27-890** or 0289/27-895. Fax 0289/27-641. E-mail: apolloniabay@myk.forthnet.gr. 30 units. A/C MINIBAR TV TEL. Dr45,200 ($151) double; Dr57,240 ($191) triple; Dr96,200 ($321) suite. Rates include breakfast. AE, DC, MC, V.

As you enter the new Apollonia Bay Hotel, dark walnut furniture contrasts dramatically with the brilliant white of the marble floor. Unlike many of the new hotels that are already crumbling at the edges, this place feels like it was built to last. There are many thoughtful details here—the trees planted in the midst of terraces for shade, the spacious bathrooms with tubs, the heavy rough-hewn ceiling timbers. There's a panoramic view of the bay from the large pool, itself just 100 meters from the edge of the sea. The guest rooms are simply furnished, and most have spacious balconies with sea views. The hotel restaurant serves a small menu of Greek dishes in addition to the substantial buffet breakfast. Elena Kousathana has been running hotels in Mikonos for more than 30 years, and her accumulated knowledge is quietly present in this fine small hotel.

Just 1½ kilometers (0.9 miles) past Ornos Beach, **Ayios Ioannis** feels more secluded and quiet than most of its neighbors. The beach here is small and pebbly, not satisfactory for true beach buffs. There are three fine tavernas on the beach, a small church, and a trail to larger Kapari Beach.

✪ Hotel Petassos Beach. Platis Yialos, 84600 Mikonos. ☎ **0289/23-437** or 0289/23-438. Fax 0289/24-101. www.vacation.forthnet.gr/petabeac.html. E-mail: petasos@myk.forthnet.gr. 82 units. A/C MINIBAR TV TEL. Dr46,500 ($155) double; Dr60,450 ($202) triple. Rates include breakfast. AE, MC, V.

Rooms here are large and comfortable, with balconies overlooking Psarrou Bay. The hotel has a good-size pool and sundeck at the edge of a precipitous drop to the sea; a Jacuzzi, gym, and sauna are just below the pool terrace. The seaside restaurant has the best view in town and a large wine list, and it serves a big buffet breakfast. A trail leads from the hotel to the nearby Psarrou Beach—in a small cove, this beach is the best-protected on the island from the predominant meltemi winds. Upon request you can take advantage of round-trip transportation from the harbor or airport, safe-deposit boxes, and laundry service. The gracious owner/operators and their well-trained and friendly multilingual staff win a star.

The sandy, crescent-shaped beach at **Platis Yialos** is just a 15-minute bus ride from Hora. It's the caïque stop for shuttles to Paradise, Super Paradise, Agrari, and Elia beaches.

Hotel Yiannaki. Ornos Beach, 84600 Mikonos. ☎ **0289/23-393** or 0289/23-443. Fax 0289/24-628. 42 units. A/C TV TEL. Dr32,000 ($107) double. Rates include breakfast. AE, DC, MC, V.

The hotel is on a small rise, overlooking the town and the beach, surrounded by a stand of trees and a small garden. The beach is 200 meters away, and there's a shortcut path that starts from the pool. A restaurant on the pool is open throughout the day; an extensive breakfast buffet is served here each morning. Rooms are basic: all have a fridge, and most have balconies with sea views.

The beach on calm Ornos Bay is especially recommended for families because of its shallow, calm water, and because it isn't a party beach. There are water-sports facilities and some good tavernas.

WHERE TO DINE

✪ Edem Restaurant. Above Panahrandou church, Hora. (Walk up Matoyianni, turn left on Kaloyera, and follow the signs up and to the left.) ☎ **0289/22-855.** Reservations recommended July–Aug. Main courses Dr2,500–Dr6,000 ($8–$20). AE, DC, EURO, MC, V. Daily noon–1am. GREEK/CONTINENTAL.

This excellent restaurant has a unique setting, where you can swim and have a drink, lunch, or dinner around a very nice pool. Edem is famous for its meat dishes, but its large menu also includes traditional Greek and continental dishes. The service is second to none.

El Greco/Yorgos. Plateia Tria Pigadia, Hora. ☎ **0289/22-074.** Main courses Dr1,800–Dr5,000 ($6–$17). AE, DC, EURO, MC, V. Daily 7pm–1am. GREEK/CONTINENTAL.

This sophisticated traditional taverna, with a large patio on central "Three Wells" Square, has a large menu that includes pastas, grilled meats, and traditional Greek specialties, including delicious eggplant boureki.

Philippi. Off Matoyianni, Hora. ☎ **0289/22-294.** Reservations recommended July–Aug. Main courses Dr3,000–Dr6,500 ($10–$22). AE, MC, V. Daily 7pm–1am. GREEK/CONTINENTAL.

You'll find this fine restaurant in a quiet garden just off the main street and Kaloyera, or you can come in the back way through the garden of the Hotel Philippi. It's one of the island's most special dining experiences, and it certainly has the most romantic atmosphere. The menu includes French classics, curry, and superbly prepared traditional Greek dishes. The wine list is also impressive.

Remvi. Hotel Belvedere, Rohari, 84600 Mikonos. ☎ **0289/25-122.** Reservations recommended July–Aug. Main courses Dr2,400–Dr4,500 ($8–$15). AE, DC, MC, V. Daily 8am–midnight. GREEK/CONTINENTAL.

The intimate Remvi (the name means something to the effect of "sitting quietly and enjoying the view") is a pleasantly surprising anomaly, a hotel restaurant that is quite exceptional. The restaurant cozily inhabits a tastefully renovated mansion with 2 centuries of history; the outside terrace enjoys a sweeping view of the town and harbor. The small à la carte menu changes substantially each day to accommodate the best and freshest local ingredients. The dishes are uncomplicated and delicious, featuring the simple flavors of Greek cuisine: the smoky aroma of roasted eggplant, the succulence of grilled fish and lamb. The wine list is short and carefully composed, with some hard-to-find treasures like the Domaine Carras Syrah and the Ktima Katzarou.

Sesame Kitchen. Plateia Tria Pigadia, Hora. ☎ **0289/24-710.** Main courses Dr1,500–Dr3,200 ($5–$11). AE, V. Daily 7pm–12:30am. GREEK/CONTINENTAL.

This small, health-conscious taverna, which serves some vegetarian specialties, is next to the Naval Museum. Fresh spinach, vegetable, cheese, and chicken pies are baked daily. There's a large variety of salads, brown rice, and soya dishes, including a vegetable moussaka, plus lightly grilled and seasoned meat dishes.

Taverna Caprice. Little Venice, Hora. ☎ **0289/26-083.** Main courses Dr1,500–Dr3,300 ($5–$11). V. Daily 6:30pm–1am. GREEK.

The Taverna Caprice, a neighbor of the justly renowned Caprice Bar, occupies a long narrow room that opens to the street on one end and the waters of the bay on the other—an ambitious wave could wash the feet of diners on the tiny back terrace. Unlike most harbor restaurants, this place isn't set up to feed hundreds each night: with room for only four tables outside and a few more inside, you can rest assured that the food won't be mass-produced. Many dishes feature local ingredients and recipes, like the appetizer sampler with onion pie, spicy Mikonian cheese, and *louza*, a local sliced meat. The menu standards like grilled fish are good, and there are some more unusual offerings like the Mikonian snails in a red-onion sauce.

MIKONOS AFTER DARK

Mikonos has the liveliest, most abundant, and most varied nightlife in the Aegean. It's a barhopper's paradise, and you'll enjoy wandering through the maze of streets looking for the right spot—and looking at everyone else looking. Don't be too disappointed if some of the places we suggest are closed or have changed their name or image; such is the nature of nightlife on an island where everything is seasonal. And be warned: Drinks in Mikonos cost more than they do in London or New York.

A perfect beginning to a long night is the view of the sunset from one of the sophisticated bars in Little Venice. The **Kastro** (☎ **0289/23-070**), near the Paraportiani church, is famous for classical music and frozen daiquiris. The classic sunset scene is the **Caprice Bar,** up the block on Scarpa, which also has a seaside perch and plays soft rock in the early evening. The **Montparnasse** (☎ **0289/23-719**), on the same lane, is highly romantic, and often plays classical music. The **Veranda** (☎ **0289/23-290**), in an old mansion overlooking the water with a good view of the windmills, is as relaxing as its name implies. **Galleraki** (☎ **0289/27-188**) also has tables near the water, and plays the latest pop music.

The "king of the scene" is **Pierro's** (☎ **0289/22-177**), very popular with gay visitors; it rocks all night long to American and European music and draws crowds in sufficient quantity to impede your progress up the narrow Odos Matoyianni. If you'd like something a little more laid back, back up and check out the **Nine Muses,** on Taxi Square. Or squeeze past the throng to the **Lotus** (☎ **0289/22-181**), for good music, good food, and an interesting scene, or the **Anchor,** which plays blues, jazz, and classic rock for its 30-something clients. Further along Matoyianni at no. 42 is **Bar Uno** (☎ **0289/26-144**), playing mostly soft rock, and populated by mostly middle-aged European clientele. **Astra,** on Tria Pigadia, is currently the place where visiting models and millionaires find each other.

Head right back toward the harbor for some wilder action. **Stavros Irish Bar** (☎ **0289/23-350**), behind Town Hall, is still among the most unrestrained places for young heavy drinkers, and nearby the **Scandinavian Bar** rivals it in the anything-goes department. And if you'd like to sample some Greek music and dancing, you're in the right neighborhood. **Thalami** (☎ **0289/23-291**), a small club underneath Town Hall, may have room for you to experience something very nearly authentic. The **Mikonos Bar** is another good place for traditional Greek music and dancing.

The other end of the harbor also has some nightlife, especially at **Remezzo Disco,** near the OTE, where you can boogie into the morning under the stars (this is an Athenian chain, and caters almost exclusively to tourists).

So, now it's well after midnight and you're still up for more. Don't worry: you haven't exhausted the possibilities. **MADD,** on Taxi Square, is only just coming alive at 1am, and the view of the port is sensational. The **Anchor Club** on Odos Matoyianni is transformed into a disco in these early morning hours, and plays loud rock.

If you're visiting between July and September, you may want to find out what's happening at the **Anemo Theatre** (☎ **0289/23-944**), an outdoor venue for the performing arts in a garden in Rohari, just above town, which presents a variety of concerts and performances.

7 Delos

The small island of Delos, just 3 kilometers (1.9 miles) off the shores of Mikonos, was considered by the ancient Greeks to be the holiest of sanctuaries, the sacred center around which the other Cyclades circled. Delos is known locally as the "brightest" island in the Cyclades, a tradition that seems to indicate both its continued significance as a sacred place and the simple fact that this is one place where you'll want to have sunglasses. It is unquestionably one of the most remarkable archaeological preserves in the world, displaying ample evidence of its former grandeur. Always a place set apart, with different rules than those of neighboring islands, in ancient times people were not allowed to die or be born on this sacred island. Today they are not

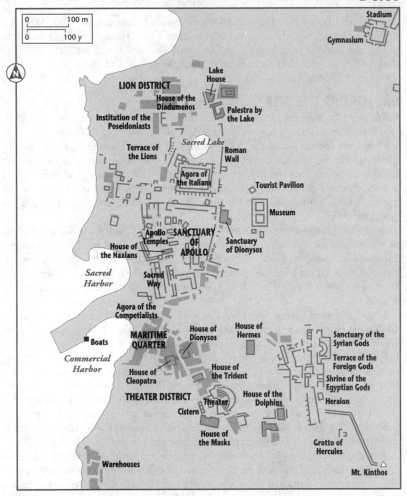

Delos

(Map labels:)

100 m
100 y

N

Stadium
Gymnasium

LION DISTRICT

Lake House

House of the Diadumenos

Palestra by the Lake

Institution of the Poseidoniasts

Sacred Lake

Terrace of the Lions

Roman Wall

Agora of the Italians

Tourist Pavilion

Museum

Apollo Temples

SANCTUARY OF APOLLO

Sanctuary of Dionysos

House of the Naxians

Sacred Harbor

Sacred Way

Agora of the Competialists

House of Dionysos

House of Hermes

MARITIME QUARTER

Sanctuary of the Syrian Gods

Terrace of the Foreign Gods

Boats

Commercial Harbor

House of the Trident

Shrine of the Egyptian Gods

House of Cleopatra

House of the Dolphins

Heraion

THEATER DISTRICT

Theater

Cistern

House of the Masks

Grotto of Hercules

Warehouses

Mt. Kinthos

---

allowed to spend the night, and the site can be visited only between the hours of 8:30am and 3pm.

The 3 hours allotted by most excursions are sufficient for only the most cursory exploration, and more than one visit is necessary to see the whole site. We recommend visiting Delos as early as possible in the day, especially in summer, when the crowds and heat become overwhelming by early afternoon. Sturdy shoes and water are necessary; a hat or cap and food are also advised. (There is a cafe near the museum, but the prices are high, the quality is poor, and the service is even worse.)

ESSENTIALS

GETTING THERE Delos can be reached by sea only. Most people visit on excursion boats from neighboring Mikonos or Tinos. The island is also a prominent stop for cruise ships and yachts. From Mikonos, organized guided and unguided excursions leave Tuesday through Sunday from the west end of the harbor; the trip takes about 40 minutes and costs Dr2,500 ($8) round-trip for transportation alone.

Sea and Sky Travel (☎ 0289/22-853) offers guided tours for Dr8,500 ($28) that depart at 9 or 10am and return at 12:30 or 2pm. From Tinos, there is an excursion during the summer months only to Delos and Mikonos for about Dr5,000 ($17) round-trip; the excursion runs Tuesday through Sunday and includes 3 hours on Delos and a short stop in Mikonos town.

EXPLORING THE SITE

Entrance to the site costs Dr1,200 ($4) for adults, Dr900 ($3) for seniors, and Dr600 ($2) for students. The site is open Tuesday through Sunday from 8:30am to 3pm, and is **closed on Mondays.** At the ticket kiosk, you'll see a number of site plans and picture guides for sale. One of the better ones is *Delos: Monuments and Museum,* by P. Zaphiropoulou (Kreve Edition), which has a well-translated text, good pictures, and a foldout map. Because the excavations at Delos have been conducted by the French School, most signs are in French, and a thorough English map and guide are especially useful.

To the left (north) of the new jetty where your boat will dock is the **Sacred Harbor,** now too silted for use, where pilgrims, merchants, and sailors from throughout the Mediterranean used to land. The commercial importance of the island in ancient times was due to the protection its harbor offered in the shelter of surrounding islands, the best anywhere between mainland Greece and its colonies and trading partners in Asia Minor.

If you're not on a tour and have the energy, you should definitely head up to ✪ **Mount Kinthos,** the highest point on the island. It offers an overview of the site and a fine view of most of the Cyclades: the neighboring island of Rinia with Siros beyond it to the west, Tinos to the north, Mikonos to the northeast, Naxos and Paros to the south. From the summit, with the islands of the Cyclades sprawled on all sides, close up and low to the horizon, you get the sense that this is indeed the center of the archipelago. On your way down don't miss the remarkable **Grotto of Hercules,** a small temple built into a natural crevice in the mountainside—the roof is formed of massive granite slabs held up by their own enormous weight. The grotto commands a fine view of the harbor and much of the archaeological site.

Just south (to the right) from the Sacred Harbor is the fascinating **Maritime Quarter,** a residential area with the remains of houses from the Hellenistic and Roman era, when the island reached its peak in wealth and prestige. Reminiscent of Pompeii, the outlines of the ancient city are remarkably preserved. Several houses contain brilliant mosaics, and in most houses the cistern and sewer systems can be seen. Among the numerous small dwellings are several palaces, built around a central court and connected to the street by a narrow passage. The mosaics in the courtyards of the palaces are particularly elaborate, and include such famous images as Dionysos riding a panther in the **House of the Masks,** and a similar depiction in the **House of Dionysos.** Further to the south is the massive **Theater,** which seated 5,500 people and was the site of choral competitions during the Delian Festivals, an event held every 4 years and comprising athletic competitions in addition to musical contests. Behind the theater is a fine arched **cistern,** which was the water supply for the city.

Adjacent to the Sacred Harbor is the **Agora of the Competialists,** built in the 2nd century B.C. when the island was a bustling free port under Rome. Roman citizens, mostly former slaves, worshipped the *lares competales,* who were minor "crossroad" deities associated with the Greek god Hermes, patron of travelers and commerce. From the far left corner of the Agora of the Competialists, the **Sacred Way**—once lined with statues and votive monuments—leads north toward the Sanctuary of Apollo. By retracing the steps of ancient pilgrims along it, you will pass the scant remains of several temples (most of the stone from the site was taken away for buildings on neighboring islands, especially Mikonos and Tinos). At the far end of the Sacred Way was the **Propylaea,** a monumental marble gateway that led into the sanctuary. In ancient times, the sanctuary was crowded with temples, altars, statues, and votive offerings.

The **museum,** open the same hours as the site, contains finds from the various excavations on the island. It displays some fine statuary, reliefs, masks, and jewelry, and is well worth a visit. Admission to the museum is included in the entrance fee to the site.

North of the Tourist Pavilion on the left is the **Sacred Lake,** where the oracular swans once swam. The lake is now little more than a dusty indentation most of the year, surrounded by a low wall. Beyond it is the famous guardian **Lions,** made of Naxian marble and erected in the 7th century B.C. (There were originally at least nine. One was taken away to Venice in the 17th century and now stands before the Arsenal there. The whereabouts of the others remain a mystery.) Beyond the lake to the northeast is the large square courtyard of the Gymnasium and the long narrow Stadium, where the athletic competitions of the Delian Games were held.

8 Tinos

161km (87 nautical miles) SE of Piraeus

Tinos is an important place of religious pilgrimage, and yet it remains one of the least commercial islands of the Cyclades and, for that reason, a joy to visit. **Panayia Evanyelistria** ("Our Lady of Good Tidings"), the "Lourdes of Greece," draws thousands of pilgrims every year seeking the aid of a miraculous icon enshrined there. Almost any day of the year you can see people, particularly elderly women, crawling from the port on hands and knees up the long, steep street leading to the hilltop cathedral. The market street of Tinos town is lined with stalls selling holy water vials, incense, candles (up to 2m long), and mass-produced icons.

The inland villages of Tinos are some of the most beautiful in the Cyclades, and every visitor to the island should take the time to explore a few of them. Many of the most picturesque villages are nestled into the slopes of **Exomvourgo,** the rocky pinnacle visible from the port, connected by a network of walking paths that make this island a hiker's paradise. In these villages and dotting the countryside, you'll see the ornately decorated medieval dovecotes for which the island is famous, and above the doors of village houses elaborately carved marble lintels. The island's beaches aren't worthy of superlatives, but they are plentiful and uncrowded throughout the summer.

The popularity of the island as a pilgrimage destination means that ferries are frequent throughout the year. Once you arrive, you'll find that the island buses are infrequent, even in summer, making a car or moped rental advisable. Don't even think about arriving without a reservation around August 15, when thousands of pilgrims travel here to celebrate the Feast of the Assumption of the Virgin.

ESSENTIALS

GETTING THERE   There are several ferries to Tinos daily from Piraeus, and two daily from Rafina; schedules should be confirmed with **tourist information** in Athens (☎ 01/171 or 01/322-2545), the **Piraeus Port Authority** (☎ 01/451-1310), or the **Rafina Port Authority** (☎ 0294/22-300). Several times a day, ferries connect Tinos with nearby Mikonos; ferries to Siros are daily in the summer, and somewhat less frequent during the winter months (Tinos has more winter connections than most

Cycladic isles due to its religious tourism, which continues year-round). There is a daily excursion in the summer from Tinos to Delos and Mikonos, returning to Tinos the same day; the cost is about Dr5,000 ($17). On Mondays, when Delos is closed to visitors, the excursion stops only on Mikonos.

There are two piers in Tinos harbor, the newer one 600 meters north of the main one (just past the children's park in the direction of Kionia). Be sure to find out from which your ship will depart; most still depart from the old pier in the town center, although this may soon change. It can happen that due to weather conditions ships will use a different pier than expected, in which case there will be an announcement by loudspeaker at the intended pier as little as 10 minutes prior to arrival—at this point you'll see a convoy of hotel buses and travelers mobilize themselves to get promptly to the other port. The **Tinos Port Authority** (marginally helpful under the best of conditions) can be reached at ☎ 0283/22-348.

VISITOR INFORMATION   The best place to go for accommodations, car rentals, island tours, or abundant information about Tinos is **Windmills Travel** (☎/fax 0283/23-398), on the water near the new port, opposite the children's park. Sharon Turner is the friendly and outgoing manager. For those planning to stay a week or longer on Tinos, she has information about houses for rent in several of the island's villages—these are a great way to see more of the island and get a taste for village life. The weekly cost is about Dr210,000 ($700) for a one-bedroom house, including car rental. Accommodations can also be arranged here for nearby Mikonos, or any of the other Cycladic islands.

GETTING AROUND   By Bus   The **bus station** (☎ 0283/22-440) is on the harbor, opposite the south (old) port. **KTEL** (the local bus company) posts its schedules here, although they're difficult to interpret (ask about bus times at Windmills Travel if the schedule is indecipherable). The buses run on time, but infrequently, making travel by bus logistically difficult.

By Car & Moped   The most reliable rental company in town is **Vidalis** (☎ 0283/23-400), just off the harbor on the main road out of town (turn at the supermarket). Car rental starts at Dr10,000 ($33) for a tiny two-door, up to Dr17,000 ($57) for a jeep; prices include full insurance. Mopeds are Dr3,000 to Dr5,000 ($10 to $17).

By Taxi   The taxi stand is on the harbor, by the south (old) pier.

FAST FACTS   There are several **banks** on the harbor—the Ethniki Trapeza (National Bank) has an ATM, one of the only ones on the island, and is open Monday through Thursday from 8am to 2pm and Friday from 8am to 1:30pm. The **first-aid center** can be reached at ☎ 0283/22-210. There's a drop-off **laundry** and **dry-cleaning** service (☎ 0283/23-765) opposite Peristerionas Restaurant, in a lane behind the Lido Hotel; open from 8am to 2pm and 5 to 9pm. For **luggage storage,** try Windmills Travel (☎ 0283/23-398), near the new port. The **police station** (☎ 0283/22-255) is at the new pier, past the Lido Hotel and the children's park. The **post office** (☎ 0283/22-247), open Monday through Friday from 7:30am to 2pm, is at the south end of the harbor next to the Tinion Hotel. The **telephone office (OTE),** open from 8am to 3pm, is on the main street leading up to the church of Panayia Evanyelistria, about halfway up on the right (☎ 0283/22-399).

WHAT TO SEE & DO

✪ **Panayia Evanyelistria Cathedral and Museums.** Tinos, 84200 Tinos. Free admission. Cathedral open daily 8am–8pm (off-season daily noon–6pm). Galleries open Sat–Sun (some weekdays during July and Aug) 8am–8pm (off-season noon–6pm).

The story of the cathedral began in 1822, during the War of Independence, when a nun at the Kehrovouniou Convent had a vision that an icon was buried on a nearby farm. The present cathedral was built on the site of the ancient church, and today you can see the miraculous icon to the left of the central aisle where it's encased in gold, diamonds, and pearls. Below the church is the crypt where the icon was found, surrounded by smaller chapels; the crypt is often crowded with Greek parents and children in white, waiting to be baptized with water from the font. Particularly interesting are the hundreds of objects in silver and gold hanging from the roof—sometimes a hand or foot, a child's crib, a house, a car, and to the right of the entrance a gold lemon tree. Each one has a story to tell, a tale of thanks for a prayer answered.

Within the high walls that surround the church are various museums and galleries, most of which are interesting primarily as curiosities. The gallery of 19th-century religious art is to the left as you pass through the main gateway; another gallery houses Byzantine icons, and to the left of the foundation offices is a fascinating display of gifts offered to the cathedral. The sculpture museum, to the right and up a flight of stairs, is one of the best galleries: it contains gifts from sculptors, many quite renowned, who studied with the help of the cathedral charitable foundation. Just below the cathedral precinct on Leoforos Megaloharis is a small **Archaeological Museum,** open Tuesday through Sunday from 8:30am to 3pm; admission is Dr500 ($1.70). The collection includes finds from the ancient sanctuary of Thesmophorion near Exomvourgo, and a sundial from the 2nd century A.D. found at the Sanctuary of Poseidon and Amphitrite at Kionia.

EXPLORING THE ISLAND

If it's a clear day, one of your first sights of Tinos from the ferry will be the pinnacle of rock towering over Tinos town, the site of the Venetian fortress of **Exomvourgo.** The fortress itself has long been in ruins, but you can still explore the remains of the fortifications and enjoy the superb view from the summit, one of the best in the Cyclades. The fortress is surrounded by sheer rock walls on three sides; the only path to the summit starts behind a Catholic church at the base of the rock, on the road between Mesi and Koumaros (you'll need to rent a car or walk from Tinos town, a distance of about 5km/3 miles). As you make the 15-minute ascent to the summit you'll pass several lines of fortification—the whole hill is riddled with walls and hollow with chambers.

The towns circling Exomvourgo are some of the most picturesque on the island, and can be visited by car or on foot (see "Walking," below). **Dio Horia** has a spring in the main square, where some villagers still wash their clothes by hand, and beautiful village houses. There is a town bus to the nearby **Convent of Kerovouniou,** one of the largest in Greece and dating to the 10th century. This was the home of Pelayia, the nun whose vision revealed the location of the island's famed icon; you can visit her cell and see a small museum of 18th- and 19th-century icons. **Loutra** is an especially attractive village with a 17th-century Jesuit monastery that contains an excellent museum of village life—implements for making olive oil and wine are on display alongside old manuscripts and maps pertaining to the island; it's open mid-June to mid-September from 10:30am to 3:30pm. **Volax** is situated in a remote valley known for a bizarre lunar landscape of rotund granite boulders—the villagers have recently constructed a stone amphitheater for theatrical productions, so be sure to ask at **Windmills Travel** (☎/fax **0283/23-398**) for a schedule of performances. Volax is also known for its local basket weaver, whose baskets are remarkably durable and attractive; ask for directions to his workshop, in one of the back lanes of the town near the Catholic church.

Tinos is famous for its **dovecotes,** stout stone towers elaborately ornamented with slabs of the local shale. The doves were an important part of the local diet, and their droppings were used as a fertilizer. Any excursion through the countryside of Tinos will reveal many of these curious structures; there are some 600 on the island, many more than 300 years old. The towns of **Tarambados** and **Smardakito** are known to have some of the most elaborate ones.

Pirgos, at the western end of the island, is one of Tinos's most beautiful villages. Renowned for its school of fine arts, the town is a center for marble sculpting, and many of the finest sculptors of Greece have trained here. The town has a small **museum,** housing mostly sculpture by local artists; it's open Tuesday through Sunday from 11am to 1:30pm and 5:30 to 6:30pm, and is located near the bus station, on the main laneway leading toward the village.

BEACHES

There's a good fine-sand beach 3 kilometers (1.9 miles) west of Tinos town at **Kionia,** and another 2 kilometers (1.2 miles) east of town at busy **Ayios Fokas.** From Tinos there's bus service on the south beach road (usually four times a day) to the resort of **Porto,** 8 kilometers (5 miles) to the east. Porto offers several long stretches of uncrowded sand, a few hotel complexes and numerous tavernas, several at or near the beach. The beach at Ayios Ioannis facing the town of Porto is okay, but you'd be better off walking west across the small headland to a longer, less populous beach. There are two good beaches at **Kolimbithres** on the north side of the island, easily accessed by car, although protection from the meltemi wind could be a problem here—the first has fine sand and a taverna, and the second (reached by a short drive on a poor dirt road across the headland) is longer, less populous, and more exposed to the wind. The lovely pebble cove at **Livada** is accessible only by a rough dirt road. Several beaches on the southwest coast (**Ayios Romanos, Ayios Petros,** and **Isternion**) are accessible by paved road.

WALKING

Tinos is a walker's paradise, with a good network of paths and remote interior regions waiting to be explored. Some of the best walks are in the vicinity of **Exomvourgo**— paths connect the cluster of villages circling this craggy fortress, offering great views and many places to stop for refreshment along the way. There isn't currently a guide to Tinos walking in English, but you can ask for information at **Windmills Travel** (☎/fax **0283/23-398**) in Tinos town: the office is planning to arrange walking tours in the future, and should be able to offer information about organized walking or about routes for you to explore on your own.

SHOPPING

The **flea market** on Odos Evanyelistria is a pleasant place for a ramble; Odos Evanyelistria parallels Leoforos Megaloharis, the main street from the harbor up to the cathedral. The colorful stalls lining the street sell icons, incense, candles, medallions, and *tamata* (tin, silver, and gold votives). You'll also find local embroidery, weavings, and the delicious local nougat, as well as loukoumia (Turkish delight) from Siros. **Harris Prassas Ostria-Tinos,** Odos Evanyelistria 20 (☎ **0283/23-893;** fax 0283/24-568), is particularly recommended for his fine collection of jewelry in contemporary, Byzantine, and classical styles; silver work; and beautiful religious objects, including reproductions of the miraculous icon. Harris is friendly, informative, and famous for the quality of his work. Near the top of the street on the left is the small **O Evangelismos Weaving School** (☎ 0283/22-894) and a store selling tablecloths, bedcovers, and other woven items produced at the school.

Those interested in authentic hand-painted icons should find the small shop of **Maria Vryoni,** the first left from the port off Leoforos Megaloharis, the second shop on the left. Maria spends at least a week on each of her works of art; they start at around Dr50,000 ($167).

There are several sculptors working in **Pirgos,** the island's center for marble sculpture. Among the most accomplished is **Antonis Hondriannis** (☎ 0283/31-470), whose studio is on the main road, downhill from the bus station. Uphill from the bus station on the main road is the studio of **Mihail Saltamanikas** (☎ 0283/31-554), a recent graduate of the Fine Arts School who also does excellent work.

WHERE TO STAY

Unless you have reservations, you shouldn't plan an overnight visit to Tinos during important religious holidays, especially **March 25** (Feast of the Annunciation) and **August 15** (Feast of the Assumption)—though a summer night under the stars wouldn't be too high a price to pay for such an experience. Summer weekends can also be very busy, when Greeks travel here by the hundreds to make a short pilgrimage to the Panayia Evanyelistria.

In addition to the following choices, you might also consider the **Porto Tango Hotel,** Ayios Ioannis, Porto, 84200 Tinos (☎ 0283/24-411 or 0283/24-415; fax 0283/24-416), an attractive place that offers many amenities. Note that its location is rather inconvenient unless you have a car.

Aeolos Bay Hotel. Ayios Fokas, Tinos town, 84200 Tinos (300m east of town on the coast road). ☎ **0283/23-339.** Fax 0283/23-086. 69 units. TEL. Dr17,000 ($57) double; Dr21,000 ($70) triple. Rates include breakfast. MC, V.

This basic seaside hotel is a good choice if you want to be within walking distance of town, but away from the noise and commotion of the harbor. The shore is just 50 meters away, but the nearest beach worthy of the name is about 1 kilometer (0.6 miles) further east. There's a pool and a restaurant serving taverna fare at reasonable prices. The simple guest rooms have dark marble floors, white walls, and small balconies (most of which overlook the bay).

Akti Aegeou Apartments. Ayios Panteleimon Beach, 84200 Tinos (5km east of Tinos town on the road to Porto). ☎ **0283/24-248** or 0283/25-523. Fax 0283/23-523. 11 units. TEL. Dr17,000 ($57) double; Dr20,000 ($67) triple. No credit cards.

The Akti Aegeou is built right on the sand of Porto Beach, one of the island's finest, and since there are only 11 apartments, it has an atmosphere of friendly informality. The place was constructed with many traditional details, like the pebble designs on the terraces, flagstone floors, and the dovecote incorporated into the restaurant. Each of the roomy apartments has a kitchenette and a balcony facing the beach; triples have a separate bedroom and sitting room. Meals are served on the pool terrace.

Avra Hotel. Tinos town, 84200 Tinos. ☎ **0283/22-242.** Fax 0283/22-176. 17 units. TEL. Dr14,300 ($48) double. Continental breakfast Dr1,000 ($3.35) extra. No credit cards.

A wooden spiral staircase leads to high-ceilinged rooms in this charming old hotel on the harbor, one of the first in Tinos when it was built in 1921. Several rooms have a view of the harbor, and three have balconies; unfortunately these front rooms also get the harbor noise, so they're not for light sleepers. Other units face a rear courtyard and share a sunny terrace filled with palms and ferns. The floors in the rooms are a cool, decorative tile, while the hallways have wooden floors—quite a curiosity on this island where marble is plentiful and trees precious. There's a suite with a small kitchen at the rear of the building that rents for Dr15,000 ($50) a night—although there's no view, it's very cozy, and feels more like an old family parlor than a hotel room.

✪ **Tinion Hotel.** Odos Alavanou 1, Tinos town, 84200 Tinos. ☎ **0283/22-261.** Fax 0283/24-754. 20 units. Dr14,500 ($48) double. Continental breakfast Dr2,000 ($7) extra. MC, V.

This venerable hotel to the right from the harbor retains an old-world charm with marble floors, dark polished wood, and lace curtains. The rooms have high ceilings, old tile floors, and handsome brass or carved walnut beds. It's on a small square, just far enough from the harbor and its late-night activity to provide a quiet night's sleep; only the rooms on the corner can be a bit noisy. The front rooms all have balconies with harbor views.

Tinos Beach Hotel. Kionia, 84200 Tinos (4km/2.5 miles west of Tinos town on the coast road). ☎ **0283/22-626** or 0283/22-627. Fax 0283/23-153. 180 units. TEL. Dr27,200 ($91) double; Dr38,000 ($127) triple; Dr44,200 ($147) suite. Children 7 and under stay free in parents' room. Rates include breakfast. AE, DC, MC, V.

The Tinos Beach is the best beachfront hotel on the island, despite its impersonal character and fading 1960s elegance. The spacious carpeted rooms all have balconies, most with views of sea and pool. Bathrooms all have half-tubs. The pool is the longest on the island, and there's a separate children's pool. Suites are especially pleasant—a large sitting room with couch opens onto a poolside balcony. There is a tennis court, although it has seen better days—weeds are beginning to sprout through the cracks.

WHERE TO DINE

As usual, avoid harbor-front joints, where food is generally inferior and service can be rushed.

✪ **Koutouki.** Paralia. ☎ **0283/24-857.** Main courses Dr900–Dr3,000 ($3–$10). No credit cards. Daily noon–midnight. GREEK.

There's usually no menu at this excellent small taverna, just a few basic ingredients, and the result is a simple meal that reminds you how delightful Greek food can be. There's only room for a few tables in the stone-walled dining room; the wicker chairs are admirably comfortable. Local cheese and wine, fresh fish and meats, delicious vegetables—these are the staples that come together so delightfully in this taverna, which demonstrates that you don't have to pay a fortune to experience cooking as a fine art.

Lefteris. Paralia. ☎ **0283/23-013.** Main courses Dr800–Dr2,600 ($2.70–$9). No credit cards. Daily 11am–midnight. GREEK.

On the harbor front, look for a blue sign over an arched entrance that leads to a large courtyard decorated with fish plaques. The menu is large and varied, offering grilled sea bass, veal stifado, and dolmades (stuffed grape leaves in lemon sauce). There's plenty of room for dancing, and the waiters often demonstrate and urge diners to join them.

Palea Pallada (old Pallada). Tinos town. ☎ **0283/23-516.** Main courses Dr1,000–Dr4,000 ($3.35–$13). AE, MC, V. Daily noon–4pm and 6:30–11:30pm. GREEK/SEAFOOD.

In a small lane immediately behind the foreign press shop on the harbor you'll find this classic taverna, named for the original "Pallada" harbor of Tinos. Equally popular with visitors and locals, the place is always lively and loud with the voices of satisfied diners. Specialties include the sharp, hard village feta served with the smooth house wine; fresh *kolios* (a long, tasty, silver mackerel); and the grilled *loukanika*, local sausage with a hint of fennel.

Peristerionas (Dovecote). Odos Paksimadi Fraiskou 12. ☎ **0283/23-425.** Main courses Dr1,600–Dr2,400 ($5–$8). No credit cards. Daily noon–3pm and 7–11:30pm. GREEK.

This restaurant is found on a small lane uphill behind the Lido Hotel, 2 blocks behind Pallea Pallada; its outdoor tables fill the walkway. It serves excellent grilled meats and fish, plus delicious *marathotiganites* (vegetable fritters with onions and dill).

9 Siros (Syros)

144km (78 nautical miles) SE of Piraeus

Having lost most of its foreign tourism to other, more glamorous Cycladic isles, Siros offers a rare opportunity to vacation as the Greeks do. Excellent food, a long tradition of popular music (known as rembetika), glorious little-known beaches, and the most vivacious island capital in the Cyclades are among the benefits of a visit to Siros.

Anything but a backwater, **Ermoupolis** is the administrative capital of the Cyclades, a thriving port that was the busiest in Greece during the 19th century. Signs of this former affluence are concentrated in the vicinity of the harbor, where neoclassical mansions abut the rocky waterfront and grandiose public buildings line spacious squares. Although the city has seen several decades of decline during which many of its finest buildings began to crumble, recent restoration efforts have brought back much of the glory of the city's heyday, and several of the most elaborate mansions have been converted to hotels and guest houses. Another sign of urban revival is a busy calendar of lively public events and some of the best food in the Cyclades.

The north end of the island is a starkly beautiful region of widely dispersed farms, terraced fields, and plentiful walking paths. The best beaches of the island are here, accessible only on foot or by boat, and the important archaeological sites of Halandriani and Kastri can both be reached by trail. The San Mihali and kopanisti cheeses are made here, as well as a delicious thyme honey; all of these can be found in the Ermoupolis open-air market.

The best months to visit Siros are May, June, and September; the worst month is August, when vacationing Greeks fill every hotel room on the island. Getting around this small island by bus is so easy and convenient that you probably won't need to rent a car or moped.

ESSENTIALS

GETTING THERE   By Plane   There are at least two flights daily from Athens. Call **Olympic Airways** at their Ermoupolis office (☎ **0281/88-018**) or in Athens (☎ **01/966-6666**) for reservations.

By Boat   Ferries connect Siros at least once daily with Piraeus, Ios, Naxos, Mikonos, Paros, and Tinos; three or four times weekly with Santorini and Samos; and once or twice weekly with Folegandros, Sifnos, Rhodes, Iraklion, and Thessaloniki. There are also daily ferries from Rafina, but you should avoid the slow cargo boats. You'll find numerous ferry-ticket offices at the pier; **Alpha Syros** (☎ **0281/81-185**), opposite the ferry pier, usually remains open until the last boat has arrived, so it can be a good place to leave your luggage if you're departing or to get information when arriving. Ferry information can be verified with the local **Port Authority** (☎ **0281/88-888** or 0281/82-690); Piraeus ferry schedules can be confirmed with **tourist information** in Athens (☎ **01/171** or 01/322-2545).

VISITOR INFORMATION   The **Hoteliers Association of Siros** operates a hotel-booking center at the pier during the summer months; it's open daily from 8am to 7pm. The **National Tourist Organization** (☎ **0281/86-725;** fax 0281/82-375) has an office at Odos Dodekanisou 10, a side street just to the left of the pier; the hours are Monday through Friday from 7:30am to 2:30pm. The people here are very friendly and helpful. There is also an Ermoupolis Web site: **www.ermupoli.otenet.gr.**

   Teamwork Holidays, on the paralia (harbor front) at Akti Ralli 10 (☎ 0281/ **83-400;** fax 0281/83-508), about 150 meters from the pier in the direction of the Hermes Hotel, is open daily from 9am to 9pm to book rooms, change money, sell Olympic Airways tickets, and arrange rental cars. They also offer a round-the-island half-day bus tour or a full-day beach tour by motorboat.

GETTING AROUND   By Bus   The **bus stop** in Ermoupolis is at the pier; the schedule is posted here, and is fairly easy to decipher. Buses circle the southern half of Siros about eight times a day between 10am and 8pm, and more frequently in summer. There are no buses to the northern part of the island. The off-season schedule is irregular, due to the fact that the buses also bring children to and from school; buses do run on time throughout the year. The fare is Dr220 to Dr330 (75¢ to $1.10).

By Car & Moped   Of the several car-rental places along the harbor in the vicinity of the pier, a reliable choice is **Siros Rent A Car** (☎ **0281/80-409**), where a small car will cost Dr16,000 ($53) per day, including full insurance. A 50cc scooter is Dr6,000 ($20) a day.

By Taxi   The **taxi station** is on the main square, Plateia Miaoulis (☎ **0281/ 86-222**).

FAST FACTS   Several **banks** on the harbor, including the Alpha Credit Bank, the National Bank, and the Commercial Bank, have ATMs. The Ermoupolis **hospital** is the largest in the Cyclades; it's just outside town to the west, near Plateia Iroon (☎ **0281/86-666**). There's a friendly drop-off **laundry/dry-cleaning** service opposite the post office on Odos Protopapadaki. For **luggage storage,** ask at Alpha Syros (☎ **0281/81-185**), a branch of Teamwork Holidays on the waterfront at the ferry pier; this office will usually remain open until the last ferry of the night departs. The **police station** (☎ **0281/82-610**) is on the south side of Miaoulis Square. The **port authority** (☎ **0281/88-888** or 0281/82-690) is on the long pier at the far end of the harbor, beyond Hotel Hermes. The **post office** is between Miaoulis Square and the harbor on Odos Protopapadaki (☎ **0281/82-596**); open Monday through Friday from 7:30am to 2pm. The **telephone office (OTE)** is on the east side of Miaoulis Square (☎ **0281/87-399**); open Monday through Saturday from 7:30am to 3pm.

WHAT TO SEE & DO
EXPLORING ERMOUPOLIS

Ermoupolis is a flourishing city, a city with a life of its own that clearly doesn't rely on tourism. In the 19th century, Ermoupolis was the busiest port in Greece, and the sophisticated neoclassical architecture of this period dominates the low-lying areas of the city in the vicinity of the harbor. The central square (**Plateia Miaoulis**) and elaborately elegant **Town Hall** seem more typical of a wealthy French provincial town than a Greek island capital, and it is this cosmopolitan quality that sets Ermoupolis apart from the relative insularity of most island towns.

   To reach Plateia Miaoulis from the port, turn inland on Odos Venizelou, near the bus station. Ringed by high palm trees and facing the imposing Town Hall, Plateia Miaoulis is the center of civic life in Ermoupolis. Outdoor theatrical and musical events are often put on here; every night the square is filled with promenading

Shopping in Ermoupolis

The shops here tend to be functional rather than funky, and there aren't any that stand out. However, just about anything you need can be found somewhere in town. The best street for shopping is **Odos Protopapadaki,** two streets from the port, which is open to car traffic and full of shops; the post office is also on this street. The town **produce market** is on **Odos Hios,** west of the main square; it's open daily, but particularly lively on Saturdays. You shouldn't leave the market without trying the local specialty *loukoumia,* better known as Turkish delight, and *halvodopita,* a sort of nougat.

Ermoupolites, and cafe chairs seem to sprout like mushrooms from every corner. On the west side of the Town Hall, beneath the clock tower, is the **Archaeological Museum.** Its tiny collection includes some fine Cycladic sculptures from the 3rd millennium B.C., two beautiful miniature Hellenistic marble heads, and Roman-era sculpture from Amorgos. Open Tuesday through Sunday from 8:30am to 3pm; admission is free.

A couple of blocks northeast of the Town Hall, you'll find the 19th-century **Apollon Theater,** a smaller version of Milan's La Scala. It's being restored, thanks to funding from the European Union. (Contact Teamwork Holidays at ☎ 0281/83-400 for information and tickets.) Northeast behind it is the lovely church of **Ayios Nikolaos,** with a green marble iconostasis carved by Vitalis, a famed marble carver of the 19th century from Tinos. (Vitalis also sculpted the monument to an unknown soldier in the garden near the entrance.) A short stroll beyond the church will bring you to the neighborhood called **Vaporia,** named after the steamships that brought it great prosperity.

Ano Siros, the taller hill seen to the left of Ermoupolis as you enter the harbor, can be visited by local bus or on foot, a half-hour hike up Odos Omirou from the main square. This medieval quarter, with an intricate maze of streets, was built by the Venetians in the 13th century. Ano Siros originally spread across the summit of both hills, where its inhabitants were protected from pirate raids. Several Roman Catholic churches stand here; the most important is the **Church of Ayios Yioryios.** The large buff-colored square building on the hilltop is the medieval Monastery of the Capuchins. Remnants of castle walls, stone archways, and narrow lanes will delight visitors.

The other hill, **Vrondado,** with its blue-domed Greek Orthodox Church of the Resurrection, was built up after the Greek immigration of 1821. Its narrow streets, large marble-paved squares, and dignified mansions lend a certain old-world charm to the bustling inner city. There's a great view of Ermoupolis and the neighboring islands from the terrace outside the Church of the Resurrection.

BEACHES

Megas Yialos, as its name states, is the largest beach on the island and the prettiest on the south coast. Its sandy beach is shaded by tamarisk trees and is especially good for families because it's gently shelved. **Agathopes,** a 10-minute walk south of Possidonia in the island's southwest corner, has a sandy beach and a little offshore islet; the beach here is not yet overdeveloped.

A few kilometers to the north, **Galissas** has one of the best beaches on the island, a crescent of sand bordered by tamarisks, but it's a bit too popular in the high season. **Armeos beach,** a short walk south of town, is less crowded and mostly nude.

Kini is a small fishing village on the west coast with two beaches on sheltered Delfini Bay, valued for its sunsets and a local family of bouzouki musicians. The best of the two beaches at Kini is the primarily nudist **Delfini beach,** 2 kilometers (1.2 miles) north of town over the headland; there's a small taverna on the beach that operates during the summer. The bus from Ermoupolis makes the trip to Kini hourly in the summer.

Lia and **Grammata,** two of the finest beaches on the island, can only be reached by boat or on foot. There is no regular boat taxi service to these beaches, although there are numerous boat owners who may be willing to take you there. For information contact **Teamwork Holidays** (☎ 0281/83-400). To get there on foot, see the descriptions directly below.

Hiking in Northern Siros

The northern part of Siros is mountainous and barren, with poor roads and widely dispersed houses. It's a wildly beautiful part of the island, and has several marked hiking trails. The region is home to dairies that produce the popular San Mihalicheese, milk, and butter that visiting Greeks love to take home.

Kastri, north of Halandriani, is thought to be one of the oldest settlements in the Cyclades, with the foundations of houses and remains of a cemetery that have provided important clues about early Bronze Age culture. A marked hiking trail to Kastri is signposted on the road to Kampos, about 4 kilometers (2½ miles) north of Ermoupolis. This trail descends steeply through terraced fields to the archaeological site, near the sea's edge; return walking time is about 2 hours.

The best **beaches** on Siros are at the north end of the island, and all are only accessible on foot or by boat. Sheltered in sandy coves, these quiet and idyllic beaches are sheltered by tamarisk and palm trees. There isn't reliable fresh water, so be sure to bring your own. The beach trails begin at Kastri, about 8 kilometers (5 miles) north of Ermoupolis; the best way to get there is by rental car or moped, since the public buses don't travel this far north and there are no public phones you can use to call a return taxi. Just before the road turns to dirt you'll see a sign for **Lia,** the longest of the northern beaches; the walk is about an hour round-trip. ✪ **Grammata,** the most beautiful small beach on the island, is situated in a palm oasis at the outlet of a natural spring. The walk in from Kampos is 2 hours round-trip; there's no shade on the trail, so try to avoid walking during the hottest midafternoon hours.

WHERE TO STAY

The small office of the **Siros Hotelier Association,** right as you come off the ferry in Ermoupolis, can help you find a room in one of the town's hotels. Accommodation rates in Ermoupolis are high, comparable with those on Mikonos. In August, when vacationing Greeks pack the island, don't even think of arriving without a reservation.

✪ **Hotel Apollonos.** Odos Apollonos 8, Ermoupolis, 84100 Siros. ☎ **0281/81-387** or 0281/80-842. 3 units. A/C MINIBAR TV TEL. Dr50,000 ($167) double. Rates include breakfast. No credit cards. Open year-round.

This mansion on the water in Vaporia has been meticulously restored and decorated by the owner; it's the best and the most expensive of the town's period hotels. Those looking for a fully authentic restoration might be disappointed—the furnishings and lighting are contemporary in style—but the overall effect is one of complete harmony between new and old, creating an atmosphere of understated elegance. The best rooms are the two facing the water at the back of the house: Both are quite spacious, and one has a loft sleeping area with sitting room below. There's a large common sitting room facing the bay, and a breakfast room facing the street. Bathrooms are large, with tile and wood floors.

Hotel Hermes. Plateia Kanari, Ermoupolis, 84100 Siros. ☎ **0281/83-011** or 0281/83-012. Fax 0281/87-412. 51 units. A/C TV TEL. Dr15,000–Dr19,000 ($50–$63) double; Dr16,500–Dr20,500 ($55–$68) triple. Continental breakfast Dr1,500 ($5) extra. AE, DC, MC, V.

The Hotel Hermes presents a bright, modern facade to busy Plateia Kanari at the east end of the harbor; what you can't see from the street is that many of the rooms face directly onto a quiet stretch of rocky coast at the back of the building. The functional and rather dull standard rooms (the lower prices given above) have carpeted floors, bathrooms with showers, and views to the street or a quiet garden in back. The 19 deluxe rooms in the new wing of the hotel are worth the extra money—every unit has a couch with fold-out bed, minibar, wood floors, bathtub, and even an extra telephone in the bathroom. Many of these rooms also have balconies perched over the bay—this stretch of coast is quiet, the water is clear, and the view of the sunrise superb. The hotel restaurant serves three meals each day, and offers quality Greek food at very reasonable prices.

Hotel Omiros. Odos Omirou 43, Ermoupolis, 84100 Siros. ☎ **0281/84-910.** Fax 0281/86-266. 13 units. A/C TEL. Dr23,000 ($77) double; Dr30,000 ($100) suite. Continental breakfast Dr2,000 ($7) extra. DC, V.

In 1988, when the work of restoration was begun, this building was in a state of near ruin; now the transformation is complete, and the Omiros has become one of the most appealing of the neoclassical mansion hotels in Ermoupolis. Rooms are furnished with elegantly simple hardwood antiques, and some details from the original building have been retained, such as marble hand basins and massive fireplaces. The architectural highlight of the building is the spiral stair that climbs through a shaft of brilliant light to the glass roof. Breakfast, drinks, and light meals are served in a small walled garden. The hotel is on a hill above Miaoulis Square—it's a steep climb from the port, so it's best to take a taxi. There is parking, although the route from the port is complex and difficult to follow; call ahead for directions.

Hotel Vourlis. Odos Mavrokordatou 5, Ermoupolis, 84100 Siros. ☎/fax **0281/88-440** or 0281/81-682. 8 units. A/C TEL. Dr24,800–Dr38,000 ($83–$127) double; Dr47,000 ($157) suite. Continental breakfast Dr2,200 ($7). MC, V. Open year-round.

On a hill overlooking the fashionable Vaporia district of Ermoupolis, the elegant Hotel Vourlis occupies one of the finest of the city's mansions. Built in 1888, the house has retained all its grandeur and charm. The fine details which have sadly been lost in many other restored mansions are here in all their glory: the painted ceilings in the front rooms are especially resplendent. Most furniture also dates to the 19th century, creating a period setting which incorporates all the comforts you expect from a fine hotel. Bathrooms are spacious, and all have tubs. The two front rooms on the second floor have great sea views; back rooms have no view and look out to a tiny back terrace. Winter guests will be glad to know that the house is centrally heated.

Ipatia Guesthouse. Odos Babayiotou 3, Ermoupolis, 84100 Siros. ☎ **0281/83-575.** 8 units, 3 with bathroom. Dr18,000 ($60) double with sea view; Dr12,500–Dr15,000 ($42–$50) double without sea view. Rates include breakfast. No credit cards. Open year-round.

This lovely restored mansion dating from 1870 is uphill from the Ayios Nikolaos Church, overlooking the bay and rocky Asteria beach. What's truly special about the Ipatia is the Lefebvre family from Philadelphia—several years ago they were steered to rooms at the aging Ipatia, fell in love with the place, and returned the next year to buy it. The high-ceilinged rooms have brass beds, stone floors, and simple Siriot furnishings. Frescoed ceilings, carved wooden doors, spotless rooms, and sloping stairs add enough charm to compensate for a little wear.

WHERE TO DINE

There are numerous excellent tavernas in and around Ermoupolis, most catering primarily to a local clientele. The **Bourba Ouzeri** and the **Yacht Club of Siros,** the oldest in the Balkans, are both excellent places for ouzo and mezedes.

Taverna Lilis. Ano Siros. ☎ **0281/88-087.** Reservations recommended. Main courses Dr1,200–Dr3,500 ($4–$12). No credit cards. Daily 7pm–midnight. Follow Odos Omirou from the center of Ermoupolis, past the Hotel Omiros, and continue straight up the long flight of steps that leads to Lilis's brightly lit terrace. If all those steps don't appeal, you can always call a taxi. GREEK/SEAFOOD.

Lilis is the best of the three tavernas in Ano Siros, the town cresting a high conical hill behind Ermoupolis. There is a stellar view from the outdoor terrace of Ermoupolis, the bay, distant Tinos, and, even farther out, the shores of Mikonos. It's highly calming to sit here as the sun sets and watch the ships moving silently into port. The food is better-than-average taverna fare—meats and fish are grilled on a wood fire, and the ingredients are predictably fresh.

To Arhontariki. Ermoupolis. ☎ **0281/81-744.** Main courses Dr900–Dr3,000 ($3–$10). No credit cards. Daily noon–midnight. GREEK.

This is the best of the tavernas in Ermoupolis center, a small place that fills the narrow street with tables precariously perched on the cobblestones. It's easy to find—just plunge into the maze of streets at the corner of Miaoulis Square between Pyramid Pizzeria and Loukas Restaurant, and weave your way left—it's 2 blocks or so in, between Miaoulis and the harbor. The menu is largely composed of specials that change nightly. It always includes a few vegetable main courses, which are subtly spiced and delicious.

✪ **To Koutouki Tou Liberi.** Kaminia. ☎ **0281/85-580.** Reservations recommended. Main courses Dr800–Dr2,500 ($2.70–$8). No credit cards. Fri–Sat 9pm–1am. GREEK.

This place has become legendary in Siros, and in the summer you'll need to reserve one of the seven or eight tables several days in advance. You'll also have to hire a taxi—even though the place is only 2 kilometers (1.2 miles) from Ermoupolis center, it's not easy to find, and your taxi driver may have some difficulty if he hasn't been here before. It may seem like a lot of trouble for a taverna, but this place is definitely worth it. There is no menu—the night's offerings are brought out to you on a massive tray, and each dish is explained in turn. The food is often innovative, making slight but significant departures from traditional recipes. The spicing is subtle, and the dishes make use of the best of what happens to be in season. The owner is also renowned locally for his bouzouki playing—early in the morning, after the last diners have finished their meals, there are sometimes impromtu traditional music sessions. Did we mention the view? It's exquisite.

SIROS AFTER DARK

In Ermoupolis, the waterfront is the best place to be at sunset. **Kidara** (☎ 0281/ 80-878) maintains a calm mood with soft rock, while the music at **Highway** is loud and gets louder as the evening continues. You can also join in the evening **volta (stroll)** around Plateia Miaoulis, or take a seat to watch it. There are, of course, several bars nearby, including the excellent **Agora** on the west side of the square. For information and tickets to a performance at the **Apollon Theater,** contact the **National Tourist Organization** (☎ 0281/86-725; fax 0281/82-375), or look out for the posters that always abound throughout the town before a big performance. There's also the outdoor **Pallas Cinema,** east of the main square, which has one nightly showing, often in English.

Ermoupolis has the only **Casino** (☎ 0281/84-400) in the Cyclades, and it's quite an elegant establishment, worth a look even if you aren't interested in gambling. The main entrance is directly opposite the bus station and ferry pier; there's another entrance on the street immediately behind the harbor. The management is British, and most of the staff speak perfect English. The entrance fee is Dr3,000 ($10), and the minimum bet is Dr2,000 ($7), although there are also slot machines that take Dr100 (35¢) coins. There's no entrance fee to the restaurant and bar, on the back street. The casino is open daily from 8pm to 4am; slot machines only are open from 12:30pm.

Siros was among the most fertile grounds for rembetika, and you will find this special music played more authentically in several venues outside town, such as **Rahanos** and **Lilis** (☎ 0281/28-087) in Ano Siros, which sometimes have late-night performances on the weekends; reservations are a must.

11 The Dodecanese

by Robert E. Meagher

The first thing to notice about this far-eastern Greek archipelago is that the Dodecanese—"the 12"—is in fact comprised of 32 islands: 14 inhabited and 18 uninhabited. They have been known collectively as "the Dodecanese" since 1908, when 12 of them joined forces to resist the recent revocation of the special status which they had long enjoyed under the sultans.

The Dodecanese are far-flung from the Greek mainland and mostly hug the coast of Asia Minor. As frontier or borderline territories, their struggles to remain free and Greek have been intense and prolonged. Although they have been recognizably Greek for millennia, only in 1948 were the Dodecanese reunited with the Greek nation.

Long accustomed to watching the seas for invaders, these islands now spend their time awaiting tourists—who, like migrating birds, show up each spring and stay until October. The coming of the tourist season awakens the islands to a pattern of life and activity largely created and contrived for the sake of drawing and entertaining outsiders. Such is the reality of island life today. As in the past, however, the islanders proudly retain their own character even as they accommodate the onslaughts of foreigners.

The islands we feature represent a considered selection from "the 12." They are all easily visited one to the other during the tourist season. The principal islands, south to north, are **Rhodes, Kos,** and **Patmos.** In between lie the lesser islands of **Simi** and **Lipsi.** All are quite barren in summer except for Rhodes and Kos, whose interiors remain fertile and forested. The spectacular historical sights, from ancient ruins to medieval fortresses, are concentrated on Patmos, Kos, and Rhodes; so are the tourists. Simi and Lipsi make for lovely getaways.

STRATEGIES FOR SEEING THE ISLANDS In planning your excursion to the Dodecanese, keep in mind that the longest tourist season is on Rhodes. So, if you're pushing the season in April, begin in Rhodes, or, if you're stretching the season into October, end up in Rhodes. In general, avoid the Dodecanese from late July through August, when they are so glutted with tourists that they nearly sink.

The three islands you are most likely to make a point of visiting—both for their own sake and as bases to explore other nearby islands—are **Rhodes, Kos,** and **Patmos.** From the mainland, all are best reached by air. Rhodes and Kos each has its own airport; Patmos is a

The Dodecanese

Ancient Lindos ❻
Asklepion ❷
Monastery of St. John
  and the Cave of the Apocalypse ❶
Monolithos Castle ❺
Panormitis Monastery ❸
Petaloudes (Valley of the Butterflies) ❹

PATMOS
Arki
Kampos Marathos
Skala
Agathonisi
Megalo Horio
Lipsi
Farmakonisi
Partheni
Levitha
LEROS
Lakki
Ksirokampos
Emborios
Arginonta
Massouri
Telendos
Mirties
KALIMNOS
Kalimnos
Psarimos
Lambi
Tigaki Kos
Mastihari
Asfendiou
KOS
Kardamena
Kefalos
Vathys
Analipsi
Astypalea
Astypalea
Yiali
Mandraki
Loutra
Emborios
Avlaki
Nisyros
Ayios Fokas
Megalo Horio
Tilos
Livadia
Nimos
Simi
SIMI Pedi
Sirna
Tria Nissia
Halki
Alimia
Mandriko
Fanes
Maritsa
Kalithea
Soroni
RHODES
Afandou
Embonas
Archangelos
Monolithos
Laerma
Lindos
Apolakia
Messanagros
Gennadio
Kattavia
Plimiri
Rhodes
Ialisos

GREECE
Athens
The Dodecanese

Saria
Diafani
Olymbos
KARPATHOS
Spoa
Piles
Karpathos
Arkassa
Armathia
Fri
← To Crete
Kassos

| 0 | 25 mi |
| 0 | 25 km |

Legend
Airport ✈
Ferry Routes _ ▬ ▬ _

short jaunt by hydrofoil from Samos, which also has an airport. The two transportation hubs of the Dodecanese are Kos and Rhodes, from which you can get just about anywhere in the eastern Aegean. Finally, if you spend any time at all in the Dodecanese, you will probably find the lure of **Turkey** eventually irresistible. It is quite easily reached from Kos and Rhodes, so you may want to build into your schedule at least a day's excursion from either of these points.

1 Rhodes (Rodos)

250km (155 miles) E of Piraeus

Selecting a divine patron was serious business for an ancient city. Most Greek cities played it safe and chose a mainline god or goddess, a ranking Olympian, someone like Athena or Apollo or Artemis or Zeus himself. It's revealing that the people of Rhodes, even then, chose **Helios,** the Sun, as their signature god—the one to watch over them, and for them, in turn, to venerate.

Indeed, millennia later, the cult of the Sun is alive and well on Rhodes, and, in return for its solar piety, the island receives on average more than 300 days of sunshine a year. What's more, Rhodes is a place of pilgrimage for sun-worshippers from colder, darker, wetter lands around the globe.

But Rhodes has more to offer its visitors than a tan. Rhodes's unique location at the intersection of east and west ensured that it would be in the thick of commerce and conflicts. The scars left by its rich and turbulent history have become its treasures. Knights, Turks, Italians—all the island's invaders—left behind objects of great beauty in the trail of devastation. Through it all, Rhodes remains beautiful. Its beaches are among the cleanest and most beautiful in the Aegean, and its interior is still home to unspoiled mountain villages and rich fertile plains.

Several days in Rhodes will allow you to gaze at its marvels as well as to bake a bit, adding, perhaps, a day trip to the idyllic island of Simi or to the luring shoreline of Turkey. If Rhodes is your last port of call, it will make a grand finale; if it is your point of departure, you can launch out happily from here to just about anywhere in the Aegean or Mediterranean.

ESSENTIALS

GETTING THERE **By Plane** **Olympic Airways** offers domestic service between Rhodes and the following Greek airports: Athens, Crete (Iraklion), Karpathos, Kasos, Kastellorizo, Kos, Mikonos, Santorini, and Thessaloniki. Reservations and ticket information can be obtained from the Olympic Airways office at Odos Ierou Lohou 9 (☎ **0241/24-571** or 0241/24-555). Flights fill quickly, so make reservations early. **Air Greece** flies twice daily to Athens, with a savings of about 10%. Tickets for Air Greece flights can be purchased at **Triton Holidays,** near Mandraki Harbor, Odos Plastira 9, Rhodes city. Call ☎ **0241/36-095** for schedules, fares, and reservations.

The Rhodes **Paradissi Airport** (☎ **0241/83-214**) is 13 kilometers (8 miles) southwest of the city and is served from 6am to 10:30pm by a bus following a complex schedule. The bus from the airport to the city center (Plateia Rimini) is Dr350 ($1.15). A taxi costs Dr1,800 ($6).

By Boat Rhodes is a major port with sea links not only to Athens, Crete, and the islands of the Aegean, but also to Cyprus, Turkey, and Israel. Service and schedules are always changing; it's essential to check with the EOT office or the Tourist Information Office and ask for their printed schedule of weekly departures. This same information, as well as tickets, is available from **Triton Holidays,** Odos Plastira 25 (☎ **0241/ 21-690;** fax 0241/31-625).

Rhodes

RHODES

Acropolis of Rhodes **8**
Archeological Museum
  of Rhodes **3**
Church of Our Lady
  of the Castle **4**
Clock Tower **5**
Mosque of Suleiman **6**
Municipal Art Gallery **2**
Municipal Baths **7**
Street of the Knights **1**

In late spring and summer there is daily hydrofoil service from Mandraki Harbor to Kos and Simi, and less predictable service to Kalimnos, Leros, Patmos, Kastellorizo, and Samos. The advantage of hydrofoils is that they make the voyage in half the time. The downside is that if the wind blows up the waves, then the sailings are canceled. There are also daily excursion boats to Simi for Dr5,000 ($17) round-trip.

Wherever it is you want to go, whether by ferry, hydrofoil, or excursion boat, schedules and tickets are available from **Triton Holidays,** Odos Plastira 25 (☎ 0241/21-690; fax 0241/31-625). Although travel agents throughout Rhodes city and island can issue air and sea tickets, we recommend Triton Holidays because they focus on the independent traveler with skill and graciousness.

VISITOR INFORMATION The **Greek National Tourist Office (EOT),** at the intersection of Odos Makariou and Odos Papagou (☎ 0241/23-655; fax 0241/26-955), gives advice about the whole island, will check on the availability of accommodations, and provides free maps, bus timetables, and copies of *Rodos News.* It's open Monday through Friday from 7:30am to 3pm. There's also a helpful **Rhodes Municipal Tourist Office** down the hill at Plateia Rimini near the port taxi stand (☎ 0241/35-945). It has information and advice on local excursions, buses, ferries, and accommodations, and offers foreign exchange minus a 2% commission. It's open May through October, Monday through Friday from 8am to 7pm and Saturday from 8am to 6pm.

GETTING AROUND Rhodes is not an island you can exhaust on foot. You need wheels of some sort: public buses, group-shared taxis, a rental car, or an organized bus tour for around-the-island excursions. The city is a different story. Walking is the best and most pleasurable mode of transport; you'll need a taxi only if you're going to treat yourself to a meal at one of the farther-out restaurants or if you're decked out for the casino and don't want to walk. Note that wheeled vehicles, except those driven by permanent Old Town residents, are not allowed within the walls. This goes for all taxis, unless you have luggage.

By Bus   There's a good public bus system throughout the island; EOT and the Tourist Information Office publish a schedule of routes and times. Buses to points **east** leave from the East Side Bus Station on Plateia Rimini, while buses to points **west,** including the airport, leave from the nearby West Side Bus Station on Odos Averof. Island bus prices range from Dr350 ($1.15) to the airport, all the way to Dr1,650 ($5.50) to Messanagros, an interior destination in the south of the island. The city bus also offers six different city tours, details of which are available from the EOT office.

By Bicycle, Moped & Motorcycle   You won't have any trouble finding two wheels, pedaled or motorized, to take you around the city and island. Petitions have been filed to reserve a strip of the newly widened major island roadways for bicycles, but until that is approved, cyclists are up against very uneven odds. Remember that you need a proper license to rent anything motorized. The **Bicycle Center,** Odos Griva 39 (☎ **0241/28-315**), rents bicycles (three-speed and mountain bikes, with baby/child seats if needed), mopeds, and motorcycles. The best-looking mountain bikes we've seen are at **Moto Pilot,** Odos Kritis 12 (☎ **0241/32-285**). Starting prices per day are roughly as follows: Dr1,000 ($3.35) three-speed; Dr1,200 ($4) mountain bike; Dr3,000 ($10) moped; Dr5,000 ($17) motorcycle. If you want a Harley, there's only one authorized rental agency, **Rent A Harley Rhodes,** Odos 28 Octobriou 20 (☎ **0241/74-925**). Rentals range from Dr22,000 to Dr38,000 ($73 to $127) a day.

By Taxi   In Rhodes city, the largest of many taxi stands is in front of the Old Town, on the harbor front in Plateia Rimini (☎ **0241/27-666**). There, posted for all to see and agree upon, are the set fares for sightseeing throughout the island. Since many of the cab drivers speak sightseer English, a few friends can be chauffeured and lectured at a very reasonable cost. Taxis are metered, but fares should not exceed the minimum on short round-the-city jaunts. For longer trips, negotiate directly with the drivers. For **radio taxis** call ☎ **0241/64-712.** There is a slight additional pickup charge when you call for a taxi.

By Car   Rhodes is up to its ears in rental-car companies. Apart from the array of represented international companies—among them **Alamo** (☎ 0241/73-570), **Avis** (☎ 0241/24-990), **Hertz** (☎ 0241/21-819), and **Interrent-EuropCar** (☎ 0241/ 21-958)—there are a large number of local companies. The latter often offer the lowest rates, but the concern here is whether, with possibly only a handful of cars, they have the resources to back you up in the event of an accident. Be very certain that you are fully covered before signing anything. An established Greek company with roughly 200 cars—reputedly the newest fleet on Rhodes—is **DRIVE Rent-a-Car** (☎ 0241/35-141), with an excellent reputation for personal service, as well as prices significantly lower than the major international companies. Prices start at about Dr13,500 ($45) per day, all-inclusive.

By Tour & Cruise   There are several operators featuring nature, archaeology, shopping, and beach tours of the island. In Rhodes city, **Triton Holidays,** near Mandraki Harbor, behind the Bank of Greece, at Odos Plastira 9 (☎ **0241/21-690;** fax 0241/31-625), is one of the largest and most reliable agencies on Rhodes and the only one offering excursions designed for the independent client. Triton offers a wide variety of day and evening cruises, hiking tours, and excursions in Rhodes, as well as to the other Dodecanese islands and to Turkey. We recommend their full-day guided tours, either their tour to Lindos (Dr7,000/$23) or their "Island Tour" (Dr8,800/$29), which takes you to small villages, churches, and monasteries, including lunch in the village of Embonas, known for its local wines and fresh grilled meat. There is also a fascinating half-day guided tour to the Filerimos Monastery, the Valley of the Butterflies, and to the ancient city of Kamiros (Dr6,000/$20). Along Mandraki Harbor, you can find excursion boats that leave for Lindos at 9am and return around 6pm (Dr4,000/$13). For an in-depth island experience, Triton Holidays also offers a combination package of car rental and hotel accommodation in four small villages around the island (Kalavarda, Monolithos, Prassonisi, and Asklepion), ranging from 4 to 10 nights.

CITY LAYOUT　Rhodes is not the worst offender in the Dodecanese, but it does share the widespread aversion to street signs. This means that you need a map with every lane on it, so that you can count your way from one place to another. We recommend the two maps drawn and published by Mario Camerini in 1995, of which the mini-atlas entitled *Map of Rhodes Town* is the one to beat. You'll wind up buying it eventually, so you might as well start out with it.

Rhodes city (population 42,400) is divided into two sections, the **Old Town,** dating from medieval days, and the **New Town.** Overlooking the harbor, the Old Town is surrounded by massive walls—4 kilometers (2½ miles) around and in certain places nearly 40 feet thick—built by the Knights of St. John. The New Town embraces the old one and extends south to meet the **Rhodian Riviera,** a strip of luxury resort hotels. At its north tip is the city beach, in the area called 100 Palms, and famed **Mandraki Harbor,** now used as a mooring for private yachts and tour boats.

Walking away from Mandraki Harbor on Odos Plastira, you'll come to **Cyprus Square,** where many of the New Town hotels are clustered. Veer left and continue to the park where the mighty fortress begins. Opposite it is the EOT office, and nearby, down the hill at Platcia Rimini, is the Rhodes Municipal Tourist Office (see "Visitor Information," above, for information on both).

FAST FACTS　The local **American Express** agent is Rhodos Tours, Odos Ammochostou 23 (☎ 0241/21-010), in the New Town; open Monday through Saturday from 8:30am to 1:30pm and 5 to 8:30pm. The **National Bank of Greece,** on Cyprus Square, exchanges currency Monday through Thursday from 8am to 2pm and 6 to 8pm, Friday from 8am to 1:30pm and 3 to 8:30pm, Saturday from 8am to 2pm, and Sunday from 9am to noon. There are other currency-exchange offices throughout the Old Town and New Town, very often with rates better than those of the banks. The **hospital** is on Odos Erithrou Stavrou (☎ 0241/22-222); you can call an **ambulance** at ☎ 166. The **Rock Style Internet Café,** Odos Dimokratous 7, opposite the Agora Stadium (☎ 0241/70-041; www.rockstyle.gr), has 17 PC terminals; open daily from 10am to 1am. **Express Laundry,** Odos Kosti Palama 5, across

---

A Helping Hand

The **Dodecanese Association for People with Special Needs** (☎ 0241/73-109; fax 0241/33-278; e-mail: dis12isil@compulink.gre) provides free minibus door-to-door service from the port, airport, and hotels—or even if you just want to go out for coffee or a swim.

from the "Sound and Light" and behind Plateia Rimini (☎ 0241/22-514), will wash (and fold, if you ask) at any temperature, using high-quality machines and only the best soaps and softeners; open daily from 8am to 10pm. The New Market Pension on Plateia Rimini will **store luggage** for Dr500 ($1.70) during the day and Dr1,000 ($3.35) overnight. The **International Pharmacy** (☎ 0241/75-331), Odos A. Kiakou 22, near the Thermai Hotel, provides worldwide medicine identification and compatibility. There is always a pharmacy open 24 hours on a rotation basis. The **police** (☎ 0241/23-849, or 100 for emergencies) in the Old Town are open from 10am to midnight to handle any complaints of overcharging, theft, swindles, or other price- or goods-related problems. A **tourist police** office (☎ 0241/27-423) on the edge of the Old Town, near the port, addresses tourists' queries, concerns, and grievances. The main **post office** on Mandraki Harbor is open Monday through Friday from 7am to 8pm. A smaller office is on Odos Orfeon in the Old Town, open daily with shorter hours.

WHAT TO SEE & DO IN RHODES CITY

Rhodes is awash in first-rate sights and entertainment. As an international playground and a museum of antiquity and of the medieval period, Rhodes has no serious competition in the Dodecanese and few peers in the eastern Mediterranean. Consequently, in singling out its highlights, we necessarily pass over sights that on lesser islands would be main attractions.

EXPLORING THE OLD TOWN

Best to know one thing from the start about Old Town: It's not laid out on a grid—not even close. There are roughly 200 streets or lanes which simply have no name. Getting lost here is not a defeat; it's an opportunity. Whenever you feel the need to find your bearings, you can ask for **Odos Sokratous,** which is the closest Old Town comes to having a main street.

When you approach the walls of Old Town, you are about to enter the oldest inhabited medieval town in Europe. It's a thrill to behold. Although there are many gates, we suggest that you first enter through **Eleftheria (Liberty) Gate,** where you'll come to Plateia Simi, containing ruins of the **Temple of Venus,** identified by the votive offerings found here, which may date from the 3rd century B.C. The remains of the temple are next to a parking lot (driving is restricted in the Old Town), which rather diminishes the impact of the few stones and columns still standing. Nevertheless, the ruins are a reminder that a great Hellenistic city once stood here and encompassed the entire area now occupied by the city, including the old and new towns. The population of the Hellenistic city of Rhodes is thought to have equaled the current population of the whole island (roughly 100,000).

Plateia Simi is also home to the **Municipal Art Gallery of Rhodes,** above the Ionian and Popular Bank (open Mon through Sat from 8am to 2pm, plus Wed from 5 to 8pm), whose collection is comprised mostly of works by modern Greek artists. One block farther on is the **Museum of Decorative Arts,** which contains finely made Rhodian objects and crafts from Rhodes and other islands, most notably Simi (open Tues through Sun from 8:30am to 3pm; admission is Dr600/$2 adults, Dr300/$1 students, and free for children). Continue through the gate until you reach the **Museum Reproduction Shop** (with a precious painted tile of the Madonna above its door), then turn right on Odos Ippoton toward the Palace of the Knights.

The **Street of the Knights** (you'll see the name Ippoton on maps) is one of the best preserved and most delightful medieval relics in the world. The 600-meter-long, cobble-paved street was constructed over an ancient pathway that led in a straight line

From the Outside Looking In

Of all the inns on the Street of the Knights, only the **Inn of France** is open daily. The ground floor houses the Institut Français, but you can see its garden and an occasional art show held in the second-floor gallery. The other inns now serve as offices or private residences and are closed to the public.

from the Acropolis of Rhodes to the port. In the early 16th century it became the address for most of the inns of each nation, which housed Knights who belonged to the Order of St. John. The inns were used as eating clubs and temporary residences for visiting dignitaries, and their facades reflect the various architectural details of their respective countries.

Begin at the lowest point on the hill (next to the Museum Reproduction Shop) at the **Spanish House,** now used by a bank. Next door is the **Inn of the Order of the Tongue of Italy,** built in 1519 (as can be seen on the shield of the order above the door). Then comes the **Palace of the Villiers of the Isle of Adam,** built in 1521, housing the Archaeological Service of the Dodecanese. The **Inn of France** now hosts the French Language Institute. Constructed in 1492, it's one of the most ornate of the inns, with the shield of three lilies (fleur-de-lis), royal crown, and that of the Magister d'Aubusson (the cardinal's hat above four crosses) off-center, over the middle door. Typical of the late Gothic period, the architectural and decorative elements are all somewhat asymmetrical, lending grace to the squat building. Opposite these inns is the side of the Hospital of the Knights, now the archaeological museum.

The church farther on the right is **Ayia Triada** (open daily from 9am to noon), next to the Italian consulate. Above its door are three coats-of-arms: those of France, England, and the pope. Past the arch that spans the street, still on the right, is the **Inn of the Tongue of Provence;** due to an explosion in 1856, it is shorter than it once was. Opposite it on the left is the traditionally Gothic **Inn of the Tongue of Spain,** with vertical columns elongating its facade and a lovely garden behind.

The **Mosque of Suleiman** and the public baths are two reminders of the Turkish presence in Old Rhodes. Follow Odos Sokratous west away from the harbor or walk a couple of blocks south from the Palace of the Grand Masters, and you can't miss the mosque with its slender, though incomplete, minaret and pink-striped Venetian exterior.

The **Municipal Baths** (what the Greeks call the "Turkish baths") are housed in a 7th-century Byzantine structure. They merit a visit by anyone interested in the vestiges of Turkish culture that still remain in the Old Town, and are a better deal than the charge for showers in most pensions. The *hamam* (most locals use the Turkish word for "bath") is in Plateia Arionos, between a large old mosque and the Folk Dance Theater. Throughout the day, men and women go in via their separate entrances and disrobe in the private shuttered cubicles. A walk across the cool marble floors will lead you to the bath area—many domed, round chambers sunlit by tiny glass panes in the roof. Through the steam you'll see people seated around large marble basins, chatting while ladling bowls of water over their heads. It's open Tuesday through Saturday from 11am to 7pm; the baths cost Dr600 ($2) on Tuesday, Thursday, and Friday, but only Dr360 ($1.20) on Wednesday and Saturday. Note that Saturday is extremely crowded with locals.

The Old Town was also home to the Jewish community, whose origins go back to the days of the ancient Greeks. Little survives in the northeast or Jewish Quarter of the Old Town other than a few homes with Hebrew inscriptions, the Jewish cemetery, and the **Square of the Jewish Martyrs** (Plateia ton Evreon Martyron, also known as Seahorse Square because of the seahorse fountain). There is a lovely **synagogue,** where services are held on Friday night; a small black sign in the square shows the way. The synagogue is on Odos Dosiadou, off the square, and is usually open daily from 10am to 1pm. This square is dedicated to the thousands of Jews who were rounded up here and sent to their deaths at Auschwitz. If you walk around the residential streets, you'll still see abandoned homes and burned buildings.

After touring the sites of the Old Town, you might want to walk around the **walls.** (The museum operates a 1-hr. tour on Tues and Sat at 2:30pm, beginning at the Palace of the Knights.) The fortification has a series of magnificent gates and towers, and is remarkable as an example of a fully intact medieval structure. Admission is Dr1,200 ($4) for adults, Dr600 ($2) for students, and free for children.

EXPLORING THE NEW TOWN

The New Town is best explored after dark, as it houses most of the bars, discos, and nightclubs, as well as innumerable tavernas. In the heat of the day, its beaches—**Elli Beach** and the **municipal beach**—are also lined. What few people make a point of seeking out but also can't miss are landmarks such as **Mandraki Harbor** (which never was and we assume never will be straddled by a colossus) and the **wannabe imperial architecture** (culminating in the Nomarhia or Prefecture) along the harbor, all of which dates from the Italian occupation. A big draw is the quite lovely park and ancient burial site at **Rodini** (2km/1.2 miles south of the city) and the quite impressive ancient **Acropolis of Rhodes** (see below) on Mount Smith.

The Acropolis of Rhodes. Open site.

High atop the north end of the island above the modern city, with the sea visible on two sides, stand the remains of the ancient Rhodian acropolis. This is a pleasant site to explore at your leisure and to enjoy a picnic, with plenty of shade available. The restored stadium and small theater are particularly impressive, as are the remains of the Temple of Pythian Apollo. Even though only several pillars and a portion of the architrave stand in place, they are provocative and pleasing, giving loft to the imagination.

SHOPPING

In Rhodes city it's the Old Town that is of special interest to shoppers. Here you'll find classic and contemporary **gold and silver jewelry** almost everywhere. The top-of-the-line Greek designer **Ilias LaLaounis** has a boutique on Museum Square. The **Alexander Shop,** a block from Odos Sokratous behind the Alexis Restaurant, offers stylish European work, elegant gold and platinum link bracelets, and beautifully set precious gems.

For imported **leather goods** and **furs** (the former often from nearby Turkey and the latter from northern Greece), stroll down the length of Odos Sokratous. Antiquity buffs should drop into the **Ministry of Culture Museum Reproduction Shop** on Odos Ippitou, open from 8am daily, which sells excellent reproductions of ancient sculptures, friezes, and tiles. True **antiques**—furniture, carpets, porcelain, and paintings—can be found at **Kalogirou Art,** Odos Panetiou 30, in a wonderful old building with a pebble-mosaic floor and an exotic banana-tree garden near the Knights Palace.

Although most of what you find on Rhodes can be found throughout Greece, several products bear a special Rhodian mark. **Rhodian wine** has a fine reputation, and on weekdays you can visit two distinguished island wineries: C.A.I.R., at its new factory 2 kilometers (1.2 miles) outside of Rhodes city on the way to Lindos; and Emery, in the village of Embonas. Another distinctive product of Rhodes is a rare form of **honey** made from bees committed to Thimati (very like oregano). To get this you may have to drive to the villages of Siana or Vati and ask who has some extra. It's mostly sold out of private homes, as locals are in no hurry to give it up. **Olive oil** is also a local art, and the best is sold out of private homes, meaning that you simply have to make discreet inquiries regarding the best current sources.

Finally, Rhodes is famed for handmade **carpets** and **kilims,** an enduring legacy from centuries of Ottoman occupation. There are currently some 40 women around the island making carpets in their homes; some monasteries are also in on the act. There's a local carpet factory known as **Kleopatra** at Ayios Anthonias, on the main road to Lindos near Afandou; and, in the Old Town, these and other Rhodian handmade carpet and kilims are sold at **Elafos,** Odos Sokratous 25, and **Royal Carpet,** Odos Apellou 15. Finally, there is "Rhodian" **lace** and **embroidery,** much of which comes not from local hands but from Hong Kong. If you can't tell the difference, ask for help or figure that what you don't know won't hurt you.

SPORTS & OUTDOOR PURSUITS

Most outdoor activities on Rhodes are beach- and sea-related. For everything from **parasailing** to **jet skis** to **canoes,** you'll find what you need at **Faliraki,** if you can tolerate everything and everyone else that you'll have to wade through to get to it.

No license is required for **fishing,** with the best grounds reputed to be off Kamiros Skala, Kalithea, and Lindos. Try hitching a ride with the fishing boats that moor opposite Ayia Katerina's Gate. For sailing and yachting information, call the **Rodos Yacht Club** (☎ **0241/23-287**) or the **Yacht Agency Rhodes** (☎ **0241/22-927;** fax 0241/23-393), which is the center for all yachting needs.

If you've always wanted to try **scuba diving,** both **Waterhoppers Diving Schools** (☎/fax **0241/38-146**) and **Dive Med** (☎ **0241/28-040;** fax 0241/61-115; www. rodos.com/divemed) offer 1-day introductory dives for beginners, diving expeditions for experienced divers, and 4- to 5-day courses leading to various certifications. Dive Med's "discover scuba" day-course is Dr12,000 ($40).

For more conservative jocks, try the **Rhodes Tennis Club** (☎ **0241/25-705**) in the resort of Elli, or the **Rhodes-Afandu Golf Club** (☎ **0241/51-225**), 19 kilometers (11.8 miles) south of the port. Fully equipped fitness centers can be found at **Body Center Rhodes** (☎ **0241/20-233**), at Odos Lindou 86, and at Busy Bodies/Women in **Motion Health Club** (☎ **0241/20-345**), at Odos Filerimou 45.

If you want to get some culture as you get in shape, information on taking traditional **Greek folk-dance lessons** can be obtained from the **Old Town Theater** (☎ **0241/29-085**), where Nelly Dimoglou and her entertaining troupe perform, or by writing the **Traditional Dance Center,** Odos Dekelias 87, 143 Athens (☎ **01/ 25-1080**). Classes run from June to early August, 30 hours per week; each week, dances from a different region are studied. There are also shorter courses available.

WHERE TO STAY IN RHODES CITY
IN THE OLD TOWN

Accommodations in the Old Town have the aura of ages past, but character does not always equal charm. There are very few really attractive options here, and they are in considerable demand, with all of the attending complications. One is that some hosts, regardless of the ethics and legalities involved, will hold you to the letter of your intent—so if you need or wish to cancel a day or more of your stay, they will do their best to extract the last drachma. And there is some hedging of bets, which means that the exact room agreed upon may at the end of the day be "unavailable." This is not to discourage you, but to urge you to be explicit and keep a paper trail.

Expensive

✪ **S. Nikolis Hotel.** Odos Ippodamou 61, 85100 Rhodes. ☎ **0241/34-561.** Fax 0241/ 32-034. E-mail: nikoliss@prometheus.hol.gr. 10 units. A/C TV TEL. Dr35,000 double ($117). Rates include breakfast. AE, MC, V. Open year-round (call ahead to confirm from Nov–Mar).

This hotel is one of a kind. Within the ancient walls, it is quite simply the only place with real finesse and class. Don't confuse this with five-star luxury: What you pay for and get here is neither grand nor sumptuous, but it is unique, and in its own way exquisite. Host Sotiris Nikolis is a true artisan with a fine eye. Here, on the site of an ancient Hellenistic agora, he has restored several medieval structures using the original stones and remaining as faithful as possible to the original style. The result is immensely pleasing (though not plush). In addition to the hotel rooms, there are four simply stunning honeymoon suites with kitchen facilities (Dr35,000 to Dr45,000/ $117 to $150), as well as four appealing though less extraordinary apartments, plus a maisonette or small family home. All units contain fridges, firm beds, and often handcrafted furniture; two suites have Jacuzzis. If you are resolved to stay within the walls of the Old Town—an unforgettable experience—and if you are willing and able to pay a premium for aesthetic taste, this is the place.

Be sure to check out the adjacent **Ancient Agora Bar and Restaurant,** where, in 1990, a 10-ton marble pediment dating from the 2nd century was found beneath the medieval foundations.

Note: Frommer's has received several spirited letters from readers describing disagreements they have had with this hotel. While continuing to recommend it, we suggest that when making a reservation, you agree in advance upon the exact accommodation held in your name, as well as upon an all-inclusive price (with breakfast and air-conditioning, if you want either).

Inexpensive

Andreas Pension. Odos Omirou 28D, 85100 Rhodes. ☎ **0241/34-156.** Fax 0241/74-285. 12 units, 6 with bathroom. Dr8,000–Dr10,000 ($27–$33) double with bathroom. V. Open Mar–Oct. When you're looking for this pension, note that Omirou 28 is between 23 and 20, not just before 29.

A relief from the cardboard walls and linoleum floors that haunt many of the town's budget choices, this exceptionally well-run pension in a restored 400-year-old Turkish sultan's house offers quite attractive rooms, some of which have panoramic views of the town. Other units have wooden lofts which can comfortably sleep a family of four. The bedrooms (with commendably firm beds) were once occupied by the sultan's harem, while the sultan held forth in room 11, a spacious corner unit with three windows and extra privacy, perfect for a guy for whom every day was a honeymoon! Hosts Dmitri and Josette serve breakfast on a shaded terrace that boasts gorgeous vistas of the town and the harbor, the best views in Old Town. A full bar with wide-screen TV is also at hand, patrolled by a pet tortoise. Laundry service is provided. Rooms 10 and 11 have the best views, while nos. 8 and 9 have private terraces.

Cava d'Oro Hotel. Odos Kistiniou 15, 85100 Rhodes. ☎ **0241/36-980.** 13 units. A/C TEL. Dr8,000–Dr13,000 ($27–$43) double. MC, V. Open Mar–Nov.

This 800-year-old structure, nearly flush against the eastern defensive wall of the Old Town, was at the time of the Knights a home within the Jewish quarter.

Rhodes Accommodations & Dining

ACCOMMODATIONS
Andreas Pension **21**
Cava d'Oro Hotel **23**
Esperia **5**
Hotel Anastasia **7**
Hotel La Luna **10**
Ibiscus **1**
Kamiros Hotel **8**
Maria's Rooms **13**
Rodos Imperial **3**
Rodos Palace **2**
Rodos Park **9**
S. Nikolis Hotel **20**
Spot Hotel **22**

DINING
Alexis Taverna **15**
Cleo's Restaurant **18**
Diafani Garden
  Restaurant **16**
Goniako Palati **4**
Iannis Taverna **17**
Kafenio Araliki **19**
Kafenio Turkiko **14**
Kioupia **26**
Kon Tiki Floating
  Restaurant **11**
Manolis Dinoris Fish
  Taverna **12**
Memories **6**
Palia Historia **24**
Salt and Pepper **25**

Legend
Lighthouse

The immediate neighborhood is today neither quaint nor scenic, but that translates into quiet, which is what you want at the end of the day. This is where Michael Palin stayed while filming the Rhodes section of his *Pole to Pole* series; if you saw that episode, you've already seen Cava d'Oro. The rooms are rustically modest and clean, with some interesting architectural features. Nearly half have balconies. There is a pleasant garden and private steps up onto the town's wall.

Hotel La Luna. Odos Ierokleous 21, 85100 Rhodes. ☎/fax **0241/25-856.** 7 rooms, none with bathroom. Dr11,000 ($37) double. Rates include breakfast. No credit cards. Open Apr–Oct. Turn off Odos Orfeos between the two halves of the Don Kichotis taverna.

This small, delightful hotel is a block in from the taverna-lined, touristy Odos Orfeos, nestled between two churches in a calm residential neighborhood. It features a large, shaded garden with bar and breakfast tables. Looking at the clean, modest rooms, all without toilet or bathtub, you may wonder why this is a prime spot in Old Town, sought after by diplomats, barons, and movie stars like Ben Kingsley and Helen Mirren. The answer is charm, which the ancient Greek poets knew to be capricious and inscrutable. It also has a lot to do with the private 300-year-old Turkish bath which more than makes up for the one you don't have in your room. This is a place for visitors who want and respect quiet; blast your radio or make a ruckus and you'll be asked to leave. Our favorite double is room no. 2 (Ben stayed in room no. 1).

Maria's Rooms. Odos Menekleous 147-Z, 85100 Rhodes. ☎ **0241/22-169.** 8 units, 3 with bathroom. Dr5,000–Dr7,000 ($17–$23) double. No credit cards. Open Easter–Oct.

This pristine little pension near the Cafe Bazaar merits high marks for both price and quality. The rooms are sparkling white and squeaky clean, and Maria is a warm and welcoming hostess.

Spot Hotel. Odos Perikleous 21, 85100 Rhodes. ☎ **0241/34-737.** 9 units. Dr9,000–Dr10,000 ($30–$33) double. Special rates offered for a stay of 2 days or longer. No credit cards.

Spotless would be a more suitable name for this small hotel. Michalis Mavrostomos, a former New York construction foreman, impeccably maintains these recently renovated rooms, which contain firm beds. By Old Town standards, this building is an infant, only 25 years old, which means there's no issue here with the damp and mold that plague many of the centuries-old structures. Located near the harbor right off Plateia Martiron Hevrcon, it provides a large communal fridge, a public card phone, and a small, pleasant inner courtyard aburst with flowers.

IN THE NEW TOWN & ENVIRONS

Unlike the Old Town, the New Town does not prohibit new construction—far from it. This means that there is a wild array of options, from boardinghouses to package-tour hotels to luxury resorts. Most are dull and some are dazzling, but the vast majority are so undistinguished that you may forget which one you're in. Cleanliness, a little comfort, and proximity to beaches and bars are what most tourists expect, so this is what you'll find.

Very Expensive

Rodos Imperial. Leoforos Ialisou, Iksia, 85100 Rhodes. ☎ **0241/75-000.** Fax 0241/76-690. 404 units. A/C MINIBAR TV TEL. Dr45,000–Dr67,500 ($150–$225) double with sea view; Dr138,000–Dr229,000 ($460–$763) executive or presidential suite. Rates include buffet breakfast. AE, DC, MC, V. Open Apr–Oct.

Located 4 kilometers (2½ miles) out of the New Town, this luxurious Aegean-style hotel, across the road from the beach, has every possible facility you might desire, plus a beach with windsurfing, sailing, jet-skiing, paragliding, and even swimming. You can stash your kids in the supervised miniclub while you're working out in the gym or taking your *syrtaki* (dancing) or aerobic lessons, and use an in-house baby-sitter while attending one of the hotel's evening shows. The rooms are spacious and comfortable, each with a large balcony—but on their own they don't have much over a top-of-the-line Holiday Inn. What you pay for here is proximity to the beach and extensive private resort facilities.

You can dine at the Marco Polo (adventurous dining with an Asian touch), the Castellania (fine traditional and international fare poolside), or the more informal Pergola. The high season brings live entertainment and fish festivals. The Imperial's amenities are too numerous to list, but include a water-sports school, tennis club, full-service health club, several freshwater pools (indoor and outdoor), and an ample shopping arcade.

✪ Rodos Palace. Leoforos Trianton, Iksia, 85100 Rhodes. ☎ **0241/25-222.** Fax 0241/25-350. www.rodos-palace.gr. 785 units, 2 presidential villas. A/C MINIBAR TV TEL. Dr52,000–Dr66,300 ($173–$221) executive double with sea view; Dr45,400–Dr58,000 ($151–$193) executive double with garden view. Rates include breakfast. AE, MC, V. Open Apr–Nov.

"Palace" is indeed the word for the largest five-star hotel in Greece, set amidst 30 acres of gardens and facing the sea just outside Rhodes city. It was decorated by the famed designer Maurice Bailey, who cut his teeth designing the sets for *Quo Vadis* and *Ben Hur*. Needless to say, this has been the uncontested king of the mountain on Rhodes for the past 25 years. It has never rested on its laurels, but is always adding to and improving what it offers, which is just about everything. It's currently constructing a new family center, a resort within a resort designed to provide the ultimate holiday for families with small children. It is simply not possible to recount the full array of accommodations, dining, entertainment, shopping, and so on offered within this world-class resort. Recommended for couples are the executive double rooms (and the corner suites for families). The largest of four pools lies beneath a massive dome constructed by Boeing—and while you're swimming, you can have a suit custom cut for you, from the finest English wool, by the hotel tailor.

The Palace's five restaurants and five bars range from the elegant La Rotisserie to the splashy poolside restaurant to the Ambrosia for more traditional Greek cuisine. The Palace provides all the amenities imaginable. The emphasis here is admittedly on sun and water, with five pools, featuring everything from water polo to scuba diving. There's also a full health center with a *hamam* (bath) and much more. And for the less aerobically inclined, you can shop yourself into a modest Greek fury here.

Expensive

✪ **Rodos Park.** Odos Riga Fereou 12, 85100 Rhodes. ☎ **800/525-4800** in the U.S. or 0241/24-612. Fax 0241/24-613. 60 units. A/C MINIBAR TV TEL. Dr38,000–Dr63,000 ($127–$210) double; Dr57,500–Dr94,500 ($192–$315) suite. Rates include breakfast. AE, MC, V. Open year-round. The hotel is only a few minutes from the Old Town and Mandraki Harbor as well as the New Town shopping and dining areas.

This superb New Town luxury hotel, with gleaming marble and polished wood interiors, enjoys a uniquely convenient yet secluded location just outside the Old Town. If you want a Jacuzzi in your room, choose one of the suites, preferably one with a superb view of the Old Town walls. If you need to work off surplus calories from the 24-hour room service or the in-house gourmet restaurant, head down to the fitness center, then get pampered with a Swedish massage, sauna, or steam bath. A dip in the outdoor pool will offer the perfect finish to your regime. For dropping anchor in the New Town, this is it, provided that cost is only a fleeting consideration.

Several excellent dining choices include Le Café (casual dining with appetizing views of the hotel's gardens and pool), the Park Side (a cafe-brasserie), and Le Jardin, where the art of Greek dining takes a timely French turn. For those who won't come in out of the air for love or money, there's an open-air grill bar. In addition to all the amenities you would expect from a first-class international hotel, there's a fully equipped gym in the health center and a most inviting outdoor pool. The biggest fringe benefit of all is the Park's location on the perimeter of the old walls, placing its guests within a short stroll to the heart of the old city.

Moderate

Ibiscus. Kos Beach, 85100 Rhodes. ☎ **0241/24-421.** Fax 0241/27-283. 205 units. A/C TV TEL. Dr18,900–Dr27,900 ($63–$93) double. Rates include breakfast. AE, DC, MC, V. Open Apr–Oct.

Fully renovated in 1998, this is a very attractive and convenient hotel within a stone's throw of the beach. The lines and decor are clean, fresh, and contemporary, with lots of light woods and marble. The spacious rooms are fully carpeted, and offer large wardrobes, ample desk areas, orthopedic mattresses, tubs and bidets, and hair dryers. Every room has a balcony, many of which face the sea. The hotel's restaurant, Lindos, has an independent reputation. This is a good, solid choice in the New Town.

Kamiros Hotel. Odos Martiou 1, 85100 Rhodes. ☎ **0241/22-591.** Fax 0241/22-349. 48 units. A/C TV TEL. Dr19,000–Dr21,000 ($66–$70) double. Rates include breakfast. AE, MC, V. Open year-round.

This renovated older hotel is well located in the heart of town overlooking Mandraki Harbor, just a few blocks from the Old Town. The guest rooms are large with high ceilings, the bathrooms especially spacious, and double-paned windows make for relatively quiet nights in spite of the hotel's central location. Fridge, hair dryer, and bathroom heater are standard. The buffet breakfast is unusually substantial. We advise staying here only if you are able to book a room facing the harbor, as some of those facing the back have unsightly views.

Inexpensive

✪ Esperia. Othos Griva 7, 85100 Rhodes. ☎ **0241/23-941.** Fax 0241/77-501. 178 units. A/C TEL. Dr8,000–Dr15,000 ($27–$50) double. Rates include breakfast. AE, DC, MC, V. Open year-round.

This fine hotel is at least one class above its cost. Nowhere in Rhodes have we found this kind of quality at such low rates. Newly refurbished, the guest rooms are tasteful and exceptionally clean, with fridge, hair dryer, and ample balcony with pleasant views—nothing spectacular, nothing unsightly. New double-glazed sliding balcony doors effectively seal the rooms off from most of the town's noise. The bar, lounge, and breakfast room are inviting, and the walled outdoor pool and poolside bar are well above average for a modest hotel. The buffet breakfast is extensive and tasty. One drawback—the beds, though new, are regrettably soft. The Esperia is located near the restaurant district, and even nearer the casino. All in all, this is a clear standout among inexpensive hotels in the New Town.

Hotel Anastasia. Odos 28 Octobriou 46, 85100 Rhodes. ☎ **0241/28-007.** Fax 0241/21-815. 20 units. Dr8,000–Dr11,000 ($27–$37) double. Rates include breakfast. AE, V. Open year-round. Just a few minutes' walk to the municipal beach and close to the restaurant district of the New Town.

If you're really set on staying in a smaller hotel, here's a convenient option. Set quietly back off the street down a green lane, this 65-year-old Italian mansion is a pleasant place. Operated for the past 20 years by George Anghelou, it has modest, clean rooms with 15-foot ceilings, giving a feeling of light and space. One air-conditioned triple is available for an extra Dr1,000 ($3.35). There's a rustic bar in the hibiscus-trellised garden, home to two venerable tortoises. You can probably negotiate an additional 25% off in winter.

WHERE TO DINE IN RHODES CITY
IN THE OLD TOWN

The Old Town is thick with tavernas, restaurants, and fast-food nooks, all doing their best to lure you into their lair, which in some cases is just where you want to be. The more brazen their overtures, the more bold you must be in holding to your course. Don't imagine, however, that all Old Town restaurants are tourist traps. Many Rhodians consider this area to have some of the best food on the island, particularly for fish.

Expensive

✪ Alexis Taverna. Odos Sokratous 18. ☎ **0241/29-347.** Reservations recommended. Appetizers Dr600–Dr2,300 ($2–$8); main courses Dr4,000–Dr7,200 ($13–$24). AE, V. Daily noon–3pm and 7pm–1am. SEAFOOD.

For more than 40 years, this fine restaurant has been the one to beat in Old Town, setting the standard by which all the other seafood restaurants are measured. Two brothers, Iannis and Constantine, today preserve the tradition established by their grandfather Alexis. Make no mistake, this is the culinary epicenter of Old Town. The list of appreciative diners over the years includes Winston Churchill, Jacqueline

Kennedy, presidents, royalty, and innumerable tourists in the know. This is one place, if you can afford it (let's say Dr36,000/$120 for two), to abandon restraint and to invite Iannis to conceive a seafood feast for you, selecting a perfect wine from his cellar that represents vineyards all over Greece. Of course, you can eat exquisitely here for much less than that. Iannis goes down to the harbor himself each day and chooses the best of the catch. Insisting on quality and freshness, he and Constantine have built their own greenhouse on the outskirts of town to cultivate organic vegetables. We started with a bounteous seafood platter, with delicately flavored sea urchins, fresh clams, and a tender octopus carpaccio. The sargos, a sea-bream–type fish, was charcoal-grilled to perfection. The creamy Greek yogurt with homemade green-walnut jam was a perfect ending for a superb culinary experience.

Manolis Dinoris Fish Taverna. Museum Sq. 14Λ. ☎ **0241/25-824.** Appetizers Dr1,600–Dr3,500 ($5–$12); main courses Dr8,500–Dr14,000 ($28–$47); fixed-price dinners Dr10,000– Dr15,000 ($33–$50). AE, MC, V. Year-round daily noon–midnight. SEAFOOD.

Housed in the stables of the 13th-century Knights of St. John's Inn, this restored building is a unique setting to enjoy delicious and fresh seafood delights. Either choose à la carte or the set menu, which includes coquille St. Jacques, Greek salad, grilled prawns, swordfish, baklavas, coffee, and brandy. In warm weather, the quiet side garden is delightful; in winter, a fire roars in the old stone hearth indoors.

Moderate
Cleo's Restaurant. Odos St. Fanouriou 17. ☎ **0241/28-415.** Fixed-price dinners Dr3,000–Dr3,200 ($10–$11). AE, MC, V. Mon–Sat 7pm–midnight. ITALIAN.

This tranquil place, with its whitewashed courtyard and elegantly furnished two-story interior, is found down a narrow lane off the noisy Odos Sokratous. Owner Romildo Fistolera, from Como, Italy, prepares the best Italian and nouvelle European cuisine in Rhodes, as well as having a superb wine selection from lesser-known boutique wineries. We savored the homemade tagliatelle with salmon sauce, and found the beef fillet with white mushroom sauce superb. Every day there is a choice of four different fixed-price three-course dinners that are especially good buys. For dessert, the creamy tiramisu is sinfully exquisite.

Inexpensive
Diafani Garden Restaurant. Plateia Arionos 3 (opposite the Turkish bath). ☎ **0241/ 26-053.** Appetizers Dr550–Dr1,100 ($1.85–$3.70); main courses Dr850–Dr2,600 ($2.85–$9). No credit cards. Daily noon–midnight. GREEK.

Several locals recommended this family-operated taverna to us. The Karpathian Protopapa family cooks up fine traditional Greek fare at bargain prices. Sitting under the spreading walnut tree in the vine-shaded courtyard, we enjoyed the potpourri of the Greek plate and the splendid *papoutsaki,* braised eggplant slices layered with chopped meat and a thick, cheesy béchamel sauce, delicately flavored with nutmeg and coriander.

Iannis Taverna. Odos Platonos 41. ☎ **0241/36-535.** Appetizers Dr450–Dr800 ($1.50–$2.70); main courses Dr950–Dr2,500 ($3.15–$8). No credit cards. Year-round daily 9am–midnight. GREEK.

For a budget Greek meal, visit chef Iannis's small place on a quiet back lane. The moussaka, stuffed vegetables, and meat dishes are flavorful and well prepared by a man who spent 14 years as a chef in New York Greek diners. His Greek plate is the best we found in Rhodes, with an unbelievably large variety of tasty foods. Portions are hearty, it's cheap, and the friendly service is a welcome relief from nearby establishments. The breakfast omelets are a great deal, too.

Kafenio Araliki. Odos Aristofanous 45. ☎ **0241/28-991.** Appetizers/snacks Dr700–Dr1,500 ($2.35–$5). No credit cards. Mon–Sat 11am–3pm and 7pm–1am. GREEK.

A *kafenio* is a place to eat small plates of savory dishes while sipping retsina or ouzo. Off the tourist circuit, this picturesque hideaway, run by two superfriendly Italian women, Valeria and Miriam, became our favorite place to sit among locals and expatriates, munching on the delightful vegetarian, fish, or meat mezedes. The upstairs gallery is especially charming, with seating either at tables or on an oriental-style platform with comfortable cushions for reclining.

Kafenio Turkiko. Odos Sokratous. No phone. Drinks/snacks Dr200–Dr600 (65¢–$2). No credit cards. Daily 11am–midnight. SNACKS.

Located in a Crusader structure, this is the only authentic place left on touristy Odos Sokratous, otherwise replete with Swatch, Body Shop, Van Cleef, and a multitude of souvenir shops. Each rickety wooden table comes with a backgammon board for idling away the time while you sip on Greek coffee or juice. The turn-of-the-century pictures, mirrors, and bric-a-brac on the walls enhanced our feeling of bygone times.

IN THE NEW TOWN & ENVIRONS
Expensive
✪ **Kioupia.** Tris village. ☎ **0241/91-824.** Reservations required. Fixed-price meal Dr10,000 ($33) per person, wines and service extra. MC, V. Mon–Sat 8pm–midnight. GREEK.

Rated by the *London Guardian* as one of the world's 10 best restaurants, this unique place offers an exquisite gourmet experience that you shall long treasure. Kioupia was founded in 1972 by the creative and artistic Michael Koumbiadis, called by Athenian society "the Colossus of Rhodes," who has discovered the true harmony in the taste of Greek traditional cuisine, using the best of local ingredients and village recipes. In the elegantly decorated, rustic old house, the meal begins with a rinsing of hands in rosewater, and then perhaps a choice from three soups, including the unusual *trahanas,* a Greek wheat-and-cheese soup. And then, another difficult choice from an amazing array of appetizers: sautéed wild mushrooms, pumpkin *beignee* (dumplings), savory braised red peppers in olive oil, accompanied by home-baked carrot bread and pastrami bread. The main dishes are equally superb—broiled veal stuffed with cheese and sprinkled with pistachio nuts with yogurt sauce, or delectable pork souvlaki with yogurt and paprika sauce on the side. For dessert, go all the way with light crepes filled with sour cherries and covered with chocolate sauce and vanilla creme. Many of the foods are prepared in a traditional wood-burning oven in clay pots, the faint smell of wood permeating the restaurant. The fixed-price meal, like the Orthodox liturgy, requires fasting, devotion, and time (roughly 3 hr.), and involves no small share of mystery.

Moderate
Goniako Palati (Corner Palace). Odos Griva 110 (corner of Griva and 28 Oktobriou). ☎ **0241/33-167.** Appetizers Dr300–Dr2,350 ($1–$8); main courses Dr1,450–Dr5,650 ($4.85–$19). AE, MC, V. Daily 7pm–midnight. GREEK.

The new Goniako Palati may not be a palace, but it is on the corner—a busy corner, something you overlook once the food arrives. Great canvas awnings spread out to cover the seating area, raised well above street level. The extensive taverna menu is basic Greek, fresh and skillfully prepared in a slightly upscale environment at reasonable prices. This is one place local New Towners go for reliable, and then some, taverna fare. The grilled swordfish souvlaki, served with a medley of steamed vegetables, was quite tasty. The saganaki here is a performance art, and delicious to boot.

Kon Tiki Floating Restaurant. Mandraki Harbor. ☎ **0241/22-477.** Appetizers Dr1,000–Dr1,500 ($3.35–$5); main courses Dr1,600–Dr5,000 ($5–$17). AE, MC, V. Daily 8am–midnight. GREEK/INTERNATIONAL.

Still floating after 34 years of serving good food, this was one of Rhodes's first decent restaurants, and it's still a great place to watch the yachts bobbing alongside while enjoying well-prepared, creative dishes, such as the sole *valevska* (fillet of sole with shrimps, crabs, and mushrooms gratinéed in a béchamel sauce). The saganaki shrimp were exceptionally tasty, served with feta cheese, local herbs, and tomato sauce. It's now open for breakfast and for a coffee or drink at the bar, if that's all you want.

Memories. Iannis Dragoumi 24. ☎ **0241/23-003.** Appetizers Dr600–Dr2,800 ($2–$9); main courses Dr1,300–Dr4,750 ($4.35–$16). MC, V. Daily noon–1am. GREEK.

This restaurant just down from the Esperia Hotel was only 3 days old when we ate here, so it's difficult to be certain whether the excellent taverna cuisine and gracious service were only due to bursts of beginners' fervor. What won't change is the exceptionally tasteful and warm ambiance and decor. The designer has a gifted eye, and the chef a discerning palate. For traditional taverna fare, this is a cut above the eateries that line the nearby streets. The party next to us had eaten here on opening night and had come back every night since. Not a bad advertisement.

✪ **Palia Historia (The Old Story).** Odos Mitropoleos 108. ☎ **0241/32-421.** Reservations recommended. Appetizers Dr800–Dr1,500 ($2.70–$5); main courses Dr950–Dr4,700 ($3.15–$16). AE, MC, V. Daily 7pm–midnight. GREEK.

Actually, this restaurant is not an old story, as it is only 10 years old—but it is already well on its way to becoming a legend. It's well worth a taxi ride from wherever you're staying. Most of the clientele is Greek, drawn by the subtle cuisine and lack of tourists. If you've maxed out on run-of-the-mill Greek taverna fare, this is one place to come to be utterly startled. The marinated salmon and capers were worthy of the finest Dublin restaurant, and the broccoli with oil, mustard, and roasted almonds was inspired. As a main course, the shrimps saganaki left nothing to the imagination. With fish, the dry white Spiropoulos from Mantinia was perfect. For a great finish, go for the banana flambé.

Inexpensive

Salt and Pepper. Odos Petridi 76. ☎ **0241/65-494.** Reservations recommended. Appetizers Dr400–Dr1,500 ($1.35–$5); main courses Dr1,500–Dr3,500 ($5–$12). V. Daily 6:30pm–midnight (closed Mon in winter). GREEK.

In this fine place frequented by discerning Greeks and the occasional fortunate tourists, genial host Spiros Diasinos succeeds in transforming Greek cooking into splendid, gourmet cuisine. He brings a selection of more than 10 mezedes to your table, each tastier than the next. We delighted in the scrumptious calamari, stuffed with rice, tomatoes, and onion. The zucchini keftedes were subtlety flavored with mint, and the beet and wild spinach salad was the best we have ever tasted. After feasting on the excellent snails in tomato sauce and the tasty black-eyed peas, we were so sated that we did not venture to try the appealing main courses, such as beef prepared in yogurt sauce. The homemade pitas, grilled on coals and served with feta-cheese spread and olive pâté, were a nice addition to the meal.

RHODES CITY AFTER DARK

Rhodes by night is brimming with energy. Outside of Athens, Rhodes claims one of the most active nighttime scenes in Greece. Granted, some of that energy is grounded in the resort complexes north of the city, but there is enough to go around.

Your own good sense is as good a guide as any in this ever-changing scene. In a city as compact as Rhodes, it's best to follow the lights and noise, not worrying about getting a little lost. When you decide to call it quits, shout down a taxi to bring you back, if you can remember where you're staying.

As a rule of thumb, the **New Town** is more lively than the Old Town. In the New Town, several **cafe scenes** are on the harbor, behind Academy Square, or on Odos Galias, near New Market. The **bar scene** tends to line up along Odos Diakonou. There are at least 100 **nightclubs** on Rhodes, so you're sure to find one to your liking. Complicating matters is a recent announcement that the police, after countless complaints of noise and mayhem until all hours, have decided to designate one area of the city for discos and bars, enabling them to stay open until whenever with impunity. When this area will be designated and where it will be is anyone's guess.

Gambling is a popular nighttime activity in Greece. Rumor has it that there's a network of private high-stakes (and illegal) gambling dens scattered throughout the city. For those who want to wager in a less subterranean atmosphere, Rhodes has had for many years one of only three legal casinos in Greece, a government-operated roulette and blackjack house adjoining the Grand Hotel. In January 1999, however, this was replaced by a much more extensive casino and hotel operated by Playboy International. The home of this new complex is the once-grand **Hotel Rodon** facing Elli Beach, which has been gutted and reconceived.

The **Sound and Light** (*Son et Lumière*) presentation dramatizes the life of a youth admitted into the monastery in 1522, the year before Rhodes's downfall to invading Turks. In contrast to Athens's Acropolis show, the dialogue here is more illuminating, though the lighting is unimaginative. Nevertheless, sitting in the lush formal gardens below the palace on a warm evening can be a pleasant and informative experience, and we heartily recommend it to those smitten by the medieval Old Town. Twice-nightly performances are scheduled according to season (check the posted schedule) and include one performance in English; they take place at Odos Papagou, south of Rimini Square (☎ **0241/21-922**). Admission is Dr1,200 ($4); free for children under 12.

We thoroughly recommend the **Traditional Folk Dance Theater,** presented by the Nelly Dimoglou Dance Company, Odos Adronikou, off Plateia Arionos, Old Town (☎ **0241/20-157**). It's always lively, filled with color, and totally entertaining. Twenty spirited men and women perform dances from many areas of Greece in colorful, often embroidered, flouncy costumes. The five-man band plays an inspired and varied repertoire, the choreography is excellent, the dancers skillful, and even the set (an open square surrounded by two-dimensional Rhodian houses) is effective. Performances take place from May through early October, Monday, Wednesday, and Friday at 9:20pm. Admission is Dr3,000 ($10) for adults and Dr1,500 ($5) for students.

EXPLORING THE ISLAND

Sun, sand, and the rest is history. That's nowhere more true than on Rhodes. Ruins and beaches—that nearly sums up what lures visitors out of Rhodes city. First things first: For the best **beaches,** head to the east coast of the island. Visitors also flock to archaeological sites identical to the three original Dorian city-states, all nearly 3,000 years old: **Lindos, Kamiros,** and **Ialisos.** Of these, Lindos was and is preeminent; it is by far the top tourist destination outside of Old Town. So we begin here with Lindos, and then explore the island counterclockwise.

LINDOS

Lindos is without question the most picturesque town on the island of Rhodes. Since Lindos has been designated a historic settlement, the Archaeological Society has control over all development in the village (God bless 'em!), and the traditional white stucco homes, shops, and restaurants form the most unified, classically Greek expression in the Dodecanese.

Be warned, however, that Lindos is often deluged with tourists, and your first visit may be unforgettable for the wrong reasons. Avoid the crush of mid-July to August, if at all possible.

There are two entrances to the town. The first and northernmost leads down a steep hill to the bus stop and taxi stand, then veers downhill to the beach. At this square you'll find the friendly, extremely informative **Tourist Information Kiosk** (☎ 0244/ **31-900;** fax 0241/31-288), where Michalis will help you from April through October, daily from 9am to 10pm. Here, too, is the commercial heart of the village with the Acropolis above. The rural **medical clinic** (☎ 0241/31-224), **post office,** and **telephone office (OTE)** are nearby. The second road leads beyond the town and into the upper village, blessedly removed from the hordes. This is the better route for people more aesthetically single-minded. Just follow signs to the Acropolis. If you want to save your feet, for Dr1,000 ($3.35) you can ride a donkey (a.k.a a Lindian taxi) all the way to the top; you'll pass their stand.

All along the way your path will be strewn with embroidery and lace which may or may not be the handiwork of local women who, in the timeless Lindian tradition, work in lace and embroidery. Embroidery from Rhodes was highly coveted in the ancient world. In fact, it is claimed that Alexander the Great wore a grand Rhodian robe into battle at Gaugemila, and in Renaissance Europe, the French ladies used to yearn for a bit of Lindos lace. Much of what is for sale in Lindos today, however, is from Hong Kong.

Finally at the top, there are from the fortress ramparts glorious views of medieval Lindos below, where most homes date from the 15th century. To the south you can see the lovely beach at St. Paul's Bay—named from the tradition that St. Paul put ashore there—along with Rhodes's less-developed eastern coastline. And, across to the southwest, rises Mount Krana, where caves, dug out to serve as ancient tombs, are thought to have been cult places to Athena well into the Christian period.

The **Acropolis** (☎ 0241/27-674) is open Tuesday through Sunday from 8:30am to 2:30pm. Admission is Dr1,200 ($4) for adults and Dr600 ($2) for students and children. This is one of Rhodes's three original Dorian acropoleis. Ensconced within the much later medieval walls stand the impressive remains of the Sanctuary of Athena Lindos, with its large Doric portico from the 4th century B.C. St. John's Knights refortified the Acropolis with monumental turreted walls and built a small church to St. John inside. Today, stones and columns are strewn everywhere as the site undergoes extensive restoration.

On your descent, as you explore the labyrinthine lanes of medieval Lindos, you will come to the exquisite late-14th- or early-15th-century **Byzantine Church of the Panayia,** still the local parish church. More than 200 iconic frescoes (dating from the 18th century) cover every inch of the walls and arched ceilings, and are being painstakingly restored at great expense. The entire right side of the interior has been restored so far, with stunning results. Be sure to spend time with these icons, many of them sequentially narrative, depicting the Creation, the Nativity, the Christian Passover, and the Last Judgement. And after you've given yourself a stiff neck looking up, be sure to look down at the extraordinary floor, made of sea pebbles.

Adjoining the Church of the Panayia is the new **Church Museum** (☎ **0244/ 32-020**), open April through October daily from 9am to 3pm; a donation of Dr500 ($1.70) is requested for admission. The historical and architectural exhibits and collected ecclesiastical items, including frescoes, icons, texts, chalices, and liturgical embroidery, comprise a surprisingly significant collection. A visit here will prove quite helpful in guiding you through the medieval town and to its almost hidden treasures.

Then, of course, there's the inviting **beach** below, lined with cafes and tavernas.

Where to Stay & Dine in Lindos & Environs

In high season, Lindos marks the spot where up to 10,000 day-trippers from Rhodes city converge with 4,000 resident tourists. Since no hotel construction is permitted, almost all of the old homes have been converted into pensions (called "villas" in the brochures) by English charter companies. In peak season, the local **Tourist Information Kiosk** (☎ **0244/31-900;** fax 0244/31-288) has a list of the homes that rent rooms. Plan to pay Dr6,000 ($20) to Dr8,000 ($27) for a double and Dr6,000 to Dr12,000 ($20 to $40) for a studio apartment.

Triton Holidays in Rhodes (☎ **0241/21-690**) books six-person villas for Dr32,000 ($107) a day in high season, including kitchen facilities (reservations are often made a year in advance). If Lindos is booked or not to your taste, consider the attractive beaches to the south at Pefkos, Lardos, or Kalathos. **Heliousa Travel** in Lardos (☎ **0244/44-057;** fax 0244/44/041) can help you find a room as well as assist with other travel needs.

You'll have a paralyzing effusion of restaurants and tavernas to choose from in tiny Lindos, and we've made our selection below. On the beach, the expansive **Triton Restaurant** gets a nod because you can easily change into your swimsuit in their bathroom, essential for nonresidents who want to splash in the gorgeous water across the way. It's also not as pricey as all the others.

Argo Fish Taverna. Haraki Beach. ☎ **0244/51-410.** Reservations recommended. Appetizers Dr650–Dr2,600 ($2.15–$9); main courses Dr1,200–Dr2,950 ($4–$10); 2-person seafood platter Dr19,900 ($66). AE, MC, V. Daily noon–11pm. Open Easter–Oct. GREEK/SEAFOOD.

Ten kilometers (6.2 miles) north of Lindos is Haraki Bay, a quiet fishing hamlet with a gorgeous, crescent-shaped pebbly beach and this excellent seafood taverna. Consider stopping here for a swim and lunch on a day trip from Rhodes to Lindos. We appreciated the freshness of the food, as well as the creative variation on a Greek salad: an addition of mint and dandelion leaves with fresh herbs, served with whole-wheat bread. The lightly battered fried calamari was tasty and a welcome relief from the standard over-battered fare. The mussels, baked with fresh tomatoes and feta cheese, were also right on.

Atrium Palace. Kalathos Beach, 85100 Rhodes. ☎ **0244/31-601.** Fax 0244/31-600. 256 units. A/C MINIBAR TV TEL. Dr22,000–Dr38,000 ($73–$127) double. Rates include breakfast. AE, DC, MC, V. Open Apr–Oct.

Located just over 4 miles out of Lindos on the long beach of crystal-clear Kalathos Bay, this luxurious resort-hotel features an eclectic architectural design—a neo-Greek, Roman, Crusader, and Italian pastel extravaganza. The inner atrium is an attractive, tropical water garden of pools and waterfalls. The beautifully landscaped outside pool complex is a nice alternative to the nearby beach, and there's an indoor pool, sauna, and fitness club to keep you busy.

Ladiko Bungalows Hotel. Faliraki, P.O. Box 236, 85100 Rhodes. ☎ **0241/85-536.** Fax 0241/80-241. 42 units. A/C TEL. Dr14,000–Dr20,000 ($47–$67) double. Rates include breakfast. MC, V.

Anthony Quinn obtained permission to build a retirement home for actors on this pretty little bay, on the road to Lindos 2 miles south of the swinging beach resort of Faliraki; he never realized his plans, but the bay retains his name. We especially enjoyed the quiet and the convenient location of this friendly family-operated lodge, with nature-lover activities such as swimming, fishing, and hiking to nearby ruins and less-frequented beaches, and its proximity (20-min. walk) to noisy and bustling Faliraki.

✪ **Lindos Mare.** Lindos Bay, 85100 Rhodes. ☎ **0244/31-130.** Fax 0244/31-131. 138 units. TEL. Dr25,000–Dr43,000 ($83–$143) junior suite for 2 with half-board plan (breakfast and dinner). MC, V.

Despite the restricting provision that accommodation is usually available only with half-board plan included, this relatively small and classy cliff-side resort hotel is a prime site to drop anchor on the east shore. The rooms are a grade up from most of the otherwise comparable luxury hotels on the coast, and the views of the bay below are heart-stopping. A tram descends from the upper lobby, restaurant, and pool area to the lower levels of attractive Aegean-style bungalows, and continues onward down to the beach area, where there are umbrellas and water sports. It's only a 2-kilometer (1.2-mile) walk or ride into Lindos, although you just might want to stay put in the evenings with the in-house social activities, such as barbecue, folklore evenings, or dancing.

✪ **Mavrikos.** Main Sq., Lindos. ☎ **0244/31-232.** Reservations recommended. Appetizers, Dr500–Dr900 ($1.70–$3); main courses Dr1,500–Dr3,400 ($5–$11). V. Daily noon–midnight. GREEK/FRENCH.

Brothers Michalis and Dimitri continue a family tradition of fine Greek and French cuisine, such as the oven-baked lamb and fine beef fillets, or the perfectly grilled and seasoned fresh red snapper. The venerable restaurant and expansive shaded terrace have retained their special rustic charm—David Gilmore of Pink Floyd fame was so furious when they brought new, modern chairs that Michalis quickly restored and returned the originals. Other notable fans have included Nelson Rockefeller and Jackie Kennedy. This is our first choice for a memorable meal in Lindos.

The Mavrikos have also opened a great ice-cream parlor, **Geloblu,** serving home-made frozen concoctions and cakes, located within the labyrinth of the old town near the church.

Sights & Beaches Elsewhere on the Island

An around-the-island tour provides a chance to view some of the wonderful variations of Rhodes's scenery. The sights described below, with the exception of Ialisos and Kamiros, are not of significant historical or cultural importance, but if you get bored with relaxing, try some. The route traces the island counterclockwise from Rhodes city, with a number of suggested sorties into the interior. Even a cursory glance at a map of Rhodes will explain the many zigs and zags in this itinerary. Keep in mind that not all roads are equal and that all-terrain vehicles are required for some of the detours suggested below. Rhodian rental-car companies usually stipulate that their standard vehicles be driven only on fully paved roads.

Ialisos was the staging ground for the four major powers that were to control the island of Rhodes. The ancient ruins and monastery on Mount Filerimos reflect the presence of two of these groups. The Dorians ousted the Phoenicians from Rhodes in the 10th century B.C. (An oracle had predicted that white ravens and fish swimming in wine would be the final signs before the Phoenicians were annihilated. The Dorians, quick to spot opportunity, painted enough birds and threw enough fish into wine jugs so that the Phoenicians left without raising their arms.) Most of the Dorians left Ialisos for other parts of the island; many settled in the new city of Rhodes. During the 3rd to 2nd centuries B.C., the Dorians constructed a temple to Athena and Zeus Polios (similar to those on Mount Smith), whose ruins are still visible, below the monastery. Walking south of the site will lead you to a well-preserved 4th-century B.C. fountain.

When the Knights of St. John invaded the island, they too started from Ialisos, a minor town in Byzantine times. They built a small, subterranean chapel decorated with frescoes of Jesus and heroic knights. Their little whitewashed church is built right into the hillside above the Doric temple. Over it, the Italians constructed the **Monastery of Filerimos,** which remains a lovely spot to tour. Finally, Süleyman the Magnificent moved into Ialisos (1522) with his army of 100,000 and used it as a base for his eventual takeover of the island.

The site of Ialisos is open daily from 8:30am to 3pm. Proper dress is required, and admission is Dr800 ($2.70). Ancient Ialisos is 6 kilometers (3.7 miles) inland from Trianda on the island's northwest coast; public buses leave from Rhodes frequently for the 14-kilometer (8.7-mile) ride.

Petaloudes is a popular tourist attraction because of the millions of black-and-white–striped **"butterflies"** (actually a species of moth) that overtake this verdant valley in July and August. When resting quietly on flowering plants or leaves, the moths are well camouflaged. Only the wailing of infants and the Greek rock blaring out of portable radios disturbs them. Then the sky is filled with a flurry of red, their underbellies exposed as they try to hide from the summer crush. The setting, with its many ponds, bamboo bridges, and rock displays, is admittedly a bit too precious. Petaloudes is 25 kilometers (15½ miles) south of Rhodes and inland; it can be reached by public bus, but is most easily seen with a guided tour. It's open daily from 8am to 6pm; admission is Dr600 ($2) from July to mid-September and Dr300 ($1) the rest of the year.

The ruins at **Kamiros** are much more extensive than those at nearby Ialisos, perhaps because this city remained an important outpost after the new Rhodes was completed in 408 B.C. The site is divided into two segments: the upper porch and the lower valley. The porch served as a place of religious practice and provided the height needed for the city's water supply. Climb up to the top and you'll see two swimming-pool–size aqueducts. The Dorians collected water in these basins, assuring themselves a year-round supply. The small valley contains ruins of Greek homes and streets, as well as the foundations of a large temple. The site is in a good enough state of preservation to imagine what life in this ancient Doric city was like more than 2,000 years ago.

Think about wearing a swimsuit under your clothes: There is a good stretch of **beach** across the street from the site, where there are some rooms to let, a few tavernas, and the bus stop. The site is open Tuesday through Sunday from 8:30am to 3pm. Admission is Dr800 ($2.70). Kamiros is 34 kilometers (21 miles) southwest of Rhodes city, with regular bus service.

Driving south along the windswept western coast from Kamiros, you will come to the late-15th-century Knights castle of **Kastellos** (Kritinias Castle), dominating the sea below. From there, proceeding south and then cutting up to the northeast, you can make your way inland to **Embonas,** the wine capital of the island and home to several tavernas famed for their fresh meat barbecues. This village is on the tour-group circuit, and numerous tavernas offer meat-and-wine feasts accompanied by live Greek music and folklore performances. If you then circle around the island's highest mountain, **Attaviros** (3,986 ft.), you come to the village of **Ayios Issidoros,** where if you're a devoted trekker you can ask directions to the summit. (It's a 5-hr. round-trip trek from Ayios Issidoros to the top of Mount Attaviros.) Otherwise, you can proceed to the picturesque village of **Siana,** nestled on the mountainside, and from there to **Monolithos,** with its spectacularly sited crusader castle perched on the pinnacle of a coastal mountain.

If, to reach the eastern coast, you now decide to retrace your path back through Siana and Ayios Issidoros, you will after many bends and twists come to Laerma, where you might consider taking a 5-kilometer (3-mile) seasonal road to the **Thami Monastery,** the oldest functioning monastery on the island, with its beautiful, though weather-damaged, frescoes. From Laerma, it's only another 10 kilometers (6.2 miles) to Lardos and the eastern coastal road, where you can either head straight to **Lindos** (see above) or take still another detour to **Asklipio,** with its ruined castle and impressive Byzantine church. The church has a mosaic-pebbled floor and gorgeous cartoon-style frescoes, which depict the 7 days of Creation (check out the octopus) and the life of Jesus.

The **beaches** south of Lindos, from Lardos Bay to Plimmiri (26km/16 miles in all) are among the best on Rhodes, especially the short stretch between Lahania and Plimmiri. At the southernmost tip of the island, for those who seek off-the-beaten-track places, is **Prasonisi** (Green Island), connected to the main island by a narrow sandy isthmus, with waves and world-class windsurfing on one side and calm waters on the other. There is lodging and food available here, including Prasonisi Club Studios. Now, back to Lindos.

From Lindos to Faliraki there are a number of sandy, sheltered beaches with relatively little development, all marked on most any island map you come across. **Faliraki Beach** is the island's most developed beach resort with dangerous levels of testosterone, offering every possible vacation distraction imaginable—from bungee jumping to laser clay shooting. The southern end of the beach is less crowded and frequented by nude bathers.

North of Faliraki, the once-healing thermal waters of **Kalithea,** praised for their therapeutic qualities by Hippokrates, have long since dried up—but this small bay, only 10 kilometers (6.2 miles) from Rhodes city, is still a great place to swim and snorkel. Mussolini built a fabulous art-deco spa here; its derelict abandonment retains an odd grandeur evoking an era thankfully long gone.

2 Simi

11km (7 miles) N of Rhodes

Tiny, rugged Simi is often called "the jewel of the Dodecanese." Arriving by boat affords a view of pastel-colored neoclassical mansions climbing the steep hills above the broad horseshoe-shaped harbor. Yialos is Simi's port, and Horio its old capital. The welcome absence of nontraditional buildings is due to an archaeological decree that severely regulates the style and methods of construction and restoration for all old and new buildings. Simi's long and prosperous tradition of shipbuilding, trading, and sponge diving is evident in the gracious mansions and richly ornamented churches scattered over the island. Islanders proudly boast that there are so many churches and monasteries that one could worship in a different sanctuary every day of the year.

During the first half of this century, Simi's economy gradually deteriorated as the shipbuilding industry declined, the maritime business soured, and somebody went and invented a synthetic sponge. Simians fled their homes to find work on nearby Rhodes or in the United States, Canada, and Australia. Today, the island's picture-perfect traditional-style houses have become a magnet for moneyed Athenians in search of real-estate investments, and Simi has a highly touted "off-the-beaten-path" resort for European tour groups trying to avoid other tour groups. The onslaught of tourists for the great part arrives at 10:30am and departs by 4pm.

ESSENTIALS

GETTING THERE   By Boat   Several **excursion boats** arrive daily from Rhodes, two of which are owned cooperatively (the *Simi I* and *Simi II*) and are booked locally in Rhodes through **Triton Holidays** (☎ 0241/21-690). Round-trip tickets are Dr4,500 ($15). The schedules and itineraries for the various excursion boats vary, but they all leave from Mandraki Harbor and stop at the main port of Simi, Yialos, with an additional stop at Panormitis Monastery or the beach at Pedi, before returning to Rhodes. Currently, there are daily **car ferries** from Piraeus, two **ferries** a week to Crete via Karpathos, and two **local ferries** weekly via Tilos, Nissiros, Kos, and Kalimnos. From late spring to summer, **hydrofoils** also skim daily from Rhodes to Simi, usually making both morning and afternoon runs.

VISITOR INFORMATION   Before your visit to Simi, check out a new and wonderfully helpful Web site launched and maintained in conjunction with Simi's independent monthly, *The Symi Visitor:* **www.symi-island.com.** Via the site's e-mail facility, you may request information on accommodations, buses, weather, and more. Webmaster Derek Donaldson says you can ordinarily expect a response within an hour. Or you can address your queries to *The Symi Visitor,* P.O. Box 64, Simi, 85600 Dodecanese. Don't ask them, however, to recommend one hotel or apartment over another; just say exactly what you're looking for and they'll provide suggestions.

The other principal source of holiday planning on Simi, from booking accommodations to chartering a boat, is the immensely resourceful George Kalodoukas of **Kalodoukas Holidays** (☎ 0241/71-007; fax 0241/71-491), just off the harbor up the steps from the Cafe Helena. Booking your room or apartment through Kalodoukas Holidays assures a wide range of options, as well as, in most cases, a some-what reduced rate. Once you've arrived on Simi, be sure to drop into the office, open Monday through Saturday from 9am to 1pm and 5 to 9pm. In summer, George plans a special outing for every day of the week, from cruises to explorations of the island. Most outings involve a swim and a healthy meal, and sometimes champagne.

There's also a Simi **tourist information kiosk** on the harbor, whose hours remain an enduring mystery. Information and a free guide pamphlet may also be obtained in the Simi **Town Hall,** located on the Town Square behind the bridge.

GETTING AROUND   Ferries and excursion boats dock first at hilly **Yialos** on the barren, rocky northern half of the island. Yialos is the liveliest village on the island and the venue for most overnighters. There's a striking (no pun intended) clock tower on the right as you enter the port, used as a local landmark when negotiating the maze of vehicle-free lanes and stairs. Another landmark used in giving directions is the bridge in the center of the harbor.

Simi's main road leads to **Pedi,** a developing beach resort one cove east of Yialos, and a new road rises up to **Horio,** the old capital. The island's 4,000 daily visitors most often take an excursion boat that stops at the Panormitis Monastery or at the beach at Pedi. **Buses** leave every hour from 8am until 11pm to Pedi via Horio (Dr200/70¢).

There are a grand total of four **taxis** on the island—leaving from the taxi stand at the center of the harbor and charging a set fee of Dr500 ($1.70) to Horio and Dr600 ($2) to Pedi. **Mopeds** are also available, but due to the limited road network, you would do better using public transportation and your own two feet. **Caïques** shuttle people to the various beaches: Emborios, Ayia Marina, Ayios Nikolaos, and Nanou; current prices range from Dr500 to Dr1,500 ($1.70 to $5) depending on distance.

FAST FACTS   For a **doctor**, call ☎ 0241/71-316; for a **dentist,** ☎ 0241/71-272. The **police station** (☎ 0241/71-11), located nearby, is open 24 hours a day. To send or retrieve **e-mail,** seek out (above "The Igloo" by the bridge) the office of *The Symi Visitor,* open daily from 8am to 8pm in summer, and Monday through Saturday from 9am to 5pm the rest of the year. You can send e-mail for a mere Dr500 ($1.70) per document. Remember, this is not a commercial venture, but a service offered by a newspaper that has its own deadlines. The **post office** (☎ 0241/ 71-315) and **telephone office (OTE)** (☎ 0241/71-212) are located about 100 meters behind the paralia (waterfront); they are open Monday through Friday from 7:30am to 3pm.

WHAT TO SEE & DO

Simi's southwestern portion is hilly and green. Located here is the medieval **Panormitis Monastery,** dedicated to St. Michael, the patron saint of seafaring Greeks. The monastery is popular with Greeks as a refuge from modern life; young Athenian businessmen speak lovingly of the monk cells and small apartments that can now only rarely be rented for R&R. The monastery has a **guest office** (☎ 0241/72-414) that provides local accommodation, ranging from Dr7,000 to Dr11,000 ($23 to $37) for a double, depending on season and type of room or apartment. The monastery itself does occasionally offer accommodation, so it's still worth a try.

The whitewashed compound has a verdant, shaded setting and a 16th-century gem of a church inside. The **Taxiarchis Mishail of Panormitis** boast icons of St. Michael and St. Gabriel adorned in silver and jewels. The combined folk and ecclesiastical museums are well worth the Dr200 (65¢) entrance fee.

The town of **Panormitis Mihailis** is most lively and interesting during its annual festival on November 8, but can be explored year-round via local boats or bus tours from Yialos. The hardy can hike here (it's 10km/6.2 miles, about 3 hr. from town), then enjoy a refreshing dip in its sheltered harbor and a meal in the taverna as reward for their labors.

In Yialos, by all means hike the gnarled, chipped stone steps of the **Kali Strate** ("the good steps"). This wide stairway ascends to Horio village, a picturesque community filled with images of a Greece in many ways long departed. Heavy-set, wizened old women sweep the whitewashed stone paths outside their homes. Occasionally a young girl or boy or very old man can be seen retouching the neon-blue trim over the doorways and shutters. Nestled between the immaculately kept homes, dating back to the 18th century, are abandoned villas, their faded trim and flaking paint lending a wistful air to the village. Renovated villas now rent to an increasing number of tourists. And where tourists roam, tavernas, souvenir shops, and bouzouki bars soon follow. Commercialization has hit once-pristine Simi, but it's still at a bearable level.

There's an excellent small **Archaeological Museum** in Horio, housing archaeological and folklore artifacts that the islanders consider important enough for public exhibition. You can't miss the blue arrows that point the way; it's open Tuesday through Saturday from 9am to 2pm. Admission is free, as is the **Maritime Museum** in the port, open daily from 10:30am to 3pm.

A Pair of Local Crafts

One local craft still practiced on Simi is **shipbuilding.** If you walk along the water toward Nos beach, you'll probably see boats under construction or repair. It's a treat to watch the men fashion planed boards into a graceful boat. Simi was a boat-building center in the days of the Peloponnesian War, when spirited sea battles were waged off its shores.

Sponge fishing is almost a dead industry in Greece. Only a generation ago, 2,000 sponge divers worked waters around the island; today only a handful undertake this dangerous work, and most do so in the waters around Italy and Africa. Working at depths of 50 to 60 meters (in the old days often without any apparatus), many divers were crippled or killed by the turbulent sea and too-rapid depressurization. The few sponges that are still harvested around Simi—and many more imported from Asia or Florida—are sold at shops along the port. Even if they're not from Simi's waters, they make inexpensive and lightweight gifts. For guaranteed-quality merchandise and an informative explanation and demonstration of sponge treatment, we recommend the **Aegean Sponge Center** (☎ **0241/ 71-620**), operated by Kyprios and his British wife, Leslie.

Crowning Horio is the **Church of the Panayia.** The church is surrounded by a fortified wall and is therefore called the kastro (castle). It's adorned with the most glorious frescoes on the island, which can be viewed only when services are held (Mon through Fri from 7 to 8am, all morning Sun).

Simi is not blessed with wide sandy beaches. Close to Yialos are two **beaches:** Nos, a 50-foot-long rocky stretch, and Emborios, a pebble beach.

A bus to **Pedi** followed by a short walk takes you to either **St. Nikolaos beach,** with shady trees and a good taverna, or to **St. Marina,** a small beach with little shade but stunning turquoise waters and views across to the islet of St. Marina and its cute church.

The summertime cornucopia of outings provided by Kalodoukas Holidays has already been mentioned; but if you want to set out on your own, be sure to pick up a copy of *Walking on Symi: A Pocket Guide,* a private publication of (guess who?) George Kalodoukas (Dr2,000/$7), outlining 25 walks to help you discover and enjoy Simi's historic sites, interior forests, and mountain vistas.

WHERE TO STAY

Many tourists bypass hotels for private apartments or houses. Between April and October, rooms for two with shower and kitchen access go for Dr7,000 to Dr12,000 ($23 to $40). More luxurious villa-style houses with daily maid service rent for Dr14,000 to Dr28,000 ($47 to $93). The best way to explore this alternative is to contact either Kalodoukas Holidays or *The Symi Visitor* Web site (see above for information on both).

The following listings are all open from mid-April to mid-October.

Aliki Hotel. Akti Gennimata, Yialos, 85600 Simi. ☎ **0241/71-665.** Fax 0241/71-655. 15 units. A/C TEL. Dr17,600–Dr19,600 ($59–$65) double without sea view; Dr21,600–Dr23,600 ($72–$79) double with sea view. Rates include breakfast. MC, V.

This well-restored sea captain's mansion, dating from 1895, is the standard by which all Simi lodging is judged. It offers elegantly styled rooms, some with dramatic waterfront views. As the Aliki has become a chic overnight getaway from bustling Rhodes, reservations are absolutely required. Five rooms have balconies.

Dorian Studios. Yialos, 85600 Simi. ☎ **0241/71-181**. 9 units. TEL. Dr9,000–Dr12,000 ($30–$40) double. No credit cards. Just up from the Akti Gennimata at the Aliki Hotel.

Located in a beautiful part of town only 10 meters from the sea, this is a rustically furnished, comfortable lodging (orthopedic beds!), with a kitchenette in every room. Some of the studios have bedrooms with vaulted beamed ceilings as well as balconies or terraces overlooking the harbor, where you can enjoy your morning coffee or evening ouzo. Five units have air-conditioning.

Hotel Nireus. Akti Gennimata, Yialos, 85600 Simi. ☎ **0241/72-400**. Fax 0241/72-404. 36 units. TEL. Dr17,000–Dr22,000 ($57–$73) double. Rates include breakfast. MC, V.

This new hotel right on the waterfront has become a popular venue for vacationing Greeks. The traditional Simian-style facade has been preserved, but the rooms are modern and comfortable. Try to get one of the 18 units that face the sea and offer stunning views; if you're fortunate, you might get one with a balcony. The rear-facing rooms now have air-conditioning.

Hotel Niriidis. Emborios Bay, 85600 Simi. ☎/fax **0241/71-784**. 9 units. TEL. Dr7,500–Dr13,000 ($25–$43) double. Rates include breakfast. No credit cards.

Satisfy your dream of having your own little place on a quiet bay with crystal-clear water. Each attractive bungalow here has a bedroom, bathroom, salon, kitchenette, and balcony facing the sea. At present, you either boat or walk (15 min. from Yialos) to this place, but owner Michalis Tsabaris assured us that sometime in the future a road will be built. With a bar on the premises and a taverna on the beach, what else could you possibly want?

WHERE TO DINE

For a respite from the crowds and traditional home cooking, you might try the tiny **Family Taverna Meraklis,** hidden on a back lane behind the Ionian and Popular Bank (☎ 0241/71-003).

Milo Petra ("The Mill Stone"). Yialos. ☎ **0241/72-333**. Fax 0241/72-194. Appetizers Dr1,900–Dr3,500 ($6–$12); main courses Dr3,500–Dr5,500 ($12–$18). V. Daily 7pm–midnight. MEDITERRANEAN.

Owners Eva and Hans converted this 200-year-old flour mill into an exquisite setting for a gourmet dining experience. Over the course of 5 years, they collected antique Greek furniture and fabrics to simply but elegantly decorate this most unusual space. (It even includes a 2,000-year-old grave visible through a glass window in the floor, which is made of pebble mosaic and rose marble.) Find an excuse to ascend to the toilet on the upper veranda to get the overall view of the wonderful interior. You may dine outdoors on the patio or inside by the open kitchen. Every day a different menu is printed. We were especially impressed by the lamb and fish dishes, using wonderful Simian hill spices, and the homemade pastas, such as ravioli Larissa, filled with potatoes and homemade cheese and served in sage butter.

Muragio Restaurant. Yialos. ☎ **0241/72-133**. Appetizers Dr500–Dr1,500 ($1.70–$5); main courses Dr900–Dr3,000 ($3–$10). No credit cards. Daily 11am–midnight. Open year-round. GREEK/SEAFOOD.

Opened in 1995, this has become a big hit among the locals, who praise the generous main courses and the quality of the food. Try the *bourekakia,* skinned eggplant stuffed with a special cheese sauce and then fried in a batter of eggs and bread crumbs. We were advised to try the extremely popular lemon lamb, but instead we chose the saganaki shrimp in tomato sauce and feta cheese, and were delighted.

Nireus Restaurant. Yialos. ☎ **0241/72-400.** Appetizers Dr800–Dr1,600 ($2.70–$5); main courses Dr1,600–Dr2,800 ($5–$9). MC, V. Daily 11am–11pm. GREEK.

We met people in Rhodes who extolled the fine cooking of Michalis, the chef of this superior restaurant located in the Nireus Hotel on the waterfront. Kudos go to his *frito misto*, a mixed seafood plate with tiny, naturally sweet Simi shrimp and other local delicacies. We also recommend the savory fillet of beef served with a Madeira sauce. They say you can't eat the scenery, but the view from here is delicious all the same.

Taverna Neraida. Town Sq., Yialos. ☎ **0241/71-841.** Main courses Dr900–Dr3,000 ($3–$10). No credit cards. Daily 11am–midnight. SEAFOOD.

Following our time-proven rule that fish is cheaper far from the port, this homey taverna has among the best fresh-fish prices on the island, as well as a wonderful range of mezedes. Try the black-eyed–pea salad and *skordalia* (garlic sauce). The grilled daily fish is delicious, and the very typical ambiance is a treat.

3 Kos

370km (230 miles) E of Piraeus

Kos has been inhabited for roughly 10,000 years, and has for a significant portion of that time been an important center of commerce and line of defense. Its population in ancient times may have reached 100,000, but today is less than a third of that number. Across the millennia, the unchallenged favorite son of the island has been Hippokrates, the father of Western medicine, who has left his mark not only on Kos but also on the world.

Today, Kos is identified with and at times nearly consumed by tourism, in which perhaps three-quarters of the island's working people are directly engaged. The scale of demand tells you something about Kos's beauty and attractions, which some visitors have done their best to diminish. But the island and its people have endured greater threats, and so will you, with a little determination and good advice.

The principal attractions of the island are its **antiquities**—most notably the Asklepion–and its **beaches.** You can guess which are more swamped in summer. But even with beaches and other natural charms, the taste of most tour groups is thankfully predictable and limited. The congestion can be eluded, if that's your preference.

You'll get the most out of Kos by learning to follow the locals, the people who live and work here. If you are in a village and see no schools or churches, and no old people, chances are you are not in a village at all, but in a resort. Kos has many such, especially along its coasts. In Kos town, the same is true of neighborhoods, and by extension, restaurants. Greek food is what Greeks eat, not necessarily what they sell.

Kos town is still very much vital. Since the island is small, it's probably better to base yourself in Kos, in an authentic neighborhood if possible, and venture out from there.

GETTING THERE   By Plane   The only scheduled flights into and out of the Kos airport are via **Olympic Airways,** whose Kos town office is at Odos Vas. Pavlou 22 (☎ 0242/28-331). Although Olympic has experimented with expanded service and may do so again, at present the only direct flights to Kos are from Athens and Rhodes. Currently, there are two flights daily from Athens, and several each week from Rhodes. Because scheduling reflects demand, it is best to consult Olympic Airways directly regarding their latest service to Kos. From **Hippokrates Airport** (☎ 0242/51-229), a bus will take you the 26 kilometers (16 miles) to the town center for Dr1,000 ($3.35), or you can take a taxi for Dr4,000 ($13). If you are flying out of Kos, Olympic will provide bus service to the airport, provided you arrive at their town center office 2 hours prior to departure.

By Boat   As the transportation hub of the Dodecanese, Kos offers, weather permitting, a full menu of seagoing options: car ferries, passenger ferries, hydrofoils (better known here as Flying Dolphins), excursion or tour boats, and caïques (converted fishing boats). Though schedules are apt to change, the good news is that you can, with more or less patience (especially in summer), make your way to Kos from virtually anywhere in the Aegean, and back again. Currently, however, the only ports linked to Kos with year-round nonstop and at least daily ferry service are Piraeus, Rhodes, Kalimnos, and Bodrum. Leros and Patmos enjoy the same frequency but with a stop or two along the way. After that, it's a matter of season and demand. The Kos harbor area is strewn with travel agents and tour operators wanting nothing more than to take you where you want to go, and in advance you can easily research current boat schedules with the Municipal Tourism Office (see below).

VISITOR INFORMATION   The **Municipal Tourism Office** (☎ 0242/24-460; e-mail: dotkos@hol.gr), on Odos Vas. Yioryiou, facing the harbor near the hydrofoil pier, is your one-stop source of information and assistance in Kos. It's open daily May through October from 7:30am to 8:30pm and November through April from 8am to 3:30pm. Hotel and pension owners keep this office informed of what rooms are available in the town and environs; you must, however, book your room directly with the hotel. Be sure to ask for a free copy of *Kos Summer*, which contains maps and a ton of useful information. If you want the latest scoop, pick up a copy of *Where and How in Kos* for Dr900 ($3). Kos also contains a regional office of the **National Tourism Organization** of Greece, with an information center on the harbor, in the old governor's mansion across from the castle at Akti Miaouli 2 (☎ 0242/29-200; fax 0242/29-201). It's open Monday through Friday from 7:30am to 3pm.

GETTING AROUND   **By Bus**   The **Kos town (DEAS) buses** offer excellent service within roughly 7 kilometers (4.3 miles) of the town center, while the **Kos island (KTEL) buses** will get you nearly everywhere else. Bus service is reduced on Sundays. For the latest fares and schedules, consult either the **town bus office,** on the harbor at Akti Kountourioti 7 (☎ 0242/26-276), or the **island bus station** at Odos Kleopatras 7 (☎ 0242/22-292), around the corner from the Olympic Airways office. The majority of DEAS town buses leave from the central bus stop on the south side of the harbor.

By Bicycle   Kos is a congenial island for less-than-competitive cyclists. Most of the island is quite flat, and the one main road from Kos town to Kefalos has all but emptied the older competing routes of traffic. Since bicycle trails are provided until you are well beyond Kos town, you can also avoid the congested east-end beach roads. But don't expect to pedal one-way and then hoist your bicycle onto a bus, because that won't work here. Rentals are available throughout Kos town and are easily arranged through your hotel. Prices vary from Dr1,000 to Dr3,000 ($3.35 to $10) per day.

By Moped   It's easy to rent a moped through your hotel or a travel agent, or, as with bicycles, to walk toward the harbor and look for an agency. Rentals range from Dr3,000 to Dr6,000 ($10 to $20) per day. Or call **Moto Rent,** Odos Kanari 49 (☎ 0242/24-583), for motorcycles; or **Moto Sport,** Odos Kanari 57 (☎ 0242/ 28-316), for mopeds and bicycles.

By Car   It's unlikely that you would need to rent a car for more than a day or two on Kos, even if you wanted to see all its sights and never lift a foot. Several companies rent cars and all-terrain vehicles—including **Autorent** (☎ **0242/28-882**), **Eurodollar** (☎ **0242/27-550**), and **Marion** (☎ **0242/26-293**). Expect to pay at least Dr20,000 ($67) per day including insurance and fuel. Gas stations are open Monday through Saturday from 7am to 7pm; for those who lose track of the day, there are always two stations open (in rotation) in Kos town on Sunday; ask your hotelier or the tourist office for directions to the one currently open.

By Taxi   To book a taxi, drop by or call the **harbor taxi stand** beneath the minaret and across from the castle (☎ **0242/23-333** or 0242/27-777). All Kos taxi drivers are required to know English, but then again we were once required to know trigonometry.

ORIENTATION   Kos town is built around the harbor from which the town fans out. In the center there is an **ancient city** (*polis*) consisting of ruins, an old city limited mostly to pedestrians, and the new city with wide, tree-lined streets. Most of the town's hotels are near the water, either on the road north to Lambi or on the road south and east to Psalidi. If you stand facing the harbor, with the castle on your right, **Lambi** is to your left and **Psalidi** on your right. In general, the neighborhoods to your right are less overrun with and defined by tourists. This area, although quite central, is overall more residential and pleasant. The relatively uncontrolled area to your left (except for the occasional calm oasis, like that occupied by the Pension Alexis) has been largely given over to tourism. Knowing this will help you find most of the tourist-oriented services by day and action by night, as well as where to find a bit of calm when you want to call it quits. Consequently, most recommended places to stay lie to your left, east of the castle.

FAST FACTS: Of the three banks offering foreign-exchange services, the **Ionian Bank of Greece,** Odos El. Venizelou, has the most extensive hours: Monday through Friday from 8am to 2pm and 6 to 8pm. For a **dentist,** contact English-speaking Dr. Fakos Miltiadis, whose office is downtown at Odos Hippokratous 7 (☎ **0242/ 28-350**). **The hospital** is very central at Odos Vas. Pavlou 32 (☎ **0242/22-300**). The **Del Mare Internet Cafe,** Odos M. Alexandrou 4a (☎ **0242/24-244;** www.cybercafe.gr), is open daily from 9am to 3am from October through April, and daily 24 hours from May through September. It serves every drink from tea to cocktails and provides computers for Dr1,500 ($5) per hour. By 1999 it plans to provide quick-cams for an additional Dr1,000 ($3.35). **Happy Wash,** Odos Mitropoleos 20, across from Ayios Nikolaos (☎ **0242/23-424**), is open May through October daily from 8am to 9pm, and November through April daily from 9am to 1:30pm and 4 to 9pm. A 12-pound load costs Dr2,000 ($7) for wash and dry; ironing is Dr400 ($1.35) per shirt or pair of pants. The **post office** on Odos El. Venizelou is open Monday through Friday from 7:30am to 2:30pm; stamps can be purchased at most tourist shops and kiosks. Across from the castle, the **tourist police** office (☎ **0242/22-444**) is open 24 hours to address any outstanding need or emergency, even roomlessness.

WHAT TO SEE & DO

Dominating Mandraki harbor, the **Castle of the Knights** stands in and atop a long line of fortresses defending Kos since ancient times. What you see today was constructed by the Knights of St. John in the 15th century and fell to the Turks in 1522. It's open Tuesday through Sunday from 8:30am to 3pm, but satisfying your curiosity is perhaps the only compelling reason to pay the minimal admission fee of Dr500 ($1.70). The castle is a hollow shell, with nothing of general interest inside that you can't imagine from the outside. Best to stand back and admire this massive reminder of the vigilance that has been a part of life in Kos from prehistory to the present.

At the intersection of Odos Vas. Pavlou and E. Grigoriou stands the **Casa Romana** (☎ **0242/23-234**), a restored 3rd-century Roman villa that straddles what appears to have been an earlier Hellenistic residence. If you have no fire in your belly for ruins, this won't ignite one. Nearby, however, to the east and west of the Casa Romana, are a number of quite interesting open sites, comprising what is in effect a small archaeological park. To the east lie the remains of a **Hellenistic temple** and the **Altar of Dionysos,** and to the west and south a number of impressive excavations and remains, the jewel of which is the **Roman Odeon,** with 18 intact levels of seats. The other extensive area of ruins is in the agora of the **ancient town** just in from Akti Miaouli. Kos town is strewn with archaeological sites opening like fissures and interrupting the flow of pedestrian traffic. Rarely is anything identified for passersby, so they seem like mere barriers or building sites, which is precisely what they were. The rich architectural tradition of Kos did not cease with the eclipse of antiquity—Kos is adorned with a surprising number of striking and significant structures, sacred and secular, enfolded unself-consciously into the modern town.

✪ **Asklepion.** Located 4km (2½ miles) southwest of Kos town. ☎ **0242/28-763.** Admission Dr800 ($2.70) adults, Dr400 ($1.35) students, free for children under 17. Oct to mid-June Tues–Sun 8:30am–3pm; mid-June to Sept Tues–Sun 8:30am–6:30pm.

Unless you have beaches on the brain, this is reason enough to come to Kos. On an elevated site with grand views of Kos town, the sea, and the Turkish coastline, this is the mecca of modern Western medicine, where Hippokrates—said to have lived to the age of 104—founded the first medical school in the late 5th century B.C. For nearly a thousand years after his death, this was a place of healing where physicians were consulted and gods invoked in equal measure. The ruins range in age from the 4th century B.C. to the 2nd century A.D. By the 6th century there were only ruins, later quarried for other projects. Systematic excavation of the site was not begun until 1902.

Kos Museum. Plateia Eleftherias (across from the Municipal Market). ☎ **0242/28-326.** Admission Dr500 ($1.70) adults, Dr250 (85¢) students, free for children under 16. Tues–Sun 8:30am–3pm.

For a town the size of Kos, this is an impressive archaeological museum, built by the Italians in the 1930s to display mostly Hellenistic and Roman sculptures and mosaics uncovered on Kos island. Although there is nothing startling or enduringly memorable in the collection, a visit reminds visitors of the former greatness of this now quite modest port town. Look in the museum's atrium for the lovely 3rd-century mosaic showing how Hippokrates and Pan once welcomed Asklepios, the god of healing, to this, the birthplace of Western medicine.

While You're Here

From the Kos Museum, you might want to walk directly across to the **Municipal Fruit Market,** then have a picnic at the foot of the oldest tree in Europe, only a short walk toward the harbor at the entrance bridge to the castle. Standing with extensive support, this is said to be the **Tree of Hippokrates,** where he once instructed his students in the arts of empirical medicine and its attending moral responsibilities.

OUTDOOR PURSUITS

As already outlined (see "Getting Around," above), the island is especially good for **bicycling,** and rentals are widely available. Guided **horseback excursions** are also available and can be booked at the **Marmari Riding Centre** (☎ 0242/41-783), which offers 1-hour beach rides and 4-hour mountain trail rides. Not surprising, Kos is awash with every sort of water sport. For sailing and yachting, call the **Yachting Club of Kos** (☎ 0242/20-055) or **Istion Sailing Holidays** (☎ 0242/22-195; fax 0242/26-777). For diving, contact the **Kos Diving Centre,** Plateia Koritsas 5 (☎ 0242/20-269 or 0242/22-782) or **Dolphin Divers** (☎ 094/548-149). **Windsurfing** is best on the north side of the island at Tingaki and Marmara, and everything you need, except the skill, may be rented there on the beach. Practically every sort of water-sport activity may be found at the resort town of **Kardamena,** including jet-skiing if you crave speed and the smell of petrol. The best **surfing** is at the furthest southwestern tip of the island on the Kefalos Peninsula near Ayios Theologos. The **Sunset Wave Taverna** rents molded plastic boards by the day for Dr1,500 ($5). For **bird-watchers,** there are at least two unique offerings on the island. Wild peacocks inhabit the forests at Skala, and migrating flamingos frequent the salt-lake preserve just west of Tingaki.

SHOPPING

Kos town is compact and the central shopping area all but fits in the palm of your hand, so you can explore every lane yourself and see what strikes you. If you've grown attached to the traditional music you've been hearing since your arrival in Greece and want some help in making the right selection, stop by either of the **Ti Amo Music Stores,** Odos El. Venizelou 11 and Odos Ipsilandou 4, where Giorgos Hatzidimitris will help you find the traditional or modern Greek music that suits you best. At either shop you may sit and listen before making a purchase.

If you're unwilling to pack another thing, you won't notice the weight of the unique handmade gold medallions at the jewelry shop of **N. Reissi,** opposite the museum at Plateia Kazouli 1 (☎ 0242/28-229). Especially striking are the Kos medallions designed and crafted by Ms. Reissi's father, which go for Dr8,500 to Dr20,000 ($28 to $67). Handcrafted gold rings, charms, and earrings are also on display.

Finally, if you're **treasure-hunting,** you must visit the mountaintop studio of Kos's most eminent artist, **Alexandros Alwyn,** in Evanyelistria (see "Exploring the Island," below). Alwyn is a painter and sculptor of international stature; his work is simply stunning and can be purchased here for a fraction of what it would cost in galleries in New York or London. Another sort of treasure to bring or send home is a **hand-painted Greek icon. Panajiotis Katapods** has been painting icons for over 40 years, both for churches and for individuals. His studio and home are on a lovely hillside little more than a mile west of Kos center at Ayios Nektarios, and visitors are welcome from April through October, Monday through Saturday from 9am to 1pm and 4 to 9pm. The way is well signposted from just east of the Casa Romana.

WHERE TO STAY

The following accommodations are open from mid-April to mid-October, unless otherwise noted. Be forewarned that Kos is not a safe drop-in location in either high or low season, as most places are booked solid in summer and closed tight in winter. Plan ahead and make a reservation well in advance.

MODERATE

Hotel Astron. Akti Kountourioti 31, 85300 Kos. ☎ **0242/23-703.** Fax 0242/22-814. 75 units. TEL. Dr14,500–Dr20,500 ($48–$68) double; Dr18,500–Dr23,500 ($62–$78) suite. Rates include breakfast. AE, MC, V. Open year-round.

This is the most attractive hotel directly on the harbor. The entrance and lobby—a mélange of glass, marble, and Minoan columns—are quite striking and suggest an elegance that does not in fact extend to the rooms and suites. All units are tasteful and very clean, with firm beds and fridges.

The pricier units include extras such as harbor views, air-conditioning, and Jacuzzis. In the larger and more expensive suites, the extra space is designed to accommodate a third person and is wasted if you intend to use it as a sitting area. The only extra worth the money, in our opinion, is a harbor view, but remember that by night you are facing the action—Kos is no retirement community. In summer, about 65% of the rooms here are allotted to package tours. The 14-meter pool, 12-person Jacuzzi, children's wading pool, and patio behind the hotel are pleasant, although diminished by the adjoining vacant lot.

Hotel Kipriotis Village. P.O. Box 206, Psalidi Beach, 85200 Kos. ☎ **0242/27-640.** Fax 0242/23-590. 1,500 beds. A/C TV TEL. Dr28,400 ($95) double; Dr37,050 ($124) apt for 2 (including breakfast). Dr3,700 ($12) extra per person for half-board plan. AE, MC, V.

If you wish to spend part of your vacation amid loads of fun-seeking Europeans with all the possible holiday facilities, try this new luxurious resort, only 4 kilometers (2½ miles) from Kos and right on the beach. Constructed as a village of sorts, the two-story bungalows and apartments surround an attractively designed activity area, which includes five pools; tennis, volleyball, and basketball courts; a state-of-the-art fitness room, sauna, hydromassage, Turkish bath, and solarium. There's a full day of supervised activities for children. With three restaurants and two bars, you never really have to leave the premises, although there is public transportation every 15 minutes into Kos town.

INEXPENSIVE

If you want a place close to both the beach and the nightlife scene, try the **Hotel Theodorou,** Odos G. Papandreou, Psalidi, 85300 Kos (☎ **0242/23-363**; fax 0242/ 23-526). The tariff is on the high side for clean but totally standard Class C accommodations; what you're paying for is the popular Psalidi Beach.

✪ **Hotel Afendoulis.** Odos Evrepilou 1, 85300 Kos. ☎ **0242/25-321.** Fax 0242/25-797. 17 units. TEL. Dr8,000–Dr11,000 ($27–$37) double. No credit cards.

Nowhere in Kos do you receive so much for so little. Nestled in a gracious residential neighborhood a few hundred yards from the water and less than 10 minutes on foot from the very center of Kos, Afendoulis offers the magical combination of convenience and calm. The rooms are clean and altogether welcoming, with firm beds. Nearly all units have private balconies, and most have views of the sea. Whatever room you have, you can't go wrong here. This is a long-established family place, and the Zikas family spare nothing to create within their walls a very special holiday community in which guests enjoy and respect one another. If you are coming to Kos to raise hell, do it anywhere else. Note that the hotel has an elevator.

Although this is likely to be many people's nonnegotiable first choice in Kos, don't despair if you haven't made a reservation. Alexis Zikas holds several extra rooms, including a two-room apartment, open and unreserved in order to accommodate such emergencies.

Hotel Giorgos. Odos Harmilou 9, 85300 Kos. ☎ **0242/23-297.** Fax 0242/27-710. 35 units. TEL. Dr5,000–Dr9,000 ($17–$30) double. Rates include breakfast. V. Open May–Oct.

This is an inviting, family-run hotel a block from the sea and no more than a 15-minute walk from the center of Kos town. Although the immediate neighborhood is not residential, the hotel enjoys a relatively quiet location. Guest rooms are modest and very clean. The carpeting is rather worn, though future plans include their refurbishment. All units have balconies, most with pleasant but not spectacular views of either sea or mountains. Each room contains a fridge, radio, and coffeemaker—and individually controlled central heating makes this an exceptionally cozy small hotel at the chilly edges of the tourist season. Convenience, hospitality, and affordability have made this a place to which guests happily return.

Pension Alexis. Odos Irodotou 9, 85300 Kos. ☎ **0242/28-798.** Fax 0242/25-797. 14 units. Dr6,000–Dr7,000 ($20–$23) double. No credit cards.

Ensconced in a quiet residential neighborhood only a stone's throw from the harbor, Pension Alexis feels like a home because it is one, or was until it opened as a guest house. The expansive rooms have high ceilings and open onto shared balconies. Most have sweeping views of the harbor and the Castle of the Knights. This is a gracious dwelling, with parquet floors and many tasteful architectural touches. Individual rooms are separated off from the halls by sliding doors, and share three large bathrooms. Room no. 4 is a truly grand corner space with knock-out views. What is now a great location will soon become perfect when the new Hippokrates Gardens are installed just across from the pension, closing the one street to cars. In summer, the heart of the pension is the covered veranda facing private gardens, where guests can enjoy breakfast and share their stories late into the night.

WHERE TO DINE

In Kos as anywhere else, there's a lot of fast food, fast consumed and fast forgotten. But there is no need to make eating on Kos a Greek tragedy. The key is to follow the locals, who know how and where not to be disappointed. Along with your meals, you may want to try some of the local wines: the dry **Lafkos,** the red **Appelis,** or the light, subtle **Theokritos** retsina.

EXPENSIVE

✪ **Petrino.** Plateia Theologou 1 (abutting the east extremity of the ancient agora). ☎ **0242/27-251.** Reservations recommended. Appetizers Dr900–Dr1,400 ($3–$4.70); main courses Dr1,600–Dr12,000 ($5–$40). AE, DC, MC, V. Mid-Dec to Nov 5 daily 5pm–midnight. GREEK.

When royalty come to Kos, this is where they dine—so why not live the fantasy yourself? Housed in an exquisitely restored, century-old, two-story stone (*petrino*) private residence, this is hands-down the most elegant taverna in Kos, with cuisine to match. In summer, sit outside on the spacious three-level terrace looking out over the ancient agora; but be sure to take a look inside (especially upstairs), because this is an architectural glory.

Although the menu focuses on Greek specialties, it is vast enough to include lobster, filet mignon, and other Western staples. But don't waste this opportunity to experience Greek traditional cuisine at its best. The stuffed peppers, grilled octopus, and *beki meze* (marinated pork) were perfection. More than 50 carefully selected wines, all Greek, line the cellar—this is your chance to learn why Greece was once synonymous with wine. The dry red kalliga from Kefalonia is exceptional, and a steal at Dr3,300 ($11).

Taverna Mavromatis. Psalidi Beach. ☎ **0242/22-433.** Main courses Dr950–Dr4,500 ($3.15–$15). No credit cards. Apr–Oct daily 11am–11pm. A 20-min. walk southeast of the ferry port, or accessible by the local Psalidi Beach bus. GREEK.

One of the best choices in town is this 30-year-old vine- and geranium-covered taverna run by the Mavromati brothers. Their food is what you came to Greece for: melt-in-your-mouth saganaki, mint- and garlic-spiced sousoutakia, tender grilled lamb chops, and moist beef souvlaki. Prices are reasonable, and the gentle music, waves lapping at your feet, and shaded back patio are delightful.

MODERATE & INEXPENSIVE

Arap (Palatano) Taverna. Platinos-Kermetes. ☎ **0242/28-442.** Appetizers Dr400–Dr700 ($1.35–$2.35); main courses Dr1,100–Dr2,700 ($3.70–$9). No credit cards. Apr–Oct daily 10am–midnight. Located 2km/1¼ miles south of town on the road to the Asklepion. GREEK/TURKISH.

Like the population of Platinos, the menu here is a splendid mix of Greek and Turkish. The pride and spirit of this unpretentious family restaurant is contagious. The menu is extensive, and we know no way of going wrong no matter which direction you take. Although there are many meat dishes, vegetarians will have a feast. The roasted red peppers stuffed with feta and the zucchini flowers stuffed with rice are splendid, as are the bourekakia (a kind of fried pastry roll stuffed with cheese). If you want to be sure to experience the "best of show," just put yourself in the hands of the Memis brothers and let them design your meal. All meals are served with home-baked, grill-toasted pita bread. Afterwards, you can walk across the street for the best homemade ice cream on Kos, an island legend since 1955. This combination is well worth the walk or taxi ride.

Olimpiada. Odos Kleopatras 2. ☎ **0242/23-031.** Main courses Dr1,000–Dr2,100 ($3.35–$7). EURO, MC, V. Daily 11am–11pm. Open year-round. GREEK.

Located around the corner from the Olympic Airways office, this is one of the best values for simple Greek fare. The food is fresh, flavorful, and inexpensive, and the staff is remarkably courteous and friendly. The okra in tomato sauce and the several vegetable dishes are a treat.

Platanos Restaurant. Plateia Platanos. ☎ **0242/28-991.** Main courses Dr1,200–Dr3,200 ($4–$8). EURO, MC, V. Apr–Oct daily noon–11:30pm. GREEK/INTERNATIONAL.

Situated in the best location in Kos overlooking the Hippokrates Tree, this restaurant is in a gorgeous building that was a former Italian officers' club, replete with arches and the original tile floor. Try reserving a place on the upstairs balcony with its impressive vista. The creatively prepared Greek specialties include shrimp in tomato sauce with feta; octopus stifado; and the unusual Hippokrates escalope, prepared with pork, cheese, mushrooms, and asparagus in a béarnaise sauce. For a change of palate, try the Indonesian fillet with pineapple and curry sauce, then an Irish coffee flambé for dessert. Cool, live saxophone and guitar music make for an all-around beautiful setting.

Taverna Ampavris. Odos Ampavris, Ampavris. ☎ **0242/25-696.** Main courses Dr700–Dr2,500 ($2.35–$8). V. Daily 5pm–2am. GREEK.

This is undoubtedly one of the best tavernas on Kos. It's outside the bustling town center on the way to the Asklepion, down a quiet village lane. In the courtyard of this 130-year-old house are served the best local dishes from Kos island. The *salamura* from Kefalos is mouth-watering pork stewed with onions and coriander; the *lahano dolmades* (stuffed cabbage with rice, minced meat, and herbs) is delicate, light, and not at all oily. The *faskebab* (veal stew on rice) is tender and lean, while the vegetable dishes, such as the broad string beans, cooked and served cold in garlic and olive-oil dressing, are out of this world. Hats off to Emanuel Scoumbourdis and his family, who operate this fine place.

☯ Taverna Ampeli. Tzitzifies, Zipari. **☎ 0242/69-682.** Appetizers Dr600–Dr900 ($2–$3); main courses Dr850–Dr2,500 ($2.85–$8); fixed-price dinners Dr1,200–Dr1,600 ($4–$5). V. Apr–Oct daily 10am–midnight; Nov–Mar daily 6–11pm. Closed Easter week and 10 days in early Nov. Just off the beach road 1km/0.6 miles east of Tingaki. Take a bus to Tingaki and walk, or take a taxi. GREEK.

This may be as close as you can come in Kos to authentic Greek home cooking, due in no small part to the fact that here Mom is in the kitchen. Facing the sea and ensconced in its own vineyard, Ampeli is delightful even before you taste the food. The interior is unusually tasteful, with high beamed ceilings, but the outside setting is even better. The dolmades are the best we've had in Greece. Other excellent specialties are the *pliogouri* (gruel), *giouvetsi* (casserole), and *revithokefteves* (meatballs); if you're less venturesome, the fried potatoes here set a new standard. The house retsina, made from the grapes before your eyes, is unusually sweet, almost like a sherry, which may come as a surprise. If you're here on Saturday or midday on Sunday, the Easter-style goat, baked overnight in a low oven, is not to be missed. Ampeli is worth going out of your way for.

Taverna Nikolas. Odos G. Averof 21. **☎ 0242/23-098.** Appetizers Dr600–Dr1,300 ($2–$4.35); main courses Dr850–Dr2,500 ($2.85–$8); fixed-price dinners Dr1,750–Dr2,600 ($6–$9), with a seafood dinner for 2 for Dr6,000 ($20). No credit cards. Daily noon–midnight. GREEK/SEAFOOD.

Known on the street as Nick the Fisherman's, this is one taverna in Kos that wasn't conjured for tourists. Year-round, it's a favorite haunt for locals, with whom you'll have to compete for one of its eight tables—until summer, when seating spills freely out onto the street. Although you can ask for and get everything from filet mignon to goulash, the point of coming here is seafood. If the Aegean has it, you'll find it here: grilled octopus, shrimp in vinegar and lemon, calamari stuffed with cheese, and mussels souvlaki, for a start. The menu is extensive, so come with an appetite.

KOS AFTER DARK

Kos nightlife is no more difficult to find than your own nose. Just go down to the harbor and follow the noise, finding your own level of preference. The **port-side cafes** opposite the daily excursion boats to Kalimnos are best in the early morning. A much more romantic alternative in the evening is the pricier, luxurious **Rendezvous Cafe,** on the east side. Here you can lounge in a striking modern environment or outdoors on the marble terrace, sipping cocktails to live piano accompaniment. **Platanos,** across from the Hippokrates Tree, has live jazz. The lively **Playboy Disco,** Kanari 2, has the most impressive light-and-laser show. On Zouroudi there are two popular discos, **Heaven** and **Calua,** with its swimming pool. If you want to hit the bar scene, try the **Hamam** on Akti Kountourioti, **Beach Boys** at Kanari 57, or **The Blues Brothers** on Dolphins Square.

EXPLORING THE ISLAND

BEACHES The beaches of Kos are no secret. Every foot of the 180 miles of mostly sandy coastline has been discovered. Even so, for some reason, people pack themselves together in tight spaces. You will know the package-tour sites from afar by their umbrellas, dividing the beach into plots measured in centimeters. **Tingaki** and

Kardamena epitomize this avoidable phenomenon. Following are a few quidelines to help you in your quest for uncolonized sand.

The beaches just 3 to 5 kilometers (2 to 3 miles) east of Kos town are among the least congested on the island, probably because they are pebbled instead of sandy. Even so, the view is splendid and the nearby hot springs are worth a good soak. In summer, the water on the **northern coast** of the island is warmer and shallower than that on the south. Because of stronger winds, however, the water is less clear. Also, the beaches are often quite shallow, allowing children a large area to play in before the water reaches their waist or shoulders. If you walk down from the resorts and umbrellas, you will find some relatively open stretches between **Tingaki** and **Mastihari.** Opposite, on the southern coast, **Kamel Beach** and **Magic Beach** are less congested than Paradise Beach, which lies between them. Either can be reached on foot from Paradise Beach, a stop for the Kefalos bus. The southwestern waters are cooler yet calmer than those along the northern shore; and, apart from Kardamena and Kefalos Bay, the beaches on this side of the island are less dominated by package tourists. Finally, for surfers or those interested in wilder environs, the extreme southwestern tip of the island, on the **Kefalos peninsula** near Ayios Theologos, offers a stretch of remote shoreline ideal for surfing and getting lost.

EXPLORING THE HINTERLANDS The most remote and authentic region of the island is comprised of the forests and mountains stretching roughly from just beyond Platani all the way to Plaka in the south. The highest point is Mount Dikeos, reaching nearly 3,000 feet. The mountain villages of this region were once the true center of the island. Only in the last 30 years or so have they been all but abandoned for the lure of more level, fertile land and, since the 1970s, the cash crop of tourism.

There are many ways to explore this region, which begins little more than a mile beyond the center of Kos town. Trekkers will not find this daunting, by car or motorbike it's a cinch, but by mountain bike the ups and downs may be a challenge. Regardless of which way you go, the point is to take your time. You might take a bus from Kos to Zia and walk from Zia to Pili, returning then from Pili to Kos town by bus. The 5-kilometer (3-mile) walk from Zia to Pili will take you through a number of traditional island villages. Sights along the way include the studio of painter-sculptor **Alexandros Alwyn** (a don't miss—see "Shopping," above); the ruins of **old Pili,** a mountaintop castle growing so organically out of the rock that you may miss it; and as your reward at day's end, a **dinner in Zia** at the **Sunset Taverna,** where at dusk the view of Kos island and the sea is magnificent. Zia also has a ceramics shop and a Greek art shop to occupy you as you wait for the last (10pm) KTEL bus to Kos town.

VENTURING OFFSHORE Two very nearby explorations offer unique opportunities. First, there are daily ferries from Kardamena and Kefalos to the small island of **Nissiros.** Nissiros is not only quite attractive, but also has at its center an active volcano which blew the top off the island in 600 B.C. and last erupted in 1873. There are also daily ferries from Kos harbor to **Bodrum, Turkey** (ancient Halikarnassos). Note that you must bring your passport to the boat an hour before sailing so that the captain can draw up the necessary documents for the Turkish port police.

4 Patmos

302km (187 miles) E of Piraeus

Architects sometimes speak of "charged sites," places where something so powerful happened that its memory must always be preserved. Patmos is one such place. It is where **St. John the Divine,** traditionally identified with the Apostle John, spent several years in exile, dwelling in a cave and composing the Apocalypse or the Book of Revelation. From that time on, the island has been regarded as hallowed ground, reconsecrated through the centuries by the erection of more than 300 churches, one for every nine residents. This is not to say that either the people of Patmos or their visitors are expected to spend their days in prayer, but it does say that the Patmians demand and deserve a heavy dose of respect for their traditions, which are so far alive and well.

If we were to compose and dedicate a piece to Patmos, it might be a suite for rooster, moped, and bells (church and goat), for these are the sounds that fill its air. Although it's a remarkably sophisticated island, it is not uncommon to see a farmer guiding his plow behind two donkeys. Patmos is wonderfully unspoiled without being remote. So many other guidebooks highlight the island's prohibitions on nude bathing and how to get around them—but the fact is, if this is a priority for you, then you've stumbled on the wrong island.

ESSENTIALS

GETTING THERE   By Plane   Patmos has no airport, but it is quite convenient (especially by hydrofoil in spring and summer) to three islands which do: Leros, Kos, and Samos. Rather than endure an all but interminable ferry ride from Piraeus, it's convenient to fly from Athens to one of these, then hop a boat or hydrofoil the rest of the way to Patmos.

By Boat   Patmos, the northernmost of the Dodecanese Islands, is on the daily ferry line from Piraeus to Rhodes—schedules should be confirmed in Athens with the **Piraeus Port Authority** (☎ 01/417-2657) or the **Rhodes Port Authority** (☎ 0241/2220). It has numerous sea links with the larger islands of the Dodecanese, as well as with the islands of the northeast Aegean. Options are limited from late fall to early spring, but from Easter through September, sea connections with most of the islands of the eastern Aegean are numerous and convenient.

VISITOR INFORMATION   The **tourism office** (☎ 0247/31-666) in the port town of Skala is directly in front of you as you disembark from your ship; it's open June through August daily from 9am to 10pm. It shares the Italianate "municipal palace" with the post office and the **tourist police** (☎ 0247/31-303), who take over when the tourism office is closed. The **port police** (☎0247/31-231), in the first building on your left on the main ferry pier, are very helpful for boat schedules and whatever else ails or concerns you; they're open year-round, 24 hours a day.

Other useful sources of information are several travel agencies on the harbor near the central square; try **Apollon Tourist and Shipping Agency** (☎0247/31-724; fax 0247/31-819), open year-round from 8am to noon and 4 to 6pm, with extended summer hours. Apollon can help you book excursion boats and hydrofoils and will arrange your lodging in hotels, rental houses, and apartments throughout the island. **Astoria Tourist and Shipping Agency** (☎ 0247/31-205; fax 0247/31-975) is also quite helpful. For the "do-it-yourselfer" in you, pick up a free copy of *Patmos Summertime.* It should be noted, however, that the map of the island provided in that publication is grossly inaccurate. Figure that out!

GETTING AROUND   By Bus   The entire island has only one bus, whose current schedule is available at the tourist office and is posted at various locations on the island. Needless to say, it can provide only very limited service—to Skala, Hora, Grikos, and Kampos—so it's probably best to think of other ways to get around.

By Moped & Bicycle   Mopeds are definitely the vehicle of choice on the island. At the rental shops that line the harbor, 1-day rentals start around Dr2,500 ($8) and go up to Dr4,000 ($13) depending on the size and power of the machine. Peter Michalis at **Australis Motor Rent** (☎ 0247/32-284) operates a first-rate shop, and is quite conscientious. You can also contact "Billis" (☎ 0247/32-218) on the harbor in Skala or Camel (☎ 0247/31-134). Bicycles are hard to come by on the island, but Iannis Apostololidis has mountain bikes for Dr1,000 ($3.35) per day at **Auto-Moto** (☎ 0247/34-115), on the harbor in Skala, as does **Theo & Georgio's** (☎ 0247/ 32-066), just behind Astoria Shipping, for Dr1,200 ($4) per day.

By Car   Two convenient car-rental offices, both in Skala, are **Auto-Moto** (☎ 0247/ 34-115), on the harbor, and **Patmos Rent-a-Car** (☎ 0247/32-203), just behind the police station. Daily rentals range from Dr8,000 to Dr15,000 ($27 to $50), depending on what kind of car you're looking for. The island has only one gas station, the **Argo** station at the east side of the harbor in Skala, open from 7am to 7pm. After that, you're out of luck.

By Taxi   The island's main taxi stand is on the pier in Skala Harbor, right before your eyes as you get off the boat. From anywhere on the island, you can request a taxi by calling ☎ 0247/31-225. As the island is quite small, it's much cheaper to hire a taxi than to rent a car.

ORIENTATION   Patmos lies along a north-south axis; were it not for a narrow central isthmus, it would be two islands, north and south. Skala, the island's only town of any size, is situated very near that isthmus joining the north island to the south. Above Skala looms the hilltop capital of Hora, comprising a mazelike medieval village and the fortified monastery of St. John the Divine. There are really only two other towns on Patmos: Kambos to the north and Grikou to the south. While Kampos is a real village of roughly 500 inhabitants, Grikou is mostly a resort, a creation of the tourist industry.

Most independent visitors to Patmos, especially first-timers, will choose to stay in **Skala** (Hora has no hotels or pensions) and explore the north and south from there. Patmos is genuinely infectious, an island to which visitors, Greek and foreign, return year after year. Consequently, on your first visit to Patmos, it makes sense to be centrally located. And, from then on, when you return, you will have no need for our advice.

FAST FACTS   The **Commercial Bank of Greece** on the harbor and the **National Bank of Greece** on the central square offer exchange services and ATMs. Both are open Monday through Thursday from 8am to 2pm and Friday from 8am to 1:30pm. You will also find an ATM where ferries and cruises dock at the main pier. For **dental emergencies,** contact Dr. Dmitra Makka-Giamaiou at ☎ 0247/33-147. The island's **hospital** (☎ 0247/31-211) is on the road to Hora. There is also a **medical clinic** (☎ 093/40-24-24) next to the **telephone office (OTE),** which is a local landmark. **Dr. Damianos Aslanvoglou,** an internist whose office is just in from the central square of Skala, can be reached at ☎ 0247/31-232 or, in an emergency, at ☎ 093/ 40-24-24. A short walk down towards the new port will bring you to **Just Like Home**

For Your Health

One essential you need to know about Patmos from the outset is that tap water is not for drinking. *Drink only bottled water.*

(☎ 0247/33-170), where a load of laundry, dried and folded, will cost Dr3,000 ($10). It's open daily until 9pm year-round, and 24 hours a day in July and August. Cold-water wash and rinse are available, as is hand washing. The **post office** on the harbor is open Monday through Friday from 8am to 1:30pm. The **tourist police** (☎ 0247/31-303) are directly across from you as you disembark at port.

WHAT TO SEE & DO

What Patmos lacks in quantity it makes up in quality. Apart from its natural beauty and its 300-plus churches, to which we can't possibly provide a detailed guide here, there are several extraordinary sights: the **Monastery of St. John,** the **Cave of the Apocalypse,** and the medieval town of **Hora.** The latter is simply there to be explored, a labyrinthine maze of whitewashed stone homes, shops, and churches, in which getting lost is the whole point.

The days and times of opening for the **cave** and the **monastery** are unpredictable, as they are designed to accommodate groups of pilgrims and cruise-ship tours rather than individual visitors. Neither is it a public place. The cave is enclosed within a convent, and the monastery is just that. It is best to consult the tourist office or one of the travel agents listed above for the open hours on the day of your visit. To visit both places, appropriate attire is required, which means that women must wear long skirts or dresses, and men must wear long pants.

The road to Hora is well marked from Skala; but if you are walking, take the narrow lane to the left just past the central square. Once outside the town, you can mostly avoid the main road by following the uneven stone-paved donkey path which is the traditional pilgrims' route to the sanctuaries above.

○ **Cave of the Apocalypse.** On the road to Hora. ☎ 0247/31-234. Free admission. Hours vary; contact the tourist office or a travel agent (see above).

Exiled to Patmos by the Roman Emperor Domitian in A.D. 95, St. John the Divine is said to have made his home in this cave, though Patmians insist quite reasonably that he walked every inch of the small island, talking with its people. The cave is said to be the epicenter of his earth-shaking revelation, which he dictated to his disciple and which has come down as the Book of the Apocalypse, or Revelation, the last book of the Christian Bible. The cave is now encased within a sanctuary, which is in turn encircled by a convent. A stirring brochure written by Archimandrite Koutsanellos, Superior of the Cave, provides an excellent description of the religious significance of each niche in the rocks, as well as the many icons in the cave. Other guides are also available in local tourist shops. The best preparation, of course, is to bone up on the Book of Revelation.

○ **Monastery of St. John.** Hora. ☎ 0247/31-234. Admission free to monastery; Dr1,000 ($3.35) to treasury. Hours vary (see above).

Towering over Skala and, for that matter, over the south island, is the medieval Monastery of St. John, which looks far more like a fortress than a house of prayer. Built to withstand pirates, it is certainly up to the task of deterring runaway tourism. The monastery virtually controls the south island, where the mayor wears a hat but the monastic authority wears a miter. In 1088, with a hand-signed document from the Byzantine Emperor Alexis I Comnenus ceding the entire island to the future monastery, Blessed Christodoulos arrived on Patmos to establish here what was to become an independent monastic state. The monastery chapel is stunning, as is the adjoining **Chapel of the Theotokos,** whose frescoes date from the 12th century. On display in the treasury are but a fraction of the monastery's exquisite Byzantine treasures, second only to those of the monastic state of Mount Athos.

OUTDOOR PURSUITS

The principal outdoor activities on Patmos are walking and swimming. The best **beaches** are highlighted below (see "Exploring the Island") and the best **walking trails** are the unmarked donkey paths which crisscross the island. You won't find jet-skis or surfboards on Patmos, although limited **water sports** are available. Paddleboats and canoes can be rented and waterskiing arranged on Agriolivada Beach at Hellen's Place, as well as on the beach at Grikos. Also at Grikos is a **summer club** where you can join in a volleyball game or play tennis (rackets and balls provided) for about Dr1,000 ($3.35) per person, per hour.

SHOPPING

Patmians are quick to lament and apologize for the fact that just about everything, from petrol to toothpaste, is a bit more expensive here. Patmos doesn't even have its own drinking water, and import costs inevitably get passed along to the customer. That said, the price differences are much more evident to the locals than to tourists.

There are several excellent jewelry shops, like **Iphigenia** (☎ 0247/31-814) and **Midas** (☎ 0247/31-800) on the harbor, though **Filoxenia** (☎ 0247/31-667) and most notably the **Art Spot** (☎ 0247/32-243), both just behind the main square in the direction of Hora, have more interesting contemporary designs, often influenced by ancient motifs. The Art Spot also sells ceramics and small sculptural works, and is well worth seeking out. Farther down the same lane you'll find **Parousia** (☎ 0247/ 32-549), the best single stop for hand-painted icons and a wide range of books on Byzantine subjects, local and general. An added bonus is that the proprietor, Mr. A. Alafakis, is quite learned in the history and craft of icon painting and can tell you a great deal about the individual icons in his shop and the diverse traditions that they represent.

The most fascinating shop on Patmos may be **Selene** (☎ 0247/31-742), directly across from the Port Authority office. The highly selective array of Greek handmade art and crafts here is extraordinary, from ceramics to hand-painted Russian and Greek icons to marionettes, some as tall as 4 feet.

WHERE TO STAY IN SKALA

There are no hotels or pensions in Hora, although Skala makes up for it. Unless you're planning to visit Patmos during Greek or Christian Easter or from late July through August, you should not have difficulty finding some suitable accommodation upon arrival, though it is always safer to book ahead. You will probably be met at the harbor by residents offering private accommodations. If you're interested in renting a kitchenette apartment or villa, contact the **Apollon Agency** (☎ 0247/31-724; fax 0247/31-819) for more information.

The following listings are open from mid-April to mid-October unless otherwise noted.

MODERATE

Blue Bay Hotel. Skala, 85500 Patmos. ☎ **0247/31-165.** Fax 0247/32-303. 26 units. TEL. Dr12,000–Dr15,400 ($40–$51) double; Dr13,500–Dr18,000 ($45–$60) suite. No credit cards.

Two unique features distinguish this hotel. First, its location on the southwest side of the harbor offers both convenience and quiet. Second, guests are requested not to smoke anywhere in the hotel except on their private balconies. The rooms are spacious, immaculate, and comfortable, and there is a special emphasis here on service. Room nos. 114 and 115 share a terrace the size of a tennis court overlooking the sea. In addition to the breakfast room, there is a private bar.

Porto Scoutari. Scoutari, 85500 Patmos. ☎ **0247/33-123.** Fax 0247/33-175. www.12net.gr/scoutari. 32 units. A/C MINIBAR TV TEL. Dr14,000–Dr32,000 ($47–$107) double. Rates include full "American brunch." AE, CB, DC, MC, V. Open year-round. Note that this hotel overlooks, but is not in, Meloï Bay—so follow the signs to Kampos, not to Meloï Bay. It's less than 2 miles from the center of Skala.

High on a bluff overlooking Meloï Bay, this new luxury hotel is seductively gracious, with the largest rooms (45 square meters) and the largest pool on the island. Ground-level suites are designed with families in mind, while upper-level suites, with four-poster beds and bathtubs, have honeymoon written all over them. The decor, a blend of reproduction antiques and contemporary design, offers elegance and comfort. Each bungalow-style suite has a kitchenette, year-round climate control, and ample private balcony. The common areas—breakfast room, lounge, piano bar, and pool—are both informal and refined. A private minibus provides local tours and transport for guests.

Romeos Hotel. Skala, 85500 Patmos. ☎ **0247/31-962.** Fax 0247/31-070. 60 units. TEL. Dr23,000 ($77) double; Dr27,000 ($90) suite. Rates include breakfast. EURO, MC, V.

Of all Skala's newer lodgings, this one in the back streets behind the OTE is especially commodious. It has a quite large pool and a quiet garden. Run by a Greek-American family from Virginia, the Romeos has spotless rooms with simple decor and country-side-view balconies. The rooms are built like semiattached bungalows on a series of tiers, with views across to Mount Kastelli. The larger honeymoon suites, with double beds, full bathtubs, and a small lounge, are another option. The only slight downside is the undeveloped lot in front of the property, hardly a factor at all once you're inside the hotel compound.

Skala Hotel. Skala, 85500 Patmos. ☎ **0247/31-343.** Fax 0247/31-747. 78 units. TV TEL. Dr20,000 ($67) double. Rates include breakfast. AE, MC, V.

Tranquilly but conveniently situated well off the main harbor road behind a lush garden overflowing with arresting pink bougainvillea, this comfortable hotel has aged like a fine wine to become an established Skala favorite. Attractive features include the beautifully landscaped garden, a large pool with an inviting sundeck and bar, a large breakfast buffet, climate control and fridges in all rooms, and personalized service. The three views to choose from are the sea, the western mountains, and the Monastery of St. John—and all are striking. At Easter or in late July and August, you're likely to be out of luck without an advance reservation, but at other times, you'll probably be able to find a room here.

INEXPENSIVE

Australis Hotel. Skala, 85500 Patmos. ☎ **0247/31-576.** 25 units. Dr10,000–Dr13,000 ($33–$43) double. Rates include breakfast. No credit cards. A 5-minute walk from the center of Skala.

On approach, you may have misgivings regarding the location of this hotel, just off the currently cluttered and somewhat unsightly new port area. But your doubts will vanish when you enter the charming hotel compound, a veritable blooming hillside oasis. Once featured in *Garden Design* magazine, the grounds are covered with bright bougainvillea, fuchsias, dahlias, and roses. The pleasant communal porch, where breakfast is served, offers delightful views of the open harbor. The guest rooms are bright, tasteful, and impeccably clean, with the best (firmest) beds we've so far found in Greece. Currently under construction are four lovely apartments ample for families, with good views of the sea and mountains. While the rates for these new apartments have not yet been determined, a one-bedroom unit for two persons is likely to be about Dr25,000 to Dr30,000 ($83 to $100) in high season (and about half that in low season). Already finished is one appealing garden studio apartment—especially quiet and cool. The owners' younger son, Peter, rents mopeds here, while the older son, Michael, has three handsome new studios over his house on the old road to Hora. Each has a well-stocked kitchen and goes for Dr12,000 ($40) per day.

Castelli Hotel. Skala, 85500 Patmos. ☎ **0247/31-361.** Fax 0247/31-656. 45 units. TEL. Dr9,000–Dr13,500 ($30–$45) double. Rates include breakfast. No credit cards.

Guests are accommodated here in two white-stucco blocks framed with brown shutters. The striking vista can be enjoyed from cushioned wrought-iron chairs on the balconies. Guest rooms, with beige tile floors, are large and spotless, while the common lounge and lobby areas are filled with photographs, flower-print sofas, seashells, fresh-cut flowers from the surrounding gardens, and other knickknacks of seaside life. Such good care and charm make this a good value.

Villa Knossos. Skala, 85500 Patmos. ☎ **0247/32-189.** Fax 0247/32-284. 7 units. Dr7,000–Dr10,000 ($23–$33) double. No credit cards.

This small white villa just off the new port is set within an abundant garden of palms, purple and pink bougainvillea, potted geraniums, and hibiscus. The tasteful bedrooms are spacious with high ceilings, and all but one has a private balcony. The two units facing the back garden are the most quiet, while room no. 7 in front has its own private veranda. A communal fridge is available in the guests' sitting room.

WHERE TO DINE IN SKALA & HORA

There are only two exceptional restaurants on Patmos, whose reputations extend well beyond the island—the **Patmian House** and the **Arhonitko**—but the island also has a large number of tavernas and estiatoria where you will be well pleased without straining your budget. Unless otherwise stated, the restaurants and tavernas listed below are open from Easter through October.

EXPENSIVE

Arhontiko Restaurant. Hora. ☎ **0247/31-668.** Reservations necessary in high season. Appetizers Dr850–Dr1,600 ($2.85–$5); main courses Dr1,000–Dr3,950 ($3.35–$13). No credit cards. Daily 7:30pm–1am. GREEK/PROVINCIAL.

French owner Ghisleine Lesvigne spent 10 years lovingly restoring this nobleman's stone villa, built originally in 1645. Exposing the ancient walls and floors revealed a templar cross, an ancient well, and ceramic implements, which now decorate the premises. The delightful ambiance, mellow lighting, and soft classical music accompany attentive service and fine cuisine. The French touch is evident in the homemade pâté, with Provençal herbs and nuts in an onion marmalade. The grilled fillet with Provençal herbs was tasty, tender, and prepared exactly as requested. The spinach with creme and basil and the gratin dauphinois were likewise memorable. The delectable, light chocolate mousse was a worthy coup de grâce to this gourmet cuisine.

✪ **Patmian House.** Hora. ☎ **0247/31-180.** Reservations recommended. Appetizers Dr800–Dr1,000 ($2.70–$3.35); main courses Dr1,200–Dr3,600 ($4–$12). No credit cards. Daily 7pm–midnight. On the back lanes behind Plateia Xanthos. GREEK/CONTINENTAL.

It shouldn't surprise you that sophisticated Hora features one of the best and most interesting Greek restaurants in the country. Set in a restored 17th-century dwelling, it has been glowingly reviewed in *Vogue, The Athenian,* and *European Travel and Life.* Victor Gouras, a Patmian gourmand who worked at Tavern on the Green and other top New York restaurants, and his talented wife, Irene, have created the perfect place for a special evening. To start, we recommend the taramosalata, gigantes (giant beans) in garlic sauce, or the tasty zucchini fritters. The varied selection of main courses includes a superb rabbit stifado flavored with juniper berries, and a Patmian vegetarian specialty, *melitzanes me revithia* (a casserole of eggplant and chickpeas). Ask the Gouras family about any fish, steak, or meat specialties of the day, and don't miss the *diples,* a honey-dipped dessert.

MODERATE

Grigoris Grill. Opposite Skala car ferry pier. ☎ **0247/31-515.** Appetizers Dr450–Dr900 ($1.50–$3); main courses Dr900–Dr2,300 ($3–$8). No credit cards. Daily 6pm–midnight. GREEK.

One of Skala's better-known eateries, this place was formerly the center of Patmian chic. We recommend any of the grilled fish or meat dishes, particularly in the low season, when more care and attention are paid to preparation. Well-cooked veal cutlets, large, tender lamb chops, and the swordfish souvlaki are favorites. Grigoris also offers several vegetarian specials.

Stefanos. Skala (new port). ☎ **0247/32-884.** Appetizers Dr600–Dr1,300 ($2–$4.35); main courses Dr700–Dr2,400 ($2.35–$8). No credit cards. Daily 6–11pm. SEAFOOD.

This unpretentious fish taverna offers very little in the way of decor except that provided by the harbor lights when the tables spill out front in the summer; equally little attention is paid to presentation and service. That said, you're here to eat—and this is where Stefanos comes through. The grilled red snapper, for Dr2,000 ($7), is extraordinary. Best to ask to see what's fresh, then leap for that. This is a real local place with lots of families dropping anchor for the evening.

INEXPENSIVE

Olympia Taverna. Hora (follow signs to Vagelis). ☎ **0247/31-543.** Main courses Dr650–Dr1,500 ($2.15–$5). No credit cards. Mon–Sat noon–2pm and 6:30pm–midnight. GREEK.

This taverna on picturesque Plateia Theofakosta, less frequented by tourists because of its low-key presence, is favored by the locals and by us for its traditional Greek home-style cooking. Try the octopus *giuvetsi* (casserole); the eggplants stuffed with meat, feta cheese, and béchamel sauce; and a slab of their famous walnut cake, all delicious and inexpensive. In summer the roof garden provides open-air dining with great views.

✪ **Pantelis Restaurant.** Skala (1 lane back from the port). ☎ **0247/31-230.** Appetizers Dr450–Dr1,200 ($1.50–$4); main courses Dr700–Dr1,700 ($2.35–$6). No credit cards. Daily 11am–11pm. GREEK.

Pantelis is a proven local favorite for no-frills Greek home cooking. Modesty aside, the food here is consistently fresh and wholesome—the basics prepared so well that they surprise you. Daily specials augment the standard menu. Portions are generous, so pace yourself, and if you're not yet a convert to the Greek cult of olive oil, speak up or order something grilled. The lightly fried calamari, chickpea soup, swordfish kebab, and roasted lamb were all up to expectation. The spacious dining hall with very high ceilings makes this a relatively benign environment for nonsmokers.

PATMOS AFTER DARK

The scene here, while not ecclesiastical, doesn't swing. Going to Patmos for nightlife is a little like going to Indiana to ski. Skala has the **Music Club 2000,** past the new port, next to the Arga station, with an air-conditioned dance hall going strong—or at least going—until 5am, as well as the **Konsolato Music Club,** to the left of the quay. Both Hora and Skala have a number of bars, which you can't miss. On a more traditional note, the **Aloni Restaurant** in Hora offers Greek music and dance performances in traditional costume every Wednesday and Saturday night in summer.

EXPLORING THE ISLAND

Apart from the seductive contours of the Patmian landscape, the myriad seascapes, and the seemingly countless churches, it's the **beaches** of Patmos that draw most visitors beyond the island's core. Don't be tempted to think of the strand between the old and new ports in Skala as a beach. Better and safer to take a shower in your room. Most beaches have tavernas on or very near the beach, as well as rooms to rent by the day or week. They're too numerous and similar to list here.

THE NORTH ISLAND

The most desirable beaches in the north lie along the northeastern coastline from Lambi Bay to Meloï Bay. The northwestern coastline from Merika Bay to Lambi is too rocky, inaccessible, and exposed to warrant recommendation. The most desirable northern beaches are located in the following bays (proceeding up the coast from south to north): **Meloï, Agriolivada,** and **Lambi.** Meloï offers some shade and good snorkeling. **Kambos Bay** is particularly suitable for children and families, offering calm, shallow waters, rental umbrellas, and some tree cover, as well as a lively seaside scene with opportunities for windsurfing, paragliding, sailing, and canoeing. Its waterside taverna also happens to serve the best lobster on the island. East of Kambos Bay at Livada, it's possible to swim or sometimes to walk across to **Ayiou Yioryiou Isle;** be sure to bring shoes or sandals, or the rocks will do a number on your feet. The stretch of shoreline from **Thermia to Lambi** is gorgeous, with crystalline waters and some rocks from which you can safely dive. The drawback here is that access is only by caïque (from Skala). Also, avoid the north coast when the meltemies (severe north summer winds) are blowing.

Where to Stay & Dine

Patmos Paradise. Kambos Bay, 85500 Patmos. ☎ **0247/32-590.** Fax 0247/32-740. 37 units. TEL. Dr15,000–Dr34,000 ($50–$113) double. Rates include breakfast. AE, MC, V. Open Easter–Oct.

Perched high above Kambos Bay, this is one of several upscale hotels on the island. The rooms are spacious and inviting, with private balconies that enjoy spectacular views. Amenities include a large terrace pool, sauna, fitness center (not that you need one if you explore Patmos on foot), and tennis and squash courts. This place is exceptionally pleasant, but for luxury accommodation on Patmos we prefer the new Porto Scoutari Hotel (see "Where to Stay in Skala," above).

Taverna Panagos. Kambos. ☎ **0247/31-570.** Appetizers Dr350–Dr700 ($1.15–$2.35); main courses Dr550–Dr1,900 ($1.85–$6). No credit cards. Mon–Sat noon–midnight. GREEK.

Just above Kambos Bay sits the sleepy village of Kambos, hosting two tavernas, this one and the one next door (Kavourakia), which a lesser detective than Sherlock Holmes might mistake for an extension. (Needless to say, there is some rivalry here.) Panagos, with its rattan chairs and checkered tablecloths, is what catches the eye, and its fare does not disappoint. The zucchini with thyme and Patmian goat in lemon sauce were excellent.

THE SOUTH ISLAND

There are two principal beaches in the south of the island, one at **Grikou Bay** and the other at **Psili Ammos.** Grikou Bay, only 4 kilometers (2½ miles) from Skala, is the most developed resort on Patmos and home to most of the package-tour holidays on the island. Psili Ammos is another story, an extraordinary isolated fine-sand cove bordered by cliffs. Most people arrive by the caïque leaving Skala at 10:30am and proceed to do battle for the very limited shade offered by some obliging tamarisks. The only way to assure yourself of a place in the shade is to arrive before 10:30am. The best way to get there is to take a taxi to Diakofti for Dr1,500 ($5) and ask the driver to point out the way to Psili Ammos, which is from there about a 30-minute trek on goat paths (wear real shoes). The caïque returning to Skala leaves Psili Ammos around 3:30pm.

Where to Stay & Dine

Joanna Hotel-Apartments. Grikos, 85500 Patmos. ☎ **0247/31-031.** Fax 0247/32-031, or 01/981-2246 in Athens. 17 units. TEL. Dr10,000–Dr16,000 ($33–$53) apt for 2 persons. Full hot breakfast Dr1,000 ($3.35) extra per person. V. Open Easter to mid-Oct.

These comfortable, relatively spacious and fully equipped apartments are situated just 200 yards from the beach. Each has a fridge, kitchenette, balcony, and fan. The layout and feel of the one-bedroom apartments is better than that of the two-bedroom apartments, in which the kitchen area is very limited. Some have air-conditioning (ask, if you want it). Room no. 15 has a large private deck enjoying a sea view, but is usually reserved for friends, clients, and guests staying 2 to 3 weeks—still, there's no harm in asking. A special feature is the attractive air-conditioned lounge with satellite TV and a bar.

Petra Apartments. Grikos, 85500 Patmos. ☎ **0247/34-020.** Fax 0247/31-035, or 01/806-2697 in Athens. 25 units. TEL. Dr24,700 ($82) apt for 2 persons. No credit cards. Open Easter–Oct.

The Stergiou family takes loving care of our favorite lodging in Grikos. If the folks aren't home, Christos and his sheepdog Lumpi will happily show you around these stylish apartments, made into one- or two-bedroom units with small kitchenettes, compact bathrooms, and verandas with wonderful views over Grikos Bay. Each is simply but carefully decorated, with the necessities of home plus some local color. It's a perfect family place, just a 5-minute walk from the beach, but with an elegant outdoor bar for the adults. It's popular with Europeans in August, so early reservations are advised.

Stamatis Restaurant. Grikos Beach. ☎ **0247/31-302.** Appetizers Dr550–Dr1,400 ($1.85–$4.70); main courses Dr900–Dr1,500 ($3–$5). No credit cards. Daily 10am–11pm. Open Easter–Oct. GREEK.

Eleni is the talented chef at this reliable restaurant located adjacent to the pier. On the covered terrace, diners enjoy drinks and consume prodigious amounts of fresh mullet while watching yachts and windsurfers. This is a very pleasant spot to let the evening unravel while enjoying delicious island fare.

Central Greece 12

by Sherry Marker

Central Greece (Sterea Ellada) is the least well defined area of the country. Unlike, for example, the Peloponnese, which is clearly set off from the rest of Greece by the Corinth Canal, or Macedonia, which has a distinct identity, Central Greece is harder to define. In fact, the name Central Greece dates only from 1821, when it was used as a shorthand term for the area of mainland Greece that had been liberated from the Turks. Today, most Greeks would agree that Central Greece stretches from Boetia and Phocis in the south to as far north as Thessaly. Some Greeks hold that Mount Olympus is the southernmost point in Northern Greece, while others consider Olympus to be the northernmost point in Central Greece.

When you set off for Central Greece, keep in mind that you will be traveling through one of Greece's most varied landscapes. There's the shore that runs along the Gulf of Corinth and the heights of Mount Parnassus. This is where Greece's most famous ancient oracle and most beautiful ancient site, Delphi, is located. There's the city of Thebes, famed for its magnificence in Mycenaean days, today an undistinguished modern town. There's the dusty plain of Thessaly and the extraordinary cliffs and promontories of the monasteries of the Meteora. And there's the lush, wooded mountain range of Mount Pelion, studded with small traditional villages. As if that weren't enough, there are famous ancient battle sites—Thermopylae and Chaironeia—and one of the famous beauty spots of Greece, the Vale of Tempe.

STRATEGIES FOR EXPLORING THE REGION If you are setting off from Athens, head via Thebes to Osios Loukas and Delphi and try to spend 2 nights in Delphi. Then head up to the Meteora for another night or two. From there, cross over to Volos and Mount Pelion, where you could easily spend a week relaxing in the mountain villages and taking in some of the best beaches. If you feel like making extra excursions en route, you'll find plenty of suggestions in what follows.

1 Delphi

178km (110 miles) NW of Athens

Delphi is the big enchilada of Greek sites. More than even Olympia, this place has everything: a long and glorious history, spectacular ancient remains, a superb museum, and a heartbreakingly beautiful

Central Greece

Aegean Sea

ALONISSOS

SKIATHOS

SKOPELOS

EVVIA

Pelion Peninsula

Pagasitic Gulf

Gulf of Evvia

Corinthian Gulf

Ionian Sea

Mt. Olympus

Mt. Pelion

Mt. Parnassus

ZAGORI

Lake Pamvotis

Litochoro
Leptokaria
Platamonas
Elassona
Tirnavos
Larissa
Ayia
Makrinitsa
Volos
Almiros
Farsala
Palamas
Karditsa
Meteora (Kalambaka)
Trikkala
Metsovo
Ioannina
Agrinio
Karpenissi
Messolongi
Patras
Lamia
Stilida
Thermopylae
Kamena Vourla
Ayios Konstandinos
Glifa
Amfissa
Arachova
Delphi
Osios Loukas
Livadia
Distomo
Orchomenos
Thebes
Eleftsina
Megara
Ayia Marina
Athens

Platamonas

25 mi
25 km
0

Delphi,
Site and Museum ❸

The Meteora
Monasteries of
Ayia Triada,
Ayios Nikolaos
Anapaphsas,
Ayiou Stefanou,
The Great Meteoron,
Roussanou,
and Varlaam ❶

Monastery of
Osios Loukas ❹

The Vale of Tempe ❷

Legend
- - - Ferry Routes
▲ Mountain

20
15
6
5
20
11
3
6
27
27
48
8a
5
1
3
44
1
8a

❶ ❷ ❸ ❹

location on the slopes of Mount Parnassus. Look up and you see the cliffs and crags of Parnassus; look down and you see Greece's most beautiful plain of olive trees stretching as far as the eye can see toward the town of Itea on the Gulf of Corinth.

Delphi is especially magical in the spring, when there's both snow and wildflowers on Parnassus—and relatively few tourists tramping around the site. But whenever you come here, you'll understand why the ancient Greeks believed that Delphi was the center of the world, the spot Apollo chose as the home of his most famous oracle.

A LOOK AT THE PAST   Pilgrims came to Delphi from all of the Greek world and much of the non-Greek world to ask Apollo's advice on affairs of state as well as small, personal matters. Unfortunately, the god's words were famously hard to interpret. "Invade and you will destroy a great empire," the oracle told Lydian King Croesus when he asked whether he should go to war with his Persian neighbors. Croesus invaded and destroyed a great empire: his own.

Delphi was also the site of the Pythian Games, the most famous festival in Greece after the Olympics. The games commemorated Apollo's triumph over his oracular predecessor here, the snaky Python. Because Apollo was the god of music, the Pythian games had more artistic contests than the Olympic Games. When you sit in the theater here, you can imagine the flute and lyre contests and the dances and plays staged every 4 years throughout antiquity to honor Apollo.

Like so many ancient sites, Apollo's sanctuary at Delphi was first neglected, then virtually forgotten, during the Christian era. Kings and generals looted Delphi of its treasures; later, locals hacked up the buildings to build their houses. The modern village of Delphi sat atop the ancient site until this century, when it was relocated just down the road so that archaeologists could help Delphi reclaim its past.

ESSENTIALS

GETTING THERE   By Bus   There are five daily buses to Delphi from the Athens bus station at Odos Liossion 260 (☎ 01/831-7096).

By Car   Take the Athens-Corinth National Highway 74 kilometers (46 miles) west of Athens to the Thebes turnoff. Continue west to Levadia. If you wish to stop at the monastery of Osios Loukas, take the Distomo turnoff and continue 9 kilometers (5½ miles) to Osios Loukas. Return to Distomo and continue via Arachova 26 kilometers (16 miles) or the seaside town of Itea 65 kilometers (40 miles) to Delphi. The approach from Itea is well worth the time, if you are not in a hurry.

VISITOR INFORMATION   Most services, such as the post office and banks, are located in the village of Delphi (population 2,500) on the obvious main street, which is named after King Paul and Queen Frederika, although no one seems to use the name. The ancient site (signposted) is about 1 kilometer (0.6 miles) out of town, on the Arachova Road.

GETTING AROUND   If you can, you should walk everywhere in Delphi. Parking places are at a premium both in the village and at the site. If you have to drive to the site rather than making the 5- to 10-minute walk from town, be sure to set off early to get one of the few parking places. Whether you walk or drive, keep an eye out for the enormous tour buses that barrel down the center of the road—and for the not terribly well marked one-way streets in the village.

FAST FACTS   You can exhange currency at the **National Bank of Greece** on the main street, which, in addition to normal weekday hours, is sometimes open from 6 to 7pm in summer; the bank has an ATM. The **police** are in the town hall on the main street. Both the **post office** and the **telephone office** are on the main street. In addition to normal weekday hours (Mon through Fri from 8am to 2pm), the post office and OTE are sometimes open Sunday from 9am to 1pm. The **tourist office** (☎ 0265/82-900), in the town hall on the main street, is open Monday through Friday from 8am to 2:30pm and sometimes reopens from 6 to 8pm in summer.

WHAT TO SEE & DO

As at Olympia, the most important thing is to begin your visit as early as possible. Note that starting your day at the museum will give you an overall understanding of the site, and you'll then be able to visualize many of the important works of art that decorated the sanctuary on your visit. *Tip:* Both the site and museum are sometimes relatively uncrowded during the hour before closing time.

The Delphi Museum. Delphi. ☎ 0265/82-313. Admission Dr1,200 ($4). Summer Mon 11am–7pm; Tues–Fri 8am–7pm; Sat–Sun and holidays 8am–3pm. Winter Mon 11am–5:30pm; Tues–Fri 8am–5:30pm; Sat–Sun and holidays 8am–3pm.

The first thing you'll see in the museum is a 4th-century B.C. **marble egg,** a copy of the yet older egg (or *omphalos*) that symbolized Delphi's unique position as the center (or naval) of the world. According to legend, when Zeus wanted to determine the earth's center, he released two eagles from Olympus. When the eagles met over Delphi, Zeus had his answer. You may still see eagles in the sky above Delphi, but more often than not, the large birds overhead are the less distinguished Egyptian vultures.

Each of the museum's 13 rooms has a specific focus: sculpture from the elegant **Siphnian treasury** in one room, finds from the **Temple of Apollo** in two rooms, finds from the Roman period (including a marble sculpture of the epicene youth **Antinous,** the beloved of the emperor Hadrian) in another.

The star of the museum, with a room to himself, is the famous 5th-century B.C. **Charioteer of Delphi,** a larger-than-life bronze figure that was part of a group that originally included a four-horse chariot. The wealthy Sicilian city of Gela dedicated this near monumental work to honor its tyrant Polyzalos's chariot victory here. The *Charioteer* is an irresistible statue: Don't miss the handsome youth's delicate eyelashes shading wide enamel-and-stone eyes, or the realistic veins that stand out in his hands and feet.

Although the Charioteer is the star of the collection, he's in good company here. Like Olympia, Delphi was chockablock with superb works of art given by wealthy patrons, such as King Croesus of Lydia, who gave the massive **silver bull** on display in the museum. And keep an eye out in the museum's last room for the tiny **bronze ornament** showing Ulysses clinging to the belly of a ram. When Ulysses and his men were trapped in the cave of the ferocious (but nearsighted) one-eyed monster Cyclops, they tied themselves to the bellies of the Cyclops's sheep. When the sheep went out to pasture, they carried the Greek heroes with them out of the cave to safety.

The Sanctuary of Apollo. Castalian Spring and Sanctuary of Athena Pronaia. ☎ 0265/82-313. Admission Dr1,200 ($4). Summer Mon 11am–7pm; Tues–Fri 8am–7pm; Sat–Sun and holidays 8am–3pm. Winter Mon 11am–5:30pm; Tues–Fri 8am–5:30pm; Sat–Sun and holidays 8am–3pm.

The Sanctuary of Apollo is immediately beyond and just above the museum. The less well known Sanctuary of Athena on the lower slopes of Parnassus is a 10-minute walk past the museum. The Castalian Spring is between the two sanctuaries. If you can't visit everything here, spend your time at the Sanctuary of Apollo, stroll to the Castalian Spring, and then cross the Delphi-Arachova Road to take a peek down at the Sanctuary of Athena. Be sure to buy a site map when you get your ticket to help you orient yourself at this sprawling site, many of whose monuments are unlabeled.

1 Roman Agora (Marketplace)
2 Votive offering of Corfu ("Bull")
3 Votive offering of Athens
   ("Victory at Marathon")
4 Votive offering of
   Lacedaemonians
5 Votive offering of Argos
   ("Seven Against Thebes")
6 Votive offering of Argos
   ("Descendants")
7 Votive offering of Argos
   ("The King of Argos")
8 Votive offering of Taras
9 Treasure House of Sikyon
10 Treasure House of Siphnos
11 Treasure House of Megara
12 Treasure House of Thebes
13 Treasure House of Boeotia
14 Treasure House of Potidaea
15 Treasure House of Athens
16 Bouleuterion (Council House)
17 Treasure House of Cnidus (Knidos)
18 Rock of Sibylla
19 Naxian Column

20 Asklepion
21 Portico of the Athenians
22 Treasure House of Corinth
23 Prytaneion
   (Magistrates' Building)
24 Treasure House of Cyrene
25 Supporting Polygonal Wall
26 Tripod of Plateae
27 Votive offering of Rhodes
28 Grand Altar
29 Spring
30 Temple of Apollo
31 Votive Tripods
32 Treasure House of Acanthus
33 Portico of Attalus
34 Shrine of Neoptolemos
35 Votive offering of Daochos
36 Club of the Cnidians
37 Kassotis Spring
38 Ischegaon–Supporting Wall
39 Votive offering of Krateros
40 Theater
41 Western Portico

Outdoor Pursuits

If you're interested in hiking or skiing, see the side trip to Parnassus, below.

As you enter the Sanctuary of Apollo, you'll be on the marble **Sacred Way,** the road that visitors here have walked for thousands of years. The road runs uphill past the remains of **Roman stoas** and a number of **Greek treasuries** (including the Sifnian and Athenian treasuries, whose sculpture is in the museum). Cities built these small templelike buildings at Delphi for several reasons: to impress their neighbors and to store riches and works of art dedicated to Apollo. Take a close look at the **treasury walls.** You'll see not only beautiful dry-wall masonry but also countless inscriptions. The Greeks were never shy about using the walls of their buildings as bulletin boards.

Alas, so many recent visitors were bent on adding their names to the ancient inscriptions, that the Greek archaeological service no longer allows visitors inside the massive 4th-century B.C. **Temple of Apollo,** which was built after the 7th- and 6th-centuries B.C. temples were destroyed. In antiquity, one of the three Pythian priestesses on duty gave voice to Apollo's oracles from a room deep within the temple. That much is known, although the details of what precisely happened here are obscure. Did the priestess sit on a tripod balanced over a chasm, breathing in hallucinatory fumes? Did she chew various herbs, including the laurel leaf sacred to Apollo, until she spoke in tongues, while priests interpreted her sayings? Perhaps wisely, the oracle has kept its secrets.

From the temple, it's a fairly steep uphill climb to the remarkably well-preserved 4th-century B.C. **theater** and the **stadium,** which was extensively remodeled by the Romans. Events in the Pythian festival took place in both the stadium and in the theater. In 1927, the Greek poet and eccentric Angelos Sikelianos and his equally eccentric wife, Eva, attempted to revive the ancient contests here (see the listing for the Sikelianos Museum, below). Today, the theater and stadium are used most summers for the **Festival of Delphi,** which, on occasion, has featured exceptionally unclassical pop music.

Keep your ticket as you leave the Sanctuary of Apollo and head along the Arakova-Delphi Road toward the Sanctuary of Athena (also called the Marmaria, which simply refers to all the marble found here). En route, you'll pass the famous **Castalian Spring,** where Apollo planted a laurel he brought here from the Vale of Tempe. Above are the rose-colored cliffs known as the **Phaedriades** (the Bright Ones), famous for the way that they reflect the sun's rays.

Drinking from the Castalian Spring inspired legions of poets in antiquity; now, poets have to find their inspiration elsewhere, as the spring is off limits, purportedly to allow repairs to the Roman fountain facade. Poets be warned: Once an antiquity is closed in Greece, it often stays closed quite a while.

North of the Castalian Spring, a path descends from the main road to the **Sanctuary of Athena,** the goddess of wisdom who shared the honors at Delphi with Apollo. As the remains here are quite fragmentary, except for the large 4th-century B.C. **gymnasium,** you may choose simply to wander about and enjoy the site without trying too hard to figure out what's what. The round 4th-century **tholos** with its three graceful standing Doric columns is easy to spot, although no one knows why this building was built, why it was so lavishly decorated—or what went on inside. Again, the oracle keeps its secrets.

The Angelos and Eva Sikelianos Museum. Admission Dr200 (65¢). Wed–Mon 8:30am–3pm.

The road that leads steeply uphill through the village of Delphi ends at the handsome stone-and-brick Sikelianos home, now a museum commemorating the work of the Greek poet Sikelianos and his American wife, Eva. An artist, writer, and, ultimately, costume designer, Eva helped her husband stage Greek tragedies in Delphi's theater in the 1920s and 1930s. The couple's attempts to revive the Pythian games was not long-lived, but their desire to make use of Greece's ancient theaters had lasting effects, as all who have seen plays performed in the theater at Epidaurus know. This museum is a pleasant place to spend an hour and see Sikelianos's manuscripts and the beautiful costumes Eva designed. Few tourists visit this elegant home, which has spectacular views from most windows, cozy fireplaces, and the best bathroom in town.

SHOPPING

Delphi used to be a good place to find nice gold jewelry, hand-loomed rugs, and antiques, but of late the nicer shops seem to have given way to rather ordinary souvenir shops. One exception: At press time, we had a report of a new **pottery** shop on the main street, selling ceramics, including some with traditional designs from the island of Siros. Also on the main street, you'll be able to get all you need in the way of postcards, groceries, and souvenirs.

WHERE TO STAY

There's no shortage of hotels in Delphi and you can usually get a room here even in July or August. Still, if you want a room in a specific price category (or with a view), it's best to make a reservation. Finally, consider staying in nearby Arachova, where the hotels are usually less crowded and the restaurants are better (see "Side Trips from Delphi," below).

Amalia Hotel. Signposted on the Delphi-Itea Rd., 33054 Delphi. ☎ **0265/82-101.** Fax 0265/82-290. 184 units. TEL. Dr42,000 ($140) double. Rates include breakfast. AE, MC, V.

Like all the Amalia Hotels, the Delphi Amalia has all the creature comforts: swimming pool, several shops, restaurants, and a vast lobby. The Amalia is outside town, above the Delphi-Itea Road, so you may not want to stay here unless you have a car. Most of the bedrooms face each other across a generous garden; nonetheless, when several tour groups are in residence, you are aware that you are not alone here.

Castalia Hotel. Vasileos Pavlou and Frederikis 13, 33054 Delphi. ☎ **0265/82-205.** 26 units. TEL. Dr24,000 ($80) double. Rates include breakfast. AE, DC, MC, V. Usually open Fri–Sun only from Jan–Feb.

The Castalia, on Delphi's main street, has been here since 1938, but was completely remodeled in 1986. Actually, it looks more "traditional" now than it did originally, with attractive projecting balconies, a white stucco facade, and some nice touches (embroideries, hand-loomed rugs) in the guest rooms. The back bedrooms have fine views over the olive plain. If the Castalia is full, the Maniatis family may suggest that you try their other hotel, the Frederikis, at Pavlou 38 and Frederikis.

✪ **Hotel Varonos.** Pavlou 25 and Frederikis, 33054 Delphi. ☎/Fax **0265/82-345.** 9 units, 8 with tub/shower, 1 with shower only. TV TEL. Dr16,000 ($53). MC, V.

This small, family-owned hotel has very clean, spare bedrooms with fine views out over the olive plain. If you can, take in the rooftop view. This is a very welcoming place: we once arrived here with an ailing gardenia plant, and the entire family pitched in to make sure that it was well taken care of during our stay. The breakfast room is pleasant; if you want to have an early breakfast, mention it at the desk the night before.

✪ **Hotel Vouzas.** Pavlou and Frederikis 1, 33054 Delphi. ☎ **0265/82-232.** Fax 0232/82-033. 59 units. TV TEL. Dr40,500 ($135). AE, DC, MC, V.

If you don't mind sacrificing the swimming pool at the Amalia, this is the place to stay—cozy fireplace in the lobby, spectacular views, and a short walk to everything you've come to see. That said, perhaps you could persuade the owners that running a wide band at eye level through the dining-room picture window is not very clever. The bedrooms and bathrooms here are very comfortable; the balconies not only have a table and chairs, but also a welcoming pot of basil.

WHERE TO DINE

Frankly, we weren't enchanted with any of our meals here; the restaurants seemed desultory at best. Let's hope things improve in the future. We suggest that you consider eating in Arachova, 10 kilometers (6.2 miles) east of Delphi, but below are some places to eat in Delphi.

Taverna Vakchos. Odos Apollonos 31. ☎ **0265/82-448.** Main courses Dr1,000–Dr3,500 ($3.35–$12). No credit cards. GREEK.

This small taverna gets many of its customers from the youth hostel next door. This means that the prices are very reasonable, the clientele casual, and the food basic.

Topiki Gefsi. Odos Pavlou and Frederikis 19. ☎ **0265/82-480.** Main courses Dr1,800–Dr4,500 ($6–$15). AE, DC, MC, V. GREEK.

This large restaurant on the main street has a good view and reasonably good food. Unfortunately, as with most establishments here, the staff is pretty sure that they'll never see you again and the service is consequently haphazard. That said, the stuffed vine leaves are quite good, and there are sometimes interesting stews on the menu. A guitar and piano duo occasionally appears in the evening.

SIDE TRIPS FROM DELPHI
ARACHOVA

The mountain village of Arachova, 10 kilometers (6.2 miles) east of Delphi, clings to Mount Parnassus some 950 meters above sea level. Arachova is famous for its hand-loomed rugs, including fluffy flokati, tagari bags, and blankets. When several tour buses stop here during the daytime, this tiny village can be seriously crowded. Don't despair: Try to come back in the evening, when the shops are still open and the cafes and restaurants give you a chance to escape from the tourist world of Delphi to the village world of Greece. There's usually an energetic evening **volta** (stroll) on main street and if you climb the steep stairs to the upper town, you'll find yourself on quiet neighborhood streets, where children play and families sit out in front of their homes.

On the main street, have a look at the weavings in Georgia Charitou's shop **Anemi** (☎ **0267/31-701**), which also has some nice reproductions of antiques. **Katina Panagakou** (☎ **0267/31-743**) has examples of local crafts as well.

For lunch or dinner here, try the **Taverna Karathanassi** by the coffee shops in the main street square with the lovely freshwater springs. You'll enjoy simple family fare, served by the Karathanassis; expect to pay about $12 for dinner. The nearby **Taverna Dasargyri,** which specializes in delicious kokoretsi (stuffed entrails), loukanika (sausages), and grills, often has an almost entirely local crowd; dinner is about $12 here as well.

If you want to stay in Arachova, the **Xenia Hotel** (☎ **0267/31-230;** fax 0267/32-175) in town, with 42 rooms, each with a balcony, has doubles at Dr21,000 ($70). The very pleasant **Best Western Anemolia** (☎ **800/528-1234** in the U.S. or 0267/31-640), on a hill just outside Arachova above the Delphi Road, has 52 rooms and charges Dr15,000 ($50) for a double Sunday through Thursday, Dr23,000 ($77) for a Friday-to-Saturday stay, and Dr33,000 ($110) for Saturday alone. The **Arachova Inn,** with 40 rooms and a cozy fireplace in the lobby, is just outside town; it charges Dr15,000 ($50) for a double. All these hotels are usually full on winter weekends, when Greeks flock here to ski Parnassus.

PARNASSUS (PARNASSOS)

Parnassus is an odd mountain: It's difficult to see its peaks from either Delphi or Arachova, although if you approach from the north, you'll have fine views of the twin summits.

The good news is that you can drive the 27 kilometers (16.7 miles) from Arachova to the **ski resort at Fterolaki,** 2,253 meters up Mount Parnassus, in about an hour. The bad news is that the road and several incipient hamlets of ski lodges built by Greeks who vacation here are spoiling the mountain's isolation and much of its beauty. If you drive to Fterolaki in summer, don't expect to find any of the cafes and restaurants open. In winter, of course, things are livelier, with a dozen ski runs, several small shops, and a **cafeteria** (☎ 0234/22-689).

If you want to hike Parnassus, there are two possibilities. You can head uphill in Delphi past the Sikelianos house and keep going. Four hours will bring you to the upland meadows known as the **Plateau of Livadi,** where shepherds traditionally pasture their flocks. As always in the mountains, it's not a good idea to make such an excursion alone. If you plan to continue on past the meadows to the **Corcyrian Cave** (known locally as Sarantavli, or "Forty Rooms"), where Pan and the Nymphs once were thought to live, or to the summits, you should check on conditions locally or with the **Hellenic Mountaineering Club** in Athens (☎ 01/ 323-4555). It's also possible to begin your ascent from Arachova, where you can get directions locally.

THE MONASTERY OF OSIOS LOUKAS

You'll probably want to see Osios Loukas en route to or from Delphi, although you could do the 96-kilometer (60-mile) round-trip via Arachova as a day excursion. If you go to Osios Loukas via Levadia, pause at **Schiste (Triodos),** where three roads cross. This is the spot where the ancients believed that Oedipus unknowingly slew his father. Things got worse: Still unknowingly, he married his mother and brought down tragedy on himself and his descendants.

Osios Loukas (the Monastery of Saint Luke) is a spectacular church and monastery founded in the 10th century, with much of what you see dating from at least the 11th century. This is not just a tourist destination: Devout Greek Orthodox visitors consider it a holy spot, something to keep in mind during your visit. This is not the place for sleeveless shirts, shorts, or a casual attitude toward the icons or the tomb of Saint Luke.

Osios Loukas is a lavishly decorated complex—not just brick but a wide variety of different jewel-like polychrome marbles were used in the buildings. Along with the mosaics at Daphne, outside Athens, and the splendid churches of Thessaloniki, Osios Loukas's **mosaics** are among the finest in Greece. If you are lucky enough to be here when the **Katholikon (Main Church)** isn't too crowded, let yourself enjoy the changing light and shadow they play on the marbles and mosaics. Then head over to the smaller **church of the Theotokos (Mother of God),** with its lovely mosaic floor. If you have time left over, sit in the courtyard and imagine what Osios Loukas would have been like when hundreds, not today's handful, of monks lived and worshipped here.

2 Thebes

87km (53 miles) W of Athens off the Athens-Corinth National Hwy.

Thebes, which Homer called "seven-gated," was one of the most important Mycenaean settlements in Greece. The Athenian dramatist Agamemnon commemorated Thebes in his play *Seven Against Thebes,* and the poet Pindar was born here. When Alexander the Great captured Thebes in 336 B.C., he leveled the town, sparing only Pindar's birthplace.

Unfortunately, several 20th-century earthquakes have also leveled a good deal of Thebes, and the new city, though energetic, is not charming. If you're pressed for time, you might give Thebes a miss altogether, although the Archaeological Museum has a fine collection. There's no good hotel here, but several really down-at-the-heels ones, so we don't recommend spending the night here. If you must, the **Dionyssion Melathron,** on Metaxa and Cadmou (☎ **0261/27-855**), is endurable. As for food, you won't starve, but if you find a superior restaurant, please let us know. We haven't, despite many attempts.

The **post office, telephone office (OTE), police** (☎ 0262/28-551), and several **banks** are on the main square.

GETTING THERE   By Car   The turnoff for Thebes, just after Eleusis, is signposted on the National Highway. Allow 2 hours from Athens, due to heavy traffic and roadwork. It's also possible to reach Thebes by taking the Athens-Salonika Highway north toward Lamia and taking the turnoff for Thebes.

By Bus   There are frequent buses departing from the Athens station, Odos Liossion 260 (☎ **01/831-7096**), to Thebes, arriving at the bus station on Odos Epaminondou in the center of Thebes (☎ **0262/275-13**).

VISITING THE MUSEUM

The Archaeological Museum. Odos Pindararou. ☎ **0262/27-913.** Admission Dr500 ($1.70). Mon and Wed–Sat 8:30am–3pm; Sun 9am–2pm.

There's only one thing to detain you in Thebes: the Archaeological Museum, which is clearly signposted. If you've come by car, try to park on one of the side streets by the museum, which has a Frankish tower in its garden. Although the collection includes a wide range of pottery, inscriptions, and sculpture, the Mycenaean objects are the highlight. There are several painted Mycenaean sarcophagi, some fine gold jewelry, and handsome body armor.

3 Two Famous Battlefields: Thermopylae & Chaironeia

THERMOPYLAE

194km (120 miles) N of Athens on the Athens-Thessaloniki National Hwy.

If you find yourself on the Athens-Thessaloniki Highway, keep an eye out for the larger-than-life-size **statue of the Spartan king Leonidas,** about halfway through the 6.4-kilometer-long (4-mile-long) Pass of Thermopylae that snakes between the mountains and the sea. One of the most famous battles in history was fought here in 480 B.C. during the Persian King Xerxes's attempt to conquer Greece. To this day, historians speculate on just how different the world might have been if Xerxes had succeeded, and Greece had become part of the Persian Empire.

A Break En Route

If you're driving from Central Greece into Northern Greece along the Athens-Thessaloniki National Highway, you may want to take a break from the road. The seaside town of **Kamena Vourla** is just off the highway and has several hotels and restaurants (most separated from the sea by a road). The **Astir Hotel Galini** (☎ **0235/22-245,** or 01/324-3961 in Athens; fax 0253/22-307) has 100 units with balconies facing either wooded hills or the sea. In summer, the hotel's pool and thermal baths are open. About a block from the Astir, the excellent **Thronio** cafe/restaurant/pizzeria (☎ **0235/22-354**) is open daily from 11am to midnight and serves delicious spaghetti carbonara and cannelloni. Although you'll be welcomed with open arms here out of season (except on weekends, when city dwellers from as far away as Athens come here), it's risky to count on getting a room in the summer unless you have a reservation.

When Xerxes invaded Greece in 480 B.C. with perhaps 100,000 men, soldiers from almost every city-state in south and central Greece rushed to Thermopylae to try to stop the Persian king's advance. The Greeks might have succeeded in holding the narrow pass of Thermopylae had not a traitor told the Persians of a secret mountain path that allowed them to turn the pass. As Leonidas and his 300-man royal guard stood and fought at Thermopylae, the main Greek force retreated south to regroup and fight another day. When the fighting at Thermopylae was over, Leonidas and his men lay dead, but the Spartan king had earned immortal fame for his heroism.

The name **Thermopylae** (Hot Gates) refers to the warm springs that bubbled here in antiquity, when the pass was considerably narrower than it is now that centuries of silt have built up the seashore. Many of Thermopylae's springs have been partly diverted to spas, such as Kamena Vourla, but unfortunately, overdevelopment has seriously undercut the former charm of the seaside towns near Thermopylae. If you want to take a fast look at the some of the springs, keep an eye out for plumes of smoke when you park near the statue of Leonidas.

CHAIRONEIA

132km (81 miles) NW of Athens on the Athens-Levadhia-Lamia Hwy.

Just north of Levadhia, the Athens-Lamia Highway passes an enormous **stone lion** that marks the site of the common grave of the Theban Sacred Band of warriors, who died here in the Battle of Chaironeia in 338 B.C. It was at Chaironeia that Philip of Macedon, with some 30,000 soldiers, defeated the combined forces of both Athens and Thebes and became the most powerful leader in Greece. It was also at Chaironeia that Philip's 18-year-old son Alexander first distinguished himself on the battlefield, when he led the attack against the superbly trained Theban Sacred Band, which fought to the last man. Philip's admiration for the Thebans' courage was such that he allowed them to be buried where they fell on the battlefield.

The lion itself, sitting on its haunches, with a surprisingly benign expression on its face, was erected by Thebes sometime after the battle. With the passing of time, the winds blew soil from the plain almost entirely over the lion. In 1818, two English antiquarians stumbled upon the lion's head; excavations in 1904 and 1905 led to the lion's restoration and re-erection here on the dusty plain of Chaironeia.

4 The Vale of Tempe & Ambelakia

326km (202 miles) N of Athens; 27km (16 miles) N of Larissa

This steep-sided 8-kilometer (5-mile) gorge between Mounts Olympus and Ossa has been famous since antiquity as a beauty spot. According to legend, this is where Apollo caught a glimpse of the lovely maiden Daphne, bathing in the Peneios River. When Apollo pursued Daphne, she cried out to the gods on nearby Olympus to save her—which they did, by turning her into a laurel tree (*daphne* in Greek). Apollo, who didn't give up easily, then plucked a branch from the tree and planted it at his shrine at Delphi. Thereafter, messengers came to Tempe from Delphi every 9 years to collect laurel for Apollo's temple.

To this day, there are laurel, chestnut, and plane trees growing in the Vale of Tempe. Unfortunately, since virtually all north-south traffic in Greece now passes through the Vale, this is no longer the sylvan spot that was once the haunt of nightingales. Still, if you're lucky enough to be here off-season, the sound of the gurgling river may be louder than that of tourists' footsteps on the suspension bridge over the gorge. The car toll is Dr500 ($1.70).

Keep an eye out for the remains of the "Kastro tis Oreas" ("Castle of the Beautiful Maiden") on the cliffs above Tempe and the little chapel deep in the gorge. Unfortunately, you won't have any trouble spotting the souvenir stands throughout the Vale, or the signs advertising a "Love Boat" cruise on the river.

If you possibly can, take an hour or two to visit the mountaintop village of **Ambelakia,** some 6.4 kilometers (4 miles) southeast of the Vale of Tempe, with spectacular views of Mount Olympus. The village is one of six in Greece to have formed the National Network of Tradition, Culture, and Community Life to attempt to preserve their traditions and base economic development on local crafts. (The other

---

The Wildflowers of Greece

Every spring, the arid Greek countryside is carpeted with a staggering variety of wildflowers. Small wonder that one of the oldest Greek poems, *The Homeric Hymn to Demeter,* celebrates meadows blooming with "roses, crocuses, lovely violets, irises and hyacinth and narcissus." Shrub roses bloom high on the Pindus Mountains of Northern Greece, there are poppies as far as the eye can see on the dusty plain of Thessaly, and the wild iris flourishes on seashores deep in the Peloponnese. Even more astonishingly, poppies and oleanders continue to bloom on hillsides and even grow from tiny cracks in the marble blocks of fallen temples during the hottest summer months.

Greeks call almost all wildflowers just that—*agria louloudia*—and don't usually bother with specific names, although they do call the wild carnation *agriogarifalo.* The ancient Greeks thought that this little pink, red, or white flower was Zeus's particular favorite, just as the laurel was beloved of Apollo.

Like many Greek flowers, the more humble broom plant, whose vibrant yellow blossoms scent much of Greece each spring, is both beautiful and useful: after the broom blooms, its stalks are gathered and made into the brooms that you see being used throughout Greece. After the orchidlike caper flowers, the capers are gathered, pickled, and used in salads, along with the dried flowers of the richly scented herb oregano, whose distinctive taste makes Greek salads so unmistakably Greek.

villages are Ia on Santorini, Panormus in Tinos, Makrinitsa on Mount Pelion, Papingo in Zagori, and Nympheon in Florina.)

Ambelakia, whose name means "vineyards" in Greek, is perched amidst old oak trees on Mount Kissavos. Astonishingly, this tiny village was an important center of cotton and silk production in the 17th century, with offices in far-off London. Today, little remains of Ambelakia's earlier wealth, but what does remain is well worth a visit: the handsome 19th-century **Schwartz House**. (It's open somewhat unpredictably, but usually from 9am to 2pm; admission is Dr800/$3.40.) The Schwartz brothers were two of Ambelakia's wealthiest merchants, and their handsome wooden house, with its overhanging balconies and elaborately frescoed interiors, is an absolute delight.

In January 1998, there were rumors that several small hotels were being built in Ambelakia, and the charming little **Nine Muses Hotel** (☎ **0495/93-405** or 041/550-774), with 12 rooms at Dr9,000 ($30) for a double, had just opened. There are two small restaurants on the main square; we've eaten in both and enjoyed their simple grills and salads. Ambelakia would be a wonderful place to spend a night or two, letting you drop out of tourist Greece and experience village Greece.

5 Mount Olympus

390km (241 miles) N of Athens; 70km (43 miles) N of Larissa

Greece's most famous mountain range, home of the Olympian gods, towers above the plains of Thessaly and Macedonia reaching 2,972 meters (9,751 ft.). From a distance, it's almost impossible to pick out Olympus's summit, Mykitas, nicknamed the "throne of Zeus," although the massive, gnarled, snowcapped range is often visible from Thessaloniki.

The first recorded successful ascent of the summit was in 1913, when two Swiss mountaineers with a local guide made it to the top. For such an imposing mountain, Olympus is surprisingly easy to climb, in large part because so many people since 1913 have climbed it. Consequently, there are a number of well-marked paths to the summit and shelters at Stavros (944m) and Spilios Agapitos (2,100m), where climbers can rest or even spend the night. In summer, these paths can be very heavily trafficked, with some elegant Greek women making the ascent in high heels.

Still, Olympus is a serious mountain and no one should attempt it alone. As always in the mountains, weather conditions can change for the worse without warning. Well into May, severe snowstorms are not uncommon on the heights of Olympus—which helps to explain why the area has been developed in recent years as a ski resort. The main town on the slopes, and the base camp, as it were, for climbers, is Litochoro.

ESSENTIALS

GETTING THERE By Bus Four buses that stop at Litochoro run daily from Athens to Katerini; seven daily buses run from Athens to Larissa, from which there is frequent service to Litochoro. All buses leave Athens from the station at Odos Liossion 260 (☎ **01/831-7059**). There are at least eight buses a day from Thessaloniki to Litochoro.

By Train There are frequent daily trains from Athens to Larissa, and Thessaloniki to Larissa; from Larissa, you can continue to Litochoro by bus. You can also take a train from Athens or Thessaloniki to the Litochoro station—but the train station is on the coast 9 kilometers (5.6 miles) from the town of Litochoro, and you have to travel on by bus or taxi. Only train lovers will want to come here this way.

By Car Take the Litochoro exit on the Athens-Salonika Highway.

VISITOR INFORMATION   The **Greek Mountaineering Club (GMC)** can be reached at ☎ **01/323-4555** in Athens, 031/278-288 in Thessaloniki, or 0352/81-944 in Litochoro. The GMC can give you information on conditions on Olympus, which is usually climbable from June 1 to October 1, and they'll let you know whether you can just turn up, or need a reservation, at one of their overnight shelters. The **Spilios Agapitos** refuge can be reached at ☎ **0352/81-800;** rates are rather flexible, but inexpensive.

Climbing information and conditions can be obtained from the **SEO (Association of Greek Climbers)** at ☎ **0352/81-944,** or the **EOS (Hellenic Alpine Association)** at ☎ **0352/81-944.** Both offices are signposted in Litochoro, and both keep irregular hours.

FAST FACTS   The **National Bank of Greece,** on Plateia Kentriki, offers currency exchange; at press time, it was planning to install ATMs. The **clinic** 5 kilometers (3 miles) outside Litochoro is signposted; in the event of a nonemergency, try to get to Thessaloniki for medical care. The **police station** (☎ **0352/81-100**) is signposted just off the central square (Plateia Kentriki) on the road up Olympus to Priona. The **post office** is on Plateia Kentriki. The **telephone office (OTE)** is just off Plateia Kentriki on the road up Olympus to Priona.

CLIMBING MOUNT OLYMPUS

If you plan to climb Olympus, you will want to check with the EOS and SEO (see above) and probably get a copy of Marc Dubin's *Trekking in Greece.* You should not attempt the climb alone; weather here can change in an instant from pleasant to life-threatening. In July and August of 1998, high winds here whipped the flames of a serious fire that burnt portions of Olympus's magnificent forests.

Here's a bit of information to give you a sense of what climbing Olympus involves. Purists will want to begin the ascent at the rapidly developing **ski resort of Litochoro,** while others may prefer to drive from Litochoro as far as **Priona** (7km/11 miles) and begin their climb there. On foot, it takes about 4 hours from Litochoro to Priona; by car, it's only an hour, but seems longer, due to the evil, twisting road. Fortunately, there's a small **cafe** at Priona, where you can reward yourself with a decent meal, or even a stiff drink.

From Priona, it's a 2-hour climb, much of it over slippery schist slopes and knobby limestone outcroppings, to the **shelter at Spilios Agapitos.** If you don't mind communal quarters, this is the place to spend the night, especially since both bedding and meals are available. Most climbers begin the final 2- to 3-hour ascent at dawn and then do the entire descent, arriving back in Litochoro before dusk. The **Monastery of Ayios Dionysos,** not far from Spilios Agapitos, is a good place to break your downward trek and enjoy the views. The monastery was destroyed by the Germans during World War II, but is now being rebuilt.

WHERE TO STAY & DINE

You can get information on the **refuges** on Mount Olympus from the EOS and SEO (see "Visitor Information," above).

As far as the dining scene is concerned, one has to conclude that climbers are not foodies. There are a number of small restaurants in Litochoro; none is worth seeking out. If you find one that is, we'd love to hear about it.

Dion Palace Resort Hotel. Litochoro Beach, 60200 Macedonia. ☎ **0352/22-731.** Fax 0352/22-735. 182 units. MINIBAR TV TEL. Dr30,000 ($100) double. AE, MC, V. Sometimes closed in winter.

This enormous beachfront resort has a main hotel building, two restaurants, a disco, shops, a fitness center, and lots of cabanas with the rooms (some private, some sharing a cabana). There are two swimming pools, one saltwater, one fresh, and all the creature comforts in the guest rooms. In summer, this is a popular family destination, and anyone with children will see why.

Mirto. Litochoro, 60200 Macedonia. ☎ **0352/81-398.** Fax 0352/82-298. 20 units. TEL. Dr20,000 ($67). MC, V.

Like a number of the newer hotels in Litochoro, the Mirto is built in a sort of pseudo-Swiss-chalet style, with lots of wood. The guest rooms have nice balconies, firm beds, and adequate bathrooms.

6 The Meteora

Kalambaka is 356km (220 miles) NW of Athens; the circuit of the Meteora monasteries is approximately 25km (15 miles)

As you drive across the plain of Thessaly, which can seem endless on a summer's day, you'll suddenly see a cluster of gnarled black rocks rising out of the plain. Some travelers have compared these crags to the mountains of the moon, but the fact is that the rock formations of the Meteora (the word means "in midair") are unique. Many geographers speculate that some 30 million years ago, all Thessaly was a vast inland sea; when the sea receded, sweeping the topsoil along, only rock formations were left behind. Over the millennia, the Peneios River and the wind carved the rock into the weird, twisted shapes that now rise some 300 meters (984 ft.) above the plain. The Meteora is especially stunning in winter, when the Pindos range is capped with snow and mists swirl around the monasteries.

When you get closer to the Meteora and see that these sheer, slippery, seemingly unscalable rocks are topped with large monasteries, you'll probably find yourself asking two questions: Why did monks settle here, and how did they build anything larger than a hut on the rocks? Small wonder that many monks believe that St. Athanasios, founder of the first monastery here, the Great Meteoron (Monastery of the Transfiguration), did not scale the rock, but was carried there by an eagle.

The first monks who came here were probably 10th-century ascetics who scaled the rocks, lived as hermits in caves, and spent their days in prayer and meditation. In fact, the word monk comes from the Greek for "alone." Over the centuries, more and more hermits and monks seeking to lead the solitary life made their way to the Meteora, until by the 14th century, there were enough monks here for St. Athanasios to found the Great Meteoron. While some monks continued to live alone and pursue the solitary religious life called "idiorrhythmic," others chose to live together and follow the cenobitic, or communal, life.

By 1500, there were 24 monasteries here, of which six—the Great Meteoron, Varlaam, Rousanou, Ayia Triada, Ayios Nikolaos Anapaphsas, and Ayiou Stefanou—are still inhabited and welcome visitors.

Visiting the Meteora is not recommended for those suffering from acrophobia, or any who might find it difficult to climb steep flights of stairs cut in the rock face. Still, even these vertiginous stepped paths are an improvement over what earlier travelers had to endure. When the English traveler Leake visited here in the 19th century, he was ferried up to the Great Meteoron in a net attached by a slender rope to a winch. Leake later wrote: "Visitors' morale was not helped by persistent rumors that the monks only replaced the homemade ropes which held the nets when they broke— usually in midair!"

Tips on Visiting the Meteora

Try to allow at least a full day here; some of the monasteries close in the afternoon, others keep abbreviated hours, and the last thing you want to do is to rush experiencing the contemplative life! Don't forget modest attire: long-sleeved shirts and skirts for women, slacks and shirts for men. If you come in winter, dress warmly, as many of the monasteries have little or no heat. Also in winter, many small restaurants and hotels may be closed. In compensation, you might get to see the Meteora at its most beautiful: covered in snow and shrouded in mists.

ESSENTIALS

GETTING THERE   By Train   There are seven daily trains from Athens's Larissa station (☎ 01/821-3882) to the Kalambaka station (☎ 0432/22-451). Allow at least 8 hours for the Athens-Kalambaka trip.

By Bus   There are seven daily buses to Trikkala from the Athens terminal at Odos Liossion 260 (☎ 01/831-1434). Allow at least 8 hours for the Athens-Kalambaka trip. There are frequent buses from Trikkala to Kalambaka. Several buses a day travel connect Kalambaka and the Meteora monasteries.

By Car   From Athens, take the Athens-Thessaloniki National Highway north to Lamia; from Lamia, take the highway northwest to Kalambaka. From Delphi, take the Lamia-Karditsa-Trikkala-Kalambaka Highway north. Allow at least 6 hours for the Athens-Kalambaka trip.

GETTING AROUND   If you don't have a car, you may want to hire a taxi to visit the Meteora monasteries. Expect to pay between Dr15,000 and Dr30,000 ($50 to $100) to visit the six monasteries usually open to the public. Your driver will wait while you visit each monastery and probably serve as a guide. Be sure you are in agreement as to how long you will have at each monastery; most drivers are content to wait 30 minutes at each one. If you want to make a longer visit, make this clear when you negotiate the fee.

FAST FACTS   At press time, the **Kalambaka National Bank of Greece** on Plateia Riga Fereou, the main square, was planning to install an ATM. The **clinic** in Kalambaka is signposted. The **police** (☎ 0432/22-109) and **tourist police** are on Odos Hadzipetrou. The **post office** is signposted off Plateia Riga Fereou. The **telephone office (OTE)** is signposted on the road out of Kalambaka to Meteora.

WHAT TO SEE & DO

The road from Kalambaka through the Meteora takes you past Ayios Nikolaos, Roussanou, the Great Meteron, Varlaam, Ayia Triada, and Ayios Stephanos. If you only have time to visit one monastery, it should be the **Great Meteoron.** Try to allow time for a leisurely visit here, so that you can chat with the monks and enjoy the stunning views through the forest of rocks from monastery to monastery. You'll find souvenir stands and places to buy bottled water or soft drinks outside each monastery.

We've listed the phone numbers for the monasteries, but don't be surprised if no one answers: telephones and the monastic life are not really compatible. Also don't be surprised if you find one or more of the monasteries closed—usually the one you've just climbed up a long series of rock-cut steps to reach.

After visiting the monasteries of the Meteora, you may find it a relief to know that there's only one church to see back in Kalambaka: the 12th-century **Cathedral of the**

Dormition of the Virgin, which is often locked. If it's open, take a look at the frescoes, which date from the 12th to the 16th centuries. You might also keep an eye out for the ancient marble blocks and column drums that the builders of this church pilfered from the earlier Temple of Apollo that once stood here.

THE METEORA MONASTERIES

Ayios Nikolaos Anapaphsas. ☎ 0432/22-375. Admission Dr500 ($1.70). Daily 9am–6pm. Often closed in winter.

This little 14th-century monastery, approached by a relatively gentle path, has splendid **frescoes** by the 16th-century Cretan painter Theophanes the Monk. Don't miss the delightful fresco of the garden of Eden, with elephants, fantastic beasts, and all manner of fruits and flowers. There's also a nice painting of the death of St. Ephraim the Syrian, which shows scenes from the saint's life, including the pillar that he lived atop for many years in the Syrian desert.

At the time of our visit, there were no monks in residence at Ayios Nikolaos, and because tour buses often rush past to get to the Great Meteoron, you may find that you have this spot all to yourself.

Roussanou. No phone. Admission Dr500 ($1.70). Daily 9am–1pm and 3–6pm.

Roussanou is relatively accessible, thanks to its new bridge. This 13th-century monastery is now a nunnery, whose inhabitants are usually much more jolly than monks. If the nuns offer you sweets while you sit in the courtyard between the refectory and the octagonal-domed church, be sure to leave a contribution in the church collection box.

The Great Meteoron. ☎ 0432/22-278. Admission Dr500 ($1.70). Wed–Mon 9am–1pm and 3:20–6pm.

Although the Great Meteoron was founded in the 14th century, most of what you see here was built in the 16th century by monks from the Holy Mountain of Mount Athos. The **church** here is especially splendid, in the form of a Greek cross inscribed on a square, topped by a **12-sided dome.** Once your eyes get accustomed to the darkness, you'll be able to enjoy the elaborate **frescoes.** If you look up to the dome, you'll see Christ, with the four evangelists, apostles, and prophets ranged below, the church fathers by the altar, and the liturgical feasts of the church year along the walls of the nave. There's also a rather bloodcurdling *Last Judgment* and *Punishment of the Damned* in the narthex.

After visiting the church, you may wish to sit awhile in the shady courtyard, before visiting the small **museum,** which has a collection of icons and illustrated religious texts. Don't miss the **wine cellar,** whose enormous wooden barrels suggest that monastic life is not all prayer and meditation.

Varlaam. ☎ 0432/22-277. Admission Dr500 ($1.70). Sat–Thurs 9am–1pm and 3:30–6pm.

A narrow bridge from the main road runs to this 16th-century monastery, which was named for a hermit who lived here in the 14th century and built a tiny chapel on this promontory. The **chapel,** considerably enlarged and decorated with **frescoes,** is now a side chapel of the main church. Varlaam's founders were two brothers from Ioannina, who found the monastery and gentle lakeside scenery there too sybaritic for their tastes. Presumably the brothers found the Meteora's harsh landscape more to their liking: according to legend, they had to drive away the monster who lived in a cave on the summit before they could settle here.

The nicest thing about Varlaam is its **garden,** and the monk who sometimes sits here and is willing to chat with visitors.

Ayia Triada. ☎ 0432/22-220. Admission Dr500 ($1.70). Daily 8am–1pm and 3–6pm.

It's not easy to say which of the monasteries has the most spectacular position, but Ayia Triada would be near the top of most lists. Perched on a slender pinnacle, reached only by laboring up 140 steps, Ayia Triada really does seem to belong to another world. The one monk who lives here is usually glad to see visitors and show them around the **church, refectory,** and **courtyard.** Don't miss the **winch,** for years used to bring supplies and visitors up here. If this monastery looks more familiar to you than the others, perhaps you remember it from the James Bond movie *For Your Eyes Only,* which was filmed here.

Ayiou Stefanou. No phone. Admission Dr500 ($1.70). Usually open Tues–Sun 9am–1pm and 3:20–6pm.

Founded in the 14th century, Ayiou Stefanou, now a nunnery, is almost on the outskirts of Kalambaka. A bridge from the main road makes it easy to get here, and the nuns usually make you feel glad that you've come. Sometimes, the nuns sell very reasonably priced embroideries.

Ayiou Stefanou was badly damaged both in World War II and in the Civil War that followed. Many priceless frescoes were defaced and others were totally destroyed, but the monastery's most famous relic was saved: the **head of St. Charalambos,** whose powers include warding off illness. There's also a small **museum** here, with ecclesiastical robes and paraphernalia.

In January 1998, the nuns were engaged in a flurry of painting and cleaning, and talked of restoring much of the monastery that had been allowed to decline. Donations are welcomed.

SHOPPING

There are a lot of tourist shops in Kalambaka (most of which close for the winter) that sell the usual carved wooden canes and spoons, ceramics, and rugs. One shop that opened in 1998 is worth a look: **Kava Nikos,** on the main drag, Odos Trikalon 114 (**☎**/fax **0432/77-881**). This small wine-and-liquor shop has a good selection of wines both in the bottle and from the barrel, and also stocks local Macedonian and Thessalian *tsiporo,* a firewater that makes ouzo look like a delicate aperitif.

WHERE TO STAY

Amalia. Outside Kalambaka on the Meteora Rd., 42200 Kalambaka. **☎ 0432/72-216.** Fax 0432/72-457. 175 units. A/C TV TEL. Dr42,200 ($140) double. Rates include breakfast buffet. Often significantly cheaper off-season. AE, DC, MC, V.

This rather handsome, large new hotel—with two restaurants, a souvenir shop, and a pool—looks almost like a small village from the road. Like most other Amalia hotels, this one is located just too far out of town to make the walk into town comfortable. The large bedrooms (most with balconies) are tastefully decorated, and bathrooms have actual shower stalls. This is a very comfortable place to stay, although you may find yourself feeling like the odd man out if all the other rooms are occupied by tour groups. On the other hand, this is a popular spot for local wedding receptions and baptisms, so you may get to spy on Kalambaka society.

Divani Motel. Outside Kalambaka on the Meteora Rd., 42200 Kalambaka. **☎ 0432/ 23-330.** Fax 0432/23-638. 165 units. A/C TV TEL. Dr25,500–Dr40,800 ($85–$136). Often less off-season. AE, DC, MC, V.

Like the Amalia, the slightly cheaper and less fancy Divani has a pool—although it doesn't hold a candle to the Amalia's fancy pool. One thing that may sway you toward the Divani: Rooms at the back with very nice balconies have especially fine views out toward the Meteora. The restaurant is perfectly decent but bland—as you'd expect, since it turns out masses of meals for tour groups, many of which are Greek.

Edelweiss. El. Venizelou 3, 42200 Kalambaka. ☎ **0432/23-966.** Fax 0432/24-733. 48 units. TV TEL. Dr15,000–Dr22,500 double ($50–$75). MC, V.

If you want to be in Kalambaka itself, this is the place to stay. The Edelweiss is new, low-key but attractive, and—a real plus—has a small swimming pool. Some rooms have views of the Meteora.

WHERE TO DINE

Gertzos. Economou 4, Kalambaka. ☎ **0432/22-316.** Main courses Dr1,500–Dr3,000 ($5–$10). No credit cards. Usually closed November 1 to Easter. GREEK.

This simple taverna has been in Kalambaka for more than 50 years, serving up the standard Greek fare, but also offering a number of dishes reflecting the owners' Greek heritage in Asia Minor. Unless it's so hot—as it can be in the summer here—that you feel you must order a cold drink, try one of the local wines.

Vachos. Plateia Riga Fereou. ☎ **0432/24-678.** Main courses Dr1,500–Dr2,700 ($5–$9). No credit cards. Usually closed Nov–Feb. GREEK.

If you want to eat outdoors, head for Vachos, which has a small garden with views toward Meteora. As at Gertzos, the food here is so well prepared that even standard Greek dishes like zucchini and eggplant stuffed with rice and ground meat taste new and different. One plus here: There are usually several tasty sweets on the menu, so you don't have to finish your meal and then search out a *zacheroplasteion* (sweet shop) for dessert.

7 Pelion

Volos is 324km (200 miles) NE of Athens

There comes a time on almost every trip when you need to take a brief vacation from your vacation. That's the time to head for the verdant hills of the Mount Pelion peninsula, whose chestnuts, apples, and fruit trees make this one of Greece's few year-round lush and verdant havens. Although it's possible to drive the circuit of Pelion's most handsome villages in a day, it seems a shame to rush through villages that preserve a sense of yesterday's leisurely pace at today's breakneck speed. If you can, spend a week here, staying in both a mountain and a seaside village. If you can't, try to spend at least 1 night here at one of the traditional settlement inns. For dinner, try one of the local specialties, such as bean soup (*fasolada*) or the spicy pepper and sausage stew (*spetzofai*).

In antiquity, Mount Pelion was thought to be the home of the centaurs, the legendary half-man, half-horse creatures who roamed the hills and dales here. Although most centaurs had a reputation for brutish behavior, the wise old centaur Chiron helped to raise Achilles, the great hero of the Trojan war; Jason, who spent so many years searching for the Golden Fleece; and Asclepius, who became the god of medicine.

Presumably the centaurs found Pelion's lush green hills, with their plane, chestnut, fruit, and olive trees, a pleasant change from the dusty plain of Thessaly. Certainly, generations of visitors have come to Pelion in search of cool breezes in summer and a glimpse, if not of centaurs, of traditional village life. Pelion's villages are among the most beautiful in Greece, shaded by enormous plane trees and watered by gushing springs. The architecture here is special, too: most of Pelion's churches are low, three-aisled basilicas, often with large porches, rather than more familiar cross-in-square design. Pelion's stone houses, many with elaborately frescoed walls, slate roofs, and overhanging wooden balconies, are among the most handsome in all Greece. In part, this is because the Pelion peninsula has been just isolated enough over the centuries to have escaped both the ravages of civil war that destroyed so many villages, and the horrors of recent development that have spoiled so many others.

In recent years, the Greek government has begun to worry that pell-mell development might threaten the beauty of Pelion's mountain and seaside villages. Consequently, the entire area now has a strict building code, and some villages, such as Vizitsa, have been declared national landmark settlements. Another, Makrinitsa, has banded together with six villages from throughout Greece to preserve local traditions and base development on local crafts and occupations. With luck these steps will help Pelion preserve its unique architecture and character.

In addition, the GNTO has established a number of "traditional settlement guest houses" by renovating abandoned village houses. These small inns give visitors a glimpse of traditional village life—and the visitors provide much-needed income for locals, who otherwise might have had to leave their beloved villages in search of work. Doubles at the traditional settlement inns are usually about Dr30,000 ($100).

ESSENTIALS

GETTING THERE By Train There are seven daily trains from Athens's Stathmos Larissa (☎ **01/362-4402**) to the Volos station (☎ **0421/24-056**). The train takes at least 6 hours.

By Bus There are frequent daily buses to Volos from two Athens terminals: Odos Liossion 260 (☎ **01/22-527**), and the corner of Grigoriou Lambraki and Lachana streets (☎ **01/831-7186**). Allow 6 hours for the trip. There are frequent daily buses from Volos to the Pelion villages. For schedules, check with the Volos bus station on Grigoriou Lambraki (☎ **0421/33-254**), or the GNTO office at Plateia Riga Fereou (☎ **0421/23-500**).

By Car Volos is the jumping-off point for touring Pelion, and it's 324 kilometers (200 miles) northeast of Athens. To get to Volos from Athens, take the Athens-Thessaloniki National Highway; allow at least 4 hours. To reach Pelion from Volos, take Eleftheriou Venizelou Boulevard, which runs from the Volos harbor northeast out of town 5 kilometers (3 miles) to Ano Volos, the suburb of Volos that is the first town on Mount Pelion.

VISITOR INFORMATION Volos (a port that could hardly be more different than the Pelion villages) is, nonetheless, the main town (the only city, actually) on Pelion. You'll probably begin your visit to Pelion in Volos—and try to get out of Volos as quickly as possible. (This isn't easy: despite its grid plan, Volos is a very confusing city to drive in.) The **Greek National Tourist Organization (EOT)** has an office on Plateia Riga Fereou in Volos, open Monday through Friday from 7am to 2:30pm (☎ **0421/23-500**).

GETTING AROUND The easiest way to visit Mount Pelion is by private car, although village buses do make their way (on a leisurely schedule) around. If you rent a car, keep in mind that the roads are narrow, and a tour bus may be heading toward you from around the next corner. Car rentals are available in Volos at **Avis,** Odos Argonafton 41 (☎ **0421/20-949;** fax 0421/32-360), and **European,** Odos Iasonos 79–83 (☎ **0421/36-238;** fax 0421/24-192).

Volos, Briefly

Although you probably won't spend much time in Volos, the **Volos Archaeological Museum** on Odos Plastira, at the east end of the harbor, has Greece's best collection of very rare—and very lovely—painted Hellenistic grave stelai, with haunting pastel images of the deceased. The museum is open Tuesday through Sunday from 8:30am to 3pm; admission is Dr400 ($1.35). Volos also has excellent **ouzo** and a number of harborside ouzeries.

FAST FACTS   The **area code** for Volos is 0421. The Pelion villages have several area codes: for Portaria and Makrinitsa, it's 0421; for Milies and Vizitsa, 0423; and for Zagora, 0426. There are several **banks** on Plateia Riga Fereou, the main square in Volos; the **National Bank of Greece** has an ATM and currency exchange. The Volos **hospital** (☎ **0421/24-531**) is signposted on Odos Plastira at the east end of the harbor. The **police** and **tourist police** (☎ **0421/27-094**) are at Odos 28 Octobriou 179. The **post office** is at Pavlou Mela 45; the **telephone office (OTE)** is at Eleftheriou Venizelou 22. As in many port towns, the OTE keeps extended hours from 6am to midnight.

WHAT TO SEE & DO

The thing to do on Pelion is to make haste slowly and enjoy the beauty of this unique region. From Volos, you can head around the peninsula in either a basically clockwise or counterclockwise fashion. Clockwise, this takes you from Volos through Ano Volos, Portaria, Makrinitsa, Hania, Zagora, Horefto, Tsangarada, Milopotamos, Miles, Vitizsa, Kato Lehonia, Agria, and back to Volos. Along the way, you'll probably make lots of stops to see the villages and to take in the spectacular views out over the Pagassitikos Gulf and Aegean. Following are some suggestions of what to watch for on your visit.

If you're very lucky, you may find someone in the cheek-by-jowl villages of **Anakasia** and **Ano Volos** who will show you the **house with wall paintings** by the well-known, early-20th-century primitive painter **Theophilos,** who was something of an eccentric. (The Theophilos House is officially open Mon through Fri from 8am to 2pm; admission is free.) Long after anyone else, Theophilos dressed in a foustanella, the old Greek national costume of a short pleated skirt, long woolen hose, and heavy wooden shoes with turned-up toes—the same costume that the guards outside the Greek Parliament in Athens still wear. If you don't find the vital villager with the key to the house Theophilos decorated, don't despair. You can see examples of his frescoes showing figures from myth and history in the Museum of Greek Folk Art, Odos Kidathineon 17, Plaka, Athens, and in the Theophilos Museum on Mytilene.

The village of **Portaria,** although only 14 kilometers (8.7 miles) out of seaside Volos, is 600 meters up on the mountainside. The central square has the fountains and plane trees that make Pelion villages so charming, as well as several cafes where you can sample the local wine and cheese.

Portaria usually has fewer visitors than nearby **Makrinitsa,** whose handsome three-story houses flank the main square, which has fantastic sunset views back toward Volos. The **Diamantis cafe** in the main square and the **Church of Ayia Triada** on the hill above the square both have examples of Theophilos's work. There are several nice traditional settlements hotels in Makrinitsa (see "Where to Stay," below).

If you're here in summer, there's no reason to stop at **Hania,** which is currently being developed as a ski center for the slopes at **Agriolefkes.** In winter, information on ski conditions is available from the **Ski Center** (☎ 0421/96-417).

Zagora, Pelion's largest village (population 3,000), has a splendid 18th-century church with a bell tower that looks almost Alpine and several buildings with the exterior porches that were built to protect people not from the summer sun, but from the winter snow. If you're here in spring, you'll smell the apple blossoms; Zagora is Greece's largest producer of apples. If you're here in summer, you might want to head south from Zagora to the fine **beaches** at **Ayios Ioannis** or **Milopotamos,** before continuing on to the villages of Milies and Vizitsa.

Milies has a splendid history. During the long years of the Turkish occupation, the school here (which you can still see today) helped to preserve Greek learning and culture. That tradition is continued today in Milies at the small **folk museum,** on the second floor of the Town Hall. Photographs, tools, household objects, and mementos from the Greek War of Independence give a glimpse of life in old Milies. Several books on Milies and Pelion in both English and Greek, as well as posters and postcards, are usually on sale here. The museum is usually open Tuesday through Sunday from 10am to 2pm, and is sometimes open other days in the afternoon; admission is free. An old mansion here is being converted into a GNTO traditional settlement inn. While you're here, check to see if the narrow gauge steam railroad from Volos to Milies is back in service, as promised in 1998.

Vizitsa, like Vathia in the distant Mani peninsula in the Peloponnese, was well on its way to becoming a ghost town when the GNTO declared the entire village (population 400) a national treasure and began to restore eight houses here as ✪ **small inns** (see "Where To Stay," below). Now there are several simple tavernas in the village, as well as the inevitable souvenir stands. The GNTO office has a small display of local items and sometimes has local weavings for sale.

It's hard not to have mixed feelings about what the GNTO has done in Vizitsa, which includes organizing **folk festivals** where traditional crafts are demonstrated. On the one hand, it's very pleasant to stay here and know that you are helping to revitalize a lovely area. On the other hand, it's hard to not worry that Vizitsa—and other Pelion villages—may end up being a kind of Greek Colonial Williamsburg: a living museum of outdoor history rather than true living communities.

BEACHES

The best beaches on Pelion are at the beach resort of **Platanias** and the smaller seaside hamlet of **Mylopotamos,** which shows signs of becoming a resort town. If you have a car, and are driving around Pelion, you will also see dirt roads leading down to a number of secluded and pleasant beaches.

WHERE TO STAY
MAKRINITSA

If you want to stay in one of Makrinitsa's traditional settlement guest houses, it's a good idea to make a reservation well in advance through one of the hotels or the main office (☎ 0421/99-250). Doubles go for Dr30,000 ($100). Reservations are particularly necessary at Easter and in early May, popular times here. All of these inns are decorated with local weavings and some old furnishings; the Sisilianou overlooks the main square, while the others are off the square.

You'll probably have to take potluck with which inn you are assigned to, but if you arrive early and case the possibilities, you can lodge a specific request at the local **GNTO** office (☎ 0423/86-373). Below is a list of the guest houses in Makrinitsa.

Archontiko Diomidi. ☎ 0421/99-430. Fax 0421/99-114. 12 units.

Archontiko Karamarli. ☎ 0421/99-570. Fax 0421/99-779. 9 units.

Archontiko Mousli. ☎ 0421/99-250. Fax 0421/99-228. 7 units.

Archontiko Pandora. ☎ 0421/99-404. Fax 0421/99-114. 5 units.

Archontiko Repana. ☎ 0421/99-548. 7 units.

Archontiko Sisilianou. ☎ 0421/99-556. 7 units.

Archontiko Theofilos. ☎ 0421/99-435. 5 units.

MILIES

The traditional guest house here is the **Archontiko Filippidi** (☎ 0423/86-714), which has eight units. There are also three other small hotels in Milies, with a total of 18 units; ask when you arrive—at present, there's no phone, fax, or reservation service that can book in advance.

VIZITSA

The Greek National Tourist Office has restored eight houses as traditional guest houses in Vizitsa. Reservations must be made through the **GNTO** at ☎ 0423/86-373. You can also inquire about reservations at the GNTO offices in Athens and Thessaloniki. In addition to the GNTO guest houses in Vizitsa, there are several other small hotels here, of which the **Vafiadi** (☎ 0423/86-765), with eight units, is especially appealing. Scheduled to open soon is Vizitsa's first luxury accommodations, the **Glorious Peleus Castle Hotel** (☎ 0423/88-671, or 01/806-3892 in Athens; fax 0423/86-661), with 11 units.

WHERE TO DINE

Although Pelion attracts a lot of Greek tourists who come back year after year, restaurants here, although perfectly pleasant, are not adventurous. Some popular local dishes include *kouneli stifado* (rabbit stew with little onions and cinnamon), various bean dishes, and *tirosomi* (cheesebread). In every village, you'll find the local restaurants on the main square; in our experience, there's no real point in searching down side streets for other places. What you see is what you get here—and it's very pleasant to sit under the plane trees on the main plateia in one of the Pelion villages.

Here are some places that we've had good meals at or heard good things about: the **Galini,** on the main square in Makrinitsa; the **Palios Stathmos** (old railroad station) in Milies; the **Georgaras, Drosia,** and **Balkonaki** in Vizitsa. Expect to pay about Dr3,000 to Dr4,500 ($10–$15) for wine and a simple meal.

13 The Sporades

by John S. Bowman

Prepared to experience some Greek islands that no one else in your crowd knows about? Then try the Sporades ("Scattered" Islands), verdant islands with fragrant pine trees growing down to the edge of golden sand beaches. The Sporades would seem to have always been natural magnets for tourists, but lacking major archaeological remains and historical associations, for a long time did not compete with other parts of Greece.

The Sporades are no longer the natural retreats they once were. Skiathos and Skopelos are the most popular islands, with excellent beaches, fine restaurants, fancy hotels, and an international following. **Skiathos** is among the most expensive islands in Greece and becomes horrendously crowded in high season, but in spring and fall remains a lovely and pleasant place. It's still worth a visit, especially by those interested in a beach vacation, good food, and active nightlife.

Skopelos is nearly as expensive as Skiathos in the high season, but isn't as sophisticated or as jaded. Its beaches are fewer and less impressive, but Skopelos town is among the most beautiful ports in Greece, and the island offers some pleasant excursions.

More remote **Skyros** seems hardly a part of the group, especially as its landscape and architecture are more Cycladic. But it has a few excellent beaches, as well as a colorful local culture, and it remains a good destination for those who want to get away from the crowds.

STRATEGIES FOR SEEING THE ISLANDS If you have only 1 to 3 days, you had better settle on just one of the Sporades. You will then be able to get a ship directly (from various ports, identified below for each island) to any of them—and a plane in the case of Skiathos and Skyros; if time is a factor, we strongly advise flying to Skiathos or Skyros.

If you do have more time, you can continue to another island via **hydrofoil** (known as "Flying Dolphins") or **ferryboat**. (Note, however, that the frequency of all connections is naturally cut back from Sept through May.)

1 Skiathos

108km (58 nautical miles) from Ayios Konstandinos, which is 166km (103 miles) from Athens

Skiathos remained isolated and agrarian until the early 1970s. Today it's one of the most cosmopolitan and attractive islands in Greece, and this rapid change has created a few disturbing ripples. Although the island's inhabitants are eager to please, in high season they can be overextended, inevitably relying on imported help, usually from Athens, who often don't care much about providing any local flavor. Meanwhile, the sheer numbers of foreigners means that some show little concern for the island's indigenous character. Skiathos town at high season has all the personality of a shopping mall. Yet Skiathos town, sometimes called Hora, does have attractive elements, and at its best seems fairly sophisticated, with the handsome Bourtzi fortress on its harbor, elegant shops, excellent restaurants, and a flashy nightlife.

The rest of the island retains much of its natural allure. For most, the main attractions are the purity of the water and the lovely fine-sand beaches. The island boasts more than 60 beaches, the most famous of which, **Koukounaries,** is considered one of the very best in Greece. If you relish sun, sand, sea, and crowds, you'll love it.

Lalaria, on the less developed north coast, much less accessible and less crowded, has magnificent rock formations and is even more beautiful. The interior of the island is densely wooded, and has several pretty monasteries; the interesting old Kastro is at the far north end.

If possible, visit before or after July 10 to September 10, when the tourist crush is at its worst and the island's population of less than 5,000 swells to over 50,000. If you must visit during high season, reserve a room well ahead of time and be prepared for the crush.

ESSENTIALS

GETTING THERE   By Plane   Olympic Airways has service daily (twice daily Apr and May, five times daily June through Sept) from Athens; contact their Athens office (☎ **01/966-6666**) for information and reservations. For the moment, Olympic does not maintain an office in Skiathos town; you must deal with them at the nearby airport (☎ **0427/22-200**). There is presently no bus service between the airport and town; expect to pay Dr1,500 ($5) by taxi.

By Boat   Skiathos can be reached by either ferryboat (3 hr.) or hydrofoil (75 min.) from Volos or Ayios Konstandinos, and there is also ferryboat service from Kimi on Evvia (5 hr.). In high season, there are four hydrofoils daily from Volos, three from Ayios Konstandinos, and service from Thessaloniki (3 hr.). There are also the hydrofoils linking Skiathos to Skopelos (30 to 45 min.), Alonissos (60 to 75 min.), and Skyros (2⅓ hr.).

In Athens, **Alkyon Travel,** Odos Akademias 97, near Omonia Square (☎ **01/ 384-3220** or 01/384-3221), can arrange bus transportation to Ayios Konstandinos as well as hydrofoil or ferry tickets. (The bus costs about Dr3,000/$10 one-way.)

For hydrofoil schedules and information, contact the **Ceres Hydrofoil Joint Service** at Piraeus (☎ **01/428-0001**), Skiathos (☎ **0427/22-018**), Ayios Konstandinos (☎ **0235/31-614**), Thessaloniki (☎ **031/547-407**), or Volos (☎ **0421/39-786**). For ferryboat information, contact the **Nomikos North Aegean Lines** in Piraeus (☎ **01/429-6740**). Ferry tickets can be purchased through several local travel agents at each port. (On Skiathos, contact the agent at ☎ **0427/22-209.**)

Hydrofoils, excursion boats, and ferries dock at the port town of **Skiathos** (also called Hora), on the island's southern coast toward the east end of the island.

VISITOR INFORMATION   The town maintains an **information booth** at the western corner of the harbor; during the summer at least, it is open daily from about 9am to 8pm. Meanwhile, private travel agencies abound and can help with most all of your requests. We highly recommend **Mare Nostrum Holidays,** Odos Papadiamandis 21 (☎ **0427/21-463** or 0427/21-464; fax 0427/21-793). It books villas, hotels, and rooms; sells tickets to many of the around-the-island, hydrofoil, and beach caïque (skiff) trips; books Olympic flights; exchanges currency; and changes all traveler's checks without commission. Katerina Michail-Craig, the charming managing director, and her staff speak excellent English, are helpful and exceedingly well informed, and have lots of tips on everything from beaches to restaurants. It's open daily from 8am to 10pm.

GETTING AROUND   By Bus   Skiathos has public bus service along the south coast of the island from the bus station on the harbor to Koukounaries (Dr300/$1), with stops at the beaches in between. A conductor will ask for your destination and assess the fare after the bus is in progress. Buses run six times daily April through November; every hour from 9am to 9pm May through October; every half hour from 8:30am to 10pm June through September; and every 20 minutes from 8:30am to 2:30pm and 3:30pm to midnight July through August.

By Car & Moped   Reliable car and moped agencies include the local **Avis** on the paralia (☎ **0427/21-458;** fax 0427/23-289; e-mail: skiathos_center@ skiathosinfo.com), run by the friendly Yannis Theofanidis; **Aivalioti's Rent-A-Car** on the paralia (☎ **0427/21-246**); and **Creator** at Papadiamandis 8 (☎ **0427/22-385**). Even for the smaller models, expect to pay Dr16,500 to Dr21,500 ($55 to $72) in high season. Mopeds start at Dr4,000 ($13) per day.

By Boat   The north coast beaches, adjacent islands, and the historic Kastro are most easily reached by caïque; these smaller vessels post their beach and island tour schedules on signs over the stem and sail frequently from the fishing harbor west of the Bourtzi fortress. An around-the-island tour that includes stops at Lalaria Beach and Kastro will cost about Dr4,000 ($13).

The Flying Dolphin agent, **Skiathos Holidays,** on the paralia, is open from 7am to 9:30pm; in high season there are as many as eight high-speed hydrofoils daily to Skopelos and Alonissos. There are also daily excursions to Skyros in high season. Call ☎ **0427/22-018** or 0427/22-033 for up-to-date departure schedules. Note that even if you have a ticket, you must appear at the agent's ticket office at least 30 minutes before the scheduled sailing to get your ticket confirmed and seat assigned. **Nomikos Lines** (☎ **0427/22-209** or 0427/22-276), at the corner of Odos Papadiamandis and the paralia, sells tickets for the ferryboats to the other islands.

FAST FACTS   The official **American Express** agent is Mare Nostrum Holidays, Odos Papadiamandis 21 (☎ **0427/21-463**; fax 0427/21-793); open daily from 8am to 10pm. There are many banks in the town, such as the **National Bank of Greece,** Odos Papadiamandis, open Monday through Friday from 8am to 2pm and 7 to 9pm, and Sunday from 9am to noon. For medical emergencies contact the **hospital** (☎ **0427/22-040**), on the coast road at the far west edge of town. A self-service **laundry** is at Odos Georgios Panora 14, 85 meters up Odos Papadiamandis, opposite the National Bank (☎0427/22-341); open daily from 8am to 2pm and 5 to 11pm. The **police station** (☎ **0427/21-111**) is about 250 meters from the harbor on Odos Papadiamandis, on the left. The **tourist police** booth is about 15 meters further along on the right. The **post office** (☎ **0427/22-011**) is on Odos Papadiamandis, inland from the harbor about 160 meters and on the right; open Monday through

Friday from 7:30am to 2pm. The **telephone office (OTE)** is on Odos Papadiamandis, inland from the harbor, on the right, some 30 meters beyond the post office; open Monday through Friday from 7:30am to 10pm, Saturday and Sunday from 9am to 2pm and 5 to 10pm (☎ **0427/22-135**).

WHAT TO SEE & DO

Skiathos is a relatively modern town, built in 1930 on two low-lying hills, then reconstructed after heavy German bombardment during World War II. The handsome **Bourtzi fortress** jutting out into the middle of the harbor is an islet connected by a broad causeway. Ferries and hydrofoils stop at the port on the right (east) of the fortress, and fishing boats and excursion caïques dock on the left (west). Two-story whitewashed villas with bright red-tiled roofs line both sides of the harbor, with the handsome church of **Ayios Nikolaos** dominating the hill on the east side; the larger church of **Trion Ierarchon** ("Three Archbishops") balances it lower on the west side.

The main street that leads off the harbor and up through town is named **Papadiamandis,** after the island's best-known son (see "The Papadiamandis House," below). Here you'll find numerous restaurants, cafes, and stores, plus services such as Mare Nostrum Holidays and the OTE.

On the west flank of the harbor (the left side as you disembark from the ferry) are numerous outdoor cafes and restaurants, excursion caïques (for the north coast beaches, adjacent islands, and around-the-island tours), and at the far corner, the broad steps leading up to the town's next level. Mounting the stairs above the Oasis Cafe will lead you to **Plateia Trion Ierarchon,** a stone-paved square around the town's most important church. The eastern flank is home to many tourist services as well as a few recommended hotels and many restaurants; beyond it the harbor-front road branches right along the yacht harbor, an important nightlife area in summer, and left toward the airport.

The Papadiamandis House. Right off main street, 50m up from harbor. ☎ **0427/23-843**. Admission Dr250 (85¢). Tues–Sun 9:30am–1pm and 5–8pm.

Alexandros Papadiamandis (1851–1911) was born on Skiathos, and after his adult career as a journalist in Athens, returned in 1908 and died in this very house. His almost 200 short stories and novellas, mostly about Greek island life, have assured him a major reputation in Greece, but his rather idiosyncratic style and vernacular language made his work difficult to translate into foreign languages. His house is more of a shrine than a museum, with his personal possessions and tools of his writing trade. (A statue of Papadiamandis stands in front of the Bourtzi fortress on the promontory at the corner of the harbor.)

BEACHES

Skiathos is famous for its beaches, and we'll cover the most important ones briefly, proceeding clockwise from the port. The most popular beaches are west of town along 12 kilometers (8 miles) of coastal highway. At most, you can rent an umbrella and two chairs for about Dr1,800 ($6) per day. The first, **Megali Ammos,** is the sandy strip below the popular package-tour community of Ftelia; so close to town and packed with the groups, it probably won't appeal to most. **Vassilias** and **Achladias** are too crowded and developed; **Tzanerias** is a slight improvement. Further out on the Kalamaki peninsula, south of the highway, **Kanapitsa** begins to excite some interest, especially among those fond of water sports; **Kanapitsa Water-Sport Center** (☎ 0427/21-298) has water and jet skis, windsurfing, air chairs, sailing, and speedboat hire. Scuba divers may want to stop at the **Dolphin Diving Center** (☎ 0427/22-520) at the big Nostos Hotel.

Across the peninsula, **Vromolimnos** ("Dirty Lake") is fairly attractive and usually relatively uncrowded, perhaps because of its unsavory name and the cloudy (but not polluted) water from which it comes; it offers waterskiing and windsurfing. **Ayia Paraskevi** is highly regarded. **Platanias,** the next major beach, is usually uncrowded, perhaps because the big resort hotels there have their own pools and sundecks. Past the next headland, **Troulos** is one of the prettiest because of its relative isolation, crescent shape, and the islets that guard the small bay. The major road north from the coastal highway here leads to the Kounistria monastery, a pretty 17th-century structure containing some beautiful icons, in a lovely spot with a nice taverna. Horseback enthusiasts should note that the **Pinewood Horse Riding Club** is located on this road.

The last bus stop is at the much ballyhooed **Koukounaries** (some 16km/10 miles from Skiathos town). The bus chugs uphill past the Pallas Hotel luxury resort, then descends and winds around the inland waterway, Lake Strofilias, stopping at the edge of a fragrant pine forest. *Koukounaries* means "pine cones" in Greek, and behind this grove of trees is a half-mile-long stretch of fine gold sand in a half-moon–shaped cove. Tucked into the evergreen fold are some changing rooms, a small snack bar, and the concessionaire for windsurfers. The beach is extremely crowded with an easy mix of topless sunbathers, families, and singles. On the far west side of the cove is the island's spartan Xenia Hotel, at present deserted. (There are many lodgings in the area, but because of the intense mosquito activity and ticky-tacky construction, we prefer to stay back in town or in a villa.)

Ayia Eleni, a short but scenic walk from the Koukounaries bus stop (the end of the line) west across the tip of the island, is a broad cove popular for windsurfing, because the wind is a bit rougher than at the south coast beaches but not nearly as gusty as the north. Across the peninsula behind the deserted Xenia Hotel, 15 to 20 minutes of fairly steep grade from the Koukounaries bus stop, is **Banana Beach** (sometimes called Krassa). It's slightly less crowded than Koukounaries, but with the same sand and pine trees. There's a snack bar or two, and chairs, umbrellas, and windsurfers and jet skis for rent. One stretch of Banana Beach is the island's most fashionable nude beach.

Limonki Xerxes, also called Mandraki, north across the tip of the island, a 20-minute walk up the path opposite the Lake Strofilias bus stop, is a cove where Xerxes brought in 10 triremes (galleys) to conquer the Hellenic fleet moored at Skiathos during the Persian Wars. It's a pristine and relatively secluded beach for those who crave a quiet spot. **Elia,** east across the little peninsula, is also quite nice. Both beaches have small refreshment kiosks.

Proceeding along the northeast coast from Mandraki, you arrive at **Megalos Aselinos,** a windy beach where free camping has taken root. It is linked to the southern coastal highway via the road that leads to the Kounistria monastery; you must continue north when the road forks off to the right toward the monastery. There's also an official campsite and a fairly good taverna. **Mikros Aselinos,** further east, is smaller and quieter, and you can reach it via a road that leads off to the left just before the monastery.

Most of the other north coast beaches are only accessible by boat, but one of these definitely rewards those willing to make the trip: ✪ **Lalaria,** on the island's northern tip, is regarded as one of the loveliest beaches in Greece. One of its unique qualities is the **Tripia Petra,** perforated rock cliffs, that jut out into the sea on both sides of the cove. These have been worn through in time by the wind and the waves to form perfect archways. You can lie on the gleaming white pebbles and admire the neon-blue Aegean and cloudless sky through their rounded openings. The water at Lalaria is an especially vivid shade of aquamarine because of the highly reflective white pebbles and marble and limestone slabs which coat the sea bottom. The swimming here is excellent, though the undertow can sometimes be quite strong. Out in the water you can admire the glowing silver-white pebble beach and jagged white cliffs above it. There are many naturally carved caves in the cliff wall that lines the beach, providing privacy or shade for those who have had too much exposure. Lalaria can only be reached by caïque excursions from the port; the fare is Dr4,000 ($13) for an around-the-island trip, which usually includes stops at one or more of the other sights along the north coast.

Skiathos's north coast is much more rugged and scenically pure, with steep cliffs, pine forests, rocky hills, and caves. Three of the island's most spectacular grottos— **Skotini, Glazia,** and **Halkini**—are just east of Lalaria. Spilia Skotini is particularly impressive, a fantastic 20-foot-tall sea cave reached through a narrow crevice, just wide enough for caïques to squeeze through, in the cliff wall. Seagulls drift above you in the cave's cool darkness, while below, fish swim down in the 30-foot subsurface portion. Erosion has created spectacular scenery and many sandy coves along the north and east coasts, though none are as beautiful or well sheltered from the meltemi as Lalaria beach.

THE KASTRO

For those preferring other pursuits, there is at least one excursion that should appeal: **Kastro,** the old fortress capital, located on the northernmost point of the island, east of Lalaria beach. Kastro was built in a remote and spectacular site in the 16th century when the island was overrun by the Turks. It was abandoned shortly after the War of Independence when such fortifications were no longer necessary. Once joined to firm ground by a drawbridge, it can now be reached by cement stairs. The remains of more than 300 houses and 22 churches have mostly fallen to the sea, but three of the churches, with porcelain plates imbedded in their worn stucco facades, still stand, and the original frescoes of one are still visible. From this citadel prospect there are excellent views to the **Kastronisia** islet below and the sparkling Aegean. Kastro can be reached on foot, a 3-hour hike from the port of Skiathos. Starting out on the uphill path just west of the harbor will take you by the monasteries of Ayios Fanourias, Ayios Dionisios, and Ayios Athanassios to Panayia Kardasi, where the road officially ends. You can also reach Kastro by **excursion caïque,** by **mule or donkey tour** (available through most travel agencies), or by **moped** via the latest road which runs to the north coast from just south of Ftelia.

SHOPPING

Skiathos town has no shortage of shops, many offering the standard wares but some offering distinctive items. The highlight for Greek crafts and folk art is **Archipelago** (☎ 0427/22-163), adjacent to the Papadiamandis House. Exquisite objects of art and folklore, both old and new, include costumes, jewelry, and sculpture. **Aris,** Odos Aglianous 4, the street opposite the Papadiamandis House (☎ 0427/22-415), sells bright, unusual dresses and flirty shirts hand-painted with lively patterns. **Galerie Varsakis** (☎ 0427/22-255), on Trion Ierarchon Square, above the fishing port, has a virtually museum-quality collection of folk antiques, embroidered bags and linens, rugs from around the world, and other collectibles.

WHERE TO STAY

Between July 1 and September 20, it can be literally impossible to find accommodations here. Try phoning ahead from Athens to book a room or, better still, book your accommodations before you leave home. Note that most of the "luxury" hotels were thrown up quickly some years ago, and some have since been managed and maintained poorly—so if you intend to stay awhile in a beach resort, we recommend you first check into one of the hotels in town and then look over the possibilities before you commit to an extended rental.

If you crave the restaurant/shopping/nightlife scene, or you've arrived without reservations at one of the resort communities, we recommend setting up base in **Skiathos town.** From here, you can take public buses to the beaches on the south coast or go on caïque excursions to the spectacular north coast. Then again, many families prefer to stay in two- to four-bedroom villas outside of the town or at hotels overlooking a beach, with only an occasional foray into town.

One of the most pleasant parts of Skiathos town is the quiet neighborhood on the hill above the bay at the western end of the port. Numerous **private rooms** to let can be found on and above the winding stair/street. Take a walk and look for the signs or ask a passerby or neighborhood merchant. All over the hillside above the eastern harbor are several unlicensed "hotels," basically rooms to rent. Inquire from passersby when you're hotel hunting and you'll be surprised at which buildings turn out to be lodgings.

By the way, the in-town hotels (Alkyon excepted) cannot provide parking, but there are possibilities at the far eastern edge of the harbor.

IN & AROUND SKIATHOS TOWN
Moderate
Also consider the **Hotel Athos,** on the "ring road" that skirts above Skiathos town (☎/fax **0427/22-4777**), which offers ready access to town without the bustle; and the **Hotel Meltemi,** on the paralia (☎ **0427/22-493;** fax 0427/21-294), a comfortable, modern place on the east side of the harbor (but avoid the front units, which can be noisy).

✪ **Hotel Alkyon.** Armoudia (at far eastern end of paralia), 37002 Skiathos. ☎ **0427/22-981.** Fax 0427/21-643. 85 units. A/C MINIBAR TEL. Dr20,900 ($70) double. Rates include buffet breakfast. AE, EURO, MC, V. Parking in adjacent area.

This should probably be the favored place for those who want it all—to be near the harbor of Skiathos town, to enjoy some shaded seclusion, and to return to a hotel with some creature comforts. It's not glitzy or luxurious, but modern and subdued; its rooms are medium sized (and offer three programs of taped music), and bathrooms are modern; there is a small pool with an adjacent bar. Best of all, it's a great place for those who look forward to a shady retreat after time in the sun.

✪ **Hotel Orsa.** Plakes, 37002 Skiathos. ☎ **0427/22-430.** Fax 0427/21-952. 17 units. TEL. Dr21,000 ($70) double. Rates include breakfast. No credit cards.

One of the most charming small hotels in town is on the western promontory beyond the fishing harbor. To get here, walk down the port west past the fish stalls and Jimmy's Bar, proceed up two flights of steps, and watch for a recessed courtyard on the left, with handsome wrought-iron details. Rooms are standard in size but tastefully decorated; most have windows or balconies overlooking the harbor and the islands beyond. A lovely garden terrace is a perfect place for a tranquil breakfast. Contact Heliotropio Travel on the east end of the harbor (☎ **0427/22-430;** fax 0427/21-952; e-mail: helio@n.skiathos.gr) for booking.

Inexpensive
The **Hotel Bourtzi,** Odos Moraitou 8 (☎ **0427/21-304;** fax 0427/23-243), an attractive choice in the middle of town, is mostly a group hotel but has a few rooms available to individuals; ask for a unit that faces the back garden.

Hotel Australia. Parados Evanyelistrias, 37002 Skiathos. ☎ **0427/22-488.** 16 units. Dr12,000 ($40) double; Dr15,000 ($50) studio with kitchen. No credit cards. Turn right off Odos Papadiamandis at the post office, then take the first left.

If you've come to Skiathos expecting some style, this plain, clean, quiet hotel is not for you. Run by a couple who lived in Australia and speak English quite well, the rooms are sparsely furnished but comfortable, with small balconies; bathrooms are small but functional, and guests can share a fridge in the hallway.

Hotel Morfo. Odos Anainiou 23, 37002 Skiathos. ☎ **0427/21-737.** Fax 0427/23-222. 17 units. TEL. Dr12,000 ($40) double. EURO, MC, V.

Looking for a slightly "atmospheric" offbeat hotel? Turn right off the main street at the National Bank, then left at the big plane tree, and find this attractive hotel on your left on a quiet back street in the center of town. You enter through a small, well-kept garden into a festively decorated lobby. The rooms are comfortable and tastefully decorated.

ON THE BEACH

Atrium Hotel. Platanias (some 9km/5 miles along the coast road southeast of Skiathos town), 37002 Skiathos. ☎ **0427/49-345.** Fax 0427/49-444. 75 units. A/C TEL. Dr30,000 ($100) double. Rates include breakfast. AE, EURO, MC, V. Parking on grounds.

This is the "class act" of Skiathos when it comes to hotels. Its location, on a pine-clad slope overlooking the sea, plus its various amenities (billiard room, fitness room, water-sports gear) make it a most pleasant place to vacation. A sandy beach is some 100 meters below and it also has a beautiful Olympic-size pool on a plaza high above the Aegean. The guest rooms are only fair-sized, but compensate with balconies or terraces that offer views over the sea; bathrooms are fully appointed. The hotel has a bar and a restaurant that serves up decent meals, outdoors if you like. There were earlier complaints about its staff and service, but we experienced only a hospitable hotel in our latest visit.

✪ **Troulos Bay Hotel.** Troulos (8km/5 miles along the coast road southeast of Skiathos), 37002 Skiathos. ☎ **0427/49-3901.** Fax 0427/49-218. 43 units. TEL. Dr23,000 ($77) double. V. Parking on grounds.

Though it's not exactly luxurious, this is our first choice of beach hotels. It's set in handsomely landscaped and well-kept grounds on the south coast's prettiest little beach. Like most of Skiathos's hotels, it's mostly used by groups. The restaurant serves good food at reasonable prices, and the staff is refreshingly attentive and truly helpful. The bedrooms are large, attractive, and comfortably furnished; most have a balcony overlooking the gorgeous beach with the lovely wooded islets beyond.

WHERE TO DINE

As is the case with most of Greece's overdeveloped tourist resorts, there's a plethora of cafes, fast-food stands, and overpriced restaurants, but there are also plenty of good and even excellent eateries in Skiathos town. Some of the more well-regarded restaurants are above the west end of the harbor, approaching and beyond Trion Ierarchon church.

EXPENSIVE

✪ **Asprolithos.** Odos Mavroyiali and Odos Korai (up Odos Papadiamandis a block past the high school, then turn right). ☎ **0427/23-110.** Reservations recommended. Main courses Dr1,500–Dr5,500 ($5–$18). AE, EURO, V. Daily 7pm–1am. GREEK/INTERNATIONAL.

An elegant ambiance and friendly, attentive service combined with superb meals of light, updated taverna fare make this one of our favorites on Skiathos. You can get a classic moussaka here if you want to play it safe, or try specialties like artichokes and prawns smothered in cheese. Their excellent snapper baked in wine with wild greens is served with thick french fries that have obviously never seen a freezer. The main dining room is dominated by a handsome stone fireplace, and there are also tables outside where you can catch the breeze.

Le Bistrot. Odos Martinou (high above western end of harbor). ☎ **0427/21-627.** Reservations recommended. Main courses Dr1,800–Dr4,800 ($6–$16). EURO, MC, V. Daily 7pm–1am. CONTINENTAL.

This intimate, continental restaurant is easily spotted along with its twin, across the street, which functions as a bar, overlooking the water. Both the bar and the dining room are lovely spaces. The full-course meals are beautifully prepared from their own stocks and sauces. Swordfish, roast pork, and steamed vegetables should be savored slowly, so you will have room for the delicious desserts.

✪ **The Windmill Restaurant.** Located on peak east of Ayios Nikolaos church. ☎ **0427/ 24-550.** Reservations recommended. Dr3,000–Dr4,000 ($10–$13). EURO, V. Daily 7–11pm. INTERNATIONAL.

The town's most special dining experience is at what is literally an old windmill, visible from the paralia. (There are several ways to approach it, but the signed one begins on the street behind the San Remo and Akti hotels at the eastern end of the harbor.) It is quite a climb, but well worth it. You couldn't ask for a more romantic setting than one of the terraces, where you can enjoy the sunset with your meal. The menu features such distinctive dishes as smoked salmon and prawn filo parcels, spareribs with barbecue sauce, and grilled chicken with bourbon glaze and chili sauce. Even the desserts are unusual—lemon-and-orange terrine with butterscotch sauce or poached pears with red-wine toffee glaze—and there are nearly two dozen wines to choose from, including the best from Greece.

MODERATE

Carnayio Taverna. Paralia. ☎ **0427/22-868.** Main courses Dr1,400–Dr3,900 ($4.70–$13). AE, V. Daily 8pm–1am. TAVERNA/SEAFOOD.

One of the better waterfront tavernas is next to the Hotel Alkyon. Favorites over the years have been their fish soup, lamb *youvetsi,* and grilled fish. The garden setting is still special, and if you're here late enough, you might be lucky to see a real round of dancing waiters and diners.

Taverna Limanakia. Paralia (at far eastern end, past Hotel Alkyon). ☎ **0427/22-835.** Main courses Dr1,400–Dr5,800 ($4.70–$19). MC. Daily 6pm–midnight. TAVERNA/SEAFOOD.

In the style of its next-door neighbor Carnayio, the Limanakia serves some of the best taverna and seafood dishes on the waterfront. We vacillate about which of the two we prefer, but we've always come away feeling satisfied after a meal in this reliable eatery.

Taverna Mesoyia. Odos Grigoriou (behind Trion Ierarchon, high above western end of the harbor). ☎ **0427/21-440.** Main courses Dr1,300–Dr2,800 ($4.35–$9). No credit cards. Daily 7pm–midnight. TAVERNA.

You'll have to work a bit to find some of the best authentic traditional food in town, as this little taverna is in the midst of the town's most labyrinthine neighborhood, above the western end of the harbor, but there are signs once you approach it. Try the "eggplant shoes" (*melitzana papoutaki*), the special chicken, or fresh fish in season. (They are straightforward in admitting when something is frozen—as some fish must be at certain times of the year, when it's illegal to catch.)

INEXPENSIVE

Kampoureli Ouzeri. Paralia (on western stretch of harbor). ☎ **0427/21-112.** Main courses Dr600–Dr3,200 ($2–$11). EURO, MC, V. Daily noon–1am. GREEK.

Although it bills itself as an ouzeri—for drinks and snacks—this is really your standard taverna, and one of the most authentic eateries in town. You can have the ouzo and octopus (which you can see drying on the front line!) combo for Dr700 ($2.35), or sample their rich supply of cheese pies, fried feta, olives, and other piquant mezedes.

Taverna To Pillion. Trion Ierarchon Sq. (to the left of the Varsakis Gallery). No phone. Main courses Dr800–Dr1,400 ($2.70–$4.70). No credit cards. Daily 7pm–1am. GRILL.

Long known as Stavros Gyros and Souvlaki, this unassuming grill (*phisteria*) with a green awning is one of our favorites in the Sporades. Outside you'll see pine tables and a chalkboard menu offering souvlaki and lamb chops. Complement your entree with a peasant salad with feta, chase it all down with soda, beer, wine, or ouzo, and you'll be ready to tackle some more sights—and at a price that few places on Skiathos can match. Delicious *and* a great value.

SKIATHOS AFTER DARK

The **Aegean Festival** presents nightly performances of ancient Greek tragedies and comedies, traditional music and dance, modern dance and theater, and visiting international troupes. Festival events take place from late June to early October in the outdoor theater at the **Bourtzi Cultural Center,** on the promontory on the harbor. (The center itself, open daily from 10am to 2pm and 5:30 to 10pm, hosts art exhibits in its interior.) Performances begin at 9:30pm and usually cost Dr4,000 ($13), half price for students; call ☎ **0427/23-717** for information.

Skiathos town has a lively nightlife scene, more concentrated on each end of the port, but many might prefer to pass the evening with a **volta** (stroll) along the harbor or around and above the Plateia Trion Ierarchon. In fact, we feel the best-kept secret of Skiathos town is the **little outdoor cafe** at the tip of the promontory with the Bourtzi fortress, a 3-minute stroll from the harbor. Removed from the glitter of the town, you can sit and enjoy a (cheap) drink in the cool of the evening and watch the ships come and go: this is the Aegean at its best.

The main concentration of **nightclubs** is in the warren of streets west of Papadiamandis (left as you come up from the harbor). The **Borzoi** is the oldest club on the island; you may want to check it out several times during the evening, which generally gets livelier toward midnight. Continue past it to find the **Banana Bar,** for "surprising dance music," on the right; then the **Admiral Benbow Club,** which offers something more soulful. Across from the Benbow Club is the flashy **Spartacus**. At the next intersection south you'll find **Kirki,** which plays jazz and blues, and the **Totem Musik Bar,** which the local young people recommend. **Vengera,** also on Polytechniou, plays "real Greek music."

Back across Odos Papadiamandis, just before the post office, along Parados Evanyelistrias you can find **Adagio,** which is discreetly gay and plays classical music and Greek ballads that allow conversation. Wander back down the main street to find **Kentavros Bar,** on the left beyond the Papadiamandis House, which plays harder rock-and-roll.

On the far west end of the harbor, **Jimmy's** promises a "getaway feeling." If you want videos with your drinks, try the **Oasis Cafe,** where the draft beer is only Dr400 ($1.35) a stein, and if there's a game of any sort being played they'll have it on the tube. Further along the old harbor, just up the steps on the far side, you'll find the

Jailhouse Cafe, which plays rock music and has a fun menu with items like Cajun-style chicken and ribs with barbecue sauce; you can even have breakfast there. **Remezzo,** on the water near the old shipyard, gets rather wild downstairs, but has a quieter upstairs if the scene is too much for you.

Movie fans might enjoy the **Cinema Paradiso,** up along the "ring road," which has two nightly showings of recent films in English, at 8:30 and 11pm; tickets are Dr1,500 ($5).

2 Skopelos

121km (65 nautical miles) from Ayios Konstandinos, which is 166km (103 miles) from Athens

It was inevitable that handsomely rugged Skopelos would follow Skiathos in its development, but it has done so a bit more wisely and at a slower pace. Its beaches are not so numerous or as pretty, but Skopelos town is one of the most beautiful ports in Greece, and the island is richer in vegetation, with windswept pines growing down to secluded coves, wide beaches, and terraced cliffs of angled rock slabs. The interior is densely planted with fruit and nut orchards. The famous plums and almonds from Skopelos are liberally used in the island's unique cuisine. The coastline, like that of Skiathos, is punctuated by impressive grottos and bays, and you'll find frequent use for a camera.

ESSENTIALS

GETTING THERE   By Plane   Skopleos cannot be reached directly by plane, but you can fly to nearby Skiathos and take a hydrofoil or ferry to the northern port of Loutraki (below Glossa) or the more popular Skopelos town.

By Boat   If you're in Athens, take a boat or hydrofoil from Ayios Konstandinos to Skopelos. **Alkyon Travel,** Odos Akademias 97, near Omonia Square (☎ 01/384-3220 or 01/384-3221), can arrange bus transportation to Ayios Konstandinos (for about Dr3,000/$10 one-way) and hydrofoil or ferry tickets. Coming from Central or Northern Greece, depart for Skopelos from Volos.

From Skiathos, the ferry to Skopelos takes 90 minutes if you call at Skopelos town, or 45 minutes if you get off at Glossa/Loutraki; the one-way fare to both is about Dr1,000 ($3.35). Ferry tickets can be purchased at the **Nomikos Lines** office on the left side coming off the dock. The Flying Dolphin hydrofoil takes 15 minutes to Glossa/Loutraki (four to five times daily; Dr2,500/$8), and 45 minutes to Skopelos (six to eight times daily, Dr2,800/$9). From Skiathos, you can also take one of the many daily excursion boats to Skopelos.

It's possible to catch a regular ferry or hydrofoil from Alonissos to Skopelos (seven times daily; Dr2,500/$8), or ride on one of the excursion boats. Expect to pay a little more on the excursion boats—but if they're not full, you can sometimes negotiate the price.

There are infrequent ferryboat connections from Kimi (on Evvia) to Skopelos. Check with the **Skopelos Port Authority** (☎ 0424/22-180) for current schedules, as they change frequently. We think hydrofoils are worth the extra expense for hopping around the Sporades.

In the port of Skopelos town, hydrofoil tickets can be purchased at the Flying Dolphin agent, **Madro Travel,** immediately opposite the dock (☎ 0424/22-300); it's open all year and also operates as the local Olympic Airways representative.

VISITOR INFORMATION   The **Municipal Tourist Office** of Skopelos is located on the waterfront, to the left of the pier as you disembark (☎ 0424/323-231);

it's open daily from 9:30am to 10pm in high season. It offers information, changes money, and reserves rooms. If you want to call ahead and arrange for a room, the **Association of Owners of Rental Accommodation** maintains a small office on the harbor (☎ 0424/24-567).

At the excellent travel agency **Skopelorama,** about 100 meters beyond the Hotel Eleni on the left (east) end of the port (☎ 0424/229-170; fax 0424/23-243), the staff can help you find a room, exchange money, rent a car, or take an excursion; they know the island inside-out, are friendly folk, and can provide information on just about anything. It's open daily from 8am to 10pm.

For those who really want to explore the island, *Walking in Skopelos,* by Birthe Leth Nielsen and Benita Schmidt (Dr1,500/$5), is an excellent guide.

GETTING AROUND   By Bus   Skopelos is reasonably well served by public bus; the bus stop in Skopelos town is on the east end of the port. There are four routes. Buses run the main route every half hour in the high season beginning in Skopelos and making stops at Stafilos, Agnondas, Panormos, the Adrina Beach Hotel, Milia, Elios, Klima, Glossa, and Loutraki. The fare from Skopelos to Glossa is Dr600 ($2).

By Car & Moped   The most convenient way to see the island is to rent a car or moped at one of the many shops on the port. A four-wheel–drive vehicle at **Motor Tours** (☎ 0424/22-986; fax 0424/22-602), for example, will run around Dr28,000 ($93), including third-party insurance; expect to pay a few thousand drachmas less for a Fiat Panda. A moped should cost about Dr4,000 ($13) per day.

By Taxi   The taxi stand is in the middle of the waterfront, and taxis will provide service to almost any place on the island. Taxis are not metered, and you should negotiate your fare before accepting a ride. A typical fare, from Skopelos to Glossa, runs Dr5,500 ($18).

By Boat   To visit the more isolated beaches, take one of the large excursion boats that visit more secluded beaches and provide a barbecue lunch. These cost about Dr12,000 ($40) and should be booked a day in advance in high season. Excursion boats operate only in the peak season to Glisteri, Gliphoneri, and Sares beaches, for about Dr1,500 ($5). From the port of Agnondas, on the south coast, there are fishing boats traveling to Limnonari, one of the island's better beaches.

FAST FACTS   There are several **ATMs** at the banks around the harbor. The **health center** is on the road leading out of the east end of town (☎ 0424/22-222). Plynthria, a self-service **laundry,** is located just past the Adonis Hotel on the upper road (☎ 0424/22-123); open Monday through Saturday from 9am to 1:30pm and 5:30 to 9pm. For any and all emergencies, contact the **police** at ☎ 0424/22-235. The police station is located up the steps to the right of the National Bank, along the harbor. The **post office,** located on the far east side of the port, up the road behind the Bar Alegari, is open Monday through Friday from 8am to 2:30pm. The only **telephone office (OTE)** on the island is in the center of the waterfront of Skopelos town; it is open Monday through Saturday from 8am to 5pm, but there are plenty of card phones. Elsewhere on Skopleos you will also find card phones or you can try a kiosk, travel agent, or hotel for telephone service.

WHAT TO SEE & DO

The ferries from Alonissos, Skyros, and Kimi and most of the hydrofoils and other boats from Skiathos dock at both Glossa/Loutraki and Skopelos town. Most boats stop first at **Loutraki,** a homely little port near the northern end of the west coast, with the more attractive town of ✪ **Glossa** high above it. We suggest you stay onboard for the trip around the northern tip of the island and along the east coast—getting a better sense of why the island's name means "cliff" in Greek—to the island's main harbor, especially if this is your first visit. You'll know why as the boat pulls around the last headland into that huge and nearly perfect C-shaped harbor, and you get your first glimpse of Skopelos town rising like a steep amphitheater around the port.

Skopelos town (also called Hora, of course) is one of Greece's most treasured towns, on a par with Hydra and Simi. It scales the steep, low hills around the harbor and has the same winding, narrow paths that characterize the more famous Cycladic islands to the south. The town's many churches add much to the fantastic effect.

Scattered on the slopes of the town are only a few of the island's 123 churches, which must be something of a record for such a small locale. The waterfront is lined with banks, cafes, travel agencies, and the like. Interspersed among these prosaic offerings are some truly regal-looking shade trees. Many of the shops and services are up the main street leading away from near the center of the paralia. The back streets are amazingly convoluted (and unnamed); the best plan is to wander around and get to know a few familiar landmarks.

The **Venetian Kastro,** which overlooks the town from a rise on the western corner, has been whitewashed, so that it looks too new to have been built over an archaic temple of Athena, and too serene to have been deemed too formidable for attack by the Turks during the War of Independence in the early 19th century.

SHOPPING

Skopelos has a variety of shops selling Greek and local ceramics, weavings, and jewelry. One of the most stylish is **Armoloi,** in the center of the shops along the harbor (☎ 0424/22-707). It sells only Greek jewelry, ceramics, weavings, and silver; some of the objects are old, and most of the handsome ceramics are made by the owners. **Nick Rodios** (☎ 0424/22-779), whose gallery is located between the Hotel Eleni and the Skopelorama agency, is from a Skopelos family who have made ceramics for three generations. His elegant black vessels, at once both classical and modern, are among the finest we've found in Greece.

EXPLORING THE ISLAND

The whole island is sprinkled with monasteries and churches, but five **monasteries** south of town can be visited by following a pleasant path that continues south from the beach hotels. The first, **Evanyelistria,** was founded by monks from Mount Athos, but it now serves as a nunnery, and the weavings of its present occupants can be bought at a small shop here; it's open daily from 8am to 1pm and 4 to 7pm. The fortified monastery of **Ayia Barbara,** now abandoned, contains 15th-century frescoes. **Metamorphosis,** very nearly abandoned, is very much alive on the 6th of August, when the feast of the Metamorphosis is celebrated here. **Ayios Prodromos** is a 30-minute hike further, but it's the handsomest and contains a particularly beautiful iconostasis. **Taxiarchon,** abandoned and overgrown, is at the summit of Mount Polouki to the southeast, a hike recommended only to the hardiest and most dedicated.

There is basically only one highway on the island, with short spurs at each significant settlement. It runs south from Skopelos town, then cuts north and skirts the west coast northwest, eventually coming to Glossa, then down to Loutraki. The first spur leads off to the left to **Stafilos,** a popular family beach recommended by locals for a good seafood dinner, which you must order in the morning. About half a kilometer across the headland is **Velanio,** where nude bathing is common.

The next settlement west is **Agnondas,** named for a local athlete who brought home the gold from the 569 B.C. Olympics. This small fishing village has became a tourist resort thanks to nearby beaches. **Limnonari,** a 15-minute walk further west and accessible by caïque in the summer, has a good fine-sand beach in a rather homely and shadeless setting.

The road then turns inland again, through a pine forest, coming out at the coast at **Panormos.** With its sheltered pebble beach, this has become the island's best resort with a number of taverns, hotels, and rooms to let, as well as water-sports facilities. The road then climbs again toward **Milia,** which is considered **the island's best beach.** You will have to walk down about half a kilometer from the bus stop, but you'll find a lovely light-gray sand-and-pebble beach with the island of Dassia opposite and water-sports facilities at the **Beach Boys Club** (☎ 0424/33-496). There are also isolated beaches between the two.

The next stop, **Elios,** is a town that was thrown up to shelter the people displaced by the 1965 earthquake. It's become the home of many of the people who operate the resort facilities on the west coast, as well as something of a resort itself. The main road proceeds on to ✪ **Glossa,** which means "tongue," and that's what the hill on which the town was built looks like from the sea. It was mostly spared during the earthquake, and remains one of the most Greek and charming towns in the Sporades. There are a number of rooms to let, a good hotel, and a very good taverna here, for those who are tempted to stay overnight. Most of the coastline here is craggy, with just a few hard-to-get-to beaches. Among the best places to catch some rays and do a bit of swimming is on the small beach below the picturesque monastery of **Ayios Ioannis,** on the coast east from town, which reminds many of Meteora. (Bring food and water.) As for the port of **Loutraki,** it's a winding 3 kilometers (2 miles) down; we don't recommend a stay there.

That ends the road tour of Skopelos, but other sites can be reached from Skopleos town by caïque. Along the east coast north of Skopelos is **Glisteri,** a small pebbled beach with a nearby olive grove offering some respite from the sun. It's a good bet when the other beaches are overrun in the summer. You can also go by caïque to the grotto at **Tripiti,** for the island's best fishing, or to the little island of **Ayios Yioryios,** which has an abandoned monastery.

The whole of Skopelos's 95 square kilometers (38 square miles) is prime for **biking,** and the interior is still waiting to be explored. There's also **horseback riding, sailing** (ask at the Skopelos travel agencies), and a number of interesting **excursions** to be taken from and around the island. Skopelorama (see "Visitor Information," above) operates a fine series of excursions such as monasteries by coach, a walking tour of the town, and several cruises. One boat excursion that might appeal to some is to the waters around Skopelos that are part of the National Marine Park; if you're lucky, you will see some of the Mediterranean monk seals, an endangered species that is being protected within this park.

WHERE TO STAY

In high season, Skopelos is nearly as popular as Skiathos. If you need advice, talk to the Skopelorama agency or the officials at the town hall. Be sure to look at a room and agree on a price before accepting anything, or you may be unpleasantly surprised. To make matters confusing, there are few street names in the main, older section of Skopelos town, so you'll have to ask for directions several times before finding your lodging.

IN SKOPELOS TOWN
Moderate
The handsome traditional-style **Hotel Amalia,** along the coast, 500 meters from the center of the port (☎ **0424/22-688**; fax 0424/23-217), is largely in the hands of groups, but should have some spare rooms in spring and fall.

Hotel Denise. 37003 Skopelos. ☎ **0424/22-678.** Fax 0424/22-769. 25 units. A/C MINIBAR TEL. Dr18,000 ($60) double. Rates include breakfast. EURO, MC, V.

One of the best hotels in Skopelos because of its premier location, clean facilities, and pool, the Hotel Denise stands atop the hill overlooking the town and commands spectacular views of the harbor and Aegean. Each of the Denise's four stories is ringed by a wide balcony. The guest rooms have hardwood floors and furniture, and most boast a view that is among the best in town. As the Denise is popular, before hiking up the steep road, call for a pickup and to check for room availability—or better yet, reserve in advance.

✪ **Hotel Prince Stafilos.** 37003 Skopelos. ☎ **0424/22-775.** Fax 0424/22-744. 65 units. TEL. Dr32,500 ($108) double. Rates include breakfast. AE, EURO, MC, V.

Charging a bit more than many of the hotels in Skopelos, this one is well worth it. The most handsome and traditional hotel on the island is about a half mile south of town. (They will give you a ride from the ferry dock.) The friendly owner, Pelopidas Tsitsirgos, is also the architect responsible for the hotel's special charm. The lobby is spacious and very attractively decorated with local artifacts. Facilities include a pool, restaurant, and bars. A large buffet breakfast is served.

Skopelos Village. About a half mile southeast of town center, 37003 Skopelos. ☎ **0424/22-517.** Fax 0424/22-958. 36 units. MINIBAR TEL. Dr32,000 ($107) bungalow for 2 persons. EURO, MC, V.

For those intending to settle in for a while, this is the place, a sort of mini-resort with its own pool, a nearby tennis court, children's playground, and room service. The buildings are tastefully constructed as "traditional island houses." Each bungalow is equipped with kitchen, private bathroom, and one or two bedrooms, and can sleep from two to six persons. Facilities include a breakfast room and snack bar. In the evening, the restaurant offers Greek meals accompanied by Greek music and dance. The hotel provides free transport to various beaches.

Inexpensive
Hotel Drossia. 37003 Skopelos. ☎ **0424/22-490.** 10 units. Dr10,000 ($33) double. No credit cards. Open July–Aug only.

This small hotel next to the Hotel Denise (see above), atop the hill overlooking the town, is for bargain-hunters. Having exceptional views, the Drossia is of the same vintage as the Denise but with slightly less expensive and less well equipped rooms. All in all, it represents good value.

Hotel Eleni. 37003 Skopelos. ☎ **0424/22-393.** Fax 0424/22-936. 37 units. TEL. Dr14,000 ($47) double. EURO, MC, V.

The Hotel Eleni is a modern hotel, set back from the coast and 300 meters from the center of the harbor. All of its rooms have balconies. After many years spent operating several pizzerias in New York, Charlie Hatzidrosos returned from the Bronx to build this establishment. His daughter now operates the hotel and provides gracious service.

Hotel Rania. 37003 Skopleos. ☎ **0424/22-486.** 11 units. TEL. Dr9,200 ($31) single or double.

Another bargain-hunter's hotel, the Rania is back of the shore, just beyond and to the left of the larger Amalia. Simply furnished rooms have balconies and are reasonably well maintained. The Rania is one of the few hotels open year-round.

IN PANORMOS

This pleasant little resort is on a horseshoe-shaped cove along the west coast, about halfway between Skopelos town and Glossa. Here you'll find several cafeteria-style snack bars and minimarkets. We recommend it as a base, especially since one of the best hotels on the island—the Adrina Beach Hotel (see below)—is just above it.

The **Panormos Travel Office** (☎ **0424/23-380;** fax 0424/23-748) is open from 9am to midnight; it has some nice rooms to let, offers telephone and fax services, exchanges money, arranges tours (including night squid fishing), and rents cars, motorbikes, and speedboats.

✪ **Adrina Beach Hotel.** Panormos, 37003 Skopelos. ☎ **0424/23-373** to 375, or 01/ 682-6886 in Athens. Fax 0424/23-372. 55 units. Dr26,000 ($87) double. Rates include breakfast. AE, DC, MC, V.

This new traditional-style hotel, 500 meters on the beach beyond Panormos, is a leading candidate for the best on the island. In addition to the main building's rooms, eight handsome "maisonettes" are ranked down the steep slope toward the hotel's private beach; these have air-conditioning and cost Dr32,000 ($107). The complex has a big saltwater pool with its own bar, a restaurant, bar, buffet room, spacious sitting areas indoors and out, a playground, and a minimarket. The rooms are large and tastefully furnished in pastels, each with its own balcony or veranda.

If you can't get a room at the Adrina, try the 38-unit **Afroditi Hotel** (☎ **0424/ 23-150;** fax 0424/23-152), a more modern choice about 100 meters across the road from the beach at Panormos.

IN GLOSSA

There are approximately 100 rooms to rent in the small town of Glossa. Expect to pay about Dr9,000 ($30) for single or double occupancy. The best way to find a room is to visit one of the tavernas or shops and inquire about a vacancy. If you can't find a room in Glossa, you can always take a bus or taxi down to Loutraki and check into a pension by the water or head back to Panormos.

Hotel Atlantes. Glossa, 37003 Skopelos. ☎ **0424/33-223.** 10 units. TEL. Dr9,500 ($32) double. No credit cards.

Owner and host Lee Chocalas, born in Mississippi but raised here, returned to this island after a 30-year absence to build this comfortable hotel, across from the bus stop. All rooms have balconies looking down on the flower-filled garden or out to sea. If Lee has no room at the inn, ask him or George Antoniou at the Pythari Souvenir Shop (☎ **0424/33-077**) in town for advice on a room to let.

WHERE TO DINE
IN SKOPELOS TOWN

You might also consider a local favorite, **Molos Taverna and Ouzeri,** near the ferry stop on the paralia (☎ **0424/22-551**). **Spiros' Taverna,** to the left as you leave the ferry dock (☎ **0424/23-146**), is a simple outdoor cafe popular for its spit-roasted chicken. And if you like crepes, don't miss **Crêperie Greca,** up from the Adonis Hotel, on the sloping street up from the waterfront bus stop (☎ **0424/23-310**).

Anatoli Ouzeri. On a hill south of town. ☎ **0424/22-851.** Main courses Dr1,200–Dr2,500 ($4–$8). No credit cards. Summer daily 8:30pm–1am. Closed in winter. GREEK.

You'll have quite a climb (or else take a taxi) to reach this diminutive ouzeri high above the town, but we think the superb food more than justifies the effort. Our meal featured several delicious mezedes, including lightly fried green peppers and an exceptional octopus salad. Specialties include *bourekakia* (fried eggplant) and fried cheese pie. *Note:* No wine is served—only *tsipouro*, a strong ouzo-like drink. If you're in luck, Yiorgios Xindaris, the rail-thin proprietor/chef, will play his bouzouki and sing classic rembetika songs, sometimes with accompanists. If you come early or late in the season, bring a sweater.

✪ **Finikas Taverna and Ouzeri.** Upper backstreet of Skopelos town. ☎ **0424/ 23-247.** Main courses Dr1,300–Dr1,650 ($4.35–$6). No credit cards. Daily 7:30pm–2am. GREEK.

Tucked away in the upper backstreets of Skopelos is a picturesque garden taverna/ouzeri dominated by a broadleaf palm. The Finikas may offer Skopelos's most romantic setting, due to its isolated location as well as its lovely garden dining area. Among the many fine courses are an excellent ratatouille and pork cooked with prunes and apples, a traditional island specialty.

Karavia Gelateria Cafeteria Snack Bar. Center of waterfront, across from the bus stop and behind the World War II monument. ☎ **0424/22-970.** Breakfast Dr600–Dr1,000 ($2–$3.35); sandwiches Dr500–Dr900 ($1.70–$3); ice cream Dr1,000–Dr1,200 ($3.35–$4). No credit cards. Daily 8am–2am. BREAKFAST/SNACKS.

The Karavia is one of the best places on the waterfront for breakfast. Its sandwiches are also good, and the ice-cream concoctions are special treats.

Platanos Jazz Bar. Beneath the enormous plane tree just to the left of the ferry dock. ☎ **0424/23-661.** Main courses Dr600–Dr1,700 ($2–$6). No credit cards. Daily 5am–3am. BAR.

For everything from breakfast to a late-night drink, try this jazz pub. Breakfast in the summer starts as early as 5 or 6am for ferry passengers, who can enjoy coffee, fruit salad with nuts and yogurt, and fresh-squeezed orange juice, all for about Dr2,000 ($7). Platanos is equally pleasant for evening and late-night drinks. All is accompanied by music from their phenomenal collection of jazz records.

Taverna Koutouki. On the main backstreet, beyond the Amalia Hotel. ☎ **0424/22-380.** Main courses Dr900–Dr2,400 ($3–$8). Daily 5:30pm–1am. GREEK.

You'll find this unpretentious, excellent-value taverna in a small grapevine-draped garden. The decor is basic, the music is traditional, the service is friendly, and the food is excellent, fresh, and hot. Some of its specialties are beef in a delicious sweet tomato sauce with garlic; meatballs; and pork stuffed with garlic.

IN GLOSSA

✪ **Taverna T'agnanti.** Glossa. ☎ **0424/33-076** or 0424/33-606. Main courses Dr1,000–Dr2,200 ($3.35–$7). No credit cards. Daily 11am–midnight. About 200m up from the bus stop. GREEK.

This is the place to meet, greet, and eat in Glossa. The food is inexpensive, the staff friendly, and the view spectacular. The menu is standard taverna style, but the proprietors make a point of using the finest fresh products and fine wines. Specialties include vegetable fritters, squid with vegetables, and chicken in wine sauce. The Stamataki and Antoniou families run this and the nearby souvenir shop Pythari; if asked, they'll even help you find a room in town.

SKOPELOS AFTER DARK

The nightlife scene on Skopelos isn't nearly as active as on neighboring Skiathos, but there are still plenty of bars, late-night cafes, and discos. Most of the coolest bars are on the far (east) side of town; follow the plentiful signs above the Hotel Amalia to find the indoor **Kirki Disco** or continue on along the beachfront to find the outdoor **Karyatis;** on the way you'll pass **Akti Panorama,** a beachside taverna that often has live Greek music. The best place for bouzouki music is **Meidani,** in a handsomely converted olive-oil factory approximately in the middle of town; it doesn't open until 11pm or so, but there's a nice little bar just up from it, or you can wander around town checking out the night scene around Platanos Square, beyond and along the paralia. Don't forget the possibility of live music at the **Anatoli Ouzeri,** above the town.

3 Skyros (Skiros)

47km (25 nautical miles) from Kimi, which is 182km (113 miles) from Athens

Skyros is an island with good beaches, attractive whitewashed pillbox architecture, picturesque surroundings, low prices—and relatively few tourists. Why? First, it's difficult to get to Skyros. To be sure, in summer there are occasional ferries and hydrofoils linking Skyros to the other Sporades as well as to ports on the mainland, but these links are either fairly infrequent and/or involve land transportation to ports that are not on most tourists' itinerary. Second, most visitors to the Sporades seem to prefer the other, more thickly forested and (thickly touristed) islands. Some of us find that Skyros's more meager tourist facilities and the stark contrast between sea, sky, and rugged terrain make it all the more inviting.

Also, many Skyriots themselves are ambivalent, at best, about developing this very traditional island for tourism. Until recently, there were only a handful of hotels on the entire island. Since 1990, however, Skyros has seen a miniboom in the accommodations/building business, and with the completion of a giant marina, it's setting itself up to become yet another tourist mecca. Don't let this deter you, however; at least for now, Skyros remains an ideal place for a getaway vacation.

ESSENTIALS

GETTING THERE   By Plane   Olympic Airways has two flights a week (daily in summer) between Athens and Skyros. Call the Olympic office in Athens (☎ 01/966-6666) for information and reservations. The local Olympic representative is **Skyros Travel** (☎ 0222/91-123 or 0222/91-600). A taxi from the airport is about Dr1,200 ($4) per person in a shared cab. A bus meets most flights and goes to Skyros town, Magazia, and sometimes Molos; the fare is Dr400 ($1.35).

By Boat   The **Lykomides Co.** offers the only ferry service to Skyros; it's owned by a company whose stockholders are all citizens of the island. In summer, it runs twice daily from Kimi (on the east coast of Evvia) to Skyros (at 11am and 5pm) and twice daily from Skyros to Kimi (at 8am and 2pm); the trip takes about 2½ hours. Off-season, there is one ferry each way, leaving Skyros at 8am and Kimi at 5pm. The fare is Dr2,000 ($7). For information, call the Lykomides office either in Kimi (☎ 0222/22-020) or Skyros (☎ 0222/91-790). The Lykomides offices also sell connecting bus tickets to Athens; the fare for the 3½-hour ride is Dr3,000 ($10). In Athens, **Alkyon Travel,** Odos Akademias 97, near Omonia Square (☎ 01/384-3220 or 01/384-3221), arranges bus transportation to Kimi and sells hydrofoil and ferry tickets.

In summer, Skyros can also be reached from several ports by the hydrofoils known as Flying Dolphins; this is easily the most convenient way to go, though a little more expensive than the ferry. (For example, whereas the ferry between Kimi and Skyros costs some Dr2,000/$7, the hydrofoil costs about Dr3,000/$10). Hydrofoil schedules both ways are: about once a week from and to Kimi; about twice a week from and to Ayios Konstandinos; about once a week from and to Volos (4½ hr.); and about twice a week from and to Thessaloniki (6-hr. ride, or 5 hr. if you get on at Moudiana, south of Thessaloniki). From other Sporades, in summer there are several trips per week between Skyros and Skiathos, Skopelos, and Alonissos (about five times a week, starting in mid-May, daily in July and August). For hydrofoil information, contact the **Ceres Hydrofoil Joint Service** at Piraeus (☎ 01/428-0001), Skyros (☎ 0222-91-600), Ayios Konstandinos (☎ 0235/31-614), Thessaloniki (☎ 031/547-407), or Volos (☎ 0421/39-786).

The tricky part of getting to Skyros by ferry from Kimi can be the connection with ferries or hydrofoils from the other Sporades islands. If they don't hold to schedule, it's not uncommon to see the Skyros ferry disappearing on the horizon as your ship pulls into Kimi. You might have to make the best of the 24-hour layover and get a room in Paralia Kimi. (We recommend the **Hotel Kimi,** at ☎ 0222/22-408, or the older **Hotel Krineion,** at ☎ 0222/22-287.)

From Athens, buses to Kimi and Ayios Konstandinos leave the Terminal B (Odos Lission 260) six times a day, though you should leave no later than 1:30pm; the fare for the 3½-hour trip is about Dr3,000 ($10). From Kimi you must take a local bus to Paralia Kimi. Ask the bus driver if you're uncertain of the connection.

The ferries and hydrofoils dock at **Linaria,** on the opposite side of the island from Skyros town. The island's only bus—sometimes they bring another over from the mainland—will meet the boat and take you over winding, curvy roads to Skyros town for Dr250 (85¢). Depending on the mood of the driver, the bus will stop at Magazia beach, immediately north below the town next to the Xenia Hotel.

VISITOR INFORMATION   The largest tourist office is **Skyros Travel Center** (☎ 0222/91-123 or 0222/91-600; fax 0222/92-123), next to Skyros Pizza Restaurant in the main market. It's open daily from 8am to 2:30pm and 6:30 to 10:30pm. English-speaking Lefteris Trakos is most helpful on many counts, offering assistance with accommodations, currency exchange, Olympic Airways flights (he is the local ticket agent), long-distance calls, some interesting bus and boat tours, and Flying Dolphin tickets.

GETTING AROUND   By Bus   The only scheduled service is the Skyros-Linaria shuttle that runs four to five times daily and costs Dr250 (85¢). Skyros Travel has a twice-daily beach-excursion bus in the high season.

By Car & Moped   A Fiat Panda costs about Dr21,000 ($70) per day, including insurance. Mopeds and motorcycles are available in Skyros, near the police station or the taxi station, for about Dr5,500 ($18) per day. The island has a relatively well developed network of roads.

By Taxi   Taxi service between Linaria and Skyros is available and costs about Dr2,400 ($8).

On Foot   Skyros is a fine place to hike. The new island map, published by Skyros Travel and Tourism, will show you a number of good routes, and it seems to be pretty accurate.

FAST FACTS   As of this writing, there is only one ATM on Skyros, at the **National Bank of Greece** in the main square of Skyros town. Because of its limited hours

(Mɪɪ ɪɪɪɪough Fri from 8am to 2pm), you are advised to bring cash and/or traveler's checks. The **clinic** is near the main square (☎0222/92-222). For emergencies, call the **police** at ☎ 0222/91-274. The police station is on the street behind the Skyros Travel Center. The **post office** is near the bus square in Skyros town; open Monday through Friday from 8am to 2pm. The **telephone office (OTE)** is 50 meters south of the bus stop. It's open Friday only, from 7:30am to 3pm, but there are card phones in town.

WHAT TO SEE & DO

The Faltaits Historical and Folklore Museum. Plateia Rupert Brooke. ☎ 0222/91-232. Free admission. Summer daily 10am–1pm and 5:30–8:30pm; in off-season, ring the bell and someone will let you in.

Located in a large, old house of the Faltaits family, this is the private collection of Manos Faltaits, and it's one of the best island folk-art museums in Greece. It contains a large and varied collection of plates, embroidery, weaving, woodworking, and clothing, as well as many rare books and photographs, including some of the local men in traditional costumes from Carnival. There's a workshop attached to the museum where young artisans make lovely objects using traditional patterns and materials. The proceeds from the sale of workshop items go to the upkeep of the museum. The museum also has a shop, **Argo,** on the main street of town (☎ 0222/92-158), open daily from 10am to 1pm and 6:30pm to midnight.

EXPLORING THE ISLAND

All boats dock at **Linaria,** a plain, mostly modern fishing village on the west coast, pleasant enough but not recommended for a stay. Catch the bus waiting on the quay to take you across the narrow middle of the island to the west coast capital, Skyros town, which is built on a rocky bluff overlooking the sea. (The airport is near the northern tip of the island.) **Skyros town,** which is called Horio and of course sometimes Hora, looks much like a typical Cycladic hill town, with whitewashed cube-shaped houses built on top of each other. The winding streets and paths that are called streets are too narrow for cars and mopeds, so most of the traffic is by foot and hoof. As you alight from the bus at the bus stop square, continue on north toward the center of town and the main tourist services.

Near the market, signs point up to the town's **Kastro.** It's a 15-minute climb, but worth it for the view, and on the way you'll pass the church of **Ayia Triada,** which contains some interesting frescoes, and the monastery of **Ayios Yioryios Skyrianos.** The monastery was founded in 962 and contains a famous black-faced icon of St. George that was brought from Constantinople during the Iconoclasm.

From one side of the citadel, the view is over the rooftops of the town, and from the other the cliff drops precipitously to the sea. According to myth, King Lykomides pushed Theseus to his death from here.

The terrace at the far (northern) end of the island is **Plateia Rupert Brooke,** where the English poet, who is buried on the southern tip of the island, is honored by a nude statue of Immortal Poetry. (Brooke died on a hospital ship off Skyros in 1915 while en route to the Dardanellese as an army officer.) The statue is said to have greatly offended the local people when it was installed; you're more likely to be amused when you see how pranksters have chosen to deface the hapless bronze figure. (The Faltaits Folklore Museum, described above, is also located near this site.)

Local customs and dress are currently better preserved on Skyros than in all but a few locales in Greece. Older men can still be seen in baggy blue pants, black caps, and leather sandals constructed with numerous straps, and older women still wear long head scarves. The **embroidery** you will often see women busily working at is famous for its vibrant colors and interesting motifs—such as people dancing hand-in-hand with flowers twining around their limbs and hoopoes with fanciful crests.

Peek into the doorway of any Skyrian home and you're likely to see what looks like a room from a dollhouse with a miniature table and chairs, and **colorful plates**—loads of plates hanging on the wall. The story behind these displays is said to have begun during the Byzantine era, when the head clerics from Epirus sent 10 families to Skyros to serve as governors. They were given control of all the land not owned by Mount Athos and the Monastery of St. George. For hundreds of years, these 10 families dominated the affairs of Skyros. With Kalamitsa as a safe harbor, the island prospered, and consulates opened from countries near and far. The merchant ships were soon followed by pirates, and the ruling families went into business with them; the families knew what boats were expected and what they were carrying, and the pirates had the ships and bravado to steal the cargo. The pirates, of course, soon took to plundering the islanders as well, but the aristocrats managed to hold on to much of their wealth.

Greek independence reduced the influence of these ruling families, and during the hard times brought by World War I, they were reduced to trading their possessions to the peasant farmers for food. Chief among these bartered items were sets of dinnerware. Plates from China, Italy, Turkey, Egypt, and other exotic places became a sign of wealth, and Skyrian families made elaborate displays of their newly acquired trophies. Whole walls were covered, and by the 1920s local Skyrian craftsmen began making their own plates for the poorer families who couldn't afford the originals.

While on the subject of local lore, we should elaborate on the famous **Carnival of Skyros.** This 21-day celebration is highlighted by a 4-day period leading up to Lent and the day known throughout Greece as *Kathari Deftera* (Clean Monday). On this day, Skyros residents don traditional costumes and perform dances on the town square. Unleavened bread (*lagana*) is served with *taramosalata* and other meatless specialties. (Traditionally, vegetarian food is eaten for 40 days leading up to Easter.)

Much of this is traditional throughout Greece, but Skyros adds its own distinctive element. Culminating on midafternoon of the Sunday before Clean Monday are a series of ritual dances and events performed by a group of weirdly costumed men. Some dress as old shepherds in dark animal skins with a belt of many sheep bells and a mask made of goatskin. Other men dress as young women and flirt outrageously. (Skyros has an age-old association with cross-dressing: it was here that Achilles successfully beat the draft during the Trojan war by dressing as a woman, until shrewd Odysseus tricked him into revealing his true gender.) Other celebrants caricature Europeans, and all behave outlandishly and rather aggressively, reciting ribald poetry and poking fun at any and all bystanders. This ritual is generally thought to be pagan in origin and causes some people to reflect on the antics of ancient Greek comedy and even tragedy ("goat song"), with men playing all the roles, and catharsis as the aim.

According to local ethnologist Manos Faltaits, there are interesting connections with similar celebrations, such as the shepherds' feasts of Sicily, Bulgaria, Austria, and northern Greece. In those places, the festivities celebrate the victory of shepherds over farmers. In Naoussa, in northern Greece, the village divides into two factions and throws stones at each other; in other places they battle with wooden swords.

Skyros is also the home of a unique breed of **wild pygmy ponies,** often compared to the horses depicted on the frieze of the Parthenon and thought to be related to Shetland ponies. The Meraklides, local Skyrians who care for these rare animals, have moved most of the diminishing breed to the nearby island of Skyropoula, though tame ones can still be seen grazing near town. Ask around and you might be able to find a Meraklide who will let you ride one.

BEACHES & OUTDOOR PURSUITS

To get to the beach at **Magazia,** continue down from Plateia Rupert Brooke. (If your load is heavy, take a taxi to Magazia, as it's a hike.) From Magazia, once the site of the town's storehouses (magazines), it's about a half mile to **Molos,** a fishing village, though the two villages are quickly becoming indistinguishable because of development. There's windsurfing along this beach, and there are some fair isolated beaches beyond Molos, with some nudist activity.

South of town, the beaches are less enticing until you reach **Aspous,** which has a couple of tavernas and some rooms to let. **Ahili,** a bit further south, is where you'll find the big new **marina,** so it's no longer much of a place for swimming. Further south, the coast gets increasingly rugged and there is no roadway.

If you're still looking for a new beach, we recommend heading back across the narrow waist of the island to **Kalamitsa,** the old safe harbor, 3 kilometers (1.9 miles) south of Linaria, which has a good clean beach and is served by buses in the summer.

The island is divided almost evenly by its narrow waist; the northern half is fertile and covered with pine forest, while the southern half is barren and quite rugged. Both halves have their attractions, though the most scenic area of the island is probably to the south toward **Tris Boukes,** where Rupert Brooke is buried. The better beaches, however, are in the north.

North of Linaria, **Acherounes** is a very pretty beach. Beyond it, **Pefkos,** where marble was once quarried, is better sheltered and has a taverna that's open in the summer. The next beach north, **Ayios Fokas,** is probably the best on the island, with a lovely white pebble beach and a taverna open in the summer. Locals call it paradise, and like all such places it's very difficult to reach. Most Skyrians will suggest walking, but it's a long hilly hike. To get here from Skyros town, take the bus back to Linaria, tell the driver where you're going, get off at the crossroads with Pefkos, and begin your hike west from there.

North of Ayios Fokas is **Atsitsa,** another beach with pine trees along it, but it's a bit too rocky. It can be reached by road across the Oros Olymbos mountains in the center of the island, and it has a few rooms to let and a **holistic health-and-fitness holiday community.** For information on its activities, contact the Skyros Centre, 92 Prince of Wales Rd., London NW5 3NE (☎ **0171/267-4424;** fax 0171/284-3063). There's a sandy beach a 15-minute walk further north at **Kira Panayia** that's a bit better.

The northwest of the island is covered in dense pine forests, spreading down to the Aegean. The rocky shore opens into gentle bays and coves. This area provides wonderful **hiking** for the fit. Take a taxi (Dr5,000/$17) to **Atsitsa.** The cautious will arrange for the taxi to return in 5 or 6 hours. Explore the ruins of the ancient mining operation at Atsitsa, then head south for about 7 kilometers (4½ miles) to **Ayios Fokas,** a small bay with a tiny taverna perched right on the water. Kali Orfanou, a gracious hostess, will provide you with the meal of your trip: fresh fish caught that morning in the waters before you, vegetables plucked from the garden for your salad, and her own feta cheese and wine. Relax, swim in the bay, and then hike back to your taxi. The ambitious may continue south for 11 or 12 kilometers (7 or 8 miles) to the main road and catch the bus or hail a taxi. This part of the road is mainly uphill, so walker beware. In case you tire or can't pry yourself away from this secluded paradise of Ayios Fokas, Kali offers two extremely primitive rooms with the view of your dreams, but without electricity or toilets (in the formal sense).

SHOPPING

Skyros is a good place for buying local crafts, especially ceramics. **Ergastiri,** on the main street, has interesting ceramics, Greek shadow puppets, and a great selection of postcards. Also popular for his handmade plates is **Yiannis Nicholau,** whose studio is next to the Xenia Hotel. Good hand-carved wooden chests and chairs made from beech (in the old days it was blackberry wood) can be purchased from **Lefteris Avgoklouris,** former student of the recently departed master, Baboussis, in Skyros town; his studio is on Odos Konthili, around the corner from the post office (☎ 0222/91-106). Another fine carver is **Manolios,** in the main market.

WHERE TO STAY

The whole island has only a few hotels, so most visitors to Skyros take private rooms. The best rooms are in the upper part of Skyros town, away from the bus stop, where women in black dresses accost you with cries of "Room! Room!" A more efficient procedure is to stop in at Skyros Travel Center (see "Visitor Information," above). The island of Skyros is somewhat more primitive in its facilities than the other Sporades, so before agreeing to anything, check out the rooms to ensure they are what you want.

IN SKYROS TOWN

✪ **Hotel Nefeli.** Skyros town, 34007 Skyros. ☎ **0222/91-964.** Fax 0222/92-061. 12 units. TEL. Dr19,000 ($63) double. Breakfast Dr1,200 ($4) extra. AE, MC, V.

One of the best in-town options is built in the modern Skyrian style. The bedrooms and bathrooms are decent sized and well appointed; many units have fine views, and the large, downstairs lobby is a welcoming space. As the Nefeli is one of the favorite choices on Skyros, you'd do well to reserve in advance.

IN MAGAZIA BEACH & MOLOS

Hotel Angela. Molos, 34007 Skyros. ☎ **0222/91-764.** Fax 0222/92-030. 14 units. TEL. Dr17,000 ($57) double.

This is among the most attractive and well-kept abodes in the Molos/Magazia beach area, located near the sprawling Paradise Hotel complex. All rooms are clean and tidy with balconies, but because the hotel is set back about 100 meters from the beach, there are only partial sea views. Nevertheless, the facilities and hospitality of the young couple who run the Angela make up for its just-off-the-beach location, and it's the best bet for the money.

Paradise Hotel. Molos, 34007 Skyros. ☎ **0222/91-220.** Fax 0222/91-443. 60 units. TEL. Dr10,500 ($35) double in the new building. Breakfast Dr1,000 ($3.35) extra.

This pleasant hotel is at the north end of Magazia beach, in the town of Molos. The older part of the hotel has 40 rooms; these more basic units run about 50% less. The newer part of the hotel has 20 rooms, which we recommend because they are better kept and have much better light. The hotel is somewhat removed from the main town, but there is a taverna on the premises and another down the street.

Pension Galeni. Magazia Beach, 34007 Skyros. ☎ **0222/91-379.** 13 units. Dr9,000 ($30) double.

The small but delightful Pension Galeni offers modest rooms, but all have private bathrooms. We like the front (sea-facing) rooms on the top floor for their (currently) unobstructed views. The Galeni overlooks one of the cleanest parts of Magazia beach.

Xenia. Magazia Beach, 34007 Skyros. ☎ **0222/91-209.** Fax 0222/92-062. 24 units. TEL. Dr28,000 ($93) double. Rates include buffet breakfast. V.

With the best location on the beach at Magazia, the Xenia offers some of the best (if not cheapest) accommodations on Skyros. The guest rooms have handsome 1950s-style furniture and big bathrooms with tubs, as well as wonderful balconies and sea views. You can get all your meals here if you so desire. Perhaps its greatest drawback is the controversial (and ugly) concrete breakwater that's supposed to protect the beach from erosion.

IN ACHEROUNES BEACH

Pegasus Apartments. Acherounes Beach, 34007 Skyros. ☎ **0222/91-552.** 8 units. MINIBAR. Dr12,800 ($43) studio for 2 persons; Dr25,800 ($86) apt for 3–5 persons. EURO, MC, V.

These fully equipped studios and apartments were built by the resourceful Lefteris Trakos (owner of Skyros Travel). They are located at Acherounes, the beach just south of the port of Linaria, on the east coast. One of the pluses of staying here is the chance to see (and ride, if you're under 15) Katerina, a Skyriot pony.

IN YIRISMATA

✪ **Skyros Palace Hotel.** Yirismata, 34007 Skyros. ☎ **0222/91-994.** Fax 0222/92-070. 80 units. TEL. Dr16,000 ($53) double. Rates include breakfast. AE, DC, EURO, MC, V.

This out-of-the-way resort—about a mile north of Molos, thus 2 miles north of Skyros town—offers the most luxurious accommodations on the island. The guest rooms are plainly furnished but comfortable, with large balconies. The beach across the road is an especially windy, rocky stretch of coastline, with somewhat treacherous water. Facilities include a lovely pool and adjacent bar, tennis courts, some air-conditioned rooms, and a well-planted garden—not to mention a soundproofed disco, the most sophisticated on the island. Twice a day, there's a minibus into town. If you want to get away from it all and enjoy some upscale amenities to boot, this might be the place for you.

WHERE TO DINE

The food in Skyros town is generally pretty good and reasonably priced. **Anemos,** on the main drag (☎ **0222/92-155**), is a good place for breakfast, with filtered coffee, omelets, and freshly squeezed juice. The venerable **O Glaros Restaurant** (☎ **0222/92-363**) serves a small selection of traditional taverna fare—regulars report favorably on the moussaka. If you're ready for pizza, try the nearby **Skyros Pizza Restaurant** (☎ **0222/91-684**), which serves tasty pies as well as other Greek specialties in generous portions.

The best **bakery** in town is hidden away up in the hills on the edge of Skyros town. Walk up along the stairs to the statue of Immortal Poetry, bear right up the white-washed stone path, and ask a local. It's tucked away, but your nose will be your guide. (They also sell their bread in the market.)

In Linaria, find **Kyria Maria,** over the headland near the power station; her fish is especially good (but ask her not to overcook it).

✪ **Kristina's Restaurant (and Rooms).** Skyros town. ☎ **0222/91-778.** Fax 0222/93-400. Reservations recommended in summer. Main courses Dr1,200–Dr3,400 ($4–$11). No credit cards. Mon–Sat 7am–4pm and 7pm–1am. INTERNATIONAL.

This restaurant (down from the taxi stand) is rather sophisticated by local standards—certainly a change from the usual fare. The proprietor/chef is Australian, and she brings a lighter touch to everything she cooks. Her fricasseed chicken is excellent, her herb bread is tasty, and her desserts, such as cheesecake, are exceptional.

There are now also eight rooms to rent, several of which can accommodate four people. A double goes for Dr15,000 ($50).

Maryetes Grill. Skyros town. ☎ **0222/91-311.** Main courses Dr1,000–Dr2,000 ($3.35–$7). No credit cards. Daily 1–3pm and 6pm–midnight. GRILL.

One of the oldest and best places in town, the Maryetes is a second-generation-run grill that's equally popular with locals and travelers. The dining room is as simple as simple gets, so what you go for is the food. We recommend the grilled chicken and meat. There's a small sampling of salads.

Restaurant Kabanero. Skyros town. ☎ **0222/91-240.** Main courses Dr1,000–Dr1,600 ($3.35–$5). No credit cards. Daily 1–3pm and 6pm–midnight. GREEK.

One of the best dining values in town, this perpetually busy eatery serves the usual Greek menu: moussaka, stuffed peppers and tomatoes, fava, various stewed vegetables, and several kinds of meat. We found the dishes tasty and prices about 20% less than most of the others in town.

✪ **Pegasus Restaurant/Cafe.** Skyros town. ☎**0222/91-123.** Main courses Dr900– Dr2,700 ($3–$9). MC, V. Daily 6pm–midnight. GREEK.

This fairly recent addition to the dining scene in Skyros town can hold its own with the best of them. Its specialties include traditional Greek rabbit stifado and lobster with spaghetti; it also offers a selection of wines from barrels. Situated in the center of town, the restaurant is enhanced by its location in a neoclassical building from 1890. Yet another venture of Lefteris Trakos of the Skyros Travel Center, it lives up to his usual high standards.

SKYROS AFTER DARK

If you've gotta dance, try the **Kastro Club** in Linaria or **Stone** on the road to Magazia. Aside from these, there are few evening diversions other than barhopping on the main street. **Apocalypsis** draws a younger crowd. **Kalypso** attracts a more refined set of drinkers who appreciate their better-made but pricier cocktails. **Renaissance** is loud and lively. **Rodon** is best for actually listening to music. And the new guy on the block, **Kata Lathos** ("By Mistake"), has gained its following.

14 Highlights of Western Greece: Epirus & Ioannina

by John S. Bowman

Evergreen slopes, deep-set rivers and lush valleys, villages of timbered houses with slate or tile roofs—this can't be Greece. But it is. It's the northwestern corner the Greeks know as **Epirus.** Plentiful rainfall, the rugged Pindos mountains, and a generally more temperate climate seem to remove this region from familiar Mediterranean Greece—at times, it almost seems Alpine. It's one of the few places in the country where you'll spend time away from the sea.

Epirus and its capital city, **Ioannina,** seem immune to the throngs who crowd the beaches and restaurants, the ferries and ancient sites, of so many parts of Greece these days. It isn't the travel-poster Greece many have come to expect, and it certainly hasn't organized itself around tourism and foreigners. Although there are plenty of hotels and restaurants, the pace of life in Ioannina and other cities, not to mention in the villages, is governed by local customs. During the off-season, for instance, places such as the post office and information offices may be closed all weekend. **Museum hours** are cut back, as are the hours of gift shops and many restaurants. And except for some staff in the hotels, better restaurants, and visitor information and car-rental offices, few people speak English, although they may speak Italian, French, or German. You may find yourself sharing a hotel with Greek commercial travelers, and it will probably be harder to find your English-language newspaper or fresh-squeezed orange juice.

A STRATEGY FOR SEEING THE REGION   Visitors to this corner of Greece will come by ship from Italy (or via Corfu), by plane from Athens or Thessaloniki, or by car or bus from other parts of Greece. We recommend basing yourself in Ioannina, a city that offers a fine mix of natural attractions, historical associations, and modern amenities.

It's easy to fill the better part of 2 days by walking around Ioannina, and you could visit Epirus's other main destination, **Metsovo,** by bus. But you really should rent a car to see most of the other attractions of Epirus—**Dodona,** the **Zagori** villages, and the cave at **Perama.** We recommend a minimum of 4 days for Epirus, 2 days for Ioannina and Dodona, 1 day for Metsovo, and 1 day for Zagori and Perama Cave.

A LOOK AT THE PAST   In its history, Western Greece and Epirus in particular have often gone in different directions from the rest of Greece. It was settled by Greek-speaking peoples about the same time

Travel Tip

Epirus is one part of Greece best visited between early June and early October, unless you really like cooler weather. In the winter, you can come up here to ski.

as other parts of Greece (ca. 2000 B.C.), and over the centuries they worshipped many of the same gods and carried on much the same culture. But there were many non-Greek peoples in this area, and this plus a natural remoteness meant that the region did not participate in the grand classical civilization. Social organization remained more tribal, led by small-time kings. The greatest of the Epirote kings, **Pyrrhus** (318–272 B.C.), was constantly making war, and his victories over the Romans outside Rome have given us the term Pyrrhic victory—because won at great cost, they came to nothing. Epirus itself was reduced to a Roman province after 168 B.C.

During the **Middle Ages,** the whole western region was constantly prey to invaders, and with the conquest of Constantinople by the Crusaders in 1204, some Greeks decided to set up a new state with Ioannina as the capital, the so-called Despotate of Epirus. It never amounted to much and soon fell under outside control. Finally it was taken over by the Turks in 1431, and soon they controlled virtually all of Greece, although the Venetians and various other Western Europeans would gain possession of parts of Western Greece.

It was near the end of this long phase that Epirus experienced its most dramatic moment in the spotlight of history, under the "Lion of Ioannina," **Ali Pasha** (1741–1822). He was born in Albania and rose to prominence fighting on behalf of the Ottoman Sultan in Constantinople. But in 1788, Ali Pasha decided to set up a virtually independent domain with his capital in Ioannina. An international celebrity in his day, visited by Byron among others, he was a cruel despot who boasted of killing 30,000 people, often in the most brutal fashion. The Ottomans tolerated Ali Pasha as long as they could, but in 1822 they sent a large force to capture him; he hid in a monastery on the islet off Ioannina but was tracked down, killed, and beheaded.

When the Greeks rose up against the Turks in the 1820s, the southern part of Western Greece, centered around Messolonghi, took an active role, but the bulk of Epirus did not join in. The southwestern district of Arta was freed from Turkish rule in 1881, but Epirus was not formally joined to Greece until after the Second Balkan War of 1913.

Epirus became a battleground twice more, against the invading Italians and Germans in World War II, and then in the Greek civil war. Since then it has enjoyed peace and quiet prosperity.

GETTING TO & AROUND EPIRUS
GETTING THERE   By Plane   Olympic Airways (☎ 01/966-6666) offers flights to Ioannina from Athens—usually two a day. At least once a day there are Olympic flights between Ioannina and Thessaloniki. Olympic also flies about once a day from Athens to Aktion, just outside Preveza on the southernmost coast of Epirus; from here you can get a bus to Igoumenitsou and Ioannina or even to the island of Lefkada, which is connected by a viaduct to the mainland.

By Boat   Igoumenitsou, on the coast opposite Corfu, is the point of entry to northwestern Greece for many people. In summer, ferries connect hourly to Corfu and less frequently to Kefalonia, Ithaka, and Paxi. Numerous ferries and ships put into Igoumenitsou go to and from ports in Italy—Ancona, Bari, Brindisi, Venice; some of these connect to Patras or Piraeus in Greece or even more distant ports such as Iraklion in Crete, or Cesme in Turkey.

In high season, there is also a ferry connecting **Astakos**—on the Ionian coast south of Preveza and north of Messolonghi—and the offshore islands of Ithaka and Kefalonia.

There are so many changes in scheduling of all these ships that it's useless to provide specific details, but if you're concerned enough to want information in advance, contact **Thalassa Travel** in Igoumenitsou, located at Odos Ethniki Antistasseos 20 (☎ 0665/23-565; fax 0665/22-506).

By Bus   The **KTEL** line (☎ 01/512-5954 in Athens; 0651/25-014 in Ioannina) enters northwestern Greece from distant points such as Athens (7½ hr.) or Thessaloniki (8 hr.).

By Car   There are several approaches to Western Greece from distant points. **From Athens,** there are two main routes. One is the inland route north via Livadia, Lamia, Karditsa, Trikkala, Kalambaka, and Ioannina. The second is via Corinth and then along the southern coast of the Gulf of Corinth to Rion, the ferry to Antirion, and then via Messolonghi, Agrinio, Arta, and Ioannina. Alternatively, you can head to the Ionian coast after Messolonghi, and go up to Igoumenitsou via Astakos, Preveza, and Parga.

The preferred route **from Thessaloniki** is via Veria west to Kozani and Konitsa and then south to Ioannina. If the former Yugoslavia has settled down enough to allow for transit, it should be possible to take the once well-traveled route from Skopje (now capital of the Former Yugoslavia Republic of Macedonia) down into Northern Greece at Florina, and from there south to Kastoria and Ioannina.

GETTING AROUND   By Bus   With enough time, you can see most of Western Greece by bus, but as always, you'll need extra hours for the little side trips. But given the many mountainous roads and curves, many might prefer to let others do the driving. **KTEL** provides bus links between virtually all points in Western Greece. Points to **Athens** and the **north, northwest,** and **northeast** (Igoumenitsou, Metsovo, Konitsa, Kastoria, and Thessaloniki) are serviced from Ioannina's **main bus terminal** at Odos Zosimadon 4 (☎ 0651/25-014). Points to the **south** (Parga, Arta, Preveza, Astakos, Messolonghi, and Patras) are serviced from a smaller **bus terminal** in Ioannina at Odos Vizaniou 19 (☎ 0651/26-286).

By Car   Having a car is probably the best way to experience the full variety of Western Greece. Distances are not all that great, but then again trips take much longer than a map might suggest because of the many mountainous and curving roads. (Mopeds or motorcycles are not advised except for the most experienced.) Western Greece doesn't offer the choice in car rentals as in more touristy parts of Greece. We have found that **Budget Rent-A-Car** in Ioannina, at Odos Dodonis 109 (☎ 0651/43-901 or 0651/45-382; fax 0651/45-382), is the best to deal with. Paul Angelis is the genial manager. But don't expect to haggle during high season, because there are a limited number of vehicles for the influx of tourists.

By Taxi   There are so many switchbacks and hairpin roads that some people might prefer to take a taxi. Agree on a fee before you set out. Each hour's drive should cost about Dr3,500 ($12); each hour's waiting, about Dr2,000 ($7). Try to get a driver who speaks at least basic English, or a foreign language you understand—and you'll get a guide in the bargain. He in turn should get a generous tip.

1 Ioannina

106km (65 miles) E of Igoumenitsou; 452km (277 miles) N of Athens

Ioannina had long been a sleepy medieval town when Greeks fleeing Constantinople after its capture by the Crusaders in 1204 arrived to make it the capital of the Despotate of Epirus. The first Despot, Michael I, started building the walls that over the next centuries would be enlarged and strengthened by various conquerors— Greeks, Italians, Serbs, and Turks—to become the quite magnificent walled old town that still exists.

ESSENTIALS

GETTING THERE   By Plane   Olympic Airlines flies to Ioannina from Athens, usually twice a day. At least once a day there are Olympic flights between Ioannina and Thessaloniki.

As of this writing, **Olympic** did not maintain an office in downtown Ioannina. Instead, you must deal with their airport office (☎ **0651/39-131**). Its hours are highly irregular and dependent on flight departures and arrivals, but they work out like this: Monday and Thursday from 8 to 11:30am and 2:30 to 9pm; Tuesday from 11:30am to 5pm; Wednesday and Friday from 11:30am to 9pm; and Saturday and Sunday from 11:30am to 5pm and 6:30 to 9:30pm. The **airport** is about 4 kilometers (2½ miles) from the center of town; it's well serviced by public buses (nos. 1, 2, and 7) from the main square, but you will probably find it more convenient to take a taxi.

VISITOR INFORMATION   Ioannina's **National Tourist Information Office** is located at Napoleon Zerva 2, opposite the far corner of the Central Square (☎ **0651/ 25-086;** fax 0651/72-148). Summer hours are Monday through Friday from 7:30am to 2:30pm and 5:30 to 8:30pm, and Saturday from 9am to 1pm; winter hours are Monday through Friday from 7:30am to 2:30pm.

In summer, the city also maintains an information booth down on the lake, to the left of the fortress and by the quay where you get the boats to Nissi, the islet (see below); it's open Monday through Saturday from 10am to 8pm.

Another helpful source of information of all kinds is **Daskalopoulos Yiannis Tour World,** Odos 28 Octobriou 13 (☎ **0651/29-667;** fax 0651/21-222).

FAST FACTS   There are numerous **ATMs** in the center of Ioannina (and also a couple in Metsovo); branches of the big national **banks** can handle all money exchanges. The basic **emergency** number for all of Greece is ☎ **100.** There is an internationally known medical school and **hospital** at **Dourouti,** some 7 kilometers (4 miles) south of Ioannina. There is another hospital at **Hatzikosta** (2km/1 mile). Other smaller cities and towns in Western Greece have clinics and plenty of trained doctors. For **Internet access,** try the Tropicana Cafe, Odos Pirsinela 8 (leading off the main square); it's in the basement and you approach it via a small alley (with the sign INTERNET CAFE). It's basically a pool room/hangout for young people, and you can rent time on the computers at Dr1,500 ($5) an hour; open daily from 10am to midnight.

Beside the main bus terminal, **Olympic Laundry,** Odos Zosimadon 6 (☎0651/ 75-504), is open Monday, Wednesday, and Saturday from 8am to 2pm; Tuesday, Thursday, and Friday from 8am to 2pm and 5 to 8:30pm. The **Tourist Police** are located at **Police Headquarters,** Odos 28 Octobriou 11 (☎ **0651/25-673**); open daily from 7am to 2am. The main **post office** is on Odos 28 Octobriou 3 (☎ 0651/ 26-437). It's open Monday through Saturday from 7:30am to 8pm; in the off-season, it's closed on Saturdays. The **telephone office (OTE)** is at the rear (right) on Odos 28 Octobriou 4; open daily from 7am to 10pm.

WHAT TO SEE & DO

Ioannina Museum. Plateia 25 Martiou (behind clock tower and the Greek Army base on Central Sq.). ☎ 0651/25-490. Admission Dr500 ($1.70). Tues–Sun 8:30–3pm.

Housed in a modern building, this fine little provincial museum has just enough to engage anyone who has come this far. Most displays are from graves and burial sites in Epirus, but the range of items extends from Paleolithic implements (including one of the oldest stone tools in all Greece) through the Bronze Age to Roman times. Various bronze works are especially interesting, as is the superb Attic-style sarcophagus dating from the 2nd to 3rd centuries A.D., with carved scenes from *The Iliad.*

But undoubtedly, the display case that will entrance most people holds some of the little lead tablets found at the **Oracle of Dodona** (see "Side Trips from Ioannina," below). People from all stations of life came to Dodona and had some desire or query inscribed on a strip of lead that was then submitted to the oracle. Today we can read these actual pleas. Some are quite practical: "Should I buy a certain property?" "Should I engage in shipping?" Others have a religious tinge: "To which god should we pray or sacrifice to get certain results?" But the most intriguing are the personals: "Is it better to marry?" "Shall I take another wife?" "Am I the father of her children?" These tablets speak to us as do few remains from the ancient world.

A STROLL AROUND THE *FROURIO:* THE WALLED OLD TOWN & CITADEL

For many of the centuries that Ioannina fell under the occupation of foreign conquerors, city walls enclosed all the most important structures. There's virtually nothing of historic or architectural importance outside the citadel except on the islet of Nissi. Originally the fortress was separated from the mainland by a moat, which was crossed by three bridges. The moat has since been filled in. An esplanade now circles the lakeside below the walls, and there are several openings in the wall, but most people will enter the walls from the **Plateia Yioryio,** which is lined by tavernas and gift shops.

A left turn inside the Plateia Giorgio gate onto Odos Ioustinianou leads (about 2 blocks) to the **Synagogue.** Dating from 1790, this white-walled synagogue, with a Hebrew inscription and a locked door, is distinctive enough to be interesting to those willing to track down someone who will let you in. (Inquire at the shop of Mrs. Allegra Matsa, Odos Anexartisias 18.) The Jewish community of Ioannina traces its origins to Jews who came here at least by the 13th century. The Germans removed all 5,000 or so in 1941 and took them to labor and extermination camps. After the war, about 150 survivors came back, but today only some 100 Jews still live in Ioannina. A small **Holocaust Memorial** is just outside the citadel, on the corner of Odos Karamanlis and Odos Soutsou.

If you continue on around the inside perimeter of the walls, you will come to a large clearing. From there, ascend a cobblestoned slope to the **Aslan Pasha Cami,** a 17th-century school with cells for Islamic scholars. Its **mosque** now houses the **Municipal Popular Art Museum.** In summer, it's open daily from 8am to 8pm; in winter, Monday through Friday from 8am to 3pm, Saturday and Sunday from 9am to 3pm. Admission is Dr600 ($2). The mosque was erected in 1618 on the site of an Orthodox church, razed by Aslan Pasha to punish the Christian Greeks for a failed revolt. Entering the mosque, observe in the vestibule the recesses for shoes. The exhibits,

Ioannina

0   200 m
0   200 y

Plateia Mavili
Citadel
Plateia Salongu
Main Bus Station
Plateia Pirrou
Stadium
Town Hall
Mitropolis
Archaeological Museum
Police Station
Secondary Bus Station
Ayia Marini

Lake of Ioannina (Pamvotis)

Legend
ⓘ Information
Ⓒ OTE
✉ Post Office

ATTRACTIONS
Boats to Island **2**
Byzantine Museum **4**
Folk Art Museum **8**
Kastro **12**
Municipal Popular Art
 Museum **3**
Old Bazaar **7**
Synagogue **5**

ACCOMMODATIONS
Hotel du Lac **14**
Hotel Galaxy **11**
Hotel Olympic **10**
Hotel Palladion **9**
Xenia Hotel **13**

DINING
La Fontantina **11**
The Pharos **1**
To Mantelo **6**

which include traditional costumes, jewelry, weapons, documents, household wares, and such, are grouped around the three major religious-ethnic communities of Ioannina: the Orthodox Greeks, the Muslims, and the Jews. There's an adjacent minaret, and when it and the mosque are illuminated each night, the scene from the lake is captivating.

In the opposite and far corner of the walled town is the innermost citadel, known by its Turkish name, **Itz Kale.** Within it are the Victory Mosque (**Fethiye Cami**); the base of a circular tower; the remains of the palace of Ali Pasha, the cruel Albanian who dominated Epirus from 1788 until 1822; and the alleged **tombs** of Ali Pasha and his wife. The Greek army long occupied this part of the citadel, but its structures have now been restored and there is an interesting **Byzantine Museum** here, located in two buildings, the virtually rebuilt **palace** and the **harem.** The former houses the icons and other church-related objects, the latter concentrates on silver work. Hours are daily from 9am to 3pm; admission is Dr500 ($1.70).

A STROLL AROUND IOANNINA

Ioannina has become a busy commercial center for all of northwestern Greece (its population is some 100,000) and its streets can be filled with vehicles of all kinds generating noise and fumes, but there are some interesting retreats from this. One is the old **Turkish Bazaar,** down near the walled town and just off the main street, Odos Averoff. Although gradually vanishing, in its tiny shops you will still see men practicing the old crafts—metalsmiths, jewelry makers, cobblers, tailors, and the like. Proceeding up Odos Averoff you come to the edge of the Central Square with the **clock tower** (on the left). Up behind this is the city's **archaeological museum** (see above). When you leave the museum, stroll across the broad terraced gardens built over the site of what was once the **walled Kastro,** where the Christians lived during the Turkish era. There was a cafe/restaurant on the far corner, but as of our last visit it was closed; perhaps new owners will revive it, because the location provides a fine view of the lake and distant mountains if you eat outdoors. Returning to the main street you are now on the **Central Square** (officially Plateia Pyrros), also with its share of cafes and restaurants.

A BOAT TRIP TO THE ISLET OF NISSI (NISSAKI)

If you have only a day in Ioannina, try to spend at least 2 to 3 hours (including an hour for a meal) on a visit to **Nissi,** the islet in Lake Pamvotis. Small boats leave from the quay below the fortress every half hour in the summer, from 6:30am to 11pm. In the off-season, service is every hour—but note that the last boat leaves the island around 10pm. The fare is Dr200 (70¢). The lake has unfortunately become over-grown with algae and is so polluted that local restaurants do not serve the fish taken from it (or so we've been assured).

The boat ride is barely 10 minutes and, day and night, provides a fine view of Ioannina. You get off in what is virtually the lobby of three restaurants—each displaying a tank filled with seafood. Resist all until you are truly ready to eat. The specialties of these restaurants include eel, frogs' legs, carp, crayfish, trout, and other imported fish.

The small village here is said to have been founded only in the 16th century by refugees from the Mani region of the Peloponnese, but its five monasteries predate this, and they are your destination. Take the narrow passage between the two restaurants, and signs are posted to your left and right. Following the signs to the left (east), you will come to the **Monastery of Panteleimon.** Although founded in the 16th century, it has been so heavily restored that little of the original remains.

The monastery houses a **small museum** devoted to the infamous **Ali Pasha,** with numerous pictures and personal items including clothing and his water pipe. It's open daily, and an attendant will come if it's closed. Admission is Dr150 (50¢). The reason for such a display in a monastery is that Pasha had taken refuge here in 1820 and was eventually killed here in 1822 by Turks. You may even be shown holes in the floor where he is alleged to have been shot from below.

Directly beside this monastery is the **Monastery of the Prodromos (St. John the Baptist),** but most people will want to move on to the western edge of the islet, fol-lowing the signs to the **Moni Filanthropinon** (also known as the **Monastery of Ayios Nikolaos Spanos**). It's sometimes referred to as the "Secret School" because of claims that Orthodox priests maintained a secret school here during the Turkish occupation. Founded in the 13th century, it was rebuilt in the 16th century, when magnificent frescoes were painted on its walls. (There's no admission, but it's customary to leave a gratuity with the caretaker.) Seldom does the public get to view such an ensemble of Byzantine frescoes so close up. Although the dim light can be a problem (bring a flashlight), you should be able to recognize such subjects as the life of Christ on the walls of the apse, God and the Apostles in the central dome, and the many saints. Most unexpected, however, are the portrayals of ancient Greek sages on the wall of the narthex as you enter—Apollonius, Aristotle, Cheilon, Plato, Plutarch, Solon, and Thucydides.

About 100 meters farther along the trail is **Ayios Nikolaos Dilios** (or **Moni Stratgopoulou**), the oldest monastery (dating from the 11th century) on Nissi. Its 16th-century frescoes are also of some interest but are in poor condition. (A small tip to the caretaker is also called for.) The fifth monastery, **Ayios Eleouses,** is closed to the public.

By now you have earned your meal on Nissi. Choose one of the restaurants (see "Where to Dine," below). And as you sip your wine, you can contemplate what such a locale means while enjoying the view.

SHOPPING

If you get the impression that every third store in old Ioannina is selling jewelry, silverware, hammered copper, and embossed brass work, you're right—these are the traditional crafts here. Many of the jewelry stores are really selling nothing but modern work in gold and silver and/or precious and semiprecious jewels. Prices are probably lower than in more cosmopolitan cities, but be wary of "antiques" that may be offered in some shops—they may be little more than 60 years old.

There's an extended cluster of jewelry and gift shops opposite the walled citadel. One of the more interesting selections of metal work (and he also has water pipes) is at **Politis Douvflis,** at Plateia Yioryio 12.

Here and there you may see embroidered clothing or woven socks, but this is not a region known for delicate needlework.

WHERE TO STAY

Ioannina and its immediate environs don't offer luxury resorts, but that's not why you come here. There are, however, several quite special hotels and plenty of more-than-adequate accommodations.

MODERATE

Another option is the **Hotel Galaxy,** Plateia Pyrros (Central Square), 45221 Ioannina (☎ **0651/25-056**; fax 0651/30-724)—it's nothing fancy, but it is convenient, clean, and cheap.

✪ **Hotel du Lac.** Leoforos Andrea Miaouli and Odos Ikkou (along the lake, half a mile right of walled citadel), 45221 Ioannina. ☎ **0651/59-100.** Fax 0651/59-200. 70 units. A/C MINIBAR TV TEL. High season Dr30,000 ($100) double; low season Dr27,000 ($90) double. Rates include buffet breakfast. AE, DC, EURO, JCB, MC, V. Open year-round. Parking on grounds. Taxis can be ordered from desk.

This hotel opened in the summer of 1998 and immediately became Ioannina's prime showplace. With its marble and woodwork, it exudes luxury; more important, its service lives up to its image. The rooms are a bit larger than in many Greek hotels and all enjoy a view across to the lake; bathrooms are state-of-the-art. When we were among the first few guests in June 1998, it was still in its start-up phase, but in addition to all the expected amenities of a first-class hotel (room service, laundry service, secretaries or baby-sitters on request, and more), it promises such extras as digital lines for computer modems, a swimming pool, and a children's pool and playground. It also plans to offer conference facilities for up to 600. If the restaurant produces meals the equal of the buffet breakfast, they should be positively sybaritic.

Hotel Olympic. Odos Melanidi 2 (1 block off Central Sq.), 45220 Ioannina. ☎ **0651/ 25-147.** Fax 0651/22-041. 54 units. A/C TV TEL. High season Dr26,000 ($87) double; low season Dr18,000 ($60) double. No credit cards. Open year-round. Parking in lot across from hotel.

For those who like to be at the center of the action, such as it is in Ioannina, the Olympic is the hotel. It has long attracted members of the foreign diplomatic corps, government dignitaries, and such. All that means nothing, of course, if you aren't made to feel welcome and comfortable, and you can be assured of both. The lobby is modest but the desk service and 24-hour room service are what count. The upper-story front rooms enjoy a view of the distant lake, and all units have small fridges. You're in the center of town, but the noise dies down by bedtime (and with air-conditioning your windows are presumably closed).

Hotel Palladion. Odos Botsari 1 (off 28 Octobriou), 45444 Ioannina. ☎ **0651/25-856** to 859. Fax 0651/74-034. 130 units. TV TEL. High season Dr17,500 ($59) double; low season Dr15,500 ($52) double. AE, DC, EURO, MC, V. Open year-round. Private parking.

We like this place for its combination of features: convenient yet quiet, a professional and helpful desk staff, no frills but good value. Rooms are of modest size and bland, bathrooms are standard issue, but everything works. (And when we asked to move from one because of lingering cigarette odor, this happened instantly and with no further questions.) There are conference facilities for up to 80 and the Palladion often hosts groups, but this won't interfere with your stay. When we last visited, the break-fast was both overpriced and "thin," but they promised to upgrade it.

✪ Xenia Hotel. Odos Dodonis 33 (up past the Central Sq.), 45221 Ioannina. ☎ **0651/ 25-078.** Fax 0651/25-089. 60 units. TV TEL. Dr25,400 ($84) double. Rates include buffet breakfast. AE, DC, EURO, JCB, MC, V. Open year-round. Parking on grounds. An easy walk from the Central Sq., or take one of the many public buses that pass by.

This was long Ioannina's finest, and although the rooms are not exceptional (but certainly tasteful and comfortable), what you get for your money is a sense of seclusion in a park setting at the very heart of town. The hotel is set well back from the street, and the bedrooms at the rear enjoy fine views. There's an outdoor cafe that allows you to relax in a park atmosphere; the indoor restaurant is highly regarded and certainly convenient if you don't care to explore Ioannina's many others. The desk will see to basic needs (laundry, car rental, excursions), there is room service, and two conference rooms can handle up to 100. The lobby and rooms have a discreet decor that will appeal to people who like an international feel to their hotels.

WHERE TO DINE
MODERATE

The Gastra Restaurant. Eleousa, along the Airport-Igoumenitsou Hwy. (7km/4.3 miles outside Ioannina; 3km/1.9 miles past the airport, just before turnoff to Igoumenitsou). ☎ **0651/61-530.** Reservations recommended in high season on weekend evenings; on Sun, you are advised to leave it to the citizens of Ioannina. Main courses Dr1,100–Dr3,500 ($3.70–$12). No credit cards. Tues–Sun 1–5pm and 8pm–1am. Open year-round. Public bus: 2. Restaurant is on the right, with large sign displaying eating implements. GREEK REGIONAL.

This is a must for all those willing to try a special type of regional cooking that involves heaping red-hot embers over a *gastra*—the conical cast-iron lid that's lowered onto the baking dish holding the food (lamb, goat, pork, or chicken), which then roasts slowly to appear on your table as an especially succulent meal. It's delicious. The restaurant also has other specialties: For an appetizer, try the *skordalia karithia* (walnut-garlic dip); for dessert, their special crème caramel.

In pleasant weather, you can eat out front in the shaded garden and watch your meal cooking in the open fireplace. In cooler times, you can sit inside the handsome restaurant. When the spirit moves, diners are encouraged to dance to the music. Come here for a leisurely experience, not just for the food. (And if it's too crowded and you need your gastra, proceed less than a mile after taking the left turn signed to Igoumenitsou to another such restaurant, the **Diogenes.**)

La Fontantina. Odos Melanidi 2 (on ground floor of Olympic Hotel, 1 block off Central Sq.). ☎ **0651/25-147.** Fax 0651/73-008. Reservations recommended on holidays and weekends in high season. Main courses Dr1,100–Dr3,500 ($3.70–$12). No credit cards. Daily 10am–midnight. GREEK/ITALIAN.

This is the house restaurant of the Olympic Hotel and has become a favorite gathering place for foreigners and Greeks who like to feel they're at Ioannina's crossroads. It's not that large, the decor is hotel classy, service is a bit standoffish, and the menu ranges from Greek standards to Italian standards. It's all tasty enough, but it's hardly *gran' cucina.* So go to take in the lively scene while you enjoy spaghetti carbonara or a steak fillet with one of the fine red wines from Northern Greece—a Naoussa, an Amyntaion, or a Carras. Florence it's not, but La Fontantina offers a taste of upscale Ioannina.

INEXPENSIVE

Pamvotis. Nissi Ioannina (the offshore islet). ☎ **0651/81-081.** Fax 0651/81-631. Main courses Dr900–Dr2,000 ($3–$7). EURO, MC, V. High season daily 11am–midnight; low season daily 11am–10pm. Ferryboat from Ioannina's lakefront. GREEK.

If you have only one meal to eat in Ioannina, it has to be at one of the restaurants on the islet out in the lake. And if you ask around as to which is the best, you'll get a different answer from everyone. In fact, they're all about the same quality, so choose one with a location that appeals. We like this one—located near the dock where the little ferries put in, so you get a lively scene along with the local specialties. (If you prefer a more natural setting, go on to the **Propodes Restaurant** at the side of the Ayios Panteleimon Monastery, which you'll want to visit. See "A Boat Trip to the Islet of Nissi (Nissaki)," above.)

You can pick your lobster, *karavides* (a cross between crayfish and shrimp), trout, or other fish of the day right out of holding tanks. If you're game, try one of the two local specialties: frogs' legs or eels. The white Zitsa Primus, a slightly sparkling white wine from the region, is a perfect accompaniment to your meal and your time on Nissi.

The Pharos. Plateia Mavili 13 (down along lakefront). ☎ **0651/26-506.** Main courses Dr900–Dr2,500 ($3–$8). No credit cards. Daily 9am–10pm. Closed mid-Oct to Mar. Bus from Central Sq. or a 10-min. walk. GREEK.

One of several restaurants set back from the lakefront, The Pharos should appeal to those who just want a good meal in a pleasant setting. In warm weather, you can sit under the awning in the square opposite; on cooler days, you can sit inside. The menu is traditional but with some variants. For an appetizer, try the fried peppers in a garlic sauce. For your main course, order whatever's being grilled that day, and get the pilaf instead of potatoes. If you're feeling ambitious, try the frogs' legs or crabs at Dr2,500 ($8).

To Mantelo. Plateia Georgio 15 (opposite the main entrance to citadel). ☎ **0651/25-452.** Main courses Dr880–Dr1,700 ($2.90–$6). No credit cards. Daily 10am–2am. GREEK.

Here's one for those who prefer their Greek tavernas to look traditional and to attract Greeks. It's a no-frills place that gives you a front-row seat on the square outside the old walled town, where all kinds of characters congregate. For an appetizer, try one of the fried-marinated dishes—peppers, squash, or eggplant. Go for any of the grilled dishes—veal, chicken, lamb—or the calves' liver. In all cases, ask for the pilaf. The taverna can feel cramped when it's crowded, but that's what makes it Greek.

2 Side Trips from Ioannina

DODONA (DODONI)

Even if you aren't the kind who chases after every classical ruin, this one is a real reward: a spectacular theater at one of the major oracles of the ancient world. In August there are performances of the classical Greek dramas; ask at travel agencies if you wish to plan your visit around them.

✪ **Dodona** is located only 22 kilometers (14 miles) from Ioannina, so it can easily be visited in about 2 hours if you have a car. The bus service is inconvenient—basically only one bus very early in the morning, and then you are stuck there for many hours; it's better to spring for a **taxi**—about Dr6,000 ($20) for the round-trip, including an hour's wait. The first 7 kilometers (4.3 miles) are on a main highway due south (signed to Arta); the turn to the left becomes (after an additional 3km/2 miles) an ascending and curving (but asphalt) road. This trip becomes part of the experience—you get the sense that you're on a pilgrimage to a remote shrine.

On arrival, you are on a plateau ringed by mountains. Admission to the sacred precincts is Dr500 ($1.70). In high season, it's open daily from 8am to 8pm; off-season, Monday through Saturday from 10am to 3pm.

The **Oracle of Zeus** at Dodona traces its roots back to the early Hellenistic peoples who had arrived in northwestern Greece by about 2000 B.C. They themselves probably worshipped Zeus, but it now appears that at Dodona there was already some cult of the earth goddess, possibly with an oracle that based its interpretations on the flights of pigeons. In any case, by about 1400 B.C., it appears that the Zeus-worshipping Greeks had imposed their god on the site and turned the goddess into his consort, Dione.

By this time, too, the priests were linking Zeus's presence to the rustling leaves of an oak tree at Dodona and were interpreting these sounds as oracular messages. The Greeks set up a shrine around this tree, at first nothing more than a protective fence. Over the centuries they built more and more elaborate structures on the site, but the first temple to Zeus was not erected here until the 4th century B.C.

Eventually the oracle spoke through the bronze statue of a youth with a whip that was stirred by the wind to strike adjacent metal cauldrons, and the reverberating sound was interpreted. Many ambitious structures, both religious and secular, were erected at Dodona, but the oracle effectively ceased functioning in the 4th century A.D.—about the time when, it is claimed by some, the original oak died. The oak now on the site of the shrine is, of course, a recent planting.

Only traces of walls are left of other structures, but the magnificent **theater** survives, albeit thanks to what was virtually a reassembling in the 19th century. The first theater was built in the 3rd century B.C. and was said to have seated 17,000. It was destroyed, but another as large replaced it in the 2nd century B.C. Later, the Romans converted it into an arena for gladiatorial contests. The theater was one of the largest on the Greek mainland and has almost the same marvelous acoustics as the famous (but smaller) one at Epidaurus. Even if you do not explore the other remains, just to sit in this theater for a while is an evocative experience.

PERAMA CAVE

Only some 5 kilometers (3 miles) north of Ioannina (the turnoff is past the airport), this cave—actually more a series of caverns—was only discovered in 1941, during World War II, when people were seeking hiding places. It has since been thoroughly developed, with electric lights, steps, and handrails that allow for a perfectly safe walk through. In high season, it's open daily from 8am to 8pm; in winter, from 9am to sunset. Guided tours set out about every 15 minutes from the well-signed entrance in Perama village; the fee is Dr1,000 ($3.35). The guides often don't speak much more English than to repeat the names assigned to unusually shaped stalagmites or stalactites and they have an annoying habit of making everyone rush through (but in fact you can linger behind and join the next group).

Whether or not Perama lives up to its boast as one of the most spectacular caves in the world, it's worth a visit if you haven't been in many such caves. *Warning:* At the very end, you must climb what seems like an endless number of steps to come out of the cave—but at least you finish at a cafe!

METSOVO

This is a traditional mountain village that has become so popular that at times the original appeal can be overwhelmed by tourism at its worst. Still, many people find it satisfying—some even find it magical. It's about a 1½-hour bus ride east of Ioannina. Although there are a couple of buses to Metsovo in the morning, there's really only one back from Metsovo in the late afternoon that allows for a day in the village—so either pay close attention to the always-changing bus schedule or, better still, rent a car. (It can also be approached by bus from the east, coming from Athens or Thessaloniki.)

The village sits at about 1,000 meters (3,300 ft.) above sea level, nestled among peaks of the Pindos mountains, so in addition to attracting day-trippers, it draws serious nature lovers and hikers from all over Greece and Europe. Overnight accommodations are often strained, especially during Greek holidays. And because there are ski slopes nearby, Metsovo is also a popular destination even during the winter.

Assuming that you'll go there on a day's excursion, what you will experience is a village that has managed to maintain a certain style of architecture; traditional customs such as clothing and dances; crafts such as weaving, embroidery, and woodwork; and several food specialties. The buildings, of course, can be seen at all times just by strolling around. They're what most of us think of as Alpine style—stone, with wooden balconies and slate roofs. Some of the older people wear traditional clothing all the time, but the fancier costumes are only worn on Sundays and holidays.

If you want to see the **dances,** July 26 is the village's feast day, but also one of its most overcrowded days. **Crafts** are on display and sale in dozens of shops up and down the main street. Some is touristy imported kitsch, but some is authentically local and handsome. The best of the latter is at the **Metsovo Folk Art Cooperative,** located about 50 meters from the Egnatia Hotel on the slope above it. The traditional **Epirote foods** can be sampled in several restaurants (see "Where to Dine," below). Disneyland it ain't, but don't go to Metsovo thinking you're discovering a quaint native village. There's even a fairly ambitious conference center in town.

There remains yet another reason to go to Metsovo. It's the center (in Greece, at least) of the **Vlach people,** who claim descent from Latin-speaking Wallachians of what is now Romania. The Vlachs were originally shepherds who followed their flocks, and many still do just that; but over the centuries, many other Vlachs have settled down in northern Greece and prospered in crafts, commerce, and trade. Some of the wealthier Vlachs have made their money from dealing in wool and other products from the flocks, and now many in Metsovo prosper from the tourist trade. Because the Vlachs wrote little of their distinctive Latin-based language down and because it's not taught in the schools, it's in danger of being lost as the new generation marry and move out of their relatively small circles. You'll find the Vlachs of Metsovo extremely congenial—and patient as foreigners constantly ask them to "say something in Vlach." (Don't expect your Latin to help much!)

In addition to walking about the village, there are several special attractions that may appeal. There's the **Museum of Folk Art** in the Arhondiko Tositsa, a 17th-century mansion that's been completely restored by Baron Michalis Tositsa, a wealthy Vlach living in Switzerland. With its paneled rooms, furniture, rugs, clothing, crafts, and domestic furnishings of all kinds, it's a superb example of how a prosperous family might once have lived in Epirus. The museum, located on a road above the main street, is open in summer, Monday through Wednesday and Friday through Saturday from 8:30am to 1pm and 4 to 6pm; in winter, it's open the same days but from 3 to 5pm only. Admission is Dr300 ($1).

Much more typical of Metsovo is the little **church of Ayia Paraskevi** on the main square, with its carved-wood altar screen, silver chandeliers, and copies of Ravenna mosaics.

And if you can handle the half-hour walk down and an hour walk back up, you can visit the restored 14th-century **Moni Ayios Nikolaos;** a signed trail for this monastery leads off from the main square. You can drive closer to it by taking the road out of the town square (signed Ioannina) and at about 1 kilometer (0.6 miles) turning down the left fork and winding downward for another 3½ kilometers (2 miles); the monastery sits up on the slope and you have to scramble up through the vineyard. The resident caretaker (a lovely lady who also has some of her own handsome weavings for sale) will allow entry during all reasonable hours (until 7:30pm in high season). Its church has some quite spectacular 18th-century frescoes (long lost until the 1950s), an iconostasis, and several icons.

WHERE TO STAY

If you want to overnight in Metsovo, there are 12 hotels to choose from. All of them are quite acceptable and all to some degree are decorated in the traditional style of the region. We can single out several.

Galaxias. On a terrace above the main square. ☎ **0656/41-123.** Fax 0656/41-124. 10 units, some with shower, some with tub. TV TEL. High season Dr17,000 ($57) double; low season Dr12,000 ($40) double. Rates include continental breakfast. EURO, MC, V.

If you want to be at the center of things, then this should be your choice—but it's for people who appreciate staying in a country inn. It's by no means a fancy hotel—the rooms are modest in size and decor, the bathrooms are just adequate. Ask for a room in the front with a view of the distant mountains. The homey atmosphere emanates from the Barbayanni family, who run this hotel and the restaurant reviewed below.

✪ **The Hotel Victoria.** About 1km (half a mile) from the main square. ☎ **0656/41-761.** Fax 0656/41-454. 37 units, some with shower, some with tub. TV TEL. Regular season Dr15,000 ($50) double; Christmas and Easter seasons Dr26,000 ($87). Rates include continental breakfast. EURO, MC, V.

If you want a more natural setting and a bit more luxury, then try the Victoria, out on the edge of town. As you approach the hotel down a steep road, the traditional Epirote style of architecture will remind you somewhat of an Alpine inn. The interior, with its generous use of natural materials and large fireplaces (functioning in winter), plus its hearty furnishings, confirm this impression. The rooms are not especially large but feel quite cozy; all have balconies and/or views. And because it's relatively new (from the late 1980s), its bathrooms are modern. The hotel maintains its own fine restaurant, but what you really come here for is the isolation and the views. In winter, it becomes a ski lodge, but either winter or summer it is highly popular with Greeks and Europeans, so reservations are advised.

Kassaros Hotel. ☎ **0656/41-800.** Fax 0656/41-262. 31 units, some with shower, some with tub. TV TEL. High season Dr18,000 ($60) double; low season Dr13,500 ($45). Rates include continental breakfast. AE, DC, EURO, MC, V.

For a location away from the square, but not as far as the Victoria, and as a favor to your budget, try the Kassaros Hotel. This is the perfect place for those who intend an extended or active stay in Metsovo, because the proprietor also runs a travel agency, Kassaros Travel, which has ski equipment or a snowmobile for rent and also has its own buses for excursions throughout Epirus.

WHERE TO DINE

Even if you spend only a few hours in Metsovo, you should try a meal at a restaurant that offers traditional Epirote fare. There are a couple decent ones along the main street, Odos Tositsa—Taverna Panormiko, Restaurant Toxotis, or Cafe Chroni Roof Garden—but the following is our favorite.

✪ **Galaxias.** In the Galaxias hotel, just above the main square. ☎ **0656/41-202.** Main courses Dr1,000–Dr2,100 ($3.35–$7). EU, MC, V. Daily noon–11pm. GREEK.

In warm weather, you can sit outdoors; in cooler weather, eat in the handsome dining room warmed by a cheerful fire. Begin a meal of the local specialties with the bean soup (*trachana*) and/or a cheese pie with leek. Move on to the spicy sausage or beef patties with leeks and celery baked in a pot. For dessert, try the baklava or yogurt but be sure to save room for one of the local cheeses, of the smoked variety (*metsovonay*), or the mild *vlachotiri*. To accompany your meal, ask for the local red wine, Katoyi, or if that's in short supply, just the house wine.

ZAGORI (ZAGORIA/ZAGOROHORIA) & THE VIKOS GORGE

For some, this might be a more appealing way to spend an extra day in northwest Greece than at Metsovo or Dodona or Perama Cave. The Zagori is the mountainous area just north of Ioannina, a region of perhaps 400 square miles. The whole region is now part of the **Greek National Park System** and has about 46 villages. These have remained virtually unchanged through the centuries. The mountainous roads can make for slow going even to visit a few sites.

Becoming a part of the national park system has put a stop to the unrestricted development that has spoiled so many locales in Greece; it's also required any new structures to be built in the traditional manner, with stone buildings and slate roofs. But it has also so cramped life that young people leave and many of the villages are now all but abandoned. The villages you'll visit tend to be interesting rather than quaint, and much of the appeal of the excursion is in the scenery and such elements as the old bridges. Some disagreement exists as to which are villages, which are hamlets, and which are mere settlements.

The region's most spectacular sight is the **Vikos Gorge,** and for those who are up to it, this can be an excursion of its own.

Getting around the Zagori without your own vehicle is all but impossible. The few buses simply don't allow you to get to more than one destination and back to

---

Trekking into the Vikos Gorge

For those who want to go into the Vikos Gorge, the lower square of Monodendri offers one of the most accessible approaches. The path down into the gorge is signed there. But even to get to where the gorge begins to open out ahead of you is a rugged 4½- to 5-hour walk—and then it would be still longer to come back up. So no one should attempt this without proper gear, supplies, and experience. The walk through the entire gorge—some 16 kilometers (10 miles)—is even more demanding. If you would like to go on even an abbreviated expedition, our best advice is to join one of the groups organized by **Robinson Travel Agency** at the edge of Ioannina on the main road to the airport, at Odos 8 Merarchias 2 (☎ **0651/29-402;** fax 0651/25-071). More experienced trekkers might prefer to contact the **Mountain Climbing Association of Ioannina** (☎ 0656/22-138) or the **Mountain Climbing Association of Papingo** (☎ **0653/41-138** or 0653/ 41-320), based in one of the Zagori villages.

Ioannina in a day. With a car you can visit one or two villages, view the Vikos Gorge from above, experience the scenery, and be back in Ioannina within 5 hours. Or you could join an organized tour (see "Trekking into the Vikos Gorge," below).

Take the main road north out of Ioannina toward Konitsa; turnoffs are clearly marked. Your first destination should be **Monodendri;** after taking the highway north for 19.4 kilometers (13 miles), just past Metamorfosi, take the right turn signed VIKOS GORGE. At about 5 kilometers (3 miles), a sign to the right indicates **Kipi;** it is well worth the brief diversion (8km/5 miles) to see the famous high-arched bridges. Usually thought of as old Turkish, they were most likely built in the 19th century for the convenience of packhorse caravans. The first, single-span one is the Kokkoros; beyond that is the three-arched Plakida Bridge. (If you have the time and inclination, another 11km/7 miles on through Kipi village leads to **Nigades,** with its strikingly handsome **Church of Ayios Yioryios,** built in 1795.) Returning to the main route, proceed about 39 kilometers (25 miles), where a sign indicates a turn right into the lower square of Monodendri.

Driving to the small parking lot on the edge of the village square, you will proceed on foot (following the sign) about 10 minutes to the lovely little 15th-century **Monastery of Ayia Paraskevi,** perched on the edge of the Vikos Gorge. The viewing areas here are well protected and this may be spectacular enough for most, but if you have no fear of heights and are sure-footed, get back on the trail above the monastery and proceed on for several hundred meters to enjoy even more spectacular views of the gorge—but also more dramatic drops from the totally unprotected and narrow path.

If you continue on the main road for about another half mile, you'll come to the upper square of **Monodendri.** (There's a short cobblestone path that connects this upper square to the lower square.) The upper square is home to several modest hotels and decent restaurants, but unless you are seeking such amenities, you need not go up there. If you want to have a meal while here, we recommend either **Katerina's Restaurant** (try her tasty chicken or meat pies!), at the top of the square, or **To Petrino Dasos,** the little taverna on the right as you come up to the square. The **Oxio,** a hotel and restaurant opposite To Petrino Dasos, is another possibility.

If you want another view of the gorge, you can drive up through the upper square and on for another 7 kilometers (4½ miles), signed to Osia; you again leave your car and walk down a stone path to what is known as the **Vikos Balcony,** offering a truly spectacular view. Local signs claim that the Vikos Gorge, at 900 meters (2,950 ft.), is "the world's deepest," but plenty of places around the world might dispute that.

Our next stop is at **Papingo.** Drivers are usually advised to retrace their entire route back to the main highway and then proceed north to the turnoff to Papingo. This is a 1½-hour drive (because you are first heading south again). If you are a bit adventurous—and more important, able to ask basic directions in Greek—you can take a perfectly fine asphalt road that cuts off half that time by going more directly to that highway. You start down from Monodendri, but at about 5 kilometers (3 miles), take the (signed) right turn and head across the flatland for Elafatopos; do not go on up to Elafatopos, however, but continue and take the left turn signed Kato Pedina; you will then come out onto the main highway; turn right and proceed some 4 kilometers (2½ miles) until a sign to the right indicates Papingo. The drive from this point on offers the kind of scenery best described by a young English traveler we fell in with, Simon, when he said, "It makes you want to stop the car and get out and applaud."

There are two villages, **Megalo Papingo** and **Micro Papingo**—"Big" and "Little" Papingo—and we recommend visiting at least the first. Many regard this as the archetypal Zagori village, with its terrain, streets, homes, roofs, public buildings, and everything else seemingly all made of the same stone. Megalo Papingo has several cafes and restaurants as well as several modest hotels; you can always be sure of a meal in Papingo, but rooms may be booked up at various times of the year—such is the reputation of the Zagori in Greece and elsewhere in Europe.

We recommend the **Hotel Koulis** (☎ **0653/41-138**). A double is Dr10,000 ($33); rates include private bathroom and breakfast. If you want something more elegant, try the **Saxonis Houses** (☎ **0653/41-615**), where a double runs Dr20,000 ($67). Rates include private bathroom and breakfast.

If you drive on another mile from Megalo Papingo, you'll come to Micro Papingo, which offers another vista. If you really want to get away from it all, stay at the little **Hotel Dias** here, with its "restaurant" (☎ **0653/41-257** or 0653/41-892); a double runs Dr10,000 ($33), but that's probably negotiable.

After all this you are now only some 60 kilometers (38 miles) from Ioannina. You can return feeling you have at least had a taste of the true Epirus.

15 The Ionian Islands

by John S. Bowman

"The isles of Greece, the isles of Greece"—when Lord Byron tossed his bouquet, he was not under the spell of today's popular Cycladic islands but of the Ionian Islands. Located off Greece's northwest coast, the Ionians offer some of the loveliest natural settings (and beaches) in the country, a fine selection of hotels and restaurants, a distinctive history and lore, and some unusual architectural and archaeological sites.

The Ionians are rainier, greener, and more temperate than other Greek islands, with a high season lasting from late June to early September. The roads are generally in good condition, even if unavoidably steep and twisting. Accommodations range from luxury resorts to quiet little rooms on remote beaches. The local cuisine and wines offer numerous special treats. Among the best are *sofrito,* a spicy veal dish; *bourdetto,* a spicy fish dish; and the Theotaki or Liapaditiko wines.

The Ionian Islands include **Corfu** (Kerkira), **Paxos** (Paxoi), **Levkas** (Lefkas, Lefkada), **Ithaka** (Ithaki), **Kefalonia** (Kefallinia, Cephalonia), **Zakinthos** (Zakynthos, Zante), and **Kithira** (Cythera, Cerigo). Meanwhile, there are many more islands in the archipelago along Greece's northwest coast, including several that are inhabited.

STRATEGIES FOR SEEING THE ISLANDS In this chapter, we single out **Corfu** and **Kefalonia,** with a side trip to **Ithaka.** With a couple of weeks to spare, you can take a ship to either Corfu at the north or Zakinthos in the south and then make your way by ship to all the others (although outside high season, you will have to do some backtracking). If you have only a week, you should fly to one and then use ships to get to a couple of the others. In either case, try to rent a car to get around the larger islands. If it comes down to visiting only one, Corfu is a prime candidate, but if you want to get off the beaten track, consider Kefalonia. All the Ionians—especially Corfu—are overrun in July and August; aim for June or September.

A LOOK AT THE PAST In the fabric of their history, the Ionian Islands can trace certain threads that both tie and distinguish them from the rest of Greece. During the late Bronze Age (1500 to 1200 B.C.), there was a Mycenaean culture on at least several of these islands. Although certain names of islands and cities were the same as those used today—Ithaka, for instance—scholars have never been able to agree on exactly which were the sites described in *The Odyssey.*

Western Greece & the Ionian Islands

Zagori
Perama
Metsovo
Paleokastritsa
Filiates
6
Ioannina
Corfu Town
Dodona
Islet
of Nissi
Trikkala
Benitses
Igoumenitsou
5
Lake
Pamvotis
Kavos
EPIRUS
**CORFU
(KERKIRA)**
Paramythia
Margariti
Lakka
Parga
E15
PAXOS
ANTIPAXOS
Arta
Zalongo
Nikopolis
*Ambracian
Gulf*
5
**To
Ancona,
Bari &
Brindisi**
Preveza
Action (Actium)
Vonitsa
Lefkas
Amfilohia
LEFKADA
Nydri
Aetos
Vassiliki
Mitikas
Agrinio
I o n i a n   S e a
Fiskardo
Frikes
Astakos
Etolikon
KEFALONIA
Vathy
E19
ITHAKA
Antirrio
Messolongi
Rio
Lixouri
Sami
*Gulf of
Patras*
Patras
Argostoli
Poros
Metaxata
Skala
9
Kyllini
PELOPONNESE
ZAKINTHOS
Zakinthos
74
Amalias
Laganas
Vassilikos
Pirgos

0   25 mi
0   25 km

GREECE
**Western Greece &
The Ionian Islands**
Athens

Legend
Ferry Routes
Mountain

Travel Tip

Kerkira is the modern Greek name for Corfu. Look for it in schedules, maps, and so on.

The islands were recolonized by people from the city-states on the Greek mainland, starting in the 8th century B.C. The Peloponnesian War, in fact, can be traced back to a quarrel between Corinth and its colony at Corcyra (Corfu) that led to Athens's interference and eventually the full-scale war. The islands then fell under the rule of the Romans, then the Byzantine empire, and remained prey to warring powers and pirates in this part of the Mediterranean for centuries. By the end of the 14th century, Corfu fell under Venice's control, and the Italian language and culture—including the Roman Catholic church—came to predominate.

With the fall of Venice to Napoleon's France in 1797, the French took over and held sway until 1815. The Ionian Islands then became a protectorate of the British; although the islands did experience peace and prosperity, they were in fact a colony. When parts of Greece gained true independence from the Turks by 1830—due in part to leadership from Ionians such as Ioannis Capodistrias—many Ionians became restless under the British. Attempts at gaining union with Greece culminated with Prime Minister Gladstone's granting this in 1864.

During World War II, the islands were at first occupied by the Italians, but when the Germans took over from them, the islands, especially Corfu, suffered greatly. Since 1945, the Ionian Islands have enjoyed tourism of a less invasive kind and a fine prosperity.

1 Corfu (Kerkira)

32km (20 nautical miles) W of mainland; another 558km (342 miles) N of Athens

There's Corfu the coast, Corfu the island, and Corfu the town, and they don't necessarily appeal to the same vacationers. Corfu the island lures those who want to escape civilization and head for the water—whether an undeveloped little beach, with a simple taverna and some rooms to rent, or a spectacular beach resort. Then there's the more civilized **Corfu town,** with its distinctive layers of Greek, Italian, French, and British elements. Finally, there's a third and little-known Corfu, the interior with its lush vegetation and gentle slopes, modest villages and farms, and countless olive and fruit trees.

Whichever Corfu you choose, it will prove to please. It was, after all, this island's ancient inhabitants, the Phaeacians, who made Odysseus so comfortable. Visitors today will find Corfu similarly hospitable.

ESSENTIALS

GETTING THERE   By Plane   Olympic Airways provides at least three flights daily from and to Athens and three flights weekly from and to Thessaloniki. One-way for each route is about Dr20,000 ($67). The Olympic Airways office in Corfu town is at Odos Polila 11, around the corner from the National Tourist Organization (☎ **0661/38-695**), but many agents all over town sell tickets.

Corfu Airport is about 4 kilometers (2½ miles) south of the center of Corfu town. Fortunately, the flight patterns of most planes do not bring them over the city. There is no public bus into town, so everyone takes a taxi; a standard fare should be about Dr1,500 ($5) but may fluctuate with the destination, amount of luggage, and time of day.

Legend
Information ⓘ
OTE ⓒ

Archaeological Museum ⑦
Ayios Spyridon Cathedral ④
Byzantine Museum ②
Ionian Academy ⑥
Museum of Asian Art ③
Palace of St. Michael & St. George ③
Synagogue ①
Town Hall ⑤

By Boat There are many lines and ships linking Corfu to both Greek and foreign ports. There are ferries almost hourly between Igoumenitsou, directly across on the mainland, and several weekly to and from Patras. During the high season there are daily ships linking Corfu to one or another ports in Italy—Ancona, Bari, Brindisi, Trieste, Venice—or to Piraeus and/or Patras. The schedules and fares vary so from year to year that it would be misleading to provide details here; deal with a travel agent in your homeland or Greece (or Italy). The ship lines involved are **Adriatica** (Piraeus ☎ 01/429-0487), **ANEK Lines** (Athens ☎ 01/323-3481), **Fragline** (Athens ☎ 01/821-4171), **Hellenic Mediterranean Line** (Piraeus ☎ 01/422-5341), **Minoan Lines** (Piraeus ☎ 01/408-0006), **Strintzis Lines** (Piraeus ☎ 01/422-5015), and **Ventouris Line** (Piraeus ☎ 01/988-9280). A typical cost for two people in a double cabin and with a (standard-size) vehicle during high season is about Dr90,000 ($300) one-way from Brindisi or Ancona to Corfu.

Corfu town is also one of Greece's official entry/exit harbors, with customs and health authorities as well as passport control. This is of special concern to those arriving from foreign lands on yachts.

By Bus KTEL offers service all the way from Athens or Thessaloniki, with a ferry carrying you between Corfu and Igoumenitsou on the mainland opposite. This mode of transportation also allows you to get on or off at main points along the way, such as Ioannina. The buses are comfortable enough, but be prepared for many hours of winding roads. The **KTEL office** (☎ **0661/39-627** or 0661/39-985) is located just off Leoforos Avramiou, up from the New Port.

VISITOR INFORMATION   The **National Tourist Office** (☎ 0661/37-520 or 0661/37-640; fax 0661/30-298) is located on the second floor of a modern building (unnumbered) on the corner of Rizospaston and Polila in the new town, a block from the post office. It's open Monday through Friday from 7am to 2:30pm; in July and August, also on Saturdays from 11am to 6pm. Also helpful is a **Municipal Tourist Office** in the reception building at the New Port, open Monday through Saturday from 6:30am to 1pm. Both offices will give you the standard brochure on Corfu with good maps of the town and island.

GETTING AROUND   By Bus   The dark-blue public buses service Corfu town, its suburbs, and nearby destinations. The semiprivate green-and-cream KTEL buses offer frequent service to points all over the island—Paleokastritsa, Glifada, Sidari, and more.

By Taxi   In and around Corfu town, a taxi is probably your best bet—sometimes the only way around, such as to and from the harbor and the airport. Although taxi drivers are supposed to use their meters, most don't, so you should agree on the fare before setting out. You may also decide to use a taxi to visit some of the sites outside Corfu town; again, be sure to agree on the fare before setting out.

By Car   There are myriad car-rental agencies all over Corfu; even so, in high season it can be very difficult to get a vehicle at the spur of the moment. If you're sure of your plans on Corfu, make arrangements with an established international agency before departing home. Otherwise, try **Greek Skies Travel Agency,** in Corfu town at Odos Kapodistriou 20A (☎ **0661/33-410;** fax 0661/36-161), or **Avanti Rent A Car,** Ethnikis Antistasseos 12A, down along the new port (☎ **0661/42-028**).

By Moped   It's easy to rent all kinds of mopeds and scooters and motorcycles, but the roads are so curvy, narrow, and steep that you should be very comfortable driving such a vehicle.

CITY LAYOUT   The **new town** of Corfu town is relatively modern and even a bit cosmopolitan. You probably won't be spending much time in this new town, except for visiting the post office or the National Tourist Office.

It's easy to spend many days wandering through the **old town,** with its *cantouni,* Greece's largest complex of picturesque streets and buildings, effectively unchanged for many centuries. The crown jewel of the old town is the **Liston,** the arcaded row of cafes where you can spend a lazy afternoon watching a cricket match on the great green of the adjacent Esplanade (or Spianada).

FAST FACTS   The official **American Express** agent for Corfu is Greek Skies Travel Agency, Odos Kapodistriou 20A (☎ **0661/39-160;** fax 0661/36-161). There are **banks** in both the Old Town and New Town; you'll find numerous ATMs on their exteriors. The **British Consul** is at Odos Menekrates 1 (☎ **0661/30-055**), at the south end of the town, near the Menekrates monument; it will take care of all British Commonwealth citizens. There is no U.S. consulate in Corfu. For general **emergencies,** dial ☎ **100.** For an **ambulance,** dial ☎ **166.** The **hospital** is on Odos Julius Andreatti, and is signed from around town.

An **Internet cafe,** the Netoikos, is on Odos Kalochairetou 14, behind Ayios Spiridon Church (e-mail: netoikos@ netoikos.gr); open daily from late morning to late evening. You can count on quick, careful, and fair-priced **laundry** or **dry cleaning** at The Peristeri, Odos Ioannis Theotikos 42 (leading from San Rocco Square on the way to the KTEL Bus Terminal). It's open Monday, Tuesday, Thursday, and Friday from 9am to 2:30pm and 5:30 to 8:30pm; Wednesday and Saturday from 9am to

2:30pm. The **police station** (☎ 0661/39-575) is at Leoforos Alexandros 19 (cater-corner from the post office). The **Tourist Police** (☎ 0661/30-265) are at Odos Xenofontos Stratigou 1 (one flight up), just off the waterfront as you walk toward Plateia Solomou and to New Fortress. The **post office** (☎ 0661/25-544) is at Leoforos Alexandros 26. It's open Monday through Friday from 7:30am to 8pm; in July and August, it's usually open for a few hours on Saturday. Now designated for assisted calls, the **telephone office (OTE)** is down at the New Port; its staff is very helpful. It's open Monday through Friday from 7:20am to 2:50pm.

WHAT TO SEE & DO
THE TOP ATTRACTIONS

Archaeological Museum. Odos P. Armeni-Vraila 1 (on the corner of Demokratias, the boulevard along the waterfront). ☎ **0661/38-124** or 0661/43-492. Admission Dr800 ($2.70); free on Sun. Tues–Sun 8:00am–2:30pm. Wheelchair accessible.

Even if you're not a devotee of ancient history or museums, you should take an hour to visit this small museum. On your way to see its masterwork, as you turn left off the upstairs vestibule, you'll pass the **stone lion** dating from around 575 B.C. (found in the nearby Menekrates tomb, along the waterfront just down from the museum). Go around and behind it to the large room with arguably the finest example of Archaic temple sculpture extant, the **pediment from the Temple of Artemis.** (The temple itself is located just south of Corfu town and dates from about 590 B.C. The remains are not of interest to most people.) The pediment features the **Gorgon Medusa,** attended by two pantherlike animals. You don't need to be an art historian to note how this predates the great classical works such as the Elgin marbles—not only in the naiveté of its sculpture but also in the emphasis on the monstrous, with the humans so much smaller.

Interesting for comparison is the fragment from another Archaic pediment found at Figare, Corfu. Displayed in an adjoining room, it shows Dionysos and a youth reclining on a couch. In this work, only a century younger than the Gorgon pediment, the humans have reduced the animal in size and placed it under the couch.

Museum of Asian Art. The Palace of St. Michael and St. George, north end of Esplanade. ☎ **0661/30-443.** Admission Dr1,000 ($3.35). Tues–Sun 8am–2:30pm.

The building itself is a great example of neoclassical architecture. It was constructed between 1819 and 1824 to serve as the residence of the Lord High Commissioner, the British ruler of the Ionian islands, to house the headquarters of the Order of St. Michael and St. George, and to provide the assembly room for the Ionian senate. When the British turned the Ionians over to Greece, this building was given to the king of Greece. As the king seldom spent much time here, it fell into disrepair, until after World War II when it was restored and turned into a museum.

The works on display are mainly from the collections of two Greek diplomats. The centerpiece of the museum is the collection of Chinese porcelains, bronzes, and other works from the Shang Dynasty (1500 B.C.) to the Ching Dynasty (19th century). There are also strong holdings of Japanese works—woodblock prints, ceramics, sculpture, watercolors, and *netsuke* (carved sash fasteners). You may not have come to Greece to appreciate Asian art, but this is one of several unexpected delights in Corfu.

Old Fort (Paleo Frourio). The Esplanade (opposite the Liston). Admission Dr800 ($2.70) adults, Dr400 ($1.35) students and seniors over 60. Tues–Fri 8am–8pm; Sat–Sun and holidays 8:30am–3pm. In summer there is a **Sound-and-Light** show several nights a week (in different foreign languages, so be sure to check the schedule) for Dr2,000 ($6.70).

Originally a promontory attached to the mainland, its two peaks—*koryphi* in Greek—gave the modern name to the town and island; the promontory itself was for a long time the main town (and appears as such in many old engravings). The Venetians dug the moat in the 16th century, enabling them to hold off several attempts by the Turks to conquer this outpost of Christianity. Each peak is crowned by a castle; you can get fine views of Albania to the east and Corfu, town and island, to the west.

The **Kalypso Star.** Old Port, Corfu town. ☎ **0671/46-525.** Fax 0671/23-506. Admission Dr3,000 ($10) adults, Dr1,500 ($5) children. In high season, trips leave daily, hourly from 10am–6pm, plus a 10pm night trip; off-season, inquire as to schedule.

The *Kalypso Star* is a glass-bottomed boat that takes small groups on trips offshore and provides a fascinating view of the marine life and undersea formations.

A STROLL AROUND CORFU TOWN

This is definitely a browser's town, where as you're strolling around in search of a snack or souvenir, you'll serendipitously discover an old church or monument. To orient yourself, start with the **Esplanade area** bounded by the Old Fort (see above) and the sea on one side; the small haven below and to the north of the Old Fort is known as **Mandraki Harbor,** while the shore to the south is home port to the **Corfu Yacht Club.**

The Esplanade is bisected by Odos Dousmani. The north part has the field known as the **Plateia,** where cricket games are played on lazy afternoons. At the far north side of the Esplanade is the Palace of St. Michael and St. George, now housing the **Museum of Asian Art** (see above). If you proceed along the left (northwest) corner of the palace, you'll come out above the coast and can make your way around Odos Arseniou above the medieval sea walls (known as the *mourayia*).

On your way you will pass (on the left, up a flight of stairs) the **Byzantine Museum** in the **Church of Antivouniotissa.** Even those who have never been especially taken by Byzantine art should enjoy its small but elegant selection of icons from around Corfu; of particular interest are works by Cretan artists who came to Corfu, some of whom went on to Venice. It's open Monday from 12:30 to 7pm, Tuesday through Saturday from 8am to 7pm, and Sunday and holidays from 8:30am to 3pm. Admission is Dr800 ($2.70).

Proceed along the coast road and come down to the square at the Old Port; above its far side rises the **New Fortress** and beyond this is the New Port. Off to the left of the square is a large gateway, what remains of the 16th-century Porta Spilia, and past the building with the tourist police is Plateia Solomou.

If you proceed left from Plateia Solomou along Odos Velissariou, on the right you'll see the 300-year-old **Synagogue,** with its collection of torah crowns. It's open on Saturday from 9am until early evening. To gain entry during the week, call the Jewish Community Center at ☎ **0661/38-802.**

This is now a good way to proceed into the section of Old Corfu known as **Campiello,** with its stepped streets and narrow alleys. You may often feel lost in a labyrinth—and you will be—but sooner or later you will emerge onto a busy commercial street that will bring you down to the Esplanade.

Heading south on the Esplanade, you'll see a bandstand and at its far end the **Maitland Rotunda,** commemorating Sir Thomas Maitland, the first British lord high commissioner of the Ionian Islands. Past this is the statue of Count Ioannis Kapodistrias (1776–1836), the first president of independent Greece. Just outside the south end of the Esplanade is a school building that once housed the Ionian Academy.

If you proceed south along the shore road from this end of the Esplanade, you'll pass the Corfu Palace Hotel (see below) on your right; then the **Archaeological**

Museum (see above), up Odos Vraila on the right. After two more blocks, off to the right on the corner of Odos Marasli, is the **Tomb of Menekrates,** a circular tomb of a notable who drowned about 650 B.C. Proceeding to the right here onto Leoforos Alexandros will bring you into the heart of the new Corfu town.

The western side of the north half of the Esplanade is lined by a wide tree-shaded strip filled with cafe tables and chairs, then a street reserved for pedestrians, and then arcaded buildings patterned after Paris's Rue de Rivoli. These arcaded buildings, known as the **Liston,** were begun by the French and finished by the British. Sit here with a cup of coffee and enjoy the passing scene.

At the back of the Liston is **Odos Kapadistriou,** and perpendicular from this are several streets that lead into the heart of Old Corfu—a mélange of fine shops, old churches, souvenir stands, and other stores in a maze of streets, alleys, and squares that seem like Venice without the water. The broadest and most stylish is **Odos Nikiforio Theotoki.** Proceeding up Odos Ayios Spiridon (at the north end), you come to the corner of Odos Filellinon and to **Ayios Spiridon Cathedral,** dedicated to Spiridon, the patron saint of Corfu. A 4th-century bishop of Cyprus, Spiridon is credited with saving Corfu from famine, plagues, and a Turkish siege. The church hosts the saint's embalmed body in a silver casket, as well as precious gold and silver votive offerings and many fine old icons. Four times a year the faithful parade the remains of St. Spiridon through the streets of old Corfu: on Palm Sunday, Holy Saturday, August 1, and the first Sunday in November.

Proceeding up Odos Voulgareos behind the south end of the Liston, you'll come up along the back of the **Town Hall,** built in 1663 as a Venetian loggia; it later served as a theater. Turn into the square it faces and enter into what seems like a Roman piazza, with steps and terraces, the Roman Catholic cathedral on the left, and, reigning over the top, the restored Catholic archbishop's residence that now houses the Bank of Greece.

From here, finish your walk by wandering up and down and in and out the various streets of Old Corfu.

SHOPPING

Corfu town has many shops selling handmade needlework and weavings, and we won't claim that **Elli—The House of Embroidery,** Odos N. Theotoki 88, the main street leading from the center of Liston (☎ **0661/26-283**), has anything all that much different in quality or pricing. But the owner, George Kantaros, is willing to tell you about his wares and discuss prices. In addition to handmade tablecloths, embroidered coverlets, and lace doilies, he sells small Greek rugs.

Standing out from the many standard souvenir-gift shops, **Antica,** Odos Ayios Spiridon 25, leading away from the north end of Liston (☎ **0661/32-401**), offers unusual older jewelry, plates, textiles, brass, and icons. **Gravures,** Odos Ev. Voulgareos 64, where the street emerges from the old town to join the new town (☎ **0661/ 41-721**), has a fine selection of engravings and prints of mostly scenes from Corfu, all nicely matted. Originals (taken from old books or magazines) can cost Dr40,000 ($135), reproductions as little as Dr2,500 ($8).

There is no end of ceramics to be found in Corfu, but we like the **Pottery Workshop,** 15 kilometers (10 miles) north of Corfu on the right of the road to Paleokastritsa (☎ **0661/90-704**), because you get to observe Sofoklis Ikonomides and Sissy Moskidou making and decorating all the pottery on sale here. Whether decorative or functional, something here will certainly appeal to your taste. The elegant **Terracotta,** Odos Filarmonikis 2, just off Odos N. Theotoki, the main shopping street (☎/fax **0661/45-260**), sells only contemporary Greek work: jewelry, one-of-a-kind pieces, ceramics, and small sculptures, some by well-known Greek artists and artisans. Nothing is cheap but everything is classy.

WHERE TO STAY

Corfu town and the island of Corfu have an apparently inexhaustible choice of accommodations, but in high season (July and Aug) many will be taken by package groups from Europe. Reservations are recommended if you have specific preferences for that period.

IN TOWN

Very Expensive

✪ **Corfu Palace Hotel.** Leoforos Demokratias 2 (along Garitsa Bay, just south of center), 49100 Corfu. ☎ **0661/39-485** to 487. Fax 0661/31-749. E-mail: cfupalace@hol.gr. 115 units. A/C MINIBAR TV TEL. High season Dr55,000–Dr71,000 ($183–$237) double; low season Dr45,000–Dr57,500 ($150–$192) double. Children up to age 12 stay free in parents' room (without meals). Rates include buffet breakfast. AE, DC, ER, MC, V. Free parking. A 5-min. walk from Esplanade.

This is a grand hotel with every creature comfort, modern business and conference services, and elegant service that lives up to its decor. It combines the most up-to-date features with a Greek feel. The landscaping creates a tropical ambiance; the lobby and public areas bespeak luxury. Neither bedrooms nor bathrooms are exceptionally large, but they are highly comfortable and well appointed. All units enjoy balconies and views of the sea. Aside from the splendid surroundings, superb service, and grand meals, the main appeal of this hotel is probably its combination of restful isolation above the bay with its proximity to the city center.

The hotel's two restaurants, the Albatross (a grill room on the poolside terrace) and the Panorama (with a view of the bay), serve both Greek and international menus; both vie to claim the finest cuisine on Corfu. Amenities include concierge, room service, laundry, newspaper delivery, baby-sitting, three pools (one for children), sundeck, tennis nearby (outdoors, lit in evening), bicycle rentals, game room, conference and banquet rooms (for up to 200), car rentals, tour arrangements, hairdresser, jewelry store, and foreign-language books. Guests can use the facilities of the nearby Corfu Tennis Club and Yacht Club and the Corfu Golf Club, 14 kilometers (9 miles) away.

Moderate

If you prefer period hotels to shiny new accommodations, consider the **Astron Hotel,** Odos Donzelot 15 (waterfront road down to old harbor), 49100 Corfu (☎ **0661/ 39-505**; fax 0661/33-708).

Arcadion Hotel. Odos Kapodistriou 44 (catercorner from south end of Liston, facing the Esplanade), 49100 Corfu. ☎ **0661/37-670** to 672. Fax 661/45-087. 55 units. TEL. High season Dr19,000 ($63) double; low season Dr13,000 ($43) double. Rates include buffet breakfast. AE, JCB, MC, V. Open year-round. Public parking lot (fee) nearby.

If you like to be at the center of a city, you can't get much closer than this: when you step out the door, the Esplanade and the Liston are 50 feet away. Admittedly, this also means that on pleasant evenings there's apt to be a crowd of young people hanging out in front of it, so it's not for early sleepers. In the mornings, however, you reclaim that area when you breakfast on the terrace. The lobby and common areas are beginning to look a bit tired; guest rooms are clean if standard in size and decor, with adequate bathrooms. This is a hotel for those who don't mind feeling they've left home.

⊙ **Bella Venezia.** Odos N. Zambeli 4 (approached from far south end of Esplanade), 49100 Corfu. ☎ **0661/46-500** or 0661/44-290. Fax 0661/20-708. E-mail: belvenht@hol.gr. 32 units. A/C TV TEL. High season Dr21,000 ($70) double; low season Dr18,000 ($60) double. Rates include buffet breakfast. AE, DC, ER, MC, V. Open year-round. Parking on adjacent streets. Within walking distance of old and new town.

Like the gold medal winner of the decathlon, this hotel may not win in any single category, but its combined virtues make it the first choice of many. The building is a restored neoclassical mansion, with character if not major distinction. The location is just a bit off center and lacks fine views, but it's quiet and close enough to any place you'd want to walk to; a decent beach is 150 meters away. The common areas are not especially stylish but do have personality. Although not luxurious, the guest rooms have an old-world charm; bathrooms are standard. There is no restaurant, but there's a colorful patio-garden for breakfast and an enclosed kiosk for light meals. Finally, its rates are below what similar hotels charge.

Cavalieri. Odos Kapodistriou 4 (at far south end of Esplanade), 49100 Corfu. ☎ **0661/ 39-041.** Fax 0661/39-283. 50 units. A/C TV TEL. High season Dr25,000 ($83); low season Dr20,000 ($67). Rates include buffet breakfast. AE, DC, MC, V. Open year-round. Parking on adjacent streets. Within easy walking distance of old and new town.

If you like your hotels in the discreet old European style, this place is for you; those who prefer glitz should look elsewhere. The Cavalieri is in an old building with a small elevator. The main lounge is Italian-velvet, its restaurant is nothing special, service is low-key, rooms are spare, and bathrooms standard. But the hotel must be doing something right, as advance reservations are usually required. Location answers for much of the appeal: ask for one of the front rooms on the upper floors, which boast great views of the Old Fort. Another draw is the rooftop garden, which after 6:30pm offers drinks, sweets, and light meals along with a spectacular view. Even if you don't stay here, it's a grand place to pass an hour in the evening.

Inexpensive

Archontiko Hotel. Odos Athanasiou 61, Garitsa (about 1.6km/1 mile from center), 49100 Corfu. ☎ **0661/36-850.** Fax 0661/38-294. 20 units. TV TEL. High season Dr12,500 ($42) double; low season Dr10,000 ($33) double. Rates do not include any meals (but breakfast is served). V. Street parking.

Here's the place for those who appreciate old buildings with unusual decor more than a fashionable location. Set one street back from the Garitsa Bay but facing a strip of park along the bay, the hotel is in a turn-of-the-century mansion and some of the rooms have original frescoed cathedral ceilings (although the furniture is a somewhat incongruous knotty pine). All units have large modern bathrooms. Suites can accommodate from three to six beds (and rates rise accordingly). You can breakfast outdoors. The neighborhood is safe and quiet and the walk into town can be pleasant.

OUTSIDE TOWN

Expensive

Corfu Holiday Palace (formerly Hilton). P.O. Box 124, Odos Nausicaa, Kanoni (some 5km/3 miles south of Corfu town), 49100 Corfu. ☎ **0661/36-540.** Fax 0661/36-551. 266 units. A/C MINIBAR TV TEL. High season Dr34,000–Dr40,000 ($113–$133) double; low season Dr20,000–Dr26,000 ($67–$87) double. Inquire at travel agents for special packages for extended stays. AE, DC, ER, MC, V. Open year-round. Free parking on grounds. Hotel offers a shuttle bus; public bus no. 2 stops 200m away; a taxi is probably more in style.

This is a grand hotel in the contemporary manner—more like a resort in the range of its facilities and amenities. Its lobby sets the tone—spacious and relaxed—while the staff is professional yet friendly. The grounds create a semitropical ambiance. In addition to the pools, there's a lovely private beach down below. The famous locale known as Kanoni is a couple hundred yards from the hotel. The island's airport is off in the middle distance—not a major problem, but we advise you to ask for a room facing the sea and not the airport.

The main restaurant serves a fixed menu for those paying for the half-board plan. There's also a bar, a casino, and a grill restaurant. Amenities include concierge, room service, laundry, baby-sitting, two pools, health club, sundeck, two tennis courts (lit at night), water-sports equipment, jogging track, bowling, billiards, table tennis, 20% discount at Corfu Golf Club 18 kilometers (12 miles) away, conference rooms (for up to 500), car-rental desk, tour arrangements, beauty salon, and boutiques.

Inexpensive

Hotel Royal. Odos Figareto 110, Kanoni (3km/2 miles from Corfu center, a few hundred yards before Corfu Holiday Palace, above), 49100 Corfu. ☎ **0661/37-512.** Fax 0661/38-786. 121 units. TEL. High season Dr14,000 ($47) double; low season Dr10,000 ($33) double. Rates include continental breakfast. No credit cards. Closed Nov–Mar. Parking on grounds. Public bus no. 2 stops 100m away, but a taxi may be easier.

This might be considered an alternative to the nearby Corfu Holiday Palace if your desire is to stay outside Corfu town but you can't afford the Palace. It's a kind of funky place: the architecture is neo-baroque, the interior decor is folksy, and the lobby is filled with traditional works of art. Bedrooms and bathrooms are standard. The most spectacular features are the three tiered pools—it's a great place to come back to with the kids after a day spent sightseeing. As with the Palace, the airport is off in the middle distance, but the noise problem adds up to a relatively small portion of a day. It's a big hotel with a family atmosphere, and you can't beat the rates.

WHERE TO DINE
IN TOWN
Expensive

If you're in a celebratory mood, you might also consider **Chambor,** Odos Guilford 71 (☎ **0661/39-031**), possibly the most elegant restaurant in town.

✪ **Venetian Well.** Plateia Kremasti (small square up from Old Harbor, behind Greek Orthodox cathedral). ☎ **0661/44-761.** Reservations recommended in high season. Main courses Dr2,000–Dr3,000 ($7–$10). No credit cards. Mon–Sat noon–midnight. Open year-round. MIDDLE EASTERN/INTERNATIONAL/GREEK.

This remains our top pick in Corfu town. Diners sit at a candlelit table in a rather austere little square with a Venetian wellhead (1699) and a church opposite. (When the weather changes, you sit in a stately room with a mural.) The atmosphere is as discreet as the food is inventive. There is no printed menu—you learn what's available from a chalkboard or from your waiter—and there's no predicting what the kitchen will offer on any given evening. Start with the dark breads and the butter-cheese spread; then move on to the mushrooms baked in a light cheese sauce. Since the chef uses seasonal vegetables, salads vary from month to month. Main courses range from standard Greek dishes such as beef *giouvetsi* (cooked in a pot) to chicken Kasmir (with yogurt, paprika, and spices). Even the wines are a bit different, such as the Corfiote white Liapaditiko.

Moderate

If you want to dine along the coast, consider **Antranik,** Arseniou 19 (☎ **0661/22-301**), located under the awnings on the seaside of the road leading from north of the Esplanade down to the New Port. **Faliraki,** at the corner of Kapodistrias and

Arseniou, below the wall, directly on the water (☎ 0661/30-392), also has a wonderful location, right on the water (although the food is standard Greek fare).

✪ **Aegli Garden Restaurant.** Odos Kapodistriou 23 (within Liston). ☎ **0661/31-949.** Fax 0661/26-268. Main courses Dr1,500–Dr3,000 ($5–$10). AE, DC, ER, MC, V. Year-round daily 9am–1am. GREEK/CONTINENTAL.

The tasty and varied menu of this old favorite attracts both residents and transients to its several locales—indoors, under the arcade, along the pedestrian mall of Kapodistriou, or under awnings across from the arcade. Try the selection of *orektika* with some of their wine or beer on tap. They take special pride in their Corfiote specialties, several of which are traditional Greek foods with rather spicy sauces: fillet of fish, octopus, *pastitsada* (baked veal), *baccala* (salted cod fish), and *sofrito* (veal). If spiciness isn't your thing, try the swordfish or prawns. Everything is done with great care, including a delicious fresh-fruit salad that you can order by itself.

Bellissimo. Plateia Lemonia (just off Odos N. Theotoki). ☎ **0661/41-112.** Main courses Dr900–Dr2,500 ($3–$8). No credit cards. Daily 10:30am–11pm. GREEK/INTERNATIONAL.

This restaurant has lived up to its promise of being a welcome addition to the Corfu scene—unpretentious but tasty. Located on a central and lovely town square, it's run by the hospitable Stergiou family. They offer a standard Greek menu with some "exotics," including hamburgers and chicken curry. Especially welcome is their "Greek sampling plate"—tzatziki, tomatoes-and-cucumber salad, keftedes (meatballs), fried potatoes, grilled lamb, and pork souvlaki, all for Dr1,600 ($5).

Gloglas Taverna. Odos Guilford 16. ☎ **0661/37-147.** Main courses Dr900–Dr2,500 ($3–$8). No credit cards. Daily 11:30am–midnight. GREEK.

You want authenticity? This is it, right on a corner in the heart of the old town, a block back from the Esplanade. You sit under a grape arbor among your fellow diners, a mixture of locals and tourists, united in their desire for a no-nonsense taverna meal. The specialties of the house tend to be off the spit or grill. Winners include souvlaki (kebab), chicken, pork, and kokoretsia (lambs' intestines roasted on the spit). The cooked vegetables—green beans, eggplant, and whatever is in season—are also tasty. Add a glass of the house red and you'll wonder why anyone wants to go to a fancier place.

CORFU TOWN AFTER DARK

Corfu town definitely has a nightlife, though many are content to linger over dinner and then, after a promenade, repair to one of the cafes at the Liston, such as the **Capri, Liston, Europa,** or **Aegli**—all of which have a similar selection of light refreshments and drinks. (Treat yourself to the fresh fruit salad at the Aegli!) Others are drawn to a candlelit table at the **Cafe Classico,** at the north end of the Esplanade, just outside the Liston. For a real treat, ascend to the rooftop cafe/bar at the **Cavalieri Hotel** (see "Where to Stay," above). Another change of scene is the **Lidos Cafe,** overlooking the beach and facilities of the Nautical Club of Corfu; it is approached by a flight of steps leading off Leoforos Demokratias, just south and outside the Esplanade. And one of the best-kept secrets of Corfu town is the little **Art Cafe,** to the right and behind the Palace that now houses the Museum of Asian Art; its garden provides a wonderful cool and quiet retreat from the hustle and bustle of the rest of the town.

If you enjoy more action, there are several nightspots along the coast to the north between Corfu town and the beach resort of Gouvia; they include **Ekati,** a typical Greek nightclub; **Esperides,** featuring Greek music; and **Corfu by Night,** definitely touristy. Be prepared to drop some money at these places.

In summer, there are frequent **concerts** by the town's orchestras and bands, mostly free, on the Esplanade. Corfu town boasts the oldest band in Greece. The **Sound-and-Light** performances are described in the listing for the Old Fort (see "What to See & Do," above). September brings the **Corfu Festival,** with concerts, ballet, opera, and theater performances by a mix of Greek and international companies. **Carnival** is celebrated on the last Sunday before Lent with a parade and a burning of an effigy representing the spirit of Carnival.

For those who like to gamble, there's a well-known **casino** at the **Corfu Holiday Palace** (see "Where to Stay," above), a few miles outside of town. Bets are a Dr1,000 ($3.35) minimum and a Dr250,000 ($835) maximum. Open nightly, it may not have the glamour of Monte Carlo, but it attracts quite an international set during the high season.

As for the younger crowd, there are any number of places that go in and out of favor (and business) from year to year. Among the more enduring up around the Esplanade are the relatively sedate **Aktaion,** just to the right of the Old Fort, and the **Tequila,** in an old mansion at Odos Kapodistriou 10, featuring the latest music. Young people seeking more excitement go down past the New Port to a strip of flashy disco bar/clubs—**Apokalypsis, Hippodrome, Point, DNA,** and **Coca Flash.** Be aware that these clubs have a cover charge (usually Dr3,000/$10, including one drink).

SIDE TRIPS FROM CORFU TOWN
KANONI/PONDIKONISI/ACHILLEION

Although these sites or destinations are not literally next door to one another and have little in common, they are grouped here because they do, in fact, all lie south of Corfu town and can easily be visited in half a day's outing. And they are all places that everyone who comes to Corfu town will want to visit, even if they go nowhere else on the island. History buffs will revel in their many associations, and even beach bums cannot help but be moved by their scenic charms.

Kanoni is approached south of Corfu town via the village Analepsis; it's well signed. Ascending most of the way, you come at about 4 kilometers (2½ miles) to the circular terrace (on the right) to the locale known as Kanoni. Make your way to the edge and enjoy a wonderful view. Directly below in the inlet are two islets. If you want to visit one or both, you can take a 10-minute walk down a not-that-difficult path from Kanoni, or you must retrace the road back from Kanoni a few hundred yards to a signed turnoff (on the left coming back).

One islet is linked to the land by a causeway; here you'll find the **Monastery of Vlakherna.** To get to the other islet, **Pondikonisi ("Mouse Island"),** you must be ferried by a small boat (always available). Legend has it that this rocky islet is a Phaeacian ship that was turned to stone after taking Odysseus back to Ithaka. The chapel here dates from the 13th century, and its setting among the cypress trees makes it most picturesque. Many Corfiotes make a pilgrimage here in small boats on August 6. It's also the inspiration for the Swiss painter Arnold Boecklin's well-known work *Isle of the Dead,* which in turn inspired Rachmaninoff's music of the same name.

There is a causeway across the little inlet to Perama over on the main body of the island (the Kanoni road is on a peninsula), but it is only for pedestrians. So to continue on to your next destination, the villa known as the **Achilleion,** you must drive back to the edge of Corfu town and then take another road about 8 kilometers (5 miles) to the south, signed to Gastouri and the villa of Achilleion. It's open daily from 9am to 4pm. Admission is Dr1,000 ($3.35). Bus no. 10, from Plateia San Rocco, runs directly to the Achilleion several times daily.

This villa was built between 1890 and 1891 by Empress Elizabeth of Austria, whose beloved son Rudolf and his lover died mysteriously (most likely a double suicide) at Mayerling in 1889. The empress identified him with Achilles, and so the villa is really a memorial to Rudolf (and her grief)—thus the many statues and motifs associated with Achilles (including the dolphins, for Achilles's mother was the water nymph Thetis). As you approach the villa from the entrance gate, you will see a slightly Teutonic version of a neoclassical summer palace. You will want to walk through at least some of the eclectic rooms. Among the curiosities is the small saddle-seat that Kaiser Wilhelm II of Germany sat on while performing his imperial chores. (He bought the villa in 1907, after Elizabeth was assassinated in 1898.)

The terraced gardens that surround the villa are now lush and tropical. Be sure to go all the way around and out to the back terraces. Only here will you see the most famous (and the most god-awful) of the statues Elizabeth commissioned (from the German sculptor Herter), *The Dying Achilles,* the 15-foot-tall Achilles that the Kaiser had inscribed: "To the greatest Greek from the greatest German." But for an even more impressive sight, step to the edge of the terrace and enjoy a spectacular view of Corfu town and much of the eastern coast to the south.

If you have your own vehicle, you can continue on past the Achilleion and descend to the coast between **Benitses** and **Perama;** the first, to the south, has become a popular beach resort. Proceeding north along the coast from Benitses, you come to Perama (another popular beach resort), where a turnoff onto a promontory brings you to the pedestrian causeway opposite Pondikonisi (see above). The main road brings you back to the edge of Corfu town.

PALEOKASTRITSA

If you can make only one excursion on the island, this is certainly a top competitor with Kanoni and the Achilleion. Go to those places for their fascinating histories; Paleokastritsa for its natural beauty.

The drive here is northwest out of Corfu town by well-marked roads. Follow the coast for about 8 kilometers (5½ miles) to Gouvia, then turn inland. (It is on this next stretch that you pass the **Pottery Workshop**; see "Shopping," above.) The road eventually narrows but is asphalt all the way as you gradually descend to the west coast and **Paleokastritsa** (24km/15 miles). There's no missing it: it's been taken over by hotels and restaurants. There are several bays and coves that make up Paleokastritsa, and some are less developed than others, although all boast sparkling-clear turquoise water. Tradition claims it as the site of **Scheria,** the capital of the Phaeacians—and thus one of these beaches is where Nausicaa found Odysseus, though no remains have been found to substantiate this.

You can continue on past the beaches and climb a narrow winding road to the **Monastery of the Panayia** at the edge of a promontory (it's about a mile from the beach, and many prefer to come here by foot). Although founded in the 13th century, nothing that old has survived, but having come this far, it's worth a brief visit, especially at sunset. It's open April through October, daily from 7am to 1pm and 3 to 8pm.

More interesting in some ways, and certainly more challenging, is a visit to the **Angelokastro,** the medieval castle that sits high on a pinnacle overlooking all of Paleokastritsa. Only the most hardy will choose to walk all the way up from the shore, a taxing hour at least. The rest of us will drive back out of Paleokastritsa (about 2.5km/1½ miles) to a turnoff to the left, signed LAKONES. There commences an endless winding and ascending road that eventually levels out and provides spectacular views of the coast as it passes through the villages of Lakones and Krini.

(*A word of warning:* Don't attempt to drive this road unless you are comfortable pulling over to the very edge of narrow roads—with sheer drops—to let trucks and buses by, something you will have to do on your way down.) Keep going until the road takes a sharp turn to the right and down and you will come to the end of the line and a little parking area. From here you walk up to the castle, only 200 meters away but seemingly longer because of the condition of the trail. What you are rewarded with, though, is one of the most spectacularly sited medieval castles you'll ever visit—you are now some 1,000 feet above sea level.

Enjoy a meal with the spectacular view at one of the restaurant/cafes on the road outside Lakones—the **Bella Vista, Colombo,** or **Casteltron.** *Be forewarned:* At mealtimes in high season, these places are taken over by busloads of tour groups. If you have your own transport, try to eat a bit earlier or later.

On your way back from Paleokastritsa, you can vary your route by heading south through the **Ropa Valley,** the agricultural heartland of Corfu. Follow the signs indicating Lakones and Pelekas (don't bother going into either of these towns). And if you have time for a beach stop, consider going over to **Ermones Beach** (the island's only golf club is located above it) or **Glifada Beach.**

Where to Stay & Dine

If you want to spend some time at Paleokastritsa, it's good to get away from the main beach. We like the 70-unit **Hotel Odysseus** (☎ **0663/41-209;** fax 0663-41342), high above the largely undeveloped cove before the main beach. A double in high season goes for Dr15,600 ($52), in low season Dr13,400 ($45); both rates include breakfast. It's open May to mid-October, and there's a pool.

On its own peninsula and both fancier and pricier is the 127-unit **Akrotiri Beach Hotel** (☎ **0663/41-237**), where an air-conditioned double in high season goes for Dr29,500 ($99), in low season Dr21,000 ($70), including buffet breakfast. All rooms have balconies and sea views. In addition to the adjacent natural beaches, there are two pools. It's open May through October.

The restaurants on the main beach in Paleokastritsa strike us as over-touristy. However, if you like to eat where the action is, the best value and most fun at the main beach can be had at the **Apollon Restaurant** in the Hotel Apollon-Ermis (☎ **0663/41-211**). Main courses are Dr1,100 to Dr3,000 ($3.70 to $10). It's open mid-April to late October daily from 11am to 3pm and 7 to 11pm.

We prefer someplace a bit removed, such as the **Belvedere Restaurant** (☎ **0663/41-583**), just below the Hotel Odysseus and serving fine Greek dishes at reasonable prices. Main courses range from Dr900 to Dr2,400 ($3 to $8). It's open mid-April to late October from 9am to midnight.

2 Kefalonia (Cephalonia)

Don't come to Kefalonia for glamour. Come to spend time in a relaxing environment, to enjoy handsome vistas and lovely countryside. This is a Greek island the way they used to be—it pretty much goes its own way while you travel around and through it. It does boast several natural wonders, a few satisfying historical buildings and archaeological sites, and many fine beaches. Kefalonia also has a full-service tourist industry, with some fine hotels, restaurants, travel agencies, car-rental agencies, the whole show. Since Kefalonia was virtually demolished by the earthquake of 1953, most structures on this island are fairly new. It has long been one of the more prosperous and cosmopolitan parts of Greece, thanks to its islanders' tradition of sailing and trading in the world at large.

Map of Kefalonia & Ithaka. Inset: GREECE, Athens, Kefalonia & Ithaka. Labels include: ATOKOS, ITHAKA, Fiskardo, Frikes, Stavros, Kioni, Anogi, Assos, Myrtos Beach, Divarata, Aetos, Ithaka (Vathy), Ithaka Strait, Ay. Evthimia, Kardakata, Melissani Cave, Sami, Dilinata, Drogarati Cave, Havdata, KEFALONIA, Lixouri, Argostoli, Lassi, Tsarkassianos, Platis Yialos, Peratata, Poros, Metaxata, Mt. Enos, Tzanata, Svorotata, Ionian Sea, Markopoulo, Skala, Katelios. Legend: Airport, Ferry Routes.

ESSENTIALS

GETTING THERE   As with most Greek islands, it's easier to get to Kefalonia in summer than in the off-season, when weather and reduced tourism eliminate the smaller boats.

By Plane   From Athens, there are at least three flights daily on **Olympic Airways** (with some flights via Zakinthos). The Argostoli office is at Odos Rokkou Vergoti 1, the street between the harbor and the square of the Archaeological Museum (☎ 0671/28-808).

The **Kefalonia airport** is 8 kilometers (5 miles) outside Argostoli. As there is no public bus, everyone takes a taxi, which costs about Dr2,500 ($8) to Argostoli and about Dr2,000 ($7) from Argostoli.

By Boat   Throughout the year there is one car-passenger ferry that leaves daily from Patras to Sami; for details, call the **Patras Port Authority** (☎ 061/341-002) or **Sami Port Authority** (☎ 0674/22-031). There is also at least one car-passenger ferry daily from Killini (out on the northwest tip of the Peloponnese) to Argostoli and Poros (on southeastern coast of Kefalonia) via the **Strintzis Line** (Athens ☎ 01/823-6011); if you haven't made arrangements with a travel agent, tickets can be bought dockside.

Beyond these more or less dependable services, during the high-season months of July and August there are usually other possibilities—ships to and from Corfu, Ithaka, Levkas, or other islands and ports—but they do not necessarily hold to the same schedules every year.

VISITOR INFORMATION   The **National Tourist Organization (EOT)** information office in Argostoli is on Odos Ioannis Metaxa, on the harbor by the Port

Authority office (☎ **0671/22-248**). It's open in high season, daily from 7:30am to 2:30pm and 5 to 10pm; low season, Monday through Friday from 8am to 3pm.

GETTING AROUND   By Bus   You can get to almost any point on Kefalonia—even remote beaches, villages, and monasteries—by **KTEL bus** (☎ **0671/22-276** or 0671/22-281 in Argostoli). Schedules, however, are restrictive and may cut deeply into your preferred arrival at any given destination. KTEL also operates special tours to several of the major destinations around the island.

The new **KTEL station** is on Leoforos A. Tritsi, at the far end of the harbor road, 200 meters past the Trapano Bridge.

By Taxi   For those who don't enjoy driving twisting mountain roads, taxis are the best alternative. If you're based in Argostoli, go up to Central (Vallianou) Square and work out an acceptable fare. A trip to Fiskardo, with the driver waiting a couple of hours, might run to Dr30,000 ($100)—with several sharers, this isn't unreasonable. Aside from such ambitious excursions, taxis are used by everyone on Kefalonia. Although drivers are supposed to use their meters, many don't, so agree on the fare before you set off.

By Car   There are literally dozens of car-rental firms, from the well-known international companies to hole-in-the-wall outfits. In Argostoli, we found both **Auto Europe,** Odos Lassis 3 (☎ **0671/24-078**), and **Euro Dollar,** R. Vergoti 3a (☎ **0671/23-613**), to be reliable. In high season, you'll find rental cars scarce, so don't expect to haggle. A compact will come to at least Dr16,000 ($54) a day (gas extra); better rates are usually offered for 3-day and longer rentals.

By Moped & Motorcycle   The roads on Kefalonia are asphalt and in decent condition, but are often very narrow, lack shoulders, and when not twisting around mountain ravines, they wind along the edges of sheer drops to the sea. That said, many choose to get around Kefalonia this way. Every city and town has places that will rent mopeds and motorcycles for about Dr6,000 to Dr8,000 ($20 to $27) per day for a two-seater.

FAST FACTS   There are several **banks** in the center of Argostoli with ATMs that can handle direct transactions with Visa or other debit and credit cards. The **hospital** (☎ **0671/22-434**) is on Odos Souidias (the upper road, above the Trapano Bridge). **Express Laundry,** Odos Lassi 46B, the upper road that leads to the airport, is open Monday through Saturday from 9:30am to 9pm. It has washing machines and driers; a modest load costs Dr600 ($2). Argostoli's **tourist police** (☎ **0671/22-200**) are on Odos Ioannis Metaxa, on the waterfront across from the Port Authority. The **post office** is in Argostoli on Odos Lithostrato, opposite no. 18 (☎ **0671/22-124**); open Monday through Saturday from 7:30am to 2pm. The main **telephone office (OTE)** is at Odos G. Vergoti 8. It's open April through September daily from 7am to midnight; October through March daily from 7am to 10pm.

WHAT TO SEE & DO

Kefalonia's capital and largest city, **Argostoli** has far and away its most diverse offering of hotels and restaurants. Staying here allows you to go off on daily excursions to the beaches and mountains, yet return to the comforts of a city. But Argostoli does not offer much in the way of old-world charm, nor many diversions. If this does not appeal, we point out some of the other "getaway" possibilities on Kefalonia.

Argostoli's appeal does not depend on any archaeological, historical, architectural, or artistic particulars. It's a city for those who enjoy strolling or sitting in a foreign land and observing the passing scene—ships coming and going along the waterfront, local people shopping in the market, children playing in the squares. There are plenty of cafes on the **Central (Vallianou) Square** and along the **waterfront** where you can nurse a coffee or ice cream. The **Premier Cafe** on the former and the **Hotel Olga** on the latter are as nice as any.

If you do nothing else, though, walk down along the waterfront and check out the **Trapano Bridge,** a shortcut from Argostoli (which is actually on its own little peninsula) to the main part of the island.

There are a couple of fine **beaches** just south of the city in the locale known as **Lassi,** which now has the numerous hotels, pensions, cafes, and restaurants that package groups love.

Historical and Folklore Museum of the Corgialenos Library. Odos Ilia Zervou (2 blocks up the hill behind the public theater and the square with Archaeological Museum). ☎ **0671/ 28-835.** Admission Dr500 ($1.70). Apr–Oct Mon–Sat 9am–2pm; off-season, by arrangement.

Many so-called folklore museums, little more than typical rooms, have sprung up in Greece in recent years, but this is one of the most authentic and satisfying. Meticulously maintained and well-labeled displays showcase traditional clothing, tools, handicrafts, and objects used in daily life across the centuries. Somewhat unexpected are the various displays revealing a stylish upper-middle-class life. Most engaging is a large collection of photographs of pre- and post-1953 earthquake Kefalonia. The gift shop has an especially fine selection of items, including hand-made lace.

SHOPPING

Interesting ceramics are for sale at **Hephaestus,** on the waterfront at Odos 21 May; **Alexander's,** on the corner of Plateia Museio—the square 1 block back from the waterfront; and **The Mistral,** Odos Vironis 6, up the hill opposite the post office, offering the work of the potter/owner.

For a taste of the local cuisine, consider a jar of Kefalonia's prized Golden Honey, tart quince preserve, or a box of almond pralines. Another possibility is a bottle of one of Kefalonia's wines. You can visit the **Calliga Vineyard** (selling white Robola and red Calliga Cava) or the **Gentilini Vineyard** (with more expensive wines), both near Argostoli, or the **Metaxas Wine Estate,** well south of Argostoli. The tourist office (see above) on the waterfront will tell you how to arrange a tour.

WHERE TO STAY

Accommodations on Kefalonia range from luxury hotels to basic rooms. During peak times, we recommend making reservations; **Filoxenos Travel** (☎ **0671/23-055;** fax 0671/28-114) can help.

EXPENSIVE

✪ **White Rocks Hotel & Bungalows.** Platys Yialos (the beach at Lassi, outside Argostoli), 28100 Argostoli. ☎ **0671/28-332** or 0671/28-335. Fax 0671/28-755. 102 units, 60 bungalows. A/C TEL. High season Dr41,600 ($139) double; low season Dr31,100 ($104) double. Rates are for either rooms or bungalows and include breakfast and dinner. AE, DC, EURO, V. Open May–Oct. Private parking. Occasional public buses go from the center of town to and from Yialos, but most people take taxis.

This is probably the most elegant hotel on Kefalonia, located a couple of miles south of Argostoli just above two beaches, one small and for hotel guests, the other larger and public. The hotel also has a new pool. On arriving, you descend a few steps from the main road to enter an almost tropical setting. The lobby is subdued and stylish, a decor that extends to the hotel's guest rooms, which are modest in size, but have first-rate bathrooms. There's a fine restaurant with views, a bar, and a TV lounge, and conference facilities can handle up to 50. The desk will take care of all your needs. The White Rocks is the kind of low-key place where people catch up on reading they've meant to do all year.

MODERATE

In addition to the following options, you might consider the 60-unit **Hotel Miramare,** Odos Metaxa 2, at the far end of the paralia (☎ **0671/25-511**; fax 0671/ 25-512); it's slightly removed from the town's hustle yet within walking distance of any place you'd want to go.

Cephalonia Star. Odos I. Metaxa 50 (along waterfront, across from the Port Authority), 28100 Argostoli. ☎ **0671/23-181.** Fax 0671/23-180. 40 units, some with shower, some with tub. A/C TV TEL. High season Dr15,000 ($50) double; low season Dr10,000 ($34) double. Rates include breakfast. MC, V. Open year-round. Street parking.

A location along the bay and balconied front rooms with fine views earns this Class C hotel more appeal than many. Rooms are standard size, bathrooms standard issue, but all are clean and well serviced. There's a cafeteria-restaurant on the premises, but except for breakfast, you'll probably want to patronize Argostoli's many fine eateries, all within a few minutes' walk. In August, a mobile amusement park has been known to set up on the quay just opposite, but then August all over Greece is a carnival.

✪ **Hotel Ionian Plaza.** Vallianou Sq. (the central square), 28100 Argostoli. ☎ **0671/ 25-581.** Fax 0671/25-585. 43 units. A/C TV TEL. High season Dr16,800 ($56) double; low season Dr12,600 ($42) double. Rates include buffet breakfast. AE, MC, V. Open year-round. Street parking.

Although it isn't quite a grand hotel, this is the class act of Argostoli and a fine deal. The lobby, public areas, and rooms share a tasteful, comfortable, and natural tone. Bedrooms are larger than most and bathrooms are modern if not mammoth. Breakfast takes place under the awning, the evening meal at the hotel's own **Il Palazzino** restaurant, indoors or outdoors; the menu has a strong Italian flavor and prices are surprisingly modest. Stay here if you like to be in the heart of a city: The front rooms look out over the central square, but as no vehicles are allowed there, it's not noisy.

INEXPENSIVE

Lakis Apartments. Odos Metaxa 3 (1 street back from waterfront, down near the Port Authority), 28100 Argostoli. ☎ **0671/28-919.** 8 units, all with shower only. High season Dr12,000 ($40) double; low season Dr6,000 ($20) double. No credit cards. Open year-round. Street parking.

Located on a quiet street midway between the central square and the waterfront, this modest hostelry offers something that most hotels can't: proprietors who speak fluent English and offer help and hospitality that no sum of drachmas can buy. Jerry and Angelina Zervos spent many years raising their family in Chicago before returning to Kefalonia. The bedrooms and bathrooms are relatively small, but everything's clean; some units have balconies. Staying here is more like being in a relative's apartment than in a remote hotel.

WHERE TO DINE

Try to taste at least one of the two local specialties: *kreatopita* (meat pie with rice and a tomato sauce under a crust) and *crasato* (pork cooked in wine). Also, try one of the island's prized white wines, the modest Robola or the somewhat overpriced Gentilini.

EXPENSIVE

Captain's Table. Leoforos Rizopaston (just around corner from Central Sq.; identifiable by its boat-model display case!). ☎ **0671/23-896.** Main courses Dr1,200–Dr4,450 ($4–$15). EURO, JCB, MC, V. Daily 6pm–midnight. GREEK/INTERNATIONAL.

This slightly upscale choice offers specialties such as the Captain's Soup (fish, lobster, mussels, shrimp, and vegetables), fillets of beef, delicate squid, and fried *courgette* (small eggplants). You could get out cheap by ordering the low end of the menu, but then why eat here? Most people dress up a bit and there is definitely a touch of celebration to meals here. It can also get crowded in high season. Go early, order a bottle of wine, and enjoy!

MODERATE

Also consider the **Old Plaka Taverna,** Odos I. Metaxa 1, at the far end of the waterfront (☎ **0671/24-849**), for modest prices and tasty Greek dishes.

La Gondola. Central Sq. ☎ **06/1/23-658.** Main courses Dr1,000–Dr3,100 ($3.35–$10). AE, EURO, MC, V. Daily 6pm–2am. GREEK/ITALIAN.

Everyone will want to eat at least one meal on the main square to experience the sense of attending a "dinner theater," with Argostoli's citizens providing the action. Frankly, all of the restaurants on the square are about the same in quality and menu, but we've enjoyed some special treats at this one. They have a "house wine" literally made by the house, and they serve a special pizza-dough garlic bread, a zesty chicken with lemon sauce, and a cannelloni that stands out with its rich texture and distinctive flavor. Both the staff and your fellow diners always seem to be enjoying themselves, so we think you will, too.

✪ **Patsouras.** Odos I. Metaxa 32 (along waterfront). ☎ **0671/22-779.** Main courses Dr1,100–Dr3,200 ($3.70–$11). V. Daily noon–midnight. A 5-min. walk from Central Sq. GREEK.

Patsouras continues to live up to its reputation as the favorite for those seeking authentic Greek taverna food and ambiance. Dine under the awnings on the terrace across from the waterfront, and try either of the local specialties, *kreatopita* (meat pie) or *crasto* (pork in wine). We found even such standards as the tzatziki and moussaka had a special zest. Greeks love these unpretentious tavernas, and you'll see why if you eat at Patsouras.

INEXPENSIVE

Portside Restaurant. Odos I. Metaxa 58 (along the waterfront, opposite Port Authority). ☎ **0671/24-130.** Main courses Dr1,000–Dr2,500 ($3.35–$8). EURO, MC, V. Apr–Oct daily 10am–midnight. GREEK.

This unpretentious taverna is what the Greeks call a *phisteria,* a restaurant specializing in meats and fish cooked on the grill or spit. Run by a native of Argostoli and his Greek-American wife, it offers hearty breakfasts, regular plates with side portions of salads and potatoes, and a full selection of Greek favorites. On special nights outside the high season they roast a suckling pig (Dr2,100/$7 a portion). It's popular with Greeks as well as foreigners, and you've got a front-row seat for the harborside activities.

ARGOSTOLI AFTER DARK

Free outdoor concerts are occasionally given in the Central Square. At the end of August, there's a **Choral Music Festival,** with choirs from all over Greece and Europe participating. There's a quite new and grand **public theater** where plays are performed, almost always in Greek and seldom in high season. Young people looking for noise and action can find a string of cafes, bars, and discos on Leoforos Rizopaston, leading away from the north side of the Central Square. They change names from year to year, but **Da Capo, Mythos,** and **Ponitiko** have been fairly steady. If your style runs more to British-style pub crawling, try the **Pub Old House,** Odos St. Metaxas 57, on a corner of tiny streets between the Central Square and the waterfront.

SIDE TRIPS FROM ARGOSTOLI
FISKARDO, ASSOS & MYRTOS BEACH

This is probably the preferred excursion for those who have only 1 day for a trip outside Argostoli. The end destination is **Fiskardo,** a picturesque port-village, which owes its appeal to the fact that it's the only locale on Kefalonia to have survived the 1953 earthquake. Its charm comes from its many surviving 18th-century structures and its intimate harbor.

You can make a round-trip from Argostoli to Fiskardo in 1 day on **KTEL** bus line (Dr1,800/$6). But with a rental car, you can also detour to the even more picturesque port-village of **Assos** (another 10km/7 miles up the upper coast road) and then reward yourself with a stop at **Myrtos Beach,** a strong candidate for one of the great beaches of Greece.

There are plenty of restaurants around Fiskardo's harbor. We recommend **Tassia's, Vassos, Nicholas Taverna,** and the **Panormos**. The latter two offer rooms as well. For advance arrangements, contact **Fiskardo Travel** (☎ **0674/41-315;** fax 0671/41-352) or **Aquarius Travel** (☎/fax **0674/41-306**). Britons may prefer to deal with the **Greek Islands Club,** which specializes in waterfront apartments and houses; its main office is at 66 High St., Walton-on-Thames, Surrey KT12 1BBU (☎ **0932/220-477;** fax 0932/229-346).

SAMI, MELISSANI GROTTO & DROGARATI CAVE

Many who come to Kefalonia arrive at Sami, the town on the east coast. The island's principal point of entry before tourism put Argostoli in the lead, Sami is still a busy port. Sami itself is nothing special, although its harbor is framed by unusual white cliffs. Of more interest to travelers are the **two caves** to the north of Sami, both of which can easily be visited on a half-day excursion from Argostoli.

The first is **Spili Melissani,** located only about 5 kilometers (3 miles) north of Sami and well signed. Proceeding through the entryway, you get into a small boat and are rowed around a relatively small, partially exposed, partially enclosed lake, whose most spectacular feature is due to the sun's rays striking the water and creating a kaleidoscope of colors. It's open daily from 9am to 6pm. Admission is Dr1,400 ($4.65). It was once believed that this water flowed underground westward to a locale outside Argostoli, Katavothres; it's now known that the flow is from Katavothres into Melissani.

On the road that leads away from the east coast and west to Argostoli (4km/2 miles from Sami), there's a well-signed turnoff to the **Drogarati Cave.** Known for its unusual stalagmites, its large chamber has been used for concerts (once by Maria Callas). You walk through it on your own; it's well illuminated but can be slippery. It's open daily from 9am to 6pm, with an admission of Dr865 ($2.90).

ITHAKA

Because of its association with Odysseus, Ithaka might seem to rate the treatment of a major destination. But it is small, not easily approached, and does not in fact offer that many touristy or historical attractions. Given its "sites" linked to the Homeric epic, however, it will appeal to certain travelers, and its rugged terrain and laid-back villages reward those who enjoy driving through the unspoiled Greek countryside.

We strongly recommend that you rent a car in Argostoli first. The boat connecting to Ithaka sails not from Argostoli but from Sami, the port on the east coast of Kefalonia; to make a bus connection with that boat, and then to take a taxi from the tiny isolated port where you disembark on Ithaka, costs far too much time. Rather, in your rented car, drive in 40 minutes from Argostoli to Sami; the boat fare for the car is Dr2,800 ($9), for each individual Dr500 ($2.70); once on Ithaka, you can drive to **Vathy,** the main town, in about 10 minutes; and now you have wheels to explore Ithaka in a day if you desire.

Vathy itself is a little port, a mini version of bigger Greek ports with their bustling touristy services. You might enjoy a cold drink or coffee and admire the bay stretching before you, but otherwise there's not much to do or see here. Instead, drive 16 kilometers (10 miles) north to **Moni Katheron;** the 17th-century monastery itself is nothing special but the bell tower offers a spectacular view over much of Ithaka. For a more ambitious drive, head north via the village of **Anogi,** stopping to view the little church in its town square, with centuries-old frescoes, and the Venetian bell tower opposite it; you proceed on via Stavros and then down to the northeast coast to **Frikes,** a small fishing village; you then take a winding road along the coast to **Kioni,** arranged like an amphitheater around its harbor.

As for the sites associated with *The Odyssey,* what little is to be seen is questioned by many scholars, but that should not stop you: after all, it's your imagination that makes the Homeric world come alive. There are four principal sites (all signed from the outskirts of Vathy). Three kilometers (1½ miles) northwest of Vathy is the so-called **Cave of the Nymphs,** where Odysseus is said to have hidden the Phaeacians' gifts after he had been brought back (supposedly to the little **Bay of Dexia,** north of the cave); known locally as Marmarospilia, the small cave is about a half-hour climb up a slope.

The **Fountain of Arethusa,** where Eumaios is said to have watered his swine, is located some 7 kilometers (4 miles) south of Vathy; it is known today as the spring of Perapigadi. The **Bay of Ayios Andreas,** below, is claimed as the spot where Odysseus landed in order to evade the suitors of Penelope. To get to the fountain, you can drive the first 3 kilometers (2 miles) by following the signposted road to south of Vathy as far as it goes; then continue on foot another 2 miles along the path (also posted).

About 8 kilometers (5 miles) west of Vathy is the site of Alalkomenai, claimed by Schliemann among others as the site of Odysseus's capital; in fact, the remains date from several centuries later than the accepted time of the Trojan War. And finally, a road out of Stavros (see above) leads down to the **Bay of Polis,** again claimed by some as the port of Odysseus's capital; in the nearby cave of Louizou was found an ancient pottery shard inscribed "my vow to Odysseus," but its age suggests only that this was the site of some hero-cult.

For lunch, we recommend **Gregory's Taverna,** on the far northeast corner of Vathy's bay (keep driving, with the bay on your left, even after you think the road may be giving out). Ideally you will find a table right on the water, where you can look back at Vathy while you enjoy your fresh fish dinner.

Most visitors will have seen what they want of Ithaka in the one day before they set off back to the little port, where you'll catch the last ferryboat to Kefalonia, usually at 5pm—but ask!

16

Highlights of Northern Greece: Thessaloniki, Mount Athos, & the Philip & Alexander Sites

by Sherry Marker

Northern Greece, with its lofty mountain ranges, deep rivers, wide plains, and profusion of little-known archaeological and historic monuments, is rapidly losing its status as one of Greece's few remaining "undiscovered" regions. Although the monasteries of the Holy Mountain of Mount Athos are still off-limits to women, improved roads mean that Athos is no longer a difficult trek from Northern Greece's largest city, Thessaloniki (Salonika). In addition, the formerly difficult-to-reach sites connected with the mighty warrior Philip of Macedon and his famous son, Alexander the Great, are now linked by good, new roads. Furthermore, the National Road from Athens to Thessaloniki makes it possible to drive between Greece's two most important cities in just 8 hours. Thessaloniki is the best place to begin your explorations of Northern Greece—and you'll find plenty to explore both in and around Greece's "Second City."

1 Thessaloniki (Salonika)

496km (310 miles) N of Athens

When a Greek tells you he's from Athens, he always sounds a bit apologetic, or regretful; Greeks from Thessaloniki, on the other hand, sound, if not smug, very pleased to be from Greece's "Second City." Thessaloniki may be second to Athens in political importance and population, but in popular songs, Thessaloniki is celebrated as "the mother of Macedonia," "the most blessed of cities," and "the city whose praises are sung."

You, too, may be tempted to sing this city's praises when you take in its wonderful situation along the broad expanse of the Thermaic Gulf. You're never far from the sea here; when you least expect it, you'll catch a glimpse of waves and boats in the distance. Alas, especially in the summer, you'll almost certainly get less pleasant whiffs of the harbor's ripe, polluted odor. If you're very lucky, you'll see Mount Olympus while you're here: pollution has increasingly obscured even that imposing landmark.

Greeks are fond of reminding foreigners that when their ancestors were painting themselves blue, or living in rude huts, Greeks were sitting in the shade of the Parthenon, reading the plays of Sophocles. Similarly, Thessalonians like to remind Athenians that when Athens languished in the long twilight of its occupation by the Romans and Ottomans, Thessaloniki flourished. It's true: Thessaloniki's strategic location on the main land route from Europe into Asia made it a powerful city during the Roman Empire—you'll see many monuments built here by the 4th-century A.D. emperor Galerius.

During the Byzantine Empire (the 4th to 15th centuries A.D.), Thessaloniki boasted that it was second only to the capital, Constantinople. That's when Thessaloniki's greatest pride, its superb and endearing churches, were built. After the Turks conquered the Byzantine Empire, Thessaloniki continued to flourish as an important commercial center and port. In the 18th and early 19th centuries, the city's Jewish community was so strong and so prosperous that some called Thessaloniki the "second Jerusalem."

Thessaloniki

Then, in August 1917, a devastating fire destroyed 80% of the city. Phoenix-like, Thessaloniki rose from the ashes. Alas, only part of the city was rebuilt according to the grand plan of the French architect Ernest Hébrard—between 1922 and 1923, 130,000 Greek refugees from Asia Minor flooded into Thessaloniki, almost doubling the city's population and leading to enormous unregulated development. Still, Thessaloniki has the broad tree-lined boulevards and parks that Athens so sadly lacks.

After World War II, and again in the 1960s, two more growth spurts left much of the city's outskirts crowded and ugly—and all too much of the city center lined with bland apartment buildings. You'll notice, however, that Thessaloniki has none of the horizon-blocking skyscrapers that have proliferated in Athens—earthquake regulations forbid this. The last major earthquake was in 1978.

Glimpses of the sea, tree-lined streets, magnificent Byzantine churches—all these make visiting Thessaloniki delightful. And there's something else here that's quite wonderful: the food. In part, this is because of the long tradition of Macedonian cuisine; in part, because this is still a city whose restaurants are supported by local customers. There are no restaurants here—as yet—that make their living off visitors.

Arch of Galerius
Aristotelous Square
Ayia Sofia Church
Ayios Dimitrios Church
Ayios Yioryios Church (Rotunda)
Cathedral (Mitropolis)
Demokratias Square
Dikasterion Square
Dioikitiriou Square
Eleftherias Square
Folk Museum
House of Ataturk
Osios David Church
White Tower

Thermaic Gulf

0   250 m
0   250 y

If you're a visitor to Thessaloniki, you'll appreciate all this. You'll also enjoy the fact that Thessaloniki's location in the virtual center of Macedonia makes it the perfect place from which to set off to the sites associated with **Philip of Macedon** and his son, **Alexander the Great.**

If you are a man, you can also take in the monasteries of **Mount Athos,** the Holy Mountain. If you are a woman, you'll have that much more time to enjoy Thessaloniki—or to sit patiently in the little port of Ouranopolis, the jumping-off point for Mount Athos, and envy those lucky enough to travel on to the Holy Mountain.

STRATEGIES FOR EXPLORING THESSALONIKI   You'll see our suggestions on exploring Thessaloniki in our "Suggested Itineraries," below. Our suggestions are really just that: suggestions. Unlike Athens, which few visitors would be bold enough to visit without seeing the Acropolis, Thessaloniki has no one "must-see" monument. Some might argue that the splendid **Archaeological Museum** fits the bill, but others would plead the case of the **Upper City (Ano Poli),** the old Turkish Quarter. Still others would recommend a loop through both the Upper City and the **city center** to take in as many Byzantine churches and Roman monuments as possible. In short, you're here to enjoy the city itself: a city filled with Byzantine churches and chapels, a city with squares built around Roman palaces, whose markets pulse with life, and whose harborside cafes and promenade refresh the weary.

ESSENTIALS

GETTING THERE   By Plane   If you're coming **from Athens,** there are usually six daily **Olympic Airways** flights to Thessaloniki, from very early in the morning until late in the evening. The flight lasts about 45 minutes and costs Dr22,000 ($73). **From the U.S.,** there are no direct flights to Thessaloniki. Connections can be made at a number of European cities, including London, Amsterdam, Brussels, Frankfort, Stuttgart, Munich, Zurich, and Vienna.

Thessaloniki's **airport** is 13 kilometers (8 miles) southeast of the city at **Mikras.** It's a 20-minute drive from the city center. A bus ride to the city costs Dr115 (40¢), and a taxi is about Dr1,500 ($5). **Budget Rent-a-Car** (☎ **031/471-491**) has an office at the airport.

A municipal bus goes between the airport and the train station every half hour and makes a stop on the northern end of Aristotelous Square, just opposite the Electra Palace Hotel. The trip takes about 30 minutes and costs Dr115 (40¢).

By Train   Five daily express trains make the trip from Athens to Thessaloniki in about 6 hours, but most are extremely crowded, without air-conditioning, and subject to various unexplained delays. If you must take a train, then let it be the overnight sleeper, which has first-class compartments for four to six passengers and sleeper compartments for four to six passengers. Nothing, however, can be done about the noisy and sometimes bumpy ride on antiquated tracks. Reservations for sleeping compartments should be made many days in advance at the Larissa train station in Athens (☎ **01/323-6747**). First-class tickets are Dr12,000 to Dr15,000 ($40 to $50); second-class, Dr8,000 ($27); sleeper supplement, Dr10,000 ($33).

In Thessaloniki, the **train station** is on Odos Monastiriou, which is the extension of Odos Egnatia west of Vadari Square, site of numerous shady bars. A taxi ride to Aristotelous Square takes about 10 minutes and costs about Dr1,000 ($3.35).

By Bus   Ten daily buses from Athens make the trip to Thessaloniki in about 7 hours, including a 20-minute stop at a roadside restaurant with toilet facilities. Buses are air-conditioned, much less expensive than the trains, and usually arrive on time. Reservations should be made in advance at the **Athens bus terminal,** Odos Kifissou 100 (☎ **01/514-8856**). A one-way fare costs Dr9,000 ($30). The buses arrive in Thessaloniki at the station opposite the train station, where there are always taxis.

By Car   From Athens, take the **National Road,** a four-lane highway that's the best in Greece, although stretches are always being repaired or widened, which leads to frequent slow-downs. The trip from Athens takes from 6 to 8 hours. Much of the drive is extremely scenic. Although there are filling stations at frequent intervals along the National Road, you often must exit to reach them.

If you're coming from other parts of **Europe,** you must take the ferry from the Italian ports of Bari, Ancona, or Brindisi to Igoumenitsou on the northwest coast of Greece, and then drive across the Pindus Mountains to Thessaloniki. The trip takes from 7 to 8 hours and is scenically spectacular. The route via Ioannina and Kalambaka to Larissa and the National Road is much less treacherous than the northern alternative through Kozani—particularly during the winter months—and is thus recommended. The southern route also will give you the opportunity to stop at Kalambaka and visit the monasteries perched on the awesome pinnacles of the Meteora (see chapter 12).

VISITOR INFORMATION   The main **Greek National Tourist Organization (EOT)** is at Aristotelous Square 8 (☎ **031/271-888** or 031/222-935); open Monday through Friday from 8am to 8pm and Saturday from 8:30am to 2pm. There's also a branch at the airport (☎ **031/471-170** or 031/473-212, ext. 215). A useful magazine to buy at virtually any newspaper kiosk is the quarterly *Pillotos,* which lists in Greek all of the cultural and entertainment goings-on in the city and has an English-language "Blue Pages" section at its end with all the important addresses and telephone numbers you could want, from the police to radio taxis to consulates, banks, bars, and cinemas.

CITY LAYOUT   Thessaloniki rests on the northern coast of the Thermaic Gulf like a somewhat lopsided turban tilted slightly to the northwest. In its center sits the city's best-known landmark, the **White Tower.** To the **east** sprawl the ever-expanding residential and suburban districts, while to the **west,** situated in the area once defined by its fortresslike Byzantine walls, is the **commercial heart** of the city.

In this latter area, bounded on the south by the harbor and on the north by the rising heights of what is called the **Ano Poli** or the **Upper City,** are Thessaloniki's most important shops, banks, agencies, hotels, restaurants, archaeological remains, and churches.

On its western edge are the shipping docks, customs building, warehouses—many now converted into the restaurants and galleries of the **Ladadika district**—the train station, and most bus terminals.

On the city center's eastern side, just north of the White Tower and outside of what was once the eastern gate, are the grounds of Aristotle University, the International Trade Fair, and the **Archaeological** and **Byzantine museums.** Between the latter and the White Tower are the **Municipal Park** and the **State Theater.**

The commercial area of the city is traversed by four main streets running on an oblique angle from the southwest to the northeast.

The largest, **Odos Egnatia,** connects Thessaloniki with both the western and the eastern areas of Northern Greece. Its two-way traffic runs straight across the northern side of the commercial district. On its western end at **Vardari Square,** it connects with roads to the west, north, and east; on its eastern end (under the name of New Egnatia), it continues on to highways leading to the **airport** and to the peninsulas of **Halkidiki** in the southeast. Along its route in the heart of the city are a host of less-expensive discount shops, cheap hotels, and modestly priced restaurants. Near its eastern end, straddling what used to be the route of the original Via Egnatia, is the **triumphal arch** built by the Roman emperor Galerius.

The city's second most important commercial route is **Odos Tsimiski,** which parallels Egnatia 2 blocks to the south and runs one-way from east to west. Along and just off its tree-shaded length are the city's most prestigious shops and department stores, as well as its post office and banks.

One block south of Tsimiski and running one-way from west to east is **Odos Mitropoleos,** so named because the Metropolitan Cathedral is situated near its center. Like Tsimiski, it has a number of the city's finest shops and boutiques.

Finally, another block to the south and running along the seaside promenade is **Leoforos Nikis.** Also one-way from west to east, it begins at the shipping docks and ends at the White Tower. Along its length is a virtually uninterrupted line of outdoor cafes and bars.

The heart of downtown Thessaloniki is the spacious expanse of **Aristotelous Square,** which borders the sea. Ringed with outdoor cafes and restaurants, it's also the site of the city's major political rallies.

Running north and south and connecting Aristotelous with the city's other major square, **Dikasterion,** is **Odos Aristotelous.** Here, along its arcaded sidewalks, are a number of bookstores and record stores.

Dikasterion Square overlooks the partially excavated Roman marketplace. The square has welcome trees, the lovely Byzantine church called Our Lady of the Copper Smiths (the Panayia Chalkeon), a restored Turkish bathhouse, and several basketball courts. Increasingly, Greek and other refugees from eastern Europe hold an informal outdoor market here. This is also where most local buses begin and end their runs to and from the heart of the city.

To the south of Dikasterion Square, across Egnatia and on either side of Odos Aristotelous, are the city's main **market areas,** where you can find flowers, fish, flip-flop sandals, and just about anything else you can think of.

To the east of Odos Aristotelous is the city's second main north-south route, **Odos Ayias Sofias.** In its center, between Egnatia and Tsimiski, is the major Byzantine church of St. Sofia on a square of the same name. Along Odos Ayias Sofias are a number of excellent clothing stores as well as, between the church and Egnatia, fast-food joints.

Running diagonally southeast from the rear of the church directly to the White Tower is **Odos Pavlou Mela,** with a number of fine bars, cafes, and patisseries; while leading directly south to Tsimiski from virtually the same point are the tree-lined pedestrian walkways of **Odos Iktinou** and **Odos Zevksidos,** site of several outdoor cafes and restaurants.

Two blocks east of the rear of Ayias Sofias Square is Thessaloniki's major pedestrian walkway, **Odos Dimitriou Gounari.** Beginning just below the Arch of Galerius and running south to Odos Tsimiski, its shop-lined length covers, for the most part, a major Roman thoroughfare leading down from the arch to the imperial palace. The area containing the palace is now partially excavated and opens westward off the pedestrian walkway into the tree-shaded park of **Navarino Square,** crowded with outdoor cafes, bars, and tavernas, and second only to Aristotelous as the city's major gathering place—although many of the artists and intellectuals who gather here would place it first.

Another 2 blocks east is **Odos Ethnikis Aminis.** While it runs one-way south from Egnatia down to the State Theater and the White Tower, it becomes a two-way street above Egnatia at **Sintrivaniou (Fountain) Square** (the former eastern gate of the city) and leads into winding roadways which run outside the ancient walls to the **Upper City.**

On the hillside leading down to Thessaloniki proper from the Upper City is the old **Turkish Quarter**—called, variously, **Ano Poli** (the **Upper City**), Eptapirgou (the Seven Gates), and Kastro (Fortress)—where some of the finest Byzantine churches are located. This is easily the most pleasant part of Thessaloniki to explore, especially the winding streets around Kalitheas Square, Odos Irodotou, Romfei Square in the district known as Koule Kafe, Tsinari Square, at the juncture of Odos Kleious and Odos Alexandras Papadopoulou, and the Seih Sou, the pine forest on the upper hills. Unfortunately, severe fires in 1997 and again in 1998 greatly damaged the pines of Seih Sou. A reforestation project has begun, but it will be years before new growth brings back Thessaloniki's "green lungs."

Just to the north of the Upper City is the **Ring Road,** which goes around Thessaloniki from the southwest to the southeast and connects the National Road from Athens with highways to Thrace and Halkidiki and the airport at Mikras along the sea to the east.

FINDING AN ADDRESS   Because of the orderly east-west, north-south arrangement of streets, finding an address in the city center is not difficult. Numbers begin at the eastern and southern ends of streets and go upwards, with even numbers on the right and odd numbers on the left. However, most Thessalonians think of addresses in terms of the cross streets or various well-known structures near them and buildings seldom have visible numbers; ask for what you want by name, not number.

Outside of the city center, particularly north of Odos Egnatia, finding what you want is difficult, as the streets begin to meander. Even with a good map, you'll probably have trouble, but take it, as the Greeks say, *"Siga, Siga"* ("Slowly, Slowly"), and you'll find your way.

MAPS   The National Tourist Organization on Aristotelous Square gives out a free booklet, *Thessaloniki and Halkidiki,* with a map of the main city streets and tourist attractions; you may find a magnifying glass useful in deciphering the map.

Two excellent guides to the city are *The Thessaloniki Handbook* (with section-by-section maps) by Christos Zafiris and *Thessaloniki* (with an excellent city-center map) by Apostolos Papagiannopoulos. Both are usually available at **Molhos's Bookstore** at Odos Tsimiski 10.

The most detailed map, but very cumbersome, is the one published by **Welcome Tourist Guides,** available at most bookstores.

GETTING AROUND   You will find that in the city center most of the attractions, restaurants, and shopping areas are easily reachable on foot in no more than 20 minutes. Otherwise, taxis are your best bet, unless you are going to the Upper City, which is a steep uphill walk, but served by bus nos. 22 and 23, which leave from Eleftherias Square. Taxis are reluctant to take this trip because there is little guarantee of a return fare down, and they may—unlawfully—refuse. But if you're in the cab before you state your destination, there's little the driver can do but take you there.

By Bus   Buses with double cars are boarded in the rear, where there is a conductor to make change and give you a ticket. Single-car buses are boarded in the front. With these, exact fare is required in the form of Dr50, Dr20, Dr10, and Dr5 pieces, which are deposited in a ticket-issuing machine situated behind the driver's seat. You should keep your ticket just in case a conductor boards the bus to check them. Fares vary according to the distance traveled and whether or not you're a student. It's up to the passenger to select the amount by pushing a button on the ticket machine. Yours will almost invariably be number 1, costing Dr75 (25¢).

By Taxi   This is your best bet except, as noted, when you want to go to the Upper City. Take along a map or have someone write out your destination in Greek, so that you can show the driver where you want to go. Rates are extremely moderate when compared to those in the U.S. A 20-minute ride should cost no more than Dr1,500 ($5). Tips are not expected. Make sure, however, that the driver turns on his meter and that, within the city limits, the rate that it uses is number 1. Number 2 is for outside the city limits, as when you approach the airport, and doubles the cost. There is an extra Dr300 ($1) charge, however, for trips from the airport. After midnight, all fares on the meter are doubled.

By Car   There is little reason to use a car within Thessaloniki. Traffic is terrible and legal parking places are almost impossible to find. But having a car for excursions into Northern Greece will allow you to see and enjoy a lot more than you would either with a bus or on a guided tour. Keep in mind that if you take a day trip, you'll spend at least an hour getting out, and another hour getting back into the city. It makes better sense to see what you want to see outside of town on your way in, or out, of Thessaloniki.

Budget Rent-a-Car has offices at the airport (☎ 031/471-491) and in the city at Odos Angelaki 15. (☎ 031/274-272 or 031/229-519), opposite the International Fairgrounds. Other rental offices are **Avis,** Leoforos Nikis 3 (☎ 031/227-126 or 031/683-300), at the western end of the harbor, opposite the docks; and **Hertz,** Odos El. Venizelou 4 on Eleftherias Square (☎ 031/224-906).

Rates vary with the model you rent, the season, and whether you want limited or unlimited mileage. Booking in advance (especially from abroad) usually gets you a cheaper rate. Nonadvance booking charges for limited-mileage cars range from Dr6,000 to Dr15,000 ($20 to $50) a day, with the rate ranging from Dr65 to Dr110 (20¢ to 35¢) per kilometer. The rental price for cars with unlimited mileage ranges from Dr60,000 to Dr150,000 ($200 to $500) for 3 days. Prices in the low season are about 20% cheaper. Remember to ask if the price quoted includes all taxes and insurance—and be sure to take full insurance if your credit card does not provide it.

If you need to park within Thessaloniki, try the free, outdoor **Municipal Parking Lot** just south of the Museum of Byzantine Culture at the eastern end of Odos Vas. Olgas. It's about a 20-minute walk from the city center, but very near the White Tower and Archaeological Museum. At night, however, it has recently become a gathering place for local transvestites.

By Boat   It's possible to take ferries and boats from Thessaloniki to a number of Aegean islands, including Crete, Santorini, Mikonos, and to the Sporades: Skiathos, Skopelos, and Alonissos. Tickets can be purchased at the following agencies: **Karaharissis,** at the corner of Odos Nikis and Odos Kountouriotou, near Eleftherias Square (☎ 031/513-005 or 031/524-444); **Polaris Travel,** Odos Pavlou Mela 22, between Odos Tsimiski and Ayia Sofia church (☎ 031/278-613 or 031/232-078); and **Zorpidis Travel,** Odos Egnatia 76, at the corner of Odos Aristotelous, second floor (☎ 031/286-812 or 031/286-825).

FAST FACTS: Thessaloniki

American Express   The office is at Odos Tsimiski 19 (☎ 031/239-797); open Monday through Thursday from 8am to 2pm and Friday from 8am to 1:30pm.

Currency Exchange/ATMs   All banks exchange currency, as do most hotels and the central post office. The major banks along Odos Tsimiski and Aristoteleos Square have ATMs.

Dentists   The two Thessaloniki dentists most preferred by foreigners are **Dr. Dimitris Sirris,** Odos Ayios Theodoras 10 (☎ 031/275-868), off Odos Ayias Sofias between Odos Tsimiski and Odos Ermou, and **Dr. Dimitra Konstantinidou,** Vas. Olgas 39 (☎ 031/815-526), east of the Municipal Park. Both are excellent and speak fluent English.

Doctors   In Greece, almost all doctors specialize and there are few who fit in with the U.S. concept of a general practitioner. An excellent English-speaking doctor who happens to be a pediatrician but can also give you general assistance and find the specialist you need is **Dr. Christos Chrysanthopoulos,** Odos Ayias Sofias 43A (☎ 031/267-292). In addition, the **U.S. Consulate** (☎ 031/266-121 or 031/260-716) has a continually updated list of recommended doctors.

Drugstores   See "Pharmacies," below.

Embassies/Consulates   The **U.S. Consulate** (☎ **031/266-121** or 031/ 260-716) is at Leoforos Nikis 59, 2 blocks west of the White Tower. It offers a bare minimum of services. The **UK/Commonwealth Honorary Consul** is at Odos Venizelou 8, eighth floor (☎ **031/278-006** or 031/269-984), by appointment only.

Emergencies   The **police hotline** (usually with English speakers) is ☎ **100.** For **first aid,** call ☎ **166.** For **car breakdowns,** call ☎ **104** (the Greek Automobile Touring Club, or ELPA). Also try the **tourist police,** 4 Dodekanisou (☎ **031/254-870** or 031/254-871), near the eastern end of Odos Tsimiski.

Hospitals/Clinics   All Greek hospitals provide virtually free care for everyone, including foreigners. However, they are terribly crowded and you may not find anyone who speaks good enough English for your purposes. There is an excellent **private clinic,** however, which takes Blue Cross/Blue Shield insurance. It's called **Ayios Loukas** (St. Luke's) and is located on the road to Panorama village northeast of the city (☎ **031/342-102** to 031/342-104). English is spoken.

Internet Access   At press time, Thessaloniki's main two Internet cafes were **Indigo Internet Cafe,** Meg. Alexandrou 53 (☎ **031/851-581**), and **Globus Internet Cafe,** Aminta 12 (☎ **031/232-901**).

Lost Property   Call the **tourist police** at ☎ 031/522-656.

Newspapers & Magazines   English-language publications are available at several kiosks in Aristotelous Square, on Odos Tsimiski, and at the excellent **Molhos Bookstore,** Odos Tsimiski 10, at the corner of Odos El. Venizelou.

Pharmacies   Pharmacies alternate late-night hours. Lists and addresses of the ones open on a particular night can be found in the local newspapers and the windows of all pharmacies.

Police   The 24-hour emergency number is ☎ **100.** The tourist police number is ☎ **031/522-656.**

Post Office   The main post office is at Odos Tsimiski 45, just east of Odos Aristotelous (☎ **031/278-924**). Hours are Monday through Friday from 7:30am to 8pm, Saturday from 7:30am to 2pm, and Sunday from 9am to 1:30pm.

Rest Rooms   All but the smallest eateries and bars have rest rooms that you can request to use without embarrassment. There are three well-kept public toilets in the central area. The best is under the dividing sidewalk on the south side of Odos Tsimiski at Odos Aristotelous. The second best is underground in the southeast corner of the Municipal Park near the White Tower. The third, clean but slightly seedy, is in Dikasterion Square, underground on the eastern side just behind the Turkish *hamam* (bathhouse). All have attendants who guard and clean the place and expect nominal tips of Dr20 (5¢) or so.

Safety   Thessaloniki is still an extremely safe city, although the influx of a rough element in recent years means that anyone walking around alone late at night should exercise caution. The only area absolutely to avoid is around Vardaris Square, where bars attract some very shady characters.

Taxis   Radio taxis in the city center can be called at ☎ **031/517-417.** See also "Getting Around," above.

WHAT TO SEE & DO

If you've already been to Athens, you probably arrived there with a pretty clear idea of what you wanted to see first: the Acropolis, the National Archaeological Museum, and Plaka head most lists. Thessaloniki also has its top attractions—the **Archaeological** and **Byzantine museums** and the superb **Byzantine churches**—but one of the great delights of visiting here is getting to know the city itself. Thessaloniki—rather than any monument or museum—is its own greatest attraction. There are lots of pleasant squares here, often near the Byzantine churches and Roman monuments you want to see, often with the shady trees that make this city so much more pleasant to visit than Athens.

Be sure to give yourself time to stroll along the waterfront (especially if the much-delayed harbor cleanup has reduced the ripe summer smell of the polluted water), time to sit in cafes across from Thessaloniki's marvelous Byzantine churches, and time to wander the streets high above the city in the old Turkish quarter, the Upper City **(Ano Poli)**. You may find that you agree with those who think that whereas Athens is a great place to visit, but not live, Thessaloniki is both a wonderful place to visit and an appealing spot to live.

SUGGESTED ITINERARIES

If You Have 1 Day

The city's two major museums—the **Archaeological Museum** and the **Museum of Byzantine Culture**—are handily located side by side near the fairgrounds. Decide whether you'd rather see the gold from the tomb of Philip of Macedon or images of life in Byzantine Thessaloniki, and be the first one through the door at the museum you choose. Then, head next door to the other museum, perhaps treating yourself en route to a coffee at a nearby cafe.

When you've finished visiting the museums, you'll probably want a serious reward, and you might stroll back along the harbor past the White Tower to the center of town for lunch and a nap.

If you feel more energetic, hop a bus or taxi up to the **Upper City (Ano Poli),** have lunch and stroll downhill—but remember: most of the churches you want to see here are closed in midafternoon.

After a nap, you might visit the churches of **Ayia Sofia** and **Ayios Dimitrios** in the city center, and see some of the Roman monuments, keeping in mind that there are cafes handily located near most of what you'll want to see. When you're ready for dinner, head to one of the restaurants in the restored warehouse district, **Ladadika,** or the always lively **Thanasis,** in the Modiano Market.

A Warning: This makes for a very full day, and you'll certainly enjoy Thessaloniki a lot more if you have more than a day here. Byzantine churches take time to find, to see, and to enjoy. Many of the frescoes and mosaics are high up on walls, or faded by time. If you possibly can, see some one day, some another day.

If You Have 2 Days

Abbreviate your first day, so that you are not trying to wipe out the city in one fell swoop. You might begin your second day with the **Upper City** and work your way downhill. Start at the **Vlatadon Monastery** and then stroll downhill, stopping at the enchanting little churches of **Osios David, Nikolaos Orphanos,** and **Profitias Elias.** Even if church architecture, mosaics, and frescoes are not your passion, you'll be

An Important Warning

Strikes that close museums and archaeological sites can occur without warning. Decide what you most want to see in Thessaloniki and go there as soon as possible after your arrival. The fact that something is open today says nothing about tomorrow. One thing to check as soon as you arrive: In June 1998, plans were announced to keep all major attractions open in summer until 7pm.

If you're here off-season, check with the **Greek National Tourist Office** (☎ 031/271-888) for the abbreviated winter hours of sites and museums. Keep in mind that the opening hours posted at sites and listed at the tourist office often vary considerably. Alas, no information is utterly reliable.

---

walking through the narrow streets of very charming old neighborhoods. If you didn't see them on your first day, take in the churches of Ayia Sofia and Ayios Dimitrios when you get back down to the city center.

Then, for a change of pace, take in the **Modiano Market,** the **Outdoor Market,** and the **Flea Market.** If you visit all three, you can buy anything from a copper bucket—to milk a sheep into—to the sheep itself. Along the way, you can nibble souvlaki, pastry, or whatever seasonal fruit catches your fancy.

In the cool of evening, you may want to take in the **arch of Galerius,** the **Rotunda,** and the **Roman agora**—in the way you can take in so much here—while relaxing at a nearby cafe.

If You Have 3 Days or More

Thessaloniki is a very lively town; it's pleasant to spend a day here simply wandering and browsing through the shops and art galleries along **Odos Tsimiski, Odos Aristotclous, Odos Ayias Sofias,** and pedestrianized **Odos Dimitriou Gounari.** Like all Greeks, the Salonikans are serious shoe-shoppers—don't miss the enormous neon high heel at Karidas Shoe Store on the Via Egnatia across from the ruined Turkish bath. Even if you think you can't face one more museum, stop in at the wonderful **Museum of Musical Instruments** and enjoy the reproductions of classical and Byzantine wind and string instruments.

Or you may want to head out of Thessaloniki to see some of the sites associated with Philip and Alexander, such as **Vergina, Dion,** or **Pella.** The easiest way to do this is to sign up for one of the efficient day trips that take in these sites (See "Organized Tours" and "Side Trips from Thessaloniki," later in this chapter). If you plan to do this by car, try to do it on your way out of town rather than as a day trip to avoid fighting your way in and out of city traffic.

THE TOP ATTRACTIONS

The Archaeological Museum. Odos Manoli Andronikou 6 (opposite the south side of the International Fairgrounds). ☎ **031/830-538.** Admission Dr1,500 ($5). Mon 12:30–7pm; Tues–Fri 8am–7pm; Sat–Sun 8:30am–3pm. Bus no. 58 from Dikasterion Sq. or bus no. 11 heading east from anywhere on Odos Egnatia.

The stars of the museum are the finds displayed in Room 9 from the tombs at Derveni and the Royal Tombs at Vergina. Most Greek (and fewer non-Greek) archaeologists think that the gold *larnax* (box) with the 16-pointed star held the bones of Philip of Macedon, the father of Alexander the Great, that the small ivory head is his portrait, and that the bronze greaves were part of his armor. The spoilsport foreign scholars think these finds belonged to another royal Macedonian—but just try telling that to any Greek, especially since the Former Yugoslav Republic of Macedonia began to lay claim to a Macedonian heritage, and tried to put the 16-point star on its flag. The 4th-century bronze crater from Derveni, with wild scenes of a Dionysiac revel, is less controversial, and absolutely superb. Once you've seen it, you'll know that the Hellenistic Greeks did not go in for understatement. While you're at the museum, check to see if the 3rd-century B.C. Derveni papyrus, which was exhibited here in 1998, is still on view. The papyrus, found in one of the Derveni tombs, seems to be a philosophical tract, and is the only substantial papyrus found in Greece. Virtually all known ancient papyrus manuscripts have been found in Egypt, whose dry climate preserved them for posterity.

Don't let these exhibits, however famous and wonderful, keep you from the rest of the museum, whose exhibits are nicely displayed to suggest the history of Thessaloniki from prehistoric days through the Roman period. These rooms are usually uncrowded, and the delicate Hellenistic glass—how could these paper-thin vessels have survived?—and Roman mosaics from private houses are quite wonderful. There's also a portrait bust of the 4th-century A.D. Emperor Galerius, whose arch is one of Thessaloniki's landmarks. Galerius looks like what he was: a brawler who entered the army as a recruit and ended as emperor.

This severe, low museum was built in 1962, and is considered to be the best example of "architectural modernism" in Thessaloniki—a sad commentary on that genre. The museum shop has postcards, guidebooks, and a number of souvenirs with the 16-point star of Macedon. The museum toilet facilities are good.

Museum of Byzantine Culture. Leoforos Stratou 2 (just west of the Archaeological Museum). ☎ **031/868-570.** Admission Dr2,000 ($7). Mon 3–9pm; Tues–Sat 11am–1pm and 5–9pm; Sun 11am–3pm. Bus no. 58 from Dikasterion Sq. or bus no. 11 heading east from anywhere on Odos Egnatia.

At present, this is the only museum in the world entirely devoted to Byzantine art and civilization. When all the exhibits here are in place, the museum will cover the 1,100-year development of Byzantine culture from its early beginnings in the Roman world through the fall of Constantinople in 1453; it will also explore the lasting influence of Byzantine culture on Greek art. Right now, exhibits on three topics have been installed: Early Christian Churches, the Early Christian City and Private Homes, and Burials and Cemeteries in the Early Christian World. As at the Archaeological Museum, the exhibits here attempt to tell the story of Thessaloniki and look at its social history through art and artifacts.

The most impressive exhibits are the 4th- to 6th-century barrel-vaulted frescoed tombs found in Thessaloniki, with frescoes showing Old and New Testament scenes, as well as scenes in Paradise. You'll see Daniel in the Lions' Den, Christ as the Fisher of Men, and blissful scenes in Paradise, where fruit, fowl, and wine are shown in abundance. The text accompanying the exhibit looks at the transition from the ancient image of the Afterworld as the Elysian Fields to the Christian images of Paradise. There are also some mosaics and elaborately carved marble panels salvaged from the church of Ayios Dimitrios after the great fire of 1917.

This museum took as long to build as some of Thessaloniki's Byzantine monuments—work began in 1989, was finished in 1993, and the museum opened in 1997. The bricks in the severe facade are meant to remind visitors of the Byzantine use of bricks—and do, although the comparison works to the detriment of this bland building. The museum bookstore usually has a range of books on Byzantine culture (sometimes including the superb catalogue of the Treasures of Mount Athos exhibit), as well as museum reproductions and postcards. The toilet facilities are good.

History 101: The Galerian Monuments

In the 4th century, the Roman empire was briefly ruled by a complicated system of two primary emperors, each of whom had an assistant—an emperor in training, as it were. The idea was that this system (known as the Tetrarchy) would make it easier to administer the vast Roman empire. In the early 4th century A.D., Galerius, one of the tetrarchs, moved his capital from Asia Minor to Thessaloniki. Then he did what no Roman, emperor or not, could ever resist—he began to build. As a good Roman, he built on a nice, neat, north-south axis flanking the Via Egnatia. The **Rotunda**, the **Arch of Galerius**, the **Palace** at Navarino Square, the **Hippodrome**, and the **Greek Agora** and **Roman Forum** are some of what survive from his ambitious building program.

The White Tower. Odos Nikis and Odos Pavlou Mela on the seaside promenade just south of the Archaeological Museum. ☎ **031/267-832.** Admission Dr800 ($2.65). Mon 12:30–7pm; Tues–Fri 8am–7pm; Sat–Sun 8:30am–3pm. Bus no. 58 from Dikasterion Sq. or bus no. 11 heading east from anywhere on Odos Egnatia.

What Big Ben is to London, or the Eiffel Tower to Paris, the 16th-century White Tower is to Thessaloniki: the city's most famous landmark. The tower was built as part of the city's defense walls, and then used as an Ottoman prison and place of execution. In 1985, the tower was restored and fitted out as a museum as part of the celebrations of the 2,300th anniversary of Thessaloniki's founding. At present, it houses a number of icons not yet on display at the Museum of Byzantine Culture, as well as exhibits on Thessaloniki's history. When the icons go back to the Byzantine Museum, there will be more exhibits here on Thessaloniki.

Right now, the most fun is the building itself, with its steep winding staircase that goes up six floors and offers terrific views out over the city and harbor. On each floor, there's a round room with alcoves, some of which were once prison cells. At the very end, there's a rooftop cafe to reward you for the climb. If you visit here in winter, you'll get an idea of just how dank and forbidding a prison this thick-walled stone tower must have been.

The Rotunda. Ayios Yioryos Sq. at Odos Filipou (1 block north of the juncture of Odos Egnatia and Odos Dimitriou Gounari, just above the Arch of Galerius). ☎ **031/213-627.** Free admission except for special events. Temporarily closed. Bus nos. 10 or 11 heading east from anywhere on Odos Egnatia.

Some say that Galerius built this massive brick-and-stone structure as his modest mausoleum, while others think that he intended it to be a temple, perhaps of Zeus. Later in the 4th century, the Byzantine emperor Theodosius the Great converted the rotunda into a church of St. George, and began the ornamentation of its 6-meter-thick walls with mosaics. When the Turks conquered Thessaloniki in the 15th century, they converted it into a mosque (you'll see one minaret left from this period), and destroyed many of the exquisite mosaics.

Just how exquisite those mosaics are is something you'll find out when the restoration work, designed to repair the damage done in the horrific earthquake of 1978, is completed and the rotunda reopens its doors. Even if the rotunda is not open when you visit, it is well worth gaping at from outside—and sometimes, if you're very lucky, the restorers will let you take a peek inside. Then you can catch a glimpse of the indigo peacocks, garlands of flowers and fruit, and blond, curly haired saints in the mosaics that cover the walls.

If possible, try to visit on a Wednesday, when the neighborhood street market stretches for blocks around the Rotunda.

The Arch of Galerius. Just below the Rotunda on Odos Egnatia and Odos Dimitriou Gounari.

If you need directions here, try asking for *ee kamara* ("the arch"), which is what Thessalonians call this hefty monument that Galerius built around A.D. 305 to celebrate a victory over the Persians a few years earlier. Originally, the arch was even larger: almost half—another entire arch—is missing. You'll see the Persians, some in the peaked caps and trousers that the Greeks and Romans found so effeminate and absurd, in the carved panels that tell the story of Galerius's battles. Until 1953, the tram line ran right under this arch, which still sits in the middle of the traffic whose fumes are steadily eroding many sculptural details.

The Palace. Navarino Sq.

Of course, Galerius built himself a palace in Thessaloniki. After all, his co-emperor Diocletian was building himself a perfectly splendid palace at Split, on the Dalmatian coast. Little remains of Galerius's palace, but even these low remains give an idea of how large this two-story palace with a large, central courtyard must have been—fit, in short, for an emperor.

The best-preserved part of the palace complex is the **Octagon,** the mysterious building that some archaeologists think may have been Galerius's throne room. Why do they think this? First, the Octagon was exceptionally richly decorated with a multicolored marble floor and interior recesses, of which one is a good deal larger than the others—in short, the ideal place for a throne. That said, it should be noted that a very similar structure built by Diocletian in Spoleto, Italy, was not a throne room, but a mausoleum.

The Hippodrome. Ippodromou Sq.

We know that the ancient hippodrome, where chariot races took place, lies under the square of the same name, because of finds made when today's apartment blocks were built here. In short, there's virtually nothing above ground to see of this ancient racetrack where, in A.D. 390, the Emperor Theodosius the Great ordered the slaughter of some 7,000 spectators. The reason: Theodosius's favorite charioteer had been lynched by a mob that supported one of his opponents. After that terrible day, the Hippodrome was abandoned and gradually covered by layers of buildings from successive eras; some say that they can still make out the oval shape of the Hippodrome in the shape of today's square.

Ippodromou Square is generally a place of evil associations: In 1566, St. Cyril was executed here by the Turks for not converting to Islam. The charming little church of St. Anthony here was, during the Turkish Occupation, a lunatic asylum. You can still see some of the manacles with which "patients" were imprisoned on view in the church.

The Greek Agora and Roman Forum. Dikasterion Sq., bounded by Filipou, Agnostou Stratiotou, Olimbou, and Makedonikis Amnis sts.

In the 1960s, workmen digging to lay the foundations of new law courts for the city of Thessaloniki came across the remains of the city's ancient Greek agora, later the Roman forum. Archaeologists took over and excavated the large complex you see today, bounded by one of the city bus terminals. As in Athens, this agora/forum was the heart of the ancient city: its commercial, governmental, social, and artistic center.

When the Romans came here they inevitably expanded the Greek agora, creating a forum that was on two levels. You can see the arched remains of the **cryptoporticus,** a retaining wall that supported part of the upper forum. The best-preserved remain here is the large **Odeum,** or Odeon, a theater where Romans enjoyed watching both musical performances and fights to the death between gladiators and wild beasts. The Odeum is sometimes used today for concerts in summer.

In modern times, the most famous monument here was the stoa with a series of statues facing the Via Egnatia, known as the *Colonnade of the Enchanted Idols,* or *Incantadas,* the name given them by Thessaloniki's then-flourishing community of Sephardic Jews. By the 19th century, much of the colonnade was lost, but a segment remained, incorporated into the courtyard of a Jewish home. When the French scholar Emmanuel Miller saw the colonnade, he knew he had to have it—and got permission to cart the remaining "incantadas" off to the Louvre, where they are to this day. If you browse in book and print shops in Thessaloniki, you'll probably see reproductions of a charming engraving of the Incantadas by the 18th-century English antiquarians Stuart and Revett.

CHURCHES

Thessaloniki's churches are a clear case of the whole being greater than the sum of its parts. Although Ayia Sofia and Ayios Dimitrios are the two best-known churches, your greatest pleasure may come from visiting the smaller churches. Therefore, we are including a number of these smaller selections in the hope that you will allow yourself the time to visit them. As you visit, try to identify those that were built in the **basilica form** (usually a rectangular church with side aisles) and those in the **cross-in-square form,** which is just what its name says.

Keep in mind that many of these churches keep irregular hours, many closing from about 1 to 5pm. In short, the best way to see them is probably on one or more morning excursions.

In Downtown Thessaloniki

Church of Ayia Sofia. Ayia Sofia Sq., between Odos Tsimiski and Odos Egnatia. ☎ **031/ 270-253.** Free admission. Daily 8am–9pm.

It's a pity that Thessaloniki's two most important churches—Ayia Sofia (Holy Wisdom) and Ayios Dimitrios (St. Demetrios)—are both heavily restored. Still, each is worth visiting for its importance in the city's history and for its fine mosaics, although both lack the pleasantly dusty ambiance of Thessaloniki's less-heavily-restored churches.

Thessaloniki's 7th-century Ayia Sofia was inspired by the emperor Justinian's famous 6th-century church of Ayia Sofia in Constantinople. Like that earlier Ayia Sofia, Salonika's namesake has an impressively large dome—in fact, this was the first church built in Thessaloniki by builders skillful enough to engineer such a large dome. The ornately carved marble columns supporting the dome were, as so often in antiquity and throughout the Byzantine era, pillaged from earlier monuments.

Fortunately, many of Ayia Sofia's original mosaics have survived. The Ascension, with an oddly-foreshortened Christ (supported by young angels), and the Virgin Mary

---

Dress Appropriately!

All these churches are places of worship where casual attire (short skirts for women, shorts or sleeveless shirts for men or women) is considered highly disrespectful. Remember to wear clothing that covers your arms and legs.

with the infant Jesus are especially fine. If you look carefully at the mosaics, you'll notice that some show only crosses and stars and have no human representations. These date from the 8th-century Iconoclastic period, when there was a ban on showing the human figure in religious art. The iconoclasts destroyed many earlier works of art, including many sacred icons—and left us with the word "iconoclast" to describe someone who destroys the past or challenges tradition.

Ayia Sofia Square is one of Thessaloniki's nicest, and most important, squares—this is where the service of Thanksgiving was held when the city was liberated from the Germans on November 2, 1944. Keep an eye out for the "red house," at 36 Ayias Sofias, built in 1925 for a wealthy industrialist, and one of few fine old houses here to have survived the fire of 1917 that gutted Thessaloniki—and, of course, severely damaged Ayia Sofia church. Across the way at 33 Ayias Sofias, now with the Terkenlis and Byzantium pastry shop on the ground floor, is another handsome Thessaloniki mansion built in the 1920s. The pastry shop is an excellent spot to rest and refresh after seeing the church of Ayia Sofia.

Church and Crypt of Ayios Dimitrios (sometimes given as Ayios Demetrios). Corner of Odos Ayiou Dimitriou and Odos Ayiou Nikolaou, 1 block north of the Roman market, at the base of the Upper City. ☎ **032/213-627.** Free admission. Church and crypt usually open Mon 12:30–7pm; Tues, Thurs, and Sat 8am–10pm; Fri 8am–11pm; Sun 10:30am–8pm. Bus nos. 22 and 23, which leave about every 10 min. from the southeast side of Eleftherias Sq., stop near the church.

Like Ayia Sofia, Ayios Dimitrios was heavily restored—in fact, almost entirely rebuilt—after the fire of 1917. Consequently, this is a church with an imposing history, some fine mosaics, but very little soul.

In the 4th century A.D., a small church was built here on the site of a former Roman bath to commemorate Dimitrios, the patron saint of Thessaloniki who refused to renounce his Christian faith and was promptly put to death in A.D. 303 by the emperor Galerius. About 100 years later, the church was considerably enlarged into its present five-aisled basilical form. After the 1917 fire, the church was rebuilt on and off from 1926 to 1949, and you can still see scorch marks from the 1917 conflagration on some of the interior walls.

Almost all the mosaics here are restorations of what was lost in 1917, but keep an eye out for the lovely original portrait of the boyish saint with two young children. (You can see other mosaics salvaged after the fire on display in the Museum of Byzantine Culture.)

The crypt, which you enter down a narrow, twisting staircase, is pleasantly mysterious, with several small anterooms and remains of the Roman baths. Particularly venerated are the spot where Dimitrios is believed to have been martyred and the spot with a holy water font. For centuries, the faithful noted a sweet scent here, and believed that a myrrh, or perfumed fluid, from the saint himself flowed from the font.

As you leave the church, have a look at the delightful chapel of St. Euthymius, built into the wall of Ayia Dimitrios. The 14th-century frescoes in the little chapel have all the verve that the heavily restored mosaics in Ayios Dimitrios lack.

The Panayia Acheiropoietos (The Church of the Virgin Made without Hands). Odos Ayias Sofia, north of Odos Egnatia. No phone.

This charming 5th-century basilica is the only church from Thessaloniki's early Christian days to have survived virtually intact, without the restorations and renovations that have changed the character of Ayia Sofia and Ayios Dimitrios. The marble columns, with their elaborate "perforated" acanthus leaf decorations, give you a good idea of the Byzantine love of the elaborate—which was achieved here by vigorous drill work. What a contrast to the mosaics, with the simple gold cross and the delicate floral and vine motifs interspersed with birds. The 13th-century frescoes showing some of the Forty Martyrs are equally appealing; those that are missing were destroyed when this church was converted to a mosque.

Due to the inexorable rise in the street level over the centuries, the church now sits below the level of today's streets and roads.

The Panayia Chalkeon (The Virgin of the Copper Workers). Dikasterion Sq. No phone.

This tiny church with its three domes looks as if it would fit nicely into a miniature village. It has some fine frescoes, but its real glory is its facade, with windows piled above windows, domes above domes. Like the Panayia Acheiropoietos, the 11th-century Panayia Chalkeon now sits considerably below Thessaloniki's modern street level. Several nearby streets still have the copper workers' shops from which, centuries ago, this church took its name. Locals call this the "red church" for its rosy bricks.

Ayios Panteleimon. Corner of Odos Egnatia and Odos Iassonidou.

This church, dedicated to one of the physician saints, is a popular place to light a candle and say a prayer for good health. The church, all that remains of a large monastery on this spot, is usually closed, but its elaborate brick and stone work makes it a delight even to glimpse from the street. If you do get inside, note how the central dome is supported by four barrel vaults, a distinctive characteristic of Macedonian churches.

In the Upper City

One of the great pleasures of visiting these churches is exploring the narrow streets of the Upper City, with its cobbled streets, wooden houses with the second floor built overhanging the first, street-side fountains, corner groceries, and cafes. In the 1960s, this area was practically falling down; now, as young Thessalonians reclaim the old quarter, an address here is considered very chic. When you come here, be prepared to get lost at least once—and probably to find a wonderful little church, or courtyard, or school yard, while you try to find your way back to your original destination.

It's very pleasant to ride up to the Upper City on bus nos. 22 or 23 from Eleftherias Square, then walk back downhill. When you get out of the bus in the Upper City, have a look at the Byzantine walls around the Acropolis and the Byzantine defense tower called the Tower of Trigoniou.

Vlatodon Monastery (also known as Vlatades). By the Gate to the Acropolis.

As you toil uphill, you'll keep seeing the overhanging walls of the substantial Vlatodon Monastery, founded in the 14th century. In the last few years, it's been substantially renovated and expanded, but the inner courtyard is still charming—and a cool spot to rest for a moment or two. If the main church is locked, don't feel too bad; the frescoes were badly damaged by the Turks, and have not been restored. By tradition, the little chapel of Saints Peter and Paul was built on the spot where St. Paul preached when he visited Thessaloniki in A.D. 50.

✪ Osios David (The Latomou Monastery). Odos Timotheou, off Odos Ayias Sofia.

We manage to get lost almost every time we come here, but always eventually find this absolutely charming 5th- or 6th-century church, with its pleasant shaded courtyard. Indeed, what a tempting fantasy to think of taking over the caretaker's job, sitting with a book in the little shelter in the courtyard, tending the flowers, and unlocking the church for visitors—who are bound to be impressed, because nothing about Osios David's simple exterior can prepare you for the glorious mosaic of the vision of Ezekiel inside. The vision shows Christ surrounded by the symbols of the four apostles (the angel, eagle, lion, and bull). If there's a finer mosaic in the city, we can't imagine what it could be. According to local lore, the mosaic spent several centuries hidden beneath a calf's skin, which prevented the Turks from finding and destroying it.

Ayios Nikolaos Orfanos. Odos Apostolou Pavlou.

Like Osios David, this seemingly unprepossessing brick-and-stone church holds an astonishing treasure: well-preserved frescoes from the 14th century, the zenith of Thessaloniki's artistic excellence. You can pick out St. Nikolaos himself, with his halo, standing in the helm of the little boat that he's guiding across stormy waters. The other frescoes, as usual in such cycles, show scenes from the Old and New Testaments, as well as depicting saints and prophets. Next to the church, part of its once-flourishing monastery, with an attractive veranda, has just been restored, and makes the traveler envy those lucky enough to live here.

Ayia Katerini. Corner of Odos Sachini and Odos Tsamadou, near the Byzantine walls.

This is another of Thessaloniki's fine 14th-century churches, built with a central dome flanked by four cupolas, and elegant brick and stone work. Now surrounded by new apartment buildings and old homes, it is a dignified reminder of one of the city's finest artistic periods. If you get inside, look for the wall painting showing the healing of the blind.

Profitias Elias. Odos Olympiados.

This substantial 14th-century church, whose elaborate brick exterior has recently been restored, is nice in and of itself, and is a fine vantage point to look out over the city. Women, who cannot visit Mount Athos, will get an idea from Profitias Elias of the cross-in-square with central dome style of many of the churches on Mount Athos.

MARKETS

The Modiano Market. The block bounded by Aristotelous, Ermou, Vasileos Irakleiou, and Komninon sts. Mon–Sat about 7am–5pm.

It's been a while since we've seen gypsies with dancing bears in the Modiano Market, although there are still gypsies aplenty, and other street musicians, here most days. You could easily spend a morning here, under the glass-roofed market that covers an entire square block, happily wandering from stall to stall and eyeing the fish, meat, fruit, vegetables, flowers, spices, and baked goods on sale. Whenever you get hungry, sit down in any one of a number of cafes or ouzo joints (including the delicious **Thanasis**).

The roofed market was built in 1922 by the wealthy Jewish merchant Eli Modiano, whose handsome family mansion at Odos Megalou Alexandrou (Alexander the Great) 65 is now the home of the **Folklore and Ethnography Museum of Macedonia.** (If you wish, take a bus or drive along both Odos Megalou Alexandrou and Odos Vas. Olgas and have a look at Thessaloniki's surviving 19th-century mansions.)

The Kapani (Vlali) Market. Bounded by Komninon, Egnatia, Aristotelous, and Menexe sts. Mon–Sat about 8am–5pm.

This market sells foods, dry goods, fabrics, and just about everything else you can think of, in a hodgepodge of ramshackle shops crowded one next to the other for as far as the eye can see. There's been a market here at least since Turkish times, and probably long before that.

The Flea Market. Odos Tositsa. Usually Mon–Sat 8am–7pm.

Just what its name implies, this market, which sprawls along Odos Tositsa, sells everything from genuine junk to genuine antiques (much more of the former than the latter). Of late, many Eastern Europeans sell their wares here, usually leather jackets, fake Leica cameras and designer watches, and an odd assortment of alarm clocks, mirrors, and socks.

The Bezesteni. Odos Venizelou and Odos Solomou. Usually Mon–Sat 9am–7pm.

It would be wonderful to have a bird's-eye view of the Bezesteni's six domes and four entrances, one on each side. This covered market, today specializing in textiles and jewelry, was built in the late 15th century by Sultan Bayezid II, and is one of the best preserved Turkish monuments in Thessaloniki. It's also a terrific place to browse and feel transported into an oriental bazaar.

MORE ATTRACTIONS

The Alatza Imaret. Dimitrion Sq., just off Odos Ayiou Nikolaou, half a block north of Odos Kassandrou, 1½ blocks north of the church of Ayios Dimitrios. ☎ **031/278-587.** Free admission. Open intermittently for exhibitions.

Along with the Bezesteni, the Alatza Imaret, a former 15th-century mosque with a poorhouse, or almshouse, is one of the best-preserved Turkish buildings in Thessaloniki. "Alatza" means "many-colored," and refers to the tiles and stones that covered the mosque in its days of glory. If you're lucky, it may be open when you visit, as exhibitions are sometimes held here.

Atatürk's Birthplace. Odos Ayiou Dimitriou 151 (8 short blocks east of the church of Ayios Dimitrios). ☎ **031/248-452.** Free admission. Daily 10am–5pm. Bus no. 22 or 23 from Eleftherias Sq. or stops along Odos El. Venizelou north to Odos Ayiou Dimitriou. Entrance through the front gate of the Turkish consulate, passport or identity card necessary.

Just behind the consulate, this modest wood-framed house was the birthplace in 1881 of Mustafa Kemal, the man who created the modern Turkish state and was its first president. Given to Turkey as a present by the Greek government in 1933, the house has been restored and furnished to reflect the way it must have been at Atatürk's birth. It contains numerous photos of the man, young and old, various letters and papers as well as cases containing the clothes and uniforms he wore. There is an excellent English-language booklet available with all the relevant information as well as photos.

Folk and Ethnological Museum. 68 Vas. Sofias. ☎ **031/850-591.** Admission Dr1,000 ($3.35). Daily 8:30am–3pm.

Be sure to call before you visit this museum, which is closed more often than it is open. That said, if it is open, the collection of costumes and items of Macedonian daily life is superb. Note that few labels are in English.

International Fairgrounds. Entrances at the corners of Odos Angelaki and Odos Tsimiski, and Odos Angelaki and Odos Egnatia. Free admission except during special exhibitions. Open irregular hours.

If you're in Thessaloniki during the September Trade Fair, you may want to take in some of the exhibits here. Usually any special exhibitions or events here are posted conspicuously throughout Thessaloniki.

Jewish History Museum (also known as the Museum of the History of the Jewish Community of Thessaloniki). 26 Vas. Irakleou. ☎ **031/275-701.** Call for hours.

This small museum in the heart of the Modiano Market uses photographs and what artifacts it has been able to assemble to portray Jewish life in Thessaloniki. In 1900, 80,000 of Thessaloniki's 173,000 inhabitants were Jews. Before World War II, there were 60,000 Jews here; 2,000 survived the death camps. Today there are almost none.

Anyone interested in contacting the Jewish community, or attending services at one of the two remaining synagogues, should phone ☎ 031/275-701.

You should be able to get information on whether the **Museum of the Jewish Presence in Thessaloniki,** in the Melka Building, corner of Odos Venizelou and Odos Ayia Mina 13, is open either from the Jewish History Museum or the Jewish community (see above). The turn-of-the-century Melka Building, formerly the Bank of Athens, was originally the home of the French-language Jewish newspaper *L'Independent.* Thessaloniki Jews established the city's first printing press in the early 1500s, and founded the city's first newspaper, *El Lunar,* in 1865.

If you are interested in learning more about the Jewish community in Greece, ask for the excellent pamphlet *Jewish Heritage in Greece* at the GNTO in Thessaloniki or Athens and keep an eye out for Niko Stavroloulakis's books *The Jews of Greece* and *Jewish Sites and Synagogues of Greece.*

Lambrakis Monument. Intersection of Venizelou, Ermou, and Spandoni sts.

On May 22, 1963, the leftist member of parliament, Grigoris Lambrakis, who had been speaking at a peace meeting, was run down and killed on this spot. Vassilis Vassilikos based his novel *Z* on Lambrakis's death; the novel was later adapted for a film by Costas-Gavras and starring Yves Montand. Lambrakis's assassination by right-wing forces and the protests that followed were part of a long series of events culminating in the dictatorship of the colonels in the late 1960s. The monument shows a bronze figure, arms upraised in supplication, flanked by a dove of peace.

✪ The Museum of Ancient Greek, Byzantine, and Post Byzantine Musical Instruments. Odos Katouni 12–14, Ladadika. ☎031/238-391. Admission Dr1,500 ($5). Tues–Sun 9am–3pm and 5–10pm.

What is it about music museums? The one in Athens is one of that city's finest small museums, and the same is true in Thessaloniki. The three floors here house beautifully displayed reproductions of stringed and wind instruments, along with marvelous photographs of depictions of the instruments from ancient vase paintings or Byzantine manuscripts. Music sometimes softly plays in the background, and there's a cafe that is sometimes open.

Museum of the Macedonian Struggle. 23 Proxenou Koromila. ☎ 031/229-778. Free admission. Tues and Thurs–Fri 9am–2pm; Wed 9am–2pm and 6–10pm; Sat–Sun 11am–2:30pm.

As its name suggests, this museum contains artifacts, uniforms, and weapons from the struggle that raged on and off from 1870 to 1919 to liberate Macedonia. The exhibits are very interesting, but there are no labels in English.

ART GALLERIES

Thessaloniki has a number of excellent art galleries that often have exhibitions well worth taking in. You can find out about them from posters in town, from the Greek National Tourist Organization in Aristotelous Square, and from the "Art Guide" listing, usually published on Mondays in *Kathimerini,* the English-language supplement to the *International Herald Tribune.* Galleries worth checking out include **Apothiki,** Odos Nikis on the waterfront (☎ 031/240-877); **Foka,** Odos Foka 17 (☎ 031/240-362); and **Metamorfosis,** Odos Tsimiski 128 (☎ 031/285-071).

In addition to these, several museums and galleries emphasize the art and life of Thessaloniki and Macedonia, with particular reference to the lively pre– and post–World War II art scene here. Most of these places keep irregular hours, and you are advised to check with the Greek National Tourist Organization in Aristotelous Square as to times. These include the **Gallery of Fine Arts,** Odos Nic. Germanou 1, inside the National Theater Building (☎ 031/238-601); the **Municipal Gallery,**

Odos Vas. Olas 162 (☎ **031/425-531**); and the **Macedonian Center of Modern Art,** International Fairgrounds (☎ **031/471-545**).

ORGANIZED TOURS

Reputable companies offering tours of Thessaloniki and of the Philip and Alexander sites include **Zorpidis Travel,** Odos Egnatia 76, at the corner of Odos Aristotelous, second floor (☎ **031/286-812;** fax 031/242-364), and **Kinissi Tour Agency,** Odos Venizelou 2 (☎ **031/241-080;** fax 031/286-824). Two agencies that offer out-of-the-ordinary tours are **Filoxenia,** Odos Tsimiski 17, fourth floor (☎ **031/280-560;** fax 031/285-170), which has "green" ecological tours to the countryside and mountaineering excursions, and **Trekking Hellas,** Odos Aristotelous 11 (☎**031/ 242-190**), which offers hiking expeditions.

OUTDOOR PURSUITS

BEACHES   Any beaches within the bay of Thessaloniki are too polluted to be entirely safe, although people do swim here. Those in the communities of Perea and Ayia Triada (16km/10 miles to 24km/15 miles along the bay east of the city) are considered reasonably safe. Just past Ayia Triada, on the headland of the bay, is the **Greek National Tourist Organization** facility of **Akti Thermaikou** (☎ **0392/ 513-52**), which also has a children's playground, changing cabins, snack bars, and tennis courts.

HORSEBACK RIDING   The **Thessaloniki Riding Club** (☎ **031/270-676**) is located in the countryside northeast of the city, off the road to the hilltop community of Panorama. Directions for getting there are too complicated for this space, but the owners speak English and can ably assist you.

JOGGING   Traffic pollution can be partly avoided by jogging along the spacious waterfront promenade east of the White Tower. It is, however, solid cement; there are no dirt footpaths anywhere in the city set aside for this purpose.

TENNIS   Within the city, outdoor courts are available at the **Poseidonion Athletic Center,** next to the seaside amusement park at the foot of Odos 25 Martiou (☎ **031/ 428-453**). Outside the city, there are courts on the beautiful, tree-shaded campus of the American-owned **Anatolia College** on the road to Panorama (☎ **031/301-071**), about a 20-minute drive. There are also facilities at **Akti Thermaikou** (see "Beaches," above).

SPECTATOR SPORTS

Like most Greeks, Thessalonians are keen soccer and basketball fans, rooting for the home teams (confusingly, Aris and PAOK have both basketball *and* soccer teams). Your best bet if you don't speak or read Greek and want to catch a game is to check with the concierge at your hotel, or at the Greek National Tourist Organization in Aristotelous Square (don't attempt this on the phone). In general, soccer games are in the spring and fall, basketball year-round. Games are held at the **Aris stadium** in the suburb of Harilaou (☎ **031/305-402**) and the much-easier-to-reach **PAOK stadium,** on Ayios Dimitrios, 2 blocks northeast of the International Fairgrounds (☎ **031/ 238-560**).

SHOPPING A TO Z

As you'd expect from Greece's second largest city, Thessaloniki has a wide variety of shops, and since the city center is quite compact, it's easy to explore the major shopping districts. As in Athens—indeed, throughout Greece—most chic clothing stores stock imported goods from Europe and America, with a very hefty import duty.

Details, Details

In Thessaloniki, old-style, pre–European Community **shopping hours,** unfathomable to foreigners, are still in force. Shops open at about 9am and close around 1:30 or 2pm for the afternoon siesta. On Tuesday, Thursday, and Friday evenings, some (but not all) reopen from about 5:30 to 8:30pm. In July, however, all shops are closed in the evening. Therefore, to be safe, plan to do your shopping in the morning.

Most of these shops will take major credit cards, but almost all, especially the smaller ones, prefer not to.

If you want to see where Thessalonians shop, take a stroll along **Tsimiski, Mitropoleos,** and **Proxenou Koromila** streets between **Odos Pavlou Mela** (the diagonal street connecting the church of Ayia Sofia with the White Tower) and the north-south vertical of **Odos Venizelou.** In this area are the city's few department stores, many boutiques selling the very latest in expensive men's and women's haute couture, shops selling jeans and casual clothing, *lots* of shoe stores, jewelry and antiques stores, several record shops selling both Greek and foreign items, the best English- and French-language book and magazine store in town, and a number of confectionery stores.

Thessaloniki also still has a number of shops selling the handiwork of local craftspeople, such as coppersmiths and jewelers. This is where you're likely to find something tempting, sometimes at what constitutes a bargain price for a foreigner. Not surprisingly, most of the shops are near the church of the Panayia Chalkeon (The Virgin of the Copper Makers) in **Dikasterion Square.**

What you won't find in Thessaloniki is anything remotely equivalent to the shops packed with souvenirs that have proliferated in Athens and on many islands. If you get a souvenir here, it's likely to be just that: something you find that will remind you of your visit, rather than a mass-produced memento.

Antiques
Relics. Odos Yioryio Lassani 3 (1 block east of the Mitropoleos Cathedral off Odos Mitropoleos). ☎ **031/226-506.** Closed Sun.

Relics offers the best variety of high-quality antiques in the city, from silver- and glassware to jewelry, ceramics, prints, art-nouveau lamps, and Victorian-era dolls. This is a serious shop with serious prices.

Art
Art Forum. Odos Nikiforo Foka 29 (off of Odos Tsimiski, 1 block east of Navarino Sq.). ☎ **031/224-060.** Mon, Tues, Thurs, and Fri 10am–2:30pm and 6–9pm. Closed July–Aug.

A rapidly emerging new gallery that shows great taste in selecting the very best of contemporary Greek art.

Terra Cotta. Odos Chrys. Smirnis 13 (1½ blocks north of the U.S. Consulate between Leoforos Nikis and Odos Mitropoleos). ☎ **031/235-689.** Fax 031/220-191. Closed Aug 1–20.

The very best gallery in Thessaloniki for paintings, engravings, and sculpture, Terra Cotta features works from all of the most famous contemporary Greek artists, such as Fasianos, as well as those of the emerging generation.

Books, Newspapers & Magazines
Apostolic Diakonta Bookstore. Ethnikis Aminis 9A, near the Archaeological and Byzantine museums. ☎ **031/275-126.**

Although this handsome bookstore specializes in books on religious matters, it also has a wide selection (in English and French, as well as in Greek) on Greece. This is a wonderful place to browse, and even if you can't afford one of the superb books of photos of Greece, you can find wonderful cards here, as well as nice reproductions of icons.

✪ **Molhos.** Odos Tsimiski 10 (between Odos El. Venizelou and Odos Dragoumi). ☎ **031/ 275-271.** Fax 031/229-738. E-mail: molho@imagine.gr.

Molhos has the best selection of foreign-language books, magazines, and newspapers in the city, and this wonderful family-run, multiple-level bookstore is a Thessaloniki institution. These people love books, and the staff can assist you in English, French, and German—and probably a great many other languages. Many of the most tempting books (including some dazzling books on Greece) are on the second floor.

Rentzis. 24 Tsimiski. ☎ **031/236-175.**

This small bookstore in an arcade between Mitropoleos and Tsimiski has a helpful staff and a good selection of English-language books on Thessaloniki and Greece.

Copper

Adelphi Kazanzidi. Odos Klissouras 12 (running off the western side of Dikasterion Sq., 1 block north of Odos Egnatia). ☎ **031/262-741.**

This family-run store has passed down its copper-working skills from generation to generation. It sells numerous finely crafted copperware items such as wine carafes, skillets, water heaters, and trays, all done on the premises and by hand.

Crafts

Skitso. Odos Grigori Palama 11 (1 block west of the intersection of Odos Pavlou Mela and Odos Tsimiski). ☎ **031/269-822.**

This store sells a delightful variety of handmade objects, mostly in wood, including puppets, ships, crosses, and children's toys.

Department Stores

Lambropoulos. Odos Tsimiski 18 (1 block west of Odos Aristotelous, at the corner of Odos Komninon). ☎ **031/269-971.**

The best in the city with five floors full of everything and anything you might want, from cosmetics to basketballs.

Fashion

For women's fashions, try the department stores such as Lambropoulos (see above) or the chic—and expensive—boutiques on pedestrian Odos Dimitriou Gounari. For men's clothing, we recommend the following store. See also "Shoes," below.

Oxford Company. 4 Palaion Patron Germanou. ☎ **031/273-087.**

This shop has a small but stylish selection of menswear (shirts, jackets, ties, slacks) made by a long-established company with branches in Athens and Volos. There are some nice photos on the walls of the family's old cotton mills in Volos.

Gifts & Souvenirs

Tanagrea. Odos Vogatsikou (1 block east of the Metropolitan Cathedral between Odos Mitropoleos and Odos Proxenou Koromila).

Here you'll find an impressive selection of handcrafted items by a stable of extremely skilled artisans employed by this well-known chain of stores, which also has outlets in Athens, Crete, and Spetsai. Offerings include ceramics, pewter, silver, leather goods, paintings, glassware, and jewelry.

Pack 'n' Send

Office supplies may sound like just what you *don't* want to think about on vacation, but if you need stationery, packing tape, scissors, or large envelopes to mail purchases home, **Spondilides,** Odos Tsimiski 24, in the stoa (☎ **031/269-825**), is the place to come.

ZM. 1 Proxenou Koromila (1 block east of Aristotelous Sq.). ☎ **031/240-591.**

Pronounced "zeeta mee," this gift shop offers three floors of expensive but well-crafted Greek souvenir items such as worry beads, pottery, folk art, rugs, toys, handcrafted caïques, prints, and a few antique silver place settings and jewelry. An extremely tempting place to browse.

Jewelry
Marina. Odos Mitropoleos 62 (1 block east of the Metropolitan Cathedral). ☎ **031/238-361.**

Specializing in gold, but not exclusively, the eponymous owner offers her own designs as well as copies of the works of famous Greek jewelers such as Lalaounis, with whom she has apprenticed.

Leather
Falli. Odos Askitou 11 (southwest corner of the outdoor market, near Odos Ermou and Odos El. Venizelou). ☎ **031/229-197.**

The best of several leather-goods shops in the area that make and sell shoulder bags, backpacks, attaché cases, and sandals. Some of these items are of very high quality and very reasonably priced. You should try to bargain.

Markets
See "Markets," earlier in this section, for the Modiano, Kapani, Bezesteni, and Flea markets.

Music
Blow Up: The Music Stores. Odos Aristotelous 8 (on the eastern side of the street, a block north of Odos Tsimiski). ☎ **031/233-255.** Fax 031/237-101. E-mail: cry@netfiles.gr.

Both this store and **Patsis,** Odos Tsimiski 39, at the corner of Odos Aristotelous (☎ **031/231-805**), have excellent selections of Greek music well displayed in their windows and on their shelves. Blow Up has literally thousands of CDs, and, according to one longtime customer, the owner here not only speaks English but also will go out of his way to help you find what you want.

   Blow Up has recently opened a second store at Odos Megalou Alexandrou (Alexander the Great) 20 (☎ **031/724-144**).

Perfume
Aroma. Odos Mitropoleos 62 (1 block east of the Mitropoleos Cathedral). ☎ **031/286-010.**

This little shop, with its enticing rows of colored perfume jars, offers a multitude of scents, copying famous perfumes or mixing ones of your own choosing at extremely reasonable prices.

Shoes
Pak. Ayias Sofias Sq. 3 (opposite the north side of Ayia Sofia church). ☎ **031/274-863.**

This shop offers a wide selection of high-quality Greek shoes—from hiking boots to high heels—at very acceptable prices. It also carries foreign brands, but these are much more expensive.

Sweets

Agapitos. Odos Tsimiski 53 (between Odos Ayias Sofias and Odos Karolou Dil). ☎ 031/279-107. Closed Sun.

In a city where sweetness is next to godliness, this venerable establishment is the best. There are a wide variety of items to choose from, all made with great, mouthwatering, high-caloric care.

Toys

Fokas. Odos Tsimiski 50 (east of Odos Ayias Sofias). ☎ **031/276-774.**

This department store has a basement filled with some adorable, Greek-made, wooden children's toys. See also **Skitso,** listed in "Crafts," above.

WHERE TO STAY

Because of Thessaloniki's long history as a center for national and international trade, its hotels have traditionally focused on serving the needs of commercial travelers rather than tourists. Most are blandly functional, and the few that aspire to elegance are almost entirely lacking in charm.

Reserve in advance during both summer and winter to avoid difficulties during the numerous trade fairs and associated cultural events. Bookings peak in September and October, when the grand International Trade Fair is quickly followed by the month-long Demetria cultural festival. During Demetria, there is often a surcharge on the regular rates. If you have trouble finding accommodations, check with the **Greek National Tourist Organization (EOT).** There's an office at the airport (☎ 031/471-170 or 031/473-212, ext. 215) and in the city center at Aristotelous Square 8, (☎ **031/271-888** or 031/222-935).

VERY EXPENSIVE

Macedonia Palace. Leoforos Megalou Alexandrou 2 (on the seafront promenade half a mile east of the White Tower), 54640 Thessaloniki. ☎ **031/861-4000.** Fax 031/868-942. 288 units. A/C MINIBAR TV TEL. Year-round Dr60,000–Dr65,000 ($200–$216). Parking Dr3,000 ($10) a day.

The Macedonia Palace is now managed by the Grecotel Group, and seems to be back on track as a luxury resort hotel after a few years of mismanagement. All the large rooms have been redone, but only in the usual Greek hotel decor, which seems to concentrate the glitz in the lobby and leave the bedrooms rather bland. All units have balconies, but if you stay here, insist on a seaside room. (Why pay all that money and not have the view?)

The Macedonia's own restaurants (one Greek, one international) are perfectly good and, as you'd expect, expensive. There are fresh- and saltwater pools in addition to the sea itself. If you can foot the bill, this is a great place to stay with kids—as many Greek families do.

EXPENSIVE

Capsis Hotel. Odos Monastiriou 18, 54629 Thessaloniki. ☎ **031/521-321.** Fax 031/510-555. 428 units. A/C MINIBAR TV TEL. Dr39,000 ($130) double. Rates include buffet breakfast. AE, DC, MC, V.

The best feature of this large 17-year-old hotel on busy Odos Monastiriou, which becomes Egnatia as it gets closer to the center of town (about 15 min. by foot), is its rooftop pool. The Capsis does a lot of convention business, so you can't expect much in the way of a personal touch, but you will get the comforts (including free parking, in-house laundry service, and a hairdresser) of a hotel that caters to businesspeople.

A Note about Rates

The rates given in this section are for high season in summer—they should be lower in winter, and higher during trade fairs and the Demetria.

The guest rooms are furnished in pale pastels and have decent reading lights, a small desk, and good-sized bathroom with hair dryer. The in-house restaurant is nothing special, although the breakfast buffet is excellent.

Electra Palace Hotel. Aristotelous Sq. 9A, 54624 Thessaloniki. ☎ 031/232-221 to 229. Fax 031/235-947. 70 units. A/C MINIBAR TV TEL. Dr32,800 ($109). Rates include American-style buffet breakfast. AE, DC, MC, V.

Overlooking Thessaloniki's main square, the Electra Palace, with its handsome, curved, arcaded facade, has the nicest location in town—except when there are noisy demonstrations in Aristotle Square. For years, this was the city's only really good hotel; sad to say, when we stayed here most recently in 1998, our small interior double bedroom had scruffy carpeting and dingy furniture, and needed serious renovations. If you do stay here, insist on one of the rooms on the fourth or fifth floors overlooking the square, as whatever redecorating efforts the hotel has engaged in of late have focused on these units. In short, this is a place that has seen better days and has been surpassed by the new Mediterranean Palace Hotel—but it does offer large rooms with balconies overlooking the square.

Hotel Astoria. Odos Salaminos 9 (at the corner of Odos Tsimiski), 54626 Thessaloniki. ☎ 031/554-902. Fax 031/531-564. E-mail: paphotels@the.forthnet.gr. 84 units. A/C MINIBAR TV TEL. Dr40,000 ($133) double. Rates include continental breakfast. AE, MC, V.

The Astoria is still one of the best hotels in town, although the Mediterranean Palace, just around the corner, is now the city's best hotel, and the Electra on Aristotelous Square has a better location. That said, the Astoria offers all the creature comforts of a businessperson's hotel: bedrooms (admittedly, with resolutely anonymous decor) and bathrooms are spacious, and there's an in-house restaurant and bar. The location just off the harbor in the Ladadika district, with its restaurants, cafes, and galleries, is only a 10-minute walk from the center of town. Staying here won't be the highlight of your visit to Thessaloniki, but you should be perfectly pleased with the service and accommodations.

Hotel Capitol. Odos Monastiriou 8, 54629 Thessaloniki. ☎ 031/516-221. Fax 031/517-453. E-mail: capitol@hol.gr. 178 units. A/C TV TEL. Dr42,000 ($140). Rates include buffet breakfast. AE, MC, V.

Friends who have stayed at this 30-year-old hotel find it less impersonal than the nearby Capsis Hotel—but missed the rooftop pool at the Capsis. There's a hotel restaurant and bar, some of the bedrooms have quite comfortable floral-print sofas and chairs, and almost all have a small desk. As at the Capsis, you're a good 15-minute walk along a busy commercial street from anything you've come to see in Thessaloniki.

Hotel Olympia. Odos Olympou 65, 54631 Thessaloniki. ☎ 031/235-421. Fax 031/276-133. 111 units. A/C TV TEL. Dr40,000 ($133). Rates include breakfast. AE, DC, MC, V. Free parking.

Like most hotels in Thessaloniki, the Olympia caters to businesspeople, but Greek families also often stay here. The bathrooms are somewhat archaic and the bedrooms are rather bland, with carpets and chairs that have seen better days (the last overhaul here was in 1980). In short, your heart won't leap up at the sight of your room here, but the Olympia's location, at the northern end of the Roman market, is convenient for visiting the city, and traffic here is less thunderous than on some of the main avenues. As always, rooms on the top floors tend to be quieter than those closer to the street—and, in this case, the flea market.

✪ **Mediterranean Palace Hotel.** Odos Salaminos 3 and Odos Karatassou, 54626 Thessaloniki. ☎ **031/552-544.** Fax 031/552-622. 118 units. A/C MINIBAR TV TEL. Dr52,000 ($173) double. American-style breakfast Dr2,500 ($8) extra. AE, DC, MC, V.

The Mediterranean Palace opened in the Ladadika district, with its tempting restaurants and cafes, in 1997, and is clearly Thessaloniki's best hotel. Rooms on the front have balconies overlooking the harbor, and virtually every unit in the house is large and furnished with comfortable beds, spiffy wall-to-wall carpeting, and cozy chairs, including some relaxing leather recliners. Many of the rooms have especially nice touches, such as decorative moldings, large walk-in closets—and if you want to make a phone call from your bathroom, this is the place to do it. As to the suites, with their large living rooms, kitchenettes, and bedrooms, we could happily live in one for months. Small wonder that the Greek magazine *Odyssey* voted this the best hotel in Thessaloniki, mentioning that this hotel "calms the souls of frazzled executives and travelers."

MODERATE

Hotel ABC. Odos Angelaki 41, 54621 Thessaloniki. ☎ **031/265-421.** Fax 031/276-542. E-mail: hotelabc@spark.net.gr. 100 units. A/C TV TEL. Dr28,900–Dr30,900 ($96–$103). AE, MC, V.

The ABC is on busy Sindrivaniou Square, across from the International Fairgrounds and a short walk from Aristotle University and the Archaeological Museum. Staff say that the windows here are "soundproof"; we'd say that the windows are "sound-proofed," but that you're still aware of traffic noises on the lower floors of this eight-story hotel. The bedrooms, many decorated in bland browns and beiges, are perfectly functional and perfectly charmless. Why stay here? The price isn't bad, and you're very close to the Archaeological Museum and the inexpensive restaurants that cater to the area's university students. The hotel's own restaurant is not worth trying.

✪ **Hotel Queen Olga.** Vas. Olgas 44, 54641 Thessaloniki. ☎ **031/824-621.** Fax 031/868-581. 148 units. A/C MINIBAR TV TEL. Dr30,000 ($100) double. Rates include continental breakfast. DC, MC, V.

The Olga is a new hotel whose good-size rooms have balconies and fully modern bathrooms. The decor is the usual pastel walls and pine beds—standard hotel stuff—but the balconies are a very nice feature. One of the pleasures of staying here is walking along the street that Thessalonians call "The Avenue of the Mansions" and looking at the elegant 19th-century buildings.

This hotel is in the eastern part of town, but buses run frequently along Vas. Olgas into the center (about a 20-min. walk).

Hotel Tourist. Odos Mitropoleos 21, 54624 Thessaloniki. ☎ **031/276-335.** Fax 031/226-865. 37 units. TV TEL. Dr18,000 ($60). No credit cards.

A friend of ours has stayed here every time she has visited Thessaloniki in the last 30 years. What she likes is that the hotel has changed imperceptibly over that time. True, there are now TVs in the rooms, but many guests prefer to gather and watch television in the communal sitting rooms, with their ornate hanging chandeliers and amazingly uncomfortable chairs. When we stayed here in January 1998, we loved our old-fashioned, high-ceilinged bedroom and tolerated the archaic bathroom (a little closet shoehorned into the room). We were less fond of the constant noise of traffic and the middle-of-the-night comings and goings to the rooms of some young, female Russian guests who described themselves as "entertainers."

Philippion. P.O. Box 19002 (in the forest of Sheih-Sou to the north of the Upper City), 56610 Thessaloniki. ☎ **031/217-406.** Fax 031/218-528. 89 units. A/C MINIBAR TV. Dr30,000 ($100) double. Rates include continental breakfast. AE, MC, V. Free parking. Take the Ring Rd. north around Thessaloniki and exit at the sign labeled PHILIPION. Shortly afterwards, another sign to the left will lead you to the hotel.

For those who cannot abide staying in any city in the summer, but still want to spend time in one, this sprawling, modern four-story hotel complex, renovated in 1992, is a good choice—although the fires of 1998 harmed the lovely surrounding forests. It overlooks Thessaloniki from a hilltop a 15-minute drive from the city center (there are hotel shuttle buses leaving every half hour), and yet is a vacation spot in its own right. The guest rooms are spacious, well appointed, and sunny, the best being on the third floor to the rear, with a view of the city.

Facilities include a pool, outdoor cafeteria, barbecue, and children's playground. The hotel restaurant is excellent, with local specialties such as mussels in hot pepper sauce; there's sometimes live entertainment in the evening. The clientele are mostly vacationing Greek families, who can be rather boisterous. The hotel's proximity to the Ring Road makes it extremely easy to reach the airport (15 min. away) and the main highways to Athens, Halkidiki, and Thrace.

INEXPENSIVE

Hotel Orestias Castorias. 14 Agnostou Stratiotou, 54631 Thessaloniki. ☎ **031/276-517.** Fax 031/276-572. 28 units. Dr9,000 ($30). No credit cards.

We were seriously tempted to stay at this small, very cheap, modest hotel across from the Roman Forum when we visited in January 1998. Room no. 27, overlooking a quiet garden, was especially tempting. What made us hesitate was that almost every guest in the hotel seemed to be part of a large group of eastern Europeans, and we had the feeling that we might be crashing a quite lively private party. We'd be eager to have an update on this hotel, whose manager assured us that we would be "comfortable and safe" at his establishment.

WHERE TO DINE

The cuisine of Thessaloniki has long been renowned throughout Greece for its delicate, aromatic character (a heritage of its historically close contact with the Levant) and the splendid variety of its game and hors d'oeuvres (*mezedes* or *mezedakia*). Recently, due to the efforts of a number of enterprising young Thessalonians, it has now become better than ever before, perhaps the finest in all of Greece.

Even in the most expensive establishments, the dress code is very casual for men, with ties and jackets rarely worn. Women, on the other hand, are often resolutely chic, in little black dresses and pantsuits. Reservations can be made, but the only guarantee that a table will be available when you arrive is if you get there before most Greeks come out to dine. If you don't want to risk waiting, try to arrive for lunch before 1pm and dinner no later than 8:30pm.

The best of Thessaloniki's dining places fall into three basic categories, which we use in our listings below: restaurants and tavernas that offer cuisine of a distinctly Thessalonian character, including game; fish tavernas; and ouzeries, which specialize almost exclusively in hors d'oeuvres. Those in the first category usually have an excellent selection of hors d'oeuvres as well, while the ouzeries may also offer more-substantial main courses.

Note: Most Thessaloniki restaurants do not accept credit cards.

The Food of Thessaloniki

Without examining the vexed question of the extent to which Thessaloniki's cuisine has been heavily influenced by Turkish cuisine, let us just observe that the use of spices, the delicate hand with fish, the wide variety of vegetable dishes, and the extravagantly rich pastries so popular in Thessaloniki are not unknown in Turkey. As any Greek will tell you, this is because the Turks, during their long occupation of Greece, absorbed—stole, actually—the secrets of Greek cuisine. Some might argue that when the Turks withdrew from Greece, they took many of those secrets with them. Others would simply say that in some parts of Greece—such as Thessaloniki—a love of cuisine and a devotion to spices lives on.

In fact, it's the spices that set Thessaloniki's cuisine apart from that of the rest of Greece. Take the peppers. The most famous Macedonian peppers are the red *florines,* originally grown in the town of Florina, but now raised throughout Macedonia. These can be either sweet, or so hot that they lift off the top of your head. We like both varieties, but we'd be a lot more relaxed when taking that first bite if we knew whether any individual *florina* were going to be sweet or pyrotechnic.

In addition to the florines, there are some *really* hot peppers traditionally grown in the Macedonian town of **Piperia** (pepper). These peppers are dried, then flaked, and the result, called *boukovo,* is sprinkled liberally into just about anything you'd care to cook. In some Thessaloniki restaurants, in addition to the salt and black pepper on your table, you'll find another shaker, of red pepper. Treat it with respect.

RESTAURANTS & TAVERNAS

Expensive

Aigli. Odos Kassandrou and Odos Ayiou Nikolaou (near the church of Ayios Dimitrios). ☎ **031/270-061.** Reservations recommended. Main courses Dr2,500–Dr4,000 ($8–$13). Surcharge of Dr2,000 ($7) when there is entertainment. No credit cards. Thurs–Sun 10pm–2:30am. Mon–Wed open only for private parties. GREEK/CONTINENTAL.

Established in 1992 in an exquisitely restored Turkish hamam (bathhouse), this is certainly the most beautiful restaurant in Thessaloniki. Indoors, one dines beneath the high double domes of the former bathhouse; outdoors, in the gardened grounds of an old, open-air cinema that sometimes shows films in summer at 9 and 11pm. The Aigli used to boast the best haute cuisine in Thessaloniki, but the management has recently decided to shift its emphasis from cooking to entertainment and to booking the entire establishment for private parties. That said, the food is still very good, and specialties include chicken kebab, Turkish dolmades, and grilled fillet of chicken breast. There is a wonderfully varied entertainment program. One night you might see a French chanteuse; on another, a group of Egyptian instrumentalists. Whatever it is, it is guaranteed to be exotic.

✪ **Krikelas.** Odos Ethnikis Antistasis 32 (an extension, going into the city from the airport, of the far eastern end of Vas. Olgas). ☎ **031/411-289.** Reservations necessary. Main courses Dr3,000–Dr4,200 ($10–$14). No credit cards. Daily 11:30am–2am. GREEK.

Renowned throughout the country since its opening in 1940, Krikelas is regularly patronized by visiting politicians, entertainment celebrities, and sports heroes, as well as by other Greeks from all walks of life. The brightly lit (and rather smoky) atmosphere is highly convivial and the food is consistently excellent.

The specialties are its mouthwatering variety of hors d'oeuvres and whatever game is in season (including quail, pheasant, rabbit, boar, and partridge). For hors d'oeuvres, try the special feta cheese, creamed with butter and hot green peppers, or the smoked Gruyère from Metsovo. An interesting regional specialty is *spetzofai,* a mixture of seasonal vegetables and pungent country sausage. For dessert, try the homemade halva with almonds. The wine list has a sumptuous variety of the very best in Greece at prices ranging from Dr2,000 to Dr5,000 ($7 to $17) a bottle.

Moderate

Kioupia. Morixbou Sq. 3–5, Ladadika. ☎/fax **031/553-239.** Reservations recommended after 9pm. Main courses Dr2,400–Dr3,500 ($8–$12). Mon–Sat 1pm–1am. GREEK.

Another small taverna in the old warehouse district, again with brick walls and wood floors, that serves excellent *stifada* (stews) baked in individual clay casseroles, *keftadakia* (meat balls), spicy *gardoubitsa* (liver and garlic), and good retsina.

Le Café. Tsimiski 12 (corner of Tsimiski and Venizelou). ☎ **031/275-625.** Fax 031/221-270. Main courses Dr1,800–Dr3,200 ($6–$11). No credit cards. Mon–Sat about 9am–1am. GREEK/CONTINENTAL.

You can get a salad, spaghetti, a sandwich, or just a coffee at this cafe, which has a curved balcony and large windows on the ground floor. Some people seem to show up here to read their morning paper and are still nibbling on the food by dinnertime. This is a nice spot to sit and read, people-watch, and eavesdrop on cellular phone conversations.

Tiffany's. Iktinous 3 (on the walkway between Odos Tsimiski and the church of Ayia Sofia). ☎ **031/274-022.** Reservations recommended after 10pm. Main courses Dr1,800–Dr4,000 ($6–$13). No credit cards. Daily 11:30am–2am. GREEK/CONTINENTAL.

This popular place, with wood paneling and pictures of old Salonika on the walls, seats about 100 and attracts an interesting mix of people—those who seem to drop in every night for a quick bite, and then the gaggles of 20-somethings who sit in the window tables and wait to be watched. We're in the distinct minority in that we find the two house specialties, bifsteki Tiffany's (stuffed with cheese and tomatoes) and *hanoym borek* (casserole of roasted chicken, ham, veal, and cheese) both rather bland. On the other hand, we had fun trying to figure out the principle behind the music here, which alternated Harry Belafonte and Greek golden oldies.

Wolves. Vas. Olgas 6 (1 block in and 2 blocks east of the Macedonia Palace Hotel). ☎ **031/ 812-855.** Main courses Dr2,000–Dr3,000 ($7–$10). No credit cards. Mon–Sat 12:30pm–1am; Sun 12:30–5pm. GREEK.

This warm, dark-wooded, old-fashioned restaurant, established in 1977, has a cook reputed among locals to be one of the best in Thessaloniki when it comes to making a delicacy out of such basic Greek fare as pastitsio and moussaka. Try the roasted red peppers from Florina as one of your hors d'oeuvres. For the main course, sample the moussaka Wolves, the oregano-flavored stewed pork, and the batter-fried codfish in garlic sauce. Or take a look in the display counter in the kitchen at whatever specialty might be available that particular day. The name of the establishment is not indicative of anything on the menu; it's simply the sobriquet of the owner's favorite English soccer club.

✪ **Zythos.** Katouni 5, Ladadika. ☎ **031/540-284.** Main courses Dr1,500–Dr3,200 ($5–$11). Mon–Sat noon–1am. GREEK/CONTINENTAL.

This was one of the first restaurants to open in the restored warehouse district, and it's still very popular with ladies who lunch, young lovers, harried businessmen, and groups of golden youths. The decor is lots of wood and brick, as you'd expect in a former warehouse—although the slim young wait staff in their chic black slacks or skirts hardly suggest warehouse workers. You can eat at the bar or at one of the tables, and we can vouch for the croquettes of vegetables, *saganaki* (fried cheese), and veggie pasta. There are usually two daily specials, including one vegetarian choice, on the menu.

Inexpensive

If you're around Aristotelous Square, **Lokanda,** at the corner of Mitropoleos and Venizelou (☎ 031/288-432), is a good spot for a coffee, stuffed croissant, or sandwich—at prices much lower than similar places in the square.

In the Upper City, head to **To Yenti,** Odos Ioannis Papareska 13, outside the gates of the Eptapirgiou prison (☎ 031/246-495), to sit under the trees, relax, and try the keftedes and other mezedes.

Corner. Odos Ayias Sofias 12 and Odos Ethnikis Aminis (a block north of the White Tower). ☎ **031/426-531.** Main courses Dr1,800–Dr3,600 ($6–$12). No credit cards. Daily about 11am–1am. PIZZA.

Locals and visiting pizza fans agree that this place serves the best pizza in town, perhaps because a wood-burning oven is used. Not surprisingly, it's a popular hangout for young Salonikans.

Kentrike Stoa. 32 Bas. Hrakleiou. ☎ **031/278-242.** Snacks Dr600–Dr1,800 ($3–$6). No credit cards. Mon–Sat noon–1am. GREEK/CONTINENTAL.

This upmarket snack-and-drinks place in the Central Market is up a winding metal staircase from the market itself. The ceiling of the snack bar is covered with parachute cloth, and jazz contends with the shouts from the market below. The languid young 20-somethings here tolerate outsiders gracefully—and are fun to spy on as they vie to impress one another.

✪ Loutros. Komninon 14 (in the Turkish bath). ☎ **031/228-895.** Main courses Dr1,200–Dr2,800 ($4–$9). No credit cards. Mon–Sat 11am–midnight. GREEK.

This tiny restaurant is in part of an old Turkish bath; you can see the arched ceiling overhead as you eat. The walls are pale yellow, hung with some nice photographs of old Salonika and some rather phallic gourds. The fried minnows (which you eat whole) and mussels are both delicious, as are the *horta* (greens) and *florines* (spicy red peppers). The music here is usually very Levantine sounding—which, in Greece, is a polite way of saying that it sounds absolutely Turkish.

✪ Thanasis. Odos Ermou and Odos Komninon 32 (just inside the Modiano Market). ☎ **031/274-170.** Reservations necessary after 10pm. Main courses Dr1,500–Dr2,200 ($5–$7). No credit cards. Daily about 7am–1am. GREEK.

The sign over the door reads H MYPOBOLOS SMYRNH (ee-me-*ro*-volos *smear*-ni) and translates as "Miraculous Smyrna," but everyone knows it equally well by the name of its marvelously genial owner, Thanasis. He and his wife and relatives labor incessantly during market hours to satisfy the cravings of a seemingly endless number of market workers, businesspeople, artists, prostitutes, actors, and various other characters from the high and low walks of Thessaloniki. The potato salad, cheese croquettes, spicy peppers with cheese, squid stuffed with cheese and rice, grilled fish and meats, and an excellent batter-fried cod (*bakaliaro*) are all wonderful, as is the mood in this tiny restaurant with photos and old prints on the walls. The music is usually very loud here, but if we could only eat at one place in Thessaloniki, this would be it.

To Makedoniko. Odos Yioryiou Papadopoulou 32 (in the Upper City, inside the arch at the western end of the walls). ☎ **031/627-438.** Main courses Dr900–Dr1,500 ($3–$5). No credit cards. Mon–Sat 9am–2am. Sometimes closed in Jan. Bus no. 23. GREEK.

You couldn't get more basically Greek than this. Rugged, rudimentary, and full of local color, To Makedoniko is a watering hole and eatery equally popular among the neighborhood working class and the downtown intellectuals, artists, and university students.

If you have the constitution to handle it, you must drink the local schnapps—*tsipouro,* a delicately perfumed but powerful variety of ouzo—with your hors d'oeuvres. While the limited menu can vary from day (or even from hour to hour), the pork *riganato* and mussels in a hot-pepper broth (*midia saganaki*) are usually on the menu.

FISH TAVERNAS

The best fish tavernas are to be found in the suburbs of Aretsou, on the eastern side of the bay past the old summer palace of the Greek royal family at Kivernio, and in the neighboring district of Nea Krini. To get to both areas from the city center, go east along the seafront drive of Megalou Alexandrou, take a right at the stoplight at Odos Themistokli Sofouli, and continue along the coast.

Be sure to ask the price of any fish you order: it's calculated by the kilo and is the most expensive thing you can eat in Greece. A good, medium-priced fish is one of the many varieties of sea bream or porgy called *sargos* or *lithrini.* The more expensive fishes are *barbouni* (red mullet) and *ksifias* (swordfish).

Expensive

Kavos. Odos Nikiforos Plastiras 59 (near the seafront road in Aretsou). ☎ **031/430-475.** Reservations recommended after 9pm. Main courses Dr1,800–Dr9,000 ($6–$30); most fish priced by the kilo. No credit cards. Daily 10am–2am. GREEK.

Somewhat more expensive than the rest of the many excellent seafood restaurants in the area, this brightly lit, no-frills taverna is known among Thessalonians as the best of its kind in the city.

Vrakos. Odos Mikras Asias 2 (in Nea Krini, in a cul-de-sac off the seafront road towards Aretsou). ☎ **031/447-991.** Reservations recommended after 9pm. Main courses Dr1,800–Dr8,000 ($6–$27). No credit cards. Daily noon–2am. GREEK.

Almost as good as the Kavos and equally as low-key. Its name means "rock," and it's so called because of its lovely location on a rocky headland on the bay, where you can dine on the terrace virtually on top of the water. Its specialty is shrimp in a hot-pepper broth.

OUZERIES

As can be gathered from the name, ouzeries are places specializing in ouzo and the mezedes, or hors d'oeuvres, that go with them. One need not, however, drink ouzo—or for that matter, any kind of alcoholic beverage—to enjoy the marvelous variety of foods they offer: octopus, meatballs, shrimp, squid, taramosalata (fish roe puréed with oil and bread), tzatziki (cucumber, yogurt, and garlic), melitzanosalata (eggplant purée), cheeses, and potato, beet, and bean salads. Since in most places you won't be able to understand the menu, it's always best to go with your waiter to look at the offerings and point out what you want.

Expensive

Aristotelous. Odos Aristotleous 8 (in a cul-de-sac between office buildings on the east side of Odos Aristotelous, just north of Odos Tsimiski). ☎ **031/230-762.** Reservations not accepted. For a variety of hors d'oeuvres, Dr2,700–Dr4,500 ($9–$15). No credit cards. Mon–Sat 10am–2am; Sun 11am–6pm. GREEK.

First on the list and the best. Highly popular with writers, artists, and everyone else in the know, Aristotelous is constantly packed during the peak lunch and dinner hours, so you should come either early or late, or you'll end up waiting at least 20 minutes. Indoor and outdoor seating areas in between high-rise office buildings contribute to the crush and somehow the charm. You can and should linger for hours, which is why it's often so hard to get a table. The variety of hors d'oeuvres is sumptuous. Try the fried zucchini and eggplant; the feta cheese mashed with hot peppers and olive oil (*ktipiti*); and, for something more substantial, the stuffed cuttlefish (*soupia*). Also delicious is the homemade halva.

Totti's. Aristotelous Sq. 3 (southwest corner fronting the sea). ☎ **031/237-715.** Main courses Dr2,700–Dr3,500 ($9–$12). No credit cards. Daily 7am–2am. GREEK.

Its outdoor dining area festooned with yellow and orange umbrellas and facing the broad east-to-west expanse of Thessaloniki harbor, this is perhaps the most soul-refreshing ouzeri in the city, particularly in the evenings when the sun sets into the sea in front of you. It's also a great place for breakfast. The food is typical ouzeri fare, but the tableware and other accoutrements have considerably more elegance, which is reflected in the price. The service, however, as the waiters take their long walks to and from the interior kitchen, can be interminable. This is but one of a number of Totti's in Thessalonika; you'll bump into others in your explorations.

Moderate

Aproopto Light. Odos Zevksidos 6 (a pedestrian walkway off the eastern end of the church of Ayia Sofia). ☎ **031/241-141.** Main courses Dr1,500–Dr3,000 ($5–$10). No credit cards. Daily noon–1:30am. GREEK.

Highly popular with professionals of the nearby State Theatre and other artistic types, this place serves excellent hors d'oeuvres as well as some main-course dishes. Its relatively small, well-decorated sidewalk and interior dining area are usually packed and rife with conviviality. Try the mussels with spinach and the leeks à la Parisienne as well as the taganaki, a cheese-and-potato dish.

THESSALONIKI AFTER DARK

Thessaloniki does not really awaken until after dark, and when it does, it seems at times as if the entire populace has come out to amuse itself. In addition to the cultural festivals held in the fall, numerous theatrical events and pop and classical concerts take place year-round. Meanwhile, the city seems festooned with enough bars and music and dance clubs to serve a population twice its size, yet all of them are crowded to the bursting point and more open every year.

While there a number of publications listing the various events, and posters splattered everywhere announcing them, they will all be Greek to you, so the best thing to do is ask for information on special events at your hotel or stop by the **Greek National Tourist Organization (EOT),** Aristotelous Square 8 (☎ **031/271-888** or 031/222-935).

ONLY IN THESSALONIKI

Taking what the Greeks call a volta (stroll) along the seaside promenade, particularly at sunset or under a full moon, is one of the great pleasures of being in Thessaloniki. Start at **Aristotelous Square,** perhaps with a coffee, a drink, or sweets at one of its many cafes, and walk east past the White Tower and toward the bright lights of the city's amusement park at the other end of the promenade, about 3 kilometers (2 miles) distant. Along **Leoforos Nikis,** which borders the promenade in the city center, are a number of cafes and bars. At the **White Tower,** there are usually peanut vendors and, occasionally, the city's only horse-drawn carriage for rent.

You might also decide to take an **hour's cruise** around the harbor on the various small boats that dock just east of the tower. Several companies make the trip, but the best of these is **Ampari Lines** (☎ 094/359-330), which has cruises scheduled every 2 or 3 hours from 12:30pm to 3am. The cost is Dr1,500 ($5). You can buy coffee, fruit juices, and beer on board.

The Performing Arts

The **State Theatre of Northern Greece** (Kratiko Theatro) has two venues. In winter, it stages plays in the **State Theatre,** which is opposite the White Tower (☎ 031/ 223-785); in summer, at the **Forest Theatre** (Theatro Dasous), an open-air amphitheater located in the forested hilltop area east of the Upper City (☎ 031/ 218-092). The company presents both ancient and modern Greek plays, as well as Greek translations of foreign plays, including those by such well-known authors as Samuel Beckett, Arthur Miller, and Tennessee Williams. Major Greek directors are brought in, and some, but not all, of the productions are quite stunning.

In summer, the Forest Theatre, which has a marvelous view of the city, also hosts lively, well-attended concerts by popular Greek singers and composers, as well as performances by visiting ballet companies.

In winter, the State Theatre occasionally gives its stage over to visiting foreign companies presenting both plays and ballets. Visitors have included the National Theatre of England and the Bolshoi Ballet.

Mention should also be made here of the outdoor **Garden Theatre** (Theatro Kypou), in the Municipal Park to the east of the State Theatre. While part of the State Theatre complex, it's rented out by various local groups who present a variety of cultural events, from music to ballets, plays, and musical comedies. All are in Greek, but some can be quite accomplished and entertaining.

The **Municipal Orchestra of Thessaloniki** performs at the **Aristotle University concert hall** on Odos Nea Egnatia, opposite the northern entrance of the International Trade Fairgrounds, from September through May (☎ 031/283-343). Its repertoire includes the works of modern Greek composers as well as the standard classics, which it plays with great distinction before a highly appreciative audience.

Festivals

THE DEMETRIA FESTIVAL   In honor of the patron saint of Thessaloniki, St. Dimitrios, whose name-day is October 26, this prestigious cultural festival runs every October and includes the Greek Film Festival as well as many theatrical and musical events, all of them performed by major and minor artists from all over the country.

THE FEAST OF SAINTS CONSTANTINE & ELENI (MAY 21)   On or around the feast of the first Christian emperor and his mother, villagers in the village of **Ayia Eleni** (80km/50 miles northeast of Thessaloniki) and at **Langadas** (12km/7.4 miles northeast of Thessaloniki) engage in *pirovassia* (fire dancing). Crowds come from all over Macedonia to see the faithful dance over a bed of hot coals. When they're done, they feast on the roasted black bull that has been sacrificed earlier in the day. Just in case you're wondering—yes, much of what's done here preserves pre-Christian rites.

THE INTERNATIONAL TRADE FAIR FESTIVAL   This takes place every year during the first 2 weeks in September and draws businesspeople from around the world. There are lots of exhibits at the international fairgrounds—and hotel rooms are very hard to find.

THE BAR, CLUB & MUSIC SCENE

In the summer, virtually all of Thessaloniki's best bars and clubs shut down. Some immediately reopen branches along a section of the road leading east along the coast, about a mile before the airport. This, plus the fact that new or newly decorated and renamed venues are constantly opening while others go out of fashion and close, makes it virtually impossible to recommend any with certainty.

There is one place, however, that we can recommended without hesitation. Not only is it both a permanent fixture of Thessaloniki nightlife year-round, but it also incorporates by far the best of the bar, music, and club scenes in the city.

✪ **The Milos.** Odos Andreadou Yioryiou 25. ☎ **031/516-945.** Cover charge varies with the entertainment, usually Dr3,000–Dr4,500 ($10–$15); drinks Dr1,200–Dr1,500 ($4–$5). The ouzeri, cafe, and galleries open from about 11am on. The clubs open at 10pm; club reservations can be made at the above number. Go west on Odos Tsimiski to its end and turn left onto Odos 28 Octobriou. At the first traffic light, turn right onto Andreadou Yioryiou and continue to the end of the street. This is quite a hike from the center, and you may want to take a cab.

Within the grounds of an old, wonderfully restored flour-mill complex, the Milos (*mee*-los) complex contains a music club for blues, folk, jazz, and pop groups, a nightclub featuring Greek singers and comedians, a bar/disco, an outdoor concert stage and movie theater, a cafe, an ouzeri, and several exhibition rooms and art galleries. Opened in 1990, it has quickly established itself as one of the top musical venues in the country and features a constant stream of talent from within Greece and abroad.

There's so much to do and see here that it's best to go early and spend the evening, eating perhaps at the ouzeri, enjoying coffee at the cafe, strolling among the exhibits, and attending one or both of the clubs. This is what the locals do, en masse, so it's best to arrive before 9pm—particularly if you want to get a place at the clubs, which open at 10pm and are mobbed.

LATE-NIGHT BITES

Since virtually every cafe and many restaurants stay open almost all night in the summer, it's not hard to find a late-night snack. Here are a couple of suggestions just in case you're in town in winter, when things tend to close down much earlier.

Corner. Odos Ayias Sofias 28 (on the east side of the street, between the church of Ayia Sofia and Odos Egnatia). ☎ **031/273-310.** No credit cards.

Open from 11am to 1am, this is where you can get, among other delicacies, the best pizza in town. Alcoholic drinks are also served. There's another **Corner** at Odos Ethnikis Aminis 6, a block north of the White Tower, behind the State Theater (☎ 031/273-039). See also "Where to Dine," above.

Xatzi. Odos Eleftheriou Venizelou 50 (just north of Odos Egnatia). ☎ **031/279-058.** No credit cards.

Established in 1908 and passed down from generation to generation, this tiny shop with seven tables is the perfect place to go for a midnight sweet. They have a superb selection of Levantine pastries and desserts (ask for the illustrated catalog) whose recipes have not changed an iota since its opening.

2 Side Trips from Thessaloniki: In the Footsteps of Philip of Macedon & Alexander the Great

Every year, more people head north to Macedonia to see the cluster of ancient sites associated with **Philip of Macedon** (382–336 B.C.) and his famous son, **Alexander the Great** (356–323 B.C.): these include **Pella, Vergina,** and **Dion.** Many of those visiting Northern Greece these days are Greeks, whose interest in things Macedonian was enormously intensified a few years ago when, just across the border, the former Yugoslavian district of Macedonia proclaimed itself a republic. How dare these non-Greeks take the name of Macedonia, Greeks asked—forgetting that their own ancestors had not considered Philip of Macedon a Greek! Most of all, Greeks were furious that Philip's best-known royal symbol—a star with 16 rays—appeared on the new Macedonia's flag. Throughout Greece, debates raged over whether the new self-styled Macedonia had imperialistic aims. For once, Greece's long-standing enmity with Turkey was virtually ignored, as Greeks painted MACEDONIA IS GREECE on virtually every road and wall in the country. Things have calmed down a bit now that the new Republic of Macedonia has changed its flag, but Greeks are still rediscovering their ancestral links with Philip, the northern king who conquered Greece in 338 B.C.

The renewed interest in Philip, Alexander, and Macedonia itself has led the Greek Archaeological Service to redouble its efforts to excavate the Macedonian royal sites and build site museums. And that, of course, means that there's much more to see above ground than there was even a few years ago.

ESSENTIALS

GETTING THERE   The only enjoyable and efficient way to see the places where Philip of Macedon and Alexander the Great lived and reigned is by car or with a tour. **Budget Rent-A-Car** has offices at the airport (☎ 031/471-491) and in the city at Odos Angelaki 15 (☎ 031/274-272 or 031/229-519), opposite the International Fairgrounds. Other rental offices are **Avis,** Leoforos Nikis 3 (☎ 031/227-126 or 031/683-300), at the western end of the harbor, opposite the docks; and **Hertz,** Odos El. Venizelou 4 (☎ 031/224-906), on Eleftherias Square. (See "Getting Around" in Thessaloniki, page 517, for more car-rental information).

Several Athens-based tour companies, such as **CHAT** and **American Express,** offer tours of Central and Northern Greece that take in the most important Macedonian sites. Reputable Thessaloniki tour companies offering tours of the Philip and Alexander sites include **Zorpidis Travel,** Odos Egnatia 76 (at the corner of Odos Aristotelous), second floor (☎ 031/286-812; fax 031/242-364), and **Kinissi Tour Agency,** Odos Venizelou 2 (☎ 031/241-080; fax 031/286-824). A day trip to Pella, Edessa, Veria, and Vergina costs about Dr30,000 ($100); an excursion to Philippa, Kavala, and Amphipolis costs about Dr22,500 ($75). The days these tours are given tend to vary and it is vital to make an advance reservation. If possible, do not visit on a summer weekend, when crowds of Greeks flock to these sites.

By Bus   If you try to visit these sites by local bus, you may feel that it is taking you longer to see them than it took Alexander to conquer the world. Still, if you have lots of time and love buses, you can visit the following sites by bus from Thessaloniki. For **Pella,** there are sometimes direct buses; failing that, take a bus to Edessa and ask to be let off at Pella. For **Vergina,** take a bus to Veria, and then a local bus to the site of Vergina. If you wish to go to Pella and continue to Vergina, you can do so by taking the Thessaloniki bus from Pella to the town of Halkidona, where you can get a bus to Veria. This may involve a substantial wait. For **Dion,** take a bus to Katerini and then

Seeing the Sites

Once you reach these sites, each is clearly marked and easy to visit. Nonetheless, wear sturdy shoes and, in summer, a hat and sunscreen.

a local bus to Dion. For up-to-date information on bus schedules and departure points, check with the **Greek National Tourist Organization** in Thessaloniki (☎ **031/271-888**); **bus information** (☎ **031/924-444**) is unlikely to have English speakers answering the phone. If you read Greek, the Thessaloniki daily newspaper *Macedonia* also lists daily bus schedules.

VISITOR INFORMATION If you're stopping in Athens or Thessaloniki before visiting these sites, drop by the **Greek National Tourist Organization (EOT)** in Athens at Odos Amerikis 2 (☎ **01/331 0561**), or in Thessaloniki at Aristotelous Square (☎ **031/271-888**), and try to get a copy of the brochure *Greece/Macedonia* and any other brochures they may have for individual sites. At each site, ask whether there is a free Culture Ministry brochure available (at press time, it was customary to give visitors brochures at Pella, Dion, and Vergina).

PELLA

40km (24 miles) W of Thessaloniki on the E86 highway to Edessa

Pella, once the capital of the Macedonian kingdom and the birthplace of Philip II of Macedon in 382 B.C. and his son Alexander the Great in 356 B.C., is easy to spot: the **archaeological site** and **museum** (☎ **0382/31-160**) are right beside the highway you take to get here. (Museum admission is Dr500/$1.65; site admission is Dr500/$1.65. Hours are Mon through Fri from 8am to 7pm and Sat, Sun, and holidays from 8:30am to 3pm.) In antiquity, Pella's situation was more appealing—a navigable inlet connected it to the broad Thermaic Gulf that borders Thessaloniki. Over the centuries, the inlet silted up, leaving Pella landlocked, but in Philip and Alexander's day, ships would have sailed here and docked at what is now a dusty plain. The city itself is thought to have covered at least 5 square miles, of which only a fraction has been excavated.

Nonetheless, there's more than enough of Pella above ground to give you an idea of this stylish city, with its large, square agora (market and civic center) bordered by colonnaded stoas and flanked by streets lined with shrines, sanctuaries, temples, and private homes. The lovely frescoes that once adorned the house walls are gone, but a number of the handsome **pebble mosaic floors** remain, both on the site and in the museum. These houses must have been exceptionally pleasant, with their gaily painted walls, handsome mosaic floors, and sheltered inner courtyards. There families could have passed an evening, perhaps discussing the Athenian playwright Euripides's *The Bacchae,* which had its premiere around 408 B.C. in the as yet undiscovered theater here.

Unfortunately, the dwelling you'd most like to see—the **palace** where both Philip and his son, Alexander the Great, were born—is not yet open to the public. Not to worry: You can drive or walk to the hilltop north of the site, peer over the wire fence, and get an idea of how large this royal home was. In fact, the palace covered 60,000 square meters—only 10,000 less than the agora itself! The view from this hill is still tremendous, but must have been truly breathtaking in antiquity, when the palace overlooked both the plain and the channel down which ships sailed, bringing supplies here from around the Mediterranean.

Pella's small **museum** is superb, especially its glorious pebble mosaics found in some of the 4th-century B.C. homes excavated here. The two best-known mosaics show a lion hunt and the god of wine, Dionysos, riding a leopard. The lion hunt is worth looking at not just for its powerful depiction of two youths and a slathering lion, but because this mosaic may show Alexander himself. Some scholars have suggested that the mosaic records the incident when the young Alexander was saved by a friend from a lunging lion. Others suspect that it's too good to be true that the mosaic actually shows that famous incident and suggest that this is simply a genre scene of a hunt. You can compare the marble bust of Alexander in the museum with the youth under attack in the lion hunt and decide whether you think they both show the young prince.

WHERE TO STAY & DINE

After you visit the site, you may want to take in **Edessa** (45km/27 miles west of Pella), a scenic cliff-top town with bubbling waterfalls and several pleasant small cafes and restaurants beside them. We've eaten at several, and can't say that we find one better than another—the real point of dining here is enjoying the rushing waterfall. This is not a good place to visit on summer weekends, when many Salonikans come here to escape the summer heat.

If it's the weekend, or if you're rushed after visiting Pella, you can grab a bite at the small roadside restaurants by the fountain beside the remains of "Baths of Alexander," a Hellenistic fountain incorporated into a Roman bath about a kilometer from Pella on the Edessa road.

As far as overnighting here, keep in mind that Edessa is a very popular year-round weekend destination for Thessalonians, that there are only about 125 hotel rooms here, and that you may have trouble finding a room if you simply appear on the weekend.

Katarraktes. Odos Karanou 4, 58200 Edessa, Macedonia. ☎ **0381/22-300.** Fax 0381/27-237. 44 units. TEL. Dr18,000 ($60) double. No credit cards.

This hotel has a nice location near the waterfall. Rooms are furnished in the usual bland Greek-hotel style: pine beds, pale walls—acceptable, but in no way memorable.

If the Katarraktes is full, you might try the 15-room **Neon** on Odos Aridea (☎ **0381/91-300**); friends of ours found it just fine for a night.

VERGINA & ENVIRONS: THE TOMBS AT LEUKADIA, THE TOWN OF VERIA & NEARBY VINEYARDS

20km (12 miles) S of Pella; 62km (38 miles) W of Thessaloniki

Vergina, just outside the hamlet of Palatitsa, is very well signposted. If you only have time to visit either the site or the museum, there's no choice here—head for the museum. If you have time for both, here's what you'll see at the **Vergina site** and **Royal Tombs Museum** (☎ **0331/92-347**). Museum admission is Dr1,200/$4; site admission is Dr500/$1.65. Hours are Tuesday through Sunday from 8:30am to 3pm.

Vergina (anciently known as Aigai) was where Philip lived when not at Pella and where he died in 336 B.C., and is the most important of the royal Macedonian sites. Preliminary excavations suggest that the palace was enormous, with an inner courtyard some 147 feet square. Around the courtyard ran a Doric colonnade; the bases of some of the 60 columns of the colonnade are still in place and give a sense of the courtyard's size. The palace also had a long airy colonnaded veranda running the length of its north side, overlooking the theater. It's quite possible that the royal family watched some spectacles in the theater from the comfort of the palace veranda.

Philip & Alexander

When Philip was born in 382 B.C., most Greeks thought of Macedonians—if they thought of them at all—as one of the rude northern tribes of barbarians who lived in the back of beyond. Macedonians, after all, were not even allowed to participate in the Panhellenic Games at Delphi. Clearly, this irritated Philip. By 346 B.C., after conquering a number of Athenian colonies and allied cities, Philip had won a place on Delphi's governing board. A few years later, in 338 B.C., despite Demosthenes's best oratorical efforts to alert the Athenians to Philip's intentions, the Macedonian king had conquered all Greece. Two years later, Philip was dead, cut down as he strolled to see a performance in the theater at his capital city of Vergina. Some said that his young son Alexander was behind the assassination, while others wondered how the unproven youth could rule Macedonia, let alone Greece.

No one, except perhaps Alexander himself, could have imagined that by the time he died at 33, he would have conquered much of the known world as far east as India. Alexander's early death makes it impossible to know what he would have done with the rest of his life, once he had no new worlds to conquer. Some scholars think that Alexander was a visionary bent not just on conquering, but also uniting the world into a "brotherhood of man." This, they suggest, is why Alexander contracted so many foreign marriages and accepted conquered princes into his retinue. Other scholars, more cynical, think that both Alexander's marriages and his use of former enemies were simply shrewd political moves. The truth probably lies somewhere in between the two theories.

In any event, after Alexander's death, his former comrades turned on one another and destroyed his empire. Within a few generations, Macedon was once more a northern kingdom in the back of beyond, living on memories of its brief period of international importance.

Unfortunately for Philip, that's not what he did on the fatal day in 356 B.C. when he was assassinated en route from the palace to take in a performance at the theater. Some said Alexander himself was behind the assassination, others simply said that the young prince was not notably grief-stricken at this father's death. You can sit in the **theater**—the only really impressive remain—and contemplate the moment when Philip realized that he was about to be struck down.

As you drive from the site to the Royal Tombs Museum, you'll notice hundreds of low mounds on the gentle hills of the Macedonian plain. These are some of the more than 300 **burial mounds** found here, some dating from as long ago as the Iron Age, but many from the time of Philip himself. Virtually all of these graves were robbed in antiquity but fortunately—and almost miraculously—the tomb identified as that of Philip himself was undisturbed for almost 2,000 years. How it was found is one of the great stories of archaeology, deserving a place beside accounts of how Schliemann found Troy and excavated the "Tomb of Agamemnon" at Mycenae.

Vergina's first excavator, the French archaeologist Leon Heuzey, prophesied in 1876 that when Vergina was fully excavated, "the importance of its ruins for Macedonia will be comparable to Pompeii." In the 1930s, the Greek Archaeological Service began to work here, and uncovered several tombs that looked like small temples. For years, the excavators nibbled away at the largest burial mound of all, the **Great Tumulus,** measuring 110 meters across and 12 meters high, containing a number of burials. One tomb they found was almost totally destroyed, another well preserved but robbed. Still, head excavator Manolis Andronikos remained convinced that he was excavating ancient Aigai, Philip's capital city, and might yet find Philip's own tomb.

Finally, in 1977—on the last day of the excavation season—Andronikos and his workers opened the massive marble gates of the last remaining tomb. As Andronikos later wrote in *Vergina: The Royal Tombs:*

> *We saw a sight which it was not possible for me to have imagined, because until then such an ossuary [container for bones] had never been found . . . all-gold . . . with an impressive relief star on its lid. We lifted it from the sarcophagus, placed it on the floor, and opened it. Our eyes nearly popped out of our sockets and our breathing stopped; there unmistakably were charred bones placed in a carefully formed pile and still retaining the colour of the purple cloth in which they had once been wrapped . . . If those were royal remains . . . then . . . had I held the bones of Philip in my hands?*

Andronikos—and virtually all of Greece—answered his question with a resounding "Yes," in large part because of the other objects found in the tomb. The gold wreaths, Andronikos felt, were too fine to belong to anyone but a king. And surely the little ivory portrait heads were the spitting image of Philip and Alexander himself. And, most persuasive of all, what about the bronze greaves (shin guards) found in the tomb? Were they not of unequal size? And was not Philip known to have legs of different length, due to an early injury?

It is difficult to overestimate the Philip-fever that swept through Greece when Andronikos announced that he had found Philip's tomb and identified Vergina as Ancient Aigai, Philip's capital city. Although some scholars have questioned whether this is, in fact, Philip's tomb, those scholars are not Greek. Greeks regard with horror any suggestion that this splendid tomb may have belonged to Arrhidaeos, the son of Philip known only for his lack of distinction.

The arched roof of the **Royal Tombs Museum** re-creates a sense of the Great Tumulus itself, as does the passageway leading into the tomb area. Each of the five tombs is protected by a glass wall, but seeing the tombs this way is the next-best thing to being able to stand inside them. Give your eyes time to get accustomed to the darkness, then enjoy the lovely decorative paintings on the facades of the temple-like tombs. And, of course, be sure to see the treasures from these tombs now on display in the Archaeological Museum in Thessaloniki.

A DETOUR IN LEUKADIA

If Vergina has whetted your appetite for royal tombs, you might consider heading north to **Leukadia,** 20 kilometers (12 miles) south of Edessa in the beautiful foothills of Mount Vermion. Be forewarned: This is one of those excursions based on suggestions such as "ask for directions in the village" and "ask if the custodian will accompany you and open the tombs." If you're lucky and find the custodian and the tombs (ask in cafes and the main square in Leukadia), you'll get to see three spectacular tombs. The 3rd-century B.C. **Great Tomb** is decorated with paintings of battles of Lapiths and Centaurs and Greeks and Persians. The **Kinch Tomb** (named after its discoverer) and the **Tomb of Lyson and Kallikles** are decorated with paintings of funeral swags of pomegranates and snakes, symbol both of the under-world (since snakes often live underground) and rebirth (because snakes shed old skins for new ones). The claustrophobic may find the descent down a dank shaft into the Tomb of Lyson and Kallikles unappealing. If the custodian does take you to see these tombs, you should slip him at least Dr1,000 to Dr1,500 ($3.35 to $5) along with your thanks.

VERIA (VEROIA) & ITS TURKISH REMAINS

If an excursion to Leukadia seems too much like work, try the nearby hill town of **Veria** (**Veroia**), 15 kilometers (9 miles) northwest of Vergina. Veria is in the throes of development, but still has a number of old streets, wood houses with overhanging bay windows, small Byzantine churches (usually locked), a 15th-century cathedral, and a good number of buildings from the Ottoman period, including a former mosque and hamam (bath). The truly devoted will wish to visit the small **Archaeological Museum** on Odos Anixeos, with finds from local sites (admission is Dr500/$1.65; hours are Tues through Sun from 8:30am to 3pm). Don't feel bad if it's closed; you'll have much more fun just wandering the streets of this old town, with its considerable Turkish remains.

Veria's restaurants serve food that is almost guaranteed to be better than that dished out around the site of Vergina. Try **Sarafopoulos** on Odos Kentrikis or **Kostalar** on Afroditis; Kostalar has the more pleasant location on a shady square.

THE NAOUSSA VINEYARDS

About halfway between Veria and Edessa, on the slopes of Mount Vermion, several vineyards are open to the public. You'll see their roadside signs announcing this. At **Naoussa,** a region famous for its wine, the **Stenimachos Winery,** run by the well-known Boutari vintners, is open to the public. Tours of the winery are given most work days and are sometimes offered in English. For information call ☎ 0332/ 42-687 or check with the **GNTO** in Thessaloniki (☎031/271-888).

WHERE TO STAY

At press time, a hotel was under construction on the Vergina-Veria road; when it is complete, it will clearly be modern and, presumably, up-to-date. Until then, Veria has a number of hotels, none enchanting, although the town itself has its pleasures.

Hotel Makedonia. Odos Kontogeorgaki 50, Veria, 59100 Macedonia. ☎/fax **031/66-902,** or ☎ 031/66-946. TV TEL. Dr18,500 ($62). No credit cards.

This is Veria's best hotel, which is to say that it is not a fleabag like some of the others, and has a quiet location. Essentially, the Makedonia has the bland ambiance of a businessman's hotel, rather than a traveler's hotel.

DION

78km (48 miles) S of Thessaloniki on the E75 highway

The **Dion archaeological site** and **museum** (☎ 0351/53-206) are outside the village of Dio, about 8 kilometers (5 miles) west of the Dion sign on the E75, the main Athens-Thessaloniki highway. *Warning:* This is a dangerous turn off the highway; reentry is also difficult. Museum admission is Dr800 ($2.65); site admission is also Dr800 ($2.65). Hours are Tuesday through Sunday from 8:30am to 3pm.

If you haven't been to Dion in a few years, you may want to know that there's good news and bad news. The good news is that excavations are continuing here, unearthing more of ancient Dion. New pathways have been constructed to help visitors tour the site, and helpful signs have gone up. The bad news is that this site, until recently one of the few left in Greece that you could wander around at will, feeling like you had just stumbled upon an ancient city, has been fenced in and tidied up with a vengeance.

Nonetheless, Dion still has a beautiful location, just outside the Vale of Tempe, in the foothills of Mount Olympus. This is an unusually green spot, with pine groves and farm fields watered by springs fed by the melting snow that clings to Olympus's peaks year-round. If you can, bring a picnic; after you visit the excavations and museum, you can linger a while at the picnic tables on the site.

Dion was founded as a religious sanctuary, and for some time was Macedonia's most important sanctuary, something of a sacred city. Later, its constant water supply led both Philip and Alexander to establish military training camps here. Philip bivouacked here before he marched south to conquer Greece, while Alexander drilled his men here before heading east to conquer Asia.

According to a story preserved by the 2nd-century A.D. biographer Plutarch, it was at Dion that Alexander, then only 8 years old, first saw Bucephalos, the handsome black stallion soon to be his favorite mount. Philip himself had bought the horse, but found that neither he nor any of his men could ride it. Alexander asked his father if he could have a go at taming the creature. Muttering that if *he* could not tame the horse, an 8-year-old hardly could, Philip nonetheless agreed to give Alexander a chance. Immediately, Alexander turned Bucephalos so that he could not see his shadow, leapt up, and galloped away. When the young prince returned from his ride, Philip said, "My son, look for a kingdom equal to you. Macedonia is too small."

Although Dion—which sits by a narrow pass between Thessaly and Macedonia—was an important military camp for first the Macedonians and then the Romans, it was not merely the Fort Bragg of antiquity. The Romans adorned Dion with a **theater** (bigger and better than the Hellenistic one, as was the Roman habit), and built **sanctuaries** to the healing god Asclepius, the nurturing goddess Demeter, and the popular Egyptian goddess Isis. In addition, of course, the Romans built **baths** here; baths being the large structures that they are, a good deal remains for you to explore. Copies of some of the statues found in the sanctuaries have been erected at the site, while the originals are safely tucked away in the museum.

There's a great deal to see at Dion, but I have to confess that some of my happiest visits here have been spent in the shade of the trees with a picnic. From here, you can make excursions onto the site, following the course of a stoa, admiring the statue of Isis seemingly admiring her reflection in a pool, and imagining the day that Alexander, all of 22 years old, mounted Bucephalos and set off to conquer the world.

The Dion **museum** is a heartening example of what a provincial museum can be when it is well funded and well cared for. An English-language video and English-language museum labels help foreign visitors understand the importance of what they are seeing, while models of the ancient site make the Dion of Philip and Alexander easy to visualize. Exhibits include statues of the children of Asclepius (lined up as though posing for a family photo), grave monuments, votive offerings, mosaics, and, best of all, a wonderful copper water organ, probably made in the 2nd century A.D., that would be the hit of any music hall today.

WHERE TO STAY & DINE

There's a string of cafes and restaurants directly across from the Dion museum; an archaeologist friend reports consistently eating well at the **Dionysos,** which serves good roast goat, loukanika (sausages), and the usual chops and salads. Expect to pay about Dr1,500 ($5) for lunch or dinner unless you go overboard on the roast goat, which is priced by the kilo and may bring your tab to Dr3,000 ($10).

Dion Palace Resort Hotel. Litochoro Beach, 60200 Macedonia. ☎ **0352/22-731.** Fax 0352/22-735. 182 units. MINIBAR TV TEL. Dr30,000 ($100) double. AE, MC, V. Sometimes closed in winter.

This enormous beachfront resort has a main hotel building, two restaurants, a disco, shops, a fitness center, and lots of cabanas with the rooms (some private, some sharing a cabana). There are two swimming pools—one saltwater, one fresh—and all the creature comforts. In summer, this is a popular family destination, and anyone with children will see why. Others may prefer the little Hotel Dion, described below.

⊙ **The Hotel Dion.** Dion, 60200 Macedonia. ☎0351/53-336. 20 units. Dr8,000 ($27) double. Rates include breakfast. No credit cards.

When we stopped here in January 1998, this little hotel was closed for the winter. Friends who stayed here this spring report that their balconied room was large, sparely furnished, and pleasant, and that the town was deliciously quiet all night—except for a few late-night motorcycles and some early-morning roosters.

3 A Side Trip from Thessaloniki: Mount Athos (The Holy Mountain)

130km (80 miles) SE of Thessaloniki

The most important thing to know about Mount Athos is that you can't just go there. And if you're a woman, you can't go there at all. (See "Permits," below). Recently, there have been mutterings that antidiscrimination regulations of the European Common Market may force Athos to open its doors; to avoid any potential complications, Mount Athos has refused any Common Market funds for restoration of monasteries. It is highly unlikely that the bureaucrats of the Common Market will prove a match for the monks of Athos and their centuries of tradition.

Many destinations are hyped as being a "step back in time" or a "glimpse of an unknown world," but both statements really are true of Mount Athos. Most monasteries here still follow the Julian calendar, which puts Athos 13 days behind the Gregorian calendar. The day is divided not into 24 equal hours, but organized according to an elaborate Byzantine scheme based on the times of sunset and sunrise; midnight, in this system, is at sunset. The flag that flies outside most monasteries is the double-headed eagle of Byzantium—symbol of the empire that fell in 1453.

Athos is very much a place of prayer and contemplation, and while some monks welcome visitors, most simply tolerate them, unless a visitor has a sincere interest in the Greek Orthodox faith and the monastic life. The monks' life focuses on prayer—usually 8 hours a day—and meditation. A local saying sums up the monks' life: "Write, read, sing, sigh, pray, keep silent."

No one is sure when monks and hermits first began to live on this rugged promontory. Some say that the place became holy when a storm blew the Virgin Mary's ship ashore here, as she was traveling from Jerusalem to Cyprus. As she stepped ashore, all the pagan idols crashed to the ground and were destroyed, a sure sign that this was a holy place.

Certainly, there were enough men of God here by 885 for the Byzantine Emperor Basil I to formally declare all Athos a "place of Quietism." The first, and still most important monastery, the **Great Lavra** or **Meyistis Lavras** ("Lavra" simply means a community of monks), was founded around 960, and others quickly followed. In 1060, an imperial decree barred "every woman, every child, eunuch, smooth faced person and female animal" from Athos, which suggests that there had been incidents of inventive nonchastity over the years. In recent years, hens have been allowed onto Athos to produce eggs, and cats to catch vermin.

Until the fall of Constantinople in 1453, successive Byzantine emperors gave the monasteries rich donations of icons and manuscripts. After the fall of Byzantium, and during the Turkish occupation of Greece, the monasteries struggled to survive; many treasures were neglected, some sold. When the traveler Robert Curzon visited Athos in 1849, he inquired about purchasing a manuscript. To his horror, Curzon later recorded in his *Visits to the Monasteries of the Levant,* a monk pulled out his knife and "cut out an inch thickness of the leaves before I could stop him."

In 1917, the execution of the Russian royal family put an end to Athos's last major source of royal patronage. In 1926, Athos was declared a "Theocratic Republic." Although it is part of Greece, it is self-governing—hence, the need for an entry permit. Today, there are 20 active monasteries, with at least that many again having closed over the centuries. There are still solitary hermits on Athos, but most monks follow a communal (cenobitic) rather than an isolated (idiorrhythmic) life. In fact, of late, monastic life has had something of a revival; Father Gabriel, gardener at the Iviron Monastery, was quoted in the July 28, 1988, Athenian newspaper *Kathimerini* as saying that "More are interested in becoming monks than we are ready to accept." According to the same story, Father Gabriel has added to his gardening duties the preparation of a computer catalog of manuscripts and icons. When asked if this would not take a very long time, he replied "We've got all eternity."

ESSENTIALS

PERMITS   To visit Mount Athos, you must be at least 21, male, and have an entry permit. To get a permit, you must have these things: a **letter of recommendation** from your embassy or consulate in Athens or Thessaloniki, and your **passport.** The United States does not charge for this; the United Kingdom and most other embassies charge about £10 (Dr5,000/$16). Getting the letter of recommendation is usually pro forma, but it's a good idea to have yourself described as a student or scholar.

Once you have the letter, take it to the **Ministry of Foreign Affairs** in Athens at 3 Akadamias, fifth floor (open Mon, Wed, and Fri from 11am to 1pm), or in Thessaloniki to the **Ministry of Macedonia and Thrace,** Plateia Dikiasterion, Room 22 (open Mon through Fri from 11am to 1:30pm). After a wait, which may be minutes or even days, you will be issued a permit for a 4-day visit to Mount Athos.

When you reach Ouranopolis, the jumping-off point for Athos, you must take your permit to the **Grafio Proskyniton** (Visitors Bureau), open daily from 8:30am to 2pm, and pay Dr7,000 ($23) for a *diamonitirion*—your passport, as it were, to Mount Athos.

Important note: The names and phone numbers of the monasteries are posted in this office; it is advisable to phone ahead to make a reservation at the monasteries where you want to stay the night.

When you reach Mount Athos, you must present your diamonitirion at the monastery/hamlet of Khilandariou, where you will be registered. Thereafter, you may be asked for your diamonitirion from time to time as you visit the monasteries.

GETTING THERE   By Car   If you drive to Mount Athos from Thessaloniki, check with the **Greek National Tourist Organization** in Aristotelous Square to see if there is road work on any of the major roads you might take, as this may help you to decide on the best route. You can take the E90 across the top of Chalkidiki east as far

What to Pack for Mount Athos

Bring sturdy shoes, long-sleeved shirts and slacks (the monks are offended by shorts and short-sleeved shirts), a hat, insect repellent, a flashlight, reading material, any prescription or nonprescription medication you might need, a map, and the best lightweight (you will have to carry it everywhere) guide you can find. If you own the archaeologically oriented *Blue Guide* to Greece, you can photocopy the excellent section on Athos to bring along. One book you may enjoy reading is Robert Byron's *The Station,* the account of his visit here in 1931.

as Stavros, and then head south along the coast to Ouranopolis, or you can head south from Thessaloniki along the airport road and then continue across the southern coast of Chalkidiki to Ouranopolis. Allow 4 to 8 hours, depending on how many stops you want to make en route.

By Bus   From Thessaloniki, take the bus to Ouranopolis from the Halkidiki terminal at 68 Karakassi. Allow 6 hours.

By Boat   However you reach Ouranopolis, you will continue from there to Mount Athos by boat. There is almost always at least one boat a day at 9:45am from Ouranopolis to Mount Athos. During the summer, there are usually more-frequent boats, as well as excursion boats that circle Mount Athos, so that those who do not wish—or are not allowed—to go ashore can see Mount Athos.

GETTING AROUND   Be prepared to do a lot of walking on Mount Athos. Feet are the preferred method of transportation. There are many footpaths on the island, and you would do well to get as good a map as you can find either in Thessaloniki or in Ouranopolis (compare maps and dates to see which is most detailed and up-to-date).

FAST FACTS   Ouranopolis, the jumping-off point for Mount Athos, has a **post office** and **telephone office (OTE);** in 1998, it was rumored to be getting a bank by 1999. **Karyes,** the main town on Athos, also has both a **telephone office (OTE)** and **post office.** It, too, is awaiting the opening of a bank—but do not count on this having happened before you visit. At present, a mobile bank van appears on an irregular schedule in Ouranopolis, so be sure to take adequate funds with you.

WHAT TO SEE & DO

Ouranopolis is the jumping-off point for Mount Athos, but unfortunately, it has become a nasty little town filled with tacky souvenir shops in recent years. However, the handsome tower immortalized in Joyce Nankivell Loch's *A Fringe of Blue* still stands (and is rumored to open soon as a museum of Byzantine art). Joyce Loch and her husband, Sydney, both Quakers, lived in Ouranopolis on and off from the 1920s to the 1960s and worked with villagers and refugees from Asia Minor. For some years, the tower was both the Lochs' home and a weaving school.

If you can't go to Athos itself, try to take one of the **boats** from Ouranopolis that cruises around the peninsula. The views of the rugged, pine-clad mountain promontory are superb, and you'll be able to see a number of the monasteries. Most look like little villages from the outside, perched on astonishingly high and sturdy stone foundations and surrounded by massive walls. Virtually all of the monasteries are built according to a similar plan, in which a **central church** (the katholikon) fronts on an arcaded courtyard, often with a bell tower. Around the courtyard are the monastic buildings, including the dining quarters (refectory or trapeza), kitchens, laundry rooms, and bedrooms (the cells).

If you do take a boat trip around Athos, and encounter rough seas, you'll understand why the Persian King Xerxes tried to cut a channel through Athos at just about the point where Ouranopolis sits today: he wanted to spare his fleet the rough seas here as he sailed north to attack Athens in 480 B.C. For centuries, scholars thought that Herodotus's story of Xerxes's canal was one of the historian's flights of fancy. The technology, the scholars said, simply didn't exist so long ago for such a massive project. In 1998, archaeologists and geologists announced that they had discovered at Ouranopolis—just where Herodotus placed it—signs of Xerxes's canal. Soundings revealed a massive channel some 65 feet wide at its base, 114 feet broad at the top, hidden beneath the 22 feet of earth that slowly filled in the canal over the centuries.

Tips on Visiting Athos

On Mount Athos, you will be walking almost everywhere you go, and staying and eating at the monasteries you have come to visit, which certainly simplifies things. "Simple" is a key word here—both your accommodations and food (Athos is a vegetarian's paradise) will be very basic. Keep in mind that although most monasteries will not accept cash offered in direct payment for food and lodgings, you can always give a donation in the church.

As always when walking in Greece, keep the danger of fires in mind, and be sure to dispose of any matches or cigarettes with care—in summer 1998, fires raged through the pine forests here for several days.

And remember, many monasteries close (and lock) their gates during the midday siesta and virtually all close (and lock) their gates at sunset.

At present, there are 20 functioning monasteries on Mount Athos. Given the rough terrain, there's no way you can visit them all during a 4-day visit—thus we mention here just the five most important monasteries. Keep in mind that if you can't visit Athos, you can see most of these monasteries from the sea. Almost all were built close enough to the water to be able to get supplies ashore with ease.

The Great Lavra   The first (ca. A.D. 960) monastery founded on Athos and hence the foremost, the Great Lavra has the red-painted katholikon church characteristic of Athos's monasteries. Its 15th-century frescoes, especially those showing exuberant singers and dancers in the Chapel of Koukouzelissa, are delightful.

The Monastery of Vatopedi   Founded only a decade after the Great Lavra, Vatopedi's long outline with red-and-white tile-roofed buildings is clearly visible from the sea.

The Monastery of Iveron   Iveron, founded in the 10th century, looks from the sea like a medieval hilltown—only the hill is actually the monastery's solid foundation.

The Monastery of Chelandari   This monastery was founded in the 12th century by St. Sabbas of Serbia. Fortunately, Sabbas's father was the King of Serbia, which guaranteed a handsome endowment. Some scholars think that the lovely frescoes in the church here were done by the same painter who decorated the walls of Ayios Nikolaos Orfanos in Thessaloniki (see page 528).

The Monastery of Dionysiou   This 14th-century monastery seems to grow right out of a rock above the sea, and has dizzily overhanging balconies, braced by rather precarious-looking wood supports. Favored by the emperor Alexios III Komnenos, Dionysiou has a superb collection of manuscripts, and an icon said to be the oldest on Athos.

WHERE TO STAY IN OURANOPOLIS

Xenia. Ouranopolis, 63075 Macedonia. ☎ **0377/71-412.** Fax 0377/71-362. 120 units. MINIBAR TV TEL. Dr31,500 ($105). AE, DC, MC, V.

This sprawling beachside resort hotel less than 5 minutes outside Ouranopolis is the nicest place to stay here. The large, tile-floored rooms have balconies (ask for a room facing the sea), most have desks and good reading lamps, and all have excellent bathroom facilities. Facilities include several restaurants, plus fresh- and saltwater pools. It offers all the creature comforts you may have missed visiting Athos.

The Northeastern Aegean Islands

17

by Mark Meagher

Dispersed along the coast of Turkey, the four islands covered in this chapter—Samos, Hios, Lesvos, and Limnos—have benefited by their remoteness from the mainland and the other Aegean islands. While the character of much of Greece has come to be dominated in recent years by mass tourism, parts of these islands remain relatively undiscovered. The crowds here tend to be concentrated in a few over-populated resorts, leaving the vast interior (and much of the coast) open to exploration. Along the coastline you'll find some of the finest beaches in the Aegean, and within the interior richly forested valleys, precipitous mountain slopes, and exquisite mountain villages. These are agricultural islands, and the staples olives, grapes, and honey are grown in abundance, providing the basis for excellent food and wine.

The influence of Asia Minor is not as evident as one might expect given the proximity of these islands to the **Turkish coast.** What you will notice immediately is the sizable Greek military presence, and large areas of each island occupied by the military are strictly off-limits (a particular annoyance to hikers and mountain bikers). Even though this military presence is a sore point with the Turks, who regularly demand the demilitarization of Limnos and stage regular flyovers in defiance of Greek airspace, travel between Greece and Turkey remains unrestricted and relations between Greeks and Turks on a personal level seem to be mostly amicable. After all, many of the islands' older inhabitants were born in Asia Minor and repatriated during the massive population exchanges of 1923, and have preserved close ties to their homeland in what is now Turkey. Many travelers use the Northeastern Aegean islands as jumping-off points to Turkey: Samos is the closest island to Turkey (only 3km/1.9 miles at the closest point) with easy access to Ephesus, Lesvos is the closest to Ancient Troy, and Limnos to Istanbul.

STRATEGIES FOR SEEING THE ISLANDS Since the distances between islands are large, island-hopping is costly and time-consuming. Add the fact that each island is quite large, and it becomes clear that you're best off choosing one or two islands to explore in depth, rather than attempting a grand tour. **Olympic Airlines'** flights between the islands are inexpensive, frequent, and fast; if you do choose to travel by **ferry,** you'll find that the departure times are more reasonable for travel from north to south, whereas traveling in the

The Northeastern Aegean Islands

BULGARIA

Kavala

Limenas (Thassos)
Makriammos
Limenaria Panayia
THASSOS

Alexandroupolis

TURKEY

Sea of
Marmara

Hora SAMOTHRAKI
Kamariotissa Mt. Fengari

Gallipoli

Aegean

Sea

GÖKÇEADA

Canakkale

TURKEY

Kornos
Mirina
Skandali
LIMNOS

Ayvalik

Pergamon

Molivos
(Mithimna)
LESVOS (Mitilini)
Eressos Petra
Skala Eressos Mandamados
Ayiassos Mitilini
Plomari

SKYROS

PSARA

Kardamila INOUSSES
Hios Town
HIOS
Mesta Piryi

Cesme

Izmir

Ephesus
Kokkari Kuşadasi
Karlovassi Vathi
Mitilini
SAMOS
Pithagorio Psili
Ammos

IKARIA

GREECE

Athens

THE NORTHEASTERN
AEGEAN ISLANDS

opposite direction usually involves departures in the middle of the night. The islands are too large and the roads too rough for mopeds to be a safe option; since the bus routes and schedules are highly restricting, you'll find that if you want to get around, it's necessary to rent a car.

1 Samos

322km (174 nautical miles) NE of Piraeus

The most mountainous and densely forested of the Northeastern Aegean isles, Samos appears wild and mysterious as you approach its north coast by plane or ferry. The abrupt slopes of hills plunging to the sea are jagged with cypresses, and craggy peaks hide among the clouds.

Unfortunately, Samos has given itself over in recent years to a highly impersonal form of mass tourism. This is mostly confined to the eastern coastal resorts—Vathi, Pithagorio, and Kokkari—which have all developed a generic waterfront of cafes, souvenir shops, and big hotels. The most interesting and beautiful villages are found in the rugged splendor of the island's interior. Difficult terrain and a remote location made these villages an apt refuge from pirates in medieval times; in this age, the same qualities have spared them from tourism's worst excesses.

Although Samos has several fine archaeological sites, the island is most notable for its excellent beaches and abundant opportunities for hiking, cycling, and windsurfing. Also, Samos is the best crossover point for those who want to visit **Ephesus,** one of the most important archaeological sites in Asia Minor.

GETTING THERE   Although ferries connect Piraeus to Samos, it's a long trip. The best way to get there is to fly.

By Plane   Olympic Airways has three flights daily (five daily in summer) between Athens and Samos. The **Olympic office** (☎ **0473/25-065**) in Vathi is at the corner of Kanari and Smirnis streets, 1 block from the bus station. From the airport, you can take a taxi to Vathi (Dr3,000/$10) or Pithagorio (Dr1,200/$4), then catch a public bus to other parts of the islands.

By Boat   The principal port of Samos is at **Vathi,** also called Samos; the other two ports are **Karlovassi** and **Pithagorio.** Ferries from the Cyclades usually stop at both Vathi and Karlovassi, although the order in which these stops are made depends on local wind conditions. There are daily boats (sometimes two) from Piraeus via Ikaria to Karlovassi and Vathi. Three to four ferries per week travel the Siros-Mikonos-Vathi route; there are also three to four boats to Paros from Vathi, and via Paros to Naxos, Ios, and Santorini. Boats to Hios and Lesvos from Vathi travel two times per week; there is also a once-weekly Rhodes-Vathi-Lesvos-Thessaloniki run. If you want to travel one-way to Turkey, there are daily Turkish ferries; a visa is required for all American, British, and Irish citizens who intend to stay for more than 1 day—be sure to inquire in advance about current visa regulations with a local travel agency. For more information on visas, see "A Side Trip to Turkey: Kusadasi & Ephesus," below. Call the **port authority** in Piraeus (☎ **01/451-1310**), Vathi (☎ **0273/27-318**), Pithagorio (☎ **0273/61-225**), or Karlovassi (☎ **0273/32-343**) for schedule information.

VATHI, KARLOVASSI & THE NORTHERN COAST

Vathi on the northeast coast and Karlovassi to the northwest are the two principal ports of Samos, and the island's largest towns. Neither is particularly exciting, and we recommend both as convenient bases rather than as destinations in themselves.

Vathi is a tired resort town, beautifully situated in a fine natural harbor. Recent development has resulted in a bland harbor front, but the old town—**Ano Vathi**—rises to the hilltops in steep narrow streets that hide a few small tavernas and cafes. Karlovassi is more interesting as a town, and is adjacent to several of the best beaches on the island, but it's spread out and offers fewer amenities than Vathi. Most tourist facilities are clustered along the water at the west end of town, forming a tiny beach resort with several hotels, restaurants, grocery stores, and souvenir shops. The old town hovers above the lower town on the slopes of a near-vertical pillar of rock; there's a cafe and a taverna here, and the lovely small chapel of Ayia Triada at the summit of the rock. Along the seafront to the east is the former industrial quarter, with rows of abandoned stone warehouses once used by a flourishing leather industry.

The **north coast** of the island is wild and steep, with high mountains rising abruptly from the water's edge. One of the most interesting areas to explore is the **Platanakia** region, known for its rushing streams, lushly foliated valleys, and picturesque mountain villages. There is also a sequence of excellent **beaches** between Kokkari and Karlovassi, with the two finest beaches on the island—✪ **Micro Seitani** and ✪ **Megalo Seitani**—a short boat excursion or somewhat long hike to the west of Karlovassi.

ESSENTIALS

VISITOR INFORMATION The **Greek National Tourist Organization (EOT)** has an office in Vathi (☎ **0273/28-582**), a half block in from the port, one lane toward the ferry pier from the main square; open Monday through Friday from 8am to 3pm, with weekend hours in high season. The EOT is staffed by local people who might be helpful if you ask nicely; they won't make room reservations by phone, but will help you find accommodations once you're at their office.

I.T.S.A. Travel (☎ **0273/23-605;** fax 0273/27-955), the agency nearest the port in Vathi, is the best and friendliest; they can help you make travel arrangements, including excursions to Turkey, find accommodations, change money at good rates, and store your luggage for free.

GETTING AROUND By Bus There's good public bus service on Samos throughout the year, with significantly expanded summer schedules. The **Vathi bus terminal** (☎ **0273/27-262**) is a block inland from the south end of the port on Odos Kanari. The bus makes the 20-minute trip between Vathi and Pithagorio frequently. Buses also travel to Kokkari, the inland village of Mitilini, Pirgos, Marathokambos, Votsalakia beach, and Karlovassi. Call for schedules.

By Boat From Karlovassi there are daily excursion boats to Megalo Seitani, the best fine-sand beach on the island. (See "Beaches," below.)

By Car & Moped We recommend **Aramis Rent a Motorbike-Car,** at the pier in Vathi (☎ **0273/23-253**), for the best prices and selection. Their least expensive car is about Dr11,000 ($37), including full insurance and 100 free kilometers; each kilometer over 100 is Dr50 (15¢). Mopeds go for about Dr3,000 to Dr6,000 ($10 to $20) a day. There are plenty of other agencies, so shop around.

By Taxi The principal taxi stand in Vathi is on Plateia Pithagora, facing the paralia. The fare from Vathi to Pithagorio is Dr2,500 ($8). To book by phone, call ☎ **0273/28-404** in Vathi, **0273/33-300** in Karlovassi.

FAST FACTS The **banks** in Vathi are on the paralia in the vicinity of Plateia Pithagora, and are open Monday through Thursday from 8am to 2pm, Friday from 8am to 1:30pm; most have ATMs. Travel agents change money at a less favorable rate, but stay open daily from 8am to 10pm. The island's **hospital** (☎ **0273/27-407** or

Vathi

ACCOMMODATIONS
Hotel Paradise **6**
Ionia Maris **1**
Pension Avli **3**
Pythagoras Hotel **2**

DINING
Christos Taverna **4**
Ta Kotopoula **5**

0273/27-426) is in Vathi. The **post office** (☎ **0273/27-304**) is on the same street as the Olympic Airways office, 1 block further in from the paralia, and 2 blocks from the bus station. The **telephone office (OTE)** is just down the street from the Olympic Airways office, in the direction of the archaeological museum (☎ **0273/28-499**). The **tourist police** (☎ **0273/81-000**) are on the paralia, by the turn into the bus station.

ATTRACTIONS

Archaeological Museum. Vathi. ☎ **0273/27-469.** Admission Dr800 ($2.70). Tues–Sun 8:30am–3pm.

This fine museum is housed in two buildings at the south end of the harbor, near the post office. The newest building houses sculpture—being much in demand, the island's best sculptors traveled all over the Hellenistic world to create their art. The most remarkable work is a massive kouros (statue of a boy), which stands a full 5 meters tall. Also impressive is the large and various collection of bronze votives found at the Heraion, illustrating its prestige in the ancient world by their value and extent.

Moni Vronta. Vourliotes. No phone. Free admission. Daily 8am–5pm. 23km (14½ miles) west of Vathi.

The 15th-century fortified monastery of Moni Vronta is on a high mountain overlooking the sea and the lovely hilltop village of Vourliotes. *Vrontiani* means "thunder on Mount Lazarus," a name resonant with the majesty of this mountain setting. There is only one monk left in the monastery, and 10 soldiers who operate a nearby surveillance post. If the gate is locked when you arrive, try knocking and one of the soldiers may be around to let you in. Ask to see the *speleo,* or cave, an old chapel in the thickness of the outer wall containing a collection of ancient objects, some from the time of the monastery's founding. To get there, continue driving uphill about 2 kilometers (1.2 miles) past Vourliotes.

TWO HILL TOWNS ON THE RUGGED NORTH COAST

Amidst the densely wooded valleys, cascading streams, and terraced slopes of Samos's north coast, many hidden villages were settled as an attempt to evade the pirates who repeatedly ravaged all settlements visible from the sea. When the threat of pirates disappeared, many of these villages were gradually abandoned in favor of their more convenient coastal counterparts. Two of the most picturesque of the surviving hill towns in this region are Manolates and Vourliotes, about 20 kilometers (12½ miles) west of Vathi.

Manolates is a 4-kilometer (2½-mile) drive uphill from the coast road. Until recently inaccessible by car, this village has seen a massive increase in tourism since the paved road was built, but it still maintains much of its character, with steep, narrow, cobblestone streets lined by stucco homes with red-tile roofs. There are several tavernas, numerous shops, and two kafenions (where the locals go).

Vourliotes was settled largely by repatriated Greeks from the town of Vourla in Turkey. It's the largest producer of wine in the region, and the local wine is among the best on the island. Walk from the parking lot at the Moni Vronta turnoff to the charming central square. Try **Manolis Taverna** (☎ 0273/93-290), on the left as you enter the square, which has good *revidokeftedes,* a delicious local dish made with chickpea flour and cheese. The proprietress, Elena Glavara, is originally from Mexico and makes a fine chili con carne. Also on the square, across from Manolis, is a small market whose displays seem not to have changed in the past 50 years. Be sure to visit the monastery of **Moni Vronta** (also known as Vrontiani), just 2 kilometers (1.2 miles) above the town (see description above).

The easiest way to visit these towns is by car; the island buses are an option if you don't mind the steep 4-kilometer (2½-mile) climb from the coast road to either of the villages. There are abundant footpaths connecting Manolates and Vourliotes with the neighboring villages, so this is an excellent place for walking—ask locally for particular routes. A great source of information for this region is **Ambelos Tours** (☎ 0273/94-136; fax 0273/94-114; e-mail: mfolas@athena.math.aegean.gr) in Ayios Konstandinos, operated by the friendly and extremely knowledgeable Mihailis Folas. You can also inquire here about several traditional houses for rent in the local villages.

A SIDE TRIP TO TURKEY: KUSADASI & EPHESUS

In high season there are two boats a day between Vathi and Kusadasi, Turkey, a popular, well-developed resort 20 minutes from the magnificent archaeological site at Ephesus; these boats also make a stop at Pithagorio. A round-trip ticket to Kusadasi runs Dr14,000 ($47), while an excursion ticket (including a guided tour of Ephesus and a same-day return) costs Dr20,000 ($67). Boats depart from both Vathi and Pithagorio. Whether you're traveling to Turkey with a one-way or a round-trip ticket, you'll need to investigate visa requirements if you're not returning the same day. Visas are granted without difficulty, but there is a charge of $45 for Americans, £5 for Irish and British citizens; Canadians, Australians, and New Zealanders don't currently need a visa. Many travel agencies sell tickets to Turkey and are able to issue visas as well; inquire at least 1 day in advance of travel, as you may need to leave your passport overnight for the visa to be processed.

BEACHES

The closest decent beach to Vathi is **Gagou,** 2 kilometers (1.2 miles) north of the pier. The best beaches on Samos are found along the north coast, the most beautiful and rugged part of the island. The busy seaside resort of **Kokkari,** 10 kilometers (6.2 miles) west of Vathi, has several beaches in rock coves as well as the crowded stretch of sand running parallel to the town's main road; to find the smaller cove beaches, head seaward from the main square. Just west of Kokkari is **Tsamadou,** a short walk down from the coast road, which offers sufficient seclusion for nudism at one end. Continue west past Karlovassi to find **Potami,** an excellent long pebble-and-sand beach with road access.

The two best beaches on the island, ✪ **Micro Seitani** and ✪ **Megalo Seitani,** are accessible only on foot or by boat; boat excursions depart daily from the pier in Karlovassi. To get here on foot, continue past the parking lot for the beach at Potami on a dirt road; the walking time to the first beach is about 45 minutes. You'll pass two obvious right turns, both of which lead to rocky coves good for sunning and swimming. The third right is marked by a cairn, and leads through a small clearing to a well-worn path; if you begin to climb steeply away from the sea on the first road, you've missed this turn. The path will bring you in a few minutes to Micro Seitani, a glorious small pebble beach in a rocky cove. On the far side of the beach, a ladder scales the cliff, leading to the continuation of the trail which will take you after an additional hour of walking to Megalo Seitani, as incredible a stretch of sea sand as any in the Aegean. Both beaches are predominantly nudist.

OUTDOOR PURSUITS

BICYCLING   There are many dirt roads and trails on Samos that are perfect for mountain biking. The only obstacles are the size of the island, which limits the number of routes available for day trips, and the fact that much of the backcountry is off-limits due to Greek military operations. Bike rentals and guided mountain-bike tours are available at **Giannis Rent-A-Bike** (☎ **0273/23-756**), on the paralia near the ferry pier, open daily from 8am to 9pm. The bikes are very high quality— aluminum frames with front or full suspension and good components—and you can request extras like helmets and toe clips. An aluminum-frame bike with front suspension is Dr3,000 ($10) per day; the full-suspension bike is Dr4,000 ($13). A guided ride is Dr4,000 ($13), including rental of a front-suspension bike.

WALKING   Some of the best walking on the island is in and around the Platanakia region of Samos's north coast, where well marked trails connect several lovely hilltop villages—Manolates and Vourliotes (see above) are among the villages on this network of trails. There is also a trail from Manolates to the summit of Mount Ambelos, the second-highest peak on Samos at 1,153 meters (3,780 ft.); the round-trip time for this demanding walk is about 5 hours. For information on walking in the Platanakia region, contact Mihailis Folas of **Ambelos Tours** (☎ **0273/94-136;** fax 0273/94-114; e-mail: mfolas@athena.math.aegean.gr) in Ayios Konstandinos.

WINDSURFING   The **Samos F2 Surfcenter** (☎ **0273/92-382;** fax 0273/92-501) on Kokkari Beach, next to Hotel Olympia Beach, rents windsurfing equipment and offers instruction at all levels. A 1-hour rental is Dr3,500 ($12), and a 1-day rental Dr8,500 ($28); this includes all equipment. A 1-week class (a total of 5 hr. on the water) is Dr20,000 ($67). The center is open daily from 10:30am to 7pm. Winds tend to be strong on this beach, which is appealing to experienced surfers but can be difficult for beginners.

WHERE TO STAY
Vathi
Hotel Paradise. Odos Kanari 21, Vathi, 83100 Samos. ☎ **0273/23-911.** Fax 0273/28-754. 47 units. A/C TEL. Dr13,000 ($43) double. Rates include breakfast. EURO, V.

Despite a central location just off the paralia and a block away from the bus station, the walled garden and pool terrace here seem a world away from the crowds and dust of Vathi. Drinks and simple Greek food are served all day at the poolside bar—the pool invites lingering, with abundant lounge chairs and umbrellas for sunning and shaded tables for a meal or drinks. All guest rooms have balconies, although the views aren't stellar; bathrooms are not large, but they do have full tubs.

Ionia Maris. Gagou Beach, Vathi, 83100 Samos. ☎ **0273/28-428** or 0273/28-429. Fax 0273/23-108. 56 units. A/C TV TEL. Dr23,000 ($77) double. Rates include breakfast. EURO, MC.

The best beachfront hotel in Vathi, the Ionia Maris has a good location and facilities but mediocre rooms. Gagou is a pleasant pebble beach 2 kilometers (1.2 miles) north of Vathi, with a small taverna; the hotel is 50 meters back from the water. There is a large pool terrace with two pools (one for children), a snack bar, and abundant umbrellas. A buffet breakfast and dinner are served daily, and full-board rates are available. The simple rooms are moderate in size, with tile floors and small balconies— units on the pool side of the hotel have an oblique view toward the sea. Two rooms are wheelchair accessible.

Pension Avli. Odos Likourgou, Vathi, 83100 Samos. ☎ **0273/22-939.** 10 units. Dr7,000 ($23) double. No credit cards. Turn in from the paralia at the Agrotiki Trapeza (just down from the Aeolis Hotel), turn left on the town's market street, and you'll see the Avli's unassuming sign directly ahead.

Although you won't find any luxuries here, you will discover the most charming and romantic pension on the island. Abundant bougainvillea fills the arcaded courtyard of this 18th-century convent, transformed into a simple pension in the 1970s. The 10 rooms open to guests occupy half the building; 10 more units are due for renovation, and may be available in the near future. The rooms are spartan, with minimal furnishings and bare walls; bathrooms are tiny and encased completely in a shell of bright orange plastic, making a shower a surreal experience.

Pythagoras Hotel. Odos Kalami, Vathi, 83100 Samos. ☎ **0273/28-422.** Fax 0273/27-955. 17 units. Dr8,000 ($27) double. MC, V. On the coast road, 600m north of the pier.

Extremely plain but comfortable, this older family hotel is on a hill overlooking Vathi Bay. Guest rooms on the side of the road can be very noisy, but the seaside units have only the sound of the surf and birds singing to contend with. Rooms and bathrooms are small, clean, and minimally furnished. The neighborhood cafe downstairs serves a good, inexpensive breakfast, and the view from the back terrace is superb.

Ayios Konstandinos
This coastal town in the heart of the Platanakia region is a great base for touring the north coast of Samos.

✪ Daphne Hotel. Ayios Konstandinos, 83200 Samos. ☎ **0271/94-003** or 0273/94-493. Fax 0273/94-594. 35 units. A/C TEL. Dr15,000 ($50) double. Rates include breakfast. V. Take the first right after turning onto the Manolates road, 19km (12 miles) from Vathi.

The Daphne is the finest small hotel on the island, with a beautiful location and amenities that you'd expect from a hotel twice the size. Artfully incised into the steep hillside in a series of terraces, the hotel commands a fine view of the stream valley leading to Manolates and a wide sweep of sea. The dining room has a massive picture window and an outdoor terrace that steps down to a large pool and an exquisite view. All rooms are moderate in size and have balconies with the same great view; all bathrooms have both shower and tub. This is a good location for walkers, with many trails nearby to Manolates and other hill towns of the Platanakia region. Make your reservations well in advance, as this hotel is filled through much of the summer by European tour groups. There is free transportation to and from the airport or the port; due to the remote location, you'll probably need a car during your stay here.

Karlovassi

✪ **Samaina Inn Hotel.** Karlovassi, 83200 Samos. ☎ **0273/35-445** or 0273/35-449. Fax 0273/34-471. 130 units. A/C MINIBAR TEL. Dr20,000 ($67) double. Rates include breakfast. MC, V.

The new Samaina Inn Hotel is built around a sequence of garden courtyards and terraces, with a large pool and separate children's pool at the center. It's extremely well managed, and our favorite of the island's big hotels. The best rooms (at the front of the building) face the sea and the town beach; others face the pool courtyard or the hills behind the hotel. Guest rooms are spacious, with marble floors and balconies; bathrooms all have tubs. There are several maisonettes: double rooms with an upstairs bedroom, many with wooden peaked ceilings and a particularly fine sea view. Other facilities include a large conference room, art gallery, jewelry shop, hair salon, tennis court, and small gym.

WHERE TO DINE
Vathi

The food in Vathi is mostly tourist-quality and mediocre; the best restaurants are to be found in the small towns. The local wines on Samos can be excellent. (As Byron exclaimed, "Fill high the bowl with Samian wine!") A preferred wine is the dry white called Samaina. There's also a delicious relatively dry rose called Fokianos. The Greeks like sweet wines, with names like Nectar, Dux, and Anthemis. Almost any restaurant on the island will serve one or all of these wines.

Christos Taverna. Plateia Ayiou Nikolaou. ☎ **0273/24-792.** Main courses Dr700–Dr2,200 ($2.35–$7). No credit cards. Daily 11am–11pm. GREEK.

This simple little taverna, under a covered alleyway decorated with odd antiques, is left off Plateia Pithagora as you come up from the port. The food is simply prepared and presented; it comes in generous portions and is remarkably good. Try the *revidokeftedes,* a Samian specialty made with cheese fried in a chickpea batter.

Ta Kotopoula. Vathi. ☎ **0273/28-415.** Main courses Dr800–Dr2,100 ($2.70–$7). No credit cards. Daily 11am–11pm. GREEK.

Ta Kotopoula is on the outskirts of Vathi, somewhat hard to find but worth the trouble. From the south end of the harbor, walk inland past the Olympic Airways office and the post office, bearing right with the road as it climbs toward Ano Vathi. Where the road splits around a large tree, about 700 meters from the harbor, you'll see the vine-sheltered terrace of this taverna on the left. The food is basic taverna fare, but the ingredients are exceptionally fresh. Local wine is available by the carafe.

Ayios Nikolaos

✪ **Psarades.** Ayios Nikolaos. No phone. Main courses Dr800–Dr4,000 ($2.70–$13). No credit cards. Daily 8am–midnight. Drive 6km (3.7 miles) east from Karlovassi, turning left at the sign for Ayios Nikolaos, and descend the treacherously narrow road to the sea. SEAFOOD.

This restaurant is on the water, and the outside terrace overlooks tide pools and a long stretch of coast to the west—it's a highly romantic setting, and a fabulous place to watch the sunset. The fish, simply prepared and cooked on a wood fire, is consistently excellent. The tastes are strong and straightforward, like the tzatziki pungent with garlic, or the melitzanosalata redolent with the smoky aroma of roasted eggplant.

Ayios Konstandinos

Platanakia Paradisos. Ayios Konstandinos. ☎ **0273/94-208.** Main courses Dr800–Dr3,000 ($2.70–$10). No credit cards. Daily 3–11pm. GREEK.

Paradisos is a large garden taverna located at the Manolates turnoff from the coast highway; it has been in the Folas family for nearly 30 years, and has been operating as a taverna for more than 100 years. Mr. Folas, the owner, worked in vineyards many years and makes his own wine from the excellent Samian grapes. Mrs. Folas's tiropita (freshly baked after 7pm) is made from local goat cheese and butter; it's wrapped in a flaky pastry. Live traditional music is performed Wednesday and Saturday nights in the summer.

VATHI AFTER DARK

The hottest disco in Vathi is **Metropolis,** behind the Paradise Hotel. For bouzouki, there's **Zorba's,** out of town on the road to Mitilini. There are several bars of various kinds on the lanes just off the port. **Number Nine,** at Kephalopoulou 9, beyond the jetty on the right, is one of the oldest and best known.

PITHAGORIO & THE SOUTHERN COAST

Pithagorio, south across the island from Vathi, is a charming but overcrowded seaside resort built on the site of an ancient village and harbor. Although this is a convenient base for touring the southern half of Samos, the town exists primarily for the tour groups that pack its streets throughout the summer. We recommend staying here for a day or two while you explore the nearby historic sites, then moving on to the more interesting and authentic villages of the north coast.

ESSENTIALS

GETTING THERE   By Plane   The Samos airport is just 5 kilometers (3.1 miles) from Pithagorio; from the airport, you can take a taxi for Dr1,200 ($4).

By Boat   Ferries from the Cyclades typically don't stop at Pithagorio, so you'll need to take a taxi or bus from Vathi. There is summer hydrofoil service between Pithagorio and Patmos, departing four times per week. Check the most current ferry schedules with the **Pithagorio Port Authority** (☎ 0273/61-225).

By Bus   The trip between Vathi and Pithagorio takes 20 minutes, and buses depart frequently. Call the **Vathi bus terminal** (☎ 0273/27-262) for current schedules.

VISITOR INFORMATION   The **Pithagorio Municipal Tourist Office** (☎ 0273/61-389 or 0273/62-274) is on the main street, Odos Likourgou Logotheti, 1 block up from the paralia; open daily from 8am to 10pm. They may help you find a room if you ask very, *very* nicely.

GETTING AROUND   By Bus   The Pithagorio **bus terminal** is in the center of town, at the corner of Odos Polykrates (the road to Vathi) and Likourgou Logotheti. The bus makes the 20-minute trip between Vathi and Pithagorio frequently. There are also four buses daily from Pithagorio to Ireon (near the Heraion archaeological site).

By Boat   Summertime **excursion boats** from the Pithagorio harbor go to **Psili Ammos beach** (on the east end of the island) daily, and to the island of **Ikaria** three times weekly. There is a popular day cruise to **Samiopoula,** a small island with a taverna and a long sandy beach.

By Car & Moped   Aramis Rent a Motorbike-Car has a branch near the bus station in Pithagorio (☎ **0273/62-267**); it often has the best prices, but shop around.

By Taxi   The taxi stand is on the main street, Likourgou Logotheti, where it meets the harbor. The fare from Vathi to Pithagorio is Dr2,500 ($8). To book by phone, call ☎ **0273/61-450.**

FAST FACTS   The **National Bank** (☎ **0273/61-234**), opposite the bus stop, has an ATM. A small **clinic** is on Plateia Irinis, next to the town hall, 1 block in from the beach near the port police (☎ **0273/61-111**). Alex Stavrides runs a self-service **laundry** off the main street on the road to the old basilica, Metamorphosis Sotiros; open daily from 9am to 9pm, in summer until 11pm. The **post office** is 4 blocks up from the paralia on the main street. The **telephone office (OTE)** is on the paralia near the pier (☎ **0273/61-399**). The **tourist police** (☎ **0273/61-100**) are on the main street.

ATTRACTIONS

Efpalinion Tunnel. Pithagorio. ☎ **0273/61-400.** Admission Dr500 ($1.70) adults, Dr300 ($1) students and seniors. Tues–Sun 8:15am–1:30pm. Located 3km (1.9 miles) northwest of Pithagorio, signposted off the main road to Vathi.

One of the most impressive engineering accomplishments of the ancient world, this 1,000-meter tunnel through the mountain above Pithagorio was excavated to transport water from mountain streams to ancient Vathi. The great architect Efpalinos directed two teams of workers digging from each side, and after nearly 15 years they met within a few meters of each other. If you can muster the courage to squeeze through the first 20 meters—the tunnel is a mere sliver in the rock for this distance— you'll see that it soon widens considerably, and you can comfortably walk another 100 meters into the mountain. Even though there is a generator that supposedly starts up in the (likely) event of a power outage, you might be more comfortable carrying a flashlight.

Heraion. Ireon. Call the Archaeological Museum in Vathi at ☎ **0273/27-469.** Admission Dr800 ($2.70) adults, Dr400 ($1.35) students and seniors. Tues–Sun 8:30am–3pm. Located 9km (5.6 miles) southwest of Pithagorio, signposted off the road to Ireon.

All that survives of the largest of all Greek temples is its massive foundation, a lone reconstructed column, and some copies of the original statuary. The temple was originally surrounded by a forest of columns, one of its most distinctive and original features. In fact, rival Ionian cities were so impressed that they rebuilt many of their ancient temples in similar style. The Temple of Artemis in nearby Ephesus is a direct imitation of the great Samian Structure. The Heraion was rebuilt and greatly expanded under Polycrates; it was damaged during numerous invasions and finally destroyed by a series of earthquakes.

BEACHES

In Pithagorio, the local beach stretches from Logotheti Castle at the west side of town several kilometers to Potokaki and the airport. Expect this beach to be packed throughout the summer. Excursion boats depart daily in the summer for **Psili Ammos,** 5 kilometers (3.1 miles) to the east. On the south coast of the island, the most popular beaches are on Marathokambos Bay. The once-tiny village of **Ormos Marathokambos** has several tavernas and a mushrooming number of hotels and pensions; its rock-and-pebble beach is long and narrow, with windsurfing an option.

A couple of kilometers further west of Ormos Marathokambos is **Votsalakia,** a somewhat nicer beach. Boat excursions leave daily from Pithagorio for **Samiopoula,** an island off the south coast with two good beaches.

WHERE TO STAY

Rooms in Pithagorio are quickly filled by tour groups, so don't count on finding a place here if you haven't booked well in advance.

George Sandalis Hotel. Pithagorio, 83103 Samos. ☎/fax **0273/61-691.** 13 units. Dr12,000 ($40) double. No credit cards. Head north on Odos Polykrates (the road to Vathi), and you'll see the hotel on your left, about 100 meters from the bus station.

Above Pithagorio, this homey establishment has a front garden bursting with colorful blossoms. The tastefully decorated rooms all have balconies with French doors. In back, the rooms face quiet hills and another flower garden, while the front rooms face a busy street and can be noisy. The friendly Sandalises are gracious hosts; they spent many years in Chicago and speak very good English.

Hotel Labito. Pithagorio, 83103 Samos. ☎ **0273/61-086.** Fax 0273/61-085. 22 units. A/C TEL. Dr17,325 ($58) double. Rates include breakfast. No credit cards.

Despite a promising facade, the Hotel Labito (and its twin, the Labito II across the street) tends toward the impersonal and plain. Still, it's tolerable if you value location and convenience over character. Set just two lanes behind the port, it does have a quiet and convenient location. Downstairs are the marble lobby and simply decorated breakfast and bar areas. Rooms are very basic; most have balconies facing the street.

WHERE TO DINE

There are few places to recommend in Pithagorio: the food is mostly mediocre to poor, and prices are higher than what you'd pay in Vathi.

Esperides Restaurant. Pithagorio. ☎ **0273/61-767.** Reservations recommended in summer. Main courses Dr1,200–Dr4,000 ($4–$13). No credit cards. Daily 6pm–midnight. INTERNATIONAL.

This pleasant walled garden is a few blocks inland from the port, and west of the main street. There are uniformed waiters and a dressier crowd here. The continental and Greek dishes are well presented and will appeal to a wide variety of palates. We resented the frozen french fries served with the tasty baked chicken, but the meats and vegetables were fresh.

I Varka. Paralia, Pithagorio. No phone. Main courses Dr1,500–Dr3,500 ($5–$14). EURO, MC. V. Daily noon–midnight. Closed Nov–Apr. SEAFOOD.

This ouzeri/taverna is in a garden of salt pines at the south end of the port. Delicious fresh fish, grilled meats, and a surprising variety of mezedes (appetizers) are produced in the small kitchen, built within a dry-docked fishing boat. The grilled octopus, strung up on a line to dry, and the pink barbounia or clear gray mullet, all cooked to perfection over a charcoal grill, are the true standouts of a meal here.

2 Hios (Chios)

283km (153 nautical miles) NE of Piraeus

"Craggy Hios," as Homer dubbed it, remains very much unspoiled—and that's why we recommend it. The black-pebble beaches on the southeast coast of the island are famous and not neglected, but there are white-sand beaches on the west coast that see only a few hundred people in a year. The majestic mountain setting of **Nea Moni,** an

11th-century Byzantine monastery in the center of the island, and the extraordinary mosaics of its chapel make for a unforgettable visit. The **mastic villages** in the south of the island are among the finest medieval towns in Greece, and the crop for which they are named (a tree resin used in chewing gum, paints, and perfumes) is grown nowhere else in the world.

Hios town is likely to be your first glimpse of the island, and it isn't a pretty sight. With its unappealing modern architecture and generic cafes, the harbor front is a disaster. Thankfully, there are a few pockets of the original town further inland which have survived earthquakes, wars, and neglect. The Kastro, the mosque on the main square, the mansions of Kampos, and the occasional grand gateway (often leading nowhere) are among the only signs of a more prosperous and architecturally harmonious past.

ESSENTIALS

GETTING THERE   By Plane   Olympic Airways has flights four times a day between Athens and Hios. There is connection twice a week with Lesvos (Mitilini) and Thessaloniki. The **Olympic office** in Hios town is in the middle of the harbor front (☎ 0271/24-515). To contact the **airport,** call ☎ 0271/23-998. If you arrive by plane, count on taking a cab into town for about Dr1,500 ($5) for the 7-kilometer (4.3-mile) ride.

By Boat   One car ferry leaves daily for Piraeus; there's also daily connection with Lesvos. There is once-a-week service to Thessaloniki, Kavala, and the Dodecanese. Excursion boats service Hios from Pithagorio on Samos three times a week (summer only). Check with the **Hios Port Authority** (☎ 0271/44-432) for current schedules and prices.

VISITOR INFORMATION   The **Tourist Information Office** on Odos Kanari 18 (☎ 0271/44-389) was closed for renovations in 1998, but should be open again by 1999; it's located on the second street from the north end of the harbor, between the harbor and the Central (Plastira) Square. It's open daily in summer from 7am to 2:30pm and 6:30 to 9pm. The **tourist police** (☎ 0271/44-428) are headquartered on Odos Neorion.

Another mine of information is **Hios Tours** (☎ 0271/29-444; fax 0271/21-333), Leoforos Egeou 84, on the harbor front. The office is open Monday through Saturday from 8:30am to 1:30pm and 5:30 to 8:30pm; it will assist with a room search, often at a discount off the published rate. Hios Tours or the tourist office will change money after the port-side banks' normal hours.

The free *Hios Summertime* magazine has a lot of useful information, as well as maps of the city. You can get abundant information off the Web by pointing your browser at **www.chios.com.**

GETTING AROUND   By Bus   All buses servicing the island leave from Hios town. The **blue buses,** which leave from the blue bus station, on the north side of the Central Park, serve local destinations. The **green long-distance buses (KTEL)** leave from the green bus station, a block south of the Central Park, near the main taxi stand. There are four buses a day to Mesta, eight a day to Piryi, five to Kardamila, but only two buses a week to Volissos and to Nea Moni.

By Car   Hios is a large island and fun to explore, so a car is highly recommended. We suggest **John Vassilakis Rent-A-Car** (☎/fax 0271/29-300), at Odos Evgenias Handri 3 (the same street as the Hotel Kyma) in Hios, or at the branch office in **Megas Limionas** (☎ 0271/31-728), about 10 kilometers (6.2 miles) south of Hios town. There's no extra charge for airport pickup.

By Taxi   Taxis are easily found at the port, though the taxi station is beyond the OTE, on the northeast corner of the central square. You can call ☎ **0271/26-379** for a cab. Fares from Hios town run about Dr4,500 ($15) to Piryi, Dr5,500 ($18) to Mesta, and Dr5,000 ($17) round-trip to Nea Moni.

By Moped   Hios is too large, and the hills too big, for mopeds—if you don't have the license to rent a genuine motorbike, go with a car.

FAST FACTS   The **Commercial Bank** (Emboriki Trapeza) and **Ergo Bank,** both at the north end of the harbor, near the corner of Odos Kanari, have ATMs; both are open Monday through Thursday from 8am to 2pm, Friday from 8am to 1:30pm. The English-speaking **dentist** Dr. Freeke (☎ **0271/27-266**) is highly recommended. The **hospital** is 7 kilometers (4.3 miles) from the center of Hios town (☎ **0271/44-306**). **Internet access** is available through Chios Compulink, Odos Venizelou 31, near Plastira Square (☎ **0271/43-894;** e-mail: drepi@compulink.gr); the rate is Dr1,000 ($3.35) per hour. There's a full-service **laundromat** just around the corner from the post office, on Odos Psichari (☎ **0271/44-801**). The **post office** is at the corner of Odos Omirou and Odos Rodokanaki (☎ **0271/44-350**). The **telephone office (OTE)** is across the street from the tourist office, on Odos Kanari (☎ **131**). The **tourist police** are headquartered at the northernmost tip of the harbor, at Odos Neorion 35 (☎ **0271/44-427**).

ATTRACTIONS

Argenti Museum and Koraï Library. Odos Koraï, Hios town. ☎ **0271/44-246.** Museum admission Dr400 ($1.35); free admission to library. Both open Mon–Thurs 8am–2pm; Fri 8am–2pm and 5–7:30pm; Sat 8am–12:30pm.

Philip Argenti is the great historian of Hios, a local aristocrat who devoted his life and savings to the recording of island history, costumes, customs, and architecture. The museum consists largely of his personal collection of folk art, costumes, and implements, supplemented with a gallery of family portraits and copies of Eugene Delacroix's *Massacre of Hios,* a masterpiece depicting the Turkish massacre of the local population in 1822. The entrance lobby has numerous old maps of the island on display. The library is excellent, with much of its collection in English and French. Those who have any interest in local architecture should ask to see the collection of drawings made by Dimitris Pikionis (a renowned 20th-century Greek architect) of the Kampos mansions and village houses—the drawings are beautiful, and have yet to be published.

✪ **Nea Moni.** Hios. No phone. Free admission to monastery grounds and katholikon; museum admission Dr500 ($1.70) adults, Dr300 ($1) students and seniors. Monastery grounds and katholikon, daily 8am–1pm and 4–8pm; museum, Tues–Sun 8am–1pm. Located 17km (10½ miles) west of Hios town.

The 11th-century monastery of Nea Moni is one of the great architectural and artistic treasures of Greece. The monastery is in a spectacular setting high in the mountains overlooking Hios town. Its grounds are extensive—this monastery was once home to 1,000 monks—but the present population has dwindled to two monks and a single elderly nun (the monks sometimes offer to give tours of the monastery, an experience not to be missed). The focus of the rambling complex is the **katholikon,** or principal church, whose nave is square in plan with eight niches supporting the dome. Within these niches are found a sequence of extraordinary **mosaics,** among the finest examples of Byzantine art—sadly, a seemingly interminable process of restoration continues to conceal the most beautiful of these behind scaffolding. You can still see the portrayals of the saints in the narthex, and a representation of Christ washing the disciple's feet. The museum contains a collection of gifts to the monastery, most of which postdate the devastating earthquake of 1881. Also of interest is the **cistern,** a cavernous vaulted room with columns (bring a flashlight), and the small **chapel** at the entrance to the monastery, dedicated to the martyrs of the 1822 massacre by the Turks (the skulls and bones displayed are those of the victims themselves).

The bus to Nea Moni is part of an island bus excursion operated by KTEL, departing from the Hios town bus station Tuesday and Friday at 9am and returning at 4:30pm. The route is Hios town to Nea Moni to Anavatos to Lithi beach to Armolia and back to Hios town; it costs Dr3,500 ($12) per person. A taxi, at Dr5,000 ($17) round-trip from Hios town, is also a reasonable option.

A DAY TRIP TO THE MASTIC VILLAGES: PIRYI, MESTA & OLIMBI

The most interesting day trip on Hios is the excursion to the mastic villages in the southern part of the island, which offer one of the best examples of medieval town architecture in all of Greece. Mastic is a gum derived from the resin of the mastic tree, used in candies, paints, perfumes, and medicines; it was a source of great wealth for these towns in the Middle Ages, and is still produced in small quantities. All were originally fortified, with an outer wall formed by an unbroken line of houses with no doors and few windows facing out. You can still see this distinctive plan at all three towns, although in Piryi and Olimbi the original medieval village has been engulfed by more recent construction.

Piryi is known for a rare technique of geometric decoration, known as *Ksisti.* In the main square this technique reaches a level of extraordinary virtuosity. The beautiful **Ayioi Apostoli** church and every available surface of every building are covered with horizontal banded decorations in a remarkable variety of motifs. At the town center is the tower for which the village is named, now mostly in ruins. It was originally the heart of the city's defenses, and a place of last refuge in time of siege.

Mesta is the best preserved medieval village in Hios, a maze of narrow streets and dark covered passages. The town has two fine churches, each unique on the island. **Megas Taxiarchis,** built in the 19th century, is one of the largest churches in Greece, and it was clearly built to impress. The arcaded porch with its fine pebble terrace and bell tower create a solemn and harmonious transition to the cathedral precinct. The other church in town, **Paleos Taxiarchis,** is located a few blocks below the main square. As the name suggests, this is the older of the two, built in the 14th century. The most notable feature here is the carved wooden iconostasis, whose surface is incised with miniature designs of unbelievable intricacy. If either church is closed, you can ask for the gatekeeper in the central square; Despina Flores of the **Messaionas Taverna** (☎ 0271/76-050) will probably know where he can be found.

Olimbi is the least well known of the three, not so spectacular as Piryi nor as intact as Mesta, but many of its medieval buildings can still be seen. There is a central tower similar to that of Piryi, and stone vaults connecting the houses.

Piryi is the closest of the three villages to Hios town, at 26 kilometers (16.1 miles); Olimbi and Mesta are both within 10 kilometers (6.2 miles) of Piryi. The easiest way to see all three villages is by car. Taxis from Hios to Piryi cost about Dr4,500 ($15). KTEL buses travel from Hios to Piryi eight times a day, and to Mesta five times a day. In 1998, the bus to Piryi cost Dr600 ($2), to Mesta Dr800 ($2.65).

BEACHES

There's no question that Hios has the best beaches in the Northeastern Aegean. They're cleaner, less crowded, and more plentiful than in Samos, and would be the envy of any Cycladic isle.

The fine-sand beach of **Karfas,** 7 kilometers (4.3 miles) south of Hios town, is the closest decent beach to the town center; it can be reached by a local (blue) bus. The rapid development of tourism in this town assures, however, that the beach will be crowded.

The most popular beach on the south coast is **Mavra Volia** ("black pebbles"), in the town of Emborio. Continue over the rocks to the right from the man-made town beach to find the main beach. Walking on the smooth black rocks feels and sounds like marching through a room filled with marbles. The panorama of the beach, slightly curving coastline, and distant headland is a memorable sight. There are regular buses from Hios town or from Piryi (8km/5 miles away) to Emborio. A short distance south is the best beach of the south coast, ✪ **Vroulidia,** a 5-kilometer (3-mile) drive in from the Emborio road. This white-pebble-and-sand beach in a rocky cove offers great views of the craggy coastline.

The west coast of the island has a number of stunning beaches. Elinda Cove shelters a long cobble beach, a 600-meter drive in from the main road between Lithi and Volissos. Another excellent beach on this road is Tigani–Makria Ammos, about 4 kilometers (2½ miles) north of Elinda; turn at a sign for the beach and drive in 1½ kilometers (0.9 mile) to this long white-pebble beach (there's also a small cove-sheltered cobble beach about 300 meters before you reach the main beach). There are three beaches below Volissos, the best of which is Lefkathia, just north of the harbor of Volissos (Limnia). Another 5 kilometers (3.1 miles) north brings you to the end of the road at Ayia Markella, a monastery overlooking a long picturesque stretch of fine sand.

The beaches of the north coast are less remarkable. Nagos (4km/2½ miles north of Kardamila) is a charming town in a small spring-fed oasis, with a cobble beach and two tavernas on the water. This beach can get very crowded, and the secret is to hike to the two small beaches a little to the east. To find them, take the small road behind the white house near the windmill. Another good beach can be found about 600 meters north of Nagos at Yiossonas.

WHERE TO STAY
HIOS TOWN

Hotel Chandris. Odos Evyenias Handri, 82100 Hios. ☎ **0271/44-401** or 0271/44-411. Fax 0271/25-768. 156 units. A/C MINIBAR TV TEL. Dr20,300 ($68) double; Dr32,000 ($107) triple. Rates include breakfast. AE, DC, EURO, MC, V.

The decor of the town's largest hotel is faded 1970s chic, a look that will thankfully be updated when the hotel began substantial renovations in the latter part of 1998. The marble entrance hall is decidedly grand, built with a solidity and scale that make this hotel unique on Hios. It's in a great location at the south end of the harbor, with water on two sides. There's a large pool facing the sea, and an expansive flagstone pool terrace. All rooms have balconies, and most have a view or at least a glimpse of the sea. Bedrooms (and bathrooms) are moderate in size, and after the renovation they'll at least be able to boast interior decor that isn't an embarrassment.

Hotel Kyma. Odos Evyenias Handri 1, 82100 Hios. ☎ **0271/44-500.** Fax 0271/44-600. 59 units. A/C TEL. Dr16,500 ($55) double. Rates include breakfast. No credit cards.

Our favorite in-town lodging was built in 1917 as a private villa for John Livanos. (You'll notice the portraits of the lovely Mrs. Livanos on the ceiling in the ground-floor breakfast room.) Though the hotel is of historic interest (the treaty with Turkey was signed in the Kyma in 1922), most of the original architectural details are gone, and the rooms have been renovated in a modern style. Many units have views of the sea, and a few have big whirlpool baths. The management, under the amiable direction of Theo Spordilis, is friendly, capable, and helpful. They also serve an excellent breakfast.

KARFAS

Karfas, 7 kilometers (4½ miles) south of Hios town around Cape Ayia Eleni, is an exploding tourist resort with a fine-sand beach lined with expensive Greek all-inclusive holiday hotels.

✪ **Hotel Erytha.** Karfas, 82100 Hios. ☎ **0271/32-060** or 0271/32-064. Fax 0271/32-182. E-mail: Erytha@compulink.gr. 102 units. A/C MINIBAR TV TEL. Dr24,400 ($81) double; Dr30,200 ($101) triple. Rates include breakfast. AE, DC, JCB, MC, V.

Built in 1990, the Erytha currently offers the most luxurious accommodations in the vicinity of Hios town. The spacious double rooms of this sprawling resort are distributed among five beachfront buildings, connected by plant-filled terraces. The outdoor breakfast area steps down to the pool terrace, which is just above a tiny cove and private beach. Guest rooms are simply furnished: All have balconies and most face the sea, although a few open onto the terraces between buildings. Bathrooms are moderate in size, and include a bathtub with shower. There are 21 studios and apartments in a separate building, but these aren't as well maintained as in the main hotel, and the kitchen facilities are very minimal: you're better off avoiding these entirely.

KARDAMILA

Kardamila, on the northeastern coast, is our choice among the resort towns because it's prosperous, self-sufficient, and untouristy.

Hotel Kardamila. Kardamila, 82300 Hios. ☎ **0272/23-353.** Fax 0271/23-354. (Contact Hotel Kyma for reservations.) 32 units. A/C TEL. Dr22,000 ($73) double; Dr28,000 ($93) triple. Rates include breakfast. No credit cards.

This modern resort hotel was built for the guests and business associates of the town's ship owners and officers, and it has its own small cobble beach. The guest rooms are large and plain, with modern bathrooms and balconies overlooking the beach. The gracious Theo Spordilis of the Hotel Kyma has taken over its management, so you can be sure the service will be good.

VOLISSOS

This small hilltop village is one of the most beautiful on the island. A fine Byzantine castle overlooks the steep streets of the town, which contains numerous cafes and tavernas. It's too far north to be a convenient base for touring the whole island, but if you want to get to know a small part of the island, you couldn't choose a better focus for your explorations.

✪ **Volissos Traditional Houses.** Volissos, Hios. ☎ **0274/21-421** or 0274/21-413. Fax 0274/21-521. 15 units. Dr11,500–Dr23,000 ($38–$77) per night. No credit cards.

The care with which these village houses have been restored is unique on this island, if not in the whole Northeastern Aegean. Stella Tsakiri is a trained visual artist, and the influence of her discerning eye is evident in every detail of the reconstruction. The beamed ceilings, often supported by a forked tree limb—a method of construction described in the *Odyssey*—are finely crafted and quite beautiful. Built into the stone walls are niches, fireplaces, cupboards, and couches. This spirit of inventiveness is also seen in imaginative recycling: a cattle yoke serves as a beam, or salvaged doors and shutters from the village become a mirror or piece of furniture. The houses and apartments are distributed throughout the village of Volissos, so your neighbors are likely to be locals rather than fellow tourists. All apartments and houses have a small but fully equipped kitchen, a spacious bathroom, and one or two bedrooms; the largest places (on two floors of a house) have two bedrooms, a sitting room, a kitchen, and a large terrace.

MESTA

The best-preserved medieval fortified village on Hios, Mesta is a good base for touring the mastic villages (see above) and the island's south coast.

Pipidis Traditional Houses. Mesta, Hios. ☎ **0271/76-029.** 4 units. Dr12,000 ($40) double; Dr13,200 ($44) triple; Dr14,400 ($48) for 4 persons. No credit cards.

These four homes, built more than 500 years ago, have been restored and opened by the Greek National Tourist Organization as part of its traditional settlements program. The apartments have a medieval character, with vaulted ceilings and irregularly sculpted stone walls (covered in plaster and whitewash). One unfortunate aspect of these authentic dwellings is the dearth of natural light: if a room has any windows at all, they're usually small and placed high in the wall. Each house comes equipped with a kitchen, bathroom, and enough sleeping space for two to six people. They're managed by the admirable Pipidis family.

WHERE TO DINE
HIOS TOWN

Hios Marine Club. Odos Nenitousi 1. ☎ **0271/23-184.** Main courses Dr650–Dr3,200 ($2.75–$14) EURO, MC, V. Daily noon–2am. GREEK.

This good, simple taverna serves the usual Greek dishes, pasta, grilled meats, and fish. Don't be put off by the ugly yellow-and-white concrete facade—the sign in front reads simply RESTAURANT-FRESCA PSARIA. It's on the bay at the edge of town, just south of the port, 50 meters beyond the Hotel Chandris.

Hotzas Taverna. Yioryiou Kondili 3. ☎ **0271/23-117.** Main courses Dr700–Dr3,400 ($2.35–$11). No credit cards. Mon–Sat 6–11pm. GREEK.

Hotzas is a small taverna that offers simple, well-prepared food, the best option in a town not known for its dining. The summer dining area is a luxuriant garden with lemon trees and abundant flowers. There's no menu, just a few unsurprising but delicious offerings each night. You won't find much fish, as most of the dishes are meat-based. This place isn't easy to find—take Odos Kountouriotou in from the harbor, and look for the first right turn after a major road merges at an oblique angle from the right; after this it's another 50 meters before the taverna appears on your left.

Theodosiou Ouzeri. Paralia, Hios. No phone. Appetizers Dr400–Dr3,500 ($1.35–$12). No credit cards. Daily 7pm–midnight. GREEK.

In the evening, many residents prefer to pull up a streetside chair at a cafe along the waterfront and eat mezedes with ouzo. Of the many ouzeries on the paralia, we like Theodosiou, located on the far right (north) side of the port, for both the scene and its menu.

LANGADA

Yiorgo Passa's Taverna. Langada. ☎ **0271/74-218.** Fish from Dr10,000 ($33) per kilo. No credit cards. Daily 11am–2am. Located 20km (12.4 miles) north of Hios town on the Kardamila road. SEAFOOD.

Langada is a fishing village with a strip of five or six outdoor fish taverns lining the harbor. Our favorite of these is Yiorgo Passa's Taverna, the first on the left as you walk down to the waterfront. Prices are low, portions are generous, and the ambiance is warm and friendly. *Note:* There are evening dinner cruises to Langada from Hios; check with **Hios Tours** (see "Visitor Information," above) about the schedule and prices.

3 Lesvos (Mitilini)

348km (188 nautical miles) NE of Piraeus

Roughly triangular Lesvos, often called Mitilini, is the third-largest island in Greece, with a population of nearly 120,000. At the tips of the triangle are the three principal towns: **Mitilini, Molivos,** and **Eressos.** Due to its remote location, Eressos is a good destination for a day trip but not a recommended base for touring the island.

Mitilini and Molivos are about as different as two towns on the same island could possibly be. Loud and obnoxious, Mitilini is a tough cousin to Thessaloniki, a port town low on sophistication or pretense, with little organized tourism and lots of local character. Molivos is a picture-postcard seaside village, a truly beautiful place, but in the summer existing only for tourism.

Not to be missed are the Archaeological and Theophilos museums in Mitilini; the town of **Mandamados** and its celebrated icon (the east coast road, between Mandamados and Mitilini, is the most scenic on the island); the remarkable, mile-long beach of Eressos; and the labyrinthine streets of Molivos's castle-crowned hill.

Getting around on Lesvos is greatly complicated by the presence of two huge tear-shaped bays in the south coast which divide the island down its center. East-west distances are great, and since bus service is infrequent this is one island where you'll definitely need a car.

GETTING THERE   By Plane   The **airport** (☎ 0251/61-490 or 0251/61-590) is 3 kilometers (1.9 miles) south of Mitilini; there's no bus to the town, and a taxi will cost about Dr1,000 ($3.35). **Olympic Airways** has three flights daily to Mitilini from Athens. There are connections 10 times weekly with Thessaloniki, three times weekly with Limnos, and twice weekly with Hios. The **Olympic office** in Mitilini (☎ 0251/28-660) is at Odos Kavetsou 44, about 200 meters south of Ayia Irinis park, just in from the southern end of the harbor. To find it, walk 300 meters south from the harbor; turn right at a large park, just before the World War II monument (a statue of a woman with sword); take the first right, and the office will be immediately on your left.

By Boat   There's one boat daily to Lesvos from Piraeus, stopping at Hios. There's one boat weekly from Rafina. One boat calls weekly from Kavala and Thessaloniki, both stopping at Limnos on the way. There are daily boats to and from Hios. In summer hydrofoils connect Lesvos with Alexandroupoli, Hios, Kavala, Limnos, Pithagorio (Samos), Samos town, the Dodecanese Islands, and Iraklion. Call the **Maritime Company** (☎ 0251/28-480) or the **port authority** (☎ 0251/28-888) for current schedules.

Once you get to Lesvos, double-check the boat schedule for your departure, as the harbor is extremely busy in the summer and service is often inexplicably irregular. Many of the ferries to Mitilini are scheduled to arrive at midnight, but can be as late as 2:30am.

MITILINI & SOUTHEAST LESVOS

With a big-city ambiance more like a mainland city than an island capital, Mitilini isn't to everyone's taste. Your first impression is likely to be one of noise, car exhaust, and crazy taxi drivers. Sadly, recent development has resulted in a generic paralia, the only signs of a more auspicious past being the cathedral dome and the considerable remains of a hilltop castle. Still, once you leave the paralia there's little or nothing in the way of amenities for tourists, a quality that can be remarkably refreshing. In the vicinity of Ermou (the market street), Mitilini's crumbling ochre alleys contain a mix of traditional coffeehouses, the studios of artisans, ouzeries, stylish jewelry shops, and stores selling antiques and clothing. Although good restaurants are notably absent in the town center, there are a few authentic tavernas on the outskirts of town.

ESSENTIALS

VISITOR INFORMATION   The **Greek National Tourist Organization (EOT)** office is in Mitilini at Odos Aristarhou 6 (☎ **0251/42-511;** fax 0251/42-512), 20 meters back from the building housing the Customs office and the tourist police, to the left (east) from the ferry quay. Hours are daily from 8am to 2:30pm, with extended hours in the high season. It offers a complete listing of hotels, pensions, and rooms throughout the island. The **tourist police** (☎ **0251/22-776**) may also be helpful.

GETTING AROUND   By Bus   There are two bus stations in Mitilini, one for local and the other for round-the-island routes. The **local bus station** (☎ **0251/ 28-725**) is near the north end of the harbor, by the (closed) Folklife Museum and across from the Commercial Bank (Emporiki Trapeza). Local buses on Lesvos are frequent, running every hour from 7am to 8pm throughout most of the year. The destinations covered are all within 12 kilometers (7.4 miles) of Mitilini, and include Thermi, Moria, and Pamfilla to the north and Varia, Ayia Marina, and Loutra to the south. The posted schedule is hard to read, but there's usually someone selling tickets who can decipher it for you. The **round-the-island KTEL buses** (☎ **0251/28-873**) can be caught in Mitilini at the south end of the port behind the Argo Hotel. There's daily service in summer to Kaloni and Molivos (four times), Mandamados (once), Plomari (four times), and to Eressos and Sigri (once).

By Car   Rental prices in Mitilini tend to be high, so be sure to shop around. A good place to start is **Payless Car Rental** (e-mail: automoto@otenet.gr), with offices at the airport (☎ **0251/61-665**) and on the port in Mitilini (☎ **0251/43-555**), near the local (north) bus station. Summer daily rates start at around Dr14,000 ($47) with 100 free kilometers; each kilometer over 100 is an additional Dr50 (15¢). Assuming an average day's drive is 150 kilometers (94 miles), add about $8.50 a day to the rental cost.

By Boat   Aeolic Cruises (☎ **0251/23-960;** fax 0251/43-694) offers daily boat excursions around the island during the high season from its port-side office in Mitilini.

By Taxi   Lesvos is a big island. The one-way taxi fare from Mitilini to Molivos is about Dr9,000 ($30); from Mitilini to Eressos or Sigri, about Dr14,000 ($47). The main taxi stand in Mitilini is on Plateia Kyprion Patrioton, a long block inland from the southern end of the port; there's a smaller taxi stand near the local bus station near the north end of the port and the (closed) Folklife Museum.

FAST FACTS   The **area code** for Mitilini is 0251, for Molivos (Mithimna) and Eressos 0253, and for Plomari 0252. There are **ATMs** at several banks on the port, including the Ioniki Trapeza and Agrotiki Trapeza (both south of the local bus station). The **Vostani Hospital** (☎ **0251/43-777**) on Odos P. Vostani, just southeast of town, will take care of emergencies. There's a drop-off **laundry** (☎ **0251/42-570**) on El. Venizelou: head south from the port, and after 200 meters you'll see it on the right. The **post office** and the **telephone office (OTE)** are on Plateia Kyprion Patrioton, 1 block inland from the town hall, at the south end of the port. The principal **taxi stand** is also on Plateia Kyprion Patrioton; Vassilis (☎ **093/718931**) is an **English-speaking driver.** The **tourist police** (☎ **0251/22-776**) are located near the EOT, left (east) from the ferry quay.

ATTRACTIONS

Archaeological Museum of Mitilini. Odos Eftaliou 7, Myrina. ☎ **0251/28-032.** Admission Dr500 ($1.70) adults, Dr300 ($1) students and seniors. Tues–Sun 8am–2:30pm. A block north of the tourist police station, just inland from the ferry pier.

This museum's extensive collection is thoughtfully presented, with many helpful explanatory plaques in English. You're greeted in the yard of the museum by massive marble lions, rearing menacingly on their hind legs, perhaps representing the bronze lion sculpted by Hephaestus which is said to roam the island and serve as its guardian. A rear building houses more marble sculpture and inscribed tablets, while the main museum contains figurines, pottery, gold jewelry, and other finds from Thermi, the Mitilini Kastro, and other ancient sites of Lesvos. A second Archaeological Museum of Mitilini is scheduled to open during the summer of 1998; it's a 10-minute walk up the hill, in the direction of the Kastro.

○ Theophilos Museum. Varia. ☎ **0251/41-644.** Admission Dr300 ($1). Tues–Sun 9am–1pm and 4:30–8pm. Located 3km (1.9 miles) south of Mitilini, on the road to the airport, next to the Theriade Museum.

One of the most interesting sights near Mitilini is this small museum in the former house of folk artist Hatzimichalis Theophilos (1868–1934). Most of Theophilos's works adorned the walls of tavernas and ouzeries, often painted in exchange for food. Theophilos died in poverty, and none of his work would have survived if it weren't for the efforts of art critic Theriade (see below), who commissioned the paintings on display here during the last years of the painter's life. These primitive watercolors depicting ordinary people, daily life, and local landscapes are now widely celebrated, and are also exhibited at the Museum of Folk Art in Athens. Be sure to take in the curious photographs showing the artist dressed as Alexander the Great.

Theriade Library and Museum of Modern Art. Varia. ☎ **0251/23-372.** Admission Dr500 ($1.70). Tues–Sun 9am–1pm and 5–8pm. Located 3km (1.9 miles) south of Mitilini, on the road to the airport, next to the Theophilos Museum.

The Theriade Library and Museum of Modern Art is in the home of Stratis Eleftheriadis, a native of Lesvos who emigrated to Paris and became a prominent art critic and publisher (Theriade is the Gallicized version of his surname). On display are copies of his published works, including the *Minotaure* and *Verve* magazines, as well as his personal collection of works by Picasso, Matisse, Miro, Chagall, and other modern artists.

Kastro. Odos 8 Noemvriou, Mitilini. No phone. Admission Dr500 ($1.70); Dr300 ($1) students and seniors. Tues–Sun 8am–2:30pm. Just past the new Archaeological Museum, turn right on the path to the Kastro.

Perched on a steep hill just north of the city, the extensive ruins of Mitilini's castle are fun to explore and offer fine views of city and sea from the ramparts. The Kastro was founded by Justinian in the 6th century A.D., and was restored and enlarged in 1737 by the Genoese; the Turks also renovated and built extensively during their occupation of the castle. In several places you can see fragments of marble columns embedded in the castle walls—these are blocks taken from a 7th-century B.C. temple

Excursion to a Mountain Village

An enjoyable destination for a day trip is the rural hamlet of **Ayiassos**, 23 kilometers (14 miles) west of Mitilini. The town, built up on the foothills of Mount Olymbos, consists of traditional gray stone houses (with their wooden "Turkish" balconies, often covered in flowering vines), narrow cobblestone lanes, and fine small churches. Here local craftsmen still turn out their ceramic wares by hand. There are excursion buses from Mitilini, or you can share a taxi (about Dr7,500/$25) for the 1-hour ride.

of Apollo by the Genoese during their rebuilding of the walls. Look for the underground cistern at the north end of the castle precinct: this echoing chamber is a beautiful place, with domed vaults reflected in the pool below. In summer, the castle is sometimes used as a performing-arts center.

A SIDE TRIP TO TURKEY: AYVALIK, PERGAMUM & ANCIENT TROY

From Mitilini, there's direct connection to Turkey via the port of Ayvalik; about 3,000 tourists make the crossing annually. Ayvalik, a densely wooded fishing village, makes a refreshing base camp from which to tour Pergamum or ancient Troy. The acropolis of Pergamum is sited on a dramatic hilltop site, with substantial remains of the town on the surrounding slopes. The complex dates back to at least the 4th century B.C., and there are significant remains from this period through to Roman and Byzantine times. It is one of Turkey's most important archaeological sites. All-inclusive tours to Pergamum with lunch, bus, and round-trip boat fare are available; inquire at Mitilini travel agencies. Ships to Turkey sail Wednesday, Friday, and Saturday. Tickets for the Turkish boats are sold by **Aeolic Cruises Travel Agency** (☎ **0251/23-960**), on the port in Mitilini. The round-trip excursion fare (returning the same day) is about Dr20,000 ($67), and a visa is not required; the fare on the Turkish boat is Dr15,000 ($50) round-trip, with an additional visa fee ($45 for Americans; £5 for Irish and U.K. citizens; no visa needed for Canadians, Australians, and New Zealanders). You may need to submit your passport 1 day in advance of departure.

WHERE TO STAY

Hotel Erato. Odos P. Vostani, Mitilini, 81000 Lesvos. ☎ **0251/41-160.** Fax 0251/47-656. 22 units. A/C TV TEL. Dr14,000 ($47) double; Dr16,000 ($53) triple. EURO, MC, V. Open year-round.

On a busy street just south of the port, this hotel offers convenience, cleanliness, and little else. Most of the small bright rooms have balconies facing the street, so noise can be a problem. The four-story hotel was converted from a medical clinic, and retains an atmosphere of institutional anonymity. On the positive side, the staff is friendly and helpful, and the noise is less than that experienced in the many port-side hotels.

Hotel Sappho. Odos Kountourioti, Mitilini, 81000 Lesvos. ☎ **0251/22-888.** Fax 0251/24-522. 29 units. TV TEL. Dr13,000 ($43) double; Dr13,600 ($45) triple. Continental breakfast Dr1,500 ($5) extra. No credit cards.

The best hotel on the port, the Sappho offers simple accommodations in a recently renovated building. Nine rooms have balconies facing the port; the rest have no balcony and face a sunny rear courtyard. All units have wall-to-wall carpets, white walls, minimal furnishings, and tiny bathrooms with showers. A breakfast room on the second floor has an outdoor terrace with a fine port view.

Villa 1900. Odos P. Vostani, Mitilini, 81000 Lesvos. ☎ **0251/23-448.** Fax 0251/28-034. 7 units. Dr9,500–Dr13,300 ($32–$44) double. Continental breakfast Dr1,400 ($4.70). No credit cards. Located 150m south of the Olympic Airways office, opposite the stadium.

The Villa 1900 is a somewhat upscale pension in a fine old house on the edge of town, about 700 meters south of the Mitilini port. The best units (room nos. 3 and 7) are quite spacious, and recall another era with their ornate painted ceilings. However, the smaller ones (room nos. 6, 8, and 9) are claustrophobic and overpriced. The remaining two rooms are plain but adequate, and offer reasonable value for your money. The house is buffered from the noise of the street by a small garden in front; a larger garden with abundant fruit trees begins at the back terrace and offers a pleasant shaded retreat. The amiable owners speak no English, but there is usually someone on hand to translate.

WHERE TO DINE

Mitilini has even more port-side cafes than your average bustling harbor town. The cluster of chairs around the small lighthouse at the point is the most scenic (as well as the windiest) of the many small ouzeries, specializing in grilled octopus, squid, shrimp, and local fish. We found the best restaurants to be a short taxi ride outside the city.

Averof 1841 Grill. Port, Mitilini. No phone. Main courses Dr600–Dr3,200 ($2–$11). No credit cards. Daily 11:30am–11:30pm. GREEK.

This taverna, located midport near the Sappho Hotel, is one of the better grills around, and one of the only restaurants in Mitilini center worth trying. It has particularly good beef dishes. Try any of their tender souvlaki or the lamb with potatoes.

O Rembetis. Kato Halikas, Mitilini. ☎ **0251/27-150.** Main courses Dr900–Dr3,600 ($3–$12). No credit cards. Daily 8pm–12am. GREEK.

Kato Halikas is a hilltop village on the outskirts of Mitilini, and although this simple taverna might be hard to find, it's well worth the effort. At the south end of the terrace you can sit beneath the branches of a high sycamore and enjoy a panoramic view of the port. The food isn't sophisticated or surprising, but it's very Greek, and the clientele is primarily local. There's no menu, so listen to the waiter's descriptions or take a look in the kitchen—there's usually some fresh fish in addition to the taverna standards. The wind can be brisk on this hilly site, so bring a jacket if the night is cool. The best way to get here is by taxi; the fare is about Dr500 ($1.70) each way.

Salavos. Mitilini. ☎ **0251/22-237.** Main courses Dr1,000–Dr3,000 ($3.35–$10). No credit cards. Daily noon–1am. GREEK.

Despite an unfortunate location on the busy airport road, this small taverna is one of the best in Mitilini. A garden terrace in back offers partial shelter from the road noise. The seafood is fresh and delicious: try the calamari stuffed with feta, vegetables, and herbs. The restaurant is very popular with locals, who fill the place on summer nights. Traveling south from Mitilini toward the airport, it's about 3 kilometers (1.9 miles) south of town on the right. Taxi fare is about Dr600 ($2) each way.

MITILINI AFTER DARK

In Mitilini, there's plenty of nightlife action on both ends of the harbor. The east side tends to be younger, cheaper, and more informal. The more sophisticated places are off the south end of the harbor. There's also the outdoor **Park Cinema,** on the road immediately below the stadium, open May through September. Don't forget that there might be entertainment at the Kastro.

MOLIVOS & NORTHEAST LESVOS

Molivos, also known by the more specifically Hellenic name "Mithimna," is at the northern tip of the island's triangle. It's a highly picturesque castle-crowned village with stone and pink-pastel stucco mansions capped by red-tile roofs, balconies, and windowsills decorated with geraniums and roses, and labyrinthine pathways.

The town has long been popular with package-tour groups, which fill the town to overflowing during the busy summer months. Souvenir shops, car-rental agencies, and travel agents outnumber local merchants in the town center, and the restaurants are clearly geared for the tourist market. Despite this, it is a beautiful place to visit and a convenient base for touring the island.

ESSENTIALS

GETTING THERE   By Bus   KTEL buses (☎ 0251/28-873) connect Molivos with Mitilini four times daily in the high season. The Molivos bus stop is between the town and the sea, just past the Municipal Tourist Office on the road to Mitilini.

By Taxi   The one-way taxi fare from Mitilini to Molivos is about Dr9,000 ($30).

VISITOR INFORMATION   The **Municipal Tourist Office** (☎ 0253/71-347), housed in a tiny building next to the National Bank on the Mitilini Road, is open Monday through Friday. **Tsalis Tours** (☎ 0253/71389; fax 0253/71-345; e-mail: tsalis@otenet.gr), on the road heading down to the sea from the National Bank, can book car rentals, accommodations, and excursions; open daily in summer from 8:30am to 9:30pm. **Communication and Travel** (☎ 0253/71-900; fax 0253/72-064; e-mail: com_travel@greeknet.com), on the road between the bus stop and the port, offers boat excursion tickets, Olympic Airways tickets, currency exchange, and Internet access; open daily from 9am to 8pm.

GETTING AROUND   By Car   There are numerous rental agencies in Molivos, and rates are comparable to those in Mitilini.

By Boat   Boat taxis to neighboring beaches can be arranged at the port or in a travel agency (see Communication and Travel, above). Rates are Dr4,000 ($13) per person round-trip with two people in the boat, or Dr2,800 ($9) per person with five people. Day excursions by boat to Kambos Beach (Dr5,200/$17 per person) depart weekly; check in travel offices for the day and time.

By Bus   Tickets for day excursions by bus can be bought in any of the local travel agencies. The destinations include Thermi/Ayiassos (Dr9,000/$30), Mitilini (Dr4,000/$13), Sigri/Eressos (Dr9,000/$30), and Plomari (Dr9,800/$33); the excursions are offered once or twice each week in the summer.

FAST FACTS   There's an ATM at the **National Bank,** next to the Municipal Tourist Office on the Mitilini Road. There's **Internet access** at Communication and Travel (☎ 0253/71-900) on the main road to the port. The **police** (☎ 0253/71-222) are up from the port, on the road to the town cemetery; the **port police** (☎ 0253/71-307) are (predictably) on the port. The **post office** (☎ 0253/71-246) is on the path circling up to the castle—turn right (up) just past the National Bank.

ATTRACTIONS

Kastro. Molivos. No phone. Admission Dr500 ($1.70), Dr300 ($1) students and seniors. Tues–Sun 8:30am–3pm.

The hilltop Genoese castle is in a better state of preservation than that of Mitilini, but it's much less extensive and thus less interesting to explore. There is, however, a great view from the walls, worth the price of admission in itself. There's a stage in the southwest corner of the courtyard, often used for theatrical performances in the summer. To get here by car, turn uphill at the bus stop and follow signs to the castle parking lot; on foot the castle is most easily approached from the town, a steep climb no matter which of the many labyrinthine streets you choose.

Mandamados Monastery. Mandamados. Free admission. Daily 6am–10pm. Located 24km (15 miles) east of Molivos, 36km (22½ miles) northwest of Mitilini.

Mandamados is a lovely village on a high inland plateau, renowned primarily for the remarkable icon of the Archangel Michael housed in the local monastery. A powerful story is associated with the creation of the icon: it is said that during a certain pirate raid (these raids were tragically common during the later middle ages), all but one of the monks were slaughtered. This one survivor, emerging from hiding to find the bloody corpses of his dead companions, responded to the horror of the moment with an extraordinary act. Gathering the blood-soaked earth, he fashioned in it the face of man, an icon in relief of the Archangel Michael. This simple icon, its lips worn away by the kisses of pilgrims, can be found at the center of the iconostasis at the back of the main chapel.

AN EXCURSION TO WESTERN LESVOS: ERESSOS & SKALA

Western Lesvos is hilly and barren, with many fine-sand beaches concealed among rocky promontories. Admirers of Sappho's poems and avid beachgoers should be sure to travel the steep and winding 65 kilometers (41 miles) between Molivos and Eressos, on the island's westernmost shore. Excursion buses (Dr9,000/$30) make this trip at least once a week from Molivos; inquire in the local tourist offices. **Eressos** is an attractive small village overlooking the coastal plain. Its port, Skala Eressou, 4 kilometers (2½ miles) to the south, has become a full-blown resort popular with Greek families as well as with gay women. This isn't surprising, since the beach here is the best in Lesvos, a wide, dark sand stretch over a mile long lined with tamarisks; a long stretch of sandy beaches and coves extends from here to Sigri, the next town to the north. Skala Eressou has a small **archaeological museum** (☎ 0253/53-332), near the 5th century basilica of Ayios Andreas, with local finds from the Archaic, Classical, and Roman periods. It's open Tuesday through Sunday from 7:30am to 3:30pm; admission is free.

BEACHES

The long, narrow town beach in Molivos is rocky and crowded near the town, but becomes sandier and less populous as you continue south. The beach in **Petra,** 6 kilometers (3.7 miles) south of Molivos, is considerably more pleasant. The beach at **Tsonia,** 30 kilometers (19 miles) east of Molivos, is only accessible via a difficult rutted road, and isn't particularly attractive. The best beach on the island is 70 kilometers (44 miles) west of Molivos in **Skala Eressos** (see "An Excursion to Western Lesvos," above).

SHOPPING

Molivos is unfortunately dominated by particularly tacky souvenir shops. To find more authentic local wares you'll have to explore neighboring towns. **Mandamados** is known as a center for pottery, and there are numerous ceramics studios here. **Eleni Lioliou** (☎ 0253/61-170), on the road to the monastery, has brightly painted bowls, plates, and mugs that are highly conventional in design. **Anna Fonti** (☎ 0253/61-433), on a pedestrian street in the village, produces plates with intricate designs in brilliant turquoise and blue. Also in Mandamados is the diminutive studio of icon painter **Dimitris Hatzanagnostou** (☎ 0253/61-318), who produces large-scale icons for churches and portable icons for purchase.

WHERE TO STAY

Hotel-Bungalows Delphinia. Molivos, 81108 Lesvos. ☎ **0253/71-315** or 0253/71-580. Fax 0253/71-524. www.gradus.com/TG/Aegean/Lesvos/A/Delphinia. E-mail: delphinia@ gradus.com. 122 units. MINIBAR TEL. Dr18,700 ($62) double; Dr31,900 ($106) 2-person bungalow; Dr39,060 ($130) 3-person bungalow. Rates include breakfast. AE, DC, V.

The best thing about this white-stucco and gray-stone resort is its panoramic setting above the Aegean. A path leads 200 meters from the hotel to a fine-sand beach and a recreation complex with saltwater swimming pool, snack bar, and tennis courts (the latter illuminated for night games). The hotel rooms are simple, with a small bathroom and shower. The 57 bungalows are more spacious: the living room has a couch that pulls out to provide an extra bed, bathrooms include a bathtub, and all units have a large terrace or balcony. Breakfast at the hotel is served in a large dining room, while the bungalows include free room service for breakfast only. The second-floor rooms in the bungalows are the most spacious, have the best views, and are the only units equipped with air-conditioning.

Hotel Olive Press. Molivos, 81108 Lesvos. ☎ 0253/71-205 or 0253/71-646. Fax 0253/71-647. 50 units. TEL. Dr21,000 ($70) double (includes breakfast); Dr30,000 ($100) studio. AE, DC, V.

The most charming hotel in town is built down on the water in the traditional style. The rooms are on the small side, but they're quiet and very comfortable, with terrazzo floors, handsome furnishings, and bathtubs with shower curtains. Some of the rooms have windows opening onto great sea views, with waves lapping just beneath. There is a nice inner courtyard with several gardens. The staff is gracious and friendly.

Sea Horse Pension (Thalassio Alogo). Molivos, 81108 Lesvos. ☎ **0253/71-630.** Fax 0253/71-374. 14 units. 12,000 ($40) double. Continental breakfast Dr1,300 ($4.35). No credit cards.

A cluster of recently built Class C hotels is set below the old town, near the beach. Among them is this smaller, homier pension. The friendly manager, Stergios, keeps the rooms (which have good views) tidy. There's also a restaurant and an in-house travel agency.

WHERE TO DINE

Captain's Table. Molivos. ☎ **0253/71-241.** Main courses Dr1,000–Dr3,000 ($3.35–$10). V. Daily 11am–1am. SEAFOOD/VEGETARIAN.

Melinda McRostie, the talented chef behind the enduringly popular Melinda's Restaurant, recently moved to the harbor in Molivos to start this new venture. Although the emphasis is now on fresh fish, the menu still offers some of the excellent vegetable dishes which were the trademark of her former establishment—try the Imam Bayeldi, a dish made with eggplant, onions, tomato, and garlic. There's live bouzouki music 3 nights a week.

Tropicana. Molivos. ☎ **0251/71-869.** Snacks/desserts Dr500–Dr3,000 ($1.70–$10). No credit cards. Daily 8am–1am. CAFE FARE.

After lunch or dinner, stroll up into the old town to sip a cappuccino or have a dish of ice cream. This outdoor cafe under a plane tree has soothing classical music and a most relaxing ambiance. The owner, Hari Procoplou, learned the secrets of ice creamery in Los Angeles.

MOLIVOS AFTER DARK

Vangelis Bouzouki (no phone) is Molivos's top acoustic bouzouki club. It's located west from Molivos on the road to Efthalou, past the Sappho Tours office. After about a 10-minute walk outside of town, you'll see a sign that points to an olive grove. Follow it for about another 500 meters through the orchard until you reach a clearing with gnarled olive trees and a few stray sheep. When you see the circular cement dance floor, surrounded by clumps of cafe tables, you've found it. Forget about the food, but have some ouzo and late-night mezedes, and sit back to enjoy the show.

Inquire at the tourist offices about summer theatrical performances in the Kastro.

4 Limnos (Lemnos)

344km (186 nautical miles) NE of Piraeus

Limnos is decidedly tame in comparison with its Northeastern Aegean neighbors. Here low hills break up the cultivated plains, circled by a rocky but gently sloping coastline. The towns are more functional than beautiful, and the beaches pleasant but not spectacular. This absence of superlatives, combined with a remote location at the edge of Asia Minor, explains the small scale of local tourism and the refreshing simplicity of village life in the principal port of Mirina.

Low on picture-postcard sights but full of small-town charm, **Mirina** is the port of Limnos and the best base for your explorations. Several of the town's restaurants and hotels cluster around a diminutive square at the port, in the shadow of the fine Ottoman castle on its lofty promontory. Connecting port and beach is the **market street,** Odos P. Kida, where you can find preserves made from the local black plums, Limnian honey (a favorite of the gods), and the famous Limnian wines—Kalavaki, a dry white (Aristotle's favorite), and the sweet Moschato. The two town **beaches—** Romeïkos Yialos and Riha Nera—are slivers of sand extending north as far as the renowned Akti Marina luxury resort, now operated as a private club. Don't miss the excellent **archaeological museum** on Romeïkos Yialos, where well-presented exhibits can serve as a prelude to your explorations of the island's archaeological sites.

Due to its remote location, Limnos is one island you'll want to reach by plane— ferry journeys can be painfully long, especially the 22-hour trip from Piraeus. Once on the island, you'll find that public bus schedules are scarce, and that a rented car or moped is the best option.

ESSENTIALS

GETTING THERE   By Plane   Olympic Airways has three flights daily between Limnos and Athens, one connection daily with Thessaloniki, and daily flights to Lesvos. Their office (☎ **0254/22-214**) is on Odos Garoufalidou, in Mirina. The **airport bus** meets all flights, and costs a reasonable Dr1,000 ($3.35); it departs from the Olympic office to the airport about 90 minutes before flight time (check with the office for the latest schedule).

By Boat   Getting to Limnos isn't much of a problem from northern Greece. It's connected by boat to Kavala four times weekly and to Lesvos three times weekly. There is infrequent service to and from Hios, Samothrace, Alexandroupoli, the Dodecanese, and Kymi (on Evvia). There is also connection with Rafina two times a week, with Piraeus three times a week, and with Thessaloniki twice a week. The schedules change often, so you'll have to contact the **Limnos Port Authority** (☎ **0254/22-225**) or the port authority or travel agency from your point of origin. Tickets for most local ferries can be purchased at **Vayiakos Travel** (☎ **0254/22-460**) on the port.

VISITOR INFORMATION   Mirina has several helpful travel agencies. **El Travel** is on a small street behind the main (taxi) square (☎ **0254/22-309;** fax 0254/22-129;

e-mail: mapet@lim.forthnet.gr); it offers accommodations and excursion booking and motorbike rental. **Petridou Travel** (☎ **0254/22-309;** fax 0254/22-129; e-mail: mapet@lim.forthnet.gr), 50 meters beyond the main square on the town's market street (Odos P. Kida), offers car rentals, accommodations booking, luggage storage, and the most bizarre mural painting of any travel agency in Greece. **Pravlis Travel** (☎/fax **0254/22-471**), on the port square, specializes in air tickets and will also book accommodations. There is an **EOT (National Tourist Organization of Greece)** office in the Eparhion, a municipal building on the road to the airport, a 3-minute walk from the central square. The location of this office will most likely change in the next year, so ask around: it's staffed by two very helpful women, and is worth seeking out. To find the office's current location, try calling the **town hall** (☎ **0254/23-736**) or the **Eparhion** (☎ **0254/22-996**).

GETTING AROUND By Bus In Mirina, the **central bus station** (☎ **0254/ 22-464**) is 3 blocks up from the main (taxi) square on the right. A schedule is posted, but you're not likely to find much on it. Except for Moudros and Kondias, most places on the island get service only once a day, usually in the afternoon. Excursion bus tours can be booked through El Travel or Petridou Travel, and include various combinations of island villages and archaeological sites. The frequency depends upon demand; tours depart at least weekly in the summer. The cost is Dr2,000 ($7) for the half-day and Dr4,000 ($13) for the full-day tour.

By Boat There are caïques on the north side of the harbor in Mirina; they offer service to the island's beaches and the grottos at Skala. You can buy tickets at most of the town's travel agencies.

By Car Car-rental prices on Limnos tend to be high compared with its Northeastern Aegean neighbors. We recommend **Myrina Rent a Car** (☎ **0254/24-476**), where a basic car costs Dr15,000 ($50) in the peak season, with full insurance.

FAST FACTS Both the **National Bank** and the **Agrotiki Trapeza,** 100 meters past the square in the direction of Romeïkos Yialos, have ATMs. There's a drop-off **laundry** (☎ **0254/24-392**) on Odos Garoufalidou across from the Olympic Airline office, next to the Hotel Astro; if it's closed, ask for help at the hotel. Continue a couple blocks past the laundry and turn left to find the **hospital** (☎ **0254/22-222**). The **post office** is on Odos Garoufalidou, 1 block toward Romeïkos Yialos from the square and to the right, just down the street from the Olympic Airlines office. The **taxi station** (☎ **0254/23-033** or 0254/22-348) marks what might conveniently be called a main square, midway along the market street. The **telephone office (OTE)** is on this square (open Mon through Fri from 8am to 1pm), as is the National Bank (open Mon through Thurs from 8am to 2pm, Fri from 8am to 1:30pm). The **tourist police** (☎ **0254/22-201**) are on the port, just down from the port police.

WHAT TO SEE & DO IN MIRINA

✪ **Archaeological Museum.** Mirina. ☎ **0254/22-990.** Admission Dr500 ($1.70), Dr300 ($1) students and seniors. Tues–Sun 8am–2:30pm. On Romeïkos Yialos Beach, next to the Castro Hotel.

This unassuming building, originally a Turkish Commandery during the Ottoman occupation, was thoroughly renovated in 1991 and now houses one of the finest archaeological museums in the Aegean. The artifacts are very well presented, and the descriptive plaques offer fascinating insights concerning the exhibits. If your appetite for exploration is whetted by the exhibits, it is possible to visit three of the island's archaeological sites by bus excursion: Poliochni, the Ifestia (sanctuary of Hephaestus), and the sanctuary of the Kaviri (see "Getting Around By Bus," above).

Kastro. Mirina. Open site. The best access path is reached via a steeply climbing road from the port, between the port police and the police station.

The Ottoman fortress that dominates Mirina from its craggy perch is easily accessible from the town, and the extensive ruins are a delight to explore. The climb from the port is long and exposed, so go in the early morning or wait for the relative cool of late afternoon. The foundations of the walls date to Byzantine times, and rock-carved inscriptions indicate that the site was once occupied by a temple to Artemis. There are numerous subterranean vaults and caves within the castle walls, so bring a flashlight. The shores of the castle's rocky promontory offer several secluded coves for bathing.

EXPLORING THE ARCHAEOLOGICAL SITES

There isn't much to see at the archaeological sites on Limnos's northern and eastern shores, but they do offer a great follow-up to the fascinating exhibits of Mirina's archaeological museum. **Kavirio,** dramatically situated on a rocky coastal promontory 10 kilometers (6.2 miles) north of the Hephaistia, is the most spectacularly placed of the three sites; only the floor plan remains of the once extensive temple. The **Hephaistia** on the island's northern shore, about 40 kilometers (25 miles) from Mirina, is the ruins of an ancient city dedicated to Hephaestus, the god of metallurgy who is said to have inhabited a volcano. Born ugly, Hephaestus was rejected by his father, Zeus, and as Milton wrote "Dropt from the zenith like a falling star, on Limnos, the Aegean isle." At the site is a Greek theater, a temple of Hephaestus, and the excavation site of a pre-Hellenic necropolis which provided many of the items now housed in the archaeological museum in Mirina. Of less interest is **Poliochni**, about 5 kilometers (3.1 miles) east of Moudros, which is still being excavated and offers little hold for the imagination. All three sites are open from 9:30am to 3:30pm, and admission is free. Some travel agencies include one or two of these sites as part of a **bus tour** of Limnos (see "Getting Around By Bus," above); the only alternative is to rent a car.

WHERE TO STAY

Castro Hotel. Romeïkos Yialos, Mirina, 81400 Limnos. ☎ **0254/22-772** or 0254/22-748. Fax 0254/22-784. 76 units. A/C MINIBAR TV TEL. Dr18,500 ($62) double; Dr21,000 ($70) double with sea view. Rates include breakfast. AE, MC, V. Located 1km (0.6 miles) north of the port.

The Castro is the best seafront hotel in Mirina, its neoclassical facade facing the sea and the narrow strip of sand called Romeïkos Yialos. The marble reception room is built on a large scale and offers a suggestion of elegance which is, unfortunately, not continued in the rest of the hotel. The rooms are plain, with wall-to-wall carpeting and more amenities than any of the neighboring hotels along the paralia. All units have balconies, although only a few actually face the water.

Hotel Ifestos. Riha Nera, Mirina, 81400 Limnos. ☎ **0254/24-960.** Fax 0254/23-623. 44 units. TEL. Dr19,000 ($63) double. Rates include breakfast. MC, V. Located 2km (1.2 miles) north of the port.

The Ifestos is in a quiet neighborhood of Mirina, surrounded by greenery. Built in 1991, the hotel facade imitates the wide arcaded porches of the town's older houses. The rooms are plain and clean; all have a small balcony or terrace and views over the neighboring gardens. The beach is a 5-minute walk, and the port a leisurely 30-minute walk.

Hotel Lemnos. Odos Arvanitaki, Mirina, 81400 Limnos. ☎ **0254/22-153.** Fax 0254/23-329. 29 units. TV TEL. Dr15,000 ($50) double; Dr19,500 triple ($65). No credit cards.

This hotel on the harbor is attractive, clean, comfortable, and quiet. Less than 100 meters from the ferry pier, it's the most convenient option if you're arriving by boat.

The owners, Harry Geanopoulos and Bill Stamboulis, spent many years in New Jersey and speak excellent English. They've also patterned their hotel on an American standard: a good night's sleep at a fair price. Breakfast (not included in the room rate) is available à la carte in the hotel cafe.

WHERE TO DINE

Mirina is not known for its restaurants. A host of fast-food places inhabit the paralia along Romeïkos Yialos Beach, but the most attractive options are on the market street or at the port.

Taverna Avra. Mirina. ☎ **0254/22-523.** Main courses Dr1,000–Dr2,500 ($3.35–$8). No credit cards. Daily 11:30am–12:30am. Next to the Port Authority, near the pier. GREEK.

Sheltered from the bustle of the port by a luxuriant grape arbor, the Avra is a good basic taverna with fair prices. There isn't a menu, so go inside and choose from the dishes displayed on the steam table. There's nothing surprising about the offerings, except perhaps the scarcity of fish in a taverna meters from the sea.

Taverna O Platanos. Mirina. ☎ **0254/22-070.** Main courses Dr1,000–Dr2,000 ($3.35–$7). No credit cards. Daily 11am–11pm. On the market street, 100m from the central square toward Romeïkos Yialos. GREEK.

O Platanos is a good, reliable taverna in an unexceptional but undeniably pleasant location. The "platanos" in question is a handsome mammoth of a tree arching above this small square on Mirina's market street, offering abundant shade during the afternoon hours. The menu is small and changes daily; the standard taverna fare is complemented by a variety of vegetables.

Appendix

A Making Your Way in Greek

The first bit of wisdom here is to admit defeat from the outset. The most we can hope for in confronting the Greek language and its complexities is to negotiate a workable surrender. In fact, there are many different kinds of Greek—the Greek of conversation in the street, the Greek used at a fashionable dinner party, the Greek used in newspapers, the Greek of a government notice, the Greek used by a novelist or a poet, and more—and they can differ from one another in grammar and in vocabulary much more than the English of, for example, a conversation at the watercooler and that of an editorial in the *New York Times.* Why that should be so is a long—and we mean *long*—story. (Much of the difficulty has arisen because Greek, like English, has a long written history in which it has been molded by influential works of literature, works that continue to be read and studied for centuries—in Greek even for millennia—so that, as in English, older words and styles of expression remain available for use even while the spoken language goes on happily evolving on its own. Also like English, Greek has kept the spelling of its words largely unchanged even though their pronunciation has changed in fundamental ways; in English this spelling lag has extended for some 5 centuries, but in Greek it is 25 centuries old. This makes it easier for us to read Shakespeare and for Greeks to read Herodotus than it would otherwise be, but it also means that Greek children, like English speakers, have a long, long row to hoe in school as they learn to spell the words they already know how to speak and to use.)

Our dilemma is further complicated by the fact that many Greek words and names have entered our language not directly but by way of Latin or French, and so have become familiar to English speakers in forms that owe something to those languages. When these words are directly transliterated from modern Greek (and that means from Greek in its modern pronunciation, not the ancient one that Romans heard as they borrowed them into Latin), they almost always appear in a form other than the one you may have read about in school. "Perikles" for Pericles or "Delfi" for Delphi are relatively innocent examples; "Thivi" for Thebes or "Omiros" for Homer can give you an idea of the traps often in store for the innocent traveler. The bottom line is that the names of towns, streets, hotels, items on menus, historical figures, archaeological sites—you name it—are likely to have more than one spelling as you come across them in books, on maps, or before your very eyes.

Sometimes the name of a place has simply changed over the centuries. If you think you've just arrived in Santorini but you see a sign welcoming you to Thira, smile, remember you're in Greece, and take heart. (Santorini is the name the Venetians used, and it became common in Europe for that reason; Thira is the original Greek name.) You're where you wanted to be. Besides, you will acquire more compassion for first-time visitors to the United States who land at JFK and find themselves welcomed to "The Big Apple."

What we offer here are a few aids to making your way in Greek. The table below will help you move from Greek signs or directions to a sense of how they should sound. This scheme for transliterating modern Greek is the one we have used throughout this book, except when we are referring to names which have become household words in English, like Athens, Socrates, Olympus, and so on. The good news here is that you won't be confused as long as you have your nose in your book; the bad news is that some confusion is probably inevitable as soon as your eyes leave the page. But it will be less. And all you have to do is to say what you are looking for, as closely as you can to the way it should sound, raising your voice at the end of the word to let your hearer know it's a question, and bingo!—you'll find you're right on the mark. Just remember that *óhi*, although it can sound a bit like "OK," in fact means "no," and that *ne*, which can sound like a twangy "nay," means "yes." To complicate matters, some everyday gestures will be different from what you are used to: Greeks nod their heads upward to express an unspoken *óhi* and downward (or downward and to one side) for an unspoken *ne*. When a Greek turns his or her head from side to side at you—and you will sometimes, despite your best efforts, have this happen—it is a polite way of signaling "I can't make out what you're saying."

One additional tip on finding your way in Greek: When you're confronting a word or name which doesn't exactly correspond to what's on your map or in your book, you can go straight to the "root" of the word, which is likely to be more or less in its middle. Greek nouns and verbs are inflected, which means that they change their forms in order to express different meanings. These changes take the form of extra letters at the beginning or the end of the word, or both, while the core or root of the word usually remains more or less unchanged at the center. And that's the thing to look for. If, for instance, the middle of the word on your map looks like the middle of the word on the sign you're looking at, then you're probably not lost.

ALPHABET		TRANSLITERATED AS	PRONOUNCED AS IN
A α	álfa	a	f*a*ther
B β	víta	v	*v*iper
Γ γ	gámma	g before α, o, ω, and consonants	*g*et
		y before αι, ε, ει, η, ι, οι, υ	*y*es
		ng before κ, γ, χ, or ξ	si*ng*er
Δ δ	thélta	th	*th*e (not as the *th-* in "thin")
E ε	épsilon	e	s*e*t
Z ζ	zíta	z	la*z*y
H η	íta	i	magaz*i*ne
Θ θ	thíta	th	*th*in (not as the *th-* in "the")
I ι	ióta	i	magaz*i*ne
		y before a, o	*y*ard, *y*ore
K κ	káppa	k	*k*eep
Λ λ	lámtha	l	*l*eap

ALPHABET		**TRANSLITERATED AS**	**PRONOUNCED AS IN**
Μ μ	mi	m	*m*arry
Ν ν	ni	n	*n*ever
Ξ ξ	ksi	ks	ta*x*i
Ο o	ómicron	o	b*o*ught
Π π	pi	p	*p*et
Ρ ρ	ro	r	*r*ound
Σ σ/ς	sígma	s before vowels or θ, κ, π, τ, φ, χ, ψ	*s*ay
		z before β, γ, δ, ζ, λ, μ, ν, ρ	la*z*y
Τ τ	taf	t	*t*ake
Υ υ	ípsilon	i	maga*z*ine
Φ φ	fi	f	*f*ee
Χ χ	chi	h	*h*ero (before e and i sounds; like the *ch*- in Scottish "lo*ch*" otherwise)
Ψ ψ	psi	ps	colla*ps*e
Ω ω	ómega	o	b*o*ught

COMBINATIONS	**TRANSLITERATED AS**	**PRONOUNCED AS IN**
αι	e	g*e*t
αϊ	ai	*ai*sle
αυ before vowels or β, γ, δ, ζ, λ, μ, ν, ρ	av	*Av*e Maria
αυ before θ, κ, ξ, π, σ, τ, φ, χ, ψ	af	pil*af*
ει	i	maga*z*ine
ευ before vowels or β, γ, δ, ζ, λ, μ, ν, ρ	ev	*ev*er
ευ before θ, κ, ξ, π, σ, τ, φ, χ, ψ	ef	l*ef*t
μπ at beginning of word	b	*b*ane
μπ in middle of word	mb	lu*mb*er
ντ at beginning of word	d	*d*umb
ντ in middle of word	nd	sle*nd*er
οι	i	maga*z*ine
οϊ	oi	*oi*l
ου	ou	s*ou*p
τζ	dz	roa*ds*
τσ	ts	ge*ts*
υι	i	maga*z*ine

B Useful Words & Phrases

When you're asking for or about something and have to rely on single words or short phrases, it's an excellent idea to use "sas parakaló" to introduce or conclude almost anything you say.

Airport	Aerothrómio
Automobile	Aftokínito
Avenue	Leoforos
Bad	Kakós,-kí,-kó*

Bank — Trápeza

The bill, please. — Tón logaryazmó(n), parakaló.

Breakfast — Proinó

Bus — Leoforío

Can you tell me? — Boríte ná moú píte?

Car — Amáxi

Cheap — Ft(h)inó

Church — Ekklissía

Closed — Klistós, stí, stó*

Coast — Aktí

Coffeehouse — Kafenío

Cold — Kríos,-a,-o*

Dinner — Vrathinó

Do you speak English? — Miláte Angliká?

Excuse me. — Signómi(n).

Expensive — Akrivós, -í,-ó*

Farewell! — Stó ka-ló! (to person leaving)

Glad to meet you. — Chéro polí.**

Good — Kalós, lí, ló*

Good-bye. — Adío or chérete.**

Good health (cheers)! — Stín (i)yá sas or Yá-mas!

Good morning or Good day. — Kaliméra.

   Good evening. — Kalispéra.

   Good night. — Kaliníchta.**

Hello! — Yássas or chérete!**

Here — Ethó

Hot — Zestós, -stí, -stó*

Hotel — Xenothochío**

How are you? — Tí kánete or Pós íst(h)e?

How far? — Pósso makriá?

How long? — Póssi óra or Pósso(n) keró?

How much does it cost? — Póso káni?

I am a vegetarian. — Íme hortophágos.

I am from New York. — Íme apó tí(n) Néa(n) Iórki.

I am lost or I have lost the way. — Écho chathí or
   Écho chási tón drómo(n).**

I'm sorry. — Singnómi.

I'm sorry, but I don't speak Greek (well). — Lipoúme, allá dén miláo elliniká (kalá).

I don't understand. — Thén katalavéno.

I don't understand, please repeat it. — Thén katalavéno, péste to páli,
   sás parakaló.

I want to go to the airport. — Thélo ná páo stó aerodrómio.

I want a glass of beer. — Thélo éna potíri bíra.

I would like a room. — Tha íthela ena thomátio.

It's (not) all right. — (Dén) íne en dáxi.

Left (direction) — Aristerá

Ladies' room — Ghinekón

Lunch	Messimerianó
Map	Chártis**
Market (place)	Agorá
Men's room	Andrón
Mr.	Kírios
Mrs.	Kiría
Miss	Despinís
My name is . . .	Onomázome . . .
New	Kenoúryos, -ya, -yo*
No	Óchi**
Old	Paleós, -leá, -leó*
	(pronounce palyós, -lyá, -lyó)
Open	Anichtós, -chtí, -chtó*
Pâtisserie	Zacharoplastío**
Pharmacy	Pharmakío
Please or You're welcome	Parakaló
Please call a taxi (for me).	Parakaló, fonáxte éna taxi (yá ména).
Point out to me, please. . .	Thíkste mou, sas parakaló, . . .
Post office	Tachidromío**
Restaurant	Estiatório
Rest room	Tó méros or I toualétta
Right (direction)	Dexiá
Saint	Áyios, ayía, (plural)
	áyi-i (abbreviated ay.)
Shore	Paralía
Square	Plateía
Street	Odós
Show me on the map.	Díxte mou stó(n) chárti.**
Station (bus, train)	Stathmos (leoforíou, trénou)
Stop (bus)	Stási(s) (leoforíou)
Telephone	Tiléfono
Temple (of Athena, Zeus)	Naós (Athinás, Diós)
Thank you (very much).	Efcharistó (polí).**
Today	Símera
Tomorrow	Ávrio
Very nice	Polí oréos, -a, -o*
Very well	Polí kalá or En dáxi
What?	Tí?
What time is it?	Tí ôra íne?
What's your name?	Pós onomázest(h)e?
Where is . . . ?	Poú íne . . . ?
Where am I?	Pou íme?
Why?	Yatí?

*Masculine ending -os, feminine ending -a or -i, neuter ending -o.
**Remember, ch should be pronounced as in Scottish loch or German ich, not as in the word church.

NUMBERS

0	Midén	17	Dekaeftá	151	Ekatón penínda
1	Éna	18	Dekaoktó		éna
2	Dío	19	Dekaenyá	152	Ekatón penínda
3	Tría	20	Íkossi		dío
4	Téssera	21	Íkossi éna	200	Diakóssya
5	Pénde	22	Íkossi dío	300	Triakóssya
6	Éxi	30	Triánda	400	Tetrakóssya
7	Eftá	40	Saránda	500	Pendakóssya
8	Októ	50	Penínda	600	Exakóssya
9	Enyá	60	Exínda	700	Eftakóssya
10	Déka	70	Evdomínda	800	Oktakóssya
11	Éndeka	80	Ogdónda	900	Enyakóssya
12	Dódeka	90	Enenínda	1,000	Chílya*
13	Dekatría	100	Ekató(n)	2,000	Dío chilyádes*
14	Dekatéssera	101	Ekatón éna	3,000	Trís chilyádes*
15	Dekapénde	102	Ekatón dío	4,000	Tésseris chilyádes*
16	Dekaéxi	150	Ekatón penínda	5,000	Pénde chilyádes*

DAYS OF THE WEEK

Monday   Deftéra
Tuesday   Tríti
Wednesday   Tetárti
Thursday   Pémpti

Friday   Paraskeví
Saturday   Sávvato
Sunday   Kiriakí

THE CALENDAR

January   Ianouários
February   Fevrouários
March   Mártios
April   Aprílios
May   Máios
June   Ioúnios

July   Ioúlios
August   Ávgoustos
September   Septémvrios
October   Októvrios
November   Noémvrios
December   Dekémvrios

MENU TERMS

arní avgolémono   lamb with lemon sauce
arní soúvlas   spit-roasted lamb
arní yiouvétsi   baked lamb with orzo
astakós (ladolémono)   lobster (with oil-and-lemon sauce)
bakaliáro (skordaliá)   cod (with garlic)
barboúnia (skáras)   red mullet (grilled)
briam   vegetable stew
brizóla chiriní   pork steak or chop
brizóla moscharísia   beef or veal steak
choriátiki saláta   "village" salad ("Greek" salad to Americans)

chórta   dandelion salad
dolmádes   stuffed vine leaves
domátes yemistés mé rízi   tomatoes stuffed with rice
eksóhiko   lamb and vegetables wrapped in filo
garídes   shrimp
glóssa (tiganití)   sole (fried)
kalamarákia (tiganitá)   squid (fried)
kalamarákia (yemistá)   squid (stuffed)
kaparosalata   salad of minced caper leaves and onion
karavídes   crayfish

*Remember, ch should be pronounced as in Scottish loch or German ich, not as in the word church.

keftédes fried meatballs
kokoretsia grilled entrails
kotópoulo soúvlas spit-roasted
chicken
kotópoulo yemistó stuffed chicken
kouloúri pretzel-like roll covered with
sesame seeds
loukánika spiced sausages
loukoumades round donut center–
like pastries that are deep-fried, then
drenched with honey and topped
with powdered sugar and cinnamon
melitzanosaláta eggplant salad
moussaká meat and eggplant casserole
oktapódi octopus
païdákia lamb chops
paradisiako traditional Greek cooking
pastítsio baked pasta with meat
piláfi rízi rice pilaf

piperiá yemistá stuffed green
peppers
revidia chickpeas
revidokeftedes croquettes of ground
chickpeas
saganaki grilled cheese
skordalia hot-garlic-and-beet dip
soupiés yemistés stuffed cuttlefish
souvláki lamb (sometimes veal) on
the skewer
spanokópita spinach pie
stifado stew, often of rabbit or veal
taramosalata fish roe with
mayonnaise
tirópita cheese pie
tsípoura dorado
tzatzíki yogurt-cucumber-garlic dip
youvarlákia boiled meatballs
with rice

Index

Page numbers in italics refer to maps.

FROMMER'S® COMPLETE TRAVEL GUIDES

Alaska
Amsterdam
Arizona
Atlanta
Australia
Austria
Bahamas
Barcelona, Madrid & Seville
Belgium, Holland &
   Luxembourg
Bermuda
Boston
Budapest & the Best of
   Hungary
California
Canada
Cancún, Cozumel &
   the Yucatán
Cape Cod, Nantucket &
   Martha's Vineyard
Caribbean
Caribbean Cruises & Ports
   of Call
Caribbean Ports of Call
Carolinas & Georgia
Chicago
China
Colorado
Costa Rica
Denmark
Denver, Boulder &
   Colorado Springs
England
Europe
Florida

France
Germany
Greece
Greek Islands
Hawaii
Hong Kong
Honolulu, Waikiki & Oahu
Ireland
Israel
Italy
Jamaica & Barbados
Japan
Las Vegas
London
Los Angeles
Maryland & Delaware
Maui
Mexico
Miami & the Keys
Montana & Wyoming
Montréal & Québec City
Munich & the Bavarian Alps
Nashville & Memphis
Nepal
New England
New Mexico
New Orleans
New York City
Nova Scotia, New Brunswick
   & Prince Edward Island
Oregon
Paris
Philadelphia & the
   Amish Country
Portugal

Prague & the Best of the
   Czech Republic
Provence & the Riviera
Puerto Rico
Rome
San Antonio & Austin
San Diego
San Francisco
Santa Fe, Taos &
   Albuquerque
Scandinavia
Scotland
Seattle & Portland
Singapore & Malaysia
Southeast Asia
South Pacific
Spain
Sweden
Switzerland
Thailand
Tokyo
Toronto
Tuscany & Umbria
USA
Utah
Vancouver & Victoria
Vermont, New Hampshire
   & Maine
Vienna & the Danube Valley
Virgin Islands
Virginia
Walt Disney World &
   Orlando
Washington, D.C.
Washington State

FROMMER'S® DOLLAR-A-DAY GUIDES

Australia from $50 a Day
California from $60 a Day
Caribbean from $60 a Day
England from $60 a Day
Europe from $50 a Day
Florida from $60 a Day

Greece from $50 a Day
Hawaii from $60 a Day
Ireland from $50 a Day
Israel from $45 a Day
Italy from $70 a Day
London from $75 a Day

New York from $75 a Day
New Zealand from $50 a Day
Paris from $70 a Day
San Francisco from $60 a Day
Washington, D.C.,
   from $60 a Day

FROMMER'S® PORTABLE GUIDES

Acapulco, Ixtapa &
   Zihuatanejo
Alaska Cruises & Ports of Call
Bahamas
California Wine Country
Charleston & Savannah
Chicago

Dublin
Las Vegas
London
Maine Coast
New Orleans
New York City
Paris

Puerto Vallarta, Manzanillo
   & Guadalajara
San Francisco
Sydney
Tampa & St. Petersburg
Venice
Washington, D.C.

FROMMER'S® NATIONAL PARK GUIDES

Family Vacations in the
National Parks
Grand Canyon

National Parks of the
American West
Rocky Mountain

Yellowstone & Grand Teton
Yosemite & Sequoia/
Kings Canyon
Zion & Bryce Canyon

FROMMER'S® GREAT OUTDOOR GUIDES

New England
Northern California

Southern California & Baja
Washington & Oregon

FROMMER'S® MEMORABLE WALKS

Chicago
London

New York
Paris

San Francisco
Washington D.C.

FROMMER'S® IRREVERENT GUIDES

Amsterdam
Boston
Chicago

London
Manhattan

New Orleans
Paris

San Francisco
Walt Disney World
Washington, D.C.

FROMMER'S® BEST-LOVED DRIVING TOURS

America
Britain
California

Florida
France
Germany

Ireland
Italy
New England

Scotland
Spain
Western Europe

THE COMPLETE IDIOT'S TRAVEL GUIDES

Boston
Cruise Vacations
Planning Your Trip to Europe
Hawaii

Las Vegas
London
Mexico's Beach Resorts
New Orleans

New York City
Paris
San Francisco
Walt Disney World
Washington, D.C.

THE UNOFFICIAL GUIDES®

Branson, Missouri
California with Kids
Chicago
Cruises
Disney Companion

Florida with Kids
The Great Smoky &
Blue Ridge
Mountains

Las Vegas
Miami & the Keys
Mini-Mickey
New Orleans

New York City
San Francisco
Skiing in the West
Walt Disney World
Washington, D.C.

SPECIAL-INTEREST TITLES

Born to Shop: Caribbean Ports of Call
Born to Shop: France
Born to Shop: Hong Kong
Born to Shop: Italy
Born to Shop: New York
Born to Shop: Paris
Frommer's Britain's Best Bike Rides
The Civil War Trust's Official Guide
  to the Civil War Discovery Trail
Frommer's Caribbean Hideaways
Frommer's Europe's Greatest Driving Tours
Frommer's Food Lover's Companion to France
Frommer's Food Lover's Companion to Italy
Frommer's Gay & Lesbian Europe
Israel Past & Present

Monks' Guide to California
Monks' Guide to New York City
The Moon
New York City with Kids
Unforgettable Weekends
Outside Magazine's Guide
  to Family Vacations
Places Rated Almanac
Retirement Places Rated
Road Atlas Europe
Washington, D.C., with Kids
Wonderful Weekends from Boston
Wonderful Weekends from New York City
Wonderful Weekends from San Francisco
Wonderful Weekends from Los Angeles